The Li'l Bronze Derby That Was!

A Remarkable Rivalry Remembered

The Newberry College Indians
Versus
The Presbyterian College Blue Hose

Chip Porter

© 2024 Chip Porter

All rights reserved. No part of this publication may be reproduced, stored in a retrieval system or transmitted in any form or by any means, electronic, mechanical, photocopying, recording or otherwise without the prior permision of the publisher or in accordance with the provisions of the Copyright, Designs and Patents Act 1988 or under the terms of any licence permitting limited copying issued by the Copyright Licensing Angency.

Cover Art: Savannah Raines

ISBN: 978-1-959563-29-7

Published by:
Maudlin Pond Press
P.O. Box 53
Tybee Island, GA 31328
www.maudlinpond.com

Contents

First Quarter The Newberry College and Presbyterian College Football Rivalry Began in 1913... A Look Back at the Teams

Second Quarter The Derby Debacle January 31, 1947 Newberry, South Carolina

Third Quarter The Bronze Derby 1947-1955

Fourth Quarter A South Carolina Football Tradition The Bronze Derby 1947-2006

Fifth Quarter Remembering The Bronze Derby Game

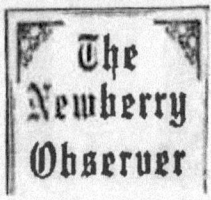

OPINION

In our view:
Derby day

Who says small-time college football isn't as good or exciting as the big time?

Those who say that have never witnessed the atmosphere, which surrounds a Newberry-Presbyterian Football game.

Saturday's 57th Bronze Derby had all the ingredients, which make college football so great. The tailgating, the pageantry, the weather and most importantly the competition.

Whether you wore Presbyterian Blue or Newberry Red, there was fun for all, and for the most part all had a good time.

Presbyterian won the Bronze Derby for a sixth straight year 42-14, and has much as it hurt the Newberry folks, they couldn't complain.

The game was played fairly. There were no push off – like that other series in South Carolina – or no 12 men on the field on a critical play. It was simply Newberry College's best against Presbyterian's best.

Newberry-PC is college football. The game has as many momentum shifts as Clemson-USC, Ohio State-Michigan or Alabama-Auburn.

But the Bronze Derby Rivalry has something all those others don't. It has two small schools giving it there all. They're not playing for bowl berths or national championships in the Bronze Derby, they're play for something more.

They play for fun, the competition and most importantly – bragging rights.

Who says small-time college football isn't as good?

Not Newberry and PC fans.

Prologue

If you were driving down Interstate 26 in South Carolina on Friday November 26, 2003 and stopped by the Waffle House in Newberry, South Carolina at Thomas Griffin Road, sat down at the counter for breakfast and picked up *The Newberry Observer* that was sitting on the counter, you may have read the article below. If you were from the midlands of South Carolina, you glanced right over it. If you were not familiar with a Blue Stocking, Blue Hose-Redskin, Indian rivalry, you read it. It's Bronze Derby week!

The Newberry Observer

The history of The Bronze Derby

From Staff Reports

A battered and well worn Bronze Derby awaits the winner of the Newberry-Presbyterian game each year. A series of scores dating back a half a century symbolizes one of the most colorful rivalries in college football.

Newberry and Presbyterian actually began their series in 1913, but it was not until the basketball season of 1947 that the passing of the Bronze Derby was born.

The following is an excerpt from *The State Magazine* in November of 1958 that describes how the Bronze Derby had its start.

"Presbyterian played at Newberry on January 30, 1947. Before the game, Presbyterian students unfurled a large banner and suspended it in prominent view on the wall of the gym behind the Presbyterian cheering section: Beat H--out of Newberry!

"When attention was riveted on the action on court, some Newberry students obtained a ladder and climbed the outside of the gym wall. Gaining access through a window, they ripped the banner off the wall and climbed back out, into the night.

"A few minutes later when the Presbyterian fans noticed the banner had been abducted, the riotous rumbling grew louder in the visitors' stands. The game ended with the Presbyterian Blue Hose getting a close 51-47 victory.

"After the game, the Presbyterian students were insistent about having the abducted banner returned. Tempers flared and a scuffle ensued. In the midst of all the commotion, a Newberry student got the prize of all spoils, a derby snatched from the noggin of one fashionable Presbyterian Yonkers.

"It would have taken a pack of bloodhounds to track down either the derby or the abductor that night."

"I heard that everybody in the student body at one time or another has taken credit for stealing that derby," said former Newberry College head coach Fred Herren to the Newberry County Touchdown Club this past Monday.

The State Magazine went on to say "Frank E. Kinard, a senior at Newberry and athletic publicity director, received a letter from Charles MacDonald, assistant professor of English and athletic publicity director at Presbyterian College. MacDonald suggested an effort be made to recover the derby and institute it as the symbol of rivalry between the Blue Hose and the Indians. Kinard presented the plan at a convocation of the Newberry student body."

The derby was recovered and the identity of the abductor was never revealed.

The derby was turned over to W.E. Turner & Son, a Newberry jewelry firm for bronzing. The hat was packaged and forwarded to a company in Columbus, Ohio, where the casting was done.

During the early years of the Bronze Derby rivalry, the hat was interchanged frequently between Newberry and PC on every athletic event. The first coming on February 28, 1947 at a basketball game in Clinton that the Blue Hose won 44-42.

For a few years, the Bronze Derby was constantly exchanged, going to the winner of each sports contest until officials and students of the two colleges decided that it would be awarded only to the winner of the Annual Thanksgiving Turkey Day Bronze Derby Game.

The game was moved from Thanksgiving after the 1992 season due to the teams and the conference moving to NCAA Division II and because that date would conflict with the playoffs.

WEARING THE DERBY — Newberry's Ike Alfred, now an assistant coach on the Newberry team, displays the coveted Bronze Derby given to the winner of the Newberry-Presbyterian game after the Indians' 21-10 victory in 1996.
— Photo special to The Observer

The article is well written and gives the reader a quick understanding of an annual tradition, a football game and its storied prize, between Newberry College and Presbyterian College. The rivalry and its trophy was much more than a football game. The rivalry began two centuries ago and culminated into a 20th-21st century football game.

A result of the 1785 Act, both Laurens County and Newberry County were formed in 1785 after the Revolutionary War. The counties were part of the Ninety Six District of South Carolina and the area was subdivided into counties with their own judicial districts. Settlers in the late 18th century in the area included immigrants from England, Germany, Scotland and Ireland. Newberry County natives had Lutheran roots from their German influence. Laurens County natives had Scotch-Irish roots in their district. Newberry became the county seat of Newberry County in 1785. Clinton, the railroad hub in adjacent Laurens County, was known as Five Points from 1785-1852. Both Newberry and Clinton were predominantly cotton producing areas. In 1793, Newberry was the site of the first cotton mill in the state of South Carolina. A population growth spurt resulted in the Clinton-Newberry area with the evolution of the cotton gin in the late 18th century coupled with the construction of the Columbia-Greenville Railroad line. Textile mills flourished in the communities. Competitive industrial baseball leagues were introduced in the mid-19th century with the advent of the textile mills and mill villages in the area. Textile (town) sponsored baseball teams taught teamwork, a sense of company and community pride, but most importantly, introduced immigrants to the new "national game." A natural competitive rivalry between the communities and neighboring mills developed.

The first Lutheran church in Newberry, South Carolina was established in 1754 in the town of Pomaria. In 1856, the General Assembly of South Carolina chartered Newberry College, a fully accredited Lutheran controlled college. Academia had arrived in Newberry, South Carolina. The first President of Newberry College was Dr. John Bachman. Today, the mission statement of Newberry College reads:

> "Newberry College prepares students in the Lutheran liberal
> arts tradition through our supportive academic community for
> lifelong intellectual and personal development, meaningful
> vocation and engaged citizenship in the global society."

The first Presbyterian church was established in Clinton, South Carolina in 1855. In 1880, Dr. William Plumer Jacobs founded The College of Clinton, influenced and under the control of the Presbyterian Church. Academia had arrived in Clinton, South Carolina. Today, the mission statement of Presbyterian College reads:

> "The compelling purpose of Presbyterian College, as a church-related college, is to develop within the framework of Christian faith the mental, physical, moral and spiritual capacities of each student in preparation of a lifetime of personal and vocational fulfillment and responsible contribution to our democratic society and the world community."

Beginning with the mission statements, the similarities between the schools are remarkable. Both liberal art colleges have maintained a small enrollment with a low student-teacher ratio. Academic standards are adhered to with above average success. Both schools have maintained a strong relationship with their respective religious affiliations. Both institutions have had a strong relationship and history with the United States military. The colleges are situated in their respective towns and maintain architecture to their appropriate original infrastructure. The citizens in both Clinton and Newberry support their respective institutions on and off the field. Volunteer efforts by the students and administration are most appreciated within the community. Both Clinton and Newberry demonstrate a historical competitive community spirit. Commitment to extracurricular activities is encouraged at both colleges and demonstrated with enthusiasm by the students and respective student-athletes.

Beginning in the late 19th century, athletic competitions between the colleges have been documented. Baseball was being played between the schools. The baseball teams were reported to be also playing "town teams." Both colleges began football programs in 1913 after the school administrations evaluated the new standardized rules eliminating violence and brutality in the rugby style sport. Football had reformed enough to reduce death and injury to student-athletes.

Goldville's 1915 baseball team posed for this picture. Back row, left to right: Archie Shieland, unidentified, Ray Rickman, Will Hamm, unidentified, Charlie O'Shields. Middle row: Boggy O'Dell, unidentified, James L. Browning, Charles Martin, Will O'Shields. Front row: Bud Mosley and Talmage Hamm.

The 1935 championship Joanna baseball team. Reading from left to right, back row: Elwyn Abrams, Cecil Farmer, Rollo Clark, Bruce Galloway, Fred Ross, Carl Farmer, Harrison. Front row: Algie Abrams, Claude Cooley, Gene Abrams, "Snow" Prater, Rudolph Prater, Rhett Abrams, Mac Brown. The bat boy was O'Dell Barrett, who was killed in action in World War II.

The campuses are only 22 miles apart. The colleges are only a 30 minute drive down Highway U.S. 76. If there is commercial traffic, it may take 35 minutes. If you encounter a tractor, it may take 40 minutes. As a result of the proximity and history between the communities, a natural rivalry was established. According to the Oxford Dictionary, a rivalry is "Competition for the same objective or superiority in the same field." In the case of athletic competition between Presbyterian College and Newberry College, I would change the definition to "Competition for the same objective or superiority ON the same field." The rivalry between the schools eventually became known as The Bronze Derby.

It's time to pause and reflect a moment before we turn the pages, not only to learn about The Bronze Derby, but remember the significance of the game to the student-athletes, administration, respective fans, alumni, Newberry and Laurens County and the State of South Carolina. Freshman that are entering both Newberry College and Presbyterian College today probably have never heard of The Bronze Derby and a Bronze Derby football game has never been played in their lifetime. The game was a Thanksgiving tradition. I was told that on the Friday after the football game, one could pick up the sports page in Boise, Idaho and an article on The Bronze Derby would be in the sports page. I checked. Wire reports went out, and for years in papers throughout the United States, The Bronze Derby was highlighted in Friday sports pages, simply because it was the only college football game played on Thanksgiving Day.

Of interest, I Googled Newberry, South Carolina and scrolled down to "What is Newberry, SC known for?" The answer was "Newberry College has a rich tradition of providing personal attention, challenging academic programs and a close-knit community that welcomes everyone… " I then Googled Clinton, South Carolina and scrolled down to "What is Clinton, SC famous for?" The answer was "The proud home of Presbyterian College… "

The community spirit regarding The Bronze Derby between Newberry and Clinton was not only resurrected, but demonstrated when I announced that I would be writing a book on The Bronze Derby. I told local editors that I would have to have an agreement between Newberry College, Presbyterian College, *The Newberry Observer, The Clinton Chronicle,* and *The Laurens County Advertiser* to proceed. Within 24 hours, everyone was on board and the project began. My book has every available and legible newspaper article on The Bronze Derby football game from Newberry and Laurens County. A historical perspective is included to remind us of social, political and economic issues at the time of The Bronze Derby football game throughout the years. The nostalgic advertisements and articles hope to bring back memories and smiles. Analysis and narrative of the games are chronicled by the actual and available county and school newspapers in a scrapbook format.

According to a December 19, 1999 feature article in *The State*, two of the top 100 sports moments of the 20th century in South Carolina occurred on Thanksgiving Day at Setzler Field in Newberry, South Carolina. One moment resulted in a game winning field goal, and the other was a result of a coaches challenge.

Jimmie Coggins, President and General Manager of Newberry Broadcasting Co., Inc. (Newberry radio station WKDK) told me that if a tiddlywinks game was scheduled today on the square in either Newberry or Clinton between Newberry College and Presbyterian College, a crowd would show up. Today, the rivalry is remembered and always will exist. The college football game became the extended rivalry between two communities. The game became an institution. The college football game is simply now *The Li'l Bronze Derby That Was!*

Chip Porter
Dum Vivimus Servimus

Dedication

To the football fans in Clinton and Newberry, Laurens and Newberry counties, and the state of South Carolina that attended the annual Thanksgiving Day Bronze Derby football game. You have represented your communities for over 100 years! A friendly fellowship was exhibited and existed between rivals. The game was always played to a capacity crowd. The students at Newberry College and Presbyterian College were home for the Thanksgiving Day holiday yet, you were there! There was beautiful weather, and even sometimes rain or snow, but you were there! Whether the game was played at Bailey Memorial Stadium in Clinton or Setzler Field in Newberry, you were there! The game was for you and your rival community! Enjoy the memories of your annual football classic!

Foreword

Those of us who are sports fans—and those of us who aren't, too—have often read or heard or said some version of "sports brings us together like nothing else." That is often and sometimes very memorably, true. Just think of the moments you have heard of, or read about, or have seen video of, or—if you are fortunate—been in person for: moments of victory and defeat, triumph and disappointment, astonishing skill and blind luck.

But the opposite is just as often—but just as memorably, sometimes even *more* memorably—true too. Athletes and coaches and fans oppose each other in those same moments, one team and its fans winning, the other team and its fan losing, with winning far more sweet because you beat your rival and losing far more bitter because you lost to your rival. If it is true that athletes, coaches and fans hate losing more than they love winning, rivalries intensify that feeling even more.

Rivalries link teams so closely that they often exist primarily in pairs: Yankees/Red Sox, Cowboys/Eagles, Celtics/Lakers, Canadiens/Maple Leafs, Manchester United/Liverpool, and so on and so on and so on. There may be no more fiercely-felt in all of American sports than college football: Alabama/Auburn, Southern Cal/Notre Dame, South Carolina/Clemson, Ohio State/Michigan, Texas/Oklahoma, Georgia/Florida, and so on and so on and so on.

Some long college football rivalries featured cherished traditional trophies: the Little Brown Jug (Michigan/Minnesota, 1903); the Old Oaken Bucket (Indiana/Purdue, 1925); the Golden Egg (Ole Miss/Mississippi State 1927); the Stanford Axe (Cal/Stanford, 1933); Floyd of Rosedale (Iowa/Minnesota, 1935) and the Paul Bunyan Axe (Minnesota/Wisconsin, 1948). (Rivalry trophies of most recent years usually feel more forced than genuine—as if every rivalry game *has* to have some tangible item to pass back and forth between loser and winner.)

But "big time" college football isn't the only, or always the best, brand of college football. As one sportswriter reminds us, sports fans should not only appreciate "huge stadiums overflowing with fans and expectations," but also those "smaller playpens where the competition and desire take second place to none." Two of those latter places in South Carolina are Newberry College, founded in 1856, and Presbyterian College in Clinton founded in 1880. Founded as church-affiliated liberal arts colleges, they are only twenty-two miles apart with roughly the same enrollment–between 500 and 1000 students–for most of the period from the 1890s through the early 2000s.

Once they adopted intercollegiate athletics, they were natural rivals in their first two sports: baseball and track and field. Though other intramural sports were encouraged and popular on both campuses, intercollegiate football was widely viewed as dangerous and was banned on all South Carolina college and university campuses except for South Carolina and Clemson until 1913. The first Newberry-Presbyterian football game, played at the South Carolina State Fairgrounds that November, began a ninety-three year football rivalry that lasted through 2006.

In early 1947 a student prank during a Newberry-Presbyterian basketball game, in a moment when both schools recognized that the natural rivalry between them in all sports was becoming more heated and less good natured than ever, set the stage for the adoption of a trophy intended to acknowledge athletic competition and school loyalty while at the same time reducing the chances that the rivalry would get out of hand.

The Bronze Derby was passed back and forth after the annual football game, the basketball series and the baseball series every year from 1947 to 1955, then restricted to the annual football game–played on Thanksgiving Day for most of its history–from 1956 to 2006.

Chip Porter's impressive chronicle of the thrilling sixty year Bronze Derby rivalry between two South Carolina colleges brings it to vivid life, both for those who remember it and those who are learning about it for the first time. It is an absorbing and lasting tribute to all those who played for The Bronze Derby and all those who cheered them on, in games where competition and desire took second place to no other games ever played.

J. Tracy Power
Associate Professor of History and College Archivist
Newberry College

The First Quarter

The Newberry College and Presbyterian College Football Rivalry Began in 1913...

A Look Back at the Teams

The Li'l 🎩 That Was!

The football rivalry between Newberry College and Presbyterian College began in 1913. The inaugural Bronze Derby game was played in 1947. Between 1913-1946, the schools played 33 football games. Presbyterian College held the edge with 20 wins while Newberry College was victorious 11 times over the 33 year period. In 1919 and 1932, the teams played to a tie. The results of the games were as follows (**Bold** denotes home team):

Year	Result	Year	Result
1913	**NC** 51 - PC 0	1913	**NC** 51 - PC 0
1915	**NC** 20 - PC 13	1916	PC 3 - **NC** 0
1917	**PC** 20 - NC 0	1919	PC 0 - **NC** 0
1920	**PC** 20 - NC 0	1921	**NC** 15 - PC 7
1922	**PC** 35 - NC 9	1923	PC 7 - **NC** 0
1924	**NC** 10 - PC 0	1925	**NC** 22 - PC 6
1926	**PC** 28 - NC 0	1927	PC 12 - **NC** 0
1928	NC 12 - **PC** 6	1929	**PC** 54 - NC 0
1930	PC 31 - **NC** 0	1931	**PC** 6 - NC 0
1932	**NC** 7 - PC 7	1933	NC 16 - **PC** 7
1934	PC 13 - **NC** 0	1935	**PC** 20 - NC 0
1936	PC 27 - **NC** 0	1937	NC 13 - **PC** 0
1938	**PC** 7 - NC 6	1939	**PC** 6 - NC 0
1940	**NC** 20 - PC 7	1941	**PC** 13 - NC 7
1942	PC 14 - **NC** 7	1943	**PC** 13 - NC 12
1944	**PC** 20 - NC 6	1945	NC 19 - **PC** 13
1946	**PC** 14 - NC 13		

The schools played each other twice in 1913. The first match-up in 1913 was played as an exhibition game on Wednesday before the traditional game between Clemson and the University of South Carolina on "Big Thursday" in Columbia, South Carolina. As a consequence of World War I, the schools did not play each other in 1914 and 1918. The following available newspaper articles look back at the beginning of a football rivalry that was second in duration in the state of South Carolina to the Clemson University-University of South Carolina football rivalry that began in 1896. The Newberry College-Presbyterian College football 93 year football rivalry began in 1913 and ended in 2006.

The Newberry Observer

Dutch MacLean: Life of a legend

Courtesy of Jay Salter of Newberry College - June 25, 2023

NEWBERRY — The name "MacLean" has been a monumental part of the Newberry College story for 110 years — first as that of a living legend, then as that of a hub of athletics and campus life. As historic MacLean Gymnasium gains new life, so should the little-known story of its incredible eponym.

Ohio-bred Fred Douglas "Dutch" MacLean (1888-1964) first entered Newberry history when he transferred from Brown University in 1913, at the behest of the Indians' first coach and one-man athletics department Raymond Thomas, who had seen him in action. The ban on football had just been lifted, and Thomas needed the best for the college's first intercollegiate squad. Though he stood only about five-foot-five, MacLean quickly made a name for himself as Newberry's first quarterback.

"He never used a leather helmet. He just wrapped a black sweatband around his head to hold his ears in, because the other guys like to pull his ears. This was in the very early days of football, back when it was rough and tumble," said Maj. Fred MacLean III, a retired Army chaplain and Dutch's grandson. "They gave him a nickname, 'the Flying Dutchman,' because when a guy would get tackled and they'd all pile on, they would pick up Dutch, throw him over the pile with the ball, and he'd hit the ground running and score. They were so effective that they outlawed that play. But the name stuck, and they shortened it to 'Dutch.'"

Along with football, Dutch MacLean lettered in baseball and basketball before graduating in 1915. That same year, a German submarine torpedoed the British liner RMS Lusitania, killing 1,195 passengers, including 123 Americans. Like many young men, MacLean was eager to fight.

"Dutch and five of his friends all got together and decided America's not getting into World War I fast enough. So, they were all going to go up to Canada and enlist," said Fred MacLean. "When he got up to Ottawa, none of the other boys showed up, but his sense of duty was so strong that it didn't matter."

Dutch MacLean joined Princess Patricia's Canadian Light Infantry, and with his strong pitcher's arm he lobbed grenades from French trenches. According to newspaper reports, he was gassed at the Battle of Vimy Ridge in April 1917 and spent six months in a London hospital. Unbeknownst to him, in the chaos of war, he was reported as killed in action. After being released from hospital, MacLean transferred to the U.S. Army, where he served until 1920. Upon returning home to Youngstown, Ohio, he surprised his family and friends with the realization that he was indeed alive.

Devastatingly, MacLean's sweetheart from Newberry, Woodie Bowman, had married another man, believing that MacLean had been killed in France.

Dutch MacLean (front row, second from left) is pictured with Newberry College Head Football Coach Raymond Thomas and the first Newberry College football team in 1913 (3-1).

"She fell in love with him, but he wasn't ready to get married. He was off to war, and they were going to get married after he came back," said Fred MacLean. "She had married after they told her that he was dead. She married a salesman, and unfortunately, as I understand it, he suffered an accidental gunshot wound while he was cleaning his gun and he died [in 1921]. After he was back teaching at Newberry, they renewed the relationship, fell in love again, and eventually they were married."

Dutch MacLean returned to Newberry in 1921 to teach English and to coach the three sports in which he excelled as a player. That year, the men's basketball team won the first of four consecutive state championships. In 1922, his football team defeated The Citadel for the first time on the brand-new Setzler Field. The following year, MacLean saw the completion of new gymnasium, which would be dedicated in his honor in 1955. His 1924 football squad achieved a season record of 8-2, which stood unmatched until 1971 and unbroken until 2006. As of 2023, Dutch remains Newberry College's longest-serving head football coach with 17 seasons.

After leaving Newberry in 1938 to pursue other callings, Dutch MacLean returned to lead the Indian Club, the athletics booster organization, from 1957-62. It was in these latter years that his grandson remembers summers and holidays visiting him in Newberry.

"You wouldn't think of a rough and tumble football player as being well-versed in Shakespeare," said Fred MacLean. "I don't remember ever seeing him without a three-piece suit, and he always had a whistle and a stopwatch. He would talk with me about the principles of character, the value of duty, the sense of what's right."

Dutch MacLean was posthumously inducted in 1976 as one of the first two members of the Newberry College Athletic Hall of Fame.

Dutch MacLean

Photo courtsey of Newberry College

FIRST P. C. FOOTBALL TEAM WAS ORGANIZED BY JACOBS IN 1913

Everett Booe, Star Player for Davidson College, Was First Coach. "Red" Thomas, of York, Captain. William P. Jacobs Assumed Financial Responsibility and Directed Efforts In Initial Season.

Early in 1913 several students at Presbyterian college, encouraged by a few who had played football in high school or in other colleges, determined to request the faculty and board of trustees the privilege of establishing inter-collegiate football at Presbyterian college. Active in this direction were J. W. C. Bell, a freshman from Arkansas, who had played high school football and later was selected all-state tackle on Coach Johnson's first team; Rufus E. Sadler of Rock Hill, who had played football at Clemson, and Wm. P. Jacobs, of Clinton, who had played football at Davidson college. Sadler dropped out of school that year and Jacobs took the leadership in circulating the petition among the students and making the request of the authorities.

The petition was granted and announcement was made at commencement, 1913, upon the condition, however, that the entry into inter-collegiate football and basketball should not involve the college in any financial loss. It became necessary, therefore, for Jacobs to personally direct the entire operation, buy the uniforms, employ and pay the coach and all other expenses.

The school had no football field and no gymnasium. Both football and basketball were played on an old plowed field, now the northwest portion of the College Plaza. The western goal-post was actually in Professor Martin's cow lot. There were no grandstands. The uniform consisted of mole-skin trousers and a cheap jersey. The players provided all other equipment. Coach Everett L. Booe coached all athletics at a salary of $800.00 a year.

Newberry defeated Presbyterian college both at the state fair and in a return game at Newberry by the identical score of 51 to nothing. Furman defeated P. C. at Greenville, 65 to 0. It was the first year in inter-collegiate football for P. C., Furman and Newberry. Only the Citadel, Carolina and Clemson had teams prior to that year. Wofford and Erskine came into the picture a year or so later.

Financially, the season was a success for P. C. and Jacobs, who financially underwrote the enterprise, did not lose, for the football season paid the coach, financed itself and also basketball and baseball.

Jacobs played quarterback, was the manager of the team, served most of the season as alternate captain with the elected captain, a freshman named Thomas, from York. Jacobs also naturally served as assistant coach. At no time during the season did Booe have a sufficient number of men out to practice to form two teams. But even under these handicaps, P. C.'s first venture was a success.

At the end of the season the first Block "P" club was formed, called the "Wearers of the P," and the first certificate was awarded to Wm. P. Jacobs. It is framed and hangs in the college gymnasium at present. Among the other players receiving football awards for the first year were: Coach Booe, honorary; J. W. C. Bell, of Arkansas; B. T. Brown, of Bishopville; Rev. Robert Woodson, of Starkville, Miss.; H. E. Hicklin, of Rock Hill, and Rev. A. H. Miller, a missionary in Africa.

FOOT BALL

NEWBERRY COLLEGE
vs.
PRESBYTERIAN COLLEGE
OF SOUTH CAROLINA

FAIR GROUNDS
Wednesday, October 29th
12 O'CLOCK

A fine battle between two strong rivals in up-State athletics.

General Admission.	50c and 75c
Grand Stand	$1.00
Individual Box Seats	$1.75
Box containing six Seats	$10.00

Tickets sold and seats reserved at Abbott's Lower Cigar Store.

Columbia, South Carolina

Courtsey of Newberry College archives

The Li'l That Was!

Pictured is the first Presbyterian College football team. The team was coached by Everett Booe. Presbyterian College went 5-3 in their inaugural season which included 2 consecutive defeats to Newberry College. Ironically, both games in 1913 ended in 51-0 scores.

Football Squad

Coach E.L. Booe was a graduate of Davidson College. A tremendous athlete who excelled at both baseball and football, Coach Booe immediately set the standard for Presbyterian College football. Presbyterian College first recognized collegiate football in 1913. In 1913, the inaugural season for football at Presbyterian College, Coach Booe led the Garnet and Blue to a 5-3 record. Presbyterian initially played both collegiate and high-school teams in their first season. The rivalries with Wofford College, Furman University and Newberry College began in 1913. Coach Booe left Presbyterian College after the 1913 season to continue his professional baseball career.

Coach Booe

The Li'l That Was!

THE FIRST FOOTBALL SEASON AT PRESBYTERIAN COLLEGE

The Blue Stocking

The letter which follows gives a resume of P. C.'s first football season, in 1913. The letter was written by W. P. Jacobs, quarterback and manager of the team, to Coach Walter Johnson in February, 1930.

Mr. Walter A. Johnson,
Presbyterian College,
Clinton, S. C.

Dear Walter:

I am giving you in this letter information in regard to the first football season at the Presbyterian College. The first season was in the fall of 1913. The coach that year was Everett L. Booe, all-Southern halfback of Davidson College. I served as assistant coach, manager and quarterback of the team. The captain of the team was a freshman named Red Thomas, from York. Incidentally, he was the best player of the team, and probably the only real football player on the team at that time. I believe I am correct in the statement that, aside from Booe, Thomas and myself, there was not a player on the entire squad who had ever played football before.

We were defeated that year by Furman in Greenville, 65 to 0; by Newberry, 51 to 0, and by Newberry again at the State Fair, on Wednesday, in advance of the Carolina-Clemson game in Columbia, by the identical score of 51 to 0. We won from Rock Hill High school, at Clinton, 26 to 0. We defeated the Anderson Fitting school, 56 to 0, at Clinton. This school has since gone out of existence. We defeated Bailey Military institute, 21 to 0, at Greenwood, and 26 to 0 in Clinton. As the final game of the season, Thanksgiving in Charleston, we defeated Charleston College, 12 to 7 — the only college game we won in the state. That year neither Erskine nor Wofford had football teams. Their first teams came the following season.

Thus our inter-collegiate standing that year in games won and lost placed us next to the bottom, and sixth from the top. It is interesting to note that the only equipment supplied by the athletic association to the players that year was a pair of moleskin trousers and a grey jersey. The players had to buy all the balance of the equipment that they had. We used no stockings.

After inducing the Board of Trustees to install football at the Presbyterian College, I employed the coach on my own responsibility, without a guarantee; gave him $800.00 salary to coach football, basketball and baseball; and the college gave him a room at the dormitory and his meals. The football season, by rigid economy, managed to pay the coach's salary, and to finance basketball and baseball. It was, incidentally, also the first

In the backfield, as I remember it, we had Red Thomas, Joe Belk, Ferdinand Jacobs, Al Brice, Buckner, Hoyt Miller and myself. In the line we had a fellow named Linton, Bill Bell, Norton, George Little, and two or three others. On the ends we had a fellow named Stephenson, and Bob Woodson. We never did have, during the entire season, enough out to practice for a full two team scrimmage.

In justice to the team, I should say, however, that we would probably have had a much stronger record had it not been for the fact that several of our most likely prospects for the team were declared ineligible at the last minute before the first game, and we never got over the crippled condition.

At that time Furman and Newberry were just starting with their first season, and while stronger than us, were

season in basketball for the Presbyterian College.

The season, as I remember it, had very few features. Thomas gained most of the ground and usually around ends; Hoyt Miller gained some ground. Thomas did most of the passing. I did most of the punting. Robert Woodson and I did most of the pass receiving. We didn't have a very good defensive team, nor did we have a good offensive team. We ran practically no interference, and aside from the individual ability of Red Thomas we didn't accomplish anything that year, except to start football. The only play in the season in which I had a part in the victory was the final Thanksgiving game at Charleston in which was a score standing 7 to 6 in favor of Charleston. I received a long pass from Thomas and scored a touchdown. It was the only game in which we were evenly matched with our competitors. The other college games we lost by an overwhelming score, and the balance of the games were nothing but high school and prep school games that we were expecting to win, weaker than the big teams. Had we played Clemson, Carolina, Citadel or Davidson that year we would have been annihilated.

We had no gymnasium, no field, no stand. We played in an old abandoned cotton field, located just east of what is now the Spencer Hall dormitory. The Wm. P. Jacobs Science hall had not at that time been built. The spectators stood around the field and took care of themselves as best they could.

Incidentally, the game we licked Charleston was the last football game the College of Charleston ever played. I remember distinctly they made me a check, as manager, that night for $180.50. This represented their losses of the day. They guaranteed us $250 for the game. We cleared nearly $200 on the trip.

Yours sincerely,
WM. P. JACOBS.

On November 23, 1922, Thanksgiving Day in Clinton, South Carolina, Presbyterian College defeated Newberry College 35-9.

The Li'l 🎩 That Was!

The Blue Stocking

"ALL FOR P. C. AND P. C. FOR ALL"

PRESBYTERIAN COLLEGE OF SOUTH CAROLINA, DECEMBER 2, 1922

Indians Bow Before Onslaught of Blue Stockings

P. C. AVENGES 1921 DEFEAT

There was jjoy in Clinton Thanksgiving night. P. C. expectations and hopes were far exceeded, for Walter Johnson's Blue Stockings completely outclassed the Newberry Indians, their traditional foes, in the annual Turkey Day encounter, which took place in Clinton this year.

Presbyterian superiority on the gridiron was proved, completely and conclusively. The 35-9 score does not give a true tale of the completeness of the Calvinist victory, as will be shown later.

The Johnsonites scored early. Newberry kicked off to the 30-yard line. Wilson gained 18 yards thru right tackle on the first play of the game. Pearce followed with 9 yards around end, and Jack paced 25 yards thru left tackle. But P. C. fumbled. However, Newberry punted forthwith, and the Presbyterian march was resumed. An 11-yard run by Pearce, a pass from Hindman to Mason for 20 yards, put the ball on the spot from where Moore bucked six yards to the first touchdown.

This march is indicative of the steady marches that led up to Blue Stocking touchdowns. The second touchdown came in the second quarter after linebucks by Hindman, Pearce, Wilson, and Moore, passes to Mason, put the ball where Wilson could buck it over. Soon thereafter, Newberry achieved her highest ambition and scored a touchdown on the Blue Stockings. Intercepting a pass on his 10-yard line, Borts raced 90 yards to the only Newberry touchdown, aided by magnificent interference from Dame Fortune. The Indians still possessed a small degree of scoring fever, for, just before the end of the first half, a bad P. C. pass from center put the ball across Presbyterian goal line in Blue Stocking hands. Newberry derived her last two points therefrom, via the safety route.

The second half was completely Calvanistic. Three touchdowns were scored by the smooth-running Johnson machine ere the conflict ended. Line bucks by Wilson, Pearce, and Moore, and passes by Hindman were instrumental in each crossbucks by Wilson, Pearce, and Moore, and passes by Hindman were instrumental in each crossing of the line. Wilson 18 yards, Moore 10 yards, Pearce 10 yards, Moore 4 yards, Wilson 3 yards, pass to Mason for 15 yards, Wilson 2 yards, Moore 2 yards, Wilson 3 yards, Moore 4 yards, every play going over right tackle, accounted for touchdown number 3. Pearce 2 yards, Moore 2 yards, Wilson 12 yards, Wilson 4 yards, pass to Mason 6 yards, Pearce 4 yards, Hindman 2 yards, Wilson 18 yards, Wilson 5 yards, Moore 10 yards, Moore 2 yards, these plays alternating between right and left tackle, gave Presbyterian touchdown number 4. Wilson returned punt 15 yds, Moore 7 yards, Pearce 5 yards, intercepted pass by Moore, Wilson 5 yards, Pearce 3 yards, Wilson 2 yards, Moore 3 yards, Mason 15-yard pass, Pearce 10 yards, all over right and left tackle and guard, give the story of the winning of touchdown number 5.

Jack Wilson, playing probably his last game for P. C., was the brilliant star of the day. Jack covered himself with glory, playing as no other half-back has ever played before on the P. C. gridiron. He bucked the line literally at will, and his return of punts was sensational. Moore, Pearce, and Hindman, were also demons at gaining ground. Mason distinguished himself by the entire game, while losing 19 yards via the same attempt. Wade, Clowney, Williamson, Mason, Brown, Bomar, Miller, and Moore, were the principle stars in the defensive line. Pearce contributed some hard tackling when occasion presented.

At forward passing Newberry was more fortunate. They completed 8 out of 25 passes, for a gain of 73 yards, making a total of four first downs during the contest. P. C. gained 495 yards from scrimmage, made 28 first donws, completed 8 passes out of 10, and punted twice during the contest. Such is the tale of Thanksgiving Day. Besides his other work Jack Wilson kicked goal after every touchdown.

Shealey, Borts, Wollet, and Eleazer were the principle Indians to distinguish themselves by defensive work, they having no chance at offensive brillian-

The Li'l That Was!

The Blue  Stocking

"ALL FOR P.C. P.C. FOR ALL"

VOLUME XI — PRESBYTERIAN COLLEGE, CLINTON, S. C., NOVEMBER 30, 1929 — NUMBER 11

Presbyterian Wins Over Newberry, 54-0

PRESBYTERIAN WINS OVER NEWBERRY

(Continued from page one)
team, the Hose pulled every play in their bunch of tricks. Passes were mixed with end runs, while Dunlap hit the line for big, consistent gains. Lateral passes and new formations were used to the bewilderment of the Indians. P. C. scored first down after first down for a total of 15 against three for Newberry, and piled up eight touchdowns.

Always wide awake, the Calvinists blocked three punts, one for a touchdown. Twice they stopped the punt of their own team-mate on the Indians' goal line, and the tackles went through the line so fast that passing was the only mode of attack open for the visitors and little of that was successful.

The feature of the game was guessing how P. C. would make extra points. They made six in eight tries. With no kicker they mixed line bucks with passes and end runs to baffle the Newberry steam.

To pick a star in the P. C. line is practically impossible. Every man played his part and deserves credit. Green ran the team well and made some beautiful runs. Dunlap did the most ground gaining through the line and got off some long runs as well. Ritchie and B. Dunlap, the other two starters in the backfield, played a fine game.

P. C.'s line worked magnificently. Capt. Beckman played his last game for P. C. and played a good one. Both Cheatham and Blakely played havoc with the opposing team's rushes, while at end Ross Lynn was down on every punt, in every play, and going at top form. Bennett did some pretty work, making two touchdowns and blocking some end runs. McNauli and McQueen played up to form.

Coach Johnson used his entire team and every available substitute as well. Senter, Walker and Truesdell all made some pretty runs against opponents, the second string line making some good opening for them.

Besides Captain Beckman, Clinton, Means, Martin and Walker played their last game for P. C. For four years these men have given their best for P. C. and played a large part in the victories.

BIG SCORE IN CLOSING GAME

Presbyterian Has No Trouble In Trouncing Indians At Homecoming Game Thursday.

In their last game of the season, their home-coming battle, and against their oldest rivals, Newberry, the Blue Stockings rose to greater heights and humbled their opponents by a 54-0 score in a great, hard fought game full of thrills.

From the beginning till the final whistle the Calvinists played "heads up" ball, moving with machine-like precision and as one rather than eleven players. An intercepted pass on the first play of the game, three downs and P. C. had a touchdown. A drive over the line made it 7-0. A few minutes later Dunlap went through the line for a 60-yard run for the second touchdown, and B. Dunlap added the extra point.

Newberry was completely outplayed in all departments of the game. Only once during the contest was the ball in P. C. territory and that was on the 40-yard line. Despite the work of the P. C. team, Newberry never gave in for an instant. They put up a dogged fight throughout, showing the best of spirit and gameness. Hutchison and Stokes played a great game for the Indians, but the Garnet and Blue was just too much to cope with.

With Jimmie Grega running the
(Continued on page four)

The Li'l That Was!

MONDAY, NOVEMBER 7, 1932

THE BLUE STOCKING

Edited By
WALKER COMBS, Jr.
Managing Editor

SPORTS

INDIANS AND BLUE STOCKINGS PLAY TO NO DECISION FRIDAY

Thrilling Game In Newberry Results In 7-7 Score. Intercepted Pass and 60-Yard Run Brings Reds' Counter. Drive Down the Field Takes Ball Over Goal For Presbyterians.

Newberry college, on Friday afternoon, succeeded in throwing a bomb into the hopes of Presbyterian college for victory, and in a game filled with the most startling breaks, succeeded in holding the Blue Stockings to a 7-7 tie.

In a battle that was alternately shifted in advantage from one to the other, Newberry first scored on a 60-yard run by Ingram after he intercepted a pass, and then in the final quarter Presbyterian drove over the tying score. While the Blue Hose gained effectively in mid-field, the Indian line was next to impregnable near the goal line, and Clary's punting enabled the Newberry men to keep their goal threatened except for two drives on the part of the Blue Hose.

In the early part of the game, Ingram took a punt on his own 10-yard line and dashed to the Presbyterian 5-yard line before finally being brought down. However, the Blue Hose held for four downs with a loss to Newberry of one yard, and succeeded in running three straight first downs, but were finally stopped.

In running three straight first downs, but were finally stopped. In the second period Presbyterian was thrown on the defensive, with Smelco getting away on one very threatening run, stopped only by Barrett. Newberry, a little later, passed over the goal line missing a chance to score. Perrin had gotten off a bad punt for 20 yards, giving the ball to the Indians on their 26-yard line. After this pass, as if all would work against the Blue Hose, Bolick fumbled, but again Newberry was forced to yield after four downs.

Opening the third quarter with a spirit that was not to be withstood, the Presbyterians marched down the field almost to the goal line. Perrin opened with a 50-yard return of the kick-off. Bolick gained seven yards through the line, and then Barrett went around left end for 10 more. Perrin, on the next play, passed to Pinson, gaining 20 yards. Again the Blue Stockings drove through for a first down, but within the final five-yard line four thrusts at the center of the line failed to put the ball across. Clary punted out of danger. P. C. again launched an offensive, but Ingram intercepted a pass from Perrin, snatching it almost from Pinson's hands, and dashed 60 yards for a score.

With the score 7-0 against them, the Presbyterians were unable to penetrate the defense set up by Newberry. Not until the fourth quarter were they able to come again within scoring distance. After several exchanges of punts, Presbyterian held, forcing Clary to punt. Reeder broke through the Newberry line and blocked the punt, trying to pick up the ball to run. However, the ball eluded him and Pinson recovered. Perrin broke off tackle for eight yards, and another of six. After two plays had failed to any considerable yardage, Perrin went over guard to the three-yard line, and Bolick added another first down. Bolick was given three tries and went over on the last attempt. Copeland's placement was perfect, to tie the score.

With both teams battling hard for the breaks, Perrin returned a punt to the Newberry 35-yard line, and then passed. Smelco, the power in the Indian offense, leaped into the air and intercepted it, ruining the Presbyterian chances to score. On the next play Newberry completed a 30-yard pass, but the game ended before they were able to take advantage of this turn.

To pick one outstanding player in the Presbyterian line, Searcy Elliott played a brilliant game. Ewing played one of the best games at tackle in his entire career, and Reeder made several attempts at blocking punts, his one successful try being responsible for P. C.'s only score.

Newberry presented a strong defense, and were able, with Ingram, to take advantage of one of their many breaks, an intercepted pass for a score. Presbyterian missed one great chance by inches, when the Newberry line proved to be a stone wall. Inspired by their home-coming day, the Indians were giving their very best.

Presbyterian made 10 first downs to Newberry's five, but counting Ingram's touchdown run, and one good run by Smelco, the yardage gained was more nearly equal.

The line-up:

P. C. (7)		Newberry (7)
Copeland	le	Pipola
Mills	lt	Gow
Elliott	lg	Richard
Harvin	c	McKenzie
Reeder	rg	Valley
Ewing	rt	Dawkins
Pinson	re	Lambeth
Perrin	qb	Ingram
Bolick	lh	Clary
Barrett	rh	Ergle
Simms	fb	Taylor

The Newberry Observer

"JUST LIKE A LETTER FROM HOME"

NEWBERRY, S. C., FRIDAY, NOVEMBER 10, 1933.

Newberry Downs P. C. Eleven

Ed Beck Dazzles Presbyterian Tacklers—Two Thousand See Contest.

Clinton, Nov. 10.—Determined to take the scalp of their biggest rival, the well-fortified Newberry Indians broke into the Presbyterian college Blue Stockins' home coming party here this afternoon and walked away to a justly deserved 16 to 7 victory before a crowd of nearly 2,000.

Twice previously the Calvinists had broken up shows arranged for old grads of their opponents, winning over Wofford and The Citadel, but they took a dose of their own bitter medicine today.

Doped to win by a slight margin, the Hosemen, previously undefeated in South Carolina and a possible claimant of the state championship, fell before the redoubtable march of the visitors, who were led by Eddie Beck, stubby ten-second halfback, who raced and wriggled his way to one touchdown and led his team in its drives up and down the field.

Newberry tallied first before the middle of the first period. Receiving a punt after the opening kickoff, they started a march on their own 40 and clicked off three first downs in a determined 60-yard parade for a touchdown, the procession ending when on a fourth down, Wyman Ingram faked a dropkick, then shot a pass into short flat territory to Ray Hewey, tackle shifted to the right flank. Lambeth, ten-second end, kicked from placement straight between the uprights for the extra point.

The Li'l  That Was!

The Blue Stocking

"ALL FOR P. C.   P. C. FOR ALL"

VOLUME XV   PRESBYTERIAN COLLEGE, CLINTON, S. C., NOVEMBER 13, 1933   NUMBER 8

INDIANS SCALP PRESBYTERIAN

Newberry Cohorts, Led By Beck, Turn Back Blue Hose, 16-7, In Home-coming Game Here Friday Before Good Crowd.

On Friday afternoon, the Newberry Indians administered the Presbyterian Blue Stockings a dose of their own medicine by breaking up home-coming day and defeated them, 16-7.

Playing before a crowd of two thousand, the Indians completely outclassed the Blue Stockings. Their two weeks' lay-off evidently put plenty of pep in them. Only in the second quarter did the Hose look anything like the team that tied Clemson. Except for that one spurt, Newberry had the situation completely in hand.

Starting off the first quarter with a bang, the Indians received a punt from P. C. and Beck immediately tore off 25 yards from punt formation. Then mixing line drives with end and passes, they drove 60 yards the field and scored on a seven pass from Ingram to Hewey. beth kicked the ball right through middle for the extra point.

Coming back in the second quarter the Hose displayed their only offensive of the afternoon. Led by P. brilliant junior quarter, they dro yards down the field and scored two-yard buck by Perrin. Horne ed the extra point. Perrin mad but 11 yards in this drive.

As the third quarter opened, looked to be back in their old but the spasm didn't last long. several exchanges of punts, New got the ball and Beck drove thr the middle of the P. C. line and s pered 28 yards to score. Lan again kicked the extra point. score put the game on ice fo Indians.

The rest of the game was d of scoring until the last minute o game. P. C. obtained possession o ball nearly on her own goal line. liday tried to pass but the Newl forwards charged through and b down the ball in the end zone f safety. P. C. kicked off from th yard line and the game ended a completion of the run-back.

Higbe, P. C.'s 145-pound half was on the spot all the after Every time he got the ball the st Newberry line seeped through threw him either on the line of s mage or for a loss. His only ga three yards was made on an off-t slant.

The lack of blocking was ent rtoo evident on the P. C. team. O runs and off-tackle plays there were always two or three Newberry players waiting to hit the runner. Furen, big right end of the Indians, was especially adept in the art of smashing the end plays before they got well started.

The play of the Indians was very versatile. Trick plays with tackles shifted to eligible positions to catch passes and tackles and ends carrying the ball kept the Hose in a quandry. The passes proved to be especially destructive. The first score came directly from a pass and the second indirectly. Beck and Ingram led the attack and were aided by Weidman and Ayoub.

P. C.'s line, which had so far this season proved very effective, showed lack of teamwork. The tackling and charging was below the usual standard and this allowed the Indians to run over them time and again. Yearout and Reeder were best in the line. Perrin was the only man in the backfield who could gain consistently with Bolick a bulwark on defense. But for these two men, the Hose would have been helpless.

The line-ups:

Newberry (16)	P. C. (7)
LE—Lambeth	Yearout
LT—Hewey	Robinson
LG—White	Corcell
C—Hite	Reeder
RG—Valley	Boggs
RT—Gibbons	Sims
RE—Furen	Forehand
QB—Ingram	Perrin
LH—Beck	Higbe
RH—Clary	Bolick
FB—Wiedman	McCulloch

Officials: Referee, Foster (Hamp-

The Newberry Observer
"JUST LIKE A LETTER FROM HOME"
International News Service
NEWBERRY, S. C., TUESDAY, NOVEMBER 13, 1934.

Blue Stockings Defeat Indians

Presbyterian College Wins From Newberry by 12 to 0 Score.

Presbyterian college cracked the strong Newberry college defense twice Friday afternoon to score a 12 to 0 victory over the Indians before a homecoming crowd of 3,000 spectators.

A dazzling aerial attack featuring riflelike shots from Bob Perrin accounted for a 56-yard march for a touchdown late in the first half, a short pass to Lee Quarterman giving the tally. Robbie Higbe returned a punt 40 yards to the shadow of the Redmen's goal on the last play of the third period and Quarterman hit the line five plays later for the second touchodwn.

Advance indications were that Ed Beck of Newberry and Capt. Harry Bolick of Presbyterian would clash in a running duel. However, Beck was throttled, Higbe's flashy work was confined to his brilliant returns of kicks and only Bolick came through with the expected all around superb performance.

His line smashing was the only consistent ground threat of the contest. P. C. met a stone wall against the tackles and ends guarded by Koch and Gibbons, Furen and Hewey, but it found the middle of the line vulnerable and launched Bolick against it time after time for appreciable yardage. He gained over center and the guards on straight bucks, delayed bucks and "outback" bucks—one step to one side to throw the defense off balance then straight through.

His blocking rated with the best seen on a South Carolina gridiron this year and his defensive work was all that could be asked. In addition to getting his full share of tackles, he intercepted no less than three passes.

Perrin's bullet-like passes provided the chief margin between the teams. He hurled them with unerring accuracy and his receivers were adept at handling them. On the other hand, the Indians had little success with overhead attack.

Ingram, the local eleven's star quarterback, was kept on the sidelines most of the time because of an injured hand and the backfield was never able to function satisfactorily without him. Beck was the chief running threat, but P. C. defense was prepared to stop his maneuvers. Twice he got away for gains of eight yards and once he clicked off six, but most of the time the Presbyterian backs closed in fast to plug the holes opened for him by his mates.

Throughout most of the contest the Indians were on the defensive. Twice they held for downs when their goal line was threatened. Vying with the versatile performance of the crack P. C. backfield was the brilliant work of the men guarding the Newberry flanks and terminals—Furen, Koch, Hood, Gibbons and Hewey. They smeared virtually every end run and off tackle play attempted by the Blue Stockings.

The Li'l That Was!

PAGE FOUR — THE BLUE STOCKING — SATURDAY, NOVEMBER 10, 1934

PRESBYTERIAN WINS ANNUAL GAME WITH NEWBERRY, 12-0

Passing By Perrin, Line Plunging By Bolick, and Brilliant Punt Returns By Higbe Feature Contest In Newberry Friday. Airtight Defense of Blue Hose Line Also Noteworthy. Beck & Co. Fail To Do Appreciable Damage In Any Part of Game.

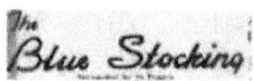

The Presbyterian college Blue Stockings inundated the fighting Newberry Indians at the latter's annual homecoming game last Friday and thereby gained sweet revenge on the Lutherans for breaking up a similar gathering on Presbyterian soil last year. A deadly passing attack, combined with short gains through the line when needed, spelled ruin for the red-jerseyed Indians, who went down under a 12-0 score.

Robbie Higbe, ael-hipped Presbyterian halfback, was the most spectacular player of the game. Time and again he received punts and brought them back almost as far as they were kicked. Ed Beck, Newberry backfield ace who reaped destruction last year in the Indians' 13 to 7 victory, was completely bottled up, however. Hardly a time did he pass the line of scrimmage for more than a yard or two, and when he did P. C.'s great defensive backs nailed him before he could get his agile legs into high gear.

With Higbe putting the ball in position for scoring drives by his long punt returns, the Blue Stockings brought into play its fine aerial attack, thus reminding rabid P. C. fans of the days of Jimmie Stamps and Charlie Wilson. With Pug Perrin flipping the forwards and a trio of able men hauling them down out of the ozone, P. C. was able to put the punch in her goal line thrusts. The Presbyterians connected with eight out of its total of fourteen aerials tried, an impressive percentage in view of the large number of attempts.

Another feature of the game was the wonderful defensive play of Harry Bolick, the burly fullback of the Blue Hose. Blocking, not usually emphasized as one of his strong points, marked him as one of the prime reasons for P. C.'s superiority over Newberry in running plays. His tackling, also, was more vicious than ever. Ever on the alert on pass defense, he was even more watchful during this engagement, as he intercepted three Indian heaves. Then, too, his line-driving was the only way in which P. C. could gain consistently through the line.

The Passing of Pug Perrin, the Union blond tornado, was especially noteworthy. His accuracy at putting just the right heat on the heaves was almost uncanny.

Another P. C. backfield man who covered himself with glory was Lee Quarterman. In blocking and defensive work he was unsurpassed on the field, while during the few times he carried the ball, he made good gains, and was credited with scoring both touchdowns.

The entire P. C. line played about the steadiest game they have exhibited this season. Led by Davis, Horne and Forehand, the forward wall hurled back every attempt of the speedy Indian backs to get past the scrimmage line.

Furen, Newberry end, was the best on defense for his team, in view of his fine work in tackling and breaking up interference. Koch, Hood, Gibbons and Hewey also helped keep P. C.'s end runs and off-tackle slants from doing much damage.

The first quarter found the two teams engaged in a punting duel, with Newberry on the defensive on account of P. C.'s superiority in offensive play. A drive to the 12-yard line was stopped early in the second period, but a few minutes later Higbe made a long punt return to midfield, where on the following play Forehand snatched a pass out of the air for a 13-yard gain.

The next play was one of the prettiest of its kind ever pulled by the Presbyterians. Perrin threw a short pass to Forehand, then ran over toward the sideline. While he was still in the air from the leap the receiver flipped it straight back to Perrin, who lifted his knees high and traversed 27 yards of Lutheran soil before he was run out of bounds. Another pass to Quarterman went to the six-yard stripe. After a couple of line plays Perrin tried his throwing arm again, and Quarterman caught the pigskin with ease, to put the Blue Stockings six points ahead.

The third quarter saw P. C. putting the Indians on the defensive again, and as the period ended Higbe ran a punt to the 11-yard line of the enemy territory. After Bolick made a first down on the one-yard line, Quarterman plunged over for the touchdown. During the remainder of the final quarter Newberry tried desperately to tally, mostly through the forward pass method. Three were completed for good gains, but many more fell incomplete, as the Lutherans failed in their attempt to stage a comeback in the closing minutes.

Presbyterian chalked up 11 first downs to five for the Indians. P. C.'s forward passes were successful eight out of fourteen times, while the Indians made only three of theirs good, out of 18 attempted.

The lineups:

Pos.	Presbyterian	Newberry
LE	Yearout	Koch
LT	Davis	Gibbons
LG	Horne	Morgan
C	Plowden	Johnson
RG	Boggs	Webb
RT	Collings	Hewey
RE	Waldrep	Furen
QB	Wilbanks	Keisler
LH	Higbe	Thomason
RH	Quarterman	Beck
FB	Bolick	Weidman

Score by periods:
Presbyterian .... 0 6 0 6—12
Newberry .... 0 0 0 0— 0

Officials: Referee, Dixon Foster (Hampden-Sidney); umpire, Otis Carter (Furman); headlinesman, Carter Newman (Clemson).

Substitutions: Presbyterian — Perrin, Holliday, Millsap, Abbott, Hutchinson, Shoemaker, Tisdale.

Newberry — Miller, Hood, Kirkland, Ingram.

PRESBYTERIAN COLLEGE, CLINTON, S. C., OCTOBER 14, 1935

The Blue Stocking

BLUE HOSE WIN THRILLING GAME

Thompson and Wilbanks Star As Calvinists Down Traditional Rivals Under Floodlights.

Walter Johnson's twentieth Presbyterian college football team scored 20 points on their Homecoming night to defeat the plucky Newberry team, who marked up 6 points themselves.

The game was the big event of a huge Homecoming day celebration and came off before a crowd estimated at 4,000. Played under the new 72,000-watt lighting system, the contest was a fitting climax to Johnson's twenty years of coaching at P. C.

The main feature of the game was the running attack shown by both teams. The Presbyterian gridiron men at last started their offense to clicking and they made many a gain thru the Indian line and also around ends. The Lutherans, on the other hand, also made many short gains from scrimmage. The P. C. touchdowns came as a result of drives down the field, while the Indians scored on an intercepted pass, with a run of 49 yards by Kirkland.

During the half Hank Wilson directed ceremonies in commemoration of Coach Johnson's twentieth year at P. C. over the amplifier which also carried play by play announcements as the game progressed.

William P. Jacobs, acting president of P. C., made a speech in praise of Johnson's past record at the college and his training of young men in high ideals and sportsmanship. He read messages of congratulation from various dignitaries from all over the state.

Several valuable gifts were presented to Johnson by various groups. A. W. Brice, of the 1915 team, the first coached by Johnson, made a presentation in behalf of the team, and James McClary placed a gift in his hands from the student body. The town of Clinton, thru Mayor Silas Bailey, and Captain Shorty Horne, for the football team, also presented gifts.

After the ceremonies a group of men from the R. O. T. C. unit staged a thrilling sham battle. The lights were turned off and the effect was quite colorful as the riflemen and machine gunners fired blanks at each other. Fireworks lit up the field from time to time during the battle.

The Blue Stockings began showing their stuff early in the game. Opening up with their passing and running attack, they started on the 46-yard line of the Indians and clicked off several gains to cross the Newberry goal finally on a 13-yard run by Bill Thompson. A pass of 13 yards, Jacobs to Higbe, was a factor in gaining the touchdown. During this march Frank Holliday, P. C. defensive back and pigskin thrower, was hurt and carried off the field.

The next period the Presbyterians displayed consistent superiority over the Indians, and after a few minutes Higbe's nice punt return put the ball on the Lutherans' 35-yard marker. With a first down in the offing, the P. C. team tried a fake reverse, with Thompson carrying the ball thru the line. Straight down the middle of the field he went, with red-shirted tacklers sprawling after him. Finally, as three of them seemingly had him hemmed in at the 10-yard line, he cut to the right and crossed the goal line untouched.

Another touch of color was added in the third period as Kirkland, Newberry back, leaped high in the air, snatched a P. C. pass, and raced down the field like an antelope for a touchdown after a 49-yard run. The try for point was wide.

During the final period Robbie Higbe made a beautiful punt return of about 40 yards, carrying the ball to the Indians' 21-yard marker. Thompson a little later passed to Jacobs, who fumbled, and Forehand recovered on the opponents' 3-yard line. Bill Thompson, with a nice hole opened for him, went over thru tackle.

During the latter part of the second period Newberry made a magnificent

P. C. 20; Newberry 6

(Continued from page one)
comeback in an attempt to score. A 46-yard march carried them to the 35-yard P. C. line, but here their attack broke down. After their score in the third period they set in to outplay the Blue Stockings for that quarter and marched to the 17-yard line. A long pass intended for Furen was deflected from the latter's hands by Wilbanks sufficiently to make him drop it.

The P. C. team showed much more power and drive than it has exhibited so far this season. With Thompson and Higbe starring on offense for the Presbyterians, the Blue Stockings registered good yardage. The P. C. defense, however, was weak in midfield, but held well enough in front of the goal. J. B. Jacobs and Wilbanks did some spectacular punting. Hutchinson, in his usual position of roving center, made some great tackles. So also did Plowden and Bradley. These two men turned in about their best performance.

The Newberry offense was good at times, but did not hold up as far as the goal line. Ed Beck and McCormish did some nifty running thru the line. Undoubtedly the best man in the Lutheran forward wall was Furen, the great end. Gibbon also played well at tackle. The Newberry team made two of the greatest goal line stands seen here in many a day as they twice held the Blue Hose for downs near the goal, once on the 1-yard line.

The line-ups:

P. C.	Newberry
LE—Bradley	Furen
LT—Collings	Gibbon
LG—Correll	Spezza
C—Hutchinson	Johnson
RG—Plowden	Webb
RT—Prather	Miller
RE—Forehand	Koch
QB—Wilbanks	Keisler
LH—Boland	McCormish
RH—Weldon	Beck
FB—Holliday	Kirkland

P. C. substitutes: Higbe, Jacobs, Thompson, Freeman, Millsap, Hipp, Abbott, Bird, Shoemarker, Beeman, McSween.

PRESBYTERIAN COLLEGE, CLINTON, S. C., OCTOBER 26, 1936

INDIANS UNABLE TO STOP BLUE HOSE VICTORY MARCH

Thompson, Jacobs and Moore Chalk Up Scores As Hose Hit Victory Stride.

PASSING ATTACK CLICKS IN SPOILING HOMECOMING

Presbyterian's crippled Blue Stockings limped through a decisive 27 to 0 victory over Newberry Friday afternoon in a colorful Indian homecoming spectacle that marked the Calvinists' second "Little Four" win of the season.

The P. C. line functioned in a smooth and potent manner and the backs shone as they executed a dazzling attack of ground and aerial warfare.

Thompson, Jacobs, Moore

Bill Thompson slipped through for a pair of touchdowns to take offensive honors, with Jacobs and Moore contributing the other two. Moore gave a powerful exhibition of blocking, running, and defensive work, and Jacobs got off some beautiful punts and passes.

The Hose touchdowns came after concentrated drives in the second and fourth quarters. Thompson, in a few runs, carried the ball over for the initial score from Newberry's 30-yard line. Weldon kicked the extra point.

Weldon was instrumental in maneuvering the pigskin in position for the second score. Moore crashed through for the touchdown and Weldon again kicked the extra point. In the final quarter, Thompson and Jacobs broke loose for long touchdown runs that swelled the total to 27. After Jacobs' score, Weldon kicked for his third placement of the game.

Empty Tepees

The Indians made two major threats, neither of which materialized. Once they advanced to Presbyterian's 10-yard line, and later in the contest to the 12, before the attack was checked. But the men from Clinton clearly outclassed their opponents in every department, rolling up 14 first downs to Newberry's eight, passing, punting, running, tackling and blocking exceptionally well.

The Blue Stockings entered the fray deprived of full strength. Dennard, Evans, Waldrep, Correll, Beeman, Bird, Ritch, and others were still suffering from injuries received in the Citadel encounter.

The Blue Stocking

PRESBYTERIAN COLLEGE, CLINTON, S. C., OCTOBER 18, 1937

NEWBERRY WINS 13-0

By Jake Penland

A superior set of backs, good punting and P. C. miscues spelled a 13-0 victory for Newberry Friday evening in a well-attended game at Johnson field, featured in Presbyterian's homecoming day program.

Aerial play filled the air as both outfits maneuvered desperately for their first scores of the season. Defensive strength kept the ball away from scoring territory in the first period. In the second, Newberry advanced to the P. C. 20 and McIntosh flipped a touchdown pass to Masters. In the third, Cooley intercepted one of P. C.'s frequent heaves and traveled 70 yards for the second and last score.

The Hosemen used the entire second half in a desperate, and oftentimes careless, attempt to score via the aerial route. Some of Horne's heaves hit their mark, but more often fell incomplete or were intercepted by an alert Indian secondary.

P. C. made its closest approach to a touchdown midway in the third quarter. Be Moore, an up-and-coming flankman, pulled down four of Horne's tosses in successive attempts to register three first downs. With the oval on Newberry's 12, Horne shot a short pass to Isom for a six-yard gain. Horne passed over the goal on the next play but no Hoseman was waiting and the threat ended. Horne inaugurated another air attack late in the period and the Presbyterians advanced to the Indian 30 before an interception gave Newberry possession of the ball.

Presbyterian made nine first downs to three for the Lutherans.

The line-ups:

	Newberry	Presbyterian
LE	Masters	Moore
LT	Matasy	Evans
LG	Hanna	Todd
C	Burnett	Henderson
RG	Harden	Strain
RT	DeBruhl	Boswell
RE	Harmon	Atkinson
QB	McIntosh	Isom
LH	Cromer	Reynolds
RH	Cooley	Hollis
FB	Haymon	Horne

Officials: Carter, referee; Foster, umpire; Reames, head linesman.

Score by periods:
Newberry .... 0 7 6 0—13
Presbyterian .... 0 0 0 0— 0

The Li'l That Was!

Monday, October 17, 1938 — THE BLUE STOCKING

Blue Hose Scalp Indians 7-6

VICTORY SNATCHED FROM DEFEAT AT CLOSE OF HARD FOUGHT GAME

Brilliant Run By Dennard and Kick By J. C. Coleman Save Rend of Blue Stockings By Hard-Fighting Newberrians.

On the flying feet of Jimmy Dennard and the educated toe of J. C. Coleman went victory for the Blue Stockings of Presbyterian college over a stubborn Newberry eleven Friday night on Johnson field. The score was 7 to 6.

Dennard, in another of his game-winning star roles, caught a Newberry punt on his own 35-yard line, cut to his left, squirmed, twisted, and sped his way 65 yards in a sensational touchdown jaunt. With Lykes Henderson on the sidelines with an injury sustained earlier in the game, the duties of attempting the extra point that meant victory or a tie went to Sophomore J. C. Coleman. He calmly took his position and, with Dennard holding the ball, split the uprights for the deciding point of the game.

Newberry presented a powerful running attack with Colangelo, a sophomore with plenty of drive, and Cooley leading the way. It was this attack which kept the Hosemen deep in their territory for the majority of the first quarter. The boys in Blue came to life in the second quarter and put the Indians on the defensive with a sharp passing attack mixed with some fancy running plays. Both teams threatened during the first half but neither had that scoring punch. The half ended with P. C. in possession of the ball deep in Newberry lands.

June Moore intercepted a pass in midfield and ran it to the Newberry 20-yard line before he was stopped. This threat bogged down and Newberry kicked out of danger. An attempted punt by Thompson was fumbled and Newberry took the ball in P. C. territory. On the first play of the final period Colangelo took the ball on a spinner and circled his own right end for eleven yards and the initial score of the game. Cooley tried for the extra point but his attempt was blocked by Kee. A few plays later the stage was set for Dennard and Coleman and they came through with flying colors. The 7 to 6 score against them did not seem to bother the Indians for they launched a threat that was stopped by a bad pass from center which went over Cooley's head and was recovered by P. C. Newberry took to the air in a vain attempt to score but the alert Blue Hose backs broke up the aerials and kept possession of the ball until near the final whistle which sounded with Newberry holding the sphere about midfield. Final score: P. C. 7, Newberry 6.

Both line-ups were studded with stars. In the Newberry backfield the work of Colangelo and Cooley was outstanding. Matasey, Masters and Johnson were stalwarts in a fast-charging. For the Blue Hose, it was Dennard, with a superb performance, the Moore brothers, who continued their bids for all-state honors with sterling performances, Large Evans, who broke up many a Newberry play, Fleischman, and Coleman, who sent that point over the bar. Meisky was a defensive power and handled the signal calling well.

The Hosemen have won two of their "Little Four" games and need only a win over Wofford to cop the honors of the small schools. They journey to Danville, Kentucky, this week-end to play the Centre college "Praying Colonels."

Monday, October 16, 1939 — THE BLUE STOCKING — PAGE THREE

  # SPORTS
FRED ALLEN, Editor THOMAS JACOBS, Asst.

Blue Hose Humble Indians, 6-0

Meisky And Moore Sparkle In Win

The Presbyterian college powerhouse met opposition a little stiffer than it expected last Friday night on Johnson field, but the see-saw battle did show that the Blue Hose outclassed the Indians of Newberry both in offense and defense, as the P. C. 6, Newberry 0 score indicates.

P. C. kicked off to Newberry, who met a P. C. stonewall defense. Newberry punted and P. C. took charge of the pigskin for a while, until the heavy Newberry line held them closely. Then Meisky put his toe to work. After about ten minutes of punt exchanges and vain thrusts at the opposing lines, P. C. pushed the ball down into Indian territory. Then Dick Meisky cannon-balled an aerial to Jane Moore from the Newberry 45. Moore hauled the oval down on the 35, then dodged, twisted, jumped and plowed past about six Newberry would-be tacklers and halted only after he had passed over the last white marker. There he applied brakes, put the ball down and watched the only chalk mark of the game go up by Presbyterian. Coleman's attempt at conversion was a little wide. The remainder of the first quarter was played in midfield.

In the second quarter Newberry took advantage of several breaks and these, combined with several fairly successful sneak plays, enabled the Indians to get within scoring distance
(Continued on page four)

BLUE HOSE HUMBLE INDIANS, 6 TO 0
(Continued from page one)
of the Blue Hose goal line. However, the Hosemen dug in and held them almost motionless. P. C. held the upper hand for most of the second quarter until Newberry again battled down to the "goal line ahoy" zone, and again the Calvinists began to take the situation in hand, as the first half ended.

Newberry received to open the second half. Colangelo took the ball on his own 10 and raced to the 40 where he was driven out of bounds by Ben Moye, hefty P. C. tackle. Again the old punting duel got under way, with Colangelo doing the toe work for Newberry and Sutton and Meisky punting the pigskin for the Presbyterians.

Sutton carried the kicking burden for P. C. during the third quarter, while Meisky was out of the game with a temporarily painful injury. Sutton was not quite as successful with his booting as were Meisky and Colangelo.

Newberry's swift passing attack and sneak plays broke into the limelight in the third quarter; that is, when they could get their mitts on the old apple. The defensive work of Kee, Evans, Moye, Sadler, Coleman, the Milam twins, Moore and Meisky, however, put a pretty good kink into the Newberry offensive. Colangelo, Coppola, and DeBruhl did the "starlight" work for the Indians.

Rock Mitchell, reserve P. C. halfback, made himself known as a driving back in the game with his powerful line smashes.

Statistics On Game
	P. C.	N'berry
Yds. gained rushing	100	90
Yardage lost	23	20
Punting average	40	42
Punt return av.	7	8
First downs	6	4
Attempted passes	11	19
Passes completed	3	5
Passes intercepted by	3	2
Yds. gained passing	55	60
Penalties against	1	9
Total yds. penalties	5	75
Fumbles by	4	2
Fumbles recov. by	1	2
Own fumbles recov.	2	1

Scoring by periods:
P. C. .... 6 0 0 0—6
Newberry ... 0 0 0 0—0
Scoring touchdown: Moore (P.C.)

CASINO THEATRE
MONDAY AND TUESDAY,
October 16 and 17
"Four Feathers"

WEDNESDAY, THURSDAY,
October 18 and 19
"Boy Friend"
"The Jones Family In Hollywood"

FRIDAY AND SATURDAY,
October 20 and 21
"Bachelor Mother"

Broadway Theatre
MONDAY AND TUESDAY,
October 16 and 17
"Way Down South"

WEDNESDAY, THURSDAY,
October 18 and 19
"Bad Lands"
"Rose Marie"

FRIDAY AND SATURDAY,
October 20 and 21
"Mountain Rhythm"

MILLING GROCERY CO.
Phone 191
WE'RE STILL FOR P. C.

The Li'l That Was!

The Newberry Observer
AND HERALD & NEWS
"Just Like A Letter From Home"

NEWBERRY, S. C., TUESDAY, OCTOBER 17, 1939 — Newberry Observer Established 1888

Newberry, S. C., Tuesday, October 17, 1939

Nazi Armies Mass for Western Blitzkrieg

Convinced his peace offensive has failed, Hitler is reported to have massed 300,000 to 500,000 German troops at each of four strategic points for a lightning attack on France. Arrows indicate expected lines of attack. The first field army headquarters is at Cologne (A); the second at Coblenz (B); the third at Bingen (C), where it is believed Hitler and Goering will take command; and the fourth at Stuttgart (D). Cross-hatched area is that seized by the Allies to date. Stippled portion indicates area into which Germany is pouring reinforcements from the Eastern front.

P. C. Passes To 6-0 Victory Over Newberry Indians

Forward Pass in First Quarter Results in Only Score; Newberry Homecoming with Erskine Sat. Night

Presbyterian College's Blue Stockings broke the Maginot line defense of the Newberry College Indians for a brief instant Friday night at Clinton and dropped the Redmen from the list of the state's undefeated teams by the score of 6 to 0.

A forward pass, Meisky to Moore, early in the first period was completed and Moore displayed a beautiful bit of shifty running to score the only tally of the game. The defeat was the first of the season for the Lavalmen, the first three games of the season resulting in scoreless deadlocks.

Both teams lived up to the expectations of their followers in the terrific battle. Numerous penalties played havoc with the scoring opportunities of the Indian offense which showed up better than at any time during the present season.

Coach Lava used every trick in his house of magic to score to no avail as the offense bogged down near pay dirt.

The battered and bruised Indian squad is now being prepared for the homecoming encounter here Saturday night, October 21, with the Erskine Seceders.

Elaborate plans are being made to set the stage for the largest crowd of the home season expected Saturday night. The squad will take the field knowing that this is the last game of the Little Four and will be out for their first victory.

Barbecue Chicken Supper
Friday Night, Oct. 20
MASONIC HALL
Prosperity, S. C.
6:00 P. M.
Price 35c
Benefit: Missionary Society
Wightman Methodist Church

ATHLETES FOOT REMEDY
Guaranteed
50c
Central Drug Store
NEWBERRY, S. C.

The Blue Stocking

Volume XXII   Clinton, S. C., October 18, 1940   Number 5

Friday, October 18, 1940   THE BLUE STOCKING

P. C. Throw Backfires

Indians Win Thrilling Game; Church Scores For Presbyterian

Interception of a daring Blue Stocking pass thrown from behind his own goal by Dick Meisky gave Newberry college a tie-breaking touchdown in the third quarter Friday night and changed the complexion of a wide open game from Presbyterian Blue to Indian Red.

Coppola, alert Newberry center, grabbed the ball intended for halfback Frank Sutton and sprinted the 12 yards to paydirt. Newberry won, 20 to 7.

Unleashing a potent passing attack in the first quarter, the Johnson-men came from behind to tie the score on Meisky's toss to Verne Church, blocking back, who charged 22 yards behind good down-field blocking. Ciolangelo, triple threater, had broken the ice for the Indians with a short touchdown pass to fullback Lewis 10 plays before.

A threat by each team in the second quarter failed to materialize. In the third quarter came Coppola's heartbreaking interception. Newberry scored once more near the end of the game when Power, a zip-snorting halfback, went over from the seven-yard line.

Lloyd Evans, junior end, and Frank Sutton, senior back, were outstanding for the Garnet and Blue Friday. The whole team appeared to have new spirit and performed brilliantly at times.

Watch Him Go!

FRANK SUTTON... will kick, run and pass for the Blue Stockings today.

Statistics

	PC	N'by
first downs	7	14
ball lost on downs	1	1
fumbles	3	1
own recovered	1	1
no. plays run	31	47
net yds. rushing	31	162
average per run	1.6	3.0
number passes attempted	10	11
number lost by interception	2	0
number completed	5	8
net yds. passing	89	113
av. yds. per pass	8.9	10.6
no. kick offs	2	3
av. yards per kick off	45	50
number kick offs returned	2	2
av. yards per kick off return	16	16
number punts	4	7
av. yds. per punt	42	38
no. punts returned	6	3
av. punt return	6	11
no. penalties	2	10
total yds. penalties	20	130
grand total— ball advanced	418	671

Score by periods:
Presbyterian   7 0 0 0 — 7
Newberry   7 0 7 6 — 20

Scoring:
Presbyterian — touchdown, Church; point after touchdown, Sutton (placement).
Newberry — touchdowns, Lewis, Coppola, Power; points after touchdown, Collangelo (2) (placements).

The Li'l That Was!

The Newberry Observer
AND HERALD & NEWS
"Just Like A Letter From Home"

TWELVE PAGES TODAY — NEWBERRY, S. C., FRIDAY, OCTOBER 11, 1940 — NEWBERRY OBSERVER ESTABLISHED 1865

Newberry Indians To Meet P. C. Here Fri.

Annual Classic to Be Played in Local Stadium—Redmen in Good Shape.

For the first time in five years the P. C. aggregation will journey to Newberry Friday night for the annual football battle between the two schools.

The Newberry-P. C. game has always been one of the most heated battles in the state. Both colleges are friendly rivals but rivals who fight to the finish for a victory. The game will begin at 8:00 on Friday night on the municipal field.

This year the competition should be very keen. Newberry has won one game, tied one, and lost one; while P. C., although losing its first three games, boasts one of its best teams in many a year. The Blue Hose have a heavy line and an elusive backfield, but the Indians will meet them with a team that has proven both its defensive power and its offensive swiftness.

Both Lewis and Corley, who were previously on the injured list will be in prime shape for the coming game and ready for action. Nick Deprim, who was slightly injured at V. M. I. will be in uniform and ready to hold his position in the line.

The defense, object of so much praise after the V. M. I. game will present a hard and experienced front for the P. C. backs to break through. The offense has been strengthened and will bear much watching Friday night.

For P. C. Miesky will be the sparkplug of the offense. However, the Blue Hose have lost several first string men due to injuries and will not be in tip top shape.

Tickets are on sale at the Central Drug Store and the advance sales indicate a sell-out. Reserve seat tickets are $1.05. All seats are reserved.

Newberry Defeats P. C., 20 To 7

Indians Go On Warpath to Take First State Game of Season

The Newberry College Indians went on the warpath to defeat the Presbyterian Blue Hose 20 to 7 Friday night in a game that kept the 4000 spectators on the edge of their seats throughout the game.

Newberry scored the first touchdown early in the first quarter but P. C. came back to tie things up before the quarter ended. The game remained tied up until the third quarter when Newberry again scored and the Indians made their third tally in the final period.

The Lavalmen had a beautiful running and passing attack, completing seven of ten tosses and racking up 14 first downs to the visitors 7.

Naval Reserve on the Job

After reporting for duty, naval reservists of the ninth naval district don their new uniforms and carry their duffle bags aboard the *Paducah* anchored off Chicago. Thousands of naval reservists throughout the country were ready to report for service.

The Blue Stocking

Distinguished For Its Progress

Volume XXIII — Presbyterian College, October 24, 1941 — Number 6

Desperate Drive Gives Hose Win

Completing three passes in rapid succession, the Blue Stockings traveled 90 yards in the final minutes of play to snatch a hard-fought game from the fire and win over an inspired Newberry team, 13-7, here last Friday night.

Jack Adams, sophomore end, grabbed Hank Caver's pass from eager Indian hands to fall safely and victoriously in the end zone on the last play of the game.

Newberry seemed assured of 7-6 triumph when, with only two minutes remaining in the game, PC was shadowing its own goal line on the six-yard stripe. It was only then that the Indians' pass defenses relaxed their vigilance, and it was then that the Hosemen struck.

After Rock Mitchell's two first downs had run the ball up to the PC 30-yard line, "Slingshot Rock" took to the air and twice connected with end Otis Weaver to place the ball on Newberry's four-yard line. Following a time out penalty, which put the ball back to the nine, Caver completed the touchdown pass to Adams. Evans converted, and there remained only time for the kick-off.

For three quarters and the better part of the fourth Newberry completely muffled the dangerous Hose aerial attack, allowing only one completion up to that time.

Presbyterian opened the scoring two minutes after the start of the second half. Morgan Randel's bad quick-kick put the ball on the Tribe's 26-yard line, and from this point Mitchell streaked around right end to score standing up. Evans' try for extra point was wide.

Late in the third period the Indians recovered a fumble in Hose territory and began their drive. Following the quarter rest period, Randel ran and passed to the Blue Stocking one-yard stripe, from where he ploughed over to knot the score. The point gave Newberry the advantage, 7-6.

Another Indian drive in the fourth was finally halted on the PC three-yard marker. End Lloyd Evans came out of nowhere to stop Randel's goal-bound run.

Herb Rollins' kick sent the Indians back into their own territory following the forced halt, and Randel's return punt went out on the PC six. From there, the Blue Stockings staged their last-minute victory spurt.

Rock Mitchell continued to spark the Hose backfield, with Rollins kicking well and Ted Dunne making good his share. Bud Collier, center, and Verne Church, moving in from his fullback post, backed up the line in a vicious manner. Ben Moye and Evans were standouts in the line.

Morgan Randel and Pat Ingram, both in the backfield, were Newberry stars.

Defensive Ace

BEN MOYE .. who smears 'em

	N'berry	PC
First downs	9	9
Yds. gained rushing	91	80
Passes attempted	2	18
Passes completed	2	4
Yds. gained passing	22	82
Passes intercepted	0	6
Number of punts	8	6
Punt average	30	37
Av. runback punts	4	8
Fumbles	7	5
Opp. fumbles recov.	3	3
Yds. lost by penalties	50	45

The Li'l That Was!

The Newberry Observer
AND HERALD & NEWS
"Just Like A Letter From Home"

TWELVE PAGES TODAY — NEWBERRY, S. C., FRIDAY, OCTOBER 17, 1941 — NEWBERRY OBSERVER ESTABLISHED 1865

Indians To Meet P C. Friday In Game At Clinton

Indians Set to Take Game Against Old Rivals

The Newberry Indians journey to Clinton Friday night where they intend to take the annual classic with their old rivals, P. C. The Indians have been hard at work all this week and expect to be at their best this week-end.

Giving added spice to the game this Friday is the long-standing rivalry between Presbyterian and Newberry. As far back as most followers of the game can remember these two teams have been at each other's throats, and in their case all pre-game dope is to be thrown to the four winds. The fact that the Indians have not had such an impressive season thus far and that the Calvinists are favored to win goes for little. Past records of these tilts are studded with upsets and never have final scores been known to lean too heavily in either direction.

Leading the Blue Hose into the conflict as their chief offensive threat will be Rock Mitchell, a diminutive senior back, who is rapidly placing himself up among the best in the state with his aerial wizardry and slippery-hipped broken-field running. In every game this season his efforts have been stand-out, his running and passing rated tops. And he'll give those bigger boys a push when honors are to be had at the close of the season.

But until the opening whistle blows, the Blue Stockings are in for some tough preparation.

Game time is set for 8 p. m. Friday, October 17.

Presbyterian's crack Reserve Officers' Training corps drill platoon will perform between halves.

Nazis' Official War Map

According to the official German caption with this radiophoto from Berlin, the map shows the Nazi battleline on the eastern front. As would be expected, at many points it shows the Germans farther advanced than is admitted by Moscow, which claims the Nazi tide has been slowed.

Priced with real moderation
Big, roomy, beautiful new 1942
STUDEBAKER CHAMPION
TOP QUALITY CAR OF LOWEST PRICE FIELD
PRICES BEGIN AT $810

- A marvel of handling ease and restful riding!
- Finest materials and craftsmanship!
- Remarkable gas and oil mileage!

Many special Studebaker features at no extra cost

MOWER MOTOR CO.
NEWBERRY, S. C.

The Blue Stocking

Distinguished For Its Progress

Volume XXIV   Presbyterian College, October 23, 1942   Number 4

Indian Scalp Dangles in PC Camp
Rollins Paces Team to Late 14-7 Win

Guards

GEORGE BRYAN

Re-acting a situation similar to that of last year, the Blue Stockings pushed over a touchdown in the closing minutes of play to break a 7-7 deadlock and defeat Newberry college, 14 to 7, in a football game played down in the Indians' hometown Friday night, October 9.

This year it was Herbert Rollins who set up the winning marker, and Droopy Atwell who lugged the ball over the final stripe. With the score tied and only minutes left to play, Rollins took a short pass on PC's own 40-yard line and then took off through a field of Newberry tacklers; he carried 58 hectic, hard yards before he was brought down on the Indian 2-yard line. From this point Atwell scored on a line plunge.

Newberry opened the scoring for the night in the initial quarter of the game. Through a series of tricky line plays, the Indians worked the ball deep into Hose territory. When the PC line stiffened on the 20-yard line, Redskin fullback Bill Quinn flipped a long pass to an end waiting in the end zone. The point after touchdown was good.

The Blue Stockings came back passing in the second quarter and with results that could not be denied. Rollins and Roddy Martin combined to do the ball-eyeing and connected receivers all the way down the field. Rollins shot an aerial to Weaver good for 40 yards to the Newberry 10, and then Martin followed suit with another to Jack Adams, who made a diving catch in the end zone to score. Ernest Jacobs' placement was good and tied the game at 7-all.

From this point until Presbyterian's final burst in the fourth quarter, the game swayed back and forth with several threats passing out just short of pay dirt.

It was an exciting game throughout and kept the spectators well on the edge of their seats.

Newberry presented a good team, stubborn on defense and with no mean ability on the offensive side. Particularly outstanding for the Indians were Quinn, Yancey and Waldrep.

As for the Blue Stockings, Herbert Rollins continued to be the shining light. He mixed good passing and running with an unusual display of punting ability. His kicks boomed for over a 40-yard average. Roddy Martin and Bill Culp, too, stood out in backfield play. Pacing the forward wall throughout the night were both ends, Jack Adams and Otis Weaver, and center Bud Collier.

ROSE'S
5c, 10c & 25c Store
Clinton, S. C.

ROYAL CLEANERS, Inc.
"Beautiful Dry Cleaning"
Phone 77
— o —
Bobby Schwanebeck
Tommy Hollis
Campus Representatives

The Li'l 🎩 That Was!

The Newberry Observer
AND HERALD & NEWS
"Just Like A Letter From Home"

SIX PAGES TODAY   NEWBERRY, S. C., TUESDAY, OCTOBER 17, 1944   NEWBERRY OBSERVER ESTABLISHED 1883

Indians, P.C. Meet Friday

Newberry's offensive skill may be the margin between two otherwise evenly matched teams when the Indians meet the Presbyterian College team in Clinton on Friday night.

This season both teams have faced some powerful foes and have come out on the short end of some big scores. The Hosemen lost to Clemson 34-0, and to Georgia 67-0. The Indians fell before the Carolina Gamecocks 48-0, and before Catawba College 34-14.

The struggle starts at 8 o'clock in Presbyterian College's Bailey Memorial stadium in Clinton, and will be the Hosemen's only game this season on their home ground.

Newberry Is Downed By P. C.

Presbyterian's Blue Stockings, capitalizing on two Newberry fumbles and driving 78 yards for a fourth period touchdown, defeated the Indians, 20 to 0, last Friday night in Clinton.

The Blue Stockings scored first, early in the first quarter right after Baker recovered Johnson's fumble on the Newberry 38. In three plays P. C. went over, with Morgan scoring from the ten-yard line. The drive was featured by a 25-yard run by Raines.

Another Newberry fumble on their own 36, this time by Mayo, was recovered by Kleckley for Presbyterian, in the second quarter.

Raines fired a pass to Kleckley for 20 yards, then came back with another aerial, this time to Dusenbury for eight. Ivey then rammed the line for five and Raines plunged over for the touchdown from the five. Gilliland's placement was good, making the score 13-0.

Newberry came storming back in the same period, driving 70 yards with a lateral from Robinson to Mayo, scoring from the nine-yard line. Robinson and Mayo took 12 plays to push the ball to the nine. The conversion attempt went wild.

Neither team scored in the third quarter, but midway in the fourth period the Blue Stockings unleashed a drive powered by Raines that carried from their own 22 across the Newberry goal.

Raines passed 15 to Dusenbury and then in three plays carried the ball to the Newberry 22. Raines again connected with Dusenbury with a pass, this time to the Newberry five. The Indians braced for a moment, holding Raines to four yards, but Ivey rammed the line for the remaining yard and touchdown.

Tonight's victory was the first of the season for P. C.

It was the last game of the season for a number of V-12 players on the Newberry team. A new group of V-12 trainees are expected to join the Newberry squad November 1.

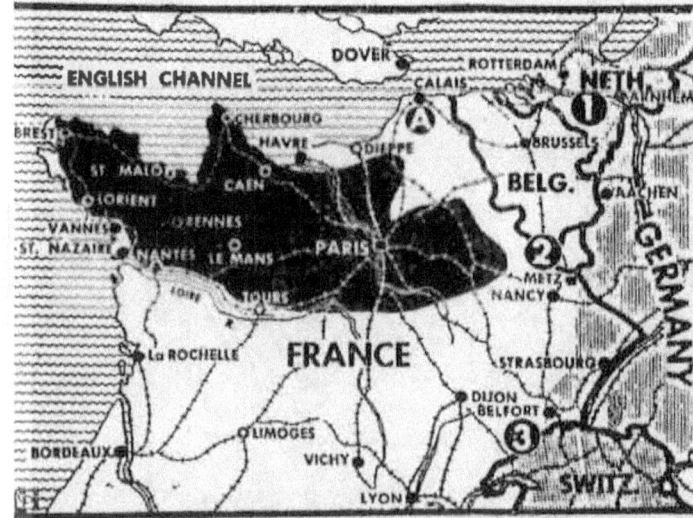

JUST BEFORE Sept. 1 the Allies had expanded their gains from the first Cherbourg beachhead to an area approximately outlined by the black section of the above map. And now after the fall of Brest comes the capture of Calais (A)—nearest of all Continental ports to England, thus giving the Allies all French ports on the north coast save St. Nazaire, La Rochelle, Lorient and Dunkerque. The latter is expected to fall at any moment. Since Sept. 1, also, the Allies have carried their push through the white areas to the current key drives which are (1) toward Arnhem and through Aachen and (2) in the Metz and Nancy areas (3) the big Belfort gap campaign. Shaded area shows battle Axis lines.   (International)

The Newberry Observer
AND HERALD & NEWS
"Just Like A Letter From Home"

EIGHT PAGES TODAY — NEWBERRY, S. C., TUESDAY, DECEMBER 4, 1945 — NEWBERRY OBSERVER ESTABLISHED 1883

The Li'l That Was!

Newberry Indians Meet Presbyterian In Game Friday

Game At 2:30 P. M.

The Newberry Indians will meet their traditional rivals, P. C., in a game of football Friday afternoon at 2:30 p. m. in the local municipal stadium. The game had originally been scheduled for 2:30 p. m., but Coach Laval considered playing a night game, to which the Presbyterians would not agree.

The Indians have had an excellent season, losing only one game, that against Fort Bragg last Thanksgiving Day.

The Newberry-P. C. Game should be one of the state's best as these rivals always put up a bitter scrap against each other than any other teams they meet.

Newberrians are urged to come out Friday and boost the Indians on to another victory.

Newberry Indians Take Final Game

Defeat P. C. Here Friday

Lose Only One Game In Season

Newberry College closed its season with a 19-13 victory over Presbyterian College of Clinton last Friday afternoon.

Newberry, under veteran coach Billy Laval, thus finished the season with a splendid record.

Presbyterian opened with a rush in Friday afternoon's game, scoring a first quarter touchdown on two passes to Beddis, an end. Newberry retaliated with a touchdown by Maxwell in the same quarter. The half ended with the score knotted at 6-6.

Newberry returned to score in both the third and fourth periods to go safely ahead, but the Blue Hose of P. C. threatened briefly in the final quarter, as Eaton, their big fullback, plunged over for another score.

The victory was Newberry's sixth in seven games this season.
Presbyterian......... 6 0 0 7—13
Newberry .... 6 0 7 6—19
Presbyterian scoring: Touchdowns, Eaton and Beddis; point after touchdown, Eaton. Newberry scoring: Touchdowns, Maxwell, Lynch and Ruth. Point after touchdown, Maxwell.

SUBSCRIBE TO THE OBSERVER

"...I'm staying in the Army!

★

THERE ARE PLENTY OF REASONS... AND HERE THEY ARE!"

PAY PER MONTH— ENLISTED MEN
In Addition to Food, Lodging, Clothes and Medical Care

(a)—Plus 20% Increase for Service Overseas. (b)—Plus 50% if Member of Flying Crews, Parachutist, etc. (c) —Plus 5% Increase in Pay for Each 3 Years of Service.

	Starting Base Pay Per Month	Monthly Retirement Income After:	
		20 Years' Service	30 Years' Service
Master Sergeant or First Sergeant	$138.00	$89.70	$155.25
Technical Sergeant	114.00	74.10	128.25
Staff Sergeant	96.00	62.40	108.00
Sergeant	78.00	50.70	87.75
Corporal	66.00	42.90	74.25
Private First Class	54.00	35.10	60.75
Private	50.00	32.50	56.25

★★★★★★★★★★★★★★★★★★★★★★★

SEE THE JOB THROUGH
U. S. ARMY
BE A "GUARDIAN OF VICTORY"
AIR, GROUND, SERVICE FORCES

ENLIST NOW AT YOUR NEAREST U. S. ARMY RECRUITING STATION
313-15 P. O. Bldg.
Spartanburg, S. C.

GIVE TO THE WAR FUND — **ROYAL CROWN COLA** REG. U.S. PAT. OFF. — GIVE TO THE WAR FUND

The Li'l That Was!

December 7, 1946 — THE BLUE STOCKING — Page Three

Blue Hose Edge Indians in Finale, 14-13

Bowles and Kaleel Are Defensive Stars

Newberry's Rock Lynch being hauled down from the rear by Hose fullback Bob Hughes, as halfback Herb Rollins comes in to give assistance, in the third quarter of the homecoming tilt last week.

The blue-shirted Hosemen wound up their most successful season in recent years as they edged Newberry, 14-13, on Thanksgiving day in Bailey Stadium.

The hard-earned win gave PC the coveted Little Four title, and a season's average of .778, as they won seven of nine tilts to lead the state standings in all games played and in points scored.

Coach McMillian's charges opened the game with both barrels as they capitalized on two Tribe fumbles to account for both their touchdowns.

The first score came early in the quarter when Maxwell, of Newberry, bobbled the ball on his own 35-yard line. Presbyterian recovering. On second down, after a pass went astray, Roger McCommons shot off left tackle for 20 yards and a first down on the Tribe 13. Hank Caver plunged to the eight, and after another pass missed, McCommons was stopped cold. "Operation Moon" rose in full splendor as Caver ran to the right and popped to Dick Kaleel in the end zone for six big points. Caver calmly converted, and the Hose led 7-0.

The eventual winning score came on a silver platter as Rush, of Newberry, was hit on his own 45-yard stripe, fumbled, and saw the ball grabbed in the air by Hose end Herb Lindsay, who galloped the 45 yards to pay dirt. Again "Operation Crossbar" was good, Caver clicking, and the score mounted to 14-0.

The enraged Indians then set out on the warpath, and scored in the second act, driving 44 yards in three plays. Frank Rush went from the PC 44 to the 29, Maxwell lost two yards off tackle, and then "Rock" Lynch, Newberry's stellar fullback hammered center, not stopping until he was over for the Lavaimen's first score. The extra point try was not good.

Just before the half the Indians tomahawked their way 50 yards to the Hose three-yard line, where the half ended the threat.

"Dusty" Scarborough, Indian guard, rushed through and blocked Rollins' kick on the Blue Hose 30, and Ray Jackson picking up the bounding ball and advancing to the 18. Four running plays later Rush circled left end for the score.

Lynch's conversion was good and the gap was narrowed to 14-13.

The crippled Hose had the breaks, but played heads-up ball in recovering six of seven Newberry fumbles, the factor that beat the tribe. Newberry was primed for the encounter, and did everything but win, rolling up 16 first downs to 5, and gaining 247 yards rushing to 32. The alert Hose rose to stop the tribe in the last stages of the melee, however, and the line particularly turned in a good performance.

CASINO THEATRE
December 9—14

Monday and Tuesday
Tomorrow Is Forever

Wednesday Only
Diary of A Chambermaid

Thursday and Friday
Never Say Goodbye

Saturday Only
Bringing Up Father

BROADWAY
December 9—14

Monday and Tuesday
Betty Co-Ed

Wednesday and Thursday
**Queen of Burlesque
Heading West**

Friday and Saturday
**Beyond Sacramento
Mr. Hex**

Prophetically, an editorial written in the November 14, 1946 edition of *The Indian*, asked Newberry College students to "Bury the hatchet" regarding the rivalry between Newberry College and Presbyterian College off the athletic playing field. Mischief between the schools was getting out of hand.

Across The Editor's Desk

IT'S TIME TO BURY THE HATCHET

For many years, Presbyterian College and Newberry College students have engaged in a rivalry that is oftentimes not too friendly. There have been incidents in the past—incidents involving the destruction of personal, school, and public property—that have led to bad feeling. Last winter, when some Newberry students boarded a chartered bus to go to Clinton for the P. C.-Newberry basketball game, that bus, containing mostly women students, was surrounded and mutilated by a group of P. C. supporters who may or may not have been P. C. students. The night before, the P. C. campus had been pretty well decorated with paint by someone with a misdirected sense of "school loyalty".

It's time to bury the hatchet! After last winter's regrettable recurrence of the long-standing vendetta, Student Body officers of both institutions got together to thrash out their problems—and there wasn't any blood shed at that meeting. The Presbyterian student officers, instead, put forth a proposal that such silly and needless destruction of property be stopped, as of immediately. The P. C. leaders further stated that, in 1947, the P. C. student body would present a Sportsmanship Trophy to that member of the Newberry College football team who showed best the elements of sportsmanship in the annual Newberry-P. C. football game. The Newberry Student Body promptly saw P. C.'s bid and raised them one—we unanimously agreed to make a presentation of such a medal to the best Presbyterian sport in '46.

Athletic rivalry is fine—it is indeed encouraged—but, it should be confined to athletics. There are few rivalries in the country that have a longer history than the one which exists between the Blue Hose and the Indians. Let's continue that rivalry, on the playing field. Let's don't do anything, either on or off that playing field, that may endanger good feeling between the two schools.

It's time to bury the hatchet!

The Second Quarter

The Derby Debacle
January 31, 1947

Newberry, South Carolina

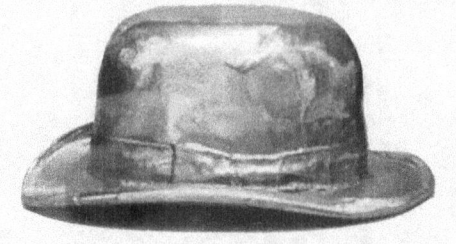

The Derby Debacle
January 31, 1947

What both Presbyterian College and Newberry College can both agree upon regarding the legend of The Bronze Derby:

On January 31, 1947, in MacLean Gymnasium on the campus of Newberry College in Newberry, South Carolina, the Newberry College Indians basketball team hosted the Presbyterian College Blue Hose in their first matchup of the season. The Blue Hose defeated the Indians 57-41. A Presbyterian College student named Jimmy Kellett attended the game wearing a derby hat in the gymnasium. A Newberry College student "obtained" his hat. Kellett returned to Presbyterian College after the game without a derby hat. What happened during and after the game became legendary to the college communities.

Presbyterian College student James Pickney Kellett, III. "Jimmy" was from Fountain Inn, South Carolina. Jimmy was a freshman at Presbyterian College and a member of Pi Kappa Phi fraternity.

The Li'l 🎩 That Was!

In addition, according to Presbyterian College:

> During the second half of the basketball game, or while driving away from the game, a Newberry College student "removed" the hat from Kelletts' head. The hat ended up in a Newberry College dormitory. A group of Presbyterian College students attempted to recover the hat and was unsuccessful. There were both heated verbal and physical exchanges between the student bodies. Kellett and his fellow Presbyterian College students returned home to Clinton, South Carolina without the derby hat.

According to Newberry College:

> At the basketball game between Presbyterian College and Newberry College, a banner was hung on the wall in MacLean Gymnasium by a group of Presbyterian College students. The banner stating "Beat the Hell Out of Newberry," did not go over well with a few Newberry College students. A select few of the students decided to remove the banner from the wall. The windows were low in MacLean Gymnasium, and with the accessibility of a ladder, from the outside, the students climbed into the gymnasium through a window and removed the banner. When the Blue Hose students discovered the banner was gone, the search for the banner began. There were both heated verbal and physical exchanges between the student bodies. During the comotion, a derby hat, worn by Presbyterian College student Jimmy Kellett was "removed" from his head. The hat disappeared into the night. Kellett and his Presbyterian College friends returned to Clinton, South Carolina without a banner or a derby hat.

Another scenario includes Newberry College student Corrin Bowers arriving at the game with his friends. He was wearing a derby hat. The hat was taken off his head by a Presbyterian College student prior to the game. During the game, the hat was retrieved by the Newberry College students and the commotion started between the students during and after the game.

Frank Kinard, editor of *The Indian*, congratulates the Newberry College student body and their overall sportsmanship at the January 31, 1947 Redskin - Blue Hose basketball game even though there was a skirmish between students.

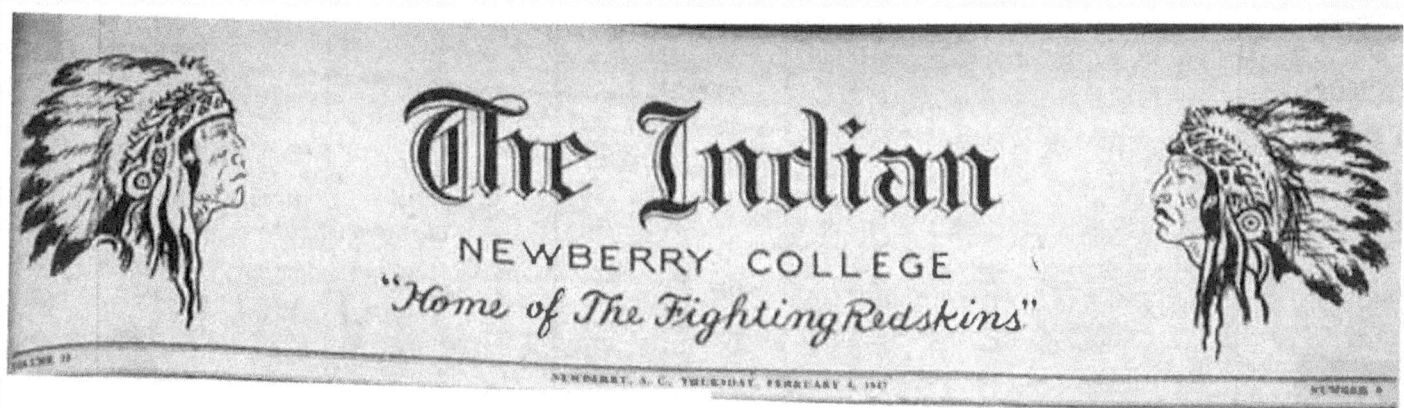

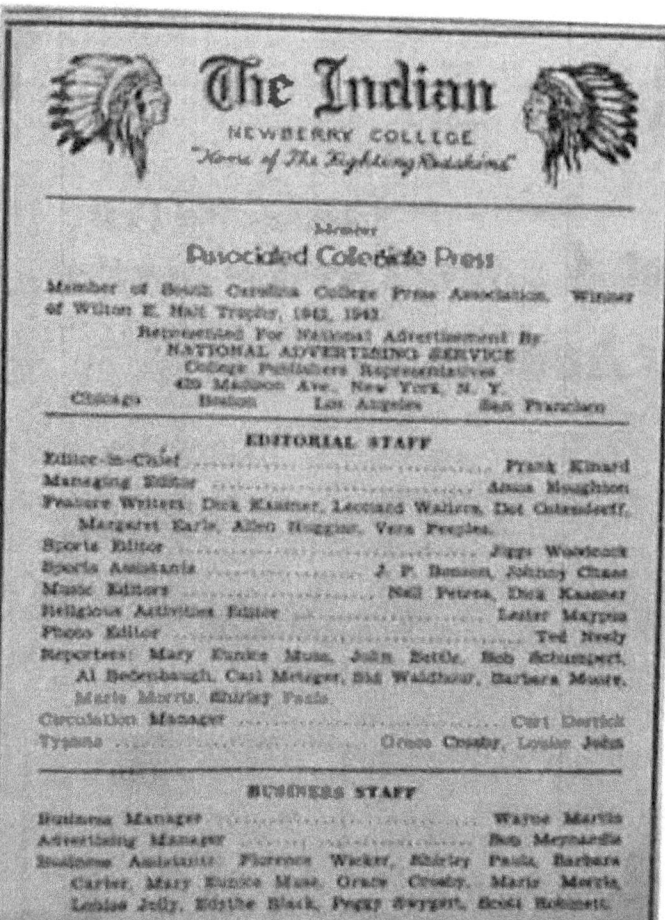

TAKE IT EASY

The Newberry student body as a whole deserves a great big pat on the back for their restrained attitude upon the occasion of the recent visit to our campus of the P. C. basketball team and a goodly 75 per cent of the P. C. student body. It is true that, because P. C. rooters were apparently under some compulsion to make themselves obnoxious both during and after the game, and because they came deliberately breaking the "good-will" agreement between the student bodies of both schools by bringing with them a large banner, several minor altercations did occur immediately after the basketball game.

However, and this is important, we should not, under any circumstances, consider our half of the agreement between ourselves and P. C. at an end. To do so would mean instant severance of athletic relations with our Little Four neighbors and none of us want that. We play P. C. again, at Clinton, on February 28. Let's all go up there and

The Li'l 🎩 That Was!

On November 21, 2023, Jay Salter, a 2019 graduate of Newberry College and External Communications Coordinator at Newberry College, published an article in *Dimensions*, the Newberry College magazine. He had the opportunity to interview Otho L. Shealy, a 1948 graduate of Newberry College. Mr. Shealy was a World War II veteran. He began his collegiate career at Newberry College, served our country in World War II, and returned to Newberry College to complete his studies after he was discharged.

DIMENSIONS

Within a few weeks of his return to Newberry, he found himself a player in what would become local lore. According to the late College archivist **Gordon Henry** (1931-2020), on Jan. 31, 1947, Newberry played rival Presbyterian College in basketball, in what would later be named MacLean Gymnasium. Legend has it that a Newberry student climbed a ladder on the outside of the building, into an open window behind the visitors' stands, and took a bowler hat off the head of a Blue Hose. Former student **Corrin Bowers** would later write that the hat was originally his, and that the whole operation was merely to recover stolen property.

"You know who helped hold the ladder?" Shealy asks. "You're looking at him! This fellow with this hat on, he was making a lot of noise. We lifted the hat out the window and I didn't know where it went to."

Several altercations ensued after the game. Soon after, Presbyterian's public relations director, Charles MacDonald, wrote **Frank Kinard '47** (1924-2021), Newberry's sports publicity director, suggesting that the hat be recovered and made into a symbol of the schools' rivalry. The hat was turned in anonymously, cast in bronze, and the Bronze Derby was born. The trophy would be passed to the victor of each meeting in basketball, baseball and football until 1956, and only in football until 2006, just before PC left Division II.

On April 22, 2014, *Blue Stocking* staff writer Olivia Alderidge interviewed Presbyterian College alumnus Reverend Jim Banbury. Reverend Banbury was editor of the Presbyterian College student newspaper, *The Blue Stocking*, during the origin of The Bronze Derby rivalry in 1947.

Recollections on the Bronze Derby with a Blue Stocking Legacy

Olivia Aldridge, Staff Writer

In the Carriage Club, a beautiful senior living community in Charlotte, NC, with picturesque views out of huge, light-filled windows, a true gem of PC's history resides, and on March 23rd, I got to meet him. Along with Dr. Brent and Bluestocking photographer Kelly Cichon, I sat down with 87-year-old Reverend Jim Banbury, 1947 to 1948 editor of the Bluestocking.

All 25 copies of the Bluestocking from Banbury's reign as editor were spread across a table, yellowed and brittle but wonderfully intact. Reverend Banbury's son Bruce pointed out a few headlines to us in particular, all regarding an object of PC lore and legend: the Bronze Derby.

According to legend (and bluehose100.com, the site commemorating 100 years of PC football and basketball), this beloved tradition began at a PC v. Newberry basketball game at Newberry, where a Newberry student, Corrin Bowers, claims the Derby was swiped from his head.

But the Banburys remember it differently.

"Jimmy Kellett was just a kid on campus that dad was friends with that wore a derby all the time; that was his trademark," Bruce said.

"That's true," Reverend Banbury piped in. "Unfortunately he went down to Newberry . . . to a basketball game we were playing, and next half of the game some guy comes by and snatches the hat . . . [there was] such a waylay of students that we couldn't get organized enough to even run after the guy. So that started it.

"We did go on their campus to see if we couldn't find it, and this was kind of dumb idea, too," he said, chuckling in remembrance. According to Banbury, about 20 PC students entered the dormitory, and emerged Derby-less after a scuffle with Newberry students.

It was the athletic director of Newberry who suggested the hat be passed to the victor of each PC v. Newberry athletic event in order to ease tensions over the theft and use the Derby as a positive symbol of the rivalry. Newberry sent the Derby to a company in Ohio to be bronzed, which Banbury claims was his suggestion to avoid tattering the hat.

Banbury embodies the experience of the Derby in more ways than one. Not only was the idea of bronzing the derby his brainchild, but as the saga of the derby unfolded, Banbury chronicled the events in The Blue Stocking. The blow by blow of each derby exchange is safely etched in The Blue Stocking records of the PC archive, including the original theft of the derby from Kellett.

Besides blowing the dust of myth from the beloved PC tradition of the derby, Banbury himself represents a tradition that we at The Blue Stocking are proud to uphold. He entered PC in 1944 after being rejected by the army on account of his poor eyesight, and proceeded to participate in campus life with the gusto of a true Renaissance man, being active in everything from his editorial duties to the football team. After graduation, he had a 25-year career in journalism before entering Presbyterian ministry. As students and writers, we hope exude the same balance and success as our 1947-1948 editor.

The PC-Newberry rivalry ended in 2006, the last year before PC changed divisions. Having defeated Newberry in this historic final battle for the Bronze Derby, we house it safely in the display cases of Templeton Gym, a memento of Jim Banbury, Jimmy Kellett, and PC days gone by.

The Li'l 🎩 That Was!

A natural rivalry had been created for 40 years prior to 1947 between Newberry College and Presbyterian College as the two schools were less than 25 miles apart in neighboring South Carolina counties. However, in January of 1947, one basketball game and a missing derby hat changed the future competitive spirit between these schools forever. The week immediately after the "Derby Debacle", a member of the Presbyterian College administration, Charles McDonald, an English Instructor and Director of Public Relations contacted Frank Kinard, the acting Sports Publicity Director and the editor of the Newberry College student newspaper *The Indian*. It was suggested and agreed upon that the derby hat needed to be recovered and should represent the competitive rivalry between Newberry College and Presbyterian College. Both administrators were instrumental and are credited for establishing the governing rules regarding the exchange of the derby hat between the schools. An exhaustive search to find the original governing rules between the schools resulted in only references in school and local newspapers pertaining to the agreement.

The idea was immediately accepted by both college administrations and students. The derby hat was eventually turned over to Frank Kinard after he spoke to the Newberry College student body. He immediately made arrangements for the hat to be bronzed. The student perpetrator at Newberry College that "removed" the hat from Jimmy Kelletts' head was never revealed or identified. The initial competitive proposal was to have The Bronze Derby competed for in basketball, baseball and football games between the two colleges. The first Bronze Derby athletic competition was scheduled for February 28, 1947 in Clinton, South Carolina. That basketball game between the Indians and the Blue Hose established and set the standard for a competitive athletic rivalry for the next 60 years.

The stories by the respective colleges are creditable, but most importantly, priceless! There is no need to prove which story is true and most accurate. The fact of the matter is that a symbol for a rivalry and long time tradition between two small colleges had originated.

MacLean Gymnasium was constructed post World War I and completed in 1923. The gymnasium was named for Fred "Dutch" MacLean, a student athlete and coach at Newberry College. Fred MacLean was on the first organized football team in 1913 at Newberry College and coached for 17 years from 1921-1938 at Newberry College. Fred MacLean also played baseball and basketball while a student at Newberry College. Coach MacLean was the first inductee into the Newberry Athletic Hall of Fame. Coach MacLean is also a member of the South Carolina Athletic Hall of Fame.

Courtesy of Newberry College archives

The Li'l 🎩 That Was!

President James O. Kinard of Newberry College and sons, James Efird (left) and Frank Efird (right). James is a Senior, Editor-in-Chief of the Indian, Assistant Editor of the Annual, President of the International Relations Club, a member of the College Singers and other student groups, and elected to "Who's Who in American Universities and Colleges." Frank is a Freshman, Photograph Editor of the Indian and Director of Athletics Publicity. Both Dr. and Mrs. Kinard, the former Miss Katherine Efird of of Lexington, are graduates of Newberry.

Pictured in the October 28, 1941 edition of *The Newberry Observer* is Newberry College President James G. Kinard with his sons James and Frank. Frank, on the right, is pictured as a freshman. In 1947, as the Sports Publicity Director of Newberry College, Frank was instrumental in developing the criteria for the symbol for athletic supremacy between Newberry College and Presbyterian College.

On February 8, 1947, the Presbyterian College newspaper *The Blue Stocking* reported on the January 31, 1947 basketball matchup between Newberry College and Presbyterian College.

Hose Trip Laval Tribe, 51-47

A late scoring rally by the Hosemen was enough to defeat a last-minute Newberry effort Thursday, January 30, in Newberry in a close thriller between two of the state's keenest rivals. Vance Logan scored 14 points for honors, but guard Roy Krouse held the Indian's high-scoring Marvin English to only four points.

The *Blue Stocking* first introduced "The Little Bronze Derby" competition between Presbyterian College and Newberry College to the Presbyterian College students and community in the February 22, 1947 edition. The derby hat was reported as part of a "tussle" between the two college's students. The derby would be awarded "After such famous trophies as the Minnesota-Michigan 'Little Brown Jug' and the Indiana-Purdue 'Old Oaken Bucket.'"

Tradition, That Is
Winner Gets "L'il Bronze Derby"

Whoever wins the game gets temporary possession of the "Little Bronze Derby."

That's the challenge facing the Blue Stocking basketball team next Friday night when they entertain their keenest rivals, Newberry's Indians, in Leroy Springs gymnasium at 8 o'clock.

Publicity departments of the two colleges this week completed plans for establishing a traditional symbol of victory, a "Little Bronze Derby," to be held by the winners of PC-Newberry football, basketball and baseball games. The plan is patterned after such famous trophies as the Minnesota-Michigan "Little Brown Jug" and the Indiana-Purdue "Old Oaken Bucket."

The derby was the subject of a "tussle" between students of the two colleges at Newberry following the first meeting of the two cage teams this season. It belonged to a PC student, but Newberry students gained possession that night. They relinquished the derby upon presentation of the trophy plan.

The derby was shipped for casting in bronze last week and will not arrive until the first week in March. However, the winner of Friday's basketball game will get the derby until the winner of the first baseball game of the season between the two schools is decided.

The two schools have been traditional rivals in sports for over 25 years.

The Li'l 🎩 That Was!

On February 20, 1947, *The Indian* introduced "The Hat" to the Newberry College community.

 **The Indian**
NEWBERRY COLLEGE
"Home of The Fighting Redskins"

ONCE AGAIN

At the risk of being repetitious, we've got something more to say about P. C. Next Friday night, the Indians will be off to Clinton to engage the Blue Hose in the season finale of the winter basketball campaign. It is our hope that large numbers of the student body will go along with the team for the game.

By that time "The Hat", the bronzed derby which is to be a symbol of athletic victory in the last contest, should P. C. publicity director Charles MacDonald, we've taken P. M. publicity director Charles MacDonald, we've taken charge of getting the hat bronzed and suitably mounted. Incidentally, now is a good time as any to express our appreciation for the cooperation of the student body in this matter. We hope that The Hat will remain on the Newberry campus indefinitely—as long as we're beating P. C.

Here's the point—Let's all go up to P. C. next week and cheer the Redskins to victory. Let's don't go up there and make ourselves obnoxious or unwelcome. The football game at Clinton last Thanksgiving Day came off without a hitch, due to your admirable behavior. The basketball game here last month was marred by a few incidents, for none of which we were to blame.

Let's don't spoil our good record.

* * * *

The Li'l 🎩 That Was!

The Indian
NEWBERRY COLLEGE
"Home of The Fighting Redskins"

NEWBERRY, S. C., THURSDAY, MARCH 8, 1947

Indian, Hose 'Derby' Award Started

"Little Bronze Derby" Be Symbol Of Athletic Feud

Presbyterian College and Newberry College have been at each other's throats, athletically, that is, for nearly half a century, and last week they had something to show for it. Borrowing a leaf from the famed Michigan-Purdue "Old Oaken Bucket" and the Stanford-California "Axe", the schools jointly announced that athletic supremacy between the two would henceforth be symbolized by "The Little Bronze Derby". Presentation of the award will be made to the victor following each meeting of the two Little Four and SIAA rivals in three major sports—football, basketball, and baseball.

Actually, the hat is still in the hands of a Columbus, Ohio, jeweler for bronze casting, but it is expected to be ready for presentation in about three weeks. It is planned to have the hat presented to the captain of the winning team by the captain of the losers at chapel exercises at the school of the victors on the day following an athletic meeting between P. C. and Newberry. Should the "Little Bronze Derby" be returned before the next meeting of the two schools, in baseball, the presentation will be made by Indian basketball captain Marvin English to the Blue Hose captain. The Stockings won the derby by virtue of their 44-42 victory over the Indians last week in the first "Little Bronze Derby" contest.

The award grew out of the "abduction" of a P. C. student's derby hat at the first basketball game between P. C. and Newberry here several weeks ago. Suggestion of the award was first made by Charles MacDonald, instructor in English and director of Public Relations at Presbyterian, in a letter to Frank Kinard, sports publicity director here. The hat was gladly surrendered by anonymous Newberry students, and was turned over to a local jewelry firm to be cast in bronze.

"The Derby" is part of a general plan to keep relations between the two colleges on a high plane, despite the bitter rivalry which exists between them. The movement was launched last winter after incidents during the basketball season threatened the severance of athletic relations between P. C. and Newberry.

The Hose and the Indians have been feuding on the athletic fields
(continued on page 2)

(continued from page 1)
since the turn of the century. Their 33-year string of football clashes—unbroken since 1913 except for the year 1918—ranks as one of the South's oldest grid vendettas, and in baseball, the two teams were bitter rivals long before football became a part of the intercollegiate scene in the South.

Frequently, in the past, impending clashes between the two schools have resulted in pre-game raiding parties on both campuses, with resultant damage to personal and school propriety and reputations. It was with the aim of eliminating such useless destruction that the student body governmental organizations initiated their cooperative movement last winter.

The Li'l 🎩 That Was!

On February 28, 1947, *The Newberry Observer* first reported and introduced The Little Bronze Derby to the Newberry community.

First Award Tonight

Newberry And P. C. Struggle Now For Little Bronze Derby

Newberry College and Presbyterian College have been a-feudin' —athletically; that is—ever since the turn of the century, with no tangible symbol of victory in their contests save the scores.

That situation was remedied today after the manner of the famed Minnesota-Purdue "Little Brown Jug" and the Indiana-Purdue "Old Oaken Bucket", according to a joint release received yesterday from the publicity departments of the two "Little Four" colleges.

Hereafter, the Fighting Redskins' and the Blue Stockings' athletic teams will know for what they struggle: A tangible symbol of victory — "The Little Brown Derby".

The award is the outgrowth of the "abduction" of a Presbyterian student's derby hat at the first meeting of the two college's basketball teams earlier this season, but the Newberry students relinquished the trophy in order to make it a traditional symbol of athletic victory.

The hat will be awarded for the first time tonight to the winner of the Newberry-Presbyterian basketball game at Clinton at 8 o'clock, but in theory only. In actuality, the derby is in the hands of a Columbus, Ohio, jeweler for bronze casting and is not expected to arrive until the first week in March. At that time, it will actually go to the winner of tonight's game.

The "Little Bronze Derby" will be enclosed in a glass case and displayed among the athletic trophies of the winning school, along with the scores of all future football, basketball, and baseball games. However, the derby may change hands again come baseball season, and the splitting of victories in the two diamond contests this spring would see a double shift in the location of the trophy.

The Newberry and Presbyterian publicity departments have made the plan applicable to each contest in all three major sports, rather than to football alone, in order to provide greater year-round interest.

The award is part of a general plan for keeping athletic relations of the two colleges on a high standard despite the keen rivalry which exists between them. The cooperative movement was initiated last winter by the student government organizations of the two colleges after "incidents" during the basketball season threatened athletic relations between the two.

On March 3, 1947, *The Newberry Observer* reported the results of the first Bronze Derby matchup between Newberry College and Presbyterian College.

Indians Lose To P. C. Team By 2 Points

In the final two seconds of a hotly contested basketball game at Clinton last Friday night, Presbyterian college's forward Vance Logan tossed a field goal, carrying the Blue Hose quintet to a 44-42 victory over the Newberry Indians to close the season for both teams.

The contest was the first of the "Bronze Derby" trophy events started by the two schools, the little derby hat going to Presbyterian.

The Alumni Bulletin

VOLUME 3 — NEWBERRY, S. C., FEBRUARY-MARCH, 1947. — NUMBER 4

Newberry And P. C. Feud For Derby

"Little Bronze Derby" Will Be Symbol of Victory To Winning Team.

Newberry College and Presbyterian College have been a-feudin'—athletically, that is—ever since the turn of the century, with no tangible symbol of victory in their contests save the scores.

That situation has been remedied after the manner of the famed Minnesota-Purdue "Little Brown Jug" and the Indiana-Purdue "Old Oaken Bucket", according to a joint release by the publicity departments of the two "Little Four" colleges.

Hereafter, the Fighting Redskins' and the Blue Stockings' athletic teams will know for what they struggle: A tangible symbol of victory—"The Little Bronze Derby".

The award is the outgrowth of the "abduction" of a Presbyterian student's derby hat at the first meeting of the two college's basketball teams earlier this season, but the Newberry students relinquished the trophy in order to make it a traditional symbol of athletic victory.

The hat was presented for the first time to Presbyterian by virtue of their 44-42 score over Newberry in the basketball game at Clinton this month, but in theory only. In actuality, the derby is in the hands of a Columbus, Ohio, jeweler, for bronze casting and is not expected to arive until sometime in March. At that time it will actually go to Presbyterian College.

The "Little Bronze Derby" will be enclosed in a glass case and displayed among the athletic trophies of the winning school, along with the scores of all future football, basketball, and baseball scores. However, the derby may change hands again come baseball season, and the splitting of voctories in the two diamond contests this spring would see a double shift in the location of the trophy.

The Newberry and Presbyterian publicity departments have made the plan applicable to each contest in all three major sports, rather than to football alone, in order to provide greater year-round interest.

Frank Kinard, '46, publicity department at Newberry, and Charles MacDonald, publicity department at Presbyterian, are to be given lots of credit for this fine plan. It will do lots to keep the athletic relations of the two colleges on a high standard despite the keen rivalry which exists between them.

The Li'l 🎩 That Was!

The Fraternal Connection of the Bronze Derby
Beta Chapter of Pi Kappa Phi
at Presbyterian College

MISS JEAN WARD
Sponsor Pi Kappa Phi Fraternity

JIMMY KELLETT
President

Colors: Gold and White   Flower: Red Rose

Pi Kappa Phi fraternity was founded at the College of Charleston on December 10, 1904, by three of its students. In 1907 Beta Chapter was established at Presbyterian College and was incorporated the same year with the purpose of becoming a national fraternity. It is the only national fraternity to be founded in South Carolina.

The Rose Ball of Pi Kappa Phi is an annual social highlight of the fraternity and is one of the most enjoyable dances of the college year at Presbyterian.

MEMBERS:
Prochaska, Howie, Morgan, Koon, Frasier, Barnhill, Estes
Seagars, W. Cruickshanks, A. Cruickshanks, Copeland, Gault, LINDSEY, WILBURN
Krouse, Perry, Scruggs, Wyman, Spurrier, Walker

PLEDGES:
D. Johnson, W. Johnson, Keith
Hipp, Fitz, Martin
Galloway, Munden, Plummer

The 1947 chapter of Pi Kappa Phi Fraternity at Presbyterian College.

Of interest, in the February 8, 1947 edition of *The Blue Stocking* was a report that Pi Kappa Phi Fraternity had elected new officers which included Jimmy Kellett who had lost his derby hat at Newberry College on January 30, 1947. Junior Cally Gault was elected Historian. Cally Gault later became the legendary Presbyterian College Blue Hose Head Coach from 1963-1984.

Pi Kappa Phi

Beta chapter of Pi Kappa Phi held its first meeting of the new semester on Wednesday of last week. New officers of the fraternity were elected, with Sanford Howie being the choice for president. Recent returnee Marvin "Skinny" Bettis was installed as treasurer. Joe Scruggs was chosen secretary; Cally Gault, historian; Frank Perry, chaplain; Herb Lindsay, warden; and Jimmy Kellett, pledgemaster.

Presbyterian College Junior, Cally Gault

The Li'l 🎩 That Was!

In 1973 Presbyterian College Head Football Coach Cally Gault said "It's the worst experience I've been in." Cally Gault was part of the "Derby Debacle" on January 31, 1947 and admitted to have participated at the debacle in Newberry.

The Laurens County Advertiser

15¢ PER COPY

"SOUTH CAROLINA'S FASTEST GROWING SEMI-WEEKLY NEWSPAPER"

VOL. NO. 89 — Laurens, South Carolina, Wednesday, November 28, 1973 — No. 42—28 Pages—2 Sections

History of . . . Bronze Derby

PRESBYTERIAN COACH CALLY GAULT— "It was the worst experience I've been in."

Although many people know of the Bronze Derby game between PC and Newberry, few know of the rivalry's past. The rivalry started back in 1913 and since then the two team's have met fifty-nine times with PC having the slight edge at 38 wins to 19.

The "Bronze Derby Game" started in 1947 with the Derby given to the winner annually. PC also holds the edge in Bronze Derby victories with 15 wins. The affair, which marks Thanksgiving in S. C., all started back in 1947 when some PC students had just attended a hotly contested basketball game with Newberry. The students, heading back to PC from Newberry, were Jim Kellett of Fountain Inn, Ed Fowler, Cally Gault, Lou Fowler, Marvin Bettis and Joe Keith and Windy Johnson. The car was leaving; a Newberry student stopped the car and grabbed Jim Kellett's derby from Ed Fowler and ran off.

The students in the car jumped out and started after the Newberry student. Fights broke out but the derby was still missing. The Sports Information Director at Newberry came up with the idea to have the derby bronzed. The students returned the derby, it was bronzed and has been given to the winner of the event ever since.

Presbyterian College Blue Hose closed out their 1973 football season on Thanksgiving Day as they played the Newberry Indians. For the Blue Hose the Thanksgiving holiday went too slowly as the Hose lost the game as well as the prize possession—the Bronze Derby.

The game, marred by bad feelings and turnovers, was played at Newberry. The Indians took a tough victory 14-3, avenging last year's defeat of 17-0. The game was a typical Bronze Derby classic with the defenses dominating the entire ballgame.

Presbyterian's defense forced Newberry into six turnovers. Three pass interceptions and three fumbles were the result of the Crusher Club's effect on Newberry's offense. Newberry's defense had their day too as they forced PC's quarterback Wally Bowen into four pass interceptions and the backfield into two fumbles.

Newberry's two touchdowns weren't the result of their defensive play but were drives of 40 and 35 yards. The first touchdown, a controversial call by the officials, was scored with just two seconds left in the first half. The controversy arose over the amount of time left in the last minutes. On third down with one yard to go for the touchdown, the Indians tried for the TD. The clock started with 25 seconds left in the half but with ten seconds left to play it stopped. The Indians used up 15 of that 25 seconds on that third down play. Newberry had no timeouts and the clock apparently should have expired, but for some reason it failed to and Newberry scored with two seconds left.

The final Newberry score came in the fourth quarter when halfback Taylor weaved his way in for an 11 yard touchdown. Presbyterian's only points came on a Buddy Gaddy field goal with twelve seconds left in the first quarter.

After the first Newberry score, the Blue Hose offense attempted a comeback, but another costly turnover closed the door. As the final gun sounded Blue Hose fans left the stadium with a feeling of failure. The game caused Coach Gault to say, "It was the worst experience I've been in."

Presbyterian ran up a total offense of 189 yards, 116 of it passing. Quarterback Wally Bowen completed seven of 22 passes. Ken Milton caught three of these for 52 yards, and flanker Norris took four passes for 64 yards. PC gained only 53 yards on the ground, 39 of these gotten by ball carrier Bob Wills on eight attempts.

This season is only a forecast of what is to come next year. And that forecast is that the Raiders are suddenly emerging as one of the more explosive 4-A teams in the state.

The Clinton Chronicle

Vol. 74—No. 48   Nov. 28, 1974, Clinton, S.C.

Coach Gault Helped Establish PC-Newberry Derby Tradition

COACH GAULT

With the big game of the State now a part of the past memory, Clemson-Carolina's attention is now turned towards Clinton, where the Blue Hose will take on the Newberry Indians in the annual Bronze Derby Classic. A big part of that history stems from the Presbyterian College Head Mentor himself, Cally Gault.

The history of the Derby started back in January of 1947 when Coach Gault was a junior at Presbyterian. On the night of the 20th the Blue Hose played Newberry in a basketball game at Newberry and Coach Gault and several students packed in a car and went to the game. Members of that bunch were Jim Kellet of Fountain Inn, S.C. (owner of the derby), Ed Fowler (wearer of the derby), Coach Gault, Lou Fowler, Marvin Bettis, Joe Keith and Windy Johnson. Presbyterian took the win (51-47) and these students started back towards Clinton. Before the fans left the Newberry campus, they wanted a particular banner that they had brought with them back from some thieving Newberry students. A scuffle broke out and the Blue Hose students left without the banner and a few minutes later without the derby. As the car that Coach Gault was riding in was leaving, a Newberry student stopped the car and grabbed the derby from Fowler and disappeared into the dorms with it.

A search by college officials turned up the derby after a few days and later Presbyterian SID Charlie McDonald came up with the idea that the derby should be bronzed and the winner of the athletic contests between the two schools would also take home the now Bronzed Derby. In recent years, the tradition has been dropped in all other contests except football. It was decided in 1956 that the Derby would be the prize awarded for the winner of the Turkey Day Classic. Since that time Newberry has been able to only hang on to the prize six times while Presbyterian has had it for 11 times. At the moment the Derby is sitting on the desk of Newberry Head Coach Fred Herren as the Indians took last year's game by a score of 14 to 3.

Talking about the Derby, Coach Gault commented, "The Derby adds some incentive to a game which really needs no incentive. It is another addition to the already fine tradition that has come to mean so much to the fans of both schools. This Derby, its possession, means something to both schools."

It will be the 27th reunion for Coach Cally Gault with the Bronze Derby when the Hose play the Indians this Thursday with kickoff time at 2:00.

PC-Newberry Broadcast

Thursday afternoon's football game for the Bronze Derby between the Presbyterian College Blue Hose and the Newberry College Indians from Johnson Field in Clinton will be broadcast over WLBG-FM starting with the pre-game show at 1:30. Kickoff is set for 2:00.

The Li'l 🎩 That Was!

George Wilkinson was a 1945 graduate of Presbyterian College, and a member of Pi Kappa Phi fraternity. While at school, he admired a hat at Adair's Mens Shop in Clinton, South Carolina. On November 11, 2006, he told the *Greenville News* "I saw that derby in the window. It cost $16.50, and I looked at it for a couple of weeks. Finally, I worked it out to where I paid the store 25 cents a week to the store for the hat. I wore that hat, and my fraternity brothers also wore the hat here and there. When I left PC in 1945, I left the hat with them. My fraternity brothers loved to take turns wearing it." On January 31, 1947, Pi Kappa Phi member Jimmy Kellett wore the derby hat to the Presbyterian College versus Newberry College basketball game. The stories have been documented. The symbol for a college rivalry was created.

Years later, Wilkinson received a true replica of the derby hat from his friendly fraternity brothers. The pictured hat was donated to the Presbyterian College archives by the family of George Wilkinson.

Presbyterian College Blue Hose

Newberry College Indians

The Third Quarter

The Bronze Derby 1947 - 1955

The Bronze Derby 1947-1955

On February 28, 1947, a month after the "Derby Debacle" on the Newberry College campus, the inaugural Bronze Derby game took place in Leroy Springs Gymnasium in Clinton, South Carolina. The game was the first of many basketball, baseball and football matchups between the Indians and Blue Hose between 1947 and 1955. The game set the tone for an overall rivalry that demonstrated athletic supremacy between the two schools. The competitive rivalry lasted for the next 60 years.

A standing room capacity crowd witnessed the Presbyterian College Blue Hose basketball team defeat the Newberry Indians 44-42. The game was tight at halftime. Early in the second half, the Indians took a commanding lead. The Blue Hose slowly worked their way back into the game. The game was tied with 10 seconds to play. Blue Hose forward Howard Willis took a shot and was unsuccessful from the corner. The ball bounced off the rim to the foul line where Vance Logan, a (sub) forward rebounded the ball and put it up with 2 seconds left on the clock for the last second, game winning points. The Blue Hose had won the inaugural Bronze Derby. The Bronze Derby would be again on the line between the two schools later in the spring of 1947 at the school's first baseball game between one another.

The Li'l 🎩 That Was!

The Clinton Chronicle

Clinton, S. C., Thursday, March 6, 1947

TRY OUR
DIXIE DOUGHNUTS and COFFEE
JOIN THE DUNKING CLUB AND LEARN
HOW TO DUNK
FRESH, TASTY, AND DELICIOUS
AT
ESSO SODA FOUNTAIN
JOE'S ESSO SERVICE
Telephone 185

Enjoy The
Drink That

"Hits The Spot"

5¢ Plus Tax

Ask for the Big Bottle

PEPSI-COLA BOTTLING CO.
GREENVILLE, S. C.

P. C. Wins Closing Basketball Game

In the final two seconds of a hotly contested basketball game here last Friday night, Presbyterian college's forward Vance Logan tossed a field goal, carrying the Blue Hose quintet to a 44-42 victory over the Newberry Indians to close the season for both teams.

The contest was the first of the "Bronze Derby" trophy events started by the two schools, the little derby hat going to Presbyterian.

The shot by Blue Hose forward Vance Willis with 2 seconds left in the game, sealed a victory by Presbyterian College to win their first Bronze Derby in 1947.

The PAC SAC 1947

Coach McMillian, Willis, Logan, Andrews, Captain Rollins, Lindsay, Krouse, Morrow, Manager Wilson

The 1947 Presbyterian College Blue Hose basketball team was the first team to win the Bronze Derby.

Leroy Springs Gymnasium, on the Presbyterian College campus, was funded and built in 1924 by a contribution from textile entrepreneur Colonel Leroy Springs. In 1929, with additional funding from Colonel Springs, a swimming pool was added to the facility. The inaugural Bronze Derby matchup, a basketball game on February 28, 1947 took place with a capacity crowd in the gymnasium.

Courtesy of Presbyterian College archives

On April 19, 1947, The Presbyterian College Blue Hose baseball team traveled to Newberry, South Carolina to play the Newberry Indians in the second Bronze Derby game. Even though the Blue Hose basketball team had beaten the Indians earlier in 1947, Presbyterian had not put their hands on the Bronze Derby as the derby hat was in the process of being bronzed and had just returned to Newberry College in time for the inaugural baseball game.

Today Is Derby Day; Hose Play Indians

Today is Derby Day!

Veteran pitcher Wade Lyle, who hurled for the Blue Stockings before the war and has a record of never having lost to a Newberry diamond team, was set today to lead his teammates in a 3 p.m. baseball defense of the traditional Bronze Derby at Newberry.

The Hosemen supposedly hold the trophy by virtue

The derby is back!

Newberry sports publicist Frank Kinard, who forwarded the derby for bronze coating by agreement between the publicity departments of the two colleges, wired late yesterday that the trophy had arrived in Newberry.

The return was too late to bring the derby here.

But today's baseball winner actually GETS the Bronze Derby!

of a thrilling 44-42 basketball win over the Indians in February, but in actuality the derby until yesterday was in the hands of an Ohio novelty firm for bronze coating. Whoever wins today's game gets the trophy

until May 3 when the two baseball teams meet again here.

Coach Larry "Coon" Weldon's diamond crew is riding the crest of a six-game winning streak (two of them exhibitions) built up over the past two weeks. The team's hitting seems on the upgrade and clutch hitting has been improving with each game.

Newberry's Indians, currently tied for leadership with Clemson in the state title race, but followed closely by the twice-defeated Hosemen, were undetermined as to their starting pitcher late yesterday.

The game assumes even more significance than winning the derby in that it may go a long way toward determining the state championship. Clemson, Newberry and Presbyterian are rated the teams to beat for the title as mid-season nears.

* * * * *

PC's crack tennis squad, hampered by an injury to the state singles titlist, Art Prochaska, but still unquestionably one of the better teams in the South, also visits Newberry today to battle the Indians.

Newberry is fielding its first intercollegiate net team in a decade and has played one match thus far, losing 7-0 to Furman.

Presbyterian now has a victory string of seven wins following a season-opener loss to strong Kalamazoo college. Bob Spurrier will be playing the number one position for the Hosemen.

To round out a full PC-Newberry day in sports, the Hose cindermen take on the Indians at Bailey stadium here at 2:00 p.m. today in the third meet of the season for the Blues.

Coach Lonnie McMillian's thinclads took the measure of Wofford by three points last week for their initial win, after dropping their opener to Clemson. Newberry lost its opener Wednesday to Furman, 87 2/3 to 38 1/3.

The Blue Stockings are featured by a standout dashman, Wallace Walkup, and "iron-man" Carl Hill, who handles assignments in the pole vault, javelin, discus, and mile relay.

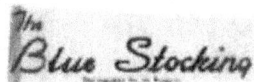

BISHOP & WALKER
"The Rexall Drug Store"

Try One of Our Famous Chocolate-Malteds
and One of Our Tasty Sandwiches

——— o ———

Visit Our Soda Fountain
We Serve the Finer Quality Hostess Ice Cream

THE BLUE STOCKING   March 29, 1947

The Li'l 🎩 That Was!

In the spring of 1947, Presbyterian and Newberry met twice in baseball. In the first meeting in Newberry, South Carolina, Newberry won 5-2 to take their first possession of The Bronze Derby. Later in the season in Clinton, South Carolina, Presbyterian College won 3-2 to reclaim The Bronze Derby. The famed prize had three owners in the spring of 1947. The next time The Bronze Derby would be competed for would be in November at the annual Thanksgiving football matchup in Newberry, South Carolina.

THE BLUE STOCKING   April 26, 1947

The Blue Stocking

Hose Nine Meets Birds, Furman, Newberry Next

Tuesday night the Hosebaseballers, now thick in the midst of the state pennant race, journey to Kingstree to take on the University of South Carolina in a night ball game there.

It will be a return game for the Hose and the Birds, as Coach Larry "Coon" Weldon's charges took the Gamecocks for a 7-3 sledding the first time the teams clashed.

Next Thursday the Blues play a return match with the Furman Hurricane here on Young field at 3:30, with the Baptists out to avenge a 7-3 licking the Hose gave them Tuesday in Greenville.

To round out the week's schedule, Newberry comes to town for the second game of the series, and the last PC chance of the school year to get back the Bronze Derby, the athletic trophy between the two schools. Newberry won possession of the hat by virtue of a 5-2 win over the Hosemen last week, and the Blues are out to take back the loss and the hat.

The team's batting average, never something to brag about, took an upsweep this week, as the Hose started to pound the ball, and really find their collective batting eyes.

Royal Cleaners, Inc.
"Beautiful Dry Cleaning"
Phone 77

Diamonds   Watches   Jewelry
J. C. Thomas, Jeweler
"It's Time That Counts"
Expert Watch Repairing
W. Main St.   Phone 89

**FOR EXPERT
SHOE REPAIRING
McIntosh Shoe Shop**

The Li'l 🎩 That Was!

The Blue Stocking

Distinguished For Its Progress

Volume XXV   Presbyterian College, May 10, 1947   Number 25

Changing Hands...

At the left is Jiggs Woodcock, Newberry's baseball captain, who is presenting the Bronze Derby to Wade Lyle, acting captain of the Hose diamond squad.

The derby was presented in chapel Wednesday, with a program that had Charles MacDonald, PC publicity director telling a short history of the derby, and giving an introduction to Frank Kinard, Newberry publicity man, who with MacDonald evolved the idea of the bronzing of the abducted derby. Woodcock was in turn introduced by Kinard, and the Newberry captain said, "... I'm going to tell the truth: it is with sincere regret and disappointment that I give this Bronze Derby to you today; but I will say one thing: that of the teams we have played, PC has been the cleanest."

The derby, a life-sized hat with a heavy bronze coating, is now reposing in state until further action can be taken on it for its preservation.

To the Victors...

The Bronze Derby came home this week in chapel Wednesday, being presented by Jiggs Woodcock, the Newberry captain.

Accepting the trophy for the Hose was Wade Lyle, standout right-hand pitcher.

In the short history of the hat, the Hose have won its possession two out of three times, taking the first derby game in basketball 44-42, losing the hat in baseball 2-5, and recovering the lid until the fall by virtue of a thrilling 3-2 triumph last Saturday.

Originally the derby belonged to Jimmy Kellett, sophomore of Fountain Inn, but it was abducted from him last winter by a Newberry student. The publicity departments of the two schools got together on a plan for the bronzing of the derby as a symbol of the 50 years' athletic competition between the two schools, and it arrived just in time to present it to Newberry after the first baseball game.

The hat goes up on the block in all three major sports, with the winner getting the derby in football, basketball, and baseball.

The Li'l That Was!

The first Newberry College athletic team to win The Bronze Derby was the 1947 baseball team. In the spring of 1947, following the inaugural basketball game, the Indians defeated the Blue Hose 5-2 to regain The Bronze Derby.

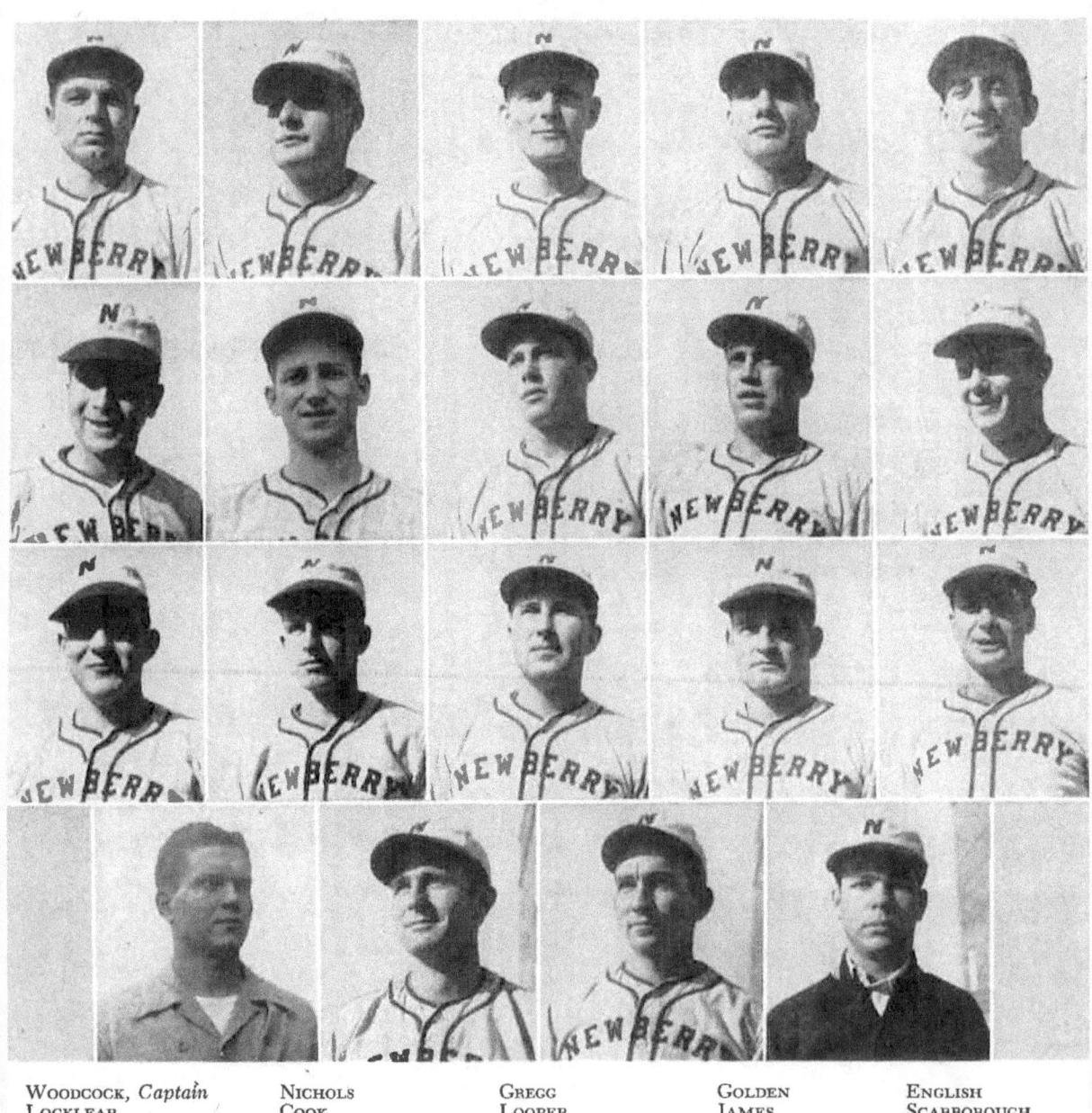

NEWBERRIAN

Woodcock, *Captain*   Nichols   Gregg   Golden   English
Locklear   Cook   Looper   James   Scarborough
Chapman   Parler   Dukes   Lynch   Coleman
Corley, *Manager*   Whitworth   Dobson   Mappus, *Manager*

The Li'l 🎩 That Was!

The Indian
NEWBERRY COLLEGE
"Home of The Fighting Redskins"

VOLUME II   NEWBERRY, S. C., THURSDAY, MAY 1, 1947   NUMBER 14

DERBY PRESENTED

MacDONALD   DERBY   WOODCOCK

The "Bronze Derby", symbol of nearly 50 years of keen athletic rivalry between Presbyterian and Newberry Colleges, made its public debut in chapel exercises here on Tuesday, April 22. The Derby was presented to Newberry baseball captain Jiggs Woodcock by Charles MacDonald of the P. C. News Bureau, acting on behalf of the Blue Stockings baseball team. The Derby, which was theoretically in the hands of the Blue Hose after their two-point basketball victory over the Indians in the first "Derby" contest, was won by the Indians, 5-2, in a baseball game with the Hose here on April 19.

The "Bronze Derby" will go on the block again Saturday, when the Indians and the Hose collide at Clinton, with the victor this time being allowed to retain the hat until the next "Derby" contest, the November 22 football game here. (Staff photo by Ted Neely).

The Li'l 🎩 That Was!

The governing rules for the athletic competition for The Bronze Derby between Newberry College and Presbyterian College were established in the spring of 1947. The chart on the next page illustrates how many Bronze Derby competitions took place between the schools from 1947-1955. For example, in the spring of 1947, Presbyterian College won the first basketball game and won the initial Bronze Derby competition. Newberry College won the first baseball game of the year and took possession of The Bronze Derby. Later in the spring, the Blue Hose won the next baseball game and they kept The Bronze Derby until the fall when the teams matched up in football. The Indians won the inaugural Bronze Derby gridiron matchup and took the trophy home to Newberry College. The next competition for The Bronze Derby would be the first scheduled basketball game in 1948. In 1956 a consensus between the schools deemed The Bronze Derby would only be competed for annually at the football game. From 1947-1955 the teams were very competitive in football, however the Newberry baseball team was dominant on the diamond. The Blue Hose were dominant on the hardcourt.

From 1947 to 1955:

- The teams competed 57 times in baseball, basketball and football.
- The Bronze Derby was exchanged 22 times between the schools.
- From 1948-1951, Newberry College won 15 (4 seasons) consecutive baseball games.
- From 1950-1955, Presbyterian College won 13 (6 seasons) consecutive basketball games.
- Presbyterian College held a slight edge over Newberry College in football winning 5 of the 9 games played. The teams played to a 7-7 tie in 1953.

1947 - 1955 Bronze Derby Game Results

	Basketball	**Baseball**	**Football**
1947	PC 44 - NC 42	NC 5 - PC 2	NC 6 - PC 0
		PC 3 - NC 2	
1948	PC 54 - NC 52	NC 5 - PC 2	PC 40 - NC 7
	NC 55 - PC 50	NC 9 - PC 2	
1949	PC 52 - NC 46	NC 4 - PC 3	NC 20 - PC 14
	NC 65 - PC 41	NC 9 - PC 6	
	NC 66 - PC 59	NC 10 - PC 6	
		NC 11 - PC 6	
		NC 10 - PC 6	
1950	PC 87 - NC 70	NC 4 - PC 3	PC 20 - NC 6
	PC 78 - NC 59	NC 9 - PC 6	
	PC 103 - NC 60	NC 12 - PC 6	
		NC 10 - PC 6	
1951	PC 87 - NC 47	NC 15 - PC 2	PC 27 - NC 0
	PC 79 - NC 59	NC 4 - PC 0	
		NC 11 - PC 0	
		NC 6 - PC 1	
1952	PC 64 - NC 51	PC 16 - NC 6	PC 14 - NC 12
	PC 76 - NC 64	NC 11 - PC 2	
		NC 14 - PC 2	
		NC 8 - PC 4	
1953	PC 98 - NC 50	NC 2 - PC 1	NC 7 - PC 7
	PC 109 - NC 69	PC 2 - NC 1	
		PC 5 - NC 1	
		NC 4 - PC 2	
1954	PC 123 - NC 51	NC 7 - PC 3	PC 20 - NC 18
	PC 150 - NC 91	NC 7 - PC 1	
1955	PC 86 - NC 82	NC 12 - PC 8	NC 20 - PC 18
	PC 111 - NC 77	NC 13 - PC 2	
Totals	PC 16 Wins	PC 4 Wins	PC 5 Wins
	NC 3 Wins	NC 25 Wins	NC 3 Wins

The Bronze Derby 1947 - 1955 Results
Wins

	Newberry	Presbyterian
Basketball 19 Games (1947-1955)	3	16
Winning %	16%	84%
Baseball 29 Games (1947-1955)	25	4
Winning %	86%	14%
Football 9 Games (1947-1955)	3	5
Winning %	33%	56%

(1 Football Tie)

Total 57 Games

Total Wins (1 Tie)	31	25
Winning %	55%	45%

The Li'l 🎩 That Was!

NEWBERRY LOSES DERBY

The Newberry Basketeers fought hard to maintain possession of the "Little Bronze Derby", symbol of athletic rivalry between Newberry and Presbyterian, in a thrill packed game which the P. C. cagers copped in the last few minutes of the game last Monday night here at the college gym.

The "Derby Game" held the enthusiastic spectators from the first jump until the final buzzer in a fast, hard game, highlighted by quick breaks, long passes, and many shots at the basket.

Marvin English and Carl Stegall were both high scorers for the Newberry cagers with 10 points each in the "Derby Game" which ended up 42 to 38 for the Blue Hose team.

The "Little Bronze Derby" will be presented to Presbyterian by the captain of the Newberry team. The next "Derby Game" will be a baseball game held in the latter part of March. Then the teams will play again in the last of the baseball season in a game which will determine the Derby's resting place until the football season next fall.

Gifts of Lasting
Permanence and Remembrance
Watch and Jewelry Repairing
FENNELL'S JEWELRY STORE
College Street

Always First With the Latest
Martha Jane
Newberry's Leading Fashion Center
1238 Main St.   Phone 893-J

T & C CLEANERS
1508 Nance Street

Our Representatives:
Ed Ott and Peg Swygert

CARPENTER'S
Women's Apparel, Dry Goods, Millinery
Newberry, S. C.

The Blue Stocking

Distinguished For Its Progress

Volume XXVII   Presbyterian College, Clinton, S. C., Jan. 15, 1949   Number 13

At Long Last

Newberry Returns Prized Derby

After being overdue for one and one-half months, the Bronze derby, symbol of athletic supremacy between Newberry and Presbyterian colleges, was returned to its normal resting place in the Library building yesterday. Five Newberry representatives presented the topper to Captains Calvert Marsh and Herb Lindsay, respective leaders of the football and basketball teams.

The Hose football eleven won the derby in the Thanksgiving slaughter of the Newberry Indians, 40-7, on Johnson field. Bill Calk, Newberry sports publicist, explained in chapel prior to the presentation that no malice was intended in not returning the hat sooner, but that a mixup had been incurred by the College registrar.

Tuesday night of this past week, the Hose basketball team captured the lid again when it edged the Indian five, 54-52, after leading at halftime, 31-15.

New arrangements were agreed upon also yesterday by the PC student body and the Newberry representatives. The plan calls for the presence of the Bronze derby at every football, basketball, and baseball contest, with the award to be made at the end of each game to the winning team.

The basketball win Tuesday night marked the fifth time PC has won the derby against five also for the Newberrians, thus evening the count between the two arch rivals.

The Li'l That Was!

The Indian
NEWBERRY COLLEGE
"Home of The Fighting Redskins"

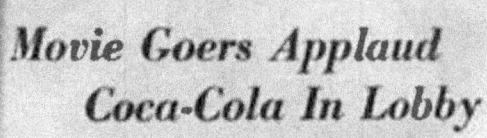

Blue Socks Nose Out Redskins Here In Cage Thriller

The Blue Stockings of P. C. nosed out the Newberry Redskins last Tuesday night, January 11 in the Newberry College Gymnasium 54 to 52. By virtue of this win the Blue Hose successfully defended their right of possession to the bronze derby.

Employing a smooth well-oiled cage machine in the first half the Hose built up a substantial 31 to 15 lead at half time. Led by Captain Lindsay and forward Groninger, P. C. apparently had the game in the bag at the half.

In the second half the Indians found themselves and began to hit the basket consistently. Coach Laval broke up his two-platoon system and put a team on the floor which not only held the Hose in check but also gradually hacked away the early P. C. lead.

Carl Stegall, star center of last year, shared top scoring honors with Al Fister, who himself, played a jam-up game. Each hit the net for 14 points. Groninger was high scorer for Presbyterian with 17 points.

STUDENTS AND FACULTY
Always Welcome
— AT —
JOHNNIE'S News and Doughnut Shop
TOASTED MALTS AND ICE CREAM

Gifts for All Occasions

Verna & Hal Kohn

VISIT THE CLARY CLOTHING CO.
See Our Fine Selection of
MEN'S CLOTHING

The Li'l That Was!

The Indian
NEWBERRY COLLEGE
"Home of The Fighting Redskins"

Indians Bag Bronze Derby

The Newberry Indian Cagers regained the Bronze Derby by virtue of their 55-50 victory over Presbyterian College, Saturday, February 19, at Clinton. Immediately after the basketball game, Captain Herb Lindsay, of the P. C. Squad, presented the prized derby to Captain Nose Poston of Newberry.

In the basketball tilt, Newberry took an early lead and maintained it throughout the game. Coach Billy Laval used successfully a two-platoon system and Newberry held a 28-19 lead at the half-time. Yaldizian was high-scorer for the night with 16 points. Groninger of P. C. was held from his average of 20 points a game to a total of 12 for Saturday night's performance. Scoring for the Indians in addition to Yaldizian were: Fister 11, Medlock 9, Stegall 6, Hodge 4, Gearns 3, Poston 3, Tarzian 2, and Stoudemire 1.

The Bronze Derby, symbol of athletic rivalry between P. C. and Newberry, is now resting in the trophy case in Holland Hall. Arrangements were agreed upon recently to present the derby to the victor immediately at the end of every football, basketball, and baseball contest.

The basketball victory Saturday marked the sixth time Newberry has won the derby against five times for the Presbyterians.

The Bronze Derby, token of athletic supremacy between Newberry and Presbyterian colleges, is shown above being exchanged for the eleventh time, since its founding two years ago. Here Captain Herb Lindsay, with his back turned, is presenting the coveted topper to Captain Bill Poston, Newberry College representative. In the background is the Newberry team which won the hat from P. C. in a heated basketball game. This marked the sixth Derby win for the Newberrians against five for the P. C. Blue Hose.—(photo by Shields)

The Li'l That Was!

The Blue Stocking

Distinguished For Its Progress

Volume XXVII   Presbyterian College, Clinton, S. C., May 21, 1949   Number 26

Indians Scalp Blue Hose, 4-2 To Keep the 'Lil Bronze Derby

Win Gives Indians State Title; Graham Leads Hose Batting

The Newberry college baseball team scored two runs in the sixth inning on two hits and an error to insure a 4-2 victory over the Presbyterian college Blue Stockings Monday on Young field. The victory also gave the Tribesmen possession of the Bronze Derby for the eighth time.

Al Fister and Billy Williams, Newberry freshmen, collaborated on a seven-hit pitching job for the winners, while their mates collected nine safeties off Lum Edwards, lone Hose hurler.

Leftfielder Harry Gambrell was the big gun for the Newberrians as he scored three times, getting two hits and monopolizing on a Hose error. Hal Graham, Hose captain and second sacker, led his teammates at bat with two hits as did Chez Burnette, who blasted a double and a single in three trips to the plate.

Two PC rallies were cut short by attempted base steals as the Hosemen scored one run in the first and third innings.

Presbyterian	ab	r	h	e
McKinney, lb	3	0	0	0
Graham, 2b	4	1	2	1
Burnette, cf	3	0	2	0
Jackson, rf	1	0	0	1
Edwards, p	3	0	1	0
Berry, ss	3	0	0	0
Copeland, lf	3	1	1	1
Weldon, c	3	0	1	0
King, 3b	3	0	0	0
Totals	26	2	7	3

Newberry   103 002 000—4
Presbyterian   001 001 000—2

McMillian Says ...

Coach Lonnie McMillian requests that track men turn in all equipment that they have drawn for the past season before leaving school. Jim Cornwell has been named the man to see.

COMPLETE OUTFITTERS FOR THE COLLEGE MAN
ADAIR'S MEN'S SHOP

McGee's Drug Store

BISHOP & WALKER
"The Rexall Drug Store"
Try One of Our Famous Chocolate-Malteds and One of our Tasty Sandwiches

The Li'l That Was!

THE BLUE STOCKING — Page Three

Hose Fight Tonight To Keep Bronze Derby

Game Set for 8:15 p.m. at Newberry; Take on Indian Five for Second Time

Rivalry—ancient and renewed—stalks the hardwoods at Newberry college tonight as the Indian quintet puts up a "squawk" to recapture the Bronze Derby from Presbyterian college's Blue Hose.

Thursday night the Hosemen scalped the Indians 52-46 to take possession of the hat, symbol of athletic supremacy between the two colleges, after a three-month rest at Newberry.

Game time is set for 8:15 p.m. in the Newberry gymnasium.

In defense of the coveted chapeau, Coach Claude Crocker of PC

will throw a fast and flashy attack at the revengeful Indians. Spearheading the PC onslaught will be All-State Forward Dwight Groninger, who is currently sporting a 14-point average in state cage circles.

Behind Groninger will be Guards Kay Hill and Paul Nye, Center Ed Thompson, and Forward Lewis Hawkins. This fivesome comprises the Hose starting lineup for the fracas.

For Newberry in their quest for the topper will be Center Ed Stegall, Guards Bill Poston and Joe Tarzian, and Forwards Al Fister and "Hank" Will in the starting berths.

Tonight's game is rated as a tossup in everybody's book. Both teams have demonstrated strong offensive spurts, and even so when such arch-rivals clash previous scores go out the gym.

Also both teams are out to tie that Derby for size and to make another notch in their Derby win column. PC has taken the topper on six occasions, while Newberry has won it nine times.

The Blue Stocking

Distinguished For Its Progress

Vol. XXVIII   Presbyterian College, Feb. 18, 1950   No. 15

The Indian
NEWBERRY COLLEGE
"Home of The Fighting Redskins"

NEWS · SPORTS · FEATURES · EDITORIALS

NEWBERRY, S. C. WEDNESDAY, FEBRUARY 11, 1953

INDIANS COP BRONZE DERBY

Remain Undefeated In State Standings

Newberry College retained possession of the "Little Bronze Derby," traditional symbol of athletic rivalry between Newberry's Fighting Redskins and the Blue Hose of Presbyterian College, last Friday evening, by out-slugging their rivals 6-8 on the local diamond.

Bug Horton, Indian ace hurler, racked up his fifth win of the season, going the route against P. C. The cool weather interfered with his usual near-hitless pitching, but it did nothing to the enthusiasm of the unusually large crowd, which was estimated as one of the largest this year.

The Indians jumped into an early lead and kept it; although in the closing frames, the Blue Hose began to tee into some of Bug's pitches and scored liberally, but not enough to counteract the locals' lead.

The Indians will face the Terriers of Wofford, Tuesday, with Boring seeking his second win of the season. In the last Indian-Terrier clash, last Monday, the locals won handily by a 9-3 final count.

PIN-POINT COLLAR
SHIRTS
BERGEN CLOTHING CO.

The Li'l 🎩 That Was!

The Blue Stocking

Distinguished For Its Progress

Volume XXVIII — Presbyterian College, Clinton, S. C., March 11, 1950 — Number 18

Blue Sox Meet Indians At Festival Wednesday

Open Baseball Season With Newberry In Bronze Derby Game at Peach Festival

Presbyterian college baseballers open their 1950 season amid peach blossoms Tuesday when the Stockings cross bats with Newberry's highly-rated Indians at Johnston, S. C.

The two ancient rivals go after the Bronze Derby for the fifteenth time when they don their spikes for a feature event in the annual South Carolina Peach Blossom festival.

Game time is set for 3 p.m., on the Johnston field.

The contest, which will pit the two teams together for the first of five scheduled meetings this season, will be the first college baseball game for South Carolina. Also it will be the first test for Presbyterian's new baseball mentor, Coach Walter Barbare.

Coach Barbare will divide the hurling duties among veteran Lum Edwards and newcomers Jake Brewer and Ankie Rowe. Each pitcher is slated to see three innings on the mound.

On the receiving end of this trio's throws will be a complete crop of newcomers—Harold Dunstan, Gerald Banks, and John McKissick—to go the rounds.

For Newberry, defending state champs, Coach Billy Laval is expected to employ his star slugger, "Snoozie" Horton. Catching the experienced lefthander will be Jack Marks.

Rounding out the PC infield will be Bob McKinney at first, either Joe Weingartner or Warren Stevenson at second, Dick Walden at shortstop, and either Bruno King or Dick Kimsey at third.

Roaming the outfield will be two of last year's returnees, Kirby Jackson and Brooks Copeland. The third starter is undetermined.

The PC team has been working out since Monday, with the pitchers and catchers getting an earlier start in February.

The Sock Says . . .

The Derby Is Weary

The Bronze Derby is tired and worn. It is overworked. And this [...] of the [...] of a [...] supremacy between [...]terian and Newberry [...] the Derby is gradually losing its significance.

In short, the coveted chapeau needs a rest.

But there is no rest—as the old saying goes—even for the weary. And this seems even truer for the symbolic topper; for it goes on auction to the higher scorer in the Presbyterian-Newberry baseball game at the Johnston Peach Blossom festival Wednesday afternoon in its seventeenth appearance since its origin in 1947.

Then to seal this, the lid is scheduled to go to the block on four more occasions this baseball season.

Isn't this overdoing a good thing?

Gone are the days when a Bronze Derby athletic contest rated a streamer headline in the daily papers of South Carolina. Nowadays it's only a formality for spirited spectators—and these fans only—to wait around after a Derby contest for the presentation of the lid to the winning team captain.

It is true that Newberry holds the upper hand in Derby competition thus far, having won the hat in 10 of 16 football, basketball, and baseball games. However, The Blue Stocking feels that the Newberry supporters and students are also aware of the fact that the Derby is playing out in significance and publicity value because it is being overworked.

Next week The Blue Stocking is going to find out just how the two student bodies stand on this question—what to do about the Derby. The Blue Stocking plans to run a cross-section poll of both campuses to check the pulses of student opinion from both sides.

In the meantime, think it over . . . This matter merits your thoughts.

THE BROADWAY
WEEK OF MARCH 13-18

Monday and Tuesday
Key to the City

Wednesday
Tension

Thursday and Friday
Mother Didn't Tell Me

Saturday
Beau Geste

THE CASINO
WEEK OF MARCH 13-18

Monday and Tuesday
Square Dance Jubilee

Wednesday and Thursday
Haunted Trails
Follow Me Quietly

Friday and Saturday
Son of Billy the Kid
Search for Danger

The Blue Stocking

Volume XXVIII — PRESBYTERIAN COLLEGE, CLINTON, S. C., MARCH 18, 1950 — Number 19

Indians Nose Blue Sox, 4-3

Stifle PC Rally in Big Ninth; Sox Open Regular Schedule Friday

Staving off a ninth inning rally by the Presbyterian Blue Sox, Newberry's state champion baseball team copped a 4-3 decision over the Sox in an exhibition ball game at the Johnston Peach festival Wednesday afternoon.

Relief hurler Pete Reiser stepped onto the mound with no outs and the bases loaded to put the quietus on the Sox spurt in the final frame. He struck out one batter, and another knocked into a double play.

The game, listed as an exhibition, was the first to be played in South Carolina collegiate circles

MEET CATAWBA FRIDAY

Friday at 3 p.m. the Blue Sox break the seal on their regular season, meeting Catawba's Indians here on Young field. Coach Barbare has not released his starting lineup yet nor his leadoff pitcher.

this season. Being an exhibition, the Bronze Derby did not go on the block as expected.

Both teams used three batteries, and both collected seven hits.

"Sug" Horton, Newberry's ace pitcher, received credit for the victory, giving up two hits in four innings. Tabbed as the loser was PC's Tommy Lide, a freshman who flipped his first college performance. The Indian batters nicked Lide for three hits in three innings.

Other PC hurlers taking three-inning flings were Ankie Rowe and Lum Edwards. Rowe gave up one hit, while Edwards allowed three.

Max Dubose, Newberry right-fielder, toted the big gun for the Indians, driving in one run in (Continued on page four)

THE BLUE STOCKING

Indians Nose Sox

(Continued from page three)
each the first and third innings. Other slugger for the Indians was Shortstop Russ Horton. He belted a three-bagger in the eighth to score the final two Newberry tallies.

For PC, it was Emmett Fulk, freshman center fielder, and Brooks Copeland, senior left fielder, who figured in the three runs scored. Fulk singled twice in two official trips to the plate, knocking in one run. Copeland contributed another score by capitalizing on a triple into center field and two bad throws to score on a round-tripper.

Copeland then scored the other marker in the ninth inning when Catcher John McKissick earned a walk to first with bases loaded

---

THE BROADWAY
WEEK OF MARCH 27—APR. 1

Monday and Tuesday
The Heiress
Olivia de Havilland and Montgomery Clift

Wednesday
Hamlet
Laurence Olivier

Thursday and Friday
Nancy Goes To Rio
Jane Powell, Ann Sothern

Saturday
Silver River
Errol Flynn, Ann Sheridan

THE CASINO
WEEK OF MARCH 27—APR. 1

Monday and Tuesday
Kidnapped
Roddy McDowall, Sue England

Wednesday and Thursday
Holiday In Havana
Desi Arnaz and Band

Red Desert
Don Barry, Jack Holt

Friday and Saturday
Mary Ryan, Detective
Marsha Hunt, John Litel

The Li'l 🎩 That Was!

The Blue Stocking
Distinguished For Its Progress

Volume XXVIII   Presbyterian College, Clinton, S. C., April 22, 1950   Number 23

Sox Seek Derby In Game Today

Waving a bat in one hand and a Bronze Derby in the other, the Newberry Indians invade the Presbyterian college campus today for the second in a series of four baseball games. Previously the Indian team edged the Blue Sox by a 9-6 score in Newberry.

Game time is set for 3:30 p.m. on Young field.

The Newberrians will bring the Bronze Derby, symbol of athletic supremacy between the two colleges, for presentation to the winning team captain. The coveted chapeau has been in Newberry hands since the last basketball engagement between the arch rivals.

In his attempt to recover the prized topper, Coach Walter Barbare will send Righthanders Lum Edwards and Ankie Rowe to the hill. Receiving the two Sox hurlers will be John McKissick and "Red" Banks.

Coach Billie Laval of Newberry will start his ace pitcher, "Sug" Horton in defense of the Derby and a brilliant record of one loss in state play.

The starting PC infield will consist of Bob McKinney at first, Joe Weingartner at second, Byron King at third, and hard-hitting "Frog" Weldon at the shortstop position. In the outfield will be Kirby Jackson, Brooks Copeland, and Regis Kinsey.

The Indian
NEWBERRY COLLEGE
"Home of The Fighting Redskins"

INVITATION: Gaver Memorial Dedication

SPORTS: From The Sidelines

NEWBERRY NINE RETAINS "BRONZE DERBY"

Indians Defeat Blue Hose Four Times This Year

The Newberry Indians defeated the Presbyterian Blue Hose last Saturday to retain the "Bronze Derby", to the tune of 12 to 5. "Bug" Horton was on the mound for the Redmen, giving up only 9 hits before being relieved in the 8th inning by Stoudemire.

Newberry's big inning came in the 7ht when 11 men went to bat. Before the combined efforts of Rowe and Lide, of Presbyterian, the Indians pushed across 7 runs.

To date the Indians have proven themselves to be the top team in the state, with a record of 15 wins and 3 losses. No doubt everyone has read Coach Laval's article in The Greenville News. We all agree that the present Newberry team is capable of taking on any college nine in this area.

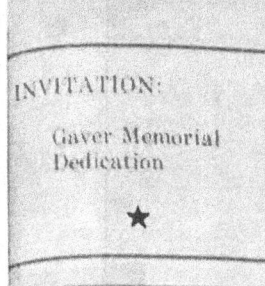

TENNIS RACKET STRINGS
DENNIS SHOE SHOP

LOVELY CRYSTAL PATTERNS by TIFFIN
THE NOVELTY SHOP
Next to Ritz Theatre

Newberry Steam Laundry & Dry Cleaning Co.
LAUNDRY DRY CLEANING
931 Main St. Newberry, S.C.

Columbia Diamond Rings
Elgin, Bulova Watches
Lunt, Towle, Manchester Sterling
Bavarian China
Glastonbury Crystal
FENNELL'S JEWELRY STORE
1102 College St.

THE WIGWAM CAFE
Fast Service
And
Beautiful Waitresses
MRS. IDA C. GRAHAM
Phone 5193

WE ARE HERE TO SERVE YOU
Home Cooked Food At Popular Prices
Open 8 A.M. - 12 P.M. Daily
THE TOMAHAWK

GILDER & WEEKS
"The Right Drug Store"
Joanna — Newberry
South Carolina

ORCHIDS GARDENIAS
ROSE CORSAGES
Dunn, See Carl Dunn. See Carl Dunn. See Carl Dunn. See
VERNA & HAL KOHN
"Your F.T.D. Florist for Thirty Years"

WHITE SWIM SHORTS
by Puritan
BERGEN CLOTHING CO.

THE MAIN STREET FLOWER SHOP
FLOWERS AND GIFTS
CORSAGES A SPECIALTY

The Li'l 🎩 That Was!

| EXAMS— HELP OR HARM? | **The Indian** NEWBERRY COLLEGE *"Home of The Fighting Redskins"* NEWBERRY, S. C., WEDNESDAY, JANUARY 17, 1951 | INDIANS RACK-UP THREE WINS |

WEDNESDAY, JANUARY 17, 1951

From The Sidelines
With HAL RICKERT

The Redskins lost their first game of the year (1951 that is) last Friday when our arch-rivals, Presbyterian, took their measure 87 to 70. Previous to then the Tribe had captured three straight intra-state victories, two of them over Little Four teams.

The team's improvement has been obvious, but it is best shown by the 63 to 60 victory over Furman, a team that had beaten Newberry earlier by 15 or 20 points.

The loss to P. C. is no disgrace. The Blue Stockings are second in the nation in scoring average and are very probably the best college team in the state. Naturally, we hated to see them cart off the "Derby" for the second straight time, but we have another basketball game with them and five baseball engagements. It won't be away too long.

The recent splurge of our basketball team is probably due to several factors. The basic factor however, is Coach Bob Tate. Tate has done a remarkable job in bringing this young team along. When the season began the squad looked "pitiful." There was little experience with only one player, Al Fister, who had started regularly last year. Charlie Stoudemire had started several games and they formed the nucleus of the team. Rounding out the squad was an assortment of Freshmen and men up from the J. V.'s.

When the team dispersed for Christmas they were winless in five collegiate games. Fister had been a disappointment; he was averaging about 14 points a game, but over half those points were foul shots. The chief reason for his inability to score with his usual consistency was possibly the fact that the team was unfamiliar to each other and that Fister plays differently than most players. He uses a "driving" game and is probably the best "foul manufacturer" in the state and one of the best in the country.

The added experience to Freshmen Neil Chrisley, Don Ardito and Bobby Bailey, and to Sophomore Art Kovacs plus their increased familiarity with each other's style of play accounts for the team improvement and the improvement of Fister. Fister has now garnered 79 points in his last three games and is averaging over 17 points per encounter.

The team has been slow getting started but they're rolling now, and should be victorious in the majority of their remaining games.

• • • • •

NEWBERRY COLLEGE BI-WEEKLY PUBLICATION

The Indian
NEWBERRY COLLEGE
"Home of The Fighting Redskins"

CHAMPS OF 1950 LITTLE FOUR BASEBALL

NEWBERRY, S. C., WEDNESDAY, MARCH 11, 1951

Indians Secure Derby, Defeat Blue Hose Twice

The Newberry baseball team brought the coveted Bronze Derby back to Newberry by defeating the Presbyterian team, 15 to 2, in the first game which was at Presbyterian.

"Bug" Horton, who has never been beaten by a South Carolina team, set the Blue Hose players down with "whiplike" quickness. His ability to put "stuff" on the ball enabled him to give up only eight hits to the P. C. team. "Bug" was in complete control of the situation from the start. He also led his team at bat by giving three triples for four trips to the plate.

Max DuBose hit a "grand-slam" home run to help the 'Tribes' scoring. Edwards got two home runs to account for the only two runs for P. C.

NEWBERRY	AB	R	H	E
Maxwell, 2b	4	3	1	0
Dukes, lf	4	2	0	0
DuBose, rf	6	2	1	0
Looper, cf	6	0	0	0
R. Horton, ss	4	3	2	0
Reames, 3b	5	1	0	0
Clements, 1b	5	0	0	0
McAllister, c	3	3	2	0
S. Horton, p	4	1	3	0
A-Bailey	1	0	0	0
Totals	41	15	9	0

The Li'l 🎩 That Was!

The Blue Stocking
Distinguished For Its Progress

Volume XXIX · Presbyterian College, Clinton, S. C., April 7, 1951 · Number 21

April 7, 1951 · THE BLUE STOCKING · Page Three

PC Meets Newberry Twice This Weekend

Rowe, Borgh Are Hose Starters In First State Competition
By HARRY DENT

Two baseball slugfests for possession of the Bronze Derby, symbol of athletic supremacy between Presbyterian and Newberry colleges, highlight the sports card in South Carolina sports circles this weekend as the two ancient rivals compete Friday and Saturday on the diamond in their first state engagements.

The first game of the two-game series will be played here on Johnson field, pitting the Indian acehurler, Sug Horton, against Blue Hose mainstay Ankie Rowe. Both made the All-State nine. On Saturday the Indian diamondeers entertain the Hosemen in Newberry in a postponed game. Both games begin at 3:30 p.m.

In the Saturday battle at Newberry, Coach Sid Varney is expected to throw another of his strong hurlers, Kelly Borgh, at the Indians. The Newberry starter has not yet been mentioned.

The winner in each of the contests will win possession of the Bronze Derby, which has been in Presbyterian hands during both the football and basketball seasons. Both teams will enter the games with good records to date. However, in seasonal play last year the Indians defeated the Blue Hose in all five encounters, going on to win the state championship.

Next week the Presbyterian team will make two home stands, one against Wofford on Tuesday and another against Erskine on Friday.

"... ON THE BLOCK"

The Li'l That Was!

The Indian
NEWBERRY COLLEGE
"Home of The Fighting Redskins"

NEWS • SPORTS • FEATURES • EDITORIALS

NEWBERRY, S. C., WEDNESDAY, APRIL 21, 1947

Indians To Meet Blue Hose Tonight; May Recover Derby
GAME TO BE AT HEDGEPATH STADIUM

The Newberry College Indians will be hosts to the Presbyterian Blue Hose tonight at 8 o'clock in the first of four games to be played between th etwo keen rivals.

To increase the color of the meeting of the two institutions, the Bronze Derby will be at stake. Newberry will be out to recapture it from the Hose who took it during the past grid season. Also to be decided will likely be the championship of the Little Four. Newberry has captured the crown for the past three seasons and is a likely holdover for this year, but P. C. presents a strong contender.

Coach McConnell will probably send "Sug" Horton to the mound to face P. C. The rest of the line-up will be regular.

The Li'l 🎩 That Was!

The Blue Stocking

Distinguished for Its Progress

Volume XXIX   Presbyterian College, Clinton, S. C., April 15, 1951   Number 22

PC Takes One, Dropped Twice

Last week-end saw the Blue Hose fall twice before the Newberry Indians and turn over to them the Bronze Derby which the PC men held through football and basketball season.

Friday the Indians rapped the Hose 15-2 in a game that saw PC pitching give up 11 walks and the home team committed six errors.

Saturday, Newberry's Pick Riser threw a two-hit shut-out at his arch-rivals as his team racked up a 4-0 victory. Riser struck out nine.

A three-run spurt in the second inning iced the game — called on account of rain after six innings — for Newberry.

Riser sparked his team's offense with two for three.

Breaking loose for six runs in the last of the eighth, Presbyterian took a 7-3 victory from the Wofford Terriers Tuesday.

Kimsey's triple with the bases loaded and Jackson's homerun highlighted the big eighth for the Blue Hose.

Fred Powers, with a triple and a single, and Bryan with a homerun and a single, paced Wofford. Kimsey and Edwards collected two hits each for the Hosemen.

BELK'S
YOUR HOME OF BETTER VALUES
Quality Clothiers and Budget Prices

ADAIR'S MEN'S SHOP
"COMPLETE OUTFITTERS FOR MEN"
CLINTON, S. C.

McGee's Drug Store

WELCOME, COLLEGE BOYS
It is a pleasure to us to serve your Printing and Stationery Needs. Everything needed for the classroom you will find here. Drop in often — it will be a pleasure to serve you.

CHRONICLE PUBLISHING CO.
Publishers -:- Printers -:- Stationers

The Broadway
WEEK OF APRIL 16-21

Monday-Tuesday
Three Secrets
Eleanor Parker, Ruth Roman

Wednesday
The Third Man
Joseph Cotten, Valli

Thursday-Friday
Bird of Paradise
Louis Jourdan, Debra Paget

Saturday
Target Unknown
Mark Stevens, Alex Nicol

The Casino
WEEK OF APRIL 16-21

Monday-Tuesday
The Lion Hunters
Johnny Sheffield

Wednesday-Thursday
The Great Plane Robbery
Tom Conway

Bordertown Trail
Sunset Carson

Friday and Saturday
Rustlers On Horseback
Alan Lane, Eddy Waller

Jungle Stampede
George Breeson

The Li'l That Was!

The Indian
NEWBERRY COLLEGE
"Home of The Fighting Redskins"

NEWS • SPORTS • FEATURES • EDITORIALS

NEWBERRY, S. C., WEDNESDAY, MAY 7, 1952

Recapture Bronze Derby; On Top Throughout Game

The Fighting Redskins avenged an earlier loss to the Presbyterian Blue Hose on Thursday, May 1, at Prosperity by toppling the Stockings 11-3. The victory brought the famed Bronze Derby back to the Newberry campus for the first time since the 1951 baseball season.

Charles Stoudemire notched his sixth victory against one defeat by scattering nine safe base blows throughout the nine innings he worked. Stoudemire was in trouble for a few innings but managed to come out unscathed in the fourth when a line drive single took a freak hop to give Welsh a three-bagger with two aboard.

The Indians took advantage of twelve free passes and launched seven hits to push across eleven scores. Charlie Berry, driving in five runs, was the main cog in Newberry's offense. Berry came up twice with the bases loaded and produced a double and a single, respectively, to drive in his runs. Webster Grayson produced two line singles in three trips for the Redskins. Leon Maxwell, who suffered an injured ankle in the fourth, and Fred Derrick also blasted doubles for the Newberry cause.

"Frog" Weldon, rifle armed P. C. left fielder, had two for five to lead the Hose at the plate. Matthews was the losing pitcher.

Newberry 203 320 01x
Presbyterian 000 300 000

Campus capers call for Coke

Commencement's a big day
... so get off to the right start.
Pause for a frosty bottle of delicious Coca-Cola
—and be refreshed.

DRINK Coca-Cola

BOTTLED UNDER AUTHORITY OF THE COCA-COLA COMPANY BY
NEWBERRY COCA-COLA BOTTLING CO.

You Are
Always Welcome
— AT —
**JOHNNIE'S
News and
Doughnut Shop**

WE HAVE
ANY KIND OF MAGAZINE
FROZEN MALT
FRIED PIES

Please enter my subscription for The 1952-53 Indian.
I ame enclosing $1.50 for my subscription.

Name _____
Address _____

The Li'l 🎩 That Was!

The Indian
NEWBERRY COLLEGE
"Home of The Fighting Redskins"

NEWS · SPORTS · FEATURES · EDITORIALS

NEWBERRY, S. C., WEDNESDAY, MAY 21, 1952

Team Wins Third Over Hose; Takes Derby, Championship

The Fighting Redskins blasted the Presbyterian Blue Stockings 11-6 on Thursday, May 15, at Clinton to capture the Little Four Championship and the right to retain the famed Bronze Derby. It was the third triumph over the Hose for Newberry this season.

P. C. jumped to an early 5-0 lead and seemed well on the way to victory until the big seventh inning when everything broke loose. Barry, P. C. hurler, had a one-hitter up until that time. The decisive blow was Bobby Bailey's four-bagger with the bases loaded. Charlie Berry promptly singled and Carl Rogers lined the third pitch out of the park for a home run, scoring Berry before him. When the smoke cleared, Newberry had six runs and six hits, including doubles by Charles DuBose and Fred Derrick. The Tribe scored four more tallies in the eighth on singles by Maxwell, Elsner, Berry, and Derrick, to put the game on ice.

Welsh and Weldon had three for five each for the Hose. Derrick, Berry, and Elsner had two hits apiece for Newberry.

Charles Stoudemire, Newberry's fourth pitcher, halted the P. C. attack and went on to notch his ninth victory against one defeat for the Redskins.

P. C. 120 200 010
Newberry 000 010 640

Stockings Stopped By Indian Power

Paced by a barrage of home runs, and the combined five-hit pitching of Wayne Boose and Charlie Stoudemire, the Newberry College Indians soundly trounced the P. C. Blue Stockings at Clinton on May 5, by the score of 14 to 1.

Ross Horton, Bobby Bailey, and Carl Rogers each hit for the circuit, and Bobby Elsner and Charlie Berry chimed in with triples, as the booming bats of the Redskins made the game a runaway.

Boose started on the hill for Newberry, and was relieved in the second by Stoudemire, who was credited with the victory. Borgh, the starting pitcher for P. C., was the loser, giving up five runs in the second.

Bobby Elsner with 3 for 5, and Ross Horton with 2 for 6 held top averages for the night. No Blue Stocking gained more than one safe blow. This was the second victory for the Indians over P. C. this season. P. C. has downed the Redskins once.

MAKE
GILDER & WEEKS
"YOUR REXALL DRUG STORE"
HEADQUARTERS
Newberry   Joanna

ODORLESS CLEANERS
1109 Friend St.
Newberry

The Li'l That Was!

The Indian

NEWBERRY COLLEGE
"Home of The Fighting Redskins"

NEWBERRY, S. C., WEDNESDAY, FEBRUARY 4, 1953

SEND YOUR RELEASE SLIPS HOME IMMEDIATELY

HAVE YOUR RELEASE SLIPS BACK BY FEB. 10

Blue Hose Take Game; Bronze Derby Remains

Poor shooting was again the factor that caused the Newberry Indians to go down in defeat at the hands of the Presbyterian Blue Hose on Thursday night. The Blue Hose, despite the absence of their star performer Dave Thompson, still had enough left to whip the Redskins 66-51.

High scorers for the Indians were Eddie Blanko with 13 and Ernie Belvin and Charlie Berry with 12 apiece. For P. C., Paul Nye, the Indians forward, was high with 24 points, and Dave Thompson's substitute, McQueen, proved his worth by ranking next with 18.

Newberry trailed by four points at the end of the first quarter, 18-14, but the Hose got hot and built a 32-16 lead with six minutes gone in the second period. Only a two-minute spurt by Indians Berry and Belvin prevented P. C. from breaking the ball game open in the first half. It closed with P. C. on top by eleven points, 34-23.

Newberry worked hard to keep within striking distance, but Nye and McQueen were too much and the third quarter closed with P. C. on top 47-33. Newberry couldn't get any closer in the last quarter and the Blue Hose couldn't build up their lead. Ernie Belvin and Ed Blanko did, however, pour most of their points thru the hoop in this last quarter, but all to no avail, with P. C. coming out on top, 66-51.

Royal Dry Cleaners
"BEAUTIFUL DRY CLEANING"
"You've tried the rest; now try the best."
1107 CALDWELL ST.   PHONE 12

The Li'l 🎩 That Was!

The Indian
NEWBERRY COLLEGE
"Home of The Fighting Redskins"
NEWBERRY, S. C., WEDNESDAY, MAY 6, 1953

Indians Retain Bronze Derby
PC, Newberry Split Games

April 21

The "Fighting Redskins" met defeat at the hands of the Blue Stockings of Presbyterian College in the first encounter between the two clubs this season, at Clinton on April 21. The score of the game was P. C. 15, Newberry 7.

The Blue Stockings were able to belt fifteen safeties off the offerings of Wayne Boose, the Indian starter, and Jimmy Haseldon, who relieved in the sixth. The Newberrians, meanwhile, could obtain only ten base hits from the slants of Borgh, Huggins, and Matthews, the three Stocking moundsmen.

Charlie Berry, Carl Rogers, and Grady Ray each had two safeties in three trips at the plate to pace the Indian batsmen, along with Bobby Bailey, who hit a home run and a single.

Center Welsh paced the P. C. attack with three singles and a double.

April 28

The P. C. Blue Hose were unable to outscore the determined nine from Newberry in the second contest between the two and came out on the short end of a 9-11 decision, at Clinton on April 28.

Dick McCarty started for Newberry and after allowing four hits and four bases on balls, gave up to Don Maxwell with one down in the third inning. After giving up four hits and two free passes, Don was relieved in the fifth by Pick Riser. Pick gave up only three hits and went on to be the winner of the game.

At the plate the Indians showed much power. Grady Ray connected for a grand-slam home run and Carl Rogers followed suit shortly afterwards with a three-run homer. Bobby Bruce was the leading hitter for the night with two hits in three times at bat. Hugh Scott, Bobby Bailey and Pick Riser were close behind with two hits apiece in four trips to the plate.

	R	H
Newberry	007 010 003—11	14
P. C.	306 000 000— 9	3

	AB	H	E
Berry	4	0	1
Maksim	5	2	2
Scott	4	2	0
Bailey	4	2	0
Riser	4	2	0
Rogers	4	1	0
Ray	5	3	0
Grayson	3	1	1
McCarty	1	0	0
Maxwell	0	0	0
Bruce	3	2	0
Totals	39	14	4

The Li'l That Was!

The Indian

NEWBERRY COLLEGE
"Home of The Fighting Redskins"

NEWBERRY, S. C., WEDNESDAY, MAY 20, 1953

Indians Win Little Four

REDSKIN REVIEW

By James Connelly

The Indians have done it again! With the smashing 10-0 shut-out of the Presbyterian Blue Hose last Saturday night, the Fighting Redskins retained both the coveted Bronze Derby, and the Little Four baseball championship, thus writing "finish" to another chapter in the saga of Newberry College baseball. During the season, the Indians defeated Erskine and Presbyterian three times each, and Wofford twice, while losing once to all three, thereby compiling a 8-3 won-lost record in "Little Four" competition, good enough for the championship, and is also around the top within state circles.

"Pick" Riser wound up his baseball career at Newberry in fine style, in allowing the Blue Hose only four safeties in the game. He was in trouble only once and that was in the first inning, as the Stockings loaded the bases. Riser eased out of that one, and preserved his shutout by making the final put-out force a runner at second.

The entire team seemed to have their slugging shoes on, as they blasted four Blue Hose pitchers for fifteen hits during the course of the evening. Slugging Bobby Bailey concluded a great year at the plate with his fine four for five performance. His average should be the best in the state. The entire team average for the season is extraordinarily high, being around or shortly above the three hundred mark, which gives weight to the reputation the team has as a hard slugging outfit.

Saturday night at Hedgepath Stadium the Newberry Indians out-hit and out-scored the Presbyterian College nine to gain possession of the Bronze Derby and sew up the championship of the Little Four Baseball Conference.

While winning the first shut-out of the season for Newberry, Pick Riser struck out three, walked one, and scattered four hits to chalk up his seventh win of the season.

Mesinheimer started on the mound for the Blue Hose, giving up eight hits, two free passes, and struck out three. He was relieved in the fourth by Brown, who gave up two hits. Johnson relieved Brown in the sixth and gave two hits. In the seventh inning, Hamilton came to the mound and allowed one hit, three bases on balls and struck out two.

Behind the plate for the Indians, Bobby Bailey was the big man with three singles and a double. Next was Mike Maksim with three singles.

NEWBERRY	AB	H	E
Berry	5	2	0
Maksim	5	3	0
Scott	2	1	0
Bailey	5	4	0
Riser	5	2	0
Rogers	5	1	0
Ray	3	0	1
Grayson	3	1	0
Bruce	4	1	0
Totals	32	15	1
PRESBYTERIAN	AB	H	E
Welsh	5	0	0
Blue	4	2	1
Hattaway	3	0	0
Huggins	1	0	0
Counts	3	0	1
Shealy	4	1	0
Carter	4	0	0
McGhee	3	0	0
Roberts	3	0	0
Dunlap	0	0	0
Mesinheimer	1	1	0
Brown	1	0	0
Parker	1	0	0
Hamilton	1	0	0
Johnson	0	0	0
Totals	34	4	2

The Li'l ⛑ That Was!

The Indian
NEWBERRY COLLEGE
"Home of The Fighting Redskins"
NEWBERRY, S. C., TUESDAY, FEBRUARY 10, 1954

★ HAPPY VALENTINE'S ★   ★ HAPPY VALENTINE'S ★

WEDNESDAY, FEBRUARY 10, 1954

REDSKIN REVIEW

By Jim Stockman

The Bronze Derby changed hands again as the Presbyterian Blue Hose whipped the Newberry Indians, 98-50. It seemed like the Indians could never get started in the first half, as they lagged behind 51-16. In the third quarter alone, the Fighting Redskins score more points than they did in the entire first half. Ed Blanko and Paul Cone led the Indians' attack with twelve and fourteen points respectively.

NEWBERRY HOTEL BARBER SHOP

The Indian
NEWBERRY COLLEGE
"Home of The Fighting Redskins"

CONGRATULATIONS F. T. A.!

CONGRATULATIONS F. T. A.!

Newberry Divides With P.C.

Last Wednesday, Lexington played host to Newberry and Presbyterian, and saw P. C. whip the Indians 6-1.

The losing pitcher was O'Cain, who now has a 1-2 pitching record. He was relieved in the fifth by Don Maxwell, who pitched 1 2-3 innings. Al Hill came in in the sixth and finished up for the Redskins.

Newberry was allowed three hits and one run on no P. C. errors.

BOX SCORE

	AB	R	H	E
Ray	3	0	0	0
Eisner	2	0	0	0
Dufford	4	0	0	1
Bailey	4	0	0	0
Maksim	3	0	0	0
Scott	2	0	0	0
Blanko	2	0	1	0
Grayson	1	0	0	0
Campbell	1	0	0	0
Rister	3	0	1	0
O'Cain	0	0	0	0
Maxwell	1	1	1	0
Hill	1	0	0	0
Haselden	0	0	0	0
Totals	28	1	3	1

Second Game

Last Friday, Presbyterian challenged the Newberry Indians on the Whitmire field but came out on the short end of the horn, by a score of 4-2.

Boose chalked up his sixth win of the season. He gave up six hits and four bases on balls, while striking out six of the men that faced him.

Newberry picked up four runs on six hits while committing six errors afield.

Leading the Newberry batters at the plate was Mike Maksim with one hit for two times at bat. Right behind him were Dufford and Rister with one for three.

BOX SCORE

	AB	R	H	E
Ray	5	0	1	2
Maksim	2	2	1	1
Eisner	3	1	0	1
Bailey	4	0	1	1
Dufford	3	1	1	1
Campbell	4	0	1	0
Scott	1	0	0	0
Grayson	3	0	0	0
Rister	3	0	1	0
Boose	4	0	0	0
Totals	32	4	6	6

The Fourth Quarter

A South Carolina Football Tradition

The Bronze Derby 1947 - 2006

Old Bailey Stadium was built in 1913 on the Presbyterian College campus. The stadium was located behind Leroy Springs Gymnasium. 27 Bronze Derby football games took place on this field between 1947-2001.

New Bailey Stadium on the campus of Presbyterian College opened for the 2002 football season and hosted 3 Bronze Derby games.

Photos courtesy of Presbyterian College archives

Historic Setzler Field on the campus of Newberry College is the oldest on-campus football field in the state of South Carolina constructed and finished in 1938. Setzler Field has hosted 30 Bronze Derby football games between 1947-2005.

Photos courtesy of Newberry College archives

November 1947

November 1	The racehorse Man 'o War, winner of the Preakness and Belmont Stakes passed away.
November 1	American college and professional Hall of Fame football player Ted Hendricks was born.
November 1	The first Aloha Week Parade was held in Hawaii.
November 2	Howard Hughes flew his wooden airplane the "Spruce Goose" for the first and last time.
November 2	The United States won the Ryder Cup golf tournament led by Ben Hogan.
November 5	British pop rock singer Peter Noone of the band Hermans Hermits was born.
November 6	"Meet the Press" debuted on NBC.
November 8	American singer-songwriter Minnie Ripperton was born.
November 11	"Gentleman's Agreement" starring Gregory Peck debuted in New York City.
November 13	Toy Caldwell, American Southern Rock musician with the Marshall Tucker Band was born.
November 15	Demonstrations in Brussels occur as a result of the soft sentences of Nazi war criminals.
November 17	An anti-communist loyalty oath implemented by Actors Guild.
November 20	Future British Queen Princess Elizabeth II married Lt. Phillip Mountbatten in Westminster Abbey in London, England.
November 20	American rock guitarist Joe Walsh was born.
November 23	Sammy Baugh, Washington Redskins quarterback, passed for 6 touchdowns against the Chicago Cardinals.
November 24	*The Pearl* by John Steinbeck was published.
November 25	The first Hollywood blacklist was created, denying employment to American entertainment professionals with Communist political ties.
November 27	Joe DiMaggio of the New York Yankees won the MLB AL Most Valuable Player Award.
November 27	The first Bronze Derby football game between Newberry College and Presbyterian College took place on Thanksgiving Day in Newberry, South Carolina. The Newberry College Indians defeated the Presbyterian College Blue Hose 6-0.

The Li'l 🎩 That Was!

The Indian
NEWBERRY COLLEGE
"Home of The Fighting Redskins"

DERBY GOES ON BLOCK

Beat PC — Indians To Shoot Works For Closing Win Over P. C.

The Bronze Derby, Symbol of 34 Years of Rivalry Between Newberry and P. C.

Game So Important That Victory Would Mean A Successful Season For Indians

Presbyterian College and Newberry College have been bitter rivals for nearly a half a century. Last year they authorized something to show for this rivalry and jointly announced that "The Little Bronze Derby" would symbolize the athletic supremacy between the two schools.

The award grew out of the "abduction" of a P. C. student's derby hat at the first basketball game between P. C. and Newberry, last winter. First suggestion of an award was made by Professor Charles MacDonald, instructor of English and director of Public Relations at Presbyterian, in a letter to the sports publicity director at Newberry. The hat was surrendered by anonymous Newberry students, and turned over to a local jewelry firm to be cast in bronze.

Presentation of the award will be made by the losers to the victor at chapel exercises following each meeting of the two "Little Four" rivals in three major sports—football, basketball, and baseball.

"The Bronze Derby" has gone on block three times since it came into existence last winter. The first time it was presented to P. C. after a 44 to 42 win over Newberry in basketball. The second time "The Derby" was recovered by Newberry after a 5 to 2 victory in baseball. The third time "The Derby" was returned to Presbyterian because of a 3 to 2 victory over Newberry in baseball. The Thanksgiving Day football game will mark the fourth time "The Derby" has been at stake.

"The Derby" is part of a general plan to keep relations between the two colleges on a high plane, despite the bitter rivalry which exists between them. The movement was launched last winter after incidents during the basketball season threatened the severance of athletic relations between P. C. and Newberry. Frequently, in the past, impending clashes between the two schools have resulted in pre-game raiding parties on both campuses, with resultant damage to personal and school property. It was with the aim of eliminating such useless destruction that the student government organizations initiated their cooperative movement last winter.

The Presbyterian "Blue Hose" and the Newberry "Redskins" have been feuding on the athletic fields since the turn of the century. Their 34 years of football ranks as one of the oldest annual contests in the South. The two teams were bitter rivals in baseball long before football became a part of the intercollegiate activity in the South.

STUDENTS AND FACULTY
Always Welcome
— AT —
JOHNNIE'S News and Doughnut Shop
FROSTED MALTS AND ICE CREAM

BRONZE DERBY COMES BACK TO NEWBERRY
MAKES SECOND TRIP HERE

Newberry College, as a result of the Thanksgiving football game with Presbyterian College, now has possession of the Bronze Derby.

It was presented to the captain of the Fighting Redskins football team on Friday, December 5, 1947, after Pat Benson gave the history of the Derby. Since it has come into existence, it has been in the hands of the Blue Hose twice; once due to a 44-42 win in basketball and again due to a 3-2 victory in baseball, and has been on the Newberry campus twice also, once due to a 5-2 triumph in baseball and now due to the Thanksgiving game.

The visitors from Roseville were presented by Pat Benson. They were Ray Banbury, the publicity director for the Presbyterians, and Tommy Todd, captain of the Hose's football team, presented the Derby to our captain, Jack Mhor.

The good spirit of Newberry toward P. C. was then shown by a cheer for the Hose led by Newberry's cheerleaders.

The Indian — Newberry College — "Home of The Fighting Redskins" — MERRY CHRISTMAS

Everybody Stops at Aunt Julia's

Wells Theatre

THURSDAY
"ROSE OF SANTA ROSA"

FRIDAY and SATURDAY
"SONG OF THE DRIFTER"
with Jimmy Wakely

OPERA HOUSE Saturday
Walt Disney's
"SONG OF THE SOUTH"
(In Technicolor)

WELLS Monday and Tuesday
The Most Honored Picture of the Decade!
"BEST YEARS OF OUR LIVES"
Myrna Loy, Fredric March, Dana Andrews and Teresa Wright

WEDNESDAY and THURSDAY
"HEART OF VIRGINIA"
Janet Martin and Robert Lowery

NOVEMBER 29-30
"IT HAD TO BE YOU"
Ginger Rogers and Cornel Wilde

DECEMBER 1-2
"FRENCH LEAVE"

COMING
"DOWN TO EARTH" and
"THE FULLER BRUSH MAN"

Indians Defeat P. C. In Turkey Day Game

Tie With P. C. For Little Four Crown. Take Possession of Bronze Derby.

In spite of a poor season, the Newberry Indians upset the Presbyterians' Blue Hose, 6-0, before a crowded stadium on Thanksgiving Day to gain a tie with P. C. in the Little Four football championship and bring the Bronze Derby to Indianland.

Tom Coleman flipped a pass to Clifford Hodge who ran the rest of the way for the only touchdown of the game in the second period on a play that covered 25 yards.

It was Coleman's passing that kept P. C. worried all during the first half. Usually the story has been that P. C. kept Newberry worried about its passing, but the Newberry coaches, Laval and Fritz, turned the tables and had Coleman doing the passing.

The game was an excellent game to watch throughout the afternoon, with excellent sportsmanship being shown by both teams.

Newberry marched 90 yards to the Blue Hose four-yard stripe on two other occasions in the second period, but both times Presbyterian held for downs. In the final period, the Indians drove 75 yards, apparently headed for another touchdown, but the Blue Hose threw back the threat on the P. C. 18-yard line.

P. C. threatened seriously only once in the game, and that was when they marched 17 yards in the third period to the Newberry 12-yard line stripe only to lose the ball on downs.

THE BRONZE DERBY

By virtue of their 6-0 win over Presbyterian College on Thanksgiving Day, the Newberry Indians now have possession of the Bronze Derby, symbol of victory between the two schools.

In the inaugural Bronze Derby football game in 1947, Newberry College defeated Presbyterian College 6-0 in Newberry, South Carolina to win their first football Bronze Derby on Thanksgiving Day.

PC
0

Newberry
6

Newberry took the Bronze Derby away from Presbyterian on Thanksgiving day at Newberry by shoving the Hose around for a 6-0 win... Coleman completed 11 of 22 passes in the first half to provide the margin of victory for the Indians... The lone score in the ball game coming on a pass from Coleman to Monts 16 yards out... Blue Hose looked sluggish, made no real offensive threat for any yardage... Bootey Ivey gave Hose supporters a thrill by intercepting a Coleman pass, and scoring from the Newberry 27, but the play was called back on a holding charge. From the Lavalmen's 20 the Blue failed to gain, ending the threat... Newberry dominated play, running up 14 first downs to the Hose's four, and gained a tie for first place in the Little Four with P. C.

The Li'l 🎩 That Was!

The Newberry Observer
AND HERALD & NEWS
"Just Like A Letter From Home"

NEWBERRY, S. C., TUESDAY, DECEMBER 2, 1947   NEWBERRY OBSERVER ESTABLISHED 1883

City Closes Down

Newberry Meets P.C. Thursday At 2:30

Newberry's observance of Thanksgiving Day will be 100% effective with all the stores of the city, the public offices, including the post-office, being closed for the day. Postal officials announce that there will be no window service, no local or rural deliveries.

A local restaurant is advertising a special turkey dinner, but with the exceptions of eating places, the town will be closed tight.

The highlight of the day's celebration will be the Newberry-P. C. football game which will be played at 2:30 p. m. on Setzler Field. Coach Bully Laval is said to "have something up his sleeve" and Newberry fans are hoping for a Blue Stocking defeat. There is no such thing as an "underdog" when P. C. and Newberry meet, as anything can happen, and as the old saying goes, "usually does."

Anyhow Newberry is set for a good observance of Thanksgiving Day and Newberrians do have many things for which to be th---

---

For Quality MEATS Visit Us
STEAKS, STEW, ROASTS, HAM, CHOPS, SAUSAGE, WIENERS, ETC.

We Are Open Daily From 8 A. M. To 10 P. M.
Sunday—9 A. M. To 8 P. M.

Come out to see us for quality meats, fresh groceries and good Gulf gas and oil, or Phone 820-J. We Deliver.

We also repair radios and small appliances.

Prompt pick-up and delivery service.

SUMMER'S RADIO & GROCERY SERVICE
College St. Ext.   Phone 820-J

FIREWORKS!   FIREWORKS!
Jobber price to retailers. Three warehouses complete with quality merchandise. Come see what you are buying and save extra 10% on warehouse delivery. Why pay more when you can buy it for less at

ATLAS FIREWORKS CO.
Write for price list or phone 9158 or 3209
229 Augusta St.   Greenville, S. C.

Newberry Indians Defeat P. C. In Turkey Day Game

Tie P. C. For Crown Of Little Four

Newberry College Indians upset Presbyterian's Blue Hose, 6-0, before a Thanksgiving Day crowd here last Thursday to gain a share with Presbyterian in the Little Four football championship.

Sub Quarterback Tom Coleman flipped a pass to sub Cliff Todd who ran the rest of the way for the only touchdown of the game in the second period on a play that covered 25 yards.

Newberry marched 90 yards to the Blue Hose four-yard stripe on two other occasions in the second period, but each time Presbyterian held for downs. In the final period, the Indians drove 75 yards, apparently headed for another touchdown, but the Blue Hose threw back the threat on the P. C. 18.

The Blue Hose threatened seriously only once in the game, when they marched seventy yards in the third period to the Newberry 12-yard stripe with Walkup and Hughes pacing a strong-running back. But the Indians threw back the threat.

Wofford's 26-20 victory over Erskine last Thursday sent the Little Four race into a two-way finale.

Pos	Newberry	Presbyterian
LE	Monts	Lindsay
LT	Vaughan	Riddle
LG	Altpater	Cushman
C	Corley	Todd
RG	Scarborough	Starnes
RT	Appling	Weir
RE	Hodges	Willis
QB	Looper	Gresham
LH	Maxwell	Walkup
RH	Seigler	Gooch
FB	Lynch	Hughes

Score by periods:
Newberry .... 0 6 0 0—6
Presbyterian ...... 0 0 0 0—0
Scoring: Newberry—Touchdown: Todd (sub).

SUBSCRIBE TO THE OBSERVER

Newberry Dumps Hose, Wins Derby Classic, 6-0

Newberry's Indians gained revenge, and the Bronze Derby Thanksgiving day at Newberry as they scalped the Hose, 6-0, scoring in the second quarter on a pass from Frank Coleman to Doug Monts, the culmination of a 53-yard scoring drive.

For 60 bruising minutes the Hosemen were played off their feet, as the Tribe racked up 14 first downs, and ran and passed for impressive yardage to outclass the sluggish Blue Stocking team.

After a scoreless first period, during which the Hose drove to the Newberry 15, only to lose the ball on downs, the Indians got into high gear, and passing the ball for ground-eating gains, they proceeded to keep the Hose in hot water for the rest of the half, pitching 22 passes and completing 11 of them. The Hose never got a sustained drive into motion, and spent the first two quarters repulsing Indian backs from the promised land, with Quarterback Billy Gresham knocking down one touchdown aerial in the end zone.

After the half-time pause, the Hose switched defenses, and the Laval crew took to running after the pass receivers were effectively covered, but were kept away from scoring territory, as the Blue Stocking line stiffened and held.

The line Hose threat came in the third period, when Fullback Bootey Ivey intercepted a Coleman aerial and trucked 27 yards for a score, but the counter was called back on a holding penalty, and four passes from the Newberry 20-yard marker proved ineffective and incomplete.

Coach Lonnie's charges ran up four first downs to the Indians' 14, ran for 53 yards to 77 for the Tribe, and completed four of 13 passes to Newberry's 12 of 29. It was the fifth defeat for the Hose this year against four wins and one tie, and left Newberry and Presbyterian in a tie for the Little Four title with two wins and one defeat apiece.

BISHOP & WALKER
"The Rexall Drug Store"
Try One of Our Famous Chocolate-Malteds
and One of our Tasty Sandwiches

―――― o ――――

Visit Our Soda Fountain
We Serve the Finer Quality Hostess Ice Cream

December 6, 1947 — THE BLUE STOCKING

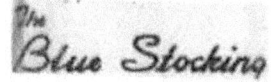

The Li'l 🎩 That Was!

The Indian
NEWBERRY COLLEGE
"Home of The Fighting Redskins"

Bronze Derby At Stake Thanksgiving Day
Old Rivals To Struggle At Traditional Contest

Indians Anxious To Retain Symbol

"The Little Bronze Derby", symbolic of the rivalry between Presbyterian College and Newberry, will be at stake in the traditional Thanksgiving Day game between the two schools in Clinton at 2 o'clock.

For nearly half a century P. C. and Newberry College have been bitter rivals. Two years ago "The Little Bronze Derby" became a symbol of this rivalry by being presented to the school which held athletic supremacy over the other.

During the first basketball game between P. C. and Newberry two years ago, a P. C. student's derby was abducted by some Newberry students. Professor Charles MacDonald, instructor of English and director of Public Relations at Presbyterian College, suggested in a letter to the sports publicity director at Newberry that the derby be made an award to the school maintaining athletic supremacy. The hat was then surrendered by anonymous Newberry students and was cast in bronze by a local jewelry firm.

The loser presents the derby to the victor at chapel exercises following each meeting of the two rivals in three major sports—football, basketball, and baseball.

Last year "The Bronze Derby" was presented to P. C. after winning over Newberry during the following baseball season, after the first game and was returned to P. C. after the second game. Because Newberry won the football game last Thanksgiving Day, P. C. presented it to Newberry again. It was retained after the first basketball game, but lost after the second basketball game. Since Newberry won the two baseball games, P. C. awarded the derby to us and we have possession of it at the present time. The football game on Thanksgiving Day will determine who will be the recipient of the derby until the basketball season.

"The Derby" is part of a general plan to keep relations between the two colleges on a high plane, despite the bitter rivalry which exists between them. The movement was launched two years after incidents during the basketball season threatened the severance of athletic relations between P. C. and Newberry.
(Continued on page four)

Bronze Derby
(Continued from page one)

Frequently, in the past, impending clashes between the two schools have resulted in pre-game raiding parties on both campuses, with resultant damage to personal and school property. It was with the aim of eliminating such useless destruction that the student government organizations initiated their cooperative movement.

The Presbyterian "Blue Hose" and the Newberry "Redskins" have been feuding on the athletic fields since the turn of the century. Their 34 years of football ranks as one of the oldest annual contests in the South. The two teams were bitter rivals in baseball long before football became a part of the intercollegiate activity in the South.

Mr. and Mrs. Rex Thomas announce the birth of a 9½ pound girl, Martha Virginia Thomas, on November 7, at the Newberry Hospital.

November 1948

November 2	United States President Harry Truman was re-elected defeating Thomas E. Dewey.
November 3	Scottish singer and actress Marie Lawrie (Lulu) was born.
November 3	Gordie Howe made his first of 23 NHL All Star appearances in Chicago Stadium at the second NHL All-Star game.
November 3	*The Chicago Tribune* published the famous headlines in error "Dewey Defeats Truman."
November 4	American humorist Will Rogers was commemorated by the United States Postal Service on a 3 cent stamp.
November 6	"Buttons and Bows" by Dinah Shore topped the *Billboard* charts.
November 6	Singer-songwriter Glenn Frey of the Eagles was born.
November 11	"Joan of Arc" starring Ingrid Bergman premiered in New York City.
November 12	Japanese Prime Minister Hideki Tojo was sentenced to death by a war crimes tribunal.
November 14	King Charles III was born at Buckingham Palace.
November 15	Louis St. Laurent became the 12th Prime Minister of Canada.
November 17	Great Britain's House of Commons voted and approved to nationalize the steel industry.
November 18	Colonel Sanders, founder of Kentucky Fried Chicken, married long time employee Claudia Price.
November 19	The Lafayette Leopards college football team was invited to play in the Sun Bowl under the condition that African American player David Showell would not play. The college team turned down the invitation.
November 20	A United States balloon reached a record height of 26.5 miles.
November 23	Dr. Frank Back patented a lens to provide zoom effects.
November 23	American Baseball Hall of Fame outfielder Hack Wilson of the Chicago Cubs passed away.
November 25	Lou Boudreau of the Cleveland Indians was named MLB AL Most Valuable Player.
November 25	The Bronze Derby was played in Clinton, South Carolina on Thanksgiving Day. The Presbyterian College Blue Hose defeated the Newberry College Indians 40-7.

The Li'l That Was!

The Blue Stocking

Distinguished For Its Progress

Volume XXVII — Presbyterian College, Clinton, S. C., Nov. 20, 1948 — Number 9

Indians Put Derby on Block Thanksgiving

Topper Token...

On auction Thursday afternoon to the highest bidder will be the Bronze Derby, symbol of athletic supremacy between PC and Newberry colleges, when the two grid powers meet on Johnson field, at 2:30 o'clock. The topper is the only such token in state collegiate rivalry, originating in 1946 at a heated Hose-Indian basketball game on a brainstorm by Charlie MacDonald, former PC publicity director. Now in the hands of Newberry, the lid will be delivered personally by the captain of the Redskin eleven, if the Hosemen are successful in their attempt to ambush the Newberry Big Chiefs.

The Li'l That Was!

End Grid Grind Thursday...

Eight finalists in the Newberry-PC clash on Thanksgiving day are pictured above in football fashion. From left to right at the top are Bob Hughes, Canton, Ga., fullback; Richard Bowles, Augusta, Ga., tackle; Dewey "Red" Riddle, Fayetteville, N. C., tackle; Milton "Booty" Ivey, Spartanburg fullback. On the bottom are Charlie Brake, Washington, Ga., center; Claude Howe, Tallahassee, Fla., center; Herb Lindsay, Greenville end; and Calvert Marsh, Orangeburg guard. All are seniors and are to be graduated in May.

November 20, 1948 — THE BLUE STOCKING

P. C. STUDENTS
WELCOME TO RODDY'S
THE PLACE IN CLINTON FOR YOUR FRATERNITY OR CLUB DINNERS

Our Latch-string Is On the Outside — Drop In Often for A Good Meal

COLD DRINKS — SPECIAL ORDERS

RODDY'S RESTAURANT
Good Meals and Service

The Li'l 🎩 That Was!

The Clinton Chronicle

Clinton, S. C., Thursday, November 25, 1948

BRONZE DERBY AT STAKE TODAY

On auction Thursday afternoon to the highest bidder will be the Bronze Derby, symbol of athletic supremacy between PC and Newberry colleges, when the two grid powers meet on Johnson field, at 2:30 o'clock. The topper is the only such token in state collegiate rivalry, originating in 1946 at a heated Hose-Indian basketball game on a brainstorm by Charlie MacDonald, former PC publicity director. Now in the hands of Newberry, the lid will be delivered personally by the captain of the Redskin eleven, if the Hosemen are successful in their attempt to ambush the Newberry Big Chiefs.

The Clinton Chronicle

Clinton, S. C., Thursday, November 25, 1948

BLUE STOCKINGS CLOSE 1948 SEASON HERE THIS AFTERNOON WITH NEWBERRY

Annual Thanksgiving Day Game Between Long-standing Rivals at 2:30. Big Crowd Expected.

Presbyterian and Newberry colleges renew their 35-year-old feud today (Thursday) when the two grid powers battle for possession of the coveted Bronze Derby, symbol of athletic supremacy between the two arch rivals, on Johnson field. Kickoff time is set for 2:30 p.m., with a large crowd anticipated for the traditional tilt which is again rated a toss-up.

The derby, the only such token in state collegiate circles, will be at stake for the ninth time, going on the block every time the two foes meet in football, basketball and baseball. Newberry holds the upper hand in the series, winning the prized topper five times in eight meetings.

This will mark the thirty-fourth grid clash between the two colleges since 1913, when football was first introduced at Presbyterian. In that time Presbyterian has taken 11 of the games, tieing two, and losing 19. All past records are forgotten, however, when Presbyterian and Newberry indulge in any sport or activity.

Missing from the Hose lineup in this final game of the season will be Ralph "Buzz" Tedards, triple threat quarterback, who underwent an appendicitis operation the past week. Other than this loss, the Stockings are reported to be in fair shape for the big Thursday encounter, as it is regarded in Little Four competition.

Filling Tedards' position at the key T-formation spot will be Bill Jolly, who alternates with Tedards at the post. Jolly is tied for high scorer on the Hose eleven with 18 points.

No ailments are reported from the Indian camp after taking the Erskine Fleet for a 14-0 ride two weeks ago. Previously, the Hose sank the Fleet by an identical score at the Presbyterian homecoming.

Most of Coach Bill Laval's hopes will be pinned on the tossing arm of Hank Witt, Indian all-stater on last season's mythical eleven, who was out when the Redskins struck through the air to down the favored Hosemen, 6-0, at Newberry last Thanksgiving.

Winding up their college football careers will be eight Hose players in the Thursday classic. Making their finales will be Bob Hughes, Canton, Ga., fullback; Milton "Footy" Ivey, Spartanburg fullback; Hosh Lindsay, Greenville end; Dewey "Red" Riddle, Fayetteville, N. C., tackle; Richard Bowles, Augusta, Ga., tackle; Calvert Marsh, Orangeburg guard; Claude Howe, Tallahassee, Fla., center; and Charlie Brake, Washington, Ga., center.

TRAINS

Electric Trains for Christmas

$11.95 to $70.45

SEE OUR TRAIN DISPLAY BEFORE YOU BUY

o

YARBOROUGH OIL CO.

WEST MAIN STREET — CLINTON, S. C.

Hose Bush Tribe, 40-7, in Finale; Derby Returns With Prized Victory

The Blue Stocking
Distinguished For Its Progress
Vol. XXVII Presbyterian College, December 1, 1948 No. 10

Striking on the ground for four long touchdown runs and two short plunges that climaxed sustained drives, the Presbyterian Blue Stockings ran amuck through a weaker Newberry grid defense Thanksgiving day to regain possession of the coveted Bronze derby and wallop their thirty-four year old foes, 40-7. Approximately 4,000 spectators jammed Bailey Memorial stadium for the rivalric Bronze derby classic, which was rated a toss-up before game time.

Receiving the opening kickoff, the Indian eleven, behind the passing arm of Hank Witt, took to the air lanes on the first play. George Fleming, Hose halfback, killed the attempted Redskin march on the sixth play of the game by intercepting an aerial and setting up the first Stocking score on the Indians' 35.

Several plays later Bob Hughes, senior fullback, cracked over from the two-yard marker. Fred Barnum, freshman end, converted as the Hosemen went ahead, 7-0.

The Hose tallied again in the opening period when Walter Gooch scooted over from the five

GEORGE FLEMING

after taking a handoff from Bill Jolly, quarterback. This ended a PC drive which had its origin on their own 44-yard line.

In the opening moments of the second quarter, Jolly, faking a lateral, raced 70 yards through the Indian defense for another score, which was nullified when a clipping penalty was called. On the following play, Allen Draughon, quarterback, hit Herb Lindsay, senior end, with a pass on the Newberry 10, but another penalty was called when Lindsay pushed a cover man to snatch the aerial.

George Fleming accounted for the third Hose six-pointer in the
(Continued on page four)

Hose Bush Tribe
(Continued on page three)
waning moments of the first half when he circled his right end on a 25-yard jaunt.

Intercepting an Indian pass on the 50 after seesawing back and forth for the first eight minutes of the second half, Walter Gooch carried the ball to the Newberry 26, where Blake Watts broke off tackle for the fourth PC marker.

Fighting off two Newberry scoring stabs in the last of the third period, the Hose finally succumbed to the only Indian score when a blocked punt, a 14-yard heave, and a final one-yard push resulted in the Redskin score.

George Fleming, taking up the Newberry kickoff two yards behind his own goal, raced the distance of the field for the fifth Hose tally and the longest run in this section of the country during the 1948 season.

On the last play of the game, Hollis Cate turned the game into a rout, scampering 47 yards for the sixth Hose score. Barnum missed his second placement of the afternoon, making the final score, 40-7, as the game ended.

A stout PC forward wall held the Indian ground attack in tack and paved the way for the strong Hose offensive play with sound line blocks and downfield aid.

The Newberry Observer
AND HERALD & NEWS
"Just Like A Letter From Home"

NEWBERRY, S. C. TUESDAY, NOVEMBER 30, 1948

The Li'l That Was!

Newberry Indians Swamped By PC

Lose Game By 40-7 Score

The Presbyterian College Blue Stockings took possession of the Bronze Derby and second place in Little Four state standings last Thursday by swamping the Newberry Indians 40-7.

The winners' scoring was featured by Halfback George Fleming's 100-yard kickoff return for a touchdown in the final period.

The lone Newberry score came just before Fleming's run, with Indian Center Bobby Jo Corley pulled into the backfield for the play, going over from the one.

Fullback Bob Hughes of Presbyterian smashed through center from the four to open the Stocking touchdown parade.

Blake Watts, halfback, circled left end for 25 yards and the second score.

In the next period Quarterback Bill Jolly went around left end for 30 yards and a touchdown.

Halfback Walter Gooch opened the second half scoring by going five yards off tackle for a touchdown.

In the final period, Newberry Hank Witt set up his Indians' touchdown with a 14-yard pass to the one. Fleming came back with his long kickoff return.

Left Half Hollis Cate climaxed the day's scoring for the victors by rounding left end for 47 yards and pay dirt.

Fred Barnam, Presbyterian end, booted four of his six extra point placement tries. Quarterback Billy Seigler kicked the extra point for Newberry.

The Presbyterian team was a hard-charging, well co-ordinated eleven. From the very start it was evident that PC was not to be denied victory. The Blue Stckings tackled hard and surely, the line was ever on the alert and the backs ran beautifully, refusing to be stopped until every inch possible was gained.

Newberry fought hard but with the exception of a final period spurt, was unable to make consistent gains against the determined Presbyterians.

Pos. — Newberry	Presbyterian
LE—Hodge	Lindsey
LT—Vaughn	Riddle
LG—Pate	Marsh
C—Corley	Howe
RG—Spence	Starnes
RT—Stone	Martin
RE—Neel	Dusenbury
QB—Seigler	Draughon
LT—Witt	Fleming
RT—DuBose	Gooch
FB—Scarborough	Hughes

Newberry .... 0 0 0 7— 7
Presbyterian ..... 14 7 6 13—40

Newberry scoring: Touchdown—Corley; point after touchdown—Seigler (placement).

Presbyterian scoring: Touchdowns—Hughes, Watts, Jolly, Gooch, Fleming, Cate. Points after touchdowns—Barnam (sub for Lindsay) 4 (placements).

OPERA HOUSE
SATURDAY
ON THE STAGE
Chicago Follies
With Chen Davis, Vickie Ray, Matthews Sisters, Miss Texas and the S. Williams Quartette

ON THE SCREEN
"Arkansas Swing"
with the Hoosier Hotshots
Added—TEX GRANGER
Admission: 25c-60c

WELLS THEATRE

MONDAY and TUESDAY
The things other girls dream about ... happen to her!

"It Had To Be You"
Ginger Rogers, Cornel Wilde
Added—PATHE NEWS
3:00, 4:53, 6:40 and 8:30

WED. and THURS.
"French Leave"
Jackie Cooper and Jackie Coogan
Added—GLAMOUR STREET
Admission: 12c-35c

It's Here! Money on your Automobile, Furniture or your Signature.

$5.00 to $2,000.00
★ ★

Special Note, Auto Dealers:
We will finance your sales, no strings attached, without recourse, no endorsements or re-purchase agreements necessary—plus attractive reserve paid date acceptance of deal. Phone 736-M.

SERVICE FINANCE CO.
1506 Main St.

Subscribe To The Newberry Observer

The Li'l ⛑ That Was!

The Indian
NEWBERRY COLLEGE
"Home of The Fighting Redskins"

Merry Christmas

Witt, Scarborough Make Indians Suffer 40-7 Loss

PC Blue Stockings Win Bronze Derby

The Newberry Indians suffered their most humiliating defeat of the season on November 25 when the P. C. Blue Stockings crushed them 40-7. That defeat entitled Presbyterian College to possession of the Bronze Derby.

The Blue Hose entered the game with a hard fighting, well-balanced eleven. There was never any doubt as to the outcome of the game even from the opening kickoff. The P. C. men scored early and increased their margin of victory rapidly as they scored almost at will.

P. C. scored twice in the first period, once in the second, once in the third and twice in the final period.

The Redskins held the Stockings somewhat in check during the third period, but in the fourth period the P. C. rock crusher rolled relentlessly onward.

The highlight of the game was Fleming's return of a Newberry kickoff the entire length of the field for a touchdown. Fleming took the ball two yards in his own end zone and ran up the left sidelines behind excellent interference 102 yards for the score.

The Indians scored their lone tally in the fourth period. DuBose returned a P. C. punt to the Hose's 15 yard line. Witt passed to Hodge on the one yard line. Hall bucked over from that point for the score.

In the 34 times that Newberry and P. C. have met on the gridiron, this game marked the widest margin of victory for either school. Previously, 27-0 had been the most one-sided score.

MITCHELL'S SANDWICH SHOP

STUDENTS AND FACULTY
WELCOME

1909 Friend St.   Phone 9199

Gifts of Lasting
Permanence and Remembrance

Watch and Jewelry Repairing

FENNELL'S JEWELRY STORE
College Street

In 1948, Presbyterian College defeated Newberry College 40-7 in Clinton, South Carolina to win their first football Bronze Derby.

November 1949

November 1	Canadian musician, composer and record producer David Foster was born.
November 1	An Eastern Air Lines flight from Boston to Washington, DC collided with a Bolivian test flight killing 55. The collision was the worst airline disaster to date.
November 2	The Netherlands recognized its former colony Indonesia as a sovereign state.
November 2	The British public was alarmed to see a member of the Royal Family, 19 year old Princess Margaret, smoking in public.
November 3	American businessman and art collector Solomon Guggenheim passed away.
November 3	American boxer and World Heavyweight Champion Larry Holmes was born.
November 6	The Greek Civil War ended after 3 years with the defeat of the communists.
November 6	70 German uranium miners were killed when the mine's powder supply blew up.
November 7	*This I Remember*, Eleanore Roosevelt's memoir of her life with Franklin D. Roosevelt was published.
November 8	"All the King's Men" starring Broderick Crawford premiered in New York.
November 8	Singer-songwriter Bonnie Raitt was born.
November 9	Tommy Caldwell of the Marshall Tucker Band was born.
November 9	Costa Rica adopts a constitution.
November 12	The Volkswagen Type 2 was introduced to the marketplace.
November 14	James Young, guitarist with the rock band Styx was born.
November 15	Actress Nancy Davis met Ronald Reagan, attempting to get her name removed from the Hollywood blacklist.
November 18	Baseball batting leader Jackie Robinson of the Brooklyn Dodgers won the MLB NL Most Valuable Player Award.
November 19	Ahmad Rashad, American sportscaster and NFL receiver with the Minnesota Vikings was born.
November 19	The Bronze Derby was played in Newberry, South Carolina. The Newberry Indians defeated the Presbyterian College Blue Hose 20-14.

The Li'l That Was!

The Blue Stocking

November 12, 1949 — THE BLUE STOCKING

Hose End Season Next Week At Newberry in Derby Contest

The Bronze Derby, a token of athletic supremacy between Newberry and Presbyterian colleges, goes on the line again next Saturday afternoon when the two athletic rivals clash at Newberry. Gametime is set for 2 p.m. on the Newberry field.

Odds favor the Blue Stockings this year, but the prevalent underdog bite narrows the gap between the two aged foes. Presbyterian has won four games while losing three, while the Newberry Indians have taken two wins against five losses. Newberry defeated The Citadel, however, who crushed the Stockings last week, 27-7.

Presbyterian will rely on the clicking heels of its famous ten-second backfield, striking out of a tricky split-T formation. Up front the Presbyterians will employ an aggressive, fast-charging line, headed by giant tackles Bozo Weir and Sam Baker.

Coach Billy Laval, of Newberry, will pin his hopes on the slinging arm of Hank Witt, 1948 all-state passing artist. Left halfback Billy Seigler, star runner, will be the other half of Laval's L-formation attack.

The Bronze Derby will highlight the occasion, the 31st meeting of the two Little Four teams. At the game's end, the winning team captain will be presented with the Derby. The winner will keep the Derby 'till the next athletic meeting between the two teams.

PC-Newberry Rivalry Dates Way, Way Back

One of South Carolina's oldest rivalries flares into 1949 football battle this afternoon at 2:30 when Presbyterian college invades Newberry for the two teams' 35th engagement.

Newberry was the second opponent on PC's first grid schedule back in 1913. And they have been after each other's athletic throats ever since.

The Blue Stockings boast a decided record superiority through the years, having won 22 games while Newberry captured 10 and two ended in deadlock. Presbyterian's total scoring punch has amounted to 465 points in the series. Newberry has notched 269.

The record, however, hardly implies the tight games that have insued in recent years. PC won, 40-7, last year for the most decisive victory in two decades. The Indians came out on top by a 6-0 count the year before that, after Presbyterian had edged through a 14-13 victor in 1946.

Typifying the intense PC-Newberry rivalry in recent years has been the Bronze Derby. This symbol of athletic superiority goes to the winner of each sports event throughout the year.

M. S. BAILEY & SON, BANKERS

Established 1886 .:. Capital $400,000.00

The Li'l 🎩 That Was!

November 19, 1949 — THE BLUE STOCKING

They'll Bow Out Today...

Eight big reasons why Coach Mac will dig deep into reserve material next season are pictured here. They're the eight Presbyterian college senior football players who will play their last game for PC this afternoon when the Hose meet Newberry in the annual Bronze Derby tilt.

They are, top row, left to right, Bob Stutts, Dick Lindsay, Bill Jolly, and Fred Yarborough.

Bottom row, Vernon Dusenbury, Claude Howe, Sam Baker, and Ralph Tedards.

(See bottom of page on their parting remarks).

They've Had It...

Eight Grid Seniors' Swan Song

When the Presbyterian Blue Hose meet Newberry this afternoon, there will be eight PC seniors who will ring down the curtain on their grid careers.

Each of them has something to say about the final whistle. They are quoted below:

Sam Baker, tackle: "It's been a great experience to play for Presbyterian. I only wish that I had four more years of my life to give it."

Vern Dusenbury, end: "I enjoyed playing for PC and especially for Coach Mac. He is one of the best coaches I have ever known. It was a great bunch of boys to play with and I wish that I could play more."

Claude Howe, center: "I've enjoyed my four years under Coach Lonnie Mac, and I don't think that I could have found a better bunch of boys to play with. I'm glad I'm still alive."

Bill Jolly, quarter: "Certainly enjoyed playing under Coach Mac. Been swell working with the fellows. They're a swell bunch of guys. Gonna miss PC and the team next year."

Dick Lindsay, end: "I know that I chose the right coach and the right school. Coach Mac teaches a lot besides just football. Enjoyed every minute of it—well, almost every minute, anyway."

Bob Stutts, guard: "Certainly enjoyed playing ball, although at times I thought I wouldn't last until the final game. If it weren't for the silly conference rules, I wouldn't mind playing a couple more years."

Buzz Tedards: "I have enjoyed playing football at PC. It just doesn't seem like my four years are up. Wish I could play more with the GOOD PC teams to come."

Fred Yarborough, back: "The four years have been lots of fun, although I enjoyed playing my freshman year most of all, 'cause anybody could play varsity then. We played everybody from Clemson to Georgia to Miami. That was when I played guard. I think I like that better than the backfield."

The Newberry Observer
AND HERALD & NEWS
"Just Like A Letter From Home"

NEWBERRY, S. C., FRIDAY, NOVEMBER 18, 1949

Bronze Derby On Block As Hosemen Invade Newberry

Witt, Watts To Vie For Scoring Honors

P. C., Indians Prepare For 36th Meeting

BLAKE WATTS, FB

Henry Witt

Setzler Field, Saturday afternoon, November 19, will be the scene of one of the bitterest contests of the year. It is a known fact that both teams look toward this game all year long and a successful season usually belongs to the victor, despite the number of other games won or lost throughout the year.

The Bronze Derby, traditional symbol of the friendly rivalry between the two schools, is at present making its home on the Newberry campus, and it is the hope of each and every true Newberrian that it will be returned to its sacred niche after the Indian-Hose altercation Saturday.

The feud between Presbyterian and Newberry dates back to 1913. Since that date the Blue Hose have copped 22 victories while losing only ten to the Redskin and tying two. The most decisive win was the 40-7 drubbing the Hose handed the Redskins last year, and it is for this reason as well as others that the Newberry eleven is especially anxious to sneak this game away from the Clinton team.

Leading scorer and ground gainer for the Tribe is aerial artist Hank "Slingshot" Witt, who only last week-end, against Erskine, completed 16 out of 24 passes for 198 yards, three of the 16 for the only Redskin scores of the game, so the Hose problem of the week is to stop "Slingshot."

The Indians will have a problem on their hands, too; it will be to stop the quartette of speedy backs that have paved the way all season for P. C.'s many scoring drives, Blake "Kilo" Watts, the leading Hose ground gainer; halfbacks Walter Gooch and George Fleming, and quarterback Billy Jolly.

Tentative starting line-ups are:

Pos.	Newberry	Presbyterian
LE	Horton	Lindsay, D.
LT	Funderburke	Weir
LG	Altpater	Honea
C	Smith	Lindsay, J.
RG	Senterfeit	Atkinson
RT	Gantz	Baker
RE	Little	Dusenbury
LH	Witt	Fleming
RH	Dubose	Gooch
QB	O'Quinn	Jolly
FB	Seigler	Yarborough

Statistics are available on both P. C.'s Blake "Kilo" Watts and Hank "Slingshot" Witt, who will be the main drives behind their respective team's offensive thrusts. Watts has gained 773 yards to date on 106 attempts to accumulate an average of 7.3 yards per try, and he will bring his record down to face the Indians, who put up Hank Witt's passing record of 70 passes completed for a total of 915 yards, or over 13 yards per pass completion, for comparison.

Both Watts and Witt exploded in their last week's games as Watts ran 15 times, piling up 164 yards, or nearly 11 yards per try, while Hank Witt connected with his receivers for 16 out of his 24 attempted passes for 198 yards, or nearly 12½ yards per pass completed. Three of these passes went for Newberry's lone TDs against Erskine, while one of Watts' runs developed into a 49-yard touchdown gallop. Come what may, the contest Saturday will be a high scoring one, with each team doing little on the defense, but concentrating on outscoring each other.

The Li'l That Was!

Blue Stocking

Distinguished For Its Progress

Volume XXVIII   Presbyterian College, Clinton, S. C., November 19, 1949   Number 8

Hose End Grid Season Today, Meet Newberry Indians at 2:30

A battle of two star-lit Little All-America and all-state candidates spotlights the Presbyterian-Newberry feature football attraction at Newberry at 2:30 o'clock this afternoon.

It's be PC fullback Blake "Kilo" Watts, the Bishopville breeze, against Indian tailback Hank Witt.

Praises of both have echoed throughout the Southeast all season. And their special talents point to a comparison of two different attack methods — running vs. passing.

Watts skips over the turf with the speed that netted him the state 440 crown in track last spring. In eight games this year the fleet fullback has covered 773 yards on 106 running attempts for an average of 7.3 yards per try.

Witt, on the other hand, prefers the airlanes. And he has proved himself to be a past-master of the atmosphere.

The Bronze Derby, symbol of athletic rivalry between Presbyterian and Newberry, originated in a baptism of fire almost three years ago.

Newberry holds the derby at present as the result of winning the final Indian-PC baseball game last spring. But the Blue Stockings are determined to snatch it back.

Presbyterian college students plan a mass invasion of Newberry for the traditional battle.

A police-escorted motorcade of (Continued on page four)

Newberry Game

(Continued from page one)
PC supporters wil swarm over the short distance separating Clinton and Newberry.

PC spirits were keyed for the occasion by a massive pep rally on the Blue Hose campus last night. Bongres and yell rallies under the the direction of head cheerleader Ju Ju Wannamaker licked up enthusiasm for the invasion.

Along Presbyterian's football front, a keyed up band of Hosemen lean toward the opening whistle. Trainers report the squad in top physical condition, and Coach Lonnie S. McMillian announced his starting lineup probably would read:

LE — Bog Ogletree; LT — Bozo Weir; LG — Frank Honea; RG — Paul Martin; RT — Sam Baker; RE — Vern Dusenbury; QB — Bill Jolly! RH — Walter Gooch; LH — George Fleming; and FB — Blake Watts.

NEWBERRY COLLEGE FIGHTING REDSKINS

From left to right are: (top row) Hance, Hatchell, Warren, Gantz, Bobby Gruhn, Whitaker, Spence, and Witt. Middle row: Senterfeit, Smith, Altpater, Norris, Hall, O'Quinn, Jones, Dubose, and Gerald Pate. Bottom row: Swygert, Reames, Burkhalter, Stokes, Blume, Horton, Seigler, and Billy Gruhn.—(photo by Price)

The Clinton Chronicle

Clinton, S. C., Thursday, November 17, 1949

Thursday, November 17, 1949

P. C. SENIORS PLAYING LAST GAME SATURDAY

Pictured above are eight Presbyterian college seniors who will be playing their last Blue Stocking football game when PC invades Newberry Saturday afternoon. They are, left to right:

First row: Fullback Fred Yarborough of Florence, Quarterback Ralph Tedards of Greenville; Center Claude Howe of Tallahassee, Fla., and End Dick Lindsay of Bennettsville.

Second row: End Vern Dusenbury of Marion, Tackle Sam Baker of Summerton, Guard Bob Stutts of Rock Hill, and Quarterback Bill Jolly of Union.

Blue Hose Close Grid Season Saturday With Newberry Rival

One of South Carolina's oldest rivalries flares into 1949 football battle when Presbyterian college invades Newberry Saturday afternoon for the two teams' 35th engagement at 2:30.

Newberry was the second opponent of PC's first grid schedule back in 1913. And they have been after each other's athletic throats ever since.

The Blue Stockings boast a decided record superiority through the years, having won 22 games while Newberry captured ten and two ended in deadlock. Presbyterian's total scoring punch has amounted to 465 points in the series. Newberry has notched 269.

The record, however, hardly implies the tight games that have ensued in recent years. PC won, 40-7, last year for the most decisive victory in two decades. The Indians came out on top by a 6-0 count the year before that, after Presbyterian had edged through a 14-13 victor in 1946.

Typifying the intense PC-Newberry rivalry in recent years has been the Bronze Derby. This symbol of athletic superiority goes to the winner of each sports event through the year.

The Blue Hose will be playing their last game of the season.

The Clinton Chronicle

Clinton, S. C., Thursday, November 24, 1949

Newberry Downs P. C.

The Newberry Indians took advantage of all the breaks which Lady Lucy could spare them (and it seemed that it was open house on luck for the Indians) as they came back in the fourth quarter to humble the Presbyterian Blue Hose 20-14.

Fred Yarborough was the big gun for the Hose as he roared to both of the Blue tallies. His power kept him in the spot light for the entire game.

Hank Witt, apparently afraid that his publicity was slipping, committed the spectators to the kind of playing which they had read about but had never quite seen from him. Witt not only displayed his passing ability but went whole hog and staged some fancy running for the usual P.C.-Newberry crowd.

Witt meant the difference in the ball game as he heaved long passes all during the game.

The straw which broke the Blue Hose' back was the 75 yard run made by an Indian back.

Presbyterian also suffered penalties when they hurt most and thus they had to give up two more possible touchdowns, which would probably have won the game for them.

Today's active people want **light refreshment**

Light, dry (not too sweet) reduced in calories. Today's Pepsi refreshes without filling.

Pepsi-Cola refreshes without filling

Pepsi - Cola Bottling Company

The Li'l That Was!

The Alumni Bulletin

VOLUME 4   NEWBERRY, S. C., DECEMBER, 1949.   NUMBER 6

Indians Annihilate P. C. Blue Stockings

Redskins Retain Bronze Derby By Virtue of 20-14 Win Over Arch Rivals.

Newberry Indians may not go to any bowl game this year, but one thing is certain, they defeated P. C., 20-14, in their annual game. That in itself is good news to many alumni.

Newberry scored twice in the final quarter to upset a highly favored Presbyterian College eleven in their annual pigskin tussle.

The half-time score read Presbyterian 7, Newberry 6. However, the Indians really came to life in the second half and were not to be denied a victory over their arch rivals.

At the conclusion of the game, the players took Coach Billy "for a ride" on their shoulders out of the stadium.

In 1949, Newberry College defeated Presbyterian College 20-14 in Newberry, South Carolina to win their second football Bronze Derby. The game was the 3rd Bronze Derby football Classic.

Newberry 20
Presbyterian 14

Nursing a heavy heart from last season's crushing 40-7 defeat handed them by the PC Hosemen, an inspired Newberry team ripped for three touchdowns and staved off several Hose jabs to take a 20-14 victory over their arch rivals.

Thrown in along with the loss to the Newberry Indians went the Bronze Derby, symbol of athletic supremacy between the two colleges.

"Forgin' Fred" Yarborough scored both tallies for the Hose, cracking over from the three in the first quarter and again from 24 yards out in the third period. Aiding him with most of the PC ball lugging was Right Half Back Walter Gooch who teamed up with Yarborough to set up both scores.

Fullback Blake "Kilo" Watts got off two good runs — one for 30 yards and another for a 25-yard romp to the double stripes which was called back.

Late in the final frame, the Hosemen began another drive toward paydirt, but this one fell short of its mark as had several previous deep thrusts.

The PAC SAC 1950

November 1950

November 1	Boston Celtics forward Chuck Cooper became the first African American to play in the NBA. In the same game, future NBA Hall of Famer Bob Cousy debuted for the Boston Celtics.
November 1	Puerto Rican Nationalists attempted to assassinate United States President Harry Truman at the Blair House in Washington, DC.
November 2	1925 Nobel Prize winner for literature George Bernard Shaw passed away.
November 4	United States troops vacate Pyongyang, North Korea.
November 4	Major League Baseball Hall of Fame pitcher Grover Cleveland Alexander passed away.
November 5	"Hour of Decision," a weekly radio show by evangelist Billy Graham, debuted on ABC Radio and has been heard every Sunday since.
November 8	The first jet to jet dogfight occurred when a United States jet shot down a North Korean jet.
November 9	Boston Braves Sam Jethroe won MLB Rookie of the Year.
November 10	The Nobel Prize for literature was awarded to William Faulkner.
November 10	American rock singer Donnie Hammond of The Atlanta Rhythm Section was born.
November 12	The first Volkswagen van was assembled in Germany.
November 13	The United States won the first world championship Bridge contest.
November 16	The UN got US government approval to issue postage stamps.
November 16	United States President Harry Truman announced an emergency crisis from the communist threat.
November 16	"Dr. Bob" Smith, co-founder of Alcoholics Anonymous, passed away.
November 19	United States General Dwight D. Eisenhower became Supreme Commander of NATO-Europe.
November 22	79 people died in a train crash in Richmond Hills, New York.
November 23	The Bronze Derby was played in Clinton, South Carolina on Thanksgiving Day. The Presbyterian College Blue Hose defeated the Newberry College Indians 20-6.

The Clinton Chronicle

Clinton, S. C., Thursday, November 23, 1950

Blue Hose and Newberry Clash In Thanksgiving Day Game

Long Standing Rivals Meet Here Today At 2:30 With Big Crowd Expected. Bronze Derby Goes On The Block.

It's Derby Day—Bronze Derby at Presbyterian college this afternoon at 2:30 when the Blue Stockings entertain Newberry in the traditional football game.

The Bronze Derby, symbol of athletic rivalry between the two colleges, goes on the block awaiting the victor. Presbyterian will be out to take it away from the Indians, who have possession of the lid as a result of baseball victory last spring.

The Blue Stockings also will be out to do a number of other things that have them feeling a triumph is imperative.

1—Get revenge for the 14-13 upset win scored by Newberry last year.

2—Close out the 1950 season with a triumphant finale.

3—Post their fifth victory of the year, thus enabling PC to finish with an even .500 record. The Hosemen so far have four wins and five defeats.

Presbyterian-Newberry is one of those keen rivalries that goes way back to 1913. The record book is full of close scores and upsets, despite the fact that PC holds a decided edge with 22 victories compared to 11 for the Indians while two games ended deadlocked.

The Blue Stockings will face today's opening whistle favored to turn the hatchet on Newberry's Redskins, who have managed to win only one game so far this fall. PC fields a sharp-cracking attack—featuring the passing of Quarterback Jack (Lefty) Walter Gooch and Halfback George Harper and the running of Fullback Fleming—which has flared to heights at times this year.

However, Newberry has a way of changing their form where this series is concerned. A high-ranking Stocking eleven had that point brought forcefully home last season when Newberry fought to victory. And Coach Lonnie McMillian says the Indians have already sent word they'll be tough to handle again this year.

McMillian also points out that the Newberry team isn't as bad as its record would seem to indicate. He says the Redskin passing has been improving all season and the kicking is good. But what he considers most is that intense feeling about this old feud which has always caused the underdog to lift himself to giant proportions.

The Li'l That Was!

The Newberry Observer
AND HERALD & NEWS
"Just Like A Letter From Home"

HERALD AND NEWS ESTABLISHED 1865 — NEWBERRY, S. C., FRIDAY, NOVEMBER 24, 1950 — NEWBERRY OBSERVER ESTABLISHED 1881

Bronze Derby At Stake Thursday At Presbyterian

Tribe, Hose Meet In 36th Football Game

DuBose Probably Start Against Presbyterian

The Newberry College Indians will be entertained by the Blue Stockings from Presbyterian at Clinton Thursday afternoon in the 36th annual clash between these two schools, who have maintained a keen spirit of rivalry since their first meeting back in 1913.

Since that memorable date, Presbyterian elevens have been successful in winning over their Lutheran opponents 22 times, while limiting the Tribe to 11 wins. Two games ended in tied scores.

Sparking the P. C. offense will be the passing of "Lefty" Harper, Hose quarterback, and backs Walter Gooch and George Fleming, who bear the brunt of the rushing chores. While for the Indians, "Chuckin' Churley" Berry will be looked to for his booming punts, as well as for his needle-threading passing ability.

Max DuBose

In the rushing department, Coach Tuck will have a surprise for the Hose, in the form of Max DuBose, who returns to the local lineup for the first time in several games. Max was saved from last week-end's tussle with Stetson, for Newberry's coach is looking toward the Turkey Day game with great longing, and will do everything he can to take the win.

Newberry has a heartening record behind it in the form of four games that were lost by margins of seven points or less, and a win over Milligan, three weeks ago. According to the "experts," P. C. is rated as a considerable favorite, in consideration of their four wins this season. "However, when Newberry and Presbyterian clash, one cannot think in terms of favorites; one can only think in terms of which team happens to get the most breaks."

P. C. is out to avenge her 20-14 loss to the Tribe last year, and the Redskins are out to repeat the upset again this year.

See it! Try it! Buy it!
NEW 1951 STUDEBAKER
Your thrifty one for '51 and many another year to come!

THE NEW COMMANDER	THE NEW CHAMPION
A truly great new V-8 sparkling with new pep and power!	Top buy and top value of the top 4 lowest price cars!

LIPSCOMB MOTOR COMPANY
1417 College Street — Telephone 107

The Newberry Observer
AND HERALD & NEWS
"Just Like A Letter From Home"

Redskins Retired Readily Following Many Fumbles

Tribe Treads Twice On Two Without Scoring

Berry To Boring Aerial Accounts For Single Score

The Newberry College Indians lost possession of the precious "Bronze Derby" at Clinton last Thursday afternoon, as they found themselves on the short end of a 20-6 final score after sixty minutes of bruising play, which was filled with unexpected occurances, like fumbles, interceptions, and long punt returns, which combined to spell the Tribe's doom, before some 3500 fans at Walter Johnson Field.

Not a single one of the scores came after any long and sustained drive, with both teams capitalizing on misques of their opponents. P. C., scoring first in last Thursday's clash, after a little more than two minutes of the game had elapsed, recovered a fumble by J. W. Jones on the Tribe's 24, and then Hollis Cate shook loose from Tribe tacklers and went the distance to score. Neely converted from placement.

The Redskins retaliated in like manner afterwards, as local end,

The Redskins retaliated in like manner afterwards, as local end, Bloss Blume recovered P. C. back, Gooch's fumble on the P. O. 25. With a fourth down staring him in the face, Charley Berry hit John Boring with an aerial for the score. The Tribe failed to convert and trailed 7-6. The score remained thus until late in the third period, when P. C.'s George Flemming took a hand-off from Sasser, who had just cradled one of Berry's punts on P. C.'s 29, and behind beautiful interference cantered the entire 71 yards separating himself from the Tribe's end zone. After a faulty placement P. C. led 13-6.

Midway in the fourth period, the Tribe drove to the P. C. 30. Redskin Berry hit an intended receiver with a bullet pass, but it was too hot to handle and bounced into the waiting arms of Hose back Sasser,

who took to his heels and didn't stop until he'd crossed the Tribe's goal line eighty yards away, for P. C.'s third and final touchdown of the game. Neely's conversion was good, putting the Blue Hose in a 20-6 lead.

The game was full of near-scores both for Newberry and P. O., with the Tribe holding a slight edge. The locals threatened mildly first as they recovered Gooch's fumble on their own 38. They advanced to the Hose 35 at which point one of Berry's passes was intercepted. Not long afterwards, Burkhalter took a P. C. punt on his own 25 and toted back to the 42. From here Newberry staged a drive that carried to the P. C. 2. Jones cutting through the line, lost the ball, which was recovered over the goal line by Gooch for a touchback.

With about six minutes to go in the first half, Newberry seriously threatened again, as Burkhalter returned a P. C. punt to midfield, and started a local drive that carried again to P. C.'s 2 yard line, with a first down and goal to go. J. W. Jones cracking the Blue Hose line again lost the precious oval, which was recovered by Starnes on the 3.

P. C. threatened soon after their third period score, following Fleming's 40-yard return to midfield. The Hose reached the local seven, at which time they attempted a

The Hose reached the local seven, at which time they attempted a field goal, which was wide to the right. This ended the Hose threat. Newberry threatened just one more time prior to the P. C. final score of the game, as they drove to the P. C. 30, where interference was ruled on a Berry pass intended for Weeks. On a play following this interference ruling Berry's pass was intercepted by Sasser and run back for a score. This was the Tribe's season finale ,and left them with a record of one win, against nine losses.

Statistics

	Newberry	P. C.
First Downs	14	11
Rushing Yds.	109	166
Passing Yds.	102	71
Total Yds. gained	211	237
Passes attempted	23	10
Passes completed	10	6
Passes intercepted	0	3
Punts	8	7
Punting average	45.1	46.4
Fumbles lost	4	2
Yards penalized	30	103
Newberry	0 6 0 0—	6
P. C.	7 0 6 7—	20

Newberry scoring: Touchdown—Boring (pass).

P. C. scoring: Touchdowns—Cate, Fleming, Sasser. Conversions—Neely (2).

The Li'l That Was!

| A VERY MERRY HOLIDAY SEASON ★ | **The Indian**
NEWBERRY COLLEGE
"Home of The Fighting Redskins" | BUY CHRISTMAS SEALS ★ |

The 1950 Newberry College Football Squad

Indians Lose Bronze Derby To P. C.

Before a crowd of about 4,000 cheering fans, the inspired Newberry Indians outplayed and outfought the P. C. Blue Hose in their best performance of the season, only to drop the contest to the Hosemen, 20-6.

The "Fighting Redskins" did just what the name implies and surpassed their Stetson performance to set the Blue Stockings back on their heels time and again.

The Newberry offense sparkled during the first half. They repeatedly crashed for first down after first down. Twice they moved the pigskin to the two-yard line, only to fumble on both occasions.

Presbyterian seemed to be stunned by the brilliance of the Indians' play, but Lady Luck smiled sweetly on the Blue Stockings on numerous occasions.

Berry hit John Boring in the end zone with a pass to put the Redskins back in the game. Weeks' conversion placement was blocked. The score stood P. C. 7, Newberry 6.

The second half was uneventful for both teams until late in the third period. Fleming took a reverse handoff from Sasser on a punt return and streaked 71 yards, twisting, turning, smacking his way down the sideline for a touchdown. The extra point attempt was blocked. P. C. led 13-6.

Newberry took the kickoff but was forced to punt. The Stockings moved the pigskin to the Newberry seven-yard line but hit a stone wall there. Neely's attempted field goal on the fourth down was wide. The Redskins took over and started churning toward pay dirt once again. A Berry pass intended for Weeks fell incomplete, but interference was ruled to give Newberry the ball o nthe P. C. 30-yard line. Berry passed again, and Sasser, defensive P. C. back, hauled the pigskin in and neatly scampered 80 yards for the final score of the day. Neely converted to make the final score P. C. 20, Newberry 6.

The Indians played their best offensive game of the year. Weeks and Jones, with the limited action of Max DuBose, hit the line for repeated gains. Berry passed for one T. D. and completed nine other aerials. The Redskins reeled off 14 first downs.

The P. C "ten-second backfield" was also hampered by the defensive play of the Indians. Claude Weeks, plucky Newberry fullback, was, by far, the deadliest tackler of the whole afternoon beside his offensive line smashing. Pate, Ulrich, Gantt, Thompson, Hance, Blume, and Cashion all turned in stellar performances in the forward wall.

The Indians closed the season in defeat, just as they opened it. Newberry followers will eagerly await the '51 season, however, which should be highly successful for the Indians.

In the spring of 1950, Charles MacDonald, former instructor of English and Director of Public Relations at Presbyterian College, wrote a short note to *The Blue Stocking*, the student newspaper at Presbyterian College. MacDonald was instrumental with the format of the Bronze Derby in 1947. He implied, once again, his hope that the Bronze Derby would eventually be awarded once a year to the winner of the annual Thanksgiving Day football game.

Letter-rip
Derby Founder Writes

Editor's note: Mr. MacDonald, now connected with the government in writing the history of World War II, is the originator of the Bronze Derby. He had the Derby bronzed and set up the rules governing its exchange. At that time he was public relations director here.

Apartment 327,
2501 Que St., N.W.
Washington, D. C.

To the Editor:

For some time I have been intending to write both you and Wallace Wilkinson to thank you for sending me The Blue Stocking and to congratulate the two of you on the excellent standards which The Sock is maintaining.

Now the Bronze Derby interest provides me with a specific occasion. First, The Blue Stocking has performed a healthy service in promoting the present discussion. Second, it was my idea at the time the Bronze Derby was instituted, that eventually it would become a trophy to be exchanged only upon the annual football game.

I note with interest the keen rivalry with Wofford. It is encouraging to see that Wofford has developed athletic teams capable of keen rivalry.

Please extend my sincerest best wishes to all at PC.

—CHARLES B. MacDONALD

The Li'l 🎩 That Was!

The Blue Stocking

Volume XXVIII — PRESBYTERIAN COLLEGE, CLINTON, S. C., MARCH 18, 1950 — Number 19

Survey Shows PC, Newberry Both Want Bronze Derby Action

A survey of both the Newberry and Presbyterian college campuses revealed this week that both student bodies are in favor of revising the regulations which govern the exchange of the Bronze Derby.

The poll was conducted by a reporter for The Blue Stocking, contacting 20 students from each college. Of the 40 students approached by the reporter, 36 replied they wanted to see action taken on the Derby policy.

The present plans call for an exchange of the coveted chapeau every time the two arch rivals meet in football, basketball, and baseball, the winner gaining possession of the lid 'til the next meeting.

Out of the poll came two prominent suggestions by students from both colleges. One called for exchange of the topper only at the annual football game, while another group backed a proposal to regulate the Derby on a point system.

In the point system, the winner in each sport in which the two meet would gain so many points toward the lid, which would be given the higher scorer at the year's end.

Next week The Blue Stocking will put the two proposals — the football exchange and point system — before both student bodies in another poll. This poll will cover approximately 800 students. Results will be carried in the next issue of The Blue Stocking.

Below follow some quotations and opinions from several of the students polled:

Henry "Hank" Witt, 1948 All-State football player from Newberry — "I've always thought the Derby should be given only in football. It's getting pretty monotonous putting it up every time we meet in the three major sports. In fact, it's been up so much lately,
(Continued on page four)

Survey Shows
(Continued from page one)
and is gonna be up so much in baseball, that I never think about it much."

Blake Watts, PC honorable mention for Little All-American in 1949 — "Football, I say, is the only time the Derby ought to be played for. This is the major sport in both schools, and since the Derby's losing out as is, I think it should be just for football."

Walter Gooch, PC three-letter athlete — "The Derby is sho' losing out in significance. I suggest we get up some system of points and award it annually instead of eight times a year."

U. G. Funderburke, Newberry football tackle — "Yeah, something ought to be done, and done fast. I'd suggest giving it to football only."

Billy Laval, Newberry athletic director — "I'm satisfied any way the boys are. It is getting a little tiresome this way, though."

Lewis Hawkins, PC basketball forward — "Naturally, I'm for the point system. Think basketball should be included. You know, the idea was conceived at a basketball game."

The Li'l That Was!

The Blue Stocking

Volume XXVIII — PRESBYTERIAN COLLEGE, CLINTON, S. C., MARCH 18, 1950 — Number 19

Students Want New Derby Policy

A cross-section poll of Newberry and Presbyterian college students taken this week by The Blue Stocking indicates that both student bodies definitely want to do something about the Bronze Derby, the overworked symbol of athletic supremacy between the two arch rivals.

Page one of this paper carries all the details of the poll and some of the prominent quotations from both student bodies. It will, therefore, suffice to say here that both Newberry and Presbyterian want action taken to restore the Derby to its proper position as a token of athletic supremacy and as a priceless piece of publicity for the two colleges to capitalize on.

Two proposals emerged from the poll—one that the topper be exchanged only at the annual football game and the other that it be exchanged annually on a point system.

In the proposed football exchange, which has as its most ardent supporter Newberry's star athlete, Henry "Hank" Witt, the winner in the Thanksgiving classic would gain possession of the chapeau 'til the next football season rolled around. Then the Derby would be placed on display during the game, and formal ceremonies with high-ranking guests on the platform would see the losing team captain present the lid to the winning captain.

The other plan offered, the point system, would surround the Derby with much the same air of dignity and ceremonies as the football exchange. However, football would be only one part of the quest for year-round possession of the hat. Here, basketball and baseball—and some even suggest all the sports the two colleges meet in—along with football would be included in the stru[ggle] for the Bronze Derby.

Points would be awarded to the winner of athletic contest between the colleges, and a[t the] end of the year the college with the high[er num]ber of points would be awarded the Derby [that] year. It would be given at the last athletic [con]test of the year, with all the year's [points] building up to this moment.

The Blue Stocking looks upon both pro[posals] being excellent substitutes for the now de[funct] system of awarding the Derby every tim[e the] two meet in football, basketball, and base[ball—] an overdose of a good thing.

The Blue Stocking's next action will be [to see] how the entire student bodies at Presby[terian] and Newberry feel about the two propos[als,] which the students prefer.

THE MEN'S SHOP

P. C.
Headquarters In Laurens

Laurens, S. C.

The Li'l 🎩 That Was!

Newberrians reflect on a Presbyterian College proposed point system and an annual presentation at either school's chapel service for the Bronze Derby. All students have heard of the prize but many have never seen it.

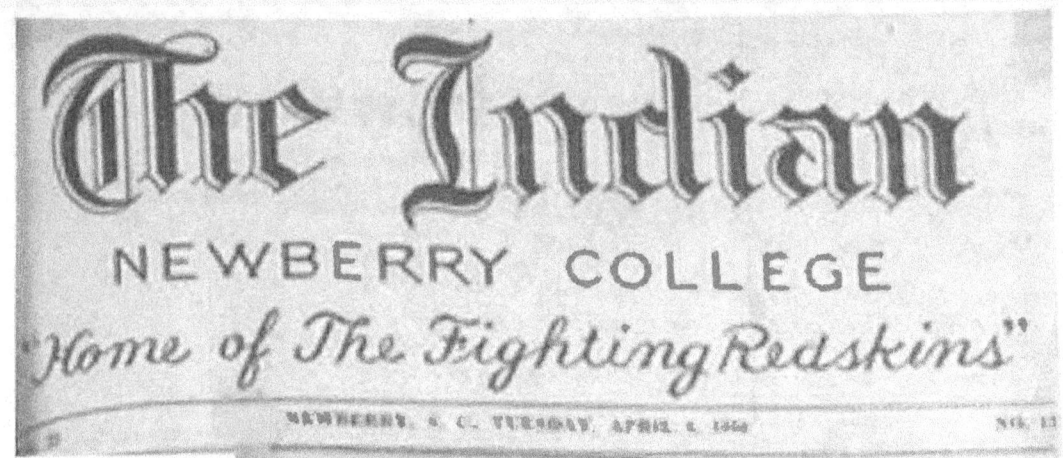

Across The Editor's Desk

THE P. C. PLAN

When that Newberry student grabbed a certain derby from the P. C. boy that night a long time ago, do you suppose he ever dreamed what would happen? We've felt, since we have had the Derby as a symbol of the rivalry between us, that every victory was really an accomplishment because we had the coveted Derby to show for it.

The procedure has been to present the Derby to the winning team after each Newberry-P. C. clash. Now those P. S.ers have had a brainstorm and are eager to revolutionize the plan. Some of them produced the idea of presenting the derby at the end of each season to the team having the largest total number of points for the games played in the particular sport. When we Indians first heard of the "P. C. Plan," we were quick to voice our hearty disapproval. Perhaps we are wrong!

Having a special chapel presentation of the Derby at the end of the season would make an occasion of it. Under our present set-up the crowds are usually stampeding for the exit at the time for the Derby to be presented. Few people ever really see the Derby being regretfully surrendered or joyously received. For that reason, one big ceremony would be an improvement.

But this business of the total number of points—would that be fair? Suppose we beat P. C. by the score of 19-18 in one football game, but in the very next game P. C. beat us by a score of 20-7. (Of course we know that P. C. wouldn't ever win, but let's just suppose!) P. C.'s total score would be larger than Newberry's but we would have won just as many games as P. C. Is the total score, then, a just measure of athletic supremacy?

Evidently, though, P. C. has thought out this plan carefully. Wouldn't it be a relief to our troubled minds to know what their plan really is? As well as we understand this new method, however, it seems that P. C. is merely attempting to make it so that they might get the Derby occasionally. We don't want to disregard the idea simply because it originated in our great rival school, and we certainly don't want to get in an undesirable rut because of our ignorance or obstinacy. We need to be open-minded and ready to accept any suggestions for betterment.

F. D.

The Li'l 🎩 That Was!

The Blue Stocking

Distinguished For Its Progress

Volume XXVIII   Presbyterian College, Clinton, S. C., April 1, 1950   Number 21

Bronze Derby Deal

• Newberry college leaders asked this week for a few weeks to think over The Blue Stocking's proposals concerning the exchange of the Bronze Derby. A report from the neighboring college shows that the student body isn't sure yet that it favors a change in policy.

The concensus at Newberry is that Presbyterian is trying to "pull the wool" over their eyes.

But this is by no means The Blue Stocking's plans. This paper is only crusading to protect the symbolism which surrounds the coveted Derby so that it will bear greater profit to both colleges in the future.

Negotiations are now in progress between the two student newspapers, and it is hoped that in the next few weeks —after the holiday period—a vote can be ready for publication from Newberry on which proposal they prefer, the point system or football exchange.

Newberry Votes Later on Proposal

Limited Time Delays Derby Vote

Newberry college will not vote on the Bronze Derby exchange 'til after the Easter holidays, an announcement from Newberry revealed today.

The Newberry student leaders gave a full chapel schedule and short notice as reasons for delay of the vote on the current issue being put before both Presbyterian and Newberry colleges.

After the holiday period, the Newberry students will hear The Blue Stocking's proposal to exchange the Bronze Derby, token of athletic supremacy between the two rivals, only annually on either a football or point system basis.

Two weeks ago the Presbyterian college student body voted in favor of the football exchange grid exchange edged the system proposal by a mare

November 1951

November 1	Roy Campanella, catcher for the Brooklyn Dodgers, won the first of his 3 MLB NL Most Valuable Player Awards.
November 1	Johnny Mercer's musical and Tony Award winning show "Top Banana" debuted in New York City.
November 1	The first military exercises for nuclear war were held in the Nevada desert by the United States.
November 3	Boston Red Sox outfielder Dwight Evans was born.
November 4	Sam Snead led the United States Ryder Cup golf team to victory over Great Britain.
November 7	American entertainer Frank Sinatra married film star Ava Gardner.
November 7	American sports journalist Chris Mortensen was born.
November 8	New York Yankee Catcher Yogi Berra won the first of his 3 MLB AL Most Valuable Player Awards.
November 8	American songwriter Larry Burnett of Firefall was born.
November 9	American actor and body builder Lou Ferrigno was born.
November 10	The first long distance telephone call without operator assistance was successfully made.
November 11	Winner of the 1981 Masters golf tournament, Fuzzy Zoeller was born.
November 11	Juan Peron was re-elected President of Argentina.
November 12	"Paint Your Wagon" opened in New York City.
November 14	American singer-songwriter Stephen Bishop was born.
November 15	Gil McDougal of the New York Yankees won MLB AL Rookie of the Year.
November 17	Great Britain developed the world's first nuclear heating system.
November 18	Former Chicago Cubs first baseman and future TV star of "The Rifleman," Chuck Connors, was the first player to oppose the major league draft.
November 19	Roy Campanella was named MLB NL Most Valuable Player on his birthday.
November 22	The Bronze Derby was played in Newberry, South Carolina on Thanksgiving Day. The Presbyterian College Blue Hose defeated the Newberry College Indians 27-0.

The Newberry Observer
AND HERALD & NEWS
"Just Like a Letter from Home"

HERALD AND NEWS ESTABLISHED 1868 — NEWBERRY, S C, FRIDAY, NOVEMBER 21, 1941 — NEWBERRY OBSERVER ESTABLISHED 1865

Blue Hose, Indians To Feature Turkey Day Festivities; Tribe Out For Upset of Year Over PC

Prized Derby At Stake, Now In Tribe Camp

Berry's Aerials Counted On For Victory Margin

Notice

Following the Newberry-P. C. game a "drop-in" for alumni and friends of the college will be held at Smith Motor Company, 1300 College Street. This buffet supper is sponsored by local alumni and members of the Indian Club in Newberry.

Paces Tribe Ground Attack

The Newberry College Indians are set for "the upset of the year" as they tackle P. C.'s Blue Hose on the Newberry College field Thursday afternoon at 2:30 p. m.

A big day has been planned with dignitaries, sports writers and sports casters to add to the usual luster of the event. A local National Guard band, together with P. C.'s band, will entertain during halftime.

To conclude the day, a buffet supper will be served at the Smith Motor Company, underwritten by friends of Newberry College.

The game is one of the top attractions of the season and draws statewide attention year in and year out. Past performances and records are tossed out the window as the rival coaches key their squads to their "zenith" for the struggle between these two perennial rivals.

Top prize in this game of games is the coveted Bronze Derby which goes to the winning team. P. C. will be out to recapture the "Derby" now held by Newberry.

The outcome will also affect the standings of the state "Little Four" championship. Wofford won the title early in the season for the fourth straight year, but the other positions won't be settled until the curtain rings down on the Newberry-Presbyterian game. Newberry could brighten up what is an otherwise dismal season by taking the game, the "Derby", and finishing as runnerup to Wofford in the "Little Four" race.

Newberry will have an added incentive, as the Indians will be seeking their initial win of the season and would like nothing better than closing the season with a win over their blue-hosed cousins from Clinton. The Indians will also be out to reverse last year's decision in a game that P. C. won by 20-6.

P. C. could end a very successful year by scalping the Indians and taking the "Bronze Derby" home with them. A win would elevate the Blue Stockings to second place in the "Little Four" and give them an even break in their ten-game slate. P. C. has already defeated Western Carolina, Davidson, Catawba and Erskine.

The game could very easily wind up in a passing duel with P. C.'s Lefty Jack Harper and Newberry's ace Charlie Berry doing the throwing. Berry is one of the leading passers among the smaller colleges and is a top candidate for Little All-American laurels.

Berry has added a new offensive punch to the Indians' attack since being forced out of the first five games due to an injury. His passing and running has resulted in four Newberry touchdowns in the last two outings against Elon and Furman.

Senior Joe Kirvin from Sumter, S. C., P. C.'s Little All-American candidate, is Harper's chief (Continued on page eight)

Sports Observer

(Continued from page five)

Newberry 13, Presbyterian 9. Yes, Harper and all!

DON'T FORGET!

Wheel Alignment is important...

SMITH MOTOR CO.
DODGE - PLYMOUTH

The Li'l 🎩 That Was!

The Newberry Observer
AND HERALD & NEWS
"Just Like a Letter from Home"

HERALD AND NEWS ESTABLISHED 1865   NEWBERRY, S. C., FRIDAY, NOVEMBER 23, 1951   NEWBERRY OBSERVER ESTABLISHED 1893

Turkey Day Tussle Set For Thursday

CLINTON, Nov. 16—It won't be a turkey hunt but a quest for the Bronze Derby when Presbyterian College invades Newberry on Thanksgiving Day.

It's the 37th renewal of an old pigskin rivalry that dates right back to 1913, the year Presbyterian first opened football shop. The Bronze Derby symbolizes that rivalry.

The Derby, the season's finale and battle against ancient foe—all of these elements mingle to make the urge for victory particularly strong. It's the type of prompting which pushes past records into the background, so that the two teams square off even no matter what the season count. Past records prove how favorites fell.

Presbyterian received a bitter taste of that on its last visit to Newberry, in 1949. A lightning backfield raced up and down the field but could only score twice, and the Indians pocketed a 20-14 upset.

History Of "Derby" Makes Good Reading

Now Possessed By Tribesmen

Presbyterian and Newberry have been rivals for nearly a half century. In 1947 they authorized something to show this rivalry. Borrowing a leaf from the famed Michigan-Purdue "Old Oaken Bucket" and the Stanford-California "Axe," the schools jointly announced that athletic supremacy between the two would henceforth be symbolized by "The Bronze Derby". Presentation of the award is made to the victor following each meeting of the two Little Four and SIAA rivals in three major sports—football, basketball, and baseball.

The award grew out of the "abduction" of a P. C. student's derby hat at the first basketball game between P. C. and Newberry in 1947. Suggestion of the award was first made by Professor Charles MacDonald, instructor of English and director of Public Relations at Presbyterian, in a letter to the sports publicity director at Newberry. The hat was surrendered by anonymous Newberry students and turned over to a local jewelry firm to be cast in bronze.

"The Bronze Derby" has gone on block many times since it came into existence. Its first presentation was to P. C. after a 44 to 42 win over Newberry in basketball.

"The Derby" is part of a general plan to keep relations between the two colleges on a high plane, despite the bitter rivalry which exists between them. The movement was launched after incidents threatening the severance of athletic relations between P. C. and Newberry took place. Frequently, in the past, impending clashes between the two schools have resulted in pre-game raiding parties on both campuses, with resultant damage to personal and school property. It was with the aim of eliminating such useless destruction that the student government organizations initiated their cooperative movement.

The Presbyterian "Blue Hose" and the Newberry "Indians", have been feuding on the athletic fields since the turn of the century. Their 39-year string of football clashes—unbroken since 1913 except for the year 1918—ranks as one of the South's oldest rivalries, and in baseball the two teams were bitter rivals long before football became a part of the intercollegiate scene in the South.

Pictured above is Max DuBose, Newberry College's senior halfback, who will play his last football game with the Redskins Thursday afternoon, in the annual Newberry-P. C. gridiron classic. Max has provided the spark for the Tribe attack every season he has played for the Indians, and has been a mainstay on the state championship baseball teams of the past two years, slamming the ball at an astronomical rate. Mobile Maxie, from Bishopville, S. C., in addition to his running prowess is an exceptional pass-receiver. He is shown above nabbing one of teammate Berry's accurate aerials. Max packs a solid 175 pounds on his compact 5'9" frame. (Observer photo by Sims Tompkins).

Seniors Play Final Game

Seven Seniors on the 1951 Football Team at Newberry College will play their last game with "The Indians" when Newberry meets Presbyterian on Setzler Field, Thanksgiving Day at 2:30 P. M. First row, left to right: Charles E. Reames, Bath, S. C., Claude L. Weeks, Charleston, S. C., Max S. DuBose, Bishopville, S. C. Second row, left to right: Faber J. Hance, Ninety-Six, S. C., Bill R. Gantz, Pampa, Tex., Booby E. Gruhn, Macon, Ga., and, Gerald S. Fate, Bishopville, S. C.

The Li'l 🎩 That Was!

The Indian
NEWBERRY COLLEGE
"Home of The Fighting Redskins"

NEWS • SPORTS • FEATURES • EDITORIALS

NEWBERRY, S. C. TUESDAY, NOVEMBER 20, 1951

Bronze Derby Is Symbol Of Newberry-P. C. Rivalry

"The Bronze Derby," symbolic of rivalry between Presbyterian College and Newberry College, will be at stake in the traditional Thanksgiving Day game between the two schools at Setzler Field.

Presbyterian and Newberry have been rivals for nearly a half century. In 1947 they authorized something to show this rivalry. Borrowing a leaf from the famed Michigan-Purdue "Old Oaken Bucket" and the Stanford-California "Axe," the schools jointly announced that athletic supremacy between the two would henceforth be symbolized by "The Bronze Derby." Presentation of the award is made to the victor following each meeting of the two Little Four and SIAA rivals in three major sports—football, basketball, and baseball.

The award grew out of the "abduction" of a P. C. student's derby hat at the first basketball game between P. C. and Newberry in 1947. Suggestion of the award was first made by Professor Charles MacDonald, instructor of English and director of Public Relations at Presbyterian, in a letter to the sports publicity director at Newberry. The hat was surrendered by anonymous Newberry students and turned over to a local jewelry firm to be cast in bronze.

"The Bronze Derby" has gone on block many times since it came into existence. Its first presentation was to P. C. after a 44 to 42 win over Newberry in basketball.

Notice

Following the Newberry-P. C. game a "drop-in" for alumni and friends of the college will be held at Smith Motor Company, 1309 College Street. This buffet supper is sponsored by local alumni and members of the Indian Club in Newberry.

"The Derby" is part of a general plan to keep relations between the two colleges on a high plane, despite the bitter rivalry which exists between them. The movement was launched after incidents threatening the severance of athletic relations between P. C. and Newberry took place. Frequently, in the past, impending clashes between the two schools have resulted in pre-game raiding parties on both campuses, with resultant damage to personal and school property. It was with the aim of eliminating such useless destruction that the student government organizations initiated their cooperative movement.

The Presbyterian "Blue Hose" and the Newberry "Indians" have been feuding on the athletic fields since the turn of the century. Their 39-year string of football clashes—unbroken since 1913 except for the year 1918—ranks as one of the South's oldest rivalries, and in baseball the two teams were bitter rivals long before football became a part of the intercollegiate scene in the South.

Plenty of Fresh FRUITS At All Times

YOUNG'S FRUIT STORE

Phone 148

LOMINICK'S DRUG STORE

Dependable Drugs

Newberry, S. C.

The Li'l 🎩 That Was!

The Indian
NEWBERRY COLLEGE
"Home of The Fighting Redskins"

NEWS | SPORTS | FEATURES | EDITORIALS

Newberry, P.C. To Battle Thanksgiving

Bronze Derby Is Symbol Of Newberry-P. C. Rivalry

SPORTS SPOTS
By Pat Dennis

THE BRONZE DERBY CLASSIC

Turkey Day and football are synonymous all over the U. S. and there will be no exception on the Newberry campus. The big game looms near with the schools' symbol of rivalry, the coveted Bronze Derby, at stake. Last year P. C. took the "Lid" and kept it through basketball season only to lose it during baseball season. Newberry is in possession of the Derby and will be fighting to keep it from falling into the hand of those "barbarians, shall we say" from Presbyterian. Keen rivalry is expected from both teams and a great game is shaping up.

In the fifth Bronze Derby football Classic in 1951, Presbyterian College defeated Newberry College 27-0 in Newberry, South Carolina to win their 3rd football Bronze Derby.

the 1952 PacSac

Hose Take Derby Battle 27-0

NEWBERRY, S. C., Nov. 22—Scoring twice on the ground and twice in the air PC romped off with the Bronze Derby as they downed Newberry College 27-0. Kirby Jackson galloped 16 yards for the first PC score and Harper connected with Cooper Tedder for the next. Ted Sasser scored the next two TD's on a pass and a 20 yard run. Neely converted on three of the four conversions. The Blue Hose saved their shutout by holding the Indians on the three yard line for two plays before time ran out.

The Li'l That Was!

The Newberry Observer
AND HERALD & NEWS
"Just Like a Letter from Home"

Tribe Tomahawks Dull; Blue Hose Humiliate Redskins In 27-0 "Bronze Derby" Clash

Derby To P. C. After Local Offense Fails

Weldon Aerials Surprise Tribe; Excells Harper

By BILL WHELAN and JIM WISEMAN

Three thousand supporters of both colleges watched an unimpressive ball game last Thursday afternoon, as Presbyterian's Blue Hose overpowered an uncoordinated Newberry College team by a final 27-0 score on Setzler field. The only Tribe threat came in the final seconds, with an Ardito-to-Reames aerial carrying 48 yards to P. C.'s 3. But the Indians were unable to carry across in the two remaining plays of the ball game.

On the ground both teams were fairly well matched with the Stockings outgaining the locals by a mere 23 yards. But in the air it was a different story. P. C.'s Harper and Weldon combined their pitching arms to cover 124 yards and two touchdowns. A last-minute pass from Don Ardito put Newberry into the game statistically, as his aerial covered 48 yards to give the Indians a 66-yard total.

Outstanding for the Blue Hose were Weldon, Sasser, Baker and Harper, on the offense, while defensive honors were copped by Neely and Kirven. For the Tribesmen, offensively, it was DuBose, Ardito, Babb and Reames, while on the defense, Thompson, Weeks and Gantt were particularly outstanding.

P. C. Kick-off

Newberrian Capps took Neely's opening kick-off on his own 12 to start a game that was expected to be a bitterly contested one. The ball changed hands four times without either team being able to penetrate beyond the midfield stripe, indicating a fine defensive game.

Berry Fumbles

On the final exchange, DuBose took Freeman's punt on his own 20 and toted to the 27. DuBose cracked through for five. The next play was disastrous as Berry fumbled and Neely recovered for the Hose on Newberry's 16, to set up the first score of the game. After an incomplete aerial, Harper ripped off to the 9. Then it was Harper again to the five and a first down. On the next play the Presbyterians hit pay dirt as Jackson skirted his own left end for the score. Neely split the uprights from placement for a 7-0 lead.

Midway in the second quarter the Stockings scored again, after the ball had changed hands five times without either team crossing the midfield stripe, and seemingly on an even footing.

Bad Gamble

This time it was a poor gamble that set up the score. Berry, quarterbacking for the Tribe, gambled on making one yard for a first down on P. C.'s 34 instead of punting out of danger. The "thin Blue line" held and P. C. took over on the 39, after tossing Reames for a five-yard loss.

On three successive plays, Walt carried to the Tribe's 49, Cox slipped through to the 47. A penalty advanced the oval to the 42. Then Baker picked up a first down to the 31. It was Baker again, this time to the 24. From here Harper flipped a pass to Tedder who scored. Neely failed to convert from the 7, where a penalty had set the Hose. The half ended shortly thereafter, with neither team being able to do much, with the score Presbyterian 13, Newberry 0.

Following Ardito's kick-off to Hoseman Weldon to P. C.'s 25, the Indians' defenses held and forced Fulk to boot to DuBose, who carried back to his own 29. But the Tribe's chances were short-lived as DuBose fumbled two plays later on the 35. The Hose were forced to punt again from Newberry's 37 when the Tribe forward wall held, the oval, booted by Fulk, going out of bounds on the Redskins' 3.

Third P. C. Score

Berry punted out of danger to Jackson who carried back eight yards to the Tribe 42. After five bruising ground plays, Harper hit end Kirven for a 14-yard gain to the 15. Harper kept and picked up to the five. Then Sasser slipped through for one, and a first down on the Indians' four. On the next play Sasser slammed over for another score. Neely's accurate placement put the Hose in a 20-0 lead.

Near the end of the third quarter Newberry took possession on their own 45 following a 29-yard Fulk punt. A pass, Berry to Morris, carried to P. C.'s 45. Babb slipped through to the 44, then Berry picked up a first down to the 43. It was Berry again to the 41 to end the third period.

On the first play of the final canto Watts intercepted a Berry aerial on P. C.'s 42. Austin picked up to the 44, then Weldon, who showed surprising aerial accuracy, hit teammate Jordan with a pass to the Newberry 42 and a first down. Weldon followed this with another pass, to Sasser, the play carrying for 42 yards and the final score of the ball game.

After two exchanges of punts, the Indians staged a mild threat, taking a Fulk punt on their own 14 and drove 20 yards before they were forced to punt. P. C. could do nothing with the ball and punted back four plays later, to Newberry's 48. After a one-yard Ardito to Reames pass, Ardito hit Reames on the P. C. 20, and Ramblin' Reames swivel-hipped to the three before he was hauled down from behind by Jackson. With but seconds to go, Babb cracked down to the one. The last play of the game followed, with an Ardito pass, intended for Davis, falling incomplete.

The game ended with good feeling on the field, among the players, despite the lopsided 27-0 score, and the "Bronze Derby" changed hands again, as the P. C. players carried the prized chapeau back to Clinton again, where it will remain until it goes on the block again during the coming basketball season.

STATISTICS

	Newberry	P. C.
First downs	7	9
Yds. rushing	99	122
Passes att.	16	14
Passes comp.	8	6
Yds. passing	66	124
Passes int. by	0	2
Fumbles	3	2
Fumbles lost	2	0
Yds. penalized	40	55
Punts	8	8
Punting av.	31.4	32.0

Presbyterian scoring: Touchdowns, Jackson, Tedder, Sasser (2); extra points, Neely, 3 (placements).

Scoring:
Newberry   0 0 0 0—0
Presbyterian   7 6 7 7—27

The Li'l That Was!

The Blue Stocking
Distinguished for Its Progress

Volume XXX   Presbyterian College, Clinton, S. C., November 30, 1951   Number 10

Stockings Scalp Indians
PC Gains Possession of Bronze Derby As Blue Romps Over Newberry, 27-0

The Presbyterian college Blue Hose mistook the Newberry Indians for turkey as they gobbled up their Bronze Derby foe by a margin of 27-0 in their annual Thanksgiving classic. The Turkey day tilt was played before more than 3,000 fans.

It was "Senior" day for PC, as all seven seniors on the football squad played a bang-up game. Halfback Ted Sasser tallied two touchdowns, Halfback Kirby Jackson and End Cooper Tedder each accounted for one marker. All-State Tackle Buddy Neely, Tackle Bo Atkinson, Guard Bob Pierce, and Quarterback Frog Weldon gave a good account of themselves in the finale.

PC's opening tally was made by Jackson, as he swept his own left end for five yards. Tedder was on the receiving end of a Jack Harper pass that covered 24 yards and the second touchdown.

In the closing minutes of the first quarter, Newberry possessed the pigskin on their own 21 yard line. Berry was called upon to try to make yardage but Pierce and Tedder roared through to tackle Berry on the 17. He fumbled and Neely recovered to give the Hose a scoring threat. After a pass play and a line crash by Harper to the five, the Ole Lefthander pitched out to Jackson for the score. Neely converted.

After Halfbacks Bootsy Cox
(Continued on page four)

passed from that point to Tedder for a 13-0 score.

It was in the second period that Halfback Sasser took over. Fullback Emmett Fulk had put the Indians deep in their own territory by a beautfiul punt that dropped out of bounds on the Newberry three. The Indians punted and then it was goalward-bound for PC as Sasser and Halfback Art Baker moved it to the 28 yard line. Harper's 12 yard pass to Tedder set the scene for Sasser. On two straight line plunges, the Brunswick halfback scored. Neely's toe made the score read 20-0.

The Hose's final tally came about after Watt had intercepted an Indian pass and had run it back to the 41. Quarterback Weldon sent Sasser to the right flank for a pass, and the fleet senior raced 41 yards, with the help of a crucial block thrown by Freshman End Joe Counts, for his second touchdown of the afternoon. After Neely converted, the final score was PC 27, Newberry 0.

The Li'l 🎩 That Was!

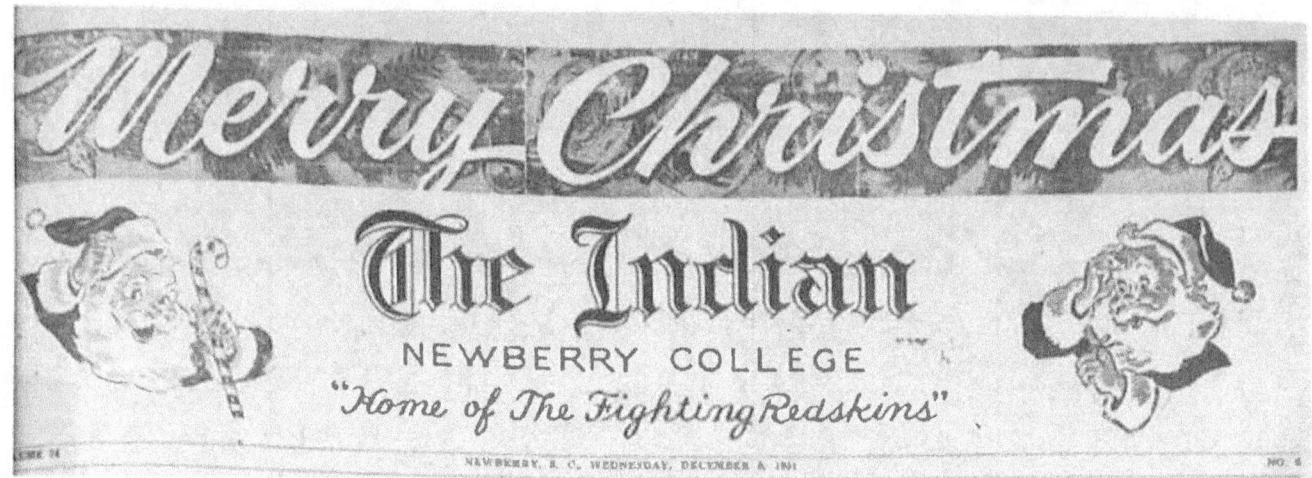

SPORTS SPOTS
By Pat Dennis

"The thing that counts most is not the size of the dog in the fight, but the size of the fight in the dog." This old adage is quite true and has a marked significance with our Fighting Redskins. Time after time our boys went up against larger, more experienced opponents, but showed a high calibre of determination and spirit on the gridiron at every outing. The season was not as successful as some of us may have wished but the squad exhibited the fighting spirit that is characteristic of Newberry College and upheld the high standards of hard, clean football. That, in itself, is an achievement of which to be proud. That old verse states this fact best. It is:

"When the one Great Scorer comes
To write against your name,
He writes not if you won or lost
But how you played the game."

Presbyterian College came up with a rousing 27-0 victory over the Redskins on Turkey Day to capture the Derby and cop second place in the Little Four Conference. Newberry tied for last place with Erskine by virtue of a 6-6 tie with the Fleet earlier in the season. Powerful Wofford took first place handily by turning back all the competition easily. It was quite a season but the most surprising incident was P. C.'s ease in scoring a 27-0 decision over the Redskins. Both teams were pretty even at game time, but Newberry got some bad breaks and mired down never to click again. P. C. reeled off two TD's in the first half and two more six-pointers in the second half to become victors for '51 in the keen rivalry of the gridiron between the two colleges.

The 1951 All-State eleven came out recently and somebody needs to wake up. Only one Newberry gridster made even the third team. This was Max Dubose in the backfield. Several others received honorable mention which was entirely inadequate for them. They were Charlie Berry, Murray Davis and Bull Thompson. How they were able to overlook such outstanding men as Claude Weeks, Charlie Reames, and Bill Brissey is too much for this columnist to understand. It just goes to show how much publicity means for a team. No sportswriter can see every team play in every game and watch every man on every play. So, what does he do? He reads and draws his conclusion from the publicity given by the newspapers. A sportswriter can play up one or two men pretty big even if they do nothing in a game. This means a lot in these mythical teams chosen every year. Our boys have received very little publicity and should have fared better as far as this All-State team is concerned.

Attention these days is turning from the gridiron to the basketball court. Now that all the old rivalries are settled between Georgia-Georgia Tech, Army-Navy, Alabama-Auburn, Tulane-LSU, and others, the limelight is on basketball. Here on the campus, football is gone and the cage season is in full swing. A couple of practice sessions against Clemson previewed the season. The Redskins were impressive against the Tigers, although not victorious. Charlie Stoudemire and Leon Maxwell were recently elected co-captains of the squad. The Indians are potentially strong and may develop into a close-knit fast working team it is capable of being. Time will tell.

See ya' after Christmas.

November 1952

November 1	"Ivy Mike," the code name of the first tested H-Bomb, was detonated in the Marshall Islands.
November 2	Larry Fink, chairman and CEO of Blackrock, was born.
November 3	Clarence Birdseye first marketed frozen peas in the United States.
November 3	American comedienne and TV star Roseanne Barr was born.
November 4	Dwight D. Eisenhower was elected President of the United States defeating Adlai Stevenson.
November 5	American Basketball Hall of Fame center Bill Walton was born.
November 8	Christine Ann Hefner, future CEO of Playboy Enterprises and the daughter of Hugh Hefner was born.
November 9	The first President of Israel, Chaim Weizmann, passed away.
November 10	Tryve Lie resigns as the first Secretary General of the United Nations.
November 12	Philadelphia A's pitcher Bobby Shantz won the MLB AL Most Valuable Player Award.
November 12	The Chicago White Sox placed outfielder Jim Rivera on a one year suspension after being convicted on a rape charge.
November 13	United States Attorney General Merrick Garland was born.
November 13	False fingernails were first marketed and sold.
November 15	American professional wrestler Randy Savage was born.
November 16	The creator of Mario, Japanese video designer Shigeru Miyamato was born.
November 17	South African President Cyril Ramaphosa was born.
November 19	Scandinavian Airlines introduced a commercial route from Canada to Europe.
November 20	Chicago Cubs outfielder Hank Sauer won the MLB NL Most Valuable Player Award.
November 20	George Axelrod's play "Seven Year Itch" premiered in New York City.
November 21	The first United States 2 color postage stamp was introduced.
November 22	A's Harry Byrd was selected MLB AL Rookie of the Year.
November 27	The Bronze Derby was played in Clinton, South Carolina on Thanksgiving Day. The Presbyterian College Blue Hose defeated the Newberry College Indians 14-12.

The Li'l That Was!

The Blue Stocking

Distinguished for Its Progress

Volume XXXI   Presbyterian College, Clinton, S. C., November 21, 1952   Number 11

Hose Terminate With Newberry

• Ozone to Be Filled With Passes

More passes may be thrown in the Presbyterian-Newberry battle here tomorrow afternoon than in any other game in the state this year.

For fans who like this razzle-dazzle type of play, the records strongly support that estimate of the situation. Here are the facts:

Both Presbyterian and Newberry have relied almost entirely upon air operations throughout the season. Together they will field four ace passers who rank with the most accurate in South Carolina. They also have two outstanding ends for receiving purposes.

The Blue StSockings, in eight games this year, have thrown 160 passes and completed 68 for 1158 yards and 13 touchdowns. But even more significant is the fact that PC passers have really taken the lid off in the past two engagements. They attempted 33 and completed 15 for 173 yards and one touchdown against Furman, then soared to a record 290 yards on 14 aerials of 26 attempted for all seven touchdowns against Western Carolina last weekend.

Quarterbacks Jack Harper and Harry Hamilton are the two slingshot artists for the Hosemen — Harper having hit on 46 of 116 attempted for 780 yards and Hamilton on 19 of 36 for another 397 yards. Their main target has been Little All-America End Candidate Joe Kirven, who has snagged 23 for 340 yards and four touchdowns.

Quarterback Charlie Berry has been the deadly-eyed sharpshooter for the Indians, with Freshman Danny Brabham stepping in with almost equal effectiveness to relieve him in the pitching duties. Big Murray Davis, one of South Carolina's very best flankmen, is the key receiver in this Newberry aerial attack and has accounted for six touchdowns.

They Stow Away Cleats

Nine Presbyterian college seniors will conclude their gridiron careers under Blue Stocking colors when they close the 1952 season against Newberry tomorrow afternoon. End Joe Kirven, of Sumter, has been acclaimed by Coach Lonnie S. McMillian as the best end he has tutored in 29 years. Center Tommy Guillebeau, of Lincolnton, Ga., has performed, like Kirven, as a team co-captain and has been outstanding both on offense and defense. Quarterback Jack Harper, of Washington, Ga., should close the book with one of the best aerial records in the nation. Fullback Emmett Fulk, of Darlington, has plunged better than three yards per try this year. Halfback Art Baker, of Sumter, also has contributed his share of the rushing yards, while Halfback Tommy Jordan, of Bishopville, has been counted on mostly for kickoff returns. Tackle Tommy Sheriff, of Orangeburg, has paced the team on defense with an average of six individual tackles per game, while giving him full support in the forward wall have been Guard Cedric Jernigan, of Fayetteville, N. C., and Guard Wade Camlin of Georgetown.

Presbyterian College, Clinton, S. C., November 21, 1952

The Li'l 🎩 That Was!

The Indian
NEWBERRY COLLEGE
"Home of The Fighting Redskins"
NEWBERRY, S. C., WEDNESDAY, NOVEMBER 19, 1952

BEAT PRESBYTERIAN

KEEP THE DERBY

Bronze Derby To Go On Block

The Fighting Indians of Newberry College will wind up the 1952 season Saturday afternoon, as they journey to Clinton to engage the Blue Stockings of Presbyterian, in an annual affair that is a highlight of the season for both teams.

As usual, when Newberry and Presbyterian meet in athletics, top prize for the victor will be possession of the Bronze Derby, symbol of athletic competition between the two schools. P. C. will be fighting to wrest possession from the Indians, who now have it as a result of their baseball victories last spring.

P. C. Air-minded

A wide-open, thrill-packed game is promised, with both teams going all-out in a effort to win. The P. C. offense is led by Quarterback Jack Harper, Back Emmett Fulk, and End Joe Kirven. The passing combination of Harper-to-Kirven has long been a thorn in the side of all P. C. opponents. Coach Lonnie McMillan has termed Kirven as the best end that he has ever coached. The senior end from Sumter, S. C., is a strong contender for All-State, and Little All-American honors. Fulk is a speedy, shifty back, who has borne the brunt of the ground-gaining for the Blue Hose this year.

Indian Offensive

The Indians can counter with an air attack of their own. Seniors Charlie Berry and Murray Davis, who will be playing their last game for the Indians, have combined their talents to give the Redskins an always-dangerous air attack. The bullet-like tosses of Berry and the sensational snagging of many of these passes by the glue-fingered Davis, have been one of the brightest spots in the Indian line-up this season. Plunging Fullback Stan Bessinger, Halfbacks Ray, Corley, and Kicklighter, together with Berry and Freshman Quarterback Dan Brabham, provide most of the punch to the Indian ground attack.

Defensive Stars

On the defensive side of the ledger, Presbyterian will be led by such stalwarts as Guillebeau and Kirven. The Indian defensive lineup boasts such veteran stand-outs as Bill Thompson, Don Maxwell, Ed Hester, Grover Davis, Frank Hartol, Bill Brissie, and End Murray Davis, one of the sixty-minute men on Coach Harvey Kirkland's squad and a strong contender for All-State honors.

Past records and performances can be thrown out the window, when making predictions concerning this game. Anything can happen and probably will. A capacity crowd is expected to be in the stands for the opening kick-off on Saturday afternoon.

When Your SHOES Need A Doctor
GO TO
DENNIS SHOE SHOP
Quality Materials and Workmanship

MAKE
GILDER & WEEKS
"YOUR REXALL DRUG STORE"
HEADQUARTERS

Newberry   Joanna

The Indian
NEWBERRY COLLEGE
"Home of The Fighting Redskins"
NEWBERRY, S. C., WEDNESDAY, DECEMBER 10, 1953 — NO. 6

ATTEND THE DANCE

MERRY CHRISTMAS

Ritz Theatre

WEDNESDAY and THURSDAY
Van Johnson, Janet Leigh, Louis Calhern
"CONFIDENTIALLY CONNIE"
Fox News and Short

FRIDAY and SATURDAY
Joel McCrea, Barbara Hale, Alex Nicol, Charles Drake
"THE LONE HAND"
(In Technicolor)
Also Two Cartoons—Cobs and Robbers, Featherweight Champs

MONDAY and TUESDAY
Elizabeth Taylor, Fernando Lamas, William Powell
"THE GIRL WHO HAD EVERYTHING"
— Extra Added Attraction —
"THE HOAXTERS"
The Inside Story of the World's Greatest Fraud

WEDNESDAY and THURSDAY
May 13 and 14
Bette Davis, Sterling Hayden, Natalie Wood
"THE STAR"
Fox News and Short

FRIDAY and SATURDAY
May 15 and 16
Randolph Scott, Patrice Wymore, Dick Wesson
"THE MAN BEHIND THE GUN"
(In Technicolor)
Also Short

MONDAY and TUESDAY
May 18 and 19
Robert Taylor, Elizabeth Taylor, Joan Fontaine
"IVANHOE"
(In Technicolor)
M. G. M. News

Blue Hose Take Bronze Derby Tilt In Last Seconds

Led by their Little All-American end, Joe Kirven, the Blue Hose rallied in the last 70 seconds of play to down the Fighting Redskins by a 14-12 score on the Presbyterian College field, Saturday, November 22.

Trailing by a 12-0 score the Blue Hose tallied twice in the final quarter for two touchdowns and the title to the coveted Bronze Derby, a symbol of rivalry between these two schools.

For the Indians, in the second quarter Charles Berry, quarterback, kept the ball and plunged through the Blue Hose forward wall for the first TD of the game. Grover Davis missed from placement and Newberry held a shaky 6-0 lead at the end of the first half of play.

In the third quarter Charles Berry threw a pass to Left End Mike Maksim, who carried the pigskin over for the Tribe. Davis missed from placement and Newberry held a 12-0 lead at the end of the third quarter. However, the Blue Hose came to life, filling the air with passes which heretofore had been ineffective. With Harper and Hamilton tossing, End Joe Kirven tallied twice for the Blue Hose. Conversions were added to both TDs, making the margin of victory for the Blue Stockings.

Newberry Steam Laundry & Dry Cleaning Co.
LAUNDRY - DRY CLEANING
934 Main St.   Newberry, S. C.

SHOP AT
ROSE'S 5, 10 & 25c STORE
FOR
Quality and Economy
COLLEGE STUDENT'S ALWAYS WELCOME

Royal Dry Cleaners
"BEAUTIFUL DRY CLEANING"
"You've tried the rest; now try the best."
1107 CALDWELL ST.   PHONE 12

B. C. MOORE & SONS, Inc.

Extend a Welcome

Newberry College Students

The Clinton Chronicle

Clinton, S. C., Thursday, November 27, 1952

Happy Thanksgiving from the Newberry Hotel

Drive safely to the Newberry Hotel Dining Room

and we will speed you on your way to the ball game after enjoying a

DELIGHTFUL THANKSGIVING BUFFET LUNCHEON

WITH ALL THE TRIMMINGS

Ralph and Elizabeth (Speake) Wilbanks

PC Beats Newberry In Last Minute Of Play

Kirven Goes Over for Final Score In Thriller, 14-12. Game Winds Up Season.

November 1953

November 3	American comedian Dennis Miller was born.
November 3	MLB Rules Committee changed the sacrifice fly rule. The rule now states a sacrifice fly is not charged as a time at bat.
November 7	WIS TV channel 10 in Columbia, South Carolina, an NBC affiliate, began broadcasting.
November 9	Cambodia gained independence from France.
November 9	The United States Supreme Court ruled that MLB is exempt from anti-trust laws.
November 9	The first king of Saudi Arabia, Ibn Saud, passed away.
November 12	A United States district judge ruled the NFL can black out TV home games.
November 12	The first Prime Minister of Israel, David Ben-Gurion, resigned.
November 13	Mexican President Andres Manuel Lopez Obrador was born.
November 17	The United States joined The United Nations in condemning Israel's raid on Jordan in October, 1953.
November 17	In MLB, The St. Louis Browns officially became the Baltimore Baseball Club, Inc.
November 19	United States Vice President Richard Nixon visited Hanoi.
November 19	The United States Supreme Court ruled 7-2 that Major League Baseball is a sport and not a business.
November 20	Scott Crossfield piloted the first aircraft to reach a speed of Mach 2.
November 24	The Brooklyn Dodgers signed Walter Alston to a 1 year contract as manager for 1954. He only signed 1 year contracts throughout his career.
November 25	An earthquake and tsunami occurred in Honshu, Japan.
November 25	The "Match of the Century" took place at Wembley Stadium in London, England. England lost 6-3, their first ever football loss to a continental team at home.
November 26	"Guys and Dolls" closed in New York City after 1200 performances and 5 Tony Awards.
November 26	New York Giants football player Harry Carson was born.
November 26	The Bronze Derby was played in Newberry, South Carolina on Thanksgiving Day. The Presbyterian College Blue Hose and Newberry College Indians played to a 7-7 tie.

The Li'l That Was!

The Clinton Chronicle

Clinton, S. C., Thursday, November 26, 1953

PC, Newberry 'Turkey Day' Game A 'Toss Up'

Presbyterian and Newberry meet Thanksgiving Day afternoon in Newberry for the South Carolina Little Three football title with a record crowd expected. There has been a ticket sellout, it is reported, from Newberry, with many Clinton fans in the stands when the whistle blows.

The game is a toss up—each team beat the third member, Wofford, by 7-6 scores.

Newberry may be accorded a slight edge on the foca that its squad is in a less injured state than the Blue Hose who are having back-le trouble because of injuries.

T quarterbacks, Lefty Harry Hamilton of PC, and Danny Brabham of Newberry.

The game will pit two fine split-

Wofford closed its season Saturday with a 49-0 loss to South Carolina in Columbia. Today's big menu in Newberry will close the season of the two teams.

Presbyterian, with its most inexperienced team in years, can post its best football record of the past seven seasons by whipping Newberry Thursday.

The Blue Stockings now boast a mark of five victories against three defeats, with those losses having been dealt by Southern Conference foes. A sixth win in the season finale would place the 1953 squad second in recent-day performances only to the 1946 eleven which won seven and lost two games.

Coach Lonnie S. McMillian entered the 1953 campaign with thin ranks which lacked experience. And throughout the season he has had to depend almost entirely upon just 23 players to carry the load. Eight, or more than one-third of these, are freshmen who stepped right out of high school into varsity play. Five others are relatively inexperienced sophomores and eight are juniors. Only two of the 23-man group are in the senior class, usually expected to provide a team's nucleus.

For Presbyterian this year it has been a case of spirit taking over when the flesh began to fail. Fight and determination brought upset wins over Wofford and Davidson, and almost clipped The Citadel. The Hosemen fought from behind a two-touchdown deficit to whip Davidson, erased another two-touchdown lead to go ahead of The Citadel momentarily toward the end of the game and came charging back in the final minute to take a tied game away from Catawba.

Team	W	L	Pct.
Newberry	7	1	.875
Presbyterian	5	3	.625
Wofford	6	4	.600

The Newberry Observer
AND HERALD & NEWS
"Just Like a Letter from Home"

The Li'l That Was!

HERALD AND NEWS ESTABLISHED 1865 — NEWBERRY, S. C., FRIDAY, NOVEMBER 28, 1953 — NEWBERRY OBSERVER ESTABLISHED 1813

Only Endzone Tickets Left For P. C. Game

The Newberry College Indians will have an idle Saturday this week, but they will be far from idle. The Redskins are being put through their paces fast and furiously in anticipation for next Thursday's "big game" of the year for them, their traditional "Little Three" clash with the Blue Hose of Presbyterian College. This year the P. C. squad will play here, and a win for the locals would not only mean the "Bronze Derby" but also their eighth consecutive victory, and their best season in years, eight wins and one loss. Ticket sales indicate the largest crowd ever to witness a football game in Newberry.

Larry B. Graves, in charge of ticket sales, reported some time ago that all tickets for the regular grandstand seats had been sold out. He stated that bleachers would be installed in the endzones, and also to extend the present stands farther down the sidelines. He reported Wednesday, that all seats in the extended portion of the stands had been sold out, and that the only seats left were in the endzones.

Tickets for these endzone seats will go on sale the first of next week at Johnnie's News Stand, Central Drugs, Lominick's Drugs, and Smith's Drugs. Tickets cost $2.50 each, and will go on a first-come-first-served basis.

placement

For the Bulldogs, expected to do more than their share, on the offense, are quarterback Frank Bickley and halfback Robert Tesenair. From last week's fine performance, we expect to see quarterback Coyt Suber, perhaps shifted to halfback, in there more often. On the defense, Frank Bickley, Bobby Dalton and Richard Bodie are expected to hold down the Devil scoring attempts.

The probable line-ups:

Pos.	Newberry	Dreher
LE	Dalton, B	Beall, E
LT	Hester, B. R	Smith, J
LG	Tedford, B.	Friedman, W
C	Summer, J.	Harrison, J
RO	Hurt, C.	Fogel
RT	Bodie, R.	Mundy, L
RE	Longshore, T L.	Baskin W
QB	Bickley F.	Miller L
LH	Tesenair, R.	Letton, J
RH	Summer, H.	Weir, R
FB	Wood, J.	Detwiler, J

The Li'l 🎩 That Was!

The Newberry Observer
AND HERALD & NEWS

Tribe Clashes Turkey Day With P. C.

Shown above are the 1953 Fighting Redskins of Newberry College who will trot onto Setzler Field Thursday afternoon, Thanksgiving Day, at two o'clock determined to: beat Presbyterian College's Blue Hose; win the Little Three crown; take top honors in state football with a record of 8 wins and one loss, and keep the Bronze Derby, symbolic of athletic supremacy. (FRONT ROW) Maksin, Davis, O., Ulrich, Heater, Harbol, Jones, E., Rogers, and Blanko; (SECOND ROW) Green, Sullivan, Ruple, Lee, Davis, P., Maxwell, Martin, and McCrory; (THIRD ROW) Tankslay, Ray, Lineberger, Robertson, Voyles, Berry, Hanselton, Reesinger, and Morris; (FOURTH ROW) Jones, R., Welch, Both, Payne, Counts, B. (dropped out), Shirley, Brabham, and Sawyer; (RIGHT ROW) Dufford, Morgan, Phillips, Cusin, Unknown (dropped out), Matthews, Russ (dropped out), Davis, R., and Hurst. (Photo by Nichols)

Sports Observer
By Bill Whelan

Pooooooor Peeeee Ceeeee!

We have high hopes of hearing the words, "Poooooor Peeeee Ceeeee" echoing across the Newberry College campus come Thursday p. m., and the Fighting Redskins of Newberry College find themselves on the heavy end of the score, if the local Tribe buckles down and plays the brand of ball of which they are capable, the Presbyterian College players and supporters will return to Clinton a lot "bluer" than when they stepped onto Setzler Field.

Contrary to opinions expressed previously, not by us, we don't believe the Indians will have much to worry about in the way of over confidence. In each game leading up to their present string of consecutive wins, they have never evidenced such a feeling, and the way Coach HARVEY KIRKLAND has been working his charges in the past two weeks, they haven't had a chance to feel over-confident.

Using Coach Kirkland's actual words, after the Indians' last win over the Red Wave of Troy Alabama, "We played the best ball club since Wofford... our passing offense gave us the two touchdowns but it was our PASS DEFENSE that was outstanding. We intercepted about five, leaving them very few completed aerials to brag about... we've been playing them one at a time, without looking ahead, but we are down to the last one. We will get ready for P. C. and for the first time since the Wofford game have all our players in good shape.

Now up to Clinton, for a chat with the Blue Hose mentor, Coach LONNIE McMILLIAN. After their 26-7 win over Western Carolina, before their week's rest, this is what he had to say: "I've just been looking at the pictures of the game and they looked bad... We missed blocking and lay assignments... Newberry will give us a sound beating if we play like that against them... we have lots of work ahead... A sleue of injuries has hit us hard... we have been lucky to win as many as we have... Newberry will have the edge, on paper."

BULLETIN!

Just before press time we received word that six P. C. players are still on the ailing list, and would at the most see "limited" action, Thursday. They include: tackles, Lee Friesson and Ernest Turner, center Frank Boulware, tackle Wayne Shoemaker, end Bobby Jackson, and halfback Landy Avant. It may be the truth, and then it may be just P. C. propaganda!

P. C. Favored

Most of the sportswriters of the state have applied the term "toss-up" to the coming game, but a few have given the nod (however slight) to the Hosemen. Not a single one, excepting us, will go as far as to say the Redskins are favored. We concede that the margin will be slim, but we cannot help but feel that the local lads will play the sox off their blue-clad rivals.

To get into facts and figures P. C. is actually favored... by nine points. Both teams have lost to Furman Newberry by 33 points and the Hose by 10 Newberry beat Catawba by 12, and P. C. only by 7. Both teams racked up one-point victories over the Wofford Terriers. They're still talking about the consecutive "flukes" up Spartanburg-way.

Presbyterian will bring a Newberry a record of five wins, and three losses... their best in seven years. They have won over Livingston State Teachers in Alabama (13-7), Wofford (7-6), Davidson (19-18), Catawba (26-19), and Western Carolina (20-7). They lost only to Clemson (7-33), The Citadel (14-20), and Furman (6-19).

The Fighting Redskins, on the other hand, have a record of seven consecutive wins, and a single loss, for the Hosemen to shoot at. After their season opener, a 0-33 loss to Furman, they came through the remainder of their games unscathed. Their victories were at the expense of Catawba (14-2), Lenoir-Rhyne (13-0), Wofford (7-6), Maryville, Tennessee (13-7), Guilford (19-7), Elon (33-6), and Troy State Teachers in Alabama (13-6).

Comparisons

The Blue Hose are thought of principally for their aerial attack, with southpaw quarterback HARRY HAMILTON doing the bulk of the chucking. Newberry too, has its aerial artist, in the form of quarterback DANNY BRABHAM In the Troy game, sub-quarterback KEN MORGAN came through with some fancy slinging to put fire into the Tribe's second string offense FELDER COOK, 3rd string P. C. quarterback, also does some fancy passing, and engineered both of the Blue Hose scores in their game with Livingston State Teachers.

In their last game, their 20-7 win over Western Carolina, P. C. evidenced a strong ground attack, running up 250 yards while holding the Catamounts to a total of only 49. W. C. on the other hand, the Cats outgained the Blue Hose 134 yards... 65 with cold weather the difference. We will pray for bitter cold weather for Thanksgiving, if that'll hold down the Hose passing attack. The Tribe's defenses will take care of the rest.

On the ground, both teams show power, with the Redskins having the advantage in this department. Fullback JOE AUSTIN is one of the power runners for the Hose, aided by the efforts of halfbacks GEORGE BLUE and GENE BUTLER. The Tribesmen also have some tricky runners in the form of halfbacks DON MAXWELL, PAUL DAVIS, and GRADY RAY, and powerful fullback STAN BERSINGER.

Defensive Set-Up

As far as weights are concerned the starting elevens of both squads will be matched pound for pound with the linemen and backs averaging 188 pounds at each position The P. C. backs, however, are heavier by less than two pounds each. To make both clubs even up, when the heavier Newberry line is brought into focus The Fighting spirit of the Indians will give them the edge Thursday afternoon, when the two teams clash on Setzler Field

Competing in all-state honors so much Tribe defensive standouts as tackle GROVER DAVIS, and guards FRANK HARROL and JOHNNY LEE The Blue Hose will set up their outstanding defensive players in the form of center FRANK BOULWARE, end JOE COUNTS, guard, WALTER YATES and line-backer GENE ALTMAN.

In closing this rambling dissertation, we should like to state that both P. C. and Newberry would very much to take this game Both teams have been known to play surprisingly well when playing each other, and anyone who would say definitely that one team or the other will win, doesn't know much about the background of either ball-club

Newberry's last win over the Blue Hose was back in 1949, when they bumped the Hosemen 30-14, after an otherwise unsuccessful season. Last year Presbyterian won by a meager one-point margin. It may be that the teams' extra point men might be called upon to be the hero and goat of the Turkey Day classic Giant GROVER DAVIS does the booting for the Tribe, while the Blue Hose have a fine placement specialist in GENE CARTER Both have kicked 10 conversions from placement so far this season.

This is probably the way the two teams will line up for the two o'clock kick-off Thursday:

Pos.	Newberry	Presbyterian
LE	Maksin (67)	Jackson (25)
LT	Rogers (69)	Turner (43)
LG	Harbol (20)	Yntra (44)
C	Heater (28)	Boulware (30)
RG	Lee (50)	Shealy (52)
RT	Davis, G (89)	Coker (80)
RE	Blanko (40)	Counts (85)
QB	Brabham (56)	Hamilton (28)
LH	Ray (31)	Butler (22)
RH	Davis, P. (82)	Blue (21)
FB	Bessinger (23)	Carter (47)

That's it, folks! We hope you've gotten your tickets already. All the good seats have been sold out. Those remaining, in the end zones, will still permit those occupying them to see plenty of red hot action. Be there, Thursday afternoon, and see the Tribesmen climaxing their 1953 season in a blaze of glory!

The Newberry Observer

Crystal Ball Sees Newberry A Winner By 20-13

(By Harry A. Littmann)

Although a phone call up to Presbyterian College on Saturday morning brought many words of woe and tears form that office's source about injured players in the Western Carolina-P. C. game on November 13, we can't help but disbelieve this source, although considered unimpeachable by this writer, who told us that five players, two of them starters, would be well below par for that coming game against our beloved Fighting Redskins on Thanksgiving afternoon.

We figure, and justifiably so that these men, especially the starters, have had ample time to recover from the supposed harm done to them by the Catamounts, who, by the way, the PC'ins whipped handily, 20-7 on November 7. Unless the injuries were of major proportions, and we don't think they were, because no release from Clinton has suggested such doings, the boys, with the aid of the PC trainer, will be ready to go on Thursday for sure. Nuff said about PC's woes and hurts!

Since the Newberry victory over Troy State on November 14, the Injuns have been practicing with their doors shut tight by Harvey Kirkland and his staff, as they try to prepare a defense for Harry Hamilton's passes. We'd like to note in all that are interested, that in the WC game Hamilton completed three of nineteen flips. Not a good average. Although the North Carolinians lost, they must have had Lefty Harry well bottled up all evening, so we'd like humbly to suggest to the Redshirts that they follow WC's footsteps and do the same thing this Thursday. Whether they follow the Catamounts or not, we feel sure that Hamilton will be forced to watch many of his plays on the ground as Messrs. Lee, Davis and Rogers go to work on him.

Rates Second

Speaking of the Seneca slinger, in statistics computed by the National Association of Intercollegiate Athletics, they show that Hamilton, in six games, is second in the country with a total of 948 yards gained through the air. In more complete statistics issued by the official service bureau of the National Collegiate Athletic Bureau, Hamilton would rank no higher than 14th. We don't want to take anything away from this fine competitor, and we must say that if Hamilton had not played his first two games against Clemson and Alabama State it is safe to estimate that he would have been nearer the leaders with over a thousand yards to his credit.

We have good news for the Newberry fans as far as injured Redskin players go. There just ain't none! Carl Rogers, great left tackle who missed the last couple of Indian games due to torn ligaments in his arm, is in perfect shape now, and is slated to start on Thursday. Only Jimmy Haselden, fullback from Summerville, may not be up to par since he has a slight knee injury at this writing. In all probabilities though, Haselden will be ready to go on Thursday, bad knee and all.

Will Miss Game

We've watched the Indians come from their 13-0 defeat at the hands of Furman the first game, and haven't missed a game in the great and exciting seven game winning streak rolled up by the Kirklandmen. Personally, we're all tuckered out from watching Injun halfbacks run touchdowns and then write stories. All sports writers get a vacation once in a while and our friend, Bill Whelan, told us that he thought it would be a good idea for me to take off for a little vacation and miss the PC game on Thursday. I agreed heartily. It's been a long season, and we have the chance to see Eberbe Neal perform in New York over the holidays and get a picture of the Siersestreet giant in action for The Observer, so, we left Wednesday via Eastern Air Lines.

Sitting up here in the room with our faithful assistant, Jim Wehle, who has been with us wherever we've been, has just taken the Crystal Ball out of hiding and is asking me to take a look at it. Hold on a minute. Ah, yes, here it is, clear, too! Newberry 20, Presbyterian 13. Eight in a row and maybe a Bowl bid New Year's Day! Happy holiday, fans.

Presbyterian Expects Rough Thursday Game

Says Redskins Would Avenge Three Losses

Clinton, Nov. 23. Tension mounts as Presbyterian and Newberry prepare to stake a full load of football honor upon the final Thanksgiving Day battle at Newberry.

Honors foremost in the balance is the championship of the Little Three conference, which neither team has held recently. The Bronze Derby, symbol of athletic rivalry between the two schools, also is a coveted prize in this annual match. And both teams are seeking their best records in recent years.

The Presbyterian-Newberry game represents one of the oldest football rivalries in the state, dating back over 38 previous clashes to 1913 and moving through two world wars without interruption. P. C. holds an edge of having won 26 against 11 Newberry victories while two ended in tied games, but the entire series has been marked by fierce competition where the unexpected has produced numerous upsets.

Sports experts matching records and statistics, have forecast the 1953 Bronze Derby edition to be one of the most colorful of this long series and one of the state's football highlights of the year.

Those who predict, generally, have given Newberry the slight nod of favorite on the basis of a consistently improving ball club which has won seven straight since losing its opener to Furman. The Indians also are fired up to avenge three straight defeats at the hands of P. C., one of the longest winning streaks of the series by either team.

Presbyterian coaches, trying to patch together a long list of injuries, are very much concerned about their prospects against Newberry. Coach Lonnie S. McMillian places the Indian backfield as a dangerous threat at all times with any one of six fast runners—headed by Quarterback Danny Brabham, Halfback Grady Ray and Fullback Stan Basinger—likely to strike for the distance at any moment.

NOW AT SINCLAIR DEALERS'

A MOTOR OIL SO GOOD YOUR ENGINE CAN OUTLAST YOUR CAR

—AND SINCLAIR GUARANTEES IT!

GUARANTEED to keep your engine in top operating condition for 100,000 miles

STROTHER C. PAYSINGER

Supplier of Sinclair Products

Newberry, S. C.

The Li'l That Was!

The Newberry Observer

Sports Observer
By Bill Whelan

Whatta Ball Game!

We were among the 3,000 or so football fans who packed Setzler Field last Thursday afternoon to watch the Fighting Redskins of Newberry College and the Blue Hose of Presbyterian College battle out the Little Three Championship to a 7-7 tie. One thing we will agree to — P. C.'s Coach LONNIE McMILLAN was right when he was quoted as saying before the game, "Newberry will have the edge, on paper." The Tribe beat the Hose in every department, except the scoring.

When two teams play a game and one emerges on the heavy end of a score, no matter how lop that team is the winner, despite statistics. But when two teams finish with the score tied, then sportswriters have the right to delve into statistics to pick a winner. We are happy to report that Newberry without question, "won" the ball game, despite the tied score.

Taking into consideration the sour looks the local Tribesmen got from Lady Luck, in the form of two fumbles on P. C.'s own-yard line; a pass interception on the Blue Hose 8, and a holding penalty that gave the Hosemen possession on the Tribe one-yard line, the score should have read Newberry 21, P. C. 0. But breaks are made, and we're taking nothing from the spunky Hosemen.

What we're using to determine the theoretical winner are the facts that the Redskins racked up 16 first downs to P. C.'s 11 ; they gained 311 yards rushing to the Blue Hose 120 , and even in P. C.'s specialty department, the Indians trailed only by 12 yards in passing -104 yards to 116-.

Newberry's linemen turned in stellar performances to a man. GROVER DAVIS broke up several of HARRY HAMILTON's aerials at the line of scrimmage. In addition to rolling blue-clad runners time after time, and booting the all-important conversion that tied the ball game. ED BLANKO and fellow-flanker MIKE MAKSIM proved efficient in smearing the at-times effective "screen pitchout" that gained considerable yardage during the afternoon. The Hosemen worked a "screen pass" successfully until the Indians got hep to it. One such play Blanko looked like a "chiropractor" working on the neck of lowering P. C. and JOE COUNTS. Another time Grover Davis sat on fullback GENE CARTER for a two-yard loss after such a screen pass. CARL ROGERS, tackle, who played for the first time in weeks, did a fine job on the defense. Peppermints of the line, however, were Newberry's two guards, FRANK HARBOL and JOHNNY LEE, both of whom played heads-up ball and got into P. C.'s backfield more than their share of times. Center ED HESTER played his usual flawless game, holding the center of the line together. His presence will be surely missed next year.

On the offense, the Tribesmen looked good (except for the fumbles) on their ground attack. Their aerial attack seemed better than usual. The highlight was, of course, PAUL DAVIS' 60-yard touchdown dash after snagging DANNY BRABHAM'S short pass. Turning in the longest ground play of the evening was GRADY RAY, who trotted 45 yards to the Blue Hose 18 early in the first period. KEN MORGAN also performed creditably when subbing for Brabham.

Two unusual plays we saw the Tribe pick out of their bag of tricks failed to impress the Blue Hose. One was a direct snap from center through the quarterback's legs to a passing back. The other was a tricky reverse going to AL MARTIN coming around from end to pass.

All we heard on the streets of Newberry Friday morning was talk about luck , fumbles , intercepted passes and "Newberry should've won that game." P. C. fans probably could give us reasons why they should've won. If it make an difference, we weren't the only ones disappointed last Thursday. Three other ball games that day (Colgate vs. Brown, Penn vs Cornell, and the traditional Parker vs. Greenville High School game, all ended in 7-7 deadlocks.

The only comment we have to make is, "It could'n been worse."

Coach of the Year!

We along with other Newberrians were quite gratified, to say the least, to learn Friday morning that Newberry's coach, HARVEY KIRKLAND, had been selected S. C.'s 1953 COACH OF THE YEAR. Giving him this designation were his fellow coaches and daily newspaper sportswriters of the Palmetto State.

Coach Kirkland came to Newberry, following TUCK McCONNELL. He had nothing to start with except a bunch of "green" kids, most of them fresh out of high school. Oh, yes, he also had a great deal of "faith" in these kids, and the ability to get as much out of them as possible. Last year was his first at the helm of the local college's gridiron machine. His boys played fine

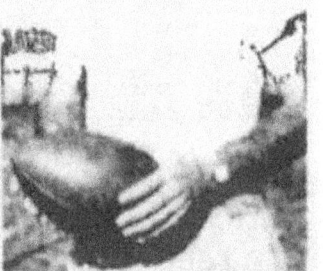

Harvey Kirkland

ball, giving tough teams scares they'll never forget. Though, the 1952 Tribe won only two games, they gained much in experience.

This year, Coach Kirkland said his boys were not ready yet but they came through with the blue chips down and, after losing the first game to Furman (as expected), they swept the remaining seven games in a row, most of them upsets. The ninth and last game of the current season was the Turkey Day thriller mentioned earlier in three columns.

Losing only four of this 1953 squad members via graduation, next year he hopes for better results from his charges. We agree wholeheartedly with his selection as COACH OF THE YEAR, and are happy that we have had the opportunity to follow the success of his team in print during the recently concluded season.

All-State Honors!

All-State honors came to six members of the 1953 Newberry College football team. Ranking highest were guard FRANK HARBOL and quarterback DANNY BRABHAM, both of whom have been mainstays on the local squad this year. Both these men made the third team.

The four Indians given Honorable Mention in the All-State selections were end MIKE MAKSIM, tackle GROVER DAVIS, guard JOHNNY LEE and fullback STAN BESSINGER. The bright thing about it is that only one of these men will be lost to the local Tribe next year. Maksim, Davis, Lee and Bessinger each have another year of football before them, and Brabham has two more. Harbol will be the only All-Stater to finis college in June

The Newberry Observer
AND HERALD & NEWS
"Just Like a Letter from Home"

Newberry 7 — Presbyterian 7

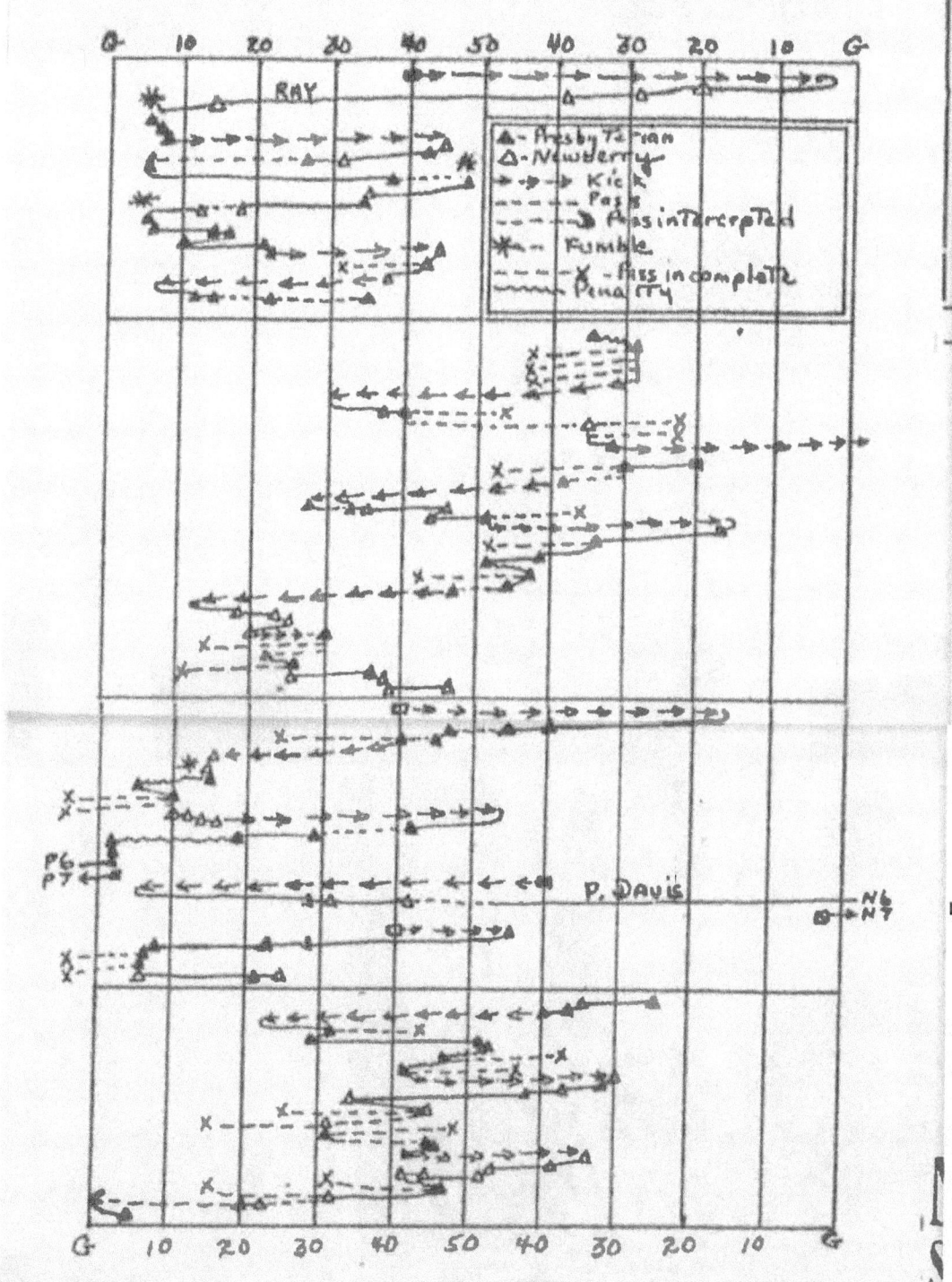

The game-o-graph above is of the Newberry-Presbyterian College game last Thursday, that resulted in a 7-7 tie on Setzler Field in Newberry. The tie left the two teams in a deadlock for the Mythical Little Three Championship, but Newberry retained the Bronze Derby, having won it in a baseball game last Spring.

The Li'l That Was!

BROADWAY Theatre

MONDAY - TUESDAY,
December 7-8
TORCH SONG
Joan Crawford

Wednesday, Dec. 9
INVASION U.S.A.

THURSDAY - FRIDAY,
December 10-11
MOGAMBO
With Gable and Gardner

Saturday, Dec. 12
SABER JET
Robert Stack - Colleen Gray

PC, Newberry Battle to 7-7 Tie

With both teams displaying terrific defensive games, PC and Newberry's Indians battled to a 7-7 season's finale tie on Thanksgiving day in Newberry with an estimated 4,000 chilled spectators looking on.

The Indians, with a big array of hard-running backs, drove twice to the PC seven-yard line, only to lose the ball both times on fumbles. This was the way most of the first half was played, with PC backed up in its own territory.

The Hosemen drove 40 yards on six plays to score midway in the third period. A 15-yard penalty took the Hose to the one-yard line where Joe Austin scored after two unsuccessful quarterback sneaks by Harry Hamilton. Gene Carter booted the extra point for PC.

PC kicked off and the Indians immediately scored in three plays. The touchdown came on a sensational Brabham to Davis pass which covered a total of 82 yards. This completed the scoring for the afternoon as both teams resisted and fought down to the wire, but to no avail.

Hamilton completed 12 of 29 passes for 116 yards to lead the Hose in their efforts offensively. Joe Austin and Curtis Freeman gained 36 and 34 yards, respectively, on the ground for PC.

On defense, guard Luther Shealy and tackle Wayne Shoemaker each had 10 individual tackles for the Blue Hose.

For Newberry, Danny Brabham, Grady Roy and Stan Bessinger were outstanding on offense and tackle Grover Davis and center Ed Hester were the defensive stalwarts.

Campus capers call for Coke

There's bedlam in the stands when the team is on a march to the goal. Keep things going! Refresh now and then with a frosty bottle of delicious Coca-Cola.

DRINK Coca-Cola

BOTTLED UNDER AUTHORITY OF THE COCA-COLA COMPANY BY
GREENWOOD COCA-COLA BOTTLING CO.
"Coke" is a registered trade-mark. © 1953, THE COCA-COLA COMPANY

Fighting Indians Retain Bronze Derby

BY DON LONG

It was a brave crowd of 3600 at Setzler Field on Thanksgiving Day to watch the Newberry Indians come from behind to tie the Presbyterian Blue Hose of Clinton, S. C., 7-7. This was the decisive game for the cherished Bronze Derby, which has been a classic between these two schools for many years. As a result of the game, Newberry is still the owner of the Derby.

In a game which was really a thriller, spectators gasped with jarring and running tackles and good runs by both backfields, but neither could muster a tally until the third quarter.

Newberry took the opening kickoff and promptly marched to the one yard line of Presbyterian before the PC'uns took over when Newberry fumbled. Injuries weren't too prevalent, but the Presbyterians got the rougher deal as far as injuries, with men hurt during the entire contest. It was one of the most colorful events ever witnessed at Newberry College; the band was excellent; the stadium was packed; and the ball clubs never let up. They really were dog-eat-dog for the whole 60 minutes, and no one was disappointed when it was over.

The Newberry Indians came through in the last half of the third quarter to tie up the ballgame and send the fans into pandemonium; both sides were waiting for that one little break which might mean another tally and the ball game. Fortunately, for the Presbyterians, Newberry couldn't muster another tally, but had the ball into scoring territroy when the game-ending whistle blew. Sports writers from all over the state were present and all agreed that this was one of the best teams ever fielded by Newberry. All were impressed with the hard running of the backs and the jarring tackles made by the staunch line of Newberry.

The entire first half was a topsy-turvy affair with neither side being able to score, but the Indians got into scoring position twice and fumbled these chances away to the Blue Hose. Both sides were on the edge as they sometimes jumped the signals and piled on to be sure that the ball was stopped. The half ended with both teams scoreless and fairly well whipped.

To open the second half, Newberry kicked off to Presbyterian and they proceeded to move down the field and send Joe Austin through the line, helped by a 15-yard penalty on Newberry. Immediately Joe Carter booted the one-pointer to send the Blue Hose out front and into a shaky 7-0 lead.

The Indians, realizing their plight, decided there was to be no more mars on their record, so Danny Brabham, quarterback, tossed to Paul Davis on the 42. He, in return, obliged with a 42 yard gallop through the entire team, twisting and turning, weaving and stiff-arming, powering his way thru, and finally outrunning about 9 PC men. Then the crowd hushed as big Grover Davis methodically added the extra point to tie the ball game at 7-all. Then it was a new ball game as far as the crowd was concerned, but the Blue Hose had done all they were capable of and time ran out when the Indians got back into scoring territory.

November 1954

November 1	General Fulgencio Barista was elected President of Cuba.
November 1	The United States Senate reprimanded Joseph McCarthy because of his slander campaigns.
November 1	Actor John Wayne married actress Pilar Pallete. He divorced his former wife earlier on the same day.
November 1	Lee Petty, with 32 of 34 top 10 finishes, won the NASCAR Grand National Championship.
November 2	United States Senator Strom Thurmond from South Carolina was the first United States Senator elected by write-in vote.
November 3	British punk rocker Adam Ant was born.
November 3	The Japanese monster Godzilla was introduced.
November 4	The Philadelphia A's announce a move to Kansas City.
November 7	A United States spy plane was shot down north of Japan.
November 8	AL approved the Philadelphia A's relocation to Kansas City.
November 8	American singer-songwriter Rickie Lee Jones was born.
November 10	"Marine Corps War Memorial" inspired by 1945 photo of Marines raising US flag in Iwo Jima, unveiled in Arlington, VA.
November 12	Ellis Island, immigration station in New York City, was closed.
November 14	Greek musician Yani was born.
November 14	Egyptian President Naguib resigned, and a state of an emergency was declared in Egypt.
November 14	Condoleezza Rice, the first African-American United States Secretary of State was born.
November 20	NFL quarterback Johnny Unitas married his high school sweetheart Dorothy Hoelle.
November 22	The United States Humane Society formed in Washington, DC.
November 23	For the first time since the 1929 crash of the United States stock market, The Dow Jones Industrial Average closed above the peak before it crashed.
November 23	Singer-songwriter Bruce Hornsby was born.
November 24	Air Force One, the first United States Presidential airplane, was christened.
November 25	The Bronze Derby was played in Clinton, South Carolina on Thanksgiving Day. The Presbyterian College Blue Hose defeated the Newberry College Indians 20-18.

November 19, 1954 — THE BLUE STOCKING — Page Three

TWITTY — YATES — BOULWARE — SHEALY — COUNTS

Blue Hose Play Host to Newberry Indians In Thanksgiving Day Bronze Derby Classic

Presbyterian Seeks Final Win

The Battlin' Blue Hose of Presbyterian College will once again meet the Newberry Indians here in Bailey Stadium in a Thanksgiving Day classic. This rivalry was begun back in 1913 and after a 7-7 tie last Thanksgiving, the Sox are ready to make this 1954 final gridiron affair, their fifth straight victory and bring their season's record to six wins and three losses.

Newberry has a good record up to date and with several key men recovering from injuries, will be up to full strength on next Thursday afternoon. Grover Davis and Danny Branham were aiding in last week's 14-14 tie with a strong Troy State eleven, but both should be ready to go by Thanksgiving.

PC, however, has showed continued improvement each week and in defeating the previously undefeated Appalachian, 14-7, boosted their record to six wins against three defeats. This victory over the North Carolinians also gave the Hosemen four victories in a row.

With an open date this weekend three days to prepare for and, the Blue Hose have a week this all-important battle and bring home the Bronze Derby plus a few scalps from the Indians.

Combining a brilliant offensive machine and an ironman defense the Blue Hose had clipped off huge hunks of yardage while opponents found great difficulty in penetrating the strong Blue Hose forward wall. Leading the running attack are halfbacks George Blue and Ken Webb, fullback Eddie Brockenbrough and quarterback Harry Hamilton. Anchoring the Blue Hose on defensive and displaying rugged football every minute are guards Luther Shealy and Walter Yates, tackles Lee Frierson and Bob Harrington, ends Joe Counts, Bob Stevens and Bob Jackson.

In the long history of the series, PC holds a decided edge on the Indians, meeting in 3 encounters, the Blue Sock teams have won 25 games while losing only eleven. The two teams have tied on three occasions and the Hosemen have completed a total of 547 points while the Indians have registered 314.

On the Block...

HAMILTON — HARRINGTON — BLUE

Eight Seniors Play Last Game

In the annual Thanksgiving football battle with the Newberry Indians, eight PC seniors will conclude their gridiron careers under Blue Stocking colors.

Halfback George Blue and center Frank Boulware have co-captained the Blue Hose this season and are among those who will show away their cleats for the last time at PC.

Both guard posts will be vacated by Luther Shealy and Walter Yates. Shealy, last year's co-captain, second team All-State, and mentioned Little All-American hails from Pacolet. Yates, a 180 pounder from Norfolk is a football lineman. He is an aggressive, spirited performer and a hard tackler.

Flankmen wearing the blue and white jerseys for the last time are Joe Counts from Brunswick, Ga., and Charles Twitty from Charlotte, N. C. Counts, an excellent pass receiver, is a ball hawk type flankman and a constant defensive threat. Twitty, one of the fastest men on the team, is also an excellent receiver and good all-around ball player.

Robert Harrington, a 205 pound senior from Mont Clare, has another year of eligibility and may perhaps see service with the Hosemen in the 1955 season.

Harry Hamilton, star back from Seneca, will also play his last game Thanksgiving Day.

The Li'l 🎩 That Was!

BAZAAR FRIDAY — **The Indian** — RAT HOP SATURDAY

NEWBERRY COLLEGE
"Home of The Fighting Redskins"
NEWBERRY, S. C., WEDNESDAY, NOVEMBER 17, 1954

Redmen Prep For PC Tilt

The Newberry College Indians will conclude their season on Thursday, November 25, as they will trade blocks and tackles with their number one rivals, the Blue Hose of Presbyterian College. In this game, as any athletic contest between the two schools, the Bronze Derby will be the prize. The "hat" is a symbol of athletic supremacy between the two schools. At present, the Derby is lodged in Holland Hall by virtue of a 4-2 baseball victory over the Blue Sox last May.

P. C. will be going all out to top Coach Harvey Kirkland's charges. The Thanksgiving Day tussel last year proved to be a real thriller as Coach Bill Crutchfield's eleven struggled hard to finally gain a 7-7 tie with the Redskins. Next week's game will undoubtedly be on the same order.

The P. C. fair-haired boys are Luther Shealy and Harry Hamilton. Shealy, a tackle from Pacolet, is co-captain of the Hose along with center Frank Boulware and a real competitor. He is rated as a strong contender for Little A-A honors. Hamilton, the Seneca southpaw is an expert passer, and it is thought that he will fill the air full of leather Turkey Day, rather than try to penetrate Newberry's great line. To help him, P. C. will have the services of halfbacks George Blue and Ken Webb. Fullback Ed Brockenbrough will do his share too in the P. C. cause.

The Newberry Indians will be in almost perfect shape for the contest. Hard-luck Stan Bessinger, who suffered an almost disastrous injury to his eye the week of the Troy State game, should be ready for plenty of action. Grover Davis, who ripped his middle finger down to the bone against The Citadel, will not be able to punt but it is thought that the big fellow will be ready for at least part-time service. Other injured men, Ed Blanko, Olin McCurry, and Danny Brabham, have come along fine and should be ready for full-time play next Thursday.

Another factor in the outcome of the game will be the emergence of some second-string players who are now pressing the regulars for their jobs. In particular, hard-running Tyler Dufford, who holds the 1954 record for long gains, a 70-yarder from Ken Morgan in The Citadel game, is one. Linemen Eddie Jones and J. P. Phillips are now capable of playing first-string ball for most any small-college team around the South. Both men were stars in the Troy and Citadel games.

Stellar performance all year from ends Ed Blanko, Mike Maksim, Hal Green, and Bobby Charpia will make them a definite threat against P. C.

It is expected that the Presbyterian Stadium will be filled to capacity for the game, and all advice is to get tickets early.

—R. A. E.

The Li'l That Was!

The Newberry Observer
AND HERALD & NEWS
"Just Like a Letter from Home"

HERALD AND NEWS ESTABLISHED 1865 — NEWBERRY, S. C., TUESDAY, NOVEMBER 23, 1954 — NEWBERRY OBSERVER ESTABLISHED 1868

Presbyterian College Makes Apologies For Friday Raid On Newberry College Campus

Evidence Of P. C. Activity

Shown above is pictorial evidence of the painting spree which took place last Friday morning at about one o'clock on the Newberry College campus. Those responsible for the damage, assumed to have been members of the Presbyterian College student body, included on their itinerary the brand new concrete block wall surrounding the local College football stadium, which they thought so much of, that they marked on it, "Home of the Blue Hose," and other phrases not shown in the first picture (TOP). Other scenes of the midnight raid, shown from top to bottom above, include the concrete Newberry College sign at the entrance to Smeltzer Hall; the College recreation building, and one end of the Science Building. Other buildings also were left with evidence of the P. C. students' artistic handiwork. (Observer Staff Photos).

Investigation Uncovers Those Responsible

College Stadium And Buildings Get Blue Paint

Students at Newberry College were quite amazed last Friday morning to find their campus aglow with freshly applied coats of blue paint, reflecting such sentiments as, "Go, P. C.," "Home of the Blue Hose," and other phrases which indicated that the damage had been done by students from arch-rival Presbyterian College at nearby Clinton.

At first feelings were high on the Indian campus, for the raid was a clear-cut violation of a "gentlemen's agreement" between students of both schools to limit their expressions of rivalry to action on the baseball diamond, basketball court and football gridiron for possession of the coveted "Bronze Derby."

The raiders from P. C. had struck swiftly. They included on their agenda the brand-new concrete block wall around the football field, the concrete "Newberry College" sign at the entrance to Smeltzer Hall, and walls of the recreation building, the administration building, a store house, and the science building. The night-watchman discovered the intruders at about 1:00 a. m. Friday, but was unable to get close enough to identify them or obtain license numbers of either of the two cars used in the spree. Had he not interrupted their activities, there is no telling how much damage would have been inflicted on the local campus.

P. C. Apologizes

When contacted by college officials, authorities at Presbyterian College stated that they knew nothing of the "raid", but that they would make every effort to identify those responsible and punish them. They also promised they would reimburse Newberry College for any damage incurred. A telephone message from P. C. this (Monday) morning indicated that those responsible for the painting orgy had been discovered and that appropriate action would be taken by Clinton's officials.

Newberry College officials informed us that officials at P. C. have been most cooperative in the matter, and expressed an attitude of friendliness to Newberry. They stated further that they hope that this incident is not misinterpreted by Newberrians, who may think that the "painters" typi-
(Continued on page two)

Bronze Derby On The Block Next Thursday

The Bronze Derby means one big event to South Carolina sports fans, the annual Presbyterian-Newberry gridiron clash. This year, the Derby day once more is scheduled for Thanksgiving afternoon, and the scene of action is P. C.'s Johnson Field at Clinton. Here the line of battle will be drawn between two of the top-ranked small college teams in the Southeast.

It builds up naturally as a headline attraction, a fact which is reflected in the unusually high rate of pre-game ticket sales both at Newberry and Clinton. All indications point to a sell-out crowd by game-time.

The Blue Hose-Indian rivalry is a football feud of long standing, dating back to 1913. Presbyterian has dominated the 30-game series to date by winning 25 games while losing only 11 and tying three. The point totals show 547 for P. C. and 314 for the Indians. In addition to the color generated by the battle of traditional rivals, there are other factors which made the game a special attraction.

Both Presbyterian and Newberry will be seeking their sixth victories of the year in this season finale. The Blue Hose have won five and lost three, and the Indian record is one of five wins, two losses and two ties. Each team has taken the count of The Citadel Cadets of the Southern Conference in earlier games this season. And both squads are eager to settle the unfinished business of last year which found the 1953 Bronze Derby game ending in an indecisive 7-7 tie.

Presbyterian
(Continued from page one)

fied the attitude of all Presbyterian College students. The students at Newberry College showed their feeling by refraining from any "acts of vengeance", permitting officials to settle matters.

Though no definite estimate of the cost to restore the campus to normalcy has been made, a rough guess has placed the amount at between $400 and $500. The scene of the painting raid was inspected by a P. C. official Friday afternoon. Members of Blue Key, Newberry College honor fraternity, visited the P. C. campus, and spoke in their chapel exercises last Friday morning, on a prearranged visit. P. C.'s Blue Key members are due to make a return visit to the Newberry chapel exercises tomorrow (Tuesday) morning. This friendly exchange of students indicates that the majority of students at both colleges hold each other in high regard, and are willing to permit their activities on athletic fields to serve as outlets for their enthusiasm and rivalry. According to reports from Presbyterian College officials, students at P. C. were just as incensed over the damage inflicted on the Newberry campus as were local students.

Deplorable Doodling

On Friday November 9, 1954, Newberry College students awoke to graffiti on their campus. Presbyterian College "Raiders of the night" visited the campus early on Friday morning, and in blue spray paint, tried to claim the campus and the entrance to Setzler Field with "Home of the Blue Hose" and other pro Presbyterian College phrases. The damage done by an isolated few from Clinton was handled with class between the 2 college communities. Presbyterian College immediately responded to the Newberry College community with an apology and paid for damages incurred. Both schools worked together in an investigation. Those involved were, in fact, identified and held accountable. Honor fraternities from each college visited the rival schools chapel service the following week and addressed the student bodies. Presbyterian College students were as appalled by the random act of vandalism as were the Newberry College students. It was stressed that the rivalry between the schools should be limited to the athletic competitions for The Bronze Derby as agreed upon in basketball, baseball and football. Both groups of student representatives told their rival students that there was great respect for their rival college community. On Thursday November, 25 1954 the traditional Thanksgiving Day game was played without a problem.

The Li'l That Was!

Blue Hose Gridmen Close Season With 20-18 Scalping of Newberry

Hamilton-to-Blue Aerial Feat Thrills Thousands at Thanksgiving Derby Game

The Blue Stocking
Vol. XXXIII Presbyterian College, Clinton, S. C., November 18, 1955 No. 10

Coming from behind in the last minutes of play on Thanksgiving Day, the flaming Blue Hose of Presbyterian scalped the Indians from Newberry, 20-18, and regained the Bronze Derby before a near capacity crowd of 4,200 on Johnson Field. Harry Hamilton's southpaw aerial to George Blue in the end zone climaxed a sensational 97-yard drive to give the Blue Hose a 20-18 advantage with only two minutes and 20 seconds left in the game.

Newberry took over on their 13 after PC had punted. With Paul Davis, Ray, and Bessinger carrying the mail overland and Brabham tosssing to P. Davis, the Indians marched 87 yards down the warpath to draw first scoring blood. Brabham received the honors as he sneaked across the double stripes from two yards out to climax the drive. Grover Davis attempted the conversion, but it was blocked by Counts of PC, leaving the Tribe with a 6-0 advantage.

Midway of the second stanza the battlin' Blue Hose started rolling toward glory land from their 47-yard line. With Hamilton tossing to Counts and Brockenbrough, Blue, and Hamilton carrying the pigskin to the 10-yard line, the Blue Hose were not to be denied a TD. In three tries Brockenbrough crashed over the double stripes into paydirt to tie the game at 6-6. The educated toe of George Blue split the uprights to give PC a 7-6 lead.

Ray took the kickoff and danced down the Newberry sidelines 47 yards before being tackled on the PC 34-yard marker. With Father Time against them, the Indians took advantage of this golden opportunity to go ahead by driving goalward in three plays after the kickoff. Morgan passed to Maksim on the five who rammed his way into the end zone to put the Indians ahead 12-7 with only seconds left in the first half. Again Davis attempted the conversion, but to no avail.

Midway of the third quarter the flaming hot Blue Hose started goalward from their own 34-yard line. With Hamilton shooting the pigskin to Counts and Twitty and Blue, Brockenbrough, and Hamilton lugging the leather on the ground, the Blue Hose were not to be denied. Hamilton sneaked across into glory land from the one to put the Blue Hose ahead 13-12. Again Blue's toe added the extra point, giving PC a 14-12 lead.

Early in the fourth quarter the Indians, with all their war paint, roared toward the land of great riches from PC's 34-yard marker. They gained possession of the pigskin on the 34 by means of a PC punt. With Dufford, Davis, and Haselden carrying the mail, the Indians had a first down on the 12. Then Dufford passed to Blanko in the end zone to put the Tribe out front, 18-14. Again Davis' attempt was not good.

On a punt exchange, Ray of Newberry dashed and danced down the sidelines 47 yards to the PC 20. From here the Indians continued on the warpath. However on the three-yard marker, the inspired Blue Hose threw up a rock-ribbed defense that stood like a stone wall. With Brockenbrough and Hamilton on the ground and Hamilton to Stevens in the air, the Blue Hose started rolling. Gene Butler, taking a pitchout, spun, twisted, and galloped 45 yards to the Newberry 29 on a spectaculer field run to set the stage for Hamilton's winning pass to Blue in the end zone. This pass was good from 27 yards out. For the first time Blue's toe failed to split the uprights, but it was not needed as PC commanded a 20-18 lead.

STATISTICS

	Newberry	PC
First Downs	11	14
Yards Rushing	168	212
Yards Passing	65	123
Total Offense	233	335
Passes Attempted	10	15
Passes Completed	5	9
Passes Intercepted by	1	0
Number of punts	4	4
Punting average	31.5	34
Fumbles	2	3
Fumbles lost	1	2
Yards Penalized	5	20
Newberry	6 6 0 6—18	
Presbyterian	0 7 7 6—20	

Newberry scoring: Touchdowns, Brabham, Maksim, Blanko. Presbyterian scoring, touchdowns, Brockenbrough, Hamilton, Blue. Conversions, Blue 2.

SELF-SERVICE LAUNDRY
S. Broad Street
Washing and Drying
Shirts and Pants Ironed

The Li'l That Was!

The Newberry Observer
AND HERALD & NEWS
"Just Like a Letter from Home"

Brabham Sneaks Across For Initial Tribe Tally

Shown above is Newberry's quarterback Danny Brabham (indicated by arrow) grimly clutching the precious pigskin as he sneaked across for the first touchdown in last Thursday's Bronze Derby football game, held at Johnson Field in Clinton. The score, occurring early in the first quarter, the first time Newberry got its hands on the ball, was the first of three tallies in the Tribe's 20-18 loss to their Blue-clad rivals from Presbyterian College. Also visible in the picture are: No. 56, Newberry guard Johnny Lee, and the following Blue Hose: No. 55, Joe Counts; No. 50, Frank Boulware; No. 45, Eddie Brockenbrough, and No. 51, Rex Harrington. Underneath No. 50 can be seen Tribe center Carl Rogers.

Extra Points Are Crucial In 20-18 P.C. Win Thursday

Three missed conversions from placement by Tribe tackle rover Davis, and a stubborn Blue Hose fourth quarter goal line stand proved to be the undoing of the Newberry College Indians last Thursday afternoon at Johnson Field at Clinton, as they fell before a pass-happy Presbyterian College eleven by a final 20-18 score. The win not only gave P. C. possession of the coveted Bronze Derby, but also gave them second place, behind Wofford, in the Little Three standings for the season.

The game was a see-saw affair from the opening whistle. Neither team was ever more than 6 points ahead of the other, and the outcome was not decided until the final five minutes when southpaw aerial artist Harry Hamilton hit halfback George Blue with a 27-yard pass that was good for a touchdown and the 20-18 lead.

The Tribesmen broke the scoring early in the initial canto as they took possession, after a Hose punt, on their own 13. Grady Ray, whose running plagued the Blue Hose all evening, broke away for 15 yards. Stan Bessinger got eight on two tries, and then Ray made enough for a first down. Option artist Danny Brabham took to the air and connected with halfback Paul Davis who carried to the P. C. 27. Ray lost 2 yards, but then Davis picked up 9. Ray powered to the 19 on a 5-yard effort. Brabham lost 7, and then Bessinger and Davis combined to move to the 14. Brabham moved to the 4, when he failed to find a receiver open. Ray moved to the 1, and then Brabham sneaked across for the score.

STATISTICS
	P. C.	Newberry
First Downs	14	11
Yds. Rush	213	168
Yds. Pass	123	63
Pass. Att.	15	10
Pass. Comp.	9	5
Pass. Int. By	0	2
Fumbles	3	2
Fumbles lost	2	1
Punts	4	6
Punts Aver.	34.7	31.3
Yds. Penalized	20	5

Davis' attempted conversion was blocked by P. C.'s Joe Counts.

P. C. Retaliates

Early in the second period, the Blue Hose took possession on their own 37 and staged a drive that stalled on the Tribe 16, where Blue fumbled and Newberry end Mike Maksim recovered to end the threat. After three plays Newberry punted, and P. C. started to roll again, from the Tribe 47. After a five-yard penalty set the Hose back momentarily, Hamilton passed to Blue for 12 yards. A second Hamilton pass, this time to Counts, moved the ball to the 31. Brockenbrough, Blue and Hamilton then stayed on the ground to move to the Newberry 2, from where Brockenbrough plowed across for the tying score. Blue's placement was good for a 7-6 Blue Hose lead.

The Tribe came back strongly, scoring in the next 42 seconds. P. C. kicked-off and Grady Ray swiveled-hipped his way on the return for 47 yards to the Hose 33. On the run nearly every P. C. defender had his hands on the elusive halfback at one time or another. Jimmy Haselden cracked center for 14 yards. Haselden got two more yards before Ken Morgan saw Maksim all alone on the five and hit him with a perfect strike. Maksim trotted across for the score. A wide conversion attempt by Davis left the Tribe in a 12-7 lead.

P. C. kicked-off to open the second half. Newberry failed to move the necessary yardage and punted to the Hose 38. Runs by Brockenbrough and three Hamilton aerials set the stage for the second Hose score of the evening, on the 2 yard line. Hamilton cracked the middle of the Newberry line for the score and a 13-12 lead. A perfect conversion by Blue extended the lead to 14-12.

Lead Changes Again

A Blue Hose punt was taken by the Indians and returned to the P. C. 38 early in the fourth quarter. Tyler Dufford, running well, picked up 15 yards. Davis and Haselden combined for 13 yards to the P. C. 19. Then Dufford, on a running pass play, found end Ed Blanko in the endzone and Newberry found itself with another score. A third missed conversion attempt left the score at 18-14, Newberry leading with 4:20 gone in the quarter.

Soon afterwards it looked as if the Tribe was about to score again. Ray took a Blue Hose punt and scampered back 33 yards with it to the P. C. 20. A pass, Brabham-to-Ray moved the ball to the 7 for the first down. But the Blue Hose line held and P. C. took over on its own 3. Then the tide of battle turned.

Three rushes produced a Hose first down. Then the Tribe was penalized five yards for off-sides. Blue snagged a Hamilton pass to his own 27. Butler took a handoff then and trotted 44 yards to the Tribe 29. A pass missed and Butler picked up two yards. Then the game broke wide open as Blue gathered in another Hamilton aerial on the Indian goal line and scored with two minutes and 21 seconds left in the ballgame. The missed placement left the final score at P. C. 20, Newberry 18.

Newberry .... 6 0 0 6—18
Presbyterian ..... 0 7 7 6—20

Newberry scoring: touchdowns, Brabham, Maksim, Blanko. Presbyterian scoring: touchdowns, Brockenbrough, Hamilton, Blue. Conversions, Blue (2).

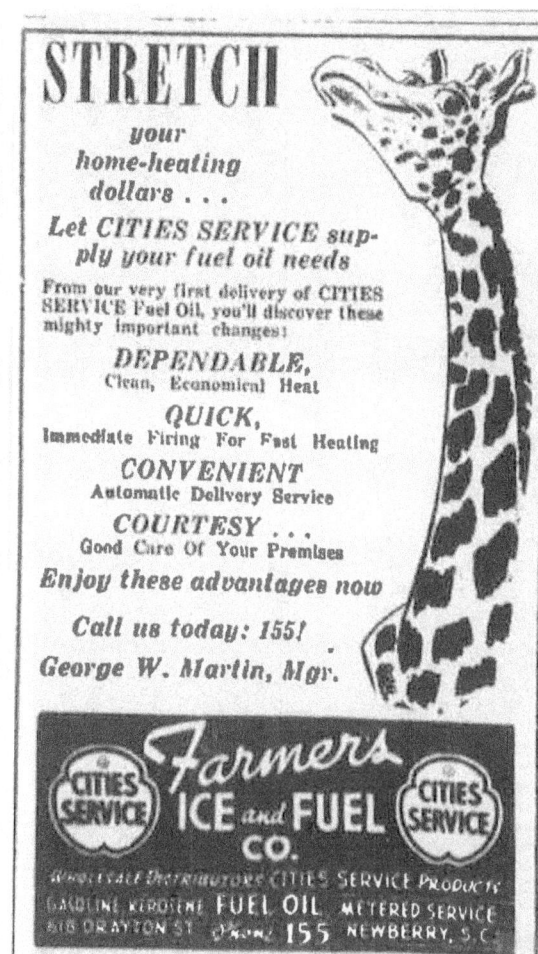

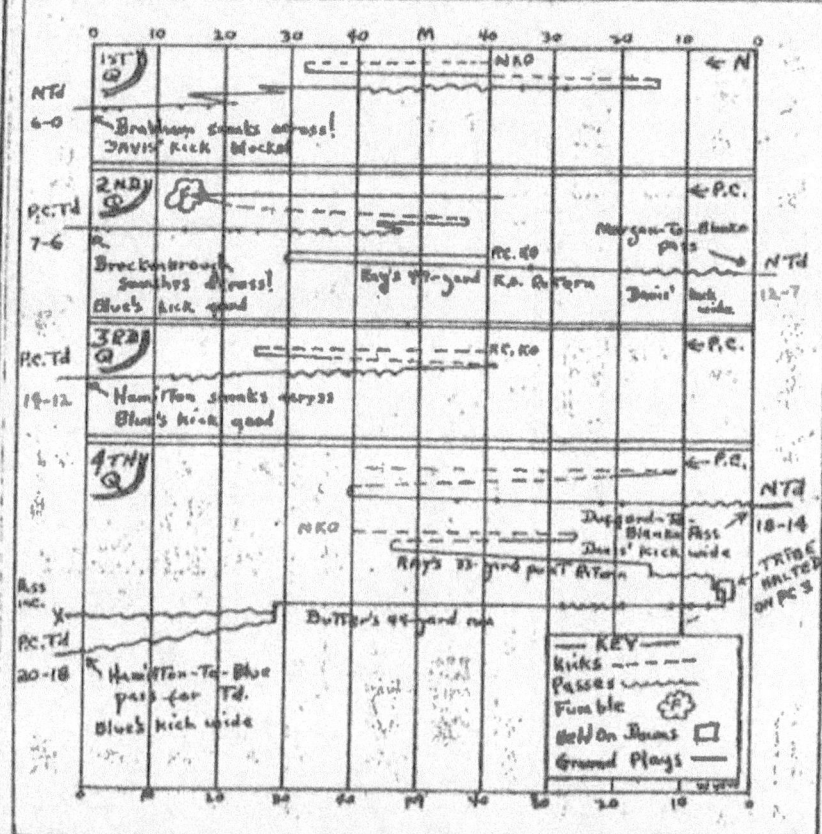

The above diagram indicates the scoring marches, quarter by quarter, during last Thursday's traditional Bronze Derby football clash between the Newberry College Indians and the Blue Hose of Presbyterian College at Clinton. No attempt has been made to follow the game play-by-play, for only the highlights of the nip-and-tuck game, won in the last three minutes by P. C. by a final 20-18 score, have been outlined.—(Observer Game-o-graph).

The Newberry Observer

Turkey Shoot!

FRESH DRESSED TURKEY HENS

12 to 14-Lb. Avg.

WEDNESDAY, NOV. 24TH

— At —

1:00 O'CLOCK P. M.

J. C. NICHOLS STORE

Hartford Road — Newberry

The Li'l That Was!

The Indian
NEWBERRY COLLEGE
"Home of The Fighting Redskins"

SEASON'S GREETINGS

SEASON'S GREETINGS

NEWBERRY, S. C., WEDNESDAY, DECEMBER 8, 1954

Tribe To Play Elks Bowl Saturday

PC Wins Bronze Derby Tilt

The P. C. Blue Hose decisioned the Newberry College Indians in the annual Bronze Derby classic on Thanksgiving Day by the score of 20-18. The game, played at Clinton this year, was close and bitterly-fought play by play, with the lead changing five times and P. C. winning on a pass from quarterback Hamilton to George Blue with less than three minutes remaining.

Newberry scored first in the first quarter on an 87-yard drive. Starting on their own 13, the Indians, led by sprints by Grady Ray and Paul Davis, and a 28-yard Brabham to Davis aerial, moved to the P. C. two, where Danny Brabham sneaked over for the score. Grover Davis' conversion attempt was blocked by P. C. end Joe Counts, and the first quarter ended 6-0-Newberry.

Midway in the second quarter, the Blue Hose began to roll for their initial touchdown, moving 52 yards in eight plays. Most of the P. C. yardage was gained in this march by Ed Brockenbrough, who climaxed the drive by crashing over from the one for the TD. George Blue, sparkplug of the P. C.'uns all afternoon, added the extra point and P. C. led 7-6 with one minute and twenty seconds remaining in the half.

Grady Ray returned the P. C. kickoff 47 yards to the P. C. 34 on a spectacular jaunt into and out of would-be Blue Hose tacklers. At least three times he appeared to be stopped but managed to wiggle loose for more yardage. On first down, Haselden picked up 15 yards up the middle, and two plays later quarterback Ken Morgan hit end Mike Makzin and he carried the oval over for the second Tribe score. The PAT try again failed with only 35 seconds remaining in the half and Newberry led 12-7.

With five minutes gone in the third quarter, Presbyterian again picked up sufficient momentum to carry them 65 yards for their second tally. Three Hamilton passes, two to Counts and one to Twitty, accounted for thirty of these yards to the Newberry 12. Brockenbrough and Hamilton quickly moved the ball to the Newberry one, and Hamilton sneaked over to put P. C. in the lead again, 13-12. George Blue again converted and P. C. was again ahead 14-12 with approximately five minutes remaining in the third period.

The Hose maintained this edge until early in the last quarter, when they got themselves in a hole by kicking out of bounds on their own 28. The Redskins came roaring back after this break with Tyler Dufford making 13 on first down, after which Paul Davis and Jimmy Haselden moved to the P. C. 12 for another first down. Then, on a running pass, halfback Dufford found end Ed Blanko in the end zone with a pass, and Newberry again moved out in front 18-14, the extra point attempt failing for the third consecutive time.

On an exchange of punts, Grady Ray again got loose for another 52 yard return to the Presbyterian 29. A Brabham to Ray pass had Newberry on the P. C. seven, first and goal, but the P. C. defenses stiffened and the Hose took over on downs at their own three.

This set the stage for P. C.'s winning 97-yard touchdown drive. After two pass plays, Hose halfback Gene Butler took a pitchout from Hamilton and twisted 45 yards to Newberry's 29, with two minutes and forty seconds left. After one incomplete pass, Hamilton hit Blue in the end zone for P. C.'s winning tally. The PAT was wide and P. C. led 20-18, with less than two minutes left to play. Three Newberry pass plays failed as time ran out and Presbyterian won 20-18, in one of the most thrilling Bronze Derby clashes ever played. All observers rated the two teams as near even as possible, with Presbyterian winning by the margin of only two extra points. Both Newberry and the Hose played alert, aggressive football, making few mistakes and playing according to plan.

Newberry ended its regular season play with a 6-3-2 record, and have one game remaining, the December 11 Elks Bowl game against Appalachian in Raleigh, N. C. P. C. completed its schedule with a 5-3 slate.

—F. C. H.

November 1955

November 1	American writer and public speaker Dale Carnegie passed away.
November 1	A bomb on a United Airlines DC-6 killed 46 over Colorado.
November 2	David Ben-Gurion formed the first Israeli government.
November 3	NFL quarterback and sportscaster Phil Simms was born.
November 3	Australia gained control of the Cocos Islands.
November 3	Ex-president of Argentina Juan Peron reportedly fled to Central America.
November 4	MLB Hall of Fame pitcher Cy Young passed away.
November 5	Date returned in "Back to the Future" by character Marty McFly.
November 5	American TV personality Kris Jenner was born.
November 6	Racial segregation was outlawed in trains and buses in the United States.
November 6	Maria Shriver, American newscaster and ex-wife of Arnold Schwarzenegger was born.
November 6	The United States won their 7th consecutive Ryder Cup golf tournament led by Chick Harbert.
November 7	Maryland Supreme Court banned segregation in public recreational areas.
November 9	Actor Rock Hudson married Phyllis Gates.
November 9	The United Nations disapproved of South Africa apartheid policies.
November 12	Eddie Arcaro, Earle Sande and George Woolf are the first three inductees in the Horse Racing Hall of Fame.
November 13	American TV host, actor and comedian Whoopi Goldberg was born.
November 19	*National Review* published its first issue.
November 21	Argentina asked Panama to return Ex-president Juan Peron.
November 22	American comedian and actor Stemp Howard of the "Three Stooges" passed away.
November 22	RCA paid Sun Records $35,000 for Elvis Presley's contract.
November 24	The Bronze Derby was played in Newberry, South Carolina on Thanksgiving Day. The Newberry College Indians defeated the Presbyterian College Blue Hose 20-18.

The Li'l That Was!

The Indian
NEWBERRY COLLEGE
"Home of The Fighting Redskins"

HAPPY THANKSGIVING — **BEAT P.C.!**

Newberry Accepts Shrine Bowl Bid

Newberry, P.C. Clash

Eight seniors, (above) are slated to turn their final home performance on Setzler Field when the Fighting Redskins take on P.C. in the Turkey Day classic. Left to right—front row—Ed Blanko, Grady Ray, Hoyt Hayes, Buddy Sullivan. Second row—Danny Brabham, Jimmy Haselden, Eddie Jones, and Harold Green. (Photo by Tom Hill)

Taking the ups with the downs, the scarlet and grey Newberry Indians are warily ready to take on P. C.'s invading Blue Hose tomorrow in the big Turkey Day contest.

On the dark and dismal side of the ledger are numerous injuries to key players, which will be a determining factor in the outcome of the final score in the fracas with the arch-rival Blue Hose.

Little All-American candidate Danny Brabham's name is on the casualty list with two broken bones in his right hand. The stellar field general missed the Stetson game and the odds stack high against his seeing action in the "Little Three Championship Battle." Mac Tant, a promising freshman fullback, also has a broken hand and will see limited or no action.

Olin McCurry, the bulwark of the Indian forward wall, has an infected leg and, after missing several days of practice, is a doubtful starter.

Jimmy Haselden, with several bruised ribs, Ed Blanko, with a twisted ankle, and Terry Dukes, with a twisted knee, are other performers who will be handicapped by painful injuries in tomorrow's tilt.

Casting a dim ray of hope on the picture, however, will be the return of Tyler Dufford to the fold and the outstanding performance of a first year man in the Stetson game.

Dufford, the fifth man in the Redskins' backfield, was sidelined for two weeks with a case of the mumps but is now well and ready to render his services to the Indians' cause.

Steve Peterson, who took over at the quarterback slot for Brabham, gave forth with a brilliant performance in the Stetson game and will be counted on to keep up the outstanding work in the Newberry-P. C. slugfest.

With a little help from Lady Luck concerning the injury situation, the Newberrians will be physically able to meet the P. C.'uns on even terms in the Turkey Day game.

Plenty of Fresh
FRUIT
At All Times
YOUNG'S FRUIT STORE

The Li'l  That Was!

HANKSGIVING · 1955

The Blue Stocking
Distinguished for Its Progress

Vol. XXXIV — Presbyterian College, Clinton, S. C., November 18, 1955 — No. 10

Hose Meet Newberry Thursday
• Bronze Derby at Stake

The Presbyterian College Blue Hose will meet the Newberry Indians on the latter's home field next Thursday afternoon and the Bronze Derby will be at stake. The Hose will be out to keep possession of the valued prize which they hold because of their victory in last year's Turkey Day duel.

Head coach Bill Cruchfield and his Battlin' Blue Hose got down to serious business Wednesday afternoon after a two-day layoff. The Hose hope to make it two straight over the Indians of Coach Harvey Kirkland.

The strong rivals have met 40 times with PC holding a decided edge in the series with 26 wins. Newberry has taken eleven games with three ending in ties. The Hose have outscored the Indians by 567 points to 332.

The Blue Hose took last year's game in the fading minutes on the strength of a scoring aerial from Harry Hamilton to George Blue. The score was set up by a fine run by PC's best broken field runner, Gene Butler, who is a returning letterman at the left halfback position.

The Hose will depend mainly on their excellent running attack. The Hose ground attack has been very efficient in grinding out huge hunks of yardage against their opponents this year. Fullback Ken Webb has been the big gun in the PC attack so far this year. His running mates are Butler and Eddie Brockenbrough.

Quarterback Felder Cook, a doubtful starter at the beginning of this season, has shown considerable improvement in his passing and running. He has also shown considerable promise as a runner and his kicks have been better than average.

The Newberry ground attack is led by veteran halfback Grady Ray. Ray was a continual thorn in the side of the Hose in last year's encounter. Ray is a former star at Camden High.

Danny Brabham, who is considered the best quarterback in the state by his coach, will be at the helm for the Indians on Thursday. Brabham is an excellent operator of the split T and this year blossomed as a competent passer.

The Blue Hose line is bolstered by two lettermen tackles and a host of fine ends. Captain Robert Harrington will be out to insure his position as a tackle on the All-State eleven. His running mate is Lee Frierson. The end positions are manned by three veterans, Ken Daughtry, Bobby Jackson, and Bob Stevens, and a transfer student of last year, Don Daniels.

There is only one letterman at the guard position, but the play of the untried men has been very pleasing. Veteran Tommy Warren, Alvis Poe, Bill Tsacrios, and Richard Shrigley will be out to stop the talented Newberry backs. The center position is well manned by George Shrigley, Jim McLauchlin, and Guy Haddix.

Against mutual foes this season the Hose have won one, lost two, and tied one. The Indians have won one, lost one, and tied two. PC has registered a win over Catawba and have suffered losses to Wofford and The Citadel. The Hose tied Stetson. Newberry has won over Wofford, lost to The Citadel, and tied both Catawba and Stetson. It all adds up to an exciting game with plenty of action.

Last week the Blue Hose lost to the Appalachian Mountaineers while Newberry and Stetson battled to a 12-12 tie. Both teams have open dates this week in preparation for their annual battle. Game time is 2:30 P. M.

Behind the Blues
By Tommy Richards

HOSE END SEASON

The Battlin' Blue Hose of Presbyterian College will draw the final curtain on the 1955 football season when they meet the Newberry Indians at Newberry Thursday afternoon at 2:30 P. M. Although the Hose record for this season has not been as impressive as the one of the '54 season, they have shown promise for the years to come.

Quite a number of new stars have been unveiled during this season. With a full year's experience the promising newcomers should offer considerable service to next year's team. Three very promising freshmen have added needed depth at the important quarterback position. Ron Isger has started more than one game this season and has shown plenty of promise as a passer and defensive ace. With a little improvement in speed Isger could be very valuable in the coming year.

The Hose team has not been short of halfbacks this season. With two returning lettermen from last year's team and the conversion of a fullback, the halfback position has been strong in both size and speed. Freshmen Tony Benson and Jerry Yoder will be around for at least three more seasons and this sounds encouraging for the Blue Hose.

Linemen who should offer considerable aid in the coming year are ends, Ted Leahy, Richard Alexander, and Don Segrest; tackles, Joe Negley, Jim Kline, and Jack Coppley; guards, Richard Shrigley, and Alvin Hampton; and centers, George Shrigley, and Marion Parrish.

COOK COMES THROUGH

Although quarterback Felder Cook was not expected to start for the Blue Hose this year, he not only started the season off as the regular quarterback but has come through in fine fashion for the P College team also. Cook has been a capable field general for the Hose this season as well as an excellent ball handler.

Cook's booming kicks have soared over the heads of opposing safety men quite a few times this year. He was not expected to be able to carry on the PC aerial attack that has been such an asset for the past few seasons. Although the Blue Hose have not relied on passing as much this year as in the past, Cook has had a better than 50% pass completion average for this year.

During a number of games Cook has shown quite an ability for carrying the pigskin. This definitely shows his versatility; as a T quarterback has very few opportunities to run the ball. All in all he has shown that the Blue Hose will not have the quarterback problem next year that they had at the beginning of this season.

Bronze Derby Symbolizes Forty Years of Rival Play

The Li'l That Was!

Behind the Blues
By Tommy Richards

HOSE END SEASON

The Presbyterian College Blue Hose ended a not too successful football season on Thanksgiving afternoon by going down in defeat before a strong Newberry eleven. Although the Hose record was not too hefty on the win side of the column, the Battlin' Blues played a fine brand of ball all season.

It seems that the PC team was plagued with tough breaks all year. The Hose had their share of the breaks this season, but they were all bad. Then there is the argument that a team makes its own breaks. This holds true to a certain extent, but only so far.

I'm not trying to make excuses for the poor season, but with just a few good breaks the Hose could have registered one of their best seasons in quite a few years. The season of 1955 is over and now all eyes are being focused on the '56 season.

With only two players being lost by graduation, the Hose should be in fine shape if all the underclassmen return. This year's play revealed quite a few promising freshmen and transfer students. The gap at quarterback has been filled and that will no longer be a problem. If all turns out as expected the Hose should compile a record worth boasting about in the 1956 season.

November 18, 1955 — THE BLUE STOCKING

WLBG
WILL BROADCAST THE
PC-Newberry
FOOTBALL GAME

Airtime is Saturday at 2:15. At mikeside are Bill Hogan and Chris Patte.

PRESENTED BY

Bank of Clinton

H. D. Payne & Co.

Canada Dry Distributors

The Blue Stocking

Distinguished for Its Progress

Vol. XXXIV — Presbyterian College, Clinton, S. C., November 18, 1955 — No. 10

The Li'l That Was!

Bronze Derby Symbolizes Forty Years of Rival Play

By LAWRENCE YOUNG

The Bronze Derby, symbol of 40 years of athletic encounters between Newberry College and Presbyterian College, has only a short history. It was first instigated in 1946 when the topper was snatched from Jimmie Kellett, former PC student, during a free-for-all after a Presbyterian victory over Newberry in Basketball.

Charles MacDonald, former PC public relations head, immediately pounced upon the incident, had the hat returned, and sent it to be bronzed by a novelty firm in Ohio.

Until last year the hat has been at stake whenever the two schools met in football, basketball or baseball. Under the influence of the public relations head, Ben Hay Hammet, the Bronze Derby has been changed to be the symbol of football rivalry between the two schools only.

On Derby Day all past records can be forgotten because no quarter will be given. Throughout the past forty years, the Battling Blue Hose have won 26, lost 11, and tied 3.

In the last three years the margin of points has not exceeded two points. The Blue Hose edged out the Indians 14-12 in the last minutes of the 1952 Thanksgiving game.

Down at Newberry on Turkey Day in 1953, the Indians tied the PC'uns 7-7. Last year Harry Hamilton and George Blue led the Hose to a 14-12 victory over the Indians.

The Li'l 🎩 That Was!

The Newberry Observer
AND HERALD & NEWS
"Just Like a Letter from Home"

HERALD AND NEWS ESTABLISHED 1893 · NEWBERRY, S. C., TUESDAY, NOVEMBER 29, 1954 · NEWBERRY OBSERVER ESTABLISHED 1865

Bronze Derby, Little Three Title Won By Tribe On Turkey Day

P. C. In 20-18 Loss; Game Is Exciting One

Conversions By Peterson Give Victory Margin

By far the largest crowd ever to pack Setzler Field at Newberry College, filling the grandstands and temporary bleachers and overflowing onto the adjacent areas, watched the Fighting Redskins of Newberry College battle their blue-clad rivals from nearby Presbyterian College to a 20-18 victory last Thursday afternoon.

The victory had two-fold significance. It gave the local Indians clear title to the Little Three football crown for 1955, and also permitted them to retain the Bronze Derby, traditional symbol of athletic supremacy between the two colleges, whose rivalry goes back 41 years. The outcome of the game was not assured until after the final whistle had blown and the entire sixty minutes were filled with the usual razzle dazzle brand of football that these two ball clubs always come up with whenever they play each other.

The presence at quarterback Danny Brabham, who played with two broken bones in his right hand, and tackle Olin McCurry, still suffering with a leg infection, meant much to the Tribe's victory, but the margin of victory, in the final analysis, was provided by the "educated toe" of sub-quarterback Steve Peterson, who converted successfully after Newberry's first two tallies.

The Tribe broke the scoring ice, with the injured Brabham directing his team 65 yards in six plays for the score. The climax came when Brabham handed off to halfback Tyler Dufford, who tossed an aerial to end Ed Blanko. Blanko's jumping snatch of the 21-yard pass gave the Tribe a 6-0 early lead, and a perfect boot from placement by Peterson made it 7-0.

Starting late in the first period, the Blue Hose drove 59 yards in 10 plays to score early in the second quarter. It was fresh halfback Tony Benson, who ran surprisingly well all afternoon, who struck pay dirt from 12 yards out to climax the drive. The attempted kick from placement for the extra point by Ken Webb failed to split the uprights and Newberry led 7-6.

The Tribe's offensive machine was fired up, however, and they scored again before the first half ended. Halfback Grady Ray's 12-yard scoring effort climaxed a 68-yard concerted march which utilized just nine plays. Another perfect conversion by Peterson left the halftime score 14-6 in favor of the Fighting Redskins.

The Hose forged into its first lead just minutes later, still in the third period. The touchdown followed a break for the Hosemen, as center George Sprigley latched on to a Tribe fumble on the Indians' 41-yard line. Just seven plays later halfback Gene Butler rambled 20 yards for the tally which put the Hose ahead 18-14. A pass for the extra point clicked but an offsides penalty nullified the point, and the subsequent attempt for the point failed, leaving the score 18-14 in favor of P. C.

The Tribe wrapped things up, starting late in the third period, when Ray raced back to the Blue Hose 43 following a short P. C. punt. Sub-fullback Hoyt Hayes picked up 17. After a five-yard penalty and a change of quarters, Ray rambled for another 10. Brabham then tossed a pass in the flat to Ray, who went for another 6 to the Hose 12. Ray was eased out of bounds on the six on the next play. Dufford picked up two, and Ray made it to the Hose half-yard marker. It was Brabham who sneaked across for the game-winning tally and a 20-18 final score.

Orren's attempted conversion failed, but the Tribe held off the Blue Hose during the remaining 11 minutes and 42 seconds of play.

Statistics

	Tribe	Hose
1st downs	18	11
Yds. rush	230	258
Yds. pass.	88	14
Tot. yds. gain.	318	272
Pass. att.	9	8
Pass. comp.	5	2
Pass. int.	0	0
Punts	4	5
Punt avg.	27.5	33
Fumbles lost	2	1
Yds. penalized	10	50

Santa's At GOODYEAR
SATURDAY, DEC. 7th
FROM 3 P. M. 'TIL 6 P. M.

Meet Santa at the Newberry Airport at 2:30 Saturday, December 7. He will have candies and toys for boys and girls! Follow Santa to the

GOODYEAR SERVICE STORE
WHERE HE WILL TALK TO ALL CHILDREN

November 1956

November 2	Hungary appealed for UN assistance against the USSR.
November 3	"The Wizard of OZ" was televised on TV for the first time on CBS.
November 3	After days of fighting, Israeli forces captured the Gaza Strip in the Suez Crisis.
November 4	200,000 Russian troops attacked the anti-Soviet movement in Budapest, Hungary.
November 5	The first African-American variety show, "The Nat King Cole Show" debuted on NBC.
November 6	President Dwight D. Eisenhower was re-elected President of the United States defeating Adlai Stevenson.
November 6	Netherlands and Spain withdrew from the 1956 Olympics in protest against Soviet aggression in the Hungarian Revolution.
November 7	The Suez Crisis ended with a cease fire.
November 8	The United Nations demanded the USSR to leave Hungary.
November 8	"The Ten Commandments" starring Charlton Heston and Yul Brynner premiered in New York City.
November 10	Henry Ford Sinclair, founder of Sinclair Oil passed away.
November 13	The United States Supreme Court ruled race separation on buses in Alabama unconstitutional.
November 14	The Hungarian revolt was put down by Soviet troops.
November 15	The movie "Love me Tender" with Elvis Presley made its United States debut.
November 16	NASCAR driver Terry Labonte was born.
November 18	CFL and NFL quarterback Warren Moon was born.
November 20	NFL New York Jets defensive end Mark Gastineau was born.
November 20	American actress Bo Derek was born.
November 21	Don Newcombe of the Brooklyn Dodgers won both the MLB NL Most Valuable Player Award and first ever Cy Young Award.
November 22	The Summer Olympics opened in Melbourne, Australia. It was the first Olympics to be held in the Southern Hemisphere.
November 22	The Bronze Derby was played in Clinton, South Carolina on Thanksgiving Day. The Newberry College Indians defeated the Presbyterian College Blue Hose 13-0.

The Li'l 🎩 That Was!

The Newberry Observer
AND HERALD & NEWS
"Just Like a Letter from Home"

HERALD AND NEWS ESTABLISHED 1865 — NEWBERRY, S. C., FRIDAY, NOV. 23, 1956 — NEWBERRY OBSERVER ESTABLISHED 1882

Newberry, P.C.

Renew Bronze Derby

SPORTS EYE of The OBSERVER
by OLLIE MOYE

Thanksgiving Day Renews Traditional Derby Battle

Thanksgiving, tradition, a bronze derby and two keyed up football squads. Put this together and the results is the traditional Thanksgiving Day festival between Newberry and Presbyterian College, with a Bronze Derby awaiting the winner.

A winner? Take your choice. Compare the teams with their previous records of this season, then forget these records. Throw all previous scores out the window, for in this Bronze Derby battle which through the years has gained state-wide fame as one of the big gridiron battles of the year, all past records are tossed out the window. It'll be a wide open affair.

Quite often a football game is decided by one big break. Such is the case in this annual affair, which this year will be the 42nd meeting of the two schools.

And speaking of breaks, the Indians are certainly due. They haven't had a decent one all season. They've truly earned the 4-2-2 mark which currently shines in the record books.

P. C. already has one break even before the game begins. Newberry's passing attack was hampered in the Stetson encounter when Quarterback Steve Peterson received a broken neck and bruised spinal cord. Without Peterson's passes, Newberry's record would be nothing to brag about today. The youngster from Tarpon Springs, Fla., himself has tossed 12 touchdown passes this season, along with setting up several other TD's with his aerials.

But despite this, the Newberry team is not discouraged. The Indians are wanting a victory in this game for Steve Peterson, and they'll be playing accordingly. But the odds are stacked against them in another way—as they'll be shooting for their fifth straight win of the season.

"They are more determined than they are happy," Coach Harvey Kirkland said of his squad. "They know they've suffered a serious blow, but they've shown a lot of determination in getting ready for this game."

Terry Dukes will be called on to handle the signal calling job, but he'll receive a lot of assistance from Scott Spears and Richard Phillips.

"Phillips and Spears will be doing the kicking, and because of the substitution rule, they'll be in a good bit of the offense," Kirkland informed.

Physically, the Indian Chief announced his team in "good shape" for the game. "We finished our heavy contact work Saturday and have devoted this week to dummy scrimmages in order to eliminate possibilities of injuries," the coach stated.

It will be the fifth Bronze Derby game for Coach Kirkland since he assumed the head coaching duties at the local college. Kirkland's record against P. C. stands at two defeats, one victory and one tie. The victory came last year when Newberry defeated P. C. here, 20-18.

Since Kirkland has been involved in the Bronze Derby game, only two points have decided the winner on three occasions. In 1952, P. C. won, 14-12; in 1953, the teams tied, 7-7, in 1954, P. C. won, 20-18; and last year Newberry won, 20-18.

So, if these past four engagements serve as a measuring stick, the game looks as a close one. But in any event, the victor will be the team that receives the breaks. Coach Kirkland hopes it's Newberry, because the Indians certainly are due one!

Newberry will be relying almost entirely on a ground game. But if you'll recall last year's meeting, quarterback Danny Brabham entered the game with a broken finger and for that reason the Indians' passing attack also was hampered. Brabham threw only one pass, and completed it for five yards. So, maybe the rushing game will pay big dividends again for the Indians.

The local squad will dress at the college and leave for Clinton in time for a short warm-up before the game.

Game Scheduled At Clinton 2:30 Thursday

South Carolina's Bronze Derby goes on the block at Clinton's Johnson Field Thursday afternoon when Presbyterian College and Newberry battle in a season-closing renewal of one of the state's oldest football feuds. A near-capacity crowd of some 4,500 fans is expected for the 2:30 p.m. kickoff.

They will come to watch two fast small-college teams clash in this 42nd game of the old rivalry which finds its symbol today in the Bronze Derby award. The series began back in 1913.

The Bronze Derby award grew out of the "abduction" of a P. C. student's derby at the first basketball game between Newberry and P. C. in 1947.

After discussions concerning the event, the hat was gladly surrendered by anonymous Newberry students and was turned over to a local jewelry firm to be cast in bronze, and to serve as a symbol of friendly relations between the two colleges.

"The Derby" is a part of a general plan to keep relations between the two colleges on a high plane despite the bitter rivalry which exists between them.

Both teams thus far have demonstrated offensive potentialities far more impressive than the record would indicate. The Blue Hose, sticking mostly to the ground, have averaged 314 yards-per-game against the combined opposition in the past nine games. Newberry has moved effectively on the ground, but its main payoff punch to date has been through the airlanes.

Newberry suffered a blow to its attack force ten days ago when star quarterback Steve Peterson sustained a broken neck while leading his team against Stetson.

Without Peterson Newberry's threat of a passing attack is virtually gone. Quarterback Terry Dukes, who took over for Peterson is a good passer, but the 150 pound quarterback prefers a running game. Dukes came in and ran the option play successfully for the Indians on several occasions. With Dukes in the game P. C. will likely put in seven or nine man forward walls with an attempt to stop the fleet Indian backs.

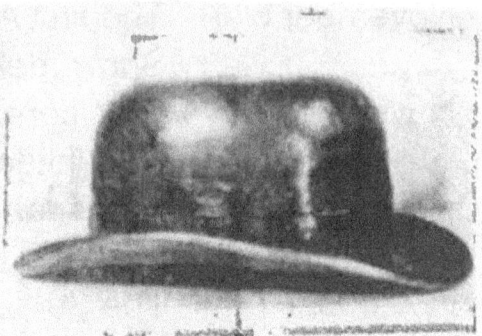

THE BRONZE DERBY: This is the Bronze Derby which is at stake Thursday afternoon when Newberry and Presbyterian College collide in the 42nd game of the state's oldest football feuds. The Indians currently are in possession of the Derby, but the results of the famed Turkey Day meeting of these teams will determine which keeps it for another year.

Halfbacks Tyler Dufford and Paul Davis who have come forth with some brilliant performances during the season, will be the work-horses for Coach Kirkland's Indians. Tyler Dufford is currently leading the Redskins in the rushing department while Paul Davis is the leader scoring-wise. The punch for those extra inches on first-down attempts will be provided by a charging fullback, freshman Ray Waters. Mr. Waters has shown amazing improvement since he was moved up to the starting eleven.

Up front a solid line made up of ace tackles Marion Lee and Olin McCurry, steady guards, Jerry Weed and Ralph Voyles, center Steve Robertson, and backing anchor men, Bobby Stokes and Jim Fraser will combine forces to stop the Blue Hose backs. Coach Kirkland has changed his defenses for the game in an effort to halt P. C. backs who have run well against all opponents this season. Special effort has been given to a pass defense which is designed to keep P. C.'s Fielder Cook from throwing.

The records show P. C. coach Bill Crutchfield ready to field a stable of hard-running backs five of whom have exceeded 200 yards rushing thus far.

Halfback Ken Webb leads the field with 485 yards, but there are others whose recent sparkle ranks them high among the Thanksgiving threats. Halfback Gene Butler has rolled up 232 yards from scrimmage in addition to last week's brilliant 79-yard punt return; fullback Billy Nalley, with 281 yards rushing, fullback Eddie Breckenborough, with 260, and halfback Raymond Johnson, with 229.

Despite quarterback Fielder Cook's superior passing record sophomore Ron Jager will get the signal-calling nod on the strength of his performance against Stetson last weekend when he directed the P. C. second unit to all five Blue Hose touchdowns.

The Indians go into the Turkey Day classic with a record of four wins, two losses and two ties.

The Li'l That Was!

The Newberry Observer
AND HERALD & NEWS
"Just Like a Letter from Home"

HERALD AND NEWS ESTABLISHED 1845 — NEWBERRY, S. C., TUESDAY, NOV. 27, 1956 — NEWBERRY OBSERVER ESTABLISHED 1853

Newberry Defeats Blue Hose 13-0 In Bronze Derby Game

Determined Newberry displayed daring desire and a devastating defense to dent Presbyterian's dream of depriving them of the Derby Thursday afternoon in the 42nd renewal of the annual Bronze Derby clash at Clinton, dashing to a 13-0 defeat of the Blue Stockings.

Especially were the Indians enthused in this annual encounter which ended their nine-game season, as they entered the melee determined to score a victory for injured quarterback Steve Peterson, who received a broken neck and injured spinal cord in the Stetson battle some two weeks earlier at Newberry.

For Newberry, it was the second straight victory in this affair, which through the years has become a tradition with much more than the outcome of the score at stake. And for Coach Harvey Kirkland, it was the second win against two losses and two ties in this series since he took over the driver's seat of the Indian grid squad.

It also marked the first time this season that P. C. has been held scoreless, and was their sixth defeat of the season against four victories.

For the Indians, it was the fifth straight victory after posting two defeats and two ties in the season's first four contests.

In this game, which always is "wide open," anything can happen and it usually does. This 1956 meeting proved to be no exception. Presbyterian outrushed the Indians almost three-to-one, out-passed Newberry nearly five-to-one, and led in the first downs department, but Newberry's determination, desire and devastating defense proved to be the deciding factor.

Here's how the statistics went: First downs—Newberry 16, P. C. 19; passes attempted—Newberry 7, P. C. 8; passes completed—Newberry 3, P. C. 1; passes intercepted by—Newberry 1, P. C. 0; yards penalized—Newberry 35, P. C. 54; fumbles lost—Newberry 3, P. C. 5; yards rushing—Newberry 161, P. C. 310; yards passing—Newberry 9, P. C. 51.

Fumbles dealt a damaging blow to the Hosemen, as Newberry turned two of five recoveries into touchdowns. Both Newberry touchdowns came the first time it got the ball in the first and second halves. And both were set up on fumbles by P. C. fullback Eddie Brockenbrough.

Junior quarterback Terry Dukes did a masterful job at running the signal-calling slot, and especially did he perform smoothly on the option play.

But the big factor for Newberry was the outstanding line performances of tackles "Bull" Lee and Olin McCurry, who crashed through the big P. C. forward wall time and time again.

Leading rushers for the Indians were halfback Tyler Dufford, with 111 yards in 11 attempts, and Paul Davis, with 53 yards in 13 carries.

Ken Webb was the big man for P. C., cracking through Newberry's line for 139 yards in 20 carries, while fullback Brockenbrough netted 73 yards in 16 attempts.

Presbyterian reached scoring position at least five times during the afternoon, but fumbles and penalties ended their threat on each occasion.

Newberry won the toss and chose to kick. Bobby Stokes' kick was taken by Isger and returned to the P. C. 29. Brockenbrough reached the 34, then Butler made it to the 36, but on the next play Brockenbrough fumbled and Ralph Voyles recovered for Newberry on the P. C. 36.

On the first play from scrimmage, Davis scooted through the line for eight to the 28 and Dukes passed incomplete. Newberry drew a five-yard off-side penalty to the 33. Then Dufford passed to Fraser for a first on the P. C. 10. Dufford notched five to the five, then bulled his way to the three on the next play. From here, Dukes circled wide around his left end for the payoff. Taylor's kick was wide to the right. Only four minutes, 30 seconds of the game had passed when Newberry scored.

P. C. took the following kick and drove 38 yards to Newberry's 27, but Dukes intercepted an Isger pass on the Newberry 15 to halt the drive. The Indians launched an offensive maneuver here that almost paid off in another touchdown, but a Dufford fumble on the P. C. 28 ended it.

As the second quarter opened, P. C. was deep in Newberry territory, but when the second stanza was only four plays old, fullback Billy Nally, in for Brockenbrough, fumbled and Dufford recovered on the Newberry 6.

Midway of the second quarter, Webb signaled for a fair catch of a Phillips' punt on the P. C. 39. Brockenbrough carried five to the 44 and Webb picked up a first on a 15-yard jaunt to Newberry's 41. Then Johnson broke loose for 12 yards and another first on the Indian 29. Johnson failed to gain, and Webb reached the 25. Webb lost to the Newberry 34 and Cook passed incomplete and Newberry had held again, taking over on downs.

With time running out in the first half, P. C. was on Newberry's 15. On a second down situation, Benson raced to the 13. Cook tried the Newberry line, but was stopped cold. Then Cook tossed an incomplete pass and Newberry took over with only a minute and 30 seconds left before intermission.

Newberry again kicked off to open the third quarter. But six plays after the kickoff, McCurry pounced on a Brockenbrough miscue on the P. C. 30 to set the stage for Newberry's second touchdown. Dukes passed to Dufford, but the senior halfback caught the ball out of bounds. Then Dufford shook away for a nine-yard gain to the 21 and Davis made it to the 16 for a first down. Davis carried again, this time for nine to the P. C. 7 and Dufford reached the two for a first. Dufford was given the ball again and this time he cracked over for pay dirt. Taylor's first kick was good, but Newberry was charged with illegal motion and penalized five yards. Taylor's second kick also was good and the Indians clung to a 13-0 lead, which stood intact at the game's ending.

BUILDING MATERIALS

See Our Complete Line Of Building Materials, Paint, And Builders Hardware. We Sell Only The Best And At Money Saving Prices. See Us Today.

Cannon Construction & Supply Co., Inc.
1732 Harris St.   Phone 1184

The Blue Stocking
Distinguished for Its Progress
Vol. XXXV — Presbyterian College, Clinton, S. C., November 30, 1956 — No. 10

Indians Take Turkey Day; Fumble Cost Hose Again

An inspired group of Newberry Indians took the annual "Turkey Day" battle from the Presbyterian College Blue Hose to the tune of a 13-0 shut-out before a chilled crowd of 4,200. The surprising Indians were determined to take the victory for their injured quraterback, Steve Peterson, who suffered a broken neck in the Stetson game.

Newberry recovered five PC fumbles to stop Hose drives and they turned two of these into touchdowns. It was the first time the Hose had been shut out this season and it was the first whitewash at the hands of the Indians since 1947.

PC's Ken Webb was the contest's leading ball carrier with 138 yards in 20 carries for a 6.9 average. Fullback Eddie Brockenbrough added 73 in 16 attempts for an average of 4.5.

Leading the way for the Indians was halfback Tyler Dufford with 111 yards in 17 carries for an average of 6.5 yards. He also completed three out of 3 passes for 51 yards. Halfback Paul Davis added 53 yards in 13 attempts.

Brockenbrough fumbled on the Hose 3 and Ralph Voyles recovered for Newberry. Davis picked up seven and then Dufford took a pitchout and passed to end Jim Fraser to the PC 10. Dufford carried twice for 7 before quarterback Terry Dukes, on an option play carried over from the three for the initial tally of the battle. Taylor's attempted conversion was no good. After 4:25 of the first period it was Newberry 6, PC 0.

Newberry started another drive but end Russ Alexander recovered their fumble on his own 27. Webb and Brockenbrough got 18. Webb spurted for 19 to the Indian 35. Benson and Brockenbrough for 7.

A penalty gave the Hose a first down. Webb picked up 7 but Nalley fumbled and Dufford recovered at the 9. Dukes kicked dead at the PC 37. Brockenbrough got 12 and Benson 15. Webb moved for 12 to the 18. Webb and Benson picked up five and Cook failed to gain. Cook passed incomplete.

Near the beginning of the second half the Hose were set back to the 3 for holding. Brockenbrough fumbled and Olin McCurry recovered at the PC 30.

Dufford and Davis got 14 for a first down at the 16. Davis picked up 9 more and Dufford moved the ball to the 2, from where he carried over for the score. Taylor converted.

Newberry took over on downs at the Hose 25. They recovered their own fumble for a 12-yard loss and Dukes kicked out at the Hose 10. PC was penalized to their own 1 from which point Cook kicked. It was partially blocked by tackle Marion Lee and Olin McCurry pounced on the ball at the 17. Dukes fumbled and Alexander recovered at the 11.

Later in the period Webb returned Dufford's quick kick to the Indian 38. Brockenbrough and Webb got 18. Butler couldn't quite hold Cook's pass, but he was out of the end zone anyway. Newberry took over on the 20 and it was only a matter of running out the clock.

The Clinton Chronicle

Clinton, S. C., Thursday, November 29, 1956

Presbyterian Gains Impressive Yardage But Get Few Scores

Even with uniforms put away for another year, Presbyterian college football fans still pondered how a team could churn out so much yardage with so little scoring to show for it.

The Blue Hose, closing their ten-game season with a 0-13 Thanksgiving Day loss to Newberry, wound up with an unimpressive four won-six lost record. Statistically, the Presbyterian offense roared with power on paper— a total of 3,138 rushing and passing yards, averaged 313 yards per game—but this attack force averaged only two touchdowns each game.

Ground action produced 2,360 of those yards, or 235 per weekend. And six Presbyterian backs individually posted rushing gains of more than 200 yards for the season.

Halfback Ken Webb, of Decatur, Ga., led the way, adding 139 yards in the final game to increase his total to 624 yards from scrimmage, an average 5.6 yards-per-carry. Halfback Gene Butler, of Conway, followed with 394 for a 4.6 average, and fullback Eddie Brockenbrough, of Charlotte, had 342 for a 5.0 average. Fullback Billy Nalley, of Central, came next with 295 and a 4.4 average; halfback Raymond Johnson, of Whitmire, posted 282 for a 4.9; and halfback Tony Benson, of Chester, with a top average gain of 6.3 yards-per-carry, accumulated a total of 219 yards.

Blue Hose passing added 778 yards during the season, mostly on the arm of quarterback Felder Cook, of Charleston. He completed 42 of 83 attempted for 561 yards. Ten passes went to end Ted Leahy, of Atlanta, for 186 yards, ten to Webb for 142 and eight to Butler for 96.

Butler led the team scoring with 41 points, followed by Webb with 27.

Newberry, in scoring its shutout victory in the season finale for both teams, retained possession of the Bronze Derby and also acquired the game football to take to the bedside of their seriously injured teammate. Quarterback Steve Peterson has been hospitalized for the past three weeks with a broken neck.

Presbyterian fumbles played a key part in the Indian triumph. Not only did they set up both Newberry touchdowns, they also helped to throttle a Blue Hose running attack which rolled for 310 yards from scrimmage during the afternoon.

Two of the five PC fumbles recovered by Newberry were inside the Presbyterian 36-yard line, the first on the 36 early in the first period and the second on the 30 at the start of the third quarter. The Indians took advantage of each to move the short remaining distances for touchdowns. Quarterback Terry Dukes sailed around his left end for three yards and the initial score, and halfback Tyler Dotford plunged two yards through center for the other tally.

The Blue Hose mounted threat after threat, only to be stopped deep in Newberry territory—twice on the 15 yard line, once on the 14 and once on the 22.

November 1957

The Li'l That Was!

November 1	American singer-songwriter Lyle Lovett was born.
November 3	The Soviet Union launched Sputnik 2. On board was the first space dog, a Siberian Husky named Laika, the first animal in space.
November 6	American actress Lori Singer of "Footloose" was born.
November 7	In the United States, *The Gaither Report* suggested to increase American missiles and fallout shelters.
November 7	"Brady Bunch" actor Christopher Knight was born.
November 10	An NFL record crowd of 102,368 in Los Angeles watched the Los Angeles Rams and San Francisco 49ers in the Los Angeles Coliseum.
November 11	One million copies of "Great Balls of Fire" by Jerry Lee Lewis were sold in the first 10 days after the song was released.
November 14	Milwaukee Braves outfielder Hank Aaron won the MLB NL Most Valuable Player Award.
November 15	The US sentenced Soviet Spy Rudolf Ivanovich Abel to 30 years and fined him $3000.
November 16	NBA Boston Celtics center Bill Russell set an NBA record for rebounds. Russell had 49 rebounds against the Philadelphia Warriors.
November 16	The University of Oklahoma Sooners win streak ended at 47 games as they lost at home to Notre Dame 7-0.
November 22	Mickey Mantle of the New York Yankees won the MLB AL Most Valuable Player Award.
November 22	Tom & Jerry debuted on "American Bandstand." The duo are better known as Simon & Garfunkel.
November 25	United States President Dwight Eisenhower suffered a minor stroke resulting in impaired speech.
November 27	Caroline Kennedy, daughter of John F. Kennedy and Jackie Kennedy was born.
November 28	Milwaukee Braves Warren Spahn won the MLB NL Cy Young Award.
November 28	The Bronze Derby was played in Newberry, South Carolina on Thanksgiving Day. The Newberry College Indians defeated the Presbyterian College Blue Hose 13-0.

The Li'l That Was!

The Newberry Observer
AND HERALD & NEWS
"Just Like a Letter from Home"

HERALD AND NEWS ESTABLISHED 1869 — NEWBERRY, S. C., FRIDAY, NOV. 20, 1959 — NEWBERRY OBSERVER ESTABLISHED 1865

Tribe, P.C. Renew Derby Battle

Setzler Stadium Site For 2 P.M. Thursday Game

South Carolina's Bronze Derby goes on the block at Newberry's Setzler Stadium Thursday afternoon when Presbyterian College and Newberry College battle in a season-closing renewal of one of the state's oldest football feuds. A near-capacity crowd is expected for the 2 p.m. kickoff.

This will mark the 43rd game of the old rivalry, which finds its symbol today in the Bronze Derby award. The series dates back to 1913—the beginning of football history at Newberry College.

The Bronze Derby grew out of the "abduction" of a P. C. student's derby at the first basketball game between Newberry and P. C. in 1947.

After discussions concerning the event, the hat was gladly surrendered by anonymous Newberry students and was turned over to a local jewelry firm to be cast in bronze, and serve as a symbol of friendly relations between the two colleges.

"The Derby" is a part of a general plan to keep relations between the two colleges on a high plane despite the bitter rivalry which exists between them.

For the Indians, this will be the third game within a period of a dozen days. The Indians played at Spartanburg September 18, and only five days later met Catawba here in a game postponed from September 26. The P. C. affair comes seven days after the Catawba game.

Newberry will be out to snap a three-game losing streak. After winning four in a row—Carson-Newman, Troy State Teachers, East Carolina and Guilford—the Indians have lost to Elon, Wofford, and Catawba.

Overall record of the Indians is four wins, four losses and a tie with The Citadel in the opening game of the season.

Presbyterian, on the other hand, will be in search of its first win of the season. Only outstanding accomplishment by the linesmen this year was a scoreless tie against powerful Lenoir Rhyne, a team which humiliated the Indians, 42-0.

But, as far as both Newberry and P. C. spectators are concerned, records are tossed out the window for this affair. It's anybody's game and usually the underdog wins. To prove this point Newberrians only have to recall last year when the Indians entered the game without the services of ace quarterback Steve Peterson, who was seriously injured in the previous affair with Stetson; and in 1955 game when quarterback Danny Brabham had a broken finger. But, the Indians emerged with victories in these past two encounters, and Coach Harvey Kirkland is in hopes he'll hang onto the Derby for a third year in a row.

Leading the scoring list for the Indians are halfback Bob Yarnall and quarterback Scotty Speares. Yarnall leads the team in rushing with 245 yards while Speares has completed 13 passes for 163 yards. End Sam Faulk has caught five passes for 177 yards and two touchdowns.

THE BRONZE DERBY: This is the Bronze Derby which is at stake Thursday afternoon when Newberry and Presbyterian College collide in the 43rd renewal of the state's oldest football feuds. The Indians currently are in possession of the Derby, but the results of the famed Turkey Day meeting of these teams will determine which keeps it for another year.

SPORTS EYE of The OBSERVER
by OLLIE MOYE

Last Wednesday Newberry's Mites and Midget football teams were host to Whitmire's Mites and Joanna's Midgets for the second annual Newberry Turkey Bowl classic.

Those who saw the game saw two bigger and more experienced teams win both games from the local elevens. Whitmire's team blanked the local Mites, 33-0, and Joanna's Midgets won the other game, 21-0.

After the game, P. K. Fuller, Newberry recreation director, talked to this writer and asked us to carry an explanation of what happened in an effort to get him "off the hook."

"Several of the mothers and fathers are on my neck about scheduling such big teams," Fuller said to us that night. "Therefore, I'd like to clear it up in the paper."

For the record, here are Fuller's remarks which appeared in last Thursday's issue of The Observer:

"As far as I'm concerned, our Mites and Midgets will never again play against outside competition because you don't ever know what you'll be playing.

"Both Joanna and Whitmire teams were bigger, older and had more experience than our boys.

"I don't believe either of the two teams played ineligible players according to Midget and Mite rules. But their programs have been in effect longer than ours and their boys are older and more experienced.

"The age limit in Midget football is 14 years old, and Joanna had several boys who were 14 years old and several others who were 13 years old. We have only two boys 13 years old on the Newberry team and the majority of our Midgets are only 12 years old.

"When I scheduled these two teams, I didn't know their boys were that much bigger than ours."

Fuller made these statements merely to explain to parents of Newberry players just why their sons did not make a better showing against their opponents. They were in no way made to reflect against the two fine teams that came here to help the local squads celebrate their Turkey Bowl classic.

However, the following letter has been received from Billy Armfield of Whitmire in defense of the Whitmire team. Types Billy:

"An article appeared in your paper last Friday concerning the outcome of the Turkey Bowl games played last Wednesday night in Newberry. I would like to answer this article and several of the statements contained therein.

"I would like to explain to the people of Newberry that the team here in Whitmire is not the bunch of ruffians as it may appear.

"I am not accusing Mr. Fuller or 'The Observer' of deliberately making Whitmire and Joanna teams look bad, but I do feel that the statements were a bit hasty. The remarks were hitting below the belt, especially when they said 'because you don't ever know what you'll be playing.' I know P. K. Fuller too well to believe that he seriously meant this to throw reflection against our boys but here in Whitmire we feel that it did, and would like to tell Newberry folks about our Mite and Midget programs.

"I think you can usually tell a team's character and sportsmanship by its coaches and in my estimation our athletic director, Rich DuBose, will rank with the best anywhere. He believes in good sportsmanship and sees that his boys practice good sportsmanship, also. None of the boys playing against Newberry was over the age limit required by Mite regulations, and all of the boys—several of which were beginners—at the game played in the game.

"Coach DuBose received word Wednesday morning concerning the size and ages of the Newberry team and immediately changed his starting lineup so that the two teams starting would be as nearly as possible of the same weight and age.

"The boys also are taught that a good sport is a person who is willing to play his best, win or lose.

"Let us clear up also the fact that we didn't ask to come to Newberry to participate in the game—Newberry asked us and Whitmire responded with the friendly willingness to help them out and at our own expense. It seems that the article which was written and the statements that were made should have been words of appreciation for Whitmire's coming rather than saying in so many words 'we're sorry we invited you and don't want you back.'

"We're not angry at anyone—just a little disgusted. We hope such an incident will never happen again, and that Mr. Fuller will forget the statements he made and invite us back again.

"Thanks very much for publishing this article for me."

Fuller offered no comments on the letter, except that "what I said about the teams being bigger, older and more experienced had a lot to do with our teams being shown up as badly as they were. Anyone who saw the games can tell you that."

The Newberry Observer
AND HERALD & NEWS
"Just Like a Letter from Home"

The Li'l That Was!

HERALD AND NEWS ESTABLISHED 1865 — NEWBERRY, S. C., TUESDAY, DEC. 2, 1957 — NEWBERRY OBSERVER ESTABLISHED 1883

Indians End Season With 13-0 Victory Over P.C.

Sloppy Field Takes Color Out Of Game

A 21-yard pass combination from quarterback Richard Phillips to end John Hudgens and a spectacular 21-yard run by halfback Bobby Rowe, who twisted and turned out of the arms of four Presbyterian tacklers, provided the necessary punch in Newberry College's 13-0 victory over P. C. Thursday afternoon on the sloppy turf of Setzler Stadium.

An estimated 3,000 partisan fans braved the drizzly weather to see Coach Harvey Kirkland's Redmen put the finishing touches to a 5-4-1 season.

In notching this fifth victory of the 1957 season, the Indians also clung to the Bronze Derby —symbol of this traditional Thanksgiving Day rivalry that began 43 years ago.

The loss was Presbyterian's eighth against one tie and Thursday's game ended P. C.'s worst season since 1937 when the Hosemen scored only three times in losing 10 straight games.

A muddy turf tended to slow down the game and take away some of the color that has come out of other similar affairs of years past. But in the end, it had provided enough action to content those who sat under the dark and dismal clouds that hung over the stadium and threatened to unload bucketfuls of rain at a moment's notice.

Phillips' pitch to Hudgens came with less than two minutes gone in the second quarter and Wyman Taylor's kick put the Indians ahead at halftime, 7-0.

Rowe, the "midget" on the Indian team that weighs 150 pounds dripping wet, put on his mud shoes and sloshed 21 yards in the final period for the clincher. Taylor's kick was wide and the 13 points already posted, proved to be the margin of victory.

In all, Kirkland used three quarterbacks during the game — Phillips, Horace Turbeville and Scotty Speares, with Phillips and Turbeville engineering the two scoring drives.

Unlike other games this season, Kirkland did not use the two platoon system. Instead, he substituted freely—allowing seniors to play as much as they possibly could.

Facing one of the heaviest lines of the year, Coach Kirkland's strategy was to employ passing tactics to catch P. C.'s defense off guard.

This paid off. The rugged P. C. defense had held the Indians to 33 yards rushing in the first half, but because of Newberry's aggressive passing attack in the initial half, the Hose changed their defense for passing and Newberry's ground game improved. The Indians netted 151 yards in the second half for a total of 184 yards rushing.

Newberry added another 102 yards in the airlanes—hitting eight of 21 aerials. Four tosses were intercepted, three by Ken Webb and a fourth by Tony Benson.

Other game statistics also were in Newberry's favor. The Indians mustered 16 first downs to six for P. C. Newberry only punted twice — averaging 27 yards each—and P. C. kicked seven times for a 29.8 average. Newberry lost one fumble—Presbyterian three.

Penalties were few and far between. Newberry had 15 yards stepped off in penalties and there were 10 against the Hosemen.

Rowe sparked the Indian ground game, picking up a net of 70 yards.

Turning in a pleasing performance in Newberry's backfield was freshman Richard Seastrunk, who notched 26 yards.

Webb and Benson saved P. C. further embarrassment by making key tackles all over the field.

The pair seemed to be where Newberry receivers weren't as they quelled the Indians' passing attack on several occasions.

The Indians kicked off at the beginning of both halves. Newberry won the toss and, oddly enough, the Tribe proved polite hosts and gave their visitors first crack at the scoring column.

P. C. didn't reach Newberry territory, however, as it had to punt from the P. C. 44. Halfback Bob Yarnall gathered in the kick on his own 19 and returned 11 to Newberry's 30. Bobby Stokes plowed through the line for five, then Webb snagged a Speares' spiral on Newberry's 42 and returned five to Newberry's 37. An off-sides penalty against the Hose made it first and 15 from Newberry's 47. The Hosemen got nowhere and Gardner's punt rolled dead on Newberry's 25. Stokes carried, reached the 27 in two attempts, and facing third down and six to go, Speares took to the air again. And again, Webb gathered in his toss—this time on P. C.'s 37.

But, as before, P. C. failed to capitalize on an interception. The Hose began moving on the ground, and sparked by a 13-yard run by Waters, P. C. reached Newberry's 34 for a first in six plays. But Barnes fumbled and Roland Rosier grabbed it for the Indians on Newberry's 31.

It was from here that the Tribe launched their first touchdown drive. Phillips passed incomplete on the first play from this point, then connected with Rowe for seven to Newberry's 37. It was third and three and Phillips took to the air again. This time, he heaved a 16-yard toss to Hudgens for a first on P. C.'s 46. Stokes and Rowe notched another first on P. C.'s 35 with respective five and six-yard runs. Rowe plowed through to the 31 and Phillips kept for one to the 30 as the first quarter ended.

On the opening play of the second quarter, Phillips tossed to Yarnall for a first on the 20. Phillips lost one on the next play, then flipped the payoff pitch to Hudgens, who was standing all alone on the right side of P. C.'s end zone. Taylor's kick was good and Newberry led 7-0 with 13:28 left in the first half.

John Temples' kick was taken by Isger on P. C.'s 10 and returned to P. C.'s 31. Messer got three to the 34 and Lee Leary recovered an Isger fumble on P. C.'s 28.

Newberry only had the ball one play as Bridges regained possession for P. C. on the 28. The Hose rolled to their own 32 and had to punt. Yarnall took the kick and returned seven to his own 44. Rowe penetrated P. C. territory to the 48. He was given the ball again, and got four more to the 44. Yarnall reached the 41 and Phillips connected with Rowe again for 10 and a first on Presbyterian's 27. Newberry was off sides and Phillips tried another pass from the 32. Benson intercepted and made a beautiful 27-yard return to Newberry's 47.

But again it was the same story. P. C.'s offense fizzled out before getting far into Newberry territory. The Hose gambled on a fourth and 12 situation on Newberry's 39. Aycock passed incomplete and Newberry took over.

The Indians began moving again, but relinquished the ball on P. C.'s 11 with 36 seconds left in the half. Stokes notched four to Newberry's 43, but that's as far as Newberry got and the Indians punted. Speares' kick rolled dead on P. C.'s 23, but on the first play from there Stokes recovered a Benson fumble on P. C.'s 30. Speares completed two passes—10 yards each to Rowe and Yarnall—to P. C.'s 10. But on a fourth down, Speares lost to P. C.'s 13 and the Hosemen took over. They ran only two plays and the half ended.

Again, Newberry kicked off to open the second half. The invaders reached their own 43 and fumbled. Rosier recovered for Newberry. Four plays later, Speares went back to punt. The snap was low and he had to run. He was hit on the P. C. 44. The Hose lost two yards in three downs and punted dead on Newberry's 25.

Stokes got one to the 26 and Phillips passed to Graham for 18 and a first on Newberry's 44. Yarnall broke loose for 14 more to P. C.'s 42 and another first. Rowe and Phillips each added four and three, respectively, to the 35. Phillips tried for three and the first, but fumbled. He recovered for no gain, then punted out of bounds on the P. C. one. Newberry was penalized five yards, however, and Phillips had to punt again. This time, his kick was six yards better than before—rolling into the end zone —but 19 yards more in favor of P. C., as the Hose then took possession on their own 20.

Three plays later found P. C. only four yards past its own 20 and the Hosemen again had to punt.

Yarnall grabbed Webb's kick on his own 44 and returned four to Newberry's 48. The Indians drove to P. C.'s eight, but were stopped cold early in the fourth stanza.

Seastrunk shook loose for nine and Coviello made the first on P. C.'s 35. Waters and Coviello added another first on P. C.'s 24 and Coviello and Phillips reached the 13 for a third first of the drive. Coviello carried four to the nine and Waters reached the eight as the third quarter ended. Phillips tried two passes on the first two plays of the final stanza, and both were incomplete. P. C. took over on the eight. Nichols pulled the Hose away from their own goal line with a 14-yard dash and a first on the P. C. 22. Nichols ran two more, but Waters lost seven to the 17 and Nichols punted.

Again the Indians threatened, but were stopped deep in P. C. territory. Rowe grabbed the punt on P. C.'s 49 and was downed on the 46. Ten plays later found the Indians facing a fourth down situation with nine to go for a first on P. C.'s 20. Turbeville tried a pass, but it was intercepted by Webb on P. C.'s five. Had Webb merely batted the ball down, the Hosemen would have had possession on their own 20.

Presbyterian only made it to their own 11 in three plays, however, and again Nichols punted. His kick was downed by Seastrunk on P. C.'s 41. This set up Newberry's second touchdown.

Rowe dashed four to the 37 and then added 11 more for a first on P. C.'s 36. Exactly four minutes remained on the clock. Waters rammed through the line for two and Seastrunk got three to the 31. That's when Turbeville handed off to Rowe, who dashed 21 yards for the touchdown. Turbeville threw a key block after the handoff to get the seaback started on his touchdown journey. But Rowe met more trouble on the route. He was rushed by four husky P. C. tacklers on the 10. All four had their hands all over him, but the shifty back spun and wiggled himself loose and went on to pay dirt safely. Stokes' kick was wide, but the damage already had been done.

With only 2:37 left in the game, P. C. got possession of the ball for the last time of the afternoon. Webb took Stokes' kick on his own four and raced 29 yards to the 33 before being stopped. Waters tried four desperate passes—one complete for five yards to Barnes—but they failed to produce even one touchdown to save face for the visitors.

Newberry took over on the P. C. 36 with 58 seconds left and Turbeville carried twice to run out the clock.

Newberry ..... 0 7 0 6—13
Presbyterian .. 0 0 0 0— 0

Newberry scoring: Touchdowns —Hudgens (21-yard pass from Phillips), Rowe (21-yard, run). Conversion—Taylor, one.

The Li'l  That Was!

The Blue Stocking
Distinguished for Its Progress

Vol. XXXVI   Presbyterian College, Clinton, S. C., December 6, 1957   No. 10

Hose Falls Newberry Prey Lose Famed Bronze Derby

By ROY FOWLER

Newberry College captured second place in the Little Three and also the coveted Bronze Derby with a 13 to 0 victory over Presbyterian College on Thanksgiving Day. The game was played on a wet, muddy field. The Bronze Derby is symbolic of victory in the annual clash between PC and Newberry.

Senior quarterback Richard Phillips passed to end John Hudgens in the second period for the first Newberry touchdown. Taylor converted after the score. Bobby Rowe dashed 2 yards for the second and final Newberry TD with three minutes remaining in the game.

Presbyterian could not seem to get their offense to click. Bob Waters, trying to get his team back into the contest with the home run pass, was constantly thrown for losses by the hard charging Newberry line. Ken Webb, whose forte is offense, ironically enough stood out on defense in the last game of his really outstanding collegiate career. The Bull from Decatur, Ga., intercepted three Indian passes and deflected two more in the end zone.

So, the curtain falls on a dismal Presbyterian College football season. However, a ray of hope shines through the gloom. This year PC will lose only five seniors, Webb, Mavromat, McLaughlin, Bowman, and Powers. These men will be missed, but Coach Jones' freshmen have gained invaluable experience; and this hard gained experience may pay off in victories next season.

About the only effort that the Hose could display this season was a 0 to 0 tie with Lenoir-Rhyne. Not since 1937 have they had such a bad season. The 1937 aggregation scored only three times in losing 10 straight. So, you see, things could have been worse, but they could also have been a lot better. Let's hope the Blue Hose jell in 1958 and produce the first winning team since 1954.

Lambda Omega Rho

NEWBERRIAN

The Li'l That Was!

newberry 13   presbyterian 0

The long ten game season reached a climax with the Redskins playing their third opponent in less than two weeks. The rain, mud, and the stubborn P. C. defenses could not halt the Redskin attack and the claim of the Bronze Derby for the third straight year.

RICHARD PHILLIPS, JOHN HUDGENS, and BOBBY ROWE were the big offensive heroes as Newberry doublecrossed the Blue Hose by sticking to a wide open offense despite the slippery conditions.

PHILLIPS connected with five passes in the Redskin's first goalward march completing the last one, for 21 yards and the score, to JOHN HUDGENS. TAYLOR added the conversion to give the Redskins a 7-0 halftime lead.

BOBBY ROWE brought the fans to their feet with a dazzling 21-yard twisting, turning, and squirming run through the entire Blue Hose squad for the final teedee in the last quarter.

Newberry took complete charge of the battle and led in every department on the statistical line-up. Offensively it was the signal calling of PHILLIPS and the running of ROWE and YARNALL, combined with the outstanding defensive determination of LEE, WEED, ROSIER, SOKEVITZ, JUMPER, LEARY, and STEPHENS, that held P. C. to six first downs and accounted for the near perfect performance by the Indians.

BOBBY ROWE eludes three of the Blue Hose on his spectacular 21-yard touchdown run.

The Li'l 🎩 That Was!

THE INDIAN
NEWBERRY COLLEGE
"Home of The Fighting Redskins"
NEWBERRY, S. C., WEDNESDAY, NOVEMBER 20, 1957 — NUMBER 5

Bronze Derby Battle--Nov. 28

With turkey on the table it's Presbyterian on the schedule for the annual Thanksgiving Day classic next Thursday, November 28, at 2:00 p.m.

Presbyterian has had a rough time all season long under new Coach Frank Jones, but have turned in some fine games, especially the 0-0 tie against Lenoir-Rhyne. Last week East Carolina sneaked past the Blue Hose in the final six sconds of the game on a 50-yard pass play and a 6-0 victory.

The 0-7-1 record may not look so hot, but when P. C. hears the word Newberry they seem to improve remarkably. For sure the Turkey Day-Bronze Derby classic will be their best game.

The Indians will put the Bronze Derby, the symbol of athletic supremacy of the two schools, on the outcome of the game. This Derby has for two years been in the Indians possession with a 20-18 victory in 1955 and the 13-0 Steve Peterson inspired victory last year.

The Bronze Derby clash has been termed as the "best small college battle in the State."

The Blue Hose will not be the only team "keyed" for the game either. About 39 scarlet and grey clad Indians have their hearts set on making this outcome of the game a favorable one—for Newberry.

CENTRAL DRUG STORE
REVLON — HELENA RUBINSTEIN COSMETICS
NORRIS — WHITMAN CANDIES
PHONE 22   WE DELIVER

We Guarantee Quality Materials and Workmanship

Dennis Shoe and Sport Shop

Schumpert's
SERVICE STATION
Phone 104
Wheel Balancing
1325 Main Street
Newberry, S. C.

November 1958

November 4	Angelo Giuseppe Roncalli of Italy became and was crowned Pope John Paul XXIII.
November 4	CBS announced the cancellation of the quiz show "The $64,000 Question."
November 4	American film producer Sam Zimblast passed away during the filming of "Ben Hur," which would win 11 Academy Awards.
November 6	MLB announced KC will play 52 night games in 1959.
November 7	Albert Freedman, the producer of the United States TV show "Twenty-One," became the first person arrested in connection with the quiz show scandal.
November 10	Soviet Premier Nikita Khrushchev indicated that the "Potsdam Agreement," an agreement between the allies' control of Berlin was out of date.
November 10	A Belgian Dominican Pope, Dominique Pire, won the Nobel Peace Prize for helping thousands of refugees after World War II.
November 10	Jewelry broker Harry Winston donated The Hope Diamond to the Smithsonian Institution.
November 12	New York Yankees pitcher Bob Turley won the MLB AL Cy Young Award.
November 13	New York City Mayor Robert Wagner announced plans to establish a new baseball league called the Continental League. The League planned to fill the void of both the New York Dodgers and Giants moving to the west coast.
November 20	Now known as The Jim Henson Company, American puppeteers Jim and Jane Henson created what is now known as Muppets, Inc.
November 21	American Baseball Hall of Fame right fielder and manager Mel Ott passed away resulting from injuries in an automobile accident at the age of 49.
November 26	Polaroid introduced its first camera in the United States.
November 27	USSR repeals war-time agreements on control of Germany.
November 27	The Bronze Derby was played in Clinton, South Carolina on Thanksgiving Day. The Presbyterian College Blue Hose defeated the Newberry College Indians 22-0.

The Li'l That Was!

THE INDIAN
NEWBERRY COLLEGE
"Home of The Fighting Redskins"

VOL. 11 — NEWBERRY, S. C., WEDNESDAY, NOVEMBER 19, 1958 — NUMBER 6

Timeout
With OZZIE HERLONG

THE BRONZE DERBY RIVALRY

(Copy from the State Magazine, article written by Charles Losemann)

Everytime the teams of Newberry and Presbyterian tangle with each other in football, the spotlight shines on the Bronze Derby, possession of which is a matter close to the hearts of Newberry and Presbyterian athletes. At this moment, the Bronze Derby reposes in the trophy case at Newberry College, but whether or not it will remain in its present storage beyond November 27, is a question to be answered when Newberry and Presbyterian clash in their Thanksgiving Day football struggle. It was during the basketball season of 1947 that the Bronze Derby had its origin as the symbol of Newberry-P. C. athletic rivalry between Newberry and Presbyterian, which began early in the century, had been growing immediately on note of student antagenism that had educators of both schools worried and considering a severance of athletic relations.

The rumpus that took place when Presbyterian's basketball team played at Newberry on the night of January 30, 1947, could have been the last straw, but for the thinking of two keen-minded college publicists who salvaged tradition from apparently ruinous events. It's a short distance, only 20 miles, between the town of Newberry, S. C. and Clinton, the Presbyterian seat of learning. This proximity of battlegrounds is favorable to bringing out the student bodies of both schools in full force when their teams meet in athletics. The Presbyterian students composed a bulky segment in the Newberry gymnasium when the Blue Hose basketball team played the Indians, on the night of the memorable melee.

Before the game started, a set of Presbyterian students unfurled a large banner and suspended it in prominent view on the wall of the gymnasium behind the P. C. cheering section. "Beat h___ Out Of Newberry!" was the fighting inscription on the banner. During a moment when attention was riveted on the action on the court, some Newberry students obtained a ladder and climbed the outside of the gymnasium wall. Gaining access through a window, they ripped the banner off the wall behind the back of the P. C. Students, and climbed back out into the night they fled, carrying the banner with them. A few minutes later when the P. C. rooters noticed that the banner had been abducted from its place on the wall, the riotous rumbling grew louder in the visitors' stands.

The game was a thrilling contest, with the Presbyterian Blue Hose getting a close, 51 to 47 victory. After the game ended, the Presbyterian students were insistent about having the abducted banner returned. Tempers flared and a scuffle ensued. In the midst of all the commotion, a Newberry student got the prize of all the spoils, a derby snatched from the noggin of one of the fashionable Presbyterian youkers. The P. C. scholar went back to Clinton bareheaded. It would have taken a pack of bloodhounds to track down either the derby or the abductor that night. During the next two days, in the aftermath of the basketball struggle and the banner and derby incidents, important events shaped up in the history of Newberry-P. C. athletic relation. Frank E. Kinard, then a senior at Newberry, editor of the school paper, The Indian, and as athletic publicity director, received a letter from Charles MacDonald, the assistant professor of English and athletic publicity director at Presbyterian College. MacDonald suggested that an effort be made to recover the derby and institute it as the symbol of rivalry between the Blue Hose and the Indians. Kinard presented the plan at a convocation of the Newberry student body. The idea of the derby serving as a laurel of victory in Newberry-P. C. games, received enthusiastic endorsement from the Newberry students. The derby was recovered and conveyed to Kinard, its return being consummated through a special committee representing the student body, so that no publicity was shed on the identity of the Newberry student who abducted it. Neither has the name of the Presbyterian student who was involved in the derby incident, been publicly revealed. The derby was turned over to the W. E. Turner and Son, a Newberry jewelry firm for bronzing. The hat was packaged and forwarded to a company in Columbus, Ohio, where the casting was done.

During the early phase of the Bronze Derby rivalry, the hat was interchanged frequently between Newberry and Clinton. The first official Bronze Derby contest was the basketball game played at Clinton, on February 28, 1947, the Blue Hose winning 44-42 on a goal shot hooped by forward Vance Logan in the last two seconds of the game. With the coming of spring and baseball season, the Indians acquired the Bronze Derby temporarily with a 5 to 2 victory over the Blue Hose on the diamond, at Newberry. A few weeks later the Presbyterian baseball team defeated Newberry 3 to 2 at Clinton. The Bronze Derby remained in the possession of the P. C. student body until Thanksgiving Day 1947 when the Indians upset a favored Blue Hose team 6 to 0 in their annual football battle.

In recent years the trophy has only been interchanged at the football contest between the two rivals, but the enthusiasm still clings to the students of each school The 11th anniversary of Bronze Derby rivalry, November 27, 1958, at Clinton, South Carolina.

Bronze Derby At Stake In Turkey Day Game

THE '58 FIGHTING REDSKINS TRY FOR A SIXTH VICTORY ON THANKSGIVING DAY.

THE INDIAN

NEWBERRY COLLEGE
"Home of The Fighting Redskins"

VOL. 11   NEWBERRY, S. C., WEDNESDAY, NOVEMBER 19, 1958   NUMBER 6

The Li'l That Was!

Two big decisions will be focused on the outcome of the Thanksgiving Day classic between the "Fighting Redsgins" and the Presbyterian "Blue Hose." Will the Indians give up the Bronze Derby or take possession of it for a fourth successive year? Who will win the Little Three Conference title since Wofford has dropped both conference contests?

These and many other questions will be presented on November 27 in Clinton, S. C., at 2:30 p.m. as the Presbyterians play host to Coach Harvey Kirkland's Tribe.

Presbyterian, riding one of the faster backfields ever seen on Dixie gridirons, carries a 5-3-1 record. Coach Frank Jones' team has really improved since the '57 campaign in which the PC'uns lost all nine contests. Jones has been haunted, just as Kirkland, by many injuries which have hampered his wing-T attack. The PC'uns are on top when the series record revealed showing that they have won 26 as compared to Newberry winning 14, and three ending in a tie. Newberry has won the Turkey Day annal for the past three years, and shut out the Hosemen 13-0 in the past two contests.

Both teams downed Wofford; Presbyterian defeated the Terriers 18-14 and Newberry rallied to a decisive 21-13 victory. Presbyterian is fresh from a 42-0 mauling of a powerful N. C. team, Appalachian, while Newberry is fresh from the Wofford victory.

Both teams downed Wofford; Presbyterian defeated the Terriers 18-14 and Newberry rallied to a decisive 21-13 victory. Presbyterian is fresh from a 42-0 mauling of a powerful N. C. team, Appalachian, while Newberry is fresh from the Wofford victory.

The Tribe will be looking for a 38th win for the Indian Chief as compared to 23 losses and eight ties since Kirkland has held the reins at the small Lutheran institution. Newberry will risk their respectable 5-3 mark against the PC'uns in the Little Thursday Classic which will answer the questions of many football fans throughout the state.

Probable starting line-ups:

Newberry
LE—Jimmie Graham (190).
RE—John Hudgens (215).
LG—Roland Rosier (185).
RG—Stanley Ross (200).
LT—Gene Hendrix (190).
RT—John Temples (195).
C—Conley Jumper (195).
LHB—Bobby Rowe (155).
RHB—Richard Seastrunk (175).
QB—Vernon Prather (170).
FB—Joe Coviello (190).

Presbyterian
LE—Ted Leahy (210).
RE—Ken Gardener (200).
LG—Billy Odgen (200).
RG—John Firby (190).
LT—Richard Shrigley (200).
RT—Bill Schofill (250).
C—Mac Copeland (205).
LHB—John Lucas (195).
RHB—Jerry Lucas (175).
QB—Bob Waters (190).
FB—Ed Foster (200).

The Li'l That Was!

The Newberry Observer
AND HERALD & NEWS
"Just Like a Letter from Home"

HERALD AND NEWS ESTABLISHED 1840 — NEWBERRY, S. C., TUESDAY, NOV. 25, 1958 — NEWBERRY OBSERVER ESTABLISHED 1882

THANKSGIVING
Indians, P. C. Battle For Derby

More than just a traditional Turkey Day football rivalry is at stake Thursday when Newberry and Presbyterian College match wits on the turf of Johnson Memorial Stadium at Clinton. Kickoff time is 2 p.m.

As coveted as this Bronze Derby symbol of athletic rivalry has become since its origin in 1947, the upcoming battle holds the added attraction of Little Three championship play.

To the victor goes the 1958 title in possibly the fastest small college league in the country.

Advance ticket sales already reflect the fierce competition expected for this 44th renewal of one of South Carolina's oldest gridiron feuds. It's rated a tossup. Both teams have won five games and lost three in traveling rugged schedule routes this season, and P. C. also has recorded a tie.

Each squad is expected to be in near top physical condition.

The Bronze Derby currently resides in the Newberry trophy case, after last year's 13-0 win in Newberry. The Indians, having also won victories in 1955 and 1956, will be after their fourth straight title.

Presbyterian has dominated the series since it started back in 1913, however, the Blue Hose winning 26 games while losing 14 and tying three. Pointwise, P. C. leads 685 to 378.

Since the Bronze Derby was established in 1947, both teams have won five games each and one contest has ended in a tie.

The Derby actually became the symbol of rivalry after a Newberry-P. C. basketball game played at Newberry early in 1947. A Presbyterian student had the derby he was wearing seized by rabid Indian supporters. It became a point of contest between the two sides, until the idea was hatched to have the chapeau dipped in bronze and set up as the laurel of victory between the two schools.

At first, the Bronze Derby was put on the block for every athletic contest between the two institutions. Then it was decided a single awarding at the annual football clash would give greater emphasis to the trophy.

Some of the top ground-gainers on the South Carolina football scene will pit their talents against each other in this 1958 meeting.

No less than seven backfield men among these two arch-rivals have amassed more than 300 yards each in previous games this season. And at least two of these bid for top rushing honors in the state this year.

Leading the Newberry attack is fullback Joe Coviello, who has raced 553 yards in 133 carries for a 4.1 per carry average. His top assistant as a ball-carrier has been halfback Bobby Howe, with 317 yards in 94 carries for a 4.9 average.

Presbyterian will field a trio of impressive runners to meet this threat. Halfback Bobby Pate has clipped off 434 yards in 92 tries for a 4.7 average, while his running mate, Tony Benson, has added 399 yards in 71 for a 5.6 average. Closing in strong immediately behind this pair is fullback Bill Hill, who has 350 yards in 60 rushes for a 5.8 after taking over a starting assignment five games ago.

Subscribe to The Observer

Nagging Backache *Sleepless Nights*

Nagging backache, headache, or muscular aches and pains may come on with over-exertion, emotional upsets or day to day stress and strain. And folks who eat and drink unwisely sometimes suffer mild bladder irritation... with that restless, uncomfortable feeling.

If you are miserable and worn out because of these discomforts, Doan's Pills often help by their pain relieving action, by their soothing effect to ease bladder irritation, and by their mild diuretic action through the kidneys—tending to increase the output of the 15 miles of kidney tubes.

So if nagging backache makes you feel dragged-out, miserable... with restless, sleepless nights... don't wait... try Doan's Pills... get the same happy relief millions have enjoyed for over 60 years. Get Doan's Pills today!

DOAN'S PILLS

Tony Benson — Bob Waters

P.C. Offense Well-Balanced Among Backfield Starters

Individual offense has been well-balanced among the four starting backfield members at Presbyterian College, the statistics report for nine games indicated today.

Presbyterian and Newberry College tangle Thursday (Thanksgiving Day) at Clinton in the annual Bronze Derby battle.

The Blue Hose added substantially to their attack totals in running up 341 yards rushing and 125 more passing against Appalachian last Saturday. And no less of a key to the rousing 42-0 victory was the outstanding defensive play which held the Mountaineers to just 29 yards rushing and 61 by air.

Halfback Bobby Pate continues to maintain his rushing leadership at P. C., with 434 yards in 92 carries for a 4.7 average. Tony Benson, his running mate at the other half, moved up to 399 yards in 71 tries for a 5.6 average. And fullback Bill Hill has the best average of all, 5.8 per carry on 350 yards gained in 60 carries.

All three have scored four touchdowns each. The position, thus, does not key on any single one of these ball carriers.

For aerial fireworks, there is quarterback Bob Waters, who has completed 38 of 80 attempts for 519 yards, three touchdowns and 47.5 per cent accuracy.

Two top leaders behind this foursome are halfback John Lucas, with 223 yards in 59 carries and quarterback Nat Cole, with 12 completions in 25 attempts for 144 yards.

Three players have snagged the majority of these passes. Pate leads with 13 receptions for 254 yards. End Paul Chastain has caught 10 for 111 yards.

The Clinton Chronicle

Vol. 59 — No. 47   Clinton, S. C., Thursday, November 20, 1958

Newberry Game
Blue Hose Look To Turkey Day

Presbyterian gridmen focused their sights this week on the Little Three championship clash with Newberry here Thanksgiving afternoon after trouncing Appalachian, 42-0, last Saturday.

A sell-out crowd is expected to pack Bailey Stadium for the Turkey-Day game, which has assumed the colorful tradition of Little Thursday throughout South Carolina. This year, not only will the Bronze Derby be at stake in the 44th meeting of these old rivals, but the 1958 title of the fast Little Three will ride on every play.

The Newberry athletic department Tuesday sent for an additional block of tickets for Indian fans, after Newberry's victory over Wofford last week prompted a sell-out of the first block given them for the opponent's side of the PC field. And Presbyterian is offering its alumni a Thanksgiving dinner special in Judd Dining Hall as a game attraction.

Both teams are expected to be at near full strength, with open dates this week-end designed to give ample time to prepare for this season finale. They'll carry good records to the kickoff.

While Newberry was knocking off Wofford, 21-14, last week to set up the Thanksgiving game as a "natural," Presbyterian treated its Parents Day crowd to a tremendous display of offensive fireworks against Appalachian.

More than 600 Parents Day visitors were among the crowd which saw the Hosemen score a pair of touchdowns in each of the last three quarters to rout the Mountaineers, 42-0. Four conversions — two kicks and a couple of two-pointers by passing and running — were added to the touchdown total.

Presbyterian made 23 first downs to 5 for Appalachian. The Blue Hose offense rolled up 341 yards rushing and 125 passing, while light defensive play limited the visitors to just 29 yards on the ground and 61 by air.

Scoring by land for PC were: Halfbacks Tony Benson and John Lucas, and Fullbacks Bill Hill and Bob Mathews. Two touchdowns came on aerials — the first a 41-yard pass from Quarterback Bob Waters to Halfback Dave Morgan, the other on a ten-yard heave from fifth unit Quarterback Pat Malone to freshman Halfback Robert Sherrell.

The Li'l 🎩 That Was!

The Li'l That Was!

The Newberry Observer
AND HERALD & NEWS
"Just Like a Letter from Home"

HERALD AND NEWS ESTABLISHED 1865 — NEWBERRY, S. C., FRIDAY, NOV. 25, 1955 — NEWBERRY OBSERVER ESTABLISHED 1853

PC Impressive In Turkey Day Victory

Presbyterian's Blue Stockings wrested both the Little Three Championship and the Bronze Derby from the Indian teepee last Thursday at Clinton with an impressive 22-0 Turkey Day victory over Newberry College.

The victory gave the Hosemen their first undisputed Little Three crown since 1946.

An estimated 4,000 spectators saw P. C. take command, after Newberry showed only about five minutes of offensive threat, and completely dominated every phase of activity.

At the mid-way point, the Indians had only amassed two first downs and a net of 16 yards rushing, while P. C. was hammering out 173 on the ground for six firsts.

Impressive in the P. C. victory was a rugged line, which itself accounted for P. C.'s second touchdown.

When the final statistics were totaled, Newberry had managed only a little more showing than it had at halftime. The Tribe had only 69 rushing to 247 for the Hose, and seven firsts to 13 for P. C.

The hosts scored touchdowns in the second, third and final quarters.

Bill Hill, a fullback, scored P. C.'s first touchdown from the one-yard line, climaxing an 82-yard drive that began when a Joe Coviello punt rolled out of bounds on P. C.'s 18. Tony Benson's 20-yard run was a key factor in the drive. Shrigley kicked the extra point and P. C. led 7-0 with a minute left in the half.

Bill Schofill, a 235-pound tackle, blocked a Coviello punt on the Newberry 26 early in the second half. The ball rolled into Newberry's end zone, but Billy Ogden, a 200-pound guard, outraced Schofill and fell on the pigskin for Presbyterian's second touchdown. Again Shrigley's kick was good and the Hosemen led 14-0.

With 7:15 left in the game, P. C. scored its third counter. Fullback Bob Mathews bounced off left guard from one foot out to climax a 35-yard drive that took nine plays. Waters passed to Benson for two points.

The Indians threatened only twice. They got the opening kickoff of the game and went to P. C.'s 20, but were stopped cold.

The Tribe's biggest threat came minutes before P. C.'s final touchdown. The Hose were fourth and 12 at their 40 and Vastine went back to punt. Copeland got off a bad snap and the ball rolled by Vastine, who finally picked it up just before Temples and Hudgens collared him at the 18.

Bob Yarnall got three and Bobby Rowe carried to the 11 in two plays. It was fourth and two, and Yarnall was stopped for no gain.

ROSIER INTERCEPTS P. C. PASS: Newberry guard Roland Rosier (No. 51) intercepts Bob Waters pass in the first quarter of last Thursday afternoon's Thanksgiving Day game at Presbyterian College, which the Blue Hose won 22-0. Rosier grabbed the ball on Newberry's 33 and returned to midfield, but Newberry was penalized to the Indian 17 for clipping on the play.—Observer Photo by Marvin (Governor) Bouknight.

Famous Warrior
Buy this Bike IN-THE-CRATE and SAVE!

Bicycle
Full 26" Size!
34.88 in the crate
3.50 Down
1.50 A Week

Put on the handle bars, pedals and saddle and it's ready to ride.. takes only 15 minutes and you've saved yourself plenty!

Hurry! Stocks Limited

Firestone Home & Auto Supplies
- Top Quality Recapping
- Quick Service

John Bultenburg, Jr., Owner
913 Main St. — Phone 575 — Newberry, S. C.

Fill 'er Up At McCOY'S
—SERVICE STATION—
"Your Old Reliable"

We Appreciate Your Business!

McCoy's Cut Rate Station
College Street — Newberry

PC Captures Bronze Derby, Little 3 Title

The Newberry Indian's rally failed in the Thanksgiving Classic to give P. C. a 22-0 victory.

Presbyterian's Blue Hose dominated every phase of play, handed Newberry's Indians a 22-0 whipping Thanksgiving Day, and won their first undisputed Little Three football championship since 1946 as well as capturing the Bronze Derby trophy which has reposed in Newberry's possession for the last three years.

It was almost no contest affair from the opening kickoff. Coach Frank Jones' Blue Stockings took command of the line play and held the whip hand all the way.

The one-sidedness of the game came as a shock to most of the 4,000 spectators who shivered in chilly 50-degree weather while the Blue Hose and Indians fought it out on the field for the 44th time.

The Indians, despite the fact that they couldn't get their offense operating on all cylinders, fought for every inch of yardage the bigger and stronger Hosemen scratched out.

Outstanding for P. C.'s forward wall were Ends Ted Leahy and John Vastine, Tackles Richard Shrigley and Bill Schofill, Guards John Firby and Billy Ogden and Center Mac Copeland.

Offensive stars for the Pe'uns were halfbacks Bobby Pate, David Morgan and Tony Benson, and fullback Bill Hill.

The men who starred on defense for Kirkland's crew were center Conley Jumper, tackles John Temples and Gene Hendrix, guard Roland Rosier, end John Hudgens and quarterback Wyman Taylor.

This was PC's first fivtory over the Indians since 1954 when the Blue Hose took a 20-18 thriller. In two of the intervening games, Newberry scored shutouts. It was 13-0 last year.

The victory was PC's 27th in the series. Newberry has won 14. They played three deadlocks.

For the PC'uns, 1958 represented a great comeback. They finished a sad campaign, Jones' first in colege coaching, at the 8-1 mark last year. The record for 1958 is 6-3-1, and it includes an 18-14 decision over the other Little Three member, Wofford.

Hill scored PC's first touchdown, going over from the one to finish off an 82-yard drive with a minute left to play in the half. The march consumed 13 plays. Ogden scored the second by winnig his man-to-man, lumbering race with Schofill to the bouncing ball in the end zone.

Fullback Bob Mathews scored the third, bouncing off his left guard into the end zone from a foot out with 7:15 left in the game. His TD climaxed a 39-yard drive that took nine plays.

Shrigley kicked two extra points, the quarterback, Bob Waters, on a fake placement try by Shrigley, passed to halfback Tony Benson for a two-pointer after the third TD.

PC opened up its first scoring march from its own 18. Pate got the Hose out of trouble with a 13-yard sprint on a trap play up the middle. Hill moved around his own left end for 12 yards on the next play and PC was at its 45. They then drove to the Newberry six. Benson put it on the one and Hill crashed over from the one after being tripped by Hudgens. Shrigley converted.

Early in the third period, Hill punted dead on the Newberry one. Fullback Joe Coviello got ten and Richard Seastrunk 11 to get the Indians out of danger, but they had to punt after being stopped at their 26.

That's when Schofill shoved his hulking figure into Coviello's punt, blocking the ball and sending it into the end zone where Ogden recovered. A bad snap from ceter caused Coviello to delay in kicking.

A 13-yard punt return by Pate to Newberry's 39 put the Hose in motion for the third TD. Waters made the first down to the 25 with a 12-yard run. Benson got four, the nJerry Lucas stepped around right end for 16 to the five. The Indians held for three downs, limiting them to four yards, but Mathews made the final yard on a wedge at right guard.

Newberry's biggest threat came minutes before PC's final tally. Tte Jose were fourth and 12 at their 40 and Vastine went back to punt.

Copeland got off a bad snap and the ball rolled by Vastine, who finally picked it up just before Temples and Hudgens collared him at the 18.

Halfback Bob Yarnall got three. Halfback Bobby Rowe slammed for four yards on two carries, with Schofill putting on the brakes each time. Then Shrigley stopped Yarnall for no gain on fourth down.

Trailing Pate in the ground gaining department for PC were Benson with 51 yards on 11 tries, Hill with 50 on nine carries, and Mathews with 40 on eight cracks. Coviello was Newberry's leader, carrying 15 times for 43 yards.

PC scoring: Hill (one plunge); Ogden (recovered blocked punt in end zone); Mathews (one plunge) Extra points: Shrigley two (placement); Benson, pass from Waters.

Presbyterian 0 7 7 8—22
Newberry 0 0 0 0—0

Merry Christmas

THE INDIAN

NEWBERRY COLLEGE
"Home of The Fighting Redskins"

The Li'l That Was!

The Blue Stocking
Distinguished for Its Progress

Volume XXXVII   Presbyterian College, Clinton, S. C., December 5, 1958   No. 11

Season's Football Statistics
(Accumulative for 10 games)

RUSHING

Player	Ydage	Attempts	Avg.	TD
Pate	521	99	5.3	4
Benson	452	82	5.5	4
Hill	403	69	5.8	5
Lucas, John	211	61	3.5	3
Mathews	125	40	3.1	3

PASSING

	Ydge	Atts.	Comp.	Pct.	Int.	TD
Waters	523	86	39	45.8	8	3
Colt	167	29	14	49.0	2	0
Isger	42	4	2	56.0	1	0

PASS RECEIVING

	Receptions	Yardage	TD
Pate	13	254	2
Leahy	11	108	0
Chastain	10	111	0

TOTAL OFFENSE (Top 3)

	Rush. Ydge.	Pass Ydge.	Total Ydge.	Plays	Avg.
Waters	14	531	545	120	4.5
Pate	521	0	521	100	5.2
Benson	452	0	452	82	5.5

PUNTING

	Yards Kicked	Times Kicked	Blocked	Avg.
Gardner	166	4	0	41.5
Yastine	1137	34	3	33.4
Drake	162	5	1	32.4
Waters	155	5	0	31.0

1957-1958 COMPARISON

RUSHING:

	Ydge.	Att.	Avg.	TD
1957—	924	348	2.7	5
1958—	1969	430	4.1	24

PASSING:

	Ydge.				R
1957—	705	112	52	46.4	8 3
1958—	746	126	5.8	46.0	11 4

PASS RECEIVING:

	Receptions	Yardage	TD
1957—	52	705	3
1958—	58	746	4

PUNTING:

	Yards Kicked	Times Kicked	Avg.	Blocked
1957—	1487	50	29.3	4
1958—	1807	57	32.8	4

Hose Claim Victory In Thanksgiving Tilt

By MARTIN CHITTY

A hard-charging line which opened the way for a bevy of speedy backs led the way for a 22-0 victory over Newberry. With the victory came possession of the Bronze Derby and the Little Three Championship.

Offensive action was led by tackles Bill Schofield and Richard Shrigley, Center Mac Copeland, and End Ted Leahy, coupled with the running of backs Bobby Pate, who streaked for 86 yards in 7 carries, Tony Benson, Bill Hill, and Bob Waters. Quarterback Bob Waters effectively called plays throughout the game.

The Hose started things rolling in the second period when Hill smashed over from the one, climaxing an 80-yard drive. Shrigley kicked good for the extra point and 7-0 Presbyterian.

PC received to start the second half, but had to kick, and Hill's boot rolled dead on the Indian one foot line. Newberry drove out to the 32, but couldn't move it any further. On fourth down Schofield broke through and blocked a punt which rolled back into the end zone and Billy Ogden recovered for the TD. Shrigley again added the extra point.

In the fourth, another drive carried to the three, and Bob Mathews drove over from there. The Blue Hose went back into a kick formation, but Waters took the ball, and flipped a pass to Tony Benson for two more points and a 22-0 final score.

	Presbyterian	Newberry
First Downs	13	4
Rush Yards	267	61
Pass Yards	54	73
Punt Avg.	39	29
Penalties	55	30
Fumbles Lost	2	2

**WHAT'S NEW
at
DILLARD'S**

SUITS - SPORT COATS - TOPCOATS - by Merit
SHOES - by Nunn-Bush, Edgerton, and Jarman
PANTS - by Hubbard
SHIRTS - by Wings

L. B. DILLARD

Serving You Since 1907

November 1959

November 1	Jacques Plante of the Montreal Canadiens became the first goaltender to wear a mask in the NHL.
November 2	Charles Van Doren admitted his appearance on the television quiz show "Twenty-One" was fixed.
November 3	David Ben-Gurion won Israel's first parliamentary election.
November 4	Chicago Cubs shortstop Ernie Banks won his second consecutive MLB NL MVP Award.
November 5	The American Football League was established with 5 teams.
November 7	Professional golfer Sam Snead led the United States in a Ryder Cup win over Great Britain.
November 10	ESPN sportscaster Linda Cohn was born.
November 11	The first cartoon episode of "Rocky and Bullwinkle" debuted on NBC.
November 12	Nellie Fox of the Chicago White Sox won the MLB AL Most Valuable Player Award.
November 16	Boston business executive Billy Sullivan was awarded an AFL franchise later branded the Boston Patriots.
November 16	Rodgers and Hammerstein's "The Sound of Music" opened on Broadway in New York City.
November 17	Future Hall of Fame outfielder Willie McCovey won the MLB NL Rookie of the Year Award.
November 17	South African firm De Beers announced development of a synthetic diamond.
November 18	"Ben Hur," starring Charlton Heston premiered in New York City.
November 19	American actress Allison Janney of "The West Wing" was born.
November 19	Ford Motor Company made a decision to stop production of the Edsel model.
November 20	The United Nations adopted the Universal Declaration of Children's Rights.
November 26	Kimberly Anne Porter was born in Richmond, Indiana.
November 26	The Bronze Derby was played in Newberry, South Carolina on Thanksgiving Day. The Presbyterian College Blue Hose defeated the Newberry College Indians 20-6.

The Li'l 🎩 That Was!

The Newberry Observer
AND HERALD & NEWS
"Just Like a Letter from Home"

HERALD AND NEWS ESTABLISHED 1866 — NEWBERRY, S. C., FRIDAY, NOV. 26, 1955 — NEWBERRY OBSERVER ESTABLISHED 1865

Indians, P. C. Battle For Derby, Little Three Title

Record Crowd Expected For 2 P. M. Kickoff Here

More than the prestige of two South Carolina football giants is at stake Thursday afternoon when Newberry College and Presbyterian tangle at Setzler Stadium here in the annual Turkey Day rivalry between the two schools. The game, which begins at 2 p.m., will be played before a record Newberry audience.

Several ingredients have been added to the menu this year to give the Thanksgiving afternoon classic more prominence than it has ever had during a colorful past.

Winner of the game not only will gain possession of the coveted Bronze Derby, symbol of the rivalry between the two schools, but also can claim the Little Three grid championship. In addition, Presbyterian brings the best record in the state (6-1) against a team that has a six-game winning streak going and an overall mark of 7-2.

This is the first time in the history of the series that both teams have entered the game with brilliant records.

The game has been a sell-out for several weeks. The 3,200 seating capacity of the stadium has been increased by about 1,800 with the addition of stands at both end zones. The college already has been assured that at least 5,000 persons will attend, and pre-game predictions are that attendance may near 6,000, since the college printed 3,000 additional standing room tickets.

The Indians, under the leadership of respected Coach Harvey Kirkland, have compiled interesting statistics in addition to the high offensive scoring.

Newberry has scored 343 points during nine games, giving the Tribe a 27-point game average and one of the highest scoring offensive units in recent years.

Fullback Richard Seastrunk claims 114 points with 19 touchdowns and holds to the undisputed lead in the Carolinas in the scoring department. Also, Seastrunk has rushed 727 yards in 160 carries, giving him a 4.5 yard per carry average. Forty yards passing boosts his offensive totals to 767 yards.

Presbyterian also has a potent offense and an individual star. The Hosemen have amassed 216 points in nine games for a 24-point per game average and have held their opponents to 118 points, an average of 13 per contest.

Halfback Bobby Pate is the individual P.C. star. He dominates the Blue Hose rushing offense with 630 yards in 116 carries for an average of 5.4 yards per try. He has scored 11 touchdowns for 66 points and leads in team pass-receiving with 14 catches and 234 yards.

Newberry has other offensive powers, and so does P.C.

In addition to Seastrunk, Newberry fans can brag of the brilliant performances of quarterback Wyman Taylor, a 135-pound senior from Sumter, who has been the spark plug of the formidable double wing-T attack. Taylor is second in the Indian scoring parade with 40 points. He has kicked 25 PATs in 26 attempts, and has himself tallied four touchdowns. His elusive ball handling is superior, a fact which is attributed by the 627 offensive yards to his credit. Taylor has punted 23 times for a 36-3 average.

P. C. also will produce an exceptional quarterback in Bob Waters, who has completed 40 of 75 aerials for 620 yards, five touchdowns and an accuracy mark of 53.3 per cent.

Rounding out Newberry's first team statistics are Jimmy Lowder of Sumter who is second in rushing with 277 yards; and Henry Team, who leads the pass receiving department with 147 yards in eight catches. Team underwent surgery recently and will miss the P.C. action.

Also featuring P. C.'s offense in addition to Pate and Waters is fullback Bill Hill, who is second to Pate in rushing and total points scored. Hill has rushed 427 yards in 97 carries for a 4.4 play average and seven touchdowns.

Progress of the Indians has been perpetual since the opening 48-0 loss to The Citadel. After the second game, the Indians fielded two units and the second team has improved tremendously with each game. The team hit a climax with a stunning 35-0 victory over Wofford recently.

Coach Kirkland, whose only comment at the beginning of the season was that his team "would be representative," has prepared his Tribe for games as each was approached. Never once has Kirkland looked past the next opponent.

Kirkland already is assured of his best record since 1935 and a victory over the Hosemen would certainly add sweeter icing to an already highly embossed cake.

Not to be forgotten, however, is the fact that Tangerine Bowl bound Blue Hose are ranked among the top 16 small college teams in the National Association of Intercollegiate Athletics.

The history making Hosemen will meet Middle Tennessee State New Year's Day in their first bowl bid.

Presbyterian will field a line averaging 210 pounds, composed of ends Jon Yustine (185) of Danville, Pa., and Paul Chastain (185) of Central; tackles Bill Schofill (235) of Ft. Valley, Ga., and Cecil Morris (215) of Hazelhurst, Ga., guards Don Bridges (200) of Decatur, Ga., and Billy Ogden (200) of Macon, Ga., and center Mac Copeand (210) of Athens, Ga. The starting backfield consists of Pate (175) of Fitzgerald, Ga., quarterback Waters (185) of Sylvania, Ga., halfback David Morgan (185) of Greenville and fullback Hill (205) of McKeesport, Pa.

An all-senior forward wall will start for Newberry, headed by pre-season All-State choice Conley Jumper (190) of Swansea at center. Others in the line are ends Jimmie Graham (205) of Johnston, and John Hudgens (215) of Lynchburg, tackles Gene Hendrix (185) of Lexington and John Temples (200) of Batesburg; guards Roland Rusier (185)

Presbyterian will field a line averaging 210 pounds, composed of ends Jon Yustine (185) of Danville, Pa., and Paul Chastain (185) of Central; tackles Bill Schofill (235) of Ft. Valley, Ga., and Cecil Morris (215) of Hazelhurst, Ga., guards Don Bridges (200) of Decatur, Ga., and Billy Ogden (200) of Macon, Ga., and center Mac Copeand (210) of Athens, Ga. The starting backfield consists of Pate (175) of Fitzgerald, Ga., quarterback Waters (185) of Sylvania, Ga., halfback David Morgan (185) of Greenville and fullback Hill (205) of McKeesport, Pa.

An all-senior forward wall will start for Newberry, headed by pre-season All-State choice Conley Jumper (190) of Swansea at center. Others in the line are ends Jimmie Graham (205) of Johnston, and John Hudgens (215) of Lynchburg, tackles Gene Hendrix (185) of Lexington and John Temples (200) of Batesburg; guards Roland Rusier (185) of Barnwell and Stanley Ross (185) of Blackville. The starting backfield will consist of fullback Seastrunk (170) of Summerville; halfbacks Jimmy Lowder (160) of Sumter and Carl Harris (185) of Florence and 135-pound quarterback Taylor.

The Turkey Day series began in 1913 and Presbyterian leads it with 27 wins. Newberry has won 14 and three have ended in ties. The worst trouncing came in 1929 when Presbyterian rolled over the Tribe, 54-0. However Newberry's first official football team of 1913 whipped them twice by identical scores of 51-0.

The Indian

NEWBERRY COLLEGE
"Home of The Fighting Redskins"

Attend The Pep Rally 7:30 pm, Fri.

Attend The Pep Rally 7:30 pm, Fri.

NEWBERRY, S. C., WEDNESDAY, NOVEMBER 11, 1959

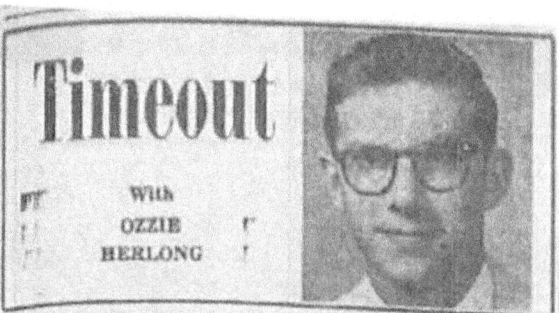

Timeout
With OZZIE HERLONG

As the football season draws to a close, the "Fighting Redskins" boast of a fine 6-2 won-loss record with two games yet to be played.

Newberry climaxes the 1959 campaign with the meeting of two Little Three Conference foes—Wofford and Presbyterian.

Coach Conley Snidows' Terriers of Wofford College started the season off slow, but have bounced back into the winning column defeating Davidson 27-20, and Furman 6-3, consecutively.

The Tangerine Bowl bound "Blue Hose" of Frank Jones lost their first contest in eight starts to the Citadel 8-0. Whether or not the Bronze Derby, which has long been a symbol of athletic rivalry between the two schools, will remain in its present storage in the trophy case at Presbyterian is a question that will be answered when the teams clash in their Thanksgiving Day struggle.

THE BRONZE DERBY: Symbol of football rivalry between Newberry College and Presbyterian College.

NICHOLS STUDIO
PHOTOGRAPHS
1311 Main St.

We Guarantee Quality Materials and Workmanship
Dennis Shoe and Sport Shop

W. E. Turner, Jeweler
Welcome, College Students
Phone 19W   Newberry, S. C.

Do You Need A
HAIRCUT?
City Barber Shop
1416 Main St.

The Li'l That Was!

The Clinton Chronicle
Volume 60 — No. 48 Clinton, S. C., Thursday, November 26, 1959

On Newberry Field
PC, Newberry to Clash Thursday in Derby Game

Presbyterian College and Newberry will clash for the Little Three championship at Newberry Thursday afternoon before a sell-out crowd of enthusiastic football fans.

It's the annual Thanksgiving engagement for the Bronze Derby, and both schools enter the game with high-scoring teams ranked among their best in history. Kickoff time is 2:00 p. m. for this 49th renewal of the old gridiron feud.

The Blue Hose sweep toward their Tangerine Bowl date on New Year's Day with a record of eight wins and a single loss. Newberry has won seven while dropping two games.

Reserved tickets for the game were sold out more than a week in advance as fan interest soared in anticipation of a wide-open contest. Both teams have well balanced attacks that score readily. In the nine previous games, Presbyterian has averaged 24 points per engagement while the Indians have averaged 27.

Two individual battles also are in prospect. On the ground PC halfback Bobby Pate, with 633 yards rushed and 66 points scored, will pit his prowess against Newberry fullback Richard Seastrunk, who has accumulated 727 yards and 114 points this season. Then, aerially, it will be a quarterback contest as Bob Waters of the Blue Hose goes against Wyman Taylor. Waters has completed 40 of 75 passes for 630 yards and 5 touchdowns, and Taylor has hit on 26 of 48 attempts for 419 yards and 1 score.

The game rates as a toss-up. Presbyterian and Newberry have played similar schedules, including five mutual opponents, and each has lost to The Citadel. Newberry's only other defeat came against Lenoir-Rhyne, which is headed for a bowl as the NAIA's top-ranked small college team.

Impressive wins by both teams in their latest engagements also have added to the build-up for this game as PC trounced Appalachian by a 34 to 0 count, while Newberry routed Wofford 33 to 6.

In the long history of this series, dating back to 1913, the Blue Hose have won 27, lost 14 and tied 2. Presbyterian shut out the Indians club last year with a 22-0 victory.

The Clinton Chronicle

Volume 60 — No. 48   Clinton, S.C., Thursday, November 26, 1959

PC Looks to Turkey Day Meeting With Newberry

Presbyterian College set football sights this week on the annual Thanksgiving finale against Newberry as this game built up into the state's highlight attraction.

A sell-out crowd already is assured for the Little Three championship clash, and each team will carry its best record in years into the game.

It rates as a toss-up. Presbyterian will move in with an 8-1 record enroute to the Tangerine Bowl. And Newberry, growing stronger each week in riding a six-game winning streak, has a 7-2 mark for the season.

High-scoring victories by both teams over strong rivals last Saturday really sent the ticket sales soaring. The Blue Hose trounced Appalachian by a 34 to 0 count, while Newberry ran roughshod over Wofford in a 35 to 0 rout.

Presbyterian scored four of its five touchdowns in the third quarter to blast the highly rated Appalachian defenses up at Boone, N.C.

Fullback Bill Hill drove 11 yards for the initial PC touchdown midway the second quarter after a 42-yard pass from Quarterback Bob Waters to End Jimmy Kolb had placed the ball in scoring position.

But it was Hill's pass interception shortly after halftime that started the avalanche. It enabled Halfback Bobby Pate to score a few plays later on a one-yard run.

Then Freshman Halfback Ronnie Hampton followed with a brilliant 95 yard runback of a pass interception which snapped the Mountaineers' most serious threat, and fumbles set up the final two scoring thrusts. Both were made by the second unit as Halfback Billy Benton swept end for one on an 11-

---

GREENACRES
On Lake Greenwood
Between Waterloo & Ware Shoals
Until November 30th
LOTS FROM $99.00 Up
EASY TERMS

Tangerine Bowl Tickets Sell Fast; Interest Rises

Tangerine Bowl tickets move quickly out of the athletic department ticket office as Presbyterian College supporters make their plans to follow the Blue Hose to Orlando on New Year's Day.

Coach Frank Jones indicated today that his office already has sold more than 800 tickets to this small college bowl classic which will pit PC against Middle Tennessee State. And Tangerine officials advise that almost 75 per cent of the Orlando stadium already has been sold out. Sixty-two per cent went before the Tennessee squad was announced as Presbyterian's opponent.

The PC athletic department received 1,200 bowl tickets, so approximately 400 remain at the two price levels of $3 and $5 each. Fans seeking tickets are urged to direct their requests to the athletic department as soon as possible.

As interest mounts, arrangements are being made for group railway transportation to Orlando—a special train out of Clinton or special coaches to leave Columbia.

Coach Jones plans to bring his players back on the practice field for at least ten days of workouts prior to Christmas. The PC squad is scheduled to arrive in Orlando on December 28 for pre-game practice sessions and to remain through the night of January 2, when the Tangerine Ball is to be held.

Presbyterian, selected almost six weeks ago as the host team for this post-season game, will make its headquarters in the San Juan Hotel in Orlando.

The Li'l 🎩 That Was!

The Newberry Observer
AND HERALD & NEWS

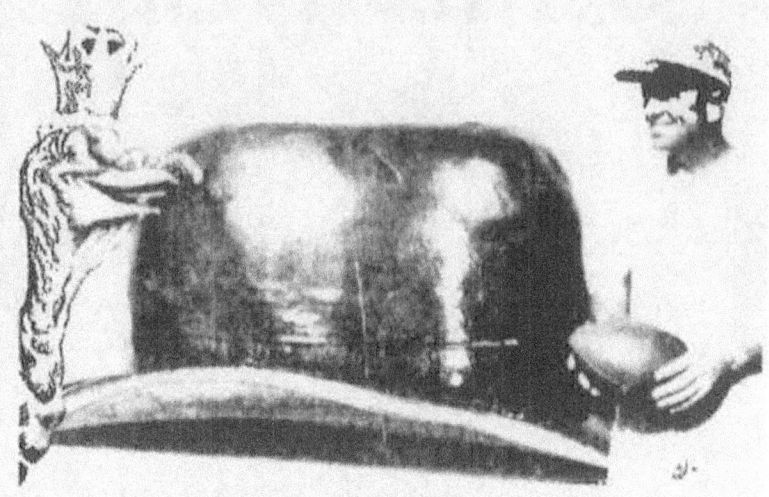

KING TURKEY AND A BRONZE DERBY CROWN: Turkey will be king of many households Thursday as another Thanksgiving Day is observed. For Newberrians, the traditional football game between Newberry and P.C. has become as much a part of the Thanksgiving observance as Mr. Turkey himself. The turkey wears his crown proudly, and so will the winning coach of the Thursday game between the Indians and Blue Hose. The Bronze Derby (center), symbol of the rivalry between these two schools, will go to the winning coach. Indian Coach Harvey Kirkland flashes a broad smile at the thought that the Derby crown might be his after the Turkey Day battle.

What's Your Opinion
Of The Newberry-P.C. Game?

MISS NITA LONGSHORE, Route 1, Kinards—I certainly hope Newberry wins it.

MISS BARBARA WARREN, Newberry College Student—I think absolutely and definitely Newberry will win because we have a much better team.

MISS FAYE WARREN, 700 Glenn St., Newberry—Newberry will win it, who else?

LARRY COCHCROFT, 818 Fair St., Newberry — I think Newberry will win because we have Seastrunk and the best line in the state.

JOHN DERRICK, Newberry College Student—P.C. has a good team, but ours is better. We'll be ready for them.

BILLY SUMMER, Newberry College Student—I believe Newberry will win it, but whichever one wins it will be a runaway.

The Li'l That Was!

The Blue Stocking
Distinguished for Its Progress

Vol. XXXVIII   Presbyterian College, Clinton, S. C., December 4, 1959   No. 9

Season Wrap-Up
Newberry Win Gives Hose 9-1 Record

Quick-thinking Bobby Pate's lateral to Ronnie Hampton proved the key play in PC's 20-6 victory over Newberry. Quarterback Bob Waters fading back to pass at his 40 found Pate in the slot at the mid-field stripe and flipped a pin-point pass to him.

Pate was immediately hit by three Indian defenders, but the alert halfback lateraled to Hampton, who was coming up after following the play, and the speedy freshman streaked over the goal. This proved to be the back-breaker for Newberry, making the score 13-6.

The Hose scored first in the first quarter, when Guard Billy Ogden intercepted a lateral at the Indian 15 and carried to the 10. Two plays later, Pate went 9 yards around end for the score. Sease converted to make it 7-0.

Neither team could get their offense rolling, and the half ended with the score 7-0.

A spirited Newberry rolled back in the second half, with HB Jimmy Lawndes and Fullback Richard Seastrunk carrying for the big yardage. Seastrunk scored from the two. A pass for two points was intercepted.

The Indians kicked off and Hill fumbled, but the Hosemen immediately recovered a Newberry fumble. Shortly thereafter Waters, Pate, and Hampton shocked the crowd with their beautiful play. Sease converted, making it 14-6.

In the fourth period, Bill Hill rolled off 50 yards in 3 plays, one of them going for 40 yards to the Newberry 5. From this point Pate slashed between guard and tackle for the score. The try for the point failed, and the final score was PC 20, Newberry 6.

Thanksgiving wrapped up the most successful PC gridiron season since 1930 when Walter Johnson's Hosemen soared to a 9-1 record.

The PC'uns began the 1959 season in a mass of thrills with squeaker victories over East Carolina 18-14, Furman 24-23, Davidson 24-21, and Wofford 27-19.

The Blue Hose defenses began to tighten and the Jones boys romped over Elon, Catawba, Tampa, Appalachian, and Newberry. The only mar of the season was the muddy 8-0 loss to The Citadel.

Aside from cheering the team, PC fans had individual heroes in the form of Bobby Pate and Bob Waters, the now famed halfback-quarterback combination.

WHITE ROSE
E. Carolina at Woodrow St.

92 Octane Regular
ONLY 29 $\frac{9}{10}$ ¢

99 Octane Premium
ONLY 32 $\frac{9}{10}$ ¢

COLLEGE CANTEEN
"Your Blue Hose Store"
BILLY and WILMA

The Li'l That Was!

The Newberry Observer
AND HERALD & NEWS
"Just Like a Letter from Home"

HERALD AND NEWS ESTABLISHED 1885 — NEWBERRY, S. C., TUESDAY, DEC. 1, 1959 — NEWBERRY OBSERVER ESTABLISHED 1855

P.C. Forgets To Play Part Of Grateful Pilgrim

Defeat Indians, 20-6, In Annual Derby Classic

Thanksgiving, originally a day when the Pilgrims shared their blessings with the Indians, was anything but that here Thursday afternoon as the Blue Hose of Presbyterian College seasoned the fatted turkey with squirts of tangerine juice and looked forward to their New Year's Day bowl bid with a glorious 20-6 victory over the Tribe.

The traditional Thanksgiving afternoon battle was played before a record crowd of 5,500 spectators under sunny skies and pleasant temperatures.

In addition to completing the season with a 9-1 record, the impressive Blue Hose also retained the Bronze Derby and clinched the Little Three grid title with a 2-0 record.

Newberry ended its season with a 7-3 mark. This is the second year Indian Coach Harvey Kirkland has won seven games since he joined Newberry College in 1952. In 1953, he compiled a 7-1-1 record and was named "South Carolina Coach of the Year."

Presbyterian will carry its flashy team to the Tangerine Bowl game with Middle Tennessee State Jan. 1.

FIRST QUARTER

Teepies' kick that opened the game was grabbed by Pate on the six, and the P. C. speedster paraded straight up the center of the field. He was brought down by Taylor on the P. C. 35. Hill found an opening for two yards to the 37, but the Hose had to punt from there after Waters had flipped two incomplete passes.

Lowder pulled Vastine's 33-yard kick out of the air on the Newberry 30 and returned it to his own 38. Harris sprinted six to the 44 and Seastrunk made his first carry of the afternoon good for two yards to the 46. Seastrunk got the call again, but missed the first and Newberry faced a punting situation. The snap from center was high, but Taylor got off a good kick that rolled dead on the P. C. three.

Pate raced to the nine. Morgan was stopped by the tough mid-section of the Newberry line, but P. C. was in motion and the Indians took the penalty. This made it second and nine on the four. Hill ran the ball out to the seven, then Waters punted.

The ball rolled through Harris' hands on the 50-yard mark and Vastine fell on it for P. C. on the Blue Stockings' 46. The Clinton invaders got only one yard and had to kick after Waters again missed his target on two successive aerials.

Lowder dropped Vastine's kick on the Newberry 10, but managed to scoop it up and traveled to the Tribe 18 before he was brought to earth. Seastrunk rammed the middle for two yards to the 20. Offense met defense on the next play and the ball recoiled straight up from the scrimmage pileup as though it had been fired from a cannon. Playing heads-up, Ogden leaped into the air, tucked it in his arms and rambled to Newberry 10 to put the Hosemen in position to score their first touchdown. Pate tried the line, but got only one yard to the nine. The next play he skirted wide to his right side and raced nine yards for the touchdown. Scase's kick was good and P. C. led, 7-0 with 8:56 left in the first quarter.

Graham caught the kickoff on his 30 and returned it seven yards. Taylor whipped an almost unbelievable lateral to Harris, who got three* to the Newberry 40. Lowder ran four more, and P. C. was penalized 15 yards giving the Tribe a first down about mid of the game. Harris ripped five to the 36, but Newberry was penalized back to the 41 for too much time, and it was second and 19. Taylor overshot Hudgens, then kept for seven to the P. C. 34, where it was fourth and three. Taylor gambled for the first, but his pass to Graham was broken up by Pate and the Hose took possession on the 34. This was Newberry's deepest penetration of the first half.

The Hose got only four yards and punted. Lowder returned the kick to the 22. Vastine crashed through and smothered Taylor for a six-yard loss on the 16, and Harris lost one to the 15. Seastrunk busted the line five to the 20, but it was fourth and 11. Taylor's punt was returned by Pate from the 40 to the 46, but P. C. was off sides and the Indians chose to kick again. This time Pate called for a fair catch on the P. C. 41 and the first quarter ended.

SECOND QUARTER

Kirkland sent in his second unit for the second quarter. Hampton and Hill got two each and Waters went back to pass. Lowder made a sensational batdown of the ball just as it was about to enter Kolb's hands on the Newberry 40. The first Newberry unit re-entered for the kick, and Waters punted dead on the Newberry 20.

Lowder failed to gain, then Yarnall added four to the Indian 24. Taylor connected with Hudgens on the 32, but P. C. was caught holding and the Indians chose instead to take the 15-yard penalty, which gave them a first on the 39. Yarnall followed with another first with a 13-yard jaunt to the P. C. 48. Four plays later, however, the Tribe punted from the 50 on a fourth and 12 situation, with Taylor's kick rolling out on the P. C. 16.

P. C. moved to the 24, but at so had to punt. Waters' kick went straight up, but took a good roll on the ground and went to the P. C. 46 before it was grounded.

Lowder fumbled, but recovered it for a one-yard loss. Taylor passed to Yarnall on the P. C. 42, and at this point Hendrix and Aber were tossed out of the game.

Taylor punted out on the nine and a new P. C. team entered the game. The Hose moved to their own 29 in seven plays, but again couldn't move against the stubborn Indian defense and punted. Yarnall took Waters' punt on the Newberry 31 and was nailed there. Seastrunk sprinted 13 for a first on the 44 and the officials gave the four minute warning. Seastrunk got the call again, this time running for six to midfield. Taylor connected with Graham for a first on the P. C. 44. Two plays later Copeland killed the drive by intercepting a Taylor pass on the 27 and returning to the 37.

One minute, 50 seconds were left in the half and Waters took to the air in an attempt to score. The P. C. quarterback completed two of eight passes, but Newberry took over on the 33 on downs with 15 seconds in the half. Harris got nine to the 42 as the half ended.

THIRD QUARTER

The Indians carried the opening kickoff of the second half all the way for paydirt. Harris caught the kick on his 10 and raced to the 23. Seastrunk managed six to the 29 and Newberry was penalized five for off-sides, making it second and nine from the 24. Taylor rolled out to pass, but elected to keep and rambled 12 for a first on the 36. Lowder broke loose on a beautiful run down the right sidelines but stepped out of bounds after a 24-yard gain. This gave Newberry a first on the 42. Seastrunk hit the line four straight times for 18 yards to the 28. Lowder circled left and for eight and a first on the 20. Lowder got five more, then Seastrunk carried three consecutive times, finally going over from the one. Taylor's pass was intercepted and Newberry trailed 7-6 with 9:33 left in the quarter.

Stephens' kick was returned by Hill from the P C 19 to the 34, where he fumbled. Bethea recovered for Newberry, but P C regained possession four plays later on the 24. The visitors had to kick from the 25 and Lowder signaled a fair catch on the Newberry 35.

Lowder carried twice to the 44, and Seastrunk got the first with a one-yard buck to the 45. Taylor kept for three to the 48 and Seastrunk reached midfield. Taylor fired a 12-yard pass to Hudgens on the P. C. 38. Lowder fumbled and Copeland recovered for P C on the 36.

Newberry's second unit was sent into the game, and the Indians drew a five-yard penalty for delaying the game, making it second and five for P. C. on their own 41. Waters passed incomplete, then hit Pate on the Newberry 45. Bethea was there to bring Pate down, but the P. C. halfback pitched out to Hampton, who lapped up the distance in rapid order for the touchdown. Scase's kick was good and P. C. led 14-6 with 58 seconds left in the quarter.

Harris returned the kick to the 25, and P. C. was penalized 15 yards for a personal foul to the P. C. 40. Harris passed incomplete, and Bethea lost seven to the 33 on the last play of the third quarter.

FOURTH QUARTER

Newberry's first team re-entered the game and Taylor's first play was an incomplete pass. Taylor kicked, and it was taken by Hampton on the Hose 30. He was hauled down on the 36. Hill carried nine to the 45, and Hampton followed with nine more to the Newberry 40 before Taylor brought him down on the Newberry five, after the P. C. fullback had sprinted 41 yards, and P. C was in position for a third touchdown. Pate got it two plays later from the four. Scase's kick was wide and P. C led, 20-6, with 12:24 left.

Hudgens was hit on the Newberry 53, after grabbing the next kickoff. Taylor fumbled and Rosier recovered for the man. Seastrunk rolled for six to the 30 and Taylor passed to Seastrunk for a seven-yard loss on the 32. It was fourth and 11 and Taylor went back to punt. The snap was over his head. Taylor picked up the ball on the three and got off a fast kick that went down to the Newberry 28 just as Vastine brought him to the ground. Taylor was shaken up, and P. C. was penalized 15 yards for roughing the kicker, giving the Indians a first on the Newberry 46. Newberry moved to the P. C. 27 in six rushing plays, then Waters intercepted a Taylor-to-Graham pass in the end zone and returned it to the P. C. 33.

P. C. was penalized back to the 11 for clipping, and Rosier crashed through and brought Hampton down on the six. P. C. had to punt from the ine and Harris returned it to the Newberry 41. But the Indians couldn't move and had to punt from the 39. Pate returned the kick 10 yards to the P. C. 31 and the Hose kept possession of the ball until Lowder intercepted Cole's pass on the Newberry 23 on the last play of the game.

For **COLDS** take **666**

Yes! You Save At McCoy's!

| REGULAR GASOLINE | **27.9¢** Gal. |
| ETHYL GASOLINE | **30.9¢** Gal. |

"DRIVE IN — FILL 'ER UP — AND SAVE"

We Appreciate Your Business!

McCoy's Cut Rate Station

College Street   Newberry

The Newberry Observer
AND HERALD & NEWS

SCENES FROM BIG THANKSGIVING DAY BATTLE AT NEWBERRY: Despite the 20-6 loss suffered by Newberry Thanksgiving Day in the traditional game with P. C. the affair produced the usual color for which it has grown famous. The

above photos depict some of the scenes that were typical of the day. Left—Coach Harvey Kirkland paces in front of the Newberry bench after the Hosemen take a two-touchdown lead. Center—Indian Halfback Jimmy Lowder (No. 47) races for a first down during the heated competition. Right—A record crowd of 5,500 persons attended the game. This shows a portion of the crowd jamming the exit after the finale had come.—Observer Photos by Marvin (Governor) Bouknight.

The Li'l That Was!

REDSKINS RACK UP SEVEN VICTORIES

With the sounding of the basketball on the hardwood floor, one is reminded that another football season has slipped into the past.

The 1959 season for the fighting Redskins was one that will be long remembered in the hearts and minds of the Indian fans. Coach Kirkland's "green team" who met Citadel early in September proved that with the correct leadership, determination, and cooperation a team can go far. In behalf of all the students of Newberry College, the INDIAN would like to say hats off to a bunch of "swell guys"!

Having only three defeats, Lenoir Rhyne, Citadel, and Presbyterian College, the "Injuns" have represented Newberry College in fine fashion.

Members of the team are John Hodgens, Lynchburg; Edgar Caddell, Moncks Corner; Willie Mickle, Ridgeway; Freddie Haley, Hartwell, Georgia; Jimmie Graham, Johnston; Jimmy Rouston, College Park, Georgia; Fred Lytle, Moncks Corner; Roger Gettys, Anderson; Maxie Knowlton, New Zion.

Also, Gene Hendrix, Lexington; Lloyd Voyles, Greenville; Donald Funston, Winter Park, Florida; John Temples, Batesburg; Charles Gaddy, Dillon; Tommy Gardner, Columbia; Stanley Ross, Blackville; Jake Hallum, Pickens, and Bobby Fore, Blackville.

Also, Jimmie Villepontesux, Jr., Moncks Corner; Mickey Stephens, Charleston; Al Freeman, Georgetown; Johnny Watson, Gatiwanta Ferry; Nick Simon, Columbia; Conley Jumper, Swansea; Ronald Corn, Greenville; Harold Douglas, Summerville; Travis Rowell, Camden.

Also, Wyman Taylor, Sumter; Bill Bethea, Dillon; Allen Wells, Baxley, Georgia; Phil Orsini, Aiken; Bobby Yarnall, Media, Penn.; Henry Team, Camden; Allen Jennings, Fairburn, Georgia; Mike Padgett, Saluda; Jimmy Lowder, Sumter; David Williams, Rockledge, Florida.

Also, Carl Harris, Florence; Tommy Truss, Baltimore, Maryland; Richard Seasirunk, Summerville; Porter Kinard, Columbia; Billy Herndon, Bennettsville; and Tommie Will, North.

Proudly We Hail—

OUR "FIGHTING REDSKINS": Throughout this season our "Fighting Redskins" have displayed outstanding school spirit and ability to come out from behind and "bring home the bacon."

The Indian
NEWBERRY COLLEGE
"Home of The Fighting Redskins"

VOL. XI — NEWBERRY, S. C., WEDNESDAY, DECEMBER 2, 1959 — NUMBER 3

MAKE
GILDER & WEEKS
YOUR
DRUG HEADQUARTERS

Newberry   Joanna

Sanitone Dry Cleaning
COMPLETE LAUNDRY SERVICE
Washed and Dried or Finished Bundles
20% Discount For Cash & Carry
The Newberry Steam Laundry & Dry Cleaning Co.
934 Main St.   Phone 319

November 1960

November 1	United States President Dwight Eisenhower indicated that the Guantanamo Naval Base in Cuba "Would be defended and he would take whatever steps were necessary because of its importance to the defense of the entire hemisphere."
November 1	Los Angeles Dodgers pitching star Fernando Valenzuela was born in Mexico.
November 1	Elvis Presley released "Are You Lonesome Tonight?"
November 1	CEO of Apple Computers Tim Cook was born.
November 2	New York Yankees outfielder Roger Maris won the MLB AL Most Valuable Player Award.
November 3	Pittsburgh Pirates Vern Law won the MLB Cy Young Award.
November 4	American comedienne Kathy Griffin was born.
November 7	Republican candidate Richard Nixon appeared on the first TV campaigning telethon, answering questions called in by viewers from 2:00-6:00 PM on ABC, CBS and NBC.
November 8	John F. Kennedy was elected United States President defeating Richard M. Nixon.
November 12	A coup against South Vietnamese President Ngo Dinh Diem was unsuccessful.
November 13	Entertainer Sammy Davis Jr. married actress May Britt in Hollywood, California.
November 13	A fire in a movie theater in Amude, Spain killed 152 children.
November 14	Ray Charles' "Georgia On My Mind" reached #1 in the United States.
November 16	Clark Gable, star of "Gone With the Wind," passed away at the age of 59 years old.
November 16	Dick Groat of the Pittsburgh Pirates won the MLB NL Most Valuable Player Award.
November 17	American actor, singer, drag queen and TV personality RuPaul was born.
November 23	American television personality and reporter Robin Roberts was born.
November 24	The Bronze Derby was played in Clinton, South Carolina on Thanksgiving Day. The Presbyterian College Blue Hose defeated the Newberry College Indians 7-6.

The Li'l That Was!

The Indian

Snag the Blue Hose — NEWBERRY, S. C., WEDNESDAY, NOVEMBER 23, 1960 — *Follow the Indians To Clinton*

Indians Meet Blue Hose On Derby Day

The 1960 Fighting Redskins

Both Newberry and Presbyterian were getting in tune this past weekend for the Turkey Day Classic to be played Thursday, November 24, in Bailey Stadium at Clinton, South Carolina.

Newberry is fresh from a 27-0 trouncing over Carson-Newman. Added incentive for a victory comes from several factors hovering in the Indian camp: (1) the Indians need this game to have their ninth consecutive winning season as their present record is 5-5, (2) the Indians want to regain the possession of the Bronze Derby, and (3) the Indians want revenge from last season's 28-6 loss.

Moreover, the Tribe will be a threat in the air and on the ground. Freshman quarterback Tom Gorman of South Plainfield, N. J., has been a passing sensation for the last few games. Already he has completed 39 passes, including six touchdown tosses, for 595 yards. Percentage-wise he has completed 51. Senior fullback Richard Seastrunk of Summerville has boosted his four-year career total to 1,719 yards. He has amassed 638 yards this season and averages 4.5 yards per carry. Two of the South's finest backs, Jimmy Lowder of Sumter and Carl Harris of Florence, flank Seastrunk. Lowder is a sophomore at the Lutheran institution where thus far this season he has totaled 598 yards rushing with a 6.7 yard per carry average. Harris, a junior, has 441 yards with a 6.1 yard per carry average. Harris leads the team in scoring with 54 points, and Lowder is second with 48.

On offense, Presbyterian, fresh from a 22-0 victory over Elon, will mix the effective passing of quarterback Bobby Joiner with the rushing onslaughts of fullback Bill Hill and halfbacks Jimmy May, Ronnie Hampton, and Billy Benton in an effort to keep this point clicking on the scoring register.

Defensively, the jolts will be on the left side of the line at the guard and tackle slots where Gordon Darby and Tommie Witt will swap leather with Presbyterian's Cilly Ogden and Sonny Dubose.

Headquarters For Fine Cosmetics

We feature cosmetics by Revlon, Yardley, Tussy, Cara Nome, Old Spice, Max Factor and hypoallergenic cosmetics by Dubarry.

MAIN STREET PHARMACY
1212 MAIN STREET • PHONE 610

REGISTERED PHARMACISTS ALWAYS ON DUTY
PHONE 610 — FREE DELIVERY SERVICE

The Clinton Chronicle
Vol. 61 — No. 47 Clinton, S. C., Thursday, November 24, 1960

THANKSGIVING

PC, Newberry to Clash Here Thursday at 2:30

Presbyterian College will seek its third straight Little Three championship when Newberry invades Johnson Field for the annual season-closing Thanksgiving clash Thursday afternoon.

The Bronze Derby, symbol of football supremacy between the two schools, also will be on the block as these two high-scoring squads answer the 2:30 p. m. kickoff. A capacity crowd is expected.

PC gridmen under Coach Frank Jones have laid seige to both the Derby and the crown of this fast small college conference for the past two years.

With a sound victory over Wofford long since under their season belts, the Blue Hose need only a triumph to retain undisputed possession of the Little Three championship.

A Newberry win, on the other hand, would end the title race in a three-way deadlock, since Wofford whipped the Indians in their 1960 contest.

Comparisons are not only odious but downright dangerous, where football scores are concerned. This is especially true in the hotly contested Little Three, where rivalries date back for almost 56 years. But as a matter of passing record, it might be pointed out that Presbyterian defeated Wofford, 21 to 7, earlier this season, after which the Terriers nosed out Newberry by a 14-13 count.

The Hosemen will be favored in this 46th engagement between the two schools. They have been rolling in high gear for the past three games and have won five of their last six encounters after dropping the first two.

(Continued on page four)

PC, Newberry

(Continued from page one)

Scores of the last two games have been especially impressive as the Hosemen trounced East Carolina, 27 to 7, and then Saturday rolled over Elon 32 to 6 as fullback Bill Hill personally accounted for 132 yards rushing.

Newberry, while less consistent this year, has produced big scoring punches to smother recent opponents. It's an explosive ball club which mauled Western Carolina 39 to 6, and then Carson-Newman 27 to 0 on the past two week-ends.

The annual Thanksgiving clash between Presbyterian and Newberry has attracted increasing attention from South Carolina fans who like to mix colorful football with their holiday activities.

The Blue Hose bested over Newberry 38 to 6 last year enroute to the post-season Tangerine bowl. And through the years, dating back to 1913, PC teams have managed to win 28 games of the series, compared to 14 for Newberry and just three that ended in ties.

Ten seniors will be playing their final ball game for the Garnet and Blue this Thursday afternoon. They are: Co-captains Bill Hill at fullback, and Jimmy Kolb at end; End Jim Vantine, tackles Billy Ogden Stone and Don Bridges, halfback Billy Benton, halfback Bruce Barnes, and center Don Aber.

The Li'l That Was!

The Newberry Observer
AND HERALD & NEWS
"Just Like a Letter from Home"

HERALD AND NEWS ESTABLISHED 1865 — NEWBERRY, S. C., FRIDAY, NOV. 25, 1960 — NEWBERRY OBSERVER ESTABLISHED 1865

Indians, Blue Hose In Annual Turkey Day Battle

Locals Hope to Salvage Winning Season, Retain Bronze Derby

The Newberry College Indians will be after a little more than the traditional Bronze Derby as they go against Presbyterian's Blue Hose in Clinton's Johnson Stadium Thursday at 2 p.m.

Coach Harvey Kirkland's lads, currently sporting a 5-3 record, will be trying to avoid a losing season, something the Indians have escaped since Coach Kirkland's initial year as Chief Indian back in 1952.

Indians Underdogs

Newberry will enter the annual classic with arch-rival PC being the favorite, but the Indian coaches think they have an advantage in comparing the two backfields and hope to exploit this for a victory.

"Coach Jones (PC's Frank) has a fine line," Kirkland informs, "and they're much bigger and faster than are we. However, we feel our backfield is better and think we have a good chance for an upset."

Newberry will take a two-game win streak into the Turkey Day brawl including their 27-0 win over Carson-Newman here last Saturday night.

PC Is 5-3

The Blue Hose, with a 5-3 record, have won three straight including their impressive 32-6 decision over Elon at Clinton last Friday.

The Indians were worked long and hard in practice Monday and Tuesday. Today (Wednesday) drills were scheduled to be light as per usual on the day prior to a game.

Newberry, by winning Thursday, could throw the Little Three championship into a three-way tie. Wofford has completed its season and lost to Presbyterian, 7-21, and beat Newberry, 14-13, in league play.

9th Winning Season

The Indians will be gunning for their ninth consecutive winning season and repossession of the coveted Bronze Derby which has been in Clinton for the past two years. Newberry's latest win over the Blue Hose was their 13-0 decision in 1957.

By way of comparative scores, PC would appear to have the edge. Other than the Wofford game they also downed Elon and East Carolina (27-7) while Newberry lost 7-0 and 21-0, respectively.

Newberry, however, has shown better against some common opponents. They lost to The Citadel, 6-19, while PC fell, 0-27. Against Catawba, the Indians won, 45-7, the Blue Hose won, 20-0.

Presbyterian lost to powerful Lenoir Rhyne 0-9 while Newberry was crushed, 12-34.

Morale High

Coach Kirkland said today (Wednesday) that the morale of the Indians was very high and that physically they were in pretty good shape with only the usual minor bruises and hurts.

Newberry's starting lineup Thanksgiving Day will probably find Edgar Caddell and Fred Hale at ends; Gordon Darby and Mickey Stephens, tackles; Tom Witt and Jimmy Houton, guards; Harold Douglas or Travis Rowell, center; Tommy Gorman, quarterback; Carl Harris and Jimmy Lowder, halfbacks; and Richard Seastrunk, fullback.

The game will mark the career finale for three of the above Indians plus a reserve player. Regulars Seastrunk, Douglas and Stephens will be playing their last game for Newberry as will tackle George Bruce.

Roaring along on a rising offensive tide that has produced five wins in the past six starts and a total of 70 points in the three most recent games, Presbyterian College will seek to extend its victory splurge against arch-rival Newberry at Clinton Thursday afternoon.

Statistical charts show the Blue Hose now averaging 253.2 yards-per-game in total offense against the eight opponents to date. Their forward spurt both yardage and point-wise received considerable acceleration with the impressive 32 to 6 triumph over Elon last Saturday night.

Fullback Bill Hill of McKees-Hill Tops

port, Pa., turned in his top performance to date by adding 152 yards to his season total, which now stands at 403 yds. in 103 carries for an average of 4.0 yards-per-carry. He's top rusher in the PC ground attack, now hitting at a team average of 161 yards-per-game.

Sophomore halfbacks Jimmy May of Greenwood and Ronnie Hampton of Kannapolis, N. C., battle for number two rushing honors. May has turned in 233 yards in 68 carries for a 3.3 average and leads team scoring with 26 points, while Hampton has added 222 in 59 tries for a 4.1 average. Halfback Billy Benton of Chamblee, Ga., follows with 180 yards in 39 for 4.7.

Good Passing

Quarterback Bobby Joiner, a junior from Macon, Ga., paces the Hose aerial game which has averaged 91 yds-per-engagement thus far. Joiner himself has accounted for 483 of the total 720 passing yards with a 54-7 per cent accuracy record that shows 41 completions in 75 attempts.

Meanwhile, showing aerial promise in his brief appearances in the last three ball games has been freshman quarterback Art Williams of Cairo, Ga. His seven completions in 12 tosses have produced 94 total yards and an accuracy mark of 58.3 per cent.

Hill and Hampton continue as top receivers for this throwing game — Hill, having 15 receptions covering 194 yards and Hampton eight for 171 yards. End Jon Vastine of Danville, Pa., dominates the punting game with a 38-yard average of 40 boots.

Fullback Hill, halfback Benton and end Vastine are the seniors listed among these individual statistical leaders. They will be surely missed next year, as will these other seven players who head into their final game as Hosemen:

End Jimmy Kolb of Sumter, tackles Billy Ogden of Macon and Hardy Ledbetter of Ridgeland, guards Bill Sease of Clinton and Don Bridges of Clinton, center Don Abee of Greenville and fullback Bruce Barnes of Concord, N. C.

The Clinton Chronicle

Vol. 61 — No. 48   Clinton, S.C., Thursday, December 1, 1960

Christmas Parade Slated for 5:00

PC Closes Good Season With 7-6 Newberry Victory

Presbyterian College wrapped up another successful football season on Thanksgiving afternoon with a 7 to 6 victory over Newberry which gave the Hosemen a stout 6-3 record for the year and their third straight Little Three championship under Coach Frank Jones.

This finish climaxed a remarkable comeback for the PC gridmen. After dropping their first two games, they roared back to take six of the next seven encounters. Jones shared credit for his success with assistant coaches, Clyde Ehrhardt, Vic Spooner, Charles Musselwhite, Billy Tiller, and Mac Copeland.

Except for the lopsided 0 to 27 loss to the Citadel after two open dates, the Blue Hose performed well even in defeat in bowing 12 to 21 to Furman and 0 to 8 to Lenoir Rhyne's top-ranked small college power.

The victories came in this fashion: 21 to 7 over Wofford, 6 to 0 over Davidson, 30 to 0 over Catawba, 27 to 7 over East Carolina, 32 to 6 over Elon, and then the 7 to 6 Bronze Derby triumph over Newberry.

The Blue Hose scored a total of 125 points during the nine games, 32 of them by halfback Jimmy May, and 30 by fullback Bill Hill. They rolled to 2,192 total yards, with Hill once more setting the pace. He plunged for 510 of the 1,377 rushing yards on 111 carries. May added 272 on 84 tries, while halfbacks Ronnie Hampton and Billy Benton had 242 and p23, respectively.

Presbyterian got 815 of its total yardage through the air. Quarterback Bobby Joiner led the way in this department, completing 45 of 88 passes covering 544 yards. His understudy, Art Williams, hit on 8 of 14 for 120 yards.

Defensively, the Blue Hose headed by such smashing linemen as tackle Billy Ogden, end Jon Vastine, and guard Sonny DuBose, limited the combined opposition to just 62 points, lowest defensive figure of any other South Carolina college.

Presbyterian won its game against Newberry on the extra point conversion of freshman end Louis Hidinger. The Hosemen scored the first time they got their hands on the ball, moving 71 yards on ten plays, with Hill crashing center for the remaining yard midway of the first quarter.

Newberry scored in the second period after a fumble by PC's May had given the Indians the ball on the Hose 23-yard line. Fullback Richard Seastrunk hit for the touchdown on a two-yard plunge, but the passing attempt at a two-point conversion failed and thereby sealed the fate of the ball game. Two desperate field goal tries by Newberry later in the game also were unsuccessful.

Indians Go Down Fighting At P. C., 7 To 6

Kirkland Suffers First Losing Season Since '52 As Hose Retain Bronze Derby

Underdog Newberry, playing inspired football, got more than its share of the breaks, but couldn't cash in when the chips were down as arch-rival Presbyterian wrapped up the Little Three Championship with a 7-6 decision at Clinton last Thursday.

The Indians pretty much dominated play in this 46th Bronze Derby classic, a much more exciting contest than the final score would indicate.

The host Blue Hose, who finished their season with six wins in nine outings, drove 71 yards for their touchdown the first time they had possession of the football. Fullback Bill Hill, who earned only 17 yards in eight carries during the afternoon, scored the six pointer from a yard out on what was PC's 10th offensive play.

Some 7:49 remained in the opening period when Lewis Ridinger came in to split the uprights on the PAT kick for what proved to be the winning point. Ridinger had previously booted only eight extra points out of 17 attempts.

The Blue Hose pushed to the Indians' 37 late in the first half, advanced to the Newberry 35 just before the third quarter ended and moved to the visitors' 41 in the game's waning moments.

However, other than these mild threats the Indians' defense contained the mighty PC attack which had scored 79 points in the three preceding games. Meanwhile, the Indian offense repeatedly knocked on the door.

INDIAN SCORE

Newberry's score came with 3:37 remaining in the half as fullback Richard Seastrunk boosted his season scoring total to 38 points with a one-and-half yard burst through the middle.

The Indians elected to go for two, but failed as halfback Carl Harris was dropped in his tracks at the two by Hill after gathering in a flat pass from quarterback Tommy Gorman.

Newberry capitalized on one of their many breaks to start this scoring move.

Guard Billy Kaigler roared through to sack halfback Jimmie May on an attempted pass causing a fumble which tackle Mickey Stephens recovered for the Indians on the PC 23.

Three of the four times Newberry had the ball previously they were forced to punt. This time, however, the Redskins weren't to be denied.

GORMAN WAS KEY

Gorman, the freshman from South Plainsfield, N. J., was the key man in the 23-yard drive. On third and eight from the 21 he found end Fred Haley open at the 12 and two plays later Haley was again the target on a six yard aerial to the three.

Seastrunk tried the PC line once, but was stopped about a yard-and-a-half short of paydirt. He made good on the next try.

The Indians just missed a score minutes later after PC had rallied to a pair of first downs before missing on a fourth down pass from their 48.

Gorman, who completed seven of 21 passes for 67 yards during the Turkey Day brawl, faded back to pass with 1:22 left in the half. He was trapped and thrown for a seven yard loss, but after sending Seastrunk back to the 48 on a draw, he hit Harris on a screen pass to the left and the junior speedster cut back across field for a 30 yard advance to the PC 13 before being hauled down from behind.

Halfback Jimmy Lowder, who had gained five yards in his only previous carry, circled end for five more to the eight and time was called with 32 seconds left.

NARROW MISS

Haley got the first down at the three with another leaping grab of a Gorman pass and freshman Rick Smith was called on for a field goal attempt with less than 10 seconds remaining.

Smith's first college try was a narrow miss, the 15-yard boot bouncing off the left upright.

Newberry came back after intermission with an inspired defense, especially against Hill and the Blue Hose passers. The PC fullback, who had rolled up 493 yards in eight previous games, managed only eight yards during the final 30 minutes.

Among the red jerseys consistently in the PC backfield all afternoon was those belonging to Indians Haley, Stephens, Kaigler and guard Tommie Witt.

The Blue Hose received a tough break after failing to move the ball and getting a tremendous punt from his 41 only to have the ball roll against the goal-line flag, barely missing going out of bounds on the one foot line.

STOPPED AGAIN

Gorman, who played on every offensive play, directed the Indians to three first downs before the drive bogged down on the Hose 32. The fresh quarterback, only promoted to the starting unit two weeks ago, sparked the move with 14 yards on four crucial occasions.

The Tribe got the ball again with one minute remaining in the third period and drove 40 yards to the PC 47 before running out of gas.

The game's outcome appeared to be decided when Hill intercepted a Gorman pass on Hose 35 with less than six minutes remaining.

PC proceeded to move into Indianland at the 41, but the Newberry line stiffened and shoved the invaders back to their own 44 in two plays.

After Hill's punt, Newberry made their final bid for victory starting at their 21 with 2:22 left.

TEMPERS FLARE

Lowder's four yards and a personal foul against PC moved the Indians forward to the 40. Seastrunk added three and Lowder got four more to the 47 as 1:50 showed on the clock.

Harris picked up a first down to the PC 40 and a few tempers flared on the play. No physical harm was done, but the clock continued to tick away during the discussion.

Referee Lou Bello signaled offsetting personal foul penalties and Newberry went into huddle. However, Bello then jogged over to the sidelines and, after conferring with the timer, the scoreboard clock was moved back 10 seconds to read 1:20.

Gorman spotted Harris in the open on the next play, but the speeding halfback let the ball slip through his fingers at the 10 yard line.

Still fighting, general Gorman sent Lowder wide to the right for 15 yards and a first at the 30. Less than a minute remained as Lowder ripped off-tackle for another first at the 24 and Gorman passed to Haley for 11 yards and the third consecutive first down at the 13.

SECOND TRY

Gorman, fading back to pass, was dumped by several blue jerseys on the 21 and, the seconds ticking away, Smith came in for his second field goal try.

Kicked as the final gun sounded, Smith's effort was far short as Hill fielded the ball on the five yard line.

Lowder, who had a 6.9 average going into the season finale, rolled up 76 yards in seven tries to top all rushers. Seastrunk was next with 61 yards in 19 carries.

Halfback Billy Benton topped the winners with 43 yards in eight attempts and May garnered 40 in 16 calls.

The loss gave Newberry a 3-6 record for the season to mark their first losing campaign since Coach Harvey Kirkland's initial year as Chief Indian in 1952.

The Blue Hose retained possession of the coveted Bronze Derby for the third straight season.

The play-by-play:

FIRST QUARTER

Captain Harold Douglas was joined by the three other senior Indians — Seastrunk, Stephens and tackle George Bruce—playing their final college game for the pre-game conference with PC Co-Captains Hill and Jimmy Kolb. Newberry won the toss and elected to receive.

Although a drizzling rain had stopped only minutes before the game time, the Johnson Stadium Field was in excellent condition and around 3,500 fans were on hand.

Lowder returned Ridinger's kickoff 24 yards to the 30. Seastrunk bulled to the 33. Gorman got a yard on rollout, but then lost three after failing to spot a pass target. On fourth and nine, Knowlton punted dead on the PC 29.

May circled end for 12 to the 41. Hill bucked to the 45. Ronnie Hampton sliced off-tackle to the 48. Joiner hit May around the Newberry 45 and the halfback advanced down to the 26 for a 26 yard gain.

Benton scooted around end behind excellent interference for 12 yards and PC's third first down at the 14. May got nine, Benton three, and May picked up another first with three yards following play. Ridinger split the uprights for a 7-0 lead.

Lowder returned the kick 26 yards to the 28. Seastrunk, with poor blocking, managed two, then three yards. Gorman couldn't find a receiver open and ran for four to the 37. With fourth and one, Knowlton punted dead on the PC 30.

Hill went up the middle for three, but Haley dropped May at the 37 for a two yard loss. Joiner hit Vastine with a 16 yarder, but after eluding a couple would-be tacklers, the Blue Hose end was surprised with a jarring tackle by Haley from behind and fumbled, Harris recovering on the Indians' 48.

Still plagued with poor blocking, Seastrunk got two. Gorman's pass was broken up. Harris gathered in a screen pass from Gorman, but lost three yards on the play. On fourth and 11, Knowlton kicked and Hampton fair catched on the 18.

Hill plowed to the 20 and Benton was stopped for no gain as the quarter ended.

SECOND QUARTER

May got two more and Hill punted on fourth and six. Lowder received the boot and was stopped after a two-yard return at the Indians' 45.

Harris recorded Newberry's initial first down with a 11-yard sprint to the PC 44. Seastrunk kept the spark burning, ripping down the middle for 15 and a first at the 29.

Seastrunk pushed to the 28, Lowder circled left, cut back for five to the 23. Gorman, back to pass, was again crowded and lost to the 25. Harris circled right for four to the 21, two yards short of the first down.

May earned six to the 27. Hill got another to the 28. Benton sliced off-tackle for five and a first at the 33. May, running wide, was thrown for a five-yard loss on the 28 by linebacker Bill Herndon shooting through. Joiner, with pressure on, overthrew May. May took a pitch-back and, attempting to pass, fumbled on a jarring tackle by Bill Kaigler, Stephens recovering for Newberry on the PC 23.

Harris lost two, Seastrunk gained four to the 21. Haley made a shoe-string grab of Gorman's pass at the 12 for a first.

Seastrunk bulled to the nine. Haley, surrounded by three defenders, made a leaping grab of Gorman's pass at the three, just inches short of a first. Seastrunk ripped 1½ yards for a first-and-goal just short of the one and bulled into the end zone on the following play.

Trying for two, Gorman passed into the flat, but Harris was dropped in his tracks at the one by Hill.

Joiner returned the kickoff to the 34. Joiner passed incomplete, but tried again to hit Kolb near the 44. On third and inches, fullback Paul Stewman pushed to the 45 for the first.

Art Williams and Joiner began alternating at quarterback with less than three minutes remaining in the half. Joiner lost seven after failing to find a receiver, but Williams hit May with a 28-yarder to the Indians' 31.

Joiner passed incomplete. May, after a pitchback from Williams, overthrew his intended receiver. Joiner, with Stephens hanging on to one arm, was charged with intentional grounding, moving PC back to their own 48. On the fourth and 15, the Blue Hose elected not to punt and a Williams' pass was broken up.

With 1:22 remaining, Gorman lost six on a pass attempt to the 44. Seastrunk garnered four on a draw. Gorman pitched a screen toss to Harris near midfield, and the fleet halfback ran to the left sideline, then cut across the field to the 13 before being hauled down from behind after the 30 yard advance.

With 22 seconds remaining, Lowder ran wide for five to the eight. Haley made another leaping grab of a Gorman pass and was up-ended on the spot at the three.

Ten seconds remained as the Indians lined up for a field goal attempt with first and goal at the three. No. 3 fullback Rick Smith's effort, his first try in college football, just missed as it bounced off the left upright on the goal post.

THIRD QUARTER

Joiner returned the second half kickoff to the 36. Hill got four and May one to the 41. Joiner passed incomplete and Hill's tremendous boot rolled into the flag at the goal nearly going out-of-bounds on the one foot line.

Seastrunk plowed up the middle for four and got five more to the 20. Gorman picked up the first with a sneak to the 21.

Gorman advanced to the 42 on an option and earned eight more after missing a handoff to Seastrunk. Gorman carried again and struggled for three for a first at the 44.

Seastrunk bulled to the 46 and then was stopped for a no gain, however PC was penalized 15 yards for a personal foul and Newberry got a first down on the Hose 38.

Gorman's pass was knocked down. Lowder ripped off-tackle for five, but Seastrunk failed to gain and Knowlton punted on fourth and five.

The punt, partially blocked by a PC lineman, was downed by an Indian inside the 10, giving the Blue Hose automatic possession on their 20.

Benton got five and Hill added another to the 28. May gained around five and fumbled forward, teammate Keith Richardson recovering at the 37.

Benton ran wide for five and picked up a first with an 11 yard burst to the Newberry 47.

May was held to one on a wide sweep. Hampton got two on another end run. May crossbucked to the 39 and Hill, on fourth and two, punted out-of-bounds at the seven.

Seastrunk hit the middle for five yards in two plays and the period ended.

FOURTH QUARTER

Lowder got loose on a wide play and appeared touchdown-bound until being bumped after gaining 33 yards by Haley in a maneuver to elude the final PC defender. Lowder fumbled on the play, but Haley recovered on the Indians' 45.

Harris garnered three, but then lost five back to the 42. An offside penalty against PC moved Newberry back up to the 48. Gorman, failing to spot a receiver, managed five to the Hose 47, but was two yards short of the first down. Knowlton's boot rolled dead on the 15.

With 11:40 remaining in the contest, May managed three yards in two tries before Hampton slipped off-tackle for seven and a first at 25.

Hill was held to three in two attempts and May could manage only two more forcing Hill to punt on fourth and five from the 30.

Travis Rowell took the short boot on the 48 and was downed at the 46. With 7:30 left, Harris got to the 49, but Gorman's pass was intercepted by Hill who fell out-of-bounds on his 30.

Williams lost three and Benton gained five to the 41. Joiner hit Hammock with a 16 yarder carrying to the Newberry 44.

Hampton advanced to the 41, but was thrown back to the 42 on the next play. Joiner, fading back to pass, was trapped on the PC 44 by Kaigler and tackle Charles Haggard. On fourth and 22, Hill punted to Harris who was stopped on the 21.

With 2:22 remaining, Lowder got four and a 15 yard personal foul penalty moved the Indians out to the 40.

Seastrunk bucked to the 43. Lowder sliced off-tackle to the 47 as 1:50 showed on the clock. Harris got five for a first at the PC 40 and a few tempers flared. Offsetting personal foul penalties were called.

The Indians broke out of the huddle with 1:10 remaining, but time was called and the clock was moved back 10 seconds. Gorman spotted Harris clear around the 10, but the perfect pitch was dropped by the speeding halfback. Lowder surprised with a wide run, earning 13 to the 30 and 1:04 remained.

Lowder picked up another first with a 12 yard off-tackle dash to the 24.

Gorman hit Haley at the 13 for the third consecutive first down and only seconds remained.

Trying to pass, Gorman was smothered at the 21 and the clock ticked on. Smith entered the game and got off his second field goal attempt as the game ended. The effort was considerably short, Hill fielding the ball around the five yard marker.

—*Mac Hill*—

On The Level

So Close And Yet So Far

The year 1960 may be remembered as the season Newberry lost the Little Three football championship by two points —Wofford, 14-12, and Presbyterian, 7-6.

"Two more points in each of those games would have made quite a difference," a dejected Harvey Kirkland sighed following the traditional Bronze Derby classic at Clinton last Thursday.

The loss to the arch-rival Blue Hose was the Indians' sixth of the season and marked their first losing campaign since Coach Kirkland's initial year at Newberry in 1952.

Bitter Pill

Missing the winning season was tough to swallow, but the pill was more bitter in that the Indians played such an inspired brand of football in the Turkey Day game, yet were denied victory.

PC Coach Frank Jones claimed his boys did not play their best. This is true, yet the fired-up performances of the Tribe was probably the key to the sub-par play of the Blue Hose.

"Our kids didn't follow instructions very well . . . we played poorly," Coach Jones announced following his sixth win in PC's ninth and final outing of the season.

"You didn't see them whooping it up, did you?" he asked after making a trip through the near silent dressing room. "They know they played a lousy game.

"Of course, it's always nice to win," Coach Jones continued, "and I'll take one-pointers any time I can get them. Yessir, 10 years from now it's just another win and nobody will remember the score.

"Newberry has a fine football team and they played well today," he added, "but, they didn't do anything we didn't expect . . . there were no surprises.

Impressive Indians

"I was especially impressed with their halfbacks (Jimmy Lowder and Carl Harris) and their ends (Edgar Caddell, Fred Haley and Willie Mickle) in today's game," Jones opined. "Of course, their fullback (Richard Seastrunk) is good as any you'll find.

"Well, here we've finished 6-3," the PC coach smiled, "and before the season started we would probably have settled for a 3-6 record. Our boys have come a long way this year and I'm really proud of them."

The Newberry Observer
AND HERALD & NEWS

The Indian

Attend Singers Concert Sunday — *Support Indians At Home*

VOL. 33 — NEWBERRY, S. C., WEDNESDAY, DECEMBER 7, 1960 — NUMBER 11

PC Retains Derby

By BILL MARJENHOFF

The Newberry College "Fighting Redskins" closed out their 1960 football season on Thanksgiving Day, losing a heart-breaker to Presbyterian College 7-6, making the "Blue Hose" the Little Three Conference Champs. The loss to Presbyterian gave the "Indians" its first losing season since 1952, the year Head Coach Harvey Kirkland came to the Lutheran institution. This year's record stands 5-6, but the "Tribe's" record since '52 is 47 wins, 33 losses, and eight ties.

Spearheading the "Indian" attack this season were senior Richard Seastrunk of Summerville and two of the state's finest running halfbacks, Jimmy Lowder of Sumter and Carl Harris of Florence. Seastrunk, averaging 4.2 yards per carry this season, led the "Redskins" in total offense with 697 yards. During his four-year career at Newberry, "Sea" has amassed a total of 1,778 yards rushing. Close behind Seastrunk in rushing was sophomore halfback Jimmy Lowder with 680 yards for a 7.2 yards per carry average. His running mate, Carl Harris, led the Tribe with 54 points to his credit. The Newberrians averaged 280 yards per game while their opponents averaged only 203. The Indians also gained approximately 1,000 more yards than their opponents this season.

Only four players will be graduated this year. They are: Richard Seastrunk of Summerville, Harold Douglas, also of Summerville, and Mickey Stephens and George Bruce of North Charleston.

BOBB'S Esso Servicenter
1523 Main St.   Phone 792

Henry's Barber Shop
Voight Dominick
Henry Barnette
College at Main—Downstairs

Royal Cleaners
"Beautiful Dry Cleaning"
1107 Caldwell   Phone 276-1411
Shirts on Hangers
"Where Quality Reigns"

CARTER'S RECORD MART
2716 College St.
Phone 276-5537
OPEN 9 A. M. to 6 P. M.
Monday - Saturday

Go where the in-crowd goes—
Go Carter's for Quality!

CLAMP'S
MEN'S AND YOUNG MEN'S QUALITY CLOTHING
AT POPULAR PRICES
1402 Main St.   Phone 276-3444

NEWBERRIAN

NEWBERRY • 6
PRESBYTERIAN • 7

End Fred Haley (84) hangs on to short Gorman pass, and almost picks up first down at Presbyterian 3-yard line.

Presbyterian got its licks in early and then fought hard defensively to nip an inspired Indian eleven, 7-6, in the 46th Bronze Derby Classic on Thanksgiving Day.

The "Bluehose" immediately ripped off 71 yards in 10 downs for the score and then booted the extra point that eventually would mean victory.

The tide began to turn when guard Billy Kaigler jolted the ball loose from the arms of a "Hoseman". Tackle Mickey Stephens recovered, and seven plays later, Newberry scored. An important play was the 9-yard over-the-middle pass from Tom Gorman to Fred Haley for a first down at the 12. Fullback Richard Seastrunk ran for 3 and Gorman hit Haley again with a short pass that just missed a first down at the 3. Seastrunk got the first down and then crashed over tackle from the 1-yard line to score. The two-point conversion attempt failed.

November 1961

November 1	The first Soviet ICBM called R-16 in the USSR and the SS-7 in the United States were put on active status.
November 2	The White House Historical Association was established by United States First Lady Jackie Kennedy.
November 2	Canadian singer-songwriter k.d. lang was born.
November 3	United Artists announced that Sean Connery would portray James Bond in "Dr. No."
November 4	With $2.00 ticket prices, American folk singer Bob Dylan made his Carnegie Hall debut in New York City.
November 8	A chartered flight carrying recruits to Fort Jackson, South Carolina, crashed while attempting an emergency landing in Richmond, Virginia. 77 of the 79 died on board.
November 8	New York Yankees pitcher Whitey Ford won the MLB AL Cy Young Award.
November 9	The Professional Golf of America eliminated the caucasians only rule.
November 9	The Beatles first met their future manager Brian Epstein.
November 11	*Catch 22* by Joseph Heller was published.
November 12	Five time Olympic gold medalist Nadia Comaneci was born in Romania.
November 15	Roger Maris of the New York Yankees won the MLB AL Most Valuable Player Award.
November 15	The United Nations banned nuclear arms.
November 16	United States President Kennedy increased military aid to South Vietnam without committing troops.
November 18	United States President Kennedy sent 18,000 "military advisors" to South Vietnam.
November 19	TV comedy star Lucille Ball married comic Gary Morton in New York City.
November 19	American actress Meg Ryan was born.
November 22	Cincinnati Reds outfielder Frank Robinson won the MLB NL Most Valuable Player Award.
November 23	The Bronze Derby was played in Newberry, South Carolina on Thanksgiving Day. The Presbyterian College Blue Hose and the Newberry College Indians played to a 7-7 tie.

The Li'l That Was!

Hose, Indians to Clash Thursday at Newberry
For Bronze Derby

The Newberry Observer
AND HERALD & NEWS
"Just Like a Letter from Home"

HERALD AND NEWS ESTABLISHED 1865 — NEWBERRY, S. C., FRIDAY, NOV. 24, 1961 — NEWBERRY OBSERVER ESTABLISHED 1835

AT NEWBERRY THURSDAY
Indians, PC Will Clash In Annual Turkey Day Bout

The Newberry College Indians close their 1961 football season here Thursday when they clash with the Presbyterian Blue Hose in the annual Turkey Day battle. Game time is 2 p.m.

This game will be the final one for three of Newberry's seniors—Co-captains Carl Harris and Johnny Watson and punting specialist Henry Tenn. David Williams and Bill Bethea are also seniors, but they have already played in their last game as both have suffered injuries that sidelined them earlier this season.

The Indians, who haven't beaten P. C. since 1957, enter this year's game with the same record that they had last year, 5-5-0. Newberry must win this game to keep from suffering a second consecutive losing season. P. C. is 3-6-0, but they defeated a strong Chattanooga team and have improved as the season progressed.

P. C. has an excellent passer in senior quarterback Bobby Joiner, who has averaged somewhere in the neighborhood of 100 yards per contest via the air lanes. But Newberry's pass defense has been one of the bright spots during the 1961 season, and they have allowed their opponents only 54.2 yards through the air per contest.

Newberry's passer is nobody to be sneezed at either. Sophomore quarterback Tom Gorman is averaging nearly 60 yards per game himself, and his ability to run the ball makes him a double threat to P. C. Gorman, an All-Conference candidate, is also the Indians total offense leader with 811 yards in 10 games. He needs only 64 yards passing against P. C. to break the school record for most yards gained passing during the school year—a record he set as a freshman in 1960.

Another All-Conference candidate, Carl Harris, will be out to break a record. Since Harris began playing football for the Indians when he was a freshman, he has not missed a single game. This adds up to 42 consecutive games. Harris will be after his 43rd consecutive game Thursday against P. C. Harris, playing three-fourths of the game with a hurt leg, gained 104 yards and averaged 6.1 yards per carry against East Tennessee last week. That brings his season total to 620 yards with 5.1 yard average.

The Newberry line will miss the services of center Travis Howell, unless the infection in his leg gets well. Howell missed last week's game and Bobby Fore, who had been playing center for only a week, did a magni...

the Colonial Stores. Coffee, sweet rolls and donuts were served by the hostesses, Mrs. C. R. Derrick and Mrs. Kenneth Hewitt.

The Li'l 🎩 That Was!

The Indian

HAPPY HOLIDAYS — NEWBERRY, S. C., WEDNESDAY, NOVEMBER 22, 1961 — BEAT P. C.

VOL. 14 — NUMBER 8

Turkey Day Game Closes '61 Season

Newberry College Fighting Redskins

Whether or not the Bronze Derby, which has long been a symbol of athletic rivalry between Newberry and Presbyterian College, will remain in its present storage in the trophy case at P. C. is a question that will be answered when the teams clash in their Turkey-day struggle.

After losing to East Tennessee, the Indian football squad sports a 5-5 winning record and stands ready to meet their arch rival on Nov. 24th. P. C. started off with a season that looked fruitless, but in their last few games, they have showed a powerful and determined team.

The fighting Redskins can not be sold short on determination either. They've been stumping teams ever since their loss to East Carolina in the last few seconds of the game.

Bill Bethea, tri-captain, who was injured for the season, has played his last year. Along with Bethea are Henry Team, star punter; and extra point holder Dave Williams, who was injured also and is out of action for the season; Carl Harris, one of the leading yardage gainers; and bulldozing fullback Billy Herndon.

The squad has worked hard to prepare for its last game. The winning air attack squad, quarterback Tom Gorman and ends Edgar Caddell and Fred Haley, are ready to score.

Other team members are Maxie Knowlton, Travis Rowell, Jimmy Routon, Jimmy Villeponteaux, Johnny Watson, Wesley Murphy, Tommie Witt, Charles Haggard, Roger Gettys, and Phil Orsini.

Also Reed Charpia, Tom Calcatuere, Jim Cockrell, Eddie Mills, Doug Robbins, Charles Partridge, Bobby Force, Jim Acker, Lloyd Shankles, Tommy Blackwell, James Fowler, Lurie Alexander, Dennis Lytle, David Hart, and Freddy Dennis.

Will we win the coveted derby from P. C. this year?

FENNELL'S
JEWELER

1505 MAIN ST.

The Student's Jeweler

Gifts For All Occasions

NICHOLS STUDIO
PHOTOGRAPHS
1311 Main St.

The Li'l 🎩 That Was!

The Newberry Observer
AND HERALD & NEWS
"Just Like a Letter from Home"

HERALD AND NEWS ESTABLISHED 1845 — NEWBERRY, S. C., TUESDAY, NOV. 28, 1961 — NEWBERRY OBSERVER ESTABLISHED 1863

Indians And P.C. Battle In Rain, Mud To 7-7 Tie

Newberry College and Presbyterian battled to a 7-7 deadlock on a soggy field here last Thursday afternoon in their annual Thanksgiving Day encounter that was hampered by an almost continuous downpour of rain.

In spite of the adverse weather conditions, however, an estimated crowd of 1,200 spectators braved the elements. The stands were blanketed with a seemingly endless cover of varied colored umbrellas.

In spite of the slippery field, Presbyterian College was able to unleash a damaging ground game which accounted for 230 yards in the rushing department.

And the Indians handled the slippery ball well to hang up an impressive passing attack with 102 yards.

P. C. was minimized to but 30 yards in the air—and the Indians could manage only 102 yards in their rushing game.

Presbyterian moved to the leadership midway of the first quarter, rolling 71 yards in 14 plays for a quick touchdown the first time they had possession. Sophomore halfback Larry Madden scored the six-pointer on a four-yard blast through the middle of the line, and Louis Ridinger added the extra point to give the Stockings a 7-0 lead.

Newberry tied the score in the third quarter to climax a drive that began when the Tribe took the opening kickoff of the second half.

Quarterback Tom Gorman's pitching arm put the Indians in scoring position with a pass to end Edgar Caddel. And two plays later, senior Carl Harris, the Tribe's rushing leader, went over for the touchdown from two yards out. Herndon kicked the all important extra point that gave the Tribe the tie.

Presbyterian had a drive underway in the early minutes of the second quarter, but it ended when Harris intercepted a Joiner pass on his own 15 and returned it to the 26.

Newberry also threatened in the second quarter, moving to the P. C. 33 before Gorman was thrown for a nine-yard loss while trying to throw, and then had a pass intercepted by Dave Harrill.

The Indians also launched a drive in the third quarter that carried them to the P. C. 18, but on a fourth down and two, Gorman was thrown for a two-yard loss and the Hose took over.

With four minutes left in the game, P. C. had moved into what looked like a sure touchdown in the Newberry 11, but a freak play killed the bid. The ball popped high in the air, behind the Blue Stockings backs, and Charlie Haggard grabbed it for Newberry.

It was the final game of the season for both teams. Newberry finished with a 5-5-1 season, and the P. C. charges posted a 3-6-1 year.

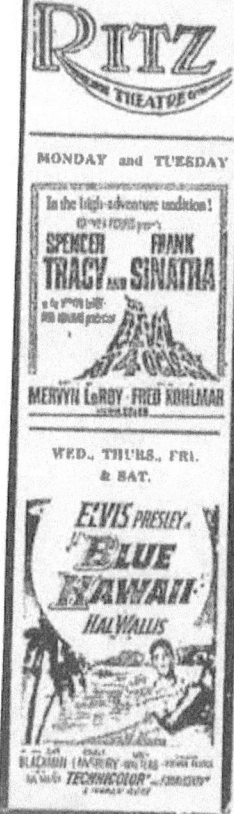

Clover Leaf Drive-In Theatre

The Drive-In now open only Friday, Saturday and Sunday until further notice.

FRIDAY & SATURDAY
"The Steel Claw"
George Montgomery
Charito Luna
Added Color Cartoon—
Bonanza Bunny

SUNDAY
"Ada"
Susan Hayward, Dean Martin, Ralph Meeker
Added Color Cartoon—
Nitwit Kelly

The Li'l 🎩 That Was!

NEWBERRY, S. C., WEDNESDAY, DECEMBER 6, 1961

"Tie For Derby"

Newberry used a pass interception and a fumble recovery to hold an eager Presbyterian team to a 7-7 tie in the traditional Thanksgiving Day clash for the Bronze Derby.

P. C. moved 83 yards to score on Larry Baddin's five-yard run the first time they got their hands on the ball. Newberry drove 95 yards with the second half kickoff, Carl Harris running one yard for the touchdown.

Late in the first period, Bill Herndon's field goal from the 15-yard stripe failed for Newberry after a blooper 11-yard punt by P. C. had given the Redskins the ball within threatening distance of the goal.

Harris intercepted a Blue Hose pass to stop a second period drive which penetrated to the Redskins' 15-yard line. Later in the game, Newberry's tackle, Charles Haggard, recovered a fumble on his 27 to stop a P. C. march that had carried to the Redskins' 11.

Presbyterian's scoring march featured seven, nine, and eleven-yard runs by Randy McCraine; a 10-yard jaunt by Larry Madden; and a seven-yard spurt by Ronnie Hampton. P. C. stayed on the ground all the way. Louis Ridinger kicked the conversion.

A 33-yard kickoff return by Harris to his own 39 started the Newberry move for pay dirt at the opening of the second half.

Several short ground gains and two passes by quarterback Tom Gorman took the ball to the goal line. Gorman passed for 12 yards to end Fred Haley and then 22 yards to the other end, Edgar Caddell, at the P. C. two-yard line. Two plays later, Harris plunged over from the one. Bill Herndon made the conversion.

The game left the two schools tied for second place in the Little Three Conference. Wofford won the loop crown, having beaten both Newberry and P. C. earlier this year.

Hatchette's Office Supplies
1206-08 Main St. Tel. 276-0404
OLIVETTI - UNDERWOOD — Sales and Service
We Rent Typewriters
Norcross Cards and Stationery — Dopp Leather Bags

Annual Thanksgiving Day Classic Brings 7-7 Tie With Newberry Foe

- **Bronze Derby Stays at PC**

Pro Footballer Hill Shows Versatility

Bill Hill, the leading ground gainer on last year's Blue Hose team at his fullback slot, played his first year of Pro Football in Canada this fall. He was one of four rookies who were kept on the Edmonton Eskimos for the entire season.

His versatility was the principal factor in his favor as he played at the positions of fullback, halfback, and end. While playing in five games this year Hill caught seven passes. Hill is planning to return next year and the Eskimos plan to use him almost exclusively at the end position for next season.

He appears to be another Presbyterian footballer with a bright future in professional athletics.

In their tradtitional Big Thursday encounter of Thanksgiving Day the Blue Hose of Presbyterian College and the Indians of Newberry College tangled in a typical encounter for the Bronze Derby. They fought fiercely to a 7-7 deadlock.

The Hose opened the scoring in the first quarter as they mounted a drive of 71 yards. It took 14 plays to cover this yardage with halfbacks Larry Madden and Ronnie Hampton and fullback Randle McCranie doing all of the carrying. Madden moved over for the score from the 6-yard line. Ridinger then booted the PAT to make the score 7-0 as the first quarter ended.

The Blue Hose continued to dominate the play until the close of the second half when the Indians mounted their first drive of any substance. This drive was killed by the interception of a Tom Gorman pass by PC linebacker "Scrap Iron" Harrill on the Blue Hose 27.

Soon after the start of the second half the Indians began to move the ball down the field with Gorman continuing to throw the ball a great deal despite the rain. This drive of 82 yards in 12 plays resulted in Newberry's only touchdown of the game. Halfback Carl Harris bulled his way over from the one-yard line for the score and fullback Bill Herndon converted the PAT to tie the score at 7 all.

During the fourth quarter both the Indians and the Blue Hose had a chance to score. Newberry moved from its own 26-yard line down to the PC 26 and a first down. There the Hose forward wall stiffened and the Indians lost the ball on downs on the Blue Hose 26-yard stripe.

From there the Hose took over and moved quickly down the field to the Newberry 11-yard line where they were halted by a mix-up on the count. Center Doyle Johnson centered the ball back to Joiner later than Joiner was expecting it and it flipped into the air. There it was grabbed off by Newberry tackle Charles Haggard.

Thus the game ended in a 7-7 tie and Presbyterian was able to retain possession of the Bronze Derby which has rested in Clinton since 1958.

The Hose showed their superior ground attack as they ground out 233 yards on the ground compared with just 99 for the Indians.

Belk's Invites All Students To Visit Our Men's Dept. for These Christmas Specials

New Dress Shirts $3.99
Wardrobe Set
Tab or Button-Down Collar Solids and Stripes

Bulky Knit Sweaters $7.99
6-Button Cardigans - All Sizes
Ivy Shades - Olive - Grey - Charcoal - Champaign

Ivy Wash and Wear
Dress Slacks $9.99
70% Orlon Acrylic - 30% Worsted Wool
Olive - Black - Charcoal - Grey - Sizes 28-40

New Ivy League
Socks 79c
75% Orlon Acrylic and 25% Stretch Nylon
Olive - Black-Red - White - Navy - Grey - Black-Brown

Wide Selection of
Ties and Belts $2.00
Christmas Gift Sets with Matching Ivy Tie and Belt

Shoes for the College Man
Italian Loafers ..... $9.95 to $12.95
Black-Olive - Black - Brown

The Blue Stocking

The Li'l That Was!

November 1962

November 1	The United States continued its arms blockade of ships bound for Cuba. The Soviet Union began dismantling missiles.
November 1	Anthony Kiedis, American rock musician and singer of The Red Hot Chili Pepper was born.
November 2	United States President John F. Kennedy addressed the nation on the resolution of The Cuban Missile Crisis.
November 3	San Francisco Warriors center Wilt Chamberlain scored 72 points against the Los Angeles Lakers.
November 3	The phrase "Country and Western Music" was replaced with "Country Music" by *Billboard* magazine.
November 3	The term "Personal Computer" appears for the first time in a New York Times technology article.
November 4	Enos, the only chimpanzee to orbit the earth, passed away from natural causes.
November 6	Ted Kennedy was elected for his first term as Senator of Massachusetts.
November 6	Saudi Arabia proclaimed the abolition of slavery.
November 6	As part of the de-Stalinization effort, a statue of Joseph Stalin was removed in Prague, Czechoslovakia.
November 7	Richard Nixon lost the election for Governor of California.
November 7	Former United States First Lady Eleanor Roosevelt passed away.
November 11	American actress Demi Moore was born.
November 15	Los Angeles Dodgers pitcher Don Drysdale won the MLB NL Cy Young Award.
November 18	American singer Barry White married Betty Smith.
November 18	Guitarist Kirk Hammett of Metallica was born.
November 19	Fidel Casto of Cuba accepted terms to remove Soviet weapons from Cuba.
November 19	Actress Jodie Foster was born.
November 20	New York Yankees Mickey Mantle won the MLB AL Most Valuable Player Award.
November 22	The Bronze Derby was played in Newberry, South Carolina on Thanksgiving Day. The Newberry College Indians defeated the Presbyterian College Blue Hose 23-0.

Who Will Acquire The Bronze Derby?

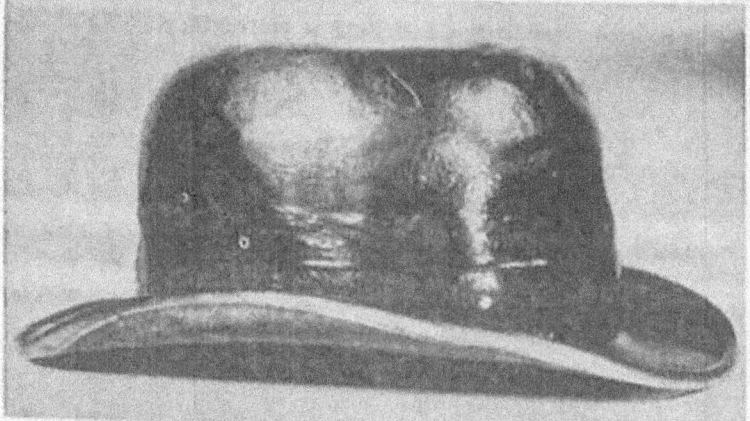

Forty-Eight-Year Rivals Clash November 22

November 22 marks the day of the forty-eighth football clash between Newberry College and Presbyterian College. These two rivals have been feuding on athletic fields since the turn of the century. They have met on the gridiron every year since 1913, with the exception of the year 1918, and are one of the South's oldest rivalries.

Because of strained relations, resulting from vandalism, athletic relations between the two schools were on the verge of severance around 1946-47. During the first basketball game be-
(Continued on page four)

Chapel Programs Lessen Rivalry?

"In order to create better relations between the two colleges," to quote the P. C. student body President, Paul Woodall, the Blue Key Chapters of Newberry and Presbyterian Colleges trade assembly programs each year. On Wednesday, November 14, Newberry College students were again delightfully entertained by P. C.'s Blue Key Fraternity. Marion Clark, who is President of the Newberry chapter, introduced Joe Harvard, President of the Presbyterian chapter. After devotions, "Brother" Paul Woodall delivered a sermon, and the Playboys played several numbers. Be-
(Continued on page four)

Forty-Eight-Year
(Continued from page one)

tween the two schools in 1947, a Presbyterian student lost his derby to anonymous Newberry students. In a letter to the sports publicity director at Newberry College, Prof. Charles MacDonald, instructor of English and director of Public Relations at Presbyterian College, suggested that the derby be used as a trophy in athletic contests. The derby was turned over to a local jewelry firm to be cast in bronze. Since then, the Bronze Derby has been given to the winner of the two schools in the three major sports — football, basketball, and track.

Since 1948, the Bronze Derby has see-sawed back and forth in football games. The scores have been as follows:

	P. C.	Newberry
1948	40	12
1949	14	20
1950	20	6
1951	27	0
1952	14	12
1953	7	7
1954	20	18
1955	18	20
1956	0	13
1957	0	13
1958	22	0
1959	20	6
1960	7	6
1961	7	7

There are things we try to say, but never
Are they said.
There are deeds we try to do, but never
Are they done.
We walk around from day to day;
And through the motions all, without a thought or careless care.
But underneath it all
In the darkness dank
    Everlasting Light
That
Blows away the ocean and puffs out all the stars.

By Janet Summers

Chapel Programs
(Continued from page one)

cause of the excellence of P. C.'s program, the Newberry chapter felt challenged to present a program, equally as entertaining, to the Presbyterian student body on Monday. The rivalry of the football field has spread to the auditorium stage. Newberry's Blue Key chapter was enthusiastically received at Presbyterian College.

BEAT PRESBYTERIAN!

Summer Study
(Continued from page two)

versity. Advanced Spanish students may enrol in certain NON-language courses which are offered only in the Spanish language. These students gain a double advantage in that they receive college credit in history, geography, or archaeology while they improve and "polish" their command of the Spanish language.

Mexico has a number of reputable institutions of higher learning from which general college credits may be transferred to American colleges. These are located in such cities as Mexico City, Monterrey, Guanajuato, Guadalajara, Saltillo, and San Luis Potosi. I hope that some

BEAT PRESBYTERIAN!

The Indian
"Voice of the Newberry College Student"

VOL. XXXV, NO. X   NEWBERRY, S. C., MON., NOV. 19, 1962   FOUNDED 1929

The Li'l That Was!

The Newberry Observer
AND HERALD & NEWS
"Just Like a Letter from Home"

NEWBERRY, S. C., FRIDAY, NOV. 23, 1962

It's Tribe vs. Hose Thursday

In Annual Thanksgiving Day Clash

Newberry will travel to Clinton Thursday to take on Presbyterian in the annual Thanksgiving Day clash with the mythical Little Three title up for grabs.

Presbyterian, who downed Wofford 3-0 for its only win, needs a victory Thursday in order to capture the mythical trophy and retain the Bronze Derby. Newberry, meanwhile, needs a victory in order to have a winning season.

The Indians, who could be undefeated if about five plays were taken out of the record books, will call on the passing of Tom Gorman and the running of halfback Phil Orsini and fullback Bill Hammond. Jimmy Lowder, senior halfback, should also be a big threat to the Blue Hose.

Gorman set a new passing mark last week when he passed for 105 yards. This gave him a total of 761 yards on the season, and breaks his old record of 695 yards. As a freshman in 1960, Gorman broke the existing passing record of 676 yards. Then as a sophomore last year he established a new record of 695 yards, and now as a junior he has done it again.

Fred Haley, Gorman's prime target, has also set a school record for pass receiving yardage. Last year Haley set the record at 289 yards, but this year he has already caught 31 passes for 393 yards. Both of these boys should add to their records this week.

Hammond, a freshman fullback, has shown up real well since the Lenoir Rhyne game. Currently he is pushing rushing leader Phil Orsini for the rushing leadership. Orsini has 425 yards, while Hammond has 423. Orsini, however, is leading in the average department, with a 4.4 avg. He also leads the team in scoring with 36 points, but Jimmy Lowder is pushing him with 30 points.

Much of the success of the backs lies in the fact that the Indians have a real strong forward wall. Anchored by tackles Tommy Witt and Charles Haggard and center Travis Rowell, the Indian line is consistent in opening up holes for the backs. They also do a good job on defense. End Roger Gettys has been playing some outstanding defensive football lately, and it was his sparkling defense which enabled the Indians to win the West Carolina game.

Other outstanding performers in the line are guards Jimmy Routon and Jimmy Villeponteaux, and end Fred Haley. This forward wall also has a fair second unit to back them up. Tackles Jim Fowler and Dennis Lynn, guards Doug Bell and Jim Acker, and linebackers Pat Merrick and Bill Greco have played outstanding ball for the second unit.

The P. C. game will be the last for 12 Newberry seniors. Tommie Witt, Charles Haggard, Travis Rowell, Jimmy Routon, Jimmy Villeponteaux, Roger Gettys, Willie Mickle, Phil Orsini, Jimmy Lowder, Maxie Knowlton, Edgar Caddell, Bobby Fore, have dedicated four years of fine ball to Newberry College.

HOW TO TRAVEL IN LUXURY WITHOUT REALLY FLYING

The exciting new '63 Chevrolet has captured the silence and effortless ease of jet flight and translated it to highway travel. Every new Chevrolet, whether it's a luxury Impala, a low-priced Bel Air or a Biscayne, now has self-adjusting brakes, a Delcotron generator to extend battery life, and the ingenious new flash-and-dry system. A test drive of a few miles will amaze you. This '63 Chevrolet is a quality automobile, built to travel with the very best. When you're driving a Chevrolet, you don't take a back seat to anyone!

CHEVROLET — The make more people depend

GO JET-SMOOTH '63 CHEVROLET - IT'S EXCITING!

Ask about "Go with the Greats," a special record album of top artists and hits and see four entirely different kinds of cars at your Chevrolet dealer's—'63 Chevrolet, Chevy II, Corvair and Corvette

Kemper Chevrolet Company
1515-17 Main Street   Newberry, S. C.   Telephone 276-1610

The Clinton Chronicle

Vol. 63 — No. 43   Clinton, S. C., Thursday, November 22, 1962

LISTEN TO
COACH CLYDE EHRHARDT
OF PRESBYTERIAN COLLEGE

On the air 15 minutes prior to each game

— ON —

WLBG

FOR BRONZE DERBY
PC Newberry to Clash Here Thursday at 2:00

Although they've won just one game this year, Presbyterian College gridmen will be battling for the Little Three championship when they entertain Newberry in the annual Bronze Derby clash here Thursday afternoon.

This small-college Thanksgiving Day classic is scheduled for 2 p. m. at Johnson Field. It's the 48th engagement of a series which ranks among the state's oldest football feud.

The Blue Hose, posting their worst season in recent years with a current record of 1-8, could recoup some measure of esteem in this final game by capturing the Little Three title. Their only victory to date came at the 3-0 expense of Wofford, the other Little Three contender, which earlier had knocked off the Newberry team.

Newberry, on the basis of a 5-3 record, is installed as a heavy favorite to deny these PC aspirations and to reclaim the Bronze Derby held by Presbyterian for the past four years. This trophy, symbol of gridiron superiority between PC and Newberry, has rested in Clinton since the Blue Hose 1958 victory, remaining through last year's 7-7 tie.

The PC-Newberry rivalry goes back to 1913, when the Indians captured the opener. Through the years, however, Presbyterian has dominated play and currently leads in the series with 29 wins against 14 for Newberry while four games have ended in ties.

Newberry will bring to Johnson Field this year one of the outstanding passers of South Carolina in Quarterback Tom Gorman. He has completed 61 passes in 121 attempts for 763 yards so far this year. Leading

THE BRONZE DERBY

the Indian running game will be Halfbacks Phil Orsini and Jimmy Lowder and Fullback Bill Hammond, each of whom averages around 4 yards-per-carry.

PC's hope in matching aerials with Gorman is sophomore Quarterback Leighton Grantham, who has compiled 254 yards on 22 completions in 61 tries while seeing only limited service. The Blue Hose are hampered by injuries in both the line and backfield, but Coach Clyde Ehrhardt looks to have Fullback Randy McCravie back in action after missing the past two games.

The Li'l 🎩 That Was!

The Indian
"Voice of the Newberry College Student"

VOL. XXXV, NO XI   NEWBERRY, S. C., WED., DEC. 5, 1962   FOUNDED 1929

Indians Retrieve Bronze Derby

By CHARLES BITTINGER

It was a chilly, but sunny, Thanksgiving afternoon. Everyone had just finished a hearty Thanksgiving dinner, and they were waiting to see who would take home the coveted Bronze Derby — Newberry College or Presbyterian College. Judging from the crowds in the stands, one could see that the Fightin' Redskins fans were more interested in claiming the derby than the Presbyterian Blue Hose fans, even though it was a home game for the Blue Hoses.

The Fightin' Redskins turned on the power early in the game to make the Blue Hose the losingest team in the state. They stumped the Blue Hoses 23-0. This gave the Indians a 6-5 record and made them the second winningest team in the state. Clemson finished up with a 6-4 record and had the best record in the state.

The Indians also wound up in an ironic three-way tie for first place in the Little Three battle. The final tally showed that Newberry beat P. C., but lost to Wofford; Wofford beat Newberry, but lost to P. C.; and P. C. beat Wofford, but lost to Newberry.

The Thanksgiving Day classic was Newberry all the way. The Indians started off the scoring early in the first quarter when the Indians' stellar quarterback Tommy Gorman recovered a fumble, just a few plays after the kickoff, by P. C.'s halfback Jimmy May. With the ball on the P. C. 26, the Indians began their long drive down the field. Finally, with 10:30 left in the period, frosh fullback Bill Hammond went over from a yard out for the TD. Charlie Haggard booted the extra point to put the Indians out in front 7-0.

The game continued. Nothing much happened on the field. One team drove, and then the other. Penalty-plagued P. C.'s longest drive carried the ball only to the Newberry 16. P. C. gave up 105 yards in penalties. Action
(Continued on page three)

Indians Retrieve
(Continued from page one)

was pretty dull until early in the third quarter. Then the Indians smashed down to the P. C. 21 and stopped. P. C. played with the ball for a while, and then Travis Rowell intercepted Bill Tyson's pass at the P. C. 42. Newberry punted after three plays, and P. C. was forced to punt after they had the ball for four plays. Fred Haley ran the ball up to the five. A personal foul on the play moved the ball up to the 25. Two plays later, after only five yards had been made, Gorman flipped one out to Haley, who caught it on the N. C. 35 and raced to the P. C. 46.

This drive started to look unsuccessful at the P. C. 28. Haggard attempted a field goal, and Newberry got another break. P. C. was penalized for being offside, and Newberry got its first and ten. It took the Indians only five plays to score with Hammond again going over for the TD. Haggard booted his second good extra point to make it 14-0.

The Indians continued in the fourth by scoring still another TD. This time Larry Eaves went over for the score. Haggard kicked another extra point, which made him three for three and the score 21-0. Jimmy Routen added the other two points when he caught a P. C. punter in the end zone. This made the final score a 23-0 shutout.

Tommy Gorman, playing one of the finest ball games in his career, completed nine out of eleven passes and finished with a total of 1,073 yards.

Coach Kirkland was most pleased with the victory as he said, "We did things right. We played our usual good football game, and we won." Many times we have played good games and still lost, as in the Lenoir Rhyne and Wofford games. The Coach said, "When I think of the way we've lost some of those games, I just shutter." He later stated, "We could have had a real fine year. I've said all along that this was one of our better clubs, and the boys proved that today. You don't beat P. C. 23-0 with a poor team."

The Newberry Observer
AND HERALD & NEWS
"Just Like a Letter from Home"

NEWBERRY, S. C., TUESDAY, NOV. 27, 1962

IN BRONZE DERBY BATTLE

Indians Are 23-0 Winners

CLINTON — The Indians used two freshmen to score three touchdowns in blanking the Presbyterian Blue Hose 23-0, taking the Bronze Derby in the annual Thanksgiving Clash for the first time since 1957, and rounding out the season with a 6-3 record.

Several senior Tribesmen finished their college football careers with outstanding play on Johnson Field.

Fred Haley, end from Hartwell, Ga., caught five passes and added 58 more yards to his record this year. Haley has set a new school record for passes caught with 36 passes and 448 yards gained this season. Haley broke his own record set in the 1961 season for 369 yards.

Halfback Jimmy Lowder, out in 1961 with a leg injury, and part of this season with a similar injury, looked like the Lowder of 1962 Thursday as he rushed for 57 yards.

Tackle Charles Haggard booted three PATs for a total of seven this season.

Center Travis Howell intercepted one pass and was in on another play where several Indian defenders wrestled with a PC receiver for the ball and the officials ruled it an interception.

Guard Jimmy Routon accounted for a safety in the fourth quarter for the Indians' final score.

Moxie Knowlton punted four times for a 39 yard average.

Phil Orsini, an academic senior, was top gainer in the game with 95 yards rushing.

Other seniors seeing action for the last time and playing heads-up ball were guard Jimmy Villeponteaux, end Roger Gettys, and end Willie Mickle. Bobby Fore and Edgar Caddell have both been out all season with injuries.

Newberry's first touchdown came just minutes after the game started. PC had elected to receive and attempted to start a drive from their own 16. Senior halfback Jimmy May fumbled on the Blue Hose 26 and Newberry quarterback Tom Gorman recovered.

On the first play PC drew a personal foul penalty and the Tribe had the ball, first and 10 at the 12. Phil Orsini hit for no gain and then picked up two yards on second down.

Gorman elected to keep on the next play and rambled through the Hose defense before finally being dropped on the two. Jimmy Lowder dived straight up the middle to the one-foot line and then freshman fullback Bill Hammond hurdled the line for the touch-

LOWDER RUSHES FOR INDIANS: Newberry College halfback Jimmy Lowder (No. 42) races to the P. C. 40 in the first quarter of the annual Thanksgiving Day Bronze Derby battle at Clinton last Thursday. The Indians won the game, 23-0.—Observer Photo by Marvin (Governor) Douknight.

down. Charles Haggard's kick was good and the Indians led 7-0.

Both teams played hard defensive ball for a while and the action was filled with fumbles and penalties.

The Tribe's second score came with 2:47 gone in the fourth quarter on a drive that began in the third quarter on the Newberry nineyard line.

Orsini took the PC punt on his five and handed off to Lowder who got out to the nine. But PC drew another penalty and the ball was placed on the 24.

Hammond drove straight up the middle to the 28 and then Lowder picked up another yard. He fumbled on this play but officials ruled that Newberry recovered.

Fred Haley then caught a Tom Gorman pass at the 35, shook loose from several defenders, and charged down the sideline to the Blue Hose 46.

Hammond hit in for three yards and on the next play Gorman elected to keep and picked up three more.

Then Lowder found a hole on the right side of the line and hit hard for seven more yards to the 32.

Hammond got two more and then Gorman was dropped at the line.

With a third and eight situation, Gorman faded deep and hit Orsini at the 26.

This gave the Tribe fourth and five and Charles Haggard attempted a field goal, but PC was offsides and the Indians had a first and 10 on the 22. Orsini went for no gain on the first play.

Then Gorman rolled left to pass, saw daylight and ran it in in the nine. Orsini picked up three and Lowder got five to the one.

Hammond hit the line, found no hole, and slid off the left side and into the end zone for the second score. Haggard's kick was good and the Indians led 14-0.

PC had the ball for four plays but a penalty cost them a first down and Louis Ridinger, their kicking specialist, punted dead on the Newberry 30 where the tribe started their last scoring drive.

Hammond bulled up the middle for four yards. Then Phil Orsini hit the line, appeared to be stopped at the 45, but broke loose and raced to the PC 18 before being dropped.

On the next play Orsini picked up four more yards and then Lowder broke loose to the four. PC drew another penalty and the ball was placed on the two.

Freshman halfback Bill Karen of Hartwell, Ga., hit up the middle for the touchdown. Haggard's kick was good and the Tribe led 21-0.

The Indians capped the scoring off with a safety in the last minutes of the fourth quarter. The Blue Hose had the ball, fourth and 26 at their own 10 and Ridinger came in to punt. A bad pass from center was hard to hold and fell into the end zone. Ridinger attempted to pick it up but guard Jimmy Routon tackled him and made the score 23-0.

The Blue Hose only threatened seriously twice, once in the second quarter and again in the fourth quarter.

In the second quarter the Hose started a drive on their own 47. Quarterback Bill Tyson flipped a pass to an end at the Newberry 40. Fullback Randy McCranie went up the middle of one and then took a pitchout from quarterback Jackie Nix and rambled to the Newberry 32.

Halfback John Ringer got three more and then halfback Ronnie Hampton ran all over the field to the 10 where he fumbled and the Indians took over.

They threatened again in the fourth quarter but a pass interception stopped them at the Newberry 37. The drive started on the PC 30.

Quarterback Leighton Grantham passed complete to end Wayne Fowler at the 42. Then he hit halfback Rut Galloway for six more. The next pass was broken up by Gorman and Lowder at the Tribe 15.

Then Grantham hit Bankhead at the 37 but several Indians went into the air in contention for the ball and the officials ruled it an interception.

GAME STATISTICS
First downs—Newberry 17, Presbyterian, 12.
Rushing yardage — Newberry, 207; Presbyterian, 63.
Passing yardage — Newberry, 76; Presbyterian, 83.
Passes — Newberry, 6-13; Presbyterian, 9-25.
Punts — Newberry, 5-39.1; Presbyterian, 7-33.
Fumbles lost—Newberry, 1; Presbyterian, 2.
Passes intercepted by—Newberry, 2; Presbyterian, 0.
Yards penalized — Newberry, 30; Presbyterian, 103.

November 1963

November 2	Ngo Dinh Diem, President of South Vietnam, was killed in a military coup.
November 5	American actress Tatum O'Neal was born.
November 7	New York Yankees catcher Elston Howard won the MLB AL Most Valuable Player Award. He was the first African-American to win the award.
November 10	NHL Detroit Red Wing Gordie Howe became the NHL all-time goal score leader.
November 10	American NFL football coach Mike McCarthy was born.
November 11	The Beatles signed a 3 show contract to appear on "The Ed Sullivan Show."
November 12	American singer and actor Robert Goulet married actress Carol Lawrence.
November 13	American football player Vinny Testaverde was born.
November 16	American tennis player Zina Garrison was born.
November 18	American college basketball player Len Bias was born.
November 18	Bell Telephone introduced the touch tone telephone.
November 22	United States President John F. Kennedy was assassinated by Lee Harvey Oswald in Dallas, Texas.
November 22	Vice President Lyndon B. Johnson was sworn in as the 36th President of the United States.
November 22	The Beatles released their second album "With the Beatles."
November 23	The long running sci-fi series "Dr. Who" debuted.
November 24	Lee Harvey Oswald was killed on live television by Jack Ruby.
November 25	President John F. Kennedy laid to rest at Arlington Cemetery.
November 25	NFL quarterback Bernie Kosar was born.
November 26	Quarterback Roger Staubach of Navy won the Heisman Trophy.
November 26	Cincinnati Reds second baseman Pete Rose won the MLB NL Rookie of the Year Award.
November 28	The Beatles "She Loves You" reached one million copies sold.
November 28	American baseball player-manager Walt Weiss was born.
November 28	The Bronze Derby was played in Newberry, South Carolina on Thanksgiving Day. The Presbyterian College Blue Hose defeated the Newberry College Indians 14-7.

the Presbyterian College magazine
Spring, 1963

Blue Hose Sports

Gault Returns As Coach

Tapping one of its former halfback stars, Presbyterian College has named Calhoun F. (Cally) Gault '48 as new athletic director and head football coach to succeed the late Clyde W. Ehrhardt.

He's getting his first good look at the 1963 prospects during a delayed spring practice session being held the first three weeks in May.

Gault, long recognized as one of South Carolina's most successful high school coaches, compiled an impressive record in ten years as football coach at North Augusta (SC) High School. His teams won class Double-A state championships in 1958 and 1961 and have compiled an overall record of 88 wins, 13 losses and seven ties. During the four-year period of 1954-58, his teams went undefeated through 42 consecutive games.

In returning to the PC campus—where he starred in football for three years, and also earned letters in basketball and baseball — Cally Gault becomes the Blue Hose' fourth athletic director in 48 years and only the sixth man to serve as head football coach. He played here under Coach Lonnie S. McMillian '21, the man who introduced T-formation football to the Southeast and the only other alumnus to serve PC as head coach.

A native of Bamberg, S. C., who grew up in Greenville, Gault received his bachelor's degree in history from Presbyterian in 1948 and a master's in education from the University of South Carolina in 1955. He coached at Mullins (SC) High early in his career, was an assistant at North Augusta when army service called during the Korean War and returned there to direct the program until PC called.

The new 35-year-old head coach is married to the former Joy Young Godfrey of Clinton. They have two daughters and a young son.

The Li'l That Was!

The Indian

"Voice of the Newberry College Student"

VOL. XXXVI   NEWBERRY, S. C., MONDAY, NOVEMBER 25, 1963   NUMBER XI

The INDIAN Wishes You A Meaningful Thanksgiving

Bronze Derby Spotlighted In Thanksgiving Game

By DAVE FEDDERN

Will the Indians retain the Bronze Derby or will it return to our rival's campus, P. C.? This seems to be the big question in everyone's mind, but more important, it rests in the minds of the football team and the coaching staff. This past week the Indians have been hitting on both offense and defense. For some fellows this is their last week of practice and the looks of relief are starting to show on some faces, but these same boys will be giving everything they have to the Turkey Day game.

This is one game where all record books, films, and scouting reports can be put into the circular file. Since this is a rival game, each team will be putting every ounce of muscle into his blocking assignment or putting on that last burst of speed and drive.

Now, let's take a look at the Blue Hose! This year P. C. posts a 2-6-1 record under the new coach Cally Gault. A lack of weight, depth, and speed is the picture PC has had during the '63 season. The halfbacks lack both experience and swiftness, but sophomores Randy McCranie and Ronnie Morris make the fullback position possibly the strongest on the team. The quarterbacking chores will be shared among three possibilities, but Leighton Grantham will probably do most of the calling. The line will not be as big as last year, but seniors Randy Fitzpatrick at guard, Frank King at tackle, and Keith Richardson at center will form strong bulwarks with their nine years of experience. Only two ends have any real game experience, however, and this will hamper the passing game. Due to the fact that P.C. is a young ball club, they usually can be counted on to make a lot of mistakes. This, I hope, will be a main factor on Thanksgiving.

Now that both teams have been reviewed, let's take a look at previous years. In the accumulative record over the years, P.C. has won 29 to Newberry's 14 wins. Four games ended in draws. The Blue Hose have racked up 640 points to the Indians' 591.

My prediction for this big game will be a big run in the Blue Hose!

During the first basketball game between Newberry and Presbyterian, a Presbyterian student lost his derby to anonymous Newberry students. In a letter to the sports publicity director at Newberry College, Prof. Charles MacDonald, instructor of English and director of Public Relations at Presbyterian College, suggested that the derby be used as a trophy in athletic contests. The derby was turned over to a local jewelry firm to be cast in bronze. Since then, the Bronze Derby has been given to the winner of the two schools in the three major sports—football, basketball, and track.

Since 1948, the Bronze Derby has see-sawed back and forth in football games.

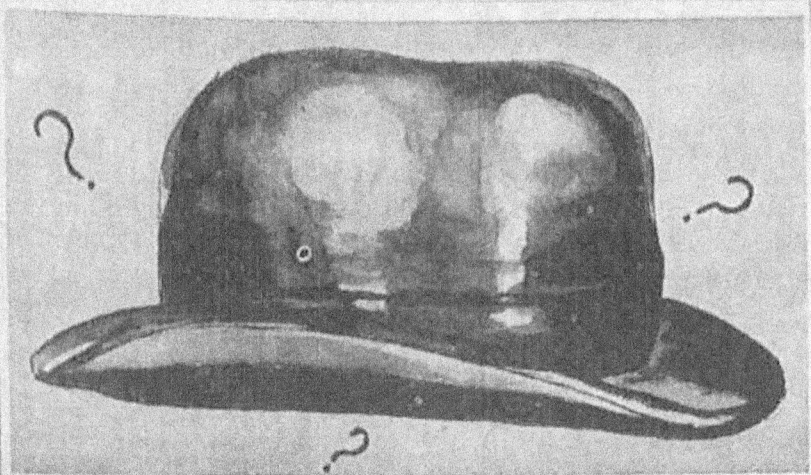

..."Snag The Blue Hose"...

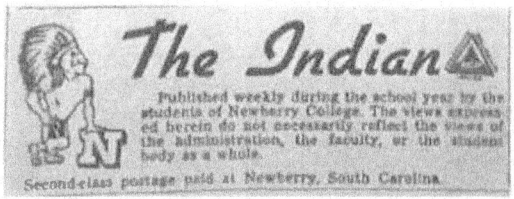

Published weekly during the school year by the students of Newberry College. The views expressed herein do not necessarily reflect the views of the administration, the faculty, or the student body as a whole.

Second-class postage paid at Newberry, South Carolina.

The Li'l That Was!

The Newberry Observer
AND HERALD & NEWS
"Just Like a Letter from Home"

VOL. 94, NO. 95   HERALD AND NEWS ESTABLISHED 1865   NEWBERRY, S. C., TUESDAY, NOV. 26, 1963   NEWBERRY OBSERVER ESTABLISHED 1885   PRICE 6¢ PER COPY

Newberry Mourns President Kennedy's Death

NEWBERRY, S. C., TUESDAY, NOV. 26, 1963

Indians Seek To Retain Bronze Derby Thanksgiving

The Newberry College Indians, after their first open date in several years, will entertain the Presbyterian Blue Hose in the annual Thanksgiving Day Bronze Derby Game on Thursday, Nov. 27. Game time is 2 p.m. on Newberry's Setzler Field.

Thursday's game will mark the twelfth time these two teams have met to decide which school gets the coveted Bronze Derby Trophy. Presently, the Indians are the possessors of this prize, as they downed P. C. 23-0, in the 1962 game.

Thursday's game will also mark the end of the careers of six fine senior Indian football players Co-Captains Tom Gorman and Fred Haley, guards Wes Murphy and Bill Grove, center Bobby Fore and end Dave Hert. Gorman and Haley will be winding up very bright four-year careers at this Lutheran institution, and both will be key figures in the Indians offensive plans this Thanksgiving.

The Blue Hose will come into Thursday's game with a 2-6-1 season record, but they are a better team than their record shows. They opened the season with a 10-0 victory over Frederick, but between that opening win and last week's 24-14 win over Troy, the Blue Hose could only manage a 14-14 tie with Davidson.

However, first year coach Cally Gault has done a tremendous job with his Blue Hose, and it seems that they may have found themselves after the Troy victory. Gault will rely basically on the powerful running of fullback Randy McCranie and halfback Don McNeill. These two boys are the leading rushers on the squad, and both are vieing for the team leadership in this department. Both have well over 300 yards rushing on the season. Gault will mix up this running game with the passing of junior quarterback Leighton Grantham, who has passed for 400 plus yards this season. Gault will also be able to call on senior Bill Tyson to direct his team offensively.

The Indian's offense will rely more heavily on the shoulders of quarterback Tom Gorman and end Fred Haley, than it has in the past games this season. The reason for this is that Bill Hammond, the Indian's leading rusher and their bread-and-butter man, will not see action in this Thursday's Turkey Day game. Hammond was one of the stars of last year's classic, scoring two touchdowns, but he was injured in the Western Carolina game and has not seen action since then. Freshman Doug Crawford from Florence will be running at the fullback position in Hammond's absence.

Hammond's absence would seem to be enough, but the Indians are also under the handicap of having their second leading rusher, Irvin Fordham, limited due to an injury. Fordham missed the WCC game, and it is not known to what extent he can be used in the Turkey Day game. Fordham has rushed for 294 yards this season and scored four touchdowns. Reed Charpia, the hero of the Lenoir Rhyne victory, will also be used lightly in the Presbyterian clash, for he has re-injured the leg that kept him out for so long this season. However, sophomore Bill Eaves has done a tremendous job of replacing Charpia. In the PCC game Eaves rushed for 77 yards, and on the season he has picked up 191 yards rushing. Sophomore halfback Joe Wren has also done a fine job filling in for Fordham. It was Wren's pile driving line bucks that produced the winning touchdown against the WCC Catamounts a week ago. Wren has also proved his worth as a pass receiver, for he has caught 11 passes for 134 yards and two touchdowns.

But again the main offensive threat of the Indians will be the passing combination of Gorman-to-Haley. So far this season, Gorman has thrown for 717 yards and seven touchdowns. Haley has caught 27 passes for 303 of these yards and two of the touchdowns. But Gorman has also proven that he can run with the ball, as evidenced in the WCC game when he picked up 88 yards in nine carries. And Haley will also be a definite asset to the Indians on both defense and offensive decoying. If everybody covers Haley, Gorman will only throw to the other fine senior end, Dave Hart, who has caught 10 passes for 175 yards and three touchdowns. Hart is also a fine defensive end, and will be extremely valuable to the Indians on Thursday.

But no matter how good the backs and ends are on Thanksgiving, the key to an Indian victory will lie with the fine forward wall of Coach Harvey Kirkland. In the last few games, the Indians forward wall has been terrific, and the fine play by these boys is one of the reasons for the Indians success lately. Since the Wofford game, the Indians have won three and lost one, and in only one of these games, did the line give up more than 100 yards rushing. WCC picked up 120 yards on the ground, and this is nothing to brag about. One of the main reasons for this success has been the inspired play of junior tackle Jim "Blimp" Fowler, Linebacker Pat Merrick, and guards Wes Murphy and Jim Acker have also done a fine job for the Indians on defense. Several freshmen have also helped in the line. Tackles Billy Arnold and Steve Robertson and linebacker Arlo Hill have come around quickly, and have been a great help to Kirkland's Indians this season.

The Li'l That Was!

The Clinton Chronicle

Vol. 64 — No. 47   Clinton, S. C., Thursday, November 28, 1963

For Bronze Derby

Hose, Indians to Clash Thursday at Newberry

Kennedy Services Monday

Presbyterian College

Coach Cally Gault Reports

Interviewed by Bill Hogan

— Over —

WLBG-AM-FM
Saturdays 12:15

Sponsored By

M. S. BAILEY & SON, BANKERS

The Newberry Observer
AND HERALD & NEWS
"Just Like a Letter from Home"

AND NEWS ESTABLISHED 1885 — NEWBERRY, S. C., FRIDAY, NOV. 20, 1963 — NEWBERRY OBSERVER ESTABLI

Indian-P.C. Bronze Derby Game At Newberry

Blue Hose Rate Favorite Role In Annual Battle

By LARRY WOLFF

Thursday is Thanksgiving Day to millions of people across the nation, but to Newberry College football players and students it is Bronze Derby Day, the day when arch rivals Presbyterian College invade Seizler Field in an escort to regain the coveted Bronze Derby.

Thursday will be the twentieth time that these two schools have settled the Bronze Derby question with a football game. Before 1947, the Bronze Derby was exchanged after every athletic event between the two schools, but in it was decided to exchange the Derby only after football games.

This year's Bronze Derby game will be no different than others in the past. We can expect anything and everything to happen. This year Newberry has a better won-lost record, going into the game with a 5-4 mark, while Presbyterian has managed a 2-6-1 record. But record and past performances are not everything in these contests, so Dunkle, a well-known football prognosticator has rated Blue Hose over the Indians by three points.

But the Indians will be relying on five fine senior players to see to it that Mr. Dunkle missed his guess. Ends Fred Haley and Dave Hart, Wes Murphy and Bill and quarterback Tom Inman will all be playing their last game for the Scarlet and Gray this Thursday, and five will be winding up brilliant careers for Coach Harland.

However, Presbyterian players will also have some incentive behind them as they go into the game. First they will also have five seniors who wish to wind up their careers on a winning note. Second, the Blue Hose would like to avenge last year's licking at the hands of the Indians. Third, they would like to present their new coach, Cally Gault, with the Bronze Derby during his first year of college coaching and fourth, they would like to end the season on a happy, winning note. In order to accomplish all these things, the Blue Hose will rely on a big forward wall and a fine running backfield in the persons of Randy McCrary and Don McNeill. They will also use the passing arm of quarterbacks Leighton Cunningham and Bill Tyson.

It is probably the passing of the Blue Hose that the Indians are most concerned about, for this has been a weakness in the past few games. In nine games this season, the Indians' forward wall has given up only
(continued on page)

Indian-PC
(continued from page one)

yards rushing, but they have given up 1123 yards passing. The Indians can counter any passing P. C. does with their formidable pass-catch combination of Tom Gorman to Fred Haley. But the Indians are somewhat worried about their running game, for several key backs are injured. Bill Hammond, the bullish fullback who has picked up 512 yards rushing this season, is a very doubtful player this Thursday. He has a knee injury. Several other Indian backs are slightly injured. Halfbacks Irvin Fordham, Reed Charpia and Joe Wren are not at full strength, and Doug Crawford, fullback replacement for Hammond, is not completely well.

Even with the above information one cannot accurately predict the outcome of a Newberry-P. C. game, especially the Bronze Derby game. The only way to find out what happens is to be in the stands Thursday.

ing when the door is opened?

4. Can you see from inside the closed door a person standing outside the door? There is a small eye that can be inserted in the door that gives a broad view of the area around the front door.

5. Is the door well lighted? Ideally this means wall fixtures mounted on both sides of the doorway. If only one light can be used, install it on the latch side of the door.

6. When guests arrive to be greeted, unwrapped, and prepared to meet other guests in the living room, are they afforded any privacy from the living room?

When a business or serviceman calls at your door, can you speak to him privately when guests are in the living room?

The Li'l That Was!

The Newberry Observer
AND HERALD & NEWS
"Just Like a Letter from Home"

NEWBERRY, S. C., TUESDAY, DEC. 3, 1963

P.C. Wins Bronze Derby With 14-7 Victory

By LARRY WOLFF

The Presbyterian Blue Hose lived up to their role as favorites in the annual Thanksgiving Day game, Thursday, and gave Coach Harvey Kirkland and his Indians a little less to be happy about during the holidays. P. C. scored early in the first quarter after a Newberry fumble and clinched the game with a long scoring pass in the fourth quarter, giving them a 14-7 victory and the Bronze Derby.

P. C.'s victory gave freshman Coach Cally Gault his first Bronze Derby in his first attempt, and enabled the Blue Hose to wind up a dismal season on a happy note. P. C.'s season record was 3-5-1, while the Indians' finished all even at 5-5.

Newberry won the toss at this year's Thanksgiving Day game, but it wasn't long before P. C. had their chance to score. Newberry's Reed Charpia returned Louis Ridinger's kick 21 yards to the Newberry 30 yard line, and the Indians got off two offensive plays before freshman halfback Jim Johnson recovered a Tom Gorman fumble on the Indians 33 yard line. From here P. C. went on to score their first touchdown of the game. P. C. drove to pay dirt on the running of fullback Randy McCranie, who picked up 25 of the 33 yards, and scored from two yards out to put P. C. ahead. Ridinger kicked the extra point and with 10:43 left in the first quarter, P. C. led 7-0.

After an exchange of punts, the Indians scored their only touchdown of the game. Halfback Neal Dufford returned a Ridinger punt 41 yards to the Presbyterian 38 yard line. Quarterback Tom Gorman then picked up 18 yards, moving the ball to the P. C. 20 yard line. Bill Eaves and Doug Crawford picked up six yards each putting the ball on the 14. From here Gorman fired a touchdown pass to halfback Joe Wren. Crawford kicked the extra point and with 2:58 left in the first quarter, the game was tied 7-7.

Newberry threatened to score twice more in the second quarter, but they could not capitalize on either of these opportunities. The first came after center Pat Merrick had intercepted a Bill Tyson pass on the P. C. 44 yard line. On two quick passes Gorman moved the ball to the 20, but a fourth down touchdown pass to Fred Haley was out of bounds. Haley caught the ball in the end zone, but the official ruled that he had one foot out of bounds, thus killing one drive.

Another Indian drive was stopped when Sammy Hagood intercepted a Gorman pass on the P. C. 15 yard line. The Indians had taken the ball on their own 42 and marched to the 36, when a P. C. player was called for roughing Indian punter Frank Herlong. This moved the ball to the 23, but then Hagood came up with his interception.

In the second half, the Indians were on defense most of the time. P. C. took the second half kickoff and marched to the Indian 25 before the defensive unit held. Louis Ridinger attempted a field goal from the 32, but the kick was low and wide. The Indians took over on the 20, but they could not move the ball.

INDIAN QUARTERBACK ENDS CAREER: Newberry College quarterback Tom Gorman (No. 12) picks up yardage in Thursday's Thanksgiving Day clash between Newberry and Presbyterian College. The game marked the end of a brilliant college career for the Indian quarterback.—Observer Photo by Marvin (Governor) Bouknight.

The Indian defensive unit held the P. C. offense at the P. C. 49 on a fourth and one situation, and this gave the Indians their first break of the third quarter. They moved the ball to P. C. 26 yard line, but could move no farther. Doug Crawford attempted a field goal from the 34, but the P. C. forward wall broke through to block the kick and P. C. recovered on its own 44. This set up the touchdown pass from Leighton Grantham to halfback Sammy Hagood, which covered 56 yards and came with 12:30 left in the game. Ridinger's kick was good and P. C. led 14-7.

After this Newberry could not generate an offense, as Gorman's passes were falling incomplete, and the P. C. defense stopped the running attack cold.

In the closing minutes of the fourth quarter, P. C. threatened to score its third touchdown, but again the Newberry defense held. This time on the one yard line. P. C. started a march on its own 31. A 47 yard pass from Grantham to Hagood sparked the drive and moved the ball to the Newberry 20 yard line. From where the Blue Hose ran out the clock with a strong running game, and nearly scored, but Newberry held on the one.

Despite the loss, there is one bright spot for the Newberry fans Quarterback Tom Gorman, who picked up 122 yards of Newberry's 169 yards total offense, gained enough yardage to put him over the 1,000 yard mark for the second straight year. His 122 yards was enough to give him 1,012 yard total offense for the year.

The Clinton Chronicle

Vol. 64 — No. 48　　　　　　　　　　　　　Clinton, S. C., Thusday, December 5, 1963

PC Ends Season With Newberry Win

Presbyterian College completed its 1963 football campaign with a two-game winning streak in downing Newberry, 14 to 7, there on Thanksgiving afternoon.

The victory enabled the Blue Hose to recapture the Bronze Derby and finish with a 3-6-1 record for the season. Following on the heels of PC's impressive 24-14 over Troy State in the previous game, it sent gridiron fans into the off-season with higher hopes for next fall.

Presbyterian went 34 yards in the first period for the game's opening score after freshman Halfback Jim Johnson recovered a Tom Gorman fumble. Fullback Randy McCranie paced the drive and finally scored from the one-yard line. End Louis Ridinger kicked the extra point.

Newberry bounced back to tie the count at 7-7 later in the quarter on a 14-yard pass from Gorman to Jim Wren in the end zone and a successful conversion.

Then, early in the fourth quarter, the Blue Hose blocked a Newberry field goal attempt, took over the ball on their own 43 and moved for the decisive touchdown. On the first play from scrimmage, Quarterback Leighton Grantham hit Sandy Hagood with a pass on the Indian 20, and the little halfback scampered the remaining yardage into the endzone. Ridinger again booted the extra point.

This performance gave Grantham the offense leadership among PC backs for the year. He passed for 460 total yards in ten games, completing 37 of 107 attempts. McCranie led the rushing with 379 yards from scrimmage for a 3.3 yards-per-carry average, while Halfback Don McNeill followed closely with 357 and a 4.4 average.

The Li'l That Was!

Reed Charpia is about to get slammed heavily to the ground by several P. C. players who are behind the Indians Dennis Lynn (70) and Doug Crawford (30). Newberry players Fred Haley (84) and Neal Dufford (20) are out of the action while Lynn and Crawford came up too late to help out.

Indian Halfback Bill Eaves is dragged down from behind by an unidentified P. C. player during the Thanksgiving Game. End Dave Hart (83) stands by helplessly as he was unable to cut off the tackle.

Presbyterian College Head Football Coach Cally Gault received the first of 14 Bronze Derby hats he and his team won in his 22 year career at his alma mater. Coach Gault led the Blue Hose on the sidelines from 1963-1984.

Assistant Sports Publicity Director Doug Robertson presents Presbyterian Head Coach Cally Gault with the coveted Bronze Derby on Thanksgiving Day.

End Fred Haley (84) and tackle Dennis Lynn (under Haley) combine to stop Presbyterian's fullback Randie McCranie (with ball) deep in Blue Hose territory during the annual Thanksgiving Bronze Derby affair. Pat Merrick (52 in background) comes up to help Haley and Lynn.

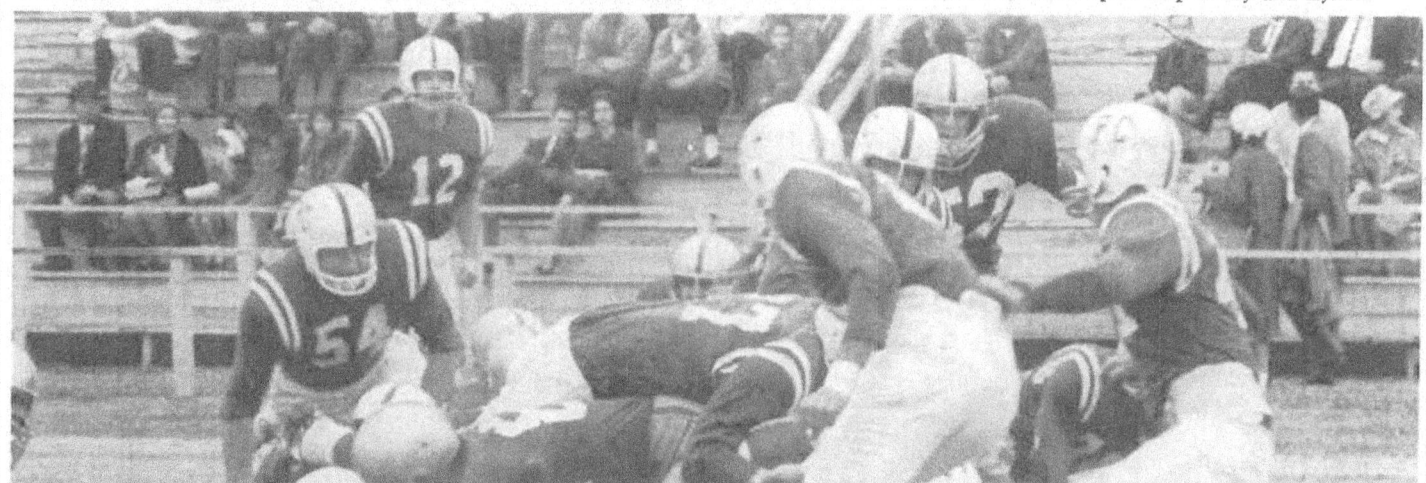

2 Turkey Day Games?

On November 28, 1963, Newberry College hosted Presbyterian College for the annual Thanksgiving Day Bronze Derby game as scheduled despite the assassinanation on November 22, 1963 of President John F. Kennedy. On November 23, 1963, The University of South Carolina Gamecocks and Clemson Tigers were scheduled to play their annual rivalry game. The game was rescheduled to Thursday November 28, 1963. It was the first and only time to date in South Carolina collegiate football history that 2 college football games were played on Thanksgiving Day. Presbyterian College defeated Newberry College 14-7 and Clemson defeated South Carolina 24-20.

November 1964

November 1	NFL Cleveland Browns running back Jim Brown became the first NFL player to rush over 10,000 yards in a career.
November 1	AFL quarterback George Blanda of the Houston Oilers attempted a record 68 passes, completing 34, in a 24-10 loss versus the Buffalo Bills.
November 2	CBS purchased an 80% share of the MLB New York Yankees for $11.2 million.
November 3	For the first time since 1800, residents of Washington, DC are allowed to vote.
November 3	United States President Lyndon Johnson was elected President of the United States defeating Hubert Humphrey.
November 10	Jimmie Dodd, actor on the "Mickey Mouse Club" passed away.
November 10	The Milwaukee Braves signed a 25 year lease to play in the new Atlanta Fulton County Stadium.
November 13	Bob Petit of the St. Louis Hawks became the first NBA player to score 20,000 points.
November 14	MLB Pittsburgh Pirates outfielder Roberto Clemente married Vera Zabala.
November 14	Red Wings Gordie Howe set an NHL record scoring 627 career goals.
November 15	Mickey Wright recorded a 62 in an LPGA event in Midland, Texas. It was the lowest competitive golf score for a professional woman golfer.
November 16	New York Mets pitcher Dwight Gooden was born.
November 18	Brooks Robinson, third baseman for the Baltimore Orioles, won the MLB AL Most Valuable Player Award.
November 18	United States FBI Director J. Edgar Hoover described Martin Luther King Jr. as a "Most notorious liar."
November 23	The Beatles released the singles "I Feel Fine" and "She's a Woman."
November 26	Alabama beat Auburn 21-14 in the 29th annual Iron Bowl.
November 26	The Bronze Derby was played in Clinton, South Carolina on Thanksgiving Day. The Presbyterian College Blue Hose defeated the Newberry College Indians 35-6.

Indians, Blue Hose Clash In Thanksgiving Day Game

By BILL HILTON, JR.

As the opening kick-off sails the length of Presbyterian College's field at 2:00 p.m. Thursday, the Newberry College Indians and the Blue Hose of P. C. will renew a seemingly age-old rivalry with their annual Thanksgiving Day game. The winner of the contest will receive the celebrated Bronze Derby which has been circulating between the arch rivals since 1948. In the last 16 duels since 1948, the Redskins have won five times, P. C. has taken eight wins, and there have been three ties. Last season the Blue Hose topped Newberry with a 14-7 score, created mostly through 104 total yards on two passes and 210 yards rushing by the Blue Hose. In contrast, the Indians collected 104 yards on eight passes and only 60 yards on the ground.

Under their new head coach, Cally Gault (graduate of Presbyterian), P. C. last season compiled a surprising 3-6-1 record. With Gault masterminding the operations again this season, and with most of last year's key players getting into top shape, the Blue Hose will undoubtedly pose a problem to the Newberry squad. Last year's backfield remains nearly intact, with fullback Randie McCranie and halfback Don McNeill doing most of the work. These two backs carried for a total of 727 yards in '63. Quarterback Leighton Grantham, who threw the bladder for 460 yards last season, will be calling the plays.

During the first basketball game between Newberry and Presbyterian, a PC student lost his derby to anonymous Newberry students. In a letter to the sports publicity director at Newberry College, Prof. Charles MacDonald, instructor of English and director of Public Relations at Presbyterian College, suggested that the derby be used as a trophy in athletic contests. The derby was turned over to a local jewelry firm to be cast in bronze. Since then, the Bronze Derby has been given to the winner of the two schools in the three major sports—football, basketball, and track.

Since 1948, the Bronze Derby has see-sawed back and forth in football games.

Last Chance To Win Prediction

This is the final week for a prediction guess. All entries must be filled out and given to Dave Feddern or deposited in the canteen before leaving for the holidays. Everyone (including girls) is invited to participate and welcomed to win $3.

NEWBERRY

P C

Name

NOTICE

Tonight at 7:00 will be the final pep rally of the 1964 season. Everyone come out and support our Fightin' Redskins. The rally will be held in front of Derrick Hall. Following the pep rally, a Hootenanny will be held, featuring many popular and talented vocal groups and soloists. Come and sing along with the rest of Newberry College. The faculty is cordially invited to attend.

The Li'l That Was!

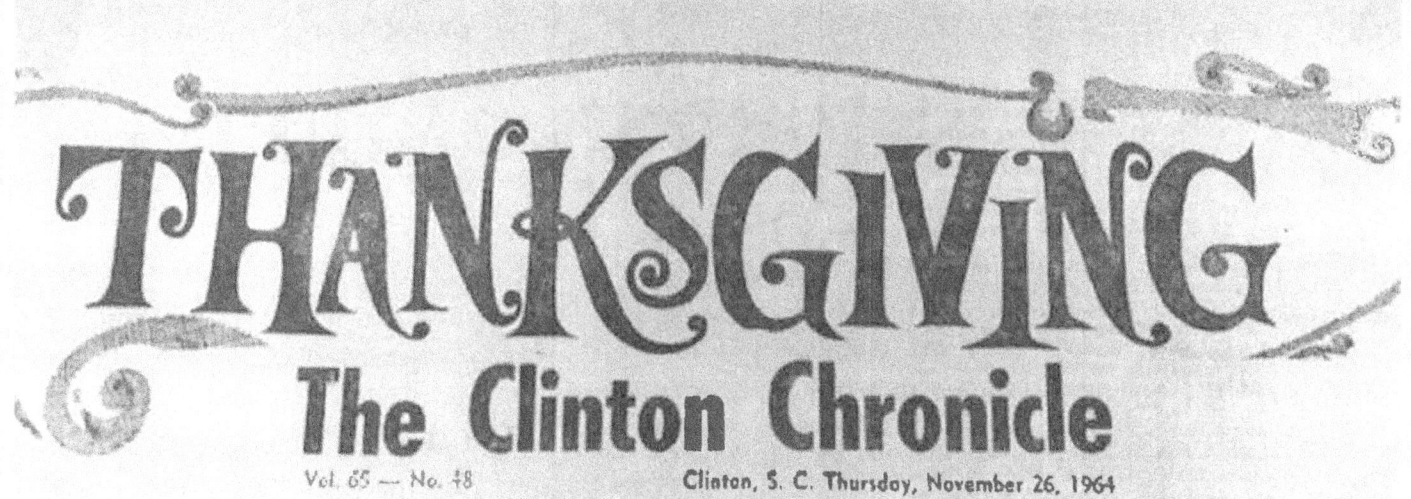

THANKSGIVING
The Clinton Chronicle
Vol. 65 — No. 48   Clinton, S. C. Thursday, November 26, 1964

Hose, Indians To Clash Thursday

The 50th meeting of Presbyterian and Newberry College football teams will be featured here Thanksgiving afternoon when the Blue Hose entertain their arch-rivals in the annual Bronze Derby clash.

Kickoff time is 2:00 p. m. on Johnson Field for this game which also will serve to honor Coach Lonnie S. McMillan, retired former coach who gave 26 years of continuous service to PC athletics.

Many alumni and friends will hit the campus early to enjoy Thanksgiving dinner served in the Presbyterian dining hall. It is scheduled from 11:00 a. m. to 1:00 p. m., with advance reservations requested.

This game will close the season for both participants. Although past records are mostly discounted in this series, the Hoseman rate as slight favorites on the basis of four wins and five losses thus far compared to Newberry's 1-8 record.

PC Coach Cally Gault, hoping to even his season at 5-all, will send an outstanding passing attack against the Indians. It is led by Quarterback Leighton Grantham of Easley, who has completed 70 of 139 passes for 915 yards in the nine games thus far. He holds the school's top individual passing record of all time and will be striving to pass the 1,000 yard mark for aerials this season.

The Blue Hose also have a deadly runner in rugged little Fullback Sam Williams. This dynamo from Monroeville, Ala., has cracked enemy defenses for 586 total rushing yards in 133 carries for a season average of 4.4 per try.

Coach Harvey Kirkland is winding up one of his most disastrous seasons since taking over at Newberry and needs a win over PC to help recapture his luster. His record of just one victory, however, fails to show the dangerous quality of his team. The past performances of Halfback Reed Charpia and Fullback Bill Hammond in particular have the Presbyterian coaches worried.

The Bronze Derby—symbol of football rivalry between PC and Newberry — has undergone a "facelifting" for the traditional game next Thursday.

Gault has had the coveted derby recased with a shiny bronze finish and mounted on a mahogany case.

The derby got its start as a prized symbol while Cally Gault was a student at Presbyterian during a heated PC-Newberry basketball game in the winter of 1947. The fast action ended on the court but not in the stands. And the derby, then a felt lid, was snatched from the head of a Blue Hose supporter by a Newberry fan.

Students from both institutions rallied for the occasion, and out of the dispute came the derby as a token of athletic superiority. The prize was dipped in bronze, and thereafter was awarded to the victorious school after contests in football, basketball and baseball.

The Bronze Derby exchange was limited to football action only in 1955 and the annual fight for possession has held the attention of South Carolina sports fans every Thanksgiving. The derby has rested on PC's shelf six of the nine years since 1955, and is currently in Blue Hose possession by virtue of last season's 14-7 PC victory.

As far as the 49-year season record is concerned, Presbyterian holds a decided edge. The Blue Hose have won 30, against 15 victories for Newberry and 4 ties.

The Li'l That Was!

The Newberry Observer
AND HERALD & NEWS
"Just Like a Letter from Home"

D AND NEWS ESTABLISHED 1865   NEWBERRY, S. C., FRIDAY, NOV. 27, 1964   NEWBERRY OBSERVER ESTABL

50th Meeting Of Indians, P. C. On Thanksgiving

The 50th meeting of the Newberry College and Presbyterian College football teams will be featured Thanksgiving afternoon when the Indians visit their arch-rivals in the annual Bronze Derby tournament.

Kick-off time is 2 p.m. on Johnson Field in Clinton.

P. C. Coach Callie Gault will be aiming for a 5-3 season record in the final game of the 1964 season. Coach Harvey Kirkland's Indians hope to make up for a 1-8 record so far this year with a victory in the long-standing feud which began in 1913.

Presbyterian leads the 49-year series with 30 wins over Newberry against 15 defeats at the hands of the Indians. There have been four ties.

The Indian offense thus far has relied on the running of senior halfback Reid Charpia of Summerville, who will make his last performance; and fullback Bill Hammond of Marietta, Ga., who has dominated all rushing statistics in the last two games since returning from the injured list.

Stalwart lineman Jim Acker, captain from St. Petersburg, Fla., and Dennis Lynn, co-captain from Greer, will see action for the last time also in this game, since graduation bells have tolled for them. Also punting specialist Frank Herlong, senior from Saluda, will make his final performance.

The big man on the Newberry forward wall will be the 1963 All-Conference center Pat Merrick, who has just received 1964 first-team center honors from N.A.I.A.'s District 26.

Appalachian, Lenoir Rhyne and Frederick have all beaten the Indians, while P. C. defeated all three common opponents. Presbyterian's big gun this year has been a passing specialist who will be trying to reach the 1,000-yard season passing mark. Quarterback Leighton Grantham of Easley needs 87 passing yards to reach the 1,000-yard club. He also will have hard-running fullback Sam Williams of Monroeville, Ala., in the backfield to balance the Blue Hose attack in the running game.

The Li'l 🎩 That Was!

Speaking of Sports

With GLEN BROWDER

PC Going To Turkey Bowl For 51st Time

Presbyterian College, already assured of the best football season since 1960, has accepted a bid to play in the Bronze Derby Bowl here Thanksgiving Day. Reports indicate the Blue Hosemen voted almost unanimously to play in the Turkey-day classic against the Indians of Newberry.

Fifty-one Year Series

The PC team will be gunning for a 5-5 season record in the final clash which will renew one of the oldest traditional rivalries in the South. The Presbyterians and Indians first met in 1913, and they played twice that year. Newberry skimmed by the Hose both times by an identical 51-0 score.

Mighty Blue Have Dominated

Since then, however, PC has pounded out its revenge, whipping the Newberrians 30 times while dropping only 15 games. The Hose also own the most one-sided victory in the series, a 54-0 shellacking in 1929. All in all, Presbyterian has scored 654 points in 49 games, allowing the Indians 421 tallies.

But what is the Bronze Derby?

About That Derby . . .

The Bronze Derby is a beaten little hat that sat on the head of a PC student 17 years ago while he watched a Hose-Indian basketball game. The game was played at Newberry in the winter of 1947, and the action was heated on the court and in the stands.

When the action on the court ended, that in the stands became eve more heated and a Newberry student grabbed the little brown derby and ran. A spirited dispute followed, which included our present head football coach, and out of the scramble came the derby as a symbol of athletic superiority between the two schools.

The derby was dipped in bronze and was ceremoniously awarded to the school which was victorious after each encounter in three sports—football, basketball and baseball.

After the first few years, the Bronze Derby ownership was decided by the traditional football game alone. Hence the name of the annual Bronze Derby gridiron clash between the Blue Hose and Indians each Thanksgiving.

PC Hopes To Give It A Home

PC currently owns the coveted prize, captured with a 14-7 victory last year. The derby has been re-covered with a bright coat of bronze, and will be displayed along the sidelines of the game here Thursday afternoon.

Smith Elliott Galloway Nix Hagood
Welsh Cape Lowrance Lokey West

Ten PC Seniors Play Final Game Against Indians Thanksgiving Day

By AL PEARCE
Co-Editor of Sports

Ten seniors will play their final game as Blue Hosemen on Thanksgiving Day in the traditional Presbyterian - Newberry clash. Gametime will be 2:00 on PC's Walter Johnson Field.

The ancient rivalry between the two denominational schools has always been billed as "the game of the year" for both teams, one in which all the stops are pulled. It is always the final regular season game for both schools and reports from the Newberry camp have it that the Indians are already anxious to get at the Hose.

For the Blue Hose of coach Cally Gault the game is also crucial because a PC win will insure a break-even season—something the Hose have not enjoyed since 1960. Not since the team of that fall posted a 6-3 record has a PC football team had at least a .500 year. Going into the final game with a 4-5 mark, the Hose may get that break-even win on Thanksgiving Day.

Newberry will be trying to salvage their second win from a season that has not been kind to coach Harvey Kirkland. Newberry has managed to win but once in nine outings, over a weak Guilford College team at home three weeks ago.

For the PC seniors it'll be their chance to take their second win in four years over their arch-rivals. Going into the game the Hose and the Indians have split exactly the past three games.

Despite their poor record going into the game, the Indians have showed signs of coming out of the slump that plagued them in the early games of the year. Coach Gault and his staff have expressed concern over stopping the three major threats in the Indians' camp — quarterback Benji Kirkland, fullback Jerry Hammond and halfback Reed Charpia.

Belk's

Manstyle Jackets ... 10.99
—Dacron-Cotton
—Water Repellent
—Machine Washable
—Wrinkle Resistant
Navy — Oyster — Light Blue
Maize

Hubbard Pants 7.99
Dacron-Cotton — Wash 'N' Wear

The Li'l 🎩 That Was!

McINTOSH'S SHOE SHOP
Catering to PC Students
for 47 Years
203 Musgrove St.

J. C. THOMAS
JEWELER
"It's Time That Counts"

Sadler-Owens Pharmacy
Stationery, School Supplies

Yarborough
Studio and Camera Shop
Phone 833-1900
Cameras - Film - Processing

The Blue Stocking

Win Over Newberry Gives PC Surprising 5-5 Record

By BILL BASSHAM
Blue Stocking Sports Writer

Coach Cally Gault's surprising Blue Hose defeated Newberry 35-6 in the Bronze Derby Classic on Thanksgiving Day to even the season's mark at 5-5. A crowd of almost 4,000 saw the Hose romp over the visitors.

Sam Williams started the scoring in the first period on a three-yard drive. Jimmy Cape kicked his first of five conversions for the afternoon. The big play in the drive was a 30-yard pass from quarterback Leighton Grantham to freshman end Richard Reed.

An interception early in the second quarter by halfback Jim Johnson set up PC's second score. Johnson carried it on a seven-yard run. PC followed with another second quarter score with Don McNeil carrying it in from the two. At the half PC led 21-0.

A fired-up Newberry held PC at bay in the third quarter, but early in the fourth quarter a screen pass to end James Smith from Jackie Nix covering 5 yards with a key block from Allen Harris resulted in a score. A few minutes later Don McNeil capped the scoring for the afternoon by making his second touchdown of the day on a thirty-yard run.

Newberry finally scored with sixteen seconds left in the game. Halfback Jim Swykert gathered in a Kirkland pass for the score. A try for a two-point conversion was no good.

Many of the PC fans were worried late in the second quarter when quarterback Leighton Grantham re-injured his knee. Grantham set a school season passing record in the game. Senior quarterback Jackie Nix from Bainbridge, Ga., who has seen most of his action this year as a defensive back, completed his career with his finest game. Nix carried the team throughout the second half—passing for one touchdown and making several key runs.

HOWARD'S PHARMACY
"YOUR REXALL DRUG STORE"
Drugs ... Fountain Service ... Gifts
ON THE SQUARE

The Newberry Observer
AND HERALD & NEWS
"Just Like a Letter from Home"

NEWBERRY, S. C., TUESDAY, DEC. 1, 1964

Indians Lose Bronze Derby To Blue Hose

By DOUG ROBERTSON

The Newberry College Indians capped a last-plagued season Thanksgiving Day at P. C., allowing the Blue Hose to keep the Bronze Derby laurel by a 35-6 romp.

A 1-8 season seemed to take its toll upon the attitude of the Indians' Thanksgiving, as the Blue Hose tallied 21 points in the first half.

Coach Harvey Kirkland sparked the team enough through a half-time conference to come back in the second half to score once and defense the Blue Hose to two touchdowns, both of which were short-yardage drives.

Newberry's only gain was made on the ground, largely through the efforts of halfback Reid Charpia who accumulated better than half of the net rushing gain. The larger hunk of the remaining yardage was gained by Joe Wrenn, junior halfback from Gaffney. Bill Hammond, fullback from Marietta, Ga., has averaged nearly 100 yards for the last two games. The scouts from P. C. apparently knew him well, since Bill picked up only 14 yards in six tries.

Benji Kirkland went through a nightmare at the quarterback position being caught behind the line three times for losses of 28 yards. His luck at the aerial attack went about the same. He completed only five passes for 29 yards out of 20 attempts and two interceptions. Benji had some trouble with overthrowing, but on three occasions the guided pigskin was just plain dropped.

Pat Merrick played an outstanding game at linebacker, accounting for most of the tackles, and his excellent pursuit of the ball carrier led to many assists.

Early in the first quarter, Blue Hose quarterback Leighton Grantham paved the way for the first touchdown by hitting freshman end Dick Reed with a 33-yard pass which brought the play within five yards of the goal. Two plays later fullback Sam Williams drove two yards for the score. Tackle Jimmy Cape kicked the extra point.

P. C.'s next teedee came late in the first period when halfback Jim Johnson intercepted a Kirkland pass on Newberry's 24-yard line. After several short passes, Johnson followed the interception with a five-yard burst over left tackle for the score. Cape again booted the extra point with his "educated toe."

The Blue Hose's last score of the first half was stimulated by Grantham, who completed several passes placing the ball on the Indians' four. Several plays, shifty Don McNeil skirted three yards to pay dirt. Cape split the uprights for the third consecutive time to send the Hose in at halftime with a 21-0 lead.

Newberry's defense picked up in the third quarter and held P. C. scoreless. Early in the fourth, Jackie Nix, replacing the injured Grantham (starting signal caller) stimulated a steady 40-yard drive down to the Newberry 10. The screen pass from Nix to Jim Smith, and, and an extra point kick by Cape made the score 28-0.

P. C.'s final touchdown came at the last of the game with a Kirkland pass intercepted by Bryan Bolcom to set up a 30-yard touchdown run by halfback McNeil.

Newberry's only score came in the final minutes, climaxing a 78-yard drive. Through Charpia's running and passing the Indians moved the ball steadily, ending the drive when the Summerville halfback hit end Donnie Swygert 11 yards away in the end zone with a well-guided pass.

Frank Herlong, senior punting specialist, played his best game of the season, averaging 37 yards in eight punts. His worst punt was 26 yards, which was pressured by a poor pass from center. His longest boot went 45 yards.

make Christmas dreams come true
-and pay year-end bills too

Deposit Weekly	Get at End of Year (50 weeks)
$ .50	$ 25.00
1.00	50.00
2.00	100.00
3.00	150.00
5.00	250.00
10.00	500.00

Open your SCN Christmas Club account now!

SOUTH CAROLINA NATIONAL
The Bank for Everybody
THERE'S AN SCN OFFICE NEAR YOU
NEWBERRY • 1119-21 BOYCE ST.

November 1965

November 1	In Cairo, Egypt, a trolley fell into the Nile River drowning 74.
November 3	Sandy Koufax of the Los Angeles Dodgers won the MLB Cy Young Award.
November 7	Pillsbury Company introduced "Poppin' Fresh" as its mascot for dough and crescent rolls.
November 8	Soap opera "Days of Our Lives" premiered on United States television.
November 8	American baseball player Jeff Blauser was born.
November 9	Willie Mays of the San Francisco Giants won the MLB NL Most Valuable Player Award.
November 9	Several northeast US states and eastern Canada are hit with a blackout that lasted for up to 13 hours.
November 12	Ferdinand Marcos was elected President of the Philippines.
November 14	Actress Judy Garland married actor Mark Herron.
November 14	The United States sent 90,000 soldiers to Vietnam.
November 15	In Central Florida, Walt Disney announced a plan for a family attraction in Orange County Florida on 27,000 acres.
November 16	Walt Disney launched Epcot Center (Environmental Prototype Community of Tomorrow).
November 17	The United Nations voted on a resolution to admit the People's Republic of China as a member.
November 18	Former United States Vice President Henry A. Wallace passed away.
November 19	ABC Radio began its weekly "Vietnam Update" report.
November 19	Kellogg's Pop Tarts were introduced.
November 22	American folk singer Bob Dylan married actress Sara Lowndes.
November 22	Muhammad Ali KO's Floyd Patterson in Las Vegas, NV to retain the World Heavyweight Boxing Championship.
November 22	The musical "Man of La Mancha" opened off Broadway, becoming a major success and ran for over 2300 performances.
November 25	NFL Hall of Fame wide receiver Cris Carter was born.
November 25	The Bronze Derby was played in Newberry, South Carolina on Thanksgiving Day. The Newberry College Indians defeated the Presbyterian College Blue Hose 6-0.

The Li'l 🎩 That Was!

The Indian
"Voice of the Newberry College Student"

VOL. XXXVIII NEWBERRY, S. C., WEDNESDAY, NOVEMBER 17, 1965 NUMBER 15

Thanksgiving Holidays
Thanksgiving recess will begin on Wednesday, November 24, after class. Classes will resume on Monday, November 29, beginning with 8:00 classes.

The big question at Thanksgiving: Will Newberry or Presbyterian become the proud possessor of the celebrated Bronze Derby?

Indians Meet PC Here For Annual Thanksgiving Clash

Newberry College Indians round out their 1965 football schedule next week in the annual Thanksgiving Day clash with arch-rival Presbyterian College. This year the game will be played on Setzler Field at 2:00 p.m.

In last season's quest for the coveted Bronze Derby, the favored Blue Hose rolled over a hapless Newberry squad 35-6. The Indians last had possession of the metal hat in 1962 when they topped PC 23-7. Prior to that, the Scarlet and Gray hadn't brought home the bacon since 1957.

1965's Turkey Day duel, however, is up for grabs, with most authorities favoring the Clinton team to win by a few points. (The Indian is not one of those who picks Newberry to lose.) PC will be going into the game with a seasonal record of 5-4, while the 'Skins sport a two win, seven loss banner. In last week's action, the Blue Hose exploded past Frederick's Lions 37-14. (Frederick defeated Newberry earlier this season) and the Indians went scoreless against West Carolina's 19-point total.

Cally Gault's Garnet and Blue team makes it debut into Carolinas Conference competition this year with last year's entire starting backfield returning. All-State quarterback Leighton Grantham — a record-breaking passer with three years' experience — heads the list. Fullback Sam Williams, who ground out over 800 yards in 1964, will be back with halfbacks Don McNeill and Wade Stewart to take the hand-offs from Grantham. Again this year the forward line will be relatively light, averaging about 175 pounds, and it will be sparked by returning lettermen Jimmy Bankhead and Joe Lawson.

Prediction Contest

In last week's football prediction contest, Nelson Merrell was closest out of a big 21 ballots with a 20-7 score in favor of West Carolina. The actual score was 19-0. Let's have a little better turn-out for the prediction of the Newberry-Presbyterian Thanksgiving Day clash. Simply turn in the blank below (or any other similar blank) to Bill Hilton, or place it in the box on the canteen counter before the holidays. The prize will be up to four free passes for this game.

This Week's Score:

NEWBERRY _____

PRESBYTERIAN _____

Name _____

Singing goes better refreshed. And Coca-Cola — with that special zing but never too sweet — refreshes best.

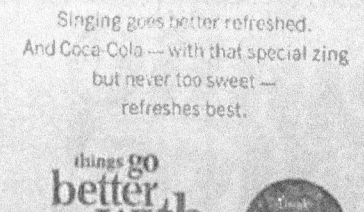

NEWBERRY COCA-COLA BOTTLING COMPANY

The Newberry Observer
AND HERALD & NEWS
"Just Like a Letter from Home"

NEWBERRY, S. C., FRIDAY, NOV. 26, 1965

Indians, Blue Hose Tangle In 54th Thanksgiving Game

The Newberry College Indians and the Presbyterian College Blue Hose tangle Thanksgiving Day in their annual battle for the Bronze Derby. Kickoff time is 2 p.m. at Newberry's Setzler Field.

This will be the 54th edition of the game of the year for both schools. Presbyterian leads the series, which began in 1913, with 32 victories and 17 losses. There have been four ties.

P. C. comes into the game highly favored. The Blue Hose have a 5-4 record, compared to Newberry's 2-7. P. C. has victories over Wofford, Elon, Furman, Troy State, and Frederick, while losing to Davidson, Lenoir Rhyne, Appalachian, and Western Carolina. Newberry's only victories have come over Catawba and Elon.

Newberry enters the game well rested with their injury list shorter than usual. While P. C. was suffering an 8-7 setback by Western Carolina, the Indians spent the whole week concentrating on P. C.

Fullback Sam Williams and quarterback Bill Kirtland lead an explosive offense for the Blue Hose. Williams, a veteran senior, has turned into a powerful and dependable runner. He led P. C. last year in rushing and has improved steadily. He and halfback Don McNeill form a hard rushing offense.

Kirtland solved a problem at quarterback left by the graduation of Leighton Grantham, an all-state performer. A small 145-pounder, Kirtland has proved to be a capable passer and a running threat.

P. C. defense, although porous at times, is led by ends

ME SCALP UM HOSE

Jimmy Bankhead and Joe Lawson. This twosome has made it hard for opposing runners to turn the corner.

Newberry, plagued by injuries all season, has been boosted by the return of two players to full time action. Defensive halfback Bill Semple, who intercepted three passes in one game this season, returns after missing the Western Carolina game due to a leg injury. Also, fullback Terry Holder, a freshman, will be running after missing five games because of a leg injury.

The Indians promise some new wrinkles to their sagging offense. Newberry has scored only one touchdown in the last three games, and only once have they scored more than two TD's in one game. Leading the offense has been halfback Bill Eaves, who has averaged four yards a carry in 60 attempts for 232 yards. Behind Eaves in rushing is freshman George Taylor, the team's leading scorer. He has gained 190 yards in 55 carries.

The starting backfield is not definite yet, but the fixture is quarterback Benji Kirkland. He leads the team in total offense, although he has rushed for -13 yards. He has completed 40 passes for 608 yards and two touchdowns.

All-conference candidates Pat Merrick and Ray Solomon lead the Newberry defense. Merrick, a linebacker, has played consistently outstanding defense, leading the team in tackles. Solomon, after a slow start, has terrorized opposing backs from his middle guard position.

THANKSGIVING
The Clinton Chronicle
Vol. 66 — No. 47 Clinton, S. C., Thursday November 25, 1965

At Newberry — For Bronze Derby
Hose, Indians to Clash Thursday

This is the one! All the marbles are at stake in the upcoming Presbyterian-Newberry football game, as the Blue Stockings shoot for their first winning season since 1960 in the traditional Bronze Derby fight at 2:00 p. m. Thanksgiving Day at Newberry.

The coveted Bronze Derby will go on the chopping block once again, with Presbyterian hoping to keep the symbol of football superiority between the old-time rivals for the third straight year. PC took last year's game 35-6, after a 14-7 upset victory by the Hose in 1963.

The Hosemen have a 5-4 record and the Indians are 2-7, but this annual meeting shows no favoritism to the favorites. PC is way out front in the 53-year-old rivalry, with 32 wins against 17 for the Newberry crowd. There have been four tie games.

For the Presbyterians, this all-important finale could leave them with the best record in the state at 6-4, after they were picked as the bottom college football squad before the season started. They lost the first two games of the campaign, then won five of the next seven.

This past week-end saw PC lose a close defensive thriller by an 8-7 count to the strong Western Carolina Catamounts, as the Cullowhee, N. C., squad hit on an 85-yard bomb to open the fourth quarter and added a 2-point conversion for the decision. It was a hard loss for the Hose, who held the upper hand the majority of the battle in their best defensive effort of the year. Quarterback Bill Kirtland put PC ahead in the third period on a 5-yard run, and Richard Reed's PAT kick made it 7-0 until the big pass play by WCC.

Kirtland is almost a certainty to capture season offensive honors for the Hosemen, since the poised rookie already has 767 yards passing going into the last game. He has compiled 58 of 117 passes, including nine touchdowns. End James Smith has taken over the pass-catching lead, with 16 receptions for 166 yards. The top ground gainer is Fullback Sam Williams, who has rushed 473 yards on 112 carries, a 4.2 average.

The Newberry Observer
AND HERALD & NEWS
"Just Like a Letter from Home"

NEWBERRY, S. C., TUESDAY, NOV. 26, 1968

Indians Blank PC, 6-0

Newberry College quarterback Benji Kirkland fired a fourth-quarter touchdown pass to freshman fullback Terry Holder last Thursday to give the Indians a 6-0 Thanksgiving Day victory over Presbyterian College in the annual Bronze Derby classic.

The touchdown pitch, which proved to be the margin of difference point-wise between the clubs in this traditional battle, came with 11:29 left in the fourth quarter.

The Indians had gone into the game as a 10-point underdog, but season performances and pre-game predictions are tossed out the window when these two clubs meet in the Bronze Derby.

"I'm glad we could win this one for these boys, I'm proud of this team," Coach Harvey Kirkland commented after the game. "This fixes our season up just wonderful."

Kirkland commented that "We felt we could stop Presbyterian's running, but we were worried about their long passes. So we gave them the short hooks and screens and wouldn't give them the long ones."

Presbyterian got only 85 yards in the rushing department, but completed nine of 16 tosses for 136 yards.

Newberry's ground hammered out 185 yards and Kirkland had three completions of 10 pass attempts for 38 yards. One of these, however, proved to be the deciding factor of the victory.

The win was the third against seven losses for Coach Kirkland, while it evened the season at 5-5 for Cally Gault's P. C. squad.

The Newberry touchdown drive started early in the final period when the Indians took a punt at the P. C. 46. Neil Dufford took the ball on a counter play and dashed off left tackle. He cut back to the right in the secondary and was brought down by P. C.'s Wade Stewart on the P. C. 13.

After Kirkland had fumbled back to the 19, the Indian quarterback faked to Holder up the middle, faked the counter and dropped back to pass. He hit Holder with a perfect pitch to the end zone.

P. C.'s most serious threat came in the third quarter. On fourth and 14 at his own 16, Jimmy Elliott returned to punt. An onrushing Indian lineman appeared to have a blocked kick in the bag so Elliott galloped out of trouble for 20 yards and a first down. One play later, fullback Sam Williams dashed 24 yards to the Newberry 30. Don McNeill raced nine yards on the first down. McNeill failed to gain on a pitchout and Bill Kirtland's pass was knocked down. The freshman P. C. quarterback fumbled the snap on fourth and one for a three-yard loss to end the threat.

DUFFORD GETS INDIAN YARDAGE: Newberry back Neal Dufford (No. 40) is shown cutting off left tackle during last Thursday's Thanksgiving Day game at Newberry with Presbyterian College. —Observer Photo by Jerry Davenport.

The Newberry Observer
AND HERALD & NEWS
"Just Like a Letter from Home"

The Li'l That Was!

FINAL SECONDS BRING KIRKLAND SMILE: The final seconds of last Thursday's Thanksgiving Day classic between Newberry and Presbyterian at Newberry's Setzler Field, brought a broad smile to the face of Newberry College Head Coach Harvey Kirkland standing next to Newberry cheerleaders. This picture was made in the final two seconds of the game which the Indians won, 6-0. —Observer Photo by Jerry Davenport.

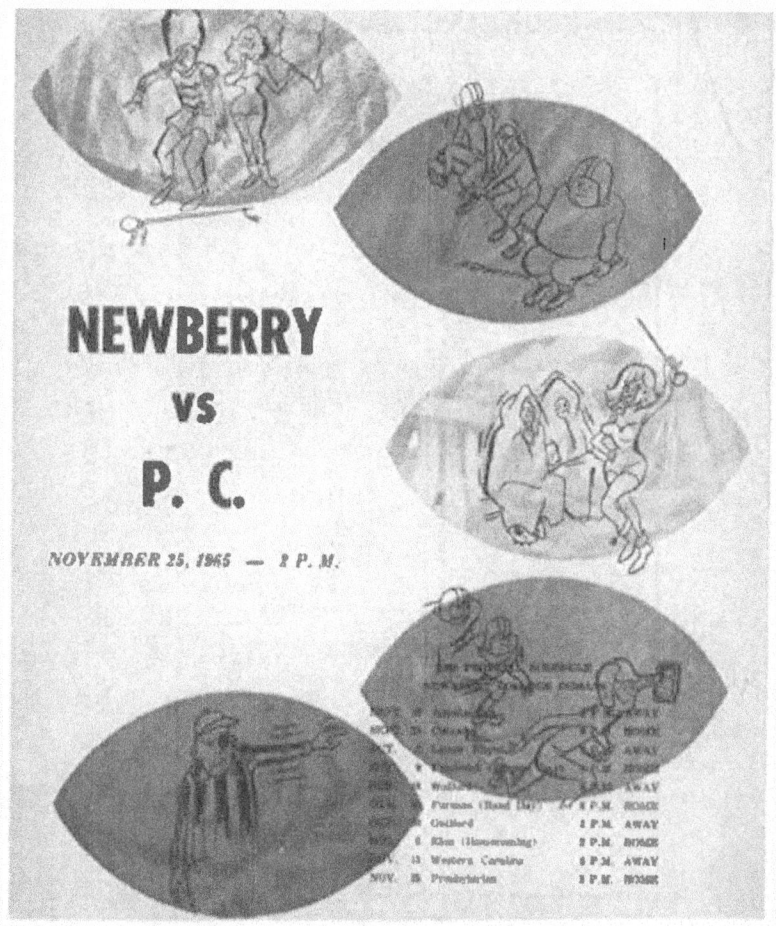

NEWBERRY VS P. C.

NOVEMBER 25, 1965 — 1 P.M.

The Li'l That Was!

In the 19th Thanksgiving Day Bronze Derby football Classic on November 25, 1965, Newberry College defeated Presbyterian College 6-0 in Newberry, South Carolina.

Quarterback Benji Kirkland (14) cuts to pick up a block from tackle Mike Hill (74) against win-hungry P.C.

The Li'l That Was!

'Skins Triumph, Take PC Derby

The Indian
"Voice of the Newberry College Student"

Christmas Formal Saturday Nite

VOL. XXXVIII — NEWBERRY, S. C., WEDNESDAY, DECEMBER 1, 1965 — NUMBER 11

Rivals 6-0 On 4th Period TD

By RICHARD HERRINGTON

An aroused tribe of Newberry Indians swept past a surprised Presbyterian team Thanksgiving Day to recapture the Bronze Derby with a 6-0 victory on a pass from quarterback Benji Kirkland to Terry Holder. The victory closed out a 3-7 season for the 'Skins of Coach Harvey Kirkland, while PC finished 5-5.

Defense was the key to the victory. Although the Blue Hose totaled 225 yards on offense, they were held to a paltry 85 yards on the ground. Senior co-captain Pat Merrick played probably his best defensive game of the season, spending more time in PC's backfield than did their halfbacks. Credited with 20 tackles and several assists, he alone was responsible with stopping one TD drive when PC needed inches for a touchdown on the Newberry 32. Merrick slammed through the forward wall to nail the runner behind scrimmage. He had help aplenty from his sidekicks, Ray Solomon and Bobby Carlton, also playing outstanding defensive games. Solomon, from his middle guard slot, tormented the PC quarterback and threw him for important losses. Carlton, one of the most underrated defensive players on the team, kept PC's halfbacks from turning the corner for big gains.

The improved blocking of tackle Mike Hill and guard Mike Collins opened numerous holes for Newberry halfbacks and allowed them to pick up good yardage. Frosh George Taylor led all runners with 98 yards in 18 attempts, and Neil Dufford, a junior, was right behind with 80 yards in 13 carries.

The first half of the struggle was scoreless, though both teams threatened. PC took the opening kickoff and moved to Newberry's 15 before giving up the ball on downs. Then Indians, too, were unable to move far, and PC received the ball again, moving to Newberry's 27 where a rough interior line held them one yard short of the first down. After taking charge, the Indians kept the Blue Hose deep in their own territory, once driving the visitors to their own two on a fine punt coverage by Gerald Beatty.

The Indians threatened midway through the second period after Beatty recovered a fumbled punt on PC's 45, but the drive culminated when Kirkland's pass on the 28 passed through Dennis Swygert's fingertips in the end zone.

For the 'Skins the final break came on their opening series in the fourth quarter when, after a 13-yard punt, Newberry had the ball on the PC 47. On the first play, Dufford scampered 34 yards down the sidelines for a first down on the 13. A pitch-out lost six yards on the next play, but Kirkland hit fullback Holder over the middle for a 19-yard scoring pass. Joby Castles missed the PAT, but six points was enough to put the Scarlet and Gray on top.

The Li'l  That Was!

The Indian
"Voice of the Newberry College Student"

Christmas Formal Saturday Nite

XXXVIII NEWBERRY, S. C., WEDNESDAY, DECEMBER 1, 1965 NUMBER 11

No One Player Was Greatest

The Indian sports staff was faced with an impossible task this week in picking a player of the week, so we decided to award the honor as it should be awarded—to the entire squad. If ever there was a supreme team effort to overcome a rival, the Thanksgiving game with PC was it.

Of course, we first notice the scoring play when quarterback Benji Kirkland passed 19 yards to punting halfback Terry Holder, who managed to fall over the goal line for the only points of the ball game. Pat Merrick was fantastic on defense and offense, making 20 individual tackles in the former role, and, along with Mike Collins and Mike Hill, opening up the PC line so that backs George Taylor and Neil Dufford could romp for 58 and 80 yards rushing, respectively. Then there was the recovery of two Presbyterian fumbles by Gerald Beatty and Chip Shealy and the tough defensive line work of the latter. Ray Solomon and Tommy McAdams, too, turned in fine defensive efforts, both of them getting in on the PC quarterback with regularity. Dennis Swygert, the rambling end, pulled down a Kirkland pass and romped on defense, and Pete Peterson is credited with deflecting a PC pass which could have made a difference. Jim Sifrit and Bobby Carlton knocked heads in their usual fashion on defense and kept the Blue Hose offense shaking like a leaf. Of course, there were others who made fine plays and contributed to the victory and they all deserve to be called the player of the week.
BH

E. B. PURCELL **KEITT PURCELL**
BEN STEWART **BOBBY UNDERWOOD**

PURCELLS
All Forms of Insurance
All Types of Loans

COME TO SEE US! PHONE 276-1422

Wertz Music & Appliance Co.
RADIO - PHONO - TV
RECORDS - TAPE
932 Lower Main

Quarterback Benji Kirkland hunts for a break in the PC line as he scoots through for a gain. The Indians won 6-0.

November 1966

November 1	The MLB NL Cy Young Award was awarded to Los Angeles Dodgers pitcher Sandy Koufax.
November 1	The NFL awarded a franchise to the city of New Orleans, Louisiana.
November 2	American actor David Schwimmer, best known for his role in "Friends" was born.
November 5	#1 on the US *Billboard* chart was "The Last Train to Clarksville" by the Monkees.
November 5	NCAA BYU quarterback Virgil Carter sets an NCAA single game passing record throwing for 513 yards versus Texas Western.
November 6	For the first time, NBC televised its complete lineup in color.
November 8	Frank Robinson of the Cleveland Indians won the MLB AL Most Valuable Player Award. He was the first player in MLB history to win the award in both the NL and AL.
November 8	Actor Ronald Reagan was elected Governor of California.
November 8	British reality actor and chef Gordon Ramsey was born.
November 8	Edward W. Brooke of Massachusetts became the first African American elected to the United States Senate.
November 11	NASA launched the Gemini 12 spaceship.
November 12	While aboard Gemini 12, United States astronaut Buzz Aldrin took the first selfie in space.
November 13	Comedian Flip Wison made his first appearance on "The Ed Sullivan Show."
November 14	Muhammed Ali TKO's Cleveland Williams in 3 rounds.
November 16	Pittsburgh Pirates outfielder Robero Clemente was named MLB NL Most Valuable Player.
November 18	MLB player Hank Greenberg married Mary Jo Tarola.
November 21	NFL Hall of Fame quarterback Troy Aikman was born.
November 22	Florida quarterback Steve Spurrier won the Heisman Trophy.
November 24	The Beatles began recording "Sgt Pepper's Lonely Hearts Club Band."
November 24	The Bronze Derby was played in Clinton, South Carolina on Thanksgiving Day. The Presbyterian College Blue Hose defeated the Newberry College Indians 28-7.

The Clinton Chronicle

Vol. 67 — No. 47   Clinton, S. C., Thursday, November 24, 1966

On Johnson Field — For Bronze Derby

Hose, Indians to Clash Thursday

Presbyterian College seeks to sustain its bid for a share of the Carolinas Conference championship in entertaining arch-rival Newberry in the season-closing Bronze Derby football game here Thanksgiving afternoon.

The Blue Hose will lineup for the 2 p.m. kickoff as slight favorites. If they succeed, it will mean a 6-4 season and the first winning record since

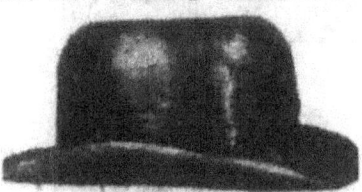

THE BRONZE DERBY

1960. And should league-leading Lenoir Rhyne lose to Catawba that same afternoon, PC will tie the Bears for the Carolinas Conference title.

Thursday's game is the 55th renewal of the PC-Newberry gridiron series, dating back to 1913 and ranking among the oldest athletic rivalries of the state. The Bronze Derby is the symbol of that rivalry, and the Thanksgiving winner will have the privilege of dis-

With Pay

Holiday For Mills

All plants of Clinton Mills will close at midnight Wednesday for a Thanksgiving holiday.

Thanksgiving Day is one of the company's designated holidays with pay for all eligible employees, officials stated. Operations will resume with the regular third shift at 12 midnight Thursday.

---

playing it in the college trophy case for the coming year.

Presbyterian will enter the game just five days after whipping, 42-29, the same Western Carolina team that defeated Newberry by a 40-0 count the previous weekend. But comparative scores go out the window for this particular contest, as PC fans learned as recently as last year, when Newberry posted a 6-0 upset. Nevertheless, the Blue Hose do hold a decided edge in the long series — 32 victories to 18 for Newberry and 4 ties.

Last Saturday afternoon's game against Western Carolina found PC turning in its most explosive performance in some time. Touchdowns came on a 64-yard pass, Bill Kirtland to Dan Eckstein; a 63-yard run by Jim Johnson; an 11-yard pass from Kirtland to James Smith; a 36-yard pass from Kirtland to Richard Reed; a 42-yard run on pass interception by Bob Hackle; and finally, a 9-yard run by Hackle.

Coach Cally Gault hopes to keep his Hosemen generating at full steam Thursday, but he has great respect for the solid Newberry defense and the effective running game led by Halfback George Taylor.

Quarterback Bill Kirtland will be attempting to extend his new school passing record while two halfbacks and a fullback battle it out for the rushing lead.

Kirtland, a sophomore from Miami, has completed 95 of 189 passes for 1,115 yards and 13 touchdowns. That's the most yardage ever compiled by a PC passer in one campaign.

The battle for the season's top rusher is up for grabs among halfbacks Dan Eckstein of Atlanta, Jim Johnson of Georgiana, Ala., and fullback Sam Williams of Monroeville, Ala. Eckstein is the front-runner after nine games with 417 yards on 87 rushes for a 4.8 average.

Williams has rushed for 408 yards on 113 carries for a 3.6 average. Then Johnson suddenly jumped into the heat of the race on the strength of last week's performance against Western Carolina when he racked up 121 yards. He has now gained 395 yards on 66 rushes for a 6.0 average.

The pass catchers still have a close race going on for the leading receiver. End James Smith of Sylvania, Ga. has 35 receptions for 438 yards and five touchdowns. However, end Richard Reed of Columbus, Ga., has more yards (447) on 31 receptions.

Reed is also the team's leading scorer with 51 points on the basis of six touchdowns, 10 of 14 conversion attempts, a two-point conversion, and one field goal.

The team has gained 2,718 yards for an average of 302 yards per game. Rushing yardage amounts to 1,409, while the passing game has added 1,309 yards.

FOOTBALL

PRESBYTERIAN
vs
NEWBERRY

Thursday, 1:45 P. M.

Air Time
— Over —

WLBG-FM

Follow The Blue Hose at Home and Away For The Entire Ten-Game Schedule

— Sponsored By —

Greenwood Mills of Joanna	D. E. Tribble Company
Lynn Cooper, Inc., Dodge Dealer	Walter Johnson Club

The Li'l  That Was!

The Indian
"Voice of the Newberry College Student"

Christmas Formal Saturday Nite

VOL. XXXVIII — NEWBERRY, S. C., WEDNESDAY, DECEMBER 1, 1965 — NUMBER 11

Indians To Face Presbyterian

By RICHARD HERRINGTON

Presbyterian College, defending Carolinas Conference Co-Champions, provide the Newberry Redskins with their next opponent on Thanskgiving Day in the traditional Bronze Derby battle. Game time is 2 pm at Newberry's Setzler Field.

The Newberry-PC clash is one of the oldest traditional battles in the area. The winner is awarded a bronze derby, the prize in a scuffle several years ago on Thanksgiving.

Newberry will have a slight scheduling advantage going into the game. The Indians of coach Harvey Kirkland have a week off to prepare for the game, while the Blue Hose of Cally Gault tangle with Western Carolina this weekend. Western Carolina defeated Newberry last week 35-0 while Presbyterian had an off date.

Presbyterian started off the 1967 season with a blaze of glory, upsetting highly regarded Lenoir Rhyne and establishing themselves as Carolinas Conference contenders. But the bottom soon fell out of their dream as the team found it hard to win again. Their fall was climaxed two weeks ago when they lost to Appalachian by seven touchdowns.

The Blue Hose gained their early victories by taking advantage of every mistake of their opponents. Their opportunist defense is led by middle guard Mickey Hampshire, who is back after sitting out the 1966 season.

Bill Kirtland, an effective runner and a dangerous passer, leads the offense from his quarterback position. He is backed by little Allen McNeil, a strong passer. Dan Eckstein is the leading ground gainer and also serves as a pass receiver from his halfback slot. The offensive line is centered around the blocking of tackle Eddie Walker and guard Jim Sullenberger.

Newberry is suffering through one of its worst seasons in the history of the school. The Indians have tasted victory only once in nine contests. They tied one game and have lost seven. The season would still be somewhat of a success if Newberry can avenge last year's 28-7 loss to PC.

Bronze Derby

The P. C. Blue Hose visit Setzler Field next Thursday to renew the Thanksgiving rivalry for the Bronze Derby. The clash will be the 53rd. between the two teams in a series which dates back to 1913. P. C. now holds a 32-16-4 edge over the Indians.

The Bronze Derby originated as the result of a highly spirited ruckus that took place when P. C.'s basketball team played at Newberry on the night of January 30, 1947. Before the game started, a group of P. C. students put up a high banner on the wall of the gymnasium, which read, "Beat Hell Out of Newberry!" During the game several Newberry students gained access to a ladder, climbed the outside of the wall, entered through the window, rolled up the banner, and exited undetected the same way they had entered. Toward the end of the contest the visitors discovered that their banner was missing! Then when the game ended and P. C. had taken a 51-47 victory, the irate visitors demanded the return of their banner. A scuffle developed and in the midst of the confusion, a Newberry student grabbed a derby off the head of a P. C. student and ran.

During the next two days, negotiations went on between the athletic publicity directors of the two schools. The result of the negotiations was that the derby was to serve as a laurel of victory in athletic contests between the two schools. The hat was returned, packaged, and forwarded to a casting company in Ohio, where the bronzing was done.

At first, possession of the Bronze Derby was determined by victories in football, basketball, and baseball, but in 1956 it was decided to award the trophy on the basis of gridiron superiority only. The Newberry showcase has been empty since P. C. defeated the Indians in the Thanksgiving battle last year. A victory next week will fill that void and double our victory total.

Awnings   Carpets

Whitaker Floor Coverings

Newberry, South Carolina

CARPETS

Paul W. Whitaker
Res. Phone 276-2202
E. Main St.
Office Phone 276-2884

Annual Bronze Derby Clash Steeped in Rich Tradition

By ROB DALTON

(The following article is reprinted from the November 19, 1965, issue of The Blue Stocking—Editor.)

The annual Bronze Derby gridiron clash on Thanksgiving Day carries 19 years of rich tradition for the two participating teams —the Presbyterian College Blue Hose and the Newberry College Indians. This year's game which is in Clinton on November 24, at 2:00 p. m., is the final game for the Blue Hose this season.

The Bronze Derby is a beaten old hat that sat on the head of a PC student some 19 years ago while he watched a Blue Hose-Indian basketball game. This game was played at Newberry in the winter of 1947. As the action on the court blazed, the stands also blazed. A Newberry student grabbed the little brown derby from the PC student's head and ran.

A spirited argument resulted in which PC's present Head Coach, Cally Gault, was involved. Out of this the beaten brown derby became the symbol of athletic superiority between the two colleges.

The derby was dipped in bronze and was ceremoniously presented to the college which was victorious after each football, basketball, and baseball game.

After the first few years, the ownership of the Bronze Derby was decided by the traditional football game each Thanksgiving.

Over the years the Blue Hose have fared well against the Indians. In 51 meetings with Newberry, PC has won 32 of them, lost 15, and tied four.

The Blue Stocking

Tribe Yields Bronze Derby to PC's Anxious Hands

PC DROPS NEWBERRY 28-7

The Newberry Indians closed out a disappointing season with a 28-7 defeat at the hands of traditional rival Presbyterian College in the Turkey Day classic. The season that began so well ended in tragedy as the Indians wound up the season with a 4-5-1 record. The only consolation was an optimistic assumption that 1967 could be the year for the long awaited return of a winning season.

The 1966 team co-captains Ray Soloman and Tommy McAdams prepared to return the Derby to Presbyterian's eager hands and to close the season with a regrettable

The Li'l That Was!

The Indian
"Voice of the Newberry College Student"

VOL. XXXIX NEWBERRY, S. C., WEDNESDAY, DECEMBER 7, 1966 NUMBER 11

Newberry, PC Battle Marks Long Rivalry

Each year on Thanksgiving Day when Newberry and P.C. clash on the gridiron, the spotlight shines on the Bronze Derby. The Bronze Derby is the symbol for football rivalry between these two teams — a series dating back to 1913 in which P. C. has the edge by 31-16-4.

The Bronze Derby originated as the result of a highly spirited ruckus that took place when P. C.'s basketball team played at Newberry on the night of January 30, 1947. Before the game started, a group of P. C. students put up a high banner on the wall of the gymnasium which read, "Beat Hell Out of Newberry!" During the game several Newberry students gained access to a ladder, climbed the outside of the wall, entered through the window, rolled up the banner, and exited undetected the same way they had entered. Towards the end of the contest the visitors discovered that their banner was missing! Then when the game ended and P. C. had taken a 51-47 victory, the irate visitors demanded the return of their banner. A scuffle developed, and in the midst of the confusion, a Newberry student grabbed a derby off the head of a P. C. student and ran.

During the next two days, negotiations went on between the athletic publicity directors of the two schools. The result of the negotiations was that the derby was to serve as a laurel of victory in athletic contests between the two schools. The hat was returned, packaged, and forwarded to a casting company in Ohio, where the bronzing was done.

At first the Bronze Derby was held up for grabs in football, basketball and baseball, but in 1956 it was limited to gridiron rivalry probably for more singular emphasis. The Bronze Derby currently rests in the trophy case in Holland Hall as a result of last year's 6-0 victory. If Newberry can cop a victory and retain the Turkey Day Topper, it will mean the first winning season for the Redskins since 1962.

Karlynn Derrick won the four dollars in the final prediction contest last week. The goal of 350 ballots was surpassed with a record 365 ballots being turned in. The sports staff thanks the fraternities, Kappa Alpha and Alpha Tau Omega, for sponsoring the contests this year, and also **Brent Shaeffer** and **Ross Webber** for their help in making last week's prediction poster.

Indians Close Season With Loss To PC

By FRANK SNYDER

Despite the fact that the 1966 Newberry Indian football team ended the season with a four win, five loss and one tie record, it was a successful year. The Indians were in the thick of the Carolinas Conference race down to the wire and had it not been for the disastrous loss to Lenoir Rhyne and the tie with Guilford, the conference championship might have been ours.

Highlights for the entire squad probably were the first two games of the season where the Big Red were underdogs. In the first game they came fom behind to down Appalachian, 15-14, and then repeated the performance in the second game by beating Catawba, 14-7. In the final game of the season and the final one ever for senior stalwarts Arlo Hill, Benji Kirkland, Neal Dufford, Barry Groce, Bobby Carlton, Steve Robinson, and the co-captains, Tommy McAdams and Ray Solomon, the Indians played their hearts out only to lose out to PC by a 28-7 count. Robertson played a particularly outstanding game against PC to close out his career.

There were many individual acolades earned during the year. First and foremost, head coach Harvey Kirkland was named N.A.I.A. District 26 Coach of the Year" for the third time. Coach Kirkland did a great job and rightly deserves the award. George Taylor, the great sophomore halfback, broke the school one-season rushing record by amassing a total of 823 yards and a high of 150 against Guilford. Friday Taylor and ferocious Dennis Swygert were named to the NAIA District 26 football team to cap the fine years both had. Swygert's forte is harassing enemy passers from his defensive end position, but when he's not doing that, he's catching passes. Dennis hauled in 16 passes this year. Both boys are returning next year, so all Indian fans can expect big things from them.

The 1966 Newberry squad was an outstanding squad and displayed the spirit and drive that is typical of all the athletic teams at NC. The student body should feel proud of them, and they can expect the same hustling tradition to continue next year.

The Blue Stocking

Presbyterian College, Clinton, S. C., December 2, 1966

Victory Over Indians Gives Blue Hose Share Of CC Title

By TOM CAIN

By defeating the Newberry Indians 28-7 on Thanksgiving Day, the Presbyterian College Blue Hose football team obtained a share of the Carolinas Conference football championship for the 1966 season.

The PC victory, coupled with a Catawba upset over Lenoir Rhyne by the score of 21-11 on the same day, enabled the Blue Hose to obtain their first conference championship or co-championship since joining the league.

PC and Lenoir Rhyne both won five games and lost two, while Catawba, who placed third by winning four and losing three, had the distinction of defeating both PC and Lenoir Rhyne.

PC's other loss was to Lenoir Rhyne by the score of 23-6, while Lenoir Rhyne was upset 21-20 by Guilford for their second loss in the conference.

Guilford finished second in the conference with a record of four wins, two losses, and one tie, while Newberry placed fourth with a record of three wins, three losses, and one tie.

Appalachian and Western Carolina tied for fifth place by winning three games and losing four, and Elon finished last after winning one game and losing six.

Reviewing the season in general, PC coach Cally Gault stated, "Sharing the crown is a tremendous compliment to the team and a very deserving reward. This group strived harder than any other group in PC's history to be a good football team."

"Striving" seems to be an appropriate word to describe the 1966 Blue Hose team, for preseason polls rated them to finish last in the Carolinas Conference race.

The Cleaning Center for PC Students...

SUNSHINE
Cleaners
... and ...
Laundry

Quality Work — Quick Service — Shirt Specialists
Expert Shoe Repair and Self-Service Washeteria
Florida Street Behind Post Office — 833-1492

The Li'l That Was!

Blue Hose footballers were urged on this season by this newly adopted embodiment of Presbyterian College athletic spirit—a Scottish kilt worn here by David Templeton of Clinton. PC is rooted in the Presbyterianism of Scotland, and this traditional garb with its knee-lnegth blue stockings presents a fitting symbol for the teams that battle on the athletic field. Presbyterian College closed its 1966 campaign last Thursday with a 28-7 victory over Newberry and a tie for the Carolinas Conference championship (with Lenoir Rhyne). The season mark of six wins and four defeats was the best PC fotball record since 1960.

The Blue Stocking

BROADWAY

FEBRUARY 17-21
DON KOTTS in

Reluctant Astronaut

Leslie Nielson, Joan Freeman, Jeanette Nolan, Arthur O'Connell.

STARTS WED., FEB. 22

The Greatest Story Ever Told

FOR SALE
1965 Volkswagen

WHITE - RADIO - EXCELLENT CONDITION

November 1967

November 1	"Cool Hand Luke" starring George Kennedy and Paul Newman was released.
November 3	The Battle of Dak To began, which became one of the bloodiest battles in the Vietnam conflict.
November 4	Pink Floyd made their American debut in San Francisco, California.
November 5	A rail crash in the United Kingdom killed 49 people. A survivor of the tragedy included Robin Gibb of the Bee Gees.
November 6	"The Phil Donahue Show" debuted on a local Dayton, Ohio television station creating the daytime talk show.
November 7	The United States launched and landed, 3 days later, Surveyor 6 on the moon.
November 7	United States President Lyndon Johnson signed a bill creating Public Broadcasting.
November 7	St Louis Cardinals Orlando Cepeda was the first unanimous MLB NL Most Valuable Player Award.
November 7	The Soviet Union celebrated the 50th anniversary of the Bolshevik Revolution.
November 7	Former United States Vice President John Garner passed away.
November 9	NASA successfully launched the Saturn V rocket.
November 9	*Rolling Stone* magazine debuted.
November 12	American boxing champion Michael Moorer was born.
November 13	American TV producer and TV host Jimmy Kimmel was born.
November 13	NFL owners approved expansion to Seattle, Washington and Kansas City, Missouri.
November 15	Boston Red Sox outfielder Carl Yastrzemski won the MLB AL Most Valuable Player Award.
November 20	Tom Seaver of the New York Mets was named MLB NL Rookie of the Year.
November 22	German tennis player and Wimbledon Champion Boris Becker was born.
November 23	The Bronze Derby was played in Newberry, South Carolina on Thanksgiving Day. The Presbyterian College Blue Hose defeated the Newberry College Indians 14-0.

Chronicle SPORTS
PC Battles Indians In Annual Classic

On the basis of records and comparative scores, Presbyterian College should be heavily favored Thursday when the Blue Hose travel to Newberry for the traditional Thanksgiving Day between the Bronze Derby rivals.

But records and such don't mean much when the Blue Hose and Indians get together. It's that kind of rivalry.

PC takes a 4-4-1 record into the game and Newberry has a 1-7-1 mark. Newberry's lone win came over Frederick (23-16), a team which tied PC 0-0 in a Virginia hurricane in the first game of the season. Newberry's tie (15-15) was with Catawba, which PC beat 21-14 in a thriller.

Newberry's losses have been to Appalachian (21-12); Lenoir Rhyne (54-6); Wofford (14-10); Jacksonville State (35-6); Guilford (51-69); Elon (24-0); and Western Carolina (35-0). In comparison, PC has beaten Lenoir Rhyne 26-9); Wofford (20-7); and Western Carolina, 10-0, last week. PC lost to Appalachian (57-18); Guilford (25-20); and Elon (21-20). PC's other loss was to Davidson (38-0), which Newberry didn't play.

Six seniors will be playing their final game for PC. They are end Richard Munn, centers Mickey Hampshire and Mel Davis, tackles Eddie Walker and Tommy Campbell and back Gene Robbins.

The series stands at 33-18 in favor of PC and Coach Cally Gault has a 3-1 record against Newberry. The Indians' last win in the series was in 1965, in an upset against a heavily favored PC team.

HEAR

CLEMSON

Vs.

SOUTH CAROLINA

SATURDAY

NOV. 25

ON

WPCC

SPONSORED BY

Baldwin Motor Co.

AIR TIME

1:45 p. m.

The Li'l That Was!

The Newberry Observer
AND HERALD & NEWS
"Just Like a Letter from Home"

NEWBERRY, S. C., FRIDAY, NOV. 24, 1967

Indians Host Blue Hose In Annual Bronze Derby Tilt

The annual battle for the Bronze Derby takes place at Newberry College's Setzler Field Thanksgiving Day. Newberry is the underdog, but old-time observers of the venerable rivalry between the Newberry Indians and Presbyterian College of Clinton, will tell you that the football form charts mean next to nothing when the two schools bump heads.

Kickoff is at 2 p. m.

It's the season finale for both clubs. A victory for Presbyterian would mean a winning season for Coach Cally Gault's charges, who are 4-4-1. Harvey Kirkland's Indians have had a rough season and stand 1-7-1. The lone success was over Frederick, and for the Indians a victory Thursday afternoon is a consummation devoutly to be wished.

A win for Newberry also would mean a return of the Bronze Derby. The trophy, a symbol of contention since 1947, now rests in Clinton as a result of P. C.'s 28-7 victory in the 1966 confrontation.

A win for Newberry also would mean a return of the Bronze Derby. The trophy, a symbol of contention since 1947, now rests in Clinton as a result of P. C.'s 28-7 victory in the 1966 confrontation.

A year earlier, Presbyterian came to Newberry as the heavy favorite on Thanksgiving Day, but went home a 6-0 loser.

The holiday tussle will be the final game for six Newberry seniors, ends Gerald Beatty and Pete Peterson, tackles Chip Shealy and Mike Collins, quarterback Ray Hesse and wingback Steve Coker. Another senior, tailback Tommy Thompson, is out with a knee injury.

The Indians have shown flashes of talent, and the possibility of a win over Presbyterian isn't wholly wishful thinking on their part. Ray Hesse has passed well when protected, and has completed 43 per cent of his throws this year. His favorite target has been Roger Hazle, 6'2" sophomore end, who has caught 30 for 440 yards. On the ground, George Taylor is an established threat and a potential game-breaker.

Presbyterian's offense is led by junior quarterback Bill Kirtland, an aerial artist who has smashed all passing records at Clinton. The Blue Hose can mount a solid running game, too, springing from a split-T sort of formation which Gault labels a "varied T."

P. C. started the season strongly but has lost four of its last six games. The loss of all-conference halfback Dan Eckstein with a fractured arm three weeks ago has weakened the Hose a bit in the pass receiving department, but doing nobly in his stead have been halfback Francis Cooper and Bob McNair, the Governor's son, who's listed as a halfback but who has been running from a split end position.

This is the 56th or the 53rd clash between Newberry and Presbyterian, depending on

This is the 56th or the 53rd clash between Newberry and Presbyterian, depending on whose records stand up under a recheck. Presbyterian says it's ahead in the series with 33 wins against 18 losses and a tie. Newberry knows it's trailing, but makes it 32-16-4 for P. C. There'll be a lot of research between this Thanksgiving and next to find out who lost track.

The Li'l 🎩 That Was!

The Indian
Voice of the Newberry College Student

Newberry Hosts PC
On Thanksgiving
Day — The
Bronze Derby Classic
Rout The Blue Hose!

PC'S DEFENSE GRABS ON—Gilstrap (No. 42) carries as the tough defense of Presbyterian moves in to help hold their 14-0 victory in the annual Thanksgiving Bronze Derby classic. (Photo by Fesperman)

Odorless Cleaners
1110 Harrington St.
(Next to Drive-In Bank)

PC Keeps Derby With Win

By DAVID HOWELL
News Sports Writer

Presbyterian College's defense came to the rescue of its injury-riddled offense as the Blue Hose defeated arch-rival Newberry, 14-0, in their traditional Bronze Derby Carolinas Conference football battle Thanksgiving Day.

Presbyterian, which started the season with a mighty roar only to wind up in a tailspin before downing Western Carolina last week, registered its fifth victory against four losses and one tie to finish with a winning season. The Indians, not as fortunate, ended their year with a 1-8-1 slate.

Left halfback Robert Hackle was the big hero for the winners. The 6-2 200-pound junior of Winnsboro scored both touchdowns by taking a 10-yard pass from junior quarterback Bill Kirtland in the opening quarter and plunging over from two yards out in the third period.

The Blue and White defense, which ran into mid-season problems, played a sterling game and harrassed Newberry's backfield. Time after time, Indian quarterbacks Bill Pritchett and Ray Hesse were flattened by onrushing linemen. They saw more than their share of the turf from the prone position and obviously weren't getting much protection from their line.

After the opening kickoff, the ball exchanged hands five times before the Blue Hose gained possession a third time. On their two previous drives, the Clinton outfit had only managed to advance as far as its own 14 and 47-yard lines, respectively.

THE STATISTICS

PC		Newberry
14	First downs	11
0	Yards rushing	74
174	Yards passing	44
17-26-3	Passes	4-21-3
6-39	Punts	9-41
2	Fumbles lost	1
54	Yards penalized	65

Presbyterian 7 0 7 0—14
Newberry   0 0 0 0—0
PC—Hackle, 10 pass from Kirtland (Horne kick).
PC—Hackle, 2 run (Horne kick).

But PC's third march was a much different tune. Francis Cooper was on the receiving end of Roger Hazel's punt and Cooper returned it 36 yards before being caught on the Indian 44. On first down, Phil Bradner got the call but Newberry was charged with a 15-yard penalty which gave the Blue Hose another first down at the Newberry 23.

An offsides penalty against PC moved the ball back to the 28, but Kirtland passed six yards to end Bobby McNair, who was tackled by Ozzie Witt. Kirtland went to the air again and lofted a four-yard aerial to Gradner. After PC was penalized five yards for backfield in motion, Pat Stogner punched out three more before Kirtland was thrown for a nine-yard loss. On third down, the Blue Hose shifted into a spread formation and Kirtland threw short to Hackle over the right side and he danced into the end zone. The drive used eight plays. Specialist Skipper Horne then split the uprights to send PC ahead, 7-0.

The second period found the ball exchanging hands on 10 occasions. It seems as if there was a cage around PC as it was never able to get out of its own territory. The Indians drove as far as the Presbyterian 20, but a 15-yard holding penalty nipped their bid for a touchdown.

Coach Cally Gault's outfit took the second-half kickoff and made believers out of the Indians. Gault obviously have given a pep talk at halftime because the Blue Hose immediately drove 79 yards to paydirt. Scratching for every inch while dominating the clock, the Hose executed 16 plays before they reached the magic stripe. Three big plays in the drive were passes by Kirtland. He hit McNair for 20 yards and had eight-yard tosses to Cooper and end Walter Sheely. Another aid was a penalty against Newberry for grabbing the face mask and the Indians were assessed half the distance of the goal.

That put the ball on the Indian five. Bradner ran for one and was stopped by end Barry Owens. Hackle picked up two more off right tackle. On second down at the two, Kirtland handed off to Hackle who drove over for right tackle again for the tally. Horne's toe was true for a 14-0 lead.

At the time, no one would have thought the scoring had ended. It seemed as if the Indians would churn out yardage only to lose valuable ground via losses.

Newberry drove as far as the PC 29 on the following kickoff but that drive stalled when Hesse was smacked behind the line again. The Indians really found themselves in trouble in the final period and only got as far as the PC 41 where they fumbled and Bill Caldwell recovered for the Blue Hose.

After four plays, Bullis was forced to punt for PC from the Newberry 36.

On their next drive, the Presbyterians marched to the Indian 25 when signal-caller Allen McNeill passed to Hackle for five yards but it was too short and 14 yards shy of a first down.

Hampered by injuries, the Blue Hose put together something of an offense to keep Newberry's defense busy while the defense controlled the game.

Henry's Barber Shop
Voight Dominick
Henry Barnette
College at Main—Downstairs

The Newberry Observer
AND HERALD & NEWS
"Just Like a Letter from Home"

NEWBERRY, S. C., TUESDAY, NOV. 22, 1967

Indians Lose to P.C., 14-0

A Thanksgiving Day gathering estimated at 6,000—including South Carolina Governor Robert E. McNair—saw Presbyterian College's Blue Hose gather in the harvest at Newberry's Setzler Field last Thursday, filling their baskets with a 14-0 decision over the Indians.

Presbyterian scored touchdowns in the first and third quarters in winning its fifth victory of the season against four losses and a tie. The loss was the eighth against one win and one tie for the Indians.

A 36-yard punt return by Francis Cooper set up P. C.'s first touchdown. After reaching the Indian 44 on the return, Phil Bradner gained six yards and a personal foul penalty moved the ball to the Indian 23. Then quarterback Bill Kirkland passed to Bradner for a first on the Indian five.

P. C. drew a motion penalty and lost six yards more, but Kirkland passed to Hackle at the Newberry 10 and the 190-pounder carried it over from there. Skipper Horne's kick for the extra point was true with 5:58 remaining in the opening quarter and the Hose had a 7-0 lead.

Newberry's deepest penetration was to the P. C. 20, but a holding penalty killed the threat. A P. C. fumble and an interception by Ozzie Witt gave the Indians possession in Blue Hose territory on two other occasions in the second period, but Newberry couldn't take advantage of the breaks.

Presbyterian opened the second half with an 80-yard touchdown drive to account for their second scoring effort of the afternoon.

The Hose completed the march in 16 plays, with three key ones on passes by Kirkland. He hit end Bobby McNair for 20 yards and had eight-yard tosses to Cooper and end Walter Shealy.

After reaching the Indian 10, P. C. accepted a penalty against the Indians for grabbing the face mask, putting the Hose on the five. Gradner ran for one and was stopped by end Barry Owens. Hackle picked up two more off right tackle. On second down at the two, Kirkland handed off to Hackle, who drove over for the score. Horne kicked the extra point for a 14-0 lead.

Kirkland, who was bothered by arm trouble earlier this season, was forced to the sidelines in the second half and saw only limited duty.

Newberry dominated play in the fourth quarter, but a fumble by sophomore quarterback Bill Pritchett and an interception by P. C.'s Steve Dishroon halted the only two promising Indian threats.

★ Parade
(Continued from page one)
15. Fogle Flashettes
16. Kemper Chevrolet Company Car No. 1
17. Newberry Mills Float
18. Speers Street School Float
19. Little Folks Kindergarten
20. Young Buick Company Car
21. Miss Newberry
22. C-P Corp. Float
23. South Carolina National Bank Float
24. Whitmire High School Band
25. Miss Whitmire High
26. Newberry-Saluda Regional Library
27. Shealy Motor Company Car No. 1
28. Rikard School Float
29. Brownies Troop 747
30. Junior Troop 748
31. Cadettes Troop 749
WALNUT STREET (beginning at the corner of Main Street)
32. Ruff Rambler Company

FLOWERS SCORES AGAINST P. C.: Newberry College halfback John Flowers (No. 45) is shown cutting the corner for yardage against Presbyterian College in last Thursday afternoon's annual Turkey Day Bronze Derby classic at Newberry, which P. C. won this year, 14-0. —Photo by Paul Savko, Newberry College.

The Li'l That Was!

The Clinton Chronicle

Clinton, S. C., Thursday, November 30, 1967   Vol. 68 — No. 48

COOPER ROMPS—Presbyterian College halfback Francis Cooper, (43), a freshman from Clemson, races for big yardage in PC's 14-0 win Thanksgiving day over Newberry. Cooper set up PC's first touchdown with a 50-yard punt return. Quarterback Bill Kirtland passed 10 yards to Robert Hackle for the TD. Hackle scored the other on a two-yard run. PC Coach Cally Gault now has a 4-1 record in the Bronze Derby classic. (Yarborough Photo)

The Li'l That Was!

1967 was the final season for legendary Newberry College Head Football Coach Harvey Kirkland. Accolades from his high school career include South Carolina High School football championships from 1948-1949 and 1949-1950. Coach Kirkland guided Summerville High School to back to back state championships. His first year as Newberry College Head Football Coach was 1952. Coach Kirkland compiled an overall record of 72-77-11 at Newberry College. As a head coach on Thanksgiving Day, Coach Kirkland was 5-9-2 competing for the Bronze Derby. A graduate of Newberry College, Coach Kirkland played both football and baseball as a student athlete. Coach Kirkland was inducted in the Newberry Hall of Fame in 1977. In 1993, Coach Kirkland was inducted in the South Carolina Athletic Hall of Fame.

Photo courtesy of Newberry College archives

November 1968

November 1	Pitcher Denny McClain of the Detroit Tigers, 31-6 in the 1968 season, was the unanimous MLB AL Cy Young Award winner and MLB AL Most Valuable Player.
November 1	The Motion Picture Association introduced a rating system (G, M, R, X).
November 4	"Wichita Lineman" was released by Glen Campbell and became the album of the year in 1969.
November 5	Richard Nixon was elected President of the United States defeating Hubert Humphrey and George Wallace.
November 9	Joe Cocker's cover of the Beatles "With a Little Help From My Friends" became a *Billboard* top hit.
November 11	John Lennon and Yoko Ono appeared nude on the cover of the "Two Virgins" album.
November 12	The United States Supreme Court declared an Arkansas law unconstitutional banning teaching evolution in public schools.
November 12	American baseball player Sammy Sosa was born.
November 13	Bob Gibson of the St Louis Cardinals won the MLB NL Most Valuable Player Award.
November 14	"National Turn in your Draft Card Day" resulted in many young Americans burning their draft cards.
November 14	The first European lung transplant was successful.
November 15	Yale University announced it was going co-educational.
November 17	The famous NFL "Heidi Game" was played. NBC cut away from the Oakland Raiders comeback victory over the New York Jets 43-32 to show the movie "Heidi" in its planned timeslot.
November 17	Beatle George Harrison made a cameo appearance on "The Smothers Brothers Comedy Hour."
November 18	American baseball player Gary Sheffield was born.
November 22	Captain Kirk and Uhura engaged in the first television interracial kiss on "Star Trek."
November 22	The Beatles released their White Album, "The Beatles."
November 28	The Bronze Derby was played in Clinton, South Carolina on Thanksgiving Day. The Presbyterian College Blue Hose defeated the Newberry College Indians 42-7.

The Li'l  That Was!

The Indian
"Voice of the Newberry College Student"

Romanoff and Juliet
Thursday - Saturday
In Little Theatre

XXXI   NEWBERRY, S. C. 29108, WEDNESDAY, NOVEMBER 20, 1968   NUMBER 11

Bronze Derby Is on the Line As Redskins Meet Blue Hose

By HAL DERRICK

The Indians will conclude this season against the Blue Hose of Presbyterian College. The annual Thanksgiving battle for the possession of the prized Bronze Derby should again be an exciting contest.

The Blue Hose run from a multiple offense. Their favorite formations are the I-set, the wing-set, and the pro-set.

Physically Newberry and PC are about equal. However, during the last four games the Blue Hose have shown much improvement.

Allen McNeil, the junior quarterback from Columbia, directs the PC offense. McNeil is an outstanding passer. End Bill Caldwell and halfback Tom Milton are McNeil's primary receivers. Phil Bradner, a senior fullback, is one of the leading rushers in the conference.

PC uses a basic fifty-defense. However they use stunts and stacks to confuse the offensive blocking assignments. Ed Paulling a 6 ft. 205 lb. senior, leads the Blue Hose defensive unit. Operating from his middle guard position Paulling has been outstanding all year.

To win the coveted Bronze Derby the Indians must play an inspired game.

The Li'l That Was!

The Indian
"Voice of the Newberry College Student"

Derby Recalls Twenty Years Of Tradition

The Newberry College Fighting Redskins travel to Clinton next Thursday to renew the annual Thanksgiving rivalry for the Bronze Derby with Presbyterian College. The clash will be the fifty-fourth between the two chools, dating back to 1913. PC holds a 33-16-4 edge over the Indians.

The Bronze Derby originated as the result of a highly spirited ruckus that took place when PC's basketball team played Newberry on the night of January 30, 1947. Before the game started, a group of PC students put up a high banner on the wall of the gymnasium, which read, "Beat Hell Out of Newberry."

During the game several Newberry students gained access to a ladder, climbed the outside of the wall, entered through a window rolled up the banner, and exited undetected the same way they had entered. Toward the end of the contest the visitors noticed that the banner was missing.

Then when the game had ended and PC had taken a 51-47 victory, the irate visitors demanded the return of the banner. A scuffle resulted and in the midst of the confusion, a Newberry student grabbed a derby off the head of a PC student and ran.

During the next two days, the athletic publicity director of the two schools negotiated for the return of the derby. The results of the negotiations was that the derby was to serve as a laurel of victory in athletic contests between the schools. The hat was returned, packaged, and forwarded to a casting company in Ohio, where the derby was bronzed.

At first, possession of the Bronze Derby was determined by victories in football, basketball, and baseball, but in 1956 it was decided to award the trophy on the basis of gridiron superiority only. The Newberry showcase has been empty since PC defeated the Indians in the Thanksgiving battle two years ago.

P.C. To Host Derby Classic

The Indians travel 20 miles up the road Thanksgiving Day to face the Presbyterian Blue Hose in the annual resumption of their oldest rivalry.

The two teams have been battling together for more than 50 years, with P.C. holding the edge in victories by a good margin. Not since 1965 have the Redskins managed to capture the Bronze Derby, which most of our students have therefore never seen.

The Hose are favored to extend their Turkey Day string to three wins, but the Tribe may find a few more scalps yet. Presbyterian has compiled a 5-4 record this season, with losses coming against such top-ranked tams as Lenoir-Rhyne, Appalachian, and Carson-Newman.

Calling signals for the Hose will be veteran Bill Kirtland, a senior who sets a new school record every time he passes. He is backed up by Allen McNeill, who has seen a lot of action this year.

The running attack is led by Dan Eckstein and Bob Hackle, both of whom double on defense. Eckstein, one of the most versatile players in the nation, is also a leading pass receiver.

Bob McNair, Kirtland's favorite target, was injured against Carson-Newman last week, and will be a doubtful starter.

Defensively, the Blue Hose are quite sound throughout, but the Indian running attack may have the best chance of bringing the Bronze Derby back to Newberry.

The Li'l 🎩 That Was!

The Newberry Observer
AND HERALD & NEWS
"Just Like a Letter from Home"

NEWBERRY, S. C., FRIDAY, NOV. 14, 1968

At Clinton
Indians-P.C. Play For Bronze Derby Thursday

'68 Hose Best P.C. Team Since '59 Tangerine Bowl

You can throw out statistics, past game scores, and season's results when the Newberry College Indians invade Bailey Memorial Stadium to battle archrival Presbyterian College in the annual Bronze Derby Classic on "Turkey Day" Nov 28. Game time is set for 2 p.m.

Going all the way back to 1913, P. C. has a decided 33-10-4 won-lost margin over the Indians. But predicting the outcome of this annual contest is as bad a job as forecasting the outcome of the Carolina-Clemson game.

The Blue Hose have a much better won-lost record this season than the Tribe, 6-4 to 3-6. PC has a chance to tie Lenoir Rhyne for the Conference Championship with a win over Newberry.

Presbyterian opened its season with a 10-0 blanking of the Quantico Marines before losing successive games to Furman by 13-9 and to powerful Lenoir Rhyne 17-7. The Blue Hose then strung together four victories in a row over Wofford, Elon, Guilford, and Catawba. Appalachian cut the Hose victory string at four by trouncing them 42-6, and nationally ranked Carson-Newman just squeezed by, 24-23. The Blue Hose were successful in their last outing, beating Western Carolina 26-19.

The spirited young Indians, picked by many not to win a single game, have 3 victories against 6 setbacks. They dropped three straight to Appalachian, Catawba and Lenoir Rhyne before picking up their first '68 win against Concord College. Wofford edged by the Tribe, 17-7, and Jacksonville State rode over them 45-10 before the Indians pulled upset victories over Guilford, 25-14, and Elon, 24-15. In Newberry's last encounter, Western Carolina blanked the Tribe, 26-0.

The Blue Hose have a talented list of stars. P.C. has in quarterback Bill Kirtland an excellent passer who sets a new school record each time he throws the ball. Halfback Dan Eckstein is a prime candidate for All-American honors on both offense and defense. Halfback Bob Hackle and fullback Phil Bradner also are steady performers.

Split-end Bob McNair is lost for this final game but Kirtland and reserve quarterback Allen McNeil have a good list of possible receivers. The Newberry defensive secondary expects a busy day, as Kirtland will definitely try to travel the air route.

By HORACE TURBEVILLE

Presbyterian College's Blue Hose, 1968 version, are one of P.C.'s best teams since the 1959 edition that played in the Tangerine Bowl.

The Blue Hose possess the best football record of any college in the state, with six wins and four losses.

P.C. has a number of outstanding personnel, including Don Eckstein, Bob Hackle, Bill Kirkland, Jim Sullenberger, Bob Hackle and McNair.

Hackle and McNair probably won't play against the Indians Thanksgiving Day. McNair, son of South Carolina Gov. Robert McNair, suffered a dislocated shoulder in the Carson Newman game and has been out since. Eckstein, halfback from Sylvan High, Atlanta, Ga., broke his arm in mid-season last year but led the team in yards rushing and passes received. He was voted by coaches for two years to the all-conference offense and defense teams. Considered a dangerous man on punt returns, Eckstein is a 9.8 dash man in track and has 52 receptions for 625 yards. He is a four-yard starter on defense and a three-year starter on offense (averaging over four yards per carry).

Hackle is a 6-2, 205-pound senior halfback from Winnsboro High. A three-year letterman, he is another capable performer on both offense and defense. A strong runner and blocker, he always gives a solid steady performance.

Quarterback Kirtland, 5-11, 160-pound senior from Coral Gables High, Miami, Fla., sets new all-time Presbyterian records each time he passes. He has completed 31 touchdown passes. His carrier record at P.C. is 255 completions for 3,339 yards and hi season record of 107 of 209 for 1322 yards and 16 touchdowns was set in 1966. He won the S. C. Player of the Week award in his first start of his career.

Sullenberger, linebacker, is a 190-pound, 5-0, senior from Garrett High, Charleston. A two-year letterman, he is quick and tough. He is a leading tackler and considered one of the best linebackers in the conference.

The fighting Redskins of Fred Herren will go into the classic as underdogs, which is nothing new to the Tribe. They have been just that in every game this season. The Indians will look to their old reliable and all-overything tailback, George Taylor, in this final game. Number 44 will long be remembered for his breaking tackles and second effort. Taylor has carried the mail for 514 yards this season, and 2,152 during his four-year career.

The Laurens Advertiser

"SOUTH CAROLINA'S LARGEST WEEKLY NEWSPAPER"

LAURENS, SOUTH CAROLINA, TUESDAY, NOVEMBER 26, 1968

PC hosts Indians

By MIKE SIMONS

The Presbyterian College Blue Hose host the Newberry Indians Thanksgiving day in the 54th renewal of the annual Bronze Derby clash, dating back to 1913.

This rivalry is one of the fiercest in all sports annals, and obtained this name in 1947 when a Newberry student snatched a derby from the head of a PC boy after a PC-Newberry basketball game, causing fights to break out all over the gym.

The derby was later dipped in bronze and awarded to the winner of each football and basketball game. It is now awarded only to the winner of the football game.

Newberry will be trying to end a two year dry spell, having last beaten PC in 1965. Last season the Hose won by a 14-0 count. Overall the series stands at 43 wins for the Hose, 18 losses and four ties.

The Indian attack is led by tailback George Taylor, who set the school's rushing mark as a sophomore. The Indians started the season off slowly, but have come around now, and pose a formidable threat.

Even though Newberry is only 4-5, this does not mean much since records can be disregarded because of the fierceness of the rivalry between the two schools.

A number of seniors will be playing their last game for the Hose, including co-captain Charlie Reid. Other senior players who will see their last action in a PC uniform are guard Bob Murray, ends Johnny Bankhead and Dowl Thompson, linebacker Bobby Byard, tackle Shell Dula and backs Dan Eckstein, Bill Kirtland and Pat Stogner. Punter Larry Bullis will also be playing in his last game for PC.

Halfback Bob Hackle and end Bobby McNair, both seniors, are injured but coaches have expressed hope that they will be back in action against the Indians. Linebacker and co-captain Jim Sullenberger has been injured all season, and will have a knee operation over the Thanksgiving holidays.

The Blue Hose fought back from a 10-0 deficit against Western Carolina, then used a last minute safety to take a 20-19 Carolinas Conference victory, and keep their title hopes alive.

With PC leading 20-17 late in the game, and the ball on their own 13 yard line, quarterback Allen McNeill ran back into the end zone on fourth down, giving the Catamounts two points, and giving PC a free kick from the 20.

Western's first scores came on a 26 yard field goal by Jimmy Corley and a two yard run by Paul Smith. Corley converted after the TD, and WC led 10-0.

Bill Kirtland hit Bill Caldwell for a nine yard scoring strike early in the second quarter, and Jerry Chandler converted to pull the Hose to 7-10.

A pass interception gave the ball to Western on their own 33, and they drove for another score, with David Lomax going over from the four. Corley again converted.

McNeill moved the Hose 88 yards for a TD with 0:55 left in the half, hitting Caldwell for a 36 yard touchdown pass. Chandler kicked to make it 14-17.

PC took the lead in the third quarter on a 21 yard pass from Bob Hackle to Dan Eckstein on the halfback pass play. The kick failed, and all the scoring was over until the late safety.

The Clinton Chronicle

Vol. 70 — No. 47   Clinton, S. C. Thursday, November 28, 1968

Thanksgiving Day
PC Hosts Tribe In Derby Battle

BY MIKE SIMONS

The Presbyterian College Blue Hose host the Newberry Indians Thanksgiving day in the 65th renewal of the annual Bronze Derby clash, dating back to 1912.

The rivalry is famed, and obtained its Bronze Derby name in 1947 when a Newberry student snatched a derby from the head of a PC boy after a PC-Newberry basketball game, setting fights to break out all over the gym. The derby was later slipped in bronze and awarded to the winner of each football and basketball game. It is now awarded annually to the winner of the football game.

Newberry will be trying to end a two-year dry spell, having last beaten PC in 1965. Last season the Hose won by a 14-0 count. Overall the series stands at 34 wins for the Hose, 28 losses, and four ties.

The Indian attack is led by halfback George Taylor, who cut the nobody running mark as a sophomore. The Indians started the season off slowly, but have come around now, posing a formidable threat.

A number of seniors will be playing their last game for the Hose, including co-captain Charlie Reid. Other senior players who will see their last action in a PC uniform are guard Bob Murray, ends Robert Hambright and Dow Thompson, linebacker Bobby Beard, tackle Shell Dula, and backs Dan Eckstein, Bill Kirtland and Pat Ziegler. Punter Larry Bedin will also be playing in his last game for PC.

Halfback Bob Hackle and Bobby McNair both seniors, are injured, but the coaches have expressed hope that they will be back in action against the Indians. Linebacker and co-captain Jim Gallenberger has been injured all season, and will have a knee operation over the Thanksgiving holidays.

WESTERN CAROLINA – PC

The Blue Hose fought back from a 14-0 deficit against Western Carolina, then used a last minute safety to preserve a 23-21 Carolinas Conference victory, and keep their fifth hope alive.

With PC trailing 20-15 late in

★★★★★★★★
Pro Scouts Watch Hackle And Eckstein
★★★★★★★★

Two professional football scouts attended Saturday night's PC-Western Carolina game and both were impressed with the two PC players they came to see, Dan Eckstein and Bob Hackle.

One scout representative Fran Polo Cowboys and the other represented several pro teams, including the Chicago Bears, Detroit Lions, Philadelphia Eagles and New Orleans Saints.

One commented, "These two boys, Eckstein and Hackle, could play for any college team in the country."

The scouts had attended the Clemson-Carolina game earlier in the day and one commented, "You know, the Clemson-Carolina game was fine but I believe this game (PC-Western) was more exciting, close wide open."

the game, and the ball on their own 41 yard line, quarterback Allen McNeill purposely ran back into the end zone on fourth down, giving the Catamounts two points, and giving PC a free kick from the 20.

Western's first scores came on a 39-yard field goal by Jimmy Curley and a two yard run by Paul Smith. Curley converted after the TD, and WC led 10-0.

Bill Kirtland hit Bill Caldwell for a nine yard scoring strike early in the second quarter, and Jerry Chandler converted to pull the Hose to 7-10.

A pass interception gave the ball to Western on their own 37, and they drove it another score, with David Lomax going over from the four. Curley again converted.

McNeill moved the Hose 66 yards for a TD with 0:15 left in the half, hitting Caldwell for a 36 yard touchdown pass, Chandler kicked to make it 14-17.

PC took the lead in the third quarter on a 25-yard pass from Bob Hackle to Dan Eckstein on the halfback pass play. The kick failed, and all the scoring was over until the late safety.

Today's active people want *light refreshment*

Light, dry (not too sweet) reduced in calories. Today's Pepsi refreshes without filling.

Pepsi-Cola refreshes without filling

Pepsi - Cola Bottling Company

The Clinton Chronicle

Vol. 70 — No. 47 Clinton, S. C., Thursday, November 28, 1968

WEATHER (Week of Nov. 21-26)
High: 67   Low: 25
(Nov. 22) (Nov. 21)
Rainfall: .01 in.

The Li'l That Was!

Gault Says Consistency Was Key To 7-4 Record

Consistency was the key to Presbyterian College's 7-4 record and a share of the Carolinas Conference football championship, according to Head Coach Cally Gault.

The Blue Hose completed their season last Thursday by bombing Newberry 42-7 in the traditional Thanksgiving Day Bronze Derby battle.

The conference win left PC with a 5-1 conference mark, the same as Lenoir Rhyne with whom the Hose share the league championship.

Coach Gault said, "We were always optimistic about this season, sometimes maybe we were too optimistic, but we felt all along that we'd have a pretty good season.

"We had thought that last year would be our year but we had so many injuries."

"This year, we consistently played good football. We were a little slack on offense at the start of the season but we played consistently overall. The boys had a good attitude in practice. They didn't go to extremes. We opened with a win and then had two losses but we didn't panic. We came back with good games against good teams, Wofford and Elon."

"Our only bad game was against Appalachian, a very good team. The cold, wet weather seemed to have an adverse affect on us although it didn't bother Appalachian."

"Three of our four losses were to teams ranked in the top 22 among the nation's small colleges. I still think we deserved to win the Furman game but that doesn't change anything."

"We will lose some fine seniors (13) this year but we try to prepare for that. Our big question now is how many non-seniors we'll lose between now and next season because of academics, service or lack of money."

Against Newberry, P.C. rolled up a 28-0 halftime edge and in general dominated the game.

All-American Dan Eckstein scored twice, once on a 14-yard pass from Bill Kirtland and then on an exciting 88-yard punt return. Kirtland sneaked over from the one for another PC score. Defensive back Elliott Poss, a sophomore, intercepted a pass and went 26 yards for a PC touchdown. Fullback Phil Bradner scored twice, on a seven-yard run and on a 16-yard pass from Allen McNeill.

The Li'l  That Was!

The Indian
"Voice of the Newberry College Student"

Support Higher Education Faculty Basketball Game Tonight, 7:30, In Gym

VOL. XXXXI — NEWBERRY, S. C. 29108, WEDNESDAY, DECEMBER 11, 1968 — NUMBER 12

CHAPMAN INTERCEPTS PASS—One of Newberry's few bright spots in the annual Thanksgiving Day battle with P. C. was Keith Chapman's interception. (Photo by Savko)

Hose Keep Topper

By BILL HILTON

The Blue Hose from Presbyterian College stuffed their Thanksgiving turkey with an easy football victory over Newberry's Fighting Redskins: Score at the final whistle was 42-7.

The win earned for PC a share of the Carolinas Conference title and also enabled them to retain possession of the celebrated Bronze Derby, the trophy which signifies the winners of the annual Turkey Day rivalry game.

Presbyterian scored in each of the first three quarters and held the lead 28-0 at the half.

The Clinton team took the opening kickoff and bulldozed 75 yards in ten plays for the first score. PC quarterback Bill Kirtland elected to pass only twice in that thrust, but the second of the throws went to right halfback Dan Eckstein, PC's Little All-American, from 14 yards out for the first TD.

When the second quarter opened, PC had the ball on its own 41, and again marched to the goal in ten plays as Kirtland carried the ball over from the one in a proverbial quarterback sneak.

Following Kirtland's effort, the Indians attempted retaliation with several passes by quarterback Gary Welchel, but the last one to fullback Jim Fulton was overthrown and PC's Elliot Poss gathered it in and raced from the 31 to the end zone to make the score 21-0.

After the next kickoff, the Tribe was virtually immobile and punted, only to regain possession of the ball on an interception. Nonetheless, PC took over the pigskin again on the 20 and hustled downfield behind the tank-like ground covering of fullback Phil Bradner. On the tenth play of the series, Bradner followed Eckstein through

(Continued on page six)

ENJOY Coca-Cola

Hose Keep

(Continued from page five)

the left tackle slot and scored easily from 19 yards out to bring the half-time score to 28-0.

In the third quarter, Newberry took the kickoff but relinquished the ball once more as PC's Bill Sloan snatched a Johnny Harbin pass to set up a nine-play series capped by second string quarterback Allen McNeill's 16-yard scoring pass to Bradner.

The rigid PC defensive line forced another Newberry punt after the sixth kickoff of the game but needed only one play to score as Eckstein grabbed the ball at the 12 and raced 88 yards for the final Blue Hose TD.

Newberry finally got on the scoreboard in the opening minutes of the fourth quarter on a fourth down, 12 yards-to-go gamble; Harbin pitched out to frosh Robert Schmidt who galloped around left end and in for the six points. Joby Castles completed the score with his usually successful PAT.

The Li'l That Was!

The Newberry Observer
AND HERALD & NEWS
"Just Like a Letter from Home"

AND NEWS ESTABLISHED 1865 — NEWBERRY, S. C., TUESDAY, DEC. 3, 1968 — NEWBERRY OBSERVER ESTABL!

P. C.'s Eckstein Breaks Another Tackle . . . Indian Harbin Gets One

Observer Photos by Paul Savko

DEFENSIVE MANEUVER: Keith Chapman (23) intercepts a pass intended for Bob McNair in the Thanksgiving Day classic played in Clinton, as the Blue Hose of Presbyterian College trounced the Newberry College Indians 42-7. —Observer Photo by Paul Savko.

The Newberry Observer
AND HERALD & NEWS
"Just Like a Letter from Home"

NEWBERRY, S. C., TUESDAY, DEC. 3, 1968

Indians Conclude Season With Unexpected 3-7 Mark

Newberry College's gridders have wound up their first season under Head Coach Fred Herren with a record of three wins and seven losses—an improvement on the 1-8-1 record of 1967 and considerably better than most experts predicted for 1968. Advance estimates of Indian victories this autumn ranged from none to one.

Newberry closed with a loss to Presbyterian College at Clinton on Thanksgiving afternoon, by a lop-sided 42-7 score. The loss, which left rival PC in possession of the coveted Bronze Derby, was a disappointment to Newberry partisans but no great surprise inasmuch as Presbyterian entered the game a heavy favorite.

A share of the Carolinas Conference title was at stake for Presbyterian in the Thanksgiving classic, and the Blue Hose clearly knew it. They piled up a 28-0 lead at the half, holding Newberry to just 25 yards of total offense in the first 30 minutes.

The Hose scored on their opening offensive series, going 75 yards in 10 plays with superback Dan Eckstein counting on a 14-yard pass from Bill Kirtland. Cruickshanks added the first of his six conversions.

Presbyterian really wrapped up the game and a share of the title (with Lenoir Rhyne) in the second quarter. The Hose engineered a three-touchdown explosion which left the Indians hanging on the ropes.

Kirtland's passes did most of the damage on the second Blue Hose drive of the afternoon, and the nifty senior quarterback went the last yard on a keeper. Almost immediately thereafter, defensive back Elliot Poss picked off a Gary Welchel pass and Presbyterian took a 21-0 lead.

With 4:19 left in the half, PC scored again to climax an 80-yard march led by fullback Phil

With 4:19 left in the half, PC scored again to climax an 80-yard march led by fullback Phil Bradner. Bradner boomed for 19 yards to the seven, then blasted across from that point. Soph quarterback Allen McNeil was at the helm throughout the drive.

McNeil also was running the Blue Hose attack in the third quarter when PC extended its lead to 35-0. On a fourth down play, he threw to Bradner for 16 yards and the score. The drive started on the Indians' 35, after another PC interception of a Welchel aerial.

The last Presbyterian touchdown was a dazzler by Eckstein, who fielded a Roger Hazel punt late in the third period, slipped through the Indians' coverage and went 80 yards down the sidelines. The run more than negated the 51-yard punt and left the Indians 42 points in the hole.

Bright spots for the Indians were hard to find, but they did get a consolation touchdown with 12:35 left in the game. They took over at the Presbyterian 40 after a bad fourth down snap to the Hose punter. Wingback Bob Schmidt swept left end for seven yards and the score, on fourth down. Freshman quarterback John Harbin steered the six-play drive, accomplishing 28 of the 40 yards on a pass to Johnnie Dawkins.

The limber-legged Roger Hazel continued his fine punting. In the fourth period he booted one 71 yards, his second-best effort of the season.

Newberry won the punting, but other statistics were less favorable. Presbyterian finished with 25 first downs to Newberry's 12 and put together 443 yards of total offense to the Indians' 137.

It was a rugged but not totally unrewarding season—for the rebuilding Indians, whose lineup was studded with talented but green freshmen and sophomores. Accustomed to the underdog role, Newberry rose above it three times in 10 tries, beating Concord, Guilford and Elon.

GREETING CARDS OF DISTINCTION BY

Gibson

You will find the right Card for everyone on your list from our wide and complete selection and

Any Christmas Cards in our stock

Imprinted

Quick Service

PEOPLES BOOK STORE
1505 MAIN ST.

The Clinton Chronicle

Hosemen Capture Carolinas Title

McNeill's Run Gives PC Derby And Crown

Prior to last week's Thanksgiving Day battle between Presbyterian College and Newberry in Clinton, Fred Herron, the Newberry coach, paid a compliment to PC Quarterback Allen McNeill. Herron called McNeill "one of the finest third down quarterbacks in this area."

Translated into layman's language, that means McNeill has a knack for coming up with a successful play at a crucial time. He's dangerous when he's backed into a corner.

So how does PC beat the Indians 27-23? Naturally, on a third down play in which McNeill ran 53 yards for the winning touchdown with 5:53 remaining in the game. Newberry, fired-up and playing a fine ball game, was leading 23-20 after a stirring comeback in which they shook off a 20-0 first quarter deficit.

PC had a lot of hardware riding on the game. Of course, there was the traditional Bronze Derby prize which goes to the winner of the Thanksgiving game. Added to this was the Carolinas Conference crown which PC had never won outright before last Thursday. A PC loss would have meant the Hosemen would have to share the crown with Lenoir Rhyne as they did in 1966 and 1968.

CONFERENCE CHAMPS

Thanks to McNeill's stunning run, the Hosemen finished with the derby and the crown and, at 8-1, their finest record since 1959 when PC had a 9-1 mark and played in the Tangerine Bowl. It also marked PC's sixth straight win, their longest win streak since that 1959 team reeled off seven straight wins in one season and nine over a two-year span.

The Blue Hose, although nursing some bruises and key injuries after a rugged game in the mud at Mars Hill the previous Saturday, scored two first quarter touchdowns before Newberry had been able to run a complete series of downs.

Tony Passarello recovered a punt at the Indian three after the ball bounced against the Newberry receiver. Tim Milton scored the first of his two touchdowns with 11:55 remaining in the first quarter. The extra point failed and it was 6-0. After the ensuing kickoff, Newberry ran one play and then Rick Medlin intercepted a Newberry pass and ran 60 yards for another PC touchdown. PC attempted a two-point conversion which failed and it was 12-0 with 8:45 left in the first quarter.

For its third first quarter touchdown, the Blue Hose went 80 yards in eight plays, capped by Milton's two-yard burst. McNeill passed to Lynn Dreger for the two-point conversion and PC had a 20-0 margin with 2:45 remaining in the first quarter.

Newberry cornerback Butch Jernigan intercepted a McNeill pass at PC's 25 to put the Indians in scoring position in the second quarter. Seven plays later, fullback Donald Garrick dived over to cut the margin to 20-6 as Passarello had blocked a conversion kick this season.

A 54-yard pass from Quarterback Tommy Williamson, a lefthanded freshman, to end Marty Pearson put the ball at PC's seven late in the first half. Garrick again burdied into the end zone from the one and the halftime score was 20-13. Newberry was back in the ball game.

In the second half, PC got only two first downs and Newberry chewed up large chunks of real estate, primarily with Williamson's passes and Garrick's runs.

With 5:35 remaining in the third quarter, Williamson sneaked over from the one to cap a 13-play, 66-yard drive. In the drive to lefthanded Hayes with rifle passes for three critical first downs. Williamson faked a pass to Hayes for the two-point conversion and ran in to tie the score at 20-20.

A 40-yard burst up the middle by Garrick put Newberry at PC's five in the fourth quarter but the Blue Hose defenders tightened up. Linebacker Bobby Norris, a junior, made three successive stops for PC. Williamson kicked a 30-yard field goal that sent Newberry ahead 23-20 with 11:40 remaining in the game.

After the teams exchanged punts and with time becoming a factor, McNeill dropped back on third down and three to go at his own 45, saw his receivers covered and started to run up the middle. McNeill cut to his left toward the visitor's sidelines at about the Newberry 40 and Dreger threw a block which took out two Newberry defenders at the 20. From that point on it was a footrace between McNeill and one Newberry defender who trailed by about five yards. McNeill went into the end zone standing and Jerry Chandler added the extra point which put PC out of field goal range at 27-23.

Still the Blue Hose had to fight down another Newberry threat but took over at its own 26 as a fourth and 10 pass from Williamson to Hayes fell one yard shy of a first down.

The win assured PC of possession of the Bronze Derby for the fifth consecutive year. It also marked Coach Cally Gault's seventh win over Newberry in eight years. The 8-1 record brings Gault's PC coaching record to 64-37-2.

The Clinton Chronicle

THE THIN DIFFERENCE — PC's 155-pound senior quarterback, Allen McNeill (No. 1), provided PC's winning margin against Newberry as he raced 55 yards late in the game. McNeill is shown above in another scrambling run in the first quarter. —(Yarborough Photo)

November 1969

November 1	The Beatles album "Abbey Road" climbed to #1 in the United States.
November 4	American actor Matthew McConaughey was born.
November 7	Yoko Ono and John Lennon released their second album "Wedding Album."
November 9	Simon and Garfunkel released their hit single "Bridge Over Troubled Water."
November 10	"Sesame Street" premiered on public television.
November 11	Singer-songwriter Jim Morrison was arrested on an airplane by the FBI for drunkenness.
November 12	The United States Army announced an investigation of Lt. William Calley for an alleged massacre of civilians in the Vietnamese village of My Lai.
November 12	Minnesota Twins star Harmon Killebrew won the MLB AL Most Valuable Player Award.
November 14	NASA launched Apollo 12.
November 15	A singing group from Gary, Indiana, The Jackson Five, made their first appearance on the *Billboard* Top 100 with "I Want You Back."
November 15	Entrepreneur Dave Thomas opened a fast food restaurant in Columbus, Ohio named Wendy's.
November 18	Joseph Kennedy, American diplomat, businessman and father of United States President John F. Kennedy, Attorney General Robert Kennedy and Senator Ted Kennedy passed away.
November 20	Brazilian Soccer star Pele scored his 1000th career goal.
November 20	MLB San Francisco Giant outfielder Willie McCovey won the NL Most Valuable Player Award.
November 21	MLB Hall of Fame outfielder Ken Griffey Jr. was born.
November 24	Lt. William Calley was charged with killing 100 civilians in My Lai, Vietnam and ordered to stand trial by court martial.
November 26	The lottery for Selective Service draftees bill was signed by United States President Richard Nixon.
November 27	The Bronze Derby was played in Newberry, South Carolina on Thanksgiving Day. The Presbyterian College Blue Hose defeated the Newberry College Indians 23-21.

The Newberry Observer
AND HERALD & NEWS
"Just Like a Letter from Home"

AND NEWS ESTABLISHED 1819 — NEWBERRY, S. C., TUESDAY, NOV. 25, 1969 — NEWBERRY OBSERVER ESTABLI

NEWBERRY, S. C., TUESDAY, NOV. 25, 1969

Tribe-P.C. Meet Thursday; Prized Derby Awaits Victor

The Newberry College Indians will close out the 1969 football campaign Thursday afternoon at Setzler Stadium in Newberry against arch-rival Presbyterian College in the annual Thanksgiving Day battle with the prized Bronze Derby as an extra bonus for the winner.

Physically, the Indians and Presbyterian College are rated "about equal." However, during the last four games the Blue Hose have shown much improvement.

Allen McNeil, the junior quarterback from Columbia, directs the P.C. offense. McNeil is an outstanding passer. End Bill Caldwell and halfback Tom Milton are McNeil's primary receivers. Phil Bradner, a senior fullback, is one of the leading rushers in the conference.

P.C. uses a basic 50-defense. However, they use stunts and stacks to confuse the offense blocking assignments. Ed Paulling, a six-foot, 205-pound senior, leads the Blue Hose defensive unit.

The last time the Bronze Derby has been at Newberry College was in 1966, when the Indians posted a 28-7 victory in Clinton.

This year's meeting will be the 55th in the series that dates back to 1913, when the Indians demolished the Hose, 51-0. Despite that initial setback, Presbyterian holds a 34-16-4 edge over Newberry.

The Bronze Derby originated as the result of a highly-spirited ruckus on the night of Jan. 30, 1947, following a basketball game between the two rival schools. Before the game got underway, several P. C. students put up a banner high on the wall of the gymnasium which read: "Beat Hell Out of Newberry."

Sometime during the game, a group of Newberry students secured a ladder, set it up against the outside wall, climbed through a window, rolled up the banner and escaped unnoticed the same way they had entered. Near the end of the game the visiting Blue Hose supporters realized that the banner was gone.

After Presbyterian had taken a 81-47 victory, the irate Hose partisans demanded the return of the banner. This prompted a scuffle, and, in the midst of the general confusion, a Newberry student snatched a derby from the head of a P. C. student and ran.

During the next couple of days, the athletic publicity directors of the two schools negotiated for the return of the derby. They finally came to the agreement that the derby should serve as a laurel of victory in athletic contests between Newberry and Presbyterian. Consequently, the hat was returned to P. C., packaged and forwarded to a casting company in Ohio, where it was bronzed.

Until 1956, possession of the Bronze Derby was determined by victories in football, basketball and baseball, but then the schools agreed to award the trophy on the basis of football superiority alone. Since then Newberry has won the Bronze Derby four times.

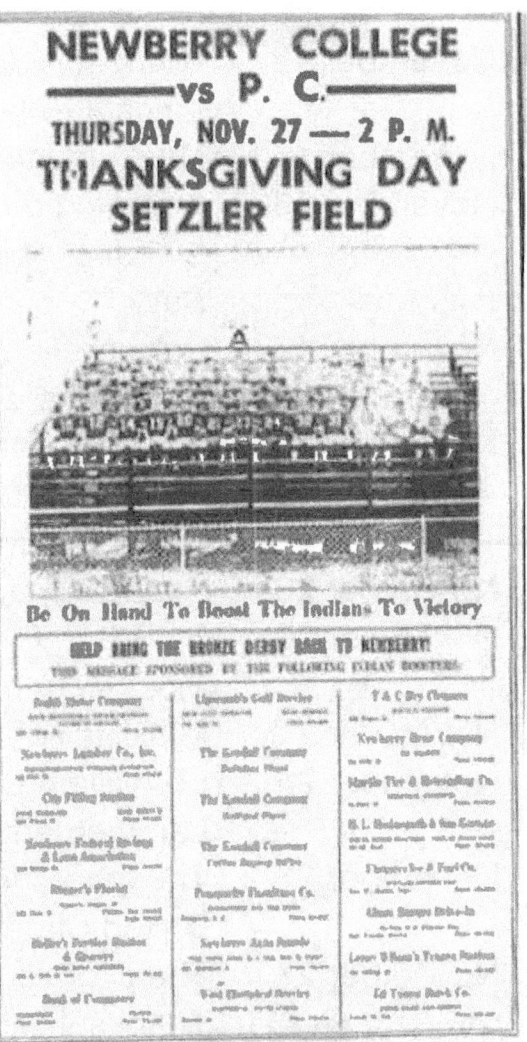

NEWBERRY COLLEGE vs P. C.
THURSDAY, NOV. 27 — 2 P. M.
THANKSGIVING DAY
SETZLER FIELD

Be On Hand To Boost The Indians To Victory

HELP BRING THE BRONZE DERBY BACK TO NEWBERRY!
THIS MESSAGE SPONSORED BY THE FOLLOWING FRIDAY BOOSTERS

The Newberry Observer
AND HERALD & NEWS
"Just Like a Letter from Home"

NEWBERRY, S. C., FRIDAY, NOV. 28, 1969

Newberry Indians Host Arch-Rival P.C. Thursday

The Newberry College Indians play host this week to their old arch-rival Presbyterian College in the annual Thanksgiving Day battle for possession of the Bronze Derby. Game time is set for 2 p.m. at Setzler Field.

Going all the way back to 1913, P. C. has a decided 34-19-4 won-lost margin over the Indians. In last year's clash the Blue Hose tied Lenoir Rhyne for the Conference Championship by whipping the Indians 42-7.

The Indians have enjoyed a much-needed recuperation period with an open date last Saturday. The previous week the Newberry team had been soundly trounced by Western Carolina 70-0. If comparison of both teams Western Carolina scores means anything, the Indians will have to put out quite an effort in order to come out on top Thursday.

Coach Fred Herren's comments on the upcoming game were as follows: "I can't imagine a team as much an underdog as we will be against P. C. on Thanksgiving afternoon. Our boys will have to feel like the turkey on the chopping block with P. C. as the pilgrim with the axe."

Herren had nothing but praise for Presbyterian's head coach, Cally Gault: "Coach Gault has done his best job since he has been at P. C., and we are looking forward to the challenge of playing against his team."

For ten Newberry College seniors the Thanksgiving Day game will be their last as members of the Indian tribe. These seniors are center Jack Boylston, guard John Castles, end David Gossess, guard Al Grunow, linebacker and co-captain Bob Hammersla, flanker and co-captain Roger Hazel, defensive back Bill Kimbrell, tackle Mike Rentz, guard Doug Solomon and end Dennis Swygert.

Although this year's Hose do not have as impressive a won-lost record as last season, they have shown surprising improvement during the latter part of the season. In their last three outings they have beaten Appalachian and Western Carolina and allowed Carson-Newman to barely squeak by them.

P. C. has one of the best quarterbacks in the area this year in Allen McNeill, who has engineered the offense and thrown for well over a thousand yards. Adding the running punch to the Blue Hose offense is fullback Phil Bradner, who has already busted his rushing mark for last season.

The defensive leader for the Clinton, S. C. team is Ed Paulling who is one of the best defensive linemen in the conference. Paulling has plenty of help from his defensive backfield which successfully put the quietus on Western Carolina's passing attack last week.

copy the guy who shops for a living!

The Li'l 🎩 That Was!

Clash to Settle Derby's Fate
Bronzed Hat Has Hectic History

The Bronze Derby, pictured at left, has not seen Newberry College since Thanksgiving 1966 when the Presbyterian football team abducted it with a 28-7 victory in Clinton.

This year, following three straight Turkey Day wins, the Blue Hose will visit Setzler Field to renew the annual battle for the symbolic topper. The meeting will be the fifty-fifth in a series which dates back to 1913, when the Indians demolished the Hose 51-0. Despite that initial setback, Presbyterian holds a 34-16-4 edge over Newberry.

The Bronze Derby originated as the result of a highly-spirited ruckus on the night of Jan. 30, 1947, following a basketball game between the two rival schools. Before the game got underway, several PC students put up a banner high on the wall of the gymnasium which read: "Beat Hell Out of Newberry."

Sometime during the game, a group of Newberry students secured a ladder, set it up against the outside wall, climbed through a window, rolled up the banner, and escaped unnoticed the same way they had entered. Near the end of the game the visiting Blue Hose supporters realized that the banner was gone.

After Presbyterian had taken a 51-47 victory, the irate Hose partisans demanded the return of the banner. This prompted a scuffle, and, in the midst of the general confusion, a Newberry student snatched a derby from the head of a PC student and ran.

During the next couple of days, the athletic publicity directors of the two schools negotiated for the return of the derby. They finally came to the agreement that the derby should serve as a laurel of victory in athletic contests between Newberry and Presbyterian. Consequently, the hat was returned to PC, packaged, and forwarded to a casting company in Ohio, where it was bronzed.

Until 1966, possession of the Bronze Derby was determined by victories in football, basketball and baseball, but then the schools agreed to award the trophy on the basis of football superiority alone. Since then Newberry has won the Bronze Derby four times.

The Indian
"Voice of the Newberry College Student"

VOL. XXXXII NEWBERRY, S. C. 29108, WEDNESDAY, NOVEMBER 19, 1969 NUMBER 12

ED YOUNG BUICK COMPANY

2800 College Street

Newberry, South Carolina

Thanksgiving Day
PC Hosts Tribe In Derby Battle

BY MIKE SIMONS

The Presbyterian College Blue Hose host the Newberry Indians Thanksgiving day in the 57th renewal of the annual Bronze Derby clash, dating back to 1913.

This rivalry is fierce, and obtained its Bronze Derby name in 1947 when a Newberry student snatched a derby from the head of a PC boy after a PC-Newberry basketball game, causing fights to break out all over the gym. The derby was later dipped in bronze and awarded to the winner of each football and basketball game. It is now awarded only to the winner of the football game.

Newberry will be trying to end a two-year dry spell, having last beaten PC in 1965. Last season the Hose won by a 14-0 count. Overall the series stands at 34 wins for the Hose, 18 losses, and four ties.

The Indian attack is led by tailback George Taylor, who set the school's rushing mark as a sophomore. The Indians started the season off slowly, but have come around now, and pose a formidable threat.

A number of seniors will be playing their last game for the Hose, including co-captain Charlie Reid. Other senior players who will see their last action in a PC uniform are guard Bob Murray, ends Johnny Bankhead and Dow Thompson, linebacker Bobby Byard, tackle Shell Dula, and backs Dan Eckstein, Bill Kirtland and Pat Stogner. Punter Larry Bullis will also be playing in his last game for PC.

Halfback Bob Hackle and end Bobby McNair both seniors, are injured, but the coaches have expressed hope that they will be back in action against the Indians. Linebacker and co-captain Jim Sullenberger has been injured all season, and will have a knee operation over the Thanksgiving holidays.

The Clinton Chronicle

NEWBERRY - PRESBYTERIAN

Annual Bronze Derby Classic

The Li'l That Was!

The Clinton Chronicle

Vol. 70 — No. 47   Clinton, S. C., Dec. 4, 1969

Gault: 'Second' Grid Season Was Successful

"I thought our second season was very successful," Presbyterian College Football Coach Cally Gault commented this week after his Blue Hose wound up their schedule with a 23-21 win over Newberry last Thursday.

"This has certainly seemed like the shortest season I've ever had and it's been one of the most enjoyable. It was encouraging to watch the young fellows come around, particularly in the latter part of the season. This was probably the youngest team PC has ever had. It's unusual to have only 27 upper classmen (six seniors) on a 60-man squad."

Gault and his coaching staff had their jobs cut out for them this year. From the end of spring practice to the start of fall practice, PC lost eight of the 22 regulars it was counting on for this season. PC brought in one of its largest contingents of freshmen and had to count on many of them. Some of them developed quickly and were instrumental in PC's strong finish.

"I'm looking forward to next season," Gault said, "I feel we're over the hump now."

After five straight losses at the start of the season, the Blue Hose had an open date. Coach Gault commented then; "We are going to forget the first five games. We are now entering a new season."

In the "new season," the Blue Hose fared very well, almost a complete turn-about from the "first" season. PC won five of its last six games, including a forfeit from Catawba because of an ineligible player.

The win over Newberry gave PC a 5-6 record and 3-2 in the Carolinas Conference. Newberry finished at 4-6 and 1-4 in the conference. PC has defeated Newberry in their last four meetings.

The Hose never trailed Newberry last Thursday but the Indians tied the score once and pulled dangerously close later in the game.

In the first quarter, PC drove 55 yards to score. Sophomore Tam Milton of Greenwood ground out 34 yards in the drive and fullback Phil Bradner, a senior, scored from four yards out with 7:40 remaining in the quarter. Sandy Cruickshanks added the extra point.

In the second quarter, Newberry recorded a PC fumble at the Blue Hose 20 and, on the next play, Newberry Quarterback Gary Welchel tagged end Roger Hazel with a scoring pass. The extra point kick tied the score at 7-7 with 3:49 remaining in the half.

PC whipped down field where Cruickshank tried a field goal on the last play of the first half but the ball hit the goal post and bounced back into the field. However, Newberry was penalized for having too many men on the field, and Cruickshank got another shot at the field goal, this time from the 13 and he boomed the 23-yarder through the uprights for a 10-7 halftime lead.

MILTON SCORES

The Hose upped the margin to 16-7 when Milton scored from the two, capping a 35-yard drive with 1:39 remaining in the third quarter.

Later in the third quarter, Newberry's Jim Fulton raced 35 yards on a trick play to pull the Indians to within two points, 16-14. Instead of going into a huddle, the Newberry linemen lined up to the left of the ball with Fulton taking a sideways throw from the center.

PC refused to rattle, however, and methodically ground out an 85-yard drive to what proved to be the winning touchdown. Tight end Bill Caldwell made a leaping catch of an 11-yard pass from Quarterback Allen McNeill to score. Caldwell was upended on his way down in the end zone but he held onto the ball for the touchdown.

CALDWELL ROMPS

A 31-yard pass play from McNeill to Caldwell was a big play in the drive. With third down and eight yards to go, McNeill hit Caldwell who rambled up the sidelines, knocking over defenders like a run-away bull. The score came with 6:10 remaining in the game.

Newberry, filling the air with desperation passes, scored with three seconds remaining in the game but couldn't pull even with the Hosemen.

The win was a tough one for the Blue Hose. They upset Western Carolina in a tough game on Saturday prior to taking to the field against Newberry on Thursday. Newberry, meanwhile, had an open date prior to the PC game.

Coach Gault commented, "We didn't have any legs out there today. We played just well enough to win. But then that's what this game's all about, winning, so I guess we can't complain."

Gault praised Newberry Coach Fred Herron, saying, "Fred had his boys well prepared. He had done a good job all season down there and he did a particularly good job in getting his boys ready for us. I thought we didn't play real well in Newberry. It was probably our worst offensive effort since our fourth ball game. However, much of this may be attributed to the fact that Newberry was well prepared and were much better than some people thought. From end-to-end, their defensive line is as tough as any we've faced and their pass defense was highly improved."

DERBY WINNERS — PC Seniors Carey Fussell (74), a tackle and fullback Phil Bradner (46) hold the Bronze Derby after defeating Newberry 23-21 Thanksgiving Day. It marked the fourth straight year that PC has won the Bronze Derby battle. Fussell and Bradner were never on the losing side in the PC-Newberry game during their collegiate years. —(Yarborough Photo)

The Li'l That Was!

The Indian
"Voice of the Newberry College Student"

Dance, Basketball, Concert, Beauties, Exams... Help!

VOL. XXXXII — NEWBERRY, S. C. 29108, WEDNESDAY, DECEMBER 3, 1969 — NUMBER 13

ROSEMAN HIT—The P. C. ball carrier carries nowhere on this play as he runs into a wall of Redskins during the Thanksgiving Derby duel. (Photo by Fesperman)

Hose Squeeze By Tribe 23-21

By HAL DERRICK

The Indians closed out the season against arch-rival Presbyterian. A valiant effort by the Indians fell short as the Bronze Derby remained at Presbyterian.

The Indians and Blue Hose exchanged punts before Presbyterian began to threaten. Following a sixty-five yard drive Phil Bradner carried the ball in for the touchdown. Sandy Cruickshanks kicked the extra point. The Presbyterian defense had completely bottled up the Indian offense.

With nearly five minutes left in the half, the Indians caused a Blue Hose fumble. Billy Koch pounced on the loose football at the Presbyterian nineteen. On the next play from scrimmage Gary Welchel dropped back and hit flanker, Roger Hazel, with a nineteen yard scoring toss. This play gave Newberry its only first down of the first half.

Presbyterian took the ensuing kickoff and drove to the Newberry eleven. With less than ten seconds left in the half, the Blue Hose attempted a field goal. Cruickshanks' kick hit the goal post and bounced off as time ran out. On a controversial call Newberry was penalized five yards for having too many men on the field. This time, five yards closer, Cruickshanks' mark was true and Presbyterian led at the half ten to seven.

Fumbling a pitch from Welchel to Garrick, Presbyterian picked up the ball deep in Indian territory. After seven plays Tom Milton took the ball in for the touchdown from the two. Cruickshanks missed the extra point.

Early in fourth period Newberry employed its play of the year. The entire team grouped at one sideline. The ball was picked up and tossed to Jimmy Fulton, who was standing in the middle of nine Indians. Fulton raced 35 yards to score as an astonished Blue Hose team watched. Castles' point after touchdown narrowed the gap to 16-14.

The Blue Hose took control after an exchange of punts and drove to score with less than three minutes left in the game. Allen McNeil hit end, Bill Caldwell, with an 8-yard scoring toss to put the game out of reach.

Gary Welchel scored from the one with only three seconds left in the game. The final score read P. C. 23 and Newberry 21.

Wash and Dry Laundry .... 14c lb.

FORMAL WEAR
RENTAL SERVICE
Rent Here For All Your Rental Service
FORMAL WEAR

Newberry Steam Laundry & Dry Cleaning Co.

834 Main Street   Phone No. 276-2240

The Laurens Advertiser

"SOUTH CAROLINA'S LARGEST WEEKLY NEWSPAPER"

LAURENS, SOUTH CAROLINA • DECEMBER 3, 1969

PC Blue Hose gridders defeat Newberry 23-21

The Presbyterian College Blue Hose, who had stunned the football world the week before with a 28-17 victory over previously unbeaten Western Carolina, ranked no. 2 among the nation's small college teams, had to pull out all the stops in order to defeat the Newberry Indians, 23-21 in the 5th Bronze Derby Thanksgiving Day game at Newberry.

The win enabled the Blue Hose to retain possession of the Bronze Derby which goes annually to the winner of this traditional Thanksgiving rivalry.

IT WAS the fourth straight over the Indians for the PC boys, gave them a 6-6 record in closing out the season, with all of their victories coming in the last six games.

It capped a remarkable comeback for Coach Cally Gault's Blue Hose who lost their first five games, some by lopsided scores, and then turned around and soundly defeated higher-ranking teams than those that had previously beaten the PC eleven.

THE BLUE HOSE led for a greater part of the game, but only a penalty against Newberry permitted Coach Gault's charges to carry a lead out to intermission.

The two teams were locked in a 7-all struggle as PC's Sandy Cruickshanks attempted a 28-yard field goal that hit the left upright and bounded away on what was supposed to be the last official play of the first half.

HOWEVER, the officials caught the Indians with 12 men on the field and from the 25 PC had another chance with time having run out on the clock. This time Cruickshank's boot was good and PC led, 10-7 at halftime.

The Blue Hose got another drive underway late in the third period after Bob Middleton pounced on a Newberry fumble at the Indian 35. They moved the ball to the two from which point Tam Milton carried the ball across, the extra point attempt was missed and the score was 16-7.

NEWBERRY came right back to score, moved to the PC 35 from which point the Indians lined up to the left of the ball. Fullback Jim Fulton took the snap and went 35 yards down the left sidelines for the touchdown. Toby Castles kicked the extra point and the score was 16-14.

The Blue Hose came right back with a long drive of their own, climaxed by a tremendous catch of an Allen McNeil pass by End Bill Caldwell who went high into the air in the end zone to grab the ball, was hit hard in mid air and crashed to the ground but held on for the score with 6:10 left to play. Cruickshanks kicked the point after to make it 23-14.

AND THAT didn't give the PC boys much to spare because the Indians made a last desperate bid that culminated in a touchdown with only three seconds to play, leaving them a scant two points short of the victors.

An interference play had moved the ball from the PC 22 to the one to put it in position for Gary Welchel to carry it across and Castles to kick the extra point.

PC SCORED first in the opening period when Phil Bradner capped a 15-yard drive by going over from the four-yard line. Tam Milton had eaten up 34 of the yards in the drive on five carries. This had come with 7:40 left in the first quarter and Cruickshanks kicked the extra point to make the score 7-0.

Newberry came back to tie the count in the second period after Bill Koch recovered a PC fumble on the Blue Hose 20-yard line.

ON THE first play afterward Quarterback Gary Welchel dropped back and fired a pass to the Indians' all-conference end, Roger Hazel, who took it for the touchdown and Castles' kick made it 7-all with 3:48 left in the half.

This set the stage for PC's go-ahead field goal by Sandy Cruickshanks and the Blue Hose were in front to stay, although the margin was shakey most of the time.

PC COACH Cally Gault had high praise for the Newberry defense, pointing out that it was as fine as any the Blue Hose have faced all year.

"We played just well enough to win," he said, "so I guess we can't complain."

The Newberry Observer
AND HERALD & NEWS
"Just Like a Letter from Home"

NEWBERRY, S. C., TUESDAY, DEC. 2, 1969

INDIANS LOSE THRILLER TO P. C.: The Newberry College Indians and Presbyterian College's Blue Hose locked horns last Thursday in Newberry in the traditional Thanksgiving Day clash and P. C. emerged with an exciting 23-21 victory. Some of the highlights of the 1969 Thanksgiving thriller are captured in the above photos. In the photo at left, fullback Jimmy Fulton races for a first down for the Indians. The center photo and right photo are somewhat related. In the center photo, Indian Coach Fred Herren discusses a matter with officials during the heat of the game. Presbyterian College just kicked and missed a field goal, but officials ruled the Indians had too many players on the field. The hand over the official's shoulder belongs to coach Herren. He appears to be shaking a finger in the official's face—but what he's actually doing is counting the players on the field. The photo at right shows P. C.'s second attempt at the field goal, this time good and later proving to be the deciding factor in the game. The boot was by P. C.'s Sandy Cruickshanks (No. 83). Zeroing in on the try to block the kick is Newberry's Dennis Swygert (No. 89). —Observer Photos.

Blue Hose Trim Tribe, 23-21, to Keep Bronze Derby

The Blue Hose of Presbyterian College retained possession of the coveted Bronze Derby during the traditional Thanksgiving skirmish at Setzler Field by a score of 23-21.

The first score came on a four yard plunge by PC fullback Phil Bradner and the extra point by Sandy Cruickshanks made the score 7-0 with 7:40 remaining in the first period.

The first Indian score came with 3:48 left in the first half as Newberry quarterback Gary Welchel threw a 19-yard touchdown pass to end Roger Hazel. Joby Castles tied the score at seven-all.

Just before the half with less than half a minute to go, PC missed a 28-yard field goal attempt but a penalty against Newberry for having 12 men on the field gave him a second chance from 23 yards out to put Cally Gault's Blue Hose ahead at the division 10-7.

After a strong defensive game by both sides during the third period PC's Tam Milton ran the ball in from six yards out, but the PAT by Cruickshanks was missed and the score was 16-7.

The surprise of the game was a 38-yard run on a quick snap by the Indians fullback Jim Fulton, and the kick by Castles made it 16-14.

After 15 plays in 75 hard yards Presbyterian's quarterback Allen McNeil threw to end Bill Caldwell for an 11-yard score and the kick by Cruickshanks gave the Blue Hose a 23-14 margin with only minutes to play.

The Indian Offense cranked up, and with less than a minute to go Gary Welchel took the ball from the Indian 20 to an Indian score in 10 plays and a total of 80 yards, Welchel scoring on a one-yard plunge. The extra point by Castles, his 16th of the season, came with only three seconds remaining and the score read Presbyterian 23, Newberry 21.

The last play of the game came with an on-side kick by the Indians which they recovered, but with no time remaining for another play the score remained 23-21 and the Bronze Derby remains in Clinton for another year.

The Blue Stocking

Presbyterian College, Clinton, S. C., Monday, December 5, 1960

POETRY IN MOTION — Blue Hose quarterback Alan McNeill moves one way, the ball falls the opposite way, and linemen from PC and Newberry travel in all directions during Presbyterian's hard-fought 23-21 victory on Thanksgiving day.

The Blue Hose ground out a hard fought 23-21 win over arch-rival Newberry in the season's final. The Hose outgained Newberry 310 yards and picked up 20 first downs to Newberry's 10. PC was hampered by pealties, losing 77 yards to the officials.

Head Coach Cally Gault has been named Carolina's Conference Coach of The Year. Gault won the honor mainly on the strength of the Hose mid-season surge. PC won 5 of its last 6 games after an 0-5 start.

Several Presbyterian players also won past-season honors. Defensive guard Ed Paulling, defensive end Johnny Bankhead and center Phil Shroyer were named All-Carolinas Conference in a vote by the Conference coaches.

The Li'l That Was!

Presbyterian College magazine

Fall, 1969

Here's what coeducation has done for the Blue Hose sidelines. In a rare off-year for PC football, these young ladies brighten the scene. From the left, kneeling: Ann Richardson of Barnwell, S. C.; head cheerleader Jean Cummings of Cartersville, Ga.; Ellen Fluharty of Asheville; Standing: Shirley Dillard of Duncan, S. C.; Frances Cox of Tallahassee; Ann Bates of Pickens, S. C.; and Ann Newton of Greenville, S. C.

November 1970

November 1	A fire at a discotheque in France killed 146. It was later discovered the emergency exits were padlocked.
November 3	MLB future Hall of Fame pitcher Bob Gibson won the MLB NL Cy Young Award.
November 3	Marxist Salvador Allende was inaugurated as President of Chile.
November 5	MLB catcher of the Atlanta Braves Javy Lopez was born.
November 6	Twins Jim Perry won the MLB AL Cy Young Award.
November 8	Tom Dempsey of the New Orleans Saints set an NFL record for a 63 yard field goal.
November 8	Director and actor Dennis Hopper and singer Michelle Phillips of The Mamas and the Papas divorced after one week of marriage.
November 9	French Army General and President of France, Charles DeGaul passed away.
November 12	American figure skater Tonya Harding was born.
November 14	The Marshall University football team were killed in an airline crash in Kenova, West Virginia.
November 17	Douglas Engelbart received a patent for the computer mouse.
November 18	Boxer Joe Frazier KO's Bob Foster to win the WBA, WBC and Ring heavyweight titles.
November 18	Cincinnati Reds catcher Johnny Bench won the MLB Most Valuable Player Award.
November 20	The United Nations General Assembly accepted membership of the People's Republic of China.
November 21	General Hafez al-Assad became Prime Minister of Syria after a military coup.
November 23	George Harrison released "My Sweet Lord" in the US.
November 24	Quarterback Jim Plunkett of Stanford won the Heisman Trophy.
November 25	New York Yankees catcher Thurman Munson won the MLB AL Rookie of the Year Award.
November 26	The Bronze Derby was played in Newberry, South Carolina on Thanksgiving Day. The Presbyterian College Blue Hose defeated the Newberry College Indians 27-23.

The Newberry Observer
AND HERALD & NEWS
"Just Like A Letter From Home"

Newberry, S. C., Tuesday, November 24, 1970

The Li'l That Was!

NEVER HAD IT
Coach Herren Considers Bronze Derby 'A Myth'

"As far as I'm concerned, the Bronze Derby is a myth," exclaimed Newberry's head football coach Fred Herren. He was owing this statement to the fact that since he has been coach at Newberry College the derby has not been in the school trophy case.

He hopes to make myth a reality Thanksgiving Day when the number one Carolinas Conference defensive team butts heads with the number one conference offensive team. The 56th meeting of the two teams is also enhanced by the enthusiasm both teams have to make this year's contest as exciting as last year's when PC won it in the last seconds on a field goal, 23-21. PC tried the field goal, but it failed; however, Newberry had too many men on the field and the Blue Hose got a second life; this time making good their try and winning the game.

Presbyterian is sporting a 6-3 record at present, and all indications are they will take the Carolinas Conference crown from Elon this year. Perhaps the biggest threat the Tribe will face is the throwing ability of quarterback Allen McNeill. Presently McNeill is averaging 160.4 yards per game in the aerial department.

But if McNeill is impressive in the passing department, the Indians pose just as big a threat in the running game with the Conference's second leading rusher Donald Garrick with 1,073 yards so far this season. Quarterback Tommy Williamson, South Carolina sports writers back of the week last week hit nine for 11 passes and three touchdowns against Samford.

"They are a very fine football team," stated Herren. "They are not the biggest or the fastest team we've played, but they are definitely one of the best. Their record speaks for itself," he continued.

"McNeill is one of the best third down quarterbacks in this area. We will have to make a minimum of mistakes to stay in the game, because they will not make very many. Bobby Norris is an outstanding linebacker and a fine football player," concluded the head coach.

The game gets underway at 2 p.m. Thanksgiving Day in Clinton.

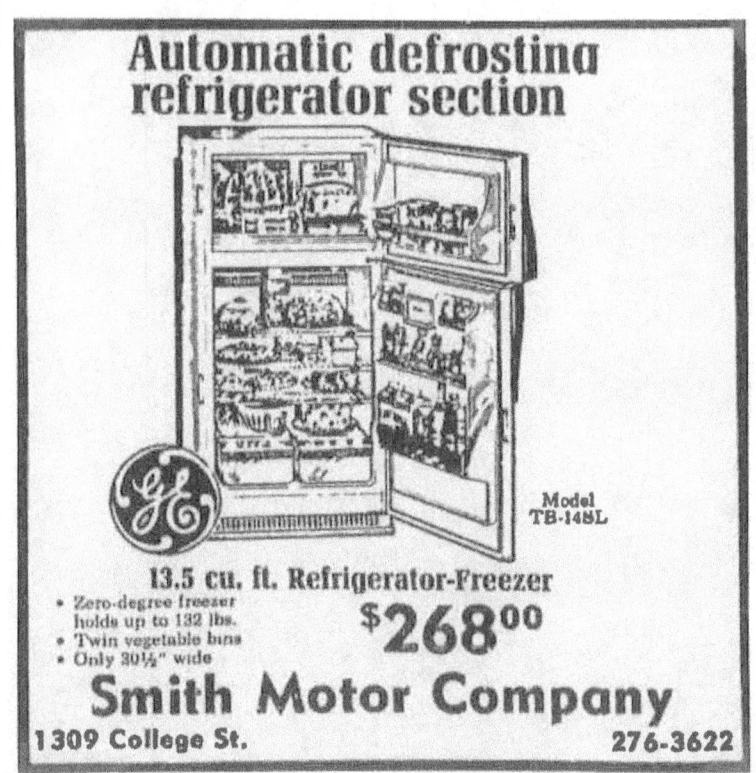

The Li'l 🎩 That Was!

The Clinton Chronicle

Vol. 71 — No. 47   Clinton, S. C., Nov. 26, 1970

Play Here Thursday Afternoon
PC, Newberry Battle For The Derby

FRED NEFF
Newberry Coach

CALLY GAULT
PC Coach

The Newberry Observer
AND HERALD & NEWS
"Just Like A Letter From Home"

The Li'l 🎩 That Was!

THURSDAY

Annual Bronze Derby Battle Is At Clinton

The Bronze Derby has not seen the Newberry College campus since Thanksgiving 1966 when the Presbyterian team abducted it with a 26-7 victory in Clinton. The Indians go after it this Thursday in the annual classic which this year is booked at Clinton.

This year, following four straight Turkey Day losses, the Indians will visit Presbyterian campus to renew the annual battle for the symbolic topper. The meeting will be the 56th in a series which dates back to 1913, when the Indians demolished the Blue Hose 51-0. Despite the initial setback, Presbyterian holds a 35-16-4 edge over Newberry.

The Bronze Derby originated as the result of a highly-spirited ruckus on the night of Jan. 30, 1947, following a basketball game between the two rival schools. Before the game got underway, several PC students put up a banner high on the wall which read: "Beat Hell Out of Newberry."

Sometime during the game, a group of Newberry students secured a ladder, set it up against the outside wall, climbed through a window, rolled up the banner, and escaped unnoticed the same way they had entered. Near the end of the game the visiting Blue Hose supporters realized the banner was gone.

After Presbyterian had taken a 51-47 victory, the irate Hose partisans demanded the return of the banner. This prompted a scuffle, and in the midst of the general confusion, a Newberry student snatched a derby from the head of a PC student and ran.

During the next couple of days, the athletic publicity directors of the two schools negotiated for the return of the derby.

They finally came to the agreement that the derby should serve as a laurel of victory in athletic contests between Newberry and Presbyterian. Consequently, the hat was returned to PC, packaged, and forwarded to a casting company in Ohio, where it was bronzed.

Until 1956, possession of the derby was determined by victories in football, basketball, and baseball, but then the schools agreed to award the trophy on the basis of football superiority alone. Since then, Newberry has won the Bronze Derby four times.

After-Thanksgiving Sale
Friday, Saturday, Monday
(Nov. 27, 28 and 30)

$12.99 — $15.99 — $17.99

(Reg. $17 to $27)

The Fashion Shoe Salon
And
Anderson's Shoe Salon

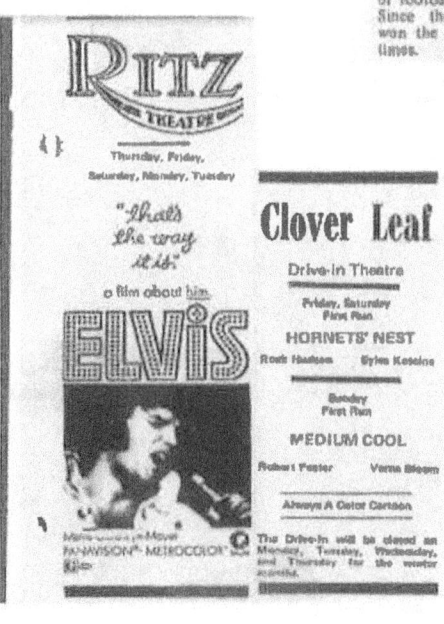

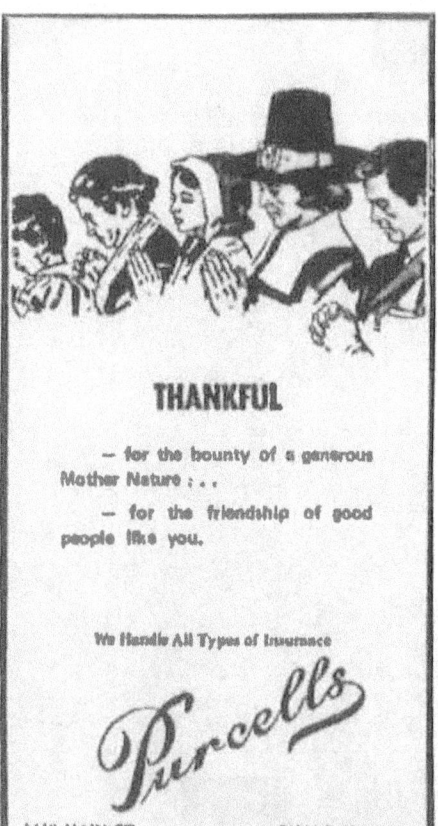

THANKFUL

— for the bounty of a generous Mother Nature...
— for the friendship of good people like you.

We Handle All Types of Insurance

Purcells

1411 MAIN ST.   PHONE 276-1423

The Li'l  That Was!

The Indian
Home of the Fighting Redskins

Eat, Drink, Be Merry! The Worst Is Coming.

VOL. XLIII — NEWBERRY, S.C. 29108, WEDNESDAY, NOVEMBER 18, 1970 — NUMBER 11

Tribe Faces Presbyterian

On Thanksgiving Day, Nov. 26, the Newberry College Indians will play the Blue Hose of Presbyterian College in a key Carolinas Conference game.

If PC can win this encounter, it will win the Carolinas Conference. If the Indians can win, however, it would help salvage a respectable season. To date PC has a 7-2 record with wins over Lenoir Rhyne, Elon, Western Carolina, Guilford, Catawba, Gardner-Webb, and Carson-Newman. Their only two losses came via the hands of Furman and Wofford.

Heading the Blue Key attack is All-Conference quarterback Allen McNeill who has completed 97 out of 206 aerial attempts for 1360 yards, a new total offense record at PC. His primary receivers are Lynn Dreger, a sophomore from St. Petersburg, Fla., who has 27 receptions, good for 425 yards, and Bill Caldwell, who has 19 receptions and 333 yards.

Tom Milton heads an impressive rushing attack with 493 yards in 150 attempts. Other names to watch for include David Eckstein and Johnny Jeselnik with 453 and 293 yards respectively.

A contributing factor in PC's success this year is a quick, responsive offensive line.

PC's offense and defense has been impressive this year but Newberry should prove to be more than a formidable foe. The "Indians" put it all together last Saturday and whipped an upstart Samford eleven 35-21. Newberry's defense, number one in the Conference and its rushing attack also number one in the conference, should provide plenty of its own fireworks during the traditional Thanksgiving game. Their 4-6 record is very misleading and PC should have their hands full as Newberry will be going for victory number five in this season's finale.

Rivalry with P. C.
Tribe Wants That Derby

The Bronze Derby, pictured at the left, has not seen the Newberry College campus since Thanksgiving 1966 when the Presbyterian team abducted it with a 26-7 victory in Clinton.

This year, following three straight Turkey Day losses, the Indians will visit Presbyterian campus to renew the annual battle for the symbolic topper. The meeting will be the fifty-sixth in a series which dates back to 1913, when the Indians demolished the Blue Hose 51-0. Despite the initial setback, Presbyterian holds a 35-16-4 edge over Newberry.

The Bronze Derby originated as the result of a highly spirited ruckus on the night of Jan. 30, 1947, following a basketball game between the two rival schools. Before the game got underway, several PC students put up a banner high on the wall which read, "Beat Hell Out of Newberry."

Sometime during the game, a group of Newberry students secured a ladder, set it up against the outside wall, climbed through a window, rolled up the banner, and escaped unnoticed the same way they had entered. Near the end of the game the visiting Blue Hose supporters realized that the banner was gone.

After Presbyterian had taken a 51-47 victory, the irate Hose partisans demanded the return of the banner. This prompted a scuffle, and in the midst of the general confusion, a Newberry student snatched a derby from the head of a PC student and ran.

During the next couple of days, the athletic publicity directors of the two schools negotiated for the return of the derby. They finally came to the agreement that the derby should serve as a laurel of victory in athletic contests between Newberry and Presbyterian. Consequently, the hat was returned to PC, packaged, and forwarded to a casting company in Ohio, where it was bronzed.

Until 1956, possession of the derby was determined by victories in football, basketball, and baseball, but then the schools agreed to award the trophy on the basis of football superiority alone. Since then, Newberry has won the Bronze Derby four times.

Lominick's Drug Store
1501 MAIN STREET — NEWBERRY, S. C.
Dial 276-3771 for Quality Service

Page 6   The Laurens Advertiser   November 24, 1970

PC-Newberry meet in Bronze Derby

The Bronze Derby has not seen the Newberry College campus since Thanksgiving 1966 when the Presbyterian team abducted it with a 26-7 victory in Clinton.

THIS YEAR, following four straight Turkey Day losses, the Indians will visit Presbyterian campus to renew the annual battle for the symbolic topper. The meeting will be the fifty-sixth in a series which dates back to 1913, when the Indians demolished the Blue Hose 51-0. Despite the initial setback, Presbyterian holds a 35-16-4 edge over Newberry.

The Bronze Derby originated as the result of a highly-spirited ruckus on the night of Jan. 30, 1947, following a basketball game between the two rival schools. Before the game got underway, several PC students put a banner high on the wall.

Sometime during the game, a group of Newberry students secured a ladder, set it up against the outside wall, climbed through a window, rolled up the banner, and escaped unnoticed the same way they had entered. Near the end of the game the visiting Blue Hose supporters realized the banner was gone.

AFTER PRESBYTERIAN had taken a 51-47 victory, the irate Hose partisans demanded the return of the banner. This prompted a scuffle, and in the midst of the general confusion a Newberry student snatched the derby from the head of a PC student and ran.

During the next couple of days, the athletic publicity directors of the two schools negotiated for the return of the derby.

THEY FINALLY came to the agreement that the derby should serve as a laurel of victory in athletic contests between Newberry and Presbyterian. Consequently, the hat was returned to PC, packaged, and forwarded to a casting company in Ohio, where it was bronzed.

Until 1956, possession of the derby was determined by victories in football, basketball, and baseball, but then the schools agreed to award the trophy on the basis of football superiority alone. Since then, Newberry has won the Bronze Derby four times.

The Li'l 🎩 That Was!

PC Edges Indians For Bronze Derby

Presbyterian College, the favorite going into the annual Bronze Derby Classic on Thanksgiving Day, had to battle from behind in the fourth quarter to overcome the aroused Newberry Indians and post a 27-23 victory that gave the Blue Hose a full share of the conference title that had never been earned by a state team in the history of the league.

Fittingly, it was the Blue Hose field leader, quarterback Allen McNeill, who provided the clincher that ended the Tribe's hopes of an upset. It came on a 55-yard excursion on a third down in the final stanza.

Trailing 23-20 following Newberry quarterback Tommy Williamson's 20-yard field goal with 11:40 left in the game, McNeill dropped back to pass on third and three at his own 45. A quick look told him Newberry had his receivers covered and he broke up the middle, cut to the right where Lynn Dreger threw a block at the 20 to wipe out two sure tackles and allow him to score standing up.

With 5:52 remaining to be played, Clinton native Jerry Chandler booted the extra-point that ended the scoring.

Newberry came back after the kickoff, however, and pushed down to the PC 35 in seven plays. There on fourth and 10, Williamson drilled a pass to sure-fingered Howdy Hays, the split end, but he was stopped short of the first down by a bare yard and PC took over to run out the clock.

The victory gave the Blue Hose the title with a perfect 5-0 conference mark and an 8-3 over-all figure. Newberry slipped to 4-7 on the year, with a 1-5 loop record.

It looked like PC would have no trouble with the visiting Indians from the beginning as the Blue Hose chalked up 20 first quarter points, despite a fight, two costly personal foul infractions, and having to go without the services of standout cornerback Elliott Poss, out with a knee injury suffered in last week's win over Mars Hill.

Newberry got in scoring position early in the second stanza when cornerback Butch Jernigan intercepted McNeill's second down pass at the PC 25. A personal foul call sent the Indians back to the Blue Hose 37 on first down, but Williamson called on Newberry leading rusher, burly tailback Donald Garrick, five times in seven plays to ram the ball down to the one on third down.

There Garrick dove over to make it 20-6 as the extra point try was blocked by Passerello, the fifth time he has blocked a conversion kick this season.

PC tried to come back on the next series, but could penetrate only as far as the Newberry 42 where they had to punt. After the punt, Williamson, behind perfect protection, lofted a strike to his end Marty Pearson open at the PC 30, and he ran on to the seven, completing a 54-yard bomb play.

It took Newberry three plays to push it across, this time from the one with Garrick once more hurdling the line to make it 20-12 at the half.

The Newberry defenders, led by Greenvillian Ken Pettus, the middle linebacker, then hurled the Hosemen back, forcing the punt.

Going into action from their own 23, the Indians struggled out to the PC 45 in six plays on the running of Garrick and Jim Fulton. Garrick broke out at that point and rambled down to the PC five, but three successive stops by linebacker Bobby Norris, who totaled 17 individual tackles on the day plus 13 assists, and end Jerry Traynham, forced coach Fred Herren's charges to attempt the field goal that gave them the lead, 23-20, for the first and last time in the game.

Henry's Barber Shop
Voight Dominick
Henry Barnette
College at Main—Downstairs

NICHOLS HANGS ON—Wade Nichols tackles a PC player in Thanksgiving Day action. (Photo by Holcombe)

GARRICK SAILS FOR GOAL—Don Garrick, guarded by Howdy Hays, tries to outrun two Blue Hose opponents in the game against Presbyterian. (Photo by Holcombe)

The Blue Stocking

Presbyterian College, Clinton, S. C., Friday, December 11, 1970

Newberry Win Gives Hose Title

by Robbie Hopkins

Presbyterian's Blue Hose, under the authority of Allan McNeill, took the Carolina Conference title on Walter Johnson Field with a 27-23 victory over the Newberry Indians on Thanksgiving Day.

At the start of the game the Hose took advantage of several Indian mistakes for touchdowns on a Frank Armstrong punt, the ball hit Newberry's Billy Cock and was recovered by Tony Passarello on the three yard line of Newberry. Tam Milton then took the handoff and ran it in for the Blue Hose's first score. Next, Rick Medlin intercepted a pass and sailed 65 yards for the second score. The third touchdown came when Tam Milton ran the ball over the goal line from the one yard line, after a terrific 80 yard drive, with 2:45 left in the first half.

The second quarter belonged all to Newberry. The Indians scored two touchdowns both by Don Garrick, the leading rusher of the game with 146 yards. The half ended with the score P.C. 20, Indians 12.

In the third period Tommy Williamson, the Indians quarterback, drove Newberry down the field and ran it in for the touchdown. The two point conversion by the signal caller game Newberry a tie with P.C. at the end of the third quarter 20-20.

At the beginning of the fourth quarter, the Indians again drove down the field, but the defense lead by All-American Bobby Norris stopped the Indians allowing only a field goal putting the score at 23-20 in favor of Newberry.

Late in the last period the Blue Hose starter a drive and on third down and five yards to go for the first down McNeill dropped back to pass. Seeing no one open McNeill set his sights for the goal line and charged down the right sideline untouched for a touchdown. Jerry Chandler converted the extra point giving P.C. the game winning score of 27-23.

Another individual game was between Newberry's Gerrick and hose's Tam Milton. Milton at the end of the game had attained the honors of scoring the most points in the conference. Milton beat Garrick by six points.

The game gave the Blue Hose and 8-3 over all record and 5-0 for the conference.

The Li'l That Was!

The Newberry Observer
AND HERALD & NEWS
"Just Like A Letter From Home"

HERALD AND NEWS ESTABLISHED 1865 — Newberry, S. C., Tuesday, December 1, 1970 — NEWBERRY OBSERVER ESTABLISHED 1*

Newberry, S. C., Tuesday, December 1, 1970 — THE NEWBERRY OBSERVER — 5-A

Hard-Luck Newberry Nipped By PC, 27-23

AN OBSERVER SPORTS REPORT

What can you say but, "Wait 'til next year?"

The most frustrating season in Newberry College's football history came to an end last Thursday afternoon. In the annual Thanksgiving Day classic at Clinton, the tie way.

Jerry Long ('68) took a pitchout and ran 24 yards for the fourth Bulldog touchdown early in the last period, and David Folk got the final score from three yards out after a 37-yard dash by Ronnie Bannister ('70).

Rader's shotgun passes moved M-C from its own 26 to the Newberry 10 in the waning moments, with prime receivers Wayne Shealy ('69), Allen Shealy ('70), Mark Counts ('69) and Mark McIntyre ('69). The Bulldogs' Greg Avedisian ('67) intercepted a pass at the goal line to snuff out the drive.

Tackle Steve Long and center Wingard Price, both '63, were the most antique of Newberry's old timers. Guard Mike Griffin ('65) was M-C's ranking veteran. Jim Kimmell, Melvin Bouknight and Mike Ware master-minded for the Bulldogs.

Indians walloped the stuffing out of Presbyterian College but lost.

Newberry excelled in all statistical departments, except the matter of points. PC had 27, Newberry 23.

It was a bitter finish to a bitter season, in which Fred Herron's young Indians won four games and lost seven. The record was far from the worst in Newberry history, but it may have been the poorest in relation to potential, and therein lies the frustration.

The Indians were contenders in every game they played. But for the toll taken by fumbles, interceptions and funny bounces, the record might well have been 8-3, 9-2, 10-1 or even (it could have happened) 11-0.

All Bad Bounces

The least Newberry might have expected, in a year when victory was a possibility every time they stepped on the field, was a winning record. It was, however, a season in which everything bounced wrong.

The Bronze Derby contest against Presbyterian last week was typical. The Indians spotted Presbyterian a 20-0 lead in the first quarter, led 23-20 in the final period, then lost it when Blue Hose quarterback Allen McNeill scrambled 55 yards for a touchdown after finding his pass receivers covered.

Reading the statistics, you can't see how PC won. Newberry had 22 first downs to 11 for their hosts. Newberry registered 424 yards of total offense, PC 248. Newberry's Tommy Williamson was a superb quarterback, PC's McNeill no better than ordinary — except, of course, for the fact that McNeill won the ball game with his desperation run, living up to his reputation as a splendid man in the clutch.

A disastrous first quarter was what really did it to Newberry in spite of a gallant come-from-behind effort. PC scored after a Blue Hose punt bounced off the Indians' Billy Koch and was recovered at the Newberry 3. They scored again after an interception at the PC 40, then put together an 80-yard drive for a 20-0 lead after only 12 minutes and 15 seconds of play.

Newberry was not to be routed, however, and recovered for two second period touchdowns. The rally was sparked by Donald Garrick's running and Williamson's passing, with Garrick getting both scores on short pops.

Brief Lead

Trailing 20-12 at intermission, Newberry tied it up late in the third quarter on a 66-yard drive, Williamson sneaking in from the one and keeping for the two-point conversion.

Williamson's 20-yard field goal early in the fourth quarter gave Newberry a 23-20 lead which lasted until McNeill's gallop out of the pocket on a third-and-3 situation with 5:52 left in the game.

The win gave Presbyterian clear possession of the Carolinas Conference crown, with a perfect 5-0 record. Over-all, the Hose won eight and lost three.

So the Indians will have to wait 'til next year for what might have been in 1970. With few losses by graduation in prospect, the outlook is perhaps the brightest ever.

Leading the 1971 returnees will be Donald Garrick, who paced Newberry to the conference rushing crown. The stocky junior tailback got 146 yards in 32 carries against Presbyterian last week, upping his season total to 1,219 yards, best in the league. He broke the school rushing record a month ago.

Losing the Hard Way

Statistical triumphs did little for the Newberry won-lost record this fall, a review of the season makes clear. The Tribe outscored its opponents 226-215 but defeated only Emory and Henry (27-8), Concord (41-6), Guilford (25-14) and Samford (35-21).

The defeats all came the hard way. Against the best and the worst of the opposition, Newberry frequently beat itself with miscues. A harbinger of things to come was the 3-0 loss to Gardner-Webb in the season's second game. Newberry lost the ball six times on fumbles.

A week later at Catawba, Newberry again lost a half-dozen fumbles plus three interceptions. Catawba won, 41-21.

Back home against Lenoir Rhyne on Oct. 3, Newberry was within striking distance in the fourth quarter, trailing only 23-19. The game wound up 37-19 in favor of the Bears.

Tussle for Wofford

Undefeated Wofford, this week within one game of the NAIA national crown, had its hands full against Newberry on Oct. 17. Newberry trailed only 17-14 in the fourth period and was marching when the first of two critical fumbles opened the door for the Terriers. Final score Wofford 31, Newberry 14.

Mars Hill beat the Indians on Oct. 24, 17-15, intercepting four Newberry passes. Elon licked the Tribe 10-6 on Nov. 7, in a game marked for the third time in the season by six lost Newberry fumbles.

Finding bright spots in so frustrating a season isn't easy, but the Indians did demonstrate a formidable offense via the triple option, and the makings of a strong passing game via freshman find Tommy Williamson.

Special

1971 Ford F103, K00160, ½ ton pickup, 6 cy., Deluxe tutone, 3 speed standard tran., 1250 LB rear springs, Custom style side, raven black and mallard green.

Reg. $3102.63

Sale Price **$2501.95**

Shealy Motor Co.

Presbyterian College magazine
Winter, 1971

Two longtime fans share Cally Gault's enthusiasm over the Bronze Derby retained in PC's last-minute Thanksgiving win over Newberry. Helping to carry the trophy off the field are Thomas Rice (left), maintenance assistant, and Willie Byrd, gymnasium custodian, whose friendships with students span 25 years.

November 1971

November 1	The World Hockey Association announced it would begin play in 1972 to compete against the NHL.
November 1	The United States mint introduced the Eisenhower dollar.
November 5	The NBA Los Angeles Lakers began a 33 game winning streak.
November 8	Led Zeppelin released "Stairway to Heaven."
November 8	The United States House of Representatives considered, but failed to pass, a proposed amendment permitting voluntary prayer in public schools.
November 9	American golfer and Open Champion David Duval was born.
November 10	Joe Torre of the St Louis Cardinals won the MLB NL Most Valuable Player Award.
November 10	The United States table tennis team arrived in China.
November 10	Vida Blue of the Oakland A's won the MLB AL Most Valuable Player Award.
November 11	Swedish director and writer Igmar Bergman married actress Ingrid von Rosen.
November 13	Mariner 9 was the first spacecraft to orbit Mars.
November 15	Intel introduced the first microprocessor, the Intel 4004.
November 20	Richard Petty won the 21st NASCAR Sprint Cup.
November 20	Women from all over the United States marched in support of abortion rights in Washington, DC.
November 21	Michael Strahan, a member of the NFL Hall of Fame, television personality and broadcaster, was born.
November 23	The People's Republic of China was seated at the United Nations Security Council.
November 24	Dan Cooper hijacked a plane and jumped out over Washington state never to be seen again.
November 25	Atlanta Braves catcher-infielder Earl Williams won the MLB NL Rookie of the Year Award.
November 25	American actress Christina Applegate was born.
November 25	Quarterback Pat Sullivan of Auburn won the Heisman Trophy.
November 25	The Bronze Derby was played in Newberry, South Carolina on Thanksgiving Day. The Newberry College Indians defeated the Presbyterian College Blue Hose 34-0.

The Li'l 🎩 That Was!

The Indian
Home of the Fighting Redskins
Cold winter ahead get that Derby!

VOL. XLIV   NEWBERRY, S.C. 29108, WEDNESDAY, NOV. 17, 1971   NUMBER 11

Rival game to decide fate of derby

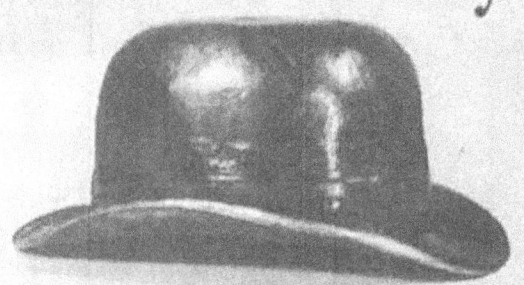

BRONZE DERBY

The Bronze Derby, pictured at right, has not been on the Newberry College campus since Thanksgiving 1966 when the Presbyterian team abducted it with a 26-7 victory in Clinton.

This year, following three straight Turkey Day losses, the Indians will visit Presbyterian tonight to renew the annual battle for the symbolic topper. The meeting will be the fifty-sixth in a series which dates back to 1915.

INTRAMURAL BASKETBALL

All organizations interested in entering a team in the Intramural Basketball program are asked to have a representative give this information to Miss Barbara Sligh, secretary of the Athletic Department. The Athletic Department is located in the basement of MacLean Gymnasium. This information should be given to Miss Sligh by December 10.

when the Indians demolished the Blue Hose 51-0. Despite the initial setback, Presbyterian holds a 35-16-4 edge over Newberry.

The Bronze Derby originated at the result of a highly-spirited rucks on the night of Jan. 30, 1947, following a basketball game between the two rival schools. Before the game got underway, several PC students put up a banner high on the wall which read: "Beat Hell Out of Newberry."

Sometime during the game, a group of Newberry students secured a ladder, set it up against the outside wall, climbed through a window, rolled up the banner, and secured it the same way they had entered. Near the end of the game the visiting Blue Hose supporters realized that the banner was gone.

After Presbyterian had taken a 51-47 victory, the irate Hose partisans demanded the return of

the banner. This prompted a scuffle, and in the midst of the general confusion, a Newberry snatched a derby from the head of a PC student and ran.

During the next couple of days, the athletic publicity directors of the two schools negotiated for the return of the derby. They finally came to the agreement that the derby should serve as a token of victory in athletic contests between Newberry and Presbyterian. Consequently, the hat was returned to PC, packaged, and forwarded to a casting company in Ohio, where it was bronzed.

Until 1956, possession of the derby was determined by victories in football, basketball, and baseball, but then the school agreed to award the trophy on the basis of football

superiority alone. Since then, Newberry has won the Bronze Derby four times.

Thanksgiving Day
Redskins to meet Blue Hose

By NEAL SHEALY

Turkey Day brings the 2 p.m. scrap between Newberry and PC for the Bronze Derby. This year's clash should be doubly exciting as Newberry is 7-2-1 on the year, and Presbyterian 7-2 with two games remaining.

The Blue Hose have the best overall team speed of anyone that Newberry has faced. PC has been ranked as high as 13th in the NAIA, and their offense leads the

Carolinas Conference in every statistic.

Quarterback Wayne Renwick leads this explosive offense. The Hosemen like to establish their running game early, and assign this task to David Eckstein, John Jeselnik, and Tam Milton Eckstein is also a favorite receiver along with Lynn Dreger.

Senior linebacker Bobby Norris, an All-American from Thomson, Georgia, heads a tough defense. Other standouts which could cause

the Indians difficulty include tackle Ted Wentzky and Tony Passarella, a safety.

PC's victories include upsets of Southern Conference foes, Furman and The Citadel, which is 2nd in the major colleges in total offense. Last week the Blue Hose were beaten by Carson-Newman 15-14 after PC had led 14-2 going into the 4th quarter. C-N has nailed down an NAIA playoff berth and is ranked 8th in the NAIA.

The 'Skins, playing on their home hunting grounds, hope to scalp our Presbyterian rivals, and return the Derby to Newberry. The Turkey Day clash will be the final game for 13 Newberry seniors.

The Li'l 🎩 That Was!

The Laurens Advertiser
"SOUTH CAROLINA'S FASTEST GROWING SEMI-WEEKLY NEWSPAPER"

LAURENS, SOUTH CAROLINA, DECEMBER 1, 1971 — NO. 25—34 PA

Despite final loss...

Presbyterian Blue Hose had successful season

Presbyterian College Thursday against Newberry helped prove that emotion plays a major role in college football. The Blue Hose, who entered the contest only 4 days after a 17-6 Homecoming victory over Mars Hill, were just not emotionally or mentally ready for the game. The Indians were ready for the game and they beat the Blue Hose every way that a team can be beaten.

It was just one of those days when nothing seems to go right. The Cool Blue Machine which was plagued all day with poor field position and turnovers just simply could not get started. For the game Presbyterian lost three fumbles and had five passes intercepted but what hurt the most was a fierce Newberry defense.

EVEN THOUGH the Cool Blue Machine only gained 37 yards total offense the first half, they trailed by a score of only 14 to 0 going into the third quarter. The turning point for Presbyterian came when halfback Tam Milton was hit on the Newberry four yard line and fumbled into the end zone. The Indians took over on the twenty and drove 80 yards for the score. That made it Newberry 21 and P. C. 0. Having to play catch up football Presbyterian's quarterback Wayne Renwick was intercepted four times in the second half.

The Indians tallied two more times giving them a 34 to 0 ball game and possession of the "Bronze Derby".

CONSIDERING everything it was an extremely successful season for the Blue Hose. They finished with an 8-3 record for the second consecutive year. Coach Cally Gault's team also beat arch rivals Furman and Wofford and upset heavily favored Citadel in Charleston.

The Blue Hose placed seven men on the Greensboro Daily News All-Conference team which is the most men Presbyterian has ever had on the team. The BlueHose saw a brillian passing combination of Wayne Renwick and Lynn Dreger emerge and an offensive line that became one of the finest in the conference.

THE DEFENSE was highlighted by the play of Bobby Norris but Coach Billy Tiller also was pleased to see tackle Ted Wentzky become a standout and possibly the next Blue Hose All-American. The defensive secondary led by Mike Apps and Ken Lister limited opponents to an average of 91.2 yards per contest through the air.

Even though the season ended on a bad note, it was a good year for a Cool Blue Machine.

The Clinton Chronicle

The Indians Were Hungry
PC Gridders Finish 8-3 Again

The Indians were just too hungry on Thanksgiving Day.

If the Pilgrims' guests on that first Thanksgiving had been as hard-eyed and hungry as Newberry's Indians were last Thursday, that probably would have nipped an American tradition in the bud.

Newberry's Indians, seeking their first win over PC after five straight losses in the Turkey Day Classic, threw a defensive wet blanket over PC's offense and ripped to a 34-0 decision. The win gave Newberry an 8-2-1 record for the season and PC finished at 8-3. It was PC's second straight 8-3 season. The 8-2-1 mark was Newberry's finest since 1925. It also was Newberry's biggest victory margin over PC since the series began in 1913 with a 51-0 Newberry win.

Comments of the Newberry players after the game gave indications of the motivation behind their splendid performance.

Marion Waters of Clinton, one of Newberry's tri-captains, had to sit out the game because of a knee injury but he was presented one of the game balls because of his inspiration to the team. He could have graduated last year but decided to return for another season of football because "I had set my goal to be on the team that beat PC. I wanted to go out with a winner."

Split End Rowdy Hays said, "I feel the same way about this game that I did against Wofford. In the past we have been beaten physically and scorewise against both. And it was unmerciful our freshman year. As a senior, I had never seen the Bronze Derby. I didn't even know what it looked like. But 8-2-1 is great, coming from where we were. We really came from nothing."

The Indians picked off five pass interceptions, running their total for the season to 41, an NAIA record. The interceptions were keys to the game, scoring one touchdown, setting up another and snuffing out PC hopes for a comeback.

PC fumbled twice inside Newberry's 10 when the score stood at 14-0. The second loss of a fumble which bounded into Newberry's end zone seemed to take the wind out of PC's sails when the Hose offense was beginning to move.

Hays scored Newberry's first touchdown on a 20-yard pass from lefthanded sophomore quarterback Tommy Williamson. Fullback Donald Garrick scored the second on a two-yard burst after a pass interception at PC's 38. A personal foul penalty against PC moved the ball on down to the 13.

The score stood 14-0 at halftime.

In the third quarter, PC recovered a Newberry fumble on a punt and had its first scoring opportunity but Newberry recovered a Tam Milton fumble at the five. Early in the fourth quarter, PC pulled a razzle-dazzle play out of its book with split end Lynn Dreger taking a reverse pitchout and passing to Milton at Newberry's 13. However two plays later, Milton was hit at the four and the ball squirted into the end zone where Newberry recovered. That was as close as PC was to get to paydirt.

The Indians were on the warpath then and swept 80 yards to score, aided by a pass interference penalty against PC. With 8:26 remaining in the game, it was 21-0.

Only a short time later, Newberry blocked a PC punt and took over at the Blue Hose six. Williamson sneaked it across and kicked the extra point for 28-0 lead. Cornerback David Sanders picked off another Renwick pass and zipped 39 yards to paydirt with 6:06 remaining in the game for the final score.

The Li'l That Was!

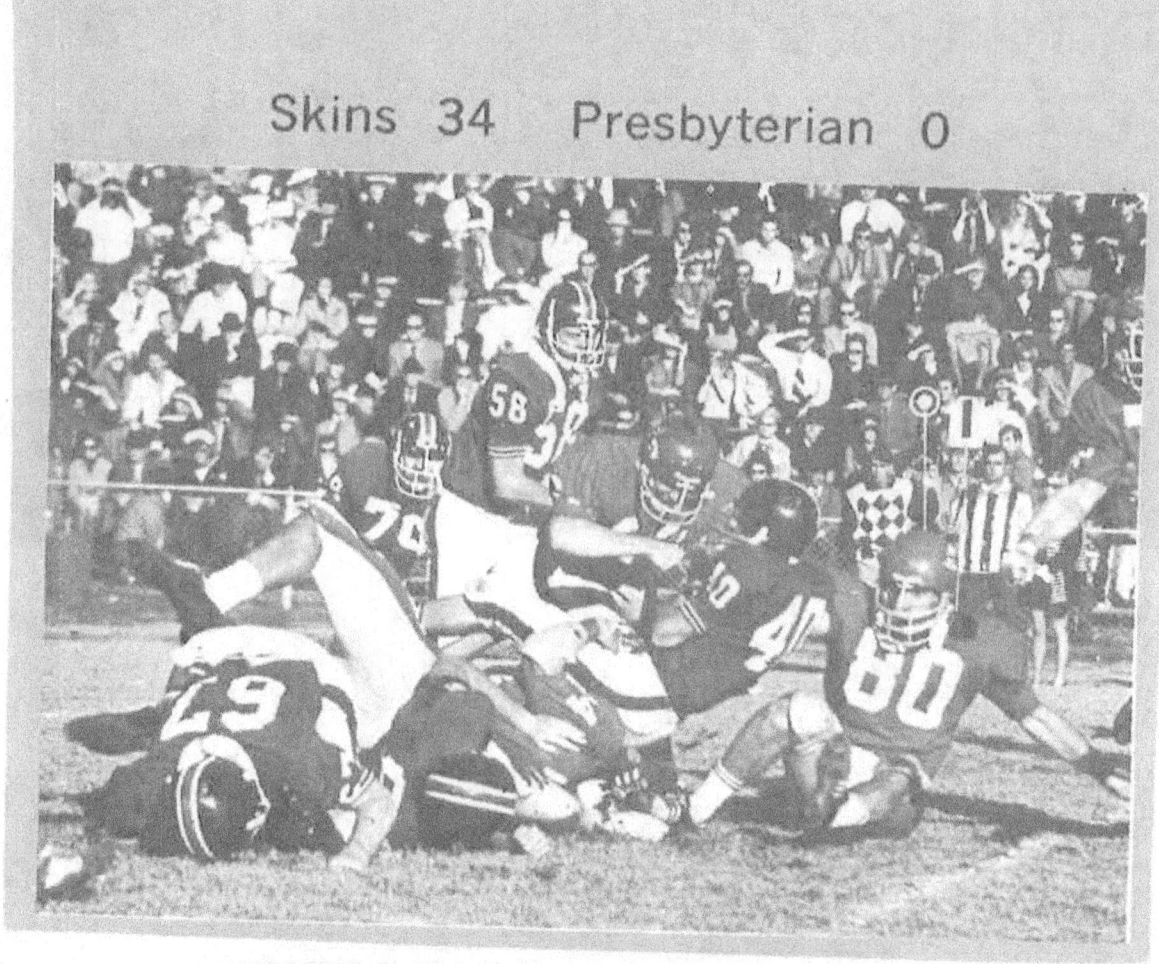

Skins 34   Presbyterian 0

NEWBERRIAN

THE MORE YOU LOOK AT IT THE BETTER IT LOOKS

Army ROTC Now Offers

$100 A Month — Take It.

The Li'l That Was!

The Newberry Observer
AND HERALD & NEWS
"Just Like A Letter From Home"

HERALD AND NEWS ESTABLISHED 1865 — Newberry, S. C., Tuesday, November 30, 1971 — NEWBERRY OBSERVER ESTABLISHED 1883

Bronze Derby Back!
Newberry Stifles PC, 34-0, For Eighth Win

Newberry College 34, Presbyterian zilch. Thus endeth the Indians' finest football season since 1924.

When the season finale was over on Thanksgiving afternoon, Fred Herren's Tribe had posted its eighth victory of the season against two losses and a tie and the treasured Bronze Derby was back in Newberry for the first time since 1965.

Not for 47 years had Newberry College experienced so successful a football season. The 1924 Indians, under Fred McLean, won eight games and lost a pair in a 10-game season.

Newberry, up against a vaunted Presbyterian offense, couldn't have been more convincing. Newberry's attack functioned smoothly for the first time in several games, and the defense was superb.

In the first half, PC's Cool Blue Machine could sputter only as far as its own 38-yard line. And although Presbyterian threatened seriously twice in the second half, the hard-hitting Indians forced fumbles and kept their

(Continued on Page 10)

SHINING SKIMMER: Fred Herren, Newberry College football coach and athletic director, tips the famous Bronze Derby in a gesture of appreciation after his Indians defeated Presbyterian College 34-0 in the Thanksgiving Day classic. The symbolic Bronze Derby came back to Newberry for the first time in six years as a result of the victory and garlanded with greenery, was the centerpiece on the Herren family Thanksgiving dinner table last Thursday night. The Indians awarded three game balls. One Herren holds went to the entire coaching staff. —Observer Photo.

★ Newberry-PC

(Continued from Page 1)

goal line intact.

It was a fine Turkey Day show for a majority of the nearly 5,000 spectators in the overflow crowd at Setzler Field, but a shocking disappointment for Cally Gault's Blue Hose and a large delegation of supporters from Clinton. The loss was PC's third against eight wins, and it gave Newberry the mythical state championship.

Everything seemed to go in favor of the Indians. They throttled PC's high-powered running and passing attack, intercepted five passes, blocked a punt, and recovered the two fumbles to shut off Presbyterian drives which might have turned the game around.

The five interceptions, four of them in the final quarter, gave Newberry an astonishing total of 41 for the season — the most ever recorded by any NAIA school in the nation.

Newberry scored in the first and second quarters, for a 14-0 halftime lead. It was still 14-0 after three periods, but the Indians turned it into a rout with 20 points in the final quarter.

The shutout was the first inflicted on Presbyterian this year. PC recorded only five first downs all afternoon and was limited to a total offense of 174 yards, only 70 of which were earned on the ground. Hose quarterback Wayne Renwick completed only seven of 23 passes, three of them to outstanding receiver Lynn Dreger.

Newberry rushed for 187 yards and added 116 more on soph quarterback Tommy Williamson's seven completions in 14 attempts. He had one intercepted, but nothing came of it. Newberry also lost three fumbles, but nothing came of those either.

It was, until the final period, a close and hard-fought contest an "old fashioned" game in that punting had a lot to do with the way things went. The Tribe's freshman kicker, Bruce Remillard, repeatedly put Presbyterian deep in the hole.

Passes Click

Newberry stopped its guests cold after the opening kickoff, then marched to a touchdown after taking the PC punt. Williamson passed twice to Howdy Hays in the drive, once for 11 yards and again for 21 yards and a touchdown. Hays went the last six yards with defenders hanging all over him.

Williamson's kick, the first of four successful conversions (his final try was blocked), gave Newberry a 7-0 lead after 4:46 had elapsed.

The lead widened in the second quarter when David Sanders picked off a Renwick pass at the PC 28. A major penalty against Presbyterian moved the ball to the 14. Two shots got only four yards, but on third and six Williamson rolled left for seven yards and a first down at the three.

On the next play, tailback Donald Garrick powered over right guard for the score with 8:57 remaining in the half.

Midway in the third period, Presbyterian finally got something going. The Hose moved to Newberry's five, but Tom Milton fumbled and Greg Hartle recovered for the Indians.

A Williamson fumble at the PC 35 late in the period gave PC another opening and the Hose moved across midfield as the fourth period began. A flea-flicker play, Renwick to Dreger and downfield to Milton, got the ball to Newberry's 15, but two plays later Milton fumbled into the end zone,

Butch Jernigan recovered for Newberry and PC was through for the season.

Garrick, who accumulated 100 yards during the game, sparked Newberry's third touchdown with a pair of fine runs. With the ball at the Tribe 21, he reeled off 24 yards and repeated for 29 more.

PC's Henry Beckham apparently intercepted a Williamson pass, but was called for interference and Newberry had a first down at the seven. Four plays later, Williamson sneaked it over for a 21-0 lead with 8:28 left in the game.

Shortly thereafter, Frank Armstrong's punt for PC was blocked by Jim Bowers and the ball went out of bounds at the PC six, 20 yards behind the scrimmage line. Williamson sneaked it in again on third and goal from the one and it was 28-0.

There was more. With about five minutes left to play, Sanders picked off his second interception of the day and sprinted 39 yards to Newberry's fifth and final touchdown. There were two more interceptions by the astonishing Indian secondary during the game's last moments, but no more scoring.

Victory in the Thanksgiving Day classic was an emotionally satisfying climax to a season marred only by defeats at the hands of Carolinas Conference champion Elon and non-conference Samford and a tie with Lenoir Rhyne.

It was the end of the collegiate football line for a dozen seniors, most of whom started out as freshmen in Herren's first year as coach in 1968.

In the four-year rebuilding period, Herren's teams have recorded 20 wins, 21 losses and a tie. They were 3-7-0 in 1968, 5-5-0 (including two forfeit wins) in 1969; and 4-7-0 in a frustrating 1970 season before shaping up this year as one of the region's finest small college teams.

Three Game Balls

After Thursday's Thanksgiving Day classic, PC's Cally Gault was terse. "We just got beat, that's all I've got to say," he remarked.

Herren was elated and voluble. "I honestly felt it would be close," he said. "I was surprised we shut them off like we did. We've had trouble making the big play all year but our guys sure made a couple today."

The Newberry defense got a definite lift, Herren felt, from the return of linebacker Ken Pettus to the lineup. Pettus had a cast removed from his knee earlier in the week.

The Indians awarded three game balls - one to the entire coaching staff, one to senior tackle Marion Waters of Clinton who watched the game on crutches, and one to secondary defensive coach Harold Wheeler whose ballhawks now own the national record for pass interceptions.

END AROUND: Newberry tight end Johnny Dawkins (81) is in a tight spot after taking handoff from Tommy Williamson. Presbyterian linebacker Stan Gruber (63), at right of picture, seems to have figured out exactly what's happening in the bit of razzle-dazzle.

The Li'l That Was!

WHOA! PC quarterback Wayne Renwick finds three reasons for not going anywhere against Newberry. The reasons are Greg Hartle (84) who has one of Renwick's legs; Keith McAlister (86) who's driving for the other leg; and Rick Sargent (73) who'll take what's left over.

The Newberry Observer

AWAY WE GO! Don Garrick, Indian tailback who rushed for 100 yards against Presbyterian, takes handoff Tommy Williamson (12) and rights gap in PC line.

The Li'l 🎩 That Was!

The Indian
Home of the Fighting Redskins

IF THE HAT FITS — Head Football Coach Fred Herren looks quite comfortable in the Bronze Derby the Tribe abducted from Presbyterian College with a 34-0 shut out in the traditional Thanksgiving clash. (Photo by Reames)

November 1972

November 1	"That Certain Summer" premiered on United States television.
November 2	Philadelphia Phillies pitcher Steve Carlton won the MLB NL Cy Young Award with 27 wins. The Phillies only won 59 games in 1972.
November 3	American singer-songwriter James Taylor married singer-songwriter Carley Simon.
November 4	Johnny Nash topped the *Billboard* charts with "I Can See Clearly Now."
November 6	In Brunswick, New Jersey, the first intercollegiate ultimate frisbee was played between Rutgers University and Princeton University.
November 7	Attorney Joe Biden was elected to the United States Senate representing the state of Delaware.
November 7	United States President Richard Nixon was re-elected, defeating George McGovern in a landslide victory.
November 8	HBO, the first "pay cable" station was launched, airing an NHL hockey game between the New York Rangers and Vancouver Canucks from Madison Square Garden.
November 8	After being re-elected, United States President Richard Nixon asked for the resignations of his cabinet in order to restructure the executive branch.
November 11	The Dow Jones Index moved above 1000 for the first time in its history.
November 12	Richard Petty won the 22nd NASCAR Sprint Cup.
November 11	The Dow Jones Index closed above 1000 for the first time in its history.
November 15	MLB Dick Allen wins AL Most Valuable Player Award.
November 16	Carley Simon released and spent 5 weeks on the top of the *Billboard* charts with the hit single "You're So Vain."
November 21	Boston Red Sox Carlton Fisk won the MLB AL Rookie of the Year Award.
November 22	The United States ended a 22 year travel ban to China.
November 23	The Bronze Derby was played in Clinton, South Carolina on Thanksgiving Day. The Presbyterian College Blue Hose defeated the Newberry College Indians 17-0.

The Li'l That Was!

The Li'l 🎩 That Was!

The Newberry Observer
AND HERALD & NEWS
"Just Like A Letter From Home"

HERALD AND NEWS ESTABLISHED 1865 — Newberry, S.C., Friday, November 24, 1972 — NEWBERRY OBSERVER ESTABLISHED 18?

Tribe Vs. Blue Hose
Bronze Derby Clash At Clinton Thursday

Just RAMBLING
NEWS OF MORE OR LESS INTEREST

THE NEXT E.Y.C. meeting of St. Luke's Episcopal Church will be Sunday, December 11. There will be no meetings November 26 or December 3.

DR. WILLIAM DAVID of Athens, Ga., will conduct services at Clayton Memorial Unitarian Universalist Church Sunday, Nov. 26, at 11 a.m. His sermon subject will be "Thankfulness In The Midst of Tragedy." The public is cordially invited.

WEATHER

From official U.S. Weather Station at City Water Filtration Plant, high and low temperatures and rainfall for the 24 hours ending at 6 p.m.

	H	L	Pct.
Nov. 20	62	44	.54
Nov. 21	65	43	.00
Nov. 22	—	34	tr.

Total rainfall for November is 2.30 inches.

The kidding around is about over, and one of the South's hottest football feuds will be resumed Thursday when Newberry College and Presbyterian College collide in the annual Bronze Derby classic.

Up to the time of the 2 p.m. kickoff in Clinton, Newberry coach Fred Herren and PC's Cally Gault will remain the most jovial of friends. Then for the next couple of hours there'll be no more Mr. Nice Guy.

At stake is more than the Bronze Derby, the symbolic hard hat which the Indians returned to Newberry a year ago by whipping the Blue Hose 34-0 in what was supposed to have been a close game.

By winning Thursday, Presbyterian can share the Carolinas Conference championship with Elon. By losing, they'll fall to third, behind second-place Newberry.

Also on the line is the prestige of owning the best season record of any college or university in South Carolina. Newberry is now 8-3-1. Presbyterian 6-3-1.

But even without those incentives, fans would be looking for the sort of knock-down drag-out contest which Newberry and PC have always put on. This will be their 58th football meeting, and is as unpredictable as most of their past encounters.

Herren and Gault were still friendly at a Kiwanis Club meeting in Newberry a few days ago. Photographers had trouble getting them to scowl at each other.

Gault left no doubt he has been smarting since the Indians licked his Blue Hose at Setzler Field a year ago. But his determined smile belied Herren's claim that Gault has thought of nothing but revenge since last year's whipping:

"That's just the kind of personality he has," said Herren. "He carries a grudge."

Gault went on smiling and said he thinks the athletic feud between PC and Newberry obligingly answered an audience question about his game plan for Thursday. "It'll be Eckstein right and Eckstein left," he replied.

His reference was to David Eckstein, the leading Blue Hose rusher. Eckstein has run for 870 yards this year and John Jeselnik has picked up another 608 yards. Gault also touts Jeselnik as probably the finest blocker in the state and, pound for pound, perhaps the best anywhere.

Quarterbacking is the key to PC's offense, as it is Newberry's. How Thursday's game goes may depend heavily on the health of the Blue Hose's Wayne Ronwick and Newberry's Tommy Williamson, who have missed a lot of play because of injuries. Both will start Thursday but neither is deemed to be at full effectiveness.

Ronwick, who has been in only six contests, is a powerful passer, throwing mostly to hot receiver Lynn Dreger. Dreger has caught 31 passes for seven touchdowns and 488 yards of offense this fall.

berry is a healthy, character-building sort of thing which calls on the participating athletes for plenty of "plain, raw courage."

Nodding to the Indians' backfield coach who came to the Kiwanis meeting with Herren, Gault said, "I've enjoyed my rivalry with Horace Turbeville and Fred — uh, Fred Whatsisname over here."

Gault told the Kiwanians he thinks both Newberry and Presbyterian have suffered some this year from "senioritis" — the mysterious malady which sometimes causes four-year veterans to play with less than 100 per cent efficiency.

He suggested that senioritis may have had something to do with Wofford College's upset victories this fall over both PC and Newberry.

"Every so often you get slipped up on," Gault said of the Wofford upsets, "and the same thing happened to Fred that happened to me. That's what Jack Peterson (Wofford coach) is supposed to do. That's what they hired him for — to get rid of Fred and get rid of me just as soon as he possibly can."

Come And Bring The Whole Family
To Welcome
Santa Claus
Santa Will Be Flying
In By Helicopter
To The
Newberry Shopping Center

Friday, November 24th — 2 P.M.

Santa Will Welcome The Children And Have Goodies For All!
Shop This Christmas With The Newberry Shopping Center Merchants Who Have Newberry's Largest Variety Of Christmas Merchandise For Every Member Of The Family.

Sentry Drug	Edward's	Wig Villa
Hub Theatre	Will Be Open Thanksgiving Day 2 P.M. - 7 P.M.	A & P
Pizza Inn	Consumer Credit	Country Clean Laundry and Dry Cleaners

The Laurens Advertiser

"SOUTH CAROLINA'S FASTEST GROWING SEMI-WEEKLY NEWSPAPER"

15¢ PER COPY — VOL. 88 — LAURENS, SOUTH CAROLINA, MONDAY, NOVEMBER 27, 1972

Blue Hose smash rival Newberry, 17-0

By DON BABB

Presbyterian College smashed archrival Newberry, 17-0, in the traditional Thanksgiving Day battle, fought this year at PC.

But this year, the win meant much more than a victory over an old rival; the win meant that the Blue Hose had finished the season with the best record of any college team in the state. Furthermore, the Blue Hose assured themselves of a co-championship in the Carolina Conference.

The superstar of the day for PC was David Eckstein, who had played the role many times before. Eckstein rushed for 152 yards, and he was responsible for PC's two touchdowns.

For the year, Eckstein amassed 1,022 yards, making him the first PC back ever to go beyond the 1,000 yard mark. His career total of 2,581 yards also set a new record.

The first of Eckstein's damaging TD's came midway in the second quarter when he plunged two yards to give PC a 6-0 lead.

With approximately twenty minutes remaining in the game, Eckstein struck again, this time electrifying the capacity crowd with a 58-yard TD romp.

As usual, Buddy Gaddy made the extra point kicks following each of Eckstein's touchdowns. In addition, Gaddy kicked a field goal from the 23 in the third quarter.

But despite the heroics of Eckstein and the sure toe of Gaddy, defense actually dominated for most of the game. And in the defensive statistics, PC again proved itself to be the superior team.

Newberry was able to total only 107 yards offensively for the day, with 87 of those negotiated by air.

In first half action, PC allowed the Indians only 30 yards on the ground; in the second half, the Indians were held to minus four yards rushing.

Renwick's first TD came about as a result of a fumble. In the second quarter, safety Mike Apps fell on a Newberry fumble on the Indians 30 yard line.

On the second play from scrimmage, John Jeselnik rambled 19 yards. Then, quarterback Wayne Renwick picked up nine more. On the next play, Renwick called on Eckstein, who dove into the end zone from the two.

Gaddy's extra point gave PC a 7-0 lead with 7:30 left in the half. Near the end of the half, PC defensive tackle Stan Gruber pounced on a fumble at Newberry's 28 yard line.

Newberry, however, rose to the occasion and PC was forced to settle for a field goal attempt; the ensuing kick was wide and the period ended with PC still out front by only seven.

However, in the second half, Newberry continued to have trouble hanging on to the football. Early in the third period, defensive end Harvey Jones recovered a Newberry fumble at the Indians 27.

A pass from Renwick to Lynn Dreger, and some hard running by Jeselnik and Eckstein, advanced the Blue Hose all the way down to Newberry's two. There, the Indians got tough.

A "busted play," hard rushing by the Indians, and a penalty resulted in the ball being moved back to the 16. Gaddy's second field goal attempt, however, was good and with the third period still young, PC led, 10-0.

With approximately five minutes left in the third period, Eckstein made his 58 yard TD sprint. Gaddy followed with the conversion; PC lead 17-0; and all the Blue Hose had to do was waste time.

WATCHING ACTION—June Moody, of Greenville, pretty PC cheerleader, intently watches the action as the Blue Hose ground out a convincing 17-0 victory over the Newberry College Indians in Clinton Thanksgiving afternoon.

ENJOYING GAME—Among the chilly but enthusiastic fans at the Presbyterian-Newberry College football game in Clinton Thanksgiving Day were State Senator and Mrs. Robert C. Lake of Whitmire. Senator Lake represents the Laurens, Union and Newberry County District, but will go into a different district January 1.

The Li'l That Was!

The Newberry Observer
AND HERALD & NEWS
"Just Like A Letter From Home"

HALD AND NEWS ESTABLISHED 1865 — Newberry, S. C., Tuesday, November 28, 1973 — NEWBERRY OBSERVER ESTABLISHED IN

Tribe Tumbles, 17-0
Hose Capture Derby, Turkey, Title Share

Diminutive Dave Eckstein and an unbending Presbyterian defense were too much for Newberry College in the annual Bronze Derby classic in Clinton last Thursday.

PC defenders shut down the Indians' offense almost completely while Eckstein who weighs something like 140 pounds – was skipping to a pair of touchdowns, one of them on a 58-yard run.

His Thanksgiving Day performance added up to 152 rushing yards in 17 carries, including non-scoring runs of 51 and 25 yards.

The outcome gave Presbyterian a share (with Elon) of the Carolinas Conference championship. The Blue Hose also recaptured the symbolic Bronze Derby won by Newberry a year ago, and earned the mythical state championship by closing their season with a 7-2-1 record, best of any South Carolina college or university.

In addition, PC took Ol' Killer, Newberry's feathered mascot whose custody had been staked on the game's outcome by Indian coach Fred Herren and his players. Killer reportedly was last seen in the care of Presbyterian's oversized line coach Billy Tiller, who was wearing an apron and a chef's hat and carrying carving utensils.

But PC's head coach Cally Gault said later, "We're not going to kill that turkey. We're going to love that turkey just like they did... Our biggest problem may be to keep him hidden from Newberry students."

Presbyterian did its Thursday afternoon carving on the field, cutting up Newberry's defense for 250 yards on the ground and 88 more aerially.

Newberry found itself backed away from the table offensively. Game statistics credited the Indians with a net of only 26 yards rushing and another 81 passing, for an anemic 107-yard total.

Turnovers helped PC send the Indians down to their fourth defeat of the season, against six wins and a tie. Newberry lost three fumbles and suffered a pair of interceptions. The errors, plus a fired-up Presbyterian defense, kept Newberry from connecting on any of its scoring chances.

The beginning looked bright for the Tribe, which in the first quarter marched to the PC 17 before stalling. Tommy Williamson's fourth down field goal try was wide to the right.

Late in the opening period, linebacker Ken Pettus gave Newberry another chance when he intercepted a Wayne Renwick pass and returned it to the Newberry 29. Hose defenders threw the Indians all the way back to the PC 48, forcing a punt.

Presbyterian took advantage of a Don Garrick fumble at the Newberry 30 for its second-quarter touchdown. Four plays later, Eckstein went over right tackle for two yards and the score. Buddy Gaddy kicked the point for a 7-0 PC lead with 7:20 remaining in the half.

PC got another chance before intermission when the Hose grabbed a fumble at the Newberry 26. But the Indians held and Gaddy's 30-yard field goal attempt was wide.

Still another fumble, on the third play of the second half, helped seal Newberry's doom. PC got the ball at the Indian 27 and moved to the five, but was hurled back to the 10-yard line, whereupon Gaddy kicked a 23-yard field goal for a 10-0 lead.

A little more than four minutes later, Eckstein shot up the middle untouched for his 58-yard touchdown sprint. Gaddy again kicking the extra point.

Eckstein's game performance gave him a season total of 1,022 rushing yards and a career total of 2,381.

Johnny Jeselnick got 49 yards in 17 tries for Presbyterian. Freshman Mike Taylor led Newberry rushers with 56 yards in 21 shots. Most of Newberry's other backs accumulated minus-yardage.

PC quarterback Renwick completed five of his 17 passing attempts and suffered two interceptions. Newberry's Tommy Williamson, who played most of the game, connected on only two of eight tries. Reserve Steve Muirhead completed six of 11.

NOWHERE TO GO: Indian quarterback Tommy Williamson bangs into a pair of Presbyterian College defenders during Thanksgiving Day action. The Blue Hose defense put heavy pressure on Williamson and reserve signal-caller Steve Muirhead.

The Clinton Chronicle

Vol. 72 — No. 48   Clinton, S. C., Nov. 30, 1972

'The Main Man'

Presbyterian College Quarterback Wayne Renwick (10) was cited by Coach Cally Gault as the key to PC's 17-0 win over Newberry last Thursday. Coach Gault said: "The coaches got the information together but it was Wayne who absorbed it all and called a near-perfect game. I doubt that I could have called that game as well as Wayne did. He absorbed a tremendous amount of he was almost like a computer in recalling the right information at the right time." In photo above Renwick stands his ground in the face of a good pass rush by Newberry. Blocking is Johnny Jeselnik (20). In photo below, Renwick (hidden behind Jeselnik) takes to Jeselnik. Other PC players shown are David Norris (76) and Tim McCorkle (41). (Photos by Jim Yarborough).

The Li'l  That Was!

The Indian
Voice of the Newberry College student

The glory is in the struggle

VOL. XLV — NEWBERRY, S.C. 29108, WEDNESDAY, DECEMBER 6, 1972 — NUMBER 12

PAGE FOUR — THE INDIAN — WEDNESDAY, DECEMBER 6, 1972

Indians lose Derby to Blue Hose

The Presbyterian College Blue Hose put it all together on Thanksgiving Day, Nov. 23, to defeat the Newberry Indians 17-0, thereby regaining the Bronze Derby. Newberry had had possession of the Derby since the 34-0 thrashing the Indians gave the Blue Hose last year.

The victory gave Presbyterian College a 7-2-1 record, the best record in the state, and a share of the Carolinas Conference championship along with Elon. Newberry's record for the 1972 football season was 6-4-1.

In the opening quarter of the game played in Clinton, both teams exchanged punts until midway in the period when Newberry drove 37 yards to the Presbyterian 17-yard line before being stopped. Tommy Williamson attempted a 35-yard field goal but the kick was wide.

Minutes later, Ken Pettus intercepted a Wayne Renwick pass and returned the ball to the Presbyterian 29-yard line. Once again the Blue Hose threw Newberry for losses, forcing a Williamson punt which the Indians downed on the one-yard line.

The Blue Hose were unable to move in the early part of the second quarter, but later in the period their first break came when they recovered an Indian fumble at the Newberry 30-yard line. Four plays later, Dave Eckstein scored from the two-yard line. Buddy Gaddy kicked the PAT giving Presbyterian a 7-0 lead with 7:20 remaining in the half.

Newberry could not come back before the half as a tough Blue Hose defense cut off the Indian running attack and forced numerous mistakes on offense.

In the third period, the Indians played even with the Blue Hose until Presbyterian recovered another Newberry fumble at the Indian 27-yard line. The Newberry defense held the Blue Hose for three plays. On fourth down, Gaddy kicked a 33-yard field goal and gave Presbyterian a 10-0 lead.

The Indians were stopped on offense by the fired-up Blue Hose and were forced to punt. A few plays later, Eckstein killed Newberry's chance for a comeback bid on a 50-yard touchdown burst. Gaddy's extra point padded the Blue Hose's victory margin 17-0.

The last Newberry threat came on a long punt return by Dusty Triplett. However, a clipping penalty nullified the run.

During the fourth quarter, Presbyterian continued to crush the Newberry running attack. The Indians, playing without a strong passing attack, could only throw two completed interceptions in the final period.

I CAN'T BELIEVE IT — The Presbyterian gridironer seems somewhat stunned as Newberry's Ken Pettus takes the ball from the Blue Hose and heads for the goal, guarded by Will Craven. Newberry lost 17-0 to the Blue Hose in the Thanksgiving clash, in which 17 Newberry seniors saw their last action for the Indians. (Photo by Reames)

The Li'l That Was!

In addition, PC took Ol' Killer, Newberry's feathered mascot whose custody had been staked on the game's outcome by Indian coach Fred Herren and his players. Killer reportedly was last seen in the care of Presbyterian's oversized line coach Billy Tiller, who was wearing an apron and a chef's hat and carrying carving utensils.

But PC's head coach Cally Gault said later, "We're not going to kill that turkey. We're going to love that turkey just like they did ... Our biggest problem may be to keep him hidden from Newberry students."

The Blue Stocking

40

In the December 19, 1999 edition of *The State* newspaper located in Columbia, South Carolina, the paper recognized Presbyterian College Assistant Coach Billy Tiller in their featured article of the Top 100 20th Century Moments in South Carolina Sports History. Entitled "Killer, We Hardly Got To Know Ya." Newberry Head Football Coach Fred Herren brought a live turkey to the game and the winner took possession of it after the game. A sign on the Newberry campus stated "Don't let Tiller Eat Ole Killer." The white turkey was sporting a red Newberry vest. Coach Tiller, a large man at 300 pounds, was seen prior to the game with an apron, cooking utensils and a chef's hat taunting the turkey. Presbyterian won the game 17-0. Presbyterian Head Football Coach Cally Gault assured everyone that the turkey would not be harmed. The #40 moment of the 20th Century in South Carolina Sports history may have been the most memorable Thanksgiving Day Bronze Derby football game for the antics outside the lines.

November 1973

November 2	The Latin American Energy Organization (OLADE) formed.
November 4	Stan Mikita of the Chicago Blackhawks scored his 1000th career goal.
November 5	Arab oil producers announce a 25 percent reduction in oil production.
November 7	New Jersey was the first Little League to allow girls to participate in youth baseball.
November 9	Apple Records released "Ringo," Ringo Starr's third album and his biggest commercial success.
November 9	Columbia Records released Billy Joels' second album "Piano Man."
November 10	American Baseball Hall of Fame broadcaster Vin Scully married Sandra Hunt.
November 11	Columbia Records released Bruce Springsteen's second album, "The Wild, the Innocent & the E Street Shuffle."
November 12	MLB Hall of Famer Hank Aaron married Billye Aaron.
November 13	Oakland A's Reggie Jackson won the MLB AL Most Valuable Player Award.
November 14	Jim Palmer of the Baltimore Orioles won the MLB AL Cy Young Award.
November 16	NASA launched Skylab 4 into space.
November 16	United States President Richard Nixon approved of construction of the Alaskan pipeline.
November 17	United States President Richard Nixon told the press, "...people have got to know whether or not their President is a crook. Well, I'm not a crook."
November 19	The New York Stock Market suffered the largest loss in 19 years.
November 21	Pete Rose of the Cincinnati Reds won the MLB NL Most Valuable Player Award.
November 21	An 18 ½ minute gap in a White House tape recording related to Watergate was revealed by Nixon attorney Fred Buzhardt.
November 22	The Bronze Derby was played in Newberry, South Carolina on Thanksgiving Day. The Newberry College Indians defeated the Presbyterian College Blue Hose 14-3.

The Li'l That Was!

The Newberry Observer
AND HERALD & NEWS
"Just Like A Letter From Home"

HERALD AND NEWS ESTABLISHED 1865 — Newberry, S. C., Tuesday, November 20, 1973 — NEWBERRY OBSERVER ESTABLISHED 18__

ARMISTEAD

CROCKER

RUSTY DAVIS

HARTLE

PENNEKAMP

SANDERS

TRIPLETT

WILLIAMSON

DERBY GAME
Last Stand For Senior Indians

YATES

For Newberry College fans, the traditional Thanksgiving Day clash between Newberry and Presbyterian is the climax of the long collegiate football season. This year for nine seniors, it is the end of their collegiate playing career.

Coach Fred Herren's Indians will face PC for the 60th time when the opening whistle sounds at 2 p.m. Thanksgiving Day, Nov. 22, at Newberry's Setzler Field.

The winner of this year's battle will get to keep the Bronze Derby, the symbol of the historic game. The hat currently is being displayed on the Presbyterian campus, since the Blue Hose won the 1972 contest 17-0. (The Derby was in Newberry after the 1971 game, when the Indians trounced the Clinton squad 34-0.)

Heading the list of the three offensive players who will suit up for the Indians for the last time on Nov. 22 is Tommy Williamson, from Thomson, Ga. The Georgia quarterback has broken the college's passing record this year by throwing the pigskin for 1,500 yards in 10 games to date to make his career record a total of 3,850 yards in four years with the Indians. He has also tallied 191 points on the scoreboard, including 13 touchdowns, 77 extra points and 12 field goals.

Dusty Triplett, who hails from Winter Haven, Fla., leads the Indians this year in pass receiving in 10 games with 25 catches good for 512 yards. He has also scored three touchdowns this season.

The third offensive senior for the Indians this year is Rusty Davis from Springfield, S. C. He is third in the pass receiving department with 29 catches worth 446 yards and three touchdowns. He also led the Indians in pass receiving in 1972 with 211 yards in 14 catches.

Six defensive players also will be missing from the line in 1974. Co-captain Greg Hartle of Newberry tops the list of defensive leaders who are playing their last game. A candidate for the professionals, he has played in the linebacker slot this year and as a defensive end in his other three seasons with the Indians.

David Sanders from Spartanburg has broken all individual interception records with a total of 24 during his four years as an Indian. Marylander Durwood Yates also will be absent next fall. He has been a three-year starter for Coach Herren and has been one of the mainstays in Newberry's defense.

Also playing their last game in the defensive line-up for Newberry are Roger Armistead, end from Clarkston, Ga.; Tom Crocker, end, Myrtle Beach; and Greg Pennekamp, end, Charleston.

The Li'l 🎩 That Was!

The Newberry Observer
AND HERALD & NEWS
"Just Like A Letter From Home"

Newberry, S.C., Friday, November 23, 1973

Full House Expected At Battle For Derby

Newberry College and Presbyterian College renew their annual football rivalry on the afternoon of Thanksgiving Day, with the treasured Bronze Derby and a lot of community pride on the line for both schools.

Kickoff will be at 2 p.m. at Setzler Field, probably before an overflow crowd.

No championship is at stake. At this stage, neither club has a winning season. But deficient won-lost records never dull interest in the yearly Thanksgiving tussle. Given decent weather, Setzler Field's 4,000 seats won't be nearly enough.

Tickets were available at the Indian Club office up to 5 p.m. Wednesday. They will go on sale at 11 a.m. Thursday at the Setzler Field ticket office.

Picking a winner is impossible. Both teams enter the final game of the season with imperfect records. Newberry is 4-5-1 and, by winning, could establish a break-even season. Presbyterian is only 3-7, and beating the Indians would salvage an otherwise lack-luster year.

So for Newberry coach Fred Herren and Presbyterian's Callie Gault, Thursday's game is a must. The two are rated as great friends except on Thanksgiving Day when they are the most bitter of competitors, and for Thursday's loser the bitterness will linger a full year.

As for the Bronze Derby, Presbyterian has it now. The Blue Hose won last year at Clinton. In 1971, Newberry won the game and the Derby at Setzler Field.

Competitiveness between Newberry and Presbyterian goes back so far that the records are unclear. Thursday's football meeting will be the 63rd for the two schools, says a Newberry College source — but Newberry records cite 37 wins for PC, 19 for Newberry and five ties. That amounts to 61 games so far.

Presbyterian's records indicate they've won 36 times, lost 18 times and tied five times. That would make Thursday's game the 60th in the long series.

Records of recent years are clearer. In the last 18 years (those in which the Bonze Derby has been exclusively a football trophy), Newberry has won only five times — in 1956, 1957, 1962, 1965 and 1971.

Whatever the over-all record, the history of the Bronze Derby is much shorter than the football series between Newberry and Presbyterian. The Derby goes back only to January, 1947, following a basketball game at Newberry.

Before the game started, several Presbyterian students put a derogatory banner on an inside wall of MacLean Gym. During the game, some Newberry scholars went up a ladder from the outside, entered a window and swiped the banner, a fact not noticed immediately by the PC partisans.

(Continued On Page 10)

Presbyterian won the basketball game, and there was a little donneybrook afterward. Blue Hose fans wanted their banner back but lost a derby hat* — snatched from the head of a PC student by a Newberry lad who grabbed the hat and ran.

In the next few days, negotiations over the derby hat took on an official note. Officers of the two schools finally agreed that the derby hat should serve as the symbol of victory in athletic contests, so the hat was returned to Presbytertain College and sent off to be bronzed. It remains in that condition today — no stiffer than when it was purchased, but a lot shinier.

For 10 years, possession of the Bronze Derby was determined by victories in football, basketball and baseball. The hat got a lot of road time between the two schools, but in 1956 the schools decided to limit its travels to once a year at the most, depending on the outcome of the Thanksgiving Day football game.

Despite its losing record this fall, Presbyterian has some potency and is booming a couple of performers as All-American material.

Stan Gruber, who plays linebacker, defensive tackle and captains the Blue Hose, gets top billing. "He should have been All-American last year and he's even better this year," Gault says of the 6'1", 213-pound lineman.

Also highly rated is defensive back Ken Lister, who specializes in returning kicks and who leads the Hose in pass interceptions over a three-year period.

Newberry has some standouts of its own — none more prominent than Greg Hartle, a Newberry native. Hartle plays both defensive end and, this year, linebacker. He's a one-man gang and worthy, say Newberry supporters, of first-string All-American honors. He made the honorable mention list last year.

NEWBERRIAN

NEWBERRY   14
PRESBYTERIAN   3

Newberry's Indians jammed across touchdowns in the second and fourth quarters to overcome their old rival Presbyterian College 14-3, in a fierce defensive struggle here on Thanksgiving Day.

Sophomore halfback Mike Taylor accounted for both TD's, driving one yard out for the first on the final play of the first half, and bolting 11 yards for the second tally with 4:31 remaining in the 63rd installment of the Bronze Derby series.

Head football coach Fred Herren had nothing but praise for the team; particularly the defensive team, led by Willie Craven, Greg Hartle, Barry Jones, David Sanders, Neal Smith and Durwood Yates.

The Newberry Observer
AND HERALD & NEWS
"Just Like A Letter From Home"

Newberry, S.C., Tuesday, November 27, 1973

WIN BRONZE DERBY
Indians Triumph, 14-3, In Game Of Turnovers

An Observer Sports Report

There was a lost fumble on the opening kickoff return, and that set the tone for Thanksgiving Day's battle for the Bronze Derby — won by Newberry College 14-3 at Setzler Field before 3,500 people.

Newberry's Rufus Johnson fumbled the ball away after a long return to start the game. Moments thereafter, the Indians' David Sanders intercepted a Presbyterian College pass. Fumbles and interceptions were that common throughout the rest of the afternoon.

There were, in all, eight pass interceptions and five lost fumbles. Newberry lost three of the fumbles but intercepted five of the passes — two by safety David Sanders who finished his college career with a total of 27 thefts. PC's John Hackett also intercepted a pair.

The result of all the raggedness was a thrill for Newberry's Coach Fred Herren. But for PC's Cally Gault it was "absolutely the worst experience I've had in 26 years of coaching."

The whole thing was an unnerving experience for both Newberry and Presbyterian fans watching the two clubs hand the ball back and forth. "Nobody can win a game like this," one observer commented midway in the second half.

But Newberry did win, balancing its season record at five wins, five losses and one tie. Presbyterian took its eighth loss against three wins, and that confirmed a rare losing season for the Blue Hose.

Newberry's Mike Taylor scored both of the game's touchdowns. PC's Ken Lister returned a punt for 41 yards and an apparent score, but it was wiped out by a clipping penalty. Lister also had another substantial return rubbed out by clipping.

It was, however, more than a game of mistakes. It was a solid defensive battle, with both clubs hitting hard as is their custom when they meet. And when the ball wasn't being exchanged inadvertently, it was being punted away — six times by Presbyterian, seven times by Newberry. So it was a lot like watching ping pong.

The Blue Hose missed a scoring opportunity early in the game when George Camp's attempt at a 35-yard field goal turned into just a low line drive into the end zone. But PC got the ball back when Newberry's Tommy Williamson authored a wild pitchout — one of three similar errors he made in the game.

That time, Buddy Gaddy kicked a 22-yard field goal with 12 seconds left in the first period to give the Hose a 3-0 lead. That, it turned out, was all the PC scoring for the day despite constant threats.

Mike Taylor scored the first Newberry touchdown with no time remaining in the half. It took a lot of slugging from inside the PC one-yard line in the last 43 seconds of play, and it wasn't clear why time remained for the touchdown.

Williamson had hit Bob Doppelheuer with a 13-yard pass to put the ball at the one. Ron Harwell was short, Williamson was short, Harwell was short again, then officials stopped the clock with two seconds left, apparently because the Hose was a bit slow in unpiling.

Newberry's timeouts were exhausted, but the clock stood still until the ball was snapped and Taylor hurled himself over left guard for the touchdown. Williamson's extra-point kick gave the Tribe a 7-3 lead.

As the second half wore on, it seemed likely that the team which scored would win. Both clubs threatened but only Newberry succeeded, taking advantage of Jim Futch's fourth-period recovery of Oral Chester's fumble at the PC 42. Mike Taylor got 35 of the 42 yards and the score.

On first down, Taylor ripped off 18 yards — the game's longest run from scrimmage. Harwell got three more to the 22, then was stopped for no gain. Williamson hit Rusty Davis with a five-yard pass to the 17, making it fourth down and two to go. Davis was hurt on the play.

Taylor was good for six yards and a first down at the 11, then picked up about a foot and a half. But on second down he took a pitchout and shot straight past right end for the touchdown. Williamson again kicked goal to establish the 14-3 score with 4:31 left in the game.

That left time for the Hose to reach the Newberry 15, where they had a first down with 3:10 to go. Wally Bowen's passes to Ken Milton, plus a pass interference call against Newberry, put the ball there. But Bowen incurred a grounding penalty, threw a pair of incomplete passes, and on fourth down, tossed one picked off by the Indians' Barry Jones.

There were only 61 seconds left at that point, yet the Indians couldn't quite use up the clock. Williamson dropped flat with the ball on fourth down, but one second still remained for a PC play from the Newberry 37. It was good for eight yards as the game ended.

It was an even kind of roughshod game in which neither team generated much offense, although it's worth mentioning that Newberry did occasionally get some effective passing off the shotgun formation the Indians used now and then to vary the triple option. They also lost a critical interception off the shotgun.

Total offense for Newberry measured 157 yards; for PC, 169.

The Indians were tabbed at minus-three yards rushing in the first half and finished up with 74 for the day, net. Mike Taylor himself registered 70 yards, but minus-readings for Williamson and others cut the team total.

Williamson completed seven of 16 passes for 83 yards.

Presbyterian had worse luck than Newberry on the ground. The Hose earned only 53 yards rushing, 116 more on seven completions in 21 passing attempts by Bowen.

The Indians registered 13 first downs, PC, 10.

The Li'l Hat That Was!

The Newberry Observer
AND HERALD & NEWS
"Just Like A Letter From Home"

HERALD AND NEWS ESTABLISHED 1865 — Newberry, S.C., Tuesday, November 27, 1973 — NEWBERRY OBSERVER ESTABLISHED 1

ON THE MOVE: Ken Lister, Presbyterian's tricky kick returner, struggles to break an unidentified Newberrians' tackle. Sailing in at the right is Indians' Rufus Johnson (34).

TWO HATS! Wearing one hat and waving another is Newberry College Coach Fred Herron, photographed atop shoulders of his players after Indians defeated Presbyterian College 14-3 at Setzler Field on Thanksgiving Day. Atop Herron's head is the Bronze Derby, traditional trophy which the victory brought to Newberry for the second time in three years.

HALT! Presbyterian's Oral Chester, on his way to nowhere. Newberry College's Roger Armistead (89) awaits him, but he's already in the firm grip of another unidentified Indian. In background is Greg Pennekamp (65).

The Indian
"Voice for the Newberry College student"

NEWBERRY, S. C. 29108, WEDNESDAY, NOVEMBER 28, 1973

TWINKLE TWINKLE, LITTLE HAT — No, the Mad Hatter is not loose, but Newberry's spirits (and head football coach Fred Herren, partially seen clutching the Bronze Derby) were flying high following the victorious recovery of that brightly burnished derby. (Photo by Reames)

Bronze Derby returns!

Newberry's Indians jammed across touchdowns in the second and fourth quarters to overcome their old rival Presbyterian College 14-3, in a fierce defensive struggle here on Thanksgiving Day.

Sophomore halfback Mike Taylor accounted for both TD's, driving one yard out for the first score on the final play of the first half, and trotting 11 yards for the second tally with 4:33 remaining in the third installment of the Bronze Derby series.

The Blue Hose got on the scoreboard on a 23-yard field goal with 12 seconds left in the first quarter.

P. C. was denied a second quarter touchdown when a 42-yard punt return by speedster Ken Lister to pay dirt was nullified by a clipping penalty.

A pass interception and 18-yard return by Safety David Sanders gave the Indians possession at their own 43 and set the stage for the first scoring threat.

Passes by Williamson keyed an advance to the P. C. 21, but Gruber went into action and halted the drive.

With Newberry on the defense again, Barry Jones captured a P. C. pass to return it to the 38-yard line, setting up Newberry's final score of the day. Neal Smith also snagged a Blue Hose pass later in the game.

The victory enabled the Indians to finish the year with a 5-4-1 record. P. C. closed the season with a 3-6 record.

Turnovers were frequent during the hard hitting contest. The alert Indian secondaries picked off five Presbyterian passes, as well as two Blue Hose fumbles. P. C. picked off three Newberry passes and took advantage of three Redskin fumbles.

The Indians were held to minus three yards rushing in the first half by the swarming P. C. defense, led by Stan Gruber, but finished the game with 74 yards rushing. Taylor gained 70 of these yards. Quarterback Tommy Williamson was true on seven of 16 passes for 83 yards.

Head football coach Fred Herren had nothing but praise for the team; particularly the defensive team, led by Willie Crayton, Greg Hartle, Barry Jones, David Sanders, Neal Smith and Dorwood Yates.

MAY I HAVE THIS DANCE? — Tommy Eaves seems to waltz the Presbyterian receiver off his feet. Newberry pranced to a 14-3 win over arch-rival PC in the annual Thanksgiving Day battle for the Bronze Derby. (Photo by Reames)

SUMMER'S RESTAURANT By-Pass 76 Phone 276-9111 *Fast Service - Low Rates*	BUDDY'S Open Air Market Mon.-Thur. 8 a.m.-10:30 p.m. Fri.-Sat. 8 a.m.-11 p.m. Sun. 10 a.m.-11 p.m.
City Filling Station 1304 Friend St. Phone 276-4395	*College Checks Cashed*

The Li'l 🎩 That Was!

The Indian
Voice for the Newberry College student
NEWBERRY, S.C. 29108 WEDNESDAY, JANUARY 23, 1974   NUMBER FIFTEEN

Second class postage paid Newberry, S. C. 29108

THINK WE CAN DO IT AGAIN?— Willie Craven shows the Bronze Derby, symbol of Newberry's supremacy in football over Presbyterian College, to Mike Harper and Stuart Leslie. The three men will be the captains of the 1974-75 Indian football squad. (Photo by Reames)

November 1974

November 2	The Atlanta Braves traded Hank Aaron to the Milwaukee Brewers for outfielder Dave May.
November 5	Former NASA astronaut John Glenn, the first American to orbit the earth, was elected to the United States Senate representing Ohio. He served in the United States Senate for 24 years.
November 6	Mike Marshall of the Los Angeles Dodgers was the first relief pitcher to win the Cy Young Award.
November 8	Elton John released the "Greatest Hits" album.
November 8	Ted Bundy victim Debi Kent disappeared in Salt Lake City, UT.
November 11	American actor Leonardo DiCaprio was born.
November 12	South Africa was suspended from the United Nations General Assembly as a result of racial policies.
November 13	Los Angeles Dodgers Steve Garvey won the MLB NL Most Valuable Player Award.
November 15	Secretariat, the racehorse who won the triple crown in 1973, became a sire. Her first foal was named First Secretary.
November 15	Universal Studios released "Earthquake" starring Charlton Heston and Ava Gardner.
November 16	Singing group ABBA began their first tour of Europe.
November 17	Bonnie Bryant became the first left handed women's golfer to win on the LPGA tour.
November 20	The United States filed an antitrust suit to break up AT&T.
November 21	After a veto by United States President Gerald Ford, the Freedom of Information Act was passed by the United States Congress.
November 24	Richard Petty won the 24th NASCAR Sprint Cup.
November 24	United States President Gerald Ford and USSR President Brezhnev agree to a framework for the SALT-II treaty to reduce each side's nuclear weapons.
November 28	MLB Commissioner Bowie Kuhn suspended New York Yankees owner George Steinbrenner for 2 years.
November 28	The Bronze Derby was played in Clinton, South Carolina on Thanksgiving Day. The Presbyterian College Blue Hose defeated the Newberry College Indians 37-7.

Turkey Day Battle's The One That Counts

They say you may as well throw out the statistics, past game scores and season's results when the Newberry College Indians invade Bailey Memorial Stadium to battle arch-rival Presbyterian College in the annual Bronze Derby classic on Thanksgiving Day, Nov. 28. Game time is set for 2 p.m.

Newberry has a 3-6 record for the season while the Presbyterian Blue Hose have a 5-5 mark and will have a winning season if they can conquer the Indians.

Coach Fred Herren will have two of his starters, quarterback Stuart Leslie and tackle Willie Craven, to replace for the game. Leslie underwent surgery last week for a malignant tumor which was discovered after he was injured in the Newberry-Elon game on Nov. 9. Craven had an operation on his knee and elbow after suffering injuries in the Mars Hill contest on Nov. 16.

On the brighter side, Ron Harwell and Rufus Johnson, who watched most of the Mars Hill game from the sidelines because of severe bruises, are expected to be at full strength. Neal Smith, who suffered a mild concussion, and Mike McGroarty, who sprained an ankle against Mars Hill, are also expected to be back in the starting lineup.

PC features a much improved team this season. Their biggest win of the season has been over powerful Elon by a score of 23-21. The Blue Hose lost to Carson-Newman this past Saturday, 21-14.

Presbyterian's offensive attack is centered around sophomore quarterback Jody Salmon, a Summerville native. Salmon's favorite receiver is Ken Milton, a junior from Greenwood.

Coach Cally Gault's other success factor is his strong defensive unit. The experienced defense is led by six seniors on the front line.

The Newberry-Presbyterian series dates back to 1913. The Blue Hose hold a decided margin, with 37 victories for them, 20 wins for Newberry, and five ties.

The ownership of the Bronze Derby for another year also rests on the outcome of the game. The Indians are the current owners of the Derby (they have only captured the Derby six times since it became the symbol of victory of the Thanksgiving Day Classic).

The Indian
Voice for the Newberry College student

VOL. XLVI NEWBERRY, S.C. 29108 WEDNESDAY, NOVEMBER 20, 1974 NUMBER TWELVE

PC GAME

The traditional Thanksgiving Day rivalry with Presbyterian will be renewed when the Blue Hose entertain the Indians Thanksgiving Day at Presbyterian College in Clinton in a 2 p.m. encounter.

PC features a much improved team this season and currently has record of five wins and five losses. Their biggest win of the season has been over powerful Elon by a score of 23-21. The Blue Hose lost to Carson-Newman this past Saturday 21-14.

Presbyterian's offensive attack is centered around sophomore quarterback Jody Salmon, a Summerville native. Salmon's favorite receiver is Ken Milton, a junior from Greenwood.

Coach Cally Gault's other success factor is his strong defensive unit. The experienced defense is led by six seniors on the defensive front. The Indians will have their hands full against a fine Blue Hose team.

The situation seems even cloudier when the Indians' physical shape is reviewed.

Stuart Leslie's condition requires additional surgery, and he will not be in the lineup against P.C. Willie Craven, who recently underwent knee and elbow surgery for injuries sustained against Mars Hill, will also read about the game.

On the brighter side, Ron Harwell and Rufus Johnson, who watched most of the Mars Hill game from the sidelines because of severe bruises, are expected to be full strength. Neal Smith, who suffered a mild concussion, and Mike McGroarty, who sprained an ankle against Mars Hill, are also expected to be back in the starting lineup.

Hopefully, the Skins can put it all together and keep the Bronze Derby here at the Berry, but a victory over the Blue Hose will be an awfully tough assignment.

It's always in, a style that has class with the ease of comfort a must by h.i.s.

The Jeans Shop
Newberry Shopping Center

The Li'l  That Was!

The Laurens County Advertiser

"SOUTH CAROLINA'S FASTEST GROWING SEMI-WEEKLY NEWSPAPER"

15¢ PER COPY

VOL. NO. 90 — Laurens, South Carolina, Monday, December 2, 1974 — No. 45—10 Pages

In Bronzed Derby classic...

Blue Hose trounce Newberry, 37-7

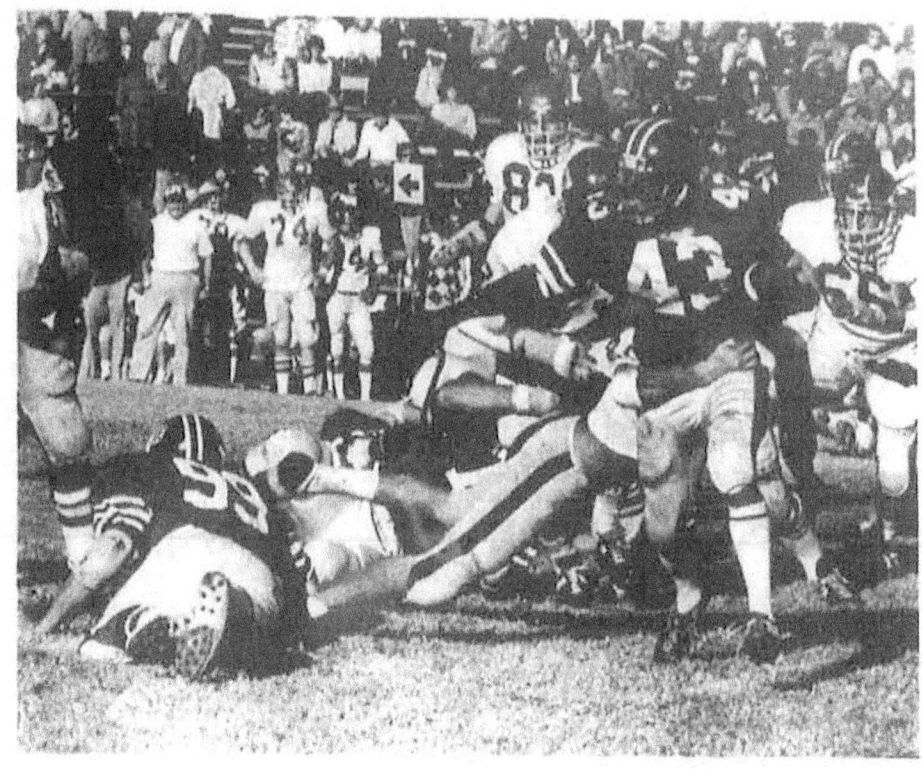

Following block... ELLIOTT PAULING—follows block laid down by Steve Farish (99) in game with Indians from Newberry.

By BRYAN SHELLEY

The Presbyterian College Blue Hose won their 39th contest over Newberry last Thanksgiving Day, retrieving the Bronzed Derby which has come to mark the annual classic. The game avenges the 3-14 loss to the Indians last year and leaves PC with a 6-5 winning season.

THREE TOUCHDOWNS in the period left the Hose in the best possible position. After Newberry failed to take the ball anywhere in their first two series, Mark Simms punted, and with 12:10 left, PC took over at their own 28. PC likewise failed on the first drive, though, the Salmon punted to the Newberry 33. But the ball was fumbled, and PC's Bruce Hill recovered. Tim McCorkle boomed for ten yards, and Steve Farish then took a pass down to the one yard line. With 8:45 left, Salmon plunged in for the six points. George Camp's boot was not good; PC led 6-0.

The Indians were again

324

halted and forced to punt. From his own 30, Mark Simms punted for 17 yards. PC had the ball inside enemy territory. Kevin Williams and Tim McCorkle each carried for 5 yards, after which Salmon hit Steve Farish at the Indian 41.

Ken Milton took a Salmon aerial for 11 yards, and the agile Blue Hose playcaller pulled a keeper good for 17 yards. Williams carried to the one yard line. After McCorkle was stopped short of the TD, Salmon kept again, popping in for a touchdown 3:25 left in the quarter. To make an even 14, he then passed to Ken Milton for the PAT.

THE VISITING INDIANS, who have never won in Bailey Memorial stadium, were again forced to punt on the next series. This time John Hackett took the ball at the 38 yard line and raced 52 yards near the Newberry ten.

Williams ran for 4 yards and McCorkle for 3 before Salmon hit Ken Milton with a pass for a touchdown. Camp's kick made it 21-0 with 13 seconds left in the first quarter.

In the second period, the Hose appeared to have another scoring drive going. After completing a pass to Elliott Pauling at the Indian 26, Salmon threw three incomplete aerials.

But with 10:25 in the quarter, George Camp kicked a field goal from 42 yards out. That was all the scoring in the second quarter. It was 24-0 at the half.

FOLLOWING a scoreless third quarter, action became ragged early in the fourth period. Salmon punted from the Blue Hose 42 deep into Newberry territory. But Kenny Brown fumbled the ball, and Trent Stockman recovered at the 16 for Presbyterian. Elmore Griffin, Salmon, and a five yard penalty brought the ball to the six yard line. With 13:30 left in the game, Salmon tossed a six-point strike to Kevin Williams, slicing across the center of the end zone. Camp's boot made it 31-0.

Halted again on the ensuing drive, Newberry punted, and PC took over near midfield. Larry Knight carried for 21 yards to the 28. Steady gains brought the ball to the 8, and with 7:35 left in the game, Salmon hit T.D. Todd with another touchdown aerial. The final Blue Hose tally was settled at 37 points.

THE INDIANS would not be held scoreless, though. Almost as suddenly as PC took command in the first period, reserve quarterback Danny Williams threw to Rufus Johnson for a 61-yard pass play that ended in the end zone. The PAT set the final score at 37-7.

Presbyterian, in one of its most outstanding offensive displays of the season, totalled 243 yards on 51 rushes and 142 yards via air. Salmon was 9 for 14 for 99 yards. Donnie Fleming was 4 for 4 for 20 yards, and freshman Mike Gill threw 2 completions in 5 tries for 23 yards.

Salmon actually had 13 net yards on 12 carries, yielding 2 touchdowns for the day. Kevin Williams had 58 yards on 12 rushes. McCorkle carried 9 times for 37 yards. Ken Milton took in his average of 4 passes (his usual for a game) for 33 yards; Farish had 49 yards on 4 receptions. Kevin Williams took one pass for 11 yards and T.D. Todd another for 8.

IT WAS A TEAM VICTORY; even the reserves looked good.

"It's good to win the last game of the year," said Coach Cally Gault of the Hose. "We played eleven games, nine of them as well as we could. I'm not so sure about the Wofford and Carson-Newman games."

Gault was asked if he felt that PC would win by a thirty point margin. "No one anticipates a big score on any game. We knew we had to start quick and get the enthusiasm out of them (Newberry). Defensively, it was one of our finer games."

Presbyterian 21–3–0–13–37
Newberry   0–0–0–7–7

UP FOR GRABS—Ken Milton of the Blue Hose tries for pass as Newberry's Barry Jones defends.

The Li'l 🎩 That Was!

The Newberry Observer
AND HERALD & NEWS
"Just Like A Letter From Home"

Newberry, S. C., Tuesday, Dec. 3, 1974

Derby Back To P.C.

The Bronze Derby went back to Clinton on Thanksgiving Day as Presbyterian's Blue Hose defeated outmanned Newberry College 37-7.

Fred Herren's Indians, crippled and below par, thus ended the season with a losing 3-7 record. The Blue Hose finished 6-5 for Cally Gault.

Newberry played it tough but couldn't cope with PC's strength and its own errors. Thus the bronzed headpiece which Newberry won as a trophy on Thanksgiving Day of 1973 was lost.

There was never any doubt about the outcome. PC led 24-0 at the half and had 37 points before Newberry scored its lone touchdown against Hose reserves late in the game.

The Indians were well below full strength, playing without quarterback Stuart Leslie and defensive tackle Willie Craven, both surgery patients. In Leslie's absence, freshman Danny Williams did the quarterbacking.

Presbyterian amassed a 21-0 lead in the first quarter, getting its first score shortly after freshman Kenny Brown fumbled a punt at the Newberry 33. Salmon sneaked across from the one, and George Camp's extra-point kick was no good.

Then a short Newberry punt gave PC the ball again at the Indian 47 and the Hose worked the ball across in nine plays, Salmon again getting the score from a yard away. His conversion pass was deflected, but Ken Milton caught it anyway for a 14-0 advantage.

John Hackett set up the third score of the period by returning a Newberry punt 51 yards to the Tribe 11.

Both teams struggled through a scoreless third period, but the Blue Hose padded their advantage in the final quarter. One score came on Salmon's six-yard pass to Kevin Williams, after Brown had fumbled another PC punt at the Newberry 16. The second, by reserves, was on Donnie Fleming's seven-yard throw to T. D. Todd. Camp made the first conversion and missed the second.

Late in the game, Newberry finally got on the board when Williams threw to Rufus Johnson for a scoring play which covered 62 yards. Tim Bunch kicked the extra point.

Newberry gained 305 yards — 153 rushing and 152 on Williams' six completions in 17 attempts.

Blackbeard's Holiday Haul

ALL YOU CAN EAT

Sunday / Monday / Tuesday / Wednesday — All You Can Eat **SHRIMP** **$3.09**
Deep fried Calabash style with French Fries, cole slaw, hush puppies OR Boiled Shrimp with cocktail sauce and crackers.

Thursday — All You Can Eat **OYSTERS** **$3.59**
With French Fries, cole slaw and hush puppies

Every Day — All You Can Eat **GALLEY FRIED CATFISH** **$2.99**
Orders to Go Regular Portions

TRY OUR COUNTRY STYLE LUNCH SERVED MONDAY THRU FRIDAY

Blackbeard's Galley
NEWBERRY SHOPPING CENTER

The Clinton Chronicle

Vol. 74—No. 48   Nov. 28, 1974, Clinton, S.C.

The Li'l That Was!

SALMON THE SLINGER—Presbyterian College's Jody Salmon prepares to fire a pass against Newberry last Thursday. Salmon passed for two touchdowns and scored two himself in pacing PC to a 37-7 victory over their arch rivals. Salmon, a sophomore from Summerville, connected on nine out of 14 pass attempts. (Photo by Bob Godlewski)

HACKETT HUSTLES—Holding the football precariously in one hand, Presbyterian College's John Hackett races down field on a 29 yard punt return which set up a Blue Hose touchdown Thursday against Newberry. (Photo by Bob Godlewski)

The Li'l 🎩 That Was!

In the 28th annual Thanksgiving Day Bronze Derby football Classic in 1974, Presbyterian College defeated Newberry College 37-7 in Clinton, South Carolina to win their 17th Bronze Derby football game.

November 1975

November 3	Chris Evert became the first tennis player to achieve the #1 ranking on the WTA rankings debut.
November 3	"Good Morning America" premiered on ABC TV.
November 4	Baltimore Orioles Jim Palmer won the MLB Cy Young Award.
November 6	The punk band The Sex Pistols performed for the first time in London, England.
November 8	NBA star Larry Bird married high school sweetheart Janet Condra.
November 10	PLO leader Yasser Arafat addressed the United Nations in New York City.
November 10	The United Nations General Assembly approved a resolution equating Zionism with racism.
November 12	Richard Petty won the 25th NASCAR Sprint Cup.
November 12	New York Mets pitcher Tom Seaver won the MLB Cy Young Award.
November 15	Ed Bruce released the hit single "Momma Don't Let Your Babies Grow Up to Be Cowboys."
November 19	"One Flew Over the Cuckoo's Nest" starring Jack Nicholson and Louise Fletcher was released.
November 19	Cincinnati Reds second baseman Joe Morgan was named MLB NL Most Valuable Player.
November 20	Spanish General and dictator Francisco Franco passed away.
November 20	Ronald Reagan announced his candidacy for the Republican nomination for President of the United States.
November 22	Juan Carlos I was proclaimed King of Spain as the monarchy was restored after 31 years.
November 26	Center fielder Fred Lynn of the Boston Red Sox was the first rookie to be named MLB AL Most Valuable Player.
November 26	A United States Federal jury found Lynette Fromme guilty of attempted assassination on United States President Gerald Ford.
November 27	The Bronze Derby was played in Newberry, South Carolina on Thanksgiving Day. The Presbyterian College Blue Hose defeated the Newberry College Indians 14-0.

The Li'l  That Was!

The Newberry Observer
AND HERALD & NEWS
"Just Like A Letter From Home"

HERALD AND NEWS ESTABLISHED 1865 — Newberry, S. C., Friday, Nov. 28, 1975 — NEWBERRY OBSERVER ESTABLISHED

Coach Of The Year

Fred Herren's Indians didn't win the South Atlantic Conference championship, but their battle for it won conference coach-of-the-year honors for the Newberry College coach this week.

His selection by his fellow coaches was announced at Elon College, N. C., information headquarters for the SAC-8 circuit.

Also announced were player selections on the SAC-8 all-conference team. Three Indians made the first team, seven the second.

First starting selections are center Det Haislip and guard Mike McGroarty on the offensive squad and freshman D. D. Boyd as a defensive back.

Defensive players named on the second team are back Neal Smith, guard Wendell Snelgrove, tackle Charlie Upchurch and linebackers Dennis Yarborough and Charlie Izzard.

Offensive players on the second team are receiver Mark Simms and running back Rufus Johnson.

FRED HERREN

Herren And Gault Cautious Optimists

WITH THE stage set for Thursday afternoon's Bronze Derby game between Newberry College and Presbyterian, both coaches were what football writers sometimes describe as "cautiously optimistic."

PC's Cally Gault called the contest "even-Steven," although his young Blue Hose have only two wins and a tie out of nine games this season.

Fred Herren of Newberry said records don't mean a hill of beans in the traditional Thanksgiving Day rivalry. His Indians are 5-4 for the season, and he's the new SAC-8 Conference's coach of the year.

Last year, the Blue Hose defeated the Tribe 37-7.

"The home team has won the last four games," Herren said, "so I just hope we can continue the tradition one more year and then break it."

Newberry has had some regrouping to do during the last 10 days. In their last game Nov. 15 at Mars Hill, the Indians lost in a muddy-field rout, 65-7.

Thursday's kickoff at Setzler Field is at 2 p.m.

Pizza Pub
Hwy. 391 at Black's Bridge Marina
Phone 364-3035

TUESDAY IS 2 FOR 1
Pizza Night

Closed Monday
Tues.-Wed.-Thurs. — 4 p.m.-10 p.m.
Friday — 4 p.m.-12 p.m.
Saturday — 12 Noon-12
Sunday — 1 p.m.-6 p.m.

Pizza, Spaghetti and Sandwiches

Blue Hose surprise Newberry with 14-0 win in Derby battle

Quarterback Jody Salmon threw one touchdown pass and ran for another score, leading the Presbyterian College Blue Hose to a 14-0 upset victory over the Newberry College Indians at Newberry Thursday afternoon in the two teams' traditional Thanksgiving Day battle.

Salmon scored on a one-yard run midway through the first period for the first Blue Hose touchdown of the afternoon, and with about five minutes gone in the third period passed six yards to halfback Elliott Pauling.

The Blue Hose did not intentionally try to run up the score. Afterall, one touchdown would have been enough. At least that is what members of the Presbyterian defensive unit had been saying all week, according to Presbyterian head football coach Cally Gault.

"Our defensive players kept telling me, 'coach, if we can get one touchdown, that'll be enough,'" Gault said. "I didn't believe them at the time, but after we scored in the first period, one of them came up and said, 'that's it, coach,' and I still didn't believe them."

But it was all true, and through the efforts of the defensive team, Salmon and a few others, the victory supplied a ton of credibility to the same often-used cliche about traditional rivalries that didn't work very well in the Clemson-Carolina game—that the records book doesn't mean anything.

Before Thursday, the Blue Hose were stumbling along with a 3-6-1 record, with both of those victories coming in the last few weeks; and things didn't look very bright for the Presbyterian squad. Meanwhile, the Indians, who went into the game in the favored role, were sporting a 8-4 record; and until a sound 7-65 thrashing at the hands of Mars Hill two weeks ago; Newberry was a contender for the South Atlantic Conference title.

If records mean nothing, neither do comparisons of personnel and injuries. Newberry's Rufus Johnson, the team's leading rusher, was suffering from a bad ankle and saw only a little action. But as if to even things up a bit, the Blue Hose left star running back Kevin Williams in Clinton.

And as in the case of most rivalries, the winner, no matter how the season has gone, suddenly has a new lease on life. After the game, Presbyterian coaches, players and fans began discussing how well this year has turned out.

Gault put it this way: "Well, you certainly can't say that when you win only three games in a year it has been a good one, but this win sure changes things quite a bit. We've had some years when we didn't win many games but won this one, and it helped us. We've had one of those situations this season where the spirit and the effort were good, but we just weren't able to win a couple of times when we should have. But we hung in there, and this makes it worth the trouble."

And Salmon, who filled the same role against Newberry as Jeff Grantz did against Clemson, though on not quite so grand a scale, even got into the act. "No doubt about it," he said, "this will give us a great start on next year since we won three of our last four. You don't forget the losses, but this is the one you remember the most."

It was Salmon, of course, whose presence on the field made the difference for Presbyterian. After Presbyterian's Alan Smith blocked a Newberry field goal attempt, following the opening kickoff, the Blue Hose took posession on their own 32, and Salmon promptly engineered the first PC touchdown.

On the first play of a nine-play, 68-yard drive Salmon passed to T.D. Todd for 22 yards and then added nine yards on a run around end. Successive runs by Pauling and Ralph McBride added nine yards to the drive, and with a third-and-one at the Newberry 20, Salmon again rolled around end for the first down.

McBride ran for eight to the 19, and Salmon again dumped a pass to Todd, this time for 18 yards to the one. Salmon went through the middle for the touchdown on the next play, and George Camp kicked the extra point, giving the Blue Hose a 7-0 lead.

The remainder of the afternoon was reminiscent of many games for Newberry head coach Fred Herren. "Yeah, it looked like a lot of games this season," he said. "A lot of chances to score, but few points."

Other than the opening drive of the game, when the Indians penetrated to the Presbyterian 18 before the field goal attempt was blocked, Newberry's greatest scoring threat came with 30 seconds left in the first half when linebacker Russell Spires intercepted a Salmon pass and returned to the Blue Hose 27.

Indian quarterback Danny Williams passed to halfback Russ Jackson for 14 yards to the 13, and another pass fell incomplete. With third down, Williams dropped back to pass for the third time and was sacked, ending the threat.

Presbyterian's second touchdown resulted from a Newberry fumble, recovered by cornerback Alex Rogers at the Indian 31. The key play in the drive was an 18 yard pass from Salmon to Tim McCorkle on a fake field goal attempt. McCorkle took the pass and drove in to the Newberry six, and from there Salmon hit Pauling with the scoring strike on the next play. Camp again added the extra point.

Newberry also had scoring opportunities in the second half, but could never manage to get the ball into the end zone. A well-executed 14-pla, drive that ended on the last play of the third quarter with a Williams fumble on fourth down at the Presbyterian 14 was the best of the opportunities.

Presbyterian 7-0-7-0—14
Newberry   0-0-0-0—0
PC-Salmon one run (Camp kick)
PC-Pauling six pass from Salmon (Camp kick)

	PC	NC
First downs	16	18
Rushing yards	174	162
Passing yards	155	105
Total offense	329	268
Passes	10-5-2	9-30-2
Punts-avg.	41	6-43
Fumbles-lost	2-2	2-2
Penalties-yards	10-75	1-15

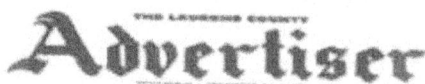

The Li'l That Was!

The Newberry Observer
AND HERALD & NEWS
"Just Like A Letter From Home"

HERALD AND NEWS ESTABLISHED 1865 — Newberry, S. C., Tuesday, Dec. 2, 1975 — NEWBERRY OBSERVER ESTABLISHED 1...

Can't Call Results Of Tribe-PC Tilt 'Upset'

CLOSE QUARTERS: PC defender Danny Grear grabs blocker Russ Jackson as Indian quarterback Danny Williams (10) looks for someplace to go.

Presbyterian's 14-0 victory over Newberry College in the annual Bronze Derby game on Thanksgiving Day was an upset, one paper said. But upset's never a good word for the outcome of that annual classic.

Experts remote from the scene may have regarded Newberry as the favorite, but close-at-hand observers know the contest is always even. It was so regarded, in advance, by PC Coach Cally Gault and Newberry's Fred Herren.

And even it was, except for the score. Newberry missed all its opportunities, but Presbyterian cashed two — on a 68-yard march in the first period and again in the third quarter after a Newberry fumble at the Tribe 30-yard line.

The loss left Newberry with a 5-5 record for the season and also did the Indians out of second place in the new SAC-8 conference. Presbyterian dropped Newberry to third by a few percentage points, although the Blue Hose now have only three wins and a tie for the entire season. They are 3-2-1 in the conference, while Newberry is 4-3.

Gault was happy for his team and astonished to find the Hose in second place after a rough season. "The defense told the offense that seven points would be enough to win," he said, "and it turned out to be true. I'm just as proud of our players as I can be."

And said Herren: "We got close a couple of times but we just didn't get any points on the board. We certainly should have got off a field goal attempt at the end of the first half, but our guys couldn't get the officials to call time out."

That lost opportunity came when Newberry's Russell Spires intercepted a pass by Jody Salmon and returned it to the PC 27 with 22 seconds left. The clock ran out.

Salmon was the key to the PC offense. He completed 1 of 16 passes for 155 yards and a touchdown. The Hose got another 175 yards rushing, and the PC defense shut off the Tribe's outside running game.

Newberry got 105 passing yards on nine completions in 20 throws, and also rushed for 163 yards, registering 18 first downs to PC's 16. Each team intercepted two passes, each recovered two enemy fumbles. It was indeed an even sort of game.

Newberry threatened on its first possession, but settled for a 36-yard field goal try by Bob McMillan when the game was only three and a half minutes old. It was blocked, and PC then mounted a 68-yard scoring march to its first score. Salmon got the touchdown on a one-yard sneak, after setting it up with a 14-yard pass to T. D. Todd. George Camp kicked the extra point.

Shortly thereafter, Newberry went goalward again but the effort ended in Alex Rogers' interception of a Danny Williams pass in the end zone. PC then put on a long advance but Neal Smith spoiled it with a Newberry interception at his six-yard line.

Two and a half minutes into the third quarter, Russ Jackson fumbled and Rogers came up with the ball at the Newberry 30. Five plays later, after a fake field goal try and a Salmon pass for a first down, Salmon scrambled around and hit Elliott Pauling with a six-yard scoring pass. Camp again converted.

Newberry wasted two more scoring chances, one of them on a drive from the Tribe six-yard line to the PC 14. That ended when Danny Williams was tossed for a loss as the third quarter ended.

The other opportunity came with 2:40 left in the game, when Newberry reached the Hose 18 on a march from the Newberry 34. PC's Rhea Faris broke that one up with an interception at the goal.

Rufus Johnson, Newberry's top rusher, was hampered by an ankle injury and played little. Kenny Brown took up the slack with a 95-yard performance in 19 carries.

ALL IN VAIN: Presbyterian receiver Steve Farish (19) has ball jarred loose by Newberry's Mike Landy (22). Hanging on farther down is Indian's Russell Spires.

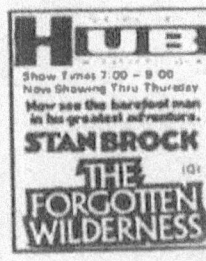

HUB
Show Times 7:00 - 9:00
Now Showing Thru Thursday
Now see the barefoot man in his greatest adventure.
STAN BROCK
THE FORGOTTEN WILDERNESS

The Li'l That Was!

Hose Keep Bronze Derby

The Bronze Derby went to Newberry last Thursday but it came back as the Presbyterian College Blue Hose downed the Indians, 14-0, in the annual Turkey Day Classic. The victory sealed second place for the Blue Hose in the first-year South Atlantic Conference finishing the season with a 3-6-1 mark and a 3-2-1 standing in the conference.

Newberry, on the other hand, suffered their third setback in the conference and finished out the season with an even 5-5 record.

Presbyterian Head Coach Cally Gault called the win "satisfying" and talked about a promise made to him before the game by the defensive squad. "They told me that if we scored just once that that would be all we would need. They did what they promised in keeping the Indians from scoring and kept them from getting deep in our territory. When they did, the squad kept them from getting any points from their work," commented Gault.

That lone touchdown that the Blue Hose defense asked for came in the first period when the Hose marched 68 yards in seven plays for the six points. A key third down pass from quarterback Jody Salmon to tight end T.D. Todd netted 36 yards and set the Blue Hose up on the Indian's one yard line. Todd, playing his last game for the Blue Hose, attempted to get into the end zone on the run but the referee ruled him short of the touchdown.

On the next play quarterback Salmon plunged the ball over from the one-yard line giving the defense the one touchdown that the squad had promised to defend. George Camp converted on the extra point and gave Presbyterian a 7-0 lead with 7:34 left to go in the first period.

That was the score when the gun sounded at the end of the second quarter as the Blue Hose and the Indians dug in on defense to thwart each others'' drives. Newberry had one opportunity to score stopped when defensive back Alan Breen blocked a field goal attempt from 35 yards out to preserve the Blue Hose lead.

The second "unnecessary" points came by way of a fake. With fourth and four to go for the first, kicker Camp came on to attempt a 41-yard field goal. Center David Penland snapped the ball back but the fake was on. Salmon got up and completed a 17-yard pass to fullback Tim McCorkle.

McCorkle worked his way to the seven-yard line before the Newberry defense was able to bring him down. On the next play from scrimmage, Salmon again went to the air and found halfback-split end Elliott Pauling alone for a six-yard pass play. Pauling, on a second effort, crossed the endzone marker for the second Presbyterian six points.

Camp came on and booted his 14th extra point of the year for a 14-0 lead with 10:44 left in the game.

The Blue Stocking, Friday, December 5, 1975, Page 4

Leroy Springs Gymnasium has seen its last inter-collegiate basketball game. One can only reminisce about the soul-rattling noise of a typical PC-Newberry game. "Lerny" may be old, but it's worth 10 points anytime!

the Blue Stocking

The Li'l That Was!

On November 27, 1975, the Newberry College Indians were defeated by the Presbyterian College Blue Hose. The final score was PC 14-NC 0. The game was the 29th Thanksgiving Day Bronze Derby football Classic.

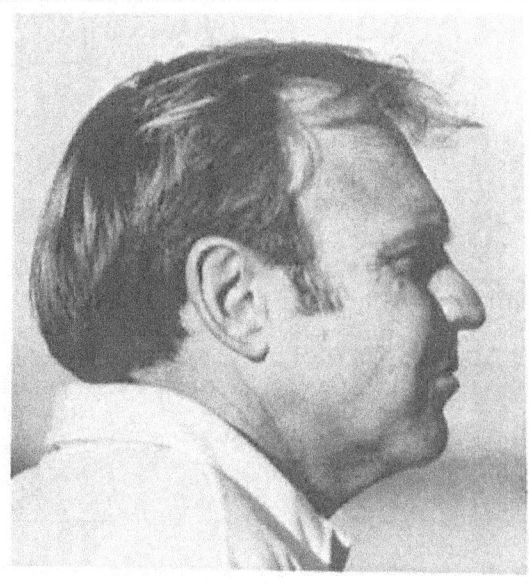

Presbyterian retained the Bronze Derby as the Indians ended the season with a 5-5 record. Twelve seniors wore the Scarlet and Grey for the final time. They were Bill Bishop, Bob Doppelheuer, Jim Fleming, Greg Fulwood, Det Haislip, Ricky Loftis, Mike McGroarty, Eddie Overstreet, Mark Simms, Neal Smith, Stanley Smith, and Jim Tucker. District 6 - NAIA all stars from Newberry are Charlie Upchurch, Charlie Izzard, McGroarty, and Haislip while SAC-8 all stars are D. D. Boyd, McGroarty, Haislip, and coach of the year Fred Herren.

The Li'l That Was!

The Indian

Voice for the Newberry College student

Newberry College

A Bicentennial College

NEWBERRY, S.C. 29108 WEDNESDAY, DECEMBER 3, 1975 — NUMBER THIRTEEN

Presbyterian retains Derby

Presbyterian College added a third period touchdown to a 7-0 halftime lead, and threw in a stingy defense to hand the Indians a tough 14-0 Bronze Derby loss Thanksgiving Day at Setzler Field.

Blue Hose premier quarterback, Jody Salmon, passed for 155 yards in ten completions of 16 attempts including one touchdown toss to lead his team in the victory. P.C. combined 168 yards rushing with Salmon's passing.

Newberry followed closely on the ground with 158 yards, while Danny Williams completed nine of 20 passes for 106 yards.

The visitors got on the board with 7:34 remaining in the first quarter on a one-yard sneak by Salmon, who directed the Blue Hose on the 68-yard scoring drive in nine plays. George Camp's extra point kick made it 7-0, P.C.

After two and one half minutes of second half play, Salmon connected with fullback Tim McCorkle on a seven-yard touchdown pass to boost the victor's lead to 14-0. Camp's PAT boot was good. McCorkle's reception came five plays after an Indian fumble at the Newberry 30, which was recovered by P.C.'s Alex Rogers.

The Indians were in scoring range several times, but failed to produce points. Kenny Brown returned the opening kickoff 65 yards to the Presbyterian 35. Seven plays later on fourth and five from the 18, Bob McMillan attempted a 35-yard field goal, but the boot was blocked by the Blue Hose' Jerry Broome.

With 22 seconds remaining in the first half, Indian linebacker Russell Spires picked off a Salmon pass on the P.C. 40, and returned it to the 26. On the first play, Williams connected with Russ Jackson for 13 yards, but two incompletions followed leaving 12 seconds on the clock. Confusion followed, and time was not called as the 'Skins wasted a golden scoring opportunity."

Late in the third quarter, the Indians mounted a drive from their own six, but the bid fell short on the visitors' 14 as the Tribe ran out of downs.

Newberry concluded their '75 campaign with a 5-5 mark overall, and a 4-3 slate in the South Atlantic Conference. The Blue Hose finished with three wins against six losses and a tie, four of the losses begin non-conference."

The Li'l That Was!

ALL FALL DOWN — The Blue Hose defense stops Longshore after the catch but fails to prevent a completion.

RIDE 'EM COWBOY — Running back Kenny Brown appears to be riding his opponent downfield as he is upended by a PC tackle. The efforts of Brown and his teammates ended in a 14-0 loss to PC's Blue Hose.

DON'T HIT ME! — Blue Hose tacklers close in as Split End Bo Longshore makes a first down catch for the Indians.

OH NO, NOT AGAIN! — Quarterback Danny Williams looks for a hole when he realizes that he must run the ball when Blue Hose defenders break through the line.

November 1976

November 2	Jimmy Carter was elected President of the United States defeating incumbent Gerald Ford.
November 3	The horror movie "Carrie" was released based on the novel written by Stephen King.
November 5	Baltimore Orioles pitcher Jim Palmer won the MLB AL Cy Young Award.
November 5	The Pittsburgh Pirates trade Manny Sanguillén and $100,000 to the Oakland A's for manager Chuck Tanner.
November 6	American football player and United States Army Ranger Pat Tillman was born.
November 7	The 1939 Oscar winning film "Gone With the Wind" starring Clark Gable and Vivien Leigh debuted on NBC. The movie was shown on 2 consecutive nights earning a 65% share of viewers.
November 9	The United Nations General Assembly condemned apartheid in South Africa.
November 9	Smokey the Bear, a black bear and resident of the Washington National Zoo, the living symbol of the United States Forest Service, passed away at 26 years of age.
November 19	American entrepreneur and co-founder of Twitter Jack Dorsey was born.
November 19	American publishing heiress Patty Hearst was freed on $15 million bail pending appeal of a bank robbery conviction.
November 20	American gymnast Dominique Dawes was born.
November 21	"Rocky" starring Sylvester Stallone premiered in New York City.
November 21	Cale Yarborough won the 26th NASCAR Sprint Cup.
November 24	American singer-songwriter Donna Summer divorced actor Helmuth Sommer after 5 years of marriage.
November 24	Cincinnati Reds second baseman Joe Morgan was named MLB NL Most Valuable Player.
November 25	American football quarterback Donovan McNabb was born.
November 25	The Bronze Derby was played in Clinton, South Carolina on Thanksgiving Day. The Newberry College Indians defeated the Presbyterian College Blue Hose 26-15.

The Li'l 🎩 That Was!

Advertiser Sports

Thanksgiving Day...
PC, Newberry vie for Derby

By DAN BRANYON

One of the state's oldest rivalries comes to a head again Thanksgiving Day in Clinton when the Presbyterian Blue Hose meet the Newberry Indians.

It will be the 63rd meeting of the two schools, the first coming back in 1913. Presbyterian boosted its lead in the series to 38-19-5 last year with a 14-0 victory.

Going into Thursday's contest, the Blue Hose hold a season record of 3-6 while the Indians are 4-5. The two will be out for more than improving records, though. Both will be out to capture the Bronze Derby.

The Bronze Derby has been a symbol of victory in athletic contests between Presbyterian and Newberry since Jan. 30, 1947.

It seems on that date that the two colleges got together in Newberry for a basketball game. Before the game started, several Presbyterian students hung a banner on the wall of Newberry's MacLean Gymnasium. The banner read "Beat Hell out of Newberry."

Sometime during the course of the game, a group of Newberry students left the gym in search of a ladder. Having found one, they set it against an outside wall, climbed through a window, rolled up the banner and escaped unnoticed the same way they entered.

Towards the end of the game, the Blue Hose realized their banner had disappeared.

After Presbyterian had posted a 51-47 win, a group of angry Blue Hose fans demanded their banner be returned. A ruckus resulted and in the midst of the confusion, a Newberry student snatched a derby from the head of a PC student and ran.

During the next few days, the two schools negotiated for the return of the derby. They finally agreed it should serve as a symbol of victory in sports events between the two.

The hat was returned to the Presbyterian campus where it was packaged and shipped to a casting company to be bronzed.

As a result of last year's Blue Hose victory, the Bronze Derby presently rests in a trophy case in PC's Ross E. Templeton Field House. Following Thanksgiving Day, who knows where it will be.

WOODEN NICKLE CONTEST STARTING SOON

HOUNDS TOOTH SPECIAL
4:30-7:30
BUDWEISER DRAFT
20¢ MUG
$1.00 PITCHER

The Newberry Observer
AND HERALD & NEWS
"Just Like A Letter From Home"
Newberry, S. C., Tuesday, Nov. 23, 1976

The Li'l That Was!

2 SECTIO

IN CLINTON

Tribe Eager For Bronze Derby Classic

Football fans across South Carolina know what Thanksgiving Day brings – the annual Newberry-Presbyterian Bronze Derby Classic. The two teams will clash for the 63rd time Thursday in Clinton and the rivalry still runs deep in both camps.

Indian coach Fred Herren described his club as having some very intense practices. "We've been working hard this week and the guys have really been intense. We just may be up for this one like no other game this year.

"It's a big game for us in more ways than one. Besides the prestigous Bronze Derby, we haven't beaten P. C. in Clinton since 1962. We don't think our record is representative of our team either. We're a better team than 4-5 and this will be our last chance to prove it. We're excited about the game and are ready to prove ourselves," concluded Herren.

Newberry and Presbyterian have had disappointed seasons record-wise. Coach Cally Gault's Blue Hose own a 3-6 overall slate and 2-4 conference record for seventh place in the South Atlantic Conference. The Indians register 4-5 overall and an even 3-3 conference showing.

But, S. C. football fans also know that records mean little when P. C. and Newberry meet on the gridiron. Statistics for the year do show how the teams match up on paper, however.

The Indians average 244 yards of total offense per game — the worst in the conference while P. C. ranks fifth in the SAC-8 averaging 293 yards per outing. The Tribe is fourth in passing offense, though, with a 121 yard average. P. C. is sixth at 109.

Newberry's defense, the strength of the Indians, is second only to Elon in total, passing and rushing defense allowing 202, 99 and 103 yards respectively. The Blue Hose hold down third in total defense stats giving up 321 yards a game, 206 of which are on the ground.

The Newberry-Presbyterian series is the oldest on the Indians' schedule dating to 1913. The trend is in P. C.'s favor as they hold down a 38-19-6 record with Newberry. Last season the Redskins lost 14-0 on Setzler Field. Newberry last claimed the Bronze Derby in '73 with a 14-3 win in Newberry.

Game time Thursday is 2 p.m. as the Indians will try to break a 13-year Presbyterian home-field jinx.

Derby's Origin Stems From Basketball Game

The "Bronze Derby" has traditionally been associated with the annual Newberry — Presbyterian Thanksgiving Day football game. Its orgin stems from a basketball game at Newberry on January 30, 1947, but the Derby finally found its place as the symbol of victory in the football rivalry between the two schools.

Before that historic game started almost 30 years ago, several Presbyterian students put up a banner on the wall of Newberry's MacLean Gymnasium which read: "Beat the Hell Out of Newberry."

Sometime during the game, a group of Newberry students found a ladder, set it up against the outside wall, climbed through a window, rolled up the banner, and escaped unnoticed the same way they had entered. Near the end of the game the visiting Blue Hose supporters realized the banner was gone. After Presbyterian had taken a 51-47 victory, the irate Hose partisans demanded the return of the banner. This prompted a scuffle, and in the midst of the general confusion, a Newberry student snatched a derby from the head of a P. C. student and ran.

During the next few days, officials of the two schools negotiated for the return of the derby. They finally agreed that it should serve as a symbol of victory in athletic contests between the two colleges. Consequently, the hat was returned to Presbyterian College, packaged and forwarded to a casting company where it was bronzed.

From 1947 to 1956 possession of the Bronze Derby was determined by victories in football, basketball and baseball, but in 1956 the schools decided to award the trophy on the basis of the winner of the Thanksgiving Day football clash.

Since then the Indians have been able to keep the Bronze Derby in Newberry only six times — in 1956, 1957, 1962, 1965, 1971, and 1973.

The Li'l That Was!

The Newberry Observer
AND HERALD & NEWS
"Just Like A Letter From Home"

Newberry, S.C., Friday, Nov. 26, 1976

Turkey Classic At Presbyterian Begins At 2 PM

SOME PEOPLE will be eating turkey at 2 p.m. this Thursday, but tradition-bound football fans in this part of South Carolina will be watching the kickoff of the annual Bronze Derby classic, a Thanksgiving Day custom which means more than turkey to Newberry and Presbyterian colleges.

This year Newberry travels to Clinton, and the Indians haven't beaten the Blue Hose on the PC field for 13 years. In fact, Newberry hasn't beaten Presbyterian anywhere since 1973 when the Tribe came out ahead 14-3 at Setzler Field.

On paper, there's little to choose between the 1976 teams. Neither club is happy with its season so far and Thursday's game is the last chance for Callie Gault's Hose and Fred Herren's Indians.

The Indians are 4-5 over-all and 3-3 in the SAC-8 conference. PC is 3-6 on the season and 2-4 in the conference. A Newberry win would mark the PC season as dismal, but should PC win, both clubs will finish 4-6 and 3-4. That eventuality would be, for Newberry, more bitter than cranberries.

Advertiser

Presbyterian's Elliott Pauling (43) breaks away for a 90-yard touchdown return of the opening kickoff during the Blue Hose' 26-15 loss at the hands of Newberry Thanksgiving Day.

Newberry tops PC; claims Derby

By DAN BRANYON

The Newberry Indians came to Clinton Thanksgiving Day in search of a hat and, sure enough, they found just what they were looking for.

The hat, of course, was the Bronze Derby, a symbol of victory in athletic contests between Presbyterian and Newberry since 1947.

Presbyterian had retained possession of the hat for the past two years by virtue of wins over their arch-rival, but the Indians were not to be denied Thursday as they whipped the Blue Hose 26-15.

The win boosted coach Fred Herren's squad to a final 5-5 mark and finished Presbyterian's season with a 3-7 mark. The Blue Hose still lead the series, which began in 1913, 36-20-5.

Elliott Pauling electrified the crowd of 4,200 Thursday when he took a handoff from Kevin Williams and returned the opening kickoff 90 yards for a touchdown. George Camp came on to add the PAT to give the Blue Hose a 7-0 lead with only 17 seconds gone off the clock.

It looked like the home team might be keeping the Derby another year when Newberry fumbled on their first possession. However, Presbyterian failed to convert on a fourth and one at the Newberry 26 to turn the ball back over to the Indians.

From there, Newberry marched steadily toward the goal until being stopped by a PC interception at the Blue Hose seven.

The Indians finally got on the board in the second quarter when Jerome Williams took a quick flat pass from quarterback Leon Williams and scampered 44 yards for a touchdown. Bob McMillan's extra point kick knotted the score at 7-7.

Later in the period, the Blue Hose got an opportunity to go ahead again when Claude Crocker picked off a Leon Williams pass to give his team the ball at the Indian 15. When they failed to move the ball, Camp attempted a 27-yard field goal that was off to the left. The score was still tied at the intermission.

The Indians got a boost on the second play of the second half when Leon Williams passed 66 yards to Kinch Edwards, a play that carried to the PC 6. Rufus Johnson dove over from the two to cap the 75-yard, five-play drive that put Newberry ahead to stay. McMillan converted with 12:50 left in the third quarter to make it 14-7.

Presbyterian failed to move the ball on their next possession, so Jody Salmon dropped back to his 10 to punt. However, the Indians blocked the kick before he could get it off and Bill Whitworth pounced on the ball in the end zone to put the visitors up 20-7.

The Blue Hose' comeback hopes were brightened later in the period when Jerry Broome recovered a fumble at the Newberry 43. Mike Taylor foiled their efforts, though, by intercepting a Salmon pass at his own three.

Newberry put the game out of reach in the final period with a 72-yard, 14-play march that consumed time the Blue Hose needed badly to catch up. It was Kenny Brown going to the outside from two yards out for the score that put Newberry up 26-7.

Presbyterian's only second half score came with 2:10 left in the game. The Blue Hose took possession at the Newberry 36 following an Indian fumble. Four plays later they got on the board when Salmon connected with Kevin Williams for a 25-yard touchdown pass play. Salmon passed to Williams again for the two-point conversion that made the final score 26-15.

Newberry   0 7 13 6 — 26
Presbyterian 7 0 0 8 — 15

Presbyterian-Pauling 90 kickoff return (Camp kick)
Newberry-J. Williams 44 pass from L. Williams (McMillan kick)
Newberry-Johnson 2 run (McMillan kick)
Newberry-Whitworth recover blocked punt in end zone (kick failed)
Newberry-Brown 2 run (kick failed)
Presbyterian-K. Williams 25 pass from Salmon (K. Williams pass from Salmon)

The Li'l 🎩 That Was!

The Newberry Observer
AND HERALD & NEWS
"Just Like A Letter From Home"
Newberry, S. C., Tuesday, Nov. 30, 1976

Indians Return That Derby To Newberry, 26-15

The fabled Bronze Derby came back to Newberry on Thanksgiving afternoon when the Newberry College Indians defeated Presbyterian College at Johnson Field in Clinton, 26-15.

It was the first win over Clinton in three years for Fred Herren's Indians, who evened their season at 5-5 and improved their SAC-8 Conference record to 4-3. Presbyterian closed with a 3-7 season and a 2-5 conference mark.

Newberry, with quarterback Leon Williams at the helm, cranked up its offense and scored with some frequency from the second period on. Presbyterian tallied on the opening kickoff, then couldn't cross the line again until only a couple of minutes remained in the game.

It was a hard-hitting game, replete with turnovers. Newberry lost three fumbles and suffered four pass interceptions. Presbyterian bobbled the ball away once and lost it three times on interceptions. But the game was spirited if not smooth.

Elliott Pauling got Presbyterian off right with a 90-yard kickoff return which, with George Camp's conversion kick, put the Indians seven points in the hole with practically no time elapsed.

The lead lasted until early in the second quarter when Jerome Williams took a quickie pass from Leon Williams and sprinted to a 44-yard Newberry touchdown. Bob McMillan's extra-point kick tied the score and it remained 7-7 at halftime.

Newberry put a lock on the outcome with a pair of touchdowns in a couple of minutes of the third period, the first coming with less than three minutes gone in the period. Leon Williams' 66-yard pass to Kinch Edwards set it up. Edwards took the ball to the PC five-yard line to complete Newberry's longest offensive gainer of the year and, a couple of plays later, Rufus Johnson went two yards for the score. McMillan then kicked Newberry into a 14-7 lead.

The Newberry defense held after the ensuing kickoff, then Tim Vinson blocked PC quarterback Jody Salmon's punt. Bill Whitworth recovered in the end zone for another Newberry touchdown and although McMillan's extra-point placement was wide, Newberry had a commanding 20-7 lead.

Presbyterian continued to threaten but couldn't put the ball over until the game was almost gone. Meantime, Newberry engineered a 14-play, 72-yard drive topped off by Kenny Brown's two-yard touchdown sweep with 7:10 left to play.

McMillan again missed his kick, but the score was a safe 26-7 and the Blue Hose touchdown with 2:10 left was no more than a consolation tally. Kevin Williams got it on a 25-yard pass from Salmon, after which the two hooked up again for a two-point conversion.

Brown led Newberry's rushers with 84 yards in 20 carries, while Jerome Williams was catching five passes for 80 yards. Leon Williams hit on 11 of his 19 passing attempts, for 210 yards. PC's Salmon was good on 14 of 24 tries for 145 yards.

In all, the Indians compiled about 400 yards of net offenses while putting on their best scoring performance of recent weeks.

The Newberry defense was outstanding all day. Mike Taylor and Mike Landy each got credit for two pass interceptions which helped keep the Blue Hose in check.

Presbyterian now leads the long-standing rivalry, 38 games to 20 with five ties or something like that. The official counts published by the two schools don't agree exactly.

The Indian
Voice for the Newberry College student

VOL. XLVI   NEWBERRY, S.C. 29108 WEDNESDAY, DECEMBER 8, 1976   NUMBER TEN

Indians Recapture Bronze Derby

Newberry wrapped up the 1976 football season with a 26-15 thrashing of Presbyterian in the annual Bronze Derby Classic Thanksgiving Day in Clinton. The win evened the Tribe's overall record at 5-5 and boosted their conference mark to 4-3 for third place in the final South Atlantic Conference standings.

Presbyterian lost the rivalry for the first time on their home field since 1962 while concluding a disappointing 3-7 overall slate and seventh place 2-5 conference record.

Coach Fred Herren's squad racked up 401 yards of total offense, including 210 through the air. Indian quarterback Leon Williams broke a Newberry season passing record by three yards with his 11 for 18 effort. The Okeechobee, Fla. senior's final performance boosted his season passing total to 1,186 yards, surpassing Tommy Williamson's old mark of 1,183 set in 1973.

Newberry crushed the Blue Hose with 21 first downs and held the home team to only ten. Freshman punter Chris Holtzclaw booted four punts for an average distance of 49.5 yards.

Teaming with Leon Williams, Jerome Williams was on the receiving end of five passes for 80 yards, including one for a touchdown.

Senior cornerback Mike Taylor picked off a pair of Jody Salmon passes, while teammate Mike Landy also intercepted a Blue Hose pass.

Presbyterian opened the game with a stuning 90-yard kickoff return by Elliott Pauling and George Camp followed with the extra point kick for a 7-0 P.C. lead.

The Indians' Williams combination struck for an early second quarter touchdown covering 44 yards. Bob McMillan's PAT kick tied the score at 7-7. Camp missed a 27-yard field goal late in the half and the score remained 7-7 at the intermission.

The Indians received the opening second half kickoff and drove 75 yards in five plays for the go-ahead touchdown by Rufus Johnson on a one-yard option run. McMillan's kick was true for a 14-7 lead. The big play of the drive was a 68-yard pass from Williams to tight end Kinch Edwards.

Four plays later, sophomore Tim Vinson blocked a Presbyterian punt and Bill Whitworth fell on the loose ball in the Blue Hose endzone for another Indian score. The extra point kick was wide, but the Tribe held a 20-7 lead with 10:49 left in the third quarter.

Kenny Brown tacked on another touchdown for Newberry midway the fourth quarter on a two-yard scamper capping a 72-yard drive in 14 plays. McMillan's kick again was wide but the Tribe led 26-7.

Presbyterian added their second touchdown with two minutes remaining on a 25-yard pass from Salmon to Kevin Williams. The Blue Hose two-point PAT pass from Salmon to Williams was complete for the 26-15 score.

November 1977

November 1	United States President Jimmy Carter raised the minimum wage from $2.30 to $3.35 an hour, effective January 1, 1981.
November 2	Philadelphia Phillies pitcher Steve Carlton won the MLB NL Cy Young Award.
November 2	Soviet General Secretary Leonid Breznev stated in a speech that the Soviet Union was ready to agree on a cease to nuclear testing.
November 5	Canadian Big Band leader Guy Lombardo passed away.
November 5	Future Texas Governor and future President of the United States George Bush married Laura Welch in Midland, Texas.
November 6	39 were killed as a result of a dam burst at Toccoa Falls Bible College in Toccoa, Georgia.
November 14	Egyptian President Anwar Sadat told the press he was willing to visit Israel.
November 16	Rod Carew of the Minnesota Twins won the MLB AL Most Valuable Player Award.
November 17	Egyptian President Anwar Sadat accepted an invitation to visit Israel.
November 17	In the Miss World Contest, Miss United Kingdom wore a $9,500 platinum bikini.
November 19	American gold medal gymnast Keri Strug was born.
November 20	Cale Yarborough won the 27th NASCAR Sprint Cup.
November 20	Egyptian President Anwar Sadat was the first Arab leader to address the Israeli legislature.
November 20	Walter Payton of the Chicago Bears set a single game NFL record rushing for 275 yards.
November 21	The first flight of the Concorde from New York to London took place.
November 21	Orioles first baseman Eddie Murray won the MLB AL Rookie of the Year Award.
November 22	Concorde passenger service between New York and Europe began.
November 24	The Bronze Derby was played in Newberry, South Carolina on Thanksgiving Day. The Presbyterian College Blue Hose defeated the Newberry College Indians 3-0.

The Newberry Observer
AND HERALD & NEWS
"Just Like A Letter From Home"

Newberry, S. C. Tuesday, Nov. 22, 1977

The Li'l That Was!

HARD HAT: The Bronze Derby will be at stake again in the Newberry-Presbyterian football game on Thanksgiving afternoon. The Derby has been awarded annually to the winner of the Indian-Blue Hose game since 1947. Newberry is the current owner as a result of a 26-15 victory over Presbyterian last year. Game time for the 66th meeting between the schools is 2 p.m. this Thursday at Setzler Field.

Newberry's Bronze Derby On The Line

When the Newberry College Indians and the Presbyterian College Blue Hose meet for the 66th time on the football field Thursday, three will be more than a victory at stake. There will be symbolic Bronze Derby, now in Newberry's possession.

The history of the Bronze Derby is much shorter than that of the football match between the two neighboring colleges (Presbyterian holds a commanding 21-40-4 edge in the series that dates back to 1913). It goes back only to Jan. 30, 1947, following a basketball game at Newberry between the two schools.

Before the game started, several Presbyterian students put up a banner on the wall of Newberry's MacLean Gymnasium which read: "Beat the Hell Out of Newberry."

Sometime during the game, a group of Newberry students found a ladder, set it up against the outside wall, climbed through a window, rolled up the banner, and escaped unnoticed the same way they had entered. Near the end of the game the visiting Blue Hose supporters realized that the banner was gone.

After Presbyterian had taken a 51-47 victory, the irate Hose partisans demanded the return of the banner. This prompted a scuffle, and in the midst of the general confusion, a Newberry student snatched a derby from the head of a Presbyterian student and ran.

During the next few days, officials of the two schools negotiated for the return of the derby. They finally agreed that it should serve as a symbol of victory in athletic contests between the two colleges. Consequently, the hat was returned to Presbyterian College, packaged and forwarded to a casting company where it was bronzed.

From 1947 to 1956, possession of the Bronze Derby was determined by victories in football, basketball and baseball. But in 1956 the schools decided to award the trophy on the basis of the winner of the Thanksgiving Day football clash.

Since then the Indians have been able to keep the Bronze Derby in Newberry only seven times — in 1956, 1957, 1962, 1965, 1971, 1973, and 1976. Newberry won the 1976 game by a 26-15 score.

The Li'l 🎩 That Was!

The Newberry Observer
AND HERALD & NEWS
"Just Like A Letter From Home"
Newberry, S. C. Tuesday, Nov. 22, 1977

2 SECT

Final Shot Thursday For 2-6-1 Redskins

The Indians prepare for their final game of the '77 slate this week as they go against rival Presbyterian College in the annual "Bronze Derby" game starting at 2 p.m. on Thanksgiving Day.

Newberry is not in the race for the SAC-8 title, but would love to defeat the Blue Hose just for the sake of morale. If the Indians should defeat PC, that would put the Blue Hose out of the race, whereas a win for PC would assure them of at least a tie for second. Currently, Coach Cally Gault's gridders are 4-2 in the conference and 6-3-1 overall. Newberry's record is 2-6-1.

Should Carson-Newman upset Elon this Saturday, the conference chase could end up in a four-way tie.

Kenny Brown, the Indian's leading rusher, suffered an ankle injury in last week's action at Mars Hill. But with the extra rest he'll get, he should be ready by next Thursday.

Coach Fred Herren gave his players a day off last Friday but said, "We'll be ready to go again on Monday."

Elliott Pauling, PC's leading rusher for three years in a row, will be tough to stop. He is currently the second leading rusher in the conference, boasting a 105.4 yards per game average. His performance last week against Carson-Newman gave him offensive player of the week honors. He rushed for 190 yards and three touchdowns, helping the Blue Hose to a 42-22 victory over the Eagles.

Seventeen seniors will be playing their last game for Newberry on Thanksgiving Day. They are Mike Landy, Batesburg; Carl Carter, Savannah; Marshall Johnson, Callison, Tony Williams, Little Mountain; Kenny Brown, West Columbia; Tony Orsini, Aiken; Trey Traylor, Carrollton, Ga.; Pat Gnann, Savannah; Jay Shelley, Columbia; Mike Austin, Orlando, Fla.; Charlie Izzard, Kershaw; Bob Brickley, Saluda; Charlie Upchurch, Savannah; Frankie Strickland, Belton; Bucky Miller, Greenville; Kinch Edwards, Simpsonville; Bo Longshore, Naples, Fla.

The Laurens County Advertiser

"SOUTH CAROLINA'S LARGEST SEMI-WEEKLY NEWSPAPER"

The Li'l That Was!

15¢ PER COPY

Vol. No. 88   Laurens, South Carolina, Monday, November 28, 1977   No. 43—16 Pages

Blue Hose capture Bronze Derby, 3-0

Presbyterian gained possession of the Bronze Derby by downing Newberry 3-0 in a defensive struggle Thanksgiving Day at Setzler Field.

The battle between the two old rivals marked the end of the 1977 grid season for both. It served to ice PC's 7-3-1 campaign, a welcome relief for coach Cally Gault and his staff after last year's disappointing 3-7 mark. They went 5-2 in the South Atlantic Conference (SAC-8), tying Mars Hill and Gardner-Webb for second in the league behind Elon.

On the other hand, the contest wrapped up a frustrating year for coach Fred Herren and the Indians. They ended up 2-7-1 and tied for last in the conference with Catawba. Five of their losses came by a total of 12 points, leaving them just shy of a good season.

The closing seconds of the game were typical of Newberry's fortunes this year. Split end Bo Longshore nabbed Jeff Tate's 57-yard pass at the two-yard line to give the Indians an opportunity to win the game with only two seconds remaining. All their timeouts spent, Tate quickly called the play that would tell the tale.

He pitched out to Bill Molony, who raced out and around right end. But PC defensive backs Derek Wessinger and David Elliott pulled up and knocked Molony out at the one, saving the day for the Clinton school.

For the Blue Hose, the winning points proved to be Larry Bridges' 36-yard field goal which came with 10:30 to go in the third quarter. A tough Indian defense along with the absense of quarterback Claude Crocker, who sustained a concussion in the first half, kept them scoreless the rest of the way.

The PC offense was held to only 109 yards rushing and 88 through the air. Running back Elliott Pauling was held to 71 yards on 26 carries, leaving him eight yards shy of the career record of 2,375 set by David Eckstein between 1969 and 1972.

They could manage only 10 first downs and ended up punting the ball away a total of 12 times.

Presbyterian's defense, their strongpoint all year long, allowed Newberry 281 total yards, 149 on the ground and 132 by passing. Though running back Kenny Brown was sidelined with a knee injury in the initial stanza, they still picked up 17 first downs.

The outcome brought the coveted Bronze Derby back to Clinton after a year's stay in Indian country. It will rest in the Ross E. Templeton Physical Education Center until the two schools challenge each other next Thanksgiving in Clinton.

PRESBYTERIAN   0 0 3 0-3
NEWBERRY   0 0 0 0-0

PC-Bridges 36 FG

The Li'l That Was!

The Newberry Observer
AND HERALD & NEWS
"Just Like A Letter From Home"
Newberry, S. C., Tuesday, Nov. 29, 1977

Big Attack But Not A Score, So Tribe Falls To Hose, 3-0

It might have been a 3-3 tie, but Newberry missed on a last-second touchdown try last Thursday at Setzler Field and Thanksgiving Day belonged to the Presbyterian Blue Hose, 3-0.

Thus the Indians, with one of the toughest teams in Fred Herren's 10 seasons at the helm, wound up with a disappointing record of two wins, a tie and seven defeats in what might as easily have been an 8-2 season.

Presbyterian finished 7-3-1, Thursday's win coming on a 36-yard field goal by Larry Bridges in the third period.

Opposition field goals have been the Tribe's curse all year long. They've lost five contests by a total of only 12 points.

Newberry played Thursday much as it has played all year — with a vicious defense and an offense which gained ground in a sometimes spectacular manner but had trouble getting across the goal line.

The Indians had about 10 chances to score against the Hose, half of them in the final period. Mistakes hurt them all afternoon — two lost fumbles, three missed field goals and four pass interceptions.

The trailing Indians never quit. As time was expiring, two passes by Jeff Tate took the ball from the Newberry 27 to the PC 41. Then with 12 second left Tate heaved a try-and-run-under-it pass to Bo Longshore, who did just that at the three-yard line while between two defenders.

With two second left, Bill Molony circled right end and almost made it, but not quite. Close to the goal, he was tripped by Derek Wessinger and shoved out of bounds by David Elliott. Time was gone, and the treasured Bronze Derby went back to Clinton with the Hose. (Newberry had taken it a year ago, 26-18.)

Defense by both clubs was superb all day. Newberry lost premier running back Kenny Brown with a first-period injury and PC's Claude Crocker collapsed with a concussion in the second quarter. It was doubtful, however, that their continued presence would have made any difference in the character of the contest.

The only score came shortly after halftime, set up by a 38-yard over-the-middle pass from substitute quarterback Mike Gill to Jesse Cason. Cason was caught at the Newberry 24, three plays gained only five yards, then Bridges executed his 36-yard placement for what turned out to be just enough PC scoring.

Newberry dominated from that point on but couldn't quite cash in. Bob McMillan, who had missed a 33-yard field goal try in the second quarter, missed two more in the final period on 31-yard and 41-yard attempts. Further damage was done late in the game by a fumble, a 15-yard penalty deep in PC territory, and a pass interception at the PC 10.

It was no comfort, but Newberry was statistically superior except in the scoring column. The Indians registered 17 first downs to 10 for the Hose and had 281 yards of total offense to 197 for PC.

Newberry collected 149 yards rushing and 132 passing, 71 of them on the three completions in its final possession. PC gained 109 yards on the ground including 71 by Elliot Pauling who carried 26 times, and got 88 aerial yards from the arms of Crocker and Gill.

The defeat, narrow as it was, nevertheless gave the Indians a 1-6 mark in the SAC-8 Conference and put them in the cellar with Catawba. PC finished 5-2 in the conference.

Coach Fred Herren proudly wears the Bronze Derby, the symbol of the Newberry-Presbyterian football game. The Indians brought the Derby back to Newberry by winning the Thanksgiving Day clash 26-15. The Bronze Derby has been awarded annually to the winner since 1956; Newberry coaches have been able to wear it only six times prior to the latest victory; in 1956, 1957, 1962, 1965, 1971 and 1973.

Bronze Derby returns to campus

The Bronze Derby returned to Newberry on Thanksgiving when the Indians downed Presbyterian 26-15 to end the season on a victorious note.

The final tally for the season was 5 wins and 5 defeats, but to Fred Herren and his grid crew the climax came on the final day of the season when they brought the Derby back for the first time since 1973.

Although the Indians won handily, it did not look as if it would be Newberry's day when a Blue Hose took the ball on the opening kick-off and returned the pigskin 90 yards to score, the extra point was good so after only 16 seconds had elapsed, PC led 7-0. But the Indians offense and aggressive defense saved the day for Newberry.

The Li'l 🎩 That Was!

12 on 12

```
    x   x   x   x   x

  x   x   x   x   x   x   x

              o

  x   x   x   x   x   x   x

    x   x   x   x   x
```

On Monday November 28, 1977, after reviewing the game film from the Thursday November 24, 1977 Thanksgiving Day Bronze Derby game, the Presbyterian College coaching staff made a call to the Newberry College coaching staff. Coach Bob Strock, defensive coach for Presbyterian, recalled that Presbyterian apologized to Newberry. With only seconds left in the game, Newberry's Bill Moloney ran to the right from the three yard line. He was stopped short of the goal line by Presbyterian College defenders Derrick Wessinger and David Elliott and went out of bounds. Time ran out of the game and PC won 3-0 and retained The Bronze Derby. The problem was that PC had 12 men on the field.

The Newberry coaching staff appreciated the telephone call. They chuckled, telling the Presbyterian coaching staff that Presbyterian had failed to notice that they (Newberry) also had 12 men on the field.

November 1978

November 2	The TV documentary "Scared Straight" narrated by Peter Faulk, debuted on TV.
November 2	Hockey player Wayne Gretzky was sold to the Edmonton Oilers after 8 games with the Indianapolis Racers of the WHA for $700,000.
November 3	The USSR and Vietnam signed a peace and friendship treaty.
November 3	"Different Strokes" debuted on NBC TV.
November 5	Masters golf champion Bubba Watson was born.
November 5	Followers of Ayatollah Khomeini attack the British embassy in Iran.
November 6	The Shah of Iran placed the country under military rule.
November 7	Boston Red Sox Jim Rice won the MLB AL Most Valuable Player Award.
November 7	Marion Berry was elected as Washington, D.C.'s first African American mayor.
November 8	American artist and illustrator, Norman Rockwell passed away.
November 10	Larry Holmes KO's Alfredo Evangelist to win the heavyweight boxing title.
November 15	An Icelandic Airlines DC-8 crash killed 183 in Sri Lanka.
November 15	Pittsburgh Pirates outfielder Dave Parker won the MLB NL Most Valuable Player Award.
November 18	American pastor and cult leader of the Peoples Temple Jim Jones died of suicide, along with his 918 members of the Peoples Temple in Jonestown, Guyana.
November 19	"The Miracle of the Meadowlands" occured as a fumble recovery and score in the closing minute by NFL Philadelphia Eagles Herm Edwards. Edwards' score with 31 seconds left resulted in a 19-17 Eagles victory over the NY Giants.
November 19	Cale Yarborough won the 28th NASCAR Sprint Cup.
November 21	Bob Horner of the Atlanta Braves won the MLB NL Rookie of the Year Award.
November 23	The Bronze Derby was played in Clinton, South Carolina on Thanksgiving Day. The Presbyterian College Blue Hose defeated the Newberry College Indians 26-0.

THE INDIAN

VOL. XLVII NEWBERRY COLLEGE Newberry, S. C. 29108 November 15, 1978 No. 7

Warning PC! Indians Swapping War Bonnet For Thanksgiving Bronze Derby

By LARRY RUCKER
(Indian Sports Columnist)

The NC football team will face PC for the 67th time Thanksgiving Day at Bailey Stadium in Clinton. The contest will not only decide an important position in the conference, but will also determine the winner of the symbolic Bronze Derby.

The origin of the Bronze Derby began back on Jan. 30, 1947, following a basketball game between the two schools. As the students gathered in the gym some PC fans decorated a wall in Newberry's MacLean Gymnasium with a banner which read: "Beat the Hell Out of Newberry."

Sometime during the game, some Newberry fans found a ladder outside, used it to gain entrance through a window, and escaped with the banner unnoticed. The PC supporters finally realized it was done near the end of the contest.

Following a 51-47 Blue Hose victory, the furious PC followers demanded the return of the banner. When Newberry declined the demand, a scuffle began between members of both schools. During the mass confusion, a NC student swiped a derby from the head of a PC student and ran.

For a period of time, the officials of both schools negotiated for the return of the derby. Following an agreement, the derby was proposed as a symbol for victory in athletic contests between the two rivalries. As a result, the derby was returned to PC, packaged and sent to a plating company where it was bronzed.

From 1947 to 1956 possession of the Bronze Derby was earned by the cumulation of victories in football, basketball, and baseball, but in 1956 the schools decided to award the derby on the basis of the winner of the Thanksgiving Day football contest.

The Indians took possession of the Bronze Derby in 1956 to start the tradition, and went on to win it in 1957, 62, 63, 71, 73, and 76. PC won the 1977 game by a 3-0 margin.

Unfortunately for the Blue Hose, the Indians are on the warpath in '78 and do not intend to be stopped Thanksgiving Day.

Indian quarterback, Eddie Pathis, appears to get a pass off in the nick of time. Tough luck Rushers! (Photo by Randy Weaver)

The Li'l 🎩 That Was!

The Newberry Observer
AND HERALD & NEWS
"Just Like A Letter From Home"
Newberry, S. C., Monday, Nov. 20, 1978

Indians Will Vie For Bronze Derby

The 12th nationally ranked Newberry College Indians will face the fifteenth nationally ranked Presbyterian Blue Hose for the 67th time — Thanksgiving Day — at Bailey Stadium in Clinton. The 2 p.m. contest will not only decide an important position in the conference, but will also determine the winner of the symbolic Bronze Derby.

The origin of the annual rivalry began back on Jan. 30, 1947, following a basketball game between the two schools. As the students gathered in the gym some PC fans decorated a wall in Newberry's MacLean Gymnasium with a banner which read: "Beat The Hell Out of Newberry."

Sometime during the game, some Newberry fans found a ladder outside, used it to gain entrance through a window, and escaped with the banner unnoticed. The PC supporters finally realized it was gone near the end of the contest.

Following a 51-47 Blue Hose victory, the furious PC followers demanded the return of the banner. When Newberry declined the demand, a scuffle began between members of both schools. During the mass confusion, a NC student swiped a derby from the head of a PC student and ran.

For a period of time, the officials of both schools negotiated for the return of the derby. Following an agreement, the derby was designated as a symbol for victory in athletic contests between the two schools. As a result, the derby was returned to PC, packaged and seint to a casting company where it was bronzed.

From 1947 to 1956 possession of the Bronze Derby was earned by the cumulation of victories in football, basketball, and baseball, but in 1956 the schools decided to award the derby soley on the basis of the winner of the Thanksgiving Day football game.

The Indians took possession of the Bronze Derby in 1956 to start the tradition, and went on to win it in 1957, 1962, 1965, 1971, 1973 and 1976.

Cally Gault's Blue Hose won the 1977 game in Newberry by a 3-0 margin on a 36 yard field goal in the third quarter. Reed Charpia's Indians will be battling on Thanksgiving Day to get the Derby back.

Tribe Ends Season In Derby Clash At P.C.

Whenever Thanksgiving Day rolls around most football teams in South Carolina have either finished their season or they are preparing for a bowl game. However, there's always one game that prevails for Newberry and Presbyterian College fans and that is the annual Bronze Derby Classic.

The two teams will clash Thursday at Bailey Memorial Stadium in Clinton. Kickoff is set for 2 p.m.

Presbyterian comes into the contest with an impressive 7-3-1 record overall and 5-0-1 in SAC-8 conference play. Newberry, under new head coach Reed Charpia, has put together a complete turnaround from last year, and come to Clinton with a 7-2 overall; their only losses being crucial SAC-8 games at Carson-Newman and Elon. The 'Skins were ranked 12th in the nation in the final NAIA poll.

Cally Gault's 15th ranked Blue Hose are led by two outstanding offensive players in quarterback Jim Spence and running back Clayton Burks, and defensive standouts Jim McCoun, Rick Porter, and Bill Sizemore. Their only losses this year have been to The Citadel and Wofford.

The Tribe will feature offensive standouts Jerome Williams, leading pass receiver, who could break a school receiving record this week, and fullbacks Rick Harward, leading scorer with 26 pts., and C. W. Wilson. Defensively, Charlie Coles, All-American candidate, and Barry Knight (interior lineman) and backs Randy Lamar and Jerry Hefney lead the attack.

Coach Reed Charpia's Indians are disappointed about not getting a playoff bid, but are still optimistic about the PC game. The possibility of a post-season bowl game is still in the air, but if the Indians do not go to one, victory in the Bronze Derby would be just as good. "It would be a nice way to end the season," said Charpia.

The Li'l 🎩 That Was!

SPORTS

The Laurens County Advertiser

Monday, Nov. 27, 1978

Blue Hose retain Bronze Derby

By DAN BRANYON

Few at the Presbyterian-Newberry football classic Thanksgiving Day afternoon could remember when playing for the Bronze Derby meant so much.

Of course, the longtime state rivalry is a "big 'un" to the two schools every year. But this Turkey Day it meant even more as both schools entered the game with winning records and nationally ranked.

The Blue Hose came in ranked 15th among NAIA schools while the Indians were 12th. The former sported a 7-2-1 mark and had a shot at a share of the South Atlantic Conference (SAC-8) lead. On the other hand, the latter was 7-2 and would have enjoyed nothing more than denying their rival the league title.

With all that at stake, the two teams lined up in a fine mist of rain at Presbyterian's Bailey Memorial Stadium. A crowd estimated at 5,000 looked on as the Blue Hose completely dominated to register a 26-0 win, their 42nd against 21 Newberry victories and four deadlocks.

The triumph assured PC possession of the Bronze Derby for another year, an 8-2-1 record, and, along with Elon, a share of the SAC-8 championship. And Coach Cally Gault believes it might earn his squad an invitation for post-season play, though nothing will be known for certain until Monday or Tuesday.

At the very outset, it appeared the Indians had come to town ready to test the hosts' noted defense. The first offensive play of the game saw quarterback Eddie Pettus hit Jacques Gilliam with a 19-yard pass that carried to the Newberry 46-yard line. But PC held at its own 45 and the visitors were forced to punt.

Later in the first period, the Presbyterian defensive unit was put to the test again. Quarterback Jimmy Spence lost the football as he was hit and the Indians took over at the Presbyterian 46. On third down and four, Pettus was dropped for a loss by defensive end Jim McCoun and once again it was time for the punting unit to enter.

The Indians found themselves in the same predicament early in the second quarter. Jeff Tate, in at quarterback, took a lick from a Blue Hose defender and coughed the ball up at his own 37. PC took charge there and marched to the end zone in eight plays.

One of the key plays in the first scoring drive came on a fourth down and four at the 31. Rather than go for the field goal, Spence dropped back and tossed a bullet to tight end Danny Thornton. Thornton made a spectacular catch and broke several tackles to move the ball to the 14.

At the 11:32 mark, Clayto Burke blasted across from the four to bring forth a bang from the cannon at the opposite end zone. Chuck Bishop tacked on the extra point kick and PC was in front 7-0.

It was another Newberry turnover that set up Presbyterian's next score. Senior linebacker Rick Porter picked off a Pettus aerial and returned to the Newberry 25. PC drove to the 10 before the Indian defense stiffened, thus bringing out Bishop to attempt a 29-yard field goal. The sophomore's kick was true to make it 10-0 with 2:47 left in the half.

Gilliam was dropped at the goal line on the ensuing kickoff to give the visitors terrible field position. But a Pettus to Gary Cali pass earned them a first down and some breathing room at the 13.

However, on the very next play, Erskine Reed stepped in front of another Pettus pass to give the Blue Hose possession at the 23. Four plays later, Bishop drilled across his second field goal, a 33-yard effort, to give his team a 13-0 halftime advantage.

A faked field goal attempt late in the third quarter allowed Presbyterian to add to its lead. Having started from the Newberry 47 following an Alan Roebuck fumble, they moved to the 29 where it was fourth and long.

Senior Larry Bridges came on in lieu of Bishop and the Blue Hose set up in field goal formation. But Spence took the snap and tossed to Burke who carried all the way to the 16. Six plays later, Burke scored from the three and Bishop added the PAT to make it 20-0 with 14:14 remaining in the game.

Only seconds later, Erskine Reed intercepted a Roebuck aerial and PC was in business again at the Newberry 31. Spence passed to Jesse Cason, who was to break the school record for receptions in one season (46) before the game was over, and he carried to the 22.

Two plays later, Burke hauled in a 22-yard pass from Spence to stretch the lead to 26-0. Bishop's kick for the extra point was no good.

The Indians finished the day with just 16 yards rushing and 101 yards total offense. On the other hand, PC racked up 282 on the ground and 113 through the air. Burke led all rushers with 70 yards in 29 attempts.

	N	PC
First downs	6	20
Yards rushing	16	282
Yards passing	85	113
Passes	8-23-4	10-18-0
Fumbles lost	2	2
Punts	7-37.1	5-44.4
Yards penalized	49	35

Newberry 0 0 0 0—0
Presbyterian 0 13 0 13—26

PC-Burke 4 run (Bishop kick)
PC-Bishop 29 FG
PC-Bishop 33 FG
PC-Burke 3 run (Bishop kick)
PC-Burke 22 pass from Spence (kick failed)

The Li'l That Was!

The Newberry Observer
AND HERALD & NEWS
"Just Like A Letter From Home"

HERALD AND NEWS ESTABLISHED 1865 — NEWBERRY OBSERVER ESTABLISHED

Newberry, S. C., Monday, Nov. 27, 1978

Hose Down Newberry, Derby Stays In Clinton

There was more at stake than a hat in the Thanksgiving Day Bronze Derby Classic, but as in years past, possession of the derby was uppermost in the minds of two long-time rivals.

In the end, however, Newberry failed in its bid to claim the metalic topper and fell 26-0 before a capitalizing Presbyterian College team at Bailey Stadium in Clinton.

Newberry's powerful defense was unable to compensate for a mistake-laden offense which lost possession six times during the game; twice on fumbles and four times with intercepted passes. The Blue Hose used the turnovers to post a 13-0 halftime margin and set up two fourth quarter touchdowns for the final spread.

The victory gave 8-2-1 P. C. a first place tie in SAC-8 competition with Elon, the two champions (both 6-0-1) having battled to a 21-21 tie earlier in the season. Newberry ended their season with a 7-3 overall mark and a 4-3 conference tally, but were ranked number 12 in the final-season NAIA poll, three steps ahead of the Blue Hose.

Bill Berry recovered a fumble and Rick Porter and Erskine Reed intercepted passes in the second period to set up a touchdown and two successful field goals to give P. C. their halftime lead.

After Berry's recovery on the Blue Hose 37-yard line, Walter Atkins capped an eight-play drive with a four-yard scoring plunge with 11:32 left in the half. Kicker Chuck Bishop added the PAT, and before the half was over booted six points worth of field goals from 29 and 33 yards.

The fourth quarter saw Joe Gan't fumble recovery set the stage for Clayton Burke's two-yard touchdown dive with 14:14 to go, and Reed's second interception of the day at the Newberry 31 set up Jimmy Spence's 22-yard touchdown pass to Burke three plays later. Bishop added another extra-point kick.

Burke led the P. C. running attack, gaining 60 yards on 29 carries as the hosts rushed for 184 yards. Newberry was limited to 25 carries for only 16 yards, their biggest threat coming when they managed to penetrate to the P. C. 40 with the help of a Blue Hose fumble.

Jessie Cason, a sophomore end, went on to claim P. C.'s single-season pass reception record in the final quarter, pulling in 46 during the season and seven against Newberry. Spence, on the other end of these passes, completed 10 out of 18 passes against the Indians to tack on an additional 113 yards.

Newberry quarterback Eddie Pettus completed eight passes in 23 attempts for 85 yards.

The game marked the second consecutive time P. C. has managed to shut out the Indians. Last year Cally Gault's Blue Hose won with a 36-yard field goal in the third quarter for the 3-0 score. Newberry won the Derby last in 1976.

The Li'l That Was!

VOL. XLVII NEWBERRY COLLEGE Newberry, S. C. 29108   December 6, 1978 No. 8

THE INDIAN

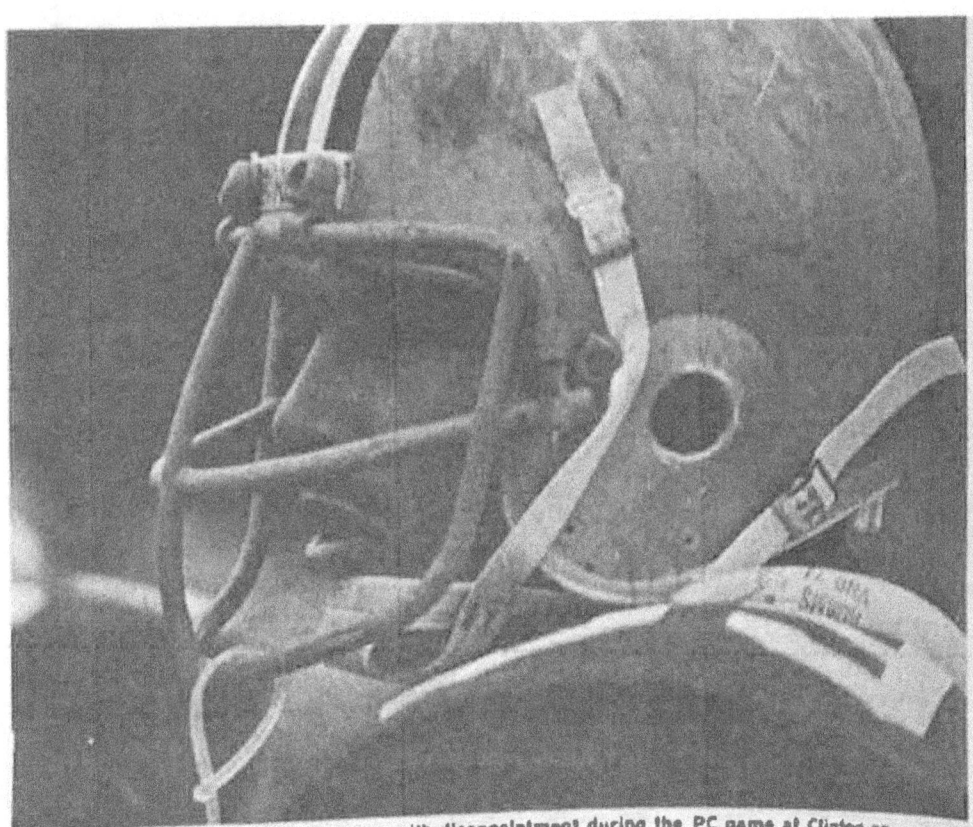

Indian Player Chris Miller looks on with disappointment during the PC game at Clinton on Thanksgiving Day. The Indians were defeated 26-0. (Photo by Randy Weaver).

Blue Hose Trounce Tribe 26-0

BY ROBERT YOUNG
(Indian Sports Writer)

NC ended a fine season on a bad note by dropping the final contest to arch-rival PC Thanksgiving Day.

This is the second straight year that the Blue Hose have taken home the Bronze Derby and they did it in a big way with a 26-0 trouncing.

The Blue Hose defense held the Tribe's usually productive offense to its poorest performance of the season. NC managed only 97 yards total offense while PC raced 184 yards on the ground and completed ten passes for 118 more.

The Skins lost two fumbles and threw four interceptions, allowing PC more than 75 yards. NC was also stifled by 44 yards in penalties.

The Blue Hose got on the board in the second quarter with a three yard run and two field goals. The two teams played between goal lines in the third period before PC exploded for two touchdowns in the final stanza. One Blue Hose score came on a two yard run with the other coming minutes later on a 2 yard pass.

Indian Coach Reed Charpia said after the game that turn overs made the difference. "It hurt a throwing three or four interceptions and losing those fumbles. We just had a bad day. PC was on the ball and they played a fine ballgame," Charpia added.

November 1979

November 1	Former United States First Lady Mamie Eisenhower passed away.
November 2	The United States government proposed making a $1.5 billion loan to Chrysler.
November 2	New York City Studio 54's owners were arrested for tax evasion.
November 4	Iranian students loyal to Ayatollah Khomeini seized 90 hostages at the US Embassy in Tehran.
November 5	Ayatollah Khomeini described the United States as "The Great Satan."
November 6	The Ayatollah Khomeini took over in Iran.
November 7	Chicago Cubs pitcher Bruce Sutter won the MLB NL Cy Young Award.
November 8	ABC TV began a late night broadcast "Iran Crisis: America Held Hostage."
November 12	United States President Jimmy Carter announced a halt to Iranian oil imports and froze Iranian assets.
November 12	American golfer Lucas Glover was born in Greenville, South Carolina.
November 13	Ronald Regan announced his candidacy for United States President.
November 15	ABC TV begins nightly broadcasts on the Iranian hostages.
November 17	*Salem's Lot*, a horror novel by Stephen King, became a two part miniseries and premiered on US television.
November 17	Iran freed most black and female US hostages.
November 17	Daniel Okrent sketched out the first draft rules for Rotisserie Baseball.
November 18	Richard Petty won the 29th NASCAR Sprint Cup.
November 19	MLB Houston Astros signed Nolan Ryan to a 4 year $4.5 million contract.
November 19	Singer-songwriter Chuck Berry was released from prison for an income tax evasion conviction.
November 22	The Bronze Derby was played in Newberry, South Carolina on Thanksgiving Day. The Presbyterian College Blue Hose defeated the Newberry College Indians 16-14.

The Li'l 🎩 That Was!

The history of a 32 year scuffle

ROBIN RUSH

A tradition at Newberry is one of the Bronze Derby. The Derby is the reward of the winner of the Newberry-Presbyterian College football game which is held on Thanksgiving Day. Did you ever wonder how this legend started? The November 19, 1969 Indian tells of the legend. It seems that the Derby is a result of a ruckus. On January 30, 1947, a group of P. C. students hung a banner on the gym wall which read "Beat the Hell Out of Newberry" before a basketball game. During the game, one of the Newberry students got a ladder and climbed through the window to get the banner. No one noticed that the banner was gone until the end of the game. After the game (which P. C. won 51-47) a P. C. student demanded the return of the banner. A scuffle began and in the middle of it, a Newberry student "snatched a derby from the head of a P. C. student and ran."

During the next couple of days, the two athletic directors negotiated the return of the hat. During their negotiations, an agreement was made between the two schools that "a derby should serve as a laurel of victory in athletic contest between Newberry and Presbyterian." After a while the hat was returned. The derby was packaged up and was sent to a casting company in Ohio. The hat was bronzed and it became the famed Bronze Derby. Until 1956, the possession of the Derby was decided by the outcome of all the games Newberry and P. C. played in football, basketball, and baseball. Now, possession is determined by the outcome of the N. C.-P. C. football game.

This year the Indian's have a chance to gain the derby back on their home field. Revenge for the P. C. victory of 1978 is in the making.

THE EPITOME OF VANDALISM: PC students hit Newberry College Friday night Nov. 16, with a blue spray paint that is not removable—The vandals painted three sides of the stadium. What was their purpose?

Newberry College has school spirit! And we use water color instead of spray paint. At least, ours is removable. Maybe, PC is unaware that water color is available on the market now.

The Li'l 🎩 That Was!

VOL. XLIX   No. 6   NEWBERRY COLLEGE   November 24, 1979

NC faces PC in Bronze Derby; 15 seniors play in final bout

DAMONE LEAPHART

Last August over 100 men reported to this campus in hopes of making this football season the best ever in Newberry College history. The men, coming from different localities and backgrounds, mixed together for the common goal of making their team a winner in 1979. Things do not always turn out as planned, however, as evidenced by this year's record. None of this really matters now though, what does matter is tomorrow's game with archrival, Presbyterian College.

Fifteen seniors will be wearing the scarlet and gray for the last time tomorrow. These seniors would like nothing better than to bring the Bronze Derby back to Newberry this year, where it belongs. The last time Newberry had the Derby was when these seniors were freshmen.

The contest between Newberry and Presbyterian is rich in tradition and has been labeled the small college equivalent of the Carolina-Clemson contest. The rivalry goes way back to the year 1913, when Newberry won the first game in the series 51-0. The Thanksgiving Day tradition evolved in the mid-fifties.

A win over Presbyterian, the NAIA number one team in the nation, would be a highlight of the 66 year rivalry. PC sports a 9-1 record coming into the contest. The 'Skins are 5-4 on the season. Records such as these, however, don't matter when it comes to the fight for the Bronze Derby. The unexpected becomes the expected in this game, and an upset is very often the rule rather than the exception.

PC brings a powerful offense, led by quarterback Jimmy Spence, to Setzler Field tomorrow. Unbelieveably, their offense has scored, on the average, twice for every three possessions. Thus, the 'Skins defense will be facing the supreme test on this Thanksgiving Day.

PC's defense has also done a good job for Coach Cally Gault. The 'Skins scoring attack will have to improve vastly over their last two performances if the Indians are to seriously challenge PC. Newberry has failed to score a point on the Blue Hose defense during the last two years, so the offense will be looking to make up for this.

The 'Skins have been practicing very hard since the Mars Hill defeat. They not only want this game for themselves, but also for school pride and for you. Yes, you, because you are Newberry College. Student support for the team this year has been inconsistent, ranging from great enthusiasm to apathy. But this is all in the past now, and the 'Skins need every bit of support that each of you can muster to win this game. The team would appreciate beyond words your staying and giving your active, real support at the game. Rumor has it that the game will be televised on cable TV. Therefore, a strong showing of students would make our cause better. PC will have their side filled; they always do. Will we be able to say the same?

A Newberry victory over PC is very conceivable. PC's lone defeat came at the hands of Wofford by a score of 23-21. Newberry defeated this same Terrier team 31-3. Furthermore, the PC players are the same ones that our senior, junior and sophomore players have beaten in each of their freshman games with the Blue Hose. So, for what promises to be an exciting football classic, do your part, and be at Setzler Field on Thanksgiving Day.

Editor's Note: There are several items of interest about the Derby tomorrow. One is that The Sandlapper has published in its November issue a history of the series, giving the same statewide publicity. Another is that, unknown members of the Blue Hose species have taken the time and "talent" to decorate the stadium for us. The Indian sincerely hopes the peachy PCs ennoy staring at their childish and destructive artwork during their defeat tomorrow.

The Li'l That Was!

Advertiser

12 The Laurens County Advertiser November 21, 1979

In Bronze Derby

Gault eyes Newberry

By SAM REGISTER

"Our immediate attention is on Newberry. They're the thing that counts right now more than anything," said Presbyterian Coach Cally Gault Tuesday. "This game is the season itself."

Gault and the Blue Hose are gearing up for this Thursday's annual Bronze Derby Thanksgiving contest against the Indians, to be played at Newberry at 2 p.m.

Although Newberry has not had the success the Hose have enjoyed this season, Gault is not underestimating the opponent.

"This game needs nothing else to make it big, like rankings or playoff berths," he said. "There is no outside incentive."

How about the Hose's number one national ranking?

"Well, there could be an extra incentive to knock us off," he said, "but we should have the extra incentive of wanting to remain where we are."

The Indians come into this Turkey Day battle, which began in 1913, with a 5-4 record, having lost its last three games to Jacksonville St., Elon, and Mars Hill. But Gault is quick to point out that Newberry was a "bruised football team" over those three games, with a total of six starters out for the Mars Hill game. All except linebacker Dennis Yarborough are expected to start Thursday's game.

The Hose have a 42-21-4 edge in the series and toppled the Indians 26-0 last year in Clinton.

Should Presbyterian beat Newberry, they will host Saginaw Valley State (Mich.) in the first round of the NAIA national playoffs. If the Hose lose to Newberry, Gault said there is a very big "if" involved whether PC gets invited or not. If they lose and still receive an invitation, there's a chance Presbyterian would have to travel to Saginaw or elsewhere to play.

Eight teams will be invited to participate in the playoffs, with the final two teams meeting Dec. 15 in McAllen, Texas for the national championship.

But for right now, Gault's thoughts are about 20 miles southeast of Clinton.

"A 5-4 record in our league is good," he said. "Newberry has proved to be a fine football team defensively and offensively. They're probably the only people that were pleased more than we were when the rankings came out."

Presbyterian will go into Thursday's game ranked second in passing offense, first in rushing offense, and first in total offense in the SAC-Eight Conference.

Junior quarterback Jimmy Spence is first in total offense in the conference, averaging 177.9 yards per contest. He is also first in passing, having hit on 96 of 157 passes for 1,427 yards and 11 touchdowns.

Burke is first in the SAC-Eight among the top three in rushing with 1,307 yards in 10 games and a 130.7 yard per game average. He is first in the conference in scoring with 90 points. Kicker Chuck Bishop is third with 57.

Jesse Cason has 44 receptions in 10 games which ranks first among conference receivers as does his 54.0 yards per game average. Tight end Danny Thornton is fourth in the conference with 22 receptions. Willie Mason is number one in the SAC-Eight in kick returns with a 29.0 average and 203 total yards. His 96-yard kick return for a touchdown highlighted the Furman game. Also tops in the conference is Hal Brannen, who has picked off seven enemy aerials.

The Bronze Derby game has been played every Thanksgiving Day since 1956. The concept of playing for the derby came about in the late 1940s when a Presbyterian student named James Kellet, whose uncle owned a clothing store in Fountain Inn, purchased a Stetson Derby from there and started wearing it for fun.

Kellet happened to be wearing it one night in 1947 when he and a group of friends went to see the Presbyterian basketball team play at Newberry. Some Newberry students put a ladder up outside the gym, climbed through the window at the top of the visitors' section, and made their way down through the crowd and one of them snatched the derby off Kellet's head and made off with it. He and his friends chased the Newberry group but Kellet went back to Clinton minus his derby.

Charles MacDonald, PC sports information director, suggested to Frank Kinard, the SID at Newberry that if the hat could be recovered it might become a symbol for athletic supremacy between the two schools.

It was decided that it would go to the winner of any athletic event between the two schools, so the derby changed hands through football, baseball, and basketball seasons from 1947 to 1955. To keep the importance of the derby from diminishing, the schools agreed in 1956 that it would be claimed only by the winner of the annual Thanksgiving Day football game.

It is noteworthy to mention that a member of the PC entourage which made the trip to Newberry that night in 1947 was a student named Calhoun Gault.

NAIA National Rankings

TEAM	1st PLACE VOTES	RECORD
PRESBYTERIAN	9	9-1-0
TEXAS A & I	7	8-1-0
KEARNEY ST. NEB.		8-1-0
WISCONSIN-RIVER FALLS		9-1-0
CENTRAL STATE OKLA.		8-1-0
WESTERN ST. COLO.		7-1-0
ANGELO ST. TEX.		7-2-0
SAGINAW VALLEY ST. MICH.		8-1-1
MARS HILL N.C.		7-1-1
FAIRMONT ST.		8-1-1
ARKANSAS-MONTICELLO		8-2-0
NORTHEASTERN OKLA.		8-2-0
OREGON COLLEGE		7-1-1
SOUTHERN COLORADO		7-2-0
OREGON TECH.		7-2-1
W. LIBERTY ST.		7-2-1
STEPHEN F. AUSTIN		7-3-0
SOUTHWEST TEXAS ST.		7-3-0
SOUTHWESTERN OKLA.		7-2-0
WISCONSIN-LACROSSE		7-2-0

This display in the lobby of Ross Templeton gymnasium is a reminder of the Blue Hose' ranking.

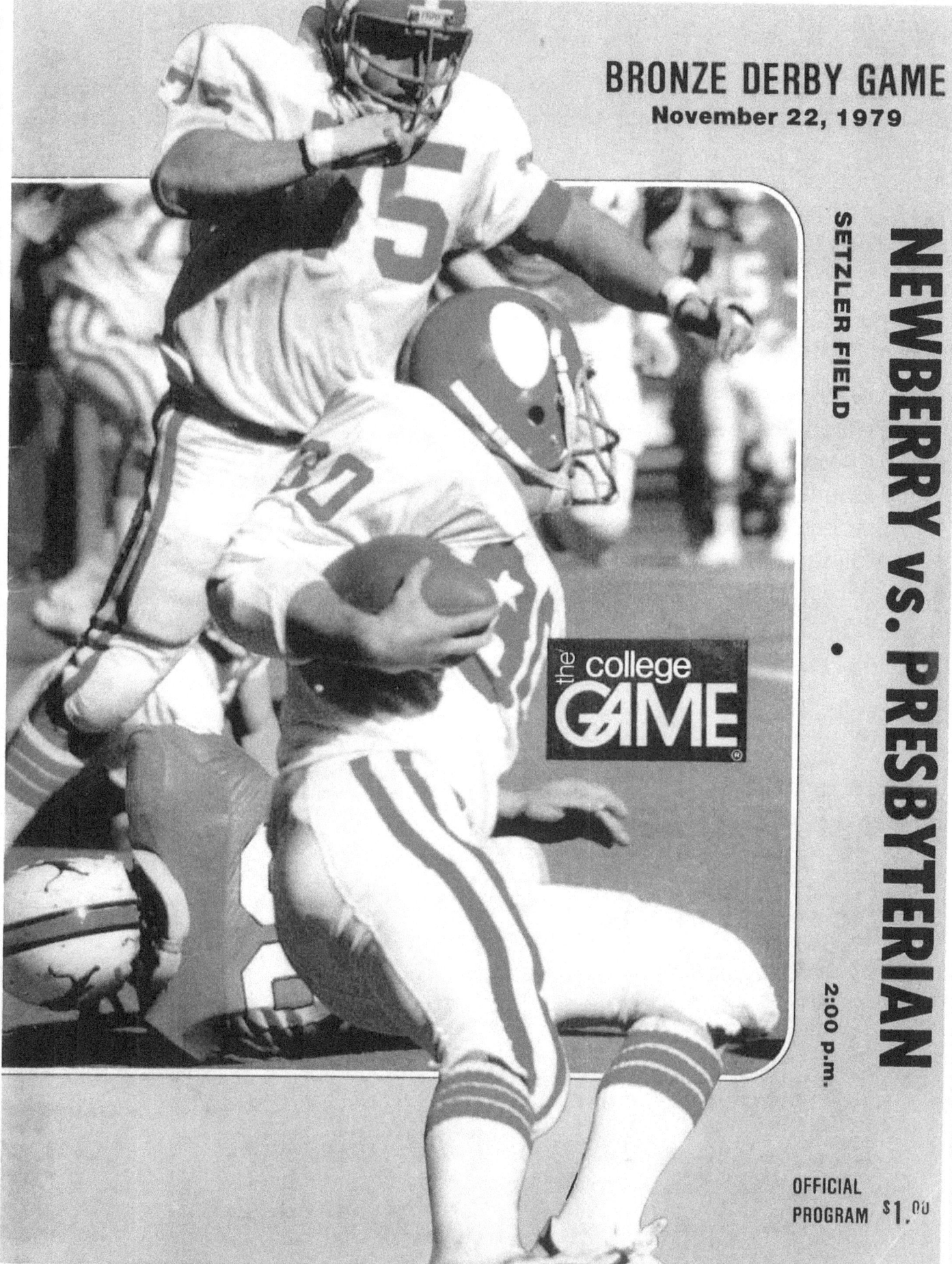

The Li'l That Was!

In 1979, Presbyterian College defeated Newberry College 16-14 on a last minute field goal by Chuck Bishop. The game was played in Newberry, South Carolina.

The Blue Stocking

Bishop Kick Lifts Hose, 16-14

The PC Blue Hose took their number one ranking and 9-1 record to Newberry on Thansgiving Day to challenge the Newberry Indians (5-4) in the annual Derby Classic. After four quarters of football, the Hose chalked up another victory as they sneaked past the Indians 16-14. PC made the most of three of six Newberry turnovers by cashing in 13 valuable points.

As usual, the Hose opened the scoring by marching 75 yards to set up a 21-yard Chuck Bishop field goal. Bishop's three pointer was his seventh of the year, breaking Sandy Cruickshank's school record of six field goals in one season. Bishop later increased his record and the score with a 22-yard field goal to give PC a 6-0 lead over the Indians. The Hose extended their lead to 13-0 when Spence scored on a two-yard run. All of PC's first three scores were set up by Newberry's turnovers.

However, Newberry, still seeking revenge for last year's 26-0 thumping from the Hose, came right back with a pair of touchdowns to take the lead. Backup quarterback Jeff Tate threw a 14-yard scoring strike to pull the Indians to within six points of PC. A battered Jimmy Spence then made his only mistake of the day as Newberry's Jimmy White intercepted Spence's pass and waltzed untouched for a 22-yard score. Newberry had the lead 14-13. All through the entire second half, the Indians had excellent field position. Their worst field position during the final half, with the exception of their last possession, was on their own 46-yard line. However, the Hoses's stubborn defense held Newberry to give PC's offense the chance it needed. Jimmy Spence, knocked out of the game twice, came back to engineer the Hose's dramatic last minute victory. Spence moved the offense 80 yards in 13 plays; but the clock was the final obstacle. Forty-seven seconds remained in the contest which now rested on the toe of kicker Chuck Bishop. The tension mounted; but Bishop's 21-yard attempt was good and the Hose were on their way to the playoffs. Bishop's three field goals gave him nine for the season, tying Tom Sexton's SAC-8 record for the most field goals in a season.

PC Completes 10-1 Season

The Li'l That Was!

Before the post-season play begins, it is only fitting to review the Hose's most successful regular season and the records that fell in the past eleven games. As the season began Coach Gault felt PC was to face its "toughest schedule ever;" the Hose seemed to disprove that fact by beating over half of their eleven opponents by more than two touchdowns. PC opened the 1979 campaign with three consecutive road games. Undaunted by the fact that they were 15 point underdogs to The Citadel opening night, the Hose outlasted the Bulldogs 21-13. Spence threw for nearly 200 yards and Burke ran for 108 yards to set the pace they would match numerous times during the season.

The Furman Paladins were the next challenge the Hose faced, but Willie Mason's 98-yard kickoff return spelled defeat for PC's second consecutive foe. The Hose defeated Lenior Rhyne, 2-0 at the time, by the score of 28-14 and moved up to sixth in the national rankings. PC fans were beginning to prepare for the SAC-8 championship; but on a rainy day the Wofford Terriers brought the Hose back to earth with a 23-21 upset of the highly favored PC team. The Wofford loss seemed to ignite the Hose as they annihilated their next five challengers, Catawba was shellacked 21-0; Elon fell 30-14; Mars Hill was creamed 34-6; Central Florida was devasted 48-0; and Gardner-Webb was dropped 21-3. The Hose then met a little stiffer competition in the "never-say-die" Carson-Newman Eagles. The Eagles got within five points of defeating the now 2nd ranked Blue Hose but the Hose defense held off Carson-Newman to give PC another victory 34-28. Following the victory over the Eagles, the Hose became the number one ranked team in the nation.

The final test PC faced was the Bronze Derby Classic versus Newberry. The comeback victory against Newberry typified the year PC had (The offense scoring the points needed and the defense coming up with the big play when needed.).

The '79 campaign saw the fall of 11 school records. 1) Jesse Cason broke his record of 46 receptions in a season by netting 48 tosses this year. 2) Chuch Bishop set new school records by kicking nine FGs in a season (ties SAC-8 record) and 36 PATS. He also set a new career record for PC fieldgoals eclipsing the old record of 10. 3) Clayto Burke set three new school records: most yards rushing in a game with over 200 yards; most yards rushing season with 1397; most yards rushing per game average with 127 yards per game (The old record was 103 yards per game.). Clayto also set two SAC-8 records, breaking the old record of 123.6 yards per game rushing average, and the record for the most net yards rusing in a season of 1360. 4) Spence broke his own record for best completion percentage by completing 62 percent of his passes (the old record was 58 percent.). The PC team set three school records: most interceptions season-28, most wins season-10, and most yards of total offense per game average-371.4. (The old records were 27,9 and 368.2 respectively.)

THE LAURENS COUNTY Advertiser

The Li'l That Was!

Playoff-bound Hose dispose of Newberry

PC's Clayto Burke carries his weight and that of about three others ...C.W. Wilson (bottom) scored the Indians opening touchdown

	Newberry	PC
First downs	14	11
Rushes-yards	37-127	55-180
Passing yards	134	75
Return yards	35	45
Passes	12-27-3	10-17-1
Punts-avg.	5-37.6	8-30.5
Fumbles-lost	5-3	2-0
Penalties-yards	10-78	3-31

By SAM REGISTER

If by chance there was someone who saw the Thanksgiving Day matchup between Presbyterian and Newberry, knowing that one of the two teams was playoff-bound but not exactly which one, it wouldn't have been an easy guess.

In fact, they would have probably chosen Newberry.

PC dominated the first quarter, but the second, third and most of the fourth quarter belonged to Newberry until Chuck Bishop's 21-yard field goal with 47 seconds remaining in the game gave the Blue Hose a 16-14 win over the Indians in the 58th Bronze Derby Classic.

Presbyterian jumped out to a 13-0 lead in the second quarter but it looked as if the team that went in the Newberry locker room at the half was not the same team that came out at the second half. It also did not help that Jimmy Spence, the SAC-Eight Player of the Year, went down late in the second quarter, reinjuring the knee that he underwent an operation on last spring for torn ligaments.

Backup quarterback Ward Gatlin filled in for Spence on the first three offensive plays of the second half, but something was definitely lacking. That something was Spence. He hobbled back in to start PC's next possession on a knee that Coach Cally Gault revealed was so heavily taped that the junior from Lexington could hardly move it.

He was unable to scramble out of the grasps of the charging defensive lineman Thursday, a Spence trademark throughout the season. He also threw an interception that went for a touchdown, something he'd never done before at PC. But with the exception of those first three plays, he was on the field throughout the second half.

"Jimmy's the kind of boy who doesn't know pain," said Gault. "He never has.

"We weren't going to play him unless the doctor gave the OK," Gault said. He told us he could play but he'd be in pain."

It was bad enough that Spence was not his usual agile self, but Clayto Burke, who went into the game having rushed for 1,307 yards this season, was having a hard time getting out of the backfield. And when he made it out of the backfield, he seldom got to the line of scrimmage. He rushed for 90 yards but it took him 34 carries. However, most of his yardage came on the Hose's final scoring drive which covered 80 yards in 13 plays and culminated with Bishop's field goal.

"Newberry was tremendous today," said Gault. "They did a tremendous job of stopping our offense. They closed Burke down and let Spence run.

"But when the chips are down—I've never seen anybody come back as well as we did. Chuck Bishop came through as he has all year."

The Indians had a little trouble on offense during the first half, sustaining three crucial penalties on their opening drive which ended at the PC 25 with a field goal that was wide to the right.

Presbyterian took over from there. A screen to Jesse Cason netted a loss of two yards and a draw play to Burke picked up one. On third and 11 Spence dropped back to pass, but finding everybody covered he scampered out of the pocket and straight up the field for a first down at the 46.

Ben Hood fumbled on the following play but Frank Kube fell on it for a three yard gain. On second and seven Spence faked a handoff to Burke and again cut upfield, rambling all the way down to the Newberry nine. But the Indian defense held and the Hose had to settle for a field goal.

The Indians used both Jeff Tate and Eddie Pettus at quarterback throughout the first half, but it was Tate who connected with C.W. Wilson in the end zone with 5:07 remaining in the first half to cut the PC lead to 13-7.

Presbyterian 3 10 0 3-16
Newberry 0 7 7 0-14

A-5,369

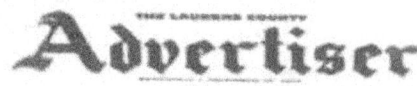

The Li'l That Was!

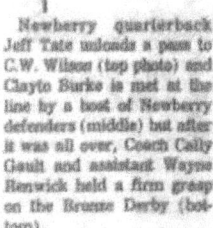

Newberry quarterback Jeff Tate unloads a pass to C.W. Wilson (top photo) and Clayto Burke is met at the line by a host of Newberry defenders (middle) but after it was all over, Coach Cally Gault and assistant Wayne Renwick held a firm grasp on the Bronze Derby (bottom).

Advertiser Sports

The Li'l That Was!

80

In the December 19, 1999 edition of *The State* newspaper located in Columbia, South Carolina, the paper recognized the 1979 Bronze Derby game as a top 100 sports moment in the state of South Carolina in the 20th Century. Presbyterian was rated the #1 team in NAIA Division 1 football heading into the game on Thanksgiving Day. Newberry College was leading 14-13 late in the 4th quarter. Presbyterian drove deep into Indian territory setting up a successful last minute 21 yard field goal by Blue Hose kicker Chuck Bishop to win the game 16-14. Chuck Bishop, the outstanding Presbyterian College place kicker, accounted for 10 points on the day. The 80th greatest moment of the 20th Century in South Carolina Sports history was a classic Bronze Derby game!

November 1980

The Li'l That Was!

November 4	Philadelphia Phillies pitcher Steve Carlton won MLB NL Cy Young Award.
November 4	Ronald Reagan was elected President of the United States defeating incumbent Jimmy Carter.
November 7	Actor Steve McQueen passed away.
November 9	Iraqi President Saddam Hussein declared holy war over Iran.
November 10	Poland acknowledged the Solidarity union.
November 12	New York City Mayor Ed Koch admitted to trying marijuana.
November 13	Gabriella Brum, 18 years old from West Germany, won the 30th Miss World. She resigned her crown the next day to marry her 52 year old boyfriend.
November 15	Pope John Paul II began a 5 day visit to West Germany.
November 15	Dale Earnhardt won the 30th NASCAR Sprint Cup.
November 17	The album "Double Fantasy" by John Lennon and Yoko Ono was released.
November 17	Country singer-songwriter Dolly Parton released "9 to 5."
November 18	Kansas City Royals George Brett won the MLB AL Most Valuable Player Award.
November 19	CBS TV banned Calvin Klein jean advertisements featuring actress Brooke Shields.
November 21	John Lennon and Yoko Ono pose nude for photographer Allan Tannenbaum.
November 21	Fire at MGM Grand Hotel in Las Vegas, Nevada killed 84.
November 21	83 million television viewers tuned into CBS as the "Dallas" episode "Who Done It" revealed who shot JR.
November 22	American actress and sex symbol Mae West passed away.
November 25	Sugar Ray Leonard regained the WBC Welterweight Boxing Championship defeating Roberto Duran.
November 26	Mike Schmidt of the Philadelphia Phillies won the MLB NL Most Valuable Player Award.
November 27	The first major role for actor Tom Hanks, "Bosom Buddies" debuted on ABC TV.
November 27	The Bronze Derby was played in Clinton, South Carolina on Thanksgiving Day. The Newberry College Indians defeated the Presbyterian College Blue Hose 28-14.

The Li'l That Was!

The Blue  Stocking

'A Century of Service to God and Man'

VOL. LXIII NO. 24   CLINTON, S.C. 29325   NOVEMBER 21, 1980

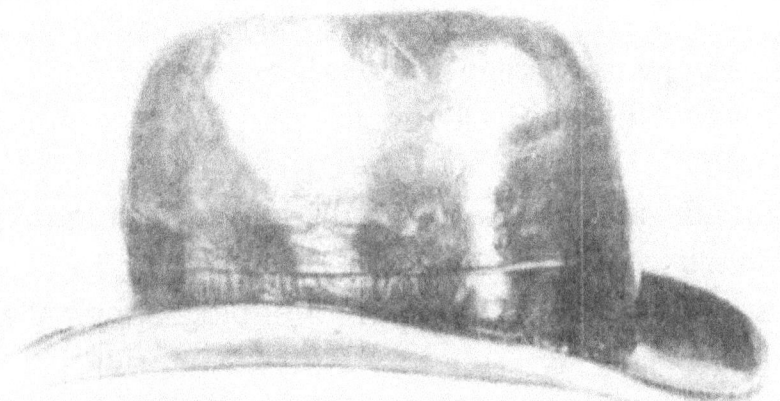

Thanksgiving Classic Continues

By Mark McCallum

On Thanksgiving Day at 2:30 p.m., when most of the campus will be at home indulging in turkey day festivities, PC's Blue Hose will be at war with their arch-conference rivals: The Newberry Indians. Although the game involves two teams that are going nowhere in post-season competition, the contest will be hard-fought as both clubs end frustrating seasons by trying to gain bragging rights in the Bronze Derby Classic. Both PC (4-6) and Newberry (3-6) are coming off losses and are looking for a rebound. The Blue Hose lead the lifetime series over the Indians, 43-21-4; PC won last year's match-up 16-14 on three Chuck Bishop field goals.

The Newberry Indians' football season mirrored the season the Blue Hose had. In numerous contests, the Indians played extremely well, only to lose. Newberry also had a rash of player injuries hinder their 1980 performance. Because of injuries to key players, the Indian offense has had to employ three different quarterbacks, most notably Eddie Pettus, and Alan Roebuck (in last week's loss to Mars Hill, Roebuck was able to move the Newberry attack from the shotgun formation). Newberry will rely heavily on fullback C.W. Wilson to guide the ground game.

Regardless of the past season, when these two teams knock heads, it is always exciting. Coach Gault, along with Newberry's Reed Charpia, will do their best to end 1980 on a winning note.

A Brief History of the Bronze Derby

By Mark McCallum

The Bronze Derby Turkey Day Classic, generally the last game played in the state and now a South Carolina tradition, is the culmination of the PC-Newberry rivalry that dates back to 1924. The Bronze Derby Trophy was first awarded in 1947 to the team from either PC or Newberry that was superior athletically; but there is more to the Bronze Derby that a trophy. It has a unique history all its own that changes with each passing year.

According to a first-hand report from Coach Gault, the legend goes somewhat as follows. During the 1946-47 basketball season, a group of PC students wore a derby hat around campus that was owned by a student's uncle. The two students most intimately involved in the tale—Lou Fowler and Jimmy Kellett—decided to wear the derby hat to the PC-Newberry basketball game at Newberry. At the game, a PC banner that raised the ire of Newberry fans was pulled down, raising the anger of the enthusiastic PC fans. The Hose won the game, but afterwards the mischief began. While leaving the game in their car, Kellett and Fowler were greeted by someone they thought they knew; however, a Newberry student reached in the car and swiped the derby off someone's head. Since tempers were already hot, the fireworks began and fights broke out in an attempt to locate the pilfered derby. The derby was later returned to PC and S.I.D. Charles McDonald suggested that it be bronzed and awarded after every PC-Newberry sports confrontation; but it was later changed and just awarded for football.

Since the inception of the award, PC has a 20-9-3 record over Newberry in football, with Newberry's last triumph coming in 1976.

The Newberry Observer
AND HERALD & NEWS
"Just Like A Letter From Home"

Newberry, S. C., Monday, Nov. 24, 1980

It's Bronze Derby Time Again Thursday

Steeped in tradition, the annual November rivalry between the Newberry Indians and the Presbyterian Blue Hose will be renewed on Thanksgiving Day in Clinton in the Bronze Derby Game at 2:30 p.m.

Both Newberry and Presbyterian will be winding up sub-par seasons, but the team records and statistics are all thrown out the window when these two neighbors get together.

The Indians, currently 3-6 on the season, will be looking to snap a three-year Presbyterian winning streak. The Tribe last collected the Derby in 1976 with a 28-15 decision but narrowly missed the coveted prize last year in a 16-14 thriller.

Presbyterian is 4-6 on the season, one that has failed to live up to pre-season expectations. The Blue Hose hold a 42-21-4 edge in the overall series.

Newberry should be about the healthiest it has been in several weeks for the contest. Wide receiver Gary Cali is expected back in the lineup after missing five games. Quarterback Eddie Pettus should get the starting nod despite suffering a broken nose against Mars Hill.

The Indians unleashed a record-setting passing attack against Mars Hill, passing 48 times in the game, and amassed 421 yars the then-second ranked Lion defense.

The Indians unleashed a record-setting passing attack against Mars Hill, passing 48 times in the game, and amassed 421 yars the then-second ranked Lion defense. Matt Deveaux, a senior wide receiver, and sophomore Bennie Mack staged an exciting exhibition as Deveaux caught eight passes for 168 yards and Mack seven for 111 yards.

Fullback C. W. Wilson leads the Indian ground attack with 495 yards rushing and a healthy 4.9 yard per carry average. Will Ottaway is back to full capacity and has 432 yards rushing and a 4.3 average. He leads the team in scoring with four touchdowns.

Newberry's defense will be lead by the nationally ranked secondary of Michael Charley, Glenn Edge, James Wyatt and Kenny Stephenson. Wyatt intercepted two passes against Mars Hill, returning one to the Lion six yard line to set up the first Indian touchdown. Wyatt and Charley each have four interceptions and Edge two out of a team total of 15.

Linebacker Mark Weeks leads the team in tackles with 42 primaries and 42 assists while tackle Darrell Croft has a total of 72 participations, defensive end Chris Miller, 67, linebacker Steve Lee 59, defensive tackle Stan Stanton 54 and assists while tackle Darrell Croft has a total of 72 participations, defensive end Chris Miller, 67, linebacker Steve Lee 59, defensive tackle Stan Stanton 54 and Wyatt 51 to lead the secondary.

The Indians have been gaining 137.6 yards per game rushing and 104.7 passing while allowing the opposition 216.6 yards rushing and only 92 passing, 15th in NAIA national stats.

However, all the statistics and team records are without meaning in this annual thriller. A victory for either team would be a fine finish to the season and a building block for 1981. The game is simply one of the best small college rivalries in the nation and always an exciting contest.

The Li'l That Was!

The Newberry Observer
AND HERALD & NEWS
"Just Like A Letter From Home"

O AND NEWS ESTABLISHED 1865   NEWBERRY OBSERVER ESTABLISH

Newberry, S. C., Wednesday, Nov. 26, 1980

Grudge Match Now In 33rd Year

RUNNER CARRIES GAME BALL: Sophomores Denise Johnson and Jerry White are simulating the beginning of a 26 mile run by White, carrying the game ball for the Newberry vs. Presbyterian football game on Thanksgiving Day. Both Johnson and White are cheerleaders for Newberry College and devised the marathon idea as a part of the Bronze Derby fever surrounding the game. White will leave Newberry's campus at approximately 11 a.m. for his run to Clinton on Thanksgiving morning.

When the Newberry College Indians travel to Clinton on Thanksgiving Day to face arch-rival Presbyterian College there will be more than a victory at stake; there will be the symbolic Bronze Derby.

Both teams will carry disappointing records to Bailey Memorial Field for a 2 p.m. contest with the Blue Hose having a 4-6 mark and Newberry fielding a 3-6 record.

The origin of the annual rivalry competition began on Jan. 30, 1947, following a basketball game between the neighboring schools. Prior to the basketball game, several Presbyterian students put a banner on the wall of Newberry's MacLean Gymnasium which read: "Beat the Hell Out of Newberry!"

During the early portion of the game a group of Newberry students found a ladder, set it up against the outside wall, climbed through a window, rolled up the banner and escaped unnoticed the same way they had entered. Near the end of the game some of the visiting Blue Hose supporters finally realized the banner had been taken.

Following a 51-47 Blue Hose victory, some of the upset Presbyterian supporters demanded the return of the banner. When Newberry fans refused to return the banner a fight began between students of both schools. During the scuffle, a Newberry student grabbed a derby from the head of a Presbyterian student and ran with it.

During the next week, officials from the two colleges negotiated for the return of the derby. It was eventually decided that the derby would serve as a symbol of victory in athletic contests between the two schools. The derby was then returned to Presbyterian College and then sent to a casting company where it was bronzed.

From 1947 to 1956 possession of the Bronze Derby was decided by victories in football, basketball, and baseball, but in 1956 the two institutions decided to award the trophy to the winner of the annual Thanksgiving Day football game.

Since then the Indians have been able to keep the Bronze Derby in Newberry only seven times — in 1956, 1957, 1962, 1965, 1971, 1973, and 1976. In the overall football series which dates back to 1913, Presbyterian holds a commanding 42-21-4 lead.

Last year the highly favored Blue Hose traveled to Newberry ranked number one in the nation by the NAIA with a 9-1 record and the SAC-8 Conference Championship under their belts. Presbyterian only needed a victory over Newberry to virtually assure themselves of a NAIA Playoff Bid.

The Blue Hose, however, found a fired up Newberry team which virtually dominated the game until a field goal in the final seconds gave Presbyterian a 16-14 come-from-behind victory.

This year's match is rated as a toss-up and as past history indicates, anything can and probably will happen on Thanksgiving Day when these two schools battle for the coveted Bronze Derby which will be watched by an estimated 7,000 plus sell-out crowd. This will be small college football at its best!

PC falls 28-20

Newberry reclaims Bronze Derby

By ELLEN ROBINSON

Newberry ended a three-year Presbyterian winning streak Thursday as the Indians defeated the Blue Hose 28-20 in the 59th annual Bronze Derby Classic at Johnson Field.

Exploding for two touchdowns in less than five minutes, Newberry first capitalized on a PC fumble recovery by Kenny Stephenson on the Blue Hose 31-yard line late in the first quarter. Quarterback Eddie Pettus capped the seven-play drive as he charged up the middle from the one to score. Jimmy Spencer's extra point gave Newberry a 7-0 edge with 12:58 remaining in the half.

THE INDIANS drew blood again about two minutes later after forcing Presbyterian to punt in four easy plays. Freshman Mike Motley took the kick at the Newberry 28 and scampered 72 yards for the second tally. Spencer booted the pigskin through the uprights to increase the lead 14-0.

Unable to make any major moves with their next possession, Presbyterian was again forced to punt. Newberry took the ball in as close as PC's 43, only to miss a field goal wide to the left.

PC, determined not to end the half without points on the board, next took advantage of a pass interference call and a screen pass-play to move the ball downfield 75 yards into the end zone. After moving out to the 36 yard-line with the penalty call, Blue Hose quarterback Jimmy Spence hit Willie Mason with a short pass. Mason, aided by some key blocking, converted the short pass into a 64-yard touchdown, with Chuck Bishop adding the extra point at the 5:04 mark.

BUT THE BLUE Hose rallied again before the half ended, as Heyward Hinton thwarted an Indian scoring drive with a pass interception at the Presbyterian 10. Unfortunately the clock ran out before the Hose could capitalize on their good fortune, and Newberry retired to the locker room on top 14-7.

After battling out half of the third quarter with neither team scoring, Newberry once again grabbed the upper hand as Chris Miller fell on a missed pitchout intended for PC's Mason on the Newberry 23. Needing only five plays to drive the ball 77 yards into the end zone, Pettus scrambled 31 yards to increase the Indian lead by six. Spencer's kick at the 8:49 mark gave Newberry a 21-7 advantage.

AT THAT POINT, two separate PC turnovers had set up two of Newberry's three touchdowns.

"Our execution has hurt us all year," said PC coach Cally Gault. "We were moving the ball well. Our running back was just looking at the seam instead of the football and instead of us going in and tying the game, Newberry got the ball and went up 21-7.

"I can't fault this team's desire, attitude or effort. We've just had problems executing and that has to be blamed on the coaching," he said.

THE GAME, however, didn't end there. Presbyterian bounced back within the following three minutes to drive the ball

> 'I can't fault this team's desire, attitude or effort. We've just had problems executing and that has to be blamed on coaching.' —PC coach Cally Gault

COOL CROWD—Braving cold, wet weather to attend the annual Bronze Derby Classic, these Presbyterian fans seem to have found a way to beat the damp in Carolina style.

The Li'l That Was!

Advertiser

> 'This ballgame gives us new life. It's great. It's been a long time coming.' —Newberry's Reed Charpia

80 yards in eight plays and cut Newberry's lead by a touchdown. Play number seven of the series featured a 22-yard completed pass from Spence to tight end Steve McCall. Freshman Lance Sanders capped the drive as he scored on a 36-yard run to the left. Bishop made his third extra point of the afternoon for a 21-14 tally.

A fourth quarter penalty for roughing the kicker against PC set up the final Newberry touchdown with 9:22 remaining to play. Electing to go for six instead of keeping the three points scored with a successful field goal, Newberry's Will Ottaway ran the ball in from the one yard line, ending a 63-yard, nine play drive. Spencer's kick was good.

DOWN BY TWO but still in the ballgame, Blue Hose reserve quarterback Paul Scott hit Randy Morris with a 21-yard touchdown pass to put Presbyterian within striking range of victory. Marching downfield 92 yards in ten plays, Presbyterian ended the afternoon with a 28-20 final after Bishop's kick failed at the :39 mark.

Presbyterian attempted a couple of unsuccessful onsides kicks, each one failing to go the full ten yards, costing the Blue Hose field position—including the last play of the game. Newberry fell on the ball, allowing the final seconds of the game to tick off the clock unnoticed.

NEWBERRY COACH Reed Charpia had more than the day's victory to celebrate because Thursday was the first time Newberry had beaten Presbyterian under his five-year leadership.

"It's great," he said of his team's 28-20 triumph, "and it's been a long time coming. I didn't want to get into a scoring battle, since PC definitely had the upper hand with Jimmy Spence. But I just can't say enough about Eddie Pettus.

"They all played super," he said. "We have been playing sort of sporadically since about the second game or so but they put it all together today. There was a real difference in the defense."

Charpia cited Motley's 72-yard punt return as the turnaround that gave the Indians a boost in spirit.

"I thought we got the momentum going our way with the long punt return," he said. "It really gave us something we needed, just as any big play will tend to swing things your way in a situation like that.

"BUT THEN THEY got the interception. The ball was perfectly thrown; it just bounced off our receiver and into their guy's hands. Then, PC started the second half with a long drive and it looked like things were swinging their way."

"This ballgame and the win here gives us new life," said Charpia. "A lot of our young people place a lot of emphasis on this win. It'll sure pull us through the off season."

ON THE OTHER HAND, Presbyterian only had three starters from last year playing against Newberry: Spence, Frank Kube and Walt Atkins. In short, the Blue Hose have been plagued by injuries this season.

"It's hard to be cohesive on offense when you've had to use as many people as we've had to this year," said Gault. "But I can't use that as an excuse. We beat ourselves in the first half and a very fine, well coached Newberry team beat us in the second half.

"We had a lot of punts not returned. Newberry just flat outdid us in punt returns and that's it. They made several third down conversions; we did not. They took advantage of their big breaks; we did not.

"And just as any Presbyterian—Newberry game, both teams started out like they were going to be penalized out of the ballpark, which is typical of this ballgame. Newberry was ready for us and they played a good game," he said. "What more can I say?"

STATISTICALLY, PC had 18 first downs to Newberry's 14 and 149 yards rushing in 38 attempts to 236 in 51. The big difference in the two teams, however, were stacked up in the passing and punt return yardages. The Blue Hose massed 206 yards through the air, completing 14 of 29 with one interception; Newberry had 38, completing 9 of 15 with one interception. Newberry took top honors in return yardage, running the ball back for 106 yards to PC's 13.

Both teams closed out the season with losing records, PC with 4-7 and Newberry at 4-6. Newberry, however, earned the right to keep the coveted bronze derby until the next PC football win or next Thanksgiving ...whichever comes first.

> 'We beat ourselves in the first half and a very fine, well coached Newberry team beat us in the second half. Newberry was ready for us and they played a good game. What more can I say?'

DERBIED CHEERS—Blue Hose cheerleaders got into the spirit of the day as they donned their own version of the bronze derby.

The Li'l That Was!

Advertiser

TOUCHDOWN?—Newberry teammates C.W. Wilson (33) and quarterback Eddie Pettus (14) engage in an endzone conference after scoring the third Indian touchdown on a 31-yard run. Although Wilson led the Indian rushing attack with 107 yards in eight attempts, Pettus accounted for two of Newberry's four touchdowns, scoring on two quarterback keeper plays.

POSSESSION REGAINED—Former Clinton Red Devil C.W. Wilson proudly displays the coveted bronze derby reclaimed by Newberry after a three-year Presbyterian winning streak.

LOOKING UP—PC ballboy Dean Long chats with senior Blue Hose quarterback Jimmy Spence on the sidelines.

The Li'l That Was!

The Newberry Observer
AND HERALD & NEWS
"Just Like A Letter From Home"
Newberry, S.C., Monday, Dec. 1, 1986

D AND NEWS ESTABLISHED 1865   NEWBERRY OBSERVER ESTABLISH

Bronze Derby Returns To Newberry As Tribe Drops Presbyterian 28-20

PURSUIT: C. W. Wilson (33) picks up some valuable age while chased by a host of Blue Hose defenders. The Tribe went on to return the coveted Bronze Derby to Newberry with a 28-20 win over PC.

TOUCHDOWN: Newberry's Will Ottaway (32) came up with a touchdown despite the efforts of Blue Hose defender Joe Mooneyhan (33) during the Tribe's 28-20 Thanksgiving Day win over Presbyterian.

The Bronze Derby is back! For the first time in four years, the Newberry Indians are again owners of the coveted hat symbolic of the victorious team in the annual Newberry-Presbyterian football game. Possession was gained by virtue of a 28-20 victory over the Blue Hose on Thanksgiving Day.

Indian coach Reed Charpia made no bones about it, "It is great to get the Derby back to Newberry, it's been four years. This is my first one and I guess the first is always the best."

Charpia's elation over the accomplishment of his team on Thanksgiving was outdone only by the elation of the team itself over the hard-earned victory. But it was earned and earned with a domination on both the offensive and defensive lines as well as by the big play.

Game observers were amazed by the total domination of the line of scrimmage by the Indians and the efforts were not unnoticed by Charpia. "Our offensive line controlled their defense. We were not sure we could do that going into the game but our kids did a super job for us," Charpia said. "The same thing goes for our defensive line. With the play we got from our linemen, we were able to do the things we wanted to do and call the plays we wanted to call." It made all the difference in the world.

Blue Hose mentor Cally Gault said, "We don't have any excuses. You've got to give Newberry a lot of credit. I felt (Eddie) Pettus had a good game for them and moved the team well. They made their third down plays and we did not; they took advantage of their breaks, we did not."

Newberry moved into the lead in convincing fashion as they took their third possession to paydirt following a key fumble recovery by Kenny Stephenson at the PC 31. Aided by a personal foul on the hosts, Eddie Pettus directed the attack and ended up carrying the ball on five of the eight plays of the scoring march. He went over from the one on a fourth down play to make it 6-0 and Jimmy Spencer's conversion pushed it to 7-0 with 12:58 remaining in the half.

The second Indian score came in much easier fashion as the defense forced PC to punt and Mike Molley scampered on a picture-perfect 72 yard return, aided by an excellent block by Chris Miller. Spencer's conversion made it 14-0 with 11:13 on the clock.

Presbyterian kept it close as quarterback Jimmy Spencer connected with Willie Mason on a 64-yard completion and the touchdown with 5:40 left to round out the first half scoring.

The teams traded second half scores with Pettus scoring on a 31-yard ramble and Will Ottaway bulling over from the one for Newberry while Lance Sanders raced 36 yards and Randy Morris caught a 21-yard pass from Paul Scott for the two Presbyterian tallies.

C. W. Wilson was the leading rusher in the contest with 107 yards in just eight carries. Pettus added 56 and Ottaway 36 as the Indians amassed 236 yards on the soggy turf.

Spence was the main Blue Hose weapon as he hit nine of 15 passes for 182 yards before being forced to the sidelines via injury in the second half. But Spence and Company were hassled all day by the Indian defense.

Miller, Mark Weeks, Darrell Craft, Steve Lee and Glenn Edge were the most visible but the entire unit was exceptional in keeping the hosts at bay. Weeks led the unit with 11 tackles while Lee had nine and Craft eight, including two sacks.

It was a happy end to a less-than-happy season for the Indians, who conclude 1980 with a 4-6 record. The bright spot is that just about all of the team returns next season with very few graduation losses. Presbyterian finished with a 4-7 mark.

374

The Blue Stocking

'A Century of Service to God and Man'

Indians Scalp Hose

By Mark R. McCallum

The Newberry Indians put the finishing touches on a disappointing Blue Hose football season by reclaiming the Bronze Derby Trophy with a 28-20 victory. Although PC's 350 yards of total offense overshadowed Newberry's 274 yards, the Indians got the yards when they counted most.

Newberry made the most of the Thanksgiving Day afternoon, jumping off to a lead they never surrendered. After a scoreless first quarter, the Indians drew first blood as QB Eddie Pettus pushed the ball across from one yard out to give Newberry a 7-0 bulge. A few minutes later, they increased their advantage to 14-0 as Mike Motley returned a punt 72 yards for the score. PC finally got on the board with a beautiful screen pass play. QB Jimmy Spence, who completed 9 of 15 attempts for 152 yards, hit Willie Mason with a short screen pass and Mason, with the aid of some fine blocking, converted it into a 64-yard scoring scamper to cut Newberry's lead in half, 14-7. The Indians regained their two-touchdown advantage when Eddie Pettus ran 31 yards for the score. PC retaliated on Lance Sanders' 36 yard burst up the middle to make the score 21-14. However, Will Ottaway scored the final Newberry TD on a one-yard play to give them a 28-14 score. With the 5'10" Paul Scott at the helm late in the game, he hit the 5'8½" Randy Morris, who brought down three passes for 59 yards, for a 21-yard TD strike as "The Midget Connection" finished out the scoring 28-20. In the game, Steve McCall had 2 receptions for 29 yards and Willie Mason had 4 catches for 72 yards; Lance Sanders rushed for 55 yards on 7 carries (a 7.8 yard average).

Note: In the Hound's Tooth sponsored Offense-Defense scrimmage, the offense took the victory with a late rally; however, conflicting reports claim that the defense won handily.

The Li'l That Was!

In 1980, Newberry College defeated Presbyterian College 28-14. The game was played in Clinton, South Carolina. The game was the 34th Thanksgiving Day Bronze Derby football Classic.

Willie Mason finds the "going" gets tough against the Indians of Newberry.

Scott Hosch makes solo tackle in the "Derby."

The Li'l 🎩 That Was!

The Indian
Voice of the Newberry College Student — December 11, 1980

Indians Defeat PC; Claim Bronze Derby

By Rodger Watson

The Newberry Indians' football team defeated the Presbyterian Blue Hose 28-20 on Thanksgiving Day in the annual Bronze Derby Classic. The Classic victory was Newberry's first since its 26-15 win in 1976. The 1980 game was played at the Bailey Memorial Stadium in Clinton, S.C.

"The PC game has been played since 1957. The basic reason for moving it to Thanksgiving Day was to accommodate for the Clemson-USC game, its rescheduling has enabled more people to attend both games (Clemson-USC and PC-NC)," according to Coach Charpia.

QB Eddie Pettus' one-yard touchdown dive completed an 8-play, 31-yard drive at 12:58 in the second quarter. Shortly afterwards, the Indians' defense forced Presbyterian to punt. A tremendous block by DE Chris Miller paved the way for a spectacular 72-yard punt return touchdown by Mike Motley. Jimmy Spencer added the extra point and Newberry led 14-0 with 11:12 left in the second period. Two possessions later the Blue Hose gave the home fans something to be jubilant about by way of a 64-yard touchdown pass from QB Spence to RB Mason at 5:40 in the second. The two-play, 75-yard drive halted all the first half scoring as Newberry lead 14-7.

During the Indians' first possession of the second half, FB C.W. Wilson's 40-yard scamper penetrated the Blue Hose territory. Two plays later QB Pettus ran 31 yards for a touchdown with 8:49 left in the third. Spencer's extra point capped the 5-play, 77-yard drive as Newberry lws 21-7. But PC refused to falter. Following Newberry's score the Blue Hose's RB Sanders trotted 36 yards to complete an impressive 8-play, 80-yard touchdown drive at 5:41 in the third. The extra point by Bishop cut the deficit 21-14 Newberry.

TOUCHDOWN!

Runs of 30 and 17 yards by FB Wilson and RB Harward, respectively, moved the Indians into Presbyterian territory early in the fourth period. Newberry discarded a 27-yard field goal by Sonny Hardman in favor of roughing the kicker penalty against PC. tB Will Ottaway came through on a fourth-and-goal play to perfect a 9-play, 63-yard drive with 9:22 left in the contest. Spencer's kick made it 28-14 Newberry. Sacks by DT Darrell Croft and DE Miller stalled the Blue Hose's offense as the Indians' rushers, led by Wilson's eight carried for 107 yards, grinded away yards and time. PC finished the scoring by executing an 8-play, 80-yard drive with :39 remaining in the game. A twenty-one yard passing play by QB Scott to WR Morris did the honors.

Although Presbyterian leads the series 22-43-4, Newberry has the coveted Bronze Derby and bragging rights — for now!

Go to the NC-PC game; support the rivalry for the Bronze Derby

NEWBERRY
vs.
P. C.

November 1981

November 1	First Class United States mail stamps increased from 18 cents to 20 cents.
November 2	American NFL football receiver Roddy White was born.
November 3	Milwaukee Brewers relief pitcher Rollie Fingers won the MLB AL Cy Young Award.
November 4	Columbia shuttle launch scrubbed with 31 seconds remaining.
November 5	Former NFL Miami Dolphin running back Mercury Morris was sentenced to 20 years for drug trafficking, conspiracy and cocaine possession.
November 6	Boxer Larry Holmes retained the heavyweight boxing title with a TKO over Renaldo Snipes.
November 11	Los Angeles Dodgers pitcher Fernando Valenzuela became the first MLB rookie to win a Cy Young Award.
November 12	Actor William Holden passed away.
November 12	A's Billy Martin was named AL Manager of the Year.
November 12	The first balloon crossing of the Pacific Ocean was completed by the Double Eagle V.
November 13	Ringo Starr released the single "Wrack My Brain" written and produced by George Harrison.
November 16	16 million daytime viewers watched Luke marry Laura on the US television soap "General Hospital."
November 16	United States President Ronald Reagan approved a covert plan to block Cuban aid to Nicaragua and El Salvador.
November 18	Mike Schmidt of the Philadelphia Phillies won the MLB NL Most Valuable Player Award.
November 19	US Steel bought Marathon Oil for $6.3 billion.
November 21	Olivia Newton John's "Physical" reached #1 on the *Billboard* music charts.
November 22	Darrell Waltrip won the 31st NASCAR Sprint Cup.
November 25	Rollie Fingers was the first relief pitcher to win the MLB AL Most Valuable Player Award.
November 26	Jazz musician Miles Davis married actress Cicely Tyson.
November 26	The Bronze Derby was played in Newberry, South Carolina on Thanksgiving Day. The Newberry College Indians defeated the Presbyterian College Blue Hose 26-23.

Gault and Charpia guests at final TD Club meeting

By STEVE SURLES

The annual Bronze Derby game — the Thanksgiving Day matchup between Presbyterian College and Newberry — was the subject of the final Laurens County Touchdown Club meeting Friday at Lakeside Country Club.

The two guest speakers were two of the main characters in the game, scheduled for 2:30 p.m. Nov. 26 at Setzler Field in Newberry.

Reed Charpia and Cally Gault, the Newberry and PC head coaches (respectively) both talked about college football and the Bronze Derby. At times, their comments were similar, but they enter the 70th meeting between the teams under radically different circumstances.

Charpia's Indians are only 3-7 on the season and are fighting to stay out of the South Atlantic Conference cellar.

GAULT'S Blue Hose are playing to sew up a share of the SAC-8 conference title. They are 5-1 and 6-4 overall.

Charpia will also be coaching his last game for Newberry. The school has announced his coaching contract will not be renewed next year.

Despite that, Charpia looks forward to the game.

"The Bronze Derby is one of college football's great rivalry games and it's one of the few games left like that still played on Thanksgiving," noted Charpia, who has compiled a 20-20 record in his four seasons at Newberry.

"It's the kind of game where anything can happen. I think last year we weren't as good as PC (Newberry won 28-20) and maybe this year the same is true, but you never know how this game will go," Charpia added.

THE FACT that it will be his last game as the Newberry coach is another unknown in the game.

"How my situation will affect Newberry is hard to tell. It may help the team. We may have some who want to win the last one for me or we may have some who don't care, but I think it'll be a good game," Charpia said.

Charpia cited several other factors which make the game and the rivalry special. He noted a similarity between the two schools and said he has a tremendous respect for the PC staff and players.

"We are so close together in many ways. We sort of have to band together with our situation. We are the only two South Carolina schools in the SAC-8 and we go through the same thing playing those North Carolina schools. We always feel cheated — we never get a S.C. official in those games," Charpia said.

"I'll say one thing, though. In my stay at Newberry, I have nothing but the most respect for the PC players, staff and school. They have some excellent players, the defense has played great all year and they've worked hard."

CHARPIA said the credit for PC's success this season is in its players and staff, a group that "put them where they are all season."

Charpia pointed out his team is not finished playing yet. Injuries, bad luck and inconsistent play have all haunted the Indians this season.

"Through the ups and downs our players have worked hard and been in nearly every game. I can't fault the players for their work this season."

Gault, who is going into his 19th Bronze Derby, spent a great deal of his time talking about football in general. He emphasized the idea that people — players, fans, coaches and everyone — shouldn't desecrate the ideals football stands for and, on a larger scale, we shouldn't desecrate the things

RIVALS AT THE TOUCHDOWN CLUB — Newberry's Reed Charpia and PC's Cally Gault were the guest speakers at the Laurens County Touchdown Club Friday. The two will meet again Thanksgiving Day in the annual Bronze Derby Classic.

the American principles stand for.

"I felt like this PC team had a destiny, but I asked one thing of them early. Don't desecrate PC football. I wanted them to be sincere, to realize football is a privilege to play," said Gault. "And we should realize how lucky we are we can live in a land with these freedoms — the freedom to be for PC or Newberry, Clemson or Carolina.

"WE ARE fortunate to have a PC-Newberry game and I hope people will not desecrate it by not being sincere," Gault added. "I'm proud of this friendly rivalry — maybe this year, with the way things are, some of the fun is out of it — but we look forward to the game. We hope we run them all over the field, but we know Newberry is tough — just like their coach."

A win by the Blue Hose would give PC at least a tie in the SAC-8 championship race with Elon.

The Touchdown Club also announced its Board of Directors and president-elect for the next year. President-elect will be Charles Wilson. Barry Whitman was named 1983 president-elect.

The Board of Directors for the coming year will be King Dixon II, Dr. Carl Wessinger and Jim Ferguson.

The Li'l That Was!

The Laurens County Advertiser

November 23, 1981

PC vets ready for Derby

By STEVE SURLES

The Presbyterian College Blue Hose football team have an unusual weekend off from competition this Saturday as they prepare for the annual Bronze Derby game with Newberry Thanksgiving Day (Nov. 26).

That change in routine gave a couple of important PC teammates two of the senior tri-captains, Steve Stalvey and Larry Owens, a chance to reflect on the 1981 season after 10 games.

The season merits consideration. Currently tied with Elon for the league championship with a 5-1 record, the Blue Hose could assure themselves of at least a tie for the title with a win over Newberry.

An Elon defeat to Carson-Newman Saturday coupled with a PC win Thursday would give the 'Hose the title outright.

"I FEEL like Newberry will always play their best game against us and that means we'll have a game to play," said Stalvey, an All District linebacker in 1980 and a native of Waycross, Ga.

Stalvey believes the 'Hose can prevail. That game is on his mind right now as is the fact that his college playing career is ending.

"I kind of have mixed emotions about it. You think how long the season is, the bumps and bruises, but then you think about playing," he said. "Newberry is so much on my mind that I think I'll have more time to miss it when the season is over."

Owens, the 213-pound offensive guard from Greenville (Carolina High) and an All SAC-8 and District selection, sounded even more sentimental about the approaching end of his playing days at PC.

"I think for me it gets sadder and sadder every week. I've been playing football since I was in the fourth grade and it's a part of me. I know I'll miss it a bunch. I guess I'd give anything if I had another year to play. Especially on this team," Owens said.

BOTH AGREE that one reason the 'Hose have had a good season with a relatively young team and a great deal of injuries has been an overall team attitude that won't allow for defeat.

"That '79 team (the year PC went to the NAIA semi-finals) was a banner year. We had raw talent. But this team has the best attitude of any team since I've been here," remarked Owens. "The seniors got together early on and decided to lead the team together. We knew we didn't have the raw talent we'd had, but we knew if we didn't have the right attitude we'd never win."

"The guys pull together," added Stalvey. "We have always seemed to pull together this season and the team morale has been great all year. It's been no trouble. It's been a big factor."

That ability to get everyone in the same world is largely a credit to senior leadership. Owens said that so many underclassmen play a big role and respect is a key.

"Little things mean so much. Especially to us linemen. Guys like Melvin (Bell), Curtis (Burton) and Lance (Sanders), they'll come back after a nice run and thank us linemen for a block. That is a little thing but they add up and everyone remembers it. It makes everyone play better."

STALVEY, who is married and planning on entering the service as a second lieutenant when he graduates, emphasizes the respect he has for the teammates and program.

"As seniors we've tried to lead the team in the ways we should. After coming off a bad year we needed some leaders and everyone has done the job," said Stalvey.

"Right now," added Owens, "we have a lot to get accomplished. We felt like Newberry worked on us last year and we want the chance to play them. It's a privilege to play for the title. We seniors all want to go out a winner. That's important to us."

The Newberry Observer
AND HERALD & NEWS
"Just Like A Letter From Home"

Newberry, S.C., Monday, Nov. 23, 1981

The Li'l That Was!

It's Derby Time Again

Thanksgiving Day normally means turkey and family dinners to most folks, except the fans of Newberry and Presbyterian colleges. To those people it's Bronze Derby Game Day, the annual football contest between the two neighbor rivals in the South Atlantic Conference.

Since 1913 the two schools have each year, with a few minor exceptions, and the game has become THE football contest in the state of South Carolina.

The story of the bronze derby, and there really is one, dates back to the 1946-47 basketball season when, as a result of some sign snitching, one Presbyterian student lost his derby in a scuffle after a heated basketball game. The two college's athletic publicity directors then got together and decided to make the pilfered derby the symbol of athletic supremacy and started a campaign to have the hat returned, bronzed, and awarded to the winner of each athletic confrontation between the two schools.

In recent years the derby has been awarded only to the winner of the annual Thanksgiving Day football game.

Of course all the normal cliches apply to the annual football classic...you can throw out all the records... this game is so intense that it doesn't matter how many games a team has won or lost. They are all true and the history of the derby game proves it out.

Presbyterian enters this year's game as the favorite with a 6-4-0 record and a 5-1 mark in the SAC-8. Newberry owns a disappointing 3-7 mark, 1-5 in the SAC-8.

While Presbyterian holds the edge in team defense, the Indians own the upper hand in offensive production. The Tribe is gaining 337.7 yards per game, fourth in the conference, and is ranked second in passing offense, 164.9 yards per game.

Presbyterian is third in team defense, allowing 265.8 yards per game while the offense is fifth at 315.9 yards per game.

Newberry is led by a pair of senior quarterbacks in Eddie Pettus and Alan Roebuck. Both are ranked in total offense and passing charts. Pettus is averaging 124 yards per game in total offense and passing for 96.3 yards per game while Roebuck is credited with 106.9 yards per game total offense and 96.8 yards per game passing.

The leading Indian rusher is junior tailback Will Ottaway who has now gained 409 yards in nine contests and caught 24 passes for 167 yards. Pettus ranks just behind Ottaway with 377 yards rushing while freshman fullback Richard Brisbon has 300 yards in just 40 carries for a 7.5 yard per carry average and three touchdowns.

Chapin product Gary Cali has caught 21 passes for 381 yards this season, the top yardage production, while split end Matt Deveaux has 26 catches for 354 yards and two touchdowns. Donald Johnson has also seen a lot of action as his seven receptions have gone for 152 yards (21.7 yards per catch) and three touchdowns.

Tailback Curtis Burton is leading the Presbyterian attack with 826 yards in 184 carries. The sophomore runner galloped for 175 yards in 35 carries in the upset of Carson-Newman last weekend. Quarterback David Waldkirch has connected on 59 of 115 attempts for 826 yards and three touchdowns this year in directing the Blue Hose attack.

Top Blue Hose receivers are split end Randy Morris, 24 receptions for 333 yards, and flanker Ronnie Hollier, 18 for 323 yards.

Overall the contest could well boil down to the team that plays the best defense. Linebackers Steve Stalvey and David Neisler lead the Blue Hose tackle charts with 101 and 80 participations respectively while cornerback Charles Ruff has six interceptions and Joe Mooneyham has four.

Indian linebacker Mark Weeks leads the Tribe's defensive charts while linebacker Arthur Atchley, tackles Stan Stanton and Darrell Croft, end Preston Threatt and safety Tim Mings have been the mainstays of the unit. Recently inserted Kevin White has come up with three interceptions within the past three games since he moved into a major role in the young Indian secondary.

Despite the dampening of the overall tone of the game this year with the premature announcement from Indian country that head coach Reed Charpia's contract would not be renewed, the two teams should still provide more of the expected, good, tough small college football come game time this Thursday at 2:30 p.m. at Newberry's Setzler Field.

The Li'l That Was!

The Newberry Observer
AND HERALD & NEWS
"Just Like A Letter From Home"

HERALD & NEWS ESTABLISHED 1865 — THE NEWBERRY OBSERVER ESTABLISHED

Newberry, S.C., Friday, Nov. 27, 1981

Tribe Keeps Bronze Derby

(Special To The Observer)

The Bronze Derby remains at Newberry College thanks to a fake field goal play that saw punter Larry Harrington race 23 yards for the winning touchdown Thursday afternoon as the Newberry Indians captured a 26-23 victory over the Presbyterian Blue Hose at Setzler Field.

As much controversy as has been stirred up prior to the game with the announcement that Indian coach Reed Charpia would not be re-hired at the end of his current contract, the controversy on the field more than matched that action. The Indians utilized a number of unusual plays to set up their win while Presbyterian mentor Cally Gault may not have calmed down yet over a key roughing the punter call in the waning moments of the game.

The Indians came up with the big play, both on offense and defense, when they needed it. Late in the third quarter it appeared that Presbyterian had finally solved the Indian defense and was on their way to a share of the South Atlantic Conference crown, but the Indians had a few final words to say about that issue. PC had come back from a 20-12 halftime deficit to assume a 23-20 lead late in the third quarter when the Indians went to work.

Barry Brown took the kickoff and set the Tribe up in business at the Newberry 25. The Indians moved out to their own 40 with a first down, but the next three plays netted only three yards, bringing up a fourth-and-seven early in the final stanza. Harrington dropped back into punt formation and lofted a short spiral, but was knocked to the ground by a Presbyterian defender. Out came the official's flag for a 15-yard penalty and the certainty in the official's mind was matched only by the wrath of Gault over the call.

Gault became incensed over the penalty, contending that the PC defender had been blocked into Harrington (which is not a penalty), but the decision stood. Gault did not, it

(See DERBY, Page 8)

Season Topper

It's ours again, Newberry players and fans yelled as the Newberry Indians won the Bronze Derby by defeating the Presbyterian Blue Hose 26-23 in an emotional battle in Setzler Field. The Bronze Derby has been "prize" for winning the Thanksgiving Day game since 1947. Thursday's victory was the first time since the 1940's that the Indians had won the coveted prize for two consecutive years. They won it in 1980, 26-23.

The Newberry Observer
AND HERALD & NEWS
"Just Like A Letter From Home"

Newberry, S.C., Friday, Nov. 27, 1981

became necessary for one Blue Hose player to restrain his head coach and the Hose ended up with another 15-yard penalty, putting Newberry on the PC 27 with a first down.

Two successive rushes, one by Will Ottaway and the other by Richard Brisbon, had the Tribe on the Hose 23, but Eddie Pettus' pass to Gary Cali failed to connect and brought up a fourth-and-six situation.

Harrington, also the holder on placements and field goals, knelt at his 30 yard line as Mickey Crocker lined up a 40-yard attempt, but as soon as the ball was snapped Harrington was on his feet and raced down the left sideline for the 23-yard touchdown jaunt. A two-point conversion attempt failed, but the Indians were on top to stay, 26-23.

The entire afternoon was the essence of college football for the 3,900 fans and statewide media. Besides the perfect weather, the football was as exciting as one could hope for at any game.

Newberry opened the afternoon with another unusual play from Charpia's bag of tricks. On their first possession of the afternoon the Indians went in for seven as Pettus lofted a 40-yard flea-flicker pass to Cali just one minute and 25 seconds after the kickoff to put the Indians on the board. Jimmy Spencer's conversion made it 7-0.

Presbyterian left no doubt that they were seeking the share of the SAC-8 title as they marched right back to score on their initial possession of the game. David Waldkirch connected with Ronnie Hollier on a 34-yard scoring pass that saw Hollier time his jump for the spiral one second better than Indian defender Kevin White. However, the conversion by John Ransom was wide and the Indians still led 7-6.

A pass interception by Joe Mooneyham got the Hose back in business at the Indian 27. The combination of Curtis Burton, Melvin Bell and Waldkirch moved the Hose into the endzone with 3:55 remaining in the first quarter with Bell vaulting over from the one. The two-point conversion failed, giving PC a 12-7 edge.

Then it was Newberry's turn. Jimmy Edwards fumbled a Harrington punt and Chris Pair covered for the Tribe at the PC 32. Brisbon and Ottaway pounded away at the Hose defense and Brisbon broke off-tackle for nine yards and the touchdown with 14:57 left in the half. Spencer again converted to make it 14-12 for Newberry.

Newberry converted a blocked field goal attempt for their next score as Ransom tried a 51-yard effort that was partially blocked. Newberry took over at their own 34 and Ottaway broke loose three plays later for a 43-yard gain to the PC 16. Five plays later Ottaway went over the top for the third Indian touchdown, but this time it was the Tribe's turn to miss the PAT leaving the score 20-12 with just 1:47 remaining in the half.

A pass interception by Tim Minges at his own 35 ended any PC threat in the first half.

Presbyterian roared back with their first possession of the second half and marched to paydirt with Ransom kicking a 31-yard field goal with 9:35 left in the third quarter. The clubs then traded interceptions with Frank Toney snaring one for the Indians and Ricky Kirkpatrick for the Hose returned to the Indian 32 after a 34-yard return. Burton shook loose on a 25-yard scamper to the Indian three and Lance Sanders took it over on the next play to give the Hose the lead. Waldkirch ran for the two-point conversion that made it 23-20 with 2:01 left in the third panel. Then the Indians went to work.

Newberry missed one late scoring opportunity when Alan Roebuck's pass was intercepted by Charles Huff at the goal line, but Kevin White returned the favor two plays later at the Hose 48. Newberry then ran the clock down to just six seconds before turning the ball over on downs and a final PC desperation pass fell incomplete and the Indians owned the day.

While the victory was sweet for Charpia and the Indians after a less than satisfactory season, it was a bitter pill for the Hose to swallow. Presbyterian finished the season with a 6-5 record, 5-2 in the SAC-8 and one game behind Elon College. Newberry's upset gave the Tribe a 4-7 mark, 2-5 in the SAC-8.

The Indians out-gained Presbyterian 365-258 in total offense. Ottaway led the 259-yard Indian ground attack with 124 yards in 18 carries while Brisbon added 58 in 10 trips. Pettus and Roebuck combined for 106 yards passing while Cali caught four spirals, for 88 yards to become the all-time career receiving leader for Newberry in total yardage. Cali concluded his career with 1,312 total yards breaking the mark of Fred Haley (1307 set between 1960-63.)

Burton led PC with 72 yards in 13 carries and Bell added 46 yards in 11 tries.

The Li'l That Was!

The Blue Stocking

VOL. LXIV NO. 26   CLINTON, S.C. 29325   DECEMBER 4, 1981

Indians Take Bronze Derby

BY MARK R. McCALLUM

On Thanksgiving Day the Newberry Indians added insult to injury as they scalped the Hose 26-23. Besides retaining the rights to the Bronze Derby for the second consecutive year, the Indians also knocked PC's conference title hopes away. (A win against Newberry would have placed the Hose in a tie with Elon for the conference championship).

In the seesaw battle which saw the lead exchanged four times, Newberry jumped out to an early lead on a forty yard pass play to Gary Cali from QB Eddie Pettus. PC came right back with a scoring strike of their own as Ronny Hollier and David Waldkirch hooked up for a 34 yard TD; however, the kick failed and PC still trailed. The Hose took a 12-7 lead on Melvin Bell's one yard run. The try for two was unsuccessful. The Indians regained the lead when Richard Brisbon burst for a nine yard score, and extended their advantage to 20-12 on Will Ottaway's one yard plunge and a missed PAT.

John Ransom's 31 yard field goal cut the Newberry lead, which fell after Lance Sander's three yard rush and Waldkirch's successful bid for a two point conversion gave PC a 23-20 cushion. Nevertheless, the Indians garnered the game early in the final frame on a 23 yard TD scamper by Larry Harrington on a fake field goal attempt.

Newberry chalked up 365 yards of total offense; 256 yards rushing compared to PC's 256 yards of total offense with 171 yards on the ground. Curtis Burton led the Hose ground game picking up 73 yards on 13 carries. Elijah Ray was PC's top receiver with two receptions for 23 yards.

PC finishes the season with a 6-5 record (5-2 conference).

The Laurens County Advertiser

LAURENS SOUTH CAROLINA

Indians end PC title hopes, 26-23

By STEVE SURLES

The Newberry College Indians, playing on an emotional peak in their final game under coach Reed Charpia, used a bizarre 75-yard touchdown drive and clutch defense in the last quarter to pull a 26-23 upset over Presbyterian College in the annual Bronze Derby Classic Thanksgiving Day at Newberry's Setzler Field.

Punter-placekick holder Larry Harrington ran a fake field goal 23 yards for the deciding touchdown and PC penalties gave Newberry some extra chances in the exciting 70th meeting between the two teams. The Thanksgiving Day crowd of 3,900 couldn't have witnessed a more hotly-contested game.

The win finishes the Newberry season at 4-7 and gives Charpia an emotional farewell to his four-year stint at Newberry. The victory gives Charpia a 21-20 coaching record at the school — the only winning mark posted by a modern-day Newberry coach.

The bitter loss ends the PC season at 6-5 and, more importantly, denies the Blue Hose a chance to tie for the South Atlantic Conference title with Elon. PC, whose only other SAC-8 loss was to Elon, finishes with a 5-2 league mark compared to Elon's 6-1 tally.

THE STORY of the game came down to some basic facts. There were the sky-high Indians, who never folded after letting a 20-12 halftime advantage evaporate into a 23-20 PC lead after three quarters. Undoubtedly, Charpia's situation motivated his players.

"The kids were ready to play," said an emotional Charpia after the game. "I'm real proud of them. I'm proud of them today and I'm proud of them for the entire season."

The second important point of the game came during the Indians' game-winning drive. PC actually forced Newberry to punt twice in the 11-play drive, but Newberry used two fake plays and 30 critical yards in Blue Hose penalties to get the touchdown.

Holder Larry Harrington took the snap on an attempted field goal with 12:30 left to play and ran untouched around the left side with the 23-yard touchdown that made the score 26-23.

The unusual scoring drive took its first weird turn when, on a fourth down-and-one situation from the Newberry 33 with :19 left in the third quarter, blocking back Larry Brisbon took the punt snap and ran six yards for a first down.

THREE PLAYS and two incomplete passes by Eddie Pettus later, PC had Newberry on a fourth-and-seven punting situation at the Newberry 43. The Indian punter, Harrington, got the punt off but a roughing the kicker penalty — plus another 15 yards on a conduct call on PC coach Cally Gault — kept Newberry's drive alive at the PC 27 with 13:47 to play.

Four plays later, on fourth-and-six, the Indians ran the fake off the field goal. The Indian defense stymied any hopes PC had of coming back in the game.

The penalties on the punting play loomed large as time slipped away from the Hose.

"I apologize to my team for losing another 15 yards on that," Gault said after the game. Gault said

INDIANS KEEP BRONZE DERBY — Newberry's Larry Harrington, who scored the winning touchdown in the Indian's 26-23 upset win over Presbyterian College, shows off the Bronze Derby

he and his staff were upset because one official ruled the play was legal, while another called for the roughing penalty.

"THE PENALTY was assessed because I was on the field," Gault said. "It wasn't because of anything I said. Maybe we went a little crazy. It sure hurt us."

The Indians used a wide-open attack all day, but had surprising success running the football. They had 259 yards on the ground (106 passing) and were able to control the line of scrimmage in key situations.

Tailback Will Ottaway ran for 124 yards on 18 carries and fullback Brisbon added 58 on 10 carries.

Newberry's first score, however, was strictly the razzle-dazzle kind when, on the fifth play from scrimmage, quarterback Pettus pitched to Ottaway.

after the game. The win ended Newberry's coach, Reed Charpia, career at the school and knocked PC out of a tie for first place for the SAC-8 championship.

Ottaway pitched it back to Pettus and the Charleston senior completed the flea flicker to a wide-open Gary Cali for a 39-yard touchdown with only 1:25 gone in the game.

Jimmy Spencer added the extra point for a 7-0 lead.

PC CAME right back on a 79-yard drive capped by a superb catch by Ronnie Hollier from David Waldkirch for a 34-yard score with 8:02 left in the quarter.

John Ransom's PAT was missed, but PC again scored when cornerback Joe Mooneyham intercepted a Pettus pass and returned it 33 yards to the Newberry 28 on the next Indian possession. Six plays later, tailback Melvin Bell dived over from the one. The two-point conversion failed and PC led 12-7.

The Li'l That Was!

Advertiser Sports

November 30, 1981 — The Laurens County Advertiser

Newberry stormed back to get 13 unanswered points in the second quarter.

The first touchdown was set up when Mooneyham and Bell collided on a punt-return attempt at the PC 32 and Newberry recovered with 1:57 left in the first quarter.

On the first play of the second quarter, Brisbon ran 10 yards untouched for a touchdown. The Newberry PAT made it 14-12.

After trading punts, PC drove to the Indian 33 before an attempted field goal was partially blocked with 6:13 left in the half.

OTTAWAY broke loose for 43 yards as Newberry went eight straight plays on the ground before scoring on Ottaway's one-yard plunge with 1:47 left in the half. PC got a break when Rodney Harris blocked the PAT.

PC had two chances in the third quarter to take control of the game.

PC's Bell opened the second half with a 55-yard kickoff return (to the Indian 45), but PC had the drive stopped at the 13, settling for a 31-yard John Ransom field goal with 9:35 left in the quarter.

Two minutes later, Jimmy Turner recovered a Newberry fumble at the Indian 45. Three plays later, a limping David Waldkirch (who sprained his ankle in the third period) ran an option play 31 yards for a score but a PC motion penalty negated the touchdown. Two plays after that, Newberry's Frank Toney intercepted a pass to kill the drive.

PC'S Rickey Kirkpatrick picked off an Alan Roebuck pass and returned the football to the Newberry 32 to regain the momentum. Curtis Burton's 26-yard run over the right side set up a two-yard score by fullback Lance Sanders with 2:01 left in the third quarter.

Waldkirch, on a keeper, added the important two point conversion and PC led 23-20.

It was the next crazy possession for Newberry that ended PC SAC-8 title hopes.

"We surely made some mistakes," Gault said. "But I guess it had to be Reed Charpia's day. His team wanted it.

"David's (Waldkirch) sprained ankle didn't beat us, other things didn't beat us — Newberry beat us. They would not be denied."

CHARPIA was particularly pleased that his team moved the football with consistency. The Indians' 365 yards of offense was 100 more a game than the Blue Hose had been allowing.

"We've played good offensive football most of the season," Charpia noted. Newberry ran its option pitches — with either Pettus or Roebuck at quarterback — to near perfection.

"We moved well today. I still think a key was our defense stopping them when we had to. Particularly in the fourth quarter. PC has a fine team and we had to stop them," Charpia said.

"I called those fake reverses and things," Charpia added with a smile. "They were a couple of asinine calls, but they worked."

And thus ended Charpia's Newberry career.

Newberry's Gary Call, a senior wide receiver, had 88 receiving yards and established a new school record for career pass receiving yards with 1,312 late in the game.

The Indian

THE VOICE OF THE NEWBERRY COLLEGE STUDENT

DECEMBER 3, 1981 — Volume LI, Number 10

Bronze Derby stays at Newberry; PC defeated 26-23

The Bronze Derby remains at Newberry College thanks to a fake field goal play that saw punter Larry Harrington race 23 yards for the winning touchdown Thursday afternoon as the Newberry Indians captured a 26-23 victory over the Presbyterian Blue Hose at Setzler Field.

As much controversy as has been stirred up prior to the game with the announcement that Indian coach Reed Charpia would not be re-hired at the end of his current contract, the controversy on the field more than matched that action. The Indians utilized a number of unusual plays to set up their win while Presbyterian mentor Cally Gault may not have calmed down yet over a key roughing the punter call in the waning moments of the game.

The Indians came up with the big play, both on offense and defense, when they needed it. Late in the third quarter it appeared that Presbyterian had finally solved the Indian defense and was on their way to a share of the South Atlantic Conference crown, but the Indians had a few final words to say about that issue. PC had come back from a 20-12 halftime deficit to assume a 23-20 lead late in the third quarter when the Indians went to work.

Barry Brown took the kickoff and set the Tribe up in business at the Newberry 25. The Indians moved out to their own 40 with a first down, but the next three plays netted only three yards, bringing up a fourth-and-seven early in the final stanza. Harrington dropped back into punt formation and lofted a short spiral, but was knocked to the ground by a Presbyterian defender. Out came the official's flag for a 15-yard penalty and the certainty in the official's mind was matched only by the wrath of Gault over the call.

Gault became incensed over the penalty, contending that the PC defender had been blocked into Harrington (which is not a penalty), but the decision stood. Gault did not, it became necessary for one Blue Hose player to restrain his head coach and the Hose ended up with another 15-yard penalty, putting Newberry on the PC 27 with a first down.

Two successive rushes, one by Will Ottaway and the other by Richard Brisbon, had the Tribe on the Hose 23, but Eddie Pettus' pass to Gary Cali failed to connect and brought up a fourth-and-six situation.

Harrington, also the holder on placements and field goals, knelt at his 30 yard line as Mickey Crocker lined up a 40-yard attempt, but as soon as the ball was snapped Harrington was on his feet and raced down the left sideline for the 23-yard touchdown jaunt. A two-point conversion attempt failed, but the Indians were on top to stay, 26-23.

The entire afternoon was the essence of college football for the 3,900 fans and statewide media. Besides the perfect weather, the football was as exciting as one could hope for at any game.

Newberry opened the afternoon with another unusual play from Charpia's bag of tricks. On their first possession of the afternoon the Indians went in for seven as Pettus lofted a 40-yard flea-flicker pass to Cali just one minute and 25 seconds after the kickoff to put the Indians on the board. Jimmy Spencer's conversion made it 7-0.

Presbyterian left no doubt that they were seeking the share of the SAC-6 title as they marched right back to score on their initial possession of the game. David Waldkirch connected with Ronnie Hollier on a 34-yard scoring pass that saw Hollier time his jump for the spiral one second better than Indian defender Kevin White. However, the conversion by John Ransom was wide and the Indians still led 7-6.

A pass interception by Joe Mooneyham got the Hose back in business at the Indian 27. The combination of Curtis Burton, Melvin Bell and Waldkirch moved the Hose into the endzone with 3:55 remaining in the first quarter with Bell vaulting over from the one. The two-point conversion failed, giving PC a 12-7 edge.

Then it was Newberry's turn. Jimmy Edwards fumbled a Harrington punt and Chris Fair covered for the Tribe at the PC 32. Brisbon and Ottaway pounded away at the Hose defense and Brisbon broke off-tackle for nine yards and the touchdown with 14:57 left in the half. Spencer again converted to make it 14-12 for Newberry.

Newberry converted a blocked field goal attempt for their next score as Ransom tried a 51-yard effort that was partially blocked. Newberry took over at their own 34 and Ottaway broke loose three plays later for a 43-yard gain to the PC 16. Five plays later Ottaway went over the top for the third Indian touchdown, but this time it was the Tribe's turn to miss the PAT leaving the score 20-12 with just 1:47 remaining in the half.

A pass interception by Tim Mings at his own 35 ended any PC threat in the first half.

Presbyterian roared back with their first possession of the second half and marched to paydirt with Ransom kicking a 31-yard field goal with 9:35 left in the third quarter. The clubs then traded interceptions with Frank Toney snaring one for the Indians and Ricky Kirkpatrick for the Hose returned to the Indian 32 after a 34-yard return. Burton shook loose on a 26-yard scamper to the Indian three and Lance Sanders took it over on the next play to give the Hose the lead. Waldkirch ran for the two-point conversion that made it 23-20 with 2:01 left in the third panel. Then the Indians went to work.

Newberry missed one late scoring opportunity when Alan Roebuck's pass was intercepted by Charles Huff at the goal line, but Kevin White returned the favor two plays later at the Hose 48. Newberry then ran the clock down to just six seconds before turning the ball over on downs and a final PC desperation pass fell incomplete and the Indians owned the day.

The Indians out-gained Presbyterian 365-258 in total offense. Ottaway led the 259-yard Indian ground attack with 124 yards in 18 carries while Brisbon added 58 in 10 trips. Pettus and Roebuck combined for 106 yards passing while Cali caught four spirals for 88 yards to become the all-time career receiving leader for Newberry in total yardage. Cali concluded his career with 1,312 total yards breaking the mark of Fred Haley (1307 set between 1960-63.)

November 1982

November 1	Honda became the first Asian company to produce cars in the United States. The Honda Accord began production in Marysville, Ohio.
November 1	Film director Martin Scorsese divorced Isabella Rossellini after 3 years of marriage.
November 1	MLB owners voted not to renew Commissioner Bowie Kuhn's contract. Kuhn would be replaced by Peter Ueberroth.
November 5	George Harrison released his 10th album "Gone Troppo."
November 7	Actress Elizabeth Taylor divorced American politician John Warner after 6 years of marriage.
November 9	Robin Yount of the Milwaukee Brewers won the MLB AL Most Valuable Player Award.
November 10	Leonid Brezhnev, General Secretary of the Soviet Union passed away.
November 12	American actress Anne Hathaway was born.
November 12	Russian KGB Chief Yuri Andropov became the new General Secretary of the Soviet Union.
November 13	Featuring over 58,000 killed or missing in the Vietnam War, The Vietnam Veterans Memorial opened in Washington, DC.
November 14	Polish Solidarity chairman Lech Walesa was freed.
November 15	Funeral services were held for Soviet President Leonid Brezhnev in Moscow's Red Square.
November 16	The NFL 57 day football strike ended after an agreement was reached.
November 17	Atlanta Braves Dale Murphy won the MLB NL Most Valuable Player Award.
November 20	At age 7, actress Drew Barrymore hosted "Saturday Night Live."
November 21	Darrell Waltrip won the 32nd NASCAR Sprint Cup.
November 21	Singer Joni Mitchell and Larry Klein were married.
November 24	Baltimore Orioles Cal Ripken Jr. won the MLB AL Rookie of the Year Award.
November 25	The Bronze Derby was played in Clinton, South Carolina on Thanksgiving Day. The Presbyterian College Blue Hose defeated the Newberry Indians 27-7.

The Li'l That Was!

The Newberry Observer
AND HERALD & NEWS

NEWS ESTABLISHED 1865 — "Just Like A Letter From Home" — THE NEWBERRY OBSERVER ESTA

Newberry, S.C., Wednesday, Nov. 24, 1982

Derby Time:
Indians' Last Chance For A Winning Season

Call it the Bronze Derby Game, the Turkey Bowl, the South Carolina Super Bowl or any other catchy name but it all boils down to one thing...Presbyterian and Newberry Colleges on the gridiron in a classic small college rivalry Thursday at 2:30 p.m. in Bailey Memorial Stadium in Clinton.

As the proverbial saying goes, you can throw out all the records, statistics and quotes from coaches or players when it comes to this particular football game, and 1982 is certainly no exception.

The Bronze Derby tradition dates back to the 1946-47 season with the now-famous theft of a derby from the head of a Presbyterian student at the basketball game in MacLean Gymnasium. In recent years the Derby is exchanged only in football and the Indians have kept the symbol of supremacy for the past two seasons.

This year's confrontation has added importance for both teams besides the possession of the Derby. For Presbyterian it is an opportunity to redeem themselves for two disappointing performances in the season-ender and a chance to claim a .500 record for 1982.

However, for the Indians it is an opportunity to finish fourth in the conference (well above the seventh place predicted by the media and coaches), and a chance for Coach Clayton Johnson's program to establish itself a winner in the first season. Newberry brings a 5-5-0 record into the game while PC is 4-5-1.

Those fans following the Indians this season know the ups and downs Johnson has faced in attempting to turn the football program around. The loss of some key personnel over the summer and building a winning attitude have given Johnson a challenge in his initial season as a college head coach, and the youth movement after the Georgia Southern humiliation has paid off handsomely.

In the last three games the Indians have drastically boosted the offensive output, churning out significant yardage and just over 40 points per game. The Tribe is coming off its best performance of the season in a 48-22 thrashing of Lenoir-Rhyne, perhaps the most improved team in the SAC-8.

Quarterback Jimmy Skipper is currently ranked fourth in the conference in total offense (120.3 yards per game) while running backs John Nesbith, Will Ottaway and Mike Motley have put the ground attack into high gear. Nesbith has gained 500 yards in his freshman season and has scored six touchdowns to lead the scoring attack.

Ottaway stepped in for Motley in the Lenoir-Rhyne game and in one half rushed for over 140 yards and scored three touchdowns to become the NAIA District 6 player of the week while Motley is perhaps the most elusive of the ball carriers and has 249 yards in just 50 carries with four touchdowns.

Skipper has completed 32 of 70 passes for 489 yards and four TD's and he has a solid receiving corps in George Taylor (20-273 yds.), Benjie Nichols (10-147 yds.), Donald J. Johnson (13-185 yds.), Joe Fields (9-168 yds) and Donald A. Johnson (9-138 yds). Taylor and Nichols give the Indians perhaps the best play in the loop at the tight end position while Fields has proven his breakaway capabilities with three touchdowns receptions.

Another plus for the Indians offense has been freshman kicker Eddie Taylor who not only punts, but has taken over the placements. Taylor has 14 conversions and four field goals to rank second on the team in scoring with 16 points.

Defensively the Indians finally put it all together against Lenoir-Rhyne with the only major letdown being the kickoff return for a touchdown.

Linebacker Mark Weeks continues to enhance his All-American chances and now

Meet The Bulldogs

Fans will have a chance to preview Newberry High School's 1982 cagers Monday, Nov. 29, when a special "Meet the Bulldogs" program gets underway at the school's gymnasium at 7 p.m.

Sponsored by the Newberry High Bulldog Booster Club, the event will introduce members of both girls and boys varsity squads, plus members of the 10th and 9th grade boys and junior varsity girls squads.

has 178 tackle participations in nine games with two sacks, six fumble recoveries and three interceptions. He was the SAC-8 defensive player of the week after the Lenoir-Rhyne game.

But Weeks got a lot of help in that victory as the front line played up to its potential and dominated the line of scrimmage, taking off some of the pressure on the secondary in the passing category.

Presbyterian started the season with a flurry after a hard-fought loss to The Citadel and appeared to be in the driver's seat for the SAC-8 title until it ran into injury problems coming down the stretch and lost decisions to Gardner-Webb (28-21) and Carson-Newman (45-14). The latter, according to observers, was almost a complete letdown by the Blue Hose although Carson-Newman was certainly smelling the playoff roses in its final contest of the regular season.

But PC has talent and coach Cally Gault is a wise veteran of the football wars and usually gets more out of his players than they expect. Curtis Burton is a proven running back with 634 yards thus far and quarterback David Waldkirch is a dangerous performer when he teams up with split end Randy Morris, 27 catches for 440 yards.

Overall the two teams are not far apart in actual yardage gained and allowed, points scored and allowed, but the Indians may have an edge in passing offense that could prove to be the difference.

The younger players on the Indian roster will be getting their first taste of the Derby rivalry, but the veterans have been there before and getting "up" for the game has never been a problem for either team.

The Indians will return a substantial nucleus next season and could be a contender in pre-season polls, but a victory Thursday would do a lot for the attitude this year and serve as a spring board for the 1983 campaign. But 1983 is 1983 and the Indians are most immediately concerned with 1982 and the Derby.

Thanksgiving Treat Before Bronze Derby

Presbyterian College has extended an invitation to all planning to attend the Thanksgiving quest for the Bronze Derby to arrive early for a day of worship and fellowship.

Morning Thanksgiving Worship has been set for 11 a.m. at Belk Auditorium on the PC campus, featuring Rev. Larry Crocker, minister of Atlanta's Morningside Presbyterian Church and 1959 graduate of PC.

A Thanksgiving turkey dinner will follow the worship at noon at the Greenville Dining Hall. Reservations are payable, $5 per adult; $3 per child under 11, but must be made in advance by calling L.V. Powell at 833-1456.

Kickoff for the Newberry-PC football contest, the 69th renewal of the heated rivalry, will be at 2:30 p.m. PC leads the series 43-23-4.

Johnson new to Bronze Derby

By BOB HENSON

The Laurens County Touchdown Club held its final regular season meeting of the year Friday at Lakeside Country Club, capping off its 11-week season.

On the agenda was a sneak preview of the upcoming Bronze Derby classic between Presbyterian and Newberry colleges on Thanksgiving Day in Clinton. On hand to discuss the game were PC head coach Cally Gault and first-year Newberry head coach Clayton Johnson.

Johnson, a former assistant coach at Elon before taking the head job at Newberry, got his turn at the lectern and said the PC-Newberry rivalry is a little new to him in his first year.

"At this point, I guess I really don't understand the rivalry," Johnson said. "Coach Gault has been really helpful, but he wines and dines you and then he gets you on the field and kicks your tail."

ALTHOUGH Johnson has never been involved in a Bronze Derby classic, he is no stranger when it comes to a game of this magnitude.

"We had the same situation when I was at Elon," he said. "We always used to play Guilford College from Greensboro, which is about the same distance from Elon as PC is from Newberry."

There is one thing, however, that he has already noticed. "When we used play Guilford, it almost always ended up in a fight after the game," he said. "On Monday night, the PC and Newberry jayvees scrimmaged with a lot of intensity, but when the game was over, everybody shook hands."

One thing that has amazed Johnson since taking the head job at Newberry is the overwhelming support for high school football in the state. "South Carolina is a good football state," he said. "There are some awfully good players, and the crowds and stadiums are simply unbelievable."

COMMENTING on his squad, Johnson called it extremely young. "We graduated 17 seniors from last year's team," he said. "Most of those came off the offense, which forced us to play young players this year.

"We have been very erratic at times, taking into consideration that we have implemented some new offensive and defensive systems," he said.

Johnson said the Indians start 10 freshman, but he also added that the team is becoming more productive.

The Indians are 5-5-0 so far in 1982, with their only remaining game being the annual affair with the Blue Hose. They finished 3-3-0 in the South Atlantic Conference.

After Johnson, it was Gault's turn at the podium. Gault shied away from discussing the game at length, but instead had a message of his own to deliver.

"Dr. (Kenneth) Orr was supposed to be here and introduce me today," Gault said. "What he was also supposed to announce was that PC would not be going to a bowl game this year. We took the same route as South Carolina, as opposed to the scenic route Clemson took."

ON A more serious note, Gault said young people in the United States today need to learn how to deal better with adversity. "Kids need large doses of success, but they also need doses of adversity so they can learn more how to adjust," he said.

No one knows more about adversity on a football field than Gault. Presbyterian has been riddled with injuries throughout the season, and Gault praised his players for handling the situation. "Our players have faced a lot of adversity this year with a lot of injuries," he said. "But that is no absolute excuse for our record this season."

The club's players of the week were also honored at Friday's meeting. For PC, the offensive player of the week was wide receiver Randy Morris, a senior from Marietta, Ga., who caught five passes for 142 yards in the 45-14 loss to Carson-Newman last Saturday.

THE outstanding defensive player of the week for the Blue Hose was Charlie Hill. The defensive end from North Augusta turned in a fine performance in the losing effort.

For Thornwell High School, the offensive player of the week was fullback Roger Hilterbrandt. The senior rushed 19 times for 83 yards as the Saints advanced in the Independent AA playoffs by downing Byrnes, 6-0.

On defense, it was Mike Green. Green, at 6-1 and 145 pounds, had a good game at defensive back and also scored the Saints' only touchdown filling in for Lewis Compton at quarterback.

The Clinton High School offensive player of the week was Kenny Wilkerson. The offensive guard rated high in his blocking assignments as the Red Devils advanced in the AAA playoffs by downing Greer, 13-0.

THE DEFENSIVE player of the week for Clinton was Darrell Young, who was credited with six solo tackles and one fumble recovery in the win.

Laurens District 55 School had two offensive players of the week. Darvin Anderson, a 6-0, 180-pound offensive guard, rated high in blocking as the Raiders were knocked out of the Division II-AAAA Upperstate Playoffs by Airport, 3-0.

The other offensive standout was Del Barksdale. The wide receiver led the team in touchdown catches and pass receptions during the season.

NEWBERRY BOSS— Clayton Johnson, the new head coach of Newberry spoke to the Laurens County Touchdown Club Friday at Lakeside Country Club. Johnson will be involved with his first Bronze Derby Classic Thursday in Clinton. (Photos by Bob Henson)

PC HEAD COACH— Cally Gault, who is in his 20th year at Presbyterian, was also on hand Friday at the Laurens County Touchdown Club. He also discussed the upcoming Bronze Derby Classic which is held on Thanksgiving Day. Last year the annual affair was won by Newberry.

The Li'l That Was!

SPORTS

The Laurens County Advertiser

A classic rivalry
Bronze Derby is Thursday

By BOB HENSON

Football fans from across the state will flock to Johnson Field in Clinton Thursday for the Thanksgiving war between Presbyterian and Newberry colleges.

The war will be for the right to take home the coveted Bronze Derby and, just as importantly, the bragging rights for the year when the Blue Hose and Indians square off at 2:30 p.m.

PC enters the clash with a somewhat disappointing mark of 4-5-1, while Newberry, under first-year coach Clayton Johnson, will bring a 5-5 record to Clinton.

MORE times than not, this game has not only been for the Derby but for the South Atlantic Conference championship as well. And usually, the rivalry produces some unpredictable results.

This year's game doesn't take on much significance from a SAC-8 perspective; the conference race was won by Carson-Newman earlier in the season.

Still, the game will be a struggle in which teams play fiercely.

"Of course, we're looking forward to the annual affair," PC head coach Cally Gault said. "It is always an exciting game."

Last year's battle proves Gault's assertion. The two teams battled evenly until Newberry prevailed when holder Larry Willington ran for the deciding touchdown in the fourth quarter on a fake field goal.

Newberry held on to its lead to post a 26-23 victory, ending PC's chance for a SAC-8 title. Tempers, as they sometimes do, flared in that last game, Gault was tagged with a 15-yard penalty for abuse of officials and being on the field of play.

That penalty, coupled with several others, proved to be a deciding factor as PC allowed Newberry to keep the eventual winning drive alive.

With the change of seasons comes a new year and a new opportunity for PC. The Hose and Gault will try to avenge last year's loss, as well as the one the year before when the Indians prevailed, 28-20.

> "We are looking forward to the annual affair. It's always an exciting game."
> ——PC Head Coach Cally Gault
>
> "We are approaching this game as if it were the 11th and final game of the season."
> ——Newberry Head Coach Clayton Johnson

THIS year's Derby should be one of the more interesting and evenly-matched games in recent years. Newberry has been averaging 270.3 yards per game on offense, while PC's offense has done slightly better at 284.6 yards per contest.

The breakdown on offense shows that Newberry has rushed for an average of 146.3 yards, with PC running for 104.5 yards per contest. In team passing, the Indians hold the edge with 124 yards to 90.1 for PC.

Both squads are even in team defense, with Newberry giving up a little more than the Blue Hose. The Indians have allowed 354.9 yards on defense to PC's 304.9 yards per game.

The defensive breakdown reveals that only 2.5 yards separate the two units in rushing defense. Newberry has given up 187.9 yards a ballgame. PC is not far behind with 189.4 yards per game.

The Blue Hose hold a definite edge in passing defense, though. PC has given up just 115.5 yards through the air, while the Indians have been touched for 167 yards.

The teams are even on paper, but all that can quickly be forgotten on Bronze Derby Day.

Newberry's Johnson is new to the PC-Newberry rivalry, since this is his first year. "From a personal standpoint, I'm not that familiar with the intensity of the rivalry," he said. "But from listening to all the coaches talk, it will be the big finale of our season.

"From a team standpoint, I'm just trying to approach the game as the 11th and final game of the season, but I'm sure there will be a lot of intensity on the part of both teams."

TURNOVERS, according to Johnson, could spell the difference between winning and losing. "Both teams are pretty evenly matched," he said. "It could come down to who makes the fewest mistakes."

It could also come down to the team that has the fewest injuries. If that's the case, PC could be in trouble. Over the course of the long season, PC has turned into the walking wounded.

At one point in the campaign, Gault was faced with the grim possibility of not having a regular starter on the offensive line.

But with the extra week of rest, Gault said his club has healed considerably. Expected to see action will be cornerback Charles Huff, who has picked off nine interceptions on the year.

Also returning will be offensive guard Robbie Way, who missed several games during the season with a bad knee and underwent arthroscopic surgery to correct cartilage damage. He saw limited action in the Carson-Newman game and should see even more against the Indians.

PUNTER Mark White should be ready to go as will quarterback David Waldkirch, who was forced out of the Carson-Newman game with a sore knee. White has been nursing a pulled hamstring muscle and a strained knee.

Another problem will be at

PRIZED POSSESSION— Newberry's Larry Willington accepts the Bronze Derby after he helped his team beat Presbyterian last year by a 26-23 score. The Indians have held the trophy for the past two years, but PC and Cally Gault will be looking to retrieve it Thursday in Clinton.

offensive center. Gone is Tommy Hancock, who had been filling in for injured starter Frank Kube. Kube should be able to play Thursday.

With the open date last week, Gault has not made any changes in his lineup, but added that the Blue Hose have been working hard on the kicking game.

"We have always worked hard on the kicking game, but we have been putting special emphasis on it during practice this week," Gault said. "The kicking game has really hurt us at times this year."

It might be easy to underestimate PC and Newberry, considering their records. But Gault said records don't show the quality of the two teams. "The records don't really reflect that," he said. "You have to take into consideration that we both lost to three of the nation's top 20 NAIA teams in Carson-Newman, Wofford and Gardner-Webb."

NEWBERRY, according to Gault, has improved over the season. "Their offense and defense both have improved," he said. "Their quarterback, Jimmy Skipper, has shown steady improvement as well."

Skipper will go into Thursday's game as the SAC-8's fourth leading offensive producer, averaging just over 126 yards per game.

On the other hand, Johnson is not worried about one particular PC; he said you must stop the whole team. "When you take a group of players who will get excited with a lot of intensity it can be tough for anybody," he said. "We must stop the whole team."

Just how well his team does that will be determined Thursday in Clinton.

The Li'l That Was!

The Blue Stocking

VOL. LXV NO. 26   CLINTON, S.C. 29325   December 3, 1982

PC Football

Derby Returned To Rightful Owners

BY TODD MORROW

In almost flawless form, the Presbyterian College Blue Hose rounded out the 1982 season by defeating the Newberry Indians 21-7. The Blue Hose, with a balanced offensive attack and a stubborn defense raised their overall record to 5-5-1. The victory for the Blue Hose also had added significance as it brought the Bronze Derby back to PC after a two year stay at Newberry College.

Senior split-end Randy Morris summed up the feelings of many of the seniors, "We had expected a better season than we had, so it was important for us to win this game to even our record, but more importantly, it gave the seniors a chance to finish their football careers on a winning note." Morris added, "Randy Hollier and I had set a goal for both of us to catch a touchdown pass in the same game. We waited until the last game, but we finally did it."

The Blue Hose offense put together a balanced attack with 200 yards rushing and 178 yards passing. David Waldkirch, who played one of his finest games as a Blue Hose, completed 9 of 13 passes for 2 touchdowns. The running attack was spear-headed by Phillip Rippy, leading the way with 64 yards on 13 carries.

In the first quarter, both teams were held scoreless by tenacious defensive efforts. The Blue Hose, however, exploded for 14 points in the second quarter. The Blue Hose first strike came on a 41 yard pass from David Waldkirch to senior flanker Hollier. Doug Culler's extra point put the Hose ahead 7-0.

After the ensuing kickoff, the Hose stopped Newberry and forced them to punt. With Charles Huff's fair catch, the Blue Hose were forced to start deep in their own territory at the 16. After a four yard run by Curtis Burton, Waldkirch hit Gordon Gaspey for a 12 yard first down completion to set up another scoring strike. A few plays later, Waldkirch hit Morris on a 67 yard touchdown pass - the longest play from scrimmage for the Hose all season. Culler's PAT gave the Hose a 14-0 advantage.

The Blue Hose seized opportunity again before the half closed when Waldkirch again hit Morris, this time for a 7 yard touchdown, however, the play was nullified by an offensive interference call. Doug Culler's 36-yard field goal attempt sailed wide to the left.

In the third quarter, the Indians got on the score board with a 1-yard plunge by Nesbith. The big play on that drive was a 23-yard run by Nesbith.

The fourth quarter began with the Hose driving 91 yards in 29 plays, eating up 6:05 from the clock. Phillip Rippy dove over the left side to cap the drive with a 1-yard touchdown. Culler's third PAT made the score 21-7. The big len enabled the Presbyterian defense, with the help of some big plays, to preserve the victory.

The Blue Hose end their season with a deceiving 5-5-1 record. Several of the Hose's losses were close games that could have gone either way. Cally Gault and his team should be congratulated for a fine year and we're looking forward to next season. The Hose should also be congratulated for bringing the Bronze Derby back where it belongs.

CURTIS BURTON breaks in the open against Newberry in the Bronze Derby Classic. The Blue Hose turned away the Indians by a score of 21-7 and retained possession of the Derby after a two year stay at Newberry. See story below.

The Newberry Observer
AND HERALD & NEWS
"Just Like A Letter From Home"

Newberry, S.C., Friday, Nov. 26, 1982

Bronze Derby Stays In Clinton

They say football is a game of inches and it couldn't have been more than one of those critters that cost the Newberry Indians the Bronze Derby in 1982. Sure, Presbyterian won the annual small college rivalry 21-7 Thursday afternoon, but one little hanky sure made a difference.

There was no doubt that, in the final outcome, Presbyterian was the better football team Thanksgiving Day in Clinton. Despite a season-long rash of injuries, the Blue Hose put forth a superlative effort to pry the coveted derby loose from a two-year Newberry domination.

However, the Indians came very close to turning the game into one of the all-time classics with a strong second half comeback effort. Trailing 14-0 at intermission the Indians staged a sterling goal line stand early in the third quarter...that is keeping Presbyterian bottled up on its own goal line. After a short punt, the Indians were in business and John Nesbith wasted no time in getting the Tribe on the board on a one-yard plunge to cut the deficit to 14-7.

Kent Larry fumbled the ensuing kickoff but Phillip Rippy recovered and got it out to the PC 9. Then a 23 play, 91 yard drive began that took up over 13 minutes, aided by a key penalty that took Newberry out of the game.

A brilliant first down call by PC saw quarterback David Waldkirch run a keeper 19 yards to the PC 28, and Rippy galloped 17 yards on the next play to get the hosts out of the shadow of their own goal line. But the Indian defense stiffened and apparently had the Blue Hose bottled up with two sacks, one by Darryl Suber and one by Frank Toney. The latter put the Hose in punting formation and the revitalized Indian attack was ready to roll.

Then came the inch and the hanky. The Indians could have done no more than barely brush the PC punter's shoe on a hard charge to block the kick, but the official covering the play elected to call roughing the kicker and the Hose were in business again at the Indian 36. Thirteen plays later the Blue Hose finally cracked the Indian defense for the clinching touchdown after Newberry had held three times inside their own three and Rippy took it over on fourth and goal from the one. Doug Culler's conversion made it 21-7.

That situation took the wind out of the Indian sails and Presbyterian was smelling victory and would not be denied.

Presbyterian earned the victory the hard way; dominating the line of scrimmage, excellent coverage in the secondary to take away the Indian passing game, a productive rushing attack, and a remarkable performance by Waldkirch at quarterback. The senior signal caller, plagued by knee injuries this year, hit two crucial passes in the first half to give PC their 14-0 lead. The first was to flanker Ronnie Hollier for 41 yards and a touchdown; the second to split end Randy Morris for 67 yards and another touchdown.

In reality, those two second-quarter tallies were all the Blue Hose needed. Rippy's fourth quarter score was merely insurance.

The Indians were not able to put together any major offensive showing in the first half. The Indians actually penetrated the Blue hose territory only on one possession and that was to the PC 43 when Nesbith fumbled after a five yard gain.

Meanwhile, Waldkirch was busy directing his team to two touchdowns in just over four minutes while the Indians looked flat emotionally.

But the second half made up for that as Newberry roared back from what must have been an inspiring halftime conversation with Coach Clayton Johnson. Eddie Taylor lofted a punt that was downed at the PC one and the Hose were unable to move it one inch from that point. John Gayton punted out to the PC 33 and Mike Motley returned to the PC 29.

Then Nesbith took over, churning out 23 yards on the first play and the freshman went over four plays later on fourth and one to cut the gap to 14-7.

Then came the 23 play drive that ended all Indian hopes of a comeback and the swarming PC defense cut short the next two Indian possessions. The hosts were able to run off the final 4:11, again aided by an obvious roughing the kicker penalty.

Overall the hosts accounted for 328 yards on offense, 178 passing and 150 on the ground despite a superior effort by senior linebacker Mark Weeks who had eight primary tackles and 20 assists to finish the season with over 20 tackle participations per game.

Newberry managed only 105 yards rushing, but the real story of the game was in the 25 yards of passing offense. Freshman Jimmy Skipper was running for his life most of the afternoon, completing just four of 14 passes and not one to a regular receiver. Will Ottaway had two catches and Nesbith two for the only action in that category.

Overall the Indians managed just 43 offensive plays while PC ran off 71.

Despite the PC overall superiority, Nesbith ended up the game's leading rusher with 56 yards in 12 carries while Ottaway tacked on 42 in 10 trips. Rippy led PC with 64 yards in 13 carries but Waldkirch hit nine of 12 passes for 178 yards and two touchdowns.

The decsion gave the Blue Hose a 5-5-1 record, 4-2-1 in the SAC-8, while the Indians closed out their first season under Johnson with a 5-6-0 record, 3-4-0 in the SAC-8.

SCORING SUMMARY
Newberry 0 0 7 0 — 7
Presbyterian 0 14 0 7 — 21.
PC-Hollier, 41 passes from Waldkirch (Culler, kick).
PC-Morris, 67 passes from Waldkirch (Culler, kick).
N-Nesbith, 1 run (Taylor, kick).
PC-Rippy, 1 plunge (Culler, kick).

The Li'l That Was!

Laurens County Advertiser

20¢ PER COPY

"SOUTH CAROLINA'S LARGEST SEMI-WEEKLY NEWSPAPER"

LAURENS, SOUTH CAROLINA

No. 43—16 Pages

PERFECT—The holiday weekend was a perfect one, Laurens County football style. On the high school level, the Saints of Thornwell High School captured a state championship by downing May River, 18-0, Friday night. Presbyterian College came away with its biggest win of the year Thanksgiving day by downing Newberry College, 21-7, to reclaim the Bronze Derby. Here, Presbyterian runner Curtis Burton is snowed under a host of Newberry tacklers. All the sports news can be found on pages 12-13 in today's Advertiser. (Photo by Bob Henson)

PC beats Newberry
Hose regain control of Derby

The Laurens County Advertiser — November 29, 1982

By BOB HENSON

It was a happy Thanksgiving Day for Presbyterian and a not so happy one for Newberry as the Blue Hose won the annual clash, 21-7, at Johnson Field Thursday.

The victory not only gave PC a 5-5-1 mark for the season, but gave the Blue Hose the coveted Bronze Derby, something they hadn't seen in two years.

It also gave the PC players and their followers something to cheer about in an otherwise disappointing season.

"This was a very courageous team that I was very proud of all year," said PC head coach Cally Gault after the game. "This team had more injuries than any other I've seen in all of my 35 years of coaching."

IT was truly a courageous performance by the Blue Hose. Offensive center Frank Kube, who has suffered the entire season with a bad knee, was a perfect example. Kube was not even supposed to play, but did anyway.

And then there was David Waldkirch. The senior quarterback had been having a miserable season up until Thursday's game, but found a little magic in his passing arm, and proved to be one of the main reasons PC came away with the win.

But in the first quarter, it was beginning to look as if neither team wanted to win. The two rivals battled in the middle of the field with neither mounting a serious scoring threat.

However, near the end of the opening period, PC started a drive at its own 38-yard line. Eight plays later with 12:49 left in the first half, the Blue Hose, behind the strong play of Waldkirch, had driven 62 yards for the game's first score.

THE scoring play came on a 41-yard touchdown pass from Waldkirch to senior split end Ronnie Hollier. On that play, Waldkirch dropped back to pass and got a strong pass rush from the Newberry defense.

Unperturbed, Waldkirch took off around left end, stopped just before crossing the line of scrimmage and spotted Hollier who was breaking across the field.

Waldkirch fired a perfect stike to him and Hollier raced untouched into the end zone. Doug Culler came on to kick the extra point to make it 7-0, PC.

After the Indians couldn't move the ball against a stubborn PC defense, the Blue Hose offensive unit got another chance, which it didn't waste.

Starting from their own 16, the Blue Hose and Waldkirch engineered another sparkling drive that covered 84 yards in five plays for their second touchdown.

Again, it was Waldkirch finding the range as he hit Randy Morris for a 67-yard touchdown. That was the longest play from scrimmage on the year for PC. On the play before, Waldkirch had tried to go to Morris, but his pass was off, setting up the scoring play.

MORRIS was running a simple out pattern, and when Waldkirch was rushed, he turned it up field and found an opening in the Indians' defensive secondary. The rest was history as Waldkirch found his man open and Morris galloped into the end zone for six points. Culler's point made it 14-0 with 8:08 left in the half.

PC would later have another chance to put more points on the board after David Neisler recovered a James Nesbit fumble at the Newberry 23-yard line.

With 5:02 left in the half, PC started another drive that would take the Blue Hose to the Newberry seven. On the eighth play of the drive, Waldkirch hit Morris in the end zone for an apparent touchdown, but the play was nullified when the officials called offensive pass interference on tight end Elijah Ray after the play was completed.

Instead of a touchdown, the Blue Hose had the ball back at the Newberry 19 after the 15-yard penalty. Two plays later, Culler tried to kick a 36-yard field goal which fell three feet short of the crossbar with only seconds remaining in the half.

A GOOD DAY— Presbyterian quarterback David Waldkirch had an outstanding game in his final day in a Blue Hose uniform for head coach Cally Gault. Waldkirch passed for 178 yards and two touchdowns in completing nine of 12 passes. Presbyterian reclaimed the coveted Bronze Derby on Thanksgiving Day by beating Newberry, 21-7 in Clinton. (Photo by Bob Henson)

NEWBERRY ran out the clock, so PC had what looked to be a comfortable 14-0 lead at the half. Things would tighten up considerably in the second half, however.

The Indians got back into the contest in the third quarter after Eddie Taylor executed a perfect, 43-yard punt which was downed on the PC one-yard line.

The Blue Hose tried to move the ball away from their own end zone, but failed to do so in three plays. John Gayton came on to punt and got away a short kick to the PC 27 that gave the Indians excellent field position.

From there, Newberry needed only five plays to cover the 27 yards for its first score. Nesbit carried the ball over from the one to make the score 14-6 with 7:18 left in the third quarter. Taylor's kick made it 14-7.

The momentum was beginning shift from PC to Newberry, but the Blue Hose came back to put together a 23-play drive that would consume 13:17 of the clock and deliver the crowning blow to head coach Clayton Johnson and the Indians.

THE DRIVE, which covered 91 yards, was kept alive when Newberry was called for roughing PC punter Gayton. That gave PC a first down at the PC 49, and as it turned out, would end any hopes Newberry might have of tying the game or winning it outright.

Phillip Rippy scored from one yard out to give the Blue Hose a commanding, 20-7 lead. Culler kicked the extra point and it was 21-7 with just 8:55 left in the game.

Newberry had two other possessions, but couldn't do anything against the PC defense. Waldkirch and company ran out the clock to post the first PC win over Newberry in two years.

After the game, Johnson turned over the Bronze Derby to Gault at midfield, and then began to answer questions from the press concerning the roughing-the-kicker penalty.

"We had to go after him (Gayton)," said Johnson. "We could have blocked it just as easily as we could have roughed him. It's just the gamble you take."

The turning point, according to Johnson, was late in the third quarter when PC fumbled the kickoff following Newberry's touchdown. That gave PC poor field position on its own nine-yard line, but the Blue Hose got a good run from Waldkirch to get out of trouble.

"That was the turning point right there," said Johnson. "We had them back there, and let them out of a hole after we had just scored. The play by Waldkirch was a big play."

Waldkirch's day was filled with big plays. The senior passed for 178 yards in completing nine of 12 passes including two touchdowns. His counterpart, Jimmy Skipper, managed just 28 yards as he completed four of 14 passes.

PC held the edge in every major statistical category. The Blue Hose racked up 21 first downs, a season high, while Newberry could only get eight.

In rushing, PC gained 150 yards to the Indians' 105. A major improvement for PC was in the turnover department. The Blue Hose didn't turn the ball over once, while Newberry fumbled the ball away one time.

So PC holds the bragging rights for at least one year. Newberry, which finished the season at 5-6, will have to wait until next year.

The Li'l  That Was!

The Indian
The Voice of The Newberry College Student
VOLUME LII, NUMBER 11 — 2100 COLLEGE ST., NEWBERRY, S.C. 29108 — DECEMBER 2, 1982

Bronze Derby Returns To P.C.

They say football is a game of inches and it couldn't have been more than one of those critters that caused the Newberry Indians the Bronze Derby in 1982. Sure, Presbyterian won the annual small college rivalry 21-7 Thursday afternoon, but one little hanky sure made a difference.

There was no doubt that, in the final outcome, Presbyterian was the better football team Thanksgiving Day in Clinton. Despite a season-long rash of injuries, the Blue Hose put forth a superlative effort to pry the coveted derby loose from a two-year Newberry domination.

However, the Indians came very close to turning the game into one of the all-time classics with a strong second half comeback effort. Trailing 14-0 at intermission the Indians staged a sterling goal line stand early in the third quarter...that is keeping Presbyterian bottled up on its goal goal line. After a short punt, the Indians were in business and John Nesbith wasted no time in getting the Tribe on the board on a one-yard plunge to cut the deficit to 14-7.

Kent Larry fumbled the ensuing kickoff but Phillip Rippy recovered and got it out to the PC 9. Then a 23 play, 91 yard drive began that took up over 13 minutes, aided by a key penalty that took Newberry out of the game.

A brilliant first down call by PC saw quarterback David Waldkirch run a keeper 19 yards to the PC 28, and Rippy galloped 17 yards on the next play to get the hosts out of the shadow of their own goal line. But the Indian defense stiffened and apparently had the Blue Hose bottled up with two sacks, one by Darryl Suber and one by Frank Toney. The latter put the Hose in punting formation and the revitalized Indian attack was ready to roll.

Then came the inch and the hanky. The Indians could have done no more than barely brush the PC punter's shoe on a hard charge to block the kick, but the official covering the play elected to call roughing the kicker and the Hose were in business again at the Indian 36. Thirteen plays later the Blue Hose finally cracked the Indian defense for the clinching touchdown after Newberry had held three times inside their own three and Rippy took it over on fourth and goal from the one. Doug Culler's conversion made it 21-7.

That situation took the wind out of the Indian sails and Presbyterian was smelling victory and would not be denied.

Presbyterian earned the victory the hard way: dominating the line of scrimmage, excellent coverage in the secondary to take away the Indian passing game, a productive rushing attack, and a remarkable performance by Waldkirch at quarterback. The senior signal caller, plagued by knee injuries this year, hit two crucial passes in the first half to give PC their 14-0 lead. The first was to flanker Ronnie Hollier for 41 yards and a touchdown; the second to split end Randy Morris for 67 yards and another touchdown.

In reality, those two second-quarter tallies were all the Blue Hose needed. Rippy's fourth quarter score was merely insurance.

The Indians were not able to put together any major offensive showing in the first half. The Indians actually penetrated the Blue hose territory only on one possession and that was to the PC 43 when Nesbith fumbled after a five yard gain.

Meanwhile, Waldkirch was busy directing his team to two touchdowns in just over four minutes while the Indians looked flat emotionally..

But the second half made up for that as Newberry roared back from what must have been an inspiring halftime conversation with Coach Clayton Johnson. Eddie Taylor lofted a punt that was downed at the PC one and the Hose were unable to move it one inch from that point. John Gayton punted out to the PC 32 and Mike Motley returned to the PC 28.

Then Nesbith took over, churning out 23 yards on the first play and the freshman went over four plays later on fourth and one to cut the gap to 14-7.

Then came the 23 play drive that ended all Indian hopes of a comeback and the swarming PC defense cut short the next two Indian possessions. The hosts were able to run off the final 4:11, again aided by an obvious roughing the kicker penalty.

Overall the hosts accounted for 328 yards on offense, 178 passing and 150 on the ground despite a superior effort by senior linebacker Mark Weeks who had eight primary tackles and 20 assists to finish the season with over 80 tackle participations per game.

Newberry managed only 105 yards rushing, but the real story of the game was in the 28 yards of passing offense. Freshman Jimmy Skipper was running for his life most of the afternoon, completing just four of 14 passes and not one to a regular receiver. Will Ottaway had two catches and Nesbith two for the only action in that category.

Overall the Indian managed just 43 offensive plays while PC ran off 71.

Despite the PC overall superiority, Nesbith ended up the game's leading rusher with 88 yards in 13 carries while Ottaway tacked on 42 in 10 trips. Rippy led PC with 64 yards in 13 carries but Waldkirch hit nine of 12 passes for 178 yards and two touchdowns.

The decision gave the Blue Hose a 5-5-1 record, 4-2-1 in the SAC-8, while the Indians closed out their first season under Johnson with a 5-6-0 record, 3-4-0 in the SAC-8.

November 1983

November 2	Michael Jackson released the best-selling album of all time, "Thriller." The album was produced by Quincy Jones.
November 2	United States President Ronald Reagan signed a bill establishing the Dr. Martin Luther King holiday.
November 3	The Nashville Network debuted on cable TV.
November 3	Jesse Jackson began his first campaign for President of the United States.
November 7	A bomb exploded in the United States Capitol causing damage with no injuries.
November 9	Amsterdam brewer Freddie Heineken was kidnapped.
November 10	Marvelous Marvin Hagler retained the world middleweight boxing title with a unanimous decision over Roberto Duran.
November 11	United States President Ronald Reagan was the first United States President to address the Japanese legislature.
November 11	British composer Andrew Lloyd Webber and Sarah Hugill divorce after 11 years of marriage.
November 11	Great Britain received its first cruise missiles from the United States.
November 13	American comedy actor from "Hee Haw," Alvin "Junior" Samples passed away.
November 17	The film "Yentl" premiered, starring, produced and directed by Barbra Streisand.
November 19	The football game referred to as the "Toilet Bowl" was played by Oregon (4-6) and Oregon State (2-8). The game ended in a 0-0 tie.
November 20	The movie "Terms of Endearment" starring Shirley MacLaine premiered in New York City.
November 20	Bobby Allison won the 33rd NASCAR Sprint Cup.
November 20	An estimated 100 million view the ABC TV movie "The Day After" about nuclear war.
November 22	Actor Michael Conrad of "Hill Street Blues" passed away.
November 23	Actress Mary Tyler Moore married Dr. Robert Levine.
November 24	The Bronze Derby was played in Newberry, South Carolina on Thanksgiving Day. The Newberry Indians defeated the Presbyterian College Blue Hose 23-0.

The Li'l That Was!

Who will win the Derby this year?

The Indian

November 17, 1983 — 2100 COLLEGE STREET, NEWBERRY, S.C. 29108 — FOUR PAGES

Tradition Abounds In Derby Game

BY BILL HATCHELL

Newberry College has a tradition that has long been celebrated in November. No, it is not Thanksgiving, although it falls on that day. It is the annual Bronze Derby Classic — The big gridiron clash of the Blue Hose from Presbyterian and the mighty Indians from Newberry.

Did you ever wonder how it all came about? It happened in 1947 as a result of a small confrontation at the Newberry-Presbyterian Basketball game that was held on the Newberry Campus that year. It seems that P.C. students had placed a banner on the gym wall, which read "Beat the hell out of Newberry!", before the start of the game. During the game one of the Newberry students obtained a ladder and climbed through a window in McLean Gym to remove the banner.

No one noticed the banner missing until the end of the hard fought game which Presbyterian won 51-47. After the game a Presbyterian student demanded that he get the banner returned to him immediately. A scuffle began in the middle of it and eventually it became a free-for-all. During the fight a Newberry student stole a Derby from the head of a Presbyterian student and ran off from the fight.

During the next couple of days, the two athletic directors negotiated the return of the hat. During the negotiations someone recommended that "a derby should serve as a laurel of victory in athletic contests between Newberry and Presbyterian." Sometime later the derby was returned to Presbyterian. It was then packaged up, so as not to destroy it, and was sent to a casting company out of Ohio. The derby was bronzed and it became the famed Bronze Derby.

Until 1956, the possession of the derby was determined by the outcome of all Newberry-Presbyterian athletic encounters. Be they baseball, basketball or football. Now, the possession is determined by the outcome of the Newberry-Presbyterian football game held annually on Thanksgiving Day.

However, the game was not always played on Thanksgiving. According to former football coach, Hravey Kirkland the game was not played on Thanksgiving before he arrived. "Before I came, the game was played on Saturday, but we got it moved on Thanksgiving Day my first year at Newberry," Kirkland explained. Kirkland became head coach in 1952. The game has been played on Thanksgiving Day ever since. "It use to be played on Thanksgiving at some point in the past but had been shifted back to a Saturday date. There is a natural rivalry between the two schools and the game on Thanksgiving just added to the meaning," Kirkland added.

Presbyterian won the game convincingly last year (21-7) and took the Bronze Derby back to Clinton with them. Second year, Newberry mentor, Clayton Johnson and his tribe aim to regain the coveted trophy back after a one year absence from the Newberry College trophy case. Presbyterian leads the overall series 44-23-4, but like the rivalries between USC and Clemson, Furman and The Citadel or any other rivalries across the nation, the record books have to be thrown out the window for this game. The game will be played on Setzler Field at 2 p.m., on Thanksgiving Day.

★ **Happy Birthday Scott** ★

The Li'l That Was!

Advertiser

SPORTS

The Laurens County Advertiser — November 23, 1983

Derby clash on tap for Thursday

By BOB HENSON

Presbyterian College head football coach Cally Gault was sitting in his office Monday afternoon talking about his annual fishing trip in the mountains. He was looking forward to it very much.

But before he can bring out the tackle and go after some trout, the veteran head mentor must get one more football game out of the way.

And that game is Thanksgiving Day when Gault's Blue Hose team travels 30 miles down the road to visit the Newberry Indians in the annual Bronze Derby Classic.

Kickoff is at 2 p.m. at Setzer Field.

PC ENTERS THE game at 5-4-1, needing a win to maintain a winning season. Newberry is in the same boat at 5-5.

No one needs to say anything about the importance of this game. Both teams know the entire state will be watching when the Hose and Indians kick it off for the 72nd time.

But excuse Gault if he seems a little laid back this week, because he's not at all. It's just his 25th Derby game as either a coach or player.

When you've been around a rivalry for that many years, you learn how to control your emotions somewhat. Still, for Gault, it's the game. There is no other.

"It's the second season," Gault said Monday. "That's the way we've always played it. Some people ask why we don't play the game on a Saturday. If we played it on Saturday, it's just another football game, and it's not just another game."

A point well taken. If you want to see 22 men fight, scratch and claw at each other for nearly three hours, finish stuffing yourself early on Turkey Day and make the trip to Newberry.

There's something about a little hat cast in bronze that makes them go crazy. It's been that way ever since it was snatched off a man's head several years ago and made the symbol of the PC-Newberry rivalry.

LAST YEAR, the Blue Hose regained control of the prized possession with a 21-7 win over the Indians at Clinton. It was a game reminiscent of past Derby games, in which the teams come out and use something new to offset the other. For PC, it was a split back set after having run out of the I for 10 previous games.

As Gault will tell you, you'd better have something new to take into this game to keep the opposing team honest if nothing else.

"The other team has more time to study film of you," he said. "You'd better have something you can use just to keep them off balance."

In the early 1970s, Newberry and Fred Herren used a crafty huddle play to score a touchdown on PC after staging an injury to set it up. In the 1960s, PC came out on one occasion and threw screen passes from a shotgun formation.

Thursday we will know what kind of surprises this year's game holds in store. You can bet there will be plenty.

In looking at the matchup, one can't really compare records because records are obsolete. As far as Gault is concerned, both teams go into the annual battle rated even because it's such an emotional rivalry.

"Oh, there have been times when they've been favored and times when we've been favored," he said. "No matter what the records are, it's an important game."

THERE ARE SO many variables to consider when looking at the pregame matchup, but one is most obvious. It will pit the SAC-8's top offense (Newberry) against the number one defense in the conference (PC).

A major part of the Indians' offense is quarterback Jimmy Skipper. Skipper, a 175-pound sophomore, has thrown for 1,256 yards and eight touchdowns this year and has set single-season records for attempts (202) and passing yards, breaking the old mark by Leon Williams in 1976 when he passed for 1,186.

Skipper only needs one more completion (he already has 90) to set a new school record in that category. Skipper has proved he can run with the football when he has to, picking up 214 yards and two touchdowns. He is averaging 147 yards of total offense per game and needs just 315 more to set a new school record.

If Skipper can't get the job done, there's always John Nesbitt and Mike Motley in the backfield. Nesbitt has rushed for 938 yards this year, while Motley is ahead with 969. Both should reach the 1,000-yard plateau easily Thursday.

Averaging 20.8 points per game is nice, but Newberry will definitely find the going much tougher against the Blue Hose defense.

PC HAS BEEN unyielding to opposing offenses over the course of the year. After being bombarded by The Citadel in the first game of the year, the Blue Hose bowed their backs and have played like the dickens on defense ever since.

In their last outing with Carson-Newman, the SAC-8 champion, the Blue Hose limited the Eagles to 232 yards, with most of those coming in the second half after the game was decided. In the first half, Carson-Newman did not pick up a first down and had just 43 yards of offense.

The week before against Gardner-Webb, PC set a new school record by allowing just 59 yards. That was almost unheard of against the Bulldogs, who showed what they could do last week by dominating Wofford.

Defense has been PC's rock all season. But in the final weeks of the season, the offense has turned around and given the defense some help.

Against Carson-Newman, the Blue Hose struck for 341 yards of offense and controlled the ball when it had to. Quarterback Ted Stephens has been directing the attack well the past three weeks and is getting good help from his receivers.

"The Carson-Newman game was obviously our best performance of the season," Gault said. "The defense has played well all year long, and the offense has started to come around, too."

THAT'S something Gault would like to see continue through Thursday so he can enjoy his fishing trip, instead of thinking about a final loss over the long winter.

BRONZE DERBY—Thanksgiving Day at Setzer Field in Newberry, one of the most intense football rivalries in college football will be renewed for the 72nd time when the Presbyterian College Blue Hose tangle with the Newberry Indians for the Bronze Derby (right). The Blue Hose have owned the Derby the past year after beating Newberry 21-7 in last year's contest at Clinton. (Photo by Bob Henson)

Monday
November 28, 1983

The Laurens County Advertiser

"SOUTH CAROLINA'S LARGEST SEMI-WEEKLY NEWSPAPER"

LAURENS, SOUTH CAROLINA

20¢ PER COPY

PC loses Derby

By BOB HENSON

Presbyterian College head football coach Cally Gault was hoping rain would not be in the forecast for Thursday's Bronze Derby game.

He had said his Blue Hose team would have to rely on quickness and speed to overtake the Newberry Indians. If it rained, his game plan of running the counter option and passing would be in serious trouble.

AS IT TURNED out, Gault was right. It not only rained, it poured. And as a result, the Blue Hose could not muster any offense against Newberry on a muddy field and wound up losing the annual struggle, 23-0, before 2,800 drenched football fans at Setzler Field.

The loss dropped PC's overall finish to 5-5-1, good for second place in the South Atlantic Conference. Newberry and head coach Clay Johnson finish with a winning mark for 1983 at 6-5.

Of course, the weather was a key factor in the game's outcome. PC was guilty of seven turnovers on the day and Newberry took full advantage of them, turning the miscues into points.

But while PC was struggling in the quagmire, Newberry was doing just the opposite. Behind the running of Mike Motley and John Nesbitt, the Indians rolled up 319 yards on a good Blue Hose defense.

Motley picked up 109 yards on 18 attempts, while Nesbitt managed 67 on 20 rushes. It pushed both of them over the 1,000-yard mark for the year, which, according to Newberry officials, is a new school record.

IT WAS A DAY of records all around for the Indians. As a team, Newberry set a new record for total offense in one season, while placekicker Eddie Taylor set a new school record with three field goals in one game, including a 45-yarder.

Newberry did play well offensively considering the terrible weather conditions. Gault acknowledged as much after it was over. "Newberry played very well today," he said. "And we didn't play as well offensively as we had hoped we would."

For a while in the first quarter, it looked as if neither team would

MUD DERBY—Presbyterian College tailback Kent Larry (40) looks to turn the corner on a wet and muddy field Thanksgiving Day during the annual Bronze Derby game at Setzler Field in Newberry. Larry and his teammates had trouble generating much offense on the wet track and wound up losing the Bronze Derby to Newberry 23-0 before some 2,800 wet fans on Turkey Day. The Blue Hose finished off their year at 5-5-1. (Photo by Bob Henson)

be able to score. A touchdown looked awfully good, as the rain got harder as the afternoon wore on.

Ironically, PC had the first prime scoring opportunity of the game when the Blue Hose drove to the Indians' 25-yard line and was faced with third and five. PC quarterback Ted Stephens tried to hit tailback Kent Larry on a screen pass but Larry couldn't hold the slippery pigskin, setting up a 41-yard field goal attempt by Doug Culler.

Culler slipped as he made his approach and couldn't get the ball up quick enough, leaving it some 15 yards short of its target with 9:07 left in the opening period. That's as close as PC got to points.

NEWBERRY ALSO blew an excellent scoring opportunity after driving from its own 20 to the Blue Hose 12, following a Jimmy Skipper pass to Donald Johnson. But the next play saw Motley cough up the ball to PC's Joe Blount on the 11.

After the Blue Hose couldn't move and punted, Newberry was stymied and kicked back to the PC three-yard line to set up a costly PC mistake. On third and 10 from the three, Stephens dropped back to pass from his own end zone and threw an interception to Newberry's Kenneth Pressley, who returned it 16 yards for the game's first score with 1:14 left in the quarter to make it 7-0, after Taylor's PAT.

The next Newberry score also resulted from a PC turnover. With 7:28 left in the half, PC's Phillip Rippy fumbled. It was recovered by Mark Kennedy at the Blue Hose 37.

The Indians' drive stalled and Taylor came on for the 45-yard field goal with 5:55 left in the half to up the margin to 10-0.

After PC took the ensuing kickoff and stalled once again, Newberry went back to work on offense and started another drive that netted more points.

SKIPPER did most of the work on the 10-play drive that covered 84 yards. On third and six from the Newberry 20, Skipper took off on a broken-field keeper and zig-zagged his way downfield, running around, through and over the PC defense for 53 yards to the PC 27 with 2:05 left in the half. Newberry immediately went to its two-minute drill and used it wisely. Runs by Motley and Nesbitt pushed the ball to the 11-yard line with 22 seconds left. Skipper's keeper lost one to the 12 and the Indians used their final timeout of the half to set up a pass that sailed over Benjie Nichols' head in the end zone, bringing up fourth and five with four seconds left.

Taylor came on and calmly booted a 28-yard field goal to send Newberry to the dressing room with a 13-0 advantage at the half.

PC was not out of the game by any means, but they damaged their comeback hopes severely in the second half with a host of turnovers, mostly interceptions.

ANOTHER TAYLOR field goal from 28 yards out with 8:21 left in the third quarter gave Newberry a 16-0 lead and all but shut the door on PC, considering the Blue Hose offensive success to that point.

With 12:39 left in the game and the rain coming down in sheets, Stephens fumbled on the PC 22 and Newberry's Kennedy had his second recovery of the day. Skipper kept to the 19 on first down to set up the game's final score.

Nesbitt took the handoff on second down and went up the middle, right over center Jim Duke for a 19-yard touchdown run with 11:58 left to play. Taylor came on to kick the point to establish the 23-0 final.

PC's miserable day offensively was evident in that the Blue Hose had just 147 yards in total offense. A lot of that can be credited to the playing conditions, but the Newberry defense also played well, stopping the Blue Hose from generating any kind of sustained drive for the most part.

And it resulted in a .500 season for Gault and PC, and the return of the Bronze Derby to Newberry, for at least one year.

The Li'l That Was!

The Newberry Observer
AND HERALD & NEWS
"Just Like A Letter From Home"

Newberry, S.C., Friday, Nov. 25, 1983

Indians Bring Bronze Derby Back To Newberry

An opportunistic offense and a bone-crushing defense boosted Newberry to a 23-0 Thanksgiving victory over archrival Presbyterian to bring the coveted Bronze Derby back to Newberry.

In a rain which soaked fans and players alike at Newberry's Setzler Field, the Indians capitalized on costly PC turnovers to set up three of their five scoring plays and end with a winning season (6-5). The Tribe finished 3-4 in the SAC-8.

Newberry had won the derby two years straight before losing it in Clinton 21-7 in 1982. The rivalry dates back to the 1946-47 season with the now-famous theft of a derby from the head of a Presbyterian student at a basketball game in MacLean Gymnasium, and PC still leads the series 44-24-4 (including basketball and baseball games).

And Thursday, as the ball slipped through PC's rain-slicked hands, Newberry played for keeps.

Newberry's defense had backed the Blue Hose into a corner early in the first quarter, and facing a third-and-10 situation inside its own 10-yard line, the visitors elected to pass. They never got the chance—exactly.

Instead, what was meant to be a long bomb squirted out of quarterback Ted Stephens' wet hands and wobbled into the arms of Newberry defensive back Kenneth Pressley.

Pressley sprinted 18 yards for Newberry's first touchdown, and Eddie Taylor added the kick to make it 7-0 with 1:14 to go.

Could be that play was the game-winner, since Presbyterian's SAC-8-leading defense played the remaining three stanzas with what appeared to be a broken spirit (PC gave up 236 yards to Newberry running backs, the most gained against the Blue Hose this year), and its offense managed only 159 yards rushing in 44 tries.

Taylor had another chance to perform his specialty in the second quarter, when Milton Pope recovered one of six PC fumbles. Four plays later, with 6:36 on the clock, Taylor booted a 45-yard field goal to put the Tribe up 10-0.

But Taylor was far from finished.

(Continued On Page 1)

Indians Bring Bronze Derby Back
(Continued From Page 1)

Newberry took its next possession 73 yards in nine plays, including a 52-yard sprint by quarterback Jimmy Skipper, and set up Taylor's 28-yard field goal with only four seconds left in the half.

In the third quarter, with 8:21 to go, Taylor made good from 26 yards out after Newberry had moved 51 yards on six plays. Mike Motley sparked the field goal-gaining drive, picking up 60 yards on four carries (including a 53-yard end sweep); and The Indians stretched the margin to 16-0.

Presbyterian sealed its fate in the final quarter when it bobbled the ball at its own 22. This time, William Worthy came up with the ball, and Newberry scored on its third play on a 19-yard scramble by John Nesbitt with 11:58 remaining in the game. Taylor's kick was good for the final spread.

Motley led all rushers with 18 carries for 109 yards, followed by Nesbitt with 20 tries for 67 yards. Both Motley and Nesbitt combined for a Newberry first by each breaking 1,000-yard season totals. The pair led Newberry to a school single-season record for total offense (3,851 yards), with Motley, a senior from Jacksonville, Fla., tallying 1,078 for the year and Nesbitt, a Mauldin sophomore, gaining 1,005.

Skipper aided the Indian cause with seven carries for 85 yards, and passed for another 83.

Newberry totaled 10 first downs, its rushing aided by three completions in seven pass attempts for 83 yards. Five punts averaged 45 yards, and the Indians lost 45 yards to four infractions and three fumbles of its own.

Presbyterian, which maintained a 5-5-1 season slate and 4-2-1 league mark, counted eight first downs. The Blue Hose completed nine of 19 passes with four interceptions for 88 yards, averaged 44.3 yards on three punts, and lost 45 yards to penalty markers.

The Li'l That Was!

The Indian
The Voice of The Newberry College Student

VOLUME LIII, NUMBER 11 — 2100 COLLEGE STREET, NEWBERRY, SOUTH CAROLINA 29108 — 4 PAGES — December 2, 1983

Indians Bring Bronze Derby Back To Newberry

Newberry recaptures coveted Bronze Derby.

An opportunistic offense and a bone-crushing defense boosted Newberry to a 23-0 Thanksgiving victory over archrival Presbyterian to bring the coveted Bronze Derby back to Newberry.

In a rain which soaked fans and players alike at Newberry's Setzler Field, the Indians capitalized on costly PC turnovers to set up three of their five scoring plays and end with a winning season (6-5). The Tribe finished 3-4 in the SAC-8.

Newberry had won the derby two years straight before losing it in Clinton 21-7 in 1982. The rivalry dates back to the 1946-47 season with the now-famous theft of a derby from the head of a Presbyterian student at a basketball game in MacLean Gymnasium, and PC still leads the series 44-24-4 (including basketball and baseball games).

And Thursday, as the ball slipped through PC's rain-slicked hands, Newberry played for keeps.

Newberry's defense had backed the Blue Hose into a corner early in the first quarter, and facing a third-and-10 situation inside its own 10-yard line, the visitors elected to pass. They never got the chance — exactly.

Instead, what was meant to be a long bomb squirted out of quarterback Ted Stephens' wet hands and wobbled into the arms of Newberry defensive back Kenneth Pressley. Pressley sprinted 18 yards for Newberry's first touchdown, and Eddie Taylor added the kick to make it 7-0 with 1:14 to go.

Could be that play was the game-winner, since Presbyterian's SAC-8-leading defensive played the remaining three stanzas with what appeared to be a broken spirit (PC gave up 236 yards to Newberry running backs, the most gained against the Blue Hose this year), and its offense managed only 159 yards rushing in 44 tries.

Taylor had another chance to perform his specialty in the second quarter, when Milton Pope recovered one of six PC fumbles. Four plays later, with 5:55 on the clock, Taylor booted a 45-yard field goal to put the Tribe up 10-0.

But Taylor was far from finished. Newberry took its next possession 73 yards in nine plays, including a 52-yard sprint by quarterback Jimmy Skipper, and set up Taylor's 28-yard field goal with only four seconds left in the half.

(continued on page 4)

December 2, 1983 — The Indian

Runningback John Nesbitt in action during the Bronze Derby game.

Bronze Derby (continued from page 1)

In the third quarter, with 8:21 to go, Taylor made good from 26 yards out, after Newberry had moved 51 yards in six plays. Mike Motley sparked the field goal-gaining drive, picking up 60 yards on four carries (including a 53-yard end sweep), and The Indians stretched the margin to 16-0.

Presbyterian sealed its fate in the final quarter when it bobbled the ball at its own 22. This time, William Worthy came up with the ball, and Newberry scored on its third play on a 19-yard scramble by John Nesbitt with 11:58 remaining in the game. Taylor's kick was good for the final spread.

Motley led all rushers with 18 carries for 109 yards, followed by Nesbitt with 20 tries for 67 yards. Both Motley and Nesbitt combined for a Newberry first by each breaking 1,000-yard season totals. The pair led Newberry to a school single-season record for total offense yards, with Motley, a senior from Jacksonville, Fla., tallying 1,078 for the year and Nesbitt, a Mauldin sophomore, gaining 1,005.

Skipper aided the Indian cause with seven carries for 55 yards, and passing for another 83.

Newberry totaled 10 first downs rushing, aided by three completions in seven pass attempts for 83 yards. Its punts averaged 45 yards, and the Indians lost 45 yards to four infractions and three fumbles of its own.

Presbyterian, which maintained a 4-6 season slate and 4-2-1 league mark, counted eight first downs. The Blue Hose completed nine of 19 passes with four interceptions for 159 yards, averaged 40 yards on three punts, and lost 45 yards to penalty markers.

LOST: One tan Members Only Jacket. Contact Bos 8-279. Reward offered.

NEWBERRY COLLEGE DIMENSIONS

VOLUME 17, NUMBER 3 — FEBRUARY 1984

The Li'l That Was!

Coach Clayton Johnson wears the Bronze Derby as his football players carry him off the field after the Indians 25-16 victory over Presbyterian in the Thanksgiving Day clash. The two squads have played for the Bronze Derby since 1947. Although the record for Derby is 14-22 in favor of the Presbyterian Blue Hose, the Indians have won the Derby game four times in the past five years. The 1983 score was 23-0. Newberry and Presbyterian have played each other 73 times since the first game in 1913; with Newberry winning 25 games and Presbyterian 44. Four games ended in ties.

November 1984

November 4	Singer Prince opened his "Purple Rain" tour in Detroit, Michigan.
November 6	Ronald Reagan was re-elected President of the United States defeating Walter Mondale.
November 6	Willie Hernandez of the Detroit Tigers won the MLB AL Most Valuable Player Award.
November 8	NASA astronaut Anna Lee Fisher was the first Mom to go into space.
November 9	Larry Holmes TKO's Bonecrusher Smith for the heavyweight boxing title.
November 9	The horror film "A Nightmare on Elm Street" premiered in the United States.
November 9	The Vietnam Veterans Memorial, "Three Servicemen" was completed in Washington, DC.
November 10	After leading 31-0 in the third quarter, the NCAA Miami Hurricanes lost to the Maryland Terrapins 42-40.
November 12	Paul McCartney released his single "We All Stand Together."
November 12	NASA astronauts recover the first salvaged satellite from space.
November 13	Ryne Sandberg of the Chicago Cubs won the MLB NL Most Valuable Player Award.
November 16	"Emergency," the 16th studio album by American band Kool & the Gang was released and won the 1985 Album of the Year.
November 16	John Lennon's "Every Man Has a Woman Who Loves Him" was released posthumously.
November 18	Terry Labonte won the 34th NASCAR Sprint Cup.
November 20	McDonald's announced the sale of its 50 billionth hamburger.
November 20	Dwight Gooden of the New York Mets was the youngest player to be named MLB NL Rookie of the Year.
November 22	American actress Scarlett Johansson was born.
November 22	Fred Rogers of PBS' "Mr. Rogers Neighborhood" presented a sweater to the Smithsonian Institution in Washington, DC.
November 22	The Bronze Derby was played in Clinton, South Carolina on Thanksgiving Day. The Newberry College Indians defeated the Presbyterian College Blue Hose 25-16.

The Li'l That Was!

The Newberry Observer
AND HERALD & NEWS
"Just Like A Letter From Home"

Newberry, S.C., Wednesday, Nov. 21, 1984

Indians Seek To Spoil PC Playoff Hopes

There will be a lot more at stake Thursday than just taking home the Bronze Derby, when Presbyterian and Newberry Colleges meet for their annual Thanksgiving clash.

The Blue Hose will be out for revenge for last year's loss of the prized hat, and ranked eighth in the nation, they will also be seeking the final berth in the NAIA football playoffs.

PC leads the series at 44-24, but last year, the Blue Hose were surprised by the Indians and lost 23-0.

There's a lot riding on the game for both teams, and the Indians would love to play the spoiler for PC's playoff hopes.

Tied with Morehead State at the number eight position, the Blue Hose hope a win would give them a chance at the playoffs against third-seeded Central Arkansas.

Morehead defeated Dubuque University, Iowa, 56-0 Sunday, after the last poll was taken. Should PC win, a special poll will be taken to determine the team for the final NAIA playoff berth.

Losses last week by both Carson-Newman, SAC-8 conference leader, and Elon College, gave the Blue Hose a chance to tie Carson-Newman for the championship of the league.

Offensively, Newberry will have to take care of Charles Huff, PC's all-star cornerback and probably the best all-around defensive back in the SAC-8 conference.

Huff, who returns kickoffs and punts in addition to his defensive duties, continues to rack up impressive defensive statistics in spite of the fact that opponents usually try to run and throw away from him.

For his career, he has 20 interceptions, three of them this season.

Quarterback Jimmy Skipper will lead the Tribe, and will have to be contained if PC hopes to win. Last season Skipper broke eight school offensive records including season records for yards passing (1,331), attempts (209) and completions (93).

This year, the junior from Cayce, has surpassed his yearly yardage with 1,599 in 10 games. He has nine more completions than last year, and with his third throw Thursday will eclipse his standard for attempts.

Skipper already holds the career passing yardage record with 3,372, surpassing Tom Gorman's 21-year old record by more than 300 yards.

John Nesbitt and Pete Bember continue to lead the Tribe's running attack and Benjie Nichols has played well in the last few games.

Skipper is not the only player going for records Thursday. Flanker Darryl Owings needs only two receptions against PC to tie the record for most receptions in a season. Also, Eddie Taylor is going for a record this time out. He needs one PAT to break the record for most PAT's in one season.

Defensively, the Tribe continues to be led by John Newkirk, Mark Kennedy, and Kenneth Pressley.

This week, the Tribe will be doing without the services of Nesbitt, who has been sidelined with a lacerated kidney.

PC feels their offense is improving every week and this will be the time for a real explosion. Newberry pulled off an upset last year, and the Indians will be out to keep that derby in their trophy case.

Call For Santa Letters

The Newberry Observer will continue a holiday tradition by again printing children's letters to Santa Claus in its annual Christmas edition, set for publication, Friday, Dec. 21.

The Observer offers an invitation to Newberry County youngsters to send their letters to Santa in care of this newspaper.

Letters may be submitted immediately, and will be accepted no later than 5 p.m. Friday, Dec. 14 to allow time for processing.

Photographs will be used with letters this year.

The Li'l That Was!

November 16, 1984 — The Voice of The Newberry College Student — Volume LLIV Number 6

Tradition Abounds In Derby Game

The Thanksgiving Day football game between Newberry and Presbyterian College has been a tradition for many many years. The tradition of the derby trophy is much more recent.

Did you ever wonder how it all came about? It happened in 1947 as a result of a small confrontation at the Newberry-Presbyterian Basketball game that was held on the Newberry Campus that year. It seems that P.C. students had placed a banner on the gym wall, which read "Beat the hell out of Newberry!," before the start of the game. During the game one of the Newberry students obtained a ladder and climbed through a window in McLean Gym to remove the banner.

No one noticed the banner missing until the end of the hard fought game which Presbyterian won 51-47. After the game a Presbyterian student demanded that he get the banner returned to him immediately. A scuffle began in the middle of it and eventually it became a free-for-all. During the fight a Newberry student stole a Derby from the head of a Presbyterian student and ran off from the fight.

During the next couple of days, the two athletic directors negotiated the return of the hat. During the negotiations someone recommended that "a derby should serve as a laurel of victory in athletic contests between Newberry and Presbyterian." Sometime later the derby was returned to Presbyterian. It was then packaged up, so as not to destroy it, and was sent to a casting company out of Ohio. The derby was bronzed and it became the famed Bronze Derby.

Until 1956, the possession of the derby was determined by the outcome of all Newberry-Presbyterian athletic encounters. Be they baseball, basketball or football. Now, the possession is determined by the outcome of the Newberry-Presbyterian football game held annually on Thanksgiving Day.

Newberry won the game convincingly last year (23-0) and took the Bronze Derby for another year. Third year, Clayton Johnson and his tribe will be going against Presbyterian as a slight underdog. The Indians may not take the derby this year, but they're going to fight for it. The game will be played at Presbyterian at 2 p.m. on Thanksgiving Day.

SPORTS

Much at stake in PC-Newberry game

By DOUG IRWIN

Every Presbyterian-Newberry football game is an important one for the two schools involved, since the coveted Bronze Derby is at stake.

But more importantly for PC this year, an NAIA playoff bid hinges on the result of the Thanksgiving Day classic.

With the help of losses by first-ranked Carson-Newman and sixth-ranked Elon Saturday, the Blue Hose (7-3, 5-1 in the conference) moved up into a tie for eighth place in the new NAIA poll with Moorhead State (Minn.). Because of the tie, the NAIA is holding out the final playoff bid until after the Newberry game. Sources indicated to PC that they will get the final spot if they beat the Indians Thursday at 2 p.m. at Johnson Field in Clinton, although an offical vote will be held to decide if the Blue Hose or Moorhead State will play Central Arkansas in Conway, Ark., Dec. 1 in the first-round of the NAIA playoffs.

For everyone involved with the Bronze Derby game — this is the 73rd meeting — nothing is needed to make it bigger than it already is. Despite Newberry winning last year's game, 23-0, in a driving rain at Newberry, PC holds the series advantage (44-24). Four games have ended in ties.

The Indians come into The Game with a 6-4 record, 4-2 in the SAC-8. Two of those losses, though, were at the hands of NCAA Division II powers — Furman, 41-7, and Georgia Southern, 41-16.

THIRD-YEAR coach Clayton Johnson has seen his team through a roller coaster year. "The opening game we had to play Furman and they beat us pretty bad. We regrouped after Furman and won three conference games. Then we got beat pretty bad by Carson Newman (44-21). We got back on the winning track but then we went down and got blown out by Georgia Southern."

Johnson said that game was a scheduling mistake because 10 top 20 teams lost that weekend and Newberry could have moved up dramatically in the NAIA polls if they could have won that weekend.

Blue Hose coach Cally Gault, who will be in his 26th Bronze Derby game Thursday, knows Newberry is no slouch: "They're as good a team as any going into the playoffs. We don't need any added importance to this game.

"We were two defensive tackles away from having a championship season," said Johnson, who is 17-15 at Newberry. "If I had a couple of players like Robert Williams and Lawrence Jackson (the outstanding PC tackles), we could have done something."

GAULT IS GLAD to have the two hulking tackles on his defensive team. Williams, Jackson, linebacker Charlie Hill and cornerback Charles Huff will all be trying to stop Indian quarterback Jimmy Skipper. The Cayce junior was 11 for 16 for 200 yards passing and two touchdowns in Newberry's 20-6 defeat of Lenior-Rhyne last Saturday. Senior tight end Benjie Nichols had five receptions for 114 yards and one touchdown.

Sophomore linebacker John Newkirk leads the Indian defense. Against Lenior-Rhyne, he had 12 primary tackles, 10 assists, a quarterback sack and a fumble recovery. Clinton's Darryl Suber is strong at nose guard.

Gault seems to sum up the great rivalry with this: "The only thing that would be unusual about this game would be that nothing unusual happens."

Two years ago when the Blue Hose won, PC came out in a split back formation after having run out of the I formation for 10 years. "They have more time to look at the game films, so you have to do something different," Gault said. "I'll tell you this. You'll never see such hitting as you'll see from this game. You'll see stars by just watching it on the sidelines."

NEWBERRY'S Johnson, who found out the meaning of the rivalry after he coached in his first two Bronze Derby games, agrees: "There's some hard hitting out there in this game. It will be an interesting game with some interesting players."

Maybe it's because of all that good Thanksgiving eating that brings out the best in the players and coaches. In any case, the turkey will have to wait Thanksgiving Day.

BRONZE DERBY GAME—Expect lots of hard hitting when Presbyterian and Newberry get together Thanksgiving Day for the 73rd Bronze Derby game in Clinton. A possible NAIA playoff bid awaits the Blue Hose if they can get by the Indians. Here, the PC defense gangs up on a Gardner-Webb runner in their 23-12 win over the Bulldogs earlier this season. (Photo by Doug Irwin)

The Li'l That Was!

Bronze Derby game
Indians finish PC

November 26, 1984 — The Laurens County Advertiser

By DOUG IRWIN

The Presbyterian College Blue Hose saw their playoff hopes dashed by Newberry as the Indians won the Bronze Derby for the second straight year, 25-16, in Clinton Thanksgiving Day.

A large crowd decided to come out in the bright holiday sunshine to see an emotionally charged and hard-hitting football game, and they were not disappointed. The 73rd annual classic lived up to its reputation.

UNFORTUNATELY for PC, the outcome ended their season at 7-4. Their probable playoff bid in the NAIA playoffs was history. Moorhead St. of Minnesota won the bid and will travel to play Central Arkansas in the first-round of the playoffs instead of PC.

Turnovers were the key to Presbyterian's disappointing loss. After Newberry had driven downfield on the strength of Jimmy Skipper's passing to take a 19-16 lead early in the fourth quarter, the Blue Hose turned the ball over three times trying to get the winning touchdown.

Running back Kent Larry fumbled after gaining almost 10 yards and a first down after the Newberry score, and the Indians recovered. The PC defense held, giving the offense another crack at winning the game. This time, on third down, PC quarterback Ted Stevens was intercepted by Anthony Hardy, who ran the ball inside the Blue Hose 10-yard line.

The PC defense made a great effort, holding Newberry on a fourth down at the one-yard line. The offense still had time to pull out another one of those miracle comebacks, but this time they had 99 yards to go and only 3:51 to do it.

After moving the ball out over the 20, Presbyterian was faced with a third and two. A Stevens pass to Harvey Blanchard was dropped, forcing a fourth and two. PC ran the option play, which had picked up a crucial first down earlier, but this time Stevens pitched the ball behind running back Jimmy Lindsey. The Newberry defense was all over the ball and the disconsolate Presbyterian team looked on as the Indians celebrated their victory.

NEWBERRY, which also finished at 7-4, was all over the ball all day, but PC got on the board first. The first quarter went scoreless, with Eddie Taylor missing a field goal attempt for coach Clayton Johnson's club. At the start of the second quarter, Lindsey went over the top from one yard out for a touchdown. Doug Culler missed the PAT for PC and the score was 6-0.

A good kickoff return gave Newberry good field position at midfield. Skipper engineered the offense down to the PC six, where he threw a six-yard scoring pass. Taylor hit the PAT, giving the Indians a 7-6 advantage.

Blue Hose running back Billy Barnes fumbled at his 25-yard line, setting up a 37-yard field goal by Taylor. Newberry led 10-6.

On the next series, Lindsey fumbled, setting up another field goal by Taylor.

The Blue Hose held onto the ball long enough on their next series for Culler to connect on a 43-yard field goal to make the score 13-9 at halftime.

Coming out customarily fired up in the second half, PC took the kickoff and drove down for the go-ahead touchdown. Lindsey finished the impressive drive on a three-yard run. Lindsey had well over 100 yards by then, but after the touchdown run, he developed cramps and played sparingly the rest of the game. PC led at that point, 16-13, which would be its last lead.

TURNOVERS plagued Presbyterian all season, but never were they more crucial than against Newberry. Still, it was a good year for Cally Gault's charges, who lost their first two games, won their next seven and lost their final two, finishing in a tie for eighth place in the final NAIA national poll.

GOING IN STYLE—Presbyterian College running back Jimmy Lindsey gains big yardage on the Newberry defense. Lindsey had well over 100 yards on the game but it was not enough to keep the Indians from upsetting the Blue Hose, 25-16, in the 73rd Bronze Derby game in Clinton Thanksgiving Day. (Photo by Doug Irwin)

The Newberry Observer
AND HERALD & NEWS
"Just Like A Letter From Home"

Newberry, S.C., Friday, Nov. 23, 1984

A Bronze Crown

Newberry College Coach Clayton Johnson wears the Bronze Derby as Indian players carry him off the field Thursday, after the Tribe defeated Presbyterian College for the second consecutive year to keep the derby. The Indians downed PC 25-16 and ended the Blue Hose's chances of a playoff berth.

Keeping Derby

Indians Kill PC Playoff Hopes

Newberry College brought home more than just the Bronze Derby from Clinton on Thursday—added to that were a second consecutive winning season and several team records.

But perhaps the most satisfying part of the day, was the Tribe's chance to play spoiler to the playoff hopes of Presbyterian College.

When the clock ran down on Newberry's 25-16 victory, the second consecutive Bronze Derby win, the Blue Hose were out of more than just the ball game. Tied for eighth with Moorhead (Minn.) State in the latest NAIA Division I poll, a PC win would have forced a special survey to determine the final berth in the eight-team national championship.

But the loss kept the Blue Hose from tying Carson-Newman for the SAC-8 championship, and eliminated their playoff hopes with four losses on the season. It also ended a season of frustration for Newberry against nationally ranked teams.

Both teams finished 7-4 on the season and 5-2 in SAC-8 play, but all of the Tribe's losses were to nationally ranked NAIA or NCAA teams. Thursday the Indians gobbled up six PC fumbles on their way to victory over their archrivals at PC's Bailey Memorial Stadium.

Converting a pair of Blue Hose turnovers to field goals, Newberry rallied to take a 19-16 lead in the fourth quarter, and then put the game away with an 11-yard pass from Jimmy Skipper to Darryl Owings with just over a minute to play.

The Indians, who forced mistakes and turned them into points, won the contest without the services of leading rusher John Nesbitt who was sidelined with a lacerated kidney

(Continued On Page 9)

The Li'l That Was!

The Newberry Observer
AND HERALD & NEWS
"Just Like A Letter From Home"

Newberry, S.C., Friday, Nov. 23, 1984

★ Indians (Continued From Page 1)

PC took an early 6-0 lead in the second period on a one-yard run by Evander Gerald, driving 53 yards after Charles Huff fielded a short punt.

Barnes broke loose for a 39-yard gain to the Newberry 14 on the first play, and would have scored had it not been for a shoestring tackle by Indian defensive back Kenneth Pressley. The Blue Hose scored six plays later, on Gerald's run off right tackle with only 1:27 gone in the second quarter. Doug Culler missed the extra point.

The Tribe came right back with a six-yard scoring pass from Skipper to Owings at the end of a 47-yard drive set up by a 38-yard kickoff return by Pete Bember to the PC 47.

Skipper passed 11 yards to Joey Spigner and 13 yards to Jim Sartin during the eight-play march, and finished it by zipping a six-yard pass to Owings between a pair of defenders for a 7-6 Newberry lead.

Two straight PC fumbles within a one and a half minute span, in the first half, led to field goals by Taylor, who was placekicking and punting despite a cast on his left arm.

The first fumble, by Billy Barnes, was recovered by Rick Gray in mid-air and returned to the PC 24. The Indians could only move two yards from there but Taylor came through on a 37-yarder to put the Tribe ahead 10-6.

Lindsey fumbled on the Blue Hose's next possession, and Leonard Benson fell on it at the PC 29. This time the Tribe gained five yards before Taylor hit a 41-yarder with 3:44 left in the half.

Culler pulled the Blue Hose to within four at halftime with a 43-yard field goal with 54 seconds left.

Trailing at intermission, the Blue Hose scored on a three-yard run by Jimmy Lindsay on their first possession of the second half to regain the lead. The Blue Hose used 11 plays to march 48 yards after Charles Huff returned the second-half kickoff 46 yards.

The highly-regarded Blue Hose defense began to weaken late in the period, and the Indians, behind Skipper and running back Bember, marched 78 yards in 13 plays for the go-ahead touchdown, a one-yard run by Bember on fourth and goal.

Bember, who finished the day with 70 yards on 28 carries, had runs of 13 and 10 yards during the drive, which consumed more than seven minutes.

The big play though, was a 24-yard pass from Skipper to Benjie Nichols. The pass was tipped by a PC cornerback, but the 6-4, 225-pound tight end still managed to catch it and batter his way to the Blue Hose nine.

Skipper hit Bember with a six-yard pass inside the one, setting up third and goal, and after Andy Guyton failed on a third down try, Bember leaped over left tackle for the score with 10:42 remaining. Taylor missed the extra point, and finished one-for-three in that department despite hitting both of his field goal attempts.

The Tribe's final score was set up when PC tried to move the ball with a hurry-up passing game that had been non-existent all afternoon, coughed up the ball for the sixth time.

Ted Stephens completed 12-yard passes to John Gayton and J.F. Lucas, and an eight-yarder to Lindsey to move the ball to the PC 36. But on a fourth and two, Stephens pitched behind Lindsey and a swarm of Indians fell on the loose ball at the 11.

Newberry Coach Clayton Johnson called a fake dive play off left guard, and Skipper found Owings open in the right corner of the end zone for the clinching TD.

The Newberry Observer
AND HERALD & NEWS
"Just Like A Letter From Home"

Newberry, S.C., Friday, Nov. 23, 1984

Winning Score

Newberry's Pete Bember (24) carried the ball 14 yards for the Tribe's go-ahead touchdown in the battle for the Bronze derby Thursday at Presbyterian College. Newberry won the game 25-16.

Indian Touchdown

Darryl Owens (9) holds the ball after catching this six-yard pass for the Indians first score at PC Thursday. The Tribe went on to win the Bronze Derby and the ball game 25-16.

The Newberry Observer
AND HERALD & NEWS
"Just Like A Letter From Home"

Newberry, S.C., Friday, Nov. 23, 1984

1984 Indians Finish Record Breaking Season

Only six other times in the history of Newberry College football have the Indians posted two consecutive winning seasons—but they did it again this year.

With their win against Presbyterian College Thursday, the Indians assured Coach Clayton Johnson as the fourth head coach with a winning career record and made him the second coach to have more than one winning season. Reed Charpia (1978-81) had a 21-20-0 mark in four years, the only other mutiple-season coach with a winning record.

The Tribe's back-to-back winning seasons occurred in 1924-25; 1938-40; 1953-54; 1956-59 (four straight); 1971-72; and 1978-79.

In addition to a winning season, the 1984 Indians broke several individual and team records, and came close on others.

The Tribe set new team records in most PAT's kicked at 28 (also a record for Eddie Taylor); most yards total offense with 3,850 in 10 games and most per game average offense with 350 for 10 games.

The Indians just missed breaking team records set in 1973 for: most points scored with 255 in 1984 (259-record), most touchdowns scored with 34 in 1984, (35 record); most yards passing with 1,965 in 1984, (1,983 record); most per game average passing 178.6 in 1984 (180.3 record); and most touchdown passes with 13 in 1984 (14 record).

Individually, team members also did well at breaking records this season.

Placekicker Eddie Taylor set the school career field goal record with 23 successful attempts, breaking the 1975-78 record of 19 set by Bob McMillan.

A junior, Taylor already owns the longest field goal record of 50 yards, set in 1983 vs. Elon; the most field goals in a single game with three; and tied the most PATs kicked in one game with six. He is currently only 12 PATs short of the career record of 75 set by Tommy Williamson, 1970-73.

Quarterback Jimmy Skipper, with 1,713 yards this year, has already broken the career passing yardage record of 3,036 yards set by Tom Gorman, 1960-63.

Skipper, in three seasons, has completed 245 of 520 passes for 3,846 yards and 23 touchdowns. His completion total is just six shy of the record of 251 completions set by Eddie Pettus, 1978-81. He has already broken his single season records for completions (105) and yards passing (1,599) set last year when he completed 93 of 209 passes for 1,256 yards.

Wide receiver Darryl Owings has tied on record, most passes caught in one game with nine against Georgia Southern several weeks ago. Three other Indians also hold that mark, the latest being Jim Sartin (a sophomore) with nine against West Georgia last year.

Owings did establish a single season receiving record, surpassing Fred Haley's 36 set in 1962. He has 37 catches for 543 yards this year, but is well short of Raphael Masters' record of 814 yards in 1938.

Defensively All-American candidate Mark Kennedy, senior defensive end, has already set a school record with five, quarterback sacks against Gardner-Webb in the second game of this season. That breaks a record held by four former Indians between 1976 and 1980 of three sacks in one game. Kennedy also has 11 fumble recoveries in his career and 30 quarterback sacks, both modern records for the Indians. His career tackle totals of just over 275 is well short of Dennis Yarborough's mark of 430 set between 1975-79.

Linebacker John Newkirk leads the Indians in tackling this year with 133 participations but is also well short of All-American Mark Weeks' record of 201 set in 1982. Weeks also holds the most participations in one game with .31 against Georgia Southern in 1982.

All-American candidate Kenneth Pressley, junior safety, has five blocked kicks this season, also believed to be a modern-day record. As far as recent records indicate, no other Indian has come close to this feat.

the Indian

The Li'l That Was!

November 29, 1984 — The Voice of The Newberry College Student — Volume LIV, Number 7

Indians Keep Derby At Home

by John Babson

The Newberry Indians invaded Bailey Memorial Field, home of the Presbyterian Blue Hose, on Thanksgiving Day for a heated match up. Not only was this a match up between two SAC-8 members but this game also determined who would win the Bronze DErby. The Indians, behind pure determination and a 4th quarter game plan, won the SAC-8 match up for the second straight year by a tune of 26-16.

The victory gave the Indians a fine 7-4 record and a fourth place finish in the SAC-8. The winning season also gave the Indians consecutive winning seasons for the seventh time in the history of Newberry football.

Newberry's win of the Bronze Derby was not an easy one. The game began slowly as neither team scored in the first quarter. The only scoring threat occurred when Newberry's Eddie Taylor, placekicker, attempted a 23 yard field goal only to see it sail wide to the left.

Presbyterian then mounted a drive in the second quarter which was keyed by a 31 yard run by Billy Barnes, fullback. After a series of plays, the Blue Hose had the ball on the Indian 1 yard line. Alexander Gerald, fullback, dove over from the 1 yardline for the TD. With the extra point attempt failing, Presbyterian led 6-0.

The Indians, not to be denied, answered right back. Pete Bember, halfback, ran the ensuing kick-off back to the Blue Hose 45 yard line to give the Indians good field position. Newberry utilized the services of Andy Guyton, fullback, and ran straight up the middle. Guyton and company left the ball on the Blue Hose 8 yard line where Jimmy Skipper, quarterback, took over. Skipper tossed a "nifty" pass to Darryl Owings, wide receiver, for the TD. Taylor was true with the extra point to give the Indians a 7-6 edge with 9:29 left in the first half.

Presbyterian then tried to answer back after the kick-off. The Blue Hose moved the ball from their 17 yard line to their 38 yard line where the Indian's defense set up their scalping ceremony which they would continue to do all day. The Indian defense scalped a Blue Hose ball carrier of the ball, and Newberry's

(See Derby P. 12)

Go Get 'Em Boys

Linebackers John Newkirk and Carl Boyd break up a pass by PC during the Bronze Derby Game on Thanksgiving Day.

Derby

(Cont'd. From P. 11)

Rick Gray recovered the fumble on the Presbyterian 35 yard line.

Newberry's offense then came on to try for another TD. The Blue Hose's defense tightened up. Newberry then called on Taylor to attempt a 37 yard field goal. Newberry led 10-6.

Presbyterian received the kick-off and once again began to drive. And once again the Newberry defense proceeded with their scalping ceremony. The Indians scalped another helpless Blue Hose ball carrier which set up another Taylor field goal. This one being from 43 yards out to give the Indians a 13-6 lead.

Presbyterian was finally able to generate a scoring drive late in the second quarter. A combination of screen passes and powerful running brought the Blue Hose to the Indian 38 yard line. Newberry defense stiffened and Presbyterian offense stalled. The Blue Hose then called Doug Cutler, placekicker, for a 63 yard field goal with 54 seconds left in the half, score 13-9, Newberry.

The second half began with Newberry kicking-off to Presbyterian. Aided by defensive back Charles Huff's 44 yard kick-off return, the Blue Hose drove to the Indian 1 foot line. But Newberry's John Newkirk, linebacker, hustled through the line to throw Presbyterian for a 3 yard loss. The Blue Hose then dove over from the 3 yard line for a TD. The kick was good and Presbyterian had a 16-13 lead.

After a series of plays, Newberry regained possession of the ball at their own 21 yard line. Newberry then put together a 79 yard march for the Bember TD. Taylor's extra point attempt was good and Newberry led 19-16 with 10:42 remaining in the game.

Presbyterian received the ensuing kick-off. But before the Blue Hose could manage a drive, Newberry's James Caldwell, noseguard, recovered a Presbyterian fumble. Newberry's offense was unable to generate anything and had to punt. With Presbyterian on their 4 yard line late in the fourth quarter, Newkirk intercepted the ball to almost seal the game.

Presbyterian got one more chance after Newberry's offense stalled. The Blue Hose took over on their 3 yard line with 2 minutes left in the game. Presbyterian drove to their 38 yard line where they faced a fourth and three situation. This would be the decisive play of the game and Newberry's head hunting defense rose to the occasion. Blue Hose Ted Stephens, quarterback, set up and attempted to run the outside option and fumbled the ball to the Indians. Newberry recovered at Presbyterian's 41 yard line.

The Indians, making sure Presbyterian understood who was boss, then calmly scored a TD when a pass from Skipper to Owings on the Indian's first play of the series. The extra point attempt by Taylor failed; nevertheless, the Indians held on for a 26-19 victory.

The victory was very important for the Indians because it allowed the Bronze Derby to remain at Newberry for a second consecutive year.

Jeff Godbee, a 5'11" 225 lb. junior offensive guard from Georgia, said "I knew we could do it all along. The coaches had been preparing us all week and telling us to follow the game plan which is exactly what we did." Godbee went on to say, "I feel that this victory is a perfect example of how much the program has improved."

Ronnie Pridgen, a 6'2" 260 lb. junior defensive tackle, said, "We don't feel any sympathy for them. All week long they were talking how bad they were going to beat us and how they were going to the playoffs, but they forgot to tell us." Pridgen went on to say, "Our offense and defense just beat their tails and that's why they aren't going to the playoffs." Presbyterian had beaten Newberry the Blue Hose would have made the playoffs. But the Indians rose to the occasion and now the Blue Hose are sitting home.

	NC	PC
First downs	15	17
Rushing yards	44-118	47-199
Passing yards	113	56
Return yards	128	98
Passes	11-20-0	4-9-1
Punts	6-30.2	1-44.0
Fumbles	1-0	5-4
Penalties	10-75	3-27

The Li'l That Was!

On November 22, 1984, the Newberry College Indians defeated the Presbyterian College Blue Hose in Clinton, South Carolina to retain the Bronze Derby. The final score was NC 25-PC 16. The game was the 38th Thanksgiving Day Bronze Derby football Classic.

The Bronze Derby Game Newberry vs. Presbyterian

NEWBERRIAN

The Li'l That Was!

The Presbyterian College Report
December, 1984

To remain as athletic director and fund-raiser for sports:

Cally Gault retires from football after 22 years

Cally Gault made the 1984 season one of his best and then retired after 22 years as head football coach.

He will continue to serve as athletic director, with additional responsibilities in athletic fund-raising as executive-director of the Walter Johnson Scotsman Club.

The 57-year-old alumnus led his last PC team to 7 wins and 4 defeats and ninth-place national ranking in the NAIA poll. It was the best finish since making the playoffs and number four rank in 1979. It also brought him the closing accolade of being named once again "coach-of-the-year" for the South Atlantic Conference.

Gault stepped down with a PC career record of 127-101-8 and a reputation for high sportsmanship as the "dean of South Carolina football coaches." He has been coach-of-the-year for the state five times and for his conference (the Carolinas, then SAC-8) on five other occasions.

"I have always considered it a privilege to coach at my alma mater," Gault said, "but now is the time to give more attention to the overall management of our broad athletic program and to the securing of more funds to help stabilize it.

"I am grateful for the fine support given to PC football by our students, faculty, administration, alumni and friends. We tried to play competitively and respectably against the good teams of our area. I also hope our program has made it apparent that there is much good in properly run intercollegiate athletics. These things have been traditional at Presbyterian, and I believe we achieved a measure of success in upholding the tradition."

President Orr praised Gault for his notable contributions to Presbyterian College and added these words:

"Cally Gault is a recognized leader in small college football. He has given PC a winning edge on the playing field while maintaining the dignity and integrity of our entire sports program. Now that he no longer has football responsibility, Cally will devote more time to the coordination and promotion of all sports. He also should be effective in raising funds for the varsity programs."

The Li'l 🎩 That Was!

The 1984 Bronze Derby victory by Newberry College was the last Bronze Derby coached by Presbyterian Head Football Coach Calley Gault. His 1963-1984 overall record with the Blue Hose was 126-100-8. In 22 seasons competing for the Bronze Derby, his record was 14-8-0.

Photo courtesy of Presbyterian College archives

November 1985

November 1	American comedy actor Phil Silvers passed away.
November 1	Nostalgia Television debuted on cable networks.
November 3	Bill Elliott won the Atlanta Journal 500 at Atlanta Raceway and became the first driver to win over $2 million in a single season.
November 9	Russia's Garry Kasparov became the youngest World Chess Champion at the age of 22.
November 11	"An Early Frost," the first AIDS themed television movie, debuted in the United States on NBC TV.
November 16	United States President Ronald Reagan and Soviet President Mikhail Gorbachev agreed to meet in Geneva, Switzerland for a summit.
November 15	A research assistant at the University of Michigan was injured when a package from the Unabomber addressed to a university Professor exploded.
November 17	Darrell Waltrip won the 35th NASCAR Sprint Cup.
November 17	Howard Stern began broadcasting on a local radio station in New York City.
November 18	Dwight Gooden of the New York Mets, the youngest 20 game pitcher in MLB history, won the MLB NL Cy Young Award. Bret Saberhagan won the MLB AL Cy Young Award.
November 18	Singer Janet Jackson married singer James DeBarge.
November 18	Paul McCartney released the film theme single "Spies Like Us."
November 19	United States President Ronald Reagan and Soviet President Mikhail Gorbachev met in Geneva, Switzerland.
November 19	Pennzoil was awarded $10.5 billion against Texaco in the largest civil suit in United States history.
November 20	Microsoft Windows 1.0 was released.
November 20	Don Mattingly of the New York Yankees won the MLB AL Most Valuable Player Award.
November 24	Egyptian commandos stormed a hijacked Egypt Air jet killing 60.
November 26	Random House bought former United States President Richard Nixon's memoirs for $3 million.
November 28	The Bronze Derby was played in Newberry, South Carolina on Thanksgiving Day. The Newberry College Indians and the Presbyterian College Blue Hose played to a 24-24 tie.

The Li'l 🎩 That Was!

ce Championship Game — Page 7 — **Bronze Derby Clash Thursday**

The Newberry Observer
AND HERALD & NEWS
"Just Like A Letter From Home"

WS ESTABLISHED 1865 — Newberry, S. C., Wednesday, Nov. 27, 1985 — THE NEWBERRY OBSERVER ESTA

NO. 142 — TWO SECTI

Indians To Play For Bronze Derby

BY MIKE MEADOW

The 7-3 Newberry College Indians will keep a Thanksgiving tradition alive this Thursday when the Tribe takes on the Presbyterian Blue Hose, who is also 7-3.

The two teams will collide for the 74th time since 1913 to do battle for the bronze derby. The Indians have held the derby for the last two seasons.

Last year, the Indians traveled to Clinton and handed the Blue Hose a 25-16 loss that knocked the Blue Hose out of the NAIA playoffs.

Last week, the Indians handed Lenoir Rhyne a loss by a 35-21 margin in their last road game of the season.

In last week's game, John Nesbitt set the career rushing record at Newberry as he carried the ball 14 times for 135 yards. Nesbitt now has 3,213 yards and 28 touchdowns in his career at Newberry.

The Indians' other fine runningback, Pete Bember, had 106 yards rushing on 13 carries in the Indians' offensive attack.

Defensively, James Caldwell had his best game of the season last week for the Indians. Caldwell had six solo tackles, seven assists, and two quarterback sacks for a total loss of -18 yards.

The Tribe also got outstanding play from its linebackers, who accounted for 27 tackles and 10 yards in loss yardage.

Both Newberry and P-C will enter the game ranked in the national poll. Newberry is ranked 14th, and the Blue Hose come into the game ranked at number 16. A loss by either team will not affect the polls, since the final NAIA poll came out on Nov. 24.

Clayton Johnson holds a 25-16 record in his fourth season at Newberry, while Elliott Poss is 7-3 in his first season at the helm of the Blue Hose.

Kickoff for Thursday's game is scheduled for 2 p.m. at Setzler Field on the Newberry College Campus.

Derby Tradition
The Newberry College Indians will be trying to keep the coveted bronze derby this Thursday in the annual Thanksgiving Day battle with Presbyterian. The Indians have won the contest the past two years under the helm of coach Clayton Johnson. — Newberry College photo.

SPORTS

The Derby
PC, Newberry renew rivalry

By Steve Owens
Sports Editor

Thursday will mark the 74th meeting of Presbyterian College and Newberry College in football's Bronze Derby Classic. If all goes according to pre-game predictions, it should also be one of the most exciting contests in the history of the rivalry.

The Blue Hose will take the top defense in the SAC-8 Conference to Newberry's Setzler Field to challenge the Indians' top-rated offense. The matchup, according to PC head coach Elliott Poss, puts the pressure on the Blue Hose offense.

"The top offense versus the top defense throws the weight upon our offense's shoulders to control the football and keep it away from them," Poss said. "That can be just as important as how well our defense plays against their offense."

Controlling the football means running it, and PC has one of the best rushers in the SAC-8 in freshman tailback Stevie Riggins. The second leading rusher in the conference, Riggins has picked up 853 yards this season for a 5.4 yard per carry average. Riggins' talent has been noticed by Newberry coach Clayton Johnson.

"WE NEED to control Riggins," the Indians' coach said. "He's going to get yardage, but I just hope he doesn't break one of those real long runs and turn the whole game around. I lay awake at night worrying about him."

Johnson said the entire PC offensive unit, which averages 323.5 yards per game, is the best he has seen in his four years at Newberry. One of his concerns is senior quarterback Ted Stephens. The conference's fourth leading passer, Stephens has thrown for 1,020 yards this season.

"We can't allow him to have a big game," Johnson said.

To slow down the PC rushing attack, Johnson will need a good game out of his defensive line, which was struck by injuries earlier in the season. The Indians currently rank seventh in the SAC-8 against the run, allowing 221 yards per game.

"Their defense is probably the one area in which they've improved the most," Poss said, noting that the Indians had played extremely good rushing teams late in the season. "We'll have to execute the block very well to move the ball on the ground against them."

NEWBERRY RETURNS an experienced secondary that ranks second in the conference. All-America free safety Kenneth Pressley and strong safety Milton Pope will try to keep the Blue Hose receivers in check, while All-District linebacker John Newkirk, the leading tackler on the team, will pressure Stephens.

The Newberry offense has provided firepower all season. Leading the balanced attack is senior quarterback Jimmy Skipper, the all-time Newberry passing leader with over 5,000 yards.

"His ability to scramble is phenomenal," Poss said. "He's made some great plays against us over a number of years. We'll have to contain him."

Leading the Indians' receiving corps are senior flanker Darryl Owings and junior wide receiver Joey Spigner. Owings, the fourth leading receiver in the conference, has accounted for 650 yards this season, while Spigner, the sixth leading receiver, has rolled up 379 yards.

But Johnson said the key for the Indians will be to establish their running game.

"That should be a real challenge because nobody has been able run the ball on PC all year," he said. "I don't want to get into the situation where PC shuts our running game down and we are forced to throw. That's what they have done to most teams this year."

TO ESTABLISH their running attack, the Indians will rely on two of the finest running backs in the conference. Senior John Nesbitt became Newberry's all-time leading rusher this season. Not only does Nesbitt rank fifth in rushing in the conference, he is currently seventh in receiving, giving the Indians a double threat out of the backfield.

Nesbitt's running mate, junior Pete Bember, is the third leading rusher in the SAC-8 with an 84.1 yard-per-game average. He also ranks fourth in scoring (6 points per game) and 10th in total offense (92.5 yards per game).

Newberry runs a multiple offense. Not only are Nesbitt and Bember used out of the split-back set, but the Indians also run out of the I-formation. In this set, Nesbitt is used as the fullback and Bember becomes the tailback. The two are a major reason the Indians average 382.5 yards per game.

The game should be a major test for the Blue Hose defense.

One of the reasons the PC defense ranks first in total team defense (248.4 yard per game average) in the SAC-8 is senior tackle Lawrence Jackson, who will be playing his final game as a Blue Hose. Jackson leads the team with 110 total tackles and 11 quarterback sacks. Senior linebacker Rodney Berry has added 100 tackles.

POSS SAID his tackles and outside linebackers will be a major force in containing Skipper.

"They will have to rush with great intensity, yet be under control at all times as we attempt to put some pressure on him," the first-year coach said. "We hope we can prevent him from making

(Continued on page 15)

DERBY TIME — Presbyterian College freshman tailback Stevie Riggins will be just one of the race horses ready to run in this year's Derby. Riggins, the second leading rusher in the SAC-8 Conference, will duel Newberry's John Nesbitt and Pete Bember for supremacy on the ground, as PC's top defense challenges the Indians' top offense. Newberry has claimed four of the last five Classics. (Photo by Steve Owens)

Game a part of Poss' life each year

Elliott Poss

By Steve Owens
Sports Editor

An impressive collection of awards adorn the trophy case in Templeton P.E. Center on the campus of Presbyterian College. However, a void between two trophies in the case is filled by a card. It reads, "Reserved for the Bronze Derby, 1985."

PC head football coach Elliott Poss said the message was placed in the case before he took over the team this season. But the card is representative of the competitive spirit inherent in the rivalry.

The Blue Hose lead the rivalry, 44-25-4, but the Indians have claimed the Derby four of the past five years. The coaches recognize the intensity of the game, summing it up in one word. Pride.

"IT'S A matter of personal pride," Poss said. "We want to bring the Bronze Derby back to PC. You feel the intensity somewhat more for this game."

Newberry coach Clayton Johnson compared the rivalry to that of Clemson and South Carolina.

"It's really a game for the fans," he said. "All the coaches and players know each other, and are on friendly terms before and after the game. But in between, it's very competitive."

The Bronze Derby Classic has special meaning to Poss. As a defensive back for the Blue Hose from 1967-1970, he enjoyed a 4-0 record against the Indians. In 1968, his sophomore year, Poss played one of his best collegiate games against the Indians in the Bronze Derby Classic.

"I had two interceptions that day, and was fortunate enough to return one for a touchdown," he recalled. "That was the only collegiate touchdown I scored."

BUT DURING his senior year, Poss injured his knee the week before the game and was unable to participate in the game. He recalled with disappointment that he did not get to play in his final college football game — the Bronze Derby Classic.

"Since 1967, nearly all of my Thanksgivings have been associated with this football game," Poss said. "It has become a part of my life on Thanksgiving Day."

Poss also said he was disappointed that PC has not had much success against Newberry over the past few years, but he expects the intensity of the rivalry to motivate his players. Poss is very familiar with that intensity. He remembers standing on the sideline his senior year, forced to watch rather than participate.

And he'll be back on the sidelines again on Thursday, hoping to add a trophy to the case.

The Li'l That Was!

| Indians, Blue Hose Tie For Derby Page 8 | Rebels, Eagles Vie For Title Page 8 |

The Newberry Observer
AND HERALD & NEWS
"Just Like A Letter From Home"

HERALD & NEWS ESTABLISHED 1885
THE NEWBERRY OBSERVER ESTABLISHED 1883
VOL. 121 – ISSUE NO. 143
Newberry, S.C., Friday, Nov. 29, 1985
ONE SECTION – 16 PAGES

Indians And Blue Hose Tie In Bronze Derby Clash

BY MIKE MEADOW

The Newberry College Indians will get to keep the bronze derby for one more year.

No, the Indians didn't win, but because they won last year and since they were the last team to win, they get to keep it.

Tom Netting blocked an Eddie Taylor 18-yard field goal attempt with time running out to keep the game knotted at 24-24.

The game, which was exciting as ever, started out to be all Newberry. The Indians scored two touchdowns in the early going, before the Blue Hose offense could get on track.

The first score of the day came on a 43-yard pass from runningback John Nesbitt to Darryl Owings. Nesbitt took the pitch from quarterback Jimmy Skipper, set up, and threw to the wide open Owings. The PAT by Taylor was good.

The Indians second score of the day came on a one-yard run by Nesbitt. The PAT by Taylor was good, and the Indians had a 14-0 lead.

The Blue Hose offense got on track in the second quarter, putting 10 points on the board just before the half.

Presbyterian runningback Riggins put the Blue Hose on the board with a 10-yard touchdown run. The PAT by Culler was good.

The Newberry lead was cut to four when Culler connected on a 45-yard field goal. Culler's three points made the score 14-10 in favor of Newberry at the half.

The Blue Hose took the lead in the second half on a nine-yard touchdown run by Barnes. The PAT by Culler was good, and P-C was up 17-14.

The final points scored by the Blue Hose were also score by Barnes. Barnes put the Blue Hose out in front by a nine on his second touchdown run of the day. The PAT by Culler was good, and P-C had a 10-point lead.

The Indians began their comeback on Taylor's 44 yard field goal. Taylor's field goal, which came late in the game, cut the P-C lead to seven.

With 5:02 remaining, Pete Bember score from four yards out to put the Indians within one. Taylor then hit his third PAT of the day to tie the score at 24-24.

The Indians final bid to score fell short as Skipper was stopped on the one yard line on third and goal from the three.

Taylor was then called to attempt an 18-yard field goal. The field goal, which was blocked, would have given the Indians their eighth win of the season.

Both teams finished the regular season at 7-3-1. Newberry was ranked 14th in the NAIA national poll and P-C came into the game ranked 18th.

Next year the game will be played Presbyterian College in Clinton.

The Li'l That Was!

The Blue Stocking
of Presbyterian College

VOL. LXXX Issue 13
Clinton, S.C. 29325
December 6, 1989

News Briefs

Picture Perfect!

The Classic Photography photos from Fall Fling weekend are in and may be viewed at the Springs Campus Center front desk. Students may order prints for $2 each through next Thursday.

Madrigal Program

The Madrigal Dinner Concerts will create a touch of 16th century "Merrie Olde England" at Presbyterian College this weekend.

It's the 20th anniversary of the PC program, one of the oldest in the Southeast, and many alumni of earlier Madrigal troupes are returning to help celebrate the occasion.

Founder-director Dr. Charles T. Gaines said reservations already have been filled for the twin evening performances this Friday and Saturday and for the dessert-concert scheduled for Sunday afternoon. All programs are being held in PC's Greenville Dining Hall, the two dinner-concerts starting at 7:30 p.m. and the dessert-concert at 2:30 p.m.

The popular presentations, an annual prelude to the Christmas season, take on notes of colorful pageantry as the PC dining facility becomes a great hall with banquet tables. A trumpet sounds its fanfare. Dressed authentically in the elaborate costumes of the ladies and gentlemen of the old English court, members of the

No Holding Back...

There was no holding back last Thursday when the Blue Hose held the Newberry Indians to a 24-24 tie. The annual Thanksgiving clash resulted in Newberry's possession of the famed Bronze Derby for another year. (Photo by Fletcher Pruitt, Jr.)

"We offer $1 discounts to PC students!"

Drug-Lo Discount Drug Center
(Across from McDonald's)
984-3541

The Li'l 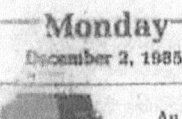 That Was!

Monday December 2, 1985

The Laurens County Advertiser

An award-winning newspaper

Published Monday and Wednesday
20¢ per copy

Vol. No. 100—Pub. No. 305050
Laurens, South Carolina
No. 46—12 Pages

PC, Newberry battle to tie

By Steve Owens
Sports Editor

NEWBERRY — More than 4,000 fans filled the stands and lined the field at Newberry College's Setzler Field Thursday to watch what was sure to be one of the most exciting Bronze Derby Classics in recent years.

Well, the 24-24 tie was exciting, but as Presbyterian head coach Elliott Poss said after the contest, it was also disappointing.

"Our players are emotionally disappointed by a tie," he said. "I think we were a little bit flat from having talked so much in the last 10 days about bringing the Derby back to PC."

The tie left the Blue Hose and the Indians tied for third place in the SAC-8 Conference with identical 4-2-1 records. Both teams also finish with overall records of 7-3-1.

Although an NAIA playoff spot was not at stake for the winner of the Thanksgiving game, both coaches spoke with pride of their teams' performances in the emotional battle. Poss noted that a 7-3-1 record earns a bowl bid at many major NCAA Division I institutions.

BUT IT was a game of domination on a partly cloudy day that marked the 74th meeting of PC and Newberry. The conference's top offense challenged the top defense. Only a blocked field goal with six seconds remaining in the game preserved the tie and sent the fans home to their Thanksgiving dinner wondering which team was better. Exciting yes, but also disappointing.

It appeared the PC defense would not be moved as Newberry head coach Clayton Johnson featured running back John Nesbitt and quarterback Jimmy Skipper rushing on the Indians' first possesion. Johnson said earlier in the week that his team would have to establish its running game to be effective, but the Blue Hose allowed just seven yards on three runs and forced a punt.

Freshman tailback Stevie Riggins opened the PC attack, rushing 11 yards on the first play from scrimmage. Six plays later, the Blue Hose faced a fourth down-and-one situation on the Newberry 34 yard line. But quarterback Ted Stephens failed to pick up the necessary yardage on a keeper, shifting the momentum to the Indians. Newberry made the most of the opportunity.

The Indians ran three sweep options to running back Pete Bember on the next possession, complementing a 17-yard completion from Skipper to junior wide receiver Joey Spigner. With 6:34 remaining in the first half, Nesbitt took the pitch from Skipper on another apparent sweep, but threw back across the field to flanker Darryl Owings who was all alone in the PC secondary and covered 43 yards for a Newberry score. Eddie Taylor's extra point gave the Indians the only score of the first half and a 7-0 lead.

NEWBERRY CONTINUED to dominate the game into the second quarter. After the Indians' defense shut down the Blue Hose offense on two successive possessions, the Newberry offense struck again.

Bember broke a 32-yard gain on a third down, and Skipper hit tight end John Casey with a 25-yard pass to move Newberry to the PC 12 yard line. Four plays later, Nesbitt capped the nine-play, 76-yard drive, with a one-yard plunge. Taylor's extra point left the Blue Hose facing a 14-0 deficit with just 8:45 remaining in the first half.

But a rejuvenated PC offense took the field on the next possession. Junior tailback Jimmy Lindsey broke runs of 41 and 16 yards as the Blue Hose quickly drove to the Newberry 16 yard line. Riggins, who was not at full strength after suffering an injured shoulder against Carson-Newman, covered those 16 yards on two runs and gave PC its first score of the game with 5:51 remaining in the half. Senior Doug Culler cut the lead to 14-7 with his 21st extra point of the year.

A late drive by the Blue Hose was sustained when Newberry was called for roughing PC punter John Gayton with 20 seconds remaining in the half. Stephens then hit Gayton with a 24-yard strike at the Newberry 29 yard line, setting up a dramatic 45-yard field goal by Culler as time expired in the first half.

ALTHOUGH POSS said the field goal, "boosted our team a great deal at the half," Johnson blamed his team's penalties for allowing the Blue Hose to get back into the game.

"We really gave them 10 points in the second quarter on the two

DIGGING IN — Blue Hose quarterback Ted Stephens looks for help as he tries to break the grasp of a Newberry tackler in the second quarter of Thursday's Bronze Derby Classic. Believe it or not, Stephens maintained his balance, but was brought down after a short gain. His efforts were not enough, however, as the Blue Hose and Indians battled to a 24-24 tie in the 74th meeting between the two teams. (Photo by Steve Owens)

personal fouls after we had stopped them," Johnson said. "It was totally ridiculous."

But the momentum stayed with the Blue Hose into the third quarter. On their opening drive of the second half, the Hose ground out 74 yards on 12 rushes, as fullback Billy Barnes scored from nine yards. Culler's extra point gave PC its first lead of the day at 17-14.

PC's top defense set up the next score, as freshman Brad Moser recovered a Skipper fumble on the Newberry 8 yard line. Barnes scored his second touchdown of the quarter two plays later, and Culler's third extra point of the game gave the Blue Hose a commanding 24-14 lead. PC fans began celebrating the apparent return of the Bronze Derby to Clinton.

Although Poss said he was surprised at how well his offense ran against the Indians in the third quarter, Johnson was not.

"They were trying to keep the ball away from our offense," Johnson said. "If that was their strategy, then they didn't feel like they could stop our offense in the first place, which I don't think they could."

JOHNSON'S OFFENSE indeed moved the ball at will against the Blue Hose defense in the final quarter. Taylor hit a 33-yard field goal to cut the lead to 24-17. The Indians scored on their next possession as well. Bember went in from four yards out to the beat of the Newberry war chant, capping a seven-play, 57-yard drive. Taylor's extra point tied the game with 5:02 remaining.

After the Blue Hose offense was shut down on three plays, the Indians received the ball on their own 48 yard line. Skipper completed a 42-yard pass to Bember, who fumbled the ball. Bember alertly ran back in bounds and recovered the fumble on the PC 7. The officials ruled that since Bember was knocked out of bounds by the PC defenders, it was legal for him to return to the field of play and recover the fumble.

Newberry faced a third-and-goal with 42 seconds remaining, but Skipper was stopped on a keeper, setting up the dramatic field goal attempt by Taylor. PC freshman defensive back Tom Netting broke through to block the 18-yard attempt that would have won the game for the Indians.

Johnson could not comprehend Netting's block.

"Something happened because it is mathematically impossible for that man to get in there and block the field goal," he said, noting that Newberry's offensive linemen should keep a specific amount of space between themselves when lining up. "You've just got to give him (Netting) credit. It was a great effort on his part."

NETTING SAID he was surprised that Taylor did not get the kick off as quickly as he had all afternoon.

"It was hard to get in there early in the game and I was getting kind of frustrated," he said. "But they cut down on (PC outside linebacker) John Terrapin and I just got a good jump on the ball and went for it."

Poss noted that the game could not detract from the pleasure he received from his first year as the head coach of the Blue Hose.

"It's been quite an experience, and I wouldn't take anything for the work and the experiences I've had with the players this year," he said.

But Clayton Johnson, whose Indians maintain possession of the Bronze Derby for another year, reflected on the day's game.

"There were some very good matchups. We dominated a couple of quarters, and they dominated a couple of quarters."

The result was excitement, disappointment and a tie.

In 1985, Newberry College and Presbyterian College played to a 24-24 tie. Newberry College retained the Bronze Derby. The game was played in Newberry, South Carolina. The game was the 40th Thanksgiving Day Bronze Derby football Classic.

Photo courtesy of Presbyterian College archives

The Li'l 🎩 That Was!

November 1986

November 1	MLB player Kirby Puckett married Tonya Hudson.
November 2	German tennis player Boris Becker won his third tournament in 3 weeks. Each tournament was won on a different continent.
November 3	Northern Mariana Islands became a Commonwealth associated with the United States.
November 3	Lebanese Magazine *Ash Shirra* broke the news of a United States secret arms sale to Iran.
November 3	John Lenon's album "Menlove Avenue" was released posthumously.
November 6	United States President Ronald Reagan signed a landmark immigration reform bill.
November 11	Houston Astros Mike Scott won the MLB NL Cy Young Award.
November 13	United States President Ronald Reagan admitted to a weapons sale to Iran.
November 15	The Beastie Boys released their debut album which became the first #1 RAP album on the *Billboard* charts.
November 15	American golfer Byron Nelson married Peggy Simmons.
November 16	Dale Earnhardt won the 36th NASCAR Sprint Cup.
November 17	Roger Clemens won the MLB AL Cy Young Award.
November 19	Boxer Muhammad Ali married Yolanda Williams.
November 19	Mike Schmidt of the Philadelphia Phillies won MLB NL Most Valuable Player Award.
November 20	The World Health Organization announced the first global effort to battle AIDS.
November 20	Comedian Steve Martin married actress Victoria Tennant.
November 22	Mike Tyson became the youngest heavyweight champion at 22 years old by defeating Trevor Berbick in the second round.
November 22	NHL player Wayne Gretzky of the Edmonton Oilers became the 13th player to score 500 goals.
November 25	Katie Cassidy, American actress of "A Nightmare on Elm Street" was born.
November 25	Jose Canseco of the Oakland A's won the MLB AL Rookie of the Year Award.
November 27	The Bronze Derby was played in Clinton, South Carolina on Thanksgiving Day. The Presbyterian College Blue Hose defeated the Newberry College Indians 35-20.

SPORTS

The Laurens County Advertiser

THANKSGIVING TRADITION — The annual Bronze Derby Classic football game has become a holiday tradition for many Presbyterian and Newberry fans, although the Indians have had the upper hand in recent years. Both teams enter the contest with 4-6 records, but will seek to cap off a disappointing year by claiming the coveted trophy. In addition, Thursday will be Bob Waters Day at PC, as the PC graduate and Western Carolina head coach will be honored at the game. (File photo)

It's Derby time again

It may be tarnished by the teams' identical 4-6 records, but this year's Bronze Derby football game could still be a classic when Newberry and Presbyterian meet Thursday in Clinton.

Records are rarely mentioned when the two teams meet in the annual Thansgiving Day contest, although the winner often has more than a long winter to look forward to. Neither team, however, will advance to post-season play this season.

Presbyterian leads the series 45-24-5, but Newberry gained possession of the Bronze Derby for five of the past six years. This year's game will mark the 75th meeting of the teams.

For sheer excitement, it will be difficult to top last year's 24-24 tie at Newberry. The Indians jumped out to a 14-0 lead, but saw that lead cut to 14-10 at halftime.

PC MAINTAINED its momentum, and roared to a 24-14 third quarter lead. But Newberry tied the game, and only Tommie Netting's block of a Newberry field goal attempt in the closing seconds preserved the tie.

The Blue Hose entered that game with a three-game winning streak, but will enter the 1986 clash attempting to break a six-game losing streak.

The Blue Hose defense has faltered in the second half of the season, but still ranks second overall in the South Atlantic Conference. The squad is allowing an average of 264.1 yards per game (150.7 rushing and 113.4 passing).

The PC offense has sputtered recently, also, and suffered its only shutout under head coach Elliott Poss' leadership when Carson-Newman took a 19-0 decision on Nov. 15.

PC managed 242 yards rushing against Newberry last year, led by Jimmy Lindsey's 85-yard effort. Stevie Riggins added 79 yards, and those two will again be counted on heavily to move the PC offense.

LINDSEY IS averaging just 59.4 yards per game his senior year, having amassed 594 yards on 116 carries. He brings a 5.1-yard-per-carry average into Thursday's game.

Quarterback Scotty Mozingo has climbed to third in the SAC-8 in passing statistics, completing 73 of 168 passes for 1,066 yards. That production is second only to Lenoir-Rhyne's Brian Bryson in the conference.

PC has slipped to fifth in the conference in total offense, averaging 317.7 yards per game. Although the rush has been the strength of Blue Hose teams in the past, the 1986 squad is averaging 205.3 yards per game — placing them fifth in the conference.

Despite its record, Newberry has lost a number of close contests this season. The Indians did show their strength in a 13-10 upset of Mars Hill earlier this season, however.

Newberry enters the Bronze Derby Classic last in the conference in total offense, averaging 303.7 yards per contest. But senior running back Pete Bember and senior quarterback Pat Bellamy make the Indians a scoring threat from anywhere on the field.

BEMBER, THE fourth-leading rusher in the conference, has gained 841 yards this season, and is averaging 84.1 yards per game.

Bellamy has completed 60 of 139 passes for 913 yards, and is averaging 114.1 yards per game. He stands just ahead of Mozingo in passing statistics.

Bellamy's favorite receiver is senior wide receiver Darryl Owings, who has 33 catches for 569 yards this season. He leads the conference, averaging 17.2 yards per catch.

Newberry ranks seventh in the conference in total defense, and is allowing 184 rushing yards per game.

The Li'l  That Was!

Special Issue
the Indian
The Voice of The Newberry College Student

2100 College St., Newberry, S.C. 29108

December 9, 1988

Volume LVI, Number 1

Derby Tradition

The Thanksgiving football game between Presbyterian and Newberry College has been a tradition for many years. However, the tradition of the Bronze Derby trophy is much more recent.

The custom began in 1947 as a result of a small confrontation at the Newberry-Presbyterian basketball game that was held on the Newberry campus that year. According to legend, a banner which read "Beat the Hell Out of Newberry" had been placed on the wall of McLean Gymnasium by PC students prior to the game. During the game, a Newberry student obtained a ladder and climbed through a gym window to remove the banner.

The confiscation of the banner went unnoticed until the end of the hard-fought game which PC won 51-47. An irate Presbyterian student then demanded the return of the missing banner. Following the demand, tempers flared and fight began which soon developed into a free-for-all on the court. In the course of the fight, a mischievous Newberry student snatched a derby from the head of PC student and ran from the fight.

In the following days, the Athletic Directors of the two schools negotiated the return of the hat. During the discussions, it was suggested that "A derby should serve as a laurel of victory in athletic contests between Newberry and Presbyterian." Sometime later, the derby was returned to PC. It was then packaged and sent to a bronzier in Ohio. The derby was bronzed, and thus was born the famed Bronze Derby.

Until 1966, the possession of the Derby was determined by the outcome of all Newberry-Presbyterian encounters. Now, the home of the Derby is decided by the result of the annual Thanksgiving Day football game. Currently, the Derby resides at Newberry following last year's game.

 Happy New Year

May your New Year be framed with love, peace and prosperity.

The Li'l That Was!

Chronicle

6-A — The Clinton, S.C., Chronicle, November 25, 1986

DISTINGUISHED ALUMNUS - Bob Waters, former Presbyterian College quarterback and highly successful head coach at Western Carolina University, will be honored at this year's PC-Newberry game Thursday. (Photo courtesy Western Carolina sports information office).

The Clinton Chronicle

SPORTS

Football, Tennis, Soccer, Auto Racing, Golf
Baseball, Volleyball, Basketball, Track, Softball

Reclaiming The Derby Tops Blue Hose Wishes

For the second consecutive year, Presbyterian and Newberry will enter their annual football meeting for the Bronze Derby with identical records.

Kickoff is Thursday at 2 p.m. at Bailey Memorial Stadium.

This year's game does not, however, match either of the past two meetings between the arch-rivals in terms of drama and prestige. This year the Blue Hose and Indians are both 4-6, suffering through disappointing seasons in marked contrast to last year, when 7-3 records by both teams prefaced a 24-24 tie on Thanksgiving Day.

The Indians have had the best of the series recently, holding the Bronze Derby since 1983. Two years ago Newberry knocked Presbyterian out of a possible NAIA playoff bid in the Indians' last visit to Bailey Memorial Stadium. PC, however, leads the all-time series standings by a 45-24-5 margin. The two neighboring private colleges have been playing one another since 1913.

Thanks to Presbyterian's current five-game losing streak, most observers will favor Newberry in this year's game. However, Blue Hose head coach Elliott Poss hopes desire for regaining possession of the Bronze Derby will stir his team to victory.

"We haven't had much success (against Newberry) in the 1980's that's for sure," Poss admits, adding, "We're working hard to bring the Derby back to PC. Our players take pride in trying to bring it home."

One of Presbyterian's all-time greats, Tangerine Bowl quarterback Bob Waters, will be on hand to aid his alma mater in that quest. Waters, the head football coach at Western Carolina University, will have the game played in his honor and will also be on hand for a post game drop-in at Springs Center immediately after the game.

A former professional quarterback for the San Francisco 49ers, Waters played and coached at PC before taking over the Western Carolina football program. His 1983 Catamounts finished as national runners-up in Division I-AA. For the past two seasons, Waters has coached at Western Carolina despite suffering from the debilitating ailment known as "Lou Gehrig's Disease."

427

The Li'l 🎩 That Was!

The Newberry Observer
AND HERALD & NEWS
"Just Like A Letter From Home"

Newberry, S.C., Monday, November 24, 1986

Bronze Derby Clash On Thursday

This year the Bronze Derby is what Jack Benny always claimed to be — 39 years old. But if it's left to senior players on the Indian football team, the only violins playing Thursday will be for Presbyterian College.

The Bronze Derby has, since 1947, gone to the winner of the Newberry vs. Presbyterian football game.

The rivalry between the two schools, however, is much older than the Derby; the football contest is now in its Diamond Jubilee year. For 75 years, Newberry and PC have played each other in football, and the current record stands at 26-44-4 with PC in the lead.

Senior Newberry College football players want to reduce that lead — they want to add another win on Thursday to make the Diamond Jubilee game a Newberry win.

Why is it so important to the seniors? Because this year, for them, the Bronze Derby is plated 14

(Continued On Page 4)

Hat's On For The Victor!
No hat is quite so becoming as the Bronze Derby — not for Newberry College coach Clayton Johnson.

★ Derby (Continued From Page 1)

kt. pride.

"Our seniors won the Derby as freshmen, and it's been here at Newberry ever since," said Nick DerCola, sports information director at the college. "There's a whole lot of pride associated with that, and our seniors want to keep that derby."

The game will be at Presbyterian College this Thanksgiving Day, Nov. 27, at 2 p.m. The Derby tradition, however, was born on Newberry's campus.

During a 1947 basketball game between the two schools, PC students placed a banner in MacLean Gymnasium: "Beat the Hell Out of Newberry". Some Newberry students (understandably offended by the sign) appropriated a ladder, climbed through a window, and absconded with the objectionable banner.

As the final minutes of the basketball game ticked away, PC fans noticed the banner was missing and demanded its return. In the scuffle that followed, a Newberry student snatched the derby off the head of a PC student and ran.

Over the next few days, officials of the two schools negotiated for the return of the derby, and finally they agreed that it should serve as a symbol of victory in athletic contests between the two colleges.

Consequently, the hat was returned to PC, packaged and forwarded to a casting company, where it was bronzed.

From 1947 to 1956, possession of the Bronze Derby was determined by victories in football, basketball, and baseball, but in 1956, the schools decided to award the trophy on the basis of the Thanksgiving Day football game.

Since then the Indians have kept the Bronze Derby in Newberry an even dozen times — 1956, 1957, 1962, 1965, 1971, 1973, 1976, 1980, 1981, 1983, 1984, and 1985.

This year's seniors want to make that an even baker's dozen — lucky '13.'

LET PC play the violins; Newberry's planning to ring that victory bell.

Another something at Newberry College that's plated 14 kt. pride.

THE NEWBERRY OBSERVER AND HERALD & NEWS — Newberry, S.C., Wednesday, November 26, 1986

The Li'l That Was!

The Newberry Observer Sports

Indians Preparing For Turkey Day Clash

BY MIKE MEADOW

The Newberry College Indians will be trying to hold on to the Bronze Derby this Thurday when they travel to Clinton to face the Presbyterian Blue Hose.

Both teams will enter the game with a 4-6 record on the season and a 4 record in the conference.

Presbyterian leads the series between the two schools with a 44-25-2 record. Last year the two teams battled to a 24-24 tie.

The last win by the Indians was in 1984 when Newberry came out on top 25-16. The last time the Blue Hose won was in 1982 by the score of 21-7.

Clayton Johnson has a 29-24-1 record as the head coach of the Indians. Elliott Poss has a 11-10-1 record as head coach of the Blue Hose.

Newberry will be led offensively by runningback Pete Bember and wide receiver Darryl Owings.

Bember has rushed for 841 yards and 10 touchdowns and Owings has 33 catches for 569 yards and one touchdown for the Indians.

Presbyterian will be led offensively by runningback Jimmy Lindsey and quarterback Scotty Mozingo. Lindsey has 594 yards rushing and three touchdowns and Mozingo has completed 73 passes for 1,066 yards and five touchdowns for the Blue Hose.

Linebackers Reggie Deas and John Newkirk, along with Drew Watson will lead the Indians defensively on Thursday.

Deas has 116 total tackles and Newkirk has 113 total tackles to lead the Indians. Watson has 73 total tackles and four interceptions so far this season.

Linebacker Rodney Berry and defensive back Kevin Caldwell will lead the Blue Hose on defense.

Berry has 82 total tackles, while Caldwell has 69 total tackles and three interceptions.

Game time for Thursday's Bronze Derby Classic is scheduled for 2 p.m. in Clinton.

EYE ON SPORTS WITH MIKE MEADOW

This week will be the last time I predict football this year. The game— Newberry vs. Presbyterian.

The annual Turkey Day Clash for the Bronze Derby will be played tomorrow in Clinton. Both teams will enter the contest with the same 4-6 record on the season.

Last year the Indians had the perfect opportunity to win the game. But a field goal attempt with time running out was blocked by the Blue Hose, leaving the game in a 24-24 tie.

This game has everything possible to make it a good game. The rivalry between the two schools, the closeness of the two schools, and two good football teams.

Presbyterian would like for the derby to return to Clinton, while the Indians would like to hold on to it for another year.

Early in the year, the Blue Hose started out 4-0. Then, after being upset by a smaller school, they then seemed to fall down hill. The Indians on the other hand, started off slow and then played several good games before they started to slide.

Fans who will attend this game on Thursday will not be disappointed. It will be hard for me to pick a winner of this contest because of the records of both schools. I guess you could say I was a chicken on Turkey Day when I decided to go with the Indians.

I think Newberry will want to keep the derby more than the Blue Hose will want to take it away: Newberry over Presbyterian.

In other local sports news, the annual Newberry High Basketball Jamboree will be played tonight (Wednesday) begining at 6:30. All three of our local teams, Newberry, Mid-Carolina, and Whitmire will participate in the event. The regular season for basketball season begins next week.

Those interested in getting a pre-season look at our high school teams should start watching in upcoming issues of THE OBSERVER.

I hope that everyone has a safe and happy Thanksgiving. And just remember, Christmas is just around the corner!

The Blue Stocking
of Presbyterian College

Hose take Derby

The PC Blue Hose football team ended its season by defeating Newberry 35-20 on Thanksgiving afternoon at Bailey Memorial Stadium.

The Blue Hose offense accumulated 482 yards, 367 of them on the ground. Tailback Jimmy Lindsey went 71 yards for a touchdown on PC's first offensive play. Lindsey and sophomore Stevie Riggins finished the contest with more than 100 rushing yards. Quarterback Scotty Mozingo was eight for 11 in the second half for 115 yards.

Defensively, the Blue Hose were without linebacker Harold Anderson, who was suspended for disciplinary reasons.

PC took a 13-0 first quarter lead on Lindsey's run and two Chris Wingo field goals. Newberry closed the halftime margin to 13-7 on Kevin Black's 21-yard touchdown pass to Joey Spigner.

The Indians took the lead briefly with 9:01 remaining in the third quarter. PC responded with a 12-play, 53-yard drive to retake the lead. Mozingo fired a short pass to tight end Glenn Jackson for the touchdown, then hit Jackson again for a two-point conversion to make the score 21-14.

Photo courtesy of The Chronicle

The Li'l That Was!

| Christmas Concert | Page 4 | Bronze Derby Decided |

The Newberry Observer
AND HERALD & NEWS
"Just Like A Letter From Home"

NEWS ESTABLISHED 1865   NO. 137   Newberry, S.C., Friday, November 28, 1986   THE NEWBERRY OBSERVER EST.   ONE SECT

Blue Hose Win Bronze Derby Battle

BY MIKE MEADOW

The Presbyterian Blue Hose kept the Bronze Derby in Clinton Thursday, as they overpowered the Newberry Indians 35-20.

Blue Hose runningbacks Stevie Riggins and Jimmy Lindsey each rushed for more than 100 yards as Presbyterian picked up more than 347 yards rushing.

The Blue Hose started off their scoring on their first play from scrimmage when Lindsey raced 71 yards for a touchdown.

Presbyterian added two field goals by place kicker Chris Wingo to make the score 13-0 after one quarter of play.

The Indians got on the board in the second quarter when Kevin Black hit a wide open Joey Spigner in the middle of the endzone for a touchdown.

With 9:01 left in the first half, the Indians took their only lead of the game. Black hit tailback Pete Bember from one yard out for the score. The score capped a six-play, 20 yard drive.

The score was set up when Blue Hose punter Jeff Alligood was unable to pull down a high snap. After the ball fell to the ground, he kicked it, which constitutes as an illegal kick. The Blue Hose were penalized 15 yards from the point of the infraction, which gave the Indians the ball on the PC 20.

After Lindsey returned the ensuing kickoff 37, and the Blue Hose ran 12 plays, PC quarterback Scotty Mozingo hit tight end Glenn Jackson with a four yard touchdown pass. After a successfull two point conversion, the Blue Hose led 21-14.

With 8:02 left in the game, Mozingo hit Del Barksdale for a 62 yard touchdown pass to seal the victory for the Blue Hose.

PC added another score late in the game when Mozingo hit Jackson for a five yard touchdown.

Newberry finished their scoring late in the game when Jim Casey scored on an 11-yard touchdown pass from Dupree. The two point attempt failed, and the game ended at 35-20 in favor of the Blue Hose.

Riggins led all rushers with 124 yards on 15 carries. Newberry runningback Pete Bember was held to only 38 yards on 12 carries.

Newberry finished the season with a 4-7 record while the Blue Hose finished a 5-6.

SPORTS

The Laurens County Advertiser

PC captures Bronze Derby with 35-20 win

By Steve Owens
Sports Editor

As they celebrated their 35-20 victory over Newberry College Thursday at Bailey Memorial Stadium, the Presbyterian College football players passed the coveted Bronze Derby around to see how it fit.

They liked the fit so much they would like to keep it awhile longer.

The victory was the first Bronze Derby Classic win for the Blue Hose since PC claimed a 21-7 win in 1982. No member of the 1986 Blue Hose squad was able to enjoy that last victory, but each savored the win as the perfect way to end an otherwise disappointing season.

"I've told our players throughout the course of this week that we really needed to get the Derby back. It's been some time," said PC Head Coach Elliott Poss. "This will give our returning players something to look forward to."

Quarterback Scotty Mozingo echoed his coach's comments that the effects of Thursday's win will not be forgotten.

"This sure caps off the season. I think it will give the team a lot of momentum going into the summer practices and next season," he said.

BOTH TEAMS entered the contest with 4-6 records, but neither Poss nor Newberry coach Clayton Johnson believed that would effect the intensity of the rivalry. Despite a five-game losing streak, PC proved them correct.

The Blue Hose defense was outstanding in the first half, shutting down Newberry on its first four possessions. The Indians did not manage a first down until 12:40 remained in the second quarter.

But the Blue Hose wasted no time in geting their offense unracked. After stopping Newberry on the opening drive, the Blue Hose took possession on their 29 yard line.

On the first play from scrimmage, senior tailback Jimmy Lindsey took a pitch from Mozingo and cut through the line before racing to the left side and leaving defenders in his wake as he covered 71 yards for the touchdown.

That score, the longest rush from scrimmage for PC this season, set off an eruption from the PC stands. Chris Wingo's extra point gave the Blue Hose a 7-0 lead with 12:40 to play in the first quarter.

PC CONTINUED its dominance on its next drive. A late hit penalty, the first of many in the contest, moved the Blue Hose to their own 41. Sophomore Stevie Riggins then broke free around the right end, and raced to the Newberry 3 before he was tripped up.

But the Newberry defense held, and PC settled for a 21-yard field goal by Wingo with 8:52 to play in the first quarter.

The penalty flags continued to fly in the first half, indicative of the rivalry between the two teams.

"This ball game is an intense rivalry," Poss said. "The officials told both coaches before the game that they were going to call it strictly, and they did. It's frustrating, but our players hung in there."

The Blue Hose were penalized 12 times for 168 yards, while the Indians suffered 10 penalties for 95 yards.

The Blue Hose drove 55 yards in 12 plays on their third possession, but the drive stalled on the Newberry 19. Wingo was called on for a 36-yard field goal, giving the Blue Hose a 13-0 advantage with 50 seconds to play in the first quarter.

A scuffle ensued near the Newberry bench with 11:42 to play in the second quarter, resulting in another personal foul penalty on the Blue Hose.

"That did tend to change the momentum," Poss said.

But the 13-play drive by the Indians ended when Eric Snipes missed a 32-yard field goal attempt with 9:32 to play in the first half.

NEWBERRY DID not have to wait long for another chance, as defensive back Sylvester Coleman picked off a Mozingo pass intended for Del Barksdale. The Blue Hose also received a facemask penalty on the play, giving Newberry possession on the PC 21.

On the next play, Indian quarterback Kevin Black hit wide receiver Joey Spigner over the middle for a touchdown. Snipes added the extra-point to cut PC's lead to 13-7.

Despite the narrow lead, PC limited the Indians to minus five yards rushing in the first half. The Indians managed 120 passing yards. The Blue Hose used an excellent performance from their offensive line to amass 241 rushing yards in the first half.

A low snap to Blue Hose punter Jeff Alligood set up the go-ahead touchdown for Newberry in the third quarter, as the Indians took possession on the PC 19.

The Indians drove to the one, where they gambled for the touchdown on fourth down. Black rolled right, but threw left to running back Pete Bember who was all alone for the touchdown reception. Snipes' kick gave the Indians their only lead of the contest, a 14-13 advantage with 9:01 to play in the third quarter.

BUT LINDSEY returned the subsequent kickoff to the PC 47, and the Blue Hose put together a 12-play, 53-yard drive to recapture the lead.

That score came on a third-down pass from Mozingo to sophomore tight end Glen Jackson with 3:04 to play in the third quarter. Jackson fell down on the play, but caught Mozingo's pass as he was on his back in the end zone. Mozingo then hit Jackson again for the two-point conversion to give PC a 21-14 lead.

With 8:02 to play, Mozingo hit Barksdale over the middle. The senior flanker split the defenders and raced 62 yards for his first touchdown of the season.

"We knew their free safety was trying to cut off our crossing patterns," Mozingo said. "I watched him come up, and Del just got open and took off when he made the catch."

Wingo added the extra-point to give PC a 28-13 lead.

The Blue Hose offense, which generated 482 yards in the contest, was not finished yet. Although he failed to complete a pass in the first half, Mozingo threw his third touchdown pass of the second half when he hit Jackson for a five-yard score with 2:29 to play to lift the Blue Hose to a 35-14 lead.

THE INDIANS added a late score when quarterback Tyrone DuPree hit tight end Jim Casey with an 11-yard scoring strike with just 25 seconds remaining, but the conversion attempt failed, giving the Blue Hose their final margin of victory and the Bronze Derby trophy.

Riggins led the 367-yard PC rushing attack with 125 yards on 15 carries. Lindsey added 115 yards on 10 carries in his final performance for the Blue Hose.

Senior linebacker Rodney Berry and junior safety Ro Lucas led the PC defense with 10 tackles apiece. Newberry earned just 244 total offensive yards.

SCORING

Newberry .... 0 7 7 6 — 20
Presbyterian .... 13 0 8 14 — 35

PC—Lindsey 71 run (Wingo kick)
PC—Wingo 21 field goal
PC—Wingo 36 field goal
NC—Spigner 21 pass from Black (Snipes kick)
NC—Bember 1 pass from Black (Snipes kick)
PC—Jackson 4 pass from Mozingo (Jackson from Mozingo)
PC—Barksdale 62 pass from Mozingo (Wingo kick)
PC—Jackson 5 pass from Mozingo (Wingo kick)
NC—Casey 11 pass from DuPree (pass failed)
Attendance—5,300.

Newberry	STATISTICS	PC
15	First downs	18
42-27	Rushes-yards	57-367
217	Passing yards	115
91	Return yards	73
3-1	Fumbles-lost	2-0
10-95	Penalties-yards	12-168

Rushing: NC, Bember 12-38, Shuler 7-26, DuPree 21-(-19), Black 2-(-18). PC, Riggins 15-124, Lindsey 10-117, Gerald 14-65, Mozingo 16-48, Alligood 1-(-7), Williams 1-4.
Passing: NC, DuPree 19-6-1-96, Black 19-9-0-121. PC, Mozingo 19-8-1-115.
Receiving: NC, Owings 6-54, Spigner 4-104, Casey 4-43, Taylor 5 1-15, Bember 1-1. PC, Jackson 4-22, Riggins 2-17, Barksdale 1-62, Herren 1-14.

LEADING THE WAY — Presbyterian College quarterback Scotty Mozingo turns upfield after breaking through the Newberry line in the first quarter of the Bronze Derby Classic Thursday at Clinton. Mozingo earned 12 yards on the effort, and the Blue Hose ground out 367 rushing yards as they took a 35-20 victory in the rivalry. The victory was the first for the Blue Hose over the Indians in four years. (Photo by Steve Owens)

PC alumnus Bob Waters honored at Derby game

The Bronze Derby Classic wasn't the only reason for excitement on the Presbyterian College campus Thursday, as the Clinton school honored one of its graduates on "Bob Waters Day."

The Western Carolina University head coach was recognized at halftime along with his family, and accepted the applause of the estimated crowd of 5,300 fans crowded into Bailey Memorial Stadium.

Waters, who is suffering from a form of Muscular Dystrophy known as "Lou Gehrig's disease," quarterbacked the 1957 Presbyterian College football team to the Tangerine Bowl, and returned to the school in 1966 as an assistant coach following a successful stint as the quarterback of the San Francisco 49ers.

He has coached Western Carolina for the past 17 years.

"Presbyterian College has a tradition of graduates who have been outstanding in the coaching field," said PC Athletic Director Cally Gault. "A hero returns home today. We are proud of Bob Waters."

PC President Kenneth B. Orr unveiled a portrait of Waters that will be permanently displayed in Templeton Athletic Center as part of the "Bob Waters Award" which will be presented to PC graduates who have provided outstanding leadership and service as coaches.

"When I came to Presbyterian College, I heard people talk about the PC spirit," Waters said. "I didn't know about it then, but I know now. I have it, and all of you here today have it."

The Li'l That Was!

Advertiser

For Barksdale
Derby win was special

By Steve Owens
Sports Editor

With one minute remaining in Thursday's Bronze Derby Classic, Blue Hose senior Del Barksdale injured his leg as Newberry kicked off following a touchdown. He limped badly as he was helped from the field.

As the Blue Hose began celebrating their 35-20 win amid the bright television lights, the Bronze Derby trophy was hoisted high above the crowd of players.

That was enough to draw Barksdale to the celebration.

The senior had waited four years to see the trophy return to Presbyterian College, and he was not about to let the opportunity to celebrate pass him by as he limped out to join his teammates.

THE SCENE typified the season endured by Barksdale and the Blue Hose. After a 4-1 start, PC began a tailspin following a loss to Elon. Players became unhappy with the situation, while the team dropped five consecutive games.

"We had a lot of problems during the season. I knew we were better than that," Barksdale said. "But this win makes the season a lot sweeter."

The 1982 Laurens District 55 High School graduate has had a lot of highlights during his career at Presbyterian, but he was also involved in an unhappy situation this season.

Being a receiver in a run-oriented program is never an easy task, but Barksdale's role had diminished as his senior season arrived. The Laurens native was named to the All-South Atlantic Conference Team in 1983.

He readily admits that his lessening role affected him at times.

"At times it did, admittedly. I was content for us to win anyway we could, but I also like to get in there and mix it up," he said. "I would have liked to have had it more."

STILL, BARKSDALE made his mark on the team. He was one of the team captains this season, and received an honor when he was named to the SAC-8 All-Academic team. As an active participant in the team's off-season weight training program, he also improved his strength under Coach Bruce Hill.

Barksdale earned the title "Most Powerful Blue Hose" last summer as decided by the team's power index which divides total poundage lifted in the squats and bench press by the player's body weight.

"That's something I take a lot of pride in. I just worked hard on it," he said. "I don't have a lot of strength, but it's proportionate to my size. That (award) is one of the things I'll remember about my career."

But the most memories will come from his playing days at Bailey Memorial Stadium.

"Football would have to encompass some of my finest times here. My freshman season was one of my finest, and the next two were very exciting because we had a shot at making the playoffs," he said. "But my senior season is always something I'll remember."

HE WILL also remember Thursday's Bronze Derby contest. With 8:02 remaining in the game, Barksdale pulled in Scotty Mozingo's pass and raced 62 yards for his first touchdown of the season.

"I was thinking about the Gardner-Webb game last year when we hooked up for a 77-yarder but I only got to the one. I knew I had to get this one in. It was also special because it was my first touchdown of the year," he said.

That catch also made the senior the leading receiver for the Blue Hose this season. He finished the year with 15 catches for 312 yards, just ahead of sophomore Eddie Rogers (14 for 285).

In addition, the 62-yard score was the team's longest touchdown pass this season.

As he pulled off his jersey and shoulder pads for the last time and limped off the field, he knew that his quest for the Bronze Derby had finally come to an end.

And his senior season looked a little bit brighter.

CO-CAPTAIN — Laurens native Del Barksdale (15) cheers on his fellow seniors as they are announced prior to Thursday's Bronze Derby Classic. Thursday's game marked Barksdale's final contest as a member of the Blue Hose team, and he went out in style by catching a 62-yard touchdown pass in the fourth quarter. (Photo by Steve Owens)

November 1987

The Li'l That Was!

November 2	George Harrison released his newest album "Cloud 9." On the same day, Paul McCartney released a greatest hit album "All the Best."
November 3	Mark McGwire of the Oakland A's won MLB AL Rookie of the Year Award leading the AL in both home runs and RBIs.
November 3	American NFL quarterback Colin Kaepernick was born.
November 4	The NBA announced 4 new franchises; Charlotte and Miami for the 1988 season and Minneapolis and Orlando for the 1989 season.
November 5	United States Supreme Court nominee Douglas Ginsburg admitted using marijuana. He later withdrew from consideration.
November 11	Roger Clemens of the Boston Red Sox won the MLB AL Cy Young Award. Steve Bedrosian of the Philadelphia Phillies won the MLB NL Cy Young Award.
November 11	Judge Anthony Kennedy was nominated for the United States Supreme Court.
November 11	Van Gogh's painting "Irises" sold for a record $53.6 million at auction.
November 12	Australian golfer Jason Day was born.
November 13	The first condom commercial appeared on British television.
November 13	MLB player Cal Ripken Jr. married Kelly Greer.
November 13	Sonny and Cher perform together for the final time on "Late Night with David Letterman" singing "I Got You Babe."
November 16	Actress Lisa Bonet married singer Lenny Kravitz.
November 17	George Bell was the first Toronto Blue Jay ever to win the MLB AL Most Valuable Player Award.
November 17	The Madonna album "You Can Dance" was released.
November 18	Andre Dawson of the Chicago Cubs was the first player to win the MLB NL Most Valuable Player Award that was on a last place team.
November 18	31 died in a fire at King's Cross, London's busiest tube station.
November 21	Actress Demi Moore married actor Bruce Willis.
November 22	Dale Earnhardt won the 37th NASCAR Sprint Cup.
November 22	Two Chicago television stations were hijacked by an unknown Pirate dressed as Max Headroom.
November 26	The Bronze Derby was played in Newberry, South Carolina on Thanksgiving Day. The Newberry College Indians defeated the Presbyterian College Blue Hose 17-15.

The Laurens County Advertiser

November 20, 1987

SPORTS

Bronze Derby
Blue Hose face challenge

By Steve Owens
Sports Editor

This year's Bronze Derby Classic will have extra meaning for the Presbyterian College Blue Hose.

As if the tradition of the annual game is not enough, the ninth-ranked Blue Hose can almost certainly lock up an NAIA playoff spot with a victory Saturday.

Standing in the way is Newberry, which will be playing its last game under the direction of head coach Clayton Johnson. PC head coach Elliot Poss knows that those circumstances could make the Indians an unusually difficult opponent.

"Newberry has played under some adversity in the past few weeks, and they are capable of beating any team in the SAC-8 as evidenced by their earlier win over Carson-Newman," Poss said. "They can pose a lot of problems for us, and we will be up against a very emotional team this Saturday."

THE BLUE Hose captured the Bronze Derby last year by taking a penalty-marred 35-20 decision. Despite collecting 482 yards of offense and limiting Newberry to 244 yards, the Blue Hose needed a pair of fourth-quarter touchdowns to shake the Indians.

As evidenced by that contest, Poss knows that statistics don't mean much in the Bronze Derby Classic.

"This will be a very hard-hitting game because of the tremendous rivalry between the two schools," he said. "Stats and records can be thrown out the window for this one."

The Blue Hose offense played well last week in a 28-8 victory over Carson-Newman, earning 325 yards of offense against the defending national champions. The Blue Hose are averaging 371 yards and 21 points per game.

The PC tailback tandem of Stevie Riggins and Steve Parsley continues to be effective. Parsley leads the team with 657 yards rushing, and Riggins has tallied 655 yards.

The Blue Hose defense is allowing an average of 260 yards and 13 points per game. The PC unit is particularly strong in the third quarter, having surrendered just 10 points during that quarter all season.

NEWBERRY WILL enter the 1987 Bronze Derby Classic attempting to break a two-game losing streak. The Indians have lost three of their last four games after taking successive wins over Carson-Newman and Wofford.

After scoring just 32 points through its first four games (including two shutouts), the Newberry offense has improved during the second half of the season. The Indians are averaging 283 yards and nearly 19 points per game.

Jerold Bell has replaced fifth-year senior Pat Bellamy as the Indians' quarterback, while senior running back Mitchell Shuler has emerged as the Indians' leading rusher.

Senior wide receiver Joey Spigner is among the conference leaders in catches and touchdowns.

The Newberry defense is allowing 26 points and just under 300 yards per game. Defensive backs Drew Watson and Kevin Reeder are both among the conference leaders in interceptions.

The Blue Hose have an opportunity to reach the high point of their season with a win over Newberry, and the PC coaching staff hopes there are more highlights to come during the 1987 season.

"For this group of players, there have been a lot of high points so far. Things just keep becoming more and more important with every ball game," Poss said.

BLUE NOTES: For Bronze Derby traditionalists, a Thanksgiving dinner will be served at the Newberry College dining hall from 11 a.m. until 1 p.m. Saturday. The cost will be $6.75 for adults and $3.75 for children under 12. No reservations are needed.

Presbyterian (7-3) at Newberry (3-7)
2 p.m., Setzler Field

Nickname: Indians
Location: Newberry, S.C.
Head Coach: Clayton Johnson
1986 Record: 4-7 (Overall)
2-5 (SAC-8)
Offensive System: Veer and Pro-I
Defensive System: Multiple 5-2
Series Record: PC leads 46-24-5

DERBY TIME — Presbyterian College fullback Evander Gerald (27) and his running mates will be in full stride Saturday at Newberry because a playoff bid may be at stake in the contest. While a victory would almost guarantee the Blue Hose of a playoff spot, a loss could place the PC team on the borderline of receiving a bid. (Photo by Steve Owens)

The Newberry Observer
AND HERALD & NEWS
"Just Like A Letter From Home"

Newberry, S.C., Friday, Nov. 20, 1987

Playoffs 1, Tradition 0 For Bronze Derby

Tradition gives way to playoffs Saturday afternoon when the Presbyterian Blue Hose challenge the Newberry Indians in the Bronze Derby game.

The Thanksgiving Day game was changed to 2 p.m. tomorrow at Setzler Field because PC has to have its record set before an NAIA playoff deadline. The Blue Hose are 7 - 3 on the season and 5 - 1 in the SAC-8 conference.

Newberry is headed in the other direction, with a 3 - 7 record on the season and 2 - 4 in the conference. The Indians lost 35 - 19 to Lenior-Rhyne last week.

This will be the last game for Indian coach Clayton Johnson who knew in the spring his contract would not be renewed.

"Presbyterian has had a great season and is looking to tie for the conference championship and get a bid to the NAIA playoffs," said Johnson, who is 32 - 32 - 1 in his career at Newberry.

"They have a very strong defensive team that is ranked in the top 10 in the country and an offense that can strike quickly. I believe it will be a typical Newberry - PC clash.

"We would like the 'Derby' back in Newberry."

The series record favors PC, 45 - 25 - 5, in a rivalry that goes back to 1913. PC won last year, 35 - 20, and the last time Newberry won was 1984, 25 - 16. PC Coach Elliott Poss is 19 - 12 - 1 in his career at the Clinton college.

The traditional Thanksgiving Day meal will be served from 11 a.m. to 1 p.m. tomorrow in Kaufmann Dining Hall. Prices are $6.75 for adults and $3.75 for children under 12.

The public is invited to dine at the college before the "Bronze Derby Classic."

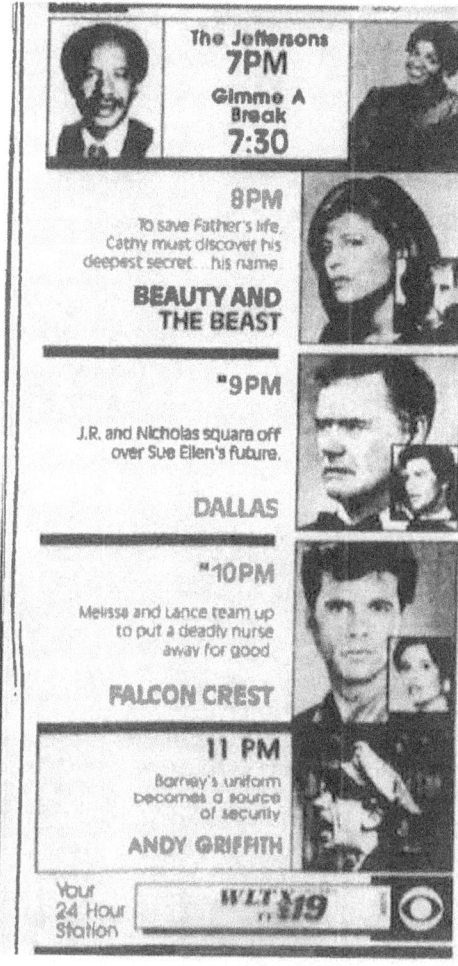

The Li'l 🎩 That Was!

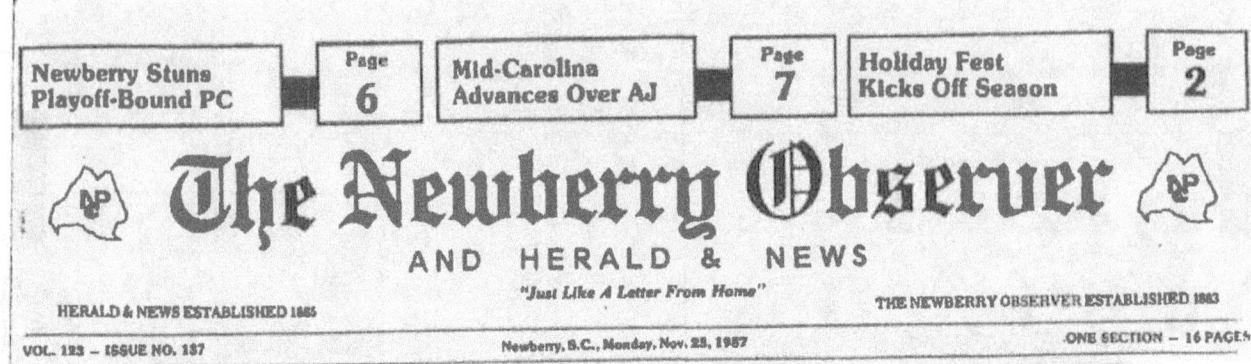

Newberry Stuns PC, 17-15, Brings Derby Home

By VIC MacDONALD

Tears flowed at the 50 yard line of Setzler Field Saturday afternoon, after the Newberry Indians' stunning 17-15 upset of their rival, nationally-ranked Presbyterian College.

Departing Newberry Head Coach Clayton Johnson, surrounded by kneeling players, and a large crowd of fans and family, tearfully accepted the Bronze Derby and the game ball in an emotional post-game celebration for the winning coach who won't be back.

Amid the congratulations, handshakes and hugs, Johnson praised the "total team effort" that defeated PC in the traditional Thanksgiving Day game, moved up this year so the Blue Hose could have their record set in time for NAIA playoff bids. PC finished its season 7-4 and second in the conference.

"It's tremendous, our defense played fantastic," Johnson said of his Indians, who capped a disappointing 4-7 season with a win which wasn't assured until the final 20 seconds.

"It was a game of big plays and we took advantage of our opportunities. It was a total team effort. We gave PC an easy one and they gave us one, it evened out."

The Bronze Derby, a symbol of the rivalry which started in 1913, "fits well," Johnson said, declining an opportunity to bad-mouth Newberry College, which told the coach in the spring his contract would not be renewed.

"There are no hard feelings. It's time for me to move on," Johnson said, although he did not know what job he would have next.

But for the moment, there were more congratulations to be accepted and pictures to be posed for with players wearing the Derby. Coach Johnson's well-worn red, Indians baseball cap was finally found, but the Derby was never far from him.

Well after 5 p.m., he was still on the field, talking to supporters, with the 17-15 still shining on the scoreboard and the sun setting behind the big Newberry College on the press box.

A half hour earlier, it looked like the Indians were going to find a way to let PC salvage a tie.

A shanked punt at the 2:44 mark gave the Blue House, down by eight, the chance for a final drive from their own 48. The Newberry faithful responded to the defense's call for noise and PC went into a hurry up offense.

Short passes got PC to the Newberry 21 and after the Blue Hose converted a fourth and three, a pass interference penalty put them on the Indian three yard line.

Junior tackle Chris Chrisley smashed PC quarterback Scotty Mozingo to the ground at the one foot line on third down, but PC running back Evander Gerald barely got the ball over the goal line with :20 left.

PC's blocked conversion late in the first half came back to haunt the Hose, who had to go for two to tie. But Mozingo's pass found Indian sophomore linebacker James Putman, who knocked it down. After the onside kick was recovered, the victory bell rang and the Derby came home.

Putman set the stage for the Indians victory at the 11 minute mark when he returned an interception to the Newberry 45. Senior running back Mitch Shuler led the offensive charge with a 34 yard run, and senior quarterback Patrick Bellamy stuck the ball over from the one at the 7:33 mark.

The touchdown, and a 30 yard Mike Hiller field goal at the start of the fourth quarter, gave Newberry its biggest lead. The scores erased a 9-7 PC lead, after a 38 yard field goal by Chris Wingo with 3:11 left in the third.

Both sides suffered from drive stopping penalties and the Indians recovered a fumble as the first quarter ended. More penalties and punts bogged down the action in the second quarter, but an interception put PC in business at the Newberry 45 late in the half.

Pass interference moved the ball to the Newberry 32 and a fourth and 16 situation set the stage for what had to be one of the wildest finishes to any half in either team's sports history.

PC's Eddie Rogers caught a pass at the :41 mark and headed for the end zone. Newberry defenders protested that they had knocked him out of bounds short of the goal, but the officials signaled touchdown. Senior linebacker John Newkirk, Newberry's defensive standout with nine tackles and 10 assists on the day, blocked the conversion.

After the kickoff, Newberry set up from its 24 with one shot at a "Hail, Mary" pass. Quarterback Bellamy lofted it to the right sideline, just before being decked by the PC rush, and senior wide receiver Terry Taylor took the tipped ball the last 30 yards for the tying, 76 yard touchdown with no time left.

Senior kicker Mike Penn's extra point sent the Indians to the locker room the leader, 7-6.

For the Indians on the day, Bellamy was four of 16 with one interception for 139 yards. Shuler gained 62 yards on the ground and Taylor caught two passes for 92 yards.

Defensively, in addition to Newkirk, the Indians were led by Chris Holschaw with six tackles and six assists and Drew Watson with seven tackles, two assists and five passes broken up.

PC's Mozingo was 15 of 30 and no interceptions for 186 yards. Derrick Smalls gained 23 yards on the ground.

Despite Saturday's loss, PC was ranked 11th in the NAIA's final national ranking released Sunday. The Blue Hose received an at-large bid to the playoffs and will host Concord, N.C., 10-0 and fifth ranked, on Saturday.

Stands In For The Bomb

...ick Patrick Bellamy stands in against the Presbyterian ..., Mary' pass with no time left in the first half of ...linemen, from left, Jessie Schwiers, Benjie Moseley, Chad Yongue, and Joe Vaughn provide the protection. The 76 yard touchdown and the conversion gave the Indians a 7 - 6 halftime lead. Observer Photo by Vic MacDonald.

THE NEWBERRY OBSERVER   Newberry, S.C., Monday, Nov. 23, 1987

The Newberry Observer Sports

Indian Defense Shines

Newberry defensive standouts John Newkirk and Chris Holsclaw lead the defensive charge that closes down a Presbyterian runner Saturday. Blue Hose runners struggled for just 69 yards on the day. Observer Photo by Vic MacDonald.

The Li'l That Was!

The Clinton Chronicle

Hose Get Bronzed
But Newberry Doesn't Cost Them A Playoff Berth

By Monte Dutton
Sports Editor

NEWBERRY—Presbyterian's 17-15 loss to the Newberry Indians Saturday was a ball of confusions, a mass of contradictions.

Heck, the game wasn't even supposed to be played on that day. The Bronze Derby Classic had been contested on Thanksgiving since World War II, at least until PC's playoff hopes forced "the classic" to be moved up five days.

Further complicating matters, the Blue Hose managed to lose this all-encompassing showdown, then receive a playoff bid anyway.

Were it not for a series of plays which can only be described as bizarre, the game could have ended in a scoreless tie. Among the strange occurrences of the day were the following:

— Presbyterian, which had run the football with some degree of success against all 10 previous opponents, somehow managed to accumulate just 79 rushing yards, in 44 attempts, against the arch-rival Indians. Playing out of the expected straight 50 defense, the Indians somehow managed to install several of their marauders as permanent inhabitants of the PC backfield.

Blue Hose head coach Elliott Poss gamely addressed the problem this way: "Newberry has got outstanding people playing on their defensive unit. They were the third-leading defense (in the SAC-8) coming into this ballgame and we knew they would be tough on defense. We were a little beat-up in the offensive line, too, but that's not an excuse in any way, shape or form."

Victorious coach Clayton Johnson answered simply, "I'll never forget how our defense played. It was fantastic."

—With a playoff berth (supposedly) on the line, Newberry pulled off a second straight derailing of an ambitious Hose team. In 1984 Johnson deprived Cally Gault's last PC team of a spot in the playoffs by crushing the Blue Hose 26-0.

—Johnson was a lame duck, having been fired nearly two weeks before by Newberry president Dr. Hubert H. Setzler Jr. Johnson's predecessor, Reed Charpia, played the Blue Hose in 1981 under similar circumstances. Newberry won 24-21.

— For the first 29 minutes of the second half, neither offense did much. Then, in the final minute, two touchdowns were scored, one for each team. Presbyterian scored on a wildly improbable fourth-down, 37-yard touchdown pass from quarterback Scotty Mozingo to split end Eddie Rogers. Rogers went up with two defenders and somehow landed in the end zone with the ball. The extra point was blocked.

—As a schoolboy might brag to his classmates, "That ain't nothing, folks." On the last play of the first half, Newberry concocted the Bronze Derby's own private Immaculate Reception. Quarterback Pat Bellamy launched his prayer toward Cleve Mueller and PC's Kevin Wade. It was answered when the ball bounced hard left, into the hands of Terry Taylor, running parallel to the play at full stride. Taylor bobbled the ball for 10 yards or so, then sprinted the remainder of the play's 76-yard course. Mike Penn kicked the PAT and Newberry led 7-6 at halftime.

—After the two teams traded field goals, a crucial mistake decided the game. Unable to sustain an orthodox attack, the Blue Hose tried some razzle-dazzle. Mozingo lateraled to Lavern Reddick at the left sideline. Reddick was supposed to hit Rogers on a bomb but was pummeled as he let the pass go. Newberry's James Putman intercepted the resulting popup, setting up Bellamy's 1-yard sneak that put the Indians up 17-9.

—Last ditch effort No. 1. Mozingo, under pressure on third-and-six, somehow got off an accurate pass to a wide-open Glenn Jackson. Jackson dropped a likely touchdown. PC punted.

—Last ditch effort No. 2. After the Blue Hose got the ball back with 2:28 left, they finally launched a sustained drive. Mozingo hit five of eight passes but it took PC 14 perilous snaps to go 53 yards. Gerald scored by the narrowest of margins on fourth-and-goal from the 1. Newberry led 17-15, with 0:20 showing on the clock. The Blue Hose went for two, hoping to salvage a tie. Mozingo drilled a quick pass toward Reddick. Putman stepped in front to bat it down. Ballgame. Celebration. Film at 11.

While the crowd at Newberry numbered considerably less than the gathering at that other rivalry in Columbia, the postgame celebration was no less intense.

The Indians presented their martyred coach with the game ball and chants of, "Heyyyy, we got duh Derrrr-bee!" Once that mob dissipated, Johnson greeted well-wishers, the derby perched atop his head, for what seemed like an eternity to the reporters assembled at his side.

Among the well-wishers were Gault, now the PC athletic director, and Bob Strock, the longtime assistant coach. Both men embraced their old rival warmly.

"I wish I could have gone out like that," Gault said.

Presbyterian at Newberry, stats

Presbyterian 0 6 3 6 — 15
Newberry   0 7 0 10 — 17

SECOND QUARTER
Pres—Rogers 37 pass from Mozingo (kick blocked), 0:41
New—Taylor 76 pass from Bellamy (Penn kick), 0:00
THIRD QUARTER
Pres—FG Wingo 38, 3:11
FOURTH QUARTER
New—FG Hiller 30, 14:45
New—Bellamy 1 run (Penn kick), 7:33
Pres—Gerald 1 run (pass failed), 0:20
Att.—4,500

	Pres	New
First Downs	16	10
Rushes-Yards	44-79	38-92
Passing Yards	156	139
Return Yards	41	6
Comp-Att-Int	15-31-1	4-16-1
Punts-Average	6-35.5	8-32.0
Fumbles-Lost	5-1	1-0
Penalties-Yards	6-45	12-98

RUSHING—Presbyterian, Smalls 7-23, Parsley 9-15, Gerald 8-15, Riggins 14-14, Mozingo 6-2. Newberry, Shuler 9-62, Jones 17-37, Bellamy 12-(-7).
PASSING—Presbyterian, Mozingo 15-30-0 156, Reddick 0-1-1 0. Newberry, Bellamy 4-16-1 139.
RECEIVING—Presbyterian, Rogers 9-128, Reddick 3-30, Riggins 2-8, Parsley 1-(-10). Newberry, Taylor 2-92, Mueller 1-9, Jones 1-38.
MISSED FIELD GOALS—Presbyterian, Wingo 46.

Playoff Tickets On Sale At PC

Advance tickets for the Presbyterian-Concord NAIA playoff game are on sale at the PC athletic department for $8, with students' tickets going for $4. On game day, all tickets are $9.

The ticket office at Templeton Center is open from 9 a.m. to 5 p.m. each day this week except Thanksgiving. The ticket office will also be open the morning of the game from 9 to 11 a.m.

Fans may call in orders (833-2820, ask for the athletic department) but the tickets must be picked up by 11 a.m. Saturday morning.

Game day tickets for the 1 p.m. contest go on sale at Bailey Memorial Stadium, beginning at 11:30 a.m.

Ticket prices and procedures are set by the NAIA.

76

The Setzler Field "Hail Mary"

After a late 2nd quarter touchdown by Presbyterian College which included a blocked extra point by Newberry College, the Indians set up on their own 24 yard line with enough time for a final play before going to the locker room at halftime. The Bronze Derby "Hail Mary" was executed by Newberry Quarterback Pat Bellamy to Cleve Mueller. But wait! The ball was tipped and landed in the hands of Newberry's Terry Taylor, who was running alongside Mueller. Taylor juggled the ball for 10 yards, gained control and was in the endzone for a 76 yard touchdown reception. The extra point was good and Newberry went to the locker room with a 7-6 lead. With time running out in the fourth quarter, Presbyterian failed on a final second 2 point conversion to tie the game. In his last game as Newberry College's Head Coach, Clayton Johnson went out a 17-15 winner.

The Li'l That Was!

NAIA ends Thanksgiving tradition

A football tradition ended this season when the Bronze Derby Classic between Newberry and neighboring Presbyterian was moved from Thanksgiving Day to Saturday, Nov. 21.

Newberry and Presbyterian football rivalry dates back 76 games to 1913 although the Thanksgiving Day play did not begin until 1950.

The move was mandated by the National Association of Intercollegiate Athletics.

The NAIA voted a change in the playoff structure in Division I earlier in the year and expanded the number of paticipants from eight to 16. This move was heavily endorsed by the membership and rapidly approved in formal voting. However, in order to maintain the playoff schedule it became necessary to begin the opening round games on Saturday, Nov. 28, rather than the first week-end in December.

Earlier in the year the NAIA national office corresponded with both Newberry and Presbyterian Colleges formally requesting the official game date be moved to Saturday, Nov. 21. Only in the event that neither team would be in a position to qualify for the playoffs under the new format would the game then be "moved" to its traditional Thanksgiving date.

By early November, it became apparent that Presbyterian would be in the playoffs; the Blue Hose were undefeated in conference play with a 4-0 mark and were 6-2 for the season.

So ended tradition.

November 1988

November 1	Staten Island ferry in New York City gets their first pay phones.
November 2	Oakland A's shortstop Walt Weiss won MLB AL Rookie of the Year Award.
November 3	TV talk show host Geraldo Rivera suffered a broken nose after a taping with skinheads.
November 3	The Soviet Union recognized the teaching of Hebrew in their local schools.
November 5	For the first time in 20 years, the Beach Boys topped the *Billboard* charts with "Kokomo."
November 5	MLB All Stars began a 7 game series with Japan All Stars in Tokyo, Japan.
November 8	George H.W. Bush was elected President of the United States defeating Michael Dukakis.
November 8	900 died as an earthquake occurred in China.
November 9	John Mitchell, Attorney General and convicted perjurer in the Watergate scandal, passed away.
November 10	Orel Hershiser of the Los Angeles Dodgers won the MLB NL Cy Young Award.
November 14	Sitcom "Murphy Brown" premiered on CBS television.
November 15	Los Angeles Dodgers outfielder Kirk Gibson won MLB NL Most Valuable Player Award.
November 16	Jose Canseco of the Oakland A's won the MLB AL Most Valuable Player Award.
November 16	Robin Givens sued boxer Mike Tyson for $125 million for libel.
November 16	Prime Minister Margret Thatcher of Great Britain began a visit to the United States.
November 19	NHL hockey player Patrick Kane was born.
November 20	Bill Elliott won the 38th NASCAR Sprint Cup.
November 20	In the first NCAA American football game played in Europe, Boston College beat Army 38-24 in the Emerald Isle Classic in Dublin, Ireland.
November 21	American Baseball Hall of Fame pitcher Carl Hubbell passed away.
November 24	The Bronze Derby was played in Clinton, South Carolina on Thanksgiving Day. The Presbyterian College Blue Hose defeated the Newberry College Indians 30-16.

The Newberry Observer
AND HERALD & NEWS
"Just Like A Letter From Home"

Newberry, S.C., Wednesday, Nov. 23, 1988

Indians To Defend Bronze Derby Thursday

The Newberry College Indians will defend the Bronze Derby Thursday in their annual Thanksgiving Day clash with rival Presbyterian.

The game will also be the final time 11 Newberry College seniors will take to the field for the Indians.

Thursday's game will be the 76th meeting between the two schools. The Blue Hose hold a 45-26-5 lead in the series which dates back to 1913.

Newberry won last year's game 17-15, and the last time the Indians won back to back victories was in 1983 and 1984.

The Indians will enter the game with a 3-7 record, while the Blue Hose enter at 2-8.

"P-C is like us," defensive coordinator Chris Worst said. "They've been playing hard all year and just not getting the breaks. They are a good football team. If we don't win this one, it's resume' time."

According to offensive coordinator John Eder, the Presbyterian defense isn't bad, especially in the defensive secondary.

"Offensively we can't beat ourselves like we've been doing," Eder said. "We've got to worry about us more than them and we can't turn the ball over."

Eder says that size for size the two teams are about equal, but the Blue Hose might be a little bit faster.

Thursday's game will be the first time Newberry Head Coach Gary Smallen has faced the Blue Hose.

Elliott Poss, in his fourth season at Presbyterian, has a 1-1-1 record against the Indians.

Kickoff for the Thanksgiving Day Classic is scheduled for 2 p.m. at Bailey Field in Clinton.

The Bronze Derby in the Hands of the Newberry Indians

The Clinton Chronicle

Wednesday, November 30, 1988

Blue Hose end five-game skid with Bronze Derby win

By Monte Dutton
Sports Editor

Presbyterian College athletic director Cally Gault is fond of saying, "If you beat Wofford and Newberry, it's a good year."

Well, 1988 was not a good year for Blue Hose football fortunes, despite wins over those two rival schools. Still, Thursday afternoon's 30-16 win over the Indians did mercifully close out a dismal 3-8 season on an upbeat note.

The win also saved PC from the dubious distinction of becoming the first Blue Hose squad ever to go winless in the SAC-8. By defeating Newberry, Presbyterian finishes with a 1-6 conference mark.

Quite literally, the Blue Hose looked like a different team in ending a five-game losing streak. Nothing symbolized that more than PC's opening score.

On third-and-11 from the Newberry 33, Indian quarterback Ron Blakely's pass to the left sideline was intercepted and returned 45 yards for a touchdown by Blue Hose senior cornerback Kevin Wade. Alex Horton's extra point gave PC a 7-0 lead with 10:10 remaining in the first quarter.

The Blue Hose struck again on their next possession, marching 80 yards in 14 plays. A 25-yard Harold Nichols-to-Eddie Rogers completion got the Blue Hose out of a third-and-18 hole, then Stevie Riggins picked up 23 yards to the Tribe 10 on second-and-seven from the 33. Derrick Smalls scored the touchdown from a yard out, and PC led 14-0 with 14:43 left in the half.

The Indians finally got on the board when all-conference defensive tackle Chris Chrisley trapped Riggins in his own end zone for a safety at the 3:56 mark.

See BLUE HOSE Page 10A

Blue Hose
Continued from Page 9A

Nichols, who completed 10 of 16 passes for 126 yards, found wide-open Glenn Jackson for a 32-yard touchdown pass at the 5:06 mark of the third period. Horton missed the extra point.

The Indians responded with their only impressive drive of the game, moving 77 yards and scoring on a 19-yard pass from quarterback Ron Blakely to Dominique Padgett. A two-point conversion attempt failed, and PC led 21-8 at the end of the third quarter.

The Blue Hose salted the game away with scores on their next two possessions. Horton booted a 42-yard field goal at the 12:04 mark and Riggins scored on a 53-yard sprint with 5:03 left in the game.

For Riggins, it was the crowning moment of an illustrious four-year career. The Walterboro native began and ended his career with touchdowns. He returned a punt for a touchdown at The Citadel in his first play in a Blue Hose uniform, back in 1985, and also scored on his last play with the touchdown against Newberry. He rushed for 104 yards against Newberry and 3,280 for his career, setting a new school record.

The game's leading rusher was Newberry's Hodie Clinkscales, with 107 yards.

A mishandled punt snap which eluded Newberry's Kevin Black almost resulted in another score but, on third-and-goal from the Newberry 11, backup quarterback Darrin McGlamry was intercepted by Newberry's Kevin Reeder, who returned it 96 yards to the PC 4. Two plays later defensive tackle Chrisley, whom Indian head coach Gary Smallen had inserted in the offensive backfield, scored from a yard out.

Smallen said, "Presbyterian did a tremendous job converting on third-and-long situations. The game started with a big bang (Wade's interception return) and went downhill from there."

Go-Getters
We Need You!

United Oil Marketers, Inc.
Convenience/Deli/Gas Chain
Now Hiring

Honest, Dependable, Self-starters to join our retail management team. Prior supervisory experience in any field a definite plus

- Full Benefits Package
- Bonus/Profit Sharing
- Advancement Opportunities

Apply in person 2:30-5 p.m. Mon-Sat
700 Fleming St., Laurens, S.C.
or call 984-6120 for appointment

NOW OPEN
Army Surplus World
Public Square-Laurens
984-3925
Hrs. Mon.-Sat. 9-6
Specializing in genuine U.S. Army
- Field Jackets
- Navy Deck Jackets
- Bomber Jackets

Everything In Camouflage
Boys' Camo Pants, Shirts & Coats
Genuine B.D.U. Pants & Shirts
Tree Bark Camo Outfits

National Guard and Armed Forces Patches,
Emblems, Ranks and Insignia
Military Boots, Back Packs, Military T-Shirts, Trunks, Foot Lockers, Military Watches, Canteens, Machetes, Pistol Belts and Much, Much More

The Li'l That Was!

The Newberry Observer
AND HERALD & NEWS

Presbyterian quarterback Hal Nichols, 9, is tackled by Indians defensive tackle Reggie Deas, 58, as Chris Holsclaw, 41, and James Putnam, 44, close in during action in Thursday's Bronze Derby game in Clinton. - Observer Photo by Vic MacDonald

After the annual Presbyterian - Newberry rivalry game on Thanksgiving Day, Newberry coach Gary Smallen and the Indians' Chris Chrisley, 74, meet with Presbyterian quarterback Hal Nichols, 9. A defensive standout, Chrisley tackled a PC runner in the end zone for a safety and switched to offense to score a touchdown as a fullback, accounting for eight of the Indians' 16 points on the day.
- Observer Photo by Vic MacDonald

Presbyterian Reclaims Bronze Derby

Presbyterian's Blue Hose beat the Newberry Indians, 30 - 16, on Thursday to take the Bronze Derby back to Clinton.

Both teams finished the season at 3 - 8 overall. Winning the Derby salvaged PC's worst season since the Hose went 1 - 9 in 1962.

PC scored first on a Kevin Wade interception of Indians' quarterback Ron Blakely. Wade ran it in 45 yards with 10:10 left in the first quarter, and the Indians never recovered.

Newberry scored on tackle Chris Chrisley's safety, nailing PC running back Stevie Riggins in the end zone.

Blakely hit Dominique Padgett with a 19 yard touchdown pass in the third quarter, cutting Presbyterian's lead to 20 - 8 with 1:08 left.

But a 42 yard field goal by PC's Alex Horton a short time later seemed to take the wind out of the Indians' sails. The score was made possible by an Indians' penalty, for having 12 men on the field. Riggins added the PC final points when he broke free for a 53 yard touchdown run with 5:03 left.

The Indians' Kevin Reeder intercepted PC quarterback Hal Nichols' pass at the goal line and returned it 96 yards to the Presbyterian four yard line.

Chrisley, an Indians' standout senior from Calhoun Falls, switched from defensive tackle to fullback, and bulled over from the one for the touchdown two plays later.

Hudie Clinkscales ran for the two-point conversion. Clinkscales, a senior from Anderson, led all rushers with 107 yards on 18 carries.

Saluda   14 30 -44
Newberry   10   7 -17

Saluda (44) -- Petina Etheridge 15, Anissa Hill 13, Daniel B. Nicholson 5, M. Jones 2.
Newberry (17) Tonia Glymph 11, Eigner 3, Ware 3.

Whitmire   11 17 -28
Clinton   12 13 -25

Whitmire (28) Kendra Agnew 20, Murphy 4, Epps 2, Stephens 2.
Clinton (25) Cheryl Floyd 14, Heaton 4, Lyles 4, Peake 2, Jones 1.

Laurens   9 16 -25
Mid-Carolina   5 17 -22

Laurens (25), Richardson 6, Hellams 4, Thompson 4, S. Wilson 4, Childers 3, Abercrombie 2, Hill 2.
Mid-Carolina (22) Dara Edwards 12, Boyd 4, Hill 2, Mathis 2, Shealy 2.

PC scalps Indians

By Steve Owens
Sports Editor

One game may not be enough to help the Presbyterian College Blue Hose team overcome the trials it has endured during the 1988 football season, but Thursday's 30-16 Bronze Derby victory over Newberry comes close.

The Blue Hose enjoyed their highest scoring performance since defeating Wofford seven games ago and even got their first defensive score of the season on the way to earning just their third win of the decade against the Indians.

"I'm proud of the way our seniors approached the football game. They gave us a lot of leadership in preparation for the game," PC head coach Elliott Poss said. "We were a little ragged at spots, but we did a pretty good job overall."

The Blue Hose had struggled with bad breaks all season long, but their fortunes turned around before 3,500 fans at Bailey Memorial Stadium. The Indians ran just five plays before Blue Hose cornerback Kevin Wade picked off Ron Blakely's pass and dashed untouched 45 yards for a touchdown.

"The overall key was when we started off and got the first touchdown off a turnover. We haven't had anything good happen to us like that in the first part of a ball game this season," Poss said. "We went into this ball game minus 12 in the turnover category. That's been a big part of this season."

A 14-play, 80-yard drive was capped by Derrick Smalls' one-yard plunge with 14:43 remaining in the first half to increase the PC lead to 14-0. Although Newberry tackle Chris Chrisley trapped Stevie Riggins in the end zone for a safety later in the second quarter, the second half would also belong to PC.

PC quarterback Harold Nichols hooked up with Glenn Jackson for a 32-yard touchdown in the third quarter, but Newberry answered with a 19-yard touchdown pass from Blakely to Dominique Padgett to trim the Blue Hose lead to 20-8.

However, PC's Alex Horton hit a 42-yard field goal, and Riggins broke free for a 53-yard touchdown run with 5:03 to play to give the Blue Hose a 30-8 advantage.

The Blue Hose finished with 300 yards of total offense while limiting Newberry to 235 yards. Riggins had 104 yards on 16 carries,

DERBY WIN — Blue Hose tailback Steve Parsley (34) kept his eyes upfield while Newberry sophomore Reggie Epps zeroed in on him during first quarter action in Thursday's Bronze Derby Classic at Clinton. The Blue Hose mixed a solid offensive attack and took advantage of Newberry errors to hand the Indians a 30-16 loss in the annual Thanksgiving Day contest. PC's offensive output was its best since the Blue Hose defeated Wofford seven games ago. Ironically, that had also been the last time the PC squad notched a victory. (Photo by Steve Owens)

while Nichols completed 10 of 16 passes for 126 yards.

Although the Blue Hose finish with a 3-8 overall mark, recapturing the Bronze Derby from Newberry (3-8) was enough to chase away some of the ghosts that haunted the team this season.

"This feels good. It's the one we wanted all year," senior flanker Lavern Reddick said.

The Li'l That Was!

In 1988, Presbyterian College defeated Newberry College 30-16. The game was played in Clinton, South Carolina. The game was the 42nd Thanksgiving Day Bronze Derby football Classic.

Photo courtesy of Presbyterian College archives

Presbyterian College running back Derrick Smalls attacks the Newberry defense in the 1988 Bronze Derby game.

Photo courtesy of Presbyterian College archives

The Li'l That Was!

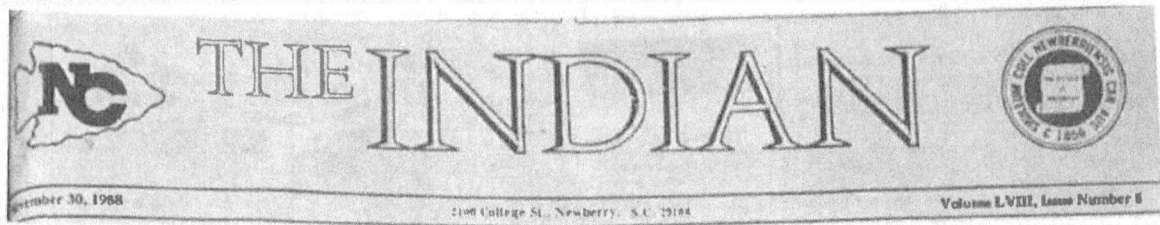

Sports

Blue Hose steal Bronze Derby from Indians

by Terry L. Stutts, Jr.

NEWBERRY

The Presbyterian Blue Hose avenged last year's Bronze Derby loss to the Newberry Indians by defeating the Indians on Thanksgiving Day '88, by a score of 30-16.

The Thanksgiving Day football game between Newberry and Presbyterian College has been a tradition since 1913, the rivalry for the Bronze Derby, however, is much more recent.

During a basketball game in 1947, a small confrontation led to the creation of the present tradition. Several PC students had placed a banner on the wall of McLean Gymnasium that proclaimed, "beat the Hell out of Newberry!". During the game, intrepid Newberry students obtained a ladder and one of them climbed through the window of the gym to remove the banner.

The missing banner wasn't noticed until the end of the hard fought match — a PC victory, 51-47. After noticing that the banner was missing, a PC student demanded that the offending banner be returned to him immediately. A small scuffle broke out and eventually grew into a free-for-all. During the melee, and unnamed Newberry student grabbed a derby off the head of a Presbyterian student and ran from the scene.

In the days that followed, the athletic directors of each school negotiated for the return of the hat. During the discussions, someone suggested that the derby serve "as a laurel of victory in athletic contests between Newberry and Presbyterian."

The derby was found and eventually returned to PC. It was then packaged up to prevent accidental destruction and shipped to a casting company in Ohio. The derby was bronzed and returned to South Carolina. Since that time, it has been known as the famous "Bronze Derby."

Until 1956, the possession of the Derby was determined by the outcome of all Newberry-PC athletic encounters. Since that time, the ownership of the Derby has been determined by the outcome of the Thanksgiving Day NC-PC football game.

This year, the Blue Hose relied on the big play, rushing for 174 yards and passing for 126 yards. The Indians could not muster a big play, but managed 131 yards on the ground and 104 yards through the air.

The Presbyterian defense put the first 6 points on the board. Kevin Wade intercepted a Ron Blakely pass and returned it 45 yards for the touchdown.

The Blue Hose then took the ball 80 yards to bring the score to 14-0. Derrick Smalls bulled 1 yard for the touchdown.

At the 3:54 point in the second quarter, Kevin Black punted to the Presbyterian 1 yard line. On the first play from scrimmage, Chris Christey caught Stevie Riggins in the endzone for a safety.

In the third quarter Glenn Jackson caught a 32 yard touchdown pass to extend the Blue Hose lead to 20-2.

The Indians tried to get back into the game, and with 1:08 left in the third quarter, Blakely hit Dominique Padgett with a 19 yard pass for a touchdown.

Presbyterian's first possession of the fourth quarter ended with a 42 yard field goal by Alex Horton to make the score 23-8.

The Blue Hose then put the game out of reach as Riggins blasted a 53 yard touchdown run.

Newberry's last attempt at a comeback was started with an interception by Kevin Renfer who returned it to the Presbyterian 4 yard line. Two plays later, Christey rambled over for a 1 yard touchdown. Hudie Chinkacales added a two point conversion making the final score 30-16.

This game brings both teams 3-8 for the season.

November 1989

The Li'l That Was!

November 1	Scandinavian Airlines was the first airline carrier to ban smoking on flights.
November 3	Lou Pinella was named manager of the Cincinnati Reds after manager Pete Rose was banned from MLB for gambling.
November 4	Demonstrations for political reform drew hundreds of thousands of people in East Berlin. The demonstrations led to the fall of the Berlin Wall.
November 7	New York City elected David Dinkins, the first African American Mayor of the city.
November 9	East Berlin opened its borders.
November 10	German citizens began demolishing the Berlin Wall.
November 15	Bret Saberhagen of the Kansas City Royals won the MLB AL Cy Young Award.
November 17	Bret Saberhagen signed a record $3 million per year contract with the Kansas City Royals.
November 18	Pennsylvania was the first state to restrict abortions after the United States Supreme court gave states the right to do so.
November 19	Rusty Wallace won the 39th NASCAR Sprint Cup.
November 19	The United States Soccer team defeated Trinidad 1-0 qualifying for the 1990 World Soccer Cup finals.
November 20	Milwaukee Brewers Robin Yount won the MLB AL Most Valuable Player Award.
November 21	A law banning smoking on most domestic airline flights was signed by United States President George H.W. Bush.
November 21	Television cameras are now permitted in the British House of Commons.
November 22	Kirby Puckett signed a record $3 million per year contract with the Minnesota Twins.
November 23	The Philadelphia Eagles defeated the Dallas Cowboys 27-0. The game was referred to as the "Bounty Bowl" as Dallas Cowboy Head Coach Jimmy Johnson accused the Eagles Coach Buddy Ryan of placing bounties on Cowboy players.
November 23	The Bronze Derby was played in Newberry, South Carolina on Thanksgiving Day. The Newberry Indians defeated the Presbyterian College Blue Hose 29-24.

The Li'l That Was!

The Newberry Observer
AND HERALD & NEWS
"Just Like A Letter From Home"

Newberry, S. C., Wednesday, Nov. 22, 1989

| Page 5 | College Page: New Arts Format | Page 6 | Sports: Indians, Hose To Clash |

Indians Prepare For Bronze Derby Clash With Presbyterian

BY MIKE MEADOW

The Newberry College Indians, riding a three game winning streak, will face the Presbyterian Blue Hose this Thursday in the annual Bronze Derby Clash.

Presbyterian comes into the game with a four game losing streak.

Both teams will enter the game with a 4-6 record on the season.

Thursday's meeting will be the 43rd time the two schools have met, with the Blue Hose leading the series with 46 wins, 26 losses, and five ties.

Presbyterian won last year's game in Clinton by the score of 30-16. Newberry has not lost to Presbyterian at Setzler Field since a 16-14 defeat in 1979.

"Hopefully, we can continue to do good things," Newberry Head Coach Gary Smallen said. "We will have to play over our heads and very emotionally and take advantage of turnovers to win."

Taking advantage of turnovers seems to be something the Indians are getting used to doing. In last week's game against Lenoir-Rhyne, Newberry capitalized in five turnovers to take a 52-30 win.

Also last week, Newberry quarterback Tim Singleton broke a 30-year-old record for most touchdown responsibilities in a season, which was set by Richard Seatrunk in 1959 in which he accounted for 20 touchdowns. Singleton broke the record on a nine yard run giving him 21 touchdowns to break the record.

"Tim has got to play well," Smallen said. "He has to play loose and make things happen on offense. The offensive line must also play well for him to do his job."

Smallen said that the special teams could also play a big factor in the game. He said that place kicker Chip Lingerfelt had worked hard during the off season, and that his foot could come into play during the game.

Last week, the Indians rushed for 318 yards in 57 attempts against Lenoir-Rhyne, but Smallen said that the Indians will do whatever it takes to win the game.

"PC will have an advantage coming into the game," Smallen said. "They have beaten the same teams we have and teams that have beaten us. That makes Newberry the underdog."

Smallen said that the crowd could play a large part in the game.

"The tradition that goes along with this game makes it one of the greatest rivalry games in small college football," Smallen said. "The fans and the crowd can come into play. Mistakes get the crowd into the game, and that makes it tougher on the players."

In game notes, Cory Patton and Maccio Montgomery have been named the players of the week by the Newberry coaches for their efforts in the last week's game.

Patton, a 6'0", 185 lb. freshman runningback carried the ball 18 times for 99 yards and two touchdowns. Montgomery, a 5'10", 235 lb. freshman defensive lineman, had two tackles for loss and one quarterback sack. He also graded out the highest in hustle and technique.

Thursday's game will kick-off at 1:30 p.m. at Setzler Field on the campus of Newberry College.

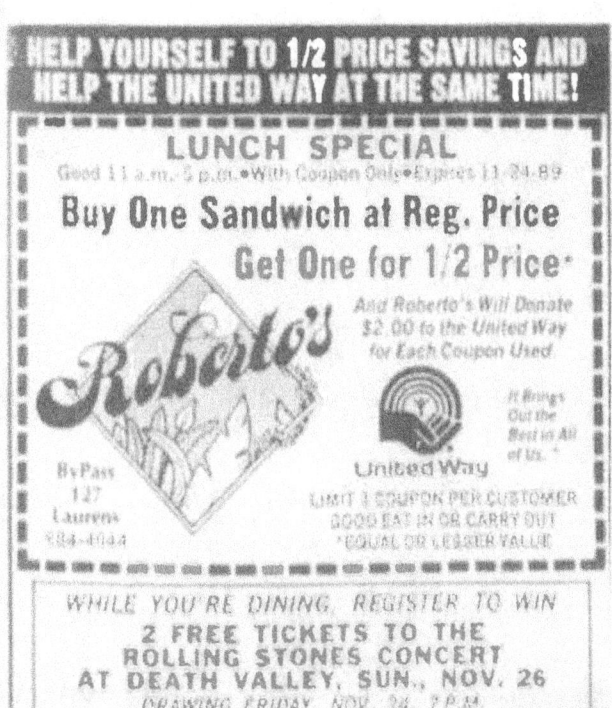

Football team fights to keep Derby

by Smokey Brown
SPORTS EDITOR

PC's Blue Hose will look to break a four game losing streak next Thursday at Newberry in the 78th meeting between the two schools.

Although PC lost its last two games to Gardner-Webb and Carson-Newman, two players set school records. Senior LaVerne Reddick set a school record for receiving yards in a season against Gardner-Webb, and his two touchdown catches against Carson-Newman puts him at the top of the SAC-8 touchdown receptions list. Reddick has 23 touchdown receptions in his career.

Quarterback Harold Nichols now owns the PC single season passing yardage record with 1778 yards, throwing 206 yards to break the mark formerly held by Jimmy Spence. Nichols also holds the season record for most completions in a season, with 135 currently.

Both PC and Newberry hold 4-6 records. Newberry has won three in a row, their last win being a 52-30 outcome over Lenoir-Rhyne. The Hose gained the Bronze Derby last year with a 30-16 win over the Indians. The Blue Hose lead the series 47-25-5 in which the first game was played in 1913.

On final play
Newberry wins Derby

By Steve Owens
Sports Editor

NEWBERRY — Presbyterian College quarterback Harold Nichols summed up Thursday's annual Bronze Derby Classic in one sentence.

"This is the weirdest thing I've ever been associated with," the senior said.

Nichols' feelings were echoes countless times Thursday afternoon at Setzler Field after Newberry quarterback Tim Singleton completed a 44-yard touchdown pass to Pat White on the final play of the game to lift the Indians to a 29-24 decision.

"We're fortunate. You can't win like that and not feel very lucky," Newberry head coach Gary Smallen said. "You throw it up there and one team is going to win on the last play. We were very lucky."

The Indians' good fortune wasn't limited to the final play. With PC holding a 24-23 lead and Newberry attempting to get into field goal range, Singleton rifled a pass out of bounds as the final seconds ticked off the scoreboard clock.

HOWEVER, THE officials put one second back on the clock, giving the Indians one final chance. Singleton found White alone at the PC 2 and the junior wide receiver fell into the end zone for his first touchdown catch of the year.

"I felt like we still had a chance with one second still on the clock. We talked about going for the middle of the field, but I saw the opening to the left side and went for it. I saw the ball, went up and got it, and came down in the end zone," White said.

"Pat said he was open all day, but I was having a bad day throwing the ball," Singleton said. "I had to get it to him once and that one counted."

While the Blue Hose defense was playing one of its best games of the season, it was the PC offense that was unable to get untracked for three quarters. Trailing 10-0, the Blue Hose dodged a bullet in the second quarter when

SCORING
PC	0	0	10	14	24
Newberry	3	7	0	19	29

N—Lingerfelt 25 FG
N—Singleton 3 run (Lingerfelt kick)
P—Sullivan 58 interception return (Horton kick)
P—Horton 37 FG
N—Singleton 26 run (Lingerfelt kick)
P—Heard 59 punt return (Horton kick)
P—Egan 18 pass from Nichols (Horton kick)
N—Singleton 13 run (run failed)
N—White 44 pass from Singleton

STATISTICS
Rushing: PC 42-61 (Smalls 12-33, Shaw 9-29, Heard 10-29); NC 49-244 (Singleton 22-148, Cummings 19-62)
Passing: PC 11-23-1—120 (all by Nichols), NC 11-28-3 153 (all by Singleton)
Receiving: PC (Egan 64, Reddick 5-46, Brinson 1-10), NC (Jeffrey 7-67 White 1-44)

junior safety Wayne Hampton picked off a pass at the PC 1 and returned it to the Newberry 29.

But the Blue Hose fumbled two plays later, one of four PC fumbles in the first half.

"We sort of shot ourselves in the foot in the first half. It was very frustrating," Nichols said. "The defense played a heck of a game and kept us in good field position. They got some key turnovers and put us in places where we should have scored, but we didn't execute well in the first half."

DEFENSE ACCOUNTED for PC's first score, a 58-yard interception return by Jason Sullivan that cut Newberry's lead to 10-7.

"Our tackle rushed him (Singleton) and made him come out of the pocket," Sullivan said. "He's a sidearm thrower and I was standing behind a lineman. When he threw it, I just stepped out and it nearly hit me in the face. I took it all the way."

Alex Horton's 37-yard field goal with 6:26 remaining in the third quarter tied the contest at 10-10, but Singleton answered with a 26-yard keeper around the left end for a touchdown seven seconds into the final quarter.

While the Blue Hose offense continued to struggle, the PC special teams provided the next score. DeNorris Heard fielded Garland Greenway's punt at the PC 41, avoided a pair of defenders and broke around the right end for a 59-yard touchdown return. Horton's PAT tied the game at 17-17 with 7:48 to play.

The Indians ran just two plays before fumbling at their own 37, giving the Blue Hose offense the chance it had been waiting for. Nichols made the most of the opportunity, hitting Billy Egan with an 18-yard scoring strike to give PC a 24-17 lead with 3:50 remaining in the game.

BUT SINGLETON rallied the Indians and scored his third rushing touchdown on a 13-yard jaunt with 2:18 to play. On the two-point conversion attempt, however, the sophomore was halted on a quarterback draw and the Indians trailed 24-23.

After recovering an on-side kick, PC ran four plays before losing possession on downs at the Newberry 43 with 37 seconds remaining. Singleton then drove the Indians for the winning points.

"I felt like we had it won," Nichols said. "If you're up by a point with that much time left, all you have to do is stop them. But this is Newberry and PC and it's a series that has been going on for a long time. A lot of strange things have happened."

The Indians finished with 397 yards of total offense, while PC managed 181 yards — including just 61 yards rushing. Senior Tyrone Lucas led the Blue Hose defensive effort with 15 tackles.

Staff photo by Steve Owens

BLUE HOSE FALL — Newberry recaptured the Bronze Derby trophy Thursday afternoon at Setzler Field, as quarterback Tim Singleton completed a 44 yard touchdown pass to Pat White on the final play of the game to give the Indians a 29-24 win. Defenses dominated the first half, but the fourth quarter belonged to the squads' offenses. The teams combined to score 33 points in the final quarter.

Sports

Poss: Newberry loss tough pill to swallow

By Rick Hendricks
Managing Editor

NEWBERRY—Perhaps last Thursday's ending to the annual Bronze Derby clash was an appropriate finish for a tough Blue Hose season.

The Newberry Indians — 44 yards away from the end zone and one tick left on the clock — won the Derby back, 29-24, on a touchdown pass from Tim Singleton to Pat White on the final play of the game.

PC's defense, which this season gave up more points than any other team in the school's football history, was unable to come through when victory was within its grasp.

The defense did, however, keep the Blue Hose in the game. "Defensively, we made some good plays and didn't really shut them down, but did keep the game close," said PC head coach Elliott Poss.

"(The final play) was a tough pill for all of us to swallow," said Poss. "The big problem was that there were (PC) players around the receiver, but we didn't go after the football as aggressively as we needed to."

The Indians built a 10-0 lead in the first half, primarily due to the inability of the Blue Hose to get their offense untracked.

"We didn't play a very good offensive game against Newberry," Poss said, citing PC's lack of execution, as well as the Indians' aggressive defensive play, for the offense's poor showing.

Newberry got the ball first in the second half, but on its fourth play from scrimmage, PC's Jason Sullivan picked off a Singleton pass and returned it 58 yards for a touchdown. Alex Horton added the PAT to bring the Blue Hose within 10-7.

The visitors tied the contest after a Newberry fumble put PC in great field position at the Indian 24. After failing to gain a first down, the Blue Hose turned to Horton, who knotted the game with a 37-yard field goal with 6:26 to go in the third quarter.

Singleton put the Indians back in front on the first play of the final stanza with his second TD — a 26-yard run. Chip Lingerfelt added the PAT to give Newberry a 17-10 lead.

DeNorris Heard got PC back within a point on his 59-yard punt return with 7:48 to play, then Horton's PAT tied the contest at 17.

The excitement was just beginning.

After the ensuing kickoff, Newberry took over at its own 37, but two plays later, PC's Tyrone Lucas recovered an Indian fumble at the 38.

Six plays later, Blue Hose quarterback Harold Nichols hit Billy Egan with an 18-yard TD pass to put PC in front for the first time. Horton's extra point gave PC a 24-17 advantage with 3:50 remaining in the game.

One minute and 32 seconds later, the Indians were back in the end zone, due to Singleton's third TD — a 13-yard run.

Newberry decided to go for a two-point conversion, but Singleton was stopped short by the PC defense and the Blue Hose led, 24-23 with just over two minutes to go.

The Indians attempted an onside kick, but failed to recover and PC was in business at the 50, needing only one first down to hold on for the win and break a four-game losing string.

Three straight runs by Heard left PC a yard short of the first down, but on fourth down, the Blue Hose elected to go for it and the Indians stopped Heard for a two-yard loss and gained possession of the football with 37 seconds left.

Newberry worked the ball to the PC 44 and it appeared that time had run out, but the officials ruled that there was still one tick left on the clock and the horn had not sounded, setting the stage for Singleton and White to win the game.

Newberry won its fourth straight contest after starting 1-6 to finish 5-6, while the Blue Hose fell to 4-7.

PC	0	0	10	14-	24
Newberry	3	7	0	19-	29

First Quarter
N-FG Lingerfelt 25
Second Quarter
N-Singleton 3 run (Lingerfelt kick)
Third Quarter
P-Sullivan 58 interception return (Horton kick)
P-FG Horton 37
Fourth Quarter
N-Singleton 26 run (Lingerfelt kick)
P-Heard 59 punt return (Horton kick)
P-Egan 18 pass from Nichols (Horton kick)
N-Singleton 13 run (run failed)
N-White 44 pass from Singleton (no attempt)

	PC	NC
First downs	10	21
Rushes-Yds.	42-61	49-244
Passing	23-11-1	28-11-3
Passing Yds.	120	153
Total Yds.	181	397
Fumbles-Lost	6-3	4-2
Penalties-Yds.	6-70	5-44

INDIVIDUAL STATISTICS
Rushing-PC, Smalls 12-33, Shaw 9-29, Heard 10-29, Brinson 5-(-1), Nichols 6-(-29). NC, Singleton 22-148, Cummings 19-62, Jeffrey 2-19, Payton 6-15.

Passing-PC, Nichols 23-11-1 120 yards. NC, Singleton 28-11-3.

Receiving-PC, Reddick 5-46, Egan 5-64, Brinson 1-10. NC, Jeffrey 7-67, Carver 1-30, Green 1-(-1), Fretwell 1-13, White 1-44.

Blue Hose defender arrives too late...
...Newberry's Pat White (2) catches game-winning pass on last play to clinch Bronze Derby win

The Clinton Chronicle

The Li'l That Was!

The Newberry Observer

Try It On, Coach
Newberry College Head Football Coach Gary Smallen holds the Bronze Derby after a last-play-of-the-game win over Presbyterian yesterday. See story and photos of the Indians' 29-24 win on Page 8. - Observer Photo by Vic MacDonald

Last Second Touchdown Lifts Indians, 29-24

Derby Returns To Newberry Campus

Taking the Hit
Presbyterian quarterback Harold Nichols, 9, will take a lick from an Indians defender after making the pitchout in yesterday's Bronze Derby game. The Indians defense played a vital role in the 29-25 win, stopping the Blue Hose on a fourth and one late in the game. - Observer Photo by Vic MacDonald

Thanks to a last second 44-yard touchdown pass from Newberry quarterback Tim Singleton to wideout Pat White, the Bronze Derby will be displayed at Newberry's Eleazer Arena until next year.

With one second remaining to play, Singleton heaved a high spiral 44-yards into the arms of White and the Indians had a 29-24 win over the Blue Hose. The chaotic play came after game officials put one second on the game clock.

The Indians' defense set the stage with 0:37 remaining in the game. On a fourth and one play at the Indian 41 the Indians stopped Presbyterian running back DeNorris Heard for a two yard loss and Newberry had the ball. Four plays later the Indians had won.

Newberry dominated the statistics, outgaining the Blue Hose 397-178 in total offense and 244-61 in rushing offense. However, Indian mistakes kept the game close. Newberry lost two fumbles and Singleton was intercepted three times.

Newberry kicker Chip Lingerfelt opened the scoring with a 25-yard field goal with 7:17 left in the first period. Singleton scored on a three yard run with 7:55 left in the half and Newberry led 10-0.

Indian miscues allowed the Blue Hose to tie the score. Jason Sullivan intercepted a Singleton pass and returned it 58-yards for a touchdown with 13:39 left in the third period.

With 6:26 remaining in that same period, the Blue Hose tied the score at 10. Newberry fumbled the ball on their own 26-yard line, Presbyterian recovered and kicker Alex Horton booted a 37-yard field goal to knot the score.

The Indians countered with 14:53 left in the game. Singleton scrambled 26-yards for a touchdown and Newberry lead 17-10.

The Blue Hose defense stiffened and with 7:48 left Newberry was forced to punt. Presbyterian deep back Heard received the ball at his own 41 and bolted 59-yards for a touchdown and the score was tied 17-17.

Presbyterian recovered a Newberry fumble with 7:01 left at the Indian 37. Six plays later Quarterback Harold Nichols found receiver Billy Egan on an 18-yard pass and the Blue Hose led 24-17.

The Indians responded with a five play, 58-yard drive. Singleton bolted around end with 2:18 left and Newberry was down 24-23. The Indians chose to go for two, but Singleton was stopped and Presbyterian led 24-23.

Newberry's defense rose to the challenge and set the stage for the classic finish.

Newberry ends the season at 5-6, riding a four game win streak. Presbyterian falls to 4-7 on the season.

And the derby? You can see it at Newberry's Eleazer Arena.

The Newberry Observer - Nov 24, 1989

The Li'l That Was!

8 THE NEWBERRY OBSERVER Newberry, S. C., Friday, Nov. 24, 1989

The Newberry Observer Sports

Late Touchdown
Newberry quarterback Tim Singleton, 4, runs in a 13-yard touchdown with about two minutes left in yesterday's Bronze Derby game, closing the Indians to within one point of Presbyterian. The Indians tried a two-point conversion to try to take the lead, but Singleton was stopped short. The late touchdown set the stage for Singleton's last-second pass to Pat White for the win. - Observer Photo by Vic MacDonald

Celebration Time
Indians receiver Pat White, 12 is held aloft seconds after catching the 44-yard touchdown pass that brought the Bronze Derby back to Newberry.
- Observer Photo by Vic MacDonald

Take a tip from Santa's elves:
WORK IT OUT NOW FOR NEXT CHRISTMAS!

Santa's elves start working a year ahead, so by Christmas, they can sit back and enjoy themselves. And that's the whole idea of Newberry Federal's Christmas Club. You can start with as little as $5.00; add to it every week or as often as you wish. Then by next October, you'll have a big check to cover Christmas!

So make this the last Christmas you worry about bills. And start your 1990 Newberry Federal Christmas Club *now!* All those elves can't be wrong.

 **N** **NEWBERRY FEDERAL SAVINGS BANK**
Banking That Works for You

In Newberry: 1330 College St. & 1735 Wilson Road 276-0732
In Prosperity: 101 N. Wheeler St. 364-2008

The Li'l That Was!

1 Second!

Late in the fourth quarter of the Bronze Derby in 1989, the Newberry College defense had stopped Presbyterian College on the Newberry College 41 yard line for a loss of possession. Presbyterian College was leading 24-23 with 23 seconds remaining in the game. Newberry ran 3 plays to the Blue Hose 44 yard line. On the third play of the drive, it appeared that time had run out and Presbyterian had won the game. The officials determined that there was one second remaining in the game. With one final desperation play in their arsenal, Newberry College quarterback Tim Singleton connected with receiver Pat White for a 44 yard touchdown pass. The Indian receiver was well covered and made an outstanding effort to get into the endzone. For players, but particularly seniors on both teams, that single second will always be remembered in their last Bronze Derby college football game. Presbyterian College quarterback and later Blue Hose Head Football Coach Harold Nichols told The Laurens County Advertiser that "This was the weirdest thing I've ever been associated with." When we were together and reflected on the game, he remembered the moment today like it had just happened minutes ago. A Newberry College Indians 29-24 win became another Bronze Derby classic!

The Li'l 🎩 That Was!

dimensions
NEWBERRY COLLEGE ALUMNI MAGAZINE
Vol. 24, No. 2 — December, 1989

WHERE THEY BELONG! --- The famous Bronze Derby and the three-year-old Bishops Trophy are pictured here residing in Newberry. The Indian football team captured both prizes by defeating Lenoir-Rhyne 52-30 for the Bishops Trophy, then pulled off the last second 29-24 win over Presbyterian on Thanksgiving Day at Setzler Field to regain the Derby. The Indians completed a 44-year "Hail Mary" pass from quarterback Tim Singleton to wide receiver Pat White with no time remaining on the scoreboard to capture the victory. Newberry finished the 1989 season with a 5-6 record including consecutive wins over Elon, Catawba, Lenoir-Rhyne and Presbyterian to close the season using mainly freshman and sophomore players at many positions.

November 1990

November 1	President George Bush compared Saddem Hussein to Adolf Hitler.
November 3	Actress Mary Martin of "Peter Pan" fame passed away.
November 4	United States Secretary of State James Baker visited American troops in Saudi Arabia.
November 4	Iraq indicated it was preparing for a dangerous war.
November 6	Singer Whitney Houston released "I'm your Baby Tonight."
November 6	Dave Justice of the Atlanta Braves won the MLB NL Rookie of the Year Award.
November 6	Iran's oil producing region suffered a major earthquake.
November 7	The first female President of Ireland, Mary Robinson was elected.
November 8	The United States sent 100,000 troops to the Persian Gulf.
November 10	The film "Home Alone" starring Macauley Culkin premiered.
November 12	The World Wide Web was first proposed by scientists Tim Berners-Lee and Robert Cailliau.
November 15	Music producers confirm that singer Milli Vanilli did not sing on their album.
November 15	United States President George H.W. Bush signed the Clear Air Act of 1990.
November 18	In women's golf, the first Solheim Cup took place. The United States team, captained by Kathy Whitworth defeated the European team, captained by Mickey Walker.
November 18	Dale Earnhardt won the 40th NASCAR Sprint Cup.
November 19	Barry Bonds of the Pittsburgh Pirates won the MLB NL Most Valuable Player Award.
November 20	Rickey Henderson of the Oakland A's won the MLB AL Most Valuable Player Award.
November 21	French President Francois Mitterrand supported a United Nations resolution that would authorize use of force in the Persian Gulf.
November 22	United States President George H.W. Bush visited United States troops in Saudi Arabia.
November 22	Margret Thatcher announced her resignation as Prime Minister of Great Britain.
November 22	The Bronze Derby was played in Clinton, South Carolina on Thanksgiving Day. The Newberry College Indians defeated the Presbyterian College Blue Hose 24-7.

The Newberry Observer
AND HERALD & NEWS
"Just Like A Letter From Home"

Newberry, S.C., Wednesday, Nov. 21, 1990

The Li'l That Was!

Eye On Sports
by Mike Meadow

The Newberry College Indians will play their final game of the season on Thursday, and also their final game under head coach Gary Smallen.

Smallen announced on Monday that he would not ask for a renewal of his contract. In his three years at the helm of the Indians, Smallen has compiled a 10-22 record at the college.

Despite their 2-8 record this season, Smallen's team has excited fans throughout the season. While some might be glad to see him go, many others are saddened that he has decided to leave.

Although his record doesn't reflect what he has done for the Newberry program, a number of young athletes have been touched by him. While talking with Coach Smallen on Tuesday he made a comment that should stick in the minds of all who have played for him.

"I have told every single young man who has ever played for me, tried out for my team, or that I have have recruited not to choose a school for a particular coach or coaching staff. Go only if you feel comfortable at that school." Smallen said. Apparently his remarks are true, as he has brought a number of young athletes to Newberry who feel comfortable with the school.

So long, Coach Smallen. It has been a pleasure working with you the past three years. Stay in touch after you leave, and from me and many others, good luck!

When the Indians face P-C Thursday, a lot could happen. The Indians will enter the game as the 10th best passing team in the nation among NAIA schools. Presbyterian will enter the game as the seventh best team in the nation in defending the pass. It should be a wild contest.

Last year the Indians won the game with no time left on the clock when Pat White caught a Tim Singleton pass in the endzone on the final play of the game.

This year's game should be just as exciting as both teams will enter the game with 2-8 records. It's not like their playing for a playoff berth, but the Bronze Derby has the same effect on the two teams.

Newberry hasn't won a game in Clinton since 1984. It is about time that Newberry does something about that.

The Indians have had a long time to get ready for this game, and ready they will be. While the announcement of Coach Smallen's leaving was made just days before the big game, the Indians players already knew what they wanted to do against P-C.

If history repeats itself, Coach Smallen should pick a victory in his last game with the Indians. In 1983 Reed Charpia resigned before the game and the Indians upset P-C 23-0. In 1987, Clayton Johnson resigned before the game and Newberry upset P-C 17-15. So what will happen this year?

The Newberry passing game will shine, and mixed in with some timely running plays will put a lot of points on the board. While the Blue Hose will probably hang tough for a while, the Newberry offense will keep the P-C defense on the field for most of the game causing a severe case of fatigue for the men in blue.

The Newberry defense will come into the game fired up instead of waiting until the second quarter, and could cause a lot of trouble for the Blue Hose.

Now, if all this happens, the Indians will have no problem bringing the Derby back home to Newberry where it belongs. If something should go wrong with this plan, the Indians will have to find a few tricks from the old medicine man to pull out the win.

I don't think the medicine man will be needed, and Coach Smallen should bring home the Derby for his last time: Newberry over Presbyterian.

CHRISTMAS TREES
Leyland Cypress, Virginia Pine, & Red Cedar
Bring family, you choose and cut
Opening Sat., Nov. 24
HALLMAN'S TREE FARM
Benny & Janice Hallman
off Amick's Ferry Rd. in Chapin
(across from Night Harbor)
See You Soon
945-7472

The Li'l That Was!

dimensions

THE QUARTERLY NEWS MAGAZINE OF NEWBERRY COLLEGE

WINTER 1990   VOL. 25 NO. 2

November — Bronze Derby!

November, 1958, The Bronze Derby Rivalry
Excerpted, State Magazine, by Charles Losemann

It was during the basketball season of 1947 that the Bronze Derby had its origin as the symbol of Newberry – P.C. athletic rivalry. P.C.'s basketball team played at Newberry Jan. 30, 1947, and before the game, Presbyterian students unfurled a large banner and suspended it in prominent view on the wall of the gym behind the P.C. cheering section: "Beat H___ Out Of Newberry!"

When attention was riveted on the action on the court, some Newberry students obtained a ladder and climbed the outside of the gym wall. Gaining access through a window, they ripped the banner off the wall behind the P.C. students, and climbed back out into the night. A few minutes later when the P.C. rooters noticed the banner had been abducted, the riotous rumbling grew louder in the visitors' stands.

The game ended with the Presbyterian Blue Hose getting a close, 51 to 47, victory. After the game, the Presbyterian students were insistent about having the abducted banner returned. Tempers flared and a scuffle ensued. In the midst of all the commotion, a Newberry student got the prize of all the spoils, a derby snatched from the noggin of one of the fashionable Presbyterian youkers. It would have taken a pack of bloodhounds to track down either the derby or the abductor that night.

Frank E. Kinard, a senior at Newberry and athletic publicity director, received a letter from Charles MacDonald, the assistant professor of English and athletic publicity director at Presbyterian college. MacDonald suggested an effort be made to recover the derby and institute it as the symbol of rivalry between the Blue Hose and the Indians.

Kinard presented the plan at a convocation of the Newberry student body. The derby was recovered and bronzed, and now is interchanged at the football contest between the two rivals.

Bronze Derby Classic 1990 — the Indians deliver! Coach Chris Johannsen finds the derby a perfect fit. He celebrates with John Thomas, 57, Russell Blackston, 74, and David Keyes, 77.

SPORTS

Indians keep Bronze Derby

By Steve Owens
Sports Editor

There were two questions surrounding Thursday's Bronze Derby Classic at Bailey Stadium.

The first was how Newberry's Indians would respond emotionally after Gary Smallen announced earlier this week that he would not return next season as the team's head coach. That answer came when the Indians scored 21 second-half points to claim a 24-7 victory over Presbyterian College.

"This one was special. This one was for Coach Smallen," said Newberry free safety Terry Moses.

Both squads struggled through an error-prone first half, making the 3,515 fans in attendance wonder if either team wanted to claim the Bronze Derby. The Blue Hose had a pair of scoring opportunities foiled by fumbles in the first half, while Newberry quarterback Tim Singleton fumbled away a second-quarter scoring opportunity at the PC 8 after a 46-yard run.

"There were a lot of breaks in the game — a lot of turnovers," said Smallen, whose team closes the season with a 3-8 mark. "The scoring opportunities were there. We were just lucky enough to be on the positive end of most of them."

Chip Lingerfelt, who earlier missed a 36-yard field goal try, connected from 41 yards out with 1:28 remaining in the first half to give the Indians a 3-0 lead.

The Blue Hose opened the third quarter with a golden opportunity. On the first play from scrimmage in the second half, linebacker Ed Healy hit Singleton and forced a fumble that Will Bedingfield recovered at the Newberry 11. But, after receiver Rader Sellers dropped a pass in the end zone on third down, Billy Bennett pushed a 27-yard field goal attempt wide to the right.

"We didn't take advantage of some opportunities in the game," PC head coach Elliott Poss said. "When we didn't do that, it seemed as if we allowed their momentum to build. It was very disappointing to end the season in that particular fashion."

After holding Newberry, the Blue Hose went back to work at their own 32. But on the first play, Michael Latham separated Eric Byrd and the football with a vicious hit, and the Indians recovered at their own 45.

Nine plays later, Dwight Cummings broke around the left end for a 13-yard touchdown run to help the Indians gain a 10-0 advantage.

As if inspired by that touchdown drive, the Indians mounted another on their next possession. Andre McCoy capped that 14-play, 80-yard march with a seven-yard reverse on the second play of the fourth quarter.

The lone bright spot for the Blue Hose came after the Indians failed to convert a fake punt deep in their own territory. PC took over at the Newberry 14, and quarterback Tim Davis connected with Rafael Traynum for a touchdown on the next play. Bennett's PAT cut the Newberry lead to 17-7 with 7:32 to play.

But, after recovering an on-side kick, the Indians added a final score with 3:35 remaining when Singleton tossed a 10-yard touchdown pass to Kelvin Jeffrey.

Newberry held a 347-281 edge in total yardage and claimed six Blue Hose turnovers. The Indians turned the ball over twice.

Oh yes, the other question surrounding the game was whether or not Poss would be back as the Blue Hose head coach after watching his team post a 2-9 record this season.

Unlike the first question, that one was as easily answered.

"That's a question I would prefer not to answer at this point in time," Poss said. "I am a graduate of Presbyterian College and I'm very fond of Presbyterian College. I'm going to be working hard for Presbyterian College in everything I do."

SCORING

Newberry	0	3	7	14—24
Presbyterian	0	0	0	7—7

N-Lingerfelt 41 FG
N-Cummings 13 run (Lingerfelt kick)
N-McCoy 7 run (Lingerfelt kick)
P-Traynum 14 pass from Davis (Bennett kick)
N-Jeffrey 10 pass from Singleton (Lingerfelt kick)

Statistics

RUSHING: Newberry 53-245 (Cummings 17-107, Singleton 16-47); Presbyterian 41-180 (Byrd 8-106, Gordon 11-52).
PASSING: Newberry 12-31-0-102 (Singleton 12-28-0-102, McCoy 0-1-0-0, Huxtay 0-1-0-0).
RECEIVING: Newberry (Carver 3-38, Jeffrey 4-33); Presbyterian (McKelvie 3-48, Sellers 2-25).

Staff Photo by Steve Owens
DERBY ACTION — Presbyterian College freshman Mason Gordon (46) tried unsuccessfully to avoid Newberry cornerback Anthony Nelson on this play in Thursday's Bronze Derby Classic at Clinton. The Indians held a slim 3-0 halftime lead, but broke the game open with three second-half touchdowns and rolled to a 24-7 victory.

The Li'l 🎩 That Was!

The Newberry Observer
AND HERALD & NEWS
"Just Like A Letter From Home"

Newberry, S. C., Friday, Nov. 23, 1990

Newberry Keeps Bronze Derby With 24 - 7 Win Over Presbyterian

BY JIM MURRAY

Covering the Newberry - P.C. football contest held in Clinton yesterday was a writer's nightmare. There were so many story angles to cover you had to keep a legal pad handy to sort them all out.

Item... Newberry Head Coach Gary Smallen resigns as head coach just before the contest, giving rise to several "win for the Gipper" stories in the papers.

Item... when we arrived at the pressbox, rumors were flying that P.C. coach Elliot Poss was about ready to step down, a story he denied in today's papers.

Item... Just prior to taking the field, a large statue of an Indian was held aloft by the players. Subsequent investigation revealed that this was the "Mandinko Warrior," an idea of Coach Johannson, brought in to spur the Indians on to victory.

Item... For the first time in what seems like eons, the weather cooperated with the contest. At game time, the weather was delightfully clear and warm, with the temperature at 74 degrees.

Item... Both teams came into the game with 2-8 records, tempting the writer to resort to any number of cliches in covering the game.. like throwing the records out, this game is for personal pride, etc., etc.,

Item...several Newberry fans were wearing T-Shirts asking the question- "Hey PC got a second?" in reference to last year's highlight film victory by the Indians in the final "second" of the contest...

Item... for the first half of the game, the two teams, which entered the contest with identical 2-8 records, played as though nobody was home, with lots of action between the 20 yard lines, but the score only 3-0 in favor of the Indians, thanks to a 41 yard field goal by Chip Lingerfelt with 10 seconds left in the half.

A seemingly different Indian team took the field in the second half. After turning back a P.C. fumble recovery at the 11 yard line, and preventing a score, the Indians marched down the field in 9 plays, and scored with 8:08 left in the third quarter, scoring on a 13 yard run by Dwight Cummings.

After an exchange of punts, the Indians again marched down the length of the field, starting at their own 20 yard line and making a 14 play, 80 yard drive that ended in a reverse by Andre McCoy from the 7 yard line. Lingerfelt's PAT was good, and with 14:16 left, the score was 17-0.

After a failed PC drive, the Indians took over at their 5 yard line. Three downs later, punter David Husky faked a punt, missing a pass attempt to Trey Castles. Presbyterian took advantage of the situation as quarterback Tim Davis threw a touchdown pass on the next play to Rafael Traynum on the next play.

After the game, Coach Smallen said "that play probably wasn't very smart, but it added some excitement to the game."

Presbyterian never threatened again. After the touchdown, an onside kick attempt failed, and the Indians took but 8 plays to score again, making the final tally 24-7.

For the game, the Indians outrushed the Blue Hose, 245-180. In the passing department, the Indians' Tim Singleton had a 12 for 31 day, totalling 102 yards. Singleton broke his single season touchdown completion record with his pass to Kelvin Jeffrey in the fourth quarter, giving him a total of 14 for the season.

Dwight Cummings led the Indian ground attack with 107 total yards in 17 carries.

After the game, a subdued Gary Smallen, with his son standing by his side, shook hands with well-wishers and spoke to several members of the media gathered around him.

"I'm happy for the kids. In the first half it could have been anybody's ball game. I'm glad for our fans. It's exciting for them to be proud of our kids; we have a great group of young men."

Asked about his future, Smallen commented that he and his young son were "going to Arizona, buy two pairs of cowboy boots, sit on the edge of the Grand Canyon, and watch the sun go down." He thought a minute, looked up and said, " This will be the halftime of my life, and we'll have to look out and see what happens in the second half."

Smallen ended his career at Newberry with a record of 11-22, but a record of 2-1 against PC.

	Newb.	PC
First downs	21	16
Rushes-yards	53-245	41-180
Yards passing	102	101
Passes	21-31-0	8-18-2
Return yards	15	51
Fumbles-lost	2-2	5-4
Punts	6-40	5-39.8
Penalties-yards	8-78	4-54

Newberry	0	3	7	14	—24
Presbyterian	0	0	0	7	— 7

New — FG Lingerfelt 41
New — Cummings 13 run (Lingerfelt kick)
New — McCoy 7 run (Lingerfelt kick)
PC — Traynum 14 pass from Davis (Bennett kick)
New — Jeffrey 10 pass from Singleton (Lingerfelt kick)
Attendance - 3,515

Individual statistics
Rushing — Newberry: Singleton 16-47; Booker 5-12, Cummings 17-107 Presbyterian: Davis 11-(minus)-3, Gordan 11-52, Burd 6-104, Eisner 12-20
Passing — Newberry Singleton 12-29-0, 102 Presbyterian Davis 8-18-2, 101
Receiving — Newberry Carver 3-36, Castles 3-19, Jeffrey 4-33. Presbyterian Sellers 2-35, McKelvie 3-48.

The Newberry Observer
AND HERALD & NEWS
"Just Like A Letter From Home"

Newberry, S. C., Friday, Nov. 23, 1990

"We Keep the Derby" High-Five
—Observer Photo by Jim Murray

Newberry College's Sean Hunter, #58, gives Indians quarterback Tim Singleton, #4, a high-five during action in yesterday's Bronze Derby win by Newberry over the Presbyterian Blue Hose in Clinton. Singleton threw one touchdown pass — his 14th on the season — in Newberry's 24-7 victory, breaking his own single-season touchdown record set last year. Indians running back Willis Fortson, #35, is in the foreground.

Travis Perry, #7, a junior running back/ wide receiver, tries to slip a Presbyterian tackler in the Thanksgiving Day Bronze Derby game at Clinton. The Indians won the Derby for the second year in a row, 24 - 7, over the Blue Hose.

A PC tackler thinks he has Andre McCoy, #14, wrapped up. But the sophomore wide receiver bounced off this tackle, reversed his field and went into the end zone for a seven-yard, fourth quarter touchdown yesterday against Presbyterian.

The Li'l That Was!

Volume LXXXV Number 7 — PRESBYTERIAN COLLEGE — CLINTON, SC 29325 — THURSDAY DECEMBER 6, 1990

Bronze Derby to Spend Year at Newberry College

by Brad Busbee
STAFF WRITER

The Bronze Derby, the coveted symbol of the P.C.-Newberry rivalry, was taken back to Newberry on Thanksgiving Day after P.C. was outscored by the Indians 24-7.

The Blue Hose fell behind at the end of the first half when a successful 41 yard field goal attempt put Newberry's first points on the scoreboard. Then, midway through the third quarter, Newberry increased their lead with a 13-yard touchdown run.

The Blue Hose were unable to score until after another Newberry touchdown gave the Indians a 17-0 lead.

The first P.C. points came with 7:32 minutes remaining in the games. Tate Davis' 14 yard pass to Rafael Trayhorn cut the Indian lead to 10 points. This touchdown was too late, however, for Newberry was able to add another 7 points with only 3:25 to play. Ultimately, this play answered the question of where the Bronze Derby would spend the year.

SUMMER JOB OPPORTUNITIES

Apply Now to work at MONTREAT!

"clubs," waterfront, auditorium, audio-visual, maintenance, child care, food service, tennis or crafts.

Montreat Summer Jobs
P.O. Box 969
Montreat, NC, 28757
(704) 669-2911

Pleated
Duckhead
slacks $16.95
Flannel & Cotton
Boxers $1.49

at

Bargain Bucks

207 Fleming Street
Laurens SC, 29360

Sports

The Clinton Chronicle

Wednesday, November 28, 1990

Indians grab Bronze Derby as both head coaches step down

By Robert Davis
Chronicle Staff Writer

Presbyterian College will have to endure another year without the Bronze Derby, as Newberry College retained the hat last Thursday with a 24-7 victory that marked the end of both head coaches' careers at the helm of their schools.

PC head coach Elliott Poss announced his resignation Tuesday, following 1990's 2-9 season.

Newberry head coach Gary Smallen announced last week that his resignation would be effective following the traditional Thanksgiving Day game with PC, and his tribe made it possible for the coach to leave with a big season-ending victory and his second consecutive Bronze Derby.

"It's been a great day," Smallen said. "I'm just tickled for the players and the fans that we were lucky enough to win today."

Both teams entered the game with 2-8 records, and a Bailey Memorial Stadium crowd of 3,515 witnessed the kind of contest one might expect from two such teams.

Exchanging punts and turnovers, PC and Newberry each found it difficult to put points on the board early.

The first of six Blue Hose turnovers came near the end of the first quarter, when following a 21-yard punt return by Quincy Eigner and a 14-yard gain by Mason Gordon, Eigner fumbled at the Newberry 23.

After forcing the Indians to punt, PC gained possession at their own 23. But two plays later Newberry got the ball back when Blue Hose quarterback Tim Davis mishandled the snap.

However, Newberry kicker Chip Lingerfelt missed a 36-yard field goal attempt to keep the game scoreless.

Following an exchange of fumbles, PC had another opportunity to get on the board first, but they also failed to convert a field goal when Billy Bennett's attempt at a 48-yarder was blocked by Alex Blizzard.

Newberry then drove into Blue Hose territory, where Lingerfelt hit a 41-yard field goal to give the Indians the first lead.

"That's the first halftime we just sat there and said we are totally out of synch," Smallen said. "We just didn't connect."

PC Head Coach Elliott Poss was dissatisfied as well with his team's performance.

"Our defense played a good first half, but we failed to take advantage of some early scoring opportunities," Poss said. Those opportunities continued to come in the second half, as Newberry fumbled on their first play from scrimmage to give PC excellent field position.

Presbyterian's Tony Robertson (47) and Keith McGriff close in on Indian...
...Newberry's Dwight Cummings (30)

Blue Hose linebacker Ed Healy caused the fumble that Will Bedington recovered when Healy broke through the Indian pass protection and hammered quarterback Tim Singleton.

The momentum PC gained soon diminished when Bennett's 27-yard field goal attempt went wide to the right.

Newberry runningback Dwight Cummings, who led all rushers with 107 yards, scored the first touchdown midway through the third quarter by racing around the left end for a 13-yard score. Lingerfelt added the extra point to put the Indians up by 10.

After forcing the Hose to punt, the visitors began a drive that would diminish PC's hopes of regaining the Bronze Derby.

Starting at their own 20 with 4:41 left in the third, Newberry used 14 plays to travel 80 yards, while erasing 5:25 off the clock.

When Andre Carter ended the drive with a seven yard TD run off the reverse, the game was into its final period.

"The long drive really hurt us," Poss said. "It took a lot out of our defense." As in many previous Bronze Derby games, last Thursday's matchup featured a rather unusual play.

Free safety Bernard Vereen collars Dwight Cummings...
...who finished game with 107 yards in 17 carries

Facing fourth and one at their own 14 yard line, with under eight minutes left in the game and nursing a 17-0 lead, Newberry faked a punt in an attempt to gain a first down.

The pass attempt failed however, and the Blue Hose capitalized by scoring on the very next play, as Davis connected with Rafael Traynum for the touchdown. Bennett added the PAT.

"That was fun wasn't it?" Smallen said of the fourth down play. "We watched a film that showed Wofford running that play, and it worked real good for them." Newberry quickly answered the PC touchdown on the following possession, as Singleton hit Kelvin Jeffrey on a 10-yard strike that closed the door on the home team.

"It's disappointing to end the season this way," Poss said. "The turning point was our failure to score in the third quarter."

The loss gave PC a final 2-9 record, while the Indians improved to 3-8, as Smallen ended his Newberry coaching career with an 11-22 record.

Poss's record at PC was 29-38-1 in his six years as head coach.

November 1991

November 2	The University of Nevada made the largest comeback in NCAA football history defeating Weber State 55-49 after being behind by 35 points in the 3rd quarter.
November 2	Jermaine Jackson debuted an anti Michael song "Word to the Badd!"
November 5	American actor Fred MacMurray of "My Three Sons" passed away.
November 6	Russian President Bori Yeltsin outlawed the Communist Party.
November 7	Magic Johnson of the Los Angeles Lakers announced he had HIV and retired from the NBA.
November 10	Bernie Kosar ended an NFL record of 308 passes without an interception.
November 12	Tom Glavine of the Atlanta Braves won the MLB NL Cy Young Award.
November 12	The twins are born in the 100th episode of the TV series "Full House."
November 13	Roger Clemens of the Boston Red Sox won the MLB AL Cy Young Award.
November 14	Michael Jackson's video "Black or White" premiered throughout the world.
November 17	The first condom advertisement aired on US television.
November 17	Dale Earnhardt won the 41st NASCAR Sprint Cup.
November 19	Cal Ripken Jr. of the Baltimore Orioles won the MLB AL Most Valuable Player Award.
November 20	Terry Pendleton of the Atlanta Braves won the MLB NL Most Valuable Player Award.
November 22	The NBA New York Knicks paid center Patrick Ewing $18.8 million for a 2 year extension.
November 23	Boxer Evander Holyfield TKO's Bert Cooper in the 7th round for the heavyweight boxing title.
November 23	Singer-songwriter Freddie Mercury confirmed publicly he had AIDS and passed away the next day.
November 24	Monica Seles set a female tennis record for $2.5 million prize money in a single season.
November 28	The Bronze Derby was played in Newberry, South Carolina on Thanksgiving Day. The Newberry College Indians defeated the Presbyterian College Blue Hose 32-17.

The Li'l That Was!

THE INDIAN

November 20, 1991 — Volume 60 Issue 6 — The student newspaper of Newberry College

Sports

November 20, 1991 — Page 8

A Thanksgiving Day Shootout: NC-PC renew rivalry

By Billy Deal
Excerpts taken from an article published in *Sandlapper*

When James Kellett was a student at Presbyterian College in the late 1940's, he acquired a sartorial habit which was to affect the destiny of one of the state's oldest athletic rivalries.

"My uncle operated a clothing store in Fountain Inn," Kellett recalls today, "and men's hats were pretty popular in those days. So, I started wearing a Stetson derby, just for fun, and I happened to be wearing it one night in 1947 when a bunch of us went to see the Presbyterian basketball team play at Newberry."

"It was a pretty exciting game, and some Newberry students put a ladder up against the outside of the gym and climbed through a window at the top of the visitor's section. They worked their way down through the crowd and one of them snatched the derby from my head and ran outside. We chased them and a few skirmishes occurred, but I ended up without my derby. We looked for it all over the Newberry campus but I finally went home hatless." (The identity of the Newberry student who swiped the hat has long since faded into obscurity.)

What might have ended as another in a series of increasingly hostile student pranks between rivals was turned into a legend by the quick thinking of cooler heads.

The Indians celebrate another Bronze Derby win. The Indians and the Blue Hose have battled it out since that infamous day in 1947. *File photo*

Charles MacDonald, Presbyterian College sports information director, suggested to counterpart Frank Kinard at Newberry College that if the derby could be recovered it might become a symbol for athletic supremacy between the schools. The idea won quick approval from the student bodies, and the hat was recovered and bronzed for posterity.

It was decided that it would go to the winner of any athletic contest between the schools, so it changed hands repeatedly through baseball, basketball and football seasons from 1947 through 1955.

Realizing that such frequent contest diminished the importance of the trophy, the schools agreed in 1956 that it would be claimed only by the winner of the annual Thanksgiving Day football game.

Perhaps the ultimate rapport occurs before the each year. The host school serves Thanksgiving lunch in its cafeteria, and fans from both schools share a meal before going out to stare at each other across 100 yards of grass with white stripes.

It is refreshing and somehow reassuring to find an athletic rivalry which combines intensity and common sense.

The cornerstone of collegiate sports is tradition and nowhere is that truer than among small colleges. With no major bowl berths available and relatively little publicity outside their own regions, small colleges take the players the big schools overlook and play a different game.

When the dust settles, someone will hoist a strange looking trophy high into the air as a symbol of victory. Friendly rivals, one hurting for the other. The true meaning of college athletics.

And that's what some folks had in mind when they covered an old derby hat in bronze in 1947.

The Li'l 🎩 That Was!

The Newberry Observer
AND HERALD & NEWS
"Just Like A Letter From Home"

NEWS ESTABLISHED 1865 — ISSUE NO. 142 — Newberry, S. C., Wednesday, November 27, 1991 — THE NEWBERRY OBSERVER ESTA... — TWO SEC...

Indians Meet Blue Hose In 44th Bronze Derby Classic

THE GAME -- Presbyterian College Blue Hose vs. Newberry College Indians Thursday, November 28, 1991, at 2 p.m. HAPPY THANKSGIVING!! Setzler Field (4,000), Newberry, South Carolina.

THE ATTRACTION -- Among one of the nation's best college football rivalries -- especially on the small college level -- it's the 44th edition of the Bronze Derby Classic.

THE RECORDS -- Presbyterian College, 3-7 overall and 3-4 in the South Atlantic Conference, comes into the game looking to rebound from last week's loss to Carson-Newman (48-20), while Newberry seeks to end a four-game losing string.

PC 1991 Schedule/Results	NC 1991 Schedule/Results
9/7 at The Citadel 10-33 L	9/7 at S. Carolina St. 7-28 L
9/21 at Furman 7-52 L	9/14 Lenoir-Rhyne 10-31 L
9/28 at Lenoir Rhyne 12-34 L	9/21 at Gardner-Webb 0-10 L
10/5 Wofford 24-42 L	9/28 at E. Tenn. St. 12-43 L
10/12 at Catawba 21-18 W	10/5 at North Alabama 7-21 L
10/19 Elon 14-38 L	10/12 Lees-McRae 41-19 W
10/26 Mars Hill 35-30 W	10/19 at Wofford 6-49 L
11/2 at Wingate 14-27 L	10/26 at Wingate 19-31- L
11/9 Gardner-Webb 10-8 W	11/2 Catawba 7-33 L
11/16 Carson-Newman 20-48 L	11/9 Elon 7-38 L
11/28 at Newberry 2 p.m.	11/28 Presbyterian 2 p.m.

THE SERIES -- This is the 80th meeting between the two intrastate rivals, with the towns of Clinton and Newberry only 22 miles apart along Interstate-26 and Route 76. Presbyterian is Newberry's longest-running series opponent, having played continuously since 1919 (a 0-0 tie). The Indians trail the series, which began in 1913 with a pair of 61-0 NC victories, to the Blue Hose by a 23-48-5 count. PC's last victory came in 1988, 30-18, in Clinton, but have not won in Newberry since 1979's 16-14 nail-biter (on a Blue Hose 21-yard field goal with :47 remaining in the game).

THE BASIC FORMATIONS -- Presbyterian's offensive system: Pro I; defensive system: 4-3 Newberry's offensive system: I/back; defensive system: 4-3.

THE COACHES -- Blue Hose Coach John Perry, a 1972 Presbyterian graduate, is in his first year at his alma mater. He has posted a school mark of 3-7 and 35-52 in eight years overall.

First-year Newberry College mentor Brad Senter, a 1975 Campbell (NC) graduate, is 1-9 at the school and overall. Senter became the football program's 15th coach in its 77-year history on December 12, 1990. He has served as an assistant on the staffs at Samford, New Mexico Highlands, North Carolina State, Duke, the now-defunct USFL's Birmingham Stallions and comes to NC from the University of North Carolina's Educational Foundation of the school's athletic department.

LAST YEAR -- Newberry retained bragging rights of the Bronze Derby Classic with a 24-7 victory in Clinton in then-Indians' Coach Gary Smallen's last game at the helm. Dwight Cummings led the NC 246-yard ground attack with 107 rushing yards of his own. He also scored one touchdown as the Indians won the Derby for the second consecutive year.

LAST WEEK -- The Indians have been idle since Nov. 9th when Elon defeated their hosts, 38-7, on a cold, wet night for Parent's Day.

PLAYER OF THE WEEK -- Senior offensive lineman Will Blackmon was selected as the team's offensive player of the week after Newberry's home loss to Elon, 38-7. The 6-2, 240-pound Blackmon (Rock Hill, S. C. (Catawba School)) recovered an Indian fumble in the end zone for his first career collegiate touchdown to give Newberry a 7-0 lead.

COLLEGE FACTS

	PC	NC
Location:	Clinton, S. C. 29325	Newberry, S. C. 29108
Founded:	1880	1856
Enrollment	1,140	762
Colors:	Garnet & Blue	Scarlet & Grey
Stadium:	Bailey Memorial	Setzler Field
(Capacity):	(5,000)	(4,000)
Nat'l Affl:	NAIA/NCAA II	NAIA/NCAA II
Conference:	South Atlantic	Independent

COMPARING 1991 STATS

	PC	NC
First Downs:	134	150
Yds. Rush/Gm:	114.8	133.4
Yds. Pass/Gm:	162.6 (123-237, 18 INT)	143.2 (137-294, 20 INT)
Tot OfGm:	277.4	276.6
Punts/Avg:	65/40.7	70/35.7
Pen/Yds.:	71/664	86/673
Fmbs/Lost:	22/12	29/15
Pts/Avg:	167/16.7	116/11.6
Opp Pts/Avg:	315/31.5	303/30.3

COMPARING 1991 LEADERS:

Rushing: PC -- Quincy Eigner, 133 atts., 550 yds., 5 TD
NC -- Louis Austin, 122 atts., 428 yds., 2 TD
Passing: PC -- Tim Davis, 83 of 169, 1,164 yds., 9 TD, 14 INT
NC -- Louis Austin, 122 of 237, 1,282 yds., 3 TD, 15 INT
Receiving: PC -- Brad Jones, 32 recp., 395 yds., 2 TD
Rader Sellers, 22 recp., 346 yds., 2 TD
NC -- Dwight Cummings, 39 recp., 438 yds., 2 TD
Defensively: PC -- Tony Robertson, 122 tkls. (70 solo), 8 for loss -- 22 yds.
NC -- Eric Houston, 93 tkls (59 solo), 3 for loss-7 yds.,
3 sacks for --22 yds.
Ricky Montgomery, 73 tackles (54 solo)
Hazel Richardson, 66 tackles (35 solo), 4 for loss--11

GRID BITS:

The Rivalry -- The PC-NC series has existed since 1913, but the Bronze Derby Classic -- established in 1947 when a Newberry student took off with a distinguished PC professor's derby -- has been the symbol of supremacy in this small-college rivalry. The Indians trail PC 17-24-3 since the Derby's inception in 1947.

Back in Uniform -- NAIA All-America (Honorable Mention) linebacker Hazel Richardson has slowly broke himself back into the NC lineup. The Sumter product was suspended after the Wofford game and didn't play for two games until the Parent's Day contest versus Elon.

No Tomorrow -- Ten NC seniors -- who have exhausted four years of athletic eligibility -- will make their last appearance in a Scarlet and Gray uniform. The Senior Class of 1992 has an opportunity to win three of four games with the Blue Hose: OL Will Blackmon (Rock Hill (Catawba)); OL Alex Blizzard (Charleston (Middleton); DB Rodney Cook (Dillon (HS)); RB Dwight Cummings (Goose Creek (HS)); OL Alex Dabney (Lancaster (HS)); DE Jason Hilton (Pauline (Dorman)); P. David Huskey (North Augusta (HS)); LB Ricky Montgomery (Columbia (HS)); QB Travis Perry (Greer (HS)); and DB Kerry Suber (Pomaria (Mid-Carolina)).

COACH SENTER ON PRESBYTERIAN

"With a predominately Pro I offensive scheme, PC has a very balanced attack. They run and pass the ball equally well.

"Their skill people are very athletic. Defensively, they play the same 4-3 as our own. They are fundamentally sound; good technique.

"To beat PC, you have to beat them with the pass because their defense is designed to stifle the running game.

"This rivalry is exciting. Personally, every game is important to me, but I feel the difference about PC-NC because the players feel it. They have been anxious to get back to practice and work hard since they know we can end the season on a positive note with a win over our rivals.

"Our goal is to play a complete football game and earn bragging rights to the Bronze Derby Classic."

ON THE AIR: Tune into the game on WKDK 1240-AM, the voice of NC athletics. Jimmy Coggins brings you the play-by-play and Steve Wait provides color commentary. The Brad Senter Show starts at 1:30 p.m. live action begins at 1:45 p.m.

Blue Hose, Indians vie for Derby

CLINTON — Presbyterian College head football coach John Perry sees a similarity between the Newberry College Indians and another, more famous football team from Columbia, S.C.

"I can relate their (Newberry) season to that of the University of South Carolina," Perry said. "In that they both started their season under adverse conditions and have gone through a metamorphosis. They were each a more unified team during the second half of their season."

Newberry (4-6), started the season under head coach Brad Senter, who resigned under controversy surrounding his professional background. New head coach Mike Taylor had little to start with as far as continuity and as a result, the Indians struggled through a winless first half of the season.

But the Newberry team that will play Presbyterian (4-6), tomorrow has won four of their last five games, setting the stage for another classic confrontation.

"This is always a big game for both schools," Perry said. "But this game will be even bigger, since this one will be the last one to be played on Thanksgiving Day."

The quest for the coveted Bronze Derby is set for a 2 p.m kickoff.

1964 BRONZE DERBY — Presbyterian running back "Rut" Galloway gains yardage during the 1964 Bronze Derby Classic. The '64 game was the second Bronze Derby Classic coached by current Presbyterian College athletic director Calley Gault. Presbyterian won 35-6.

November 29, 1991

The Laurens County Advertiser
An Independent Newspaper Founded in 1885/South Carolina's Award-Winning Semi-Weekly Newspaper

SPORTS

PC returns to Bronze Age

◆ By Neal Crotts
Sports Editor

NEWBERRY — Following Presbyterian College's game with Newberry on Thanksgiving Day, Blue Hose head coach John Perry tipped his hat, and that hat was a Bronze Derby.

Perry's team fought off a late charge by the Indians of Newberry College to take a 32-17 win in the Bronze Derby Classic, one of the state's oldest and richest rivalries.

After taking a 16-0 lead in the first half on a 39-yard run by Mason Gordon and a 10-yard pass from Tim Davis to Chris Griffin, the Blue Hose let Newberry back in the game in the second half, allowing Newberry to come within 5 points early in the fourth quarter.

"We came back out and were talking about wanting to set the stage offensively with the first drive, and dern if we didn't let the momentum slip away. But then the defense had their back to the wall and came through with big plays two times," Perry said.

And big plays they were. With the score 22-17 and with over seven minutes left in a game, the Indians drove into PC territory looking for the go-ahead score. But Jeff Wilson stepped up to make an interception on third-and-six to take away that scoring opportunity.

Then, on Newberry's next possession, it was Tony Robertson's turn to take the ball away.

As Newberry quarterback Louis Austin dropped back to pass, Robertson slipped in front of the Indian receiver and picked off the pass at the Indian 38-yard line and returned the ball to the 16-yard line. One play later, Mason Gordon had scored his second touchdown of the afternoon to give PC a comfortable lead with just over two minutes remaining.

Gordon, who has seen limited playing time in the latter part of the season due to injuries, set a new single-game personal best with 164 yards rushing on 28 carries.

"Mason Gordon is that kind of player, he's just been hurt. That's a dimension we didn't have — breaking tackles in a few ballgames and running over people — when he was out of there. I hope that's a sign of his future," Perry said.

Considering the future in light of the past, Perry was optimistic about what the win, which improved the team's record to 4-7, will mean to the Blue Hose.

"We are certainly finishing on a high note. We were picked to finish last in the conference and we finished tied for fourth. We've got to feel good about that.

"It's not a championship, it wasn't a winning season percentage-wise, but it was a winning season in attitude and turnaround, and in confidence and feeling good about yourself. I just hope we carry all that over to next year," Perry said.

Along the way, the Blue Hose out-gained Newberry, 286 yards to 216, including an 8-of-22, 152-yard passing performance by quarterback Tim Davis. Davis connected on two touchdowns, the 10-yard strike to Griffin and a 25-yard pass to Rader Sellers in the second half.

The PC special teams also recorded two safeties in the game. The first came on the last play of the first half when Tony Nelson was tackled in the end zone, and the second on a blocked punt with under a minute left in the game.

The Clinton Chronicle

Bronze Derby returns to Presbyterian

Game 11

The Results
Presbyterian 32
Newberry 17

By Rick Hendricks
Editor

NEWBERRY—If you stayed for just the first 14 plays of last Thursday's contest between Presbyterian College and Newberry, you might have left with the impression that it was going to be a long day for the Blue Hose.

Newberry mistakes turned the annual Bronze Derby game in PC's favor, however, and John Perry's team left Setzler Field with a 32-17 win.

The victory closed out Perry's initial season as Blue Hose mentor with a 4-7 record.

Fullback Mason Gordon could claim a lot of credit for the win over Newberry, as the sophomore from Due West gained 164 yards on 28 carries and scored two touchdowns.

After the game, Gordon was giving the credit to his offensive line for his success.

To whoever the credit goes, Gordon's second carry, after a six minute drive by Newberry to open the game ended in a fumble by Indian quarterback Louis Austin that was recovered by senior defensive tackle Will Bettisfield, was the play that swung the momentum back in PC's favor.

PC had recovered the ball at the Newberry 46 and Gordon rushed for 7 yards on his first carry.

On his second carry, Gordon got loose in the Newberry secondary and rumbled 39 yards for a TD. Alex Horton's PAT was good and PC led 7-0, with 8:23 to go in the first quarter.

Near the end of the opening quarter, the Blue Hose got the ball after a Newberry punt at their own 29.

On the first play from scrimmage after the punt, PC junior quarterback Tim Davis hit sophomore tight end Brad Jones on a 32 yard-pass play to move the Blue Hose to the Newberry 39.

As the second quarter began, Davis and Jones were at it again, this time on a 13-yard pass play to the Newberry 22.

Gordon followed with a 14-yard run to the 8, and two plays later, Davis hit freshman running back Chris Griffin with a 10-yard TD pass. Horton again added the extra point, and PC's lead was 14-0 with 13:28 to go in the first half.

After the next Newberry drive ended in a punt, PC started at its own 2, then proceeded to control the ball for 19 plays and over seven minutes.

The Blue Hose got as close as the Indian 2, but the drive proved to be an exercise in futility as PC fumbled and turned the ball back over to Newberry.

Presbyterian did get on the board again before halftime, however, as Blue Hose punter John Plasky, the South Atlantic Conference's top punter, kicked the ball to Newberry's Tony Nelson at his own 1.

Nelson fumbled the ball, retrieved it, then attempted to run it back, but was tackled in the end zone for a safety and a 16-0 PC halftime lead as time expired in the second quarter.

The Blue Hose got the ball first in the second half, but a Davis interception by Newberry's Eric Houston was returned to the PC 1.

Indian running back Dwight Cummings did the rest, scoring the TD on a 1-yard run. The extra point by Jason Arnold was good and Newberry had cut PC's lead to 16-7 less than two minutes into the second half.

A 31-yard punt return by Newberry's Jason Gambrell to the PC 26 with 9:02 to go in the third quarter put the Indians in good scoring position again. The Blue Hose defense stiffened and Newberry had to settle

See DERBY Page 13

Photo by Fletcher Pruitt, Jr.
PC coach **John Perry**, center, wears the Bronze Derby...
...during celebration of Blue Hose win over Newberry

Derby

Continued From Page 11

for a 37-yard field goal from Arnold, but had trimmed the lead to 16-10 with 6:27 remaining in the third quarter.

PC responded this time, however. After the ensuing kickoff, Newberry was called for a personal foul and the Blue Hose started with good field position at their own 44.

Eight plays later, the Blue Hose were back in the end zone, as Davis hit Rader Sellers with a 26-yard strike. Newberry coach Brad Senter and his players howled after Sellers caught the ball, then fumbled it out of bounds, but the officials ruled that Sellers had possession long enough.

The Blue Hose went for a two-point conversion, but Davis' pass to Jones fell incomplete and PC's lead was 22-10 with 2:45 to go in the third quarter.

A personal foul penalty was assessed against PC after the ensuing kickoff this time and Newberry started out at its own 49. Eight plays later, on the third play of the fourth quarter, Newberry's Willis Fortson, a graduate of Clinton High, scored on a 5-yard run. Arnold's extra point was good and the Indians were back within a touchdown, 22-17, with 14:11 to go in the contest.

PC moved into Newberry territory during its next drive, but Davis was intercepted again, this time by Maccio Montgomery, who returned the ball to the Indian 47.

Newberry could not move the ball, however, and punted the ball back to PC.

The Blue Hose were buried deep in their own territory and the Indians took over at the PC 41 with 8:19 to play.

Three plays into the drive, Blue Hose sophomore defensive back Jeff Wilson intercepted an Austin pass and on Newberry's next drive, junior linebacker Tony Robertson picked off another Austin pass.

Robertson, who had 17 tackles on the day, intercepted the pass at the Newberry 38 and returned it to the Indian 16 with 2:33 to play.

Gordon settled the issue on his next carry, capping his day with a 16-yard TD run. PC went for two and was successful as Davis threw a complete pass to Jones. That increased the Blue Hose lead to 30-17 with 2:25 to play.

PC added another score with under a minute left to play in the game, as the Blue Hose blocked a Newberry punt out of the end zone for a safety to make the final 32-17.

"We certainly finished the season on a high note," Perry said after the contest.

He was clinging tightly to the Bronze Derby, which will come back to Clinton after a two-year absence.

The Blue Hose accomplished another milestone Thursday, ending an 11-year winless streak at Newberry.

Sports
The Newberry Observer
Newberry, S.C., Friday, Nov. 29, 1991

Bronze Derby Back To Clinton

BY VIC MacDONALD

A touchdown pass that wasn't caught.

A safety with no time on the clock.

A 265-pound lineman running with an interception.

All these become part of the Bronze Derby Legend now in the 44-year grudge game between Newberry and Presbyterian Colleges.

The visiting Blue Hose took the trophy, formerly the derby of a PC enthusiast snatched by rowdy Newberry students at a 1947 basketball game, back with them to Clinton for the first time in three years.

But they had a scare. Newberry had the ball at its 36 and driving

with three minutes left trailing by just six points. Then, disaster struck.

PC linebacker Tony Robertson, a plague to the Indians offense all day, picked off a Louis Austin pass, ran it 22 yards and the rout was on.

PC's workhorse running back, Mason Gordon, 164 yards on the day, blasted over from the Indians 16. Blue Hose quarterback Tim Davis, 152 yard passing on the day, tossed a two-point conversion with 2:33 left to put the game out of Newberry's reach -- 30 - 17.

Presbyterian tacked on an exclamation point -- a safety after a David Huskey blocked punt out of the endzone with :54 -- to seal their first Bronze Derby victory for first-year coach John Perry.

It was Presbyterian's second safety of the game -- Newberry punt returner Tony Nelson muffed a high spiral and wound up tackled by PC players with no time on the clock at the end of the first half. Newberry was down by a 16 - 9 margin at halftime.

A fired-up defense led the Newberry charge in the second half, as Eric Houston intercepted

Presbyterian running back Mason Gordon, #46, carries the ball for the Blue Hose

Newberry's Michael Latham, #97, breaks up a pass at the goal line against PC.

Davis at the 13:39 mark of the third quarter and ran the ball back 36 yards to the PC one.

Newberry senior Dwight Cummings blasted the ball into the endzone from there, and Jason Arnold's PAT closed the gap. Arnold nailed a 37-yard field goal with 7:01 left in the third, after Jason Gambrell returned a PC punt to the enemy's 26 yard line.

Presbyterian ran the score to 22-10 with a gift touchdown late in the third quarter. Rader Sellers took a 25-yard pass from Davis, bobbling it out of the back of the endzone, but getting credit for a TD catch. The two-point conversion failed.

Newberry put together its best drive in the late third and early fourth quarter, aided by a PC personal foul penalty for hitting out of bounds. Two Austin to Kelvin Jeffery passes drove the ball into PC territory.

Willis Fortson, a Clinton High standout now playing for Newberry, capped the drive with 14:26 left in the game with a five yard TD run. Arnold added the PAT.

That set the stage for a mid-fourth quarter standoff featuring a pass interception and 12 yard run by Newberry's giant lineman Maccio Montgomery with 11:27 left. The Indians offense could not get going and Huskey punted.

PC punted back two minutes later and the Indians were in business again before Austin threw another interception. The Indians defense held again forcing another PC punt with 4:47 left.

A 13 yard Austin to Cummings pass gave the Indians' fans hope for another miracle comeback, like the 1989 game won by Newberry at Setzler Field with a no-time-on-the-clock touchdown pass.

It wasn't to be. PC this time turned in the last minute heroics with the Robertson interception and 10 points in the last two and half minutes of the game.

"In order to be a successful team, you've got to play football on every snap," Newberry's first-year head coach Brad Senter said.

"We never learned how to do that," he said of the 1-10 Indians. "It's my fault, but I can promise you, we'll take care of that in the spring."

Presbyterian wrapped up a 4-7 season with the Derby victory. "How about that defense in the second half," PC head coach Perry yelled to his players and fans gathered around him for prayer at mid-field.

Cummings led the Indians attack with 82 yards on 20 carries for the day. Austin, a junior wide receiver pressed into action as quarterback in the season's second game after the Indians lost four potential starting quarterbacks to bad grades, transfer and injuries, ran for 73 yards and threw for 56.

Kelvin Jeffery, Newberry's all-time leading receiver, caught three passes for 22 yards and Trey Castles added 21 yards receiving.

Leading the defense with his inspired play, 5-7 junior linebacker Eric Houston led the team with 14 tackles. Ricky Montgomery had 10.

Junior linebacker Hazel Richardson, playing after a suspension, had nine tackles, two sacks and a fumble recovery. He also led the team in "victory dances" after defensive plays.

Both teams were guilty of considerable taunting and occasional near fights as the intensity of the rivalry surfaced.

PC leads the series of games between the two schools, dating to 1913, by a 48 - 27 - 5 margin.

The Li'l 🎩 That Was!

The Newberry Observer
AND HERALD & NEWS
"Just Like A Letter From Home"

NEWS ESTABLISHED 1869 — ISSUE NO. 148 — Newberry, S. C., Friday, Nov. 29, 1991 — THE NEWBERRY OBSERVER ESTAB... — ONE SEC...

Presbyterian College vs. Newberry College
November 28, 1991
Setzler Field, Newberry
Attendance 3,625
BRONZE DERBY CLASSIC (EST. 1947)

Score by Quarters	1	2	3	4	Final
Presbyterian Blue Hose (4-7)	7	9	6	10	32
Newberry Indians (1-10)	0	0	10	7	17

Team	Qtr.	Time	Play	Score/NC-P
Presbyterian	1	8:23	Mason Gordon 39 run (Alex Horton kick)	0-7
Presbyterian	2	13:28	Chris Griffin 10 pass from Tim Davis (Horton kicked)	0-14
Presbyterian	2	0:00	Nelson tackled in end zone for safety	0-16
Newberry	3	13:21	Dwight Cummings 1 run (Jason Arnold kick)	7-16
Newberry	3	6:27	Arnold FG37	10-16
Presbyterian	3	2:45	Rader Sellers 25 pass from Davis (two-point conv. failed)	10-22
Newberry	4	14:11	Willis Fortson 5 run (Arnold kick)	17-22
Presbyterian	4	2:25	Gordon 16 run (Davis to Brad Jones 2-pt conversion)	17-30
Presbyterian	4	:54	David Huskey point blocked out of end zone for safety	17-32

Time of Game: Kick off 2:00; End of Game: 4:37; Total Elapsed Time: 2:37

	NBY.	PRESBY.
First Downs	14	4
Rushing	9	9
Passing	5	5
Penalty	0	0
Rushing Attempts	48	43
Yards Gained Rushing	204	184
Yards Lost Rushing	44	50
Net Yards Rushing	160	134
Net Yards Passing	56	152
Passes Attempted	21	22
Passes Completed	6	8
Had Intercepted	2	2
Total Offensive Plays	69	65
Total Net Yards	216	286
Average Gain Per Play	3.1	4.4
Return Yards	103	31
Fumbles: Number-Lost	4-1	6-1
Penalties: Number-Yards	7-63	5-45
Interceptions: Number-Yards	2-48	2-22
Number of Punts-Yards	6-189	6-262
Average Per Punt	31.5	43.7
Punt Returns: Number-Yards	6-55	2-9
Kickoff Returns: Number-Yards	5-92	5-88
Possession Time	N/A	N/A
Third-Down Conversions	N/A	N/A
Sacks By	4-30	2-12

The Li'l That Was!

Blue Hose take Bronze Derby home, Indians complete season

By Andrew Dodd
Sports Editor

Thanksgiving 1991 will be remembered by many Newberry football followers as the day the Bronze Derby left their possession for the first time in three years as a result of Presbyterian College's 32-17 victory over the arch-rival Indians.

Down only 22-17 late in the fourth quarter the Indians, trying to replay their dramatic victory the last time the teams met on Setzler Field, moved inside the Blue Hose territory with under four minutes to play only to have a PC defender steppe in front of a Louis Austin pass to end the come-from-behind effort.

The Blue Hose threw salt into the Indian's wounds by capitalizing on the turnover, scoring on a Mason Gordon, who finished the game with 167 yards rushing, 16 yard scamper with only 2:25 remaining.

The Indians, down 16-0 at the half, outscored the Blue Hose 17-16 in the second half thanks to two turnovers from Presbyterian.

Newberry first got on the board with 13:21 left in the third quarter as Dwight

The Indians show their excitement prior to their game against arch-rival Presbyterian. The Blue Hose regained the Bronze Derby with a 32-17 win.
File photo

Cummings banged his way in from one yard out. Jason Arnold's PAT cut the Indians deficit to 16-7.

Arnold pulled the 'Skins to within 16-10 later in the third with a 37-yard field goal.

But that is as close as the Indians would get on this day.

After a PC touchdown gave them a seemingly secure 22-10 lead, Willis Fortson's early fourth quarter touchdown set the scene for the Indian's final opportunity.

Senior Eric Houston, who led the defensive unit with a game-high 14 tackles, summed up the Indians disappointing 1-10 finish, "We had opportunities all year. It was either a case of the defense playing well and the offense not showing up or vice-versa."

The game marked the end to thirteen Indian careers: Will Blackmon, Alex Blizzard, Rodney Cook, Gary Counts, Dwight Cummings, Alex Dabney, Jason Hilton, Eric Houston, David Huskey, Kelvin Jeffrey, Rickey Montgomery, Travis Perry, and Kerry Suber.

November 1992

November 3	Singer Whitney Houston released "I Will Always Love You."
November 3	Bill Clinton was elected President of the United States defeating incumbent President George H.W. Bush.
November 3	Representing the state of Illinois, Carol Mosely-Braun was elected the first African American woman in the United States Senate.
November 3	Senator Diane Feinstein of California was elected to the United States Senate and became the longest serving female until her death in 2023.
November 5	American NFL football receiver Odell Beckham Jr. was born.
November 5	American chess grandmaster Bobby Fisher defeated Russian Boris Spassky to win the "Revenge Match of the 20th Century." The unofficial match took place in Belgrade.
November 8	300,000 people gather and protest against racism in Berlin, Germany.
November 10	Actor and author Chuck Connors of "The Rifleman" passed away.
November 11	The Church of England approved the ordination of female priests.
November 13	Riddick Bowe won the undisputed world heavyweight boxing crown over Evander Holyfield with a unanimous point decision in Las Vegas, Nevada.
November 15	Alan Kulwicki won the 42nd NASCAR Sprint Cup.
November 17	"The Bodyguard" soundtrack was released by Arista records and won the 1993 *Billboard* Album of the year.
November 18	The film "Malcom X" starring Denzel Washington and Angela Bassett was released. The film was directed by Spike Lee.
November 20	Windsor Castle, the home of Queen Elizabeth, caught fire.
November 23	American actress and singer Miley Cyrus of "Hannah Montana" fame was born.
November 23	The 10 millionth cell phone was sold.
November 23	Roy Acuff, American country fiddler and singer passed away.
November 24	A Boeing 734 crashed into a mountain in China killing 141.
November 26	Alabama defeated Auburn in the 57th Iron Bowl in Birmingham, Alabama.
November 26	The Bronze Derby was played in Clinton, South Carolina on Thanksgiving Day. The Newberry College Indians defeated the Presbyterian College Blue Hose 14-0.

The Li'l 🎩 That Was!

Newberry College
The Newberry Observer

VOLUME NO. 128 – ISSUE NO. 139   Newberry, S. C., Wednesday, Nov. 25, 1992   ONE SECTION – 12 PAGES

Newberry Indians determined to bring home Bronze Derby Nov. 26 in last Thanksgiving Day match

The November 26 Bronze Derby contest between Newberry College and Presbyterian College marks the end of an era. This will be the final game on Thanksgiving Day for the two long-time rivals.

In the future, the Newberry-Presbyterian game will be scheduled earlier in the season to allow for post-season play. According to Jack Williams, athletic director at Newberry, the schools are going to try to schedule this game as the final game of the season. However, next year's game is scheduled in September. Williams hopes the 1994 schedule can match up the Newberry vs. Presbyterian game as the final of that season and start a new tradition.

The game will be played on Blue Hose turf this year. Kick off time is 2:00 pm. The Blue Hose currently have custody of the celebrated derby, but Mike Taylor and the Indians are determined to bring it home. All Newberry fans are encouraged to wear red to the game.

History of the Bronze Derby

When James Kellett was a student at Presbyterian College in the late 1940's, he acquired a sartorial habit which was to affect the destiny of one of the state's oldest athletic rivalries.

"My uncle operated a clothing store in Fountain Inn," Kellett recalls today, "and men's hats were pretty popular in those days. So, I started wearing a Stetson derby, just for fun, and I happened to be wearing it one night in 1947 when a bunch of us went to see the Presbyterian basketball team play at Newberry."

"It was a pretty exciting game, and some Newberry students put a ladder up against the outside of the gym and climbed through a window at the top of the visitor's section. They worked their way down through the crowd and one of them snatched the derby from my head and ran outside. We chased them and a few skirmishes occurred, but I ended up without my derby. We looked for it all over the Newberry campus but I finally went home hatless. (The student who swiped the hat has long since faded into obscurity.)

What might have ended as another in a series of increasingly hostile student pranks between rivals was turned into a legend by the quick thinking of cooler heads.

Charles MacDonald, Presbyterian College sports information director, suggested to counterpart Frank Kinard at Newberry College that if the derby could be recovered it might become a symbol for athletic supremacy between the schools. The idea won quick approval from the student bodies and the hat was bronzed for posterity.

It was decided that it would go to the winner of any athletic contest between the schools, so it changed hands repeatedly through baseball, basketball and football seasons from 1947 through 1955. Realizing that such frequent contests diminished the importance of the trophy, the schools agreed in 1956 that it would be claimed only by the winner of the annual Thanksgiving Day football game.

Perhaps the ultimate rapport occurs before the game each year. The host school serves Thanksgiving lunch in its cafeteria, and fans from both schools share a meal before going out to stare at each other across 100 yards of grass with white stripes.

It is refreshing and somehow reassuring to find athletic rivalry which combines intensity and common sense.

The cornerstone of collegiate sports is tradition and nowhere is that truer than among small colleges. With no major bowl berths available and relatively little publicity outside their own regions, small colleges take the players the big colleges look over and play a different game.

When the dust settles, someone will hoist a strange looking trophy high into the air as a symbol of victory. Friendly rivals, one hurting for the other. The true meaning of college athletics.

And that's what some folks had in mind when they covered an old derby hat in bronze in 1947.

Written by Billy Deal

477

The Li'l That Was!

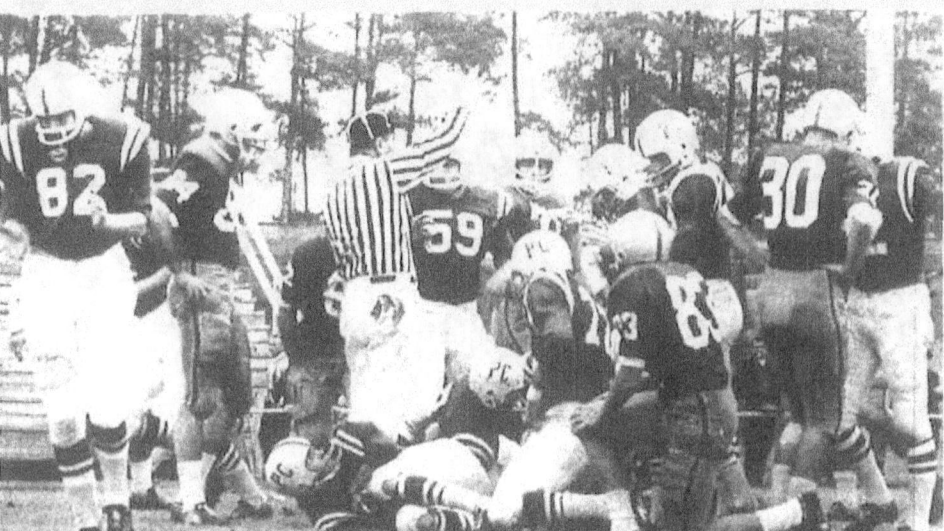

1963 BRONZE DERBY — Presbyterian College's Jim Johnson (on ground at referee's feet) just recovered a Newberry fumble during the 1963 Bronze Derby Classic, which was current Presbyterian athletic director Calley Gault's first as head coach. Presbyterian won 14-7.

November 25, 1992 The Laurens County Advertiser

Bronze Derby full of Classic memories for Gault

By Russ Pace
Sports Editor

CLINTON — What began as a friendly rivalry between two small colleges located 20 miles apart has become part of Laurens County Football lore that generations of fans look foward to each year as much as ... well, the dressing and pumpkin pie.

For the past 49 Thanksgiving Days, Newberry College and Presbyterian College have drawn the line of scrimmage and dared each other to cross. Records, streaks or statistics don't matter. Who's favored doesn't come into play. What matters is now. Each snap of the ball can be the play that etches another mark in the history of this greatest of Laurens County football traditions.

But traditions are often mortal and with the passing of this, the 50th Thanksgiving Day Bronze Derby Classic, the epitaph is written. No longer will the final game of the regular season between Newberry and Presbyterian College be played on Thanksgiving Day.

The reason is progress. Presbyterian will play full-time next season as a member of NCAA Division II. For reasons of possible playoff berths and other considerations, the Classic must go.

Which leaves followers of the Classic with just one alternative. Following the game, when the final gun is sounded and the players walk off the field and the crowd disperses for the warmth of fire places and the fellowship of family, memories of the tradition will have to serve in place of anticipation. There will be no more Thanksgiving Days like tomorrow.

One participant in tomorrow's Bronze Derby Classic who has had a part in various Classics since 1944 is Presbyterian College Athletic Director Calley Gault. Gault played in the series from 1944 to '47, then became a part of the tradition as head coach of the Blue Hose from 1963 through '84. Since his retirement from coaching, he has overseen the game as Presbyterian College's AD.

Gault has seen the series from the inside, and shares some of his most memorable occasions.

"The first thing I always say about the Bronze Derby is that only the unusual things happen during these games," Gault said. "If unusual things were going to happen to our football team it would happen on the day of the Classic.

"In 1963, we won the game on a shovel pass run from a shotgun formation. It was an unusual call, but it worked. Then in '77, on what should have been the last play of the game, Newberry completed a long pass down to our three-yard line. There was a lot of motion going on before the snap of the next play, but we stopped them cold and won the game.

"After the game when we were on the bus, one of my assistant coaches told me that we had 12 men on the field and that it was our illegal man that made the game-saving tackle. Well, I went fishing that weekend, but decided to call (then Newberry head coach Fred Herron) Fred and tell him about the mistake, but we weren't going to forfeit. No sir, we won the game and that was that.

"Well I got in after fishing and Fred called me and asked me if I had looked at the game films yet. I told him had not and then he tells me that when I do, to count the men on the field during the final sequence.

"It seems we both had 12 men on the field and that was the end of that," Gault recalled.

Pre-game antics by both teams involved in such a rivalry are just as big a part of the tradition as the game itself. Perhaps the most memorable example of this is the saga of "Killer the Turkey."

It seems Newberry picked the pride of someone's Turkey farm and announced that the winner of the Classic that year would get the prized Tom as a prize.

The local media hyped the event, and the Turkey was named "Killer." But some Presbyterian coaches had plans of their own for Killer.

The late Billy Tiller, a robust 300 pound assistant coach arrived to the game prior to the Newberry squad dressed in chef's attire, complete with apron, a hat as well as a knife and serving fork. Tiller approached the teathered turkey in front of the Newberry sideline and began to prode Killer with tenderizing jabs with his utensils just as the Indians made their way to their bench.

Newberry's first look at Tiller chasing Killer around and around with a large fork was enough to freeze them in their tracks, throw them mentally off balance and off track enough for a 17-0 Presbyterian win.

Rumor has it that Killer was saved from the oven and sent out to stud somewhere in Clinton. However, recent findings indicate that Tiller finally caught Killer and the rest was, well ... gravey.

The Bronze Derby

All-time scores in the Thanksgiving Day games

1943 — PC 46, Newberry 7	1957 — Newberry 13, PC 0	1968 — PC 42, Newberry 7
1944 — PC 6, Newberry 0	1958 — PC 22, Newberry 0	1969 — PC 23, Newberry 21	1982 — PC 21, Newberry 7
1945 — Newberry 19, PC 13	1959 — PC 20, Newberry 6	1970 — PC 27, Newberry 23	1983 — Newberry 23, PC 0
1946 — PC 14, Newberry 13	1960 — PC 6, Newberry 0	1971 — Newberry 34, PC 0	1984 — Newberry 25, PC 16
1947 — Newberry 6, PC 0	1961 — PC 7, Newberry 7	1972 — PC 17, Newberry 0	1985 — PC 24, Newberry 24
1948 — PC 40, Newberry 7	1962 — Newberry 23, PC 0	1973 — Newberry 14, PC 3	1986 — PC 35, Newberry 20
1949 — Newberry 20, PC 14	1963 — PC 14, Newberry 7	1974 — PC 37, Newberry 7	1987 — Newberry 17, PC 15
1950 — PC 20, Newberry 6	1964 — PC 35, Newberry 6	1975 — PC 14, Newberry 0	1988 — PC 30, Newberry 16
1951 — PC 27, Newberry 0	1965 — Newberry 6, PC 0	1976 — Newberry 26, PC 15	1989 — Newberry 29, PC 24
1952 — PC 14, Newberry 12	1966 — PC 28, Newberry 7	1977 — PC 3, Newberry 0	1990 — Newberry 24, PC 7
1953 — PC 7, Newberry 7	1967 — PC 14, Newberry 0	1978 — PC 26, Newberry 0	1991 — PC 32, Newberry 17
1954 — PC 20, Newberry 18		1979 — PC 16, Newberry 14	
1955 — Newberry 20, PC 18		1980 — Newberry 28, PC 20	
1956 — Newberry 13, PC 0		1981 — Newberry 26, PC 23	

THE BLUE STOCKING

The Li'l That Was!

Blue Hose fans bid farewell to Thanksgiving tradition

by LeJeanna Maddox
MANAGING EDITOR

For the past 47 years, PC Athletic Director Cally Gault has scheduled his Thanksgiving Day festivities around a different kind of tradition. And although it is often painful to watch a tradition drift into the recesses of memory, he'll have to do so this Thanksgiving Day, as PC faces Newberry in the final Thanksgiving Turkey Day Bronze Derby Classic.

The Thanksgiving Day rivalry began in 1943, and since that time three generations of upstate SC football fans have placed football at the top of their holiday agendas. Last year, the PC-Newberry match-up was one of only four games to be played in the entire nation on Thanksgiving Day.

The end of the tradition comes in the wake of PC's transition from NAIA athletic standing to NCAA Division II status. The NCAA regular season ends the second week in November. A Thanksgiving Day game could, therefore, interfere with NCAA playoff games and would, in any case, make the season too long.

"Most of us don't want to move the game," explained Gault, "but we realize the necessity. You just don't limit any team's playoff chances."

The PC-Newberry rivalry will always be unique, however. Erase "Thanksgiving Turkey Day" from the title, and you are still left with "Bronze Derby Classic." What, after all, is a bronze derby, and why do we name a football game after it?

The term originated as a result of an incident during a PC-Newberry basketball game in January of the 1946-47 season. A number of PC students travelled to Newberry for the game, carrying with them a banner bearing the message, "Beat the Hell Out of Newberry."

"They put the banner across the back of the gym over the student cheering section," explained Gault, who was a student at PC at the time. During the game, however, a group of Newberry students obtained a ladder, climbed up the outside wall of the gym, reached through the window, and pulled the banner out. Once the game ended and the PC students realized what had happened, they were determined not to return to Clinton without their stolen banner.

Scuffles and earnest searching ensued. In the midst of the chaos, a Newberry student reached through a car window and snatched a derby - a type of hat- from the head of a PC student. Everyone then forgot about the banner and concentrated all efforts on reclaiming the beloved derby.

"The derby had been worn at some time or another by every resident of Smyth Dorm. We took turns wearing it to class," explained Gault, who was sitting in the car from which the derby was stolen.

All searches proved futile, and the Blue Hose fans returned to Clinton without their banner or their derby. Incidentally, they did return with a 51-47 victory in the game, if that was any consolation.

Although some of the names and events of the ensuing two weeks remain undisclosed, we do know that PC's athletic publicity director and assistant professor of English, Charles MacDonald, sent a letter to Frank Kinard, the editor of the Newberry College newspaper. MacDonald proposed that the derby be instituted as a symbol of the athletic rivalry between the two schools. Kinard presented the idea to the Newberry student body, who enthusiastically lent their support of the idea.

"The derby was returned and bronzed," added Gault, "and has since served as a symbol of sports supremacy."

For several years, the trophy was up for grabs at every athletic confrontation between the schools. Then it was decided to award it only once each year to the winner of the annual Thanksgiving Day contest.

So while the Thanksgiving Turkey Day Bronze Derby Classic will bid farewell next week, the Bronze Derby Classic will live on. In the future, the game will likely be played near the beginning of the season. The schools will continue to battle for possession of the trophy.

This year's game will begin at 2:00 pm on Thanksgiving Day here at Bailey Stadium. The coveted Bronze Derby will be delivered to the field by the Golden Knights, a US Army Parachute Team.

Blue Hose Head Football Coach John Perry shows off the coveted Bronze Derby. The final Bronze Derby Thanksgiving game will be next Thursday.

photo by Kim Gibson

The Li'l That Was!

The Newberry Observer
AND HERALD & NEWS
"Just Like A Letter From Home"

Newberry, S.C., Friday, Nov. 27, 1992

Last Bronze Derby on Thanksgiving

PC Hosts Landmark Game

BY GENA EVANS

It is said that all good things must come to an end. Yesterday at Clinton, something did -- a tradition which to some meant "Thanksgiving" as much as turkey, dressing, and sweet potato pie.

The Newberry College/Presbyterian College football game has been played on Thanksgiving Day since 1943. Now because of NCAA playoffs, the game will have to be moved.

Newberry College Athletic Director Jack Williams says that although the game won't be on Thanksgiving, it will continue to be the Carolina-Clemson of small college football. Next year, the game will be played on September 18.

However, Williams says he hopes that the following year, a new tradition will be born. One which pits the Indians and the Blue Hose on the last game of the season.

Williams says he is saddened to see the tradition come to an end. He stresses, though, that the intensity of the game will not end.

"There will always be a special rivalry with P.C., whether it is on Thanksgiving, in September or in June," Williams said.

Fans of the two schools are especially sad that the game is being moved. "I guess that I will have to start cooking Thanksgiving dinner again," longtime Indian fan Sara Shealy said.

Newberry College players give Head Coach Mike Taylor a victory ride after Thursday's 14-0 win over Presbyterian. Taylor, a former Newberry College player himself, said that win was one that was hard to describe.

Players Will Always Remember This Game

BY AMBER EAVES AND MIKE MEADOW

Not even the muddy conditions at Presbyterian's Bailey Memorial Stadium could dampen the spirits of a victorious Newberry College Indian team as they recaptured the Bronze Derby trophy.

In the 81st meeting of the two schools, Newberry's 14-0 victory ended a season of emotional ups and downs. With the arrival of a new head coach, only weeks before the season opener, the Indians went from an 0-4 team at the beginning of the season, to a team that won five of their last seven games.

For the senior leaders on the Indian team, a win at this last Thanksgiving Day Bronze Derby clash completed what has been, for them, a four year history of staff changes, consistent community support... a range of positive and negative experiences. Yet, despite their less-than-perfect record of the past four seasons, these seniors will revel in the fact that they captured the Bronze Derby three of the last four times that the series was played on Thanksgiving Day.

THE NEWBERRY OBSERVER Newberry, S.C., Friday, Nov. 27, 1992

Sports

The Newberry Observer

*Player Remember

(Continued From Page 1)

These emotions were evidenced in the words of senior offensive lineman Jerry Wright as he reflected on his last season:

"Man, it's great (winning the Bronze Derby). Ever since I've been here, we've beat PC three out of four times and I think this program is in the right direction. At the beginning of the season, we just weren't used to the coaches and they weren't used to us and it just took us some time to develop everything... if he (Coach Taylor) would have been here during the summer, I really believe during the spring that we would be undefeated, probably."

Wright, considering this his final game, had a message for next year's Indian team:

"It's lookin' good. When we only lose two out of the last seven games, everybody's pumped up for next year and I can't wait to get back and see my boys play. I just wish them all luck."

Another player who will have much to remember about this game is senior Tim Singleton. Singleton, who sat out last season, was moved from quarterback to an all-purpose back mid-way through the season. Singleton had only positive reflections on the move that changed his senior season.

"You can't express the great feeling that we have. We worked hard. Coach Taylor enstilled nothing but hard work in us and it paid off. Well, I had little second thoughts at first (about his position change), but it helped the team... that was the bottom line, and that's what we were trying to do."

Singleton too, had words for his legacy players.

"I'd like to tell them to do nothing but work hard, have discipline, and get that education because that is what we are here for."

For Coach Mike Taylor, though, the win against Presbyterian was a personal victory as well as a coaching success.

"It's hard to describe. I don't think our season was so rocky... we started out bad, and we finished up great. Finishing 5-6 is like ending up a mile from where we started from. I'm proud, I'm glad to be here and I'm proud to be associated with these guys."

With this season's five wins, Taylor, himself a Newberry Indian alum, turned around a dispairing Indian team that finished 1-10 last season.

Fans who endured cloudy conditions through most of the game were glad to see rays of sun that finally peeked through the parting clouds. It seemed that the sun came out to accompany the Indians to victory at the close of the game. Perhaps the Newberry faithful traveling home noticed the two parallel rainbows that could possibly signify the bright future in store for Newberry College football.

The Li'l That Was!

Bronze Derby

(Continued From Page 1)

Mrs. Shealy and her husband, Charles, have been attending the "Bronze Derby" on Thanksgiving for over 40 years. They were there when the derby was stolen in 1947 and they were there yesterday when the last Thanksgiving battle occurred.

Mr. and Mrs. Shealy say they have many special memories of the Bronze Derby. However, they say that their favorite memory was when their son played on the 1965 Indian team which beat PC 6-0.

Mr. Shealy's sister, Elizabeth Shenly, also has fond memories of the traditional battle. She lived in New York for 40 years and has only attended three of the Thanksgiving classics including this one.

However, she did have a Thanksgiving tradition of her own. "Every Thanksgiving when I lived in New York, I would call the *New York Times* sports department and ask them about the Newberry-PC game," Ms. Shealy said.

Other fans have equally vivid memories on the classic dual.

Former Newberry players Neal Dufford and Jimmy Graham have been active Indian supporters since they've ended their playing careers. Dufford has a fond memory of a win at Newberry, but he also remembers losing at PC.

Graham also remembers a loss to PC in 1959 when he played for the "Fighting Redskins". In fact, he says that it is his favorite Bronze Derby memory.

"In 1959 both Newberry and PC had good records coming into the game. The winner was going to get a bid to play in the Tangerine Bowl, which is really something for a small college team," Graham said.

"Anyway, it was a hard fought game, and in the end, PC won," Graham continued.

Wayne and Becky Saville are also dyed-in-the-wool Newberry fans. They've been to 16-straight Thanksgiving matchups and say they are sure the rivalry will continue.

The most treasured Thanksgiving Day memory for the Savilles is the 1989 clash. In that game, Newberry quarterback Tim Singleton found receiver Pat White in the end-zone with one second on the clock to give the Indians the win.

Saville says, though, that the media has misinterpreted the play. "The papers and TV kept saying that it was a "Hail Mary" pass and it wasn't," Saville stated emphatically.

"A 'Hail Mary' pass is when you throw the ball up and pray someone catches it. Tim Singleton saw Pat White and threw the ball to him. That's not a 'Hail Mary'," Saville added.

Coaches and former coaches from Newberry and Presbyterian alike also treasure the game. In a special banquet held Wednesday night in Clinton commemorating the tradition, former Newberry Coach Fred Herren and former PC Coach, now Athletic Director, Cally Gault brought back to life memories of the days when they coached against each other.

Episodes such as the "Don't let Tiller get Killer" game and Gault's famous sideline tap-dance were some of the events remembered by the two coaches.

Current Newberry Coach Mike Taylor and PC skipper John Perry are also former players. They told the players that the memories made in the game, would be ones they would keep forever.

They also told the crowd, that although the players may not appreciate the significance of playing in the last Thanksgiving match-up, that one day they will. "You don't really appreciate this game until you get out of it," Coach Taylor said.

Some people who aren't too devastated that the game is being moved are the players.

Sophomore linebacker Quintard Tucker said before the game that he thinks moving the game may be a good idea. "In some ways, moving the game is good because the players will get to go home and spend Thanksgiving with their families," Tucker said.

He added, though, that no matter when it's played the matchup between PC and Newberry will remain a battle of wills. "As long as there's that Bronze Derby, as long as there's that little bronze hat, we'll be playing with the same intensity as before," Tucker said.

Senior defensive tackle Muccio Montgomery agrees with Tucker that moving the game may be better in the long run. However, he also said that Newberry will always be motivated to play Presbyterian

"This is like a bowl game. It's more than a football game -- it's pride," Montgomery said.

The pride that motivated the Indians on that muddy field on that chilly Thanksgiving afternoon, and in fact, that motivated them through the entire tumultuous season, catapulted the team into history. It was a game and a season few will ever forget.

Now the Thanksgiving dual for the Bronze Derby will go the way of Big Thursday, the band concert at Willowbrook Park, and the Fourth of July picnic at Jolly Street. All memories that will last a lifetime.

THE NEWBERRY OBSERVER   Newberry, S.C., Friday, Nov. 27, 1992

Sports
The Newberry Observer

Newberry College players pile on runningback Eric Green after his 24 yard touchdown run late in the fourth quarter to secure a 14-0 win over Presbyterian in the last Bronze Derby game played on Thanksgiving between the two schools.

The track was messy in Bailey Stadium on Thanksgiving Day...
...as Presbyterian dropped the final Bronze Derby holiday game to Newberry
Photo by Fletcher Pruitt Jr.

Newberry reclaims Derby, 14-0

By Rick Hendricks
Editor

Game 11

The Results
Newberry 14
PC 0

A year ago, the Bronze Derby was a perfect fit as coach John Perry capped his first season as Blue Hose mentor with a 32-17 victory over Newberry.

This past Thursday, amid the hype of the final Bronze Derby Classic to be played on Thanksgiving, missed opportunities spelled doom as Presbyterian dropped a 14-0 decision to the Indians in Clinton.

As Perry lamented after the contest, which left his team with its second consecutive 4-7 mark, "This game was very typical of four or five others this year."

There were numerous times throughout the game when it appeared the Blue Hose were ready to break through, only to have a penalty or turnover stall their efforts.

After PC won the toss and deferred, Newberry took possession at its own 27 after the opening kickoff.

On the Indians' first play from scrimmage, Tim Singleton fumbled the pitch from Newberry quarterback Andy Thomason. **Brett Turner** recovered for PC at the Newberry 21 with 14:42 to go in the first quarter.

Five plays later, PC tailback **Mason Gordon** seemingly scored from 4 yards out, but the Blue Hose were called for holding to negate the score.

On the very next play, Blue Hose quarterback **Tim Davis** was intercepted by Tony Nelson at the Newberry 3 to snuff out the PC threat.

Presbyterian's defense stifled the Indian offense during the ensuing possession, and Newberry was forced to punt.

Blue Hose punt return specialist **Corey McKelvie** caught the punt at his own 26, then fumbled and Newberry recovered at the PC 23 with 10:23 to go in the first quarter.

A 17-yard run by Thomason moved Newberry to the Blue Hose 1, then two plays later, Eric Green scored the game's first touchdown. Jason Arnold kicked the extra point and the Indians led, 7-0, with 8:45 remaining in the first quarter.

PC proceeded to move the ball during its ensuing possession. The Blue Hose started the drive at their own 29, then moved 63 yards in 12 plays before the drive stalled at the Newberry 8.

Kicker Alex Horton came on to attempt a 25-yard field goal at the 2:16 mark of the first quarter, but it was no good and Newberry's 7-0 lead was safe for the time being.

The Indians took over at their own 20. On the second play of the drive, tempers flared and unsportsmanlike conduct penalties were called against both teams. The incident also resulted in the ejection of senior defensive lineman Turner.

The Indians were moving into PC territory as the second quarter began, but Tyron Phillips intercepted a Thomason pass at the Blue Hose 23, then returned it 19 yards. An unsportsmanlike conduct penalty against Newberry resulted in PC having a first down at the Indian 43.

The Blue Hose failed to move the ball, however, but a **Kevin Eby** punt pinned Newberry deep in its own territory at the 5.

A 22-yard run by Green and a 20-yard jaunt by Willis Fortson, a Clinton High graduate, helped get the Indians out of that hole.

The Blue Hose defense again rose to the occasion and forced Newberry to punt.

PC took possession of the ball at its own 18 with 9:31 to go in the first half.

The Blue Hose retained possession until only 36 seconds remained in the half.

Fifteen plays produced 48 yards, but PC could get no closer than the Newberry 34.

The Indians took their 7-0 lead to intermission.

A 25-yard return by Phillips to open the second half gave PC good field position at the Blue Hose 41.

A 38-yard pass from Davis to Chris Yonce moved Presbyterian to the Newberry 33, then two plays later, Gordon, who gained 119 yards on the day, got loose for a 14-yard gain to the Indian 20.

PC moved to the Newberry 11, but faced fourth-and-two from that spot, so Perry again called on Horton. This field goal attempt was from 28 yards out, but was no good to leave the Indian lead intact with 9:30 remaining in the third quarter.

Newberry retained possession and again moved into Blue Hose territory before a 25-yard loss on a fumble killed the drive.

PC took over at its own 31 after a Newberry punt with 2:20 to go in the third quarter. On the fourth play into the drive, Davis completed an 11-yard pass to Ron Palmer to move PC into Newberry territory at the Indian 46.

Two plays later, a Davis pass hit Steve Gorrle in the hands and bounced into the hands of Indian Lamar Thompson as the third quarter expired.

Newberry was forced to punt several plays following the Blue Hose turnover, then PC took over at its own 16. Passes from Davis of 10 and 18 yards to Palmer and McKelvie, respectively, helped the Blue Hose again advance.

Two plays later, Palmer fumbled a pass from Davis and Thompson recovered for Newberry at the 50 with 11:10 to go in the contest.

The Blue Hose would not threaten again, but after giving the ball up on downs with 2:28 remaining, Green scored his second TD of the day from 24 yards out to clinch the win. Arnold's PAT was good and the Indians held the upper hand in recapturing the Derby, 14-0, with 2:16 left in the game.

Newberry ran out the clock, then team members and coaches crossed the field to the PC sideline to claim the Derby.

PC finished the season with a 4-7 slate, while Newberry closed its season at 5-6, winning five of its last seven contests.

"We kept getting the ball back and had opportunities to play ourselves back into the game," said Perry.

Despite the loss and the identical record in 1992 as in 1991, the coach said he does not think the Presbyterian College program has been set back.

"The program's got a bright future," he said. "We've seen a lot of improvement with some of the young kids this season. A good recruiting year will be important for us."

Newberry	7	0	0	7-14
Presbyterian	0	0	0	0-0

The Clinton Chronicle

December 2, 1992

The Li'l That Was!

THE NEWBERRY OBSERVER   Newberry, S.C., Friday, Nov. 27, 1992

Sports
The Newberry Observer

Indians Reclaim Bronze Derby With 14-0 Win

BY MIKE MEADOW

Despite conditions that only a pig would love, the Newberry College Indians brought home the Bronze Derby for first year head coach Mike Taylor.

Heavy rains Wednesday night and early Thursday morning left the field at Bailey Memorial Stadium a sloppy mess for the final Thanksgiving Day battle between the Indians and the Blue Hose.

A skirmish at midfield following the coin toss set the tone for one of the most exciting Newberry - PC games in history.

Newberry took the opening kickoff on their own 21 yard line and on the first play from scrimmage Tim Singleton fumbled and Presbyterian recovered.

On third and 10 from the Newberry 10, Tim Davis's pass was intercepted by Tony Nelson at the Newberry three yard line and returned to the eight. An unsportsman like conduct penalty gave the Indians the ball on their own 16.

Four plays later, Corey McKelvie fumbled a Hap Greenway punt and the Indians had the ball on the Presbyterian 23.

With 8:45 left in the first quarter, Eric Green bounced over the top of the Blue Hose line for a one yard touchdown. Jason Arnold added the PAT to give the Indians a 7-0 lead.

Presbyterian's only scoring threat on the first half came late in the first quarter when Alex Horton's 25 yard field goal was wide to the right.

PC drove to the Newberry 23 late in the second quarter, but their drive stalled and they were forced to punt with :38 left to play in the first half.

On their first drive of the second half, the Blue Hose drove to the Newberry 12 in 10 plays. On fourth and two, Horton's 28 yard field goal hit the right crossbar and was no good to end another PC threat.

Neither team managed to move the ball in the fourth quarter and the Indian defense managed to keep the Presbyterians on their side of the 50 for the entire forth quarter.

After stopping the Blue Hose on downs with 2:28 left in the game, Green broke over the middle and raced 24 yards for his second touchdown of the day. Arnold's PAT gave the Indians a 14-0 lead with only minutes left in the game.

Newberry's defense once again held the Blue Hose to only four plays and the Indians killed the rest of the clock on three plays to secure the win.

"We had a bunch of guys come up here and play with guts today because we had guys hurt, and they played over and above their ability and we made things happen," Newberry College Head Coach Mike Taylor said. "They moved the football and they can say how they should have done this and should have done that, but we did it. They're a good football team, and I know they are hurting over there but I'd rather them be hurting than me."

The Indains started out the season losing their first four games, but bounced back to win five of their last seven.

Taylor said that the turning point of the season was the 66-16 loss early in the season.

"You just can't get any worse than that. Our guys understood, we told them on Monday we weren't going to punish then or beat them to death, we were going to go out and keep working and try to get better, and that's what they did. They know we were on their side. We didn't blame them, we said we're all screwed up, let's go ahead and keep working."

With the sloppy conditions of the field, Taylor had an unusual message for his players before the game.

"At least it's not cold," Taylor said. "that's what I told them. I said it's raining like bats, but at least it's not cold. I said I wouldn't go out there if it was cold.".

Presbyterian out gained Newberry 272 to 205 in total yardage, but the big key to the game was PC's four tournovers to Newberry's two.

Tim Adams, a senior on the Newberry squad reflected on his final season.

"It's the best feeling in the world. We worked awfully hard and the guys hung in their through thick and thin, the coaches got on and I think we wanted this game more than anything, to go out on a winning fashion. Hey, that's the season right there," Adams said, "

The Indians finished the season with a 5-6 record, four wins better than last year's 1-10 team.

The Newberry Observer — Friday, Nov. 15, 2002 ■ PAGE 15

—Observer file photo

VICTORY RIDE — Newberry College seniors hoisted first year head coach Mike Taylor on their shoulders after the Indians stunned Presbyterian, 14-0, in the 1992 Bronze Derby Game. It was the last time the two rivals played for The Bronze Derby on Thanksgiving Day.

Flashback to 1992

Indians win Derby back
Newberry shuts out Blue Hose in historic game

■ Mike Meadow

Despite conditions that only a pig would love, the Newberry College Indians brought home The Bronze Derby for first year head coach Mike Taylor with a 14-0 victory over rival Presbyterian College.

Heavy rains Wednesday night and early Thursday morning left the field at Bailey Memorial Stadium in Clinton a sloppy mess for the final Thanksgiving Day battle between the Indians and the Blue Hose.

A skirmish at midfield following the coin toss set the tone for one of the most exciting Newberry-PC games in history.

Newberry took the opening kick-off on their own 21-yard line and on the first play from scrimmage Tim Singleton fumbled and Presbyterian recovered.

On third-and-10 from the Newberry 10, Tim Davis's pass was intercepted by Tony Nelson at the Newberry three and returned to the eight. An unsportsmanlike conduct penalty gave the Indians the ball on their own 16.

Four plays later, Corey McKelvie fumbled a Hap Greenway punt and the Indians had the ball on the Presbyterian 23.

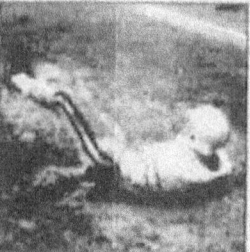
—Observer file photo

MUDDY VICTORY — A Newberry player slides in the mud after the Indians beat rival Presbyterian 14-0 in the last Bronze Derby Game played on Thanksgiving Day.

With 8:45 left in the first quarter, Eric Green bounced over the top of the Blue Hose line for a one-yard touchdown. Jason Arnold added the PAT to give the Indians a 7-0 lead.

Presbyterian's only scoring threat on the first half came late in the first quarter when Alex Horton's 25-yard field goal was wide to the right.

PC drove to the Newberry 23 late in the second quarter, but the drive stalled and they were forced to punt with :36 left in the first half.

On their first drive of the second half, the Blue Hose drove to the Newberry 12 in 10 plays. On fourth-and-two, Horton's 24-yard field goal hit the right crossbar and was no good to end another PC threat.

Neither team managed to move the ball in the fourth quarter and the Indians' defense managed to keep the Blue Hose on their side of the 50 for the entire fourth quarter.

After stopping the Blue Hose on downs with 2:28 left in the game, Green broke over the middle and raced 24 yards for the game-clinching touchdown of the day.

"We had a bunch of guys come up here and play with guts today because we had guys hurt, and they played over and above their ability and we made things happen," Taylor said. "They moved the football and they can say how they should have done this and should have done that, but we did it. They're a good football team and I know they are hurting over there but I'd rather them be hurting than me."

— Mike Meadow followed and covered the Indians for the Newberry Observer in 1992.

The Li'l  That Was!

NEWBERRY COLLEGE
D·I·M·E·N·S·I·O·N·S

Vol. 27 No. 1   The Quarterly Alumni Magazine   Fall 1992

On the Cover

Coach Mike Taylor is carried away by members of the Indians football team after winning the Bronze Derby back from Presbyterian College. The score was 14-0.

This is the last game the two rivals will play on Thanksgiving Day.

Photo by Pam Royal, courtesy of The State newspaper.

September 1993

September 2	Pearl Jam and En Vogue are headline winners at the 19th annual MTV Video Music Awards.
September 4	Mats Wilander of Sweden defeated fellow Swede Mikael Pernfors in a marathon 4 hour US Open tennis final.
September 4	MLB one handed pitcher Jim Abbott of the New York Yankees threw a no-hitter against the Cleveland Indians.
September 5	Noureddine Morceli ran a world record mile at 3 minutes 44 seconds.
September 7	The late night talk show "The Chevy Chase Show" debuted on FOX television. It was canceled 6 weeks later.
September 6	Jerry Lewis raised $46 million in his 28th "Muscular Dystrophy Telethon."
September 8	MLB proposed switch to a three division format was approved by the AL.
September 9	Israel and the Palestine Liberation Organization mutually recognized one another.
September 10	Actress Loretta Young at 80 years old married 85 year old costume designer Jean Louis.
September 10	Boeing celebrated production of their 1000th 747 jumbo airplane.
September 10	The TV show "The X-Files" debuted on FOX television.
September 11	Steffi Graf won the US Open Women's Tennis Championship.
September 11	Country singer Merle Haggard married Theresa Ann Lane.
September 12	Pete Sampras won the US Open Men's Tennis Championship.
September 12	"Ironside" and "Perry Mason" actor Raymond Burr passed away.
September 13	The Oslo Accords, a peace agreement initiated by Norway, recognized an Israeli and Palestine peace agreement.
September 15	Singer Meatloaf released "I'd Do Anything For Love." The song reached #1 in 28 countries.
September 16	American pool player Wille Mosconi passed away.
September 16	American US Open champion golfer Bryson DeChambeau was born.
September 16	The television show "Frazier" debuted on NBC TV.
September 17	The last Russian troops left Poland.
September 18	The Bronze Derby was played in Newberry, South Carolina. The Presbyterian College Blue Hose defeated the Newberry College Indians 30-13.

Reflections...
On The Bronze Derby Classic

BY JACK WILLIAMS

Wait a minute! The schedule says this is the Newberry vs. Presbyterian Bronze Derby Classic. That can't be right! It's 5:30 in the afternoon, and it's not dark outside...it's 87 degrees and sunny, not 43 degrees and raining...it's baseball dominating the sports page, not the NFL play-offs.

It can't be the Indians vs. the Blue Hose, Newberry vs. PC, tradition vs. tradition -- there's no turkey defrosting in the refrigerator!

It's September. Newberry and Presbyterian are about to go at it for the Bronze Derby. When was the last time Newberry and P.C. went after each other and it wasn't the last game of the season on Thanksgiving? (Oh, sure, NAIA Playoffs disrupted the series in 1979 and 1987.) But you have to go back to 1956 when Catawba was able to sneak in a game after the battle with Newberry, but the Bronze Derby game has always been on Thanksgiving.

The Rivalry

I've only been involved with the "THE RIVALRY" since 1983, and I have enjoyed Newberry's 6-3-1 record against the Hose in the past 10 years -- but what I have always enjoyed about the series are the STORIES...

Ah, the stories! Let's put Cally Gault and Fred Herren in a room and just let a tape recorder run. A turkey named Killer or 12 men on the field would surely be mentioned...how about the one-second pass in 1989 when Newberry won...what of John Perry (Class of '73, PC) winning his first chance at the Bronze Derby in 1991 and Mike Taylor (Class of '76, Newberry) turning the tables by winning his first chance at the coveted derby in 1992.

"If it's not broken, don't fix it!" is a wise old saying. However, due to a changing climate in college football, the Thanksgiving part of the classic is now over.

Is it still a classic?

Absolutely. True Newberry and Presbyterian fans know that! The emotion will always be there, along with Wayne and Becky Saville who haven't missed a Newberry-PC game for the past 14 years.

Is September the best time for the Classic? The majority of those in the know will say, "Put the football down in Joanna and have some guys in red and some guys in blue square off...You'll get a crowd!"

It is known that officials at both schools are trying to get the game moved to the second Saturday of November as a season-ending climax. This would be appropriate and probably the best thing for both schools.

Anyway...Buying a frozen turkey at the grocery store may be easier in November. We are still suggesting tailgaters serve turkey sandwiches before the game, though. For an outstanding football series with deep roots in Thanksgiving, we consider it highly appropriate!

Derby Duel May Be First Win For Tribe Or The Blue Hose

Newberry and Presbyterian will renew the annual Bronze Derby rivalry .. but not on Thanksgiving.

Last Turkey Day, Newberry stole the Derby away at Clinton on the last rivalry game scheduled for the holiday. NCAA scheduling makes it nearly impossible to schedule a regular season game that late in the season anymore.

So, the Tribe and the Blue Hose will square off this Saturday at Setzler Field, 7 p.m. kickoff, with the Derby still at stake.

"It's going to feel a little different at first," said Mike Taylor, Newberry head coach, "but remember -- you have a '73 Presbyterian graduate and a '76 Newberry graduate squared off here. I would imagine the word pride will be mentioned very prominently in our talks this week."

There are on-going discussions on how the rivalry game can be re-scheduled for the second Saturday in November -- to keep the late season flavor of the series, which started in 1947, alive.

Missed opportunities and penalties were the main culprits in Newberry's 14-10 loss to Lenior-Rhyne last Saturday night at Setzler Field. This Saturday night's contest will be the last night game of the season at the Indians' stadium.

The Blue Hose come into the game with the same 0-2 record as the Indians, dropping a 17-16 game last Saturday at Charleston Southern. PC lost 20-17 at home to Fairmont State to open the season.

Entering his third season at the helm at the rival school from Clinton, John Perry welcomes back a Blue Hose team blessed with great experience in a number of places -- with several critical exceptions.

"Overall, we will try to climb over the hump (consecutive 4-7 records the last two years) this year. We must depend on some new faces, but if they have some success early, we could have a good year."

On defense, a Newberry County player is mentioned in Perry's plans for improvement. Senior cornerback Quincy Eigner from Mid-Carolina is listed as one of seven returning starters, headed by a secondary which highlights four starters. Along with Eigner, Tyron Phillips (seven interceptions last season), Todd Shearer and Jeff Wilson anchor the defense.

At running back, the Blue Hose have two weapons, Mason Gordon and Steve Gorie, but they must work with an untested group of quarterbacks. Senior Corey McKelvie and junior Todd Wofford lead the receiving corp for PC.

The Presbyterian roster also features Newberry players Eric Moore, a sophomore at tailback, and Wylie Rucker, a freshman at defensive back.

Sports

The Clinton Chronicle — Wednesday, September 22, 1993

Derby comes back to Clinton

By Rick Hendricks
Editor

Game 3

The Results
Presbyterian College 30
Newberry College 13

NEWBERRY—The 82nd renewal of the Bronze Derby battle between Presbyterian College and Newberry College featured a number of firsts.

Saturday night's contest represented the first Bronze Derby Classic not played on Thanksgiving Day in 50 years.

But the most important first in the 30-13 decision for the Blue Hose was that it was PC's initial victory of the season following two disappointing losses.

"We were an awfully frustrated football team," said a soaked and excited Blue Hose coach John Perry after the game. "We gained a lot of confidence...this is as big a rivalry as there is."

The difference in Saturday's win versus the prior two losses, said the coach, was that his team "got some breaks in our favor. We set the tempo early in the game with that long drive."

Indeed.

Led by freshman quarterback Randy Sullivan, who was making his first start after taking over in the second half for injured QB Chris Smith against Charleston Southern, the Blue Hose got on the board quickly.

PC took the opening kickoff and moved 69 yards in 11 plays.

Tailback Mason Gordon capped the drive with a 3-yard run and Frank Jordan's PAT gave the Blue Hose a 7-0 lead with 9:27 to play in the first quarter.

The Indians responded with a drive of their own after the ensuing kickoff. Taking the ball at its own 24, Newberry marched 76 yards in 13 plays. Indian quarterback Andy Thomason scored on a 2-yard run to get Newberry on the board. Jason Arnold added the extra point to tie the game at 7 with 3:56 to go in the quarter.

The teams remained deadlocked until about the 10-minute mark of the second quarter.

See DERBY Page 11

Derby
Continued From Page 10

Blue Hose cornerback Quincy Eigner recovered a Newberry fumble at the Indian 47 with 10:05 to go in the first half.

On the first play from scrimmage after the turnover, Sullivan hit fullback Steve Gorrie with a screen pass. Gorrie did the rest, outrunning the Indian defense to the end zone for the score. Jordan missed the PAT, but PC led 13-7 with 9:54 to go in the first half.

Again, Newberry came right back with a score of its own.

After the ensuing kickoff, the Indians took over at their own 27 and moved 73 yards in 9 plays. Fullback Tremayne Washington capped the drive with a 4-yard run to knot the score at 13. Arnold missed the PAT to leave the game tied, 13-13, with 6:21 to go in the first half.

It was PC's turn to respond, taking over at its own 30 after the ensuing kickoff and moving 70 yards on 9 plays in just a little over 3 minutes.

Gorrie, who played the game of his career with 167 yards rushing on 31 carries plus another 82 yards receiving, scored his second TD to put PC up for good. The sophomore scored from 4 yards out, then freshman Sparky Vaughn made the first PAT of his career to give the Blue Hose a 20-13 advantage with 3:52 remaining in the second quarter.

PC would score once more before halftime.

On Newberry's first play after the ensuing kickoff, PC linebacker Antonio Merriweather recovered a poor pitch by Thomason to give the Blue Hose the ball at the Indian 22.

Presbyterian would not score a TD on this possession, but Vaughn's first career field goal — a 26-yarder — put PC up 23-13 at the half.

The second half belonged to Gorrie and the Blue Hose defense.

Gorrie gained about 100 of his rushing yards in the second half, in part because poor field position in the final two quarters caused a conservative approach offensively by the PC coaching staff.

"We were determined not to mess up," said Perry.

Sullivan said the Blue Hose kept going to Gorrie because "that's what the defense was giving us."

The young QB tended to underestimate his own performance. Like any smart signal caller, Sullivan credited the play of the Blue Hose offensive line.

As did Gorrie. "The offensive line opened up some great holes."

Perry was very impressed with Sullivan's play in his first start. "Randy was tremendous," said the coach. "If he had a bad play, I don't know what it was."

For the record, Sullivan was 10-of-18 through the air for 157 yards and 1 TD, while rushing 7 times for 12 yards.

The Blue Hose defense came up with some big plays in the second half to keep Newberry off the scoreboard.

PC's defense, in fact, scored the clinching TD with 29 seconds to go in the game.

Newberry fumbled, and Blue Hose linebacker Damond Carr scooped up the loose ball and ran 39 yards for a touchdown. Vaughn added the PAT to give PC its final 30-13 margin.

"I think we wanted the Derby a lot more than they did," summed up Gorrie after the contest.

The Newberry Observer
AND HERALD & NEWS

"Just Like A Letter From Home"

Newberry, S. C., Monday, Sept. 20, 1993

PC Fullback Bulls Hose To Victory And Bronze Derby

BY VIC MacDONALD

Whoever took control of the second half -- that's who would win the game Saturday night at Setzler Field.

The prediction came from a man who should know -- retiring Presbyterian College athletic director Cally Gault, honored for his years of service to college athletics at halftime of the annual Newberry-Presbyterian Bronze Derby clash.

Gault, the winningest coach at PC in his 22 year history with the Hose, knows his football. His coaching in the Bronze Derby clash, much of it against former Indians coach Fred Herren, is legendary. His view this night, too, was right on -- PC held a 23-13 lead at the half and made it stand up for a 30-13 win in the 87th Derby Duel.

"Both teams just could not get it together," Gault said after being recognized by NC President Dr. Ray Bost at midfield. "You couldn't stop us. We couldn't hold anybody. That extra point will be big."

As it turned out, Jason Arnold's missed PAT in the second quarter -- the senior placekicker also missed a field goal -- wasn't the margin of victory. But neither team scored in the second half until Hunter Spivey fumbled the Indians' last gasp and Damond Carr rambled 39 yards for a touchdown.

Coming with 29 seconds left, the TD wasn't necessary -- Newberry could not erase a 10 point lead with dying seconds on the clock. For PC it was sweet revenge for last year's 14-0 home loss to an Indians' squad under a first-year head coach.

"We've had a lot of adversity. But this stands alone," PC coach John Perry exulted to his kneeling players at mid-field.

Clutching the Bronze Derby taken from its ceremonial stand, Perry yelled, "How 'bout that 32!" -- PC fullback Steve Gorrie, a sophomore from Snellville, Ga., took what the Indians defense offered and rambled 167 yards on 31 carries. He caught four passes for 82 yards.

Along with senior tailback Mason Gordon who suffered a pinched nerve, Gorrie fueled a PC offense that held the ball in the critical last three minutes of the game,

and had the game in hand. But when the drive finally stalled, Newberry's last gasp came with 55 seconds when the defense held PC on a fourth and one at the Indians' 15.

Unfortunately, there is no 10 point play. When Eric Green dropped a pass, Newberry's hopes for a quick score faded, but a catch moved the ball out to the 40. That's when the back-breaker happened -- freshman Spivey had the ball knocked loose and no one could touch Carr on his way to the endzone -- and a PC celebration.

Newberry's last serious threat came with eight minutes left and the ball at mid-field. A Thomason run and Skinner catch moved it to PC's 21 and Green went ahead for an important first down.

But, decked as he threw, Thomason tossed one of two interceptions on the night and stayed down for a while.

Thomason had suffered a shoulder injury in the SC State game but came back strong on game day last week against Lenoir-Rhyne. The sophomore quarterback ran for 29 yards against PC. The Hose freshman quarterback Randy Sullivan threw for 157 yards in his first start.

As the fourth quarter started, Heath Taylor's defense had stymied PC in its own territory forcing a third and six that the Hose could not convert. Just before, Nathan Broome's punt had pinned PC back at its own two yard line.

During the third quarter, untimely penalties hurt Newberry drives. A completion from Thomason to Steve Campbell -- the ball hit Campbell and his PC defender at the same time and bounced straight up with Campbell catching it coming down -- was negated by a hold. A PC interception ended that drive and put the Hose at mid-field.

On its first drive of the second half Newberry made it to the PC 21, converting a fourth and one. But the drive bogged down on a sack and Arnold missed a 35-yard field goal try. That, in Indians' coach Taylor's mind, was the game's turning point.

And it seemed to bear out ex-coach Gault's halftime observation -- "PC better hold them," he said. "This is a great rivalry."

"Gorrie won the game by himself," a frustrated Newberry coach Mike Taylor said. His team slipped to 0-3 for the second time at season-start in his two years at the Indians' helm.

Taylor said his defense appeared to be afraid, at times, to tackle Gorrie.

Taylor scoffed at the idea of a well-played first half -- compared to a scoreless second half.

PC had its scoring spurt at the end of the first half -- a Gorrie touchdown with four minutes left was followed by an Antonio Merriweather fumble recovery; the Tribe coughed it up five times on the night, losing three.

The fumble gave the Hose field position at the Newberry 22. The defense denied a PC first down bid on third and nine from the 11, forcing a Sparky Vaughn field goal. The quick 10 points broke a 13-13 tie with just 1:36 left in the half.

"We moved the ball on them," Taylor said. "We had a dropped pass on second and long, then we missed the field goal. That was the game right there."

PC's win overshadowed a stellar performance by Newberry's Eric Green -- 116 yards on 21 carries. Green almost single-handedly ran the ball into position for a Tremayne Washington four yard TD run in the second period. NC quarterback Andy Thomason dived over from the two for Newberry's first period score.

But Gorrie's two touchdowns -- a 47 yard pass and a four yard run -- along with Gordon's burst from three yards out on the opening series of the game, along with Vaughn's 26 yard field goal, sealed Newberry's fate.

Dean Skinner caught five passes for 53 yards to keep Newberry moving down the stretch, but key errors kept the Indians out of the endzone. Thomason's 86 yards through the air along with Spivey's 49 yards on two completions in a relief role proved the Indians could travel through the air for most of the game.

"We don't know how to finish anything," Taylor said.

With three minutes left, leading by 10, the Hose were driving to mid-field behind Gorrie's running

The Newberry Observer
AND HERALD & NEWS
"Just Like A Letter From Home"

Newberry, S. C., Monday, Sept. 20, 1993

PC Celebrates 1st Win

BY GENA EVANS

"Whoorip, there it is," the Presbyterian College Blue Hose football team exclaimed as the Bronze Derby was presented to them Saturday evening following the team's 30-13 win over Newberry.

The joy and jubilation on the visitors' side of Setzler Field was in sharp contrast to the dismay and despair of the Indians.

The victory, the first either team has had all season, was especially sweet for the three members of the Blue Hose squad who are from Newberry County.

Mid-Carolina High School graduate Quincey Eigner is a senior cornerback for P.C. He was also one of the team captains for the game.

He said that this win was one of the highlights of his life.

"This is just fantastic. It is great to beat Newberry, and especially in front of all these people I know. It just feels wonderful," he said.

Eric Moore, a sophomore reserve running back for the Blue Hose, is a graduate of Newberry High School.

He said that this win was extraordinarily exciting for him. "This game was more exciting for me than any other just because I knew more people here than at other away games. It feels really great to beat Newberry because I consider P.C. to be my home now," Moore said.

P.C. freshman Wylie Rucker, former quarterback at Newberry High, is being red-shirted this season. But he was on the sidelines Saturday as his team played in his hometown.

According to Rucker's mother, he was enjoying the game, even if he wasn't playing.

(Continued On Page 7)

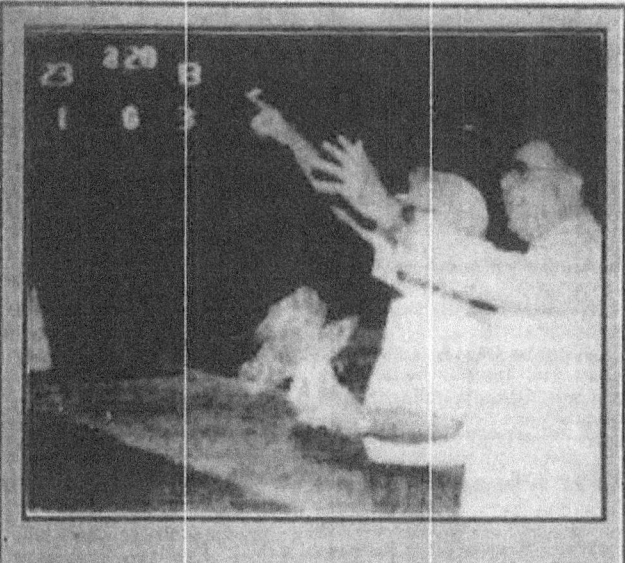

PC's retiring Athletic Director Cally Gault and Newberry President Dr. Ray Bost signal to the NC fans as the scoreboard reflects the halftime score in the annual Bronze Derby clash Saturday night.

(Continued From Page 1)

"Wylie's been standing at the back of the sideline, talking to everyone on the 'chain gang,' who are all from Newberry," Harriett Rucker said.

Rucker's brother, Brandt, was also on the Blue Hose team, but he decided to not play this year, and concentrate on his pre-law studies.

Mrs. Rucker said that living in Newberry, and pulling against the hometown team, has not been as difficult as it could have been.

"We are lucky that we have understanding friends. We pull for Newberry at every other game, but when these two teams play, we have to root for P.C.," she said.

Her husband John said that the game was good, not just because it matched two arch-rivals, but also because they were evenly matched teams.

"It's fun being at a game where the teams are so similar and so close together," Rucker said at halftime. "No matter who wins, it will be fun."

And for the Presbyterian Blue Hose and their fans it certainly was. The players took turns wearing the Bronze Derby at midfield.

For the Newberry Indians, there is the welcome news that for the past five games between Newberry and Presbyterian, the visiting team has won. Newberry, 14-0 winners at Bailey Stadium last year on Thanksgiving, will play P.C. in Clinton next year.

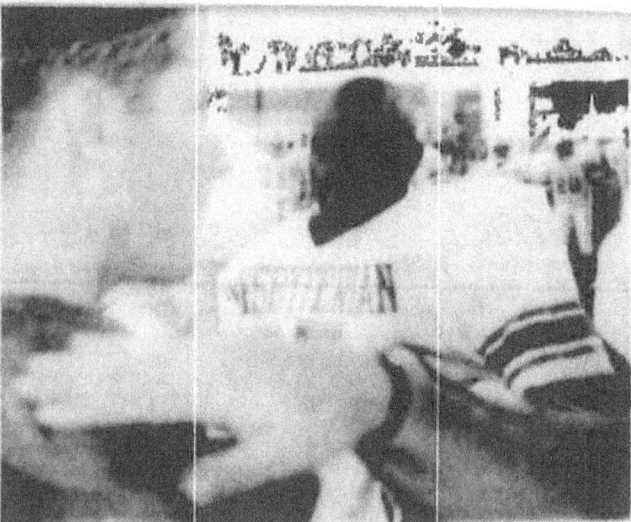

Mid-Carolina's Quincey Eigner

... serves as a captain for the Presbyterian Blue Hose during the coin-toss before Saturday's Derby Duel at Setzler Field.

SPORTS

Gorrie leads successful Derby mission

PC may have turned season around with resounding 30-13 decision

By Monte Dutton
Sports Editor

NEWBERRY — It's kind of unusual during the month of September to see the kind of celebration Presbyterian College's football team enjoyed Saturday night.

Then again, it's kind of unusual to see the Bronze Derby Classic played in September.

Led by the stirring performance of sophomore fullback Steve Gorrie, the Blue Hose defeated Newberry 30-13, effectively putting the futility of the season's first two weeks behind them.

And if in fact Presbyterian does recover from its 0-2 start to have a successful season, mark this in bold face: It happened here, on the Indians' Setzler Field.

Linebacker Damond Carr put the exclamation point on a powerful team statement with a 39-yard fumble return with 29 seconds to play, turning the already joyous PC bench into an ecstatic revel of dancing fools.

"It just bounced up into my hands," said Carr as his teammates passed the bronze headwear around nearby. "This means a lot. Coming into this season, I thought we could go 11 and 0. Right now, I think we can win the next eight."

Whoa, there. Let's take them one at a time, fellows. This is a team coming off two 4-7 seasons.

Gorrie — who rushed for 167 yards, caught 82 yards worth of passes and scored twice — also considered it far more than just a garden-variety win.

"It's really a big turnaround for this ballclub," he said. "We wanted it more than (Newberry) did, and we went out there and took it (the derby) from them."

Lest Gorrie's words seem a bit brash, it should be noted that Newberry head coach Mike Taylor concurred with every syllable.

"I felt like Gorrie won the game by himself," said Taylor. "He ran all over us. He's a heck of a fine player. We had some opportunities to tackle him, but I guess he was so good we were afraid of him. He punished us so bad we didn't want any part of him. That's what it looked like.

"That Steve Gorrie was a man among men," Taylor added. "I'm proud to see him play."

Freshman quarterback Randy Sullivan, still learning the nuances of doing his own laundry, proved that directing the Blue Hose offense comes naturally. Sullivan, who directed PC's fruitless comeback at Charleston Southern the previous week, played so well that listed starter Chris Smith never stepped onto the field. Sullivan completed 10 of 18 passes for 157 yards.

"Randy Sullivan, still a true freshman in his second ballgame, and I don't know if he had one single bad play," said Presbyterian head coach John Perry. "He had a lot of good ones. To be that young and

Staff Photo by Monte Dutton
INDOMITABLE — Presbyterian College fullback Steve Gorrie (32), said Newberry head coach Mike Taylor, was "a man among men" against the Indians Saturday.

Staff Photo by Monte Dutton
HEADLESS — Presbyterian's Antonio Merriweather steps up to make the stop on Newberry runner Tremayne Washington.

The Li'l That Was!

Advertiser

OFF THE BLOCK — Newberry College running back Eric Green (25), the Indians' leading rusher, cuts off blocker Sammy Gary's block on PC's Quincy Eigner (35). *Staff Photo by Monte Dutton*

---

not have bad plays is tremendous."

Both teams scored on their first possessions and both teams missed their second extra points. Other than that, the outcome was decided by Presbyterian's ability to make big plays and the likewise inability of Newberry to convert its ample opportunities.

After the two teams combined for 3 points in the first half (PC led 23-13), the second half settled into a pattern of failed Newberry scoring opportunities and long, time-consuming PC drives led by Sullivan and Gorrie.

"We've got to grow up or we're going to have a miserable year," said Taylor.

◆ See DERBY, Page 12A

◆ Derby

(Continued from Page 11A)

his 0-3 Tribe. "I don't know what to do about our football team because we don't know how to finish anything."

Taylor could easily have been describing the PC losses to Fairmont State and Charleston Southern.

What made the difference against Newberry? Could it have been something as simple as Cally Gault's oft-cited "fighting Blue Hose spirit"?

One and the same, said second-generation Blue Hose tackle John Edwards: "That's exactly what it was. We had intensity tonight, where the last couple of weeks we didn't."

"We cranked it up, we came in here with a mission to do, and we did it.

"Last year we weren't ready to play, and we were this year. That's what it boiled down to."

Newberry had won the final Thanksgiving Day edition of the game by a score of 14-0 in Clinton last year. The most recent game lifts Presbyterian's edge in the series to 49-28-5. The two teams began playing in 1913.

Newberry tailback Eric Green rushed for 116 yards and quarterback Andy Thomason passed for 86, but the competitiveness in terms of total offense yards (PC 378, Newberry 330) was an almost insignificant factor.

"We took the ball the length of the field to open up the second half," said Taylor. "We got it down there and drop a pass (before a missed field goal). That was the football game right there. We had to convert right there and make it 23 to 20.

"Then that drive in the fourth quarter would've been real interesting, wouldn't it?"

The latter drive ended with 5:21 remaining when Bernard Versen intercepted a Thomason pass on second-and-six from the PC 11.

Presbyterian	7	16	0	7—30
Newberry	7	6	0	0—13

P—Gordon 3 run (Jordan kick)
N—Thomason 2 run (Arnold kick)
P—Gorrie 47 pass from Sullivan (kick failed)
N—Washington 4 run (kick failed)
P—Gorrie 4 run (Vaughn kick)
P—Vaughn FG 26
P—Carr 39 fumble return (Vaughn kick)

	P	N
First downs	17	19
Rushes-yards	54-225	51-195
Passing yards	157	135
Passes C-A-I	10-18-0	12-23-2
Fumbles-lost	3-3	5-3
Punts-avg.	5-34.6	4-39.5
Penalties-yds.	7-45	5-40
Possession time	29:46	30:14

RUSHING: Presbyterian, Gorrie 31-167, Gordon 11-32, Yonce 5-14, Sullivan 7-12; Newberry, Green 21-116, Washington 7-35, Thomason 15-29, Hedgepeth 6-14, Broadwater 1-3, Smith 1-(-2).
PASSING: Presbyterian, Sullivan 10-18-0 157; Newberry, Thomason, 10-19-2 86, Spivey 2-4-0 49.
RECEIVING: Presbyterian, Gorrie 4-62, Yonce 3-31, Edwards 1-23, McKelvie 1-16, Jones 1-5; Newberry, Skinner 5-63, Campbell 2-11, Green 2-29, Castles 1-23, Sellers 1-14, Washington 1-5.

Attendance: 3,568.

THE BLUE STOCKING

"Give the people the light, so they may find the way."

Volume LXXXVIII Number 2 — PRESBYTERIAN COLLEGE — Clinton, South Carolina 29325 — October 7, 1993

Blue Hose football team suffers two tough losses

by Everett Catts
SPORTS EDITOR

Close but no cigar is a cliche which has been fitting for PC's 1993 football season. The Blue Hose are 1-4 (0-1 SAC), and all four of their losses have been by a margin of a touchdown or less.

On September 18, the Blue Hose defeated Newberry 30-13, regaining the Bronze Derby which they had lost last year. Steve Gorrie rushed for 168 yards on 31 carries and scored two touchdowns, on on a 47-yard reception, and another on a three-yard run. The PC offense punished Newberry, racking up 257 yards rushing and a total of 414 yards combined. Freshman Randy Sullivan, starting quarterback, was 10 for 18, passing for 157 yards. At halftime, the Blue Hose led Newberry 23-13. The Blue Hose defense allowed only two Newberry touchdowns and held the Indians scoreless in the second half. Interceptions by Todd Shearer, Jeff Wilson, and Bernard Vereen, and fumble recoveries by Quincy Eigner, Antonio Merriwether, and Damon Carr killed four Newberry drives in the last two quarters. Carr picked up the ball and ran 39 yards for a touchdown that broke Newberry's back with 29 seconds left.

On September 25, the Blue Hose played at Lenoir-Rhyne in their first conference game of the season. Lenoir-Rhyne led 10-7 at halftime. In the third quarter, PC took the lead with two Sparky Vaughn field goals and shut out Lenoir-Rhyne. In the fourth quarter, the Bears came back and tied the score at 20 with 4:50 remaining. PC had a chance to win with five seconds left, but Vaughn's 25-yard field goal attempt was blocked. In the first overtime, Sullivan scored on a one-yard run, but the Bears tied the score at 27-27, forcing a second overtime. In the second overtime, L-R scored and recovered a PC fumble, ending the game with a 34-27 loss.

On October 2, the Blue Hose lost to Wofford, 20-13. At halftime, the Terriers led 13-3, and PC's only scoring came on a Frank Jordan 40-yard field goal. In the third quarter, Jordan added a 39-yard field goal, making the score 20-6. In the final quarter, PC rallied. Randy Sullivan's four-yard pass to Chris Yonce made it a 20-13 Wofford lead. But PC's second drive was stopped when Sullivan was sacked on fourth down with 48 seconds left, giving Wofford the ball and the win.

Head Coach John Perry commented on the two losses, saying, "We had a chance to win all of our games, but we've just come up short."

The Li'l That Was!

November 1994

November 1	The NBA Chicago Bulls retired Michael Jordans #23 jersey.
November 2	The NFL announced that 2 expansion teams, the Carolina Panthers and the Jacksonville Jaguars, would be added to the league.
November 3	Sony released the first Playstation console.
November 3	Susan Smith, who had claimed her 2 children were carjacked, was arrested for murder.
November 3	A 4 minute 23 second total eclipse occurred in South America.
November 3	Small forward Glen Robinson signed a 10 year $68 million rookie contract with the Milwaukee Bucks, the highest rookie contract to date.
November 4	The first conference that focused on the commercial potential of the internet took place in San Francisco.
November 5	At 45 years old, George Foreman won the boxing heavyweight championship.
November 5	The space probe Ulyssus completed its first passage behind the sun.
November 5	Tony Rominger set a world record traveling 34.4 miles in one hour on a bicycle.
November 8	Singer and entertainer Sonny Bono was elected to the United States Congress.
November 8	In the United States House of Representatives, a 54 seat swing from the Democratic Party to the Republican Party resulted from the midterm elections. It was the largest swing since 1946.
November 9	Chandrika Kumaratunga was chosen the first female President of Sri Lanka.
November 10	Spanish golfer Jon Rahm was born.
November 11	American college basketball coach Frank McGuire passed away.
November 11	Olympic gold medalist track star Wima Rudolf passed away.
November 11	Microsoft founder Bill Gates purchased Leonardo da Vinci's "Codex" for $31 million.
November 12	Mark Martin won the 1994 Hooters 500 at Atlanta Motor Speedway and claimed his 14th career Winston Cup Series victory.
November 12	The Bronze Derby was played in Clinton, South Carolina. The Presbyterian College Blue Hose defeated the Newberry College Indians 24-13.

The Li'l That Was!

November 11, 1994 — The Laurens County Advertiser

An Independent Newspaper Founded in 1885/South Carolina's Award-Winning Semi-Weekly Newspaper

SPORTS

Hose, Newberry battle for Bronze Derby

♦ By Dave McCallum
Sports Editor

At first glance, you see two teams with identical 4-6 records and their only apparent incentive is to end the year on the winning note.

Then, you find out the two combatants are Presbyterian and Newberry which can mean only one thing in this area — it's Bronze Derby week.

The bitter rivals meet for the 83rd time Saturday at Bailey Memorial Stadium for a 2 p.m. clash. PC holds the series edge at 48-29-5, including last year's 30-13 victory at Newberry.

"It's one of those tradition-type rivalries which has gone on for years," Blue Hose coach John Perry said. "It's always a hard-fought game and it doesn't really matter what the teams' records are coming in."

This year's annual get-together could be a high-scoring affair considering both teams are averaging around 26 points a game, while the defenses are yielding about the same (PC-26.6, Newberry 29.3).

"Newberry is a lot like us in many respects," Perry said. "They've had their ups-and-downs all year and have had trouble lining up the same guys each week.

"They are a talented football team."

Newberry's pro-I offense is led by the tandem of tailback Keath Porterfield and quarterback Nathan Broome.

Porterfield needs only 137 yards against the Blue Hose to reach the 1,000-yard mark for the season.

"Their running game is really strong," said Perry. "They're a true option team who takes advantage of what you give them.

"We have to be able to find a way to slow Porterfield down, but because Broome has done a good job since he replaced their starter we have to be wary of him, too.

"Their offense has really come around with him (Broome) in there."

Leading the PC defensive charge will be pre-season All-South Atlantic Conference selection Antonio Merriweather, who recorded 10 tackles in last week's 33-24 loss to Gardner-Webb.

Merriweather has totalled 76 tackles — tops on the team. Teammate Jon Ory posted eight stops in last week's loss.

Presbyterian's defense will be minus one starter, defensive back Elton Pollack, who had knee surgery earlier this week.

Newberry's defense, led by defensive end Tracy Gooding, will present its own set of problems for a PC offense led by quarterback Randy Sullivan and fullback Steve Gorrie.

The Indians' will show a shade-50 look in an attempt to slow down Gorrie who rushed for a career-high 169 yards last week and had 167 against NC last year.

On the year, Presbyterian is averaging 371 yards total offense, headlined by 241 yards per game rushing.

"They (Newberry) really pursue the ball well," Perry said. "They've had some injury problems, but they've played solid football.

"They're a lot bigger than we are, so we can't just line up and play smash-mouth with them. We'll need to come up with ways to maintain control of the ball and keep it away from their offense."

Presbyterian keeps Bronze Derby

Hose uses late rally

♦ By Chris Burgin
For The Advertiser

The derby stays home! Thanks to the solid play of the Presbyterian defense, the coveted "Bronze Derby" will remain in Clinton for another year, following Saturday's 24-13 win over archrival Newberry.

PC finishes its season at 5-6 and strings together two straight wins over Newberry for the first time since the 1978 and 1979 campaigns when the Blue Hose had a string of three straight against the Indians dating back to 1977.

Saturday's game was not the offensive explosion many of the 3,579 fans that turned out for the 83rd renewal of the "Bronze Derby" clash, expected going in, as neither team crossed the goal line in the first half.

As a matter of fact, the only scoring came in the final five minutes of the second quarter

♦ See PC, Page 10A

HOSE FLYER — Presbyterian running back Steve Gorrie dives over a pile of Newberry defenders for a touchdown in PC's 24-13 victory Saturday at Bailey Memorial Stadium. The victory ensured the Blue Hose would keep the coveted Bronze Derby for a second consecutive year. PC finished its season at 5-6.
Photo by Dale Knight

The Li'l That Was!

Advertiser

November 16, 1994 — The Laurens County Advertiser

An Independent Newspaper Founded In 1885/South Carolina's Award-Winning Semi-Weekly Newspaper

SPORTS

◆ **PC**

(Continued from Page 9A)

on field goals by each squad.

PC's Brian Gorney opened the scoring with a 27-yard field goal with 4:45 remaining.

Newberry's Jeff Martin kicked a 20-yarder with six seconds remaining to tie the game at halftime.

The Indians, 4-7, who shot themselves in the foot with mistakes all game long, committed a big penalty on their first play from scrimmage.

After forcing Presbyterian to punt on the opening possession, the Indians went to the air as quarterback Hunter Spivey found wideout Steve Campbell for an apparent touchdown, but the pass was called back for offensive pass interference.

Newberry would punt it back to the Blue Hose without crossing midfield.

The second half was a tale of two quarters.

The third quarter belonged to Newberry, as it took a 13-3 lead into the fourth.

The Indians scored the game's first touchdown just 1:06 into the second half when tailback Keath Porterfield rambled in from two yards.

The plunge capped a a three-play, 59-yard drive with the big play coming on Spivey's 45-yard option run to PC's 14.

Newberry increased their lead to 10 when Martin connected on his second field goal, this one from 18 yards, with 1:36 left in the third.

Luckily for Blue Hose fans the fourth quarter belonged to Presbyterian, as the Blue Hose scored three times, including two touchdown passes from Randy Sullivan to Kevin Lindler.

The first, a 30-yarder, cut the deficit to 13-10 and the second, a 29-yarder gave PC a 17-13 lead with 10:18 remaining.

Presbyterian then salted the game away, as Steve Gorrie, capped a seven-play, 36-yard drive, with a one-yard plunge to make the score 24-13.

Gorrie, who was named to the South Atlantic Conference's first team offense, finished with 99 yards on 23 carries.

The Blue Hose were outgained on the ground by the Indians, 280-198.

Newberry	0	3	10 0	- 13
PC	0	3	0 21	- 24

PC—Gorney 27-yd FG
N—Martin 20-yd FG
N—Porterfield 2-yd (Martin PAT)
N—Martin 18-yd FG
PC—Lindler 30-yd pass from Sullivan (Gorney PAT)
PC—Lindler 29-yd pass from Sullivan (Gorney PAT)
PC—Gorrie 1-yd run (Gorney PAT)

	PC	N
First downs	22	17
Rushes-yards	60-198	40-280
Passing yards	220	143
Passes C-A-I	12-19-0	8-24-1
Fumbles-lost	1-0	4-4
Penalties-yds.	8-75	8-65

RUSHING: PC, Gorrie 23-99, Yonce 13-51, Sullivan 16-41, Grant 5-9, Griffin 2-2; Newberry, Spivey 10-128, Porterfield 20-101, Washington 7-32, Broome 1-18.

PASSING: PC, Sullivan 12-18-0—220, Yonce 0-1-0—0; Newberry, Spivey 8-24-1—143.

RECEIVING: PC, Yonce 3-52, Wofford 3-45, Lindler 2-59, Thorpe 2-24, Vickery 1-35, Gorrie 1-5; Newberry, Campbell 3-49, Broome 1-29, Broadwater 1-23, Washington 1-18, Skinner 1-12, Hedgepath 1-12.

Photo by Dale Knight

STAYING PUT — The prized Bronze Derby will be staying in Clinton for another year following Saturday's 24-13 Presbyterian victory over archrival Newberry. It marks the first time in 16 years PC has kept the coveted trophy for at least two consecutive years. The Blue Hose won three straight over NC from 1977-79.

10A Wednesday, November 16, 1994

Sports
The Clinton Chronicle

Hose explode

Presbyterian comeback leaves Derby in Clinton

Game 11

The Results
Presbyterian 24
Newberry 13

By Rick Hendricks
Editor

Presbyterian exploded for 21 fourth-quarter points Saturday en route to a 24-13 victory over arch-rival Newberry in the annual Bronze Derby Classic in Clinton.

For almost three quarters, the Blue Hose offense, in particular, seemed to be functioning in a fog and PC trailed, 13-3, with 1:36 to play in the third stanza.

A Newberry field goal that stretched the Indian lead to 10 points seemed to serve as a partial wake-up call for the Blue Hose offensive unit.

"Their eyes got big when they got down 13-3," PC head football coach John Perry said.

A 24-yard pass from sophomore quarterback Randy Sullivan to senior receiver Todd Wofford moved PC into Newberry territory after the ensuing kickoff following what turned out to be the Indians' last score of the contest.

Early in the fourth quarter, five plays into the drive, Sullivan connected with junior receiver Kevin Lindler on a 30-yard scoring pass to narrow the Newberry advantage. Freshman kicker Brian Gorney added the PAT to close the Indian lead to 13-10 with 14:35 left in the game.

After the defense forced Newberry to punt, the Blue Hose took over at their own 22 and were back in the end zone minutes later when the Sullivan-Lindler connection worked again — this time on a 29-yard TD strike. Gorney's PAT gave Presbyterian a 17-13 advantage with 10:18 left in the game.

Newberry got good field position after the ensuing kickoff, but on the Indians' second play from scrimmage, PC senior linebacker Damond Carr intercepted a Hunter Spivey pass and returned it 13 yards to the Newberry 36.

Carr said his pickoff was redemption, of sorts.

"In the first half, I dropped one (an interception)," the senior said. "I knew they were trying to draw us (the linebackers) up and dump it to the tight end behind us. I just figured out they were going to run that play and watched the quarterback and he threw it my way."

Carr said it meant a lot to him to come up with the interception in his final game for the Blue Hose —

See EXPLODE Page 11A

Explode

Continued From Page 10A

particularly in the Bronze Derby Classic.

"We were up 17-13 and somebody had to make a big play," he said.

Aided by a 17-yard scamper by Sullivan and a 15-yard jaunt by junior fullback Steve Gorrie, the Blue Hose quickly moved into scoring position again following Carr's interception.

Gorrie's 1-yard plunge extended PC's lead. Gorney's PAT gave the Blue Hose a 24-13 advantage with 6:30 remaining.

Newberry got another chance, however, but again turned the ball over as freshman linebacker Michael Cook recovered a fumble for PC at the Blue Hose 33 with 5:14 left in the contest.

Presbyterian held onto the ball for the remainder of the contest and captured its second straight Bronze Derby Classic.

The late comeback was due to the fact that PC "started getting a lot of breaks," according to Sullivan.

Perry said another factor was the play of the defense, which did a good job of keeping the Blue Hose in the game in the first half.

"The defense played great," said Sullivan. "We had a lot of three-and-outs and they kept us in the game."

The quarterback said the offense was "sluggish" at the beginning of the contest, while Newberry seemed to be very fired up to play.

"They were pumped up and we came out sort of flat," said Sullivan.

Gorrie said the Indians had a good game plan and were keying on him initially.

As the game wore on, he said, "the pass set up the run and the offense got clicking, then the defense was enthused about what the offense was doing."

Gorrie said the Blue Hose didn't block as well as they were capable of in the first half.

"We finally got a wake-up call with the field goal and the fact they didn't have 25 or 30 points," said the fullback.

Gorrie said the season has been a roller coaster, as the Blue Hose wound up 5-6 on the year, but it was "great to end the season with a win."

Perry said it is difficult to point to exactly what led to the PC comeback.

"Your character shows in those situations," said the Blue Hose coach. "We just wore them down."

Presbyterian wound up totalling 418 yards of offense — 198 on the ground and 220 through the air.

Sullivan completed 12-of-18 passes for 220 yards and 2 touchdowns.

Gorrie led the ground game with 23 rushes for 99 yards and a touchdown.

Altogether, the Blue Hose defense made 8 tackles for loss in the contest.

Blue Hose Notes: PC's victory over Newberry gives Presbyterian a 49-29-5 advantage in the long-time rivalry...Perry is 7-4 against the Indians in his head coaching career, 3-1 at PC...Gorney extended his streak of successful extra points to 29...Lindler's TD catches were the first and second of his career at Presbyterian...The Blue Hose won 4-of-6 outings at Bailey Memorial Stadium, but won only 1-of-5 contests on the road.

Presbyterian head football coach John Perry...
...With Derby in hand after Blue Hose defeated Newberry

Photo by Fletcher Pruitt Jr.

Newberry	0	3	10	0	-13
Presbyterian	0	3	0	21	-24

Second Quarter
PC-FG Gorney 27
N-FG Martin 20

Third Quarter
N-Porterfield 2 run (Martin kick)
N-FG Martin 18

Fourth Quarter
PC-Lindler 30 pass from Sullivan (Gorney kick)
PC-Lindler 29 pass from Sullivan (Gorney kick)
PC-Gorrie 1 run (Gorney kick)

	Newberry	PC
First Downs	17	22
Rushes-Yds.	40-280	60-198
Passing	24-8-1	19-12-0
Passing Yds.	143	220
Total Yds.	423	418
Fumbles-Lost	4-4	1-0
Penalties	8-65	8-75

INDIVIDUAL LEADERS

Rushing--Newberry, Spivey 10-128, Porterfield 20-101, Washington 7-32, Broome 1-18, Broadwater 2-1; PC, Gorrie 23-99, Yonce 13-51, Sullivan 16-41, Grant 5-9, Griffin 2-2.

Passing--Newberry, Spivey 24-8-1 143 yds.; PC, Sullivan 18-12-0 220 yds, Yonce 1-0-0 0 yds.

Receiving--Newberry, Campbell 3-49, Broome 1-29, Broadwater 1-23, Washington 1-18, Skinner 1-12, Hedgepath 1-12; PC, Lindler 2-59, Yonce 3-52, Wofford 3-45, Vickery 1-35, Thorpe 2-24, Gorrie 1-5.

The Li'l That Was!

The Li'l 🎩 That Was!

The Newberry Observer
AND HERALD & NEWS
"Just Like A Letter From Home"

Newberry, S. C. Monday, Nov. 14, 1994

Presbyterian's 4th Quarter Attack Sinks The Indians

Presbyterian College unleashed an offense spurt and took advantage of five Newberry turnovers to beat the Indians 24-13 Saturday in the annual Bronze Derby Classic at Clinton.

Newberry took a 10-point lead into the fourth quarter but could not hold it. Presbyterian's 21 fourth quarter points were more than enough to overcome a Newberry offense that fumbled four times, losing all four.

The win improved PC to 5-6 on the season; Newberry fell to 4-7. The Blue Hose have won the Bronze Derby, symbol of football supremacy between the neighboring colleges for two seasons; the last time Newberry won the Derby was 1992, the last time the game was played on Thanksgiving. The Classic now is scheduled as the last game of the season for the traditional rivals.

PC leads the series 49-29-5.

Newberry settled for a 20-yard field goal after driving to the PC one-yard line in the third quarter, and that was the end of the scoring on the afternoon for the Indians. The Tribe had hit on a 20-yard field goal in the second quarter, and the half had ended 3-3. Newberry scored a TD on its first drive of the second half, but lost two other scoring chances in the third quarter on fumbles.

Presbyterian's offense then struck in the fourth quarter on two touchdown passes and a TD run by Steve Gorrie.

Keath Porterfield led Newberry on the ground, rushing 20 times for 101 yards, and quarterback Hunter Spivey added 128 yards on 10 rushes. Gorrie ran 23 times for 99 yards for Presbyterian.

Randy Sullivan passed 18 times, completing 12 for 220 yards for the Blue Hose. Spivey completed just eight of 24 passes for 143 yards, and threw the key fourth quarter interception that sent the PC offense on its way to the game-winning explosion.

Presbyterian scored its first touchdown on the second play of the fourth quarter, while Newberry had an 80-yard touchdown pass on the first play of the game called back for offensive pass interference.

The Indians were penalized eight times for 65 yards by an officiating crew from the South Atlantic Conference, of which Presbyterian is a member school.

	New	PC
First downs	17	22
Rushes-yards	40-260	60-198
Passing	143	220
Comp-att-I	8-24-1	12-19-0
Fumbles-lost	4-4	1-0
Punts-avg.	5-43.4	8-37.6
Return yds	0	68
Penalties-yards	8-65	8-75
Time of Poss.	23:32	36:28

Newberry	0	3	10	0	-13
Presbyterian	0	3	0	21	-24

PC — FG Gorney 27
N — FG Martin 20
N — Porterfield 2 run (Martin kick)
N — FG Martin 19
PC — Lindler 30 pass from Sullivan (Gorney kick)
PC — Lindler 29 pass from Sullivan (Gorney kick)
PC — Gorrie 1 run (Gorney kick)

INDIVIDUAL STATISTICS
RUSHING Newberry, Porterfield 20-101, Spivey 10-128, Washington 7-32, Broome 1-18, Broadwater 2-1. PC, Gorrie 23-99, Yonce 13-51, Sullivan 16-41, Grant 5-9, Griffin 2-2.
PASSING: Newberry, Spivey 8-24-1-143. PC, Sullivan 12-18-0-220, Yonce 0-1-0-0.
RECEIVING: Newberry, Campbell 3-49, Broome 1-29, Broadwater 1-23, W. shington 1-18, Skinner 1-12, Hedgepath 1-2. PC, Lindler 2-59, Yonce 3-52, Wilford 3-45, Vickery 1-35, Thorpe 2-24, Gorrie 1-5.

THE BLUE  STOCKING

"All for PC   PC for all"

Volume LXXXIII, Number 4   PRESBYTERIAN COLLEGE   Clinton, South Carolina 29325   November 22, 1994

PC to keep Bronze Derby following Newberry win

by Everett Catts
STAFF WRITER

Sitting on the PC bench was the sacred Bronze Derby, the hat that marks the rivalry between Presbyterian and Newberry, schools that are 20 miles apart. In the 83rd battle between the two squads, the Blue Hose fought to keep the derby at home for two straight years for the first time since 1986. Although PC held a 49-28-5 overall record against the Indians coming into the game, the home team had not won the Bronze Derby Classic since 1989. Last year, the Blue Hose won in Newberry, 30-13.

After three unsuccessful offensive possessions, PC finally got on the board with Brian Gorney's 27-yard field goal. Gorney had attempted a 45-yarder, but it was blocked by Newberry's Karras Cohen. On the Indians' next possession, Earl Guidry recovered a Keith Porterfield fumble at the PC 24-yard line. Unfortunately, the Blue Hose could do nothing offensively and punted the ball away. Newberry's Jeff Martin kicked a 20-yard field goal to tie the score at 3-3 and to end the first quarter.

While PC's offense remained stagnant, the Indians tacked on a touchdown and another field goal to give them a 13-3 edge at the end of the third quarter.

But like the quick switch of a light bulb, the Blue Hose went on a scoring spree. Twenty-five seconds into the fourth quarter, PC found the endzone when wideout Kevin Lindler caught a 30-yard pass from quarterback Randy Sullivan, capping a 67-yard, five-play drive. On their next possession, the Hose drove 78 yards in seven plays and tallied another seven on Lindler's 29-yard reception. The TD gave the Blue Hose a 17-13 lead. Set up by Damond Carr's 30-yard interception return 53 seconds later, PC increased its lead to 24-13 on Steve Gorrie's one-yard scamper. Another Blue Hose score by Chris Griffin was called back by a penalty, and the game ended with PC on top, 24-13.

The defense was the story of the game, recovering all four Indian fumbles and shutting out Newberry in the fourth quarter. Although the Indians racked up 423 total yards, they were held scoreless in ten possessions. Leading the defense was Carr, who had eight tackles, a broken up pass, an interception and a tackle for a loss. PC had eight tackles for a loss, three by Jon Ory.

Offensively, the Blue Hose were led by Gorrie's 99 rushing yards on 23 carries, and Sullivan's 220 yards passing (12 of 18, 2 TD's and no INT's).

"The Bronze Derby is a big game for us. I've been associated with it as a player, spectator or coach for 25 years. The players get into it and realize how big it is, and how important it is. It makes the winner better than the loser with recruiting, spring practice and the next season, having won the ball game," said head coach John Perry.

Perry also commented on his players' pride and confidence in bouncing back to win after a loss, something the Blue Hose did on four occasions.

"I think because of the way our season went, it really showed the team's character. We lost a couple of heartbreakers against Elon and Gardner-Webb. If you don't overcome those games emotionally, you could send your season into a tailspin. But our team bounced back," Perry added.

In the previous week, PC lost one of those "heartbreakers", as Gardner-Webb took the lead with 37 seconds left, and later ran back an interception for a touchdown, stopping the Blue Hose's comeback attempt and winning 33-24. Gorrie led PC on the ground with 169 yards rushing, while Sullivan threw for 184 yards in the air. Antonio Merreweather led the Blue Hose defense with ten tackles.

Back on October 29 PC bounced back from two straight losses by crushing Wingate 49-14. The Blue Hose scored twice on interception returns by Carr and Tyron Phillips, and PC's offense racked up 403 yards rushing. Sullivan, Chris Yonce, Terrance Grant and Griffin had 121, 102, 96 and 72 yards, respectively.

PC finished the season 5-6 overall and sixth in the SAC-8 (2-5). Enabled by a tough line led by second team All-SAC center Chris McGaha, the Blue Hose offense averaged a school record 375 yards per game. McGaha helped open holes up the middle for Gorrie, who was PC's lone first team All-SAC selection and rushed for 989 yards in ten games (99 ypg), both second in the SAC-8.

Representing the Blue Hose defense on the second team were Merreweather, who had 82 tackles (seventh in SAC-8) and six tackles for a loss, and Phillips, who had 65 stops, four interceptions and seven passes broken up, and ranked second in the SAC-8 in kickoff returns (23.5 yards per return).

THE INDIAN

Newberry College, Newberry, SC   Nov. 17, 1994, Vol. 66, No. 3

Team unity and school spirit: not enough for PC

By: NARA SELLERS
Sports Editor

Team unity and school spirit are two emotions that could be felt at the start of the Newberry vs. Presbyterian Bronze Derby game. "We all need to pull together as a team in order to win," expressed junior wide receiver Willie Sellers. The Indians went into the game with a record of four wins and seven losses. The Blue Hose were only one game up on the Indians with a record of five wins and six losses. Both teams had the strive and heart to win, but only one team could be the winner. "We have four starters out but they have been replaced by some strong players," said defensive player Jeramiah Jones. So far it hasn't effected our game in a negative way." The Indians have played a good season despite the four starters that are out with knee injuries.

Because both teams were matched defensively and offensively, each player knew that the winning team would be the team with the most heart, strive and dedication. Sophomore quarterback Hunter Spivey felt that Newberry could win the game if they put it all together." Did they put it all together? According to Presbyterian fullback Steve Gorrie, the Indians played a good game just not good enough.

The tension was high and the overall moral of the crowd was incredible. But the Derby stays in Clinton for now, but the team is looking forward to next year when they can bring it back to Newberry. The Indians left Blue Hose territory with a loss of 24-13.

Sophomore wide receiver Rico Cannon and junior wide receiver Willie Sellers discuss upset of the Bronze Derby game. -- Photo by Nara Sellers

Calling All Sports Writers!

If you enjoy sports and enjoy writing about sports The Indian wants YOU! See any staff member for more information.

November 1995

The Li'l That Was!

November 3	British actor John Orchard of "M*A*S*H" passed away.
November 3	The Boston Celtics lost to the Milwaukee Bucks 101-100 in the first game at FleetCenter in Boston, Massachusetts.
November 3	The Portland Trail Blazers lost to the Vancouver Grizzlies 92-80 in the first game at Rose Garden in Portland, Oregon.
November 3	The Toronto Raptors beat the New Jersey Nets 94-79 in the first game played at SkyDome in Toronto, Canada.
November 5	Canadian Prime Minister Jean Chretien survived an assassination attempt.
November 5	American actor Edward Egan of "The French Connection" passed away.
November 5	The Toronto Grizzlies beat the Minnesota Timberwolves 100-98 OT in the first game played at General Motors Place.
November 5	While taking questions from reporters on Air Force 1, United States President Bill Clinton emphasized American commitment to Israel and the peace process.
November 6	Owner Art Modell officially announced that the NFL Cleveland Browns were moving to Baltimore, Maryland.
November 6	Israel buried their 5th Prime Minister of Israel Yitzhak Rabin. The Prime Minister was assassinated by an extremist who opposed peace with the Palestines.
November 6	American actress Aneta Corsaut, better known as Helen Crump on "The Andy Griffith Show" passed away.
November 7	The Howard Stern radio show premiered in Pittsburgh, Pennsylvania. In addition, Stern released his book *Miss America*.
November 10	"Ace Ventura : When Nature Calls" is released and became the #1 movie in November.
November 10	In Nigeria, playwright and environmental activist Ken Saro-Wiwa is hanged along with 8 other supporters by government forces.
November 11	"Fantasy" by Mariah Carey was the #1 song on the *Billboard* Top 100
November 11	"Mellon Collie and the Infinite Sadness" by The Smashing Pumpkins was the #1 album on the *Billboard* Top 100.
November 11	The Bronze Derby was played in Newberry, South Carolina. The Newberry College Indians defeated the Presbyterian College Blue Hose 9-8.

The Li'l  That Was!

Ready To Break An Indians' Record

Junior runningback Keath Porterfield, #20, is on the verge of breaking a Newberry College football record that has stood for 25 years. With 1,212 yards rushing for the season, Porterfield finished Saturday's game against the Carson Newberry just seven yards away from the season rushing record, held by Don Garrick. Porterfield, from Lexington, topped the 1,000 yard mark two weeks ago against Catawba, and his 144 yards against the highly regarded Eagles defense put him in a position to set a new single-season rushing record this Saturday against Presbyterian; the Bronze Derby game is 2 p.m. at Setzler Field. Porterfield has said his goal for the season was to run for at least 1,300 yards against Newberry opponents.

Newberry vs. PC -- Ball Run Starts Activities

Seasons of sports overlapping at Newberry College means the Indians will be on the basketball court Friday night and the gridiron Saturday afternoon, as roundball starts and football ends for the season.

Starting the annual activities will be the Clinton to Newberry "Game Ball Run" sponsored by fraternities. Businesses have donated to this event based on the miles that will be run, and proceeds will benefit the Boys Farm in Newberry.

Alpha Tau Omegas from Newberry and Pi Kappa Alphas from Presbyterian are participating this year. The ATOs will run about 15 miles in this year's event. Presidents of both colleges will present the money at halftime.

Not to be outdone in their community service, the members of the Newberry College baseball team assisted with the annual NC vs PC Blood Drive Monday at MacLean Gym. But it's football that takes the center stage for this weekend.

The annual Bronze Derby game against Presbyterian will be at 2 p.m. Saturday at Setzler Field. In addition to a chance to bring back the bronzed hat symbol of bragging rights between the two church-supported neighbor schools, a win by Newberry will highlight a record-breaking performance by junior runningback Keath Porterfield.

He will break the single-season rushing record, which has stood since 1970 when it was set by Indians' runner Don Garrick, with just seven more yards. The record could fall on Newberry's first possession of the game, as Porterfield has been the Tribe's "go-to" player this season, a 4-6 campaign for Newberry.

The Indians had their fi... game mid-season winning str... snapped 39-30 by Car... Newman last week. The Indi... had lost five straight before... Eagles, seventh ranked in t... nation in NCAA Division II, sl... down the Tribe's offense in t... fourth quarter. A Newbe... touchdown that would have m... it a three-point game inside...

(Continued On Pag...)

The Newberry Observer
AND HERALD & NEWS
"Just Like A Letter From Home"

final minute was called back by a procedure penalty.

Porterfield's 144 yards rushing against the Eagles put him in a position to shatter Garrick's record with a good performance against the Blue Hose. In his senior season, Porterfield can look at breaking the career rushing mark for the Indians -- he gained just under 1,000 yards last year, and the career mark is 3,244 by John Nesbitt (1982-85).

The Hose, 6-4 on the season, bring in their own high-powered back, senior Steve Gorrie, already a 1,000 yard rusher and holder of PC rushing records.

in the crowded sports schedule at the local Lutheran college, volleyball action for the season ends tonight (Nov. 8) with the Lady Indians hosting Southern Wesleyan (7 p.m. at Eleazer Arena).

And then, Friday night, the Newberry College men's basketball team warms up Bronze Derby weekend with a 7 p.m. game against Crossfire, an exhibition team which brings a Christian message to its games. Proceeds benefit the Crossfire Ministry.

The Porterfield-Gorrie match-up could be the story of the game as both teams want to salvage their seasons by taking the Bronze Derby, which PC kept last season by defeating Newberry. The Indians last won the Derby in 1992, the last time the traditional rivalry game was played on Thanksgiving. Since traditions die hard at Newberry, turkey sandwiches and turkey barbecue may be the food of choice at the tailgating before and after the "Turkey Day" contest.

November 10, 1995 — The Laurens County Advertiser

SPORTS

Blue Hose look to retain Bronze Derby

By Dave McCallum
Sports Editor

It stands alone as far as games go for Presbyterian coach John Perry.

And only three words need be spoken to get the blood boiling on both sides — Presbyterian versus Newberry.

The old-time combatants meet for the 84th time Saturday at 2 p.m. in Newberry for the coveted Bronze Derby. PC leads the series 50-28-5.

"It's a big game in many respects — for our institution, the players, the alumni, the proximity of the schools (20 miles) and the rivalry which has developed over the years," said Perry whose squad has won the last two meetings including a 24-10 decision a year ago in Clinton.

PC, 6-4, will enter the Setzer Field turf red-hot with a four-game winning streak in tow including a 34-20 road victory over Gardner-Webb last week.

Newberry, 4-6, had a four-game win streak of its own snapped last Saturday in a 39-30 loss to Carson-Newman.

Perry says playing Newberry last makes the Blue Hose's schedule tough and unique at the same time.

"It's tough because we're coming off seven emotion-charged league games where we've been trying to win a

◆See PC, Page 11

◆ PC

(Continued from Page 9)

championship and then there's Newberry," he said. "Newberry, as an independent, puts its whole year on their two rivalries — us and Wofford.

"Even though, we've been through the league schedule with a lot of emotion we realize we have to step it up one more week and be at a high emotional pitch.

"There have been a lot of people come before us playing for the Bronze Derby and we've tried to convey that point and how important a game it is to people around here. Our kids, who have played in this game the last couple of years, know the importance."

The game could be one with some offensive fireworks. PC is averaging 24.6 points per game, while Newberry is coming off a 30-point performance a week ago against Carson-Newman.

The Indians' I-formation attack is led by standout tailback Keath Porterfield.

Porterfield, who needs only seven yards to set a school record for rushing yards, netted 138 in the loss last week.

"He's a big kid who runs hard and fast," Perry said. "We have to try and not let him get in the seams and do damage."

Quarterback Hunter Spivey engineers the offensive unit. When the Indians go to the air, Spivey looks to wide receivers Ike Allred and Rico Cannon.

Defensively, Newberry will give the Blue Hose a shade-50 look which features some beef up front, Perry said.

SPORTS

November 15, 1995 · The Laurens County Advertiser

PC loses to Newberry in Derby battle

By Dave McCallum
Sports Editor

The game and the Bronze Derby which goes to the victor was seemingly in hand for Presbyterian with two minutes left Saturday afternoon at archrival Newberry.

However, like the muddy Setzler Field, both slipped from the Blue Hose's grasp, as Newberry rallied for nine points in the final 1:35 to steal a 9-8 victory over PC.

"Obviously this is a very tough loss," said Presbyterian coach John Perry whose squad finished its season at 6-5. "We apparently have the game won and then lose it.

"The guys played hard. We did what we wanted to: we just fumbled the football."

After Newberry's Keath Porterfield scored with 1:35 remaining to cut the deficit to 8-6, PC recovered the onsides kick and looked set to run out the clock for the victory.

The Blue Hose coaching staff, after quarterback Randy Sullivan downed the ball at NC's 43, decided to give the ball to reliable fullback Steve Gorrie on second down.

Gorrie, though, was striped of the ball and Newberry recovered at its 45.

"It was a heartbreaker," said Gorrie, PC's all-time leading rusher with 3,486 yards. "It is certainly not the way I wanted to go out in my final game.

"I thought I was down on the play (fumble), but the officials made the call and that is their job."

Newberry, without any timeouts, then went to the air and quarterback Hunter Spivey connected on a 34-yard strike to tight end Willie Sellers to PC's 11.

After three plays, Indian freshman kicker Matt Deaton booted the game-winning 24-yard field goal with 25 seconds remaining.

"This kind of thing has happened time and time again in this series," said Perry. "It just didn't work out for us Saturday.

"Our defense, our offense and special teams played well considering the field conditions.

"Newberry is a good football team and they hung in there the entire game."

The contest was played much of the time in rain and muddy conditions.

PC went on top on Newberry's second possession when the Indian center snapped the ball through the end zone for a safety and a 2-0 Blue Hose advantage.

Presbyterian upped its cushion to 5-0 on the final play of the quarter when junior placekicker Chris Kinert booted a 32-yard field goal.

Kinert's kick, the first of two, capped an 11-play, 38-yard scoring march.

Gorrie, who finished with 82 yards on 24 carries, did much of the damage netting 16 yards on the probe.

The score stayed that way until midway in the third quarter when Kinert split the uprights from 30 yards for an 8-0 Blue Hose advantage.

The field kick culminated a short four-play, 18-yard march which was set by freshman cornerback Troy Gamble's fumble recovery.

Newberry, 5-6 and winner of four of its last five games, didn't get untracked until late in the contest.

The Indians got on the board when Porterfield rambled 16 yards to cap a 10-play, 84-yard march.

Spivey's two-point pass attempt fell incomplete leaving PC on top 8-6.

NOTES

In addition to his career rushing record, Gorrie set single season marks for points (122) and touchdowns (20). He led the Blue Hose in receiving for all four of his seasons at Clinton.

Kinert tied the single-season percentage record for point-afters hitting all 18 of his attempts. Sandy Cruickshanks and Chris Wingo hit 21 straight in 1968 and 1986, respectively).

PC's offense set a new school single-season record for total offense averaging 381.6 yards per game. The mark eclipsed the one Presbyterian established last year.

Photo by Dale Knight

AIR BATTLE — Presbyterian defensive Troy Gamble (33) attempts to break up a pass intended for Newberry's Rico Cannon during the Bronze Derby game Saturday in Newberry. The host Indians kicked a 25-yard field goal in the closing seconds to nip PC, 9-8, and reclaim the Bronze Derby. The Blue Hose finished their season at 6-5.

The Newberry Observer
AND HERALD & NEWS
"Just Like A Letter From Home"

Newberry, S. C., Monday, Nov. 18, 1996

The Li'l That Was!

The Derby Comes Home!

—Observer Photos by Vic MacDonald

Newberry College players, above, celebrate the return of the Bronze Derby to Setzler Field Saturday afternoon after a 9-8 win over Presbyterian College. Head Coach Mike Taylor, below, was hoisted to the shoulders of his players with the Derby, symbol of "bragging rights" between the church-supported neighboring colleges, in a wild post-game celebration at mid-field.

Late Field Goal Lifts NC, 9-8

BY VIC MacDONALD

Matt Denton's 24 yard field goal with 17 seconds left brought the Bronze Derby home to Newberry College Saturday in a thrilling 9-8 Indians' win.

The freshman from Lancaster said in a wild post-game celebration on a rain-soaked field that he had been in pressure situations before in high school but he admitted to being scared this time. He said all the Indians' players knew going in the importance of this game for the Newberry seniors.

"You know the tradition," Denton said, "but you don't really know it 'til you're out there."

Keath Porterfield's 16 yard TD run with 1:35 left in the game set the stage for the winning points. Porterfield ran through a PC defensive back at the five and dragged defenders with him into the endzone, falling over from the one.

"It was the toughest

(Continued On Page 7)

The Li'l That Was!

The Newberry Observer
AND HERALD & NEWS
"Just Like A Letter From Home"

ESTABLISHED 1865 — Newberry, S. C., Monday, Nov. 13, 1995

(Continued From Page 1)

touchdown I ever made. But I was determined there was no way I would go down less than three yards away," Porterfield said. "I knew I couldn't cut because of the wet field."

For the game, Porterfield's 95 yards gave him 1,307 on the season, topping Don Garrick's 1,219. Garrick didn't mind; he and buddies at an Indian Club dinner afterward it's surprising the record stood for 25 years. "If that record was never broken," the former runningback now an Orangeburg businessman and active Indians' supporter said, "we're not recruiting right."

Garrick still holds the record for career carriers, although he expects Porterfield to top that mark, too, and the longest run from scrimmage -- 90 yards.

Porterfield broke the record with two carries on Newberry's first possession in a monsoon-like first quarter opening of the game, and coach Mike Taylor already had decided the game would not be stopped.

"This isn't basketball or baseball where they stop the game for records," Taylor said.

Three quarters of soggy, sloppy football later, Taylor said he didn't even watch Deaton's field goal attempt -- a cheerleader told him it was through the uprights.

As PC got the ball back with 17 seconds left, Taylor stood away from his team while Porterfield tried to distract him and two players sneaked from behind with an ice-filled water cooler. Not until :05 would Taylor let them splash his rain-soaked jacket with the ceremonial "coach dunking," and he walked back to the team who ran onto the field.

They hoisted Taylor, clutching the Bronze Derby, onto their shoulders.

Talking about the game's wild finish, the Indians' coach said he'd already decided to on-side kick and try to get in a position for the win before trying for a two-point conversion after Porterfield scored. The two-point pass that would have tied the game fell short to Rico Cannon after junior quarterback Hunter Spivey somehow avoided a blind side PC rusher.

"I told the team we're going for two but don't panic -- we're going to on-side kick anyway. We had a tough time getting to that point," Taylor said.

PC recovered the onside kick but two plays later quarterback Randy Sullivan handed off to Steve Gorrie, PC's most reliable runner -- who fumbled.

"I thought I was down but the officials made the call and that's their job," Gorrie said of the critical mistake with just 51 second left. Gorrie closed out his PC career as the college's all-time leading rusher, 3,486 yards, and top TD maker, 42. For the game, the NC defense held him to 83 yards -- Gorrie's PC career to date had 14 100 plus yards games.

"It was a heartbreaker. It is certainly not the way I wanted to go out," Gorrie said.

But even after the Gorrie fumble, NC was a long way from a win -- with no timeouts. It took a Spivey to tight end Willie Sellers 34 yard reception to set up the winning field goal. Sellers, a senior from Florence, was one of five receivers who caught Spivey passes for a total of 104 yards through the air on the treacherous Setzler Field turf.

For PC's Randy Sullivan, the yardage was better -- 127 through the air -- but he was intercepted three times -- twice by Shawn Wylie and once by Tony Sullivan - and his longest completion, 50 yards to Ben Power, resulted in a Power fumble at the end of the play, recovered by Jason Gambrell.

Newberry actually fumbled more than PC -- five losing two -- while the Blue Hose fumbled twice and lost both. But the PC miscues were most costly - Tracy Gooding, senior defensive lineman, was credited with recovering Gorrie's critical late fumble.

"For Tracy Gooding and Ron Reese, this is their 43rd game starting. That's got to be a record, certainly a Newberry record. That ought to be written up somewhere," Taylor said after the game.

About the Bronze Derby, Taylor said its importance is as a symbol of the football rivalry. "It's ended up 2-2 the last four years. This is one people will talk about for a long time. ... This is a proud team," the Indians' coach said. "Our guys did the job when it had to be done."

With a 5-6 season now behind them, the Indians look back to a disastrous second half at Mars Hill as the time they turned things around. Since then, Taylor said after Saturday's Derby-winning game, "We're 5-1."

PRESBYTERIAN VS. NEWBERRY
SCORING SUMMARY

Score by quarters	1	2	3	4	Final
Presbyterian	5	0	3	0	8
Newberry	0	0	0	9	9

1st Quarter
PC, 5:32, safety -- bad snap, 2-0
PC, :01, Kinert 32 yd. FG, 11-39, 5-0.

3rd Quarter
PC, 7:37, Kinert, 30 yd. FG, 4-18, 8-0.

4th Quarter
Newberry, 1:35, Porterfield, 10 yd TD, Spivey Complete, 10-84, 8-8.
Newberry, :17, Deaton, 24 yd. FG, 5-45, 8-9.

STATISTICS

	Newberry	Presbyterian
First Downs	12	13
Rushing	6	8
Passing	5	3
Penalty	1	2
Rushing Attempts	41	45
Yards Gained Rushing	161	143
Yards Lost Rushing	30	13
Net Yards Rushing	131	130
Net Yards Passing	104	127
Passes Attempted	26	23
Passes Completed	10	8
Had Intercepted	0	3
Total Offensive Plays	67	68
Total Net Yards	235	257
Average Gain Per Play	3.5	3.7
Fumbles Number Lost	5-2	2-2
Penalties Number Yards	8-96	5-43
Number of Punts Yards	8-312	6-204
Average Per Punt	39.0	39.0
Punt Returns Number yards	1-7	4-39
Kickoff Returns Number yards	1-7	2-41
Interception Returns No Yards	3-30	0-0
Fumble Returns. No. Yards	2-0	2-0
Possession Time	28:51	31:09
Third-Down Conversions	0 of 14	4 of 17
Sacks by No Yards	0-0	0-0

Sports
Newberry Observer

Bronze Derby

Newberry Observer - Nov 13, 1995

Willie Sellers, #86, is doubled up by PC defenders on this pass play in Saturday's Bronze Derby game. Later, Sellers grabbed a 34 yard pass that moved the Tribe to field goal range with :17 left to play — the FG gave Newberry the 9-6 win over Presbyterian.

Newberry College's Keith Porterfield, #20, gained 95 yards on a muddy Setzler Field Saturday to become the single-season rushing leader in Indians' football history. He scored his 14th touchdown of the season with 1:30 left in the Bronze Derby game.

The Clinton Chronicle

14A Wednesday, November 15, 1995

Sports

Late fumble costs Hose in Bronze Derby game

Sometimes, it's just not meant to be.

Ahead 8-0 with two minutes left in the game, Presbyterian College seemingly had won the 84th meeting between the Blue Hose and the Indians of Newberry College.

A touchdown and field goal by the Indians in the final 1:35, however, gave Newberry a dramatic come-from-behind victory over Presbyterian, snapping the Blue Hose's four-game winning streak.

Keath Porterfield capped a 10-play, 87-yard drive with a 16-yard touchdown run at the 1:35 mark of the fourth period to pull Newberry within 8-6.

The drive featured a successful 14-yard pass from quarterback Hunter Spivey to wide receiver Ike Allred on a fourth-and-8 play from the PC 28.

After the Indians' two-point conversion attempt failed on an incomplete pass, Newberry tried and failed to recover an onside kick, giving Presbyterian possession at the Newberry 43.

On PC's second play from scrimmage, the Indians, who were out of timeouts, recovered a fumble to give them new life.

Five plays later, including a 34-yard pass from Spivey to tight end Willie Sellers, freshman placekicker Matt Deaton booted a 24-yard field goal to give Newberry a 9-8 advantage with just 17 seconds remaining on the clock.

"Obviously, this is a very tough loss," PC head coach John Perry said. "We apparently have the game won and then we lose it. The guys played hard. We did what we wanted to; we just fumbled the football at the wrong time of the game."

The win gave Newberry the Bronze Derby for the first time since 1992. After dropping the first five games of the season, Newberry won five out of six to close the year at 5-6.

For Presbyterian, the 1995 campaign comes to a close at 6-5, marking the first winning season since the 1987 Blue Hose went 8-5.

The Blue Hose's five losses in 1995 came by a total of 15 points.

The Blue Hose took a 2-0 lead at the 8:32 mark of the first quarter when a poor snap sailed over the head of Newberry punter Joe Huntley and out of the end zone for a safety.

Junior placekicker Chris Kinert put Presbyterian ahead 5-0 on the final play of the opening period with a 32-yard field goal.

In the third quarter, freshman safety Troy Gamble recovered a Newberry fumble, giving the Blue Hose a first down at the Indian 18.

Three rushing plays resulted in 6 yards, setting up Kinert's second successful field goal of the afternoon, this one covering 30 yards to extend PC's lead to 8-0 with 7:37 left in the

See FUMBLE Page 15A

Fumble

Continued From Page 14A

third period.

"It just didn't work out for us today," Perry said. "Our defense played well, our offense played well, and the special teams played well considering the weather and field conditions. Newberry is a good football team. They hung in there the entire game."

Despite the loss, Presbyterian leads the all-time series, which began in 1913, between the two schools by a 50-29-5 count.

Blue Hose senior fullback Steve Gorrie, who rushed for 82 yards on the day, exits the Presbyterian program as the school's all-time leader in career rushing yards (3,486) and touchdowns (42).

In 1995, the Snellville, Ga., native rushed for 1,312 yards while setting the school single-season marks for touchdowns with 20 and points with 122.

"Today was a heartbreaker," Gorrie said. "It is certainly not the way I wanted to go out. I've enjoyed every minute of my time here at Presbyterian, but it went by so fast. I've got a lot of memories which I will never forget."

Kinert matched a school single-season record for point after touchdown percentage by successfully kicking all 18 of his extra point attempts.

Kinert joins Sandy Cruickshanks (18-for-18 in 1968) and Chris Wingo (21-for-21 in 1986) in the PC record book.

The Li'l That Was!

The Blue Stocking
The Newspaper of Presbyterian College

Vol. 91, No. 5 — Friday, December 8, 1995 — Free

Gridders post 6-5 season record

Football team ends season with disappointing Bronze Derby loss

by Jeff Walker
Staff Writer

The Indians of Newberry College ended Presbyterian's reign as king of the Bronze Derby on a muddy, rain soaked field on Saturday, November 11th. The final score of the less than enjoyable outing was 9-8.

"Obviously this is a tough loss. We apparently had the game won and then we lost it," said a disappointed Coach Perry.

The Blue Hose controlled the ball for the majority of the contest. In the opening quarter PC lit up the scoreboard first with a safety when a Newberry snap sailed over the punter's head and out of the endzone. Then with one second remaining in the first quarter, junior place kicker Chris Kinert kicked a 32 yard field goal to put PC ahead 5-0, a lead which they took to the locker room at halftime.

Kinert added another field goal late in the fourth quarter to give PC a 8-0 advantage, but the Hose noticeably lost momentum with about three minutes remaining in the game. Newberry drove the length of the field and scored a touchdown with 1:35 on the clock, but failed to convert on their two point conversion attempt.

After a failed onside kick attempt, the Blue Hose regained possession, and it seemed that their only objective would be to "run out the clock." With so little time remaining, it was feasible for the Hose to let the clock expire, and so on first down quarterback Randy Sullivan took a knee. On second down, however, the call went to senior fullback Steve Gorrie. After plowing ahead for a few yards, Gorrie was hit hard and in the shuffle coughed up the ball. The Indians recovered the fumble with about 52 seconds left in the ballgame and quickly drove deep into PC territory. As time expired, Newberry booted a 24

> "Obviously, this is a tough loss. We apparently had the game won, and then we lost it."
>
> —Head coach John Perry

yarder through the uprights to clinch a 9-8 win and the Bronze Derby.

Though PC still leads the series by a 50-29-5 mark, this loss was quite disappointing and cast a bit of a shadow on an otherwise successful season. The Hose will play Newberry at home next year.

"It was a heartbreaker. It is certainly not the way I wanted to go out, but I enjoyed every minute of it. I've got a lot of memories which I will never forget," said senior fullback Steve Gorrie.

The 1995 season included the setting of several new team and individual records. PC opened the season with an untainted 2-0 record and went on to set a school record for total offense with an average of 381.6 total yards per game. Ultimately, the Blue Hose concluded the season with a 6-5 overall record and their first winning season since 1987. Senior Steve Gorrie, who rushed for over a thousand yards this season, will leave PC as the all-time leader in career rushing yards (3,486), and touchdowns (42).

The Li'l  That Was!

FRIDAY

Bronze Derby GAME DAY Special Section

INSIDE Students attend teaching KATE. PAGE 5

The Newberry Observer

Just like a letter from home.

NOVEMBER 14, 2003   NEWBERRY, S.C.

What a muddy day

I'll never forget the Bronze Derby game that tore up my boots.

1995. Derby Day. Setzler Field. The day, the place where every Indian fan wants to be. Presbyterian is coming to town, and we're ready for them.

The only problem this year, it's raining. And it's been raining. And the sidelines are starting to puddle up.

Common wisdom is, it never rains on Derby Day. For a long while, when the Derby game was played on Thanksgiving, that seemed to be true. It was cold, mind you. Thanksgiving just seems to usher in the cold weather, like the day after ushers in the Christmas buying season. It's been bone-chillin' on Thanksgiving, Derby Day, around here. But you'd warm up at the Thanksgiving meal served in Kauffman Hall, and go out braced against the elements with turkey and dressing, and black coffee.

Everybody would be sitting under blankets, or wrapped in parkas. As the game wore on, the temperature dropped, and shadows overtook the playing field - Derby Day could be down right miserable.

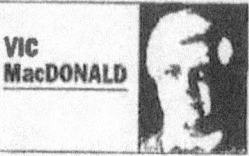
VIC MacDONALD

Actually, last year was colder and wetter than I remember in 1995, but no less a thrilling game.

It was a foregone conclusion at the beginning of that season's finale that Keath Porterfield would become the all-time career rushing leader for Newberry. Seems like (remember, I'm recalling all this with a 50-year-old memory) that he got the record early in the game, sloshing through turf that was getting more and more soupy.

Both teams slugged it out between the 20s that day, as defense ruled. PC was leading 8-6 as the clock waned. We were going home a loser.

No. Wait. They fumbled. All they had to do was run out the clock. And, the unthinkable, they fumbled. Newberry's got it!

But we're too far from pay dirt. It'll never happen then, it did.

The offense got clicking.

The stage is set -- for all Indians' fans' hearts to be broken. We will never hit this field goal. It's not cosmically possible that we're going to win this game, that PC is going to hand over this victory. That - hold on, it's good! NC 9, PC 8.

The sidelines exploded. Some how the Derby got exchanged (PC's 24-13 win the year before). It was the first of three straight Mike Taylor-led Newberry wins of the Bronze Derby.

And it was the best 9-8 football game I ever saw. As the game ended Mike walked way out of the team box into vast mud puddle. Porterfield came over to him, tried to keep his attention while somebody else tried to pour a cooler of water over him. Mike wouldn't have any of it.

"I'll give you $100," I shouted, trying to encourage the players to douse their coach. He wouldn't let it happen.

Win, with some dignity.

The final horn sounded. I was ankle deep in mud. I pulled one boot out of the thick muck, and my boot disintegrated.

The soul was flapped off. The stitching around it no

■ MUD BOWL

Continued from page 3B

into the turf again. I had to get going, everybody was celebrating, the Derby was getting passed around, from head to head.

I must get out onto the field! Virtually bootless, I made my way into the throng. (Only later did I realize, those guys were wearing cleats.) Amongst the celebrating players you know how hard they had worked to get this prize - just four years before, Newberry was a 1-10 team, going nowhere. Football was seriously considered for extinction at Newberry

College.

Then, they brought in a new coach. His first team went 5-6, won the last Derby game played on Thanksgiving (14-0 at Presbyterian — I've always coveted one of those "I was there ..." T-shirts). Things looked like they were headed in the right direction.

Finally, exhausted, I fell into the room in the Casey Center that's now the Presidential Dining Room. Some Indian Club folks were there - - more than anything I just needed a chair. I downed a Bud (maybe two), saw C.A. Dufford come in with his jacket and overshirt off, underneath he wore a white T-shirt with something on the back — you know those drawings of the

mischievous boy looking over his shoulder as he takes a wee-wee, just guess what he was wee-weeing on.

I laughed. I said "shoo, what a Derby game" with all the rest of the Indian Club people. I think even Greg Hartle showed up, looking like he could still roam the gridiron in that fearsome defense.

I listened to the clanging of the Victory Bell. I watched the sky turn black outside — you just didn't want to leave.

You wanted to soak it all up. Our Indians had won, the Derby was back where it belonged. Newberry was back on track.

'Til next year.

THE INDIAN

Newberry College, Newberry, SC — November 20, 1995

Newberry holds out to the very end to come back with a win

By Shawndrea Stafford, Guest Writer

Newberry came into the game with high expectation and hopes of a Bronze Derby victory, but the PC Blue Hose had other ideas. PC started a defensively strong game deflating the hopes of a Newberry victory. Then the Indians shot themselves in the foot when a bad snap and a penalty on a punt gave PC a safety and good field position.

In the first half the Indians defense did not allow the Blue Hose to get into the end zone but PC scored a field goal giving them a 5-0 lead. Senior cornerback Shawn Wylie made two interceptions in the first half. "We had to win, regardless. It was a must win situation so that we can continue with high expectations for next season," said Wylie.

Coming out for the second half both teams had hopes of improving their game. PC scored another field goal giving themselves an 8-0 edge over the Indians. Tension was mounting for the Indians. "We had to score somehow, we couldn't lose. Either offense or defense had to score quick. I felt as long as we went into the fourth quarter with three or seven points I knew we could win," said senior line backer Ronald Reese.

The fourth quarter crunch had Newberry praying for a miracle. Never giving in, the sun started to shine for the Indians. With good ball management and support from the fans the Indians running back, Keath Porterfield, scored with less than two minutes left in the game. The two point attempt which would have tied the game failed giving PC renewed hope for a victory. Newberry's defense had other ideas. A fumble recovery by Senior cornerback Jason Gambrell gave the Indians another chance to win the game. Quarterback Hunter Spivey connected with tight end Willie Sellers to give the Indians good field position. The Blue Hose defense did not allow the Indians to get into the end zone. Freshman kicker Matt Deaton came through for the Indians by kicking a field goal with 21 seconds left in the game.

According to Shawn Wylie, "No one player won the game for us. Winning the Bronze Derby was a team effort." "Very intense game," said Sellers, "the team that won the game was the team that never stopped believing."

The Indians don't let the weather keep them from beating PC and winning the Bronze Derby.
Photo By Amy Goldman

The Li'l 🎩 That Was!

Take A Knee PC

Late in the fourth quarter, with Presbyterian College leading 8-0 in the 48th meeting of The Bronze Derby, Newberry College drove 87 yards and scored with 1:35 left in the game. The Indians 2 point conversion failed. An onside kick attempt failed by Newberry, giving the ball to the Blue Hose at the Newberry 43. Newberry was out of timeouts. Instead of killing the clock by taking a knee, The Blue Hose fumbled on their second play of the drive and Newberry recovered the loose ball. Five plays later, which included a 34 yard pass from Newberry quarterback Hunter Spivey to tight end Willie Sellers, Newberry freshman placekicker Matt Deaton kicked a game winning 24 yard field goal to beat the Blue Hose 9-8. Soon after, a most popular t-shirt appeared on the campus of Newberry College stating, "Take a Knee PC."

November 1996

November 1	The Philadelphia 76ers lost to the Milwaukee Bucks 111-103 in the first game at CoreStates Center in Philadelphia, PA.
November 1	Shaqille O'Neil made his debut with the NBA Los Angeles Lakers.
November 2	Miami Heat's head coach Pat Riley became the 8th NBA coach to win 500 games as the Miami Heat defeated the Indiana Pacers 97-95.
November 3	At 18 years old, Kobe Bryant of the NBA Los Angeles Lakers made his NBA debut.
November 3	NFL San Francisco 49'ers wide receiver Jerry Rice became the first player in NFL history to reach 1000 receptions.
November 4	The British singing group The Spice Girls released their first album "Spice."
November 5	Bill Clinton was re-elected President of the United States defeating Bob Dole.
November 5	California voters re-elected singer entertainer Sonny Bono to the United States Congress.
November 5	New York Yankees shortstop Derek Jeter won the MLB AL Rookie of the Year Award.
November 6	Los Angeles Dodgers outfielder Todd Hollandsworth won MLB NL Rookie of the Year Award.
November 7	Ex-NFL running back and winner of the Heisman Trophy Mike Rozier was shot several times in his hometown of Camden, New Jersey.
November 9	Evander Holyfield upset Mike Tyson by KO to regain the WBA Heavyweight boxing title.
November 10	Terry Labonte won the 46th NASCAR Sprint Cup.
November 11	Atlanta Braves pitcher John Smoltz won the MLB NL Cy Young Award.
November 12	Saudi Arabia and Kazakhstan commercial airliners collide over India killing 349 people.
November 13	Padres Ken Caminiti is 4th unanimous winner of the MLB NL MVP.
November 14	Singer Michael Jackson married Debbie Rowe.
November 16	American golfer Phil Mickelson married Amy McBride.
November 16	The Bronze Derby was played in Clinton, South Carolina. The Newberry College Indians defeated the Presbyterian College Blue Hose 21-10.

Sports
The Newberry Observer

Game Notes
Newberry, PC Renew Brown Derby Rivalry

Newberry Observer - Nov 13, 1996

vs.

Seeking to avenge last year's heart-breaking loss -- 9-8 at Setzler Field on a field goal with :17 left in the rain-soaked game -- Presbyterian takes a 5-5 record into its home Bailey Memorial Stadium against the 6-4 Newberry Indians.

The Tribe comes off a disappointing 13-0 loss at Carson-Newman. PC won 21-20 over Gardner-Webb last Saturday. Both were South Atlantic Conference games.

Newberry has a 5-2 record against SAC foes in its first season back in the conference. A win would leave Newberry tied for second in the conference, but the Indians are not eligible for SAC recognition in the football standings until 1997.

Presbyterian is 4-3 this season against SAC foes. The Blue Hose could solidify third, if their game with Newberry counted in the final SAC standings. The conference, however, does not recognize Newberry games as wins or losses for other SAC teams -- until next season.

Either way, there are bragging rights on the line. The winner takes the fabled Bronze Derby, symbol of football superiority in this series since a Newberry student snatched it from the head of a PC student after a basketball game. Ironically, the two teams play each other in roundball next week -- PC is here Nov. 20 in the Indians' first home game, a 5:30 and 7:30 p.m. men's and women's doubleheader in Eleazer Arena.

The home-and-home series goes to Presbyterian -- the pre-season No. 1 men's team in the South Atlantic Conference -- Nov. 27. It was at the last NC-PC game in Clinton that a fight broke out in the stands and was captured on videotape to be broadcast nationwide on ESPN.

It happened shortly after PC honored its football team at halftime of the basketball game, which was attended by a large number of Newberry football players. Several Newberry players were charged with disorderly conduct and fined in municipal court in Clinton.

No basketball players were involved in the fracas at Clinton. There are rarely any fighting incidents at Newberry-Presbyterian football games, either.

But both gridiron teams will want to win for the sake of their programs. Presbyterian wants another winning season. Newberry, already assured of its first winning season since 1984, wants to make a case at 7-4 for an at-large bid to the NCAA Division II football national championship playoffs.

Derby game: Presbyterian and Newberry have met on the gridiron 84 times. The Blue Hose own a 50-29-2 lead in the series, but the Derby spent last season in Newberry. The first meeting between the two schools was in 1913 when the Indians shut out the Blue Hose 51-0. The actual battle for the Derby in football did not begin until 1947.

That season the Indians defeated PC 8-0. Since then, the Blure Hose have won the Derby Battle 26 times to the Indians' 19, and there have been four deadlocks. The Bronze Derby is reputed to have started at a basketball game between the two teams. The Derby at that time was awarded to the winner in any athletic event between the two schools, until the 1947 football season.

Record-holders: NC senior runningback Keath Porterfield owns the career rushing record, and added 65 yards against a tough Carson-Newman front line to add to it. He has 3,314 yards in his four year career. The game against PC is his last for the Indians.

Another senior, Rico Cannon, has the opportunity to put himself in the record books. The Easley native has 11 career touchdown receptions -- that ties him at the top of the career ladder with Darryl Owings (1984-86) and Jerome Williams (1976-78).

His next career TD reception will give him the career lead. Going in to the Carson-Newman game, Cannon was the second leading receiver in the South Atlantic Conference.

Senior QB Hunter Spivey has eight TD passes this season, to tie his career high set last season. His next TD pass will give him a new career best. Spivey leads an Indians offense that averages 23.6 points per outing.

Defensively, NC has given up just 151 points this season, a 15.1 points per game average. A major contributors is senior Stanley Clay, who leads the team in sacks. The defensive back has snuck into the opposing team's backfield three times for sacks totalling 18 total yards lost.

Clay can also cover the opposition's receivers pretty well -- he leads the team in interceptions with four and has returned two for scores.

Tough on third down: If you have a third down against the Indians, you may be in trouble. NC has limited the opposition to only 34 percent (50-145) on third down plays; the offense has converted 43 percent of the time (58 of 135) on third down.

Junior linebacker Brian Rutherford was the team's leading tackler against Carson-Newman -- his 15 tackles were the most for an Indians this season. Rutherford is second on the team with 48 tackles to senior linebacker Doug Knight with 53 unassisted tackles.

Winning record: The Indians six wins this season under Clayton Johnson assures the football team of its first winning mark since 1984. The Tribe was second in the old SAC that year. NC has the chance to duplicate that feat with a win over Presbyterian this Saturday. Kickoff at Bailey Memorial Stadium (capacity 5,000) is set for 1:30 p.m.

Last season: Newberry won a thriller -- battling back from an 8-0 fourth quarter deficit, Newberry got a late TD from Keath Porterfield and a 24-yard field goal from freshman kicker Matt Deaton to win with just 17 seconds on the clock. With less than a minute to play, Newberry's Jason Gambrell recovered a PC fumble and set up Deaton's game winner.

Not content to just run out the clock, PC handed off to its career leading rusher Steve Gorrie -- 3,486 yards in three seasons and 42 touchdowns -- who fumbled.

The Li'l 🎩 That Was!

The Newberry Observer
AND HERALD & NEWS
"Just Like A Letter From Home"

ESTABLISHED 1865 — Newberry, S.C. Friday, Nov. 15, 1996

Newberry College plays Presbyterian College for The Bronze Derby Saturday in Clinton. The game starts at 1:30.

Newberry-Presbyterian: It's Derby Time

Newberry will travel to Clinton for a 1:30 p.m. showdown with Presbyterian. Up for grabs is one of college football's oldest rivalries meeting in The Bronze Derby. The Derby has used Newberry as it's home for the past season after the Indians nine to eight comeback victory over the Blue Hose last year.

"There's a different feeling in the air when you step off the bus and get on the field to play PC," head Coach Mike Taylor said. "Both teams will play extra hard and both teams have something to play for. PC will be playing for a winning record and we want to win our seventh game of the season."

For the Indians to win they will have a better offensive production than they had last week at Carson Newman. The sixth-ranked Eagles held the Indians to 220 yards and did not allow the Indians to score a point. The last time the Indians were shut out was in 1993 when South Carolina State turned the trick, said a Newberry College release.

"We have to get our confidence back on offensive after last week," Taylor said. "We don't have a chance to win when we have that kind of offensive production."

"I thought our defense played fairly well. We lost our composure some there in the third quarter, but we were able to regain it and hung in with a good football team. Our defense has the mentality that giving up 13 points last week was to much to help us win the game."

Presbyterian is coming off an exciting 21-20 win over Gardner-Webb. The game was not decided until the last few seconds of the game, when the Blue Hose blocked a field goal to turn back the Bulldogs.

"PC is a good football team and they are playing well right now," Taylor said "They did the things they had to do last week to win the game. They are very effective at throwing the football, especially on the boot leg and sprint out passes. We have seen it before, but PC has been doing it a long time and they are very good at it."

"Defensively, they have some good defensive linemen. We couldn't block them last year when they were freshmen, and now they are sophomores and are even better. They also have very good linebackers and cornerbacks."

The Indians (6-4) will be going for their seventh win of the season. The last time the Indians won seven games was back in 1984 when Newberry went 7-0-4.

"Winning seven games would be a great accomplishment for this team and these seniors," Taylor said. "They came in here as freshmen and won 2-9-, then 4-7 and last year 5-6. Also, wining the last game of the season gives you something to talk about. The seniors feel good because they won their last game, and it gives the younger players something to build on for next season."

The Newberry Observer
AND HERALD & NEWS
"Just Like A Letter From Home"

Newberry, S.C. Monday, November 18, 1996

NC Seniors Keep Derby In Newberry

By: Jim Murray
Special To the Observer

It was "Senior Day" at Bailey Field in Clinton for the Newberry College Indians as they defeated the Presbyterian College Blue Hose 21-10 to retain the Bronze Derby for the trophy case at Eleazer Arena.

The Indians were led on offense by Seniors Ike Allred, who caught two touchdown passes, including one that featured a highlight film 45 yard run after a routine catch; by Senior Rice Cannon, who set a career touchdown passing record with a 48 yard play on the Indian's first possession, by Senior running back Keath Porterfield, who ran for 148 yards on 28 carries to add to his all time career rushing record; by Senior quarterback Hunter Spivey, who directed the Indian offense.

On defense, senior linebacker Jeremiah Jones and cornerback Stanley Clay seemed like they were in on every tackle that the Indians produced during the day. Senior Doug Knight's fumble causing tackle led to a Newberry score late in the game.

As he spoke to the team after the game, Newberry Coach Mike Taylor gave specific praise to his senior players, pointing out that these were the first that he had recruited to Newberry, and that they went out as winners in a game that potentially means the most to the Indian program.

"I especially want to mention Ike Allred... he will remember his college career on that catch and run play for us. Twenty years from now, they will remember this game, and remember this win."

The game was played on a clear, cold, windy day, conditions which may have caused the offenses for both teams to clog up and sputter, or so it seemed. The score at the first half was 7-7, after a end of half that featured scores by both teams early, then several series of frustrating turnovers and missed opportunities for both teams.

The Indians scored on their opening possession, driving to a score when Spivey connected to Rice Cannon on a 48 yard scoring pass. In addition to the school record for Cannon, Spivey established a personal-best record for touchdown passes with the play.

Presbyterian answered with a 90 yard drive that ended when Chris Smith threw 3 yards to Vic Vickery in a drive that established PC's passing game, which caused Newberry problems for most of the afternoon.

"The Bronze Derby game, as a freshman and in your early years it's not a big deal, but it is when it's the last game of your career."
— Indian quarterback Hunter Spivey

At the half, Newberry had 204 yards total offense, 50 of those coming from Keath Porterfield. The Blue Hose put up 164 yards in offense for the half, most of those coming through the air, with Chris Smith getting 125 yards on 8 completions.

The Blue Hose took the lead in the third quarter on a Kris Keinert field goal, which came after the Indians were called for a pass interference penalty that gave the Hose the ball first and goal on the three yard line. The Blue Hose could not get the ball in and Keinert kicked the ball through for a 20 yard effort.

Newberry came back for keeps when senior Doug Knight caused and freshman Doc Moore recovered a PC fumble and Hunter Spivey connected with Ike Allred on a 21 yard pass.

Allred added six points in the last quarter to close out the scoring when he caught a pass at the Blue Hose and rumbled in to complete a

[Continued On Page 10]

*NC vs PC
Continued From Page 1

68 yard play. Allred was not to be denied on the play, in which he ran through what seemed to be most of the blue-shirted Presbyterian defense.

The win was the seventh this season for the Indians, marking the first time in 12 years that an Indian football team has notched that many victories. The Indians were not eligible for any conference standing or awards this year.

Carson Newman will be the SAC-8 conference champions, ending with a 6-1 record, followed by Catawba with a 5-2 mark. PC and Elon tied for third with identical 4-3 conference records.

Nice Fit

Newberry College senior linebacker Doug Knight tries on the Bronze Derby after the Indians claimed the hat for another year with a 21-10 victory over Presbyterian College Saturday in Clinton.

One Of Two

Senior wide receiver Ike Allred belly flops across the PC goal line to complete a 46-yard reception from quarterback Hunter Spivey. It was the first of his two touchdowns catches on the day for Allred.

Sports

The Clinton Chronicle

Wednesday, November 20, 1996, 1B

Newberry College retains Bronze Derby

By Richard Farmer
Staff Writer

Four Newberry seniors teamed up in their final collegiate game to carry the Indians to a 21-10 victory over Presbyterian College Saturday at Bailey Memorial Stadium in Clinton in the 85th meeting of the two teams.

Quarterback Hunter Spivey, tailback Keith Porterfield, wide receiver Ike Allred and flanker Rico Cannon led the Indian charge and combined for 362 yards total offense and three touchdowns as the Indians claimed the Bronze Derby for the second year in a row.

With the victory, Newberry carried the Derby east, some 25 miles down U.S. 76 where it's been since last season's 9-8 Indian victory. PC now leads the overall series 50-30-5.

Newberry came out smoking by beginning the day's scoring just three minutes into the game when Spivey found Cannon streaking down the middle of the field.

Cannon turned on the afterburners, creating a 48-yard touchdown from a routine screen pass and leading Newberry to a 7-0 lead.

See DERBY Page 4B

Derby

Continued from Page 1B

Several minutes later, PC accepted a punt from Newberry, downing the ball in the end zone. A penalty against Presbyterian halved the distance to the goal and the Blue Hose found themselves 90 yards from paydirt.

But senior tailback Vasio Smith led the PC attack, gaining 24 yards on the drive with runs of 12, 10 and 2 yards. On the afternoon, Vasio Smith gained 27 yards on 8 carries, while spelling junior tailback Terrance Grant who gained just 40 yards on 17 attempts for his day's work.

But PC answered decisively with the 13-play, 90-yard drive capped by a 3-yard pass from senior quarterback Chris Smith to senior fullback Vick Vickery.

Junior kicker Chris Kinert added the extra point and PC pulled even at 7-7.

The remainder of the first half turned into a mistake-laden puntfest with both schools throwing interceptions and Newberry adding a fumble at the PC 16 with under a minute left to play before intermission.

PC opened the third-quarter scoring when Kinert connected on a 20-yard field goal with 10:41 remaining.

The 9-play, 68-yard drive ended with PC holding the lead for the first time on the afternoon by a score of 10-7.

Several minutes later, with the Blue Hose facing a third-and-19 situation from their own 40, Newberry defensive back Doug Knight caught a scrambling Chris Smith from behind and knocked the ball loose.

With 5:14 left in the third quarter, Newberry was just 44 yards from the lead.

Seven plays later, Allred dove into the end zone after catching a 17-yard pass from Spivey, putting the Indians up for good.

On the ensuing drive, it took Newberry just four plays to get the ball back when Chris Smith threw an interception on first down from the PC 37.

Newberry put the contest out of reach midway through the final quarter when Allred caught a short slant pass over the middle and raced downfield, scoring on a 66-yard jaunt.

With just 5 minutes remaining and up by two scores, the Newberry sidelines erupted in celebration while the PC sidelines simply stood and stared.

On its next possession, a do-or-die situation, PC failed to make headway and was forced to punt with 4:02 remaining.

Newberry had but from there to kill the clock and seal the victory.

Something New *is coming to you* from your local radio station stay tuned to this Spot *& listen to* **WPCC • 1410 AM**

November 20, 1996 — The Laurens County Advertiser

SPORTS

The Laurens County Advertiser
An Independent Newspaper, Founded In 1885/South Carolina's Award-Winning Semi-Weekly Newspaper

PC sees Allred in loss to Newberry

♦ By Dave McCallum
Sports Editor

For the second straight year, the Bronze Derby will not reside in the Presbyterian College trophy case.

Fourteen unanswered points by Newberry in the second half secured a 21-10 Indians victory over their archrival and ensured the coveted trophy would back in Newberry by nightfall Saturday.

PC, which dropped a 9-8 decision to the Indians last year, not only saw the Derby slip from its hands but also saw its year end with a losing record.

The Blue Hose, playing its final game under head coach John Perry, finished its season at 5-6. Perry resigned his position late Monday afternoon in a prepared statement.

Despite its second straight loss to Newberry, PC still owns a whooping margin in the overall series at 50-30-5.

Presbyterian led 10-7 early in the third quarter when Chris Kinert booted a 20-yard field goal.

From that point on, though, the Blue Hose saw nothing but red, as in Newberry receiver Ike Allred.

Allred, a senior, latched on to a

♦See ALLRED, Page 15A

♦ Allred

(Continued from Page 13A)

17-yard scoring pass from Hunter Spivey with 2:48 left in the third quarter for the go-ahead score. The TD strike capped a seven-play, 44-yard scoring march.

Allred, who finished with three catches for 93 yards, then put the contest out of reach late in the game.

He hauled in a Spivey pass at Newberry's 48, then broke two tackles at PC's 45 en route to a 66-yard scoring strike. Matt Deaton's point-after made it a 21-10 contest with 5:04 left.

The visiting Indians, who finished 7-4, looked ready to make quick work of Presbyterian in the early going.

Newberry struck quickly on the game's opening drive when Spivey hit Rico Cannon on a 48-yard scoring pass. Deaton's point-after made it 7-0 with 11:57 remaining in the first quarter.

On the day, Spivey completed 11-of-15 passes for 189 yards and the three scores.

Despite Newberry's opening salvo, PC battled its way back to even late in the opening quarter.

Senior quarterback Chris Smith, playing his final contest, tossed a three-yard scoring strike to tight end Vic Vickery off a nifty fake. Kinert's PAT deadlocked the game at 7-all with 2:38 left in the first.

Smith's touchdown pass culminated a 13-play, 90-yard probe. On the day, Smith was 15-of-31 passing for 255 yards.

November 1997

The Li'l That Was!

November 1	"Titanic" premiered, directed by James Cameron and starring Leonardo DiCaprio and Kate Winslet.
November 1	Negro Leagues Baseball Museum and The American Jazz Museum opened in Kansas City, Missouri.
November 1	Nebraska head football coach Tom Osbourne won his 250th game with a 67-7 win over Oklahoma.
November 2	Rodgers & Hammerstein's "Cinderella" with Whitney Houston, Brandy Norwood and Bernadette Peters premiered live on ABC.
November 3	American horse racing legend "Willie" Shoemaker retired.
November 3	American journalist and TV host Wally Bruner of "ABC News" and "What's My Line" passed away.
November 3	California law ends affirmative action.
November 3	Boston Red Sox shortstop Nomar Garciaparra won MLB AL Rookie of the Year Award.
November 4	Shania Twain released her album "Come on Over," becoming the *Billboard* Album of the Year in 1999.
November 5	Hours after retiring as manager of the Baltimore Orioles, Davey Johnson was named MLB AL Manager of the Year.
November 6	San Francisco Giants manager Dusty Baker was named MLB NL Manager of the Year.
November 10	Artist Peter Max pleaded guilty to tax fraud.
November 11	The MLB Cy Young Award winners were both from Canadienne teams. Roger Clemens of the Toronto Blue Jays won the AL Award. Pedro Martinez of the Montreal Expos won the NL Award.
November 12	American basketball sportscaster Dick Vitale signed an ESPN contract.
November 13	"Lion King" opened on Broadway in New York City.
November 13	Ken Griffey Jr. of the Seattle Mariners won the MLB AL Most Valuable Player Award.
November 14	American horse racing jockey and Hall of Fame member Eddie Arcaro passed away.
November 15	Actor William Shatner married model Nerine Kidd.
November 15	The Bronze Derby was played in Newberry, South Carolina. The Newberry College Indians defeated the Presbyterian College Blue Hose 28-22.

The Li'l 🎩 That Was!

The Newberry Observer
AND HERALD & NEWS
"Just Like A Letter From Home"

Newberry, S.C. Friday, November 14, 1997

Old Rivals Clash Saturday For Bronze Derby

By LISA WHEELER
Staff Writer

Newberry College does not want a golden medallion to commemorate this 50th anniversary.

It wants bronze — more specifically, the Bronze Derby.

The Newberry College Indians will meet the Presbyterian Blue Hose at Setzler Field Saturday at 2 p.m. to battle over the coveted symbol of football superiority in the rivalry between the two schools.

Newberry and Presbyterian began bumping shoulder pads and helmets in 1913.

However, the annual contest did not actually heat up until 1947.

The tradition of the Bronze Derby started not at a football game, but unfolded instead in a basketball arena.

> **Class of 1940 wins 'Miniature Bronze Derby', page 12**

On Jan. 30, the two schools met at Newberry College to play hoops.

According to records, a couple of zealous Presbyterian fans hung a banner that was not particularly flattering to their opponents.

During the game, several Newberry College students propped a ladder against the gym, climbed through a window, took the banner and disappeared.

Presbyterian won the game 51-47.

The Presbyterian fans wanted the banner returned, their Newberry counterparts refused, and a fight broke out in the ranks.

While fists and insults flew, a young Newberry College student snatched a hat from his opponent's head and ran.

A short time later, Frank E. Kinard, a senior at Newberry College and athletic publicity director, received a letter from Charles MacDonald, assistant professor of English and athletic publicity director at Presbyterian College.

He suggested that officials at Newberry find the hat and use it as a symbol of the rivalry between the two schools.

After a discussion during a convocation at Newberry, the derby was recovered and bronzed.

Now, whichever team wins the

➡ **Continued on page 3**

Photo provided by Newberry College
Indians Coach Mike Taylor talks with his players after last year's victory over Presbyterian College.

Derby
(Continued From Page 1)

gridiron match-up each year takes the trophy home.

The Indians' Bronze Derby record stands at 20-27-3, with an overall record against the Blue Hose of 30-50-5.

Last year, Newberry won the derby.

Newberry College's Head Coach Mike Taylor said Thursday every game between the two schools is a toss up, and Saturday's is no exception.

"The only thing I know is that you don't know," he said. "The thing is, to me, there is never a favorite in this football game. One year, we could be favored and they win. The next year, we can be evenly matched and we win."

Taylor said if people just went by the season statistics, Presbyterian is favored in Saturday's game. He said Presbyterian College has a new coaching staff that has done an outstanding job with the team this year.

"They are outstanding on defense and do not make mistakes in their kicking game," Taylor said. "They have struggled some on offense because of having young players. But I see an ability for them to break out and have a big play at any time."

He said that for the Indians to win, they have to have a strong defense, not giving up the big play.

Taylor said giving up the big play, such as a blocked kick and dropped punt, has been his team's downfall all year.

He said the Indian offense has to move the ball with running and passing plays.

"The key to the game is to keep PC off balance," Taylor said. "They are ranked in the top 10 for the conference in scoring defense. If their defense gets locked in, it will be hard to shake them."

He said the strategies for both teams will be different from last year because of Presbyterian's new coaching staff and Newberry's loss of key players in the line up.

He does not have the 200-pound tailback and the speed of the linebackers that he had last year, he said. But regardless of the final score, the Bronze Derby game is special to him and, more importantly, to his players, the coach said.

"To me, this rivalry is the ultimate players' game," he said. "Both teams get excited about and charged for the game. When you walk on the field, you can feel the electricity in the air on both sides."

The Li'l That Was!

The Laurens County Advertiser
Published Wednesday and Friday
Laurens, South Carolina

PC's rally comes up short

By Brad Bryant
Sports Editor

After a half Saturday afternoon it appeared the 50th annual Bronze Derby game, pitting Newberry College against Presbyterian, was going to be nothing more than a bronze blowout as the Indians raced out to a 21-0 lead.

However, that all changed in the second half as the Blue Hose mounted a furious rally, only to see its effort come up just a bit short as Newberry held on for a 28-22 victory.

"I was rather proud of the team for fighting back the way they did," Presbyterian Head Coach Daryl Dickey said. "We spotted them 28 points, but just couldn't come all the way back. But I was proud of the effort they gave."

The Blue Hose saw nearly everything it tried in the first half backfire, while the Indians could do no wrong. In building its 21-point advantage, Newberry amassed over 300 yards in the first half, while Presbyterian managed less than 100.

But things were a complete reversal in the second half as the Blue Hose took advantage of two Newberry mistakes in the third quarter to spur its comeback.

"PC played hard and made the plays they had to in the second half," Newberry Head Coach Mike Taylor said. "It was amazing we held on at the end."

The Indians got off to a good start when they took the opening kickoff and drove 66 yards in seven plays for a touchdown. Vic Gilmore got the score on a three yard run. After Matt Deaton's extra point, the Indians were up 7-0 just two minutes and 50 seconds into the game.

The lead grew to 14 points before the end of the first quarter when Gilmore scored again from six yards out. The touchdown was set up by a Presbyterian turnover at its own 25-yard line. From there, the Indians used just three plays to get the score. Deaton was again good on the extra point attempt.

It appeared the Blue Hose was going to limp in at halftime just down by two touchdowns; however, Newberry had other plans.

♦ See HOSE, Page 14

♦ HOSE

(Continued from Page 13A)

Gilmore, with his third touchdown of the half, capped an eight-play 75-yard drive that took up just a minute and 28 seconds. Gilmore scored on an eight-yard run with just :44 left in the half to put the Indians up 21-0, following Deaton's extra-point kick.

Things didn't start much better for the Hose in the second half, after the offense was stymied on its first possession.

The Indians then quickly responded with a seven-play 83-yard drive that was finished off by quarterback Jack Murdock's 54-yard touchdown pass to Josh Pierce.

Following Deaton's point-after kick, the Indians were up 28-0 with 10:17 left in the third quarter. However, things would drastically change for Newberry.

"At halftime we told the guys this was PC-Newberry College and not to let up," Taylor said. "We came out and stuffed them and then we go down to make it 28-0. But after that things started going bad."

The rout appeared as if it was going to continue as the Indians' defense got another stop and the offense promptly took over and was driving without resistance. But Presbyterian's Lee Hannah stepped up for the Hose to pull down an interception in the endzone.

Starting from its own 20-yard line, the Blue Hose drove 80 yards in 14 plays to score on quarterback Blake Wilkey's five-yard run. Chris Kinert added the extra point, making the score 28-7 with 1:19 to go in the third quarter.

After successfully executing an on-sides kick, the Presbyterian offense went to work again.

Wilkey used just seven plays to move the Blue Hose 60 yards in 1:25 to post the team's second touchdown in less than two minutes. Eric Godfree got the score on a five-yard reception of a pass from Wilkey to make the score 28-14, following Kinert's extra point.

"We made a coaching mistake on the kickoff and they recovered the on-sides kick and then just stuck it in there," Taylor said. "They dropped into that two-minute offense and we didn't see the ball much after that."

After an exchange of possessions, the Blue Hose continued to capture more momentum. The defense came through forcing a punt that Troy Gamble returned 48 yards to the Newberry 21-yard line.

From there Presbyterian used just two plays to score its third touchdown of the half. Wilkey again threw for the score, this time hitting Ben Power with a 21-yard pass. On the extra point attempt the Indians were flagged for a personal foul, putting the ball at the one-yard line. The Blue Hose then opted to go for two and Terrance Grant crossed the goal line, pulling Presbyterian to within six points at 28-22 with 7:23 left in the game.

The Blue Hose made one last attempt at winning the game, driving deep into Indian territory. However, the threat ended when Wilkey's pass on fourth down sailed through the endzone.

"I told them at the half they needed to respond to the challenge they were being presented," Dickey said. "I told them they needed to take pride in the way they were representing Presbyterian College. And they did that. They fought back, but they came up just a little short."

Wilkey finished the game with a season-high 26 completions in 53 attempts for 287 yards. Grant was the Hose's leading rusher with 64 yards on 20 carries.

Newberry was led by Gilmore, who finished with a season-high 210 yards on the ground. Murdock finished the day 8-of-18 for 183 yards.

Presbyterian finished the game with 361 yards, while Newberry had 454.

The loss was the third straight for the Hose, which ended the season at 5-6. The victory ended Newberry's season with a 4-7 record.

The Li'l That Was!

The Newberry Observer
AND HERALD & NEWS
"Just Like A Letter From Home"

Newberry, S.C. Monday, November 17, 1997

Newberry Keeps Derby

By HAMPTON FULLER
Special Correspondent

The Newberry Indians won their third straight Bronze Derby title Saturday with a 28-22 victory over archrival Presbyterian.

But it was a victory they had to earn.

With a 28-0 cushion over the Blue Hose, the Indians thought they had the game wrapped up, but the Blue Hose rallied late in the third quarter to score 22 unanswered points.

It was the type of rally that sent shivers down Newberry Coach Mike Taylor's spine.

"At half-time, we told the guys that this was PC-Newberry College, and not to let up," he said.

The Indians, however, had things under control, at least the first half of play. With 12:10 to play in the first quarter, tailback Vic Gilmore scored three yards out on a running play. Matt Deaton's PAT was good. The drive covered seven plays for 66 yards, and the score was Newberry 7, Presbyterian 0.

Gilmore scored again with 11:10 left in the first quarter on a play from six yards out. Deaton's PAT was good. The drive covered three plays for 25 yards. Newberry was up by 14.

The only scoring that came in the second quarter of play was from Vic Gilmore and company. He scored on an eight-yard run with 44 seconds left to go in the half. The PAT was good by Deaton. The drive covered eight plays for 75 yards and concluded the first half, with the home team up by 21 points.

The second half was, however, a different ball game. The Indians scored their last touchdown on a Jack Murdock to Josh Pierce passing play that covered 54 yards. Deaton's PAT was good. The drive covered seven plays for 83 yards and occurred with 10:17 left in the third quarter. Newberry was up by 28 points.

The Blue Hose then began to come alive. They scored 22 unanswered points.

It started on a Blake Wilkey quarterback keeper as he raced for the end zone on a five-yard run. Chris Kinert's PAT was good. The drive covered 14 plays for 80 yards. The score happened with 1:19 left in the third quarter, and the score went to Newberry 28, Presbyterian 7.

The fourth quarter scores came from the visitors. With 14:54 left in the game, Eric Godfree caught a five-yard pass from Wilkey. The PAT was good by Kinert. The drive covered seven plays for 60 yards, and the score was Indians 28, Presbyterian 14.

Continued on page 6

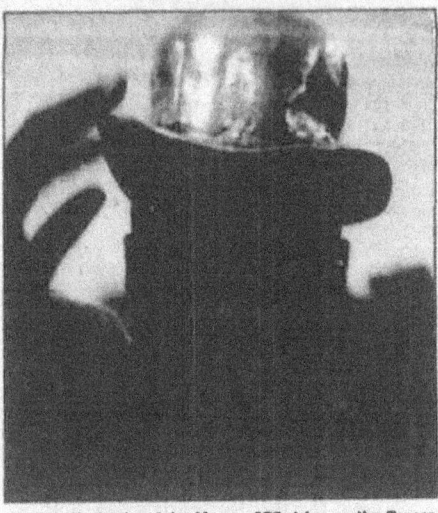
Senior linebacker John Moore, #73, tries on the Bronze Derby after Newberry's victory Saturday.

Indians
(Continued From Page 1)

The final touchdown occurred with 7:23 left in the game. Wilkey threw a 21-yard pass to Ben Power. The Blue Hose went for two and made it, courtesy of Terrance Grant.

The final score was Newberry 28, Presbyterian 22.

Presbyterian "played hard and made the plays," said Newberry Head Coach Mike Taylor.

"We dropped passes, and they did as well," he said. "It was amazing how we held on to win it at the end.

"The game-saver was when Lorenzo McFadden made the big play, when he got in and made the quarterback sack. That pushed them back and made them score from further out."

Runningback Josh Pierce, #34, takes home a 54-yard pass from quarterback Jack Murdock for an Indian touchdown.

Newberry College President Peter French presents alumnus George Scruggs of Virginia with a miniature of the Bronze Derby during half-time at Saturday's game. The award honored Scruggs' graduating class of 1940.

Sports

The Li'l  That Was!

Wednesday, November 19, 1997, 1B

The Clinton Chronicle

Newberry takes 50th Bronze Derby

By Rick Hendricks
Editor

NEWBERRY—Newberry's Indians thought they were in for a walk in the park after the first five minutes of the 50th Bronze Derby, but wound up in a bloodbath and hung on to beat Presbyterian College, 28-22.

Less than 4 minutes into the annual rival clash, Newberry held a 14-0 lead and with 3:26 to go in the third quarter, the Indians scored their fourth touchdown and led 28-0.

"We were embarrassed in the first half," said Presbyterian head football coach Daryl Dickey. "They physically took it to us on both the offensive and defensive lines."

But as out of the game as the Blue Hose were, they made a dramatic comeback that fell just short.

Presbyterian quarterback Blake Wilkey put up some big passing numbers in the game, particularly in the second half. Wilkey established new single game records for completions and attempts with 26 and 53, respectively.

Wilkey's passing numbers were by necessity, as the Blue Hose running game was ineffective in the second half.

Presbyterian rushed for 64 yards in the first half, but only 10 in the third and fourth quarters.

"We couldn't run a lick in the second half," said Dickey.

But Wilkey, to coin a phrase, was "en fuego."

The Blue Hose QB was 23-of-45 in the second half for 271 yards and 2 TDs through the air and also ran in another.

"Blake made a couple of completions and gained some confidence, plus our receivers made some great catches," said Dickey.

Presbyterian's comeback started when Lee Hannah intercepted a Jack Murdock pass late in the third quarter.

Wilkey's 5-yard run with 1:19

See DERBY Page 2B

Photo by Fletcher Pruitt Jr.

Blue Hose receiver Ben Power (16)...
...catches TD pass during PC's second half comeback that fell short in Bronze Derby

Work begins for Dickey

Presbyterian College head football coach Daryl Dickey has his first season behind him.

Now the true work begins.

"We've got a lot of work to do," Dickey said after Saturday's 28-22 loss at Newberry. "We'll find out how good coaches and recruiters we are — half of coaching is recruiting."

The Blue Hose have some big holes to fill.

"We're going to have a big signing class," said Dickey. "There will be a lot of opportunities for playing time."

One of the places that will get a lot of attention will be the offensive line, where Presbyterian loses three of five starters.

The Blue Hose also need to recruit strong skill position players.

The Blue Hose coach said he expects next year's senior class to provide strong leadership.

After the team's strong 4-2 start, Presbyterian won only one of its last five games.

"We might have worn down and ran out of gas," said Dickey.

He said there is a lot of parity in the South Atlantic Conference, underscoring the need to be mentally and physically strong every week.

"It's a very competitive league," Dickey said.

Derby

Continued from Page 1B

left in the third quarter capped a 14-play, 80-yard drive to get the Blue Hose on the board.

Chris Kinert added the PAT to trim the Newberry lead to 28-7.

Presbyterian proceeded to recover an onside kick on the ensuing kickoff.

Starting at their own 40, the Blue Hose moved 60 yards in seven plays — the last of which was a 5-yard touchdown pass from Wilkey to Eric Godfree.

Kinert's second extra point cut the Indians' advantage to 28-14 with 14:54 left in the game.

The Blue Hose failed to score on their next possession, but Troy Gamble's 48-yard punt return with 7:34 left in the game gave Presbyterian the ball at the Newberry 21.

Two plays into the drive, Wilkey hit Ben Power for a 21-yard TD pass.

Kinert kicked the PAT, but Newberry was cited for a personal foul penalty, so Dickey took the point off the board and decided to go for two.

"I had already decided I was going to go for the win," said Dickey. "I wasn't going to play for overtime. The odds were better then."

Senior Terrance Grant, playing in his final game for the Blue Hose, appeared to be stopped on the two-point conversion attempt, but he spun around into the end zone to cut Newberry's lead to 28-22 with 7:23 remaining in the game.

The Indians worked the ball deep into Presbyterian territory on their ensuing drive, but a 43-yard field goal attempt to put the game away was missed and the Blue Hose were still alive.

Travis Smith and Wilkey hooked up on a 42-yard pass play that moved the ball to the Newberry 14, but two plays later, Wilkey was sacked for a 10-yard loss.

Wilkey threw two incomplete passes that turned the ball over to Newberry on downs, allowing the Indians to run out the clock and earn their third straight Bronze Derby victory.

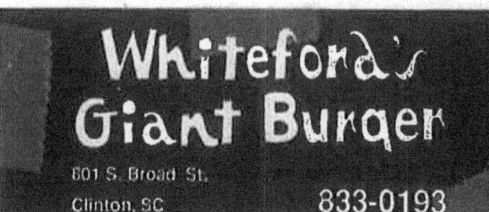

Whiteford's Giant Burger
801 S. Broad St.
Clinton, SC
833-0193

The Li'l That Was!

DIMENSIONS

Vol. 31 No. 1   Newberry College Alumni Magazine   Spring 1997

Ike Allred models the Bronze Derby for the press after the Presbyterian game.

Hunter Spivey goes back for another pass during the Presbyterian game.

FOOTBALL TEAM WINS THE BRONZE DERBY

The Indians defeated staunch rival Presbyterian in a hard fought 21-10 victory to take possession of football's Bronze Derby. The Indians made their first score three minutes into the game when Hunter Spivey connected with Rico Cannon for a 48-yard touchdown pass. The Blue Hose came back late in the first period to even the score at 7-7. In the third quarter Presbyterian went ahead briefly with a 20-yard field goal, but a pass from Spivey to Ike Allred put the Indians back in the lead. With just five minutes left in the game Allred caught a 12 yard hook pass from Spivey and made an unbelievable run. Running away from the defensive back, he broke three tackles, and ran 48 yards for the final score.

DIMENSIONS

Vol. 32 No. 1 — A Magazine for Alumni and Friends of Newberry College — Spring 1998

The Li'l That Was!

Newberry College
ATHLETICS

INDIANS KEEP BRONZE DERBY IN GOLDEN ANNIVERSARY WIN

Newberry ended the 1997 football season with a 28-22 victory over Presbyterian in the 50th annual Bronze Derby game and earned the honor of keeping the derby in Newberry for the third consecutive season. This three-year winning streak over the Blue Hose is the first since the 1955-57 seasons.

Newberry jumped out to a 21-0 halftime lead behind three touchdowns from **Vic Gilmore**, who finished the game with a career-high 210 yards rushing.

Newberry extended the lead to 28-0 in the second half when Josh Pierce took a Jack Murdock pass and turned it into a 54-yard touchdown.

That final score turned out to be significant, as the Blue Hose scored three consecutive times to close the lead to 28-22 mid-way through the final quarter. Newberry managed to hold off the PC comeback as Jeff Taylor knocked away a fourth down pass with only a minute left in the game.

The Derby game started in 1947 and the Blue Hose hold a 27-21-3 lead in the "Battle for the Derby," but the Indians have now kept it for three consecutive seasons.

Snatched from the head of a visiting Blue Hose fan 50 years ago, the Bronze Derby represents one of the oldest intercollegiate rivalries in South Carolina. Wearing the derby is senior Brion Rutherford. Photo by Ted Williams.

The Bishop's Trophy symbolizes the contest between the colleges of the ELCA North Carolina and South Carolina Synods. Five different Indians scored touchdowns in this South Atlantic Conference romp.

NEWBERRY ALSO KEEPS BISHOP'S TROPHY

Newberry also went into the game with Lenoir-Rhyne hoping to keep the Bishop's Trophy in Newberry for the third consecutive season. The Indians built a 14-7 halftime lead and cruised in the second half to defeat the Bears 49-23. Five different Indians scored touchdowns in this South Atlantic Conference romp and the Indians racked up a season-high 324 yards on the ground.

The battle for the Bishop's Trophy began in 1987 and the Bears hold a seven to four lead in the battle, but the Indians have won the

Section compiled by Darrell Orand, director of sports information

November 1998

November 1	The European Court of Human rights was established.
November 1	San Francisco 49ers quarterback Steve Young and wide receiver Jerry Rice set an NFL record with 80 career touchdowns in a game against the Green Bay Packers. The duo passed Miami Dolphins Dan Marino and Mark Clayton.
November 2	NFL quarterback Jordan Love was born.
November 3	Juvenile releases "400 Degreez", the 1999 year end #1 R&B / Hip Hop Album.
November 3	All 6 incumbent South Carolina United States Congressional Representatives won re-election.
November 6	Actor Tony Curtis of "Some Like it Hot" married Jill Vandenberg. It was his 6th and final marriage.
November 9	German actress Ursula Reith of "Willie Wonka & The Chocolate Factory" passed away.
November 9	Capital punishment in the United Kingdom was completely abolished for all capital offenses.
November 9	The largest civil settlement in United States history resulted as brokerages were ordered to pay $1 billion to United States NASDAQ investors to compensate for price fixing.
November 10	American Baseball Hall of Fame pitcher Hal Newhouser passed away.
November 10	"Star Trek: Insurrection" starring Patrick Srewart and directed by Jonathan Frakes premiered in the United States.
November 12	The Vice President of the United States Al Gore signed the symbolic Kyoto Protocol.
November 13	New York Knicks William "Red" Holzman, American Basketball Hall of Fame Coach passed away.
November 13	Michael Trudeau, son of Pierre Tudeau passed away.
November 14	Former NBA Chicago Bulls player Dennis Rodman married actress Carmen Electra.
November 14	American football wide receiver DeVonta Smith was born.
November 14	American tennis player Sophia Keniin was born.
November 14	The Bronze Derby was played in Clinton, South Carolina. The Presbyterian College Blue Hose defeated the Newberry College Indians 45-14.

Advertiser

SPORTS

Blue Hose brings Derby back to Presbyterian

Cunningham and Smith lead record-setting day that ends in lopsided victory

By Brad Bryant
Sports Editor

With the Bronze Derby firmly in his grasp, Presbyterian head football coach Daryl Dickey celebrated what possibly was the brightest moment in his young head coaching career.

The second-year coach had just witnessed his team neatly package a record-setting afternoon that ultimately resulted in the Blue Hose blowing out rival Newberry, 45-14, in the annual season-ending battle for the Bronze Derby.

"I'm just happy that our seniors were able to go out on such a positive note and end the season like we did," said Dickey, whose team finished the year at 8-3. "We had a tremendous season — it's just a shame we're not going to keep playing. I think the team is worthy of making the playoffs. This team deserves to play on."

Although the Blue Hose will not be going to the postseason, despite winning its final four games, the team used Saturday as a showcase of just how good it is.

Several players wrapped up record-setting seasons with record-setting games, including the lethal passing combination of quarterback Todd Cunningham and receiver Travis Smith.

Cunningham, who had already set the school's single-game passing record with a 358-yard effort against Elon earlier this season, shattered that mark with 409 yards passing against the Indians. Also, despite playing in only seven games, Cunningham set Presbyterian single-season records in yards with 2,080 and touchdown passes with 24.

"Todd has made a tremendous impact," Dickey said. "I knew how good Todd was the day we signed him. He had to learn the offense before he stepped in — and he still hasn't mastered it, but it's going to be fun having him around three more years."

On the day, Cunningham completed 20-of-33 passes and threw a record six touchdown passes, four of which went to Smith.

"I didn't know I was going to come in and play as quickly as I did," the freshman Cunningham said. "I just got the opportunity to step in, the team was behind me and I just tried to do what I could."

Smith was equally impressive on the day, catching nine passes for 266 yards and four scores. Smith, who had already established the single-season record for receptions, also established marks Saturday for most yards in a game, most yards in a season and also tied the single-game mark of touchdown receptions with four.

"What a football player Travis Smith is," Dickey said. "The thing about Travis is he also has a 3.0 gpa at our school. He's a guy you love to be around. He brings so much to this football team as far as character, ability and making plays."

Besides the individual marks, the 8-3 record Presbyterian finished with is the best among all college teams in South Carolina this year, while it also is the best record for Presbyterian since 1979.

Pres. 45 / Indians 14

"To have the best season we've had in some 20 years and to get the Bronze Derby back (after three years) is a good feeling," Dickey said. "And we've got the best record among all our colleges — we're excited about that. It's something our seniors can hang their hats on for a long time."

The Blue Hose got Saturday's season finale off to a good start when the duo of Cunningham and Smith struck on Presbyterian's first offensive play.

After the Blue Hose defense had forced a three-and-out on Newberry's first possession, Cunningham and company took over at their own 43-yard line.

On the first play, the freshman dropped back and perfectly lofted a pass down the right sideline that Smith hauled in despite being double covered and then scampered into the endzone.

The point after attempt was wide, but the Blue Hose had a 6-0 lead just 1:30 into the game.

◆ See HOSE, page 13 A

◆ HOSE
Continued from Page 11

After another defensive stand, Presbyterian was on the move again, going from its own 48-yard line to the Newberry 21. But the drive ended when Cunningham was flushed from the pocket and was then picked off by Demedthrus Davis.

However the Indians didn't have the ball long as Michael Scornavacca intercepted a Dustin Coates pass at the Newberry 38-yard line just two plays later.

Again the Blue Hose came up empty on the drive as John Redding's field goal try sailed wide, leaving the score 6-0 with 6:25 to go in the opening period.

Newberry finally mounted a good drive the next time it had the ball, moving from its own 20 to the Presbyterian 39, but Scornavacca ended the drive once again with an interception at the 6-yard line.

Starting from there, the Blue Hose offense traveled 94 yards in seven plays to take a 13-0 lead.

Ryan Knight started the drive with a 29-yard run. Then Cunningham had completions to Di Young, Brad Boleman and Ben Power to move his team to the Newberry 13-yard line. From there, Cunningham got the score when he found Power over the middle who got into the endzone after making a low catch of a pass that was slightly behind him.

"I just get the ball out there," Cunningham said. "The receivers make all the catches and runs. I just have a great corps of receivers."

After an exchange of possessions, the Blue Hose offense went to work again with another long drive midway through the second quarter.

Starting from its own 16-yard line, Presbyterian moved 84 yards with Cunningham and Smith ending the possession with their second touchdown of the day. This time the score covered 46 yards and gave the Blue Hose a 19-0 lead.

Newberry answered with an impressive drive of its own, moving 67 yards in just over 4:30 to get back into the game.

Trokya Bates got the touchdown when he hauled in a 25-yard pass from Coates to make the score 19-7 at the half and give the Indians some momentum.

Newberry continued to try to turn things around in the third quarter when Tony Sullivan intercepted Cunningham on the first play of the second half to give the Indians the ball at the Presbyterian 37-yard line.

Newberry had moved inside the 25 when senior defensive back Troy Gamble turned the game around. The All-South Atlantic Conference candidate stripped Newberry's Vic Gilmore as he ran up the middle and then went 79 yards for a touchdown, which, after Redding's kick, gave the Blue Hose a 26-7 lead. The fumble return also set a school record as the longest fumble return for a score, eclipsing the old record of 40 yards set in 1923 by P.H. Bomar in a 7-3 win over South Carolina.

"He sort of had the ball on his hip and wasn't protecting it very well," said Gamble, who was named All-American a season ago. "I just grabbed at it and it came out and I started running. When I didn't hear a whistle blow, I knew we had another touchdown."

The Indians tried to keep the game close as they moved 74 yards in 14 plays and got a touchdown on Coates' 3-yard option keeper on the ensuing possession. After the extra point, the Indians were back to within 12 points at 26-14 with 7:03 to go in the third quarter.

But the Blue Hose answered right back when Smith and Cunningham hooked up once more. The time the reception covered 44 yards as Smith out-jumped a Newberry defender and then waltzed into the endzone.

Redding's point after made the score 33-14 with 5:51 to go in the third period.

After dodging a bullet when Newberry's Deonte Huntley interception return of a Cunningham pass for a touchdown was nullified by an interference call, the Blue Hose began to roll the next time it had the ball.

Brad Boleman moved Presbyterian deep into Newberry territory, picking up 13 yards on a reverse. Then Cunningham found Smith once again.

Smith did most of the work on his fourth touchdown of the day, catching a short pass in the flat and juking through numerous Newberry defenders on his way to a touchdown that covered 35 yards.

The extra point was no good, but the Blue Hose was up 39-14 with 12:59 to go in the game.

"We're capable of exploding on offense," Dickey said. "We've known our football team was capable of a season like this and today they just went out and made the plays. It's a shame they can't play some more this year."

The Blue Hose's final touchdown was set up by a Lee Hannah interception as the senior defensive back caught a tipped pass, making sure to get his feet down before falling out of bounds along the sidelines at the Newberry 15-yard line.

Ben Power got the final score of the day when he hauled in 8-yard pass from Cunningham with 8:16 to go in the game.

Gamble, who is the back-up kicker, was asked to try the extra point, but his attempt was wide, leaving the Blue Hose in front 45-14.

Presbyterian finished the game with 490 yards of offense while Newberry had 333. Although the Indians were able to move the ball at times, they suffered seven turnovers (five interceptions and two fumbles), virtually locking up the top spot in the nation in turnover ratio for Presbyterian. The Blue Hose had three turnovers, all coming on interceptions.

"We haven't won this in three years," Cunningham said. "This was the first time for the seniors. I'm happy for the team. They got out of here with a win over Newberry. It's a great way to end the season."

The Li'l That Was!

Bronze Derby returns to Clinton, 45-14

By Rick Hendricks
Editor

Presbyterian College convincingly returned the Bronze Derby to Clinton Saturday, blasting Newberry 45-14 at Bailey Memorial Stadium.

The win was the eighth of the season for the Blue Hose and capped a 6-1 performance in South Atlantic Conference play.

PC head football coach **Daryl Dickey** said getting the Bronze Derby back and winning the eighth game were equal in importance.

"I think we've proven we're an exciting team to watch," said Dickey. "We laid an egg last year and I'm sure (Newberry head coach Mike Taylor) will use this next year."

The victory was also marked by record-setting performances by freshman quarterback **Todd Cunningham** and sophomore wide receiver **Travis Smith**.

Cunningham broke the single-season record for passing yardage with his 22-for-30, 409-yard, six touchdown effort.

The freshman finished the season with 2,082 yards to break assistant coach **Harold Nichols'** mark of 1,898 yards, which was set in 1989.

Cunningham also broke the single-season mark for touchdown passes in a season with 24, eclipsing **Roddy Martin's** mark set in 1942.

"Todd makes play after play," said Dickey.

On the receiving end of nine of Cunningham's passes Saturday was Smith, who broke **Lavern Reddick's** single-game mark with 266 receiving yards.

Photo by Rick Hendricks

Presbyterian quarterback Todd Cunningham (8)...
...looks for a receiver during 409-yard performance against Newberry.

The performance also gave Smith over 1,000 yards in receptions for the season on 58 catches.

Smith's four TDs on Saturday gave him 16 for the year.

"Travis is a tremendous football player," said Dickey. "He just makes catch after catch."

The Blue Hose racked up 490 yards of total offense against the Indians, while PC's defense forced seven Newberry turnovers.

Presbyterian got on the board just a minute and a half into the game.

Newberry took the opening kickoff but did nothing with it and the Blue Hose took over at their own 43.

On the first play from scrimmage, Cunningham spotted Smith streaking down the right sideline and hit him with a 57-yard touchdown pass.

John Redding missed the PAT, but the Blue Hose had the early advantage, 6-0.

Late in the first quarter, Cunningham got the Blue Hose back in the end zone with a 13-yard scoring pass to **Ben Power**.

Redding's extra point gave PC a 13-0 lead with 2:53 remaining in the

See DERBY Page 2B

Derby

Continued from Page 1B

first quarter.

The Blue Hose built their lead to 19-0 with 4:33 remaining in the first half.

Cunningham and Smith hooked up for another touchdown — this one covered 54 yards — to get PC on the board again.

Redding missed the extra point.

Newberry finally answered, driving 67 yards in 12 plays for its first score of the day.

A 25-yard pass from Indian quarterback Dustin Coats to Trokya Bates gave Newberry its first TD just 42 seconds before halftime.

Matt Deaton booted the extra point to cut the Blue Hose lead to 19-7.

The second half started with big defensive plays on both sides of the ball, but **Troy Gamble** forced a Vic Gilmore fumble and returned it 79 yards for a touchdown.

Redding booted the PAT to give Presbyterian a 26-7 lead.

"We needed a play and Troy made one for us," said Dickey. "What a job he's done all year."

Newberry responded with a 74-yard drive for its second touchdown of the day.

Coats ran the ball in from 4 yards out to get the Indians back on the scoreboard.

Deaton's PAT was good and Newberry had trimmed PC's lead to 26-14 with 7:03 left in the third quarter.

The Blue Hose responded immediately, moving 59 yards in four plays for another score.

This drive was also capped by a Cunningham-to-Smith connection from 44 yards out.

Redding's PAT increase PC's advantage to 33-14 with 5:51 to go in the third quarter.

Early in the fourth quarter, Cunningham and Smith hooked up on a 35-yard scoring pass to all but insure the Blue Hose victory.

Redding's PAT attempt was no good, but PC held a 39-14 lead with 12:59 remaining in the game.

Presbyterian scored its final touchdown with 8:16 left in the game when Cunningham hit Power with an 8-yard scoring pass.

Gamble's PAT was missed, but the Blue Hose held a 45-14 advantage.

Senior weakside linebacker **Brandon Moore** said he couldn't have imagined a better way to end his career with the Blue Hose.

"This is the way I wanted it to end up," said a beaming Moore after the game. "We emphasized not coming out flat like last year."

Moore said he doesn't think it has sunk in that he has played his final game for PC.

"I probably will about spring practice time," he said.

Dickey said the Blue Hose will have a number of big shoes to fill next year.

"We'll have a difficult time replacing those seniors," he said. "It will be a big challenge."

The Clinton Chronicle

Wednesday, November 18, 1998,

THE BLUE STOCKING
THE NEWSPAPER OF PRESBYTERIAN COLLEGE

VOLUME 94, NUMBER 6 — WEDNESDAY, NOVEMBER 25 1998 — FREE

The Li'l That Was!

Football Team Wins Awards, Bronze Derby

by Jeff Walker
Sports Editor

The Blue Hose football team finished 8-3 overall and 6-1 in the SAC this season. This is the best finish since 1979 when PC finished 11-2 and finished the regular season ranked #1 in NAIA. The Blue Hose even had a postseason award, including the Bronze Derby back from Newberry this year.

Head Coach Darryl Dickey was named the 1998 SAC Coach of the Year. Freshman quarterback Todd Cunningham was named the SAC Offensive Freshman of the Year. He set the Blue Hose single-season passing yardage mark and the single season touchdown mark. Troy Gamble, Lee Hannah, Travis Smith were all named to the First Team All-SAC. Keith Sargent, Rod Hammond, Toby Davis, Duane Thompson and Jeremy Joyner were named to the Second Team All-SAC. Gamble was selected to represent the Blue Hose at the 1999 Snow Bowl held on the North Dakota St. campus in Fargo, North Dakota. He will represent the East team. The game is slated for January 9, 1999.

The Blue Hose brought home the Bronze Derby on November 14, against rival Newberry. PC pounded the hosts 45-14. Cunningham hit Smith and Power on 52 yard and 13 yard touchdown passes in the first quarter. Cunningham hit Smith again in the second quarter on a 54 yard touchdown strike. PC took a 19-7 lead into halftime. Gamble recovered a fumble and scampered 79 yards up the sidelines for a touchdown to put the Blue Hose up 26-7. Cunningham found Smith two more times in the second half for touchdowns. The first touchdown was a 44 yard strike and the second touchdown was a 34 yard strike. Cunningham hit Power for the final blow of the game on a 8 yard touchdown pass.

Cunningham finished the game 20 of 30 for 409 yards and six touchdowns. Smith led the receiving corps with nine catches for 266 yards and four touchdowns. Ryan Knight led the rushing attack with four carries for 42 yards. The Blue Hose offense had 23 first downs and 466 total yards. The defense held Newberry to 333 total yards. Leading the defense was Thompson with 14 total tackles. Hannah and Harris each had two interceptions and Brooks had one interception. Gamble recovered two fumbles.

The Blue Hose defeated Garner-Webb University 38-9 on November 7. PC jumped out to a 17-0 halftime lead. Scoring all of their points in the second half. Gamble returned a punt 27 yards for a touchdown. Hannah returned an 18 yard interception for a touchdown to give the Blue Hose a 14-0 lead. With 35 seconds left before halftime, John Redding kicked a 33 yard field goal. The Blue Hose offense got cranked up in the second half. Cunningham hit one of his favorite targets, Rex Power on a 22 yard touchdown pass, one minute into the second half giving PC a 24-0 lead. Garner Webb answered back with a five minute drive. Cunningham got hot after the Garner Webb touchdown. He hit Brad Bozeman for two touchdown passes. One a 78 yard and the other a 50 yard touchdown pass to give the Blue Hose a 38-9 win at Boiling Springs, North Carolina.

PC tallied 411 yards of total offense and the defense held Gardner Webb to under 200 yards of total offense. Cunningham finished the game 18 of 33 for 343 yards with three touchdowns and one interception. Bozeman had five catches for 200 yards. Power had five catches for 60 yards. Knight led the ground game with 11 rushes for 58 yards. The defense sacked Gardner Webb's quarterbacks six times. Davis led the defense with 13 total tackles.

On Parent's Weekend, the Blue Hose crushed Wingate University 45-17. Cunningham hit Smith for a nine yard touchdown pass. Redding hit a 36 yard field goal to give PC a 10-0 lead after the first quarter. Wingate answered with a 39 yard field goal early in the second quarter. Cunningham hit Smith again on a 34 yard touchdown pass. Wingate came back and hit on a 42 yard pass play close the gap to 17-10. The Blue Hose scored a touchdown with 35 seconds left in the second quarter on a Cunningham 24 yard touchdown pass to Power. PC took a 24-10 halftime lead. Cunningham hit Smith for his third touchdown pass of the day on a 19 yard strike. With four minutes left in the third quarter, Cunningham ran into the end zone on a 11 yard sneak. Dean came in the game to replace Cunningham and hit Smith on a 57 yard touchdown pass play.

The Blue Hose offense had 436 total yards, along with 21 first downs. The defense held Wingate to 371 total yards and to 15 first downs. Cunningham finished the game with 16 of 26 for 210 yards with one interception and four touchdown passes. Smith had eight catches for 144 yards and four touchdowns. Power caught seven passes for 102 yards and one touchdown. Wilson and Bozeman led the rushing attack with 48 and 41 yards respectively. Gamble led the defense with 12 tackles and recovered one fumble. Hannah and Tyler each had an interception.

For the season the Blue Hose led the nation in turnover margin with +2.27 turnovers per game. The passing game finished thirteenth in the nation with 267 yards per game. The pass efficiency defense finished eighth in the nation with a rating of 86.3.

Cunningham finished the season 129 of 227 for 2,082 yards with 24 touchdowns and 11 interceptions playing in only seven games this season. Smith had 38 receptions for 1,069 yards and 16 touchdowns. Power caught 37 passes for 697 yards and nine touchdowns while Bozeman caught 30 receptions for 556 yards and five touchdowns. Knight led the ground game this season with 119 carries for 439 yards and one touchdown. Wilson carried the ball 78 times for 310 yards and scored four touchdowns. Redding finished the season six of ten on field goal attempts. On defense, Todd Huffman led the team in total hits with 93. Gamble and Davis had 85 and 76 hits respectively. Hannah led the team with eight interceptions and Gamble had four interceptions. Brandon Moore led the team with seven sacks.

The Li'l That Was!

In 1998, Presbyterian College defeated Newberry College 48-14. The game was played in Clinton, South Carolina. The game was the 52nd annual Bronze Derby football Classic.

NORTH AMERICA'S HOSPITALITY DISH

LOCATED AT
8 SO. BROAD ST.
CLINTON, S.C.
833-0824

COL. HARLAND SANDERS ORIGINAL RECIPE

WHITEFORD'S GIANT BURGER

Good Food
Fast Service

Phone 833-1930
801 S. Broad St.
Clinton, S.C.

by Jeff Walker
Sports Editor

The Blue Hose football team finished 8-3 overall and 6-1 in the SAC this season. This is the best finish since 1979 when PC finished 11-2 and finished the regular season ranked #1 in NAIA. The Blue Hose swept many postseason awards, including the Bronze Derby back from Newberry this year.

Head Coach Darryl Dickey was named the 1998 SAC Coach of the Year. Freshman quarterback Todd Cunningham was named the SAC Offensive Freshman of the Year. He set the Blue Hose single season passing yardage mark and the single season touchdown mark. Troy Gamble, Lee Hannah, Travis Smith were all named to the First Team All-SAC. Keith Sargent, Rod Hammond, Tony Harris, Duane Thompson and Jeremy Joyner were named to the Second Team All-SAC. Gamble was selected to represent the Blue Hose at the 1999 Snow Bowl held on the North Dakota St. campus in Fargo, North Dakota. He will represent the East team. The game is slated for January 9, 1999.

The Blue Hose brought home the Bronze Derby on November 14, against arch rival Newberry. PC pounded the Indians 48-14. Cunningham hit Smith and Power on 87 yard and 13 yard touchdown passes in the first quarter. Cunningham hit Smith again in the second quarter on a 53 yard touchdown strike. PC took a 19-7 lead into halftime. Gamble recovered a fumble and scampered 79 yards up the sidelines for a touchdown to put the Blue Hose up 26-7. Cunningham found Smith two more times in the second half for touchdowns. The first touchdown was a 44 yard strike and the second touchdown was a 35 yard strike. Cunningham hit Power for the final blow of the game on a 8 yard touchdown pass.

Cunningham finished the game 20 of 30 for 400 yards and six touchdowns. Smith led the receiving corps with nine catches for 266 yards and four touchdowns. Ryan Knight led the rushing attack with four carries for 42 yards. The Blue Hose offense had 23 first downs and 490 total yards. The defense held Newberry to 333 total yards. Leading the defense was Thompson with 14 total tackles. Hannah and Harris each had two touchdowns and Brooks had one interception. Gamble recovered two fumbles.

The Scarlet & Gray

Newberry College, Newberry, SC — Volume 1, Number 4 — November 20, 1998

College Jazz Ensemble has new CD — Page 3

One student's opinion about MTV — Page 4

PC recaptures Bronze Derby 45-14

BY Hampton Fuller
Reporter

For the 87th time in history, the Bronze Derby match between Presbyterian College and Newberry College was held Saturday at Bailey Stadium in Clinton, S.C. The Blue Hose of Presbyterian snapped a three-game losing streak to Newberry and handed the Indians a 45-14 loss. Due to three fumbles and three interceptions lost to PC the Indians were denied their fourth straight year of keeping the Bronze Derby.

PC scored first when Travis Smith caught a 57 yard pass from Todd Cunningham. They would scored again with 2:53 left in the first quarter off of a Ben Power 13 yard reception from Cunningham to put PC ahead 13 to 0. At the 4:53 mark of the second quarter, Smith caught a 54 yard pass from Cunningham and PC extended its lead to 19 points. The Indians finally got on the scoreboard with 42 seconds left to go in the first half on a Dustin Coates 25 yard pass to Trokya Bates.

PC scored first in the second half on a fumble recovery: Troy Gamble picked up the loose ball and rumbled 79 yards for the touchdown. Newberry got its second and final score in the third quarter on a 4 yard run by Coates.

With 5:51 to go in the third quarter, Smith of PC caught a 44 yard bomb from Cunningham to put the Blue Hose up 33 to 14. In the fourth quarter, Smith scored again on a 35 yard pass from Cunningham. Then with 8:16 to go in the game, Ben Power caught an eight yard pass from Cunningham. After the game, Coach Taylor said: "It all came down to turnovers, and poor pass defence- we had five passes intercepted, and we had three fumbles; add all that up, and you get a good tail whipping." The Indians finished their winning season at 6-5, 3-4 SAC.

November 1999

November 1	NFL Hall of Fame Running back Walter Payton passed away.
November 1	The *New York Post* reported that the television show "Judge Judy" had surpassed "Oprah" in viewership.
November 1	American NASCAR driver John Sears passed away.
November 3	The Los Angeles Lakers defeated the Vancouver Grizzlies 103-88 in the inaugural game in the STAPLES Center in Los Angeles, California.
November 6	Australians voted to keep the British monarch as their Head of State.
November 6	"Smooth" by Santana featuring Rob Thomas topped the *Billboard* Top 100.
November 6	Anthony "Snooty" Jones, bassist of Humble Pie passed away.
November 7	Dale Jarrett won the NASCAR Winston Cup Series Championship.
November 7	Tiger Woods won the inaugural World Golf Championship American Express Championship held in Sotogrande, Spain. Tiger defeated Miguel Angel Jimenez on the first extra hole of a playoff to win $1 million.
November 7	Tony Stewart won his second NASCAR race, The Checker Auto Parts Dura Lube 500 in Avondale, Arizona.
November 8	Tenor Andrea Bocelli released the world's best-selling classical studio album by a single artist, "Sacred Arias."
November 8	The 19th James Bond movie, "The World is Not Enough" premiered in Los Angeles, California starring Pierce Bronson.
November 10	"Pokemon: The First Movie - Mewtwo Strikes Back" premiered.
November 12	An earthquake measuring 7.2 on the Richter scale was centered in Turkey.
November 12	Chipper Jones of the Atlanta Braves won MLB NL Most Valuable Player Award.
November 13	Lennox Lewis defeated Evader Holyfield for the undisputed heavyweight boxing championship.
November 13	American singer Donald Mills of The Mills Brothers passed away.
November 13	"Toy Story 2," starring Tom Hanks and Tim Allen debuted in the United States.
November 13	The Bronze Derby was played in Newberry, South Carolina. The Presbyterian College Blue Hose defeated the Newberry College Indians 45-35.

The Li'l That Was!

FRIDAY | Freedom of Information Scorecard | Battle for a Bronzed Hat | 50¢
♦ Opinion, Page 4 | ♦ Sports, Page 14

The Newberry Observer

NOVEMBER 12, 1999 — *Just like a letter from home.* — NEWBERRY, S.C.

Battle for Bronze

Staff Reports

Newberry and Presbyterian look to salvage seasons that both teams thought would go better when the long-time rivals square off this Saturday afternoon at Setzler Field.

The Indians seek revenge for last season's 45-14 drubbing at the hands of the Blue Hose. PC, after having sophomore QB Todd Cunningham of Irmo named the pre-season All-SAC first teamer at signal-caller, was looking for an offensive banner year. The player Cunningham beat out for the pre-season honor -- Newberry's Dustin Coats, a junior from W. Columbia's Airport High.

For the most part, the Blue Hose offense has produced -- PC scored 40 points against Carson-Newman but lost the upset and a potential hold on first place in the conference on a late Eagles TD run. The Blue Hose ran up 51 points on the conference's cellar-dweller, Tusculum. Other impressive performances were 41 points against W. Georgia (but the defense gave up 40), 40 points against Charleston Southern, 49 points against the University of Virginia - Wise, and 43 points against Wingate.

Against the South Atlantic Conference's stiffest defense, however, the Blue Hose -- like Newberry -- has struggled, managing 10 points against Catawba (which held Newberry to three points) and 20 against Gardner-Webb (a team Newberry beat, 34-31).

Newberry's best offensive output of the season was 39 points against Wingate, only to lose a disappointing home game, 42-39.

Newberry QB Coats threw for three TDs last week against Carson-Newman, giving him 35 for his career -- a new school record. The previous record was held by 1999 Newberry College Hall of Fame inductee Jimmy Skipper (1982-85), who threw 37 TDs passes in his career.

Coats has 4,290 yards passing and is just 1,001 yards short of that career record. Records in attempts (182 short) and completions (87 short) should fall next season for Coats. The red-shirt junior could graduate or he could opt to come back for a fourth season with the Indians.

Coats' 1,899 yards passing this season is the second highest single-season total in Newberry history -- he is 186 yards away from a new single-season passing record. Coats threw for 230 yards last week against Carson-Newman; on the season, Presbyterian is allowing an average of 212.4 yards per game, the worst pass defense average in the conference. (Newberry is allowing 184.4 ypg by its opponents.)

Newberry's offense had possibly its best game of the season against top-ranked Carson-Newman, outgaining the Eagles 398 to 339 yards. The 31 points scored was the second highest surrendered by C-N this season. The problem was four turnovers, all converted into points -- 35 of C-N's 45 points came off TOs.

The Game at a Glance

The Battle for the Bronze Derby -- Newberry Indians vs. Presbyterian Blue Hose, Nov. 13, 2 p.m. at Setzler Field, Newberry College (5,000 capacity).

• Records: Newberry, 5-5 (3-4 in the South Atlantic Conference); Presbyterian, 6-4 (3-4 in SAC)

• Series: Presbyterian leads, 51-31-5.

• Last week: Newberry is coming off a 45-31 loss to Carson-Newman, the #1 teams in NCAA Division II; PC dropped a 31-20 decision to Gardner-Webb.

• Last season: In the storied history of the Bronze Derby, the win by PC was their first in four years -- since 1980, Newberry holds a 11-7-1 edge in the series. The Blue Hose won at home, 45-14, showing their offensive firepower on the first play of the game -- a 57-yard Todd Cunningham to Travis Smith TD pass.

• Back-to-Back ?: If the Indians win, it will give them a 6-5 record, identical to last season's mark. The last time NC had consecutive winning seasons was the 1984 & 85 season -- the Tribe was 7-4 in 1984 and 7-3-1 in 1985. Newberry defeated PC in 1984, 25-16, and tied the Blue Hose, at 24, in 1985.

The Li'l That Was!

The Laurens County Advertiser SPORTS

An Independent Newspaper Founded in 1895/South Carolina's Award-Winning Semi-Weekly Newspaper

Staying Put
PC wins battle for Bronze Derby

TWO IN A ROW – PC head coach Daryl Dickey raises the Bronze Derby for the second straight year after his team won 45-35 Saturday.

Staff photo by Brad Bryant

Advertiser

ON THE RUN – Presbyterian quarterback Todd Cunningham fires a pass during Saturday's annual Bronze Derby game. The sophomore quarterback helped the Blue Hose to a 45-35 victory in the season finale.

Staff photo by Brad Bryant

◆ By Brad Bryant
Sports Editor

In a game seemingly between two one-armed, defenseless heavyweights trading blows, the Presbyterian College football team got off the canvas one final time and delivered a knockout punch Saturday afternoon as the Blue Hose came away with a 45-35 victory over rival Newberry to win the 88th meeting of the Bronze Derby game.

Both teams found themselves against the ropes at times on Saturday but Presbyterian proved it had more offensive fire power and just enough defense to close the season on a positive note and give the PC program back-to-back winning seasons for the first time since the 1984 and '85 campaigns.

"This is a better victory than it was last year," said PC head coach Daryl Dickey, who got his second win in a row over the Indians. "Our football team started the year with great expectations but we've been up and down a little. We wanted to finish the year the way we started so this was a great victory."

Saturday's effort somewhat epitomized the Blue Hose's year as the team opened up leads of 21-7 and 35-14 only to see Newberry come storming back to avoid a scene like last year's 45-14 massacre.

"I give Newberry a lot of credit for fighting the way they did," said Dickey, whose team finished the year 7-4 overall and 4-4 in the South Atlantic Conference. "They're a well-coached team and they came ready to play. I have a lot of respect for Coach (Mike) Taylor and his program."

But in a game that captured the essence of a football rivalry, which included such happenings as defensive linemen from both PC and Newberry returning interceptions for touchdowns in the game's first 18 minutes, the Blue Hose showed it had just enough to pull off the victory.

"Strange things happen at a graveyard and that's where we are right now," said Dickey, referring to the cemetery that lies just beyond Newberry's Stezler Field. "Two linemen score touchdowns on interceptions – how about that for a strange ball game."

Not only was the game

◆ See **DERBY**, page 16A

Blue Hose outguns Indians, hangs on to Derby

◆ DERBY

Continued from page 14A

strange but it also served as an offensive showcase. The two teams combined for more than 800 yards of total offense, with PC gaining 492. Presbyterian quarterback Todd Cunningham just missed setting the school career record for yardage as he finished his sophomore season completing 17 of 32 passes for 284 yards and a pair of scores. Six of Cunningham's completions went to Travis Smith, who had 105 receiving yards.

But the true offensive standout for the Blue Hose was another sophomore, running back Donald Wilson, who rushed for 123 yards and two touchdowns as well as caught a 43-yard scoring pass from Cunningham.

"Donald really came to play today," said Dickey, whose team rolled up 208 yards on the ground. "He did a tremendous job. Today I told him this was going to be his springboard because he is going to be a great player for us."

Meanwhile, the Blue Hose defense was exposed for 330 yards by the Indians but did manage to produce four turnovers, including 6-0, 295-pound Keon Talbert's 35-yard interception return for a touchdown.

"The defense did a good job," Dickey said. "We gave a little bit but we made some key plays."

The Blue Hose opened the game in fine fashion, taking the opening kickoff and driving 59 yards in three plays to take an early 7-0 lead.

Wilson was the workhorse on the drive, notching carries of 14 and seven yards on the ground. He then got into the end zone when Cunningham threw him a middle screen in which he ran through and spun away from would-be tacklers on his way to the 43-yard score.

John Redding added the point after as PC was in front 7-0 just 1:13 into the game.

Presbyterian then went for the early kill, attempting an onside kick which the Blue Hose recovered.

However, the momentum quickly changed when Newberry defensive end Nick Whitner stepped in front of a Cunningham screen pass and returned it 32 yards untouched for a touchdown.

After B.J. Griffin's extra point kick, the game was tied at 7-7 just 1:28 into the contest.

The furious pace slowed a bit as the two exchanged punts on their next possessions; however, PC was back in the scoring column the next time it got the ball.

Capping a 60-yard, seven play drive, Wilson got his second touchdown of the day diving over from a yard out. Cunningham set up the score by lofting a pass down the sidelines that Smith

Staff photo by Brad Bryant
OVER THE TOP — PC running back Donald Wilson dives over the pile and into the end zone for one of his three touchdowns.

hauled in for a 50-yard gain on a third-and-20 play that got the Hose down to the three-yard line. Two plays later Wilson went in as PC moved in front 14-7 with 5:41 to go in the opening period.

Presbyterian had one more scoring opportunity in the first period; however, a 36-yard field goal effort by Redding was no good.

It didn't matter though as Talbert put the Blue Hose up 21-7 with his interception return in the opening minutes of the second period.

The play was very similar to Whitner's return as Talbert stepped in front of a screen pass. Instead of having a clear path to the end zone, though, Talbert bounced off of several Newberry players, eventually running over an Indian at the goal line as he lumbered in for the score.

Trailing 21-7, Newberry wasn't ready to fold. On the Indians' next possession they drove 68 yards in nine plays to pull within a touchdown.

Quarterback Dustin Coats provided the score when he lofted a pass to Jeff Tucker, who had gotten behind the PC defense. After the 31-yard pass play the score was 21-14 with 8:29 to go in the opening half.

PC, though, came right back with a staggering blow of its own. Cunningham's passing and Wilson's running moved the Blue Hose 52 yards in seven plays, as Wilson got his third touchdown of the day on a rush from four yards out.

While Wilson did have 30 yards rushing in the drive, it was Cunningham's passing that proved invaluable as he picked up two first downs with his three completions, including two that came back-to-back to convert a second-and-19 situation.

Newberry tried to add one more touchdown just before the half as Coats drove his team to the PC 15-yard line; however, Josh Pierce fumbled on a carry up the middle and Brandon Stewart recovered to preserve PC's 28-14 lead at intermission.

Newberry got the ball to start the second half and quickly moved to the Blue Hose 40-yard line.

But the drive stalled. Newberry tried to keep things going, opting to go for it on fourth and one, but the PC defense came through with the stop to give the ball back over to the Blue Hose.

Wilson then picked up where he left off, carrying six straight times down to the Newberry 22-yard line.

Then after an eight-yard Cunningham completion to Brad Boleman, Wilson carried for eight yards down to the three-yard line. From there Cunningham rolled to his right and found Jerome Bryant in the end zone for the score. Redding's point after put the Blue Hose up 35-14.

But just like it had in the first half, Newberry came battling back. Two possessions later, Newberry's leading rusher Vic Gilmore finally got on track, breaking up the middle for a 36-yard touchdown run that made the score 35-21.

After PC was unable to move the football, Coats capped a 13-play, 58-yard drive with a nine-yard touchdown completion to Adrian Pigford on a third-and-goal play to make the score 35-28.

"I was worried," Dickey said, remembering how he felt after Newberry's second straight touchdown. "Coach Taylor said his team had learned to fight for 60 minutes and that thought kept going through my mind. I knew they were going to come back but I didn't know to what extent and I didn't know if we could answer."

Fortunately for Dickey and the Blue Hose, the PC offense could answer. After Newberry's touchdown, the Blue Hose moved down the field and got a 42-yard field goal from Redding to take a 38-28 lead.

The PC defense then came through on the next series, sacking Coats twice and forcing a fumble on the second one which the Blue Hose's Nick Harris recovered at the Indians' 18-yard line.

From there running back Paul Freeman needed only two carries to find the end zone, the second of which was from 13 yards out as he fought his way in for the score. Redding's point after kick was again good as PC had moved in front 45-28 with 5:54 to go in the game.

"It was tremendous for us to come back like we did," Dickey said. "We were really proud of our football team for how they responded."

But like any Blue Hose lead this year, its security wasn't safe until the final gun. Newberry added one final touchdown when Coats hooked up with Pigford on a 34-yard score with 4:22 remaining but that was all the Indians could manage as the Blue Hose offense ran out the clock.

"We wanted to finish on a real positive note," Dickey said. "We've got an extremely young football team and I think the best years are ahead for this program. We're excited about the future and I'm glad we finished the way we did so we can springboard into next year."

The Newberry Observer

Just like a letter from home.

NOVEMBER 15, 1999 — NEWBERRY, S.C.

The Li'l That Was!

Celebrate with a Teammate

Photo by Vic MacDonald

Senior wide receivers Adrian Pigford, #21, and Jeff Tucker, #14, celebrate Tucker's 32-yard touchdown catch in the first quarter of the Newberry - Presbyterian Bronze Derby football game Saturday at Setzler Field. Pigford also caught two TD passes from Indians' quarterback Dustin Coats, as he and Tucker, a former standout at Chapin High School, played in their final game for Newberry College – a 45-35 loss to rival Presbyterian. The play of Pigford and Tucker at the wide receivers position was a major reason why Coats was nearly able to throw for a school-record in single-season yardage. The Indians entered the game needing 186 yards passing to set the new record; they got 181 in passing yards against Presbyterian.

The Li'l That Was!

The Newberry Observer

NOVEMBER 15, 1999 — *Just like a letter from home.* — NEWBERRY, S.C.

PAGE 8 Monday, Nov. 15, 1999

Derby Winners' TD

Photo by Ted B. Williams

Presbyterian's Donald Wilson, #34, dives into the endzone with one of his two touchdowns on the afternoon in the Blue Hose's 45-35 win Saturday at Setzler Field. Wilson led the PC offensive attack with 121 yards rushing and a 43-yard pass reception.

Derby Duel Goes to PC

Staff reports

Presbyterian College turned four Newberry turnovers into 14 points on the way to a 45-35 win Saturday over the Indians to close out the college football season.

PC's win keeps the Bronze Derby in Clinton for another season. The Blue Hose finish the campaign 7-4, 4-4 in the South Atlantic Conference; Newberry ends at 5-6, 3-5 in the conference.

Donald Wilson led the Blue Hose with 121 yards and two rushing TDs on 21 carries. Vic Gilmore led Newberry's attack with 108 yards and a score on 20 carries. The TD was Gilmore's career 32nd; he needs just two more in his senior season to become the Indians' career leader.

With the Blue Hose leading 45-28, Newberry tried for a comeback as junior QB Dustin Coats hit senior wide receiver Adrian Pigford from 34 yards out. That would be all the scoring for the Indians, however, as Newberry failed to recover the on-side kick and PC was able to run the clock down to the final :21. Newberry took over on downs, and Coats completed his final two passes.

But it was not enough, as Newberry failed to bring home the Bronze Derby for the second straight year.

Presbyterian had taken a 35-14 lead on a Todd Cunningham to Jerome Bryan pass from four yards out. The tally came after Newberry's Josh Pierce came up inches short on a critical fourth and one attempt.

The Tribe sliced into that lead as Gilmore broke free from 37 yards out. With the run, Gilmore went over 1,000 yards for the season, and became just the second NC player to rush for more than 1,000 yards twice in his career.

Newberry cut PC's lead even more when Coats hooked up with Pigford on a 10 yard scoring toss with more than 12 minutes left to play.

The Blue Hose offense then went on a 6:11 drive that ended in John Redding booting a 43-yard field goal. PC was the beneficiary of another Newberry turnover when Coats was hit inside the Indians' 20. It took just two plays for Paul Freeman to scoot in and push the PC lead to 45-28, too much for the Indians to overcome.

Senior defensive end Nick Whitner got the score knotted at seven in the first quarter when he stepped in front of a Cunningham pass and rambled 32 yards for a TD. PC later returned the favor, as defensive tackle Keon Talbert intercepted a Coats' pass at the line of scrimmage and ran in 35 yards.

Coats' 32-yard scoring strike to senior wide receiver Jeff Tucker (from Chapin) cut PC's lead to 21-14. It was the 36th scoring pass of Coats' career; he holds the school record.

THE BLUE STOCKING

THE NEWSPAPER OF PRESBYTERIAN COLLEGE

VOLUME 95, NUMBER 6 — **TUESDAY, NOVEMBER 23, 1999** — **FREE**

Football falls to Gardner-Webb, clenches Bronze Derby

by Hank Coleman
Sports Editor

Presbyterian College's football team lost a week ago during PC's annual Parents' Weekend against visiting Gardner-Webb University 31-20 in South Atlantic Conference action in Bailey Stadium.

The Bulldogs jumped out to a seven point lead in the first quarter until PC came right back with a 61-yard touchdown pass from sophomore quarterback Todd Cunningham to junior wideout Travis Smith to bring the score within one point. Gardner-Webb went into the locker room at halftime after two more unanswered touchdowns, bringing the score up to 21-6.

In the second half, the punishment continued as the Bulldogs added a touchdown and a field goal to their score. The Blue Hose managed to come alive a little too late near the end of the game with two touchdowns, but they could not come any closer to winning. Cunningham completed 23 out of 41 passes for 292 yards and two touchdowns while leading the team in rushing with 73 yards on 18 carries. Smith led the receiving with 134 yards on seven catches and a touchdown. Gardner-Webb rolled over the Blue Hose with a total of 500 yards of offense compared to just 104 yards rushing for PC.

Presbyterian College's football team rebounded after the loss by winning the annual Bronze Derby game against rival Newberry College this past Saturday at the Indians' field. PC won its second consecutive Bronze Derby by a score of 45-35, ending the season with an overall record of 7-4 and a conference record of 4-4.

It did not take long for PC to jump on the Indians when Cunningham passed the ball to Donald Wilson for a 43-yard touchdown on the opening drive. Newberry College quickly tied the score on an interception. Then, PC scored two more touchdowns with another pass to Wilson and an interception of their own that was run into the end zone 35 yards by sophomore defensive tackle Keon Talbert. Wilson's third touchdown of the day and a catch by sophomore Tank Bryant pushed the Blue Hose lead to 35-14. PC ended its scoring for the game with a field goal by senior kicker John Redding and a ten yard run by junior running back Paul Freeman for a final score of 45-35. Wilson led the Blue Hose with 121 yards on 21 carries and three touchdowns. Todd Cunningham finished the game with 284 passing on 17 of 32 attempts.

The Scarlet & Gray

Study abroad — Page 3

Basketball season — Page 5

Indians give up Bronze Derby

By HAMPTON FULLER
Reporter

The 88th annual Bronze Derby Game was held in Newberry between the Newberry Indians and the PC Blue Hose. The Blue Hose retained the trophy for the second year in a row, winning 45-35.

PC drew first blood on a Donald Wilson 43 yard reception from Todd Cunningham with 13:42 to go in the first quarter. Newberry returned the favor on a Nick Whitner 32 yard interception return with 13:32 remaining, tieing the game 7-7.

At the 5:41 mark, Wilson scored again from 1 yard out, giving them a 14-7 advantage.

Then at the 12:22 mark of the second quarter, Keon Talbert returned a 35 yard interception for a touchdown. Then with 8:29 to go in the half, Jeff Tucker scored on a 32 yard pass from Dustin Coats.

PC scored the last touchdown of the first half on a Wilson 4 yard run, giving them a 28-14 halftime lead.

In the third quarter, PC scored first on a Cunningham to Jerome Bryant 4 yard pass with 7:50 to go. Newberry responded with 3:59 to go on a Vic Gilmore 37 yard run to cut PC's lead to 35-21. Then Newberry went on a comeback quest, with Adrian Pigford scoring on a 10 yard reception from Coats with 12:07 to go in the game. PC was unable to get the ball in the end zone on its next drive; however, Chris Redding kicked a 47 yard field goal, which extended PC's lead to 10. Three minutes later, PC's Paul Freeman scored from 13 yards out. 45-28

The final touchdown ended up being scored by the home team, on a 34 yard pass from Coats to Pigford with 4:22 left in the game. 45-35.

After the game, Coach Taylor said that "the field goal was big because it kept PC from scoring yet another touchdown. However, we turned the ball over twice inside the 20 yard line, which took us out of scoring opportunities."

The Newberry football team finished its season 5-6 overall, 3-5 in the South Atlantic Conference.

November 2000

The Li'l That Was!

November 1	Miami Heat coach Pat Riley became the second coach in the history of the NBA to reach 1000 wins with a 105-79 victory over the Orlando Magic. Lenny Wilkens was the first to achieve the 1000th NBA win milestone.
November 2	The first crew of the International Space Station arrived on board.
November 4	Limp Bizkit had the top album in the United States, "Chocolate Starfish and The Hot Dog Flavored Water."
November 5	Austrian-American fashion designer Etienne Aigner passed away.
November 5	Jeff Burton won his 11th career NASCAR race at the 2000 Checker Auto Parts Dura Lube 500 in Avondale, Arizona.
November 5	The top film in the United States was "Charlie's Angels."
November 7	R. Kelley released "TP-2.com" which became the *Billboard* Album of the Year.
November 7	"Florida, Florida, Florida," became his famous saying as NBC journalist Tim Russert announced the outcome of the 2000 United States Presidential election.
November 7	George Bush became President of the United States defeating Al Gore. The controversial result was resolved by the United States Supreme Court.
November 7	Representing the state of New York, former United States First Lady Hillary Clinton was elected to the United States Senate.
November 7	In Wamego, Kansas, The United States Drug Enforcement Administration discovered one of the country's largest LSD labs in a converted missile silo.
November 10	Atlanta Braves shortstop Rafael Furcal won MLB NL Rookie of the Year Award.
November 11	The Florida Gators defeated the USC Gamecocks 41-21.
November 11	155 snowboarders and skiers died when a railway caught fire in an alpine tunnel near Kaprun, Austria.
November 11	Mike Weir of Canada became the eventual winner of the World Golf Championship American Express Championship in Sotogrande, Spain.
November 11	The Bronze Derby was played in Clinton, South Carolina. The Presbyterian College Blue Hose defeated the Newberry College Indians 34-27.

Sports

The Clinton Chronicle
Wednesday, November 15, 2000

Blue Hose keep Bronze Derby for another year

By David Hays
For the Chronicle

"We gave them one to remember."

That's how Presbyterian quarterback Todd Cunningham summed up what will likely be the last Bronze Derby game ever played at Bailey Memorial Stadium.

Terry Meng's second touchdown catch of the day with 26 seconds left gave the Blue Hose a 34-27 victory over Newberry Saturday in the 89th meeting of the rivalry. PC finished 26-10-1 against the Indians at Bailey Stadium and is 53-31-5 overall in the historic series.

Know The SCORE PC

| Presbyterian | 34 |
| Newberry | 27 |

The school officially began its public fund-raising drive to build a new stadium at another location on campus during halftime of Saturday's game.

The new facility is expected to be ready in time for the 2002 season.

The euphoria of Saturday's victory didn't last long, however, because Valdosta State's win over West Georgia that evening ended PC's hopes for a playoff berth.

The Blue Hose finished with their best record since 1979, winning their last six games for an 8-2 mark (6-1 South Atlantic Conference.) But Catawba (10-0), Valdosta State (10-1), Delta State (10-1) and West Georgia (10-1) will represent the South Region in the Division II playoffs.

It was the final game for seniors receivers Di Young, Travis Smith and D.J. Humphries, offensive linemen Damien Jackson and Jason Fox, kicker John Redding, defensive tackle Adam Cresswell, and cornerbacks Roderick Gambrell and Michael Scornavacca. Gambrell was unable to play due to an ankle injury.

Saturday's game proved the old adage that you can "throw out the records" when rivals play. Newberry wound up 4-7, 1-6 in the conference. But the Indians gave PC all it wanted.

"It doesn't matter what the records are or what the stats are. When two rivals meet, it's going to be a dogfight," Cunningham said. "Every time we scored, they would come back and hit us right back in the mouth."

"Give Newberry a lot of credit for playing hard and playing to win like they did," Blue Hose coach Daryl Dickey said. "Whenever these

Mr. Smith doffs the derby
Photo by Fletcher Pruitt Jr.

Presbyterian wide receiver Travis Smith from Dublin, Ga., playing in his last game as a Blue Hose, celebrates PC's 34-27 last-minute victory over rival Newberry College last Saturday at Bailey Memorial Stadium.

The Clinton Chronicle

two teams get together, it's a big rivalry and you can throw everything out. They came in here to win."

The statistics didn't mean much. Presbyterian outgained the Indians 505-191 in total offense, but Newberry stayed in the game due to punt, kickoff and interception returns for touchdowns.

The Blue Hose needed two scoring drives in the fourth quarter to win the game. Newberry had just scored its only offensive touchdown when Shawn Carnes bulled in from the 6 to pull the Indians within 21-19 with 9:54 left. Max Grant batted down Newberry's two-point conversion pass.

Presbyterian answered with an 18-play, 83-yard drive which took seven minutes and 39 seconds off the clock. Paul Freeman scored on a 3-yard run, but Redding missed the point after for a 27-19 lead with 2:15 to go.

Vic Gilmore returned the ensuing kickoff 97 yards for a touchdown and Dustin Coats passed to Chad Tackett for the game-tying two-point conversion with 1:58 left, a shocker which evened the score at 27.

The Blue Hose knew what they had to do in the final two minutes.

"We went to five wides and just worked it down the field," said Cunningham. "I just took what they gave me and the receivers made plays.

"Coach told me, 'Be smart. We have two minutes and three time-outs, even if it takes six yards at a time. We're going to get down the field.'"

Cunningham opened the drive with a 9-yard pass to Kevie Smith, who was body-slammed at the end of the play for an additional 15-yard personal foul penalty to the Indians 49. Travis Smith caught 14- and 10-yard passes to keep the chains moving.

Facing third-down and 15, Cunningham hit Meng on a crossing pattern from 16 yards out for the game-winner. Meng and Travis Smith each ran short "scissors" routes to opposite sides, and Meng got open to the left.

"All I could see was the end zone and I knew I had to get there," said the red-shirt freshman, who had one man to beat after catching the pass inside the 10.

"Todd gave me a perfect ball. All I could think about was getting into the end zone, using my speed, the little bit I've got, to get in there."

Presbyterian booted the ball

See BLUE HOSE Page 4B

Rothar gets rough
PC sophomore linebacker Russell Rothar from Ft. Lauderdale, Fla., had another big game for the Blue Hose in the season-ending victory over Newberry College. Rothar had four unassisted tackles and nine assisted to lead the Presbyterian defense. Despite having an 8-2 season mark, the Blue Hose will not be going to the playoffs.

The Clinton Chronicle

Blue Hose

8-2 Blue Hose won't be in playoff field

Continued from Page 1B

away from Gilmore on the ensuing kickoff, giving the Indians possession at their 29. On the next play, tackle Keon Talbert sacked Coats and forced a fumble. Defensive end Nacomma Maxwell, as he did against Carson-Newman, clinched the victory with a fumble recovery.

"I thought our team really sucked it up in the fourth quarter," said Dickey. "Offensively, the last two drives were tremendous. Eighteen plays, seven-and-a-half minute drive. Then to lose the lead again, and take it down in under two minutes and score was a tremendous accomplishment."

The Blue Hose won despite a less than stellar performance by Harlon Hill Trophy candidate Cunningham who completed 17 of 32 passes for 275 yards and three touchdowns but was intercepted four times. At one point early in the fourth quarter, Cunningham was only 9 of 22 passing.

"I didn't play well at all," he admitted. "I think that is probably one of the worst games I've ever played. The team rallied around me and found a way to win."

Newberry's Sentelle Peake opened the scoring with a 46 yard punt return.

But the Blue Hose pulled even when Cunningham scrambled away from the rush and found Meng open in the right corner of the end zone from 29 yards out with 4:14 left in the first quarter.

"I was a little nervous at first," Meng said. "I was going to make sure I was in bounds. I almost didn't catch up with the ball."

The Indians regained the lead when Tyrone Rouse returned his first career interception 81 yards for a touchdown. But B.J. Griffin missed the point after.

Cunningham scrambled 10 yards for a touchdown on the third play of the second quarter to give PC a 14-13 lead.

An important momentum swing came late in the first half after Newberry had driven to the Blue Hose 14. Coats fumbled on the next play and Ryan Bowers recovered.

Two plays later Cunningham threw the longest touchdown pass of his career, an 88-yarder to Travis Smith. The All-American caught the sideline toss near midfield, broke a tackle and raced to the end zone for a 21-13 lead with 1:19 left in the first half.

"He put the ball in the right spot and I tried to catch the ball and outrun everybody else," said Smith, who caught eight passes for 169 yards to finish his brilliant career with school records in catches (183), yards (3,095), and receiving touchdowns (34).

Losing leading rusher Donald Wilson to a right ankle injury in the first half didn't help the Blue Hose offense, which struggled in the third quarter and was held to a missed field goal.

Newberry opened the fourth quarter with an 11-play, 74-yard scoring drive, setting the stage for the dramatic final 10 minutes.

"The four years went by pretty fast," Smith said, looking back on his career. "I don't think there could be any better way to go out, winning a close game. It would have been better if we could have blown them out. But you remember the close ones better and they taste a little bit sweeter."

The members of Presbyterian College's football team did all that they could do Saturday by defeating Newberry 34-27 for the Bronze Derby, but their bid for postseason play fell short Sunday as the NCAA Division II Football Championships field was announced.

Catawba College (10-0), the top seed in the South Region will host State University of West Georgia (10-1) this Saturday in Salisbury, N.C., in one South Region first round game.

The other first round matchup will include Delta State University (10-1) hosting Valdosta State University (10-1) on the same date. Earlier this year, Delta State defeated Valdosta State 45-35 at home on October 7.

Presbyterian College (8-2) entered the final week of the regular season with a #6 region ranking. Tuskegee, who was ranked #4, had decided not to participate in the NCAA postseason this year giving the Blue Hose an "unofficial" #5 ranking.

Saturday's 45-35 win by Valdosta State over West Georgia helped to eliminate PC's chances of a postseason bid.

Presbyterian running back Donald Wilson fights his way for some yards during Saturday's game with Newberry. PC won the annual Bronze Derby with a last-minute touchdown.

The Li'l That Was!

The Laurens County Advertiser

Presbyterian wins battle for Bronze Derby
Late touchdown pass lifts Blue Hose to third-straight win in the series

By Rich Browne
Staff Writer

Despite taking an eight-point lead into the fourth quarter on Saturday in the 54th annual Bronze Derby Classic, Presbyterian College found itself forced to score twice in the closing minutes in order to hang on to the Bronze Derby for the third year in a row.

The Indians of Newberry College would cut PC's lead to two with 9:54 left in the game when their fullback Shawn Carnes broke through the center of the Blue Hose line on 2nd and 3 from the PC 6 to score. Going for two to tie the game, Indian quarterback Dustin Coats' pass was batted down in the end zone by Max Grant.

PC would respond with junior quarterback Todd Cunningham engineering an 83-yard drive on 18 plays to put the Blue Hose back up by eight. Junior running back Paul Freeman was the work horse of the drive, carrying the ball eight times, with the last carry going off tackle from three yards out to score. A bad snap from center on the point after attempt caused kicker John Redding's boot to go wide left, which left the door open for Newberry.

The Indians' Vic Gilmore, the senior running back who had been considered doubtful for the game due to injuries, took the ball at his own 3 yard line on the ensuing kickoff and ran all the way back up the field to score a 97-yard touchdown return. A successful two-point conversion threw the game back into a tie with less than two minutes remaining.

Cunningham, who had been struggling all afternoon and had been picked off four times, put PC's two-minute offense into high gear and moved the ball 73 yards on eight plays, finding freshman wide receiver Terry Meng crossing the center of the end zone with a go-ahead touchdown pass with 26 seconds left in the game. This time, Redding's point-after kick was good.

Newberry would try to stage another miracle comeback but quarterback Coats would fumble on the first play from scrimmage and the Blue Hose's sophomore defensive end Nacomma Maxwell covered it to give PC control of the ball on the Newberry 21 with 14 seconds on the clock and, effectively, end the game.

It had been a long afternoon for the Blue Hose who, despite leading statistically, found themselves fighting for the lead.

Despite stopping the Indians on their first drive and forcing a punt, PC fell behind in the game in the first period as Newberry's Sentell Peake took the punt on PC's first possession and returned it 46 yards for a touchdown with 7:52 left.

The Blue Hose, however, bounced back as junior running back Donald Wilson powered PC down to the Indians' 21 before a leg injury forced him from the game. On 3rd and 18 from the Newberry 28 after being pushed back 10 yards by a penalty, Cunningham scrambled and, as coverage broke down, floated a pass to Meng in the corner of the end zone for the score. Redding's point after kick was accurate and the Blue Hose had tied the game at 7-7 with 4:14 left in the first.

The Indians were forced to punt after its next series, although a pair of off-setting penalties had prompted a re-kick that was nearly blocked near the Newberry goal line, and PC had possession at the Newberry 43.

Forced to scramble as the Indian defensive front put pressure on him, Cunningham threw one incomplete pass. On second down, Newberry defensive back Tyrone Rouse picked off the first of four interceptions of Cunningham and returned it 81 yards for another Indian touchdown.

The point after attempt kick went wide right but Newberry owned a 13-7 lead going into the second

Photo by Dale Knight
VICTORY — Presbyterian College wide receiver Travis Smith raises the Bronze Derby high above his head Saturday evening.

PC just misses playoffs

The Presbyterian College football team did all they could do Saturday in defeating Newberry 34-27 for the Bronze Derby, but their bid for postseason play fell short as the NCAA Division II Football Championship pairings were announced Sunday.

Catawba College (10-0), the top seed in the South Region will host State University of West Georgia (10-1) this Saturday Nov. 18 in Salisbury, N.C. in one South Region first round game. The other first round match-up will include Delta State University (10-1) hosting Valdosta State University (10-1) on the same date. Earlier this year, Delta State defeated Valdosta State 45-35 at home on Oct. 7.

Presbyterian College (8-2) entered the final week of the regular season with a no. 6 region ranking. Tuskegee, who was ranked fourth, had decided not to participate in the NCAA postseason this year giving the Blue Hose an unofficial no. 5 ranking. Saturday's 45-35 win by Valdosta State over West Georgia help to eliminate PC's chances of a postseason bid.

period.

Without Wilson's services, Cunningham turned to junior running back Joseph Bell to provide the main offensive thrust for the Blue Hose on the ensuing drive. Senior wide receiver Di Young provided 26 yards in the seven-play drive when he took a reverse back around right end.

On 2nd and 9 from the Newberry 11, Cunningham was flushed from the pocket and scrambled into the end zone to score. Redding's successful point-after kick put the Blue Hose up 14-13 with 13:46 left in the first half.

After Newberry was forced to punt, Cunningham would suffer his second pass interception, giving the Indians the ball back at their own 25. Newberry failed to capitalize on the turnover as Coats bobbled two snaps and the Indians ended up punting again.

PC went nowhere on its next series and Newberry took over on the touchback at its own 20 after the Blue Hose punt.

The Indians then mounted a serious scoring threat, moving the ball down to the PC 14 before Coats fumbled the snap and PC's strong safety Ryan Bowers recovered the loose football at the PC 7. Throwing from his own 12, Cunningham found Blue Hose wide receiver Travis Smith open around the PC 38 and Smith streaked the rest of the way down the sideline to score on an 88-yard pass reception with 1:19 left in the half. With Redding's kick, PC took a 21-13 lead into the break.

Neither team was able to score in the third period with the only threat coming when a 40-yard field goal attempt by PC's Redding fell wide to the right.

Newberry's Gilmore was the leading rusher in the game, picking up 88 yards on 19 carries. PC's Freeman had 65 yards on 16 carries, followed by Cunningham with 64 yards on 12 carries, Wilson with 53 yards on seven carries, and Bell with 39 yards on 11 carries. Cunningham was 17-for-34 in the passing department for 275 yards while getting sacked twice and throwing four interceptions. Newberry's Coats would pass 13 times, completing seven for 77 yards but would suffer four sacks.

Saturday's game was the last Bronze Derby Classic that will be held in the venerable Bailey Memorial Stadium.

Built in 1928, Bailey Stadium will be replaced by a new football facility that PC expects to open in the fall of 2002.

MONDAY

Goodyear Honors Soil District
♦ Business -- Page 5

Indians Nearly Nip Blue Hose
♦ Sports -- Page 8

The Newberry Observer

NOVEMBER 13, 2000 — *Just like a letter from home.* — NEWBERRY, S.C.

PAGE 8 Monday, November 13, 2000 -- The Newberry Observer

Sports

PC Nips Newberry In Final Seconds

By Vic MacDonald
Editor

Presbyterian was playing the final Bronze Derby game at Bailey Memorial Stadium. The Blue Hose needed a win to qualify for the NCAA Division II national playoffs. They were trying to finish second in the South Atlantic Conference.

The Newberry Indians were playing for pride.

And with :26 left on the clock it looked like the two old rivals -- Saturday was their 89th meeting on the gridiron -- were headed to overtime. But PC's Houdini-like quarterback Todd Cunningham had one more trick to pull out of the hat, a slant pass to Terry Meng that covered the last 17 yards of Newberry real estate into the endzone, giving PC a 34-17 Bronze Derby win. After a celebration pile-up in the corner of the endzone, the Blue Hose booted through the final point.

Newberry's final possession of the hard-fought battle ended with a fumble. The last-second PC touchdown negated an electrifying 97-yard kick-off return for a touchdown by Vic Gilmore, playing his final game for Newberry. The Indians career leader in rushing yardage finished with 88 tough yards, one of his best outputs of the season which was virtually ended after a shoulder injury in the second game against Furman.

"I really don't care about them," said a dejected Newberry head coach Mike Taylor of all the incentives Presbyterian had for winning the game. "I care about our kids. I've always said if we met in Joanna and played in a pasture (against Presbyterian) we'd play hard."

Taylor credited his defense with its best game of the season, even though the statistics didn't show it. The high-powered Presbyterian offense gained 505 yards on 82 offensive plays. Newberry had just 50 offensive plays.

But the Indians kept the game in doubt until the end with special teams play and plays in the defensive secondary. In addition to Gilmore's 97-yard kick return followed by Chad Tickett's two-point conversion pass reception which tied the game, Sentell Peake scored the game's first TD on a 46-yard punt return. Senior Tyrone Rouse added an 81-yard interception return for a score. Newberry's other touchdown was on a six-yard burst up the middle by Lexington's Shawn Carnes in the fourth quarter.

"I thought we were headed for overtime, and I liked our chances in overtime," Taylor said. "Penalties hurt us, we turned the ball over and we gave up a long touchdown pass."

Travis Smith's 88-yard touchdown reception from Cunningham with just 1:19 left in the first half was the longest scoring play of the game. Cunningham also scored an 11-yard rushing TD and threw 29 yards to Meng in the first quarter for another PC score. Paul Freeman also tallied a three-yard TD run against the Indians. It was enough for PC's third straight Bronze Derby win.

Photo by Vic MacDonald
Senior Vic Gilmore, #3, outruns PC defenders for a 97-yard kickoff return for a TD with 1:58 left in Saturday's Bronze Derby game in Clinton. The two-point conversion following the touchdown tied the score at 27.

PC wins last Bronze Derby Game at Bailey Memorial

The Blue Stocking — NOVEMBER 17, 2000

Presbyterian College redshirt freshman wideout Terry Meng (Campobello, SC) caught his second TD catch of the day with :26 seconds remaining to give the Blue Hose a 34-27 win over Newberry College in the annual Bronze Derby Classic Saturday afternoon.

The game was in doubt down to the last play as Newberry fought back after every Blue Hose score to keep the game close.

PC took a 21-13 lead into the fourth quarter only to see Newberry's junior fullback Shawn Carnes (W. Columbia, SC) scored from six yards out to cut the lead to 21-19 with 9:54 remaining. Newberry missed the two-point conversion as Indian quarterback senior Dustin Coats' (W. Columbia, SC) pass was deflected by PC's junior defensive back Max Grant (Ridgeville, SC) in the endzone.

The Blue Hose took advantage and marched 83 yards on 18 plays as junior halfback Paul Freeman (Lawrenceville, GA) scored on a three-yard run to give PC a 27-19 lead with 2:15 remaining. On the ensuing kickoff, Newberry's senior tailback Vic Gilmore (Denmark, SC) ran 97 yards for a TD to pull the Indians to within 27-25 with 1:58 remaining.

Coats found sophomore running back Chad Tackett (Swansea, SC) in the endzone for a two-point conversion to tie the game at 27-27.

PC's junior quarterback Todd Cunningham (Irmo, SC), who struggled for most of the day, stepped up with 1:51 remaining and led the Blue Hose on a 73-yard drive on eight plays and found wideout Meng for a 17-yard TD reception to give PC a 34-27 lead.

The game was still in jeopardy with :20 seconds remaining when PC's junior defensive tackle Keon Talbert (Greenville, SC) sacked Coats, who fumbled on the Newberry 24 yard line and Blue Hose sophomore defensive end Nacomma Maxwell (Hartwell, GA) recovered the fumble to end the last Indian threat.

Special teams was the name of the game early for the Indians as junior wideout Sentell Peake (Union, SC) returned a 46-yard punt for a TD to give Newberry a 7-0 lead at the 7:52 of the first quarter. After a Cunningham to Meng touchdown, Newberry's senior defensive back Tyrone Rouse (Edgefield, SC) picked off one of four Cunningham passes on the day and returned it 81 yards for a TD and a 13-7 Indian lead in the first quarter.

PC came back in the second quarter as Cunningham ran for a 11-yard TD run and found senior wideout Travis Smith (Dublin, GA) for a 88-yard TD strike to put PC ahead 21-13 at the half. PC dominated the game on offense, outgaining the Indians 291 to 104 in the first half.

For the game, PC gained 505 yards of total offense while holding the Indians to 191 yards.

PC was led by Smith who caught eight passes for 169 yards and one TD while Freeman led the ground attack with 64 yards and one TD on 16 carries.

PC gained 230 yards on the ground on the day while Cunningham passed for 275 yards and three TD's on 17-of-32 passes, but was picked off four times. Newberry was led by Gilmore who ran for 81 yards on 19 carries including 71 in the second half while Coats passed for 77 yards on seven-of-13 completions, but fumbled five times.

Presbyterian improves to 8-2 overall and 6-1 in the SAC while Newberry falls to 4-7 overall and 1-6 in the league. The 6-1 mark for the Blue Hose is the best league record since the 1998 team also went 6-1. PC's 8-2 overall mark is the best record by winning percentage since 1979 when the Blue Hose went 10-1. Today's game was the last Bronze Derby game on PC's home field, Bailey Memorial. PC plans to build a new stadium that will be ready by the 2002 season. The Blue Hose own a 26-10-1 mark on their home field versus Newberry dating back to the 1928 season.

The Li'l 🎩 That Was!

Newberry College
The Scarlet & Gray

Holly Hopple, Homecoming Queen 2001

Volume 3 Number 5 — Friday, November 9, 2001

Bronze Derby is Up For Grabs

Paul Gable
Sports Editor

July 4, 1776. December 25th. January 1st. November 10th. Not all days are created equal, so don't let the football players of Newberry College and Presbyterian College tell you that November 10th isn't circled on their calendars because it is. The reason? The Bronze Derby will once again be up for grabs. On November 10, on the campus of Newberry College, football fans will be treated to the 54th Annual Bronze Derby clash between Newberry and Presbyterian. The Blue Hose enter the contest looking to win the Bronze Derby for the fourth straight year. Fans will remember that PC won the contest, 34-27 last year, as the Blue Hose torched Newberry's defense for 230 yards on the ground and 275 yards through the air. How did this annual competition get its roots and what makes this game so important, not only to those involved but to the townspeople of each town?

Amazingly, the Bronze Derby established its roots right here on the Newberry College campus. It is said that the Bronze Derby began on January 30, 1947, when the Blue Hose traveled to Newberry, for what many thought would be a friendly game on the hardwood. During the basketball game, several Newberry students ripped PC's banner off the wall and fled into the night. After the game, which PC won 51-47, Presbyterian students demanded their sign to be returned and a shoving match broke out. It is said that during the fight, one Newberry student grabbed a derby from the head of a PC student. For several days, talks between a Newberry student and a Presbyterian student raged on what to do with the derby, if it ever were recovered. The idea of the derby serving as a prize for victory in Newberry-PC games received a warm reception from Newberry students. The derby was later recovered, however, the identity of the thief was never revealed. The derby was turned over to a Newberry jewler firm for bronzing, before being sent to an Ohio company for casting.

Presbyterian College won the first annual Bronze Derby clash, as the Blue Hose won a basketball game 44-42 on February 28, 1947. This year's Bronze Derby contest promises to be a thriller, as both teams come in with not only bragging rights at stake, but chances to improve their seasons. PC, who owns the rivalry with a 53-31-5 record, held off Tusculum last week, 48-41. Cunningham had a record setting day, as he tossed for the South Atlantic Conference record, 542 yards and 3 touchdowns.

Cont. Page 7 ▶

Derby from pg. 1
The Indians, on the other hand, enter the game on a four game skid, following a 10-0 loss last week against Lenoir-Rhyne. A win against the Blue Hose will save the season for Newberry.

Game time is set for 2:00 at Setzler Field on the campus of Newberry College.

November 2001

November 3	The top song on the *Billboard* Hot 100 in the United States was "Family Affair" by Mary J. Blige.
November 3	In NCAA football, Arkansas beat Ole Miss 58-56 in Oxford, Mississippi. The game was the longest game in NCAA history going 7 overtime periods.
November 3	Going 8 for 8, Steve Smith of the San Antonio Spurs played his first game against the Portland Trail Blazers after being traded from the Trail Blazers. He tied an NBA record for most 3 point field goals in a game without a miss.
November 3	The top album by various artists was, "God Bless America: For the Benefit of the Twin Towers Fund."
November 4	"Harry Potter and the Philosopher's Stone" debuted in London, the first film adaptation of the book series by J.K. Rowling, starring Daniel Radcliffe.
November 4	"West Wing" and "Sex in the City" collected Emmy Awards for the 2001 television season.
November 4	American tennis star Serena Williams won the WTA Tour Championship in Munich, Germany. Lindsey Davenport defaulted in the final match due to a knee injury. It was Serena Wiliams' first season ending title.
November 4	The Arizona Diamondbacks won their first MLB World Series defeating the New York Yankees. Randy Johnson and Kurt Schilling shared MVP honors.
November 6	The TV series "24" debuted on FOX TV starring Keiffer Sutherland.
November 6	Crude oil reached record lows as major non-OPEC oil producers surge in their oil production.
November 7	Tim McGraw, Lee Ann Womack and Toby Keith collected awards at the 35th Country Music Association Awards.
November 7	The supersonic commercial aircraft Concorde resumed service after a 15 month evaluation of a July, 2000 crash killing 100 passengers.
November 10	Ken Kesey, author of *One Flew Over the Cuckoo's Nest* passed away.
November 10	The Bronze Derby was played in Newberry, South Carolina. The Presbyterian College Blue Hose defeated the Newberry College Indians 31-24.

The Li'l 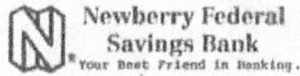 That Was!

The Newberry Observer

FRIDAY — American Profile Magazine ♦ Inside — Every Friday's issue of The Observer — Newberry Federal Savings Bank, Your Best Friend in Banking.

Just like a letter from home.

NOVEMBER 9, 2001 — NEWBERRY, S.C.

—Presbyterian College

Presbyterian will try to beat Newberry for the fourth year in a row when the two rivals hook up for the 90th time this Saturday. Not since the Blue Hose won five straight from 1966-'70 has either school won more than three straight.

Indians hope to end streak at three in Bronze Derby

By WILL VANDERVORT
SPORTS EDITOR

Daniel Norris admitted he knew nothing about the Newberry-Presbyterian rivalry when he first came to Newberry C... But it didn't take long for the ... 260-pound tight end to find out why the rivalry is so heated.

Norris said a Blue Hose defensive end took a cheap shot at him in his first Bronze Derby game and from that point on he has always hated the Indians' biggest rival.

"The guy sucker punched me in the gut. I'm not the classiest player by no means, but I don't take cheap shots at anyone," said the ... Elgin High ... "...from that point on it has been a revenge thing. In this game there is no forgive and forget."

One thing Norris and his teammates haven't forgotten is PC's

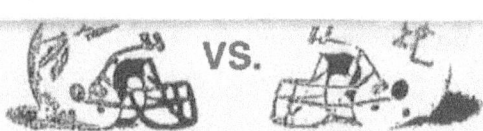

Newberry (4-6, 0-6) vs. Presbyterian (6-3, 4-2), 2 p.m.
Setzler Field, Newberry

three straight wins over Newberry. The Indians will try not to become the first school in the rivalry to lose four straight games in 32 years. From 1966-1970, the Blue Hose controlled the Bronze Derby.

Last year, Presbyterian beat Newberry 34-27 on a 17-yard touchdown pass from Todd Cunningham to Terry Meng on a slant pass with 26 seconds left in the game.

"(We) want to go out on a winning note," said fullback Shawn Carnes. "When I look back on my last year, I want to say it was a successful season. It can be as long as we beat PC."

Beating the Blue Hose might be as tough as ever for Newberry. Thanks to Cunningham and his rifle arm, PC is averaging a SAC best 327 yards per game through the air. They have won three straight games, including wins over Carson-Newman and Tusculum. A win on Saturday means the Hose would finish second in the SAC race.

"We will have to play our best game of the season to beat them," said Newberry coach Mike Taylor. "They're confident enough in their offense that they can answer just about anything you might throw at them."

PC coach Tommy Spangler knows his team will be favored, but at the same time he isn't worried about his players overlooking the Indians.

"Newberry is probably the most physical football team we have seen since I have been here," said Spangler, who spent four seasons as an assistant to Daryl Dickey before taking over as head coach this year. "Their offensive line blocks well and their defense will really get after you.

"Once it all starts all the pre-game hype will be over and it will come down to who executes the best."

Carnes remembers the last time Newberry beat PC, he was being red-shirted as a freshmen. That afternoon, the Indians held off a late charge from Presbyterian for a 28-22 victory.

"I was excited even though I wasn't on the field," said the Lexington native. "You could feel the emotions of the game and it got me pumped up.

"I'd like to feel that again, but in this game you're always wondering what is going to happen next so it keeps you nervous."

The Newberry fullback, who has rushed for 302 yards for an

see RIVALRY, page 13

RIVALRY
continued from page 10

average of 4.9 yards a carry, knows the Indians' offense must control the clock and score points to be successful.

"We have to hold on to the ball and make it a 60-minute game," he said.

Taylor, who said the PC game is always his favorite one to coach, knows his team's success rides not just on ball control, but also on how they handle the pressure.

"Our defense can't panic when they make a catch or a big play. They are going to get their share, but we have to be able to make clean tackles and make sure they don't get any extra stuff," he said.

"The thing they do best is catch the ball and turn upfield for long gains, we are going to have to limit those things and stay within our assignments."

Norris said winning the PC game is important to this year's senior class. Like a volcano, he is about to erupt from all the tension.

"Between the (coaches), players and friends it just gets larger and larger," he said. "Our focus is straight and strong for this weekend and our confidence is at a very high level.

"This is a game that is always played well. It is like taking two pitbulls and throwing them in the ring."

Not a bad analogy from a guy who at one point knew nothing about Newberry-PC.

The Li'l 🎩 That Was!

The Blue Stocking
Presbyterian College's Student Newspaper - "Friend or foe, we write the news as it goes."

Vol. 97, Num. 8 — Wednesday, November 28th, 2001 — FREE

A History Lesson: Things you never knew about Presbyterian College
The Bronze Derby, a PC Tradition

photo by Hank Coleman

PC plays Newberry College for the Bronze Derby every year.

Weekly Web Poll:
Do you think that there is a place for cell phones at college?

A) No, it does not enhance learning and there is no need for it at school.
B) No, because people miss use them by taking calls during classes, etc.
C) Yes, it is beneficial especially for the purpose of safety.
D) Yes, it is esential tool that students need and use everyday.

Cast your vote at
http://www.presby.edu/bluenews

Newberry vs. Presbyterian
November 10, 2001
2:00 p.m.
(Bronze Derby)

The Clinton Chronicle

PC seniors win all four Bronze Derby Classics

By David Hays
For The Chronicle

NEWBERRY - The Bronze Derby fits quite nicely on the heads of Presbyterian's seniors.

This year's senior class became the first since 1970 to win four straight against Newberry, holding off the Indians 31-24 Saturday to win the 55th annual Bronze Derby game.

As seniors Edmound Ellison, Max Grant, Keon Talbert and company tried on the Bronze Derby in front of the television cameras, classmate Todd Cunningham talked about beating Newberry for four consecutive years.

"They're all special," the Irmo native said. "Four years winning the Bronze Derby, the senior class has done a great job. It's the first time in 20 or 30 years PC has been able to do this."

"I heard it hasn't been done in a long time," added Grant, a defensive back. "I am really proud of all the seniors. Sometimes when you win two years, you lose the hunger. But we stayed hungry and we got them all four years that I was here."

The seniors also tied the class of 1980 for most victories with 30.

"What can you say about the senior class," said Blue Hose head coach Tommy Spangler. "Thirty wins in four years and we still have one game left (at Furman Nov. 24). It's a great finish to a great career for a lot of them. And now we'll get ready for Furman and see what happens."

"I am really proud of that (the 30 wins), too, because when we came in we brought a lot to the program," said Grant, who like most of the seniors got limited playing time in 1998.

"There was a time when the program was down. Maybe we just came in at the right time. My freshman year we really had some good seniors that helped start this. And we finished it up."

The circumstances surrounding Saturday's Bronze Derby game was similar to last year when Presbyterian had a far better record and seemed superior on paper. But as Spangler said last weekend as has about every coach before him, "When rivals meet, you can throw out the records."

Last November, PC beat the Indians 34-27 on Terry Meng's touchdown catch with 26 seconds left to complete one of its best seasons at 8-2. This year's victory, also by a touchdown, gives the Blue Hose a 7-3 record while Newberry finishes its second consecutive season at 4-7.

Newberry's strategy was clearly to keep PC's offense off the field as much as possible. Its game plan worked as the Indians won the time of possession battle 36:30 to 23:30.

Newberry controlled the clock in the first half behind running back Chad Tackett, who had 18 carries for 119 yards and a touchdown. Winning the time of possession battle 19:31 to 10:38, the underdog Indians trailed only 14-10 at halftime.

"Newberry had a good plan early and we were off-balance a little bit," Spangler said. "We settled down and started moving the ball. I thought the key to the game was the defense's play early in the third that created some good field position. We got some points and were able to go up by a few touchdowns, enough to pad the lead. They made a good run at the end."

A seven-yard sack by defensive tackle Ellison and an interception by linebacker Russell Rothar turned the game Presbyterian's way in the third quarter, setting up 10 points.

Ellison's sack ended Newberry's first possession of the second half, then Ben Creasman returned the ensuing punt 31 yards to the Indians 40. PC settled for Michael Wright's 34-yard field goal for a 17-10 lead with 10:54 left in the third quarter.

A few minutes later, Newberry quarterback Brian Shealy threw his second costly interception of the day. After Maurice Gibbs had returned an interception for a

Derby, Page 3B

D.J. spins another hit
PC wide receiver D.J. Humphries grabs one of his seven catches on this touchdown reception against Newberry College Saturday. Humphries led the Blue Hose offense with 126 yards receiving and helped PC grab its fourth consecutive Bronze Derby victory.

Interception
Blue Hose strong safety Ryan Bowers leaps for an interception as linebackers Isaac Gibson (33) and Russell Rothar (44) eye the ball during Saturday's 31-24 Bronze Derby victory over Newberry. PC will take a 7-3 overall record and 5-2 SAC mark into a matchup against Furman Nov. 24.

Recovery — Photo by Fletcher Pruitt Jr.
PC linebacker Isaac Gibson picks up a loose ball during the Blue Hose's 31-24 win over Newberry College. The Blue Hose defense forced four turnovers, including three interceptions, and sacked Newberry quarterback Brian Shealy three times on their way to securing the Bronze Derby trophy.

Derby

From 1B

touchdown in the first half, Rothar picked off a pass at the Indians 35 and returned it to the 15. Three plays later, Cunningham threw an 11-yard scoring strike to D.J. Humphries to make it 24-10 with 5:15 left in the third quarter.

Four minutes later, PC increased its lead to 31-10 when Barrett Fleming caught a tipped pass for a 12-yard touchdown. Cunningham completed 11 of 15 passes in the third quarter.

The fourth period brought back memories of Nov. 3 when Tusculum scored three unanswered touchdowns to cut a 45-17 deficit to 45-38. The Blue Hose eventually won, 48-41, and they held on again Saturday. But Newberry made things interesting by putting together scoring drives of 90 and 86 yards. Tackett scored on a 3-yard run with 10:48 to go and Shealy threw a 25-yard touchdown pass to Michael Bailey at the 4:05 mark.

Presbyterian ended the threat when Meng caught one third-down pass and Steve McCoy got open for a 19-yard reception on another third down, enabling the Blue Hose to run out the clock.

"He (McCoy) threw his hand up and I saw him," said Cunningham, who avoided a sack on the play. "I threw it to him. He made a big catch (at the Newberry 39). Third and eight, we knew if we got a first down the game was over, and that is what happened."

The Blue Hose took a 7-0 lead with 3:53 left in the first quarter when Shealy, being dragged down in the backfield by Tony Gaines, threw an ill-advised, desperation pass right into the arms of Gibbs. The 6-foot-4, 260-pound defensive end returned it for an easy 24-yard touchdown.

The sophomore said it was his first touchdown since "Pop Warner." Gibbs, who played defense and some tight end in high school, returned a fumble for an apparent touchdown against West Georgia on Sept. 1, but the ball was blown dead. This touchdown counted.

"When we played West Georgia I picked it up and ran it back, and they said it was down. This time, it felt so good," Gibbs said. "I saw Nacomma (Maxwell) come running in and bowl me over. That felt so good."

Cunningham threw passes of 32 yards to McCoy and 25 to Humphries to set up PC's second touchdown, a 4-yard keeper by Cunningham for a 14-0 lead with 11:04 left in the second quarter.

But Newberry dominated the rest of the half, scoring on B.J. Griffin's 44-yard field goal and Tackett's 4-yard run. And while PC regained control in the third quarter, the Indians wouldn't go away.

"They have a good, ball control offense. They limited our touches today," Cunningham said. "But I thought our defense played well. They were on the field a lot. They played a lot of snaps. So I knew they were tired toward the end of the game, but they found a way to hang in there."

Presbyterian improved to 54-31-5 all-time against Newberry, including a 33-20-2 record since the teams started playing for the Bronze Derby in 1947. With the victory, the Blue Hose also returned to Don Hansen's Football Gazette NCAA Division II poll at No. 25.

Newberry had 23 first downs to PC's 22 and was outgained only 397-387 in total offense.

It was another effective day for Cunningham, whose two touchdown passes gave him an NCAA Division II second-best 107 for his career. He trails only Valdosta State's Chris Hatcher, who had 116.

Cunningham completed 33 of 53 passes for 377 yards, including seven for 126 yards to Humphries. He spread the rest of his completions around to Meng, McCoy, Fleming, Kevie Smith, Donald Wilson, Derrick Keith, Chris Charles, Artie Swinton and Tim Pope.

Cunningham also became the all-time leader in NCAA Division II history in career total offense. He now has 11,235 yards of total offense in 38 career games. He breaks the former record held by Wingate University's Vernon Buck (1991-94) of 11,224 yards of total offense set during his career.

Humphries broke another school record, passing Travis Smith for receiving yards in a season. He finished atop the South Atlantic Conference with a school-record 85 catches, 1,211 yards, and 121.1 yards per game.

Rothar led the Presbyterian defense with 14 tackles. Defensive backs Ben Creasman and Ryan Bowers, and linebacker Isaac Gibson were in on 10 tackles apiece.

Shealy was 12-for-24 for 187 yards and three interceptions for Newberry while Tackett, playing with a deep thigh bruise, finished an impressive effort with 177 yards on 29 carries. Tackett finished third on Newberry's all-time single-season rushing list with 1,210 yards for the season, nine yards short of second place.

The Blue Hose finished tied for second in the SAC with Tusculum and Carson-Newman at 5-2, trailing only Catawba (6-1). Newberry finished 0-7 in the league.

The Newberry Observer

MONDAY — NOVEMBER 12, 2001 — *Just like a letter from home.* — NEWBERRY, S.C.

- NHS Bashes the Beach — Sports, Pages 6 & 7
- Praising Veterans — Editorial, Page 4

PC makes clutch plays to keep Derby

Blue Hose seniors first class since 1970 to win four

By WILL VANDERVORT
SPORTS EDITOR

It was a perfect ending to a not-so-perfect day for Presbyterian quarterback Todd Cunningham.

Clinging to a seven-point lead with 1:52 remaining and facing a third down-and-eight from his own 42, Cunningham found Steve McCoy open in the Newberry zone for 19-yards and a game-clinching first down. With just one time out left, the Indians couldn't stop the inevitable. The Blue Hose's seniors became the first class since 1970 to win the Bronze Derby four times with a 31-24 victory Saturday at Setzler Field.

Though he threw for 377 yards and two touchdowns, the Indians' rattled the Harlon Hill candidate—Division II's version of the Heisman Trophy—forcing him to throw two second-quarter interceptions, while sacking him three times. But when the game was on the line, Cunningham delivered like all great players do.

"It was big," said PC coach Tommy Spangler, referring to the first down reception. "Todd was looking left and didn't see anything. He looked back across the middle and found McCoy. It is just Todd, he threw it off balance and didn't make a good throw, but McCoy was there and made a nice

see BRONZE DERBY, page 7

—photo by Will Vandervort
Presbyterian wide receiver D.J. Humphries (13) pulls in a Todd Cunningham pass for a third quarter touchdown, while Newberry's Terry Scipio (34) can only watch. The Blue Hose seniors became the first class in the rivalry to win four Bronze Derby's since 1970.

—photo by Will Vandervort
Newberry quarterback Brian Shealy (14) delivers a first quarter pass in the Indians' 31-24 loss to Presbyterian in the 55th Annual Bronze Derby Saturday at Setzler Field.

The Newberry Observer

MONDAY — NHS Bashes the Beach ♦ Sports, Pages 6 & 7 | Praising Veterans ♦ Editorial, Page 4

NOVEMBER 12, 2001 — *Just like a letter from home.* — NEWBERRY, S.C.

BRONZE DERBY

continued from page 6

catch to get the first down.

"There is no question that if we don't make the first down and punt it back, they have a lot of momentum."

Newberry, which finished the season 4-7, stole momentum from the Blue Hose with two fourth quarter touchdowns. The Indians reeled off back-to-back scoring drives of 90 and 86 yards to erase a 31-10 deficit.

"Maybe some of the guys thought the game was over, but I knew it wasn't," said Spangler. "(Newberry) is a good football team and is a lot better team than what their record indicates."

The Indians moved within two scores after Chad Tackett capped a 90-yard, nine-play drive with a two-yard run with 10:48 left in the game. After the Newberry defense held Presbyterian on its next possession, the offense went back to work.

Red-shirt freshman Brian Shealy directed the Indians 86 yards in 12 plays, with the Batesburg native finishing the drive by lofting a perfect 25-yard pass to Michael Bailey in the right corner of the PC end zone. After B.J. Griffin's point after, Newberry found itself trailing just 31-24 with 4:05 left in the game.

"Coaches told us to do what we have been doing all day and put the game away," said Presbyterian wide receiver D.J. Humphries. "We made some plays, (Newberry) took me away, but we had other guys step up and make plays and that is the way it has been all year."

Besides McCoy's game-winning catch, Terry Meng—who caught the 17-yard winning pass in last year's game—also came up with a clutch third down reception three plays earlier to keep the clock moving.

"That is the thing about our offense, we have a lot of good wide receivers," said Cunningham. "We spread the ball around and they all make great catches and step up in big situations."

By going two-for-two on third down, on the game's final drive, the Blue Hose were able to run out the final 3:52.

"I liked our chances right there because we had a lot of momentum," said Newberry head coach Mike Taylor. "But they convert on a couple of plays they need to convert."

Presbyterian got the scoring started thanks to its defense. After the Blue Hose offense managed minus three yards on its first three possessions, the defense took matters into its own hands.

Marcus Gibbs intercepted a Shealy pass and raced 24 yards untouched for the touchdown and a 7-0 lead with 3:53 left in the first quarter. Gibbs' interception was set up thanks to a strong pass rush, which forced the Newberry quarterback to throw an ill-advised pass.

Cunningham completed an eight-play, 80-yard drive with 11:04 left in the second quarter, when he went in from four yards out for a 14-0 lead.

Newberry answered the PC score on its next possession. Behind the running of Tackett, the Indians moved the ball to the Blue Hose 28, where Griffin's 44-yard field goal made the score 14-3, and sparked life on the Indians' sideline.

Todd Geter recorded his school record 10th interception of the year when he picked Cunningham off on the next series, setting up the offense at the PC 49.

Five plays later, Tackett ran in from four yards out, pulling Newberry within 14-10. The key play came, when Shealy hit Kendall Brown with a pass across the middle, which the freshman took to the Presbyterian 15 on the first play of the drive.

"I admire our kids, they wouldn't go away," said Taylor. "We are not the most talented team in the world, but I can't complain about their work ethic, how they play and their character."

Indians' defensive tackle J.R. Brown ended a possible scoring opportunity for the Blue Hose late in the second quarter. The big lineman showed some finesse by diving and intercepting a deflected Cunningham pass at the Newberry nine.

After being held to 176 yards in the first half and watching Newberry double up the time of possession, Presbyterian's offense started to find its rhythm in the third quarter.

Michael Wright started things with a 35-yard field goal for a 17-10 advantage. The defense later intercepted Shealy, thanks to Russell Rothar, setting up the Presbyterian offense at the Newberry 15. Three plays later, Cunningham connected with Humphries from 11 yards and a two-touchdown lead.

On the Blue Hose's next possession, Cunningham got his second touchdown pass of the afternoon as he connected with Barrett Fleming from 16 yards.

"Luckily we played well in the third quarter to pad the lead just enough," said Spangler. "It was a great game and Newberry hung in there and fought and our guys fought."

—photo by Will Vandervort

Chad Tackett (36) out runs Presbyterian's Ben Capers (5) to the end zone during Saturday's Bronze Derby. Tackett scored the second quarter touchdown from four yards and pulled Newberry within four, 14-10.

Staying Put

Presbyterian keeping Bronze Derby for fourth straight year

By Brad Bryant
Sports Editor

Presbyterian College quarterback Todd Cunningham knew if the Blue Hose continued to run its offense, things would eventually click. After four years and better than 10,000 yards, who would doubt him?

Cunningham and his teammates finally got their offense going and had just enough to hold off Newberry for a 31-24 victory in the annual Bronze Derby game Saturday.

"Newberry wasn't doing anything in particular. We just couldn't find a rhythm early," Cunningham said. "This offense is a rhythm offense and you have to find (a rhythm) to be successful. We had a couple of turnovers that hurt us but in the second half we kind of got in a rhythm."

Hose 31
Indians 24

While the offense never produced the big play the Blue Hose have become accustomed to of late, PC did have enough firepower to get the job done. Cunningham, in his final meeting with Newberry, completed 33 of 53 passes for 377 yards. He did throw two interceptions but was also responsible for three touchdowns, completing scoring passes to D.J. Humphries and Barrett Fleming. Cunningham also ran in a touchdown from four yards out.

The Blue Hose misfired on their first three possessions of the game and had their final two of the half end with Cunningham interceptions. But sandwiched in-between were an 80-yard scoring drive and defensive score as Maurice Gibbs returned an interception 24 yards for a touchdown.

While Presbyterian did build a 14-0 lead in the game's first 19 minutes, Newberry was able to take advantage of PC's offensive struggles in the second quarter to pull within four, at 14-10, by halftime.

The third quarter belonged to Cunningham, though, as he led his team to 17 points in the period and put the game out of reach.

The Blue Hose defense, which spent most of the game bending but not breaking, surrendered a pair of fourth quarter touchdowns to allow Newberry to close the gap. But Cunningham, with a pair of third down conversions, managed to run the final four minutes off of the game clock.

"This is a good way to end the year," said Cunningham. "We do have one game left when we go to Furman (on Nov. 24) but this is something we can carry into the offseason."

The game is truly something Presbyterian can build on as it was the Blue Hose's fourth straight victory in the long-standing series. This year's PC senior class is the first since 1970 to sweep the Indians.

"They're all special but it's great to win the Bronze Derby all four years," Cunningham said. "This senior class has done a great job."

Although the Blue Hose entered the game as a heavy favorite, it appeared Newberry, which finished its season winless

■ See PC, page 11A

■ PC
Continued from Page 9

in the South Atlantic Conference, was primed for an upset. Presbyterian netted (-3) yards on its opening possession and had to punt the ball away.

However, the Indians' offense couldn't match the defense's intensity as quarterback Brian Shealy fumbled on Newberry's third play from scrimmage. PC's Edmund Ellison recovered the ball, giving the Blue Hose possession at the Newberry 37.

But once again the Blue Hose offense struggled as Cunningham threw incomplete on first and second down and was then sacked for a three-yard loss on third down, forcing another punt.

Both offenses continued to sputter as the two teams continued to trade punts back and forth.

It appeared the Indians might finally get something going when running back Chad Tackett broke free for a 23-yard gain that got Newberry out of a hole and gave the team a first down at the PC 30-yard line.

On the next play Shealy came under a heavy rush when he dropped back to pass.

As he was being dragged down, he tried to throw the ball away but, instead, the pass went straight up in the air. Gibbs snagged the ball and raced 24 yards into the end zone for the game's first score.

Michael Wright added the point after kick for the Blue Hose, giving PC a 7-0 lead with 3 minutes and 53 seconds remaining in the opening quarter.

Newberry got the ball back on its own 30 and once again found some success. After Tackett pushed the Indians out to midfield with a 30-yard gain on first down, he went up the middle for two yards on a fourth-and-one play from the PC 41 to keep the drive alive. Tackett followed the conversion with three more carries, giving the Indians a first down at the Presbyterian 28. But after Tackett came up short of the first-down marker on a third-and-six play, Newberry opted to try to get on the scoreboard with a field goal. B.J. Griffin's 37-yard attempt sailed wide right, though, leaving the Blue Hose on top 7-0 with 13:23 remaining in the first half.

Starting from the Blue Hose 20-yard line, Cunningham began to find some offensive rhythm. On first down he threw for 12 yards to Steve McCoy and then followed the completion with a 10-yard run out to the PC 42-yard line.

Cunningham then moved his team into scoring position with a 32-yard pass play to Fleming down to the Newberry 26. Facing third and 13 at the Newberry 29 after a holding penalty, Cunningham spotted his favorite target, Humphries, on a 25-yard pick up down to the Indians' four-yard line.

On the next play Cunningham went up the middle for Presbyterian's second touchdown of the game. Wright's PAT kick was good, giving the Blue Hose a 14-0 lead with 11:04 remaining in the first half.

Just when it appeared Presbyterian was ready to deliver a knock-out punch, Newberry came battling back.

The Indians took the ensuing kickoff and methodically moved 56 yards in 10 plays to set up a 44-yard field goal from Griffin. Tackett did most of the damage, rushing for 35 yards on just three carries.

Shealy also had a key run in the drive, which ended with Newberry cutting the Blue Hose's advantage to 11, at 14-3, with 6:28 remaining in the opening half.

The Blue Hose tried to respond as Cunningham, starting from his own 35-yard line, threw complete to Tim Pope for an 11-yard gain. However, on the next play Cunningham was sacked for a five-yard loss. Then on second and 15, Newberry's Todd Geter came up with an interception at the Blue Hose 49-yard line.

> "They're (Bronze Derby wins) all special but it's great to win the Bronze Derby all four years. This senior class has done a great job."
> —Todd Cunningham

The Indians wasted little time taking advantage of the turnover, covering the 49 yards in five plays for their first touchdown of the game. Tackett got the score, going in from four yards out. Shealy provided the biggest play of the drive, completing a 34-yard pass to Kendal Brown on first down.

After Griffin's PAT kick, the score remained 14-10 going into halftime. PC did have one more scoring opportunity before the end of the second quarter; however, Cunningham was intercepted by J.R. Brown at the Newberry nine.

After PC's defense forced a three-and-out from the Indians to open the second half, the Blue Hose went back to work.

After Ben Creasman's 31-yard punt return set up PC at the Newberry 40, Cunningham threw to Chris Charles for an 11-yard gain on first down. Kevie Smith then hauled in an eight-yard pass and Cunningham picked up a first down with a two-yard run.

The drive stalled there but Wright kicked a 35-yard field goal to push the Blue Hose's lead to 17-10 with 10:54 remaining in the third quarter.

Presbyterian's defense continued to play well in the period, not giving up a first down on Newberry's next possession, and then Russell Rothar came up with an interception to give the Blue Hose the ball at the Newberry 15-yard line. From there PC needed just three plays to find the end zone as Cunningham connected with Humphries on an 11-yard scoring toss.

Wright's point after gave PC a 24-10 lead with 5:15 remaining in the third quarter.

"Our defense was great to get us turnovers," Cunningham said. "They gave us the ball back and that's what we ask them to do. And they stopped them when we had a couple of turnovers."

Sensing a chance to put the game out of reach, the PC defense quickly forced Newberry to punt, giving the ball back to the Blue Hose at their own 32-yard line.

Cunningham quickly moved Presbyterian down the field, throwing 48 yards to Humphries on second down. After runs from Charles and Wilson, Cunningham passed to Fleming for a 16-yard score.

Wright again was good with the PAT, giving the Blue Hose a 31-10 advantage with 1:31 remaining in the third quarter.

Newberry, however, wouldn't quit. Shealy led his team on a pair of lengthy fourth-quarter scoring drives. The first was capped by a two-yard Tackett run and the second culminated in a 25-yard touchdown pass to Michael Bailey.

After the pass to Bailey, the Indians had moved within seven points at 31-24 with 4:05 remaining in the game.

What once seemed like a runaway was a ball game again as Cunningham was left with the task of trying to run out the clock and preserve the win.

After a six-yard run by Wilson on first down, Cunningham picked up a first down with a four-yard completion to Terry Meng on third and four.

Faced with third and eight from the PC 42-yard line, Cunningham threw to McCoy for a 19-yard gain to give the Blue Hose a fresh set of downs and enough plays to run out the clock.

"Newberry played a good game," Cunningham said. "They came to play today. But we just found a way to win."

Presbyterian finished the game with 397 yards while Newberry had 387. The Blue Hose had 377 yards through the air and rushed for just 20 yards on 20 carries. The Indians were much more balanced as Shealy was 12-of-24 passing for 187 yards. Newberry rushed for 200 yards, which included 177 from Tackett.

Presbyterian will get this week off before wrapping up its season on Nov. 24 with a game against NCAA Division I AA power Furman. Kickoff for that game is set for 2 p.m.

November 2002

The Li'l That Was!

November 2	New York Rangers player Mark Messier moved into 2nd place on the all-time NHL games played list playing his 1616th in a 3-2 Rangers loss against the St. Louis Blues.
November 6	12 people were killed in a fire onboard a train headed for Vienna from Paris.
November 6	Alan Jackson and Martina McBride walked away with annual honors at the 36th Country Music Association Awards.
November 7	Iran prohibited advertising of products from the United States.
November 8	The United Nations Security Council approved Resolution 1441 forcing Iraq and Saddam Hussein to disarm or face "Serious consequences."
November 9	Singer Sheena Easton married John Minoli.
November 11	Belgium tennis star Kim Clijsters defeated United States tennis star Serena Williams to win the season ending WTA Tour Championship at STAPLES Center in Los Angeles, California.
November 13	Eminem released the single "Lose Yourself." It was the first RAP song to win an Academy Award for Best Original Song.
November 13	Saddam Hussein and Iraq agreed to the United Nations Security Council Resolution 1441.
November 14	The film "Harry Potter and the Chamber of Secrets" was released, based on the second book from J.K Rowling.
November 14	Argentina defaulted on a $805 million payment to the World Bank.
November 14	The United States House of Representatives voted not to create a special commission to investigate the September 11 attack.
November 15	Former Beatle Ringo Starr was inducted into to Percussive Arts Society Hall of Fame.
November 15	Hu Jintao becomes the General Secretary of the Central Committee of the Communist Party of China.
November 16	The SARS virus was first detected in China.
November 16	Saddam Hussein said that he had to accept United Nations Resolution 1441 "Because the United States and Israel had shown their claws and teeth and declared unilateral war on Iraq."
November 16	The Bronze Derby was played in Clinton, South Carolina. The Presbyterian College Blue Hose defeated the Newberry College Indians 14-10.

The Li'l  That Was!

The Newberry Observer

Just like a letter from home.

MONDAY — Vic MacDonald: Indians' fan couldn't be prouder of team — Sports: Blue Hose hold off NC

NOVEMBER 18, 2002 — NEWBERRY, S.C.

Officials take away shot

Newberry falls to PC as refs fail to put ball in play

Will Vandervort
Sports Editor

CLINTON — Newberry College head football coach Mike Taylor didn't want to take anything away from Presbyterian's 14-10 victory Saturday in the 55th Annual Bronze Derby. However, he believed his Indians deserved one last chance to end the Blue Hose's recent dominance in the longstanding series.

As Presbyterian attempted to run out the clock on its last possession, Taylor and his staff argued that the on-field officials wasted valuable seconds in spotting the ball and starting the game's 25-second play clock. To top things off, Blue Hose quarterback Zach Ellis fumbled the snap while trying to take a knee on fourth down, which should have given the Indians the ball just inside the Presbyterian 45-yard line with a second to go.

However, the officials let the clock run out, sparking a series of shoving matches between players, while the officials escaped to their dressing room.

"We should have had one more play," said Taylor, who could only watch as Presbyterian won the Bronze Derby for the fifth straight year. "The officials choked the call. The chances are slim and none of us completing (a pass for a touchdown), but it happened in 1989. It was the last play of the game this thing was won. We kicked a field goal on about the last play in 1989. It was possible."

It was a possibility Newberry's players and coaches believed they deserved.

"If we had had one more chance, we would have scored on that play," said senior defensive end Rodrick Elkins. "We were up enough and had enough intensity. I'm quite sure we would have scored."

"This hurts real bad. A lot of players are hurt right now because we knew we had the game," said cornerback Todd Geter.

Despite the game's ending, Taylor acknowledged his team should have taken care of business when it had the chance.

"We had some opportunities in the second half and we didn't do it," he said. "(Presbyterian) won the football. I'm not going to take anything away from them. I congratulate them on that.

"But I will tell you this. That was a gutless display by the officials of our conference on that last play. I might get reprimanded and I might get fined, but I will tell you one thing, I am right. I am right. That was gutless."

The Indians (1-10, 0-7 in the SAC) had several chances in the fourth quarter to over take Presbyterian, but failed to convert. Twice in the last six minutes, Newberry received the ball near midfield, and both times they came away with no points to show for it.

TOUCHDOWN — Newberry quarterback Brian Shealy keeps on an option play to score the Indians' lone touchdown in Saturday's 55th Bronze Derby at Bailey Memorial Stadium in Clinton.
— Staff photo by Vic MacDonald

After getting the ball at their own 35-yard line, the Indians converted one fourth down play before bogging down at their own 47 three plays later. After holding the Blue Hose (8-3, 5-2) to a three-and-out, Newberry got the ball back at its own 43-yard line with 2:55 left. On fourth-and-five from the 48, quarterback Brian Shealy over threw receiver Kendal Brown at the Presbyterian 41, ending the Indians' last chance to get back the Derby.

"We did a lot of good things today, but we just could not capitalize on it. All you can do is try," said linebacker Jarrod Riddle.

The Indians, who were heavy underdogs coming in, tried all afternoon. Despite falling behind 14-3 on an Ellis five-yard run just before the half, Newberry didn't give up. For the most part, the Indians played a complete game for the first time since the second week of the season.

■ See DERBY, page 7

■ DERBY
Continued from page 6

Presbyterian, which had 150 total yards at half-time, was held to just 51 yards of offense in the second half, and to just 10 in the fourth quarter. The Newberry offense out gained the Blue Hose 2-to-1 in the final 30 minutes, and had sustained drives during the game of 67, 60, and 36 yards against the SAC's top-rated defense.

"This is PC. This is the most important game of the year," Taylor said. "You win here, you're 1-0. Our guys sold out for us today. We failed to convert a couple of times in the second half when we needed to, and I feel for these guys because they played so hard.

"Our guys really wanted to win this football game. They gave Newberry College and me personally all I wanted this year. This is a 1-10 football team that I don't feel like is 1-10, because they gave us great work all year long. I'm proud of these guys. I'm proud of these guys."

The Blue Hose stopped Newberry's third drive of the second half when strong safety Ryan Bowers intercepted a Shealy pass at the PC nine-yard line on a deflection from defensive lineman Tony Gomez. But two plays later, Newberry's Brian Rose returned the favor, intercepting Ellis and returning it nine yards to the Blue Hose eight-yard line.

Shealy scored with 3:46 left in the third quarter, when he kept the ball on an option to the right for an eight-yard touchdown to make the score 14-10.

Terry Meng's 70-yard punt return, aided by a personal foul, set Presbyterian up at the Newberry three with a chance to put the game away with 11:55 remaining. But C.J. O'Bryant fumbled the ball while trying to go over the top on third-and-goal from the one, allowing Newberry's Ray Cooper to recover it in the end zone for a touchback. O'Bryant's fumble was one of four Blue Hose turnovers in the second half, but thanks to their defense — which limited Newberry to 190 total yards — the Indians were only able to capitalize on one. Presbyterian forced three Newberry turnovers in return.

"We turned it over, I don't know how many times, but the defense played lights out like they have the past four wins," said Ellis. "You have to give it up to them. I don't know how many points they have been giving up, but it hasn't been too many."

The way Presbyterian started the game, the Indians' chances of winning the game looked bad. On the game's first possession, Ellis directed the Blue Hose down the field 69 yards in five plays to take a 7-0 lead just two minutes in.

The 6-foot-1, 190-pound sophomore from Tifton, Ga., connected with O'Bryant on a 41-yard pass play to move the ball to the Newberry 23-yard line, and then teamed up with Meng on an 18-yard scoring play on third down-and-five. Meng caught the ball on the right sideline, broke a would-be tackle and tightroped the sideline for the score.

Newberry answered with its best drive of the season — in terms of plays — with a 19-play, 67-yard drive, consuming nine minutes and 34 seconds. Justin Freeman kicked the Indians' first field goal of the season — a 25-yarder — to make the score 7-3 with 14:55 left in the first half.

After an exchange of punts, Ellis gave the Blue Hose a 14-3 advantage with his 3-yard scramble with 4:56 left to the half. The Presbyterian quarterback, who improved to 4-0 as a starter, set up his own score with a 15-yard scramble on third-and-one to the Indians' 10-yard line.

	NC	PC
Newberry	0 3 7 0	— 10
Presbyterian	7 7 0 0	— 14

Scoring Summary
PC: Terry Meng 18 pass from Zach Ellis (Ryan Noll kick), 12:39 1st.
NC: Justin Freeman 25 field goal, 14:55 2nd.
PC: Ellis 5 run (Noll kick), 4:46 2nd.
NC: Brian Shealy 8 run (Freeman kick), 3:46 3rd.

	NC	PC
First Downs	13	6
Rushing	41-85	60-73
Passing	105	126
Passes	9-28-3	7-14-1
Punts	6-38.8	6-34.7
Fum / lost	3-0	4-3
Pen / yards	4-19	5-68
Time of Poss.	33:31	26:30

Individual Statistics
Rushing: NC — Brandon Carnes 1-21, Daniel Gray 18-67, Shealy 16-19, Titus Davis 6-0, Jimmy Overstreet 4-1, Ben Jones 1-(6). PC — Carey Mitchell 19-38, C.J. O'Bryant 18-35, Meng 2-10, Ellis 8-6, Chris Charles 1-1, team 3-(-7).
Passing: NC — Shealy 9-25-3, 105. PC — Ellis 7-14-1, 126.
Receiving: NC — Kendal Brown 5-62, Michael Bailey 3-39, Ben Jones 1-5. PC — Tim Pope 3-43, O'Bryant 1-41, Henry Easton 1-19, Meng 1-18, Ryan Mobley 1-6, Kip McAlister 1-(-1).

562

PC downs Newberry to end year

by T. Roberts
Staff Writer

The Blue Hose played their final game of the season last Saturday. When all was said and done, the Blue Hose emerged with a rain soaked, wind swept victory. Terry "touchdown factory" Meng notched PC's first score on a nice pitch and catch from Zach Ellis. Ellis later in the game scampered in from five yards out. Ryan Noll sent both extra point attempts through the up rights. The PC defense played tough, forcing the Indians to snap the ball nineteen times for 67 yards on their only touchdown drive.

What was truly important was that PC

Zach Ellis slides past a defender into the endzone.

achieved its fifth straight victory over Newberry. There isn't a single player on this years team that has ever lost to Presbyterian's arch rival. That is quite an accomplishment. There have been blow outs, and close calls, games that came down to the last play. However, on Saturday, The Blue Hose were content to run the ball, grinding out yards while wearing down the Newberry defense and eating the clock with Corey Mitchell and CJ O'Bryant.

PC leaned heavily on its stout defense lead by Ryan Bowers, Russ Rothar, Seth Murdock, Isaac Gibson, and Quentin Davis. Bowers and Rothar both had interceptions, while Davis had one, yet the play was called back due to penalty. The Blue Hose front four kept steady pressure on Newberry's quarterback all day long. Naconma Maxwell and Isaac Gibson left a permanent impression. More than once the friends and roommates up ended the hapless Newberry ball carrier with big time hits, much to the delight of the PC crowd.

The weather certainly put a damper on pregame festivities. Tailgating was down substantially and the many stu-

C.J. O'Bryant prepares to meet a defender.

dents opted to stay in bed (many recovering from Friday nights festivities, no doubt). However that didn't stop the die hards from coming and cheering on, not just the Blue Hose football team, but also their friends and roommates.

The redshirt freshmen made their appearance known. Decked out in kilts and body paint, they screamed and supported their teammates through the freezing weather. No one really knew what was spelled out on their chests, but more than likely, it wouldn't get past the copy editor.

One almost felt sorry for the dejected Newberry players, especially the seniors. Several of Newberry's players (those not trying to start fights), could be seen lingering on the field trying to

Terry Ming runs for the TD.

take in what it means never to have beaten Presbyterian. Never to have held the infamous Bronze Derby. Never to have beaten their arch rival.

THE LAURENS COUNTY Advertiser
Laurens, South Carolina

Blue Hose battle back, keep Bronze Derby

Presbyterian College quarterback Zach Ellis (Tifton, Ga.) threw three touchdown passes and ran for one more as the Blue Hose came back with 14 points in each of the last three quarters to defeat Newberry College 42-14 on Senior Day at Setzler Field in South Atlantic Conference football action. The game was the Battle for the Bronze Derby and the 92nd meeting between the two schools. PC has won the Derby game for six consecutive years, setting a series record for an unbeaten span.

Newberry (3-7, 2-5 SAC) came out strong in the first quarter. On the fifth play from scrimmage, Ellis was intercepted by senior defensive lineman Robert Holley (Union), who returned the pass 32 yards for a touchdown to give the Indians a 7-0 lead. Holley came up big again three plays later when he recovered a Corey Mitchell (Dalzel) fumble to put Newberry on the PC 38 yard line.

Newberry quarterback Mazi Drummond (Greer) was intercepted in the end zone by Quintin Davis (Sumter), one of five PC interceptions on the day. PC went five plays and out on the next drive before receiver Tymere Zimmerman (Bennettsville) hooked up with receiver on a wide receiver reverse pass to Derrick Higgins (Darlington) for a 48-yard touchdown. The catch gave Higgins a share of the school record for touchdown catches in a single season, tying him with Zimmerman from this year and Louis Austin from 1990. The Indians broke the school record for passing yards in a season with 2,539 and setting a new mark for passing touchdowns with 22.

The Blue Hose (4-6, 2-5 SAC) then shutout the Indians for the remainder of the game. On the first play of the second quarter, Ellis ran in a five-yard touchdown scamper to get the ball rolling for PC and close the gap to 14-7.

Less than 10 minutes later, running back Jared Southerland (Plantation, Fla.) ran in a three-yard scamper to tie the game after a Ryan Noll (Monroe, Ga.) extra point. The game was tied at the half at 14-14.

Drummond fumbled on the third play in the third quarter, setting up a short field for PC on

■ See Derby, page 15A

■ Derby
Continued from Page 14A

the Indians' 36. Five plays later, Ellis found a wide open Brett Wilhoit (Johnson City, Tenn.) up the left sideline for a lead the Blue Hose would not relinquish.

Two plays later, Drummond lost another fumble, part of a seven turnover day, and setting up more great starting field position for the Blue Hose on the Indians' 22. Newberry committed an illegal substitution penalty on fourth and four, giving PC a free first down at the 11 yard line.

The Blue Hose punched it in again two plays later on a Southerland rush, his second score of the day to put PC up 28-14.

Southerland led all rushers with 93 yards rushing with no negative carries.

PC tacked on a pair of Ellis to Tim Pope (Ninety-Six,) touchdowns in the fourth quarter to create the game's final margin. PC held Newberry to 279 yard of offense while racking up 402 yards of offense on the day. The Blue Hose were six-of-seven in the red zone and possessed the ball for 37:57 in the contest.

Drummond ran for 70 yards and threw for 108, while Ellis finished 18-for-31 for 212 yards.

Newberry's Kendal Brown (Cross) had 48 yards receiving, giving him 2,013 for the year. He is Newberry's all-time leading receiver and the 14th receiver in the South Atlantic Conference to cross the 2,000-yard mark.

Pope led PC with 94 yards receiving.

Defensive back Donny Stamper (Colbert, Ga.) led PC with eight tackles. Stewart Young (Union) had a pair of interceptions, while three other PC defenders had a pick in the contest.

Holley finished with a sack, the fumble recovery and the interception for Newberry. Linebacker Terrance Leverett (Ware Shoals) made 15 tackles for the Indians, giving him 112 for the season to lead the team and give him 11.2 per game for the season.

Both teams are finished with their seasons.

Newberry's three wins was two better than last year and the pair of conference wins is the most since 1999.

Presbyterian's losing season is its first since 1997 and the team's four wins are the fewest since the 1992 campaign.

November 2003

The Li'l That Was!

November 1	The Royal Mail in the United Kingdom was delayed due to unofficial strikes.
November 1	Arkansas beat Kentucky 71-63 in 7 overtimes in Lexington, Kentucky. The game tied an NCAA record for the longest game in college football history.
November 1	The first Gay Pride parade took place in Taipei, China.
November 4	Toby Keith released his 8th album "Shock'n Y'all" and became the 2004 *Billboard* album of the Year.
November 5	The third Matrix movie, "The Matrix Revolution," opened worldwide.
November 5	The ninth case of mad cow disease was reported in Japan.
November 5	Gary Ridgeway, the Green River Killer, confessed to the murder of 48 women in Seattle, Washington.
November 5	Singer Bobby Hatfield of the Righteous Brothers passed away.
November 6	The United States changed the nickel design for the first time since 1938.
November 6	United States Senator John McCain objected to President Bush's plan to reduce troops in Iraq.
November 6	Four people were murdered in a motorcycle shop in Chesnee, South Carolina. The murders went unsolved for 13 years and was finally solved in 2016.
November 7	Doctors indicated there is enough evidence to warrant licensing cannabis for the treatment of multiple sclerosis.
November 8	St. John's University football coach John Gagliardi became college football's all-time winningest coach with 409 wins passing Eddie Robinson of Grambling University.
November 9	American actor Art Carney of "The Honeymooners" passed away.
November 11	Singer Josh Groban released his second album "Closer" which went to #1 on United States charts and became his biggest seller.
November 11	Toyota became the world's second largest car producer behind General Motors.
November 14	The United Kingdom introduced identity cards, which were intended to eventually become compulsory.
November 15	The Bronze Derby was played in Newberry, South Carolina. The Presbyterian College Blue Hose defeated the Newberry College Indians 42-14.

The Li'l ⛑ That Was!

MONDAY
NOVEMBER 17, 2003

The Newberry Observer
Just like a letter from home.

NEWBERRY, S.C.

INSIDE — March of Dimes honors Newberry companies — PAGE 2
INSIDE — Adult Ed presents first Hispanic GED diplomas — PAGE 3

ews? Call 276-0625 (ext. 106 after business hours) or email us at sports@newberryobserver.com

No 'Lady Luck'

Newberry loses Derby for sixth straight year

Will Vandervort
Sports Editor

When Presbyterian wide receiver Tim Pope caught Zach Ellis' deflected pass in the right corner of the endzone with 5:49 left in the 57th Bronze Derby Saturday, it demonstrated the kind of afternoon it was for Newberry College.

Ellis' pass was originally intended for Brett Wilhoit, but the pass was a little behind the 6-foot-1 wideout. As Wilhoit tried to adjust to the pass, he knocked it up in the air, where three Indians ran to the deflected pass and appeared poised to make the interception.

But on this day "Lady Luck" proved she was on Presbyterian's side. Even with all the red jerseys hanging around the ball, it dropped right into the waiting arms of Pope for the Blue Hose final score in a 42-14 victory at Setzler Field.

the credit has to go to them."
After falling behind 14-0 not even seven minutes into the game, Presbyterian (4-6, 2-5 in the South Atlantic Conference) never lost its focus and fought off two more potential Newberry scores to rally with 42 unanswered points of its own.

"Coach (Tommy Spangler) told us to stay in the game and keep our heads up," said Blue Hose quarterback Zach Ellis, who threw three touchdown passes and completed 18-of-31 passes for 212 yards. "We kept playing hard. This was the last game of the year. This was for the 'Derby'."

Newberry (3-7, 2-5) appeared as if it was going to run away with its first win in South Carolina's second oldest series in six years when defensive end Robert Holley returned an interception 32 yards just two minutes and two seconds into the game. On Presbyterian's next possession, Holley got his second

OUT OF THEIR REACH — Newberry College wide receiver Derrick Higgins tries to haul in a th... quarter pass from quarterback Mazi Drummond in Presbyterian's 42-14 victory Saturday. It w... the sixth straight year Newberry has failed to get its hands on the coveted Bronze Derby.

— Photo by Ted B. Williams / Special Correspond...

The Indians drove to the PC eight, but defensive back Quentin Davis picked off Mazi Drummond's pass to Derrick Higgins at the one yard line, returning it 25 yards up the left sideline. No one knew at the time, but Davis' pick was a sign of things to

would have been hard to dig out of that," said Spangler.
Newberry stopped the Blue Hose on the ensuing possession and got the ball back in great field position when Philip Bernardi shanked his first punt 11 yards to the Indians' 41. After an 11-yard

Drummond pitch on an ... around, pulled up and th... a perfect pass to Higgins w... easily scored on the 48-y... play.

With 8:26 still remaining ... the first quarter, the Ind... had a 14-0 lead.

"We came out strong ...

■ DERBY
Continued from page 5

after we got up. In rivalry games like this, you just can't do that."
The Blue Hoses finally got on the scoreboard when Ellis ran in from five yards out on the first play of the second quarter to make the score 14-7. Ellis' touchdown capped a three-play, 37-yard drive, highlighted by a 25-yard pass to Barrett Fleming to the Indians' five-yard line.

Newberry answered the PC score with a 53-yard drive of its own on the ensuing possession, but when Drummond tried to hit Higgins with the home run ball from the Presbyterian 36, he was again intercepted. This time by Stewart Young at the Blue Hose eight. It was the Indians last real scoring threat of the afternoon.

"I don't know how many interceptions we had on the day...but they did a good job," Spangler said. "We made (Newberry) go the distance and we didn't give up a lot of big plays."
Presbyterian tied the game, 14-

14, with 4:44 left in the first half as fullback Jared Southerland barreled in from three yards out to cap a nine-play, 63-yard drive.
In the second half, the turnover bug again hit Drummond as he coughed up the ball on Newberry's first possession and the Blue Hose recovered at the Indians' 36. It didn't take PC long to turn the fumble into points as Ellis found Wilhoit wide open on a 20-yard touchdown pass to make the score 21-14.

On Newberry's next offensive play, the Presbyterian defense got another turnover as defensive end Dwayne Howell stripped Drummond and recovered the loose ball at the Indians' 22. Five plays later, Southerland dove into the endzone from three yards out and with 10:12 still left in the third

quarter PC had a 28-14 lead.
"We played the best quarter of football we played all year, and then we played the worst three quarters we've played all year," said Willis. "I don't know the last time we had that many turnovers, but it has been a while."

The Blue Hose, which finished the afternoon with 402 yards, upped the score to 35-14 with 10:29 left in the fourth quarter as Ellis found Pope slanting inside for a 10-yard score.

As for Newberry, it couldn't recover from seven turnovers, including five interceptions — three from Drummond and two from junior Brian Shealy. The offense managed just 279 total yards and got no deeper than the PC 22 the rest of the afternoon.

MONDAY

INSIDE
March of Dimes honors Newberry companies
PAGE 2

INSIDE
Adult Ed presents first Hispanic GED diplomas
PAGE 3

The Newberry Observer

Just like a letter from home.

NOVEMBER 17, 2003 — NEWBERRY, S.C.

Quarter by Quarter

—Staff photo by Will Vandervort
Newberry's Leo Reed keeps PC's Zach Ellis in the pocket.

1 Key Moment: Wide receiver Tymere Zimmerman hits Derrick Higgins on a wide receiver reverse pass that resulted in a 48-yard touchdown and a 14-0 Newberry lead. With the catch, Higgins earned a share of the school record for touchdown catches in a single season with eight.

The man: Newberry defensive end Robert Holley, who stepped in front of a Zach Ellis pass and returned the interception 32 yards for the Indians' first touchdown of the game. He later recovered a fumble.

First Quarter Score
Newberry 14
Presbyterian 0

—Staff photo by Will Vandervort
Presbyterian quarterback Zach Ellis scores a touchdown.

2 Key Moment: Down 14-7, Presbyterian's Stewart Young intercepted Newberry quarterback Mazi Drummond at the Presbyterian eight yard line. That interception stopped a drive that could have put Newberry ahead 21-7.

The man: Zach Ellis was the man in the second quarter, as the Blue Hose redshirt sophomore hit the endzone from five yards out for Presbyterian's first score of the game. Minutes later, Ellis hit Barrett Fleming for an 11-yard strike that set up a 3-yard touchdown run by Jared Southerland.

Second Quarter Score
Newberry 14
Presbyterian 14

—Photo by Ted B. Williams
PC's Jared Southerland runs for some of his 93 yards.

3 Key moment: On Newberry's first possession of the second half, Newberry quarterback Mazi Drummond fumbles after scrambling for a first down at his own 32-yard line. Drummond's fumble setup Presbyterian's go-ahead score, and what turned out to be the game-winner.

The man: On Presbyterian's second offensive possession, Southerland scored from three yards out to stretch Presbyterian's lead to 28-14. After coming in with less than 200 yards rushing on the season, the PC fullback finished with a game high 93 yards.

Third Quarter Score
Presbyterian 28
Newberry 14

—Photo by Ted B. Williams
PC players hold up the Derby for sixth straight year.

4 Key Moment: On third and four with just over three minutes left in the game, Drummond hit Kendal Brown for a 1-yard gain that not only kept the drive alive, but gave Brown 48 yards total for the game. Brown's 48 yards gave him 2,116 for the year and made him the all-time leading receiver and 15th receiver in the South Atlantic Conference to eclipse the 2,000 yard mark.

The man: Presbyterian's wide receiver Tim Pope, who caught a pair of touchdown passes to create the final margin of victory.

Final Score
Presbyterian 42
Newberry 14

PC running game too much

Will Vandervort
Sports Editor

The are several areas where Newberry College lost the Bronze Derby for a sixth straight year Saturday, but none of them are more glaring than the rushing statistics.

Presbyterian dominated both sides of the line of scrimmage, and the game's rushing statistics prove it. The Blue Hose, which averaged just 89.1 yards a game on the ground coming in, amassed 190 yards on 49 carries, while Newberry netted just 75 yards on 23 carries, with quarterback Mazi Drummond getting 70 of those yards.

"They didn't surprise me at all," said Newberry head coach Zak Willis about PC's running game. "They're a good football team and I knew they were good coming in. I told people all along we would struggle to beat them, and I think they thought I was just poor mouthing.

"(Presbyterian) has a good football team. They have character, quality and seniors that want to win and believe they can. We now have to go out and develop that in our program."

■ Saturday's first. Defensive end Robert Holley and wide receiver Tymere Zimmerman both had first for Newberry in Saturday's 57th Bronze Derby.

Holley lived a defensive linemen's dream, when he returned a Zach Ellis pass 32 yards for the game's first touchdown. It was Holley's first career touchdown in his last college game.

Tymere Zimmerman, who tied a school record for receiving touchdowns in a season last week, threw his first career touchdown pass, when he hit Derrick Higgins in stride for a 48-yard touchdown pass on an end around in the first quarter.

Sports
The Clinton Chronicle
Wednesday, November 19, 2003

Bronze Derby is Presbyterian's again

All you need is one: Junior wide receiver Tim Pope (1) needs just one hand to haul in this touchdown pass in the fourth quarter of PC's 42-14 win over Newberry Saturday in the annual Bronze Derby game. Pope scored twice in the fourth quarter to help put away the Indians. At right, Red shirt senior Maurice Gibbs dons the derby as a young fan reaches for a look.
— Photos by Fletcher Pruitt Jr

By David Hays
For The Chronicle

NEWBERRY — The Newberry Indians felt this was the year they would finally take the Bronze Derby back for the first time in six years. The Presbyterian Blue Hose said, "Not so fast!"

Presbyterian made a loud and clear statement Saturday that they still own the Bronze Derby, rallying from an early deficit to score six unanswered touchdowns in a 42-14 victory.

PC was not the clear favorite against Newberry for the first time in several years and was actually viewed as the underdog by many after clinching their first losing season since 1997.

Then the Blue Hose played a sloppy first quarter and fell behind 14-0. And they could have been down three touchdowns.

"I knew Newberry had a good team to begin with. I know a game lasts a long time. But being down 21 points to a team like Newberry would have been tough," PC coach Tommy Spangler admitted.

The Blue Hose somehow hung in the game, then heroes started coming to the forefront. PC scored twice in the second quarter for a 14-all halftime tie, then dominated the second half in front of more than 3,200 fans at Setzler Field.

Quentin Davis and Stewart

that set up touchdowns. Freshman Jared Southerland rushed for 93 yards and scored the first two touchdowns of his career. And Zach Ellis recovered from an embarrassing early interception to throw three touchdown passes, two to Tim Pope and one to Brett Wilhoit.

Presbyterian closed a disappointing season 4-6 overall and 2-5 in the South Atlantic Conference (SAC) though all its losses were by a touchdown or less. PC actually outscored its opponents 267-190.

Newberry rebounded from last year's 1-10 season to finish 3-7 overall, 2-5 in the SAC with a new coaching staff and several talented transfers including former Clemson signees receivers Tymere Zimmerman and Derrick Higgins.

"They were probably the favorites. We had a lot more motivation," said Presbyterian defensive back Young, who had two of PC's five interceptions.

"Usually we are the better team going in and everybody expects us to blow them out," said lineman Tony Gaines, part of a defense that forced seven Newberry turnovers. "This year we were about even (record-wise). But people thought they had the better athletes and that we were the underdogs."

"We train all year to develop mental toughness," Spangler said. "We sometimes make it physically hard to develop mental toughness. Down 14-0 early in the game on the road against a good Newberry team, our guys showed we had some mental toughness. We didn't panic."

The game started badly for PC. On the fifth play, defensive

Young kept the Blue Hose in the game with early interceptions. Dwayne Howell and Chad Burgess caused fumbles

Hose, Page 13A

The Clinton Chronicle

Hose

From Page 10A

lineman Robert Holley stepped in front of the intended receiver, picked off an Ellis screen pass and returned it 32 yards for a touchdown.

Two plays later, PC's Corey Mitchell fumbled and Holley recovered at the Blue Hose 42. But Presbyterian dodged a bullet when Davis stayed in front of Higgins and intercepted Mazi Drummond's underthrown pass at the 1.

PC continued to struggle, however. All-SAC punter Philip Bernardi uncharacteristically shanked an 11-yarder. Two plays later, Zimmerman took a reverse pitch from Drummond and hit Higgins in perfect stride into the end zone from 48 yards out to make it 14-0. There was an air of confidence on the Newberry sideline.

"We haven't had an easy season," Gaines said. "We knew that if we could stick together, we could get it done. We played like a team today. Everybody stayed up and we got it done."

PC waited until the final play of the first quarter to make its first big offensive play when Ellis threw a 25-yard pass to Barrett Fleming to the 5. On the next snap, Ellis faked a handoff to fullback David Behrendson and ran to the right corner of the end zone to cut it to 14-7.

The Indians responded with another promising drive when Higgins went up high over two defenders to make an athletic 28 yard grab. Then Zimmerman caught a 16-yarder to move the ball into PC territory, giving the two receivers five catches for 118 yard.

But the tide began to turn when Young outjumped Higgins for an interception inside the Blue Hose 10, quelling what would be Newberry's final threat. And Zimmerman and Higgins would be held to just one reception combined the rest of the game.

Later in the second quarter Presbyterian began finding running room up the middle with Ellis racing 13 yards on a draw, and Southerland plowing 18 yards to the Indians 28. Six plays later, Southerland scored from the 3. Noll's PAT tied it at 14 with 4:44 left in the half.

The Blue Hose defense continued its turnover mode into the second half. On the third play after the break, Burgess stripped the ball from Drummond. Donny Stamper recovered it at the Newberry 36.

"I saw him come back across the grain. I had to take him out," said Burgess, getting his first taste of the Bronze Derby rivalry as a freshman defensive back.

PC capitalized but not without Ellis rifling a fourth-and-5 pass to Fleming at the Indians 20. On the next play, a blown coverage left Wilhoit wide open and Ellis found him in the left side of the end zone.

The Blue Hose continued to build unstoppable momentum. On Newberry's next offensive play, Howell sacked Drummond, forced a fumble and then fought for the recovery at the Indians 22.

Newberry's defense continued to make mistakes. After forcing PC to attempt a field goal, the Indians were flagged for an illegal substitution giving the Blue Hose a first down at the 11. Southerland scored on a two-yard run to make it 28-14 with 10:12 left in the third.

PC broke the game open in the fourth. Ellis set up a touchdown with a 58-yard strike to Pope, who had beaten Deonte Hundley deep. Two plays later, from the 10, Ellis pump faked and hit Pope in the right corner of the end zone.

Quasi Gary's interception set up the Blue Hose's final score. Ellis again found Pope, who caught a seven-yard scoring pass that went through Newberry defensive back Donovan Fludd's hands.

Burgess and Young added interceptions in the final minutes.

"The defense was outstanding today. In big games, you've got to play big," Burgess said.

"They had to do a trick play to score on us in the first half," Young said. "We were pretty much blanketing their receivers. That was nice, especially with the big names that they had."

The Blue Hose once again got to celebrate on the field and pass around the Derby. Several players tried on the bronzed hat.

"We need to get an extra large," linebacker Isaac Gibson said, with a laugh.

"We needed it. It's good for the program," Spangler added. "It gives our guys some confidence. It helps your recruiting. It's a great way to finish."

It was the final game for seniors Davis, Howell, Gibson, Gaines, Greg Witt, Terry Meng, Chris Charles, Hamp Eadon, Mike Hill, Maurice Gibbs, Michael Jacobs, Steve McCoy and Joey Tucker. The senior class finished 27-15.

November 2004

November 1	American country singer Craig Morgan released the 2005 *Billboard* Song of the Year "That's What I Love About Sunday."
November 1	Terry Knight, American rock producer and singer for Grand Funk Railroad, was murdered by his daughter's boyfriend. He was defending her during a domestic dispute.
November 1	"She Will Be Loved" by Maroon 5 was the #1 song in the United States.
November 1	Mac Dre, American Rapper and Hip Hop pioneer, passed away.
November 2	The Arizona Diamondbacks announced that former New York Met Wally Backman would become their manager.
November 2	George W. Bush was re-elected as President of the United States defeating John Kerry.
November 3	In the middle of a players strike, the NHL canceled the All Star game scheduled for February, 2005 in Atlanta, Georgia.
November 4	The Charlotte Bobcats of the NBA played their first game in franchise history losing to the Washington Wizards 104-95.
November 4	The New York Mets named Willie Randolph as their new manager.
November 4	The Philadelphia Phillies named Charlie Manuel as their new manager.
November 5	The hit movies "Alfie" and "The Incredibles" were released in the United States.
November 5	Three days after hiring Wally Bachman as their new manager, the Arizona Diamondbacks fired him and hired Bob Melvin. On November 2, The New York Times had reported that Bachman had recent criminal convictions including drunk driving. An investigation by The Diamondbacks confirmed the story.
November 6	"Over and Over" by Nelly featuring Tim McGraw was the #1 song in the United States.
November 6	Retief Goodsen was the eventual winner of the PGA Tour Championship winning $6 million at East Lake CC in Atlanta, Georgia.
November 6	The Charlotte Bobcats of the NBA recorded their first franchise win with a 111-100 win over the Orlando Magic.
November 6	The Bronze Derby was played in Clinton, South Carolina. The Newberry College Indians defeated the Presbyterian College Blue Hose 28-25.

The Newberry Observer

Newberry at Presbyterian College • 1:30 p.m. • Bailey Memorial Stadium, Clinton

Indians look to rescue season with Derby win

Newberry coach wants to erase shame of last year's 42-14 loss

Paul Gable
Sports Editor

When Zak Willis was named head football coach at Newberry College he established three goals for his program.

Perhaps, the biggest of which was to beat Presbyterian in the annual Bronze Derby clash.

In the early going of last year's Bronze Derby contest, the Newberry faithful had much to cheer about as they saw the Indians race out to a 14-0 lead under Willis.

However, by the time the game was over, they were shocked following a 42-14 loss to Presbyterian.

While a complete year has passed since that day, the head coaches of both schools have not forgotten it.

During Newberry College's Media Day earlier this season, Newberry head coach Zak Willis said, "That game is everything. I have never been as ashamed as I was following that game. I knew it would be hard to beat them, but we flat out got beat."

As for Tommy Spangler,

LOOKING FOR SOME HEAD GEAR— Newberry College hopes Lady Luck is on its side this Saturday as they look to take the Bronze Derby against PC after six straight losses in the rivalry.

head coach of Presbyterian (5-4, 4-2) he admits that he began thinking about this year's game shortly after last season's.

"I have been real concerned since last year's game. Newberry is coached well and they have good players, but it still comes down to who plays the best. We have been fortunate to beat them the last six times straight, but sooner or later that streak will end. We caught some breaks last year, but we are not 42-14 better than Newberry. We are expecting a close game and hoping that it will be a classic Bronze Derby game," Spangler said.

Much like last year's game, the main event will feature two teams in different directions, as Presbyterian is tasting success in conference action, while Newberry is 3-6 overall, 0-6 and have not won since knocking off Division I-AA Coastal Carolina University back in September. However, both coaches admit that you can throw the records out when the Bronze Derby is up for grabs.

"Newberry College is playing good football, they have got good players and they are dangerous. They are playing better than an 0-6 conference team and they are due to win a game. I know they will give us their best effort and you can throw records and everything else out the window come Saturday. Newberry has

to be disappointed with their season, but a win over us would make their season," Spangler said.

For Newberry, a win could save their season.

"In order to turn this program around, you have to win this game. Last year, they blew us off the field completely," Willis said.

Newberry will enter in the midst of a six-game losing skid, however, four of those games have been decided in the final minute.

"It has been tough, but you have to remain persistent. Luck has to turn around at some point and we are hoping it will happen Saturday," Willis said.

The game will feature a rather interesting match-up between Newberry's explosive offense and Presbyterian's dominant defense, which leads the conference.

Indian quarterback Josh Stepp and wide receiver Tymere Zimmerman will face a stiff challenge from Blue Hose defenders Chad Burgess and Quasi Gary.

"They have an explosive offense. Josh Stepp is dangerous with his arm and feet and he has got weapons. I have been impressed with Tymere Zimmerman. He is a tremendous leader and a good young man. We cannot worry about how good we are on defense, or else we could give up 40-plus points to Newberry. We can't let Josh Stepp have a career day," Spangler said.

Willis stated that the key for Newberry is to execute and stop the Blue Hose's run attack.

"We have to try and execute. We want to play mistake-free football and if we do that, that in itself will be a victory. Presbyterian is a solid football team and they do not make mistakes. We need to stop their running game and that is the key for us," Willis mentioned.

Kickoff is set for 1:30 p.m. at Presbyterian College on Saturday.

HOW THE INDIANS SEE IT

Willis

"In order to turn the program around, you have to win this game. Last year they blew us off the field and that has been a motivator. Presbyterian is solid and they make no mistakes. They are just a solid football team and the key for us is to stop the run game."

— Zak Willis
Newberry head coach

HOW THE BLUE HOSE SEE IT

Spangler

"Newberry College has been playing some good football... They are due to win a game and I know we will get their best effort. They have to be disappointed with not winning a conference game, but a win over us would make their season. We have been fortunate to beat them the last six times."

— Tommy Spangler
Presbyterian head coach

NEWBERRY'S KEYS TO VICTORY

1. Play field position

The winner of a game like this usually wins the battle of field position. Both teams will start tremendous punters and kickers Saturday so whomever is more successful getting off and covering kicks will help the defense a great deal. It will be important for Newberry to make the right decisions in the kicking game. Field goals and extra points must be made and punts need to be solid this Saturday. The Indians cannot afford to give Presbyterian strong field position to start their drives with. A mistake of that nature could doom Newberry's chances.

2. Play with emotion and heart

The first quarter and a half of last year's Bronze Derby game was great for Scarlet and Gray fans. The rest...well, let's not discuss that. Newberry has been close to picking up a conference win in every game, including Carson-Newman. A win against archrival PC would give the Indians a conference win and would make their season, but it can only be accomplished by playing with emotion, heart and wanting it more than the Blue Hose. Newberry is a fine football team and have been all season long. They need to find that emotion that they played with against CCU this Saturday.

3. Get the offense going

The Presbyterian defense will focus on NC quarterback Josh Stepp and wide receiver Tymere Zimmerman. With that said, the Newberry running attack will have to come ready to pull out all the stops and pick up some big yardage. The Indians need to open up the playbook and not become so predictable this Saturday. When fans know what plays are coming, you have got some problems. Would it really kill to run a reverse or a little option? Newberry has to get the offense going this week and they will need solid outings from everyone, including the running backs.

Things to Know

- **When:** Saturday
- **Time:** 1:30 p.m.
- **Where:** Bailey Memorial Stadium, Clinton.
- **Records:** Presbyterian 6-4, 4-2; Newberry 3-6, 0-6.
- **Interesting fact:** Presbyterian has won the last six outings.
- **Interesting fact II:** This is the Palmetto State's second oldest rivalry.
- **Interesting fact III:** No current Indian player has won the Bronze Derby. Only assistant coach Ike Allred has won it as a Newberry Indian.
- **The Series:** Presbyterian holds a 56-31-5 edge, including the last six meetings.
- **Rankings:** Neither team is ranked.
- **Nicknames:** Newberry Indians; Presbyterian Blue Hose.
- **Last week:** Newberry lost to Mars Hill; Presbyterian beat Wingate.
- **Last year:** Newberry jumped out to a quick 14-0 lead, but the Blue Hose picked up the win by a count of 42-14.
- **Coaches:** Zak Willis for Newberry; Tommy Spangler for Presbyterian.

ADVANTAGE

	Newberry		Presbyterian
OFFENSE			
QBs	Josh Stepp is now the all-time leader in three categories for the Indians in his first year. He will face a strong test from PC, but expect him to be up for the challenge.	✓	Zach Ellis has tossed for well over 1,000 yards this season and continues to get better each time out. As Ellis goes, so goes the Blue Hose offense. If he has time, look out.
RBs	The running game was missing last week. Deshon Roddell and Gerard Jackson will have to bring it this Saturday.	✓	Corey Mitchell leads the ground attack and Corey Fidler is right behind him. These guys are effective when they run the football.
O-Line	These guys continue to play well each time out. They are over the injuries and now it's time to show that all the hard work is paying off.	✓	These guys have done a solid job of protecting Ellis and giving him time to get passes off.
WR	Tymere Zimmerman keeps setting records; Antwan Surratt and Charles Brandon are quality wide outs. Corey Boswell caught a TD pass last week.		Tim Pope and Kip McAlister lead this unit. Pope is well over 700 yards, while McAlister is nearing 500. They will need a big day.
DEFENSE			
D-Line	These guys played well last week. They will have to get pressure going early.	✓	These guys have put the clamps down on opposing teams. They do not give up many points in a contest and lead the SAC in scoring defense.
LBs	Terrance Leverett wants the Bronze Derby, but he can't do it all by himself. Look for others to help him this week.		David Behrendsen can stop runners and quarterbacks cold in their tracks. He is PC's Terrance Leverett.
D-Backs	These guys shut down Mars Hill's best receiver a week ago. Jonathan Lyles had a great game last week. This group stacks against stiff competition. This is a push.		Chad Burgess and Quasi Gary lead this unit. Both have combined for well over 10 picks on the season and they know how to shut down receivers. This is truly a push to be decided on the field.
SPECIAL TEAMS			
Kicking	Hyatt Lubbins is a good kicker and has shown it as of late this season. Punter Jeff Williams is truly one of the best in America and is a true NFL prospect.	✓	Rachel Hyatt Nutt has been great this season and last week he made two big field goals against Wingate. At one point he was perfect on PATs this year.

The Li'l  That Was!

The Li'l 🎩 That Was!

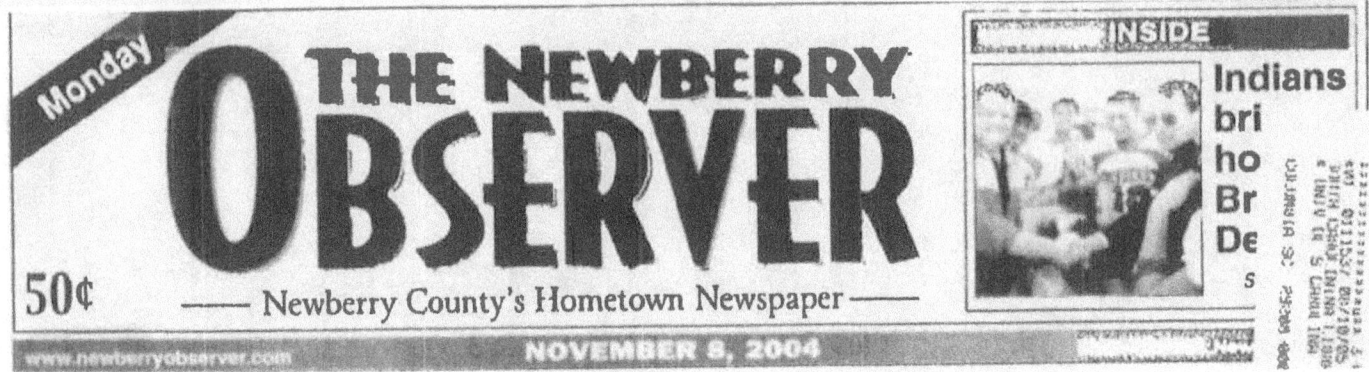

Indians deliver the final insult to PC, reclaim Bronze Derby

Paul Gable
Sports Editor

When fans of Newberry College look back on the 2004 football season, they will see only one win in the South Atlantic Conference, but odds are good it will be the one that will be remembered for years to come.

With Saturday's 28-25 come-from-behind victory over rival Presbyterian College, the Indians improve to 4-6, 1-6 on the season and reclaim the Bronze Derby for the first time since 1997. The win eased memories of last year's 42-14 loss.

"This win is for everyone who has ever worn a Newberry College jersey. This is the biggest win this school has ever had and I just want to thank all the fans for sticking with us," said a soaked, but pleased, Newberry College coach Zak Willis.

The win was due, in part, to some last-minute heroics by the Indians.

Following a blocked punt, Presbyterian took the lead for the first time in the game after quarterback Zach Ellis hit Steve McCoy for a 33-yard touchdown to put the Blue Hose ahead 25-21 with 2:12 left in the game. After an interception on the ensuing drive after the touchdown, Newberry forced the Blue Hose three-and-out, giving the Indians one final shot at the game with 1:12 left. Indian quarterback Josh Stepp led the Indians on a seven-play, 59-yard drive, finding sophomore wideout Corey Seawell for the 3-yard TD pass with 22 seconds left in the game.

"You can't put this into words. It was a total team effort and it makes everything we have worked for worth it this year. This is a huge win for Newberry," said Stepp, who finished the game 28-of-43 for 223 yards, three touchdowns and one interception. Stepp also rushed the ball 13 times for 62 yards.

Seawell echoed those same thoughts.

"This is a great feeling. This is what we worked for and nothing in the world could be better than this right now," Seawell said.

Much like last year's contest, the Indians came out and struck first, reeling off 14 points including a 24-yard touchdown pass from Stepp to Charles Brandon and a 2-yard touchdown pass from Stepp to Tmere Zimmerman.

Presbyterian got into the ballgame early in the second quarter, putting up a 42-yard field goal from Ryan Noll and cutting the deficit to 14-3 heading into the lockers.

Presbyterian took the opening kickoff to start the second half and drove 80 yards on 10 plays with Ellis nailing halfback Jay Freeman for a 14-yard touchdown—cutting the lead to 14-10 with 10 minutes left to play in the frame.

The Blue Hose defense forced Newberry to cough the ball up, and looked to take the lead as they drove deep into Indian territory. Newberry's defense had other plans, and Emil Gibson intercepted an Ellis pass and tossed the ball to teammate Deonte Hundley, who rumbled 40 yards for the score to put the Indians out in front 21-10.

Presbyterian refused to back down, mounting a comeback of their own in the fourth quarter. A 2-yard touchdown run by Andreas Wright capped a seven-play drive that spanned 62 yards. The Blue Hose converted on the two-point attempt to cut the deficit to 21-18.

Gerard Jackson led the run attack for Newberry, picking up 76 yards on 15 carries. Zimmerman hauled in nine grabs for 79 yards and Brandon caught seven passes for 69 yards for the Indians, who finished with a total of 378 yards.

Newberry looks to finish the season on a two-game win streak when they travel to Webber International in Florida next Saturday.

BACK WHERE IT BELONGS — Newberry College football coach Zak Willis, left, and college president Dr. Mick Zais, right, were all smiles following Newberry's 28-25 victory over Presbyterian for the coveted Bronze Derby Saturday afternoon.

CLAWING FOR A FEW MORE YARDS — Newberry College quarterback Josh Stepp, with ball, tries to fight off a Presbyterian defender who has a hand on Stepp's helmet en route to Newberry's 28-25 win over the Blue Hose Saturday.

The Clinton Chronicle

Wednesday, November 10, 2004

The Li'l That Was!

Bronze Derby finally a fit for Newberry

Hose lose by 3 in final seconds

By David Hays
For The Chronicle

It looked like Steve McCoy and Stewart Young were going to be heroes in the last game of their Presbyterian football careers.

McCoy blocked a punt, setting up the go-ahead touchdown pass that he caught with 1:58 left to give the Blue Hose their first lead in Saturday's Bronze Derby battle at Bailey Memorial Stadium. Then Young intercepted a Newberry pass on the next play and it appeared PC was on its way to a seventh consecutive victory over its arch rival.

But the Indians got the ball back with 1:20 left, and ended years of frustration when Josh Stepp threw a 3-yard scoring pass to freshman Corey Seawell with 22 seconds remaining to give Newberry a 28-25 victory. It was only Seawell's seventh catch of the season.

"The hardest part was fighting so hard to get back in it, then having it (the lead), and then letting it go," said PC head coach Tommy Spangler. "I told the guys (after Young's interception) that it's not over. I knew they had three time outs."

It was jubilation for the Indians, whose last victory over Presbyterian was in 1997. Not only were they riding a six-game losing streak against PC, they had lost their last six games coming into Saturday's action. Four of those losses were by a touchdown or less.

There were enough big plays in the last 2:57 to fill a whole game. Newberry (4-6, 1-6 South Atlantic Conference) had driven to the Blue Hose 41, but was forced to punt with a 21-18 lead. The Blue Hose (6-5, 4-3)

High and low: Blue Hose defensive end Nick Willis (30) leaps after Newberry quarterback Josh Stepp (11) during PC's 28-25 loss to the Indians in the Bronze Derby game Saturday at Bailey Memorial Stadium. — Photo by Fletcher Pruitt Jr.

Newberry	28
Presbyterian	25

figured to get the ball deep in their own territory. But McCoy, Justin Jones and Quasi Gary burst into the backfield with McCoy cleanly blocking the Jeff Williams punt. The ball rolled out of bounds at the Newberry 37.

"The hole opened up and I got a good jump on it and executed the block," McCoy said. "Luckily the punter came straight for me and I got a hand on it."

Two plays later, PC quarterback Zach Ellis was flushed out of the pocket to the right, and McCoy got separation from his defender near the goal line. Ellis threw a 33-yard strike to McCoy, who made the catch and slid into the end zone. Ryan Noll's point after gave the Blue Hose a 25-21 lead with 1:58 left.

But momentum switched back to Newberry's side when freshman Alex Haynes returned the ensuing kickoff 60 yards to the PC 33. Then on the next play, Young stepped in front of intended receiver Tymere Zimmerman, intercepted the ball at his 29 and returned it 6 yards. Derrell Doe's rush forced Stepp to hurry the throw right into Young's hands.

"They had been running that route pretty much all game," Young said. "The way our defense was designed today was to shut that down. He (Zimmerman) maybe caught two of them out of about 10. I really didn't think they would throw it again. But I anticipated it anyway, got inside, and the ball looked so big coming right to me."

But 1:52 still remained in the game and the Indians had three time outs. Jay Freeman ran three yards to the 38. Adam Scott sacked Ellis on second down; then Donavin Fludd broke up a deep pass intended for Justin Durant. That forced the Blue Hose to punt, and Newberry took over at its own 41 with 1:20 to go.

"It's kind of hard to call plays when you're up four and are pinned deep (in your own territory)," Spangler said. "You know you can't take a knee, so you just try to run some conservative plays and we just didn't execute."

Stepp completed passes of 11 and 9 yards, then found Zimmerman for a 21-yard gain to the PC 16. Stepp hit Charles Brandon with a 13-yard sideline pass to the 3. Then on second and goal, he found Seawell on a slant to the middle of the end zone. It was Newberry's first offensive touchdown since its second possession.

The Indians scored on their first two possessions in the 93rd meeting between the two schools. Newberry took the opening kickoff and drove 83 yards in eight plays with Stepp throwing a 24-yard scoring pass to Brandon. Zimmerman's 3-yard scoring catch made it 14-0 with 7:19 left in the first quarter.

While the Blue Hose defense settled down, Ellis struggled in the first half. He completed only six of 17 passes for 60 yards and was intercepted twice. PC's

Hose, Page xxA

Protected: The Blue Hose offensive line gives quarterback Zach Ellis plenty of time to throw during PC's 28-25 loss Saturday to Newberry. — Photo by Fletcher Pruitt Jr.

Hose

From Page 7A

only offense in the half was Noll's season-best 42-yard field goal with 12:21 left in the second quarter.

The Blue Hose opened the second half with a 10-play, 80-yard scoring drive. Ellis completed all four passes, including a 14-yard scoring throw to Freeman. The sophomore avoided a tackle inside the 10, then dived to the pylon in the right front corner of the end zone.

Newberry built its lead to 21-10 with 1:41 left in the third when Emil Gibson intercepted a tipped pass at his 47, returned it 13 yards, then as he was being tackled, flipped the ball to cornerback Deonte Hundley who took the ball the final 40 yards.

PC pulled within 21-18 with nine minutes left in the game on Andreas Wright's 2-yard scoring sweep to the left corner. Tim Pope caught the two-point conversion pass, adjusting to a throw over the opposite shoulder.

But in the end, the Blue Hose suffered their third SAC loss by a touchdown or less.

"Considering where we came from at 0-2 and how we played, we accomplished a lot," Spangler said, referring to season-opening losses to NAIA Cumberland College and 52-7 at Furman. "We could have very easily won at Catawba, at Mars Hill, and this game. We gave ourselves an opportunity to win every conference game late and we just didn't today."

Ellis completed 24 of 44 passes for 282 yards and two touchdowns. Freeman led PC's ground game with 69 yards on 13 carries, and McCoy led all receivers with eight catches for 118 yards. Defensively, safety Kevin Molony led the Blue Hose with 12 tackles, while Young broke up four passes and defensive end Sherman Burnett three.

Stepp completed 28 of 43 passes for 223 yards. PC had a 403-378 edge in total offense. Newberry was penalized 13 times for 141 yards. Spangler tried to be positive as he talked to his team after the game.

"I told them, you've got to be careful. Don't just put the weight of this game on our shoulders. Let's look at the whole season. We have a lot of things to feel good about," Spangler said.

"You're naturally going to be a little down. But if we think back at what we accomplished, we beat Carson-Newman, we beat Wingate when they were ranked, and we beat a real good Tusculum team. We are not going to think any less of our football team simply because of a three-point loss."

Newberry claims Bronze Derby with last-second win

Newberry College quarterback Josh Stepp's three-yard touchdown pass to wideout Corey Seawell in the final seconds lifted the Indians to a 28-25 victory over host Presbyterian College in the 58th edition of the Bronze Derby Classic held at Bailey Memorial Stadium Saturday afternoon.

With the win, the Indians snap a six-game losing streak in the series, the longest losing streak by either school. PC ends the season with a 6-5 overall record and 4-3 mark in the South Atlantic Conference. Newberry ends the season with a 4-6 overall record and 1-6 mark in league play.

The Blue Hose, trailing 21-10 entering the fourth quarter, fought back with a pair of touchdowns to retake the lead at 25-21 with 2:12 remaining in the game. Sophomore Andreas Wright got the first Blue Hose score from one-yard out at the 9-minute mark followed by a 33-yard touchdown pass from quarterback Zach Ellis to wideout Steve McCoy.

On the ensuing Indian drive, PC's cornerback Stewart Young intercepted Stepp at the PC 29 yard line to end the Indian scoring threat. The Blue Hose were unable to keep the ensuing drive alive and punted the ball away that Newberry's Antwan Surratt returned 17 yards to setup the Indians on the Newberry 41 yard line which led to Stepp's game-winning drive.

In the first half, Newberry jumped out to a 14-0 lead in the first quarter thanks in part to a pair of touchdown passes by Stepp the first to wideout Charles Brandon for 24 yards and then to wideout Tymere Zimmerman from two yards out. PC got on the scoreboard at the 12:21 mark of the second quarter when senior place-kicker Ryan Noll connected on a 42-yard field goal capping a five-play, 28 yard drive.

In the second half, PC took the opening kickoff and drove 80 yards on 10 plays with Ellis finding halfback Jay Freeman for a 14-yard touchdown strike to cut the lead to 14-10 with 10 minutes to play in the third. After Newberry's next drive stalled, PC took over first-and-10 at its eight yard line. The Blue Hose drove into Indian territory at the 40 yard line before Newberry's left defensive tackle Emil Gibson intercepted an Ellis pass and tossed the lateral to teammate Deonte Hundley for a 40-yard touchdown to put the Indians ahead 21-10 with 1:40 left in the third quarter.

Stepp completed 28-of-43 passes for 223 yards and three touchdowns while Zimmerman caught nine passes for 79 yards and one score. Defensively, the Indians were led by defensive back Corky Howell who tallied 11 total stops and defensive end Tony Ransom who registered eight total stops and three sacks on the day.

PC's offense was led by Ellis who completed 24-of-44 passes for 282 yards and two touchdowns, but threw four interceptions on the day. PC's McCoy led the receiving corps with eight catches for 118 yards and one touchdown while free safety Kevin Molony tallied a career-high 12 total stops for the defense

THE BLUE STOCKING

THE STUDENT NEWSPAPER OF PRESBYTERIAN COLLEGE

Monday, November 29, 2004 — Volume 100, Issue 5

SPEAKMAN ON SPORTS

By Stephen Speakman
SPORTS EDITOR

For this week's edition of "Speakman on Sports," I'd like to say a few words about this year's Bronze Derby game against Newberry College. For anyone not familiar with the outcome, Presbyterian College was defeated by Newberry College by the score of 28-25. In what turned out to be a very exciting end to the game (along with entire fourth quarter for that matter), the lead shifted from Newberry to Presbyterian and then back to Newberry within about a two minute span. I don't know that there's anything much more that one can say except that it was a hard loss for everyone involved: fans, coaches, and players alike.

After the game, I found myself searching for an explanation about how the team's play during the opening minutes of the first half. Quite simply, the team looked flat and uninspired. I had expected that the team would be revved up for a rivalry game and that the opening minutes would be filled with a strong and emotional effort. While Newberry came out firing on all cylinders, there was obviously something lacking for Presbyterian. Maybe it was nerves; I don't know, but the defense started slowly and the offense could not sustain a drive for the entire first half of the game.

That being said, things did improve for the Hose, and I was impressed with the way the Hose kept fighting. Despite a terribly slow start on offense, the defense stepped up their play after the first several drives and kept the game well within striking distance. Time after time the defensive unit made big stops, providing great opportunities for the offense to chip away. Unfortunately, the late surge by the offense was not enough to secure the win. A defense that had been leaned on the entire game finally cracked. It was disappointing seeing the Indians drive 59 yards for a game winning touchdown, especially since, on the preceding drive by the PC offense, all that PC needed was a single first down to secure the victory. The inability of the offense to convert the first down really summed up what kind of a day, and even more so, what kind of a year it was for the team. So close, and yet not quite there...

November 2005

November 1	Burt Bacharach released his album "At This Time" which won a 2006 Grammy Award for Best Pop Instrumental Album.
November 1	The International Olympic Committee announced South Korea and North Korea will field a united team at the next Olympics.
November 2	American actress Jean Carson, who portrayed Daphne, one of the fun girls on the "Andy Griffith Show" passed away.
November 2	23 killed and over 150 wounded in clashes between opposition supporters and police in the Ethiopian capital of Addis Abba.
November 3	New York Yankees outfielder Matt Lawton tested positive for steroids and was suspended for the first ten games of the 2006 season.
November 4	In MLB, two retired and former players are announced that they will be returning to their old teams as coaches. The Milwaukee Brewers announced that Hall of Famer Robin Yount would return as a bench coach. The New York Yankees announced that Ron Guidry would return as their new pitching coach.
November 4	Top movies released in the United States included "Chicken Little" and "Jarhead."
November 4	Arthur Hastings Wise was executed by lethal injection in South Carolina. Wise had murdered 4 fellow employees at a lawn mower parts manufacturing facility in Aiken, South Carolina.
November 4	A-ha released their album "Analogue."
November 5	Scoring on each of their 7 possessions in the first half, #1 Southern California defeated Stanford 51-21. Quarterback Matt Leinart threw for 4 touchdowns.
November 5	Winner of 5 Emmy Awards from "Santa Barbara," "Another World" and "Guiding Light," musical composer Rick Rhodes passed away.
November 5	2004 Indianapolis 500 winner Buddy Rice married Michelle Noonan.
November 5	In the NFL, the Philadelphia Eagles suspended wide receiver Terrell Owens for "conduct detrimental to the team." Owens complained to the team for not recognizing his 100th career touchdown reception. In addition, he criticized the play of Eagles quarterback Donovan McNabb.
November 5	The Bronze Derby was played in Newberry, South Carolina. The Presbyterian College Blue Hose defeated the Newberry College Indians 38-7.

PC reclaims Bronze Derby

THE LAURENS COUNTY Advertiser
Laurens, South Carolina

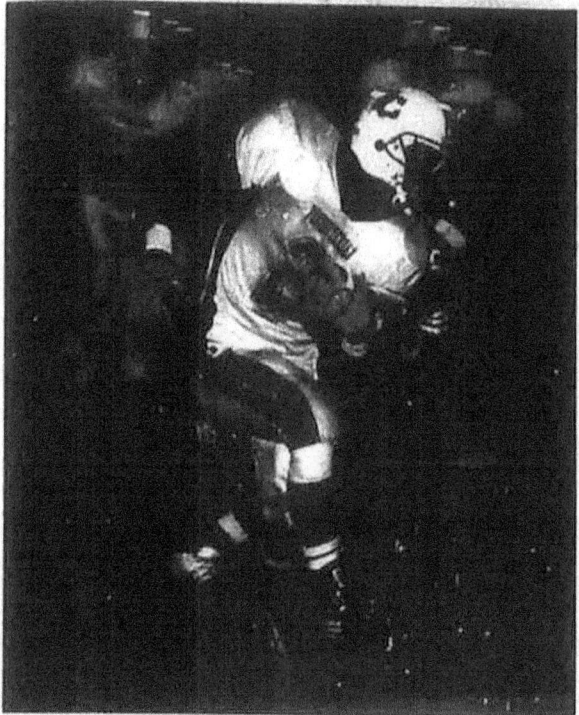

Photo by Dale Knight

DEUCE'S WILD — PC's Chetyuane Reeder (2) makes a move during a 38-7 victory over Newberry for the Bronze Derby Saturday night.

By John Clayton
Managing Editor

NEWBERRY — Presbyterian senior defensive back Arthur Middleton was just part of a blue and white mob moving toward midfield late Saturday night at Setzler Field.

"Where's that hat at?" Middleton called out as the mob oozed toward the Bronze Derby, which PC had just reclaimed for the seventh time in nine years with a lopsided 38-7 victory over rival Newberry in the 59th meeting for the coveted trophy.

Moments later, Middleton was the cat in the hat, mugging for photos with teammates, but with even more to celebrate than simply a victory in PC's storied rivalry with Newberry. That win, coupled with a loss earlier in the day by Valdosta State vaulted the Blue Hose to the top of the Southeast Region poll and earned PC a first-round bye in the regional playoffs.

"There was a lot at stake — not just the Bronze Derby and bragging rights, especially with the Valdosta State loss," said PC head coach Tommy Spangler. "Our guys stepped up and answered the challenge. We told them they could be the No. 1 team in the region and play like it, and they did."

The win over Newberry capped a near-perfect season by the Blue Hose (10-1 overall, 7-0 South Atlantic Conference), which advanced to the NCAA Division II Playoffs for the first time in school history and claimed the program's first SAC Championship since 1979.

And it was close to a near-perfect performance — one that left Newberry head coach Zak Willis a bit awed.

"This is a special team," Willis said of PC. "They're a lot like the Furman teams I played on back in the 1980s and that's the highest

■ See **PC**, page 10A

■ **PC**

Continued from Page 9A

compliment I can pay any team."

PC senior quarterback Zach Ellis connected on 27 of 39 passes for 292 yards and three touchdowns, including two to Justin Durant, to lead the Blue Hose.

PC wasted little time establishing an early lead that a stingy defensive effort would make stand up for the rest of the game. The Blue Hose took the opening kick and drove 60 yards in seven plays, capping it with a 19-yard touchdown pass from Ellis to Durant and a 7-0 with 11:55 to play in the first quarter. Less than two minutes later, James Mitchell recovered a blocked Newberry punt in the end zone for a 14-0 lead.

Meanwhile, the PC defense set about holding the SAC's top-ranked offense, which was averaging 406 yards per game, in check. PC limited the Indians (5-4, 4-3) to 183 yards of total offense. Preseason all-conference quarterback selection Josh Stepp was limited to just 12 of 27 passing for 103 yards with one interception.

"We knew we were going to see the best offensive team we'd seen all year," said PC defensive back Quasi Gary. "We studied, prepared all week and then came out and executed. We knew we weren't going to win the lip contest, but we came in and played hard and gave it our all."

PC's only miscue of the night set up Newberry's only score. Poised for what appeared to be third first-quarter touchdown at the Newberry 5-yard-line, the Blue Hose fumbled a shotgun-snap, which was recovered by Newberry sophomore defensive end Antoine Morgan and returned 65 yards to the PC 20. Four plays later, Titus Davis scored on a 3-yard run to cut the PC lead to 14-7 with 12:17 left in the second quarter.

But the Blue Hose responded to its second-quarter misstep with 24 unanswered points in the second half. Ellis connected with Brett Wilhoit on a 44-yard bomb with 9:41 left in the third and found Durant again from 11 yards out to extend the PC lead to 28-7 with 56 seconds remaining in the quarter.

A 29-yard field goal from Andy Schlimmer and a 3-yard run by freshman Chetyuane Reeder, who led all rushers with 96 yards on 20 carries, padded PC's lead and stoked its momentum headed toward the playoffs.

After a bye-week, PC will host the Albany State-Central Arkansas winner on Nov. 19.

"I just hope we can keep it going, but knowing our guys, they're going to keep focused and stay humble," said Spangler.

The Li'l 🎩 That Was!

THE BLUE STOCKING
THE STUDENT NEWSPAPER OF PRESBYTERIAN COLLEGE
Thursday, November 10, 2005 — Volume 101, Issue 4

PC Crushes Newberry; Regains Bronze Derby
By Stephen Speakman

In what was a fitting end to a stellar regular season by the Blue Hose football team, Presbyterian College soundly defeated rival Newberry on Saturday night, November 5th, 2005 by the score of 38-7. Not only did the victory return the coveted "Bronze Derby" to its rightful home in Clinton, South Carolina, but with the victory, PC finished the regular season undefeated in the SAC with a record of 7-0. The team completed the regular season with a 10-1 record overall, and now will move into Division II playoffs next Saturday.

Presbyterian College quarterback Zach Ellis led the PC offense with 292 yards on 27 of 39 passing. Wide Receivers Chris Pope and Justin Durant led the receiving corps with 8 catches for 93 yards and 7 catches for 70 yards, respectively.

Chetvaune Reeder led the way on the ground attack for the Hose, taking 20 carries for 96 yards. Tailback Corey Fidler added 10 carries and 40 yards on the ground as well as made 6 receptions for 29 yards, acting as a potent double threat option for Ellis and the PC coaching staff.

Presbyterian led the way in every meaningful statistical category on offense, outpacing the Newberry Indians in first downs (24-13), rushing yards (108-80), passing yards (292-103), number of offensive plays (75-59), and time of possession (32:59-27:01).

The Blue Hose offense performed well in third-down situations, converting 10 of 16 third down attempts. They also capitalized on their red-zone opportunities, finishing drives with a score on 4 out of 5 trips to the red-zone.

Presbyterian College's defensive unit performed excellently for the Hose. Antwan Thomas led the team with 8 tackles, Justin Jones finished the night with 7, and Terrance Blake added 6 in what was a very strong defensive effort. Newberry's offense was limited to only 183 total yards and went the entire second half without scoring. The only big play by Newberry came after a Zach Ellis fumble on the Newberry 8 yard-line which was returned all of the way to the Presbyterian College 20 yard-line. The ensuing drive resulted in the only Newberry score of the night.

When asked about the game, Senior defensive back Arthur Middleton said, "We were ready for them all week. We had a game plan that we talked about and the offense and defense were executing—going in and doing their jobs to make it a success.

"There wasn't anything outstanding. It's just been the same attitude: expecting to get it done; expecting to go in there and win."

The Blue Hose now move into Division II playoff action. Their first playoff game will be held at Presbyterian College's Bailey Stadium on Saturday, November 19th.

November 2006

The Li'l That Was!

November 2	Shakira became the first female artist to win Record of the Year, Album of the Year and Song of the Year at the 7th Latin Grammy Awards.
November 3	The "Fruitcake Lady," Marie Rudisil passed away.
November 3	The film "Borat: Cultural Learnings of America for Make Benefit Glorious Nation of Kazakhstan" was released.
November 4	The University of Georgia Bulldogs lose to Kentucky 24-20. It is the first time the Bulldogs lose to both Vanderbilt and Kentucky in the same season since 1973.
November 5	Saddam Hussein, the former President of Iraq, and his codefendants were sentenced to death for their role in the massacre of the 148 Shi'as in 1982.
November 5	Tony Stewart won the Dickies 500 at Texas Motor Speedway in the Chase for the NEXTEL Cup.
November 6	Kenny Chesney, Carrie Underwood and Keith Urban were winners at the 40th Country Music Association Awards.
November 6	In MLB, Oakland A's coach Ron Washington was named manager of the Texas Rangers.
November 6	Paul Azinger was named the captain of the 2008 Ryder Cup Team.
November 7	Keith Urban released his album "Love, Pain & The Whole Crazy Thing."
November 7	NASCAR race car driver Jeff Gordan married actress Ingrid Vandebosch.
November 7	Bryan Pata, defensive end for the NCAA Miami Hurricanes, was shot and killed after leaving practice. Years later, the murder was solved and discovered to be a former teammate.
November 7	Sugarland released their album "Enjoy the Ride."
November 7	Boston Braves baseball pitcher Johnny Sain passed away.
November 9	British singer-songwriter David Bowie performed on stage in New York City for his final time.
November 9	American journalist Ed Bradley of CBS passed away.
November 11	Shoppers stood in line for hours for the new Sony PS3 console.
November 11	The Bronze Derby was played for its final time in Clinton, South Carolina. The Presbyterian College Blue Hose defeated the Newberry College Indians 10-0.

The Li'l 🎩 That Was!

On November 3, 2006, Sports Editor Paul Gable's article "Bronze Derby Night is Monday for TD Club" appeared in the *Newberry Observer*. It was beginning to sink in that The Bronze Derby would be played for the final time in Clinton, South Carolina.

Emotions are sure to be running high Monday night as the Newberry County Touchdown Club will relive memories from the last 60 years of the **Bronze Derby** Clash. Fans may remember that the **Bronze Derby** clash pits rivals Newberry and Presbyterian together.

The meeting is set to begin at 7:30 at Community Hall in downtown Newberry, and among other things, Newberry College head football coach Zak Willis will offer his view on the big game, which could be the last one played.

Also on tap, former Indians standouts Dennis Swygert and Dusty Triplett will offer their memories of the game with the Blue Hose.

Swygert played in the 1960's, and has worked as an assistant coach at Summerville High School. Triplett is also a former player, and he has been a high school coach at various stops, including Strom Thurmond High School.

Also, the Touchdown Club will honor high school Players- of-the-Month from the three area high schools, along with three players from Newberry College.

Kickoff for the **Bronze Derby** game is slated for 1:30 p.m. next week at Presbyterian College in Clinton, and SCETV will televise the game live.

On November 8, 2006, former Newberry College football players reflected on The Bronze Derby in *The Newberry Observer*.

The names and faces have changed during the course of time, but anyone who has played in the **Bronze Derby** game can recall with vivid detail what transpired during the game.

Newberry College's Will Blackmon, Dusty Triplett, Dennis Swygert, Ike Allred and Matt Dewitt are no exception. All five had both good and bad memories during their playing days when the annual game rolled around.

"For small college football, the **Bronze Derby** game is our Clemson and Carolina, and that is how we viewed it. We don't run down the hill and touch the rock like they do at Clemson, and we don't come out to 2001 like they do at South Carolina, but for us, the game had the same emotion," said Blackmon, a former offensive lineman. "When I played, we looked forward to three games-opening day, Carson-Newman and the **Bronze Derby**."

Blackmon said on his recruiting visit to Newberry, he attended the **Bronze Derby** game, and he gained an appreciation for the rivalry.

"I know that some of the smaller schools have a rivalry, but nobody has the tradition and rivalry like Newberry and Presbyterian. When I played for Newberry, it was just another game that we got up for, but one you wanted to win. I have always had a high respect for Presbyterian, and when I played, we beat them twice in my four years. It is a great rivalry, and I just hate that it is not played on Thanksgiving anymore," Blackmon said.

Many fans have compared the **Bronze Derby** game to that of Army-Navy, but as far as Triplett is concerned, there is no comparison, and he should know, having played in both games during his collegiate career.

"I want to publicly make my vote for the most intense rivalry. Every year about this time all the T.V. shows and talk radio hosts talk about the biggest rivalry in college football. They talk about Ohio State and Michigan, they talk about Oklahoma and Texas, Southern California and Notre Dame, and very rarely do they mention Clemson and Carolina. Ultimately within the top two is Army-Navy, and I can understand that because there are more veterans from the services than there are alumni from any two colleges that will get together. Both schools reek of pride, and it is a tremendous rivalry game. In 1970, I played in that game, and we lost, and I am OK with it. Our lives continued, and we were so glad to be away from the Academy. But in 1973, my last football game, we got beat by Presbyterian, and I am upset about that," Triplett told the gathering at the Newberry County Touchdown Club Meeting earlier this week.

Swygert echoed those same thoughts reminiscing on his playing career with the Scarlet and Gray.

"I hadn't had a lot of humorous experiences against PC. We played them four times, and we got our butts kicked three times, which means we won one," Swygert said.

With that said, he did remember his last football game against the Blue Hose, which came on Thanksgiving Day in 1969.

"My last football game on Thanksgiving Day in 1969 sticks with me. We were not very good, and we came into that particular game 3-6. Our two games before PC, we went up to Western Carolina and lost 50-0, and the next week, Elon came in and beat us 56-21. Those were our two games before we played PC. PC, on the other hand, went to Western Carolina and beat them. Here we are on a downward slide, and here comes PC fresh

The Li'l That Was!

off this super victory. It was a mismatch, but sometimes a mismatch does not turn out like it should. Coach Herrin brought in a real good freshman class. Halftime we are in the football game, and we get into the third quarter, and it's a good football game. We are leading and we have PC backed up to the concession stand, and I am going to make a big play. They have 4th-and-12, and I know I can block this kick. I almost blocked the last one, and I knew I would block the kick. We lined up, ball is snapped, the kicker gets the ball and everything is going good. I know what is going to happen. I am going to come in and do what my coaches have taught me. High school players, don't ever leave your feet because here I am, everything is good, I am perfect in form and I came in flying full speed ahead. The kicker takes the ball, tucks it and runs 19 yards for a first down. I went flying through the end zone. Sometimes life gives you a second chance. We clawed, scrapped and fought back. We came back, and we got the lead. We are ahead 21-20 and we are down to the last two minutes. PC has to drive toward the concession stand, which should have been a clue. They get a first down at our 18-yard line. Three plays later, they have fourth-and-10 from our 18-yard line. They got nothing, and they have to kick a field goal. They bring the field goal kicker on, and I am going to make a big play. We line up, and I know I can get my hand on the ball. I come in and get a piece of it. The yellow flag came out, and we had 12 men on the field. They kicked it and they beat us 23-21. Coach Herrin had a lot of freshmen on that team, and they were a good group. The player that was the 12th man, unfortunately was a freshman. Two years later, those same freshmen that made that mistake, PC came in and they looked good, but on that Thanksgiving Day in 1971, Newberry took those pretty blue uniforms and dropped them. The score was 34-0," he said.

For Dewitt, who graduated in 2002, there will never be anything like the games against his arch-rival.

"It still eats me up to this day that I never had a chance to win it. It must really mean something if after all this time I am still upset because I never got to say I helped win the **Bronze Derby**. My most gut wrenching moment was my junior year when we lost in the final 30 seconds at their place," Dewitt said.

To the fans, it may be just another game, but for Dewitt, the **Bronze Derby** game was a way of life during his career.

"The biggest thing I can remember is people always asking about the game against Presbyterian regardless of what time of the year it was. We could have played a Division I-A opponent at Newberry, and all the local people wanted to know was whether or not we were ready for the **Bronze Derby** game. Honestly, it can be a burden for the players to win it, because they hear about it so much, and people try to make it bigger than the game. All you want to do is win it for your school, but you feel this pressure to win it for your team, your school and the town. It can be a bit much," the former offensive lineman stated.

For Allred, the game has a special meaning, as he capped his collegiate career with a victory over the Blue Hose.

"We were down 10-7, and I caught two touchdown passes to help us win 21-10. What is special to me is the very last time I ever touched the ball, Hunter Spivey threw it to me at Presbyterian. If you are going to go out, that is the way to do it. The game seems to always have heroes come out that you don't expect," Allred said.

The current assistant coach also echoed Dewitt's quote that the game could seem like it was bigger than life.

"The game is talked up so much that it is a rivalry, whether the players feel that way or not. Everybody feels it is a big game, but as far as we are concerned, we need to approach all the games like it's Presbyterian. Personally, I just feel that there is too much hype surrounding the game," Allred said.

Regardless of what happens this season, odds are good that the players who participate in the 60th **Bronze Derby** game will have plenty of stories to share, especially if it is the final one.

On November 8, 2006, *The Newberry Observer* asked "Could This Be The Last Bronze Derby Game?"

For 59 seasons, both Newberry College and Presbyterian College have met on the football field, competing for a battered and wellworn derby.

However, this season-the 60th-could be the final clash between these two for quite some time. That's right.

When these two teams strap up at 1:30 p.m. Saturday at Bailey Memorial Stadium on the campus of Presbyterian College, it could be the final **Bronze Derby** game. The reason?

Among other things, the fact that the Blue Hose are moving to the Big South Conference and Division IAA next season.

The annual game, which features a **bronze derby** going to the winner, has been played every year since 1947, and actually got its start in 1913 with the Indians picking up a 51-0 win. With that said, the teams did not begin passing the **Bronze Derby** until the basketball season of 1947.

According to both parties, there is a desire to keep the traditional game active in the near future.

Bee Carlton, director of athletics for Presbyterian College, said that his school already had seven road games, meaning that if the two teams were going to play it was going to be at Presbyterian rather that at Newberry, where it was to be played. Carlton said that a contractual agreement for a return trip to PC by Newberry could not be reached.

"We have played for all these years, and we asked them if they could come here. Right now, every game I have on the schedule is an away game. In the normal rotation of things, it would be our turn to go to Newberry, but we really need them to come here," said Carlton, who played for Presbyterian from 1972-1976.

However, Andy Carter, Newberry College's Director of Athletics, states there was no discussion of financial considerations.

"Here's the facts. It is our rotation for them to come here. Bee Carlton asked me and told me that they had too many road games next year, and if we could come there. I said that generally comes with a financial consideration, and he said they were unwilling to do that so I was unwilling to go. Is there a desire on our part to play? Absolutely, but not to be taken advantage of, and so there is a standard operating procedure that if you play someone at their place an extra time that there is a financial consideration. I am not going to go over there for two years in a row for free, and that is where it stood. My comment was that I guess we are not going to play, and he was OK with that. I don't have any ill feelings toward him or PC at all, but this is a two-way street. You can't lay the facts out there and say they are willing and we are not. We have moved forward, and our schedule is full, but if they want to play us, the next game will be at Newberry College or there will be a financial consideration that I'll have to agree to for us to go to their place," Carter said.

When asked about financial considerations, Carlton said, "We have played Charleston Southern home and away without any financial considerations. It is my desire to continue the home and away series with Newberry, but they have their considerations. It takes two to tango."

Carter fired back, saying that Newberry College was not going to give Presbyterian revenue for no compensation.

The Li'l 🎩 That Was!

"I think it is important that if this thing does not continue, people understand why. Do I think Bee Carlton wants to keep this thing going? I don't know, but I think he does. Do we? I am pretty sure we do, but at what point does it cease to make sense? Do we give them the game at their place every year with no financial considerations? Do we continue to play them when they have double scholarships? The whole thing is not as easy as saying you have to keep playing. It is an important relationship to try to do everything we possibly can to try and salvage, but at some point, the equation may end up being that it is never played again, and that is unfortunate. The only way to make it reality is to go over there and give them an extra game at home. I would not do that to anyone if they owed us a game, and if the shoe was on the other foot, I would not expect anyone else to do that for anyone. That is a high level of expectations for low level of return. Nobody is going to give you a home game," Carter said.

Carter continued by saying that his first year at the helm, Newberry had five home games and made $30,000 a game. Last year, the two teams played at Newberry and Newberry made approximately $40,000 on the **Bronze Derby** game alone.

"So we are going to give them revenue for no compensation?" Carter asked.

The **Bronze Derby** game this season will be televised live on SCETV, and it has traditionally been a well-attended event.

Neither Carter or Carlton would rule out that this is the final contest between the two rivals.

"I truly hope this is not the last one. We are hoping we can pick it up after a year or

· See DERBY, page 3B

Continued from page 1B

two away, but all the pieces have to come together for both teams. We will continue to talk, and we will see where we are down the road," Carlton said.

As for Carter's thoughts, if the series is going to continue, it will be with the two teams either playing at Setzler Field or Newberry receiving a financial consideration for playing at Presbyterian.

"The way the NCAA does postseason, we get more points for playing in region Division II teams so playing them win or lose does not help us with a postseason opportunity. Saying all that, it is still something worth keeping, but you have to consider two, three or four years down the road, with a full recruiting cycle and double scholarships than what we have. Does it make sense to do it? That decision will not be made by me alone. There are others who will weigh in on the decision. There are those who say you play it regardless of what it does to you or what benefits it gives you. Right now, the ball is in their court and they owe us a game. There is a way to get it at PC, but they are unwilling to do it. Will it ever be played again? Look, forever is a long time, so it probably will. Everyone has a decision to make here. Their decision is to play at their place, and my decision was not for free. We are all big people, and we all make our decisions, but for them to say they were willing to keep it going is true under their terms with no benefit to Newberry College. If they were willing to keep it going, they'd play us here at Newberry College next year," Carter said.

Presbyterian head football coach Tommy Spangler said he was unsure if this would be the last **Bronze Derby** game.

"I don't know if this will be the last one for good, but it will be for a little bit. We are headed in a different direction for a few years, and there should be more reason for a rivalry. It should be more than close proximity. It's a great rivalry, but I am not sure we are recruiting the same kind of kids anymore. They've beaten us on some kids, and we've beaten them. I don't know if the rivalry is like it was once was. The rivalry is there, but who knows if it's still as big as it once was. It's a fun game for our kids, and it didn't work out. I think they wanted us to pay them, and we are not quite into the paying business yet. I don't think there's any negativity to that, and I think it will happen sooner than people think," Spangler said.

The Li'l That Was!

On November 10, 2006, *The Newberry Observer* reflected on the Newberry-Presbyterian College rivalry and the complications of Presbyterian College moving to NCAA Division I.

As you probably already know, the 60th **Bronze Derby** is for all the marbles. Newberry College-Presbyterian College. Forget Clemson and South Carolina. The only game that matters for people who graduated from Newberry or that school in Clinton is the one that will kickoff tomorrow at 1:30 p.m. at Bailey Memorial Stadium, and based on all the media reports from various outlets, including this one, it will be the last, which we have already touched on. You also might recall that we said Wednesday we would not enter the debate of who is to blame, but the whining is really starting to get old already. Forget all the talk about this and that, but instead let's talk about the Blue Hose and their move to Division I-AA. Odds are very good that when they began to put all the pieces together, they knew that there was a very good chance that they would have to travel to the likes of Furman, Coastal Carolina, Gardner-Webb, etc., and yes, they have seven games currently on their roster for next season, and they are on the road. They didn't have any problem appearing snooty in their report, which happened to be leaked on several Web sites, but when they have to travel, boy oh boy here come the tears. That brings us to tomorrow's game. You may have read Wednesday in our commemorative issue that the game was to be played at Newberry next year, but the Blue Hose wanted the Indians to travel, to which Newberry Director of Athletics Andy Carter said, OK, but let's talk about a financial consideration since you owe us a home game. Presbyterian Director of Athletics Bee Carlton would have none of that, and for that reason, he has been referred to as a grinch by several loyal Scarlet and Gray fans. Excited players. Excited fans. Great crowds. Classic rivalry. Yeah, we don't need any of that anymore do we? Some things you do for the good of the game. For intracounty football, and-cover your ears Carlton-because it's just fun. When these last two teams played each other the last two years there have been record crowds. Several at Presbyterian have said that they are not in the paying business yet, and that's fine, but how about we at least put everything out on the table. At worst, if you want to play at your place, split the gates. You'll be making money in your thumpings at Coastal Carolina and Furman. Carlton harps on the fact that the Blue Hose have seven away games. What in the world did you expect to have happen-everyone would come to your place to play? Nope. Instead, you'll be what Newberry's squad used to be-everyone's Homecoming opponent next year. And as for the tears about playing at CCU, Gardner Webb and Charleston Southern, you'll be required to make those trips when you join the Big South Conference, and if I am not mistaken, you've already made the trip to CSU before. Perhaps, it is best that tomorrow could be the final meeting. I don't know, but I do know that if you're a fan of either one of these institutions of higher learning, you need to be at Bailey Memorial Stadium tomorrow. See you at the game.

The Li'l 🎩 That Was!

On November 13, 2006, *The Newberry Observer* reflected on The Bronze Derby for the final time after the game was played at Bailey Stadium on November 11, 2006 in Clinton, South Carolina.

About 60 years ago, a Presbyterian College student, George Wilkinson, went into Adair's Men Shop in Clinton and started making payments of 25 cents to then owner Mr. Mac Adair each week until he had paid off the total sum of $16.50 for a derby-yes, that derby-to wear around the campus and town.

When Wilkinson's derby was stolen off a fellow fraternity brother's head during a melee at the Jan. 31, 1947, basketball game between the two schools at Newberry College, it was decided upon its return, a few days later, to make this a trophy that would go to the winner between the two schools in then, every sport.

The first couple of "Derby Games" seemed to garner little press as stories about Santa Claus making a visit to downtown Clinton in a few days seemed to be of more interest to the reader in the Clinton Chronicle.

On Nov. 11, 2006, however, plenty of interest was involved as a sea of several thousand Newberry College Indian fans, dominantly clad in red, seemed to take over Bailey Memorial Stadium in what was perceived to be the final 'Derby Day" for quite some time.

In the "Burning of Atlanta" scene in "Gone with the Wind," Rhett Butler (Clark Gable) tells Scarlet O'Hara (Vivien Leigh) to "take a good look my dear. It's a historic moment you can tell your grandchildren about-how you watched the Old South fall one night."

The "Old South" didn't fall Saturday, but fans from both sides agreed that neither Newberry nor Presbyterian Colleges- or themselves- would ever be the same again with the ending of this annual rivalry.

During the history of the Derby series, there have been very few meetings, if any, that Adair, Sandy Cruickshanks or Jimmie Coggins hasn't been in attendance.

Cruickshanks (who has missed maybe two Derby games in his lifetime), called his final PC football game Saturday after 25 years of broadcasting. Friday, he told about how he "was born in June and then got wrapped up in a blanket that Thanksgiving to go to the game."

Adair, whose father sold the original derby, said that he had "a lot of good memories and a lot of bad memories" in this rivalry as he was waiting outside the same men's store he now owns.

Coggins, the "Voice of the Indians," can recall fondly "childhood memories, student memories, adult memories

· See MEMORIES, page 9

Continued from page 8

and now, media memories as a broadcaster," of so many great games that "I hate to see coming to an end."

Presbyterian College has decided to leave their present affiliation with the South Atlantic Conference and move up to Division I next year where they will now face the likes of Coastal Carolina and Charleston Southern on a yearly basis.

"PC has decided to move on to bigger and better things," said Newberry County Sheriff Lee Foster.

"To discontinue this game is a tradition that's cheating the people," said Jerry Chitty. "It's an atrocity for this to stop."

"This is a sad day for small college football that a rivalry like this has to end," said David Duffie of Ninety Six. "Both towns look forward to this every year, and it's hard to imagine a season without the **Bronze Derby**."

There seems to be a 180- degree difference though in how Newberry people feel about the future of playing the Blue Hose.

"I wish we could keep the series going," said Keith Harmon. "Maybe we could be each other's opening game as this is like a South Carolina- Clemson rivalry and it ought to keep going." B.L. Brown sees differently.

"I don't care if we don't ever play them again in any sport of any kind, at any time nor at any place...theirs or ours," he said.

As the final seconds of Saturday's 10-0 win by the Blue Hose were ticking off, Georgia B. Thomason of Clinton looked up at the sky that was a shade of "PC Blue" and believes it was fate that earned them the win. "This is a beautiful day," she said. "This win was meant to be."

WPCC's Chris Burgin was glad to see PC play a whole game of what "we've only seen them play in spurts this year."

Mr. Wilkinson, after watching the game from the comfort of the President's Box, described what the spirit of winning The Derby truly means:

"It's for the schools, the character of the guys and the sportsmanship of the rivalry," he said. "It's for the history of the two schools as they have about 300 years of existence between them. This is just great for both schools. I'm sorry to not see them playing each other next year as it is ending a wonderful tradition," he concluded.

(Editor's Note- Wilson Senn included the following personal comment: "Tradition" seemed to be the noun that was used repeatedly over the past week about the rivalry whether someone was clad in Newberry or Presbyterian colors. 'Ironic' might be the best adjective for me at least. The late Wilson W. Harris covered the first **Bronze Derby** game for the Chronicle, the paper he was owner and publisher of. Harris was my grandfather and my namesake.)

The Li'l That Was!

THE LAURENS COUNTY Advertiser

Wednesday November 15, 2006

Vol. No. 122-Pub. No. 306000 — Laurens, South Carolina

Photo courtesy of Steve Owens

POPE'S HAT — Chris Pope (13) celebrates his team's 10-0 win over Newberry Saturday afternoon with the Bronze Derby

Advertiser

FIDLER ON THE MOVE — PC's Corey Fidler (39) gains yardage in Saturday's 10-0 win over Newberry for the Bronze Derby.
Photo courtesy of Steve Owens/PC

Bronze age

PC saves best for last in 10-0 win for Derby

By John Clayton
Managing Editor

The Bronze Derby will be staying at Presbyterian indefinitely.

Presbyterian used a steady running game and stubborn defense to end rival Newberry's bid for a perfect season and retain the Bronze Derby with a 10-0 victory Saturday afternoon at Bailey Memorial Stadium.

It was the 60th and perhaps final edition of the Bronze Derby rivalry game. PC owns a 35-22-3 advantage in the Derby series and now owns the Derby for the foreseeable future. The two teams will not meet in 2007 — the first time they have not played one another since 1918.

The defeat, however, was more costly for the Indians, who lost what was thought to be the No. 1 seed from the Southeast Region in the Division II playoffs, their bid at a perfect season as well as the Bronze Derby. Newberry hosts Albany State as a No. 3 seed this Saturday in the opening round of the playoffs.

PC (7-4 overall, 5-2 SAC) will be at home, but not without some degree of satisfaction in a dominating, season-ending performance.

"We did a lot of the same things we did all year," said PC offensive lineman Blake Hudson. "Overall, I think we just came out to play today and that was the difference."

PC's defense, ranked No. 1 in the South Atlantic Conference, made Chis Pope's 5-yard touchdown reception from Grayson Mullins just before the half stand up. Carl Stevenson added a 20-yard field goal, capping a 15-play, 87-yard drive with 13:23 left in the game to give PC a 10-0 lead.

Senior running back Corey Fidler returned after missing several games due to injury to rush for 101 yards on 17 carries. Fidler was the key factor in several second-half drives that kept Newberry's vaunted offense off the field.

"I really can't ask for anything more," Fidler said of the end of his college football career. "I'm glad things worked out like they did — I tore my quad before the Tusculum game and didn't know if I'd get back or not."

Fidler came back with a big performance, but so did PC's entire rushing offense, rolling up 297 yards on the ground with on 64 rushes as the Blue Hose racked up 24 first downs while holding the Indians to just six.

Meanwhile, the PC defense held Newberry, the top-ranked offense in the South Atlantic Conference to 97 yards total.

Harrassed for much of the day, Josh Stepp completed just 7 of 23 passes for 29 yards. The Newberry ground game fared little better with just 68 yards on 24 attempts.

"First down was the biggest key to our success," said PC defensive back Kevin Molony. "We kept them in second-and-long and third-and-long and that allowed us to do what we wanted to do."

With its ground game clicking and its defense keeping Newberry off balance, PC was able to control the clock, running 70 plays from scrimmage and keeping the ball for more than 37 minutes. Newberry had the ball for just over 22 minutes and ran 48 plays from scrimmage.

It was a performance more dominating than the score might indicate — and PC Head Coach Tommy Spangler said he saw it coming.

"I could sense it in warmups," Spangler said. "If there's such thing as a look in the eye, they had it."

The only regret from Spangler and his players is that this performance came too late to deliver a second straight SAC title. A win in near-miss losses at Catawba or against Wingate earlier in the season could have made Saturday's Bronze Derby game a conference championship game as well.

"It definitely would have tasted better had we beaten Catawba," Spangler said.

GAME NOTES: Newberry (10-1, 6-1) will be making its first NCAA playoff appearance this weekend. Newberry announced that has contacted the NCAA and is exploring a change of its mascot by the fall of 2008. In return, the NCAA lifted its ban on the Indians' hosting of NCAA playoff games because of "Indians" nickname

The Li'l That Was!

Sports
The Clinton Chronicle
Page 8A — Wednesday, November 15, 2006

That's gotta make 'em mad
Newberry College loses for first time this season -- and it's to the Blue Hose

By David Hays
For The Chronicle

The best team in the history of Newberry College football could not wrestle the Bronze Derby away from the Presbyterian Blue Hose.

The Indians entered Saturday's backyard showdown ranked No. 9 in NCAA Division II, were 10-0 and averaging 35 points per game. Having already clinched their first South Atlantic Conference title, this is by far the best season in 93 years of Newberry football.

But the defending SAC champion Blue Hose rose to the challenge. The scoreboard read Presbyterian 10, Newberry 0. But the final score did not reflect PC's dominance in front of 5,982 fans at Bailey Memorial Stadium.

"In my 10 years and that's been over 100 games, this is probably the best football game we've played collectively," Blue Hose head coach Tommy Spangler said.

Presbyterian had overwhelming edges in total offense (366-97), first downs (24-6), time of possession (37:36 to 22:24), and plays ran from scrimmage (77-48).

Newberry, led by one of the nation's top quarterback-receiver duos in All-American candidates Josh Stepp and Tymere Zimmerman, were averaging 422.5 yards per game. PC held Stepp to 7-of-23 passing for a measly 29 yards. Zimmerman caught one pass for nine yards. Arie "Ate" Haynes, the SAC's leading rusher, was held to 23 yards.

The Indians faced 15 second and long plays and 12 third and long situations. PC had eight tackles for loss in the game and held Newberry to just two yards per play. With the shutout, Presbyterian won the SAC team defensive scoring title (11.2 points per game). Newberry's previous lows for the season were 23 points and 255 yards.

"I think our first downs were probably the key to our defense today," Blue Hose defensive back Kevin Molony said. "Getting them in second and long and third-and-long allowed us to do a lot more as far as staying in the zone. We didn't have to depend on the blitz. We controlled their running game, which was actually our biggest worry coming in."

The Indians had been averaging 213 yards on the ground per game but were held to 68.

"It was a team effort," PC safety Chad Burgess said. "The defensive line kept him (Stepp) in the pocket. The DBs and linebackers, we just stayed in our zones and tried to shut down the receivers."

The final score reflects Presbyterian's defensive dominance but doesn't show how impressive the offense was. The Blue Hose chewed up large chunks of real estate on the ground. PC rushed 63 times for 297 yards. The Blue Hose had 20 plays of nine or more yards, mostly on the ground.

Corey Fidler returned from injury to pick up his first 100-yard game of the season, leading PC with 101 yards on 17 carries. S.J. Worrell added 81 yards on 16 attempts. Chetyuane Reeder had seven carries for 36 yards. The Blue Hose used an effective mix of misdirection plays, inside handoffs and receiver end-arounds including Chris Pope's six carries for 40 yards.

"We knew how powerful their offense was," said PC quarterback Grayson Mullins, who needed to complete only six passes for 69 yards including the game's only touchdown to Pope. "We knew we needed to move the ball on offense to keep their offense off the field.

Game Results
Presbyterian 10
Newberry 0

Our defense played a heck of a game. What can you say? They kept us in games all year."

The offensive line did its part too, opening up large holes.

"We knew we were going to have to run the ball and hold on to the ball," guard Blake Hudson said. "We wanted to keep our defense off the field. We just basically went out there

Derby, Page 10A

Pass defense: Presbyterian linebacker Cheyenne Kenner (45), a redshirt senior from Canton, N.C., closes in on Newberry quarterback Josh Stepp, a transfer from Furman University. A stifling Blue Hose defense shut down an Indian offense that was averaging 35 points a game. — Photo by Fletcher Pruitt Jr.

PC pass: Presbyterian College wide receiver Terrance Butler (1), a sophomore from Surfside Beach, lays out to catch a pass from Grayson Mullins in action Saturday against Newberry College. Presbyterian ended Newberry's perfect season with a 10-0 win. — Photo by Fletcher Pruitt Jr.

The Clinton Chronicle

Stevenson bangs it through: Presbyterian kicker Carl Stevenson (17), a redshirt sophomore from Alamo, Ga., kicks a 20-yard field goal to give the Blue Hose a 10-0 lead with 13:23 left in the third quarter. The PC defense held Newberry to just three first downs in the third quarter.
— Photo by Fletcher Pruitt Jr.

Derby

From Page 8A

just pounding away, pounding away. The running backs did a great job hitting the holes hard, making great cuts and hanging on to the ball. We just came to play today. We did our jobs."

Fidler was glad to be back on the field after missing four games with a torn quad muscle.

"I was worried a little bit because I hadn't been in a game situation in about five weeks," the senior said. "I was a little worried about how I was going to run. But I guess it's like riding a bike. I think hands down our offensive line had its best game of the year. It was so easy for me and S.J. and Chetyuane to run pretty much anywhere we wanted. They made it happen today."

Spangler sensed that the game could be special.

"I could sense it in warm-ups. With that look in their eyes and their demeanor, I have never seen our football team look quite like that. We may not be the better team on paper, but we were (better) today. This game is played with heart and this game is played with 11 guys playing as one."

But the bottom line is the Indians (10-1, 6-1 SAC) will continue to play into the Division II playoffs. And PC (7-4) will not, having finished in a second-place tie with Wingate at 5-2. Had the Blue Hose been able to win at Catawba the previous week, the Bronze Derby would have been for the SAC title.

"We had a difficult loss last week and it was a test of our character to come out this week against the best team in the Southeast," Molony said of Newberry. "I think we proved we have good character on this team and on the coaching staff. It (the Catawba loss) hurts. It's definitely in the back of our minds right now."

The Indians will make their first-ever trip to the playoffs Saturday when they host Albany State, Ga.

A first-quarter interception by Newberry's Cliff Crockett put the ball at the Blue Hose 31 and five plays later, the Indians were on the 12. But Justin Jones intercepted Stepp to end the threat. It was only the third interception thrown by Stepp this season. Newberry would not threaten again.

PC's offense asserted itself in the second quarter with a 72-yard drive that included five consecutive plays of 10 yards or more. But the Blue Hose stalled at the 8, and Carl Stevenson missed a 25-yard field goal wide left.

PC got the ball back with 2:41 left in the first half and drove 73 yards in 11 plays. Mullins hit Terrance Butler with an 18-yard pass down the middle to the 5. On second-and-goal from the 5, Mullins rolled right and threw a pass toward the end zone that was tipped away.

On the next play, Mullins rolled right again and the defense followed. But Mullins stopped after a few steps, planted, and threw back to the left. Pope had broken away from Temarcus Thompson, was wide open, and caught the 5-yard scoring pass in the "B" of "Blue Hose" in the end zone. Stevenson's extra point made it 7-0 with just four seconds left in the half.

"We ran it the play before and we saw what they do on defense," Mullins said. "We knew it was going to be open. It was a great call by the coach. It was well executed by the team. The offensive line gave me plenty of time and he made a good catch."

At halftime, PC had a 14-2 edge in first downs and was ahead 194-52 in total offense.

"I had the best halftime speech I ever had. I didn't say anything," Spangler said.

The Blue Hose held Newberry to just three first downs in the third quarter and started the scoring drive that would put the game away. Stevenson hit a 20-yard field goal to make it 10-0 with 13:23 left.

Newberry would get just one more first down the rest of the game.

"We are a good football team and we came to play. That's what it comes down to," Hudson said.

It might be the final game in the Newberry-Presbyterian football rivalry. Presbyterian ends the series with a 35-22-3 record in the Bronze Derby series since its outset in 1947. Overall, Presbyterian concludes the 95-game rivalry with an all-time series advantage of 58-32-5.

It would be the final games for seniors Fidler, Hudson, offensive lineman Mitchell Anthony, tight end Eric Bendig, receivers Pope and Brett Wilhoit, and defensive standouts Cheyenne Keener, Derrell Doe, Burgess and Jones.

"Keener, Jones, Doe and Burgess have been a part of the best defenses we've ever had here at Presbyterian," Spangler said.

The Li'l 🎩 That Was!

On November 13, 2006, *The Newberry Observer* reflected on an outstanding performance by Presbyterian College. Newberry College was flat, and both the score and performance cost the Indians a bye in the playoffs.

However, this was the final time you'd get to play the Blue Hose, and when he took the job, one of the four goals for Willis was to reclaim the **Bronze Derby**.

Why would you not put that same emotion and attitude into beating your rival one final time and bringing the **Bronze Derby** back home?

Asked if the rivalry mattered, Willis responded, "Not really, to me," he said. "To be honest, this state is preoccupied with rivalries, which maybe is why only

two national champions have come out of South Carolina."

Um, someone forgot to tell that to PC, who now leaves the Division II ranks as the title holder to the **Bronze Derby**.

Willis, did, however, acknowledge that the Indians came out flat, which prompts a question of why.

Newberry's running attack, which had been strong was held to 68 total yards on 24 touches. PC rushed for 297 yards on 64 touches.

Astranger who did not know which team came into the game ranked in the top 10 would have been stunned to discover that the Blue Hose did not win the SAC championship. He would have been startled to know that the Indians came into the game with one of the best offenses in America.

"I thought their defense just played great today," Willis said. "They just did a great job all the way around, and all the credit goes to them. We had a bad day, and they had a great day."

PC's defense demanded a solid passing game and Newberry's aerial attack was anemic.

All-American quarterback Josh Stepp was 7-of-23 for 29 yards and an interception.

Now, I realize that Newberry is not the first team that Presbyterian has beaten this year, but it was in the manner that the Indians were beaten that is the story.

The setback drops Newberry to 10-1, and the championship rings have already been ordered. Newberry is still in the national rankings, and they still have a chance to do big things in the playoffs, but the performance took the bloom off the season.

Let's hope that the loss serves as a wake-up call this week.

Nothing but questions. That is what Newberry College football fans, the coaches and players have after watching an un-inspired performance Saturday against the Presbyterian Blue Hose, in which the Indians fell 10-0 in the 60th and final game between the two.

The biggest question that was asked by many was, "How can you not get up for your biggest rival?"

We all knew several things going into Saturday's game.

For starters, we knew that the Indians were the SAC champs, and that there was no way the Blue Hose could steal that away.

Secondly, we knew that this was the final meeting between the two. In other words, the losing team was going to have to drive the 24 miles to see what the trophy looked like.

Finally, there was a bye week before their first playoff game for the Indians if they won.

One would think that the last two would have been enough to fire up the boys in white, but instead, they opted not to show mentally and, instead, lost spectacularly.

Presbyterian had a lot to do with the Indians' futility on offense and defense, but only once did Newberry look the part of the team that won the conference crown.

The 10-0 score does not do justice to the Blue Hose's domination.

Instead, as the saying goes, the proof is in the pudding.

Newberry was shutout for the first time under head coach Zak Willis, held to under 100 yards and picked up just six first downs, one of which came thanks to a penalty. You can say what you want to about referees and such, but they played little role in Newberry's inability to make plays or stop the same three running plays on defense (odds are good the defenders for Newberry saw the trap in their sleep Saturday).

Perhaps, the best question of all is simply: "What happened?"

After quarterback Josh Stepp was intercepted in the first quarter, Newberry's offense seemed to vanish, and instead the Indians ran plays that they hadn't run at any point prior to Saturday.

To top it off, the defense shifted from its usual 4-4 look to a 3-3-5 that did little to stop the running attack that the Blue Hose offered.

Contrasting the Indians of Saturday with the Indians of a week earlier is a confounding puzzle. How can a team play so well one game and be so dominated the next? Perhaps emotion?

There is no doubt that against Lenoir-Rhyne, Newberry put everything they had into the game, as a win locked up the SAC crown.

The Li'l That Was!

The Bronze Derby Win

On January 12, 2007, the Presbyterian College newspaper The Blue Stocking reported on the last Bronze Derby game played between Newberry College and Presbyterian College.

By Lauren Joyce

After ninety-five consecutive years, the Presbyterian College Blue Hose defeated the Newberry Indians 10-0 in their final Bronze Derby. Their meeting this Saturday ended a long standing tradition between these two heated rivals.

In the win, Presbyterian shut out a dynamic Newberry offense that averages over 400 yards a game. Newberry quarterback, Josh Stepp, and receiver, Tymere Zimmerman, have led the Indians to a 10-1 record (6-1 SAC), but PC's defense held the Indians to a mere 97 yards of total offense.

Presbyterian also shined on offense, leading Newberry in every statistical category. At the helm of the Presbyterian effort, quarterback Grayson Mullins completed fifty percent of his passes for 69 yards. His completion to Chris Pope put PC on the scoreboard 7-0 with just seconds left in the second quarter. Carl Stevenson tacked on the extra point and later hit a 20 yard field goal to make the score 10-0.

On the ground, senior Corey Fidler led the Blue Hose with 101 of the team's 297 yards. He earned his first 100 yard game of the season.

The Blue Hose held the Bronze Derby coming into the game, after last year's 38-7 victory over Newberry. Still, Newberry stood alone atop the Southern Athletic Conference (SAC) standings Saturday and had already claimed the regular season championship. When these two teams stepped on the field, the records were thrown out the window and a dogfight ensued.

"Some of the best games these two teams have played have been in the Bronze Derby. It's always an important game for both Newberry and PC," said Newberry Athletic Director, Andy Carter.

The history of the Bronze Derby dates back to January 30, 1947, when during a post-game scuffle between PC and Newberry students at a basketball game, a derby was stolen from the head of a PC student. Because of the proximity of the two schools to each other, both schools decided to clean up the passionate rivalry. Before the rivalry got out of hand, it was decided to award a bronzed version of the derby to the winner of PC/Newberry athletic contests. For a few years, the derby exchanged hands to the winner of every PC/Newberry game, but later, it was decided the derby would only be handed out after football games.

PC Athletic Director, Dr. Carlton said, "It's a game, but it's more than a game. How can you quantify a rivalry like this, like Carolina/Clemson or Ohio State/Michigan?"

At 1:30 this past Saturday at Bailey Memorial Stadium, a chapter of the PC/Newberry rivalry closed, and now, Presbyterian holds the Bronze Derby indefinitely.

"Indefinitely"

On November 15, 2006, John Clayton, managing editor of *The Laurens County Advertiser* got straight to the point. "The Bronze Derby will be staying at Presbyterian College indefinitely." A 10-0 win over undefeated Newberry College was certainly a classic Bronze Derby football game and one of the best. The 2006 edition of the Newberry College Indians may have been the greatest football team in their storied school history. Presbyterian College, the number 1 defense in the South Atlantic Conference, prevailed over the top ranked offense in the South Atlantic Conference. The Blue Hose held Newberry College to only 97 yards in total offense. *The Laurens County Advertiser* also reported Presbyterian College Head Football Coach Tommy Spangler commenting that in his career at Presbyterian College, "... It may have been the best collective effort ever." The 60th Bronze Derby football game may be the last matchup between Newberry College and Presbyterian College in football as a result of the move by Presbyterian College to NCAA Division 1. Presbyterian College holds the all-time advantage with a 36-21-3 in Bronze Derby football action since 1947.

On November 25, 1992 in *The Laurens County Advertiser*, legendary Presbyterian College Blue Hose Head Football Coach Cally Gault made a prophetic statement. "The first thing I say about The Bronze Derby is that only unusual things happen during these games. If unusual things were going to happen to our football team, it would happen on the day of the Classic." On November 11, 2006, a 6-4 Presbyterian College Blue Hose football team and its defense rose to the occasion defeating the undefeated South Atlantic Conference Champion Newberry Indians 10-0. In 2006 the Newberry Indians won their first ever South Atlantic Conference Championship in program history. Head Coach Zak Willis guided the team to its first ever appearance to the NCAA Division II playoffs. In possibly the final match-up between the schools, The Bronze Derby is now in the possession of Presbyterian College "Indefinitely," the result of a tremendous collective effort by the 2006 Blue Hose football team in Clinton, South Carolina.

The Fifth Quarter

Remembering The Bronze Derby Game

Newberry College Indians

vs.

Presbyterian College Blue Hose

All Time Series Results

Presbyterian College Blue Hose

vs.

Newberry College Indians

All Time Football Series

Presbyterian leads series, 57-33-5
(**Bold** Team Denotes Home Team)

Newberry College Home Games	48
Newberry Wins at Home	23 47.9%
Presbyterian College Home Games	47
Presbyterian Wins at Home	32 68.1%

1913	**NC** 51 - PC 0		1913	**NC** 51 - PC 0
1915	**NC** 20 - PC 13		1916	PC 3 - **NC** 0
1917	**PC** 20 - NC 0		1919	PC 0 - **NC** 0
1920	**PC** 20 - NC 0		1921	**NC** 15 - PC 7
1922	**PC** 35 - NC 9		1923	PC 7 - **NC** 0
1924	**NC** 10 - PC 0		1925	**NC** 22 - PC 6
1926	**PC** 28 - NC 0		1927	PC 12 - **NC** 0
1928	NC 12 - **PC** 6		1929	**PC** 54 - NC 0
1930	PC 31 - **NC** 0		1931	**PC** 6 - NC 0
1932	**NC** 7 - PC 7		1933	NC 16 - **PC** 7
1934	PC 13 - **NC** 0		1935	**PC** 20 - NC 0
1936	PC 27 - **NC** 0		1937	NC 13 - **PC** 0
1938	**PC** 7 - NC 6		1939	**PC** 6 - NC 0
1940	**NC** 20 - PC 7		1941	**PC** 13 - NC 7
1942	PC 14 - **NC** 7		1943	**PC** 13 - NC 12
1944	**PC** 20 - NC 6		1945	NC 19 - **PC** 13
1946	**PC** 14 - NC 13			

The Li'l 🎩 That Was!

Bronze Derby Football Results

Year	Result	Year	Result
1947	**NC** 6 - PC 0	1948	**PC** 40 - NC 7
1949	**NC** 20 - PC 14	1950	**PC** 20 - NC 6
1951	**PC** 27 - NC 0	1952	**PC** 14 - NC 12
1953	**NC** 7 - PC 7	1954	**PC** 20 - NC 18
1955	**NC** 20 - PC 18	1956	NC 13 - **PC** 0
1957	**NC** 13 - PC 0	1958	**PC** 22 - NC 0
1959	PC 20 - **NC** 6	1960	**PC** 7 - NC 6
1961	PC 7 - **NC** 7	1962	**NC** 23 - PC 0
1963	PC 14 - **NC** 7	1964	**PC** 35 - NC 6
1965	**NC** 6 - PC 0	1966	**PC** 28 - NC 7
1967	PC 14 - **NC** 0	1968	**PC** 42 - NC 7
1969	PC 23 - **NC** 21	1970	PC 27 - **NC** 23
1971	**NC** 34 - PC 0	1972	**PC** 17 - NC 0
1973	**NC** 14 - PC 3	1974	**PC** 37 - NC 7
1975	PC 14 - **NC** 0	1976	NC 26 - **PC** 15
1977	PC 3 - **NC** 0	1978	**PC** 26 - NC 0
1979	PC 16 - **NC** 14	1980	NC 28 - **PC** 14
1981	**NC** 26 - PC 23	1982	**PC** 27 - NC 7
1983	**NC** 23 - PC 0	1984	NC 25 - **PC** 16
1985	**NC** 24 - PC 24	1986	**PC** 35 - NC 20
1987	**NC** 17 - PC 15	1988	**PC** 30 - NC 16
1989	**NC** 29 - PC 24	1990	NC 24 - **PC** 7
1991	PC 32 - **NC** 17	1992	NC 14 - **PC** 0
1993	PC 30 - **NC** 13	1994	**PC** 24 - NC 13
1995	**NC** 9 - PC 8	1996	NC 21 - **PC** 10
1997	**NC** 28 - PC 22	1998	**PC** 45 - NC 14
1999	PC 45 - **NC** 35	2000	**PC** 34 - NC 27
2001	PC 31 - **NC** 24	2002	**PC** 14 - NC 10
2003	PC 42 - **NC** 14	2004	NC 28 - **PC** 25
2005	PC 38 - **NC** 7	2006	**PC** 10 - NC 0

60 Total Bronze Derby Football Games

Presbyterian College	36 - 21 - 3
Newberry College	21 - 36 - 3

Newberry College Head Football Coach
Bronze Derby Records

Years	Coach	W	L	T
1947 - 1949	Billy Laval	2	1	0
1950 - 1951	Tuck McConnell	0	2	0
1952 - 1967	Harvey Kirkland	5	9	2
1968 - 1977	Fred Herren	3	7	0
1978 - 1981	Reed Charpia	2	2	0
1982 - 1987	Clayton Johnson	3	3	1
1988 - 1990	Gary Smallen	2	1	0
1991	Brad Senter	0	1	0
1992 - 2002	Mike Taylor	4	7	0
2003 - 2006	Zak Willis	1	3	0

Presbyterian College Head Football Coach
Bronze Derby Records

Years	Coach	W	L	T
1947 - 1953	Lonnie McMillan	4	2	1
1954 - 1956	Bill Crutchfield	1	2	0
1957 - 1961	Frank Jones	3	1	1
1962	Clyde Ehrhardt	0	1	0
1963 - 1984	Cally Gault	14	8	0
1985 - 1990	Elliott Poss	3	2	1
1991 - 1996	John Perry	3	3	0
1997 - 2000	Daryl Dickey	3	1	0
2001 - 2006	Tommy Spangler	5	1	0

Newberry College Head Football Coach Overall Records

Years	Coach	W	L	T
1913	Raymond Thomas	3	1	0
1914	Joe Parrish	5	3	1
1915	William Shaw	2	5	0
1916	James Driver	5	2	0
1917	Robert Pfohl	0	6	0
1919 - 1920	L.C. Sullivan	2	11	2
1921 - 1937	Dutch MacLean	43	95	11
1938 - 1949	Billy Laval	45	61	5
1950 - 1951	E.R. McConnell	1	18	1
1952 - 1967	Harvey Kirkland	72	77	11
1968 - 1977	Fred Herren	46	54	4
1978 - 1981	Reed Charpia	21	20	0
1982 - 1987	Clayton Johnson	33	32	1
1988 - 1990	Gary Smallen	11	22	0
1991	Brad Senter	1	10	0
1992 - 2002	Mike Taylor	47	73	0
2003 - 2006	Zak Willis	39	25	0

Presbyterian College Head Football Coach Overall Records

Years	Coach	W	L	T
1913	Everett Booe	5	3	0
1914	Erling Theller	4	1	1
1915 - 1940	Walter Johnson	101	104	19
1918	Gilford Shaw	2	0	0
1941 - 1953	Lonnie McMillan	61	58	2
1954 - 1956	Bill Crutchfield	13	14	1
1957 - 1961	Frank Jones	24	22	3
1962	Clyde Ehrhardt	1	9	0
1963 - 1984	Cally Gault	126	100	8
1985 - 1990	Elliott Poss	29	38	1
1991 - 1996	John Perry	29	37	0
1997 - 2000	Daryl Dickey	28	15	0
2001 - 2006	Tommy Spangler	54	52	0

The Bronze Derby Overall Results
Wins

	Newberry	Presbyterian
Basketball	3	16
(1947-1955)		
Winning %	16%	84%
Baseball	25	4
(1947-1955)		
Winning %	86%	14%
Football	21	36
(1947-2006)		
Winning %	35%	65%
(3 Football Ties)		
Total 108 Games		
Total Wins	49	56
Winning %	45%	55%

What are my top 10 Bronze Derby Games?

(in no particular order)

- 1987   Blue Hose   15   **Indians**   17   (Football)

  The Bronze Derby Hail Mary!

- 2006   **Blue Hose** 10   Indians   0   (Football)

  The final Bronze Derby football game.

- 1989   Blue Hose   24   **Indians**   29   (Football)

  One second lasts a lifetime!

- 1947   **Blue Hose** 44   Indians   42   (Basketball)

  The inaugural Bronze Derby basketball game.

- 1995   Blue Hose   8   **Indians**   9   (Football)

  Take a knee PC!

- 1947   Blue Hose   2   **Indians**   5   (Baseball)

  The inaugural Bronze Derby baseball game.

- 1979   **Blue Hose** 16   Indians   14   (Football)

  PC's finest football team kicks its way to the playoffs.

- 1963   **Blue Hose** 14   Indians   7   (Football)

  Cally Gault wins his Bronze Derby head coaching debut.

- 1985   **Blue Hose** 24   **Indians**   24   (Football)

  The most exciting tie!

- 1972   **Blue Hose** 17   Indians   0   (Football)

  Ol' Killer leaves with PC Coach Tiller.

What were yours?

The Li'l 🎩 That Was!

The Bronze Derby By the Numbers

1	The Bronze Derby was the annual and only South Carolina Thanksgiving Day Classic football game lasting from 1947-1992. The series ended in 2006.
2	Thanksgiving Day games in 1963 in the state of South Carolina. USC-Clemson moved their game to Thanksgiving Day as a result and respect of the assassination of President John F. Kennedy.
3	Total number of Bronze Derby football games played at new Bailey Stadium on the campus of Presbyterian College.
5	Total number of ties in football from 1913-2006. Of interest, the ties took place on Setzler Field in Newberry, South Carolina.
5	Harvey Kirkland had the most Bronze Derby wins by a Newberry College Head Football Coach.
7	Total number of Bronze Derby players from Presbyterian and Newberry College who have won the Jacobs Blocking Award.
9	Total number of Presbyterian College Head Coaches that participated in The Bronze Derby.
10	Total number of Newberry College Head Coaches that participated in The Bronze Derby.
12	In 1977, math classes at both Presbyterian and Newberry College may have failed to offer addition past 11! The final Bronze Derby play involved 12 players on offense versus 12 players on defense!
14	Total number of Bronze Derby wins by Presbyterian College Head Football Coach Cally Gault.
14	Number of Bronze Derby football games that were not played on Thanksgiving Day. Beginning in 1993 -2006, the game was played on a date other than Thanksgiving Day.
16	Total Presbyterian College Bronze Derby basketball wins between 1947-1955.
19	Total times The Bronze Derby was competed for in basketball between 1947-1955.
21	Total Newberry College football Bronze Derby wins.

22	Mileage between the campuses of Presbyterian College and Newberry College via Highway 76.
22	Number of times The Bronze Derby was exchanged between the schools from 1947-1955.
22	Most appearances in the Bronze Derby by a Head Coach was by Presbyterian College Head Football Coach Cally Gault.
25	Total Newberry College Bronze Derby baseball wins between 1947-1955.
27	Total number of Bronze Derby football games played at old Bailey Stadium on the campus of Presbyterian College.
29	Total times The Bronze Derby was competed for in baseball between 1947-1955.
30	Total number of Bronze Derby football games played at Setzler Field on the campus of Newberry College.
33	Total 4th quarter points scored in the 1989 Bronze Derby.
36	Total Presbyterian College football Bronze Derby wins.
40	Per The State, #40 of the top 100 South Carolina 20th century sports moments happened at Setzler Field as a white turkey named "Ol' Killer" made a cameo appearance.
46	Total number of Thanksgiving Day Bronze Derby games. The turkey day football tradition ended in 1992.
54	Overall career winning percentage by Presbyterian Head Football Coach Cally Gault.
57	Total number of Bronze Derby baseball, basketball and football games competed for between the schools from 1947-1955.
60	Total times The Bronze Derby was competed for in football between 1947-2006.
64	Overall Bronze Derby winning percentage by Presbyterian College Head Football Coach Cally Gault.
65	Overall Bronze Derby football winning percentage by Presbyterian College.
76	Yardage of the 1987 Newberry College "Hail Mary."
76	2 lane highway between Clinton and Newberry, South Carolina.

The Li'l 🎩 That Was!

80	Per The State, #80 of the top 100 South Carolina 20th century sports moments happened at Setzler Field when a 21 yard final second field goal solidified Presbyterian College as the #1 rated team in NAIA Division 1 football and a playoff berth.
83	Presbyterian College Head Football Coach Tommy Spangler winning percentage leading all Bronze Derby Head Coaches.
108	Number of baseball, basketball and football Bronze Derby games played between 1947-2006.
126	Total career wins by Presbyterian Head Coach Cally Gault.
1913	The first football matchup between Presbyterian College and Newberry College saw the Indians prevail over the Blue Stockings 51-0 at the South Carolina State Fairgrounds.
1947	The first Bronze Derby game took place at Leroy Springs Gymnasium in Clinton, South Carolina. The final basketball score was Presbyterian 44 Newberry 42.
2006	The final football matchup between Presbyterian College and Newberry College. The final score was PC 10-NC 0.
2007	Presbyterian College moved to NCAA Division 1.

It's Like Kissing Your Cousin!
The Bronze Derby Ties

Both the Newberry College and Presbyterian College football teams work so hard throughout the year and look forward to their annual Thanksgiving Day rivalry game. Prior to 1947, the teams played to 2 ties. Both tied games were played in Newberry, South Carolina.

In 1919, the teams battled to a 0-0 tie.

In 1932, the teams played to a 7-7 tie. Early in the game, Newberry intercepted a Blue Stocking pass. A 60 yard rush from scrimmage by Newberry quarterback Ingram resulted in a 7-0 lead. A defensive battle commenced throughout the game. Late in the fourth quarter, Newberry was forced to punt, and the punt was blocked by the Blue Stockings. Six rushes later, Presbyterian scored and the extra point was good. With little time left in the game, Newberry ran out of time and the game ended in the series second tie.

1947 was the inaugural Bronze Derby football game. The Bronze Derby was competed for on the football field 60 times. There were 3 ties in the 60 Bronze Derby match-ups. Coincidentally, each of the ties also occurred at Setzler Field on the campus of Newberry College.

In 1953, the teams played to a 7-7 tie. The game was the first Thanksgiving Day tie of the rivalry. The Blue Hose defense was backed up in their territory throughout the first half. Midway through the third period, Presbyterian quarterback Joe Austin scored on a quarterback sneak. After kicking off to the Indians, Newberry scored 3 plays later on a 62 yard pass from Brabham to Davis. The fourth quarter went scoreless. Newberry retained The Bronze Derby as a result of a 4-2 win in baseball earlier in the spring.

In 1961, the teams played to a 7-7 tie. In a driving rain, the Blue Hose opened the game with a 14 play 71 yard drive. Halfback Larry Madden scored from 6 yards out. The PAT was good. The Presbyterian offense was done for the day. Early in the second half, Newberry drove 62 yards in 12 plays for a touchdown and PAT. Indians quarterback Tom Gorman showcased his throwing ability despite the rain on the drive. Halfback Carl Ellis went over from the one yard line for the Indians only score of the day. Presbyterian College retained possession of The Bronze Derby as a result of their 1960 7-6 win over the Indians in Clinton, South Carolina.

In 1985, two 7-3 teams, both ranked in the NAIA Division 1 national polls (Newberry #14, Presbyterian #18) played to a 24-24 tie. The Indians got off to a fast start with Newberry scoring 2 touchdowns in the first quarter. The first score resulted when running back John Nesbitt took a pitch from quarterback Jimmy Skipper and connected on a 43 yard touchdown pass to Darryl Owens. The PAT was good. Newberry then scored on a one yard run by Nesbitt. Presbyterian finally got on the board with a 10 yard run by Steve Riggins. The PAT was good. After a late second quarter 45 yard field goal by the Blue Hose, the teams went into halftime with Newberry leading 14-10.

The second half may have been one of the most exciting halves in Bronze Derby history. The Blue Hose opened the scoring with a 9 yard touchdown by fullback Billy Barnes. The PAT was good. Barnes then scored another rushing touchdown and with a successful PAT, the Blue Hose were up by 10, 24-14. Newberry began their comeback with a successful 44 yard field goal. With 5 minutes remaining in the game, Newberry's Pete Bember scored from 4 yards out. The PAT tied the game. The Blue Hose failed to move the ball after the ensuing kickoff. Newberrry then drove the ball inside the Blue Hose 5 yard line and failed to convert on third down. A field goal by Newberry would win the game in the final second. The field goal was blocked by the Blue Hose defense. Newberry College retained possession of The Bronze Derby as a result of their 1984 25-16 win over the Blue Hose in Clinton, South Carolina.

Presbyterian College student-athletes that played in both the Presbyterian College - Newberry College football rivalry and the NFL.

Above: Larry Weldon, K 1945-1945 Washington Redskins

Below: Paul Moore, W/R 1940-1941 Detroit Lions

Photos courtesy of Presbyterian College archives

Presbyterian College student-athletes that played in both the Presbyterian College - Newberry College football rivalry and the NFL.

Above: Ken Webb, FB 1958-1962 Detroit Lions
1963 Cleveland Browns

Below: Bob Waters, QB 1960-1963 San Francisco 49ers

Photos courtesy of Presbyterian College archives

Presbyterian College student-athletes that played in both the Presbyterian College - Newberry College football rivalry and the NFL.

Above: Jimmy Elliott, P 1967 Pittsburgh Steelers

Below: Jimmie Turner, LB 1984 Dallas Cowboys

Photos courtesy of Presbyterian College archives

Presbyterian College student-athletes that played in both the Presbyterian College - Newberry College football rivalry and the NFL.

Above: Charles Huff, DB 1987 Atlanta Falcons

Below: Lawrence Jackson, G 1987 Atlanta Falcons

Photos courtesy of Presbyterian College archives

Arguably, the greatest student-athlete to play in the Newberry College-Presbyterian College football rivalry may have been Heath Benedict. Heath transferred as a red shirt freshman to Newberry College in 2004 from the University of Tennessee. An offensive tackle, Heath collected 2 Jacobs Blocking Awards in 2006 and 2007. Overall, he collected 13 total All-American honors in his collegiate career. He played in the 2008 Senior Bowl after his career at Newberry College, the only Division II player to participate. Heath was projected to go no higher than the 4th round in the 2008 NFL draft. Unfortunately, in March of 2008, the 6'6" 335 pound NFL prospect was found lifeless in his family's home in Jacksonville, Florida. An autopsy revealed that Heath died of complications from an enlarged heart that had never been detected. Although Heath never played a down in the NFL, he deserves to be mentioned as a Newberry College player that "would" have played in the NFL. His achievements at Newberry College on and off the field will always be remembered. In 2008, Heath was inducted into the Newberry College Athletic Hall of Fame.

Photo courtesy of Newberry College archives

Newberry College student-athletes that played in both the Presbyterian College - Newberry College football rivalry and the NFL.

Above: Gregory Hartle, LB 1974-1976 St. Louis Cardinals

Below: Herb Spencer, LB 1987 Atlanta Falcons

Photos courtesy of Newberry College archives

The Bronze Derby Jacobs Blocking Award Winners

In 1928, William P. Jacobs, Jr. of Presbyterian College introduced the Jacobs Blocking Award, an award to the best blockers in the state of South Carolina. The award was initially given on a statewide basis, and later was recognized in regional conferences including the ACC, SEC, SAC and the SoCon.

The following student-athletes not only won this most prestigious award, but also participated in The Bronze Derby.

Year	Name	College	Award
1972	Johnny Jeselnik	Presbyterian College	State Winner
1979	Roy Walker	Presbyterian College	State Winner
1985	Jeff Godbee	Newberry College	State Winner
1996	Bruce Estes	Presbyterian College	SAC Winner
1997	Ryan Keese	Presbyterian College	SAC Winner
2005	Marcus Brisbone	Presbyterian College	SAC Winner
2006	Heath Benedict	Newberry College	SAC Winner

William Plumer Jacobs III and Hugh Jacobs pictured in 2001 in front of the Jacobs Blocking Award display at Presbyterian College.

Photo courtesy of Presbyterian College archives

The Li'l 🎩 That Was!

Monte Dutton is a graduate of Furman University and a long time resident of Clinton, South Carolina. An author and sportswriter, Monte spent over 20 years writing and reporting on NASCAR. He is a longtime local sports editor in the midstate, and was grateful to reflect on The Bronze Derby.

"I've attended a lot of rivalries: Clemson-South Carolina, Oklahoma-Texas, Red Sox-Yankees…

None compares even remotely to the once-annual game for The Bronze Derby between Newberry and Presbyterian. It wasn't bigger. It wasn't better. It was unique, and it's one reason Thanksgiving is my favorite holiday.

It was never played in front of more than 4,000 fans. Many students went home for the holiday. That made room for others to visit Clinton or Newberry. I went to the game every year when I came home from Furman. I wouldn't have missed it for the pro games in Detroit or Dallas, or a guest spot with Johnny Carson.

PC and Newberry. Turkey Day and football. One and inseparable.

Every daily newspaper in the state was there. Now, there are rarely papers at any of the games the two schools play.

The Bronze Derby had luminaries, dignitaries and regional celebrities. Clemson and Carolina head coaches watched on the sidelines. The governor was often there.

The Bronze Derby had personalities. Cally Gault and Fred Herron were old school. They were friends. They got together for lunch or dinner when their paths crossed. The defensive coordinators, Billy Tiller and Steve Robertson, were larger than life, too… literally.

One year, Tiller and Robertson played the game for a large white turkey named Killer. Tiller dressed like a chef on the sideline. *The Clinton Chronicle* ran a photo of Tiller, brandishing his butcher knife with the bird after the Blue Hose prevailed. The front page headline read: "Tiller Gets Killer!"

The beginning of the end was when the rivals joined the NCAA Division II, which required the availability of Thanksgiving weekend for playoff games.

The death knell rang when Presbyterian College developed delusions of grandeur and joined Division I. The Blue Hose and Wolves (*nee* Indians) burned all the bridges on U.S 76 and stopped playing.

If I'm in a sentimental mood, my eyes still moisten.

Folks made the pilgrimage to see The Bronze Derby because they wanted to be there. I never talked to a sportswriter who didn't love it. We'd arrive early and have turkey and dressing in the dining hall. After the game, Gault and Herren would hold court, win or lose. Players would remain on the field, win or lose.

If we had to lose, I'm glad we lost to them boys over yonder.

It was friendly. It was sportsmanlike. The rivals were like the old cartoon of Ralph Wolf and Sam Sheepdog. They'd scrap all day, then clock out and go home.

How's the family, Ralph?

It's not like that anymore. Life's not like that anymore."

The Li'l That Was!

Randy Randall is a 1975 graduate of Presbyterian College and has seen his share of Bronze Derby football games. Randy worked for over 30 years in various capacities at Presbyterian College. Randy was the first women's basketball coach for The Blue Hose. He also served as Director of Alumni Relations and Director of Student Affairs while at PC. For the last twenty years, he has served the community he loves, and is the current Mayor of Clinton, South Carolina. Randy was excited to share memories of his Thanksgiving Day tradition.

"I attended Bronze Derby football games from the fall of 1971 until they ended in 2006. My wife Kim and I always joked for many years that The Bronze Derby game simplified Thanksgiving Day. For many years, before we had children, our families in Washington, Georgia and Columbia, South Carolina always asked what we were doing for Thanksgiving. The answer was easy. 'We are going to the Bronze Derby!' We always attended the Thanksgiving Day event at PC and Newberry. We even attended the games after our move to NCAA Division II as the game was no longer played on Thanksgiving Day. When it was played on Thanksgiving Day, it was the only football game in the state or anywhere close by for many years, so you saw folks from all over the state. My mother-in-law Cathy Byers was a huge Clemson fan. She always said that some people hated Carolina and some people hated Clemson, but everybody loved the Blue Hose!

As I celebrate my 7th decade, my memories become less accurate, but much more interesting. I'm sure that the truth and my imagination meet somewhere out there. When I was a student, I was at Newberry when Coach Billy Tiller wore a chef's hat and had a big fork and knife and a real turkey named "Killer." We won that 1973 game!

I began doing the public address at Bailey Stadium for Presbyterian College football in 1978. I had fun announcing the games every other year. A few games stick in my memory. One was the year (1977) that PC beat Newberry in Newberry by stopping them short of the endzone on the last play. PC Head Coach Cally Gault and Newberry Head Coach Fred Herren were very good friends and two of the finest men that I have ever known. Coach Gault was watching film of the game and realized that PC had 12 men on the field on the last play of the game. He called Coach Herren to confess, and Coach Herren told him to look at Newberry on the last play of the game. Ironically, Newberry had 12 men on the field on the last play. The two old friends had a great laugh.

Of course, we must remember the game at Newberry in 1979 when PC was trying to maintain its #1 NAIA Division 1 ranking and a trip to the NAIA playoffs.

I remember PC quarterback Jimmy Spence getting hurt and returning to the game to inspire victory. In the fourth quarter, Newberry was driving when PC's Erskine Reed separated the ball from a Newberry player resulting in a PC fumble recovery. Chuck Bishop kicked a last second field goal to win the game. It was great to be a Blue Hose that day!

Then, the final Bronze Derby game (2006), was played on a Saturday in Clinton. Newberry was in possession of The Bronze Derby as a result of their 2005 victory. I was calling the game in the pressbox. P-Nut Dowdle was sitting beside me operating the 40 second clock and John Kay was my spotter. During the week before the game, our good friend John Paul Whitaker from Newberry was up to mischief. A flooring contractor from Newberry, John Paul must have been in Clinton the week of the game. John Paul took a polaroid picture of himself wearing The Bronze Derby. He and P-Nut Dowdle were great friends. John Paul snuck into P-Nut's house and put his picture of himself wearing The Derby on P-Nut's refrigerator. Later in the week he called me to remind me that Newberry was undefeated and their offense was scoring 30 points a game. I told him that would make whooping them so much better! The game was hard fought, and The Blue Hose won 10-0 in a close low scoring game. How sweet it was!

There are more stories, but I am probably already on Chip Porter's cutting room floor. The Bronze Derby game was a classic between two class acts, two neighbors… two friends."

The Li'l 🎩 That Was!

John Clayton is the editor of *The Laurens County Advertiser* and a Staff writer at WordSouth. A graduate of Wofford College, John is a longtime resident of South Carolina. John has become a mentor to me regarding my writing projects, but most importantly, has become a friend that I can call to answer that sticky question and for literary guidance. John was elated to reflect on The Bronze Derby.

"The Bronze Derby isn't physically lost.

But metaphorically? That's another question.

Both the trophy and the game between Presbyterian and Newberry was a quintessential symbol of college football's backroads that lead to places like Carson-Newman, North Greenville, Bluefield State and Mars Hill.

And maybe it's a symbol of something that has been lost in the dash for cash college football has become.

PC fans got a small taste of that past in 2023 when the Blue Hose upset old rival Wofford in Spartanburg. The Terriers no longer play at quaint old Snyder Field. It even isn't there anymore, gone the way of the first Bailey Memorial Stadium at PC.

But gosh, that game - a come - from - behind 23-20 PC win - seemed to have the once familiar vitriol of the school's NAIA Division and NCAA Division II days together.

As heated as that rivalry was, The Bronze Derby game took it to another level - in part due to the 30-minute drive between the two schools on Highway 76.

As a fan, and my fathers son, I spent part of more than one Thanksgiving Day at "Old Bailey," watching the annual rivalry game, including a couple as my cousin, John Cann, suited up for Cally Gaults' Blue Hose.

As a sports writer, I covered the final two editions of The Bronze Derby, crowding once into Newberry's tiny Setzler Field press box with the late, great *Charleston Post and Courier* columnist Ken Burger in 2005 (a 38-7 PC win) and the final game at PC in 2006 (a 10-0 PC victory).

PC headed to what was then NCAA Division I-AA after that, and the rest is a story of an athletic program that has struggled to find its footing in Division I.

And as someone who attended neither PC nor Newberry, I wonder if it was all worth it. I wonder if packing the old bronzed derby away in a back room was worth a little more time on ESPN chyron.

As I get older, I do romanticize those "good ol' days" a little more, I guess, but I remember folks standing around the field at Old Bailey because no seats remained on Thanksgiving. They were there because it mattered then, and it could matter again, even as the landscape of college football is less and less recognizable.

Big-time college football will be what it will be in the next five years - super conferences and NIL deals and all of that.

But small college football will have to become something different, too, and perhaps decision makers should look to the past, embrace those old regional rivalries and travel those backroads once again."

The Li'l 🎩 That Was!

Vic MacDonald is the editor of *The Clinton Chronicle* and longtime resident of the South Carolina midstate. Vic is a 1975 graduate of Newberry College. He covered The Bronze Derby for both *The Newberry Observer* and *The Clinton Chronicle*. Vic has always demonstrated a community passion in his editorials and news coverage. Vic was excited about my book, and was gracious to share the following on The Bronze Derby:

"When my wife and I got married, our first dance song was Thomas Rhett's "Die a Happy Man." It was a happy day, and you know what could be another happy day for real football fans? September 12, 2026.

I have a personal connection to that day because, you see, my community journalism retirement date is October 1, 2026. It was 2025 - October 1 is our anniversary, so easy date to remember, and that's my 50 years in journalism - but I have the desire and the financial need to work a year after that. So, the one and last thing that could allow me to "die a happy man" would be, if on September 12, 2026, Presbyterian College and Newberry College would meet again on the gridiron. And, I could be there - I don't even care where - with my cameras in tow.

And the reason I pick that date is two-fold: this will require serious negotiation, and based on the 2024 football schedule, it seems like the most logical Revival of the Bronze Derby Day.

Bear with me. On Sept. 14, 2024, Newberry will host Keiser. That same day, PC hosts Virginia Lynchburg. So, you see, no conference entanglements.

And, I hear you, "but Vic, it's not THANKSGIVING" - that ship has sailed, for a multitude of reasons. Better - I believe - to make the Bronze Derby, if not the FIRST game of the season, at least early in the season. I'm not a math genius but, I betcha, a Presbyterian - Newberry game would out-draw in attendance the Newberry-Keiser and PC-VA Lynchburg games COMBINED.

Because you see, People Remember.

Even if today's students have no clue.

They remember when two teams, 20 miles apart, played each other - really, in multiple sports - and they both were really good.

They remember that these two teams and schools REALLY didn't like each other. PC was snooty. Newberry took just anybody (witness: me). Maybe, PC's feeling in that regard, that NC was underclass, has something to do with the fact that they won a stunning 7 out of the last 9 Bronze Derby games. They lead the series by TWENTY.

You know, it's not really a rivalry if the same team wins all the time.

So, PC got too big for their breeches. As a recent infamous PC football coach once told his players, why not do it my way, y'all have never won anything doing it your way. That's a LIE of Presidential proportions, of course; but he was looking at PC's Division I record which, in football, is dismal.

Now, that's not to say PC can't compete in D1. It's women's basketball team made the Big Dance, until they got buzz-sawed by the best team in the country. But, for me personally, it was a bucket list moment - the first time ever I sat courtside at a D1 championship series sporting event - and let me tell you, it was cool.

Sportswriters who do it all the time do it a disservice, by taking it for granted.

We, too, got spoiled all those years taking the Bronze Derby Game for granted.

The thing I remember most, how close the scores were.

Just a quick glance at the overall record showed me just a few 30-point wins (1971, 1974, 1998) and of course the darkest day in Newberry history, 54-0 PC at Clinton in 1929.

The time I was at Newberry it was: Newberry 34-0 in Newberry 1971; PC 17-0 in Clinton 1972; Newberry 14-3 in Newberry; PC 37-7 in Clinton 1974; and I probably was hanging around the co-eds in 1975 - PC 14-0 in Newberry.

After that, we had Newberry 26-15 in Clinton in 1976; and (the year my first wife graduated in June and we got married in September) PC 3-0 in Newberry 1977.

We knocked around a couple of places and landed back in Newberry in the

The Li'l 🎩 That Was!

1980s and 1990s - and I covered the Derby for *The Newberry Observer*. By the last time the game was played on Thanksgiving, my wife had persuaded me that going to Jacksonville to visit her parents was good for our family; and I missed the final Turkey Day game.

But, my heart was there.

After a while, you know, life happens. You stay loyal to your school - and many people enjoy going to every game every weekend - but that is not my journey.

I've fallen away from Newberry, through no fault of theirs.

I do remember 2006.

The Indians travel to PC's brand new stadium. It is raining. I am on the visitor's sideline and look across at the vast home crowd. There on the front row were chest-painted PC "boys" spelling out NUCK FEWBERRY. I took a picture. I've always had the philosophy - take the picture, decide later whether to use it. So, Monday, a nice hole opened up on our front page and the picture slid right in there (with some kind of sarcastic caption). Publication day, I got a visit from one of our church ladies: "Victor," she said - that's what they all call me - "you do know what that spells?" Yes.

"Aren't you ashamed?" No.

Because, it's the perfect example of young people who simply do not like each other, probably for the dumbest of reasons. And besides, they had no right to treat us like that. Especially since we didn't think of it first.

Game over. I get a great shot of Mike Taylor stalking out to midfield to discuss "strategy" with the refs, who were not our friends that day - I don't even know PC's coach but I probably do now, some of them never even leave the city.

Newberry headed to the field house - this is it, the last one ever, they couldn't bring home the Derby. One player does a U-turn in front of me - I know where he's going, and he has sinister intent. I one-arm bear-hugged him (I was much stronger in my younger days) and probably kept him away from a confrontation with the Clinton Police Department.

"Let me go."

"Not a chance."

Well, at least that's the way I remember it.

I've been to that stadium many times since then - PC put dorms on its old football field and tore down the smoke stack; I've even shot lacrosse in the "new" stadium; they have a bicycling event there, "Flight of the Dove," a hospice fund-raiser; we had a microburst there during one Blue Hose football game and there was the most beautiful ever rainbow over the field - but I was in my car driving away. A young PC staffer got a picture of it - I could have won an award for that picture (dang, this place has never been lucky for me).

I don't consciously do it, but whenever I see PC play football, I think something is missing. I remember Thanksgiving Dinner in the Newberry dining hall. I remember Greg Hartle knocking out running backs, until somebody (probably a PC player) went low on his knee. I remember the young ladies I courted at those games - my children with me at Settler Field. I remember Fred Herren and Cally Gault. I remember the graveyard cheer.

I remember that I was Editor of one of the best small college newspapers in the country - and the young women who were Editors before me set it on that path. I remember Gordon Henry.

And I remember that, once upon a time, Team Clinton won at the Newberry College campus in pretty much every SC Science Olympiad they ever competed in. Then, it went to (ugh) The Citadel. Talk about full circle, the next time there is an SC Science Olympiad, it will be at Presbyterian College.

I almost dropped my dentures when I saw that announcement.

It is, as photographers say, a photo-rich environment.

I probably was tangentially connected somehow to PC winning 6 Derby games in a row, 1998-2003; and the 1985 24-24 tie.

I remember how these games were always gritty and close.

The Li'l 🎩 That Was!

Mostly I remember the absolutely great picture one of our photographers made of an Indian - with a muscled forearm and a tight hand grip - holding that crazy, glowing in the late afternoon sun hat aloft above everybody else. I remember how it looked on Cally Gault's head or Fred Herren's head - when coaches were less concerned about appearances and more about their school's spirit. The Bagpipes. The Tomahawk Chop. It would always be there because both schools wanted it, they wanted to compete, they wanted to challenge their athletes, they wanted their coaches to rise to the challenges, they wanted their student bodies involved and their fans rabid. Until, they didn't.

We took it for granted.

We took it all for granted."

Jimmie Coggins is President and General Manager of Newberry Broadcasting Company, Inc. (Newberry radio station WKDK). Since 1982, Jimmie has been the radio voice of both Newberry High School and Newberry College football. Jimmie is tremendously active in the Newberry community. Jimmie was inducted in the Newberry Athletic Hall of Fame in 2013. Jimmie was so excited to be included in my book chronicling a special small college rivalry and shared some of his special memories of The Bronze Derby:

"My Bronze Derby memories date back to my childhood. My family's Thanksgiving dinner family gathering was just that....dinner. We knew that we would not eat our dinner until after The Bronze Derby game was completed and we celebrated at night.

I remember a lot of the games as a teen because I was the remote boy for the radio station. I set up the equipment and ran the equipment for the broadcast. While attending Newberry College, I attended all of the games as a student. In 1982, I began broadcasting both Newberry College and Newberry High School football. I broadcast both the Thanksgiving Day match-ups and those later Division II match-ups that were not played on Thanksgiving Day.

In 1963, President John F. Kennedy was assassinated on the Friday before Thanksgiving. The annual Clemson-South Carolina game was scheduled for Saturday. The game was rescheduled the next week on Thanksgiving Day. Two collegiate games were played on Thanksgiving Day in 1963 in South Carolina.

In 1989, it appeared time had expired and the game had ended. The clock had run out, but no horn had sounded. The officials huddled and one second was placed on the clock. Newberry got an extra play. On the final play of the game, Newberry scored on a long touchdown pass resulting in a final second Newberry 29-24 win.

I will never forget the 1995 "Take a knee PC" game. PC was leading very late in the fourth quarter. Newberry had no time outs. All PC had to do was take a knee to run out the clock. PC fumbled the ball resulting in a turnover. Newberry kicked a field goal moments later to win the game 9-8.

In 2004, Newberry traveled to Clinton for the annual rivalry game. Newberry warmed up prior to the game at Clinton High School. The team showed up at the stadium just in time for the coin flip. Newberry defeated PC 28-25.

Two years later in 2006, Newberry returned to Clinton undefeated with a 10-0 record and their best team in school history. Newberry did the same thing and warmed up at Clinton High School. When they got to the stadium, they got off the buses lacklusterly and it seemed they didn't have that pep in their step. Those of us that were at the stadium saw the tremendous Newberry crowd that had shown up, maybe more scarlet and gray than PC blue. Newberry came out flat and lost the game. I think if they had come early and done their normal warmup, they probably would have gotten that enthusiastic feeling from the crowd and maybe have gone on to win that game.

Such fond memories of Cally Gault, Fred Herren and Coach Harvey Kirkland with their supporting staff. They would put on quite a show before the game on Thanksgiving Day. The most memorable was in 1972 when the team's line coaches, Steve Peterson and Billy Tiller met at midfield in chef's outfits ready to carve a turkey.

The rival broadcasting teams even started a tradition and competed for a turkey. Sandy Cruickshaw, PC's play by play man won more turkeys than I did!

It was just a marvelous, marvelous time for us all.

It's a crying shame that they don't play anymore."

Whoops!

In 1947, Charles McDonald from Presbyterian College and Frank Kinard of Newberry College are credited for developing the governing rules for The Bronze Derby. Both the schools and the communities embraced the rivalry. When competing in basketball, baseball and football, the rules stipulated that The Bronze Derby would represent the athletic competitive rivalry between Presbyterian College and Newberry College. The winner of the competitions would be awarded the prize. In the November 18, 1955 edition of *The Blue Stocking*, it was reported by Ben Hammet, head of Presbyterian College Public Relations, that beginning in 1956, The Bronze Derby would only be competed for only on the football field. The voice of the students at both Presbyterian College and Newberry College made an impact in the early 1950's regarding the ultimate decision to compete for The Bronze Derby on the football field. Throughout documenting the history of The Bronze Derby, a repetitive theme occurred and is displayed annually in the school newspapers. To educate incoming students regarding the rivalry football game, the history of The Bronze Derby was printed year after year. It was certainly assumed that the schools would compete against each other for years to come.

Fast forward to 2006. Whoops! As a result of Presbyterian College making the transition to NCAA Division 1, the final football matchup between the NAIA Division I and NCAA Division II rivals Presbyterian College and Newberry College took place. A 10-0 victory by Presbyterian College over undefeated Newberry College certainly did not disappoint any fan of this storied rivalry. Ironically in 1952, Charles McDonald made a revelation when he wrote a letter to the *Blue Stocking* indicating that his preference for the competitive rivalry between the schools would have been limited to an annual football game. Today, Presbyterian College is currently in possession of an iconic symbol in South Carolina athletic history. The sixty year Bronze Derby football rivalry between Newberry College and Presbyterian College abruptly ended on November 11, 2006.

The Li'l 🎩 That Was!

Emphasis prior to 2007 was placed on the move by Presbyterian College to compete in the NCAA Division 1. Historical knowledge regarding the game and impact on the student-athletes, alumni and communities was evaluated. The move to NCAA Division 1 by Presbyterian College was a complicated process. Alumni, staff and former board members of Presbyterian College explained to me the complexities involved in the final decision. Ultimately, a Bronze Derby alternative not involving football could and still can be implemented. The original governing rules had been established in 1947. Historically, an amendment to the original governing rules was made in 1955. Another amendment certainly could have been made for athletic competition in baseball and basketball between the schools after the final 2006 Bronze Derby football game was played.

If both college administrations agreed to honor the original governing rules of The Bronze Derby prior to 2007 and amend accordingly, four games could have been included in this rivalry. As a result of football not being played after 2006, the 4 games that have been played between the schools include:

Baseball	3/17/2007	**Newberry**	11	Presbyterian	2
Baseball	3/17/2007	**Newberry**	5	Presbyterian	4
Baseball	3/18/2007	Newberry	7	**Presbyterian**	9
Basketball	11/4/2010	Newberry	61	**Presbyterian**	83

No women's basketball competition between the colleges has taken place since 2006. The Bronze Derby has never been competed for by a women's basketball team.

From 1947-2006, 108 athletic competitions in basketball, baseball and football for The Bronze Derby have taken place. Forty-eight basketball and baseball games took place between 1947-1955. Sixty football games took place between 1947 and 2006. Traditionally played on Thanksgiving Day, football became and was known as The Bronze Derby.

Years have quickly gone by since the last Bronze Derby football game was played. Times have changed and are now complicated. There is a new generation, new administrations, scheduling problems, NCAA rules, coupled with pressures from the press, fans and alumni. An effort between schools, fans, the press and alumni to resurrect the football rivalry is periodically encouraged and reviewed by administrations.

A rivalry is simply competing for a prize. The Newberry College Indian-Presbyterian College Blue Hose rivalry began at a fair and ended in despair. Beginning in 2007, new rivalries for both schools were invented. Inventing a competitive spirit between schools has been proven to be difficult. The storied history of The Bronze Derby is the standard for not only an athletic competition between schools, but a friendly competitive spirit between communities. On March 20, 2024, during a nationally televised women's basketball game, ESPN sportscaster Courtney Lyle made an observation that both Newberry and Laurens counties have recognized for over 120 years. The Presbyterian College women's basketball team were seconds away from winning their first NCAA Division 1 tournament game. Lyle told the nation that "This team (Presbyterian College) is playing for not just Presbyterian, but the Clinton community. They (The Presbyterian College women's basketball team) feel a responsibility because they have felt the support that the community has put around them." If Newberry College had been playing in that game, with the same circumstances and result, I am confident the same exact statement would have been made.

The prize will never be forgotten by their respective communities and alumni. In a few short years, the prize will only be read about. In future generations, the prize will only be referred to as *The Li'l Bronze Derby That Was*!

Acknowledgements

Special thanks, in no particular order, to a fabulous group of enthusiastic individuals that helped guide me on a sixty year journey of The Bronze Derby. No matter what colors we wore, we all had in common the memory and history of The Bronze Derby. A special thank you to Tracy Power, Associate Professor of History and Director of the Newberry College Archives. Tracy and his colleagues in Wessels Library at Newberry College provided me unlimited access to resources available for research and publication. In addition, Tracy's researching efforts are most appreciated. As a graduate of Presbyterian College, I was welcomed with open arms by everyone on the Newberry College campus and in the city of Newberry. Reflecting on my journey, I am elated with the contacts I have made. What is most important, I now call them my friends!

Steffi Hiltgen	Public Services Librarian, Wessels Library, Newberry College
Reid Austin	Director, Wessels Library, Newberry College
Steven Knapp	Executive Director, Newberry County Museum
Jimmie Coggins	President / General Manager WKDK Radio
Randy Randall	Mayor, Clinton, South Carolina
Foster Senn	Mayor, Newberry, South Carolina
Orion Griffin	Editor, The Newberry Observer
Monte Dutton	Author and Sports Editor, Clinton, South Carolina
Vic MacDonald	Editor, The Clinton Chronicle
John Clayton	Editor, The Laurens County Advertiser
Kimberly Porter	Motivator and editor
Sarah Leckie	Archives and Technical Services, James H Thomason Library, Presbyterian College
Walter Shealy	Chairman / CEO Shealy Consulting Group and Black Grove LLC
Staff	Newberry County Library
Staff	Laurens County Library

Photo Credits

Title page	Used with permission from Newberry College Archives
Content page	Used with permission from Presbyterian College Archives
Page 1	Used with permission from Presbyterian College Archives
Page 11	Used with permission from Newberry College Archives
Page 34	Used with permission from Presbyterian College Archives
Page 52	Used with permission from Presbyterian College Archives
Page 53	Used with permission from Presbyterian College Archives
Page 54	Used with permission from Presbyterian College Archives
Page 90	Used with permission from Presbyterian College Archives
Page 243	Used with permission from Presbyterian College Archives
Page 249	Used with permission from The Clinton Chronicle
Page 251	Used with permission from Presbyterian College Archives
Page 279	Used with permission from Presbyterian College Archives
Page 301	Used with permission from Presbyterian College Archives
Page 312	Used with permission from Presbyterian College Archives
Page 361	Used with permission from Presbyterian College Archives
Page 560	Used with permission from Newberry College Archives

The Li'l 🎩 That Was!

Newspaper articles and pictures are cited and used with permission by:

The Newberry Observer

THE LAURENS COUNTY Advertiser

The Clinton Chronicle

The Blue Stocking

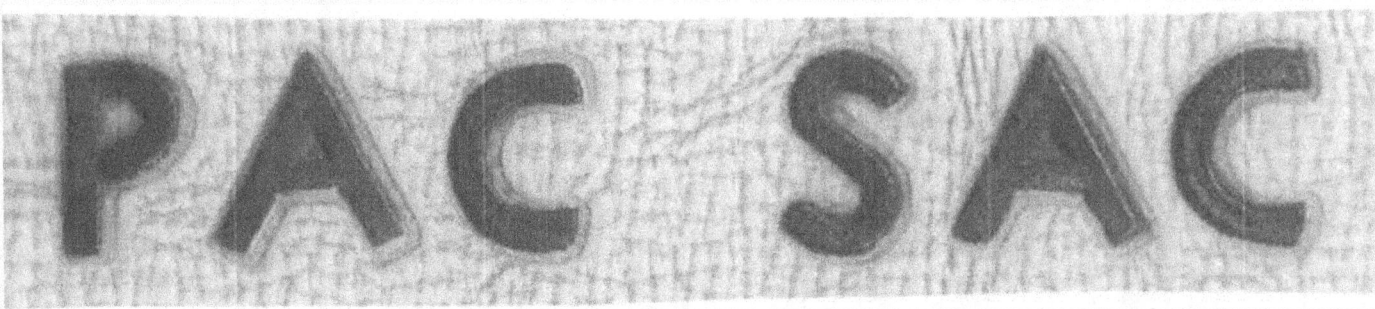
PAC SAC

Newspaper articles and pictures are cited and used with permission by:

The Presbyterian College Report

The Indian
NEWBERRY COLLEGE
"Home of The Fighting Redskins"

The Alumni Bulletin

NEWBERRY COLLEGE DIMENSIONS

NEWBERRIAN

The Newberry College Scarlet & Gray